The Cambr
Literar

MW01156493

VOLUME 3

The Renaissance

This volume is the first to explore as part of an unbroken continuum the critical legacy both of the humanist rediscovery of ancient learning and of its neoclassical reformulation. Focused on what is arguably the most complex phase in the transmission of the Western literary-critical heritage, the book encompasses those issues that helped shape the way European writers thought about literature from the late Middle Ages to the late seventeenth century. These issues touched almost every facet of Western intellectual endeavour, as well as the historical, cultural, social, scientific, and technological contexts in which that activity evolved. From the interpretative reassessment of the major ancient poetic texts, this volume addresses the emergence of the literary critic in Europe by exploring poetics, prose fiction, contexts of criticism, neoclassicism, and national developments. Sixty-one chapters by internationally respected scholars are supported by an introduction, detailed bibliographies for further investigation and a full index.

GLYN P. NORTON is Professor of French Literature and the Willcox B. and Harriet M. Adsit Professor of International Studies at Williams College, Williamstown, Massachusetts. He has published widely on French Renaissance literature and criticism, and on Franco-Italian literary relations in the Renaissance. He is author of *Montaigne and the introspective mind* (1975), *The ideology and language of translation in Renaissance France and their humanist antecedents* (1984), and numerous articles in such journals as *Publications of the modern language association of America, Romanic review, The Journal of medieval and Renaissance studies, Comparative literature studies, Modern language quarterly*, and *Italica*.

The Cambridge History of
Literary Criticism

GENERAL EDITORS

Professor H. B. Nisbet
University of Cambridge
Professor Claude Rawson
Yale University

The Cambridge History of Literary Criticism will provide a comprehensive historical account of Western literary criticism from classical antiquity to the present day, dealing with both literary theory and critical practice. The *History* is intended as an authoritative work of reference and exposition, but more than a mere chronicle of facts. While remaining broadly non-partisan it addresses, where appropriate, controversial issues of current critical debate without evasion or false pretences of neutrality. Each volume is a self-contained unit designed to be used independently as well as in conjunction with the others in the series. Substantial bibliographic material in each volume provides the foundation for further study of the subjects in question.

VOLUMES PUBLISHED

OTHER VOLUMES IN PREPARATION

The contribution of Professor Peter Brooks, *Yale University*,
to the setting up of Volume 3 is gratefully acknowledged.

The Cambridge History of
Literary Criticism

VOLUME 3

The Renaissance

Edited by

GLYN P. NORTON

CAMBRIDGE
UNIVERSITY PRESS

CAMBRIDGE UNIVERSITY PRESS
Cambridge, New York, Melbourne, Madrid, Cape Town,
Singapore, São Paulo, Delhi, Tokyo, Mexico City

Cambridge University Press
The Edinburgh Building, Cambridge CB2 8RU, UK

Published in the United States of America by
Cambridge University Press, New York

www.cambridge.org
Information on this title: www.cambridge.org/9780521317191

First published 1999
Reprinted 2004
First paperback edition 2006

A catalogue record for this publication is available from the British Library

Library of Congress Cataloguing in Publication data

ISBN 978-0-521-30008-7 Hardback
ISBN 978-0-521-31719-1 Paperback

For
Ian McFarlane

Contents

Notes on contributors

Michael J. B. Allen is Professor of English and Italian at the University of California, Los Angeles. He is the author of *Marsilio Ficino: the 'Philebus' commentary* (1975), *Marsilio Ficino and the Phaedran charioteer* (1981), *The Platonism of Ficino: a study of his 'Phaedrus' commentary, its sources and genesis* (1984), *Icastes: Marsilio Ficino's interpretation of Plato's 'Sophist'* (1989), *Nuptial arithmetic: Marsilio Ficino's commentary on the fatal number in book* VIII *of Plato's 'Republic'* (1994), *Plato's third eye: studies in Marsilio Ficino's Metaphysics and its sources* (1995), and *Synoptic art: Marsilio Ficino on the history of Platonic interpretation* (forthcoming). He is also co-author of *Sources and analogues of Old English poetry*, with Daniel G. Calder (1976) and co-editor of *First images of America*, with Fredi Chiappelli and Robert L. Benson (1976), *Shakespeare's plays in quarto: a facsimile edition of copies primarily from the Henry E. Huntington Library*, with Kenneth Muir (1981), and *Sir Philip Sidney's achievements*, with Dominic Baker-Smith and Arthur F. Kinney (1990).

Ann Blair is Assistant Professor of History and of History and Literature at Harvard University. She specializes in the history of Renaissance science and is the author of *The theater of nature: Jean Bodin and Renaissance science* (1997). She is also the editor of *The transmission of culture in early modern Europe*, with Anthony Grafton (1990).

Christopher Braider is Associate Professor of French and Italian at the University of Colorado, Boulder. He is the author of *Refiguring the real: picture and modernity in word and image, 1400–1770* (1993). His most recent published article is ' "Cet hymen différé": the figuration of authority in Corneille's *Le Cid*' (1996). He has also published articles on interart problems in such journals as *Poetics Today* and the *Yearbook of Comparative and General Literature*.

Marina S. Brownlee is Class of 1963 College of Women Professor of Romance Languages at the University of Pennsylvania. Her principal publications include *The poetics of literary theory: Lope de Vega's 'Novelas a*

Marcia Leonarda' and their Cervantine context (1981), *The status of the reading subject in the 'Libro de buen amor'* (1985), and *The severed word: Ovid's 'Heroides' and the 'novela sentimental'* (1990). She is also the co-editor of *Romance: generic transformation from Chrétien de Troyes to Cervantes*, with Kevin Brownlee (1985), *The new medievalism*, with Kevin Brownlee and Stephen G. Nichols (1991), and *Cultural authority in Golden Age Spain*, with Hans Ulrich Gumbrecht (1995).

Colin Burrow is a Fellow and University Lecturer in English at Gonville and Caius College Cambridge. He has published widely on the relations between Classical and Renaissance literature. He is the author of *Epic romance: Homer to Milton* (1993) and *Edmund Spenser* (1996). He is presently preparing an edition of Shakespeare's poems and sonnets for the Oxford Shakespeare.

Terence Cave is Professor of French Literature at the University of Oxford and Fellow of St John's College Oxford. His work includes *Devotional poetry in France c. 1570–1613* (1969), *The cornucopian text: problems of writing in the French Renaissance* (1979) (French translation, 1997), *Recognitions: a study in poetics* (1988). He is also the translator and editor of the Comtesse de Lafayette's *The Princesse de Clèves* (1992) and editor of *Ronsard the poet* (1973) and of George Eliot's *Daniel Deronda* (1995) and *Silas Marner* (1996).

Marga Cottino-Jones is Professor of Italian at the University of California, Los Angeles. Her publications include *An anatomy of Boccaccio's style* (1968), *Metodi di critica letteraria americana* (1973), *Order from chaos: social and aesthetic harmonies in Boccaccio's 'Decameron'* (1982), *Introduzione a Pietro Aretino* (1993), and *Il dir novellando: modello e deviazioni* (1994). She has also co-edited *Boccaccio: secoli di vita; atti del Congresso internazionale Boccaccio 1975*, with Edward F. Tuttle (1978) and *The architecture of vision: writings and interviews on Cinema / Michelangelo Antonioni*, with Carlo di Carlo and Giorgio Tinazzi (1996). She is the author of numerous articles on the literature and criticism of the Italian Renaissance and is at work on a study of Italian Renaissance artistic and literary views of women.

Nicholas Cronk is Fellow and Tutor in French, St Edmund Hall, and Faculty Lecturer in Eighteenth-Century French Literature in the University of Oxford. His publications include an edition of Voltaire's *Letters concerning the English Nation* (1994), and articles on Molière, Voltaire, and Diderot. He has also published various articles on seventeenth-century French poetic theory, including 'The singular voice: monologism and

French classical discourse', *Continuum* (1989). His study *The classical Sublime* is forthcoming.

Hugh M. Davidson is Commonwealth Professor of French Literature, Emeritus, at the University of Virginia. He is the author of *Audience, words, and art: studies in seventeenth-century French rhetoric* (1965), *A concordance to the 'Pensées' of Pascal*, with P. H. Dubé (1975), *The origins of certainty: means and meanings in Pascal's 'Pensées'* (1979), *A concordance to Pascal's 'Les Provinciales'*, with P. H. Dubé (1980), *Blaise Pascal* (1983), and *Pascal and the arts of mind* (1983). He has authored many articles on seventeenth-century French literature, especially the topic of rhetoric.

Joan DeJean is Trustee Professor of French at the University of Pennsylvania. Her work includes *Scarron's 'Roman comique': a comedy of the novel, a novel of comedy* (1977), *Libertine strategies: freedom and the novel in seventeenth-century France* (1981), *Literary fortifications: Rousseau, Laclos, Sade* (1984), *Tender geographies: women and the origins of the novel in France* (1991), *Fictions of Sappho, 1546–1937* (1989), and *Ancients against moderns: culture wars and the making of a 'fin de siècle'* (1997).

Martin Elsky is Professor of English at the CUNY Graduate School and at Brooklyn College. He is also coordinator of the Renaissance Studies Program at the CUNY Graduate School. He is the author of *Authorizing words: speech, writing, and print in the English Renaissance* (1989), and has written articles on Donne, Herbert, Jonson, Bacon, and Milton. He is currently working on a monograph about Ben Jonson's country house poems in relation to family and local history during the dynastic consolidation of the English countryside. He is also working on the ecclesiological sources of Erich Auerbach's literary history of Europe.

Floyd Gray is Professor of French at the University of Michigan. He has published extensively on Rabelais and Montaigne and is the author of *Le style de Montaigne* (1958), *Rabelais et l'écriture* (1974), *La poétique de Du Bellay* (1978), *La balance de Montaigne: exagium / essai* (1982), *La Bruyère amateur de caractères* (1986), *Montaigne bilingue: le latin des 'Essais'* (1991), and *Rabelais et le comique du discontenu* (1994). He is also the editor of *Montaigne, textes d'Albert Thibaudet, établis par F. Gray* (1963) and *Anthologie de la poésie française du XVIe siècle* (1966).

Roland Greene is Professor of Comparative Literature and English at the University of Oregon. He is the author of *Post-Petrarchism: origins and innovations of the Western lyric sequence* (1991), *Unrequited conquests:*

love and empire in the colonial Americas (1999), and co-editor (with Elizabeth Fowler) of *The project of prose in early modern Europe and the new world* (1997).

Robert Griffin is Emeritus Professor of French and Comparative Literature at the University of California, Riverside. His publications include *Coronation of the poet: Joachim du Bellay's debt to the trivium* (1969), *Clément Marot and the inflections of poetic voice* (1974), *Ludovico Ariosto* (1974), *Rape of the lock: the mythology of Gustave Flaubert* (1984), *Gustave Flaubert: early writings* (1991), *Apocalypse of / de Chiokoyhikoy*, with Donald A. Grinde, Jr. (1997). He is also the author of over seventy essays on authors ranging from Homer to Joyce.

Elizabeth Guild is Newton Trust Lecturer in French at the University of Cambridge. Her recent essays include ' "Le Moyen de faire de cela un grand homme": the Abbé de Choisy and the unauthorized body of representation' (1994), ' "Et les interpréter là où elles n'exhibent que leur mutisme', in *(Ré)interprétations sur le seizième siècle*, ed. J. O'Brien (1995), 'Adultery on trial: Martin Guerre and his wife, from judge's tale to the screen', in *Scarlet letters: fictions of adultery from antiquity to the 1990s*, ed. N. White and N. Segal (1997), and 'Montaigne's commerce with women: "jusques où va la possibilité?" ', in *The texture of Renaissance knowledge*, ed. P. Berry and M. Tudeau Clayton (forthcoming).

Fernand Hallyn is Professor of French Literature at the University of Ghent, Belgium. His principal publications are *Formes métaphoriques dans la poésie lyrique de l'âge baroque en France* (1975), *La structure poétique du monde: Copernic, Kepler* (1975), English translation (1990), *Paradigmes dans les études littéraires* (1979), *Onze études sur la mise en abyme* (1980), and *Le sens des formes: études sur la Renaissance* (1994). He is also the editor of *Méthodes des textes: introduction aux études littéraires* (1987) and *Les 'Olympiques' de Descartes: études et textes réunis par Fernand Hallyn* (1995). His edition of *Metaphors in science / métaphores scientifiques* is forthcoming.

Timothy Hampton is Associate Professor of French, Comparative Literature, and Italian Studies, and Chair of French at the University of California, Berkeley. His publications include *Writing from history: the rhetoric of exemplarity in Renaissance literature* (1990) and various essays on literature and politics in the European Renaissance. He was the editor for *Yale French Studies* of *Baroque topographies: literature, history, philosophy* (1991) and is currently at work on a study of literature and nationhood in the French Renaissance.

Theo Hermans is Professor of Dutch and Comparative Literature at University College London. He is the author of *The structure of modernist poetry* (1982), *Door eenen engen hals: Nederlandse beschouwingen over vertalen, 1550–1670* (1996), and *Translation in systems* (1998). He is also the editor, co-editor, or translator of *The manipulation of literature: studies in literary translation* (1985), *Second hand: papers on the theory and historical study of literary translation* (1985), *Studies over Nederlandse vertalingen: een bibliografische lijst* (1991), *The Flemish movement: a documentary history, 1780–1990*, editor with Louis Vos and Lode Wils (1992), *From revolt to riches: culture and history of the Low Countries 1500–1700: international and interdisciplinary perspectives*, editor with Reinier Salverda (1993).

George Hoffmann is Associate Professor of French at Boston University. He is the author of *Montaigne's career*, forthcoming with Clarendon Press. His principal essays include ' "Neither one nor the other": how scholastic logic can help explain Panurge's marriage question', *Etudes rabelaisiennes* (1990), 'The Montaigne monopoly: revising the *Essais* under the French *privilège* system', *Publications of the Modern Language Association of America* (1993), 'Monsters and modal logic among the French naturalists of the Renaissance', *South Central Review* (1993).

George K. Hunter is Emily Sanborn Professor of English, Emeritus, at Yale University, Honorary Professor at the University of Warwick, and Fellow of the American Academy of Arts and Sciences. He has written extensively on Elizabethan drama and is the author of *Shakespeare, the later comedies* (1962), *John Lyly: the humanist as courtier* (1962), *Lyly and Peele* (1968), *Dramatic identities and cultural traditions: studies in Shakespeare and his contemporaries* (1978), and *English drama 1586–1642: the age of Shakespeare* (volume VI in *The Oxford history of English literature*) (1997). His editions include Shakespeare's *All's well that ends well* (1959) and *Macbeth* (1967), Marston's *Antonio and Mellida* (1965), *Antonio's revenge* (1966), and *The malcontent* (1975), John Lyly's *Campaspe* and *Sappho and Phao* (1992), F. P. Wilson's *The English drama 1485–1585* (1969), *John Webster* (1969) (with S. K. Hunter), and *A casebook on Shakespeare's 'Henry IV'* (1970).

Daniel Javitch is Professor of Comparative Literature at New York University. He is the author of *Poetry and courtliness in Renaissance England* (1978), *Cantus interruptus in the 'Orlando furioso'* (1980), and *Proclaiming a classic: the canonization of 'Orlando furioso'* (1991) (Italian translation, 1998). He is also the co-editor of *Comparative literary history as discourse: in honor of Anna Balakian* (1992), with Mario J. Valdes and A. Owen Aldridge.

Michel Jeanneret is Professor of French Literature at the Université de Genève. He has also served as Visiting Professor at Harvard University, Princeton University, the University of California, Irvine, and the University of Washington. His principal publications include *Poésie et tradition biblique au XVIe siècle: recherches stylistiques sur les paraphrases des psaumes de Marot à Malherbe* (1969), *La lettre perdue: écriture et folie dans l'œuvre de Nerval* (1978), *Des mets et des mots: banquets et propos de table à la Renaissance* (1987), English translation (1991), *Le défi des signes: Rabelais et la crise de l'interprétation à la Renaissance* (1994), *Perpetuum mobile: métamorphoses des corps et des œuvres, de Vinci à Montaigne* (1997), English translation (forthcoming). He is also the author of numerous essays on Rabelais, Montaigne, sixteenth-century poetry, Renaissance hermeneutics, La Fontaine, Nerval, and the Geneva School of Criticism.

William J. Kennedy is Professor of Comparative Literature at Cornell University. His publications include *Rhetorical norms in Renaissance literature* (1978), *Jacopo Sannazaro and the uses of pastoral* (1983), and *Authorizing Petrarch* (1994). He is also co-editor of *Writing in the disciplines* (1987, 1991, 1995) and the author of numerous articles on Italian, French, and English literature from Dante to Milton and on literary theory. His book on *The site of Petrarchism* is forthcoming.

Jill Kraye is Senior Lecturer in the History of Philosophy at the Warburg Institute. She is the associate editor of *The Cambridge history of Renaissance philosophy* (1988) and has recently edited and contributed to *The Cambridge companion to Renaissance humanism* (1996) and two volumes of *Cambridge translations of Renaissance philosophical texts* (1997). She was also the joint editor of *Pseudo-Aristotle in the Middle Ages* (1986) and *The uses of Greek and Latin* (1988). She has published a number of articles on the influence of classical philosophy in the early modern period.

Ullrich Langer is Professor of French at the University of Wisconsin, Madison. His books include *Rhétorique et intersubjectivité: 'Les Tragiques' d'Agrippa d'Aubigné* (1983), *Invention, death, and self-definitions in the poetry of Pierre de Ronsard* (1986), *Divine and poetic freedom in the Renaissance: nominalist theology and literature in France and Italy* (1990), and *Perfect friendship: studies in literature and moral philosophy from Boccaccio to Corneille* (1994). He is also co-editor of *What is literature? France 1100–1600*, with F. Cornilliat and D. Kelly (1993) and *Anteros*, with J. Miernowski (1994).

John Logan is Literature Bibliographer at Princeton University. He is a specialist on Longinus in the Renaissance and seventeenth century. His essays include 'The poet's central numbers' (1971), 'Longinus', in *Ancient writers: Greece and Rome* (1982), 'Montaigne et Longin: une nouvelle hypothèse' (1983), and 'La Fontaine, Plato, and "La cigale et la fourmy"' (1986). He is currently working on a comprehensive study of Longinus in the Renaissance and seventeenth century.

Jonathan Mallinson is Lecturer in French at the University of Oxford, and Fellow of Trinity College Oxford. He is the author of *The comedies of Corneille: experiments in the comic* (1984) and of numerous articles on French theatre and prose fiction of the seventeenth century. He is also the editor of Molière's *L'Avare* (1988) and *Le Misanthrope* (1996).

Lawrence Manley is Professor of English at Yale University. His principal publications include *Convention, 1500–1750* (1980) and *Literature and culture in early modern London* (1995). He is also the editor of *London in the age of Shakespeare: an anthology* (1986).

David Marsh is Professor of Italian at Rutgers University. He is the author of *The Quattrocento dialogue: classical tradition and humanist innovation* (1990), and of *Lucian and the Latins: humor and humanism in the early Renaissance* (1998); and is the translator of Leon Battista Alberti, *Dinner pieces* (1987) and of Giambattista Vico, *The new science* (1998).

John Monfasani is Professor of History at The University at Albany, State University of New York. His principal publications include *George of Trebizond: a biography and a study of his rhetoric and logic* (1976), *Collectanea Trapezuntiana. texts, documents, and bibliographies of George of Trebizond* (1984), *Fernando of Cordova: a bibliographical and intellectual profile* (1992), *Language and learning in Renaissance Italy: selected essays* (1994), and *Byzantine scholars in Renaissance Italy. Cardinal Bessarion and other emigrés: selected essays* (1995).

Michael Moriarty is Professor of French Literature and Thought at Queen Mary and Westfield College London. His publications include *Taste and ideology in seventeenth-century France* (1988), *Roland Barthes* (1991), and *Semiotics of world literature* (1996).

Ann Moss is Professor of French at Durham University. Her principal publications include *Ovid in Renaissance France: a survey of the Latin editions of Ovid and commentaries printed in France before 1600* (1982), *Poetry and fable: studies in mythological narrative in sixteenth-century France* (1984), and *Printed commonplace-books and the structuring of Renaissance thought* (1996).

Glyn P. Norton is Willcox B. and Harriet M. Adsit Professor of International Studies and Professor of French Literature at Williams College, Williamstown, Massachusetts. His publications include *Montaigne and the introspective mind* (1975) and *The ideology and language of translation in Renaissance France and their humanist antecedents* (1984). He has contributed numerous essays on French Renaissance literature, Franco-Italian literary relations in the Renaissance, on Dante, Boccaccio, and Rousseau to journals such as *Publications of the Modern Language Association of America*, *Romanic Review*, *Modern Language Quarterly*, *Comparative Literature Studies*, *Journal of Medieval and Renaissance Studies*, and *Italica*. He is currently completing a book on *Eloquence beside itself: the theory and art of improvisation in the French Renaissance and neoclassical text*.

Marjorie O'Rourke Boyle is a cultural historian living in Toronto, Canada and a widely known specialist in the rhetoric of religion. She is the author of *Erasmus on language and method in theology* (1977), *Christening pagan mysteries: Erasmus in pursuit of wisdom* (1981), *Rhetoric and reform: Erasmus' civil dispute with Luther* (1983), *Petrarch's genius: pentimento and prophecy* (1991), and *Divine domesticity: Augustine of Thagaste to Teresa of Avila* (1997). Her most recent literary criticism is *Loyola's acts: the rhetoric of the self* (1997).

James A. Parente, Jr. is Professor of German, Scandinavian, and Dutch at the University of Minnesota. He is the author of *Religious drama and the humanist tradition: Christian theater in Germany and the Netherlands, 1500–1680* (1987). He is also co-editor of *Literary culture in the Holy Roman Empire, 1555–1720*, with Richard Erich Schade and George C. Schoolfield (1991) and editor of *Socio-historical approaches to early modern German literature* (1993). He has published several essays on early modern German literature, and especially on neo-Latin writers, in such journals as *The German Quarterly*, *Daphnis*, *Humanistica Lovaniensia*, *Sixteenth Century Journal*, and *Central European History*. His current research focuses on early modern sexuality; German, Dutch, and Scandinavian humanism; and Latin drama in early modern Europe.

Richard Parish is Professor of French at the University of Oxford and Fellow of St Catherine's College Oxford. He is the author of *Pascal's 'Lettres provinciales': a study in polemic* (1989), *Racine: the limits of tragedy* (1993), and a forthcoming study of Scarron's *Le Roman comique*. He is also the editor of Molière's *Le Tartuffe* (1994) and of Racine's *Bérénice* (1994) and *Phèdre* (1996). He is currently at work on a general book on French seventeenth-century Catholic writing.

Anne Lake Prescott is Professor of English at Barnard College, Columbia University. She is the author of *French poets and the English Renaissance* (1978) and *Imagining Rabelais in the English Renaissance* (1998). She is co-editor of the Norton Critical Edition of Edmund Spenser and has published widely on Ben Jonson, Marguerite de Navarre, Sir Philip Sidney, and David (the king and poet).

Catharine Randall is Associate Professor of French at Fordham University. Her publications include *Subverting the system: D'Aubigné and Calvinism* (1990), *(Em)bodying the word: textual resurrections in the martyrological narratives of Foxe, Crespin, de Bèze, and d'Aubigné* (1992), and *Simon Bouquet: imitations et traductions de cent dixhuict emblesmes d'Alciat (Bibliothèque Nationale de France, ms. Fr. 19.143)*, with Daniel Russell (1996). She is also the author of the forthcoming *Creating from constraint: Calvinist aesthetics in early modern Europe*.

Timothy J. Reiss is Professor of Comparative Literature at New York University. His books include *Towards dramatic illusion* (1971), *Tragedy and truth* (1980), *The discourse of modernism* (1982, 1985), *The uncertainty of analysis* (1988), *The meaning of literature* (1992), and *Knowledge, discovery and imagination in early modern Europe* (1997). *The meaning of literature* was awarded the 1992 Forkosch Prize in intellectual history. Books forthcoming are *Patterns of personhood in ancient and medieval Europe*, *Mirages of the selfe*, and *Against autonomy*.

François Rigolot is Meredith Howland Pyne Professor of French Literature and Chair of Renaissance Studies at Princeton University. His principal publications include *Les langages de Rabelais* (1972, 1997), *Poétique et onomastique* (1977), *Le texte de la Renaissance* (1982), *Les Métamorphoses de Montaigne* (1988), *Louise Labé Lyonnaise ou la Renaissance au féminin* (1997). *Le texte de la Renaissance* was awarded the Gilbert Chinard Literary Prize in 1982. He is also the editor of Louise Labé's complete works (1986) and Montaigne's *Journal de voyage* (1992) as well as the author of many articles on French Renaissance literature.

Diana Robin is Professor of Classics and Director of Comparative Literature and Cultural Studies at the University of New Mexico. She is author of *Unknown Greek poems of Francesco Filelfo* (1984) and *Filelfo in Milan: writings, 1451–1477* (1991). She has also translated and edited Laura Cereta (1469–99) in *Collected letters of a Renaissance feminist* (1997), and is co-editor of *Redirecting the gaze: women and third-world cinema* (1998). She is currently at work on a book on women writers and print culture in sixteenth-century Venice.

Daniel Russell is Professor of French at the University of Pittsburgh. His publications include *The emblem and device in France* (1985) and *Emblematic structures in Renaissance French culture* (1995). He has written numerous essays on the art and theory of the emblem, Rabelais, Montaigne, and Marguerite de Navarre and is the co-editor of *Emblematica*. He is presently at work on a book on the reception-orientated history of book illustration in early modern France.

Paul Salzman is Senior Lecturer in the School of English, La Trobe University, Melbourne, Australia. He is the author of *English prose fiction, 1558–1700: a critical history* (1985) and the editor of two volumes of early prose fiction for Oxford World Classics, as well as a selection of Aphra Behn's poetry and prose. He is presently completing a book about the writing of 1621.

Michael Schoenfeldt is Associate Professor of English at the University of Michigan. He is the author of *Prayer and power: George Herbert and Renaissance courtship* (1991). He is currently completing a book for Cambridge University Press entitled *Bodies and selves in early modern England*.

Joshua Scodel is Associate Professor of English and Comparative Literature at the University of Chicago. His publications include *The English poetic epitaph: commemoration and conflict from Jonson to Wordsworth* (1991) as well as essays on Francis Bacon, John Donne, John Milton, and Cavalier love poetry in such journals as *Criticism*, *Comparative Literature*, *English Literary History*, *Studies in Philology*, and *Modern Philology*. He is Associate Editor of *Modern Philology* and is currently at work on a study of moderation and excess in early modern English literature.

Debora Shuger is Professor of English at the University of California, Los Angeles. Her publications include *Sacred rhetoric: the Christian grand style in the English Renaissance* (1988), *Habits of thought: religion, politics, and the dominant culture* (1990), *The Renaissance Bible: scholarship, subjectivity, and sacrifice* (1994). She is also co-editor of *Religion and culture in Renaissance England* (1997), with Clair McEachern.

Peter Skrine is Professor of German at the University of Bristol. He is the author of *The Baroque: literature and culture in seventeenth-century Europe* (1978) and of *A companion to German literature*, with Eda Sagarra (1997). He has also authored a number of essays on the Baroque literary period, including 'Deutsches Barock und englische Sprachcultur' (1981), 'James VI & I and German literature' (1989), 'James I and Martin

Opitz' (1990), 'Gryphius in Italy' (1994), 'The Greek tragedies of Hans
Sachs' (1995), and 'Christian Weise' (1996).

Wesley Trimpi is Professor of English at Stanford University. He is widely
known for his work on English Renaissance poetics and is the author of
Ben Jonson's poems: a study of the plain style (1962), *Muses of one mind:
the literary analysis of experience and its continuity* (1983). His essays
include 'The practice of historical interpretation and Nashe's "Brightnesse
falls from the Ayre" ', *Journal of English and Germanic Philology* (1967),
'The meaning of Horace's *ut pictura poesis*', *The Journal of the Warburg
and Courtauld Institutes* (1973), 'Horace's "ut pictura poesis": the argument for stylistic decorum', *Traditio* (1978), and 'Reason and the classical premises of literary decorum', *The Independent Journal of Philosophy*
(1988).

John O. Ward is a Senior Lecturer in History at the University of Sydney,
where he has taught all aspects of medieval history since 1967. His books
include *The Middle Ages* (1977), *The Vézelay chronicle*, with John Scott
(1992), *The sorcery trial of Alice Kyteler: a contemporary account (1324)*,
with Sharon Davidson (1993), and *Ciceronian rhetoric in treatise, scholion,
and commentary* (1994). He is the author of numerous studies in the history of rhetoric and Latin, specializing in the medieval and Renaissance
periods. Among his essays: 'The commentator's rhetoric: from antiquity
to the Renaissance: glosses and commentataries on Cicero's *Rhetorica*', in
*Medieval eloquence: studies in the theory and practice of medieval rhet-
oric*, ed. J. J. Murphy (1978), 'Renaissance commentators on Ciceronian
rhetoric', in *Renaissance eloquence: studies in the theory and practice
of Renaissance rhetoric*, ed. J. J. Murphy (1983), and 'Quintilian and
the rhetorical revolution of the Middle Ages', *Rhetorica* (1995). He is
currently at work on several other projects involving Cicero's *De inventione*
and the pseudo-Ciceronian, *Ad Herennium*.

Richard Waswo is Professor of English at the Université de Genève. His
books include *The fatal mirror: themes and techniques in the poetry of
Fulke Greville* (1972), *Language and meaning in the Renaissance* (1987),
and *The founding legend of western civilization: from Virgil to Vietnam*
(1997).

Valerie Worth-Stylianou is a Senior Lecturer in French at King's College
London. One of her main areas of research is the relationship between
translation and other forms of writing in the Renaissance. Her major
publications include *Practising translation in Renaissance France: the
example of Etienne Dolet* (1988), and editions of Claude de Taillemont,

La tricarite (1556) (1989), with G.-A. Pérouse, F. Lecercle, and D. Fenoaltea, of Racine, *Alexandre le Grand* (1991), with M. Hawcroft, and of the *Cassell guide to literature in French* (1996). She is also the author of various articles on Amyot, Du Bellay, Montaigne, and issues in Renaissance translation, among the latter 'Reading monolingual and bilingual editions of translations in Renaissance France', in *Translation and the transmission of culture*, ed. J. Beer and K. Lloyd-Jones (1995). Her forthcoming book is titled *Confidential strategies: the evolving role of the 'confident' in French classical drama (1635–1677)*.

Introduction

Glyn P. Norton

Criticism and crisis are etymological friends. Throughout history, literary criticism and cultural crisis have tended to follow convergent trajectories. Renaissance humanism, above all, was responsible for generating a language that would not only reflect the cultural crisis at hand, but base that crisis in its own distinctiveness as a period.[1] The deepest, most central impulses of humanism are thus critical. If, as Frank Kermode asserts, crisis 'is a way of thinking about one's moment, and not inherent in the moment itself',[2] then one may infer that crisis, and with it criticism, speak in a discourse peculiar to this temporal displacement. The critical temper, in its cultural as well as literary dimension, fixes the Renaissance view of time squarely within the Greek concept of κρίσις [*krisis*] as designating a moment both of *separation* and of *decision*. The present volume has as its chief aim to register the discourse – the voices and modulations, as it were – of this moment.

The process by which Renaissance humanists sought to apply their systematic scholarly judgement to the encyclopaedia [*decision*] together with their sense of a time ripe for cultural reappraisal and self-identity [*separation*] is at the fulcrum of the literary-critical initiative that extended throughout the sixteenth and seventeenth centuries. The scale of this enterprise is complex and multiform. Strongly resistant to chronological segmentation as it is to enshrinement in ordered, self-contained units of critical activity, any history of reading – and that, arguably, is what this volume undertakes to scan for the period in question – founders on the temptation to 'read' the literary past as an edifice of integrated building stones, permanently set in critical mortar and in danger of collapse when the canon inscribed on those blocks is reconfigured by successive generations. Ian McFarlane has drawn attention to the pitfalls of trying to freeze the literary map for a period in which the world picture was shaped by a convergence of syncretist and sometimes muddled strands of thought

---

[1] On the Renaissance view of time and Petrarch's role in shaping those notions, see Donald J. Wilcox, *The measure of times past: pre-Newtonian chronologies and the rhetoric of relative time* (Chicago: University of Chicago Press, 1987), pp. 153–86.
[2] Frank Kermode, *The sense of an ending: studies in the theory of fiction* (New York: Oxford University Press, 1967), p. 101.

linking together the domains of science, theology, classical scholarship, cosmogony, rhetoric, poetics, and philosophy.[3] A sense of critical moment intersected with each of these fields, helping to sharpen and focus the distinctive profile constructed by Renaissance thinkers to account for the rift of a *medium aevum* – the cultural divide through which the Renaissance saw its identity framed in a distant, yet revitalized classical past. Small wonder that visions of fatherland, national identity, and vernacular culture could flourish and be refracted through the prism of the classical landscape, a place whose permanence was preserved in memory acting both as a fictive and as an actualizing resource.[4] The 'places' so rooted in the memories and obsessions of Renaissance thinkers looking across to the familiar scapes on the far side of the medieval divide were no less textual than they were topographic. The distant inhabitants of those places – the texts through which ancient culture was transmitted – continued to speak across time and space to a culture bent on inscribing its collective self-identity within a paradox: the assertion that antiquity, dead, interred, poignantly removed in time, remains in conversational touch with a present drawn into an ongoing dialogue with textual artefacts. Literary-critical reappraisal together with a sense of critical moment and dialogue are coextensive postures in the Renaissance mind. What Thomas Greene has referred to as Petrarch's 'self-subverting confession' of temporal and spatial estrangement from the Homeric past, 'Quam longe absis intelligo' ['I realize how far from me you are'], enacts if nothing else the engagement of the critic with his materials, the immanence of distant textual topographies within a vocal present.[5] Petrarch's addressee is fully within audible range of his voice.

It is scarcely surprising that the Renaissance literary critic tends frequently to read texts as though they are participants in an act of conversation. Criticism is pre-eminently a mode of discourse and thus frequently dialogic in structure. As a consequence, Renaissance literary-critical texts commonly occur in a framework of discussion and affirmation of distinctiveness from other critical positions. The light they presume to shed on rediscovered texts is contingent on an uttered darkness against which that light is profiled, a 'middle' age which sets irrevocably the terms of the dialogue and promotes a sense of larger cultural self-identity. It is difficult to overstate the degree to which this emerging self-identity constitutes a sea change in the cultural awareness of the early modern period. In his

[3] I. D. McFarlane, *Renaissance France* (London and Tonbridge: Ernest Benn, New York: Barnes & Noble, 1974), p. 7.
[4] Compare Simon Schama, *Landscape and memory* (New York: Alfred A. Knopf, 1995), pp. 14–15, 517–38.
[5] Thomas M. Greene, *The light in Troy: imitation and discovery in Renaissance poetry* (New Haven and London: Yale University Press, 1982), p. 29.

analysis of this phenomenon, Stephen Greenblatt situates the process – what he terms 'self-fashioning' – within the hypothesis that self-identity is achieved only within a framework of alterity, the presence of an alien structure whose stress lines lead to a new configuration of self-representing features both for the individual and the culture at large.[6]

The plan of the present volume owes much to the above paradigm. Renaissance readers and literary critics, from the more unsystematized intuitions of the early periods of the sixteenth century to the formalizing tendencies of the seventeenth century, found it hard to discuss and interpret literature without marking their separation from earlier critical positions. On the premise that literary criticism is linked to a sense of moment and thereby separation from what has gone before, the essays contained herein record to varying degrees the changes on the literary map initiated by humanist culture. These shifts embrace philosophies of language, approaches to reading and interpretation, the crafting of poetics as a tool for describing how texts function, the refinement and expansion of literary forms, polemical rivalries, aesthetics, structures of thought, and the postulate that all literary criticism is situational, shaped by its own contextual habitat.

Reading and interpretation

Poetics, taken in its widest sense as a taxonomy for describing works of prose and poetry alike, is rooted in a distinctive set of conditions having to do with notions of language, reading, and interpretation. The Renaissance contribution to the history of poetics is doubtless its single most important legacy to the discourse of modern literary criticism; hence, the scale of its coverage in the second part of the present volume. This achievement, however, has as much to do with an awareness of how reading occurs within a distinct linguistic environment as it does with the quest for a meaningful taxonomy to describe how the text is put together. Indeed, it is doubtful that any understanding of Renaissance poetics could take place without first addressing the issues broached in the first part of this survey, namely, the revolution heralded by far-reaching reappraisals of the way language functions and how readers read in an age that so unblushingly advertised and promoted its own critical significance. The field of textual philology became the main beneficiary of an erosion in the deeply held belief – in scholastic thought – that words are representational pointers that help inventory the objects of cognition. Renaissance thinkers, prominent among them Lorenzo Valla, laid the groundwork for

---

[6] Stephen Greenblatt, *Renaissance self-fashioning from More to Shakespeare* (Chicago and London: University of Chicago Press, 1980), p. 9.

this revolution by giving technical expression to Petrarch's sense of historical distance by revealing language in general, and Latin in particular, to be subject to historical transformation. Reading and, by extension, interpretation engage their practitioners in the discovery that strategies of meaning inhere in the cycle of change to which all languages are subject. Discourse is specific to the time and milieu that help generate it. In turn, this revolution in the way scholars described the semantic process of secular texts set into play conditions that led eventually to a radical reappraisal of approaches to sacred texts. From its inception, Reformist doctrine tended to undermine the long-established belief that sacred literature is made accessible to readers by a fourfold methodology giving high profile to the allegorical interpretation of truths revealed in divine statement. Once again, scholastic thought would see its most cherished assumptions arraigned as Evangelical reformers, chief among them Erasmus, viewed revelation as an ongoing discourse emerging, *mutatis mutandis*, through a restorative attention to the process of utterance, of speech [*sermo*] over the atomized particles [*verba*] contained within it. At the very core of this doctrine was the assertion that rhetoric rather than philosophy, discourse rather than intellection, helps bring the reader into communion with the Divine by demystifying the tools of scriptural analysis and by renewing the potency of statement mediated from God to Man through Christ the Logos.

To read, in this developed Evangelical view, was to practise conversation and, therefore, to be drawn into open-ended theological dialogue with the Scriptures and through them, with the Creator. Evangelical approaches to the text helped thereby to ensure that reading and interpretation would always be subject to constant re-reading and reinterpretation, never closed to further refinement. Every reading implied a strategy for contemporizing the text and adapting it to new cultural climes and contexts. Criticism, while always tied to an act of rupture, also re-enacted the discovery of an originating document. In the case of poetics, no more compelling originating voices could be found than those of Aristotle, Horace, Cicero, and Quintilian.

In a real sense, these four poetico-rhetorical theorists of antiquity spoke in converging and overlapping registers to literary critics of the sixteenth and seventeenth centuries. The work of transmission by which Renaissance readers assimilated the texts of these ancient theorists tended to betray the contemporary interests of a rhetorical culture unable to separate issues of form from those of expression and content. Above all, these texts fed into what is arguably the predominant poetic issue of the entire period, that of imitation. And to the degree that commentators on these works tried frequently to construct a unitary theoretical dialogue from their critical distinctiveness as texts – Horatian tenets conflated with

Aristotelian ones, Ciceronian proposals with those of Quintilian – the instances of commentary themselves worked to actuate their own significance as vehicles of imitation. They were their own best promotion of the activities so single-mindedly championed in the wider arena of speculative writing on poetics. In Cinquecento Italy, Aristotelian scholarship, especially that practised at Padua in the 1540s, superposed on an entrenched Horatian tradition a fragmented and even distorted view of the *Poetics*, using such Aristotelian tenets as probability and *catharsis* to work through the interpretative issues raised in the *Ars poetica*. In time, the linkage of the *Poetics* to relevant sections of the *Ars* was accompanied by the tendency to use Aristotle's treatise to help craft a typology of genre outside the classifying structures defined by the Stagirite. Part of a much older, more tenacious exegetical tradition, readings of the Horatian text as early as the late fifteenth century likewise exhibited a syncretism in which commentators poached on aspects of the Ciceronian programme to reveal explicit correlations between the missions of poet and orator. Humanists as diverse as Cristoforo Landino, Josse Bade, Aulo Jano Parrasio, and Denys Lambin were each unable to isolate the *Ars poetica* from the refracted voices of Aristotle, Cicero, Quintilian, and (in the case of Lambin) even Plato. Commentary is nurtured on acts of critical emulation and reassessment, a dialogue with antecedent texts. With the early fifteenth-century recovery of the Latin rhetorical canon (Cicero, Quintilian, and the *Rhetorica ad Herennium*), the stage was set not only for the pursuit of a discourse that would harmonize the interests of poetics with those of euphonious prose style (the *dictamen prosaicum*), but invest that discourse in the pedagogical initiatives of the Renaissance classroom.

Poetics

Nothing distinguished poetics more, perhaps, during this period of humanism's cultural hegemony than the scope of its aesthetic prerogatives. No longer classed among the restrictive medieval domains of natural and moral sciences, poetry came to assume the panoply of political, rhetorical, scientific, philosophical, artistic, and moral achievement. The texts so often the catalysts of these issues were, for the most part, written in Latin by Italian writers. Girolamo Vida's *De arte poetica* (1527) was, much like Horace's *Ars*, a poem about poetry. Its syncretist focus drew together the various strands of Horatian concern with the exemplarity of the past, the development of a rhetorical system through which literary expression could be imitated and formalized, and the apotheosis of the Poet as intercessor with the Divine. Writers like Fracastoro, Minturno, Scaliger (albeit a Franco-Italian), and Viperano expanded and refined these principles by addressing the poetic text both as macro- and as micro-structure, a composite of elements from a larger artistic vision, yet fashioned around discrete replicable forms and methods. Playing a central role in this incorporative approach to poetry was Julius Caesar Scaliger, whose *Poetices libri septem* (1561) contained the first attempt to formalize literary-critical method as a comparison of spatially juxtaposed texts. The result is a theoretical resonance that transforms the act of literary criticism into a work of transmittal in the profoundest sense.

As writing came to be seen increasingly as a demonstration of artistic effect and a reworking of textual models, imitation began to assume a place both of pedagogical dominance in the Renaissance classroom and of theoretical ascendancy within works and manuals on poetics, namely, with such Latinists as Dolet, Omphalius, Ricci, and Vida. With the canonizing of Petrarch's *Rime sparse* by Pietro Bembo in the early 1500s and by other later commentaries, a vernacular poet was brought into the vanguard of imitative models, taking his place in the pantheon of ancient authors and establishing his exemplary status with respect to later generations of aspiring poets. Petrarchism quickly took root as the predominant poetic discourse of the lyric in Italy, France, and England and frequently drew the reader into the deeper philosophical question of how source texts migrate from their point of origin, appropriated by a contemporary poetic voice. As a full-blown poetic agenda, imitation emerged from the older, more entrenched humanist fascination with *interpretatio* [translation] as a creative activity. Central to the writings of Salutati, Bruni, Manetti, and, later on, of Dolet and Humphrey, translation embraced a notion of language and culture founded on the conviction that a textual past is a replicable artefact. Imitation together with translation referred to activities that address the phrasing, wording, and expressive resources of source and target texts (in rhetorical terms, their *elocutio*). Textual appropriation, however, was not limited to compatibilities of style. With the burst of attention directed at Horace's *Ars poetica* and at the Ciceronian *œuvre* in the early 1500s, the process of 'recovering' a textual past carried with it the prerogative of 'finding' [*invenire*] those larger units of expression in which style functions: the subject-matter or materials of invention. Retrieved so as to promote a new creative project, these materials tended to be viewed as the mechanisms through which new, but not wholly original, subjects are contemporized in the language and culture of the 'inventor'. Eventually, the notion of invention, with its technical allegiance to the fields of rhetoric and dialectic, would assert its autonomy from this restrictive environment by legitimizing imagination as an agent of composition.

The belief in a migration of words [*translatio verborum*] and cultures [*translatio studiorum*] across the medial span of the Middle Ages was arguably the most tenacious principle to shape the complex of cultural, social, psychological, and intellectual forces that came together in the Renaissance classroom. Under humanist tutelage, the same process of textual rediscovery and transmittal that had made philology the authoritative scholarly method in early modern culture led to the equally forceful assumption that schools are primarily in the business of teaching a mastery of discourse and through it a fashioning of selfhood. This assumption, of course, survived largely intact from the pedagogical formats handed down in the mature rhetorical works of Cicero and in Quintilian's *Institutio oratoria*. As a student, to move from the assimilation of rhetoric's technical inventory to the status of practitioner served like no other activity, perhaps, to erase the boundaries between discourse, epistemology, and ontology. To speak was, concurrently, to know, and to know carried with it the assumption of accrued authenticity within the circle of humanist citizenry. With Justus Lipsius, late in the sixteenth century, this development culminated in the presciently neoclassical assertion: 'the style reveals the man'. And so it was that the Renaissance classroom became the primary site for the critical examination and assimilation of literary texts in a process which, in turn, set into play a process of self-awareness, the student absorbed in the critical interrogation of authors whose resonance was amplified through his own power of utterance and identity.

Without the focal place accorded to rhetoric in the Renaissance classroom, it is doubtful whether rhetorical approaches to literary expression could have had such a radical impact on the discourse of poetics. The principal issues shaping literary criticism were invariably those related to the view that texts are vehicles of persuasion. The tendency to view poetic writing as a branch of rhetoric was less a failure to emancipate poetics from the constraints of metre, cadence, and formal structure than it was the means to establishing a critical vocabulary whose versatility would extend with equal ease to prose and poetic genres alike. Indeed, recent thinking has tended to confirm that for the so-called 'grands rhétoriqueurs' distinctions between prose and verse were largely secondary to the goal of uncovering new expressive reserves in speech, of enhancing thought itself through the power of cadence. Instead of pitting the art of 'Second Rhetoric' against mainstream poetics whose sights are fixed on more transcendent poetic issues, the concerns of the 'rhétoriqueurs' could be viewed as part of a gathering critical momentum which, during much of the sixteenth and seventeenth centuries, would seek to create coalitions between levels and modes of style, varieties of cadence, and contexts of ideology. Speakers and writers, inclusive of the literary critic, could be classed politically, philosophically, and theologically by their adopted voice. Concepts of style implied a set of strategic choices which embed aesthetics within the tastes and tendencies of the surrounding culture.

Quite apart from their assignment to a typology of utterance, such terms as 'Attic', 'Asiatic', 'plain', 'middle', and 'grand' tended to reflect, as Debora Shuger confirms in the present volume, the ideological climate in which they had evolved.

To the extent that cadence and euphony were in the service of an imagined audience – a receptor agent responsive to rhetorical effects – it was probably inevitable that the exchange between text and audience (that is, the reader) be seen in terms of its relative authenticity as a creative event. For that event to appear authentic, poetics needed to base the process on the premise that words have the power to make things seem present, to enact a credible fiction. Again, the arts of poetry and prose were poaching here on common ground as *ekphrasis* and a host of other related terms for literary description were reworked from the ancient rhetorical stockpile and used to define the visualizing potential of all utterance, whether poetry or prose. Some of the most eloquent literary theorists of the age (Scaliger, Castelvetro, Dolce, Tasso, Sidney, Dryden), not to mention an array of art theoreticians (Alberti, Dufresnoy, Félibien, Bellori, de Piles), all grappled with the prescriptive analogy between painting and poetry, although, like so many other instances of Renaissance Horatian criticism, this was based on a profound misreading of the *Ars*. In the case of Sir Philip Sidney's *An apology for poetry*, this analogy was at the centre of a searching reappraisal of aesthetic conception and the projection of mental images on to a written surface. The noetic power of poetry, its capacity for making palpable the products of inner contemplation, was thought to transfigure the very environment of literature, enabling it to bring the audience into direct communion with visible truths. And never far away was the injunction underpinning all rhetorical poetics: the call to stir emotions. It was precisely this concern with the affective impact of literature that gave rise to some of the period's most thoughtful meditations on the mechanisms of reader response, none of these more compelling than that surrounding Longinus and sublimity.

There is little question that what contributed most to the Renaissance text's air of modernity was its preoccupation with the status of the reader as the recipient of the literary utterance. The analogy with the orator/audience in the rhetorical tradition was paramount in helping articulate the dynamics between writer and reader during the early modern period. What made this analogy especially meaningful, however, was not its mere allusiveness as an image, but its emergence from the most ponderous typology of utterance ever devised: the rhetorical *paideia*. As a way of viewing and articulating the world, rhetoric depended on the resources of classification. Both at the point of delivery and of reception a statement was shaped by the particular strategy invested in its presentation, its formal arrangement according to the *genera dicendi*. Transposed to the realm of literature, rhetorical formalism, therefore, provided Renaissance theoreticians with a structural framework around which to build a tax-onomy of genre or, as it is frequently called, of 'kind'.

The perils of addressing questions of genre loom conspicuously over any survey of Renaissance literary criticism. The period's unflagging energy for dipping back into ancient inventories of 'kind' (whether Aristotelian, Horatian, or conventionally rhetorical), coupled with its inventive verve and tendency to amplify and conflate the recipes for generic types, makes any enquiry into genre-systems, at least in surveys like the present one, an unsatisfactory, if not risky, undertaking. Alastair Fowler has argued convincingly that generic categories are under the continual stress of modification from the very works which purport to mime their configurations in the first place.[7] This lack of fixity is inherent in the nomenclature itself, prompting a recent thinker on genre to refer to the 'statut bâtard' [hybrid status] of generic terminology.[8] Terms collude with the very history of the forms they propose to designate, thereby ensuring that 'kind' is, at best, an acculturated norm, what Rosalie Colie calls '*ideas* of form, established by custom and consensus'.[9]

Clearly, the attempt at genre coverage in the present survey is not intended to be exhaustive, nor could it be. Colie's analysis of the elasti-city of generic schemes during the Renaissance – what she terms their 'inclusionism' – amply justifies the more limited coverage given here to the major generic groupings. Such uncanonical forms as Rabelaisian narrative, for instance, resist formulation precisely because they represent intern-ally a dispersion of the normative, a multiplication and intermingling of generic 'kinds'. The forms represented here, on the other hand, constitute for the most part the prevailing classes of literary structure, though the genres of dialogue and essay are arguably uncanonical in their resistance to methodology. What is especially striking about this coverage is the way the various studies tend to corroborate Colie's assertion that the Renaissance genre-system 'offers us not a second world but an array of ways to look at the real world, offers us a special way to make of culture a *common place*'.[10] In the lyric, many of the same ontological questions implicit in the rhetorical *paideia* – questions having to do with identity, subjectivity, the shaping of individual consciousness through interpretation of the physical world – extend its versatility as a literary form. The epic, though ostensibly derived from Aristotelian patterns, gradually found

---

[7] Alastair Fowler, *Kinds of literature: an introduction to the theory of genres and modes* (Cambridge, MA: Harvard University Press, 1982), pp. 170–90.

[8] Jean-Marie Schaeffer, *Qu'est-ce qu'un genre littéraire?* (Paris: Seuil, 1989), p. 65.

[9] Rosalie L. Colie, *The resources of kind: genre-theory in the Renaissance*, ed. B. Lewalski (Berkeley: University of California Press, 1972), p. 128.

[10] *Ibid.*, p. 119.

itself by the 1550s absorbed in a process of self-renewal and refinement, with Giovambattista Giraldi Cintio and Giovanni Battista Pigna each endorsing the acculturated value of the romance as against the anachronistic strictures of ancient epic. The very debates to which these efforts gave rise led to searching discussions of the nature of epic and its susceptibility to theoretical formulation.

And nowhere was genre a subject of more protracted dispute than in notions of tragedy, where questions of vernacular appraisal, political and ethical topicality, and the transfiguration of the inner being all grappled with the intersection of ancient rules and contemporary habits of thought. The case of Elizabethan England and the vitality of its dramatic production, however, was not easily contained in any allegiance to theoretical definition or prescriptive technical format. Here, the affective appeal to audience tended to override or at least limit the kinds of theoretical speculation to which continental commentators on tragedy were given, resulting in a genre that reflected the homogeneous expectations of the masses rather than conformity to any critical template. This tendency led inevitably to an indigenous dramatic form whose objectives were centred on the moral, and hence frequently political, interaction of the characters rather than on adherence to an overarching neoclassical design. It is probably a mark of the theoretical vitality of literary 'kind' that few issues were settled in the attempt to canonize definitions. The most telling example of this resilience, it would appear, is that of comedy which, by the time of Molière, had been so thoroughly hybridized that no consensus ever developed over the aesthetic criteria of this genre so indebted to a diverse literary tradition. The English scene once again accentuates this subversion of structural uniformity by promoting such dramatic amalgams as the history play and the tragicomedy.

Other 'kinds' of literature, notably the dialogue and the essay, though for internal reasons conforming less to a stylistic format, were likewise the product of an age that viewed language as a vehicle of discussion. Discussion, in turn, engendered images of competing voice. And while dialogue by the late sixteenth century had all but abandoned its heuristic mediation of truth, the essay ensured that the sustaining principles of dialogue, namely, its open form and spirit of enquiry, would be carried over in the seventeenth century to a new literary form: the art of conversation. At the other end of the literary spectrum were the epigram and emblem, both serving to concentrate the action of truth rather than disperse it, as with the dialogue and essay. Each of these shorter poetic forms, associated as they were with notions of inscribed space and abbreviated truth, tended to highlight the characteristic Renaissance dabbling with mnemotechnic devices and the retrieval of knowledge as a medium of visual presentation. By the seventeenth century the epigram had become one of the principal formats for wit and satire, thereby demonstrating how 'kinds' of literature were sometimes capable of cross-pollination.

Nowhere was such generic permeability more keenly expressed than in the long Renaissance experimentation with prose narrative whose very variety reflected the complex ideological, social, and aesthetic forces both of high and low culture, leading in the seventeenth century to greater formalization and generic self-consciousness together with a drift away from the idealized heroic fiction prevalent in the courtly and epic traditions. The site from which critical speculation on prose fiction reverberated during the period was that of Italy, most especially the work of Boccaccio. In a sense, the scope of Boccaccio's *œuvre*, ranging from his high-minded Latin treatises, moralistic and didactic in tone, to the *Decameron*, escapist in its adoption of rhetoric and aesthetics as ends in themselves, helped set the terms of the literary-critical debate that would invigorate theories of prose fiction in the sixteenth and seventeenth centuries. The litmus test for fiction – doubtless based partly in the rediscovery of Horace's *Ars poetica* and the Peripatetic compromise of the useful and the pleasurable [*utile dulci*] – lay both in its parabolic message and in its affective power as art. Thus, in France, where the home-grown *fabliau* and *exemplum* already hinted at these dual narrative obsessions, assimilation of the *Decameron* was not restricted to its status as escapist literature, but also brought to the work's interpretative history values of moral justification and earnestness. Inevitably, this attempt to reconcile the extremes of fictional artistry and imagination with a sense of fiction as redolent of life and ethical progression led to searching enquiries into truth and verisimilitude as ingredients of longer and shorter prose fiction. Many of these reappraisals were carried out in the prefaces of the chivalric romance (namely, the *Amadis* series) and would assert themselves even more vigorously in seventeenth-century England where, as earlier on in France, they helped adumbrate the political context of civil strife into which the nation had fallen. Both in the French and English contexts, theoretical commentary on the nature of prose fiction would, by the end of the seventeenth century, culminate in greater attention to defining the novel as an increasingly autonomous class of fiction (as distinct, say, from the *nouvelle* and the romance). The latter genres, of course, flourished in Italy throughout the Cinquecento and the Seicento; however, the preponderance of critical writing dates from the Cinquecento. Sharply defined theoretical lines developed both around the *novella* and the *romanzo*, with the former grounding itself in the Aristotelian tradition and the latter in eloquence and a latent Quintilianism. And though the examples of prose romance in the Cinquecento are outnumbered by their poetic counterpart, an independent 'poetics' of romance versatile enough to encompass prose as well as poetry is in place by the end of the sixteenth century. In the case of Spain, its relative cultural isolation during the period resulted in a much more openly self-conscious strain of writing on prose fiction than is the case in England, France, or Italy. A fascination – indeed, obsession – with the affective power of rhetoric gave to such seminal works as Quevedo's *Buscón*, Gracián's *Criticón*, and Cervantes' *Quijote* a subjective edge, structured around the interplay of truth and appearance. As a consequence, these works mark the power of prose fiction to initiate literary-critical discourse with itself, to interpret its generic character through its own narrative process.

Contexts of criticism

Much about literary-critical awareness has to do with the issue of timeliness or, as it was frequently represented in the iconography of the period, of *kairos* and *occasio*, of the moment ripened for action and seizure. Discourse in early Sophist thought was viewed as an event that took place largely in the situational framework of *empeiria* or experience – in a venue of experimentation, as it were. The modern linguistic notion that all utterance emerges from a context of situation is heavily indebted to this view, adopted and refined by Latin rhetoricians and present in a wide array of Renaissance poetic and theoretical settings from early meditations on speech emitted 'from time' [*ex tempore*], notably with Nicolaus Beraldus (1534), to neoclassical concepts of *bienséance*. It is fitting, therefore, that the present survey address those factors that shaped the environment in which critical reflection on literature took place, linking it to encircling socio-political conditions as well as to the intellectual climate.

In Italy, the immediacy of the humanist initiative was most visible, for it was there that the crumbling vestiges of ancient civilization were seen in relationship to the acts of philological archaeology through which that civilization was replenished. This convergence of a recumbent, decaying monumentality and the revitalizing scrutiny of language and historical analysis helped bring to the Italian city-states the values of civic humanism in all its permutations. In this environment, literary-critical scholarship tended to flourish as a tool of civic oligarchy and patronage, a discourse of the academies and schools helping to underwrite the dual commitment of the literary scholar as critic and political *engagé*.

Many of these same conditions were transplanted, in turn, into that most Italian of French Renaissance cities, Lyons, situated at the crossroads of a mercantile culture and an intellectually vigorous élite, yet less constrained by the coercive presence of such institutions as Church and crown. This climate of intellectual ferment, coupled with an energetic printing community and ongoing exposure to Italian humanist thought, made Lyons well suited as a conduit for literary-critical activities, especially those that required the stimulus and imprint of a rival vernacular culture with which to interact. In Paris the air was decidedly more fractious, with the development of a strongly independent humanist community whose influence made its heterodox views seem a direct affront to the entrenched presence of court and university, the latter embodied by that mouthpiece of theological officialdom, the Sorbonne. Nonetheless, this environment also witnessed some of the most compelling literary experimentation of the entire age as the poets of the so-called Pléiade managed so deftly to turn their linguistic and poetic innovation into a project of national scope. The idea of an institutionalized culture, aloof and serene, based in certain shared national aspirations for language and literary scholarship found, however, less receptive ground in Tudor-Stuart London where a mercantilist ethos informed literary and other cultural pursuits. The consequences of this amalgam were far-reaching and creative. Reformist thought, economic prosperity and well-being, and the growth of a mobile merchant class open to learning and to religious reform helped promote an urbane, richly fertile medium for those activities central to the humanist educational agenda. An ideal of easy urbanity, derived in part from Castiglione's Courtier, permeated the range and variety of literary activities, turning the metropolis into a market-place where polite and popular culture found common ground. Free-ranging yet emanating from a single generative centre (metropolitan London), these activities were as noteworthy for their lack of institutional empowerment as their Germanic counterpart was for its affiliation to organized bodies of literary promotion and the corresponding absence of any single generative centre.

As a consequence, German-speaking contexts of literary scholarship tended to reflect the geographical and cultural dispersion of the Holy Roman Empire itself. While humanism was a thriving intellectual enterprise in these areas (as witnessed by such figures as Melanchthon, Camerarius, and Vadianus), its form was largely that of an epistolary community whose literary discussions and activities took place through correspondence. Institutional venues for these activities consisted of the courts (both secular and ecclesiastical), municipal grammar schools, and literary sodalities, the latter developing in the seventeenth century into the so-called language societies, whose aims embraced literary, linguistic, and ethical concerns. Unlike the phenomenon of the French salon, these confraternities tended to be male-dominated and occasionally parochial in their agendas.

In each of these regions of emerging national identity (granted, in the case of Italy and German-speaking Europe, a more retarded process), literary production and criticism were deeply entangled in other sociopolitical developments. Almost without exception literary discourse bore the imprint of the dominant political structure of the society in which it evolved. Patronage and the sustaining environment of mercantilist and courtly life ensured that literature, while viewed as a commodity, would reflect the collusion of a tacit, censorial presence (the patron) with an emancipated poetic voice (the writer). In England, these trends were eventually displaced as literary sponsorship shifted from the court to the country in the late seventeenth century. In France, on the other hand, the court tended to exercise its autarchic role while contributing directly to the emergence of a cultural space (the salon) that stimulated literary criticism in its most elemental form – as an act of discrimination based on the free flow of dialogue. Salon culture embodied the propensity of the age for discussion and conversation, hastening, in turn, the advancement of criticism as a separate, yet presumptive branch of all literary endeavour. Such common features as there were in the socio-political make-up of European culture during the sixteenth and seventeenth centuries all tended to centre on the production and marketing of the literary text. More than any other factor, perhaps, the printing-press transformed the environment and culture of reading on an international scale, first in Germany in the mid-fifteenth century followed quickly in Italy and the rest of Europe, where it became a humanist archaeological tool by the 1470s. Accordingly, textual editing became early on its chief beneficiary, but as entrepreneurial instincts began to take hold, the momentum for industrialization and technological advance accelerated not only the democratization of the reading public, but the marketing strategies required to reach that public. The result was the creation of a book trade whose rapid empowerment as a vehicle of social change exposed it both to institutional regulation and to often strident engagement with the voices of ideological and, especially where biblical scholarship was concerned, literary-critical dissent.

Voices of dissent

These conflicts were played out along a wide-ranging front, but one located within the period's sense of critical separation from its own past. The most primitive, if not the most radical, of these dissenting voices was that which sought to question the prevailing cultural and linguistic authority of Latinism. Together with his humanist peers, an otherwise committed Latinist like Lorenzo Valla promoted a view of language which, while it advertised the structural monolith of Latinity and its grammar, also recognized language systems as inherently dynamic. By implication, this view enabled vernacular tongues to describe their component parts as participating in the generative growth of all language, and thus to gain enhanced prestige. And with vernacular linguistic prestige came not only audible claims on behalf of the 'mother' tongue, but even more significantly, the authorizing of a literary culture produced and nurtured entirely within the vernacular idiom.

These issues permeating the debates over Latinity and vernacularism – were classical models to be imitated or transcended? – surfaced openly in the early 1500s when the so-called Ciceronians (among them such writers as Castellesi and Delminio) championed the *tempus perfectum* of their namesake as the exemplary age of style not only for all good Latinists, but for the fledgling vernacular culture bent on emulating as well as distancing itself from an admired source. Ciceronianism, however, remained a vulnerable target for the heterodox artillery well into the seventeenth century and beyond. The voices of dissent pressed relentlessly in on the forces of formalism and stylistic/philosophical orthodoxy embodied by Cicero and, to an even greater extent, by Aristotle. The assault was strenuous, initiated by Poliziano in the late 1400s and carried on by Erasmus as the champion of linguistic *facilitas*. With such intellectual giants as Vives and Ramus the theatre of battle was widened to encompass the dominant intellectual superstructure of late medieval scholasticism and, more pointedly, the legacy of Aristotle. It was a battle which, ironically, replayed polemical positions with respect to 'ancient' and 'modern' writers already well rehearsed during the era of the Ciceronian *tempus perfectum*. But it was those very heterodox voices of the sixteenth-century humanist community (Erasmus, Vives, and Ramus among others) which helped reformulate the terms of deeply felt cultural antithesis that were embedded in the proto-modern positions of vernacular writers and served to foreshadow the later quasi-institutionalized debates of neoclassical society and the 'Quarrel of Ancients and Moderns'.

In some ways, it could be argued that the Ciceronian position with its advocacy of philosophical and rhetorical orthodoxy exemplified a linguistic and intellectual community in which, traditionally, authority, and thereby legitimacy, were conferred only on the male voice. Access to the educational system which served as the institutional validator of literary-critical discourse was a privilege that largely excluded the participation of women. Thus, with few exceptions, literary criticism in early modern Europe tended to limit women's role in the theoretical dialogue on letters until well into the seventeenth century. To be sure, the so-called *querelle des femmes* made it possible to focus, in France at least, on representations of women in the entrenched misogyny of male writing, but it did little to advance the authority of women as practitioners and critics of letters. With the rise of salon culture in the seventeenth century, however, and its promotion of the art and rhetoric of conversation, women were accorded a venue within which they could participate fully and equally in literary-critical dialectic. From this context there emerged, with such notable figures as Marguerite Buffet and Madeleine de Scudéry, a limited attempt to include women in the circle of those who wrote about literature, more especially the genre of the novel. It is thus not unreasonable to view this growing critical participation as a direct consequence of the heterodox climate of late medieval society which initiated the long, querulous challenge to male cultural authority and its representation of women. This challenge culminated in the 1620s in the authoritative work of Marie de Gournay, whose *Egalité des hommes et des femmes* (1622) recognized the creative potential and investment of women in the enterprise of letters.

Structures of thought

The tradition of liberal humanism that would eventually shape the intellectual currents of eighteenth-century European thought derived, with few exceptions, from the Renaissance capacity for reinvigorating the philosophical codes through which antiquity had interpreted its world. These codes were instrumental in helping to promote literary discourse as a critical language steeped in the prevailing thought structures of the age.

The most pervasive of these intellectual endeavours was unquestionably that of Neoplatonism, fashioned largely by a fifteenth-century Florentine intelligentsia led by Marsilio Ficino and Giovanni Pico della Mirandola and, through the poetic vitality of its myths, validating the power of the literary imagination. As a philosophico-theological movement, Neoplatonism was rooted in cosmological and metaphysical issues of wide scope, but ones which engaged poets and philosophers alike in confronting the informing Idea behind all contemplative activity. The forces of Aristotelian formalism were once again finding themselves arraigned, this time by a cluster of aesthetic and philosophical concepts whose expression was non-systematic, linked to such intuitional themes as ascent towards the Divine. Through this ascent to ever higher levels of poetic and philosophical cognition, the creative potential of poetry was imagined to lie in its cosmographic magnitude and capacity for embodying the physical and ethereal harmonies of the universe. To the extent that such visions of the poet seemed to portray him as a reader and interpreter of the 'book of nature', it was inevitable that an alliance be forged between the interests of literature and those of Natural Philosophy. But as the so-called 'new science' led to the kinds of rationalist, geometrical, and empirical constructions that we have come to associate with such figures as René Descartes, the practice of poetry, and, indeed, of literature in general, was no longer viewed as preparatory to the study of physical laws and scientific method. Quite the contrary, by the second half of the seventeenth century, the domains of received language and an ascendant symbolic language like mathematics were already marked by divergent interests and objectives.

The trend towards scientific cosmographic poetics in the late sixteenth century was not entirely unconnected to the emerging revival and re-examination of classical philosophical movements. Lucretius, after all, was known not only for his interpretation of the 'nature of things' and their reduction to philosophical and scientific intelligibility, but for transcribing that intelligibility in poetic images. In fact, it was Denys Lambin's authoritative commentary on the *De rerum natura* (1563–4) that would foster the growing interest among Renaissance authors in composing scientific didactic poetry. Lucretius's rediscovery of Epicureanism as a philosophical system, despite the disapproving scrutiny of orthodox Christian thinkers, was eventually ratified by a succession of mid-seventeenth-century writers, all bent on reclaiming the scientific and ethical integrity of Lucretian thought and its correlation with the emerging mechanistic science of Galileo, Descartes, and Hobbes. In more literary contexts Lucretius's luminous transcriptions of classical myth held immediate appeal for the Pléiade poets, though philosophical doctrine, when it did surface in their work, was frequently little more than a distillation of such well-worn clichés as *carpe diem* and *parvo vivere*. In the case of Stoicism, a similar rehabilitation was under way with powerful voices like those of Justus Lipsius, Francisco de Quevedo, and Guillaume Du Vair engaged in searching out fundamental compatibilities between Stoic and Christian doctrine. Framed in its own distinctive discourse, Neostoicism, with its tersely phrased periods and pointed prose style, came to embody the underlying harmony of an ethical system endowed with distinctive resources of expression and utterance. It is no doubt a measure of the integrity of these philosophical systems (Stoicism and Epicureanism) that it was virtually impossible to separate their structures of thought from the language through which those structures resonated. Their distinctiveness as ethical schemes derived from their ability to make a philosophy of language responsive to codes of behaviour; discourse was empowered to confer identity and to shape particular views of the world through a corresponding grammar. On the religious front, Calvinism and Jansenism each developed a particular discourse that had both ontological and institutional consequences, embracing both the scrutiny of self and the establishment of communal exclusivity (Geneva and Port-Royal) as the venue of faith within a postlapsarian world. Once again, both movements would be known by the prevailing resonance of their own rhetoric.

Neoclassicism

The conviction that ontology and discourse form a unitary process, though explicitly and implicitly supported in most of the philosophical and theological enquiries of the sixteenth and seventeenth centuries, was not exclusively a speculative problem. It spoke, perhaps, more emphatically to the entire repertory of literary-critical issues and conventions which have been grouped under the somewhat imprecise heading of 'neoclassicism'. The current survey, it should be stressed, has resisted the temptation to engage in any taxonomical housekeeping. Rather, it has assembled five ostensibly disparate perspectives on neoclassical values as they relate to literary-critical problems: Cartesian aesthetics, rhetoric in neoclassical France, combative classicism in England, principles of judgement, and Longinian sublimity. What links these perspectives is the underlying assumption that neoclassical discourse reflects not so much a codification of conditions and norms as the isolation of a single text within the unstable time line of language and culture. Thus words, texts, and those who produce them are emblems of their own transience, what James Boyd White refers to as 'the reconstitution of culture in a relation shared between speaker and audience'.[11] This is not to say that the pursuit of the normative and the conventional was not a neoclassical concern; most certainly it was. Rather, it was the focus of that pursuit on the exemplarity of ancient models (aesthetic, ethical, stylistic) together with the imitative conversion of those models into the temporizing contexts of early modern society that seemed to expose the notion of classical 'purity' to the more relativistic stresses of taste, custom, appropriateness, judgement, and decorum. In a word, neoclassicism could not escape a struggle that seemed to pit rationalism against what Vladimir Jankélévitch called 'le pathos d'incomplétude' ['the emotion of the inconclusive'], the nostalgic sense that time is fragmentation and thus immune to reductionist schemes.[12] One of the most intriguing aspects of neoclassical thought lay in its ability to meld quite comfortably a state of fixed values (the normative world of classical antiquity and its codes) with the shifting time-line of the present in which norms seemed to teeter on the brink of their own ineffability, if not their eventual extinction (the *nescio quid*, the *je ne sais quoi*, and the *presque rien*). The Cartesian and Pascalian visions each experimented with these alternatives, the one systematic, reductive, rationalist, seeking general truths, the other indeterminist, drawn to metaphysical disproportions, anguished, unable to embrace totalities.

In aesthetic terms, the pursuit of beauty was certified in the neoclassical era as a return to the prescriptive certainties of classical antiquity. In this sense, it became easy to articulate a philosophical doctrine of art that ascribed fixed paradigms and dogmas to the process of artistic creation.

---

[11] James Boyd White, *When words lose their meaning: constitutions and reconstitutions of language, character, and community* (Chicago: University of Chicago Press, 1984), p. 4.
[12] Vladimir Jankélévitch, *Le je-ne-sais-quoi et le presque-rien*, 3 vols. (Paris: Seuil, 1980), vol. 1, *La manière et l'occasion*, pp. 11–12.

Instances of such aesthetic dogmatism are legion, linked as they are to the pursuit of structural harmonies and rationalist patterns of thought. Yet, even at the generative heart of neoclassical rationalism itself – namely, Cartesian method – an obsession for deducing the underlying laws, for instance, of cadence and euphony (in music and poetry) and their effect on the receptor mechanisms shifted eventually towards an intimation of disarray, a *non plus ultra* beyond which attempts at quantitative measurement found themselves disabled. In letters to Marin Mersenne in late 1629 and early 1630 Descartes seemed to hedge his earlier views on measurable aesthetics with a more relativistic, perhaps deepened, sense of the temporizing qualities of experience, taste, and memory as they relate to the fashioning of beauty. Quintilian's atechnical *alogos tribe* in Book x, it is recalled, refers to speech that is generated from a temporal moment [*ex tempore*] and as such occurs at the instant of emancipation from the quantifiable technical agenda of his first nine books. Its authenticity is measured by its timeliness, its calibration to the particular circumstances of a particular moment and a particular place. In France, the pursuit of an adequate discourse for neoclassicism took shape around the incursive presence of rhetorical ideals in all aspects of social, intellectual, and aesthetic engagement. Rhetoric – arguably that most temporizing of arts – aspired to be the vehicle of a rationalist programme of cognition; its limitations (as also its aesthetic potential) lay in the fact that its taxonomy of forms was subject to the transformations of the here and now, what ancient rhetoricans called the *empeiria* or the experiential. Discourse of the *empeiria* was a discourse of finite persuasion, of an audience brought together in a forensic moment; it was thus revelatory only to the extent that the circumstantial is revelatory, only within that cluster of dispositions that comprise taste, appropriateness, probability, and present experience. The aesthetics of the *je ne sais quoi* served only to validate this transitoriness. An estrangement between rationalist thought and the activities of poetry and eloquence seemed unavoidable and it ultimately came with the latter's demotion as mere products of the imagination by Bernard Le Bovier de Fontenelle in 1688.

On the English scene, these issues were played out with far greater verve, if in a less philosophically integrating fashion than were their continental equivalents. Lacking the deep-rooted institutional framework of French neoclassicism, English literary-critical experiments tended to emulate the classical past without the pretence of recovering a monolithic inventory of codes and rules on which to pattern literary achievement. Indeed, a concept like 'imagination', so reviled in the purist aesthetics of French classicism, seemed to open the door for critics like Puttenham and Sidney to integrate a sense of aesthetic regulation with intrinsic poetic gifts of insight and visualization. With Ben Jonson, the prescriptive structures of classical antiquity performed only limited service to the formulation of new codes, allowing him to champion aesthetic doctrines that were shaped by the transitoriness of present-day custom and convention. To a society whose legal system was rooted in principles of customary law – of non-statutory, convention-based practice – aesthetic norms and rules were viewed, predictably, as part of an evolutionary process rather than as an unassailable classical legacy. It was not surprising, therefore, that Miltonian poetics, though in many ways anti-conventional, should validate the mission of the Poet from within a body of thought (namely, Ciceronian rhetoric) based in the immediacy of forensic performance and charismatic engagement with the reader/audience. If nothing else, the arena of the *empeiria* was agonistic and conflictual; it predicated rhetorical appropriateness on the rhetorician's personal vision of what is suitable, a posture tending to isolate him in his mission and promoting the value of aesthetic irregularity which was to be canonized among later English literary critics.

It is now conventionally held that Milton's views of a poet-prophet may owe much to his familiarity with Longinus's treatise *On the Sublime*. If, indeed, they do, they would help explain Milton's connection with a poetic tradition that was not only charismatic, but disjunctive in the way it seemed occasionally to work at cross purposes with neoclassical formalism. Like Quintilian's commitment to a transcendence of prescriptive rhetoric in Book x – the Longinian thunderbolt, as it were – Miltonian aesthetics seemed to locate rapture within a discourse of separation, ravishment, and transfiguration of the poet/orator. In its assault on the deepest recesses of the artistic temperament, such aesthetics embodies the very premise of disjuncture on which the present summary was initiated. For an era self-consciously aware of its own critical distinctiveness, Longinian poetics brought the discourse of criticism during the period in question to an appropriately new critical moment, legitimizing the claims of insight and inspiration. The immediacy of this literary-critical moment was enriched through the awareness that the criticism and interpretation of literature is at bottom a dialogue between shifting aesthetic values and the still luminous literary achievement of classical antiquity.

*

The present volume seeks to encompass those issues which, for more than two hundred years from the end of the Middle Ages to the beginning of the eighteenth century, helped rekindle and refine the literary-critical legacy of the classical past. I am deeply indebted to Ian McFarlane for the part he has played in helping me to organize the array of topics in a way that highlights their linkage and underlying allegiance to the literary-critical continuum during this period of great creative energy and significance.

For their guidance and scholarly intuition at crucial stages of the project, my heartfelt thanks go to Ilona Bell, Hugh M. Davidson, Alastair Fowler, Anthony Grafton, Paul Holdengräber, Jill Kraye, John D. Lyons, John F. Reichert, David L. Rubin, and Wesley Trimpi. For their patient, informed, and diplomatic assistance in countless aspects of the editorial, development, and production process, I thank Linda Bree, Josie Dixon, Terence Moore, Camilla Erskine, and Adam Swallow, all of the Cambridge University Press. For their gifts of sight and insight at the stages of editing and indexing, I am deeply grateful respectively to Ann Lewis and Barbara Hird. For her careful and attentive assistance during an early phase of the editing, I thank Diana Elvin. In the final months of preparation, Walter J. Komorowski and Rebecca Ohm Spencer of the Sawyer Library, Williams College, and John Logan of the Princeton University Library provided invaluable technical help in clearing up lingering bibliographical questions. And to Marjorie Allen who shared at a crucial juncture in the collaborative effort that produced the index, I also express my thanks.

My gratitude goes to the President and Trustees of Williams College for their support over the years and to Francis C. Oakley for his unswerving endorsement of this project and constant encouragement, not to mention the quality and depth of his scholarly judgement which, in places, has left its mark. To Will and Harriet Adsit, the benefactors of the Willcox B. and Harriet M. Adsit Professorship of International Studies, I acknowledge fondly their great generosity and unqualified support of humanistic studies. To my wife, Victoria, whose gifts of recall and insight have served on countless occasions to prompt my own reflection, my thanks are immeasurable.

To each of the contributors to the present volume I owe special recognition for their signal co-operation, for their patience and unstinting good cheer during the long pauses, and for the illuminating way in which they have brought their collective expertise to such a complex and wide-ranging sweep of literary-critical issues. This achievement bears witness, above all, to their distinction both as scholars and critics and to their shared commitment to the value of the undertaking.

Finally, for their gracious and unflagging support in helping to guide this project through the complexities of the editorial process towards a successful conclusion, I offer my profound, though somehow inadequate, appreciation to Peter Brooks and Kevin Taylor.

One final coda. The reader of this volume will no doubt be struck by the recurrent indebtedness of so many contributors to Bernard Weinberg's *A history of literary criticism in the Italian Renaissance* and to his pioneering editions of the principal critical treatises of the Cinquecento. Few bodies of literary analysis ever earn the lasting tribute of monumentality, but surely none is more deserving than Weinberg's study and editions. The luminosity of his scholarship has not dimmed over the years and, as this volume attests, continues to invigorate critical dialogue and bring us back to fundamental theoretical issues about great writing. It is arguable whether the present work could ever have ripened to its own critical moment without such scholarly precedence.

Reading and interpretation:
an emerging discourse of poetics

Theories of language

Richard Waswo

The Renaissance – as the name of a cultural movement and a period – enjoys the still-lasting distinction of self-creation. Not since Athena sprang full-grown from the forehead of Zeus (or Sin from Lucifer's, in Milton's version) has an epoch so self-consciously defined itself, along with and against the preceding one, for all posterity. The humanists' cultural self-flattery was of course expanded and intensified in the later nineteenth century by Jakob Burckhardt, whose particular praises of the artistic, idealistic, and individualistic energies of the period continue to command allegiance and stimulate debate today.[1] Most periods are obliged to make do with what posterity makes of *them* – no contemporaneous residents ever labelled themselves 'antique', or 'medieval' – or get designated merely by the decimal tyranny of the calendar (the Mauve Decade; the twelfth century) or by the dynastic accident of a long reign (Victorian England; Carolingian France). Other periods may *try* to name themselves, as our own seeks to call itself 'postmodern', only to produce continual dispute over the contents of the label, and the additional irony that its inventor (Jean-François Lyotard) did not use it as an exclusive 'period' designation.

But no such disputation or irony ever seemed to afflict the earlier generation of Italian humanists (from Petrarch through Leonardo Bruni and Coluccio Salutati to Poggio Bracciolini and Lorenzo Valla) who decided that they were the midwives of the 'rebirth' of a classical culture incontestably superior to that of their own time and place. In their manifold efforts to make this culture live again, in literature, education, and politics, these writers disputed mainly with each other. And although such efforts generated their own forms of doubt and pathos, the confidence that they were worth making remained absolute. Almost no one quarrelled with the enterprise itself, which was to revivify the Golden Age of Republican and/or Imperial Rome. No one joked about this enterprise until it had succeeded so far as to produce its own excesses; and even then, when in 1528 Erasmus subjected the slavish reproduction of Ciceronian prose style to some mild ridicule, he aroused a small tempest of outrage.

[1] See William Kerrigan and Gordon Braden, *The idea of the Renaissance* (Baltimore: The Johns Hopkins University Press, 1989).

The inventors of the 'Renaissance', along with their sixteenth-century heirs, took it and themselves with no small degree of humourless seriousness.

For they were embarked on a kind of crusade, to recover and repossess a part of (what they were newly defining as) the cultural and political past. The crusade was focused, from first to last, on language: the purification of classical Latin from barbarous, 'medieval' accretions; the establishment of complete, correct, and 'authentic' classical texts, including especially those in ancient Greek, a language unknown to the Western 'Middle Ages' (and to Petrarch); and the constant production of grammars, rhetorics, editions, commentaries, and translations of all kinds that were the pedagogical vehicles for these aims and the insurance of their continuation. The humanists were, famously, philologists, and their acute attention to linguistic forms and usages had ultimately revolutionary consequences in the conceptualizing of three related but distinct branches of Western thought: history, religion, and philosophy. The first two revolutions were achieved, and constitute part of our present modernity; the third remained merely proposed, a challenge that awaited our own age to become as controversial as it was then.

History as the radical discontinuity between the present and the past was what emerged from the humanist observation of the differences between classical and medieval Latin – hence the Occident's still standard periodization of itself into the ancient, the medieval, and the modern. From the focus on the changes in the vocabulary and grammar of Latin grew a wider awareness of changes in the very institutions of Western culture: its legal systems, its government, its Church. Philology thus produced modern historicism, a move towards long-term structural and causal explanations for the discrete events listed in the earlier chronicles of *res gestae* – 'drum and trumpet history', in the words of one of the best studies of this transformation.[2] The textual passions of the humanists, their desire to return *ad fontes* – initially the ancient Greek texts that all the Roman writers knew – also came to focus on the West's most sacred text, renewed the study of ancient Hebrew, and thus made possible the Protestant Reformation. As conceived by the great reformers, in precise analogy to the humanist recovery and purification of classical texts, their 'revolution' was to be the recovery of the prior and purer practices of the early Christians, purged of the corruptions thereto accreted over the centuries in the Roman Church. The reformers read these practices out of the original languages of the Bible, and made the dissemination, translation, and interpretation of that book into a matter of (eternal) life or death.

---

[2] Donald R. Kelley, *Foundations of modern historical scholarship: language, law, and history in the French Renaissance* (New York: Columbia University Press, 1970), p. 9.

There is a paradox in these two successful revolutions, which will be repeated in the case of the third and aborted one, and which has particular importance for literary criticism. The Renaissance reconceptions of history and of religion were based on the observance of change, first in language, then in various institutional practices. But the aim of the resultant programmes – of Latin pedagogy, of Protestantism, and of literary neoclassicism – was precisely to arrest those observed changes. Change – 'innovation' was the always pejorative English term for it in the sixteenth century – was not generally seen as desirable, even and especially by those who were most concerned to effect it. Revolutions justified themselves, as they usually have since, by a discourse of purgation and return to an idealized prior state of things: the prose of Cicero (not Peter of Spain); the doctrines preached in the New Testament (not those in papal decrees); the composition of epics (not chivalric romances). What was observed could not be approved, except in reverse; the only good change was a change back to something presumably better *because* nearer to the 'sources'. It took a whole century of argument (the seventeenth) to arrive at the notion that change was itself desirable, under the since tyrannical appellation of 'progress'. The decisive step, still, was the distance discovered by the Renaissance between whatever 'sources' were postulated and us, hence the necessity of a 'rebirth'.

And the decisive field of this discovery was the social practice that subtended all forms of culture: language itself, but above all, writing. What had begun in the nostalgic admiration felt by Petrarch and the earliest humanists for both the political and stylistic achievements of the Romans became, by the middle of the fifteenth century, the basis for a philosophical enquiry into language that would constitute the first fully conceptualized alternative to the way it had been regarded since Plato and Aristotle. This challenge was formulated first and most explicitly in the work of Lorenzo Valla. Not incidentally, Valla's best-known achievement today remains his unmasking of the forgery known as the 'Donation of Constantine'.[3] The way in which he demonstrated the falsity of the document, which other contemporaries merely suspected, was a consummation of the historical revolution and a beginning of the philosophical one. Deeply acquainted with the Latin usages of late antiquity, Valla could show that both the diction and the grammar of the purportedly fourth-century document did not exist before the eighth or ninth. The recognition of lexical, grammatical, and morphological change created the discipline of historical philology; the recognition of semantic change produced a new and powerful sense of language itself as a historical phenomenon. The

---

[3] Christopher B. Coleman (trans.), *The treatise of Lorenzo Valla on the Donation of Constantine* (New Haven: Yale University Press, 1922).

written record had its own history, was produced in its own moment; its meanings were not immune from time. It was the distinction of Valla to pursue the implications of this recognition – that language is a social practice that has a history – through his revival of Quintilian's rhetoric and into an attempt to redefine the nature and procedures of philosophy itself.

This proposed (and unconsummated, until this century) revolution in philosophy has been described by its principal diagnostician as the 'deontologizing' of language.[4] This is nothing less than the radical reformulation of the relationship that had been presumed, since Plato and Aristotle (via whom it was long established in scholastic thought), to supply language with meaning: the relation between *res* and *verba*, things and words. The traditional understanding of this relation was that words acquired meaning by standing for things, and it had long been formalized as the referential theory of meaning and the correspondence theory of truth. That is, words have meaning, and propositions are true, if they correspond to (or reflect, or represent) whatever is taken to be pre-existent 'reality' – either concepts in the mind or objects in the world or both together. In the extremest form of this position, taken by medieval speculative grammarians, or *modistae*, the structure of the universe and of the mind are regarded as simply congruent with that of the eight parts of speech; other, and subtler, medieval philosophers found no such automatic correspondence, and disputed at length about exactly how words could stand for things.[5] But that they did so was not a matter of dispute: language could only be seen as making sense, 'signifying', by locating that sense in an a priori ontological order of some sort.

But this kind of order became much more difficult to postulate once the facts of linguistic change became, as they did for Valla, the focus of attention. His catalogue of such changes in the usages of Latin, called the *Elegantiae* (c. 1440), which he reworked and expanded over much of his career, became one of the most influential, frequently reprinted and abridged, textbooks of the period. In it, Valla invents the inductive, descriptive approach to grammar that will become the method of comparative philology in the nineteenth century and of linguistics in the twentieth. That is, he surveys actual usages; he does not prescribe rules, thus reversing the traditional procedure and incurring the bewildered wrath of

[4] Salvatore I. Camporeale, 'Lorenzo Valla, "Repastinatio, liber primus": retorica e linguaggio', in *Lorenzo Valla e l'umanesimo italiano*, ed. O. Besomi and M. Regoliosi (Padua: Antenore, 1986), pp. 217–39.
[5] The first chapter of Martin Elsky, *Authorizing words: speech, writing, and print in the English Renaissance* (Ithaca and London: Cornell University Press, 1989), is a good, concise survey of this material, citing most standard authorities, to which should be added Norman Kretzmann's article on the 'History of semantics', in *The encyclopaedia of philosophy*, ed. Paul Edwards (New York: Macmillan, 1967), vol. VII.

some of his contemporaries, notably Poggio Bracciolini.[6] Most importantly, in this text that virtually defines the humanist programme to recover
the stylistic grace and semantic precision of ancient Latin, Valla regards
the meaning of words as determined not by ontological correspondence,
but by their manifold relations to other words and by their uses in historical contexts.

This practice, itself revolutionary, receives in Valla's most ambitious
philosophical work, extant in three versions (1431–53) but generally
known as the *Dialecticae disputationes*,[7] theoretical analysis and conceptual justification. In the course of a root-and-branch attack on Aristotelian scholasticism (*Dialecticae*, Book 1), Valla submits the venerable
dichotomy of *res* and *verba* to almost total dissolution. Proceeding from
the twin paradoxes that written words are themselves 'things', and that
the word 'thing' can signify any or all things and words, Valla collapses the
entire distinction that allowed meaning to be exiled from language into
some pre-constituted object-world. 'It makes no difference', he writes,
'whether we say, what *is* wood . . . or, what does "wood" . . . *signify*.' He
collapses being into meaning, ontology into semantics – for what the thing
is, is simply what the word means. There is no separate ontological realm
to which words must correspond – for the use of the word constitutes
that realm. So the central philosophical question for Valla becomes 'what
kind of *word* is *x*'? – that is, what work does it do in common usage? This
question elevates the semantic determinant of *consuetudo loquendi*,
which Valla found in Quintilian (and used as a leitmotiv in all his writing),
into a principle which invalidates the referential theory of meaning and
the correspondence theory of truth, a principle that is 'nothing other than
Wittgenstein's "grammar of the word" '.[8] In this radical reconception
of philosophy, language 'is not a sign or copy of pre-extant things', but
rather the cognitive process of concept-formation that identifies those
things in the first place – for Valla 'the second, specifically *human* creation
of the world, the model of reality'.[9]

Such a radical revision of received ideas about what language and philosophy are and do, presented with iconoclastic delight in texts of extreme

[6] Their quarrel on the issue is analysed by Salvatore I. Camporeale, *Lorenzo Valla:
umanesimo e teologia* (Florence: Istituto Palazzo Strozzi, 1972), pp. 180–92. For the text
of the *Elegantiae*, see E. Garin's edition and reprint of the 1540 Basle edition of the *Opera
omnia* (Turin: Bottega d'Erasmo, 1962), 2 vols.

[7] All the versions are now consultable in the critical edition of Gianni Zippel, *Laurentii
Valle repastinatio dialectice et philosophie*, 2 vols. (Padua: Antenore, 1982). The version
most circulated in the period was that in Valla's 1540 *Opera omnia*.

[8] Camporeale, 'Repastinatio', p. 233. Other parallels between the language philosophies of
Valla and the later Wittgenstein are noted by Richard Waswo, *Language and meaning in
the Renaissance* (Princeton: Princeton University Press, 1987), pp. 103–4.

[9] Hanna-Barbara Gerl, *Rhetorik als Philosophie: Lorenzo Valla* (Munich: W. Fink, 1974),
p. 65.

difficulty, did not fail in Valla's time, in Wittgenstein's, and in our own, to generate often vehement controversy. More important, however, than the debates then or now about the nature and validity of Valla's efforts, are the historical consequences of his assault on the assumed and ancient relation between *res* and *verba* that made the latter but the representational shadows of the former. Though Valla's revolution in philosophy itself remained only posited,[10] his practice of interpreting texts, enormously diffused and influential through the agency of the *Elegantiae*, provided a working model of how language conveys meaning without corresponding to some ontology. And this working model established as practice the fundamental humanist opposition to the scholastics, which consisted in regarding language as 'a cultural artifact rather than an abstract philosophical instrument'.[11] The largest consequence, in short, of the challenge posed to the old *res/verba* relation, both by Valla's explicit theoretical assault and the implicit habit of treating usage and history as semantic determinants, was simply that it could no longer be merely assumed. Having been denied, it had to be (and endlessly was) reasserted. The scholastics decontextualized language, removing it from its actual existence in society and time in order to make it a more transparent sign of a prior ontology. Valla deontologized language, in order to replace it in the actual social contexts of its history and use, finding its meaning precisely in this use, and not in some postulated elsewhere. Most subsequent humanists did both: appropriating Valla's practices (and his tastes), and yet insisting on the ancient conception that these practices contradicted.

The contradictions are apparent in many sixteenth-century grammarians who follow what one scholar calls a 'mixed approach' to their subject: on the one hand, they analyse it in the humanist way as a semantic determinant, treating *verba* as meaningful without recourse to *res*; on the other hand, they continue the scholastic way of classifying the universe 'with a one-to-one correspondence between names and things'.[12] Almost any writer on language in the sixteenth century will exhibit some degree of oscillation between conceiving it explicitly as referential and treating it implicitly as constitutive of its own meanings. But referential to exactly what, and exactly how? These problems were inherent from the beginning in the whole Platonic/Aristotelian postulation of separate realms, *res* and *verba*, that had somehow to be linked; the nature of the link, and just what

---

[10] It was understood neither then nor now, as Camporeale (*Umanesimo e teologia*, p. 169) observed. No account of it, for example, save a brief defence by Lisa Jardine (p. 179) of his innovative dialectical procedure of examining the 'grammar' of words, is to be found in *The Cambridge history of Renaissance philosophy*, ed. C. B. Schmitt *et al.* (Cambridge: Cambridge University Press, 1988).

[11] Elsky, *Authorizing words*, p. 36.

[12] G. A. Padley, *Grammatical theory in western Europe, 1500–1700: the Latin tradition* (Cambridge: Cambridge University Press, 1976), pp. 30–9.

it was with, furnished the central arguments between the medieval realists and nominalists, and were the entire preoccupation of the *suppositio* theorists. Along came Valla to abolish the separation and the theoretical need for a link, and the new discipline of historical philology to find the meaning of words in contexts of use. Here, of course, no *final* determination of meaning was possible; it could only be interpreted and reinterpreted in the endless chain of glosses on glosses evoked by Montaigne in 'De l'expérience'.[13] Final, determinate, and unchanging significance was what the old correspondence theory promised (no matter that it had and has still eluded fulfilment), and the desire for this seemed to intensify in the seventeenth century as a direct result of its having been gravely and continually threatened, first by humanism and second by the Reformation, in the preceding century and a half.

The intensity of the desire may be gauged by two powerful forms of resurgent interest in reasserting the old view; only now, after the threat, it required argument of another sort. One such sort had long existed in the mystical speculations of the Neoplatonic and hermetic traditions, which found ancient Egyptian hieroglyphs to be allegorical of the structure of the universe. Similarly, and more directly relevant to the embattled study of Scripture mandated by the Protestant Reformation, the cabbalistic tradition could find the whole world symbolically encoded in the twenty-two consonants of the Hebrew alphabet. The prestige of the latter was enhanced for many by identifying it with the language of Adam, whose naming of the animals (Genesis 2: 19–20) was almost universally regarded as a perfect form of ontological correspondence, since, as one English commentator put it in 1608, 'names were given at the first according to the severall properties and nature of creatures'.[14] During the sixteenth century, Johann Reuchlin, Henry Cornelius Agrippa, Guillaume de Salluste du Bartas, and Alexander Top were among the promoters of Hebrew as the origin of all languages (now, after Babel, all corrupted) and the perfect, perhaps recoverable, model of the intrinsic connection between words and things.[15] Here was one way to reassert (if not to explain) the connection that kept words the infallible signs of the essential nature of things: it was ordained by God. The trouble was, like Eden, it was since lost, and so required rather daunting processes of restoration, available to initiates only after years of study.

Facing this problem, and sharing this desire for an ultimate guarantee that language conformed to reality, some seventeenth-century speculators decided it would be simpler just to invent a language – that is, a sign-system

[13] Michel de Montaigne, *The complete essays*, trans. D. M. Frame (Stanford: Stanford University Press, 1958), pp. 815–18.
[14] Quoted by Waswo, *Language and meaning*, pp. 284–5.
[15] These writers and others are reviewed by Elsky, *Authorizing words*, pp. 139–46.

– that would, infallibly, do so. Hence the various proposals for a 'universal character', some kind of transparent and unambiguous hieroglyphics that would encode once and for all everything in the world. To do this, of course, required that everything in the world be conceptually classified. The extent to which this new endeavour (which was pursued sporadically until the end of the eighteenth century) was the last gasp of the old scholastic assumption that *verba* stood for *res* is manifest in the fact that the classifications made in the fullest proposals 'were but emended versions of the logical categories of Aristotle'.[16] These, regarded as the given order of reality, were what the invented graphic notations would represent – clearly and universally, by analogy with numerals and algebraic equations. Thus the lost link between *res* and *verba* once ordained by God might be reforged by men, repairing the ruins of Babel. The motivation of this project, the extent to which it was made necessary by the whole humanist insistence on language as a socio-historical product, is stated by its best-known exemplar, Bishop John Wilkins. The problem, as he sees it, is precisely the fact of history: it is that 'Letters and Languages' were not invented by 'Rules of Art', but instead were all derived from some original, 'or else, in a long tract of time, have, upon several emergencies, admitted various and *casual alterations*; by which means they must be liable to manifold defects and imperfections'.[17] The defects are these: polysemy, metaphors, idioms, synonyms, grammatical irregularities, differences between orthography and pronunciation – in short, all the features that make natural languages natural, which had largely furnished the subject-matter of humanist rhetoric and philology, and had been everywhere at issue in all the arguments the Renaissance had produced about translation and biblical interpretation. Wilkins and his ilk wished to end the wrangling in the most traditional way, by firmly reattaching words to the order of things, which would give them fixed and final meaning. But ordinary words were, now, seen as hopeless for this purpose, and so were abandoned in quest of a sign-system that would obey rules and correspond forever to the order of reality.

Such projects, of course, came to nothing; but in the poignancy of their desire to escape the human world of society and time, they recall Wittgenstein's sadness at the end of the *Tractatus*, where, after doing at a higher level of abstraction pretty much what Wilkins was seeking – laying down the conditions of a symbolic system that would clearly record what is the case in the world – he concluded that most of the human world could not

[16] James Knowlson, *Universal language schemes in England and France 1600–1800* (Toronto: University of Toronto Press, 1975), p. 101. This work is a complete and cogent survey of the field.
[17] *An essay towards a real character and a philosophical language* (London: Samuel Gellibrand and John Martin, 1668), p. 19.

thus be spoken about.[18] Reasserting the correspondence of *res* and *verba* in mystical hieroglyphs or in an invented, rationally transparent, graphic code did not do the job. The other seventeenth-century form of the same reassertion, however, had quite apparently spectacular success. This was nothing less than empirical science. Francis Bacon's famous analysis of the 'Idols' that prevented our accurately knowing the world had included the same kind of objections to the deficiencies in natural languages remarked by Wilkins.[19] But Bacon was not thereby seduced into the invention of an artificial language to do what natural ones failed to; his own *abecedarium naturae* is a purely heuristic metaphor, which, he insists, 'should by no means . . . be received for true and fixed division of things. For this would be to profess that we know the things which we inquire; since no one can divide things truly who has not a full knowledge of their nature'.[20] For Bacon, there is not any *given* order of nature precisely because it remains to be discovered by the great instauration of the experimental method it was his business to promote. Since we do not know this order yet, we cannot possibly devise a language that will refer to it. Bacon's whole programme, of course, is predicated on the absence of correspondence between language, the mind, and reality, and the whole aim of the programme is to restore it. The mind is to be purged of its errors, and natural language to be pruned of all its misleading figurative concepts and expressions, so that, as the cumulative result of whole communities of enquirers, a gradual and correct description of the world will emerge. As one scholar observes, the Royal Society will take on this necessarily never-ending 'task of maintaining the correspondence between word and thing'.[21] And just this task will also be accepted by Hobbes and Locke.

Considered with respect to the theory of language, the Renaissance, often regarded as the birthplace of linear, progressive modernity, seems rather to make a great circle, ending pretty much where it began, triumphantly reasserting the ancient referential view against all the challenges to it that had arisen. Valla's philosophy and the humanist discovery of time in the usages of Latin had radically historicized language, finding its meaning in its social uses and not in its referents. The seventeenth century, both at its margins (of mystical speculation) and in its mainstream (empirical science and rationalist philosophy) reontologized language with a vengeance. Only the ontology was different (in the mainstream) – no longer an a priori

---

[18] Ludwig Wittgenstein, *Tractatus logico-philosophicus* (London: Kegan Paul, Trench, Trubner, 1933), § 7.

[19] Francis Bacon, *The advancement of learning*, ed. G. W. Kitchin (London: Dent, 1915), pp. 132–4; *Novum organum*, vol. I, pp. 39–44, 59–60, in *Works*, ed. J. Spedding, R. L. Ellis, and D. D. Heath, 14 vols. (London: Longmans, 1857–74), vol. IV, pp. 53–5, 60–2.

[20] *Works*, vol. V, p. 210.   [21] Elsky, *Authorizing words*, p. 179.

order made visible in grammar, but an order to be painstakingly discovered that languages would have to be disciplined in order to reflect.
The correspondence between *res* and *verba* had been transformed from
an assumption into a purpose, with a concomitant and crucial change in
how its achievement could be recognized. The question of the criteria for
judging when correspondence had occurred hardly arose under the old
assumption (since it was what was assumed), except for medieval logicians
who became thereby obsessed with the forms of the syllogism as the only
reliable (indeed, tautological) guarantor of truth. But the criterion under
the new purpose was unmistakable: a statement about the world corresponded to it when it could successfully predict what would happen in it.
The new criterion was the ability to control material phenomena – to
replicate experiments and accurately predict their outcomes. And this
new enterprise of knowledge as power succeeded, of course, beyond even
Bacon's wildest dreams.

That such success at control was, indeed, a validating criterion for the
correspondence theory of truth has been persuasively denied by some historians of science;[22] but the referential view of language thus presupposed
continues, and continued throughout the Renaissance, to dominate most
formal discussion of literature. For example, the sixteenth century's most
systematic and influential treatment of literary theory, which synthesizes
the period's recovery of and arguments about Aristotelian *mimesis* and
Horatian didacticism, grounds it explicitly in the representational theory
of language. Words are simply pictures of things as they exist, and in
fiction, as they don't exist; what words mean in both cases is whatever
they stand for.[23] The ontological status of such things is not of much concern to literary theorists, as it was to logicians and philosophers; they
assume the process of representation and focus their attention on its purposes: to please and instruct. And this kind of attention, to the psychological effect of written words on readers, was the way in which literature
was assimilated to the ancient art of rhetoric, the oratorical persuasion
of hearers.

Although neither in textbooks of rhetoric nor in literary theory did this
kind of attention modify the old referential assumptions about language
itself, it did modify them in the most hotly contested arena of dispute
about interpretation: the biblical. Both Erasmus and Luther found in
Scripture a kind of meaning that was not referential at all, but was rather
constituted by the emotional impact of words on readers. They developed

---

[22] Thomas S. Kuhn, *The structure of scientific revolutions*, 2nd edn (Chicago: University of
    Chicago Press, 1970); Paul Feyerabend, *Against method* (London: New Left Books,
    1976).
[23] Julius Caesar Scaliger, *Poetices libri septem* (Geneva: Jean Crispin, 1561; facs. reprint
    Stuttgart: Frommann-Holzboog, 1987), pp. 1, 346–7.

a new kind (and stimulated a new industry) of biblical exegesis in which semantics is not representational, but affective and performative. Thus to apprehend language not merely as changing the mind, but moving the will, had consequences for profane literature far greater than those of the period's explicit theories. The revolution in linguistic philosophy that the Renaissance proposed was consummated only in its practice. That, however, is another story.

2

Renaissance exegesis

Michel Jeanneret

Debates on hermeneutics play a prominent role in Renaissance intellectual life. How should one read in order to grasp the full meaning and value of a text? What issues should the commentary address? Whether applied to the Bible or to ancient poetry, these questions arise constantly.[1] Two very different methods are at work. One considers that old texts are still relevant and alive; interpretation, in this case, stresses examples worth imitating or hidden meanings that will affect readers' morals or beliefs. The other is more historically minded and attempts to understand a work according to its cultural context, as a witness to a lost civilization. Let us consider these two methods – allegorical and philological – in turn.

Among the Fathers of the Church there arises a principle that will command biblical exegesis throughout the Middle Ages: the Scriptures have several simultaneous meanings. Each episode or statement is normally endowed with four stratified senses: the literal or historical meaning, its connection with the teaching of Christ, its moral value and finally its spiritual or eschatological dimension.[2] The designations of these four steps can vary and their order can change, but two rules remain firm: (a) the hidden senses are superior to the obvious story; (b) this grid imposes a compulsory method on the commentary.

In the Middle Ages this 'quadruple interpretation', with its mechanical procedures, was applied early on to pagan literature and, more particularly, to ancient myths. The most spectacular illustration is the systematic unfolding of Ovid's *Metamorphoses* according to the fourfold method. In its different versions, Latin or French (from the early fourteenth century till around 1530), the *Ovide moralisé* aims thus at making ancient mythology appear compatible with Christian truth: Phaëton

---

[1] See Gisèle Mathieu-Castellani and Michel Plaisance (ed.), *Les commentaires et la naissance de la critique littéraire. France/Italie (xive–xvie siècles)* (Paris: Aux Amateurs de Livres, 1990); Lee Patterson and Stephen G. Nichols (ed.), *Commentary as cultural artifact, The south Atlantic quarterly* 91, 4 (1992); Jean Céard, 'Les transformations du genre du commentaire', in *L'automne de la Renaissance*, ed. Jean Lafond and André Stegmann (Paris: Vrin, 1981), pp. 101–15.

[2] See Henri de Lubac, *Exégèse médiévale. Les quatre sens de l'Ecriture*, 4 vols. (Paris: Aubier, 1959–64).

represents Lucifer and his revolt against God; Diana is a figure of the Trinity, and so on.[3]

Allegorical reading was particularly active in Italy, where (there being no gap between the Middle Ages and the Renaissance) it continued well into the sixteenth century. In his *Genealogia deorum gentilium* (1350–74) Boccaccio credits myths with something like three different meanings, relating to history, natural phenomena and ethics. Two centuries later, mythographers like Lilio Giraldi, Natale Conti, and Vincenzo Cartari still follow the same method.

Towards the end of the fifteenth century, the idea that ancient texts conceal hidden revelations was given new vigour in the Neoplatonist circle of the Medicean Academy.[4] Philosophers like Marsilio Ficino and Pico della Mirandola were fascinated by mystery; in nature as well as in ancient poetry, in pagan fables as in the Bible, there lies much more than meets the eye. The more enigmatic a sign is, the deeper and richer it is likely to be. The belief that profane garments veil metaphysical truths was founded on the assumption that primitive poets – Orpheus, Homer, Pythagoras – were divinely inspired and, like prophets, had access to supernatural knowledge. In that early age, when Gods shared their secrets with men, poetry, natural philosophy, and theology were one and the same. Homeric tales and Olympian stories may seem frivolous, occult traditions and hermetic symbols may appear incompatible with Christianity, but they are to be read as figurative and coded messages.

The doctrine of parallel revelation, common among Renaissance Neoplatonists, was to strengthen this conception of reading as unveiling. The divine truths that God shared with his prophets and apostles, available to us in the Bible, were thought to have also been indirectly conveyed to a few magi in the pagan world. Similarities between Plato and Moses, Socrates and Christ, Orpheus and David were considered proofs of the profound unity of the two traditions. Either because the Sages were not aware of the true content of their message or because they meant to conceal it from profanation by the crowd, their discourse is misleading. But it is the scholars' task to extract the sacred from the profane, the edifying from the morally dubious. In their commentaries on Homer, Virgil, or the Orphic hymns, Florentine exegetes like Ficino, Cristoforo Landino, and Angelo Poliziano bring to light a wealth of moral advice and metaphysical

[3] See Jean Seznec, *The survival of the pagan gods: the mythological tradition and its place in Renaissance humanism and art* (New York: Harper Torchbooks, 1961); Ann Moss, *Poetry and fable: studies in mythological narrative in sixteenth-century France* (Cambridge: Cambridge University Press, 1984).

[4] See Edgar Wind, *Pagan mysteries in the Renaissance* (Harmondsworth: Penguin Books, 1967); D. P. Walker, *The ancient theology: studies in Christian Platonism from the fifteenth to the eighteenth century* (London: Duckworth, 1972); Frances A. Yates, *The occult philosophy in the Elizabethan age* (London: Routledge & Kegan Paul, 1979).

revelations. Trojan epics, Aesopic fables, Greek tragedies may seem to be untrustworthy channels to convey the True and the Good, but fiction might turn out to be more suggestive than abstract and analytical statements. And has not the Bible, with its prophecies and parables, used exactly the same means? Ultimate mysteries cannot but be transmitted indirectly, 'through a glass, darkly' (1 Corinthians 13: 12).

Furthermore, the parallel proved to be a powerful way to lend ancient poetry a badly needed respectability. Plato had banished the poet, as a liar, from his Republic and the Church held pagan tales as false and immoral. Interpreted as allegories, they appeared to be loaded with useful knowledge, edifying examples, or religious revelations. To moralize and Christianize seemed the best way to defend the past and adapt it to the new culture.

The targets and methods of philology could not be more different.[5] Here, the first objective is to reconstruct the genuine version of an antique text, either biblical or classical. Through the critical study of the manuscript tradition – identifying the oldest source, eradicating the interpolations and the copying errors – scholars aim at no more and no less than just editing the correct original text.

Nonetheless in many cases philologists add their own contribution: either a running commentary or, more and more, merely marginal notes or footnotes. Interventions by editors like Poliziano, Joseph Scaliger, and Henri Estienne are selective and technical. To explain, for them, is to make sure the literal sense and the author's intention are understood; whereas allegorists favour polysemy, philologists work at dispelling ambiguities in order to secure one single and clear meaning. To achieve this, they analyse the words and grammar, thus harking back to the model of antique commentaries. They elucidate allusions to the historical background – scientific or religious ideas, geographical or political references, and so on. Notes also carry information on the likely sources of a given passage (the Greek paradigm behind the Latin text) as a clue to its meaning. Finally, attention is often drawn to stylistic, rhetorical, or prosodic peculiarities; literary qualities are also adduced as examples for students to follow.

A basic principle underlies this philological research: a given work or statement is best understood as the product of a specific milieu and time – hence the vital role of chronology and the urgency of tracking down anachronisms. As Lorenzo Valla showed, proper reading – along with all types of historical investigation – depends on a rigorous analysis of the linguistic and semantic means available at the time, since words and structures provide the precise framework within which knowledge and

---

[5] See Anthony Grafton, *Joseph Scaliger: a study in the history of classical scholarship*, 2 vols. (Oxford: Clarendon Press; New York: Oxford University Press, 1983–93).

signification take place. To read according to the new demands of philology is to look for the specificity of a text and of its cultural environment. The condition for understanding is not so much to assimilate as to put the object at a distance and admit to its difference. For the first time, a sense of alterity and loss – an acknowledgement that the past was gone and that cultures were transient – was shifting the process of reading into the field of historical enquiry.

Were then allegory and philology incompatible? Not necessarily. Historical rigour did not need to deprive the work of all relevance or productivity for present readers. Though it might be distant, a text was not dead and might well continue to provide valid models, moral or aesthetic. Thus critical analysis and personal involvement were frequently encountered in close proximity until the end of the sixteenth century.[6] In the same way, we, as readers, often combine historical and timeless criteria.

In another sense, however, the two methods are contradictory and tend to diverge. What current value an old text may have is left more and more implicit, for modern readers to discover by themselves. Scholarly editions serve this purpose: rather than impose a foregone interpretation, they furnish readers with the tools for building up their own commentary. The notes allow them first to grasp the historical meaning and then, on a more tentative basis, to gain access to its latent values. Encyclopaedic and anonymous erudition distrust allegory in order to open another, more personal route to a work's hidden substance.

The dismantling of allegory is taken one step further by the hermeneutics performed among 'Evangelical' theologians – the predecessors of the Reformers. Let us look briefly at Erasmus's and Jacques Lefèvre d'Etaples's method applied to biblical exegesis.[7]

Quadruple interpretation is endorsed in so far as it acknowledges the Scriptures' polysemy, but it is also rejected as too mechanical; divine Truth is so plentiful, so beyond human reason, that it resists systematization. Similarly, philology is considered both good and insufficient: good, because God's Word is the very pillar of religious experience and has to be restored in all its purity and integrity; insufficient, because science and its external tools cannot but be subordinated to the power of faith. It is more important to believe than to understand, and to establish direct contact with the Truth than to rely on mediators. Whatever intervenes between God and the faithful, either the erudition of scholars or ready-made and formalized grids, is bound to alter the radiance of divine revelation.

---

[6] See Anthony Grafton, 'Renaissance readers and ancient texts: comments on some commentaries', *Renaissance quarterly* 38, 4 (1985), 615–49.

[7] See Guy Bédouelle, *Lefèvre d'Etaples et l'intelligence des Ecritures* (Geneva: Droz, 1976); de Lubac, *Exégèse médiévale*, vol. IV; Terence Cave, *The cornucopian text: problems of writing in the French Renaissance* (Oxford: Clarendon Press, 1979).

The meaning of the Bible can be neither exhausted nor totalized, and requires a constant quest for the spiritual riches that lie beneath the surface. Paul's saying, 'the letter kills but the Spirit gives life' (II Corinthians 3: 6), is central to Erasmian exegesis. The Ancient Alliance and Judaic rituals as such are dead wood; they will only reveal their depth if read as prophecies of Christ's message of love. The New Testament may be more readily accessible, but it too contains an endless and permanently adaptable wealth of lessons and promises. It might be more fruitful, Erasmus says, to read pagan fables allegorically than to read the Scriptures literally.

Reading is a state of mind. It requires humility and a complete availability to the Spirit's guidance. The aim is to achieve, as it were, spiritual symbiosis with the Sacred Word, to understand and absorb it more through intuition, faith, and love than through intelligence and knowledge. For the Christian to be infused and transformed by the reading process, he will meditate the Scriptures and intimately unfold their secrets. In the same way as Christ interiorized and regenerated Hebraic Law, the faithful instil a new life and relevance in the Bible, that in turn revives them. Here, interpretation, meditation, and prayer are one and the same.

About 1530–50, French intellectuals participate in this Evangelical mood. As readers or as writers, either religious or profane, they readily adopt the principle of deep-searching but unsystematic interpretation. Rabelais's position is typical. His invitation to the reader to look for the 'substantific marrow' of his narrative (Prologue to *Gargantua*, c. 1534) is not a joke: there is undoubtedly a treasure of religious, ethical, and political thought and certainly a profound wisdom to be drawn from his books. But no certainty is ever given to the interpreter. The mixture of serious and burlesque, the demystification of the authorial persona, the ambiguities of his signals, all these ruses, which continue to preoccupy present-day commentators, are as many challenges to the reader: there is much to be deciphered between the lines, but how and what? It is as though Rabelais were appropriating the freedom and endlessness of biblical exegesis.

Yet Rabelais's stance as regards meaning is equivocal. Is the truth difficult to grasp because it is complex and demands effort, or because it is out of reach and, perhaps, even absent? One wonders if the Evangelical model has not been appropriated by scepticism, and if interpretation, in human matters at least, does not lead to doubt and epistemological resignation. This uncertainty is revealed in the recurrent patterns of his narratives. Episodes, particularly in the *Third* and *Fourth books*, are divided into two phases: first an event or a discourse with enigmatic signs, then a pause in which the characters discuss and try to explain what they have just seen or heard. But these hermeneutical debates regularly erupt into disagreements: opinions clash as if there were as many solutions as interpreters. Methods seem incompatible, individual peculiarities disperse the unity of the message, the quest for an ideological community succumbs to the opacity of signs. Marguerite de Navarre's *Heptaméron* (published posthumously 1558/59) uses a similar alternating structure – a series of short stories, each followed by the hearers' commentaries – to illustrate the same difficulties. Whereas the unitary *logos* of the Scripture, however mysterious, leads to ever deeper convictions, secular interpretation no longer controls the circulation and dissemination of meaning. All this points to a crisis, or at least a problematization of hermeneutics. Narratives like Rabelais's or Marguerite's treat interpretation as one of their themes; they set up characters who are in the position of readers and are faced with the challenge of trying to understand. Meaning appears to drift in suspension, dependent on the addressees' initiative.

There is a further indication of the crisis: fiction, here, is established as an appropriate medium to reflect on hermeneutics. To explore the theoretical problems posed by interpretation, Rabelais and Marguerite adopt a narrative and playful mode, with its paradoxes and imaginary scenarios.[8] In one sense, this may be seen as a means to escape the issue by placing it in the reader's lap or as another aspect of the antischolastic campaign against the excesses of method. In another sense, however, the writer appears to construct fictional models in order to lift the question from the realm of rational categories; the heuristic power of narrative is called upon to imagine new interpretative procedures and investigate other approaches to truth.

The proximity or even assimilation of fiction and commentary is a natural consequence of literary imitation – a practice that dominates all writing activities at the time. To imitate a work of the past is to rewrite it by actualizing its latent resources and exploiting its present values; the imitator both submits to an old model and adapts it to a new culture, making it accessible and relevant. It is therefore to be expected that imitation include a measure of commentary and that commentary be instilled in the text of the previous work, to such a degree that the primary discourse and its explication become indistinguishable. For Erasmus, the best exegesis of the Bible is by way of paraphrase, that is understanding through rewriting, amplifying, and re-creating.

Among the different possible procedures of transformation and reactivation through interpretation, translation plays an unexpected but significant role. (*Interpretatio*, in Latin, means both interpretation and translation.) For obvious reasons, humanists were keen on translating, but many were hostile to a word-for-word rendering.[9] Theoreticians often

[8] See Michel Jeanneret, 'Commentary on fiction, fiction as commentary', *The south Atlantic quarterly* 91, 4 (1992), 909–28.
[9] See Glyn P. Norton, *The ideology and language of translation in Renaissance France and their humanist antecedents* (Geneva: Droz, 1984).

claimed that to reproduce mechanically a text without seizing its deep meaning is to betray it. To avoid this, one has first to assimilate it and to extract its essence from the inside. Like imitation, translation has to rethink the text and necessarily comprises a degree of interpretation in order to make it understood. On examination, it appears that many translators actually weave explanations into the fabric of the foreign text: a brief commentary, or a more expansive interpolation, can clarify an allusion or make a difficult passage intelligible. Between commentary and translation – two pillars of the humanist syllabus – the boundary is often blurred.

Interpretation, in such situations, is hardly distinguishable from the object interpreted. Michel de Montaigne provides us with another example. His *Essais* originate in reading notes, in remarks scribbled in the margins of the classics, in comparisons between diverse authors. In keeping with a habit familiar among the literate, Montaigne annotates, discusses, and glosses the books of his library. Henceforth, the emergence of his own individual voice is only a question of degree. An increased amount of reflection and a refusal to submit himself to any authority shape what could have been a mere commentary into an independent work. But the structure of commentary remains omnipresent in the *Essais* and serves to propel the writing forward.[10] Whether Montaigne explains a quotation or recontextualizes it in order to appropriate it, whether he approves of it or rejects it, his discourse unfolds parallel to another's discourse. He may also suspend this exchange and gloss himself instead of other authors: the *Essais* repeatedly turn back on to themselves, in order to explain, criticize, or complete what has just been said. Either transitive or reflexive, commentary is at the core of Montaigne's book – a condition that does not prevent it from also being one of the most personal works of the Renaissance.

Commentary, then, takes on diverse forms and statuses. On the one hand, it reinforces its distinctness. Relegated to the margins, the end of a passage, or the bottom of a page, it is unambiguously presented as a metadiscourse and puts the resources of philology to work for a text that it explicates without altering it. A radical distinction between primary and secondary is observed. While the gloss and criticism keep a low profile, the text commented on acquires prestige and progressively rises to the rank of classic: it enters into the canon of literary works. The separation of scholarship from 'creation' is a long process which, from the sixteenth century onward, will produce a favourable environment for the birth of the concept of 'literature'. We thus arrive at the complete dichotomy of the

[10] See André Tournon, *Montaigne, la glose et l'essai* (Lyons: Presses Universitaires de Lyon, 1983).

nineteenth century with, on one side, the literary masterpiece venerated as an irrational, inimitable, unchanging, and almost sacred object and, on the other side, academic knowledge claiming the opposite properties of objectivity, rigour, and dependency.

But such a divorce in the sixteenth century is far from having been finalized. As we have seen, the borders between discourse and metadiscourse are often fluctuating or non-existent, so that traces of commentary appear in unexpected contexts and even in fiction. Interpretation will not be confined to an inferior role, but imposes itself as one of the avenues of creation. A work is always another work's commentary; there is no ontological difference between understanding the other and realizing the self. The Renaissance thus affirms what deconstruction has recently established through other means: the opposition of the 'original' and the 'derivative', of the primary substance and the supplement, is based on a metaphysics that separates forces which are, on the contrary, in constant interaction.

3

Evangelism and Erasmus

Marjorie O'Rourke Boyle

The publication of an emended Greek text of the New Testament with a parallel Latin translation in 1516 established Erasmus as the premier evangelical humanist. The Complutensian Polyglot Bible was the first such printed, although it was not published until 1520 for lack of a licence. It was an unprincipled edition by competent philologists but religious conservatives, who subordinated their linguistic skills to ecclesiastical orthodoxy and the Vulgate version. Erasmus's edition secured the approval of Pope Leo X, the prestige of Johann Froben's press, and the applause of learned readers. Lorenzo Valla had inaugurated philological scholarship with corrections to the Vulgate edition. Erasmus surpassed all predecessors in Greek textual criticism, establishing the text that would dominate New Testament studies until the nineteenth century. He would issue four revisions.[1] Scripture was to be correct, Erasmus insisted in a methodological preface, for 'the theologian derives his name from divine oracles, not from human opinions'.[2]

Countering the speculative and controversial scholasticism that prevailed, Erasmus would provide knowledge of the original sources of theology as his principal purpose. As he outlined his method, by collating variants of the Greek New Testament he produced what he considered the definitive text. Although he consulted manuscripts broadly, he relied consistently only on several, unwittingly not the best available, but only determined so in modern research. Erasmus advanced beyond dependence on New Testament manuscripts, however, by appropriating patristic citations as sources of Scripture. Methodically he identified confused homonyms, corrupt assimilations, and intentional changes. Erasmus invented the principle of the harder reading, and explored inference and even

---

[1] Lorenzo Valla, *Collatio Novi Testamenti*, ed. A. Perosa (Florence: Sansoni, 1970); *Biblia complutense*, 6 vols. (Alcalá: Arnão Guillen de Brocar, 1514–17); Erasmus (ed.), *Novum Testamentum*, in *Opera omnia*, ed. J. LeClerc (hereafter abbreviated LB), 10 tomes in 11 vols. (Leiden: Petrus Vander Aa, 1703–6), vol. VI. See Jerry H. Bentley, *Humanists and holy writ: New Testament scholarship in the Renaissance* (Princeton: Princeton University Press, 1983); Erika Rummel, *Erasmus' annotations on the New Testament: from philologist to theologian* (Toronto: University of Toronto Press, 1986).

[2] *Ratio verae theologiae*, in *Ausgewählte Werke*, ed. H. Holborn with A. Holborn (hereafter abbreviated H) (Munich: C. H. Beck, 1964), p. 305.

conjecture in reconstructing the text. His translation intended to be accurate, lucid, and idiomatic Latin; he corrected the Vulgate for clarity, style,
and grammar. It endeavoured to preserve the integrity of the classical language while respecting the simplicity of the apostolic tongue. In his annotations Erasmus laboured to explain or clarify sentences troublesome by
their obscurity or ambiguity, without deviation from the sense of the text.
He relied on the judgement of patristic authorities, initially exposing more
than 600 passages, augmenting those in subsequent editions.[3]

The second edition of 1519 introduced the alteration that was paradigmatic for his humanism, for the correction of a single word presaged a
Christian society. That word was *logos*, which means both 'speech' and
'method', and in John 1: 1 names the divine Son. The Vulgate had rendered
'In the beginning was the Word'. Erasmus from historical evidence, philological argument, and liturgical practice translated 'In the beginning was
the Conversation'.[4] He acknowledged that 'Discourse' would have been
perfect, but rejected *oratio* as inappropriate for divine incarnation in Christ
because of its feminine gender.[5] It was the choice of *sermo* that Erasmus's
detractors seized to secure ecclesiastical opposition, to marshal civic power,
and to incite public outrage. They accused him of changing tradition and
even of correcting the gospel, although the earliest sources reported *sermo*
and the evangelist wrote *logos* not *verbum*. Despite their false allegations,
his critics correctly perceived the importance of his alteration.[6]

In defence Erasmus transformed philology into a theological method
by arguing that the denotations of *verbum* as a word, a brief saying, and
the verb as a part of speech could not satisfy the denotation of *logos* as
'speech'. In Latin *logos* was more correctly, appropriately, and customarily translated as *sermo* than *verbum*.[7] The importance of his alteration
was that the paradigmatic Logos was Christ: 'He is called Speech [*sermo*],
because through him God, who in his own nature cannot be compre-
hended by any reasoning, wished to become known to us'. Through the
eternal pronouncement of this Speech, God created the universe, populated with angelic intelligences and human beings, as an admirable text
through which he could insinuate himself into creaturely affections. God
spoke again to people more solidly and familiarly in the incarnation of

---

[3] Erasmus, *Opus epistolarum*, ed. P. S. Allen *et al.* (hereafter abbreviated EE), 12 vols.
(Oxford: Clarendon Press, 1906–58), vol. III, pp. 380–1. Bentley, *Humanists and holy
writ*, pp. 112–98.
[4] Erasmus, *Novum Testamentum* 336A–338A; *Annotationes in Novum Testamentum*, LB,
vol. VI, 335A–337C.
[5] Erasmus, *Annotationes* 335C.
[6] Marjorie O'Rourke Boyle, *Erasmus on language and method in theology* (Toronto:
University of Toronto Press, 1971), pp. 3–31.
[7] Erasmus, *Annotationes* 335A–C; *Apologia de 'In principio erat sermo'*, LB, vol. IX,
113B,E,F, 114A, 121D, 122D.

his Son. Such Speech as eternally and incorporeally proceeding from the paternal mind transcended human experience. As a voluntary operation of the divine nature, its eloquence differed from organic vocalization.[8]

Yet divine speech was analogous to human speech, since the Son was not a terse utterance but the sufficient and copious medium of revelation. Copious language even among humans was a 'divine virtue'.[9] As revelation Christ was speech not word, no longer abstracted, as in the Vulgate version, from the contexts of discourse and audience. Distinctive from the traditional doctrine of the Logos was Erasmus's concept of Christ as the complete oration of the Father. 'Christ is for this reason called *logos*, because whatsoever the Father speaks, he speaks through the Son'. It had a suggestive precedent in a single sentence of the first Christian theologian, Irenaeus; only that translation was inadequately *verbum*. Since theological discourse was to imitate Christ as Speech, the implication of Erasmus's alteration was ultimately a rhetorical rather than grammatical culture. Just as ancient iconography had sculptured Christ in figures copied from statues of classical orators, so did Erasmus adopt rhetoric as the excellent vocation: because it was the role God himself had assumed to teach in the voice of flesh the lessons of wisdom.[10]

Although grammatical knowledge did not make a theologian, neither did its ignorance.[11] Erasmus corrected the scholastic neglect and abuse of grammar by requiring a classical trilingual education and by commending its utility. Vocabulary was a principal part of learning.[12] The comprehension of the mysteries of Scripture often depended on knowing the nature of the thing designated.[13] Knowledge was double: of things and of words. The name was the index of the reality, 'for things are only intelligible to us through vocal signs'.[14] The translation and interpretation of Scripture was a grammatical task requiring diligent erudition not divine inspiration.[15] The scholastics, boastful of their ignorance of language, pretended to intuit bare reality but quibbled sophistically about the particles of speech.[16] In the trivium grammar should precede logic, for a mastery of languages was the better foundation for theological truth. Theologians should be trained from infancy in clear and accurate speech through memory and imitation.[17]

[8] Erasmus, *Paraphrasis in evangelium Joannis*, LB, vol. VII, 499B–F.
[9] Erasmus, *De duplici copia verborum ac rerum*, LB, vol. I, 3B.
[10] Erasmus, *Annotationes* 335C; Boyle, *Erasmus on language*, pp. 24–6.
[11] Erasmus, EE, vol. II, p. 325.
[12] Erasmus, *De recta latini graecique sermonis pronunciatione dialogus*, ed. M. Cytowska, in *Opera omnia* (hereafter abbreviated ASD) (Amsterdam: North Holland, 1971), vol. I–4, p. 43.
[13] Erasmus, *Ratio verae theologiae*, p. 185.
[14] Erasmus, *De ratione studii*, ed. J.-C. Margolin, ASD, vol. I–2, p. 113.
[15] Erasmus, EE, vol. I, p. 410.   [16] Erasmus, *De ratione studii*, p. 113.
[17] Erasmus, *De pueris instituendis*, ed. J.-C. Margolin, ASD, vol. I–2, pp. 70, 48, 49, 66.

Although speech proceeded from the animal instinct of imitation, in exhibiting the ascendancy of spirit it manifested the superiority of humanity over animality. By speech a person revealed the divine image and indwelling. It was the sign of understanding, a reflection of character, a mark of virtue. The creation of humanity in the divine image, with the gift of revelation through speech, imitated the eternal generation and temporal incarnation of the Logos as the paternal discourse: 'What in divine affairs is the Father generating from himself the Son, is in us the mind, the seat of thought and speech [*sermo*]. What in that case is the Son being born from the Father is in us speech [*oratio*] issuing from the spirit.' Just as the gift of Speech to creation mediated God to humanity, so the gift of speech in creation mediated humanity to God. The paradigmatic Logos, who perfectly resembled and revealed the Father, was impressed in the human spirit and expressed in its speech. When humans spoke truly, they expressed their divine resemblance in a bond of filiation, repeating in the temporal order the eternal Speech. Unfeigned speech aligned human expression with its spiritual origin in the Logos, who perfectly revealed his own origin in the speaking Father. Good language was thus the imitation of Christ. Erasmus's critique of scholasticism as barbaric or babyish fundamentally indicted its inhumanity or immaturity in failing to imitate the divine creation and generation.[18]

A prominent model for Scripture was Augustine's metaphor of divine baby-talk.[19] The theologian's role in scholasticism, which Erasmus derived from his speculation,[20] became the elevation of its imagery to ideas by dialectic. Erasmus replaced that contemplative ideal with a discursive one. Acknowledging that divine wisdom babbled to accommodate human infancy, he nevertheless urged a maturation to its sublimity.[21] The method of such aspiration was not philosophical but rhetorical, the apprehension of wisdom by speech not intellection. Its accomplishment was through the imitation of eloquent authors, classical and patristic. Grammar was not norm but tradition, the usage of Latin speakers and writers; but only of the best of them, defined humanistically as the learned and virtuous. Imitation was not simulation but emulation, surpassing the master's style by cultivating native beauty in harmony with contemporary life. Against the Ciceronians, who replicated classical diction, Erasmus argued that in Christian eloquence the selection of vocabulary was governed by propriety: attention to the subject and its audience. Meaning

---

[18] Boyle, *Erasmus on language*, pp. 48, 39–44, citing Erasmus, *Lingua*, ed. J. H. Waszink, ASD, vol. IV–IA, p. 93.

[19] Augustine, *In evangelium Iohannis tractatus* CXXXIV 7.23, ed. R. Willems (Turnhout: Brepols, 1954), pp. 80–1.

[20] Erasmus, *Hyperaspistes diatribae adversus servum arbitrium Martini Lutheri*, LB, vol. X, 1495D.

[21] Erasmus, *Enchiridion militis christiani*, H, p. 34.

was also contextual, requiring consideration of the entire composition: sentences and not merely words.[22] The discrimination of the apt word for communicating reality was to be strengthened by correct pronunciation and proper orthography.[23]

Christ as the Saviour of humanity was the renovator of speech, by disclosing unperceived reality and conferring new significance on known reality. 'In Christ everything is created anew and vocabulary wholly transformed.'[24] Just as he had restored creation as Speech, so would Erasmus restore it through speech. The discipline of grammar was in service to rhetoric and the republic. The gift of speech was 'the principal reconciler of human relationships'[25] conferred by the Creator 'so that people might live together more agreeably'.[26] By persuasion the human orator imitated the divine Saviour in a revival of the classical doctrine of the therapeutic Logos. Erasmus promoted the power of language to transform society, like the classical rhetors in the tradition of Isocrates who had declared language the agent of civilization. Scholastic barbarism he criticized as dividing and dispelling the commonwealth into factions.[27] Which, Erasmus posed, was proper theological method – humanism or scholasticism – when 'in this kind of philosophy, located more truly in dispositions than in syllogisms, life is more than disputation, inspiration more than erudition, transformation more than reason?'[28]

Erasmus heralded a Christian society constituted by Scripture. Baptism conferred a common citizenship that admitted all persons without discrimination of age, sex, or class to the theological profession.[29] True oratory was simple, and nothing was truer or simpler than Christ its paradigm. Method was extremely easy to master, and Erasmus offered a short cut for learners. Piety was essential as a filial disposition, a pure and simple faith docile to the Scriptural mysteries. Erasmus advocated exegesis from the original languages rather than from translations, appealed to patristic authorities, and applied the secular disciplines. Theologians needed an average ability for discerning the significance of the text through grammar, and, moreover, a clean and elegant style. Among hermeneutical rules he advised consideration of the variations of speech – not only what was said, but to whom, with what diction, at what time, on what occasion – and of the context of a passage, what preceded and followed it. For the interpretation of obscure sayings he recommended the collation and comparison of passages. An important method for disclosing the hidden

---

[22] Erasmus, *Dialogus cui titulus, Ciceronianus, siue, De optimo dicendi genere*, ed. P. Mesnard, ASD, vol. I-2, esp. pp. 636–48, 650, 656.
[23] Erasmus, *De recta . . . pronunciatione*.   [24] Erasmus, *Enchiridion*, p. 96.
[25] Erasmus, *Querela pacis*, ed. O. Herding, ASD, vol. IV-2, p. 63.
[26] Erasmus, *Lingua*, p. 43.   [27] Boyle, *Erasmus on language*, pp. 47–8, 53–5.
[28] Erasmus, *Paraclesis*, H, pp. 144–5.   [29] *Ibid.*

sense of Scripture was allegory, as treating the mystical body. Allegory was divine pedagogy, for Christ adopted it in his parables to exercise human sluggishness, so that the difficulty of discerning his meaning would yield to the pleasure of its comprehension. Pleasure was endorsed as the classical motivation for learning.[30] Allegory was also efficacious in its polysemous accommodation to the needs of various readers.[31]

Theology was to be metamorphic speech, converting persons to Christ. For the transformation of humanity it was to be focused on him as the paradigm of language: 'The special sighting of theologians is to expound Scripture wisely; to render its doctrine according to faith, not frivolous questions; to discourse about piety gravely and efficaciously; to wring out tears, to inflame spirits to heavenly things.' It was visceral not intellectual discourse. Christ he imagined diagrammatically as a sighting [*scopus*] intact at the centre of concentric circles that represented the social estates.[32] Like a commonplace, Christ was the singular point of reference to which the various arguments derived from the topics of Scripture were to be referred for verification and meaning. He was the plentiful and summary principle from which the theologian invented his eloquence. Erasmus contrasted the simplicity of the Logos and the loquacity of scholasticism, his concord and their factionalism. In such tension of unity and multiplicity he desired the simplicity of a devout consideration of Scripture as containing full wisdom in compendium.[33]

The sufficiency of Christ rendered theology 'very easy and available to everyone'.[34] Scripture vividly represented the living image of his mind more fully present than would his very apparition.[35] The person in the sixteenth century reading the Bible beheld God more effectively than did Moses in the burning bush.[36] The text was real presence. Scripture engaged human affairs with the social requirements of education and government, so that it was rhetorically purposeful. Ordinary Christian conversation was to be drawn from it: the farmer singing at the plough, the weaver humming to his shuttle, the traveller relieving his weariness. Few could achieve erudition, but all could be pious, and more boldly as Erasmus stated, 'No one is prevented from being a theologian'.[37] His humanist ideal was dramatized in a colloquy at an emblematic villa among laymen, who feasted on the interpretation of Scripture, then dispersed to the real village for acts of apostolic charity.[38] Human speech

---

[30] Erasmus, *Ratio verae theologiae*, pp. 280, 179–80, 181, 182, 196–7, 284, 260, 262.
[31] Erasmus, *Paraclesis*, pp. 141–2.
[32] Erasmus, *Ratio verae theologiae*, pp. 180, 193, 202.
[33] Boyle, *Erasmus on language*, pp. 92–5. [34] Erasmus, EE, vol. III, p. 364.
[35] Erasmus, *Paraclesis*, p. 149. [36] Erasmus, *Ratio verae theologiae*, p. 179.
[37] Erasmus, *Paraclesis*, pp. 142, 145.
[38] Erasmus, 'Convivium religiosum', in *Colloquia*, ed. L.-E. Halkin, F. Bierlaire, R. Hoven, *et al.*, ASD, vol. I–3, pp. 231–66.

mediated persons in social harmony, just as Christ the Logos was not a single word in isolation but a complete speech to an audience.

The public airing of scholarly dispute about his translation *sermo* alarmed Erasmus, however. Retracting his invitation of theology as a profession for everyone, he restricted it to the learned.[39] Nothing, therefore, upset his evangelical humanism more than the evangelical assertion of Luther, and a substantial objection was its publicity as fomenting sedition. Their conflict formally manifested the doctrinal issue of the will towards grace, but it entailed more fundamentally cultural issues of language and method. Erasmus, arguing classically from a comparison of scriptural texts, composed a diatribe in the deliberative genre. His choice coincided with his epistemological Scepticism (Ciceronian not Cartesian) in disputed questions. Luther undercut the entire discussion by responding in the juridical genre, with a competitive epistemological Stoicism, to condemn rhetoric itself as a theological method.[40]

Luther redefined the linguistic norm from humanist eloquence to ordinary speech, a consensus of popular usage. Like Erasmus he was determined about correct signification, but his culture was wholly grammatical. Not the persuasion of rhetoric but the assertion of grammar was the standard. His biblical hermeneutics had two criteria: grace and grammar. The interior criterion was the unique gift of the Spirit, by which the manifest meaning of the text for Christians seized believers. The exterior criterion was the universal constituent of nature, by which the intellect apprehended the manifest meaning of the text in itself. That criterion was the ordinary usage of speech as expressing innate intelligence, the norm nominalism had established in logic against scholasticism. Luther's appeal was to a manifest Scripture whose 'words are simple and their meaning simple'. Since revelation lacked any inconsistency, there was 'no need of an interpretation to resolve any difficulty'. Luther's hermeneutics was anti-hermeneutical: not the private interpretation of Scripture, as Protestant belief is frequently misstated, but rather no interpretation of Scripture.[41] Although Luther like Erasmus initially encouraged the daily reading of Scripture by commoners, with developing concern for its misinterpretation he retreated to the security of the catechisms he composed. Those he authorized to disseminate the official creeds of the state churches and to inculcate orthodoxy in the public by memorization and recital.

[39] Boyle, *Erasmus on language*, pp. 5–8.
[40] Marjorie O'Rourke Boyle, *Rhetoric and reform: Erasmus' civil dispute with Luther* (Cambridge, MA: Harvard University Press, 1983).
[41] Marjorie O'Rourke Boyle, 'The chimera and the spirit: Luther's grammar of the will', in *The Martin Luther quincentennial*, ed. G. Dünnhaupt (Detroit: Wayne State University Press for *Michigan Germanic studies*, 1985), pp. 23–4. Citing Luther, *De servo arbitrio*, in *Luthers Werke in Auswahl*, ed. O. Clemen, 6 vols. (Berlin: Walter de Gruyter, 1960), vol. IV, p. 229.

Although schooling, thus literacy, significantly increased, bibles were scarcely assigned, so that there was no causation between the Lutheran Reformation and the popular reading of Scripture. It was the spiritualists who favoured personal reading and judgement of the Bible; Luther condemned that as heresy. His catechetical programme thus tacitly conceded the ambiguity of Scripture.[42]

In principle he had strenuously opposed ambiguity with his cardinal doctrine of Scriptural 'clarity'. Allegorical interpretation he judged illicit unless the language and reality of the passage so transgressed an article of faith as to compel such a resort. As his 'invincible argument' Luther stated that 'vocabulary ought to remain in the usage of natural signification, unless the contrary is demonstrated'. An interpreter must otherwise 'always adhere to the simple and plain and natural signification of words that grammar and the habit of speech, which God created in man, maintain'. The violation of that rule would render Scripture so flimsy that a trope could sophistically dismiss an article of faith, rendering nothing certain. Luther's insistence on the literal sense of the text as understood by ordinary usage was the corollary of his epistemological demand of 'absolute certitude for establishing consciences'. Theologians were to obey the 'universal Latin tongue' defined as 'grammatical and plain meaning'. The classical accommodation to audience that distinguished Erasmus's interpretation of Christ's own pedagogy Luther condemned as dangerous and defiling. For Luther, Scripture was to be maintained 'in the purity of its powers' without any interpretation, which he frankly declared 'human dung'. Exegesis was confusion; text was clarity. His own volumes on Scripture intended merely to observe, record, and transmit meaning in literal *mimesis*.[43]

Although Luther considered grammar the most advantageous science for theology, grammar was a human invention. It merely exposed the literal sense of Scripture as universally apprehensible by the human intellect; it could never reveal its spiritual sense as apprehending believers. Grammar was not, as in Erasmus's humanism, propaedeutic to piety, for the natural and supernatural orders were in Luther's theology absolutely dichotomous. Erasmus and Luther differed concerning the definition of grammar as a consensus of erudite or popular usage, its province as the tropological or literal sense, its status as a sacral or secular discipline, and its function as constitutive of or auxiliary to theology.[44] Beyond grammar,

---

[42] Richard Gawthrop and Gerald Strauss, 'Protestantism and literacy in early modern Germany', *Past and present* 104 (1984), 31–43.

[43] Boyle, 'The chimera and the spirit', pp. 25–6. Luther, *De servo arbitrio*, pp. 195, 248; *Rationis Latomianae confutatio*, in *D. Martin Luthers Werke*, 58 vols. (Weimar: H. Bohlau, 1883–), vol. VIII, pp. 91, 119, 103.

[44] Boyle, 'The chimera and the spirit', p. 27.

they divided over rhetoric: theology as persuasive discourse or assertive word, with Erasmus adopting and Luther rejecting a rhetorical culture. Protestant translations into the vernacular favoured the clarity of an assertive 'Word'.[45] The Council of Trent regressively authorized the Vulgate translation for Catholic use,[46] silencing the paradigmatic translation *sermo* and with it Erasmus's humanist ideal. It could not terminate humanist method, which founded modern critical scholarship.[47]

---

[45] The Latin translation by Théodore de Bèze, *Biblia sacra*, used *sermo*, following John Calvin, *Commentarius in evangelium Ioannis*, in *Opera quae supersunt omnia*, ed. E. Reuss *et al.*, Corpus reformatorum 75 (Brunswick: C. A. Schwetschke, 1863–1900), vol. XLVII, cols. 1–3.

[46] *Concilium tridentinum*, ed. Societas Goerresiana, 2nd edn, 13 vols. (Freiburg: Herder, 1961), vol. V, pp. 91–2.

[47] For Erasmus's historiographical fortune see Bruce Mansfield, *Phoenix of his age: interpretations of Erasmus c. 1550–1750* (Toronto: University of Toronto Press, 1979); Mansfield, *Man on his own: interpretations of Erasmus c. 1750–1920* (Toronto: University of Toronto Press, 1992).

4

The assimilation of Aristotle's *Poetics* in sixteenth-century Italy

Daniel Javitch

Italian men of letters in the mid-sixteenth century were the first to promulgate the idea that Aristotle's *Poetics* was a central and traditional text of ancient poetic theory. One of the ways they did so was by conflating and harmonizing Aristotle's treatise with Horace's *Ars poetica*, the one text which had enjoyed a relatively uninterrupted fortune in Western Europe as a digest of ancient poetic art. Vincenzo Maggi (Madius), one of the very first Cinquecento commentators on the Greek treatise, maintained that Horace's epistle to the Pisos was a stream flowing from the Aristotelian spring of the *Poetics*. Maggi actually appended a commentary on the *Ars poetica* to the one he provided on Aristotle's *Poetics* in order to reveal Horace's 'obscure and subtle imitation' of the Greek philosopher's treatise. This fictive genealogy was meant, in turn, to make uniform and therefore more authoritative two ancient views of poetry that were, indeed, quite different.

Aristotle's view of poems in terms of the inherent or internal requirements of their forms was a minority view in the ancient world. Most ancient critics (Horace, among them) measured the effectiveness and value of a poetic work in terms of external standards of truthfulness and of morality, and not by the degree to which it contributed to realizing what Aristotle took to be its particular form and function. Moreover, the rhetorical orientation of these critics made them preoccupied with the conditions imposed by the audience and not, as was Aristotle, with the composition of coherent structures which produced certain emotions because of inherent and objective properties.[1] This can explain why the *Poetics* was largely neglected in antiquity. It exerted surprisingly little influence. As D. A. Russell has pointed out, Aristotle's effect with regard to subjects considered literary came almost entirely through his *Rhetoric*.[2] Neoptolemus of Parium appears to have been one of the intermediate

---

[1] For the distinction between Aristotle's formal approach to poetry and mainstream 'ethical criticism' in the ancient world see James Coulter, *The literary microcosm: theories of interpretation of the later Neoplatonists* (Leiden: Brill, 1976), esp. pp. 7–19. For a more synoptic accounting of Aristotle's *Poetics* in the context of Renaissance commentary, see Marga Cottino-Jones's survey essay in the present volume (pp. 566–77).

[2] D. A. Russell, *Criticism in antiquity* (Berkeley: University of California Press, 1961), p. 43.

Hellenistic sources through which some Aristotelian ideas, that may have already been commonplace, were transmitted to Horace. However, modern scholars (*pace* Maggi and subsequent amalgamators) have not been able to demonstrate that Horace used the *Poetics* directly in the *Ars poetica*, and have revealed, on the contrary, the incompatibilities of the two theories.

The marginality that Aristotle's treatise acquired in late antiquity became even more pronounced in the Middle Ages. The accurate Latin translation William of Moerbeke made of the text in 1278 was virtually ignored. The refraction of it that does seem to have appealed to medieval thinkers was Averroes' 'Middle Commentary on the *Poetics*', as translated by Hermann the German in 1256. Averroes' interpretation of tragedy as the art of praise (aiming to incite virtue), and of comedy as the art of blame (aiming to castigate vice) transformed Aristotle's poetic into one that conformed more easily with existing notions about the rhetorical methods and moral aims of poetry. In fact, because the kind of ethico-rhetorical terms into which Averroes recast Aristotle's poetics reflected prevailing notions of poetry well into the sixteenth century, Averroes' commentary on the *Poetics* was published, reprinted, and coexisted along with Giorgio Valla's 1498 Latin translation of Aristotle's text (the first to be published), and the 1508 Aldine printing of the Greek original.[3]

With the reacquisition of the Greek language in the course of the fifteenth century, and the recuperation of original Greek texts, learned Italians no longer had to depend on medieval refractions of the *Poetics*. Manuscripts of Aristotle's Greek text were being copied, were circulating, and were being studied in Italy as early as the 1470s. By 1480, or shortly thereafter, Angelo Poliziano was referring to the *Poetics* in his university lectures, as had Ermolao Barbaro before him. In fact, Poliziano appropriates some of Aristotle's views on *mimesis* in the reflections on comedy with which he begins his commentary on Terence's *Andria*.[4] Yet despite the availability of the Greek text, and, eventually, of Giorgio Valla's (less

---

[3] Both a useful account and an English version (of excerpts) of Hermann the German's translation of Averroes' 'Middle Commentary' can be found in *Medieval literary theory and criticism c. 1100–c. 1375: the commentary tradition*, ed. A. J. Minnis and A. B. Scott (Oxford: Clarendon Press; New York: Oxford University Press, 1988), pp. 277–313. The *editio princeps* of Averroes' commentary was published in 1481 and a reprint appeared in 1515. See Charles E. Butterworth's translation and edition of Averroes' *Middle Commentary* on Aristotle's *Poetics* (Princeton: Princeton University Press, 1986). On the ongoing influence of this commentary in the Renaissance see Bernard Weinberg, *A history of literary criticism in the Italian Renaissance*, 2 vols. (Chicago: University of Chicago Press, 1961), vol. I, pp. 352ff.

[4] See Angelo Poliziano, *La commedia antica e l' 'Andria' di Terenzio*, ed. R. L. Roselli (Florence: Sansoni, 1973). On Poliziano's knowledge of the *Poetics* and the dissemination of the text at the end of the Quattrocento see Vittore Branca, *Poliziano e l'umanesimo della parola* (Turin: Einaudi, 1983), pp. 13–15, 32–3.

than reliable and incomplete) Latin translation of it in 1498, the evidence suggests that Aristotle's theory had little relevance and value for its readers. It is telling that Giorgio Valla's own treatise on poetry, his *De poetica* (largely devoted to metrics), was much more indebted to Diomedes' *Ars grammatica* than to Aristotle, cited by Valla only occasionally and mostly for his views on the origins of drama.[5] Even after Aldus published the Greek text in 1508 (as part of an anthology entitled *Rhetores graeci*!), it had little impact. To be sure the *Poetics* was not dismissed or totally disregarded in Italy, as it was in other parts of Europe ('it has not much of good fruit', Juan Luis Vives would declare not untypically in his *De disciplinis* (1536), 'being wholly occupied in the observation of ancient poems, and in those subtleties, in which the Greeks are most pestiferous, and . . . inept to boot'), but interest in the treatise only begins to grow once the Italians become more familiar with ancient Greek tragedy. It is hardly accidental that Alessandro de' Pazzi, the first writer to provide a relatively reliable Latin translation of the *Poetics* (composed in 1524; published in 1536) was also responsible for the first Latin and then vernacular translations of Sophocles and Euripides.

Pazzi's translation served to make Aristotle's text more accessible but only somewhat more intelligible. In the dedication to his first tragedy *Orbecche* (1541) Giovambattista Giraldi Cintio (whose own use of the *Poetics* will be discussed shortly) indicates how obscure and perplexing the text was to contemporary readers. Beyond Aristotle's characteristic obscurity, the treatise, writes Giraldi, 'remains so cryptic and dark that it takes much effort to understand his definition of tragedy'.[6] It was at this very moment that the first sustained exegesis of the *Poetics* began. Bartolomeo Lombardi's lectures on the *Poetics* at Padua in 1541, continued by Vincenzo Maggi (who also lectured on the text at Ferrara in 1543), inaugurate a series of explications and retranslations by professors connected to the school of Aristotelian philosophy at Padua. With the appearance of Francesco Robortello's *Explicationes* (1548), the first of the commentaries to be published, a real upsurge of interest in the *Poetics* begins to manifest itself. Robortello's commentary was followed by Bernardo Segni's first Italian translation of the treatise in 1549, and then a series of rival commentaries which mark as well as contribute to the full assimilation of Aristotle's theory in the latter half of the Cinquecento: the *Explanationes* of Lombardi and Maggi in 1550; Pietro Vettori's

---

[5] Giorgio Valla's *De poetica* appeared as the thirty-eighth book in his encyclopaedic *De expetendis ac fugiendis rebus opus* published posthumously at Venice in 1501. On this treatise see E. N. Tiegerstedt, 'Observations on the reception of Aristotle's *Poetics* in the Latin West', *Studies in the Renaissance* 15 (1968), 7–24.

[6] See Giraldi's dedication to his *Orbecche* in *Trattati di poetica e retorica del Cinquecento*, ed. B. Weinberg (Bari: Laterza, 1970), vol. I, p. 411.

Commentarii in 1560; and Castelvetro's Italian commentary in 1570.[7] The authority that the *Poetics* begins to acquire is also reflected in mid-century literary disputes, for example the anonymous *Giuditio sopra la tragedia di Canace e Macareo* published in Lucca in 1550. This polemic against Sperone Speroni's *Canace* (composed in 1542) for not complying with Aristotle's rules for tragedy initiates the first of a series of Italian literary quarrels in the second half of the sixteenth century in which conformity to the rules set forth in the *Poetics* is the main ground of contestation.[8]

Although the value and authority that the *Poetics* began to enjoy in the mid-century had to do with the fact that Aristotle's approach and method corresponded to the new orientations of some Italian critics and writers, there was a marked effort, nonetheless, to assimilate Aristotle's view of poetry to prevailing conceptions of that art. This required diminishing or simply overlooking the discrepancies between the ethico-rhetorical pre-occupations that characterized mid-century poetics with Aristotle's differ-ent concern with the poem's internal and formal aspects. One way this was accomplished was by conflating Aristotle's directives with those of Horace in the *Ars poetica*, still the main source of poetic theorizing in this period. As Weinberg and others have shown, this conflation led to a frag-mentation of Aristotle's theory so that the qualitative parts of tragedy as well as concepts like unity and probability which, in the *Poetics*, had been interconnected, were isolated to correspond with different parts of Horace's verse epistle, and consequently lost their original meaning.[9] The rhetorical orientations of the conflators – their primary concern with the relation of the poem with, and its impact on, the audience – marked their interpretation of Aristotle's concepts and also facilitated their efforts to reconcile these concepts with Horatian rules. For instance, interpreters modified Aristotle's call for probability [*eikos*], a concept which bears on the logical sequence and intelligibility of a plot, into a requirement of verisimilitude, a notion that bears on the relation of what the poet represents to the beliefs of the audience. Already in Francesco Pedemonte's *Ecphrasis in Horatii Flacci Artem poeticam* (1546), the earliest effort

---

[7] For a detailed account of the reception and exegesis of the *Poetics* in the mid-century see Bernard Weinberg, *A history of literary criticism*, vol. I, pp. 349–423. For more summary accounts see Baxter Hathaway, *Marvels and commonplaces: Renaissance literary criti-cism* (New York: Random House, 1968), pp. 9–19; and Enzo Turolla, 'Aristotele e le "Poetiche" del Cinquecento', in *Dizionario critico della letteratura italiana*, ed. V. Branca (Turin: UTET, 1974), pp. 133–9.

[8] The *Giuditio* had, for a long time, been attributed to Bartolomeo Cavalcanti but Chris-tina Roaf has made a convincing reattribution of the authorship to Giraldi. See her 'A sixteenth-century *anonimo*: the author of the *Giuditio sopra la tragedia di Canace e Macareo*', *Italian studies* 14 (1959), 49–74.

[9] See Marvin Herrick, *The fusion of Horatian and Aristotelian literary criticism 1531–1555* (Urbana: University of Illinois Press, 1946); and Weinberg, *A history of literary criticism*, vol. I, pp. 111–55; and also Antonio Garcia Berrio, *Formacion de la teoria literaria moderna: la topica horaciana en Europa*, 2 vols. (Madrid: CUPSA, 1977–80), vol. I *passim*, but esp. pp. 457–89.

to find parallels between Horace and Aristotle, the latter's demand for probability (1451a36ff.) is connected to Horace's statement that 'ficta voluptatis causa sint proxima veris' ['fictions meant to please should be close to the truth', *Ars poetica* 338]. When Robortello elaborates on Aristotle's concepts of the probable and the necessary he too equates *to eikos* with 'secundum verisimile' which he ties to his all-important requirement of winning the credibility of the audience.[10] To be fair to the sixteenth-century commentators, what Aristotle meant by probability was not totally unconnected with rhetorical ideas of the credible and plausible, but he wanted it to bear chiefly on the logic and coherence of plot structure and it is that primary meaning that the commentators lose sight of.

The four qualitative parts of tragedy – *muthos, ethos, dianoia, lexis* – were similarly modified to conform to a rhetorical or didactic bias. *Ethos*, for example, which in the technical sense Aristotle uses in Chapter 15 (1450b.8–10) indicates what kind of choice a person makes (and by that choice is qualified as a *good* woman, man, slave), is translated by Cinquecento commentators as 'mores' in Latin (and 'costume' in Italian) and thereby acquires the sense of 'character traits' as defined by age, sex, nationality, as well as disposition. In other words, 'mores' or 'costume' is closer to the sense *ethos* has in Aristotle's *Rhetoric* (3.7.1408a25–29) than it does as a part of tragedy where it is always an indication of choice. Given, moreover, the desire of most commentators to find corroborated in the *Poetics* their own conception of poetry as a medium of moral edification, they assumed that Aristotle shared their view that poetry served its ethical function through its revelation of character. *Ethos* therefore becomes associated with the delineation of exemplary moral types.[11] As a result commentators were more prone to emphasize Aristotle's concern with characterization according to universally accepted notions of ethical behaviour, *harmotton*, the second of four criteria he demands of *ethos* (at 54a22). Even Castelvetro, who adamantly opposed the idea that Aristotle advocated the representation of exemplary characters, considered the credibility of characterization of utmost importance and devoted a lengthy discussion to the observance of 'convenevolezza' (as he translated *harmotton*), especially in the representation of women.[12]

---

[10] One finds this parallel repeatedly: for example, Francesco Lovisini's commentary on the *Ars poetica* (1554) also conflates Aristotle's probability with Horace's *proxima veris*. For Robortello's equating of *to eikos* with verisimilitude see his *Aristotelis de arte poetica explicationes* (Florence: L. Torrentino, 1548; facs. reprint Munich: W. Fink, 1968), pp. 86–9, 93. For Cicero's possible conflation of the two notions see Kathy Eden, *Poetic and legal fiction in the Aristotelian tradition* (Princeton: Princeton University Press, 1986), pp. 115ff.

[11] See, for example, how Trissino's discussion of *ethos* (Weinberg (ed.), *Trattati di poetica*, vol. II, p. 62) projects on to Aristotle's term the meanings it was given by Dionysius of Halicarnassus.

[12] For Castelvetro's discussion of *convenevolezza* see *Poetica d'Aristotele vulgarizzata e sposta*, ed. W. Romani, 2 vols. (Bari: Laterza, 1978–9), vol. I [1978], pp. 422–5.

For those who wished to find a moralistic function in Aristotle's view
of poetry, *catharsis* offered a good deal of scope, especially since Aristotle
left it quite open to interpretation. As Stephen Halliwell observes about
various Cinquecento definitions of *catharsis*,

> Whether the emphasis was placed on acquiring fortitude or resistance against
> the assaults of misfortune, as it was by Robortello; or on the administration by
> tragedy of a conscious moral lesson, as it was by Segni and Giraldi; or on pity
> and fear as a means of helping us to avoid *other* dangerous emotions (anger,
> lust, greed, etc.), as it was by Maggi and others – in all these cases, a much
> more direct and explicit effect is posited than anything which can reasonably
> be thought to have been Aristotle's meaning.[13]

Catharsis did serve to corroborate that, for Aristotle, as for many of his
sixteenth-century readers, the end of poetry was to persuade its readers to
behave, or avoid behaving, in certain ways. However, the rhetoricization
and moralization of the *Poetics* that such readings of *catharsis* serve to
document have been over-emphasized by Bernard Weinberg and other
literary historians. In fact, because of the influence of Weinberg's *History
of literary criticism in the Italian Renaissance*, the so-called distortion
of Aristotle's theory to make it fit mainstream ethico-rhetorical poetics
has been taken to be the most characteristic feature of its reception in
the late Renaissance. In comparison, too little attention has been given to
the innovations in late Renaissance theory that accompanied the assimilation of the *Poetics*. The most important of these developments was that
sixteenth-century writers and theorists built upon Aristotle's theory of
tragedy to define more fully as well as to distinguish all the relevant poetic
genres. They maintained that such a comprehensive system of the genres
had already been conceived by the Stagirite when, in fact, they were the
ones who invented it. Aristotle's treatise gained currency and authority in
the middle decades of the sixteenth century precisely because its method
and orientation eminently suited this new need to conceive of poetry in
terms of the form and functions of its various genres.

In their respective histories of Italian Renaissance criticism Spingarn[14]
and Weinberg mislead their readers when they maintain that the Italian
theorizing about poetic genres that emerges in the middle decades of the
sixteenth century stemmed directly from the recovery and exegesis of

---

[13] Stephen Halliwell, *Aristotle's poetics* (Chapel Hill: University of North Carolina Press,
   1986), pp. 300–1. For a comprehensive account of later sixteenth-century theories of
   catharsis see Baxter Hathaway, *The age of criticism: the late Renaissance in Italy* (Ithaca:
   Cornell University Press, 1962), pp. 205–300. See also T. J. Reiss's observations on
   catharsis in 'Renaissance theatre and the theory of tragedy', in the present volume; esp.
   pp. 241–4.
[14] Notably, Joel E. Spingarn's *Literary criticism in the Renaissance* (New York: Macmillan,
   1899).

Aristotle's *Poetics*. There is more reason to believe that it was the new need to classify and define poetry according to its genres that led to such unprecedented interest in the *Poetics*. Weinberg's view that the development of poetic genre theory (or indeed of all poetic theory) is a history of the recuperation and iteration of Aristotle has been particularly influential. It has reinforced the erroneous idea that generic codification and theory have always been with us, and that the sixteenth-century efforts to define and reflect upon the various genres was a continuation of a tradition rather than the new development it actually was.

Aristotle's treatise had a discernible, and in some cases, even a decisive impact on early genre theory. That, however, does not mean that it was responsible for the genesis of such theory. The *Poetics*, it should be borne in mind, is not the systematic genre theory that was gradually projected on the text by Cinquecento commentators and interpreters. Aristotle does provide elements for building a theory of generic classification, but that systematic theory was never fully erected by him. Recent studies of the *Poetics* remind us how little generic theorizing there is in the treatise, aside from the analysis of tragedy, and how partial that theorizing is.[15] If, since the mid-sixteenth century, the treatise has been perceived as a more comprehensive genre theory, this was due to the desire of early interpreters to read into the Greek text a more fully developed generic system than Aristotle had provided, or to evolve from it a comprehensive analysis of the traditional genres. Aristotle's announcement, at the beginning of he *Poetics*, that the different kinds of *mimesis* can be distinguished according to their means, their objects, and their modes, and his very brief discussion of the last two categories, were used as the basis for a generic grid in which tragedy, epic, and comedy were given dominant places, but which could also be made to accommodate genres either disregarded by or unknown to Aristotle.

Consider, for example, Aristotle's classification of the modes of enunciation at the beginning of Chapter 3 (48a20). Richard Janko's translation captures some of the complexity of the original:

Again, a third difference among these [kinds] is the manner in which one can represent each of these things. For one can use the same media to represent the very same things, sometimes (a) by narrating (either (i) becoming another [person], as Homer does, or (ii) remaining the same person and not changing), or (b) by representing everyone as in action or activity.[16]

---

[15] On the sketchiness and incompleteness of Aristotle's generic distinctions see Thomas Rosenmeyer, 'Ancient genre theory: a mirage', *Yearbook of comparative and general literature* 34 (1985), p. 79. See also Stephen Halliwell, *Aristotle's poetics*, pp. 254–65.

[16] Aristotle, *Poetics*, with the *Tractatus coislinianus*, reconstruction of *Poetics* II, and the fragments of the *On poets*, trans. R. Janko (Indianapolis and Cambridge: Hackett, 1987), p. 3.

It is unclear whether the division Aristotle makes is bipartite or tripartite, but beginning with Robortello's 1548 commentary, the tripartite interpretation – that is, that there were three modes of *mimesis*, dramatic, narrative, and mixed – became the dominant one among sixteenth-century exegetes. Robortello also assumed that the pure narrative mode was instanced in dithyramb, even though neither in this passage nor in what immediately follows does Aristotle say anything about dithyrambic poetry. This misreading – already challenged by Maggi's claim that Aristotle disregarded dithyrambic poetry – was due to the fact that Robortello and other interpreters after him took Aristotle's laconic remarks to corroborate Plato's comments on the differences between *diegesis* and *mimesis* in Book III of his *Republic*.[17] That Plato had a different agenda and different views from Aristotle did not deter Robortello from conflating the two, especially since he presumed that Aristotle regularly appropriated the ideas of his old teacher. Plato brings up dithyrambic poetry as an instance of pure *diegesis* when he divides *mimesis* into three modes. Robortello therefore presumes that the category of pure narrative, about which Aristotle says nothing, refers to dithyrambic poetry.[18]

Aristotle's statements are often so generalized, or so inexplicit or so elliptical that they could be and were made to subsume meanings they were clearly not intended to have. In the passage from Chapter 3, cited above, the text was ambiguous enough to be read as part of an initial effort to erect a generic grid that would accommodate the various kinds of poetry that Greece had produced, whereas Aristotle's intent seems rather to have been to narrow the focus of his enquiry to the modes of *mimesis* of human action. To be sure, Aristotle does provide, in his first three chapters, elements for building a more comprehensive genre theory. But one needs to distinguish what he says in those chapters, from the sort of systematization that late Renaissance Italian readers projected on them.

These readers appreciated Aristotle's analysis of the qualitative parts of tragedy (that is, the four out of the six that are discussed in Chapters 6–20: plot, characterization, thought, and diction) as a method of defining the basic features of a genre, and they appropriated it to define genres that Aristotle had ignored or barely considered. The first genre to receive this sort of analysis was comedy. As sixteenth-century commentators frequently remind us, Aristotle left no substantive definition of comedy, or if he did, as was promised at the beginning of Chapter 6, it was subsequently

---

[17] See Robortello's *Explicationes*, pp. 24–5. For Plato's distinction between *mimesis*, *diegesis*, and a third mixed mode see *Republic* (3.392c and ff.).

[18] Such a misreading may not seem significant until one realizes that it inaugurates the fiction that drama, epic, and lyric were distinguished by Aristotle, a fiction that is still alive and well in René Wellek and Austin Warren, *Theory of literature*, 3rd edn (New York: Harcourt, Brace & World, 1956), pp. 227–8.

lost. This did not prevent Robortello, or Giraldi, or Trissino or, later, Riccoboni from projecting, each in a different way, what they imagined the fuller Aristotelian definition might be. Robortello's codification of comedy, the first of these reconstructions to be published (in 1548), was appended to his commentary on the *Poetics* along with similar 'explicationes' on satire, the epigram and the elegy.[19] While Robortello drew occasionally on some of the commonplaces about comedy from Donatus's *De comoedia* and other ancient sources, the crucial difference between his codification of comedy and what was said about it in prior Terence-centred commentary was his analysis of the qualitative parts of comedy, a transposition, in very abbreviated form, of Aristotle's analysis of the plot, characterization, thought, and diction of tragedy (Robortello's remarks about the fifth qualitative part, spectacle, which Aristotle does not discuss, were drawn from Vitruvius). In comparison to the summary distinctions between tragedy and comedy formulated by the ancient grammarians such an appropriation of Aristotle's qualitative analysis allowed for a more methodical comparison of the two genres, already evident in Robortello's considerations of the differences that plot, characterization, and diction assume in comedy, in comparison to tragedy. Moreover, the priority and specificity that Robortello accorded to his analysis of the comic plot, reflecting Aristotle's own privileging of plot, already began to provide a sense of the internal workings of comedy and therefore of its particular form which is not to be found in earlier Terence-centred discussion of comedy.[20]

Robortello's 'trattatelo' on comedy served as an example of how Aristotle's qualitative analysis of tragedy could be progressively extended to define both traditional as well as modern genres ignored by Aristotle. Thus from the 1550s to the 1570s one finds such codifications of modern genres like the *romanzo* and the *novella*, but also of traditional genres disregarded by Aristotle, like the dialogue.[21] Even Aristotle's profile of

[19] It was entitled 'Explicatio eorum omnium quae ad comoediae artificium pertinent', and has been reprinted along with the other short treatises in Weinberg (ed.), *Trattati di poetica*, vol. I, pp. 516–29. Trissino's codification of comedy is to be found in the sixth division of his *Poetica*, also reprinted in Weinberg's *Trattati di poetica*, vol. II, pp. 57–76. Antonio Riccoboni's *De re comica ex Aristotelis doctrina* (1579) is reprinted in Weinberg (ed.), *Trattati di poetica*, vol. III, pp. 255–76.

[20] For a dissenting position, namely that the norms extrapolated from ancient and humanist commentary on Terence's comedies did anticipate the rules of comedy formulated by neo-Aristotelian theorists, see Marvin Herrick, *Comic theory in the sixteenth century* (Urbana: University of Illinois Press, 1950).

[21] Giovanni Battista Pigna acknowledged borrowing Aristotle's method of analysing the qualitative parts in *I romanzi* (1554), one of the first codifications of chivalric romance (see p. 65). Francesco Bonciani defines the *novella* in terms of its characteristic 'favola', 'costume', 'sentenza', and 'dizione' in his *Lezione sopra il comporre delle novelle* (1574). Carlo Sigonio devises qualitative parts for the dialogue to give a legitimate Aristotelian profile in his *De dialogo liber* (1562).

epic, the one other genre besides tragedy that is defined in the *Poetics*, was largely filled out by sixteenth-century interpreters. Thanks to their elaboration of Chapters 23 and 24 (see 'Italian epic theory' in the present volume) it has subsequently been believed that these two brief chapters constitute a fully articulated theory of epic.

This codification of both ancient and modern kinds of poetry reflects a pronounced need to map out and systematize poetic discourse. Aristotle's *Poetics*, as suggested earlier, acquired such unprecedented relevance precisely because its method and orientation eminently suited the new need to define poetry in terms of the form and function of its various genres, and of their differences. But the new value Aristotle's treatise acquired was also due to other cultural needs that it served to fulfil. One of these was a need to break away from or supersede what can be called the master author-centred poetics of Renaissance humanism. Given the centrality of *imitatio* in the humanist poetics of the fifteenth and early sixteenth centuries, respective kinds of poetry were usually identified with the ancient authors considered its pre-eminent practitioners and models. Writers aspiring to compose an epic poem, or a comedy, or any of the recognized poetic kinds were usually asked to imitate the one or two master authors in that kind. Naming the acknowledged master author of a genre – say, Virgil for epic, Terence for comedy, Horace for satire – virtually sufficed to indicate the norms of that genre.

The generic codification that emerges in the mid-Cinquecento clearly expanded this very narrow poetic canon by formulating norms not based on the example of one master author, but on the generic practice over time. Not that these new genre-specific arts cease altogether from invoking the practice of master authors, but they tend to refer to several authors, and cite their works to exemplify particular features of a genre, not the genre as a whole.

G. B. Giraldi Cintio's pioneer *Discorso . . . intorno al comporre delle comedie e delle tragedie* (published in 1554; composed as early as 1543) well illustrates how such codification enabled an enlarging of the canon that had been established by the poetics of *imitatio*. As the title indicates, Giraldi codified comedy as well as tragedy, and he did so, in imitation of Aristotle, by considering the plot, characterization, thought, and diction of each genre, but concurrently. When he formulates norms for these qualitative parts of tragedy and comedy (devoting most of his discussion to plot) he often starts off with prescriptions drawn from the *Poetics*, but these prescriptions are regularly made to include examples of post-Aristotelian practice, not only Roman but modern, which inevitably stretch what Aristotle had originally prescribed. The modification of Aristotle's principles to accommodate modern needs, and especially to justify his own dramatic practice, is particularly noticeable in Giraldi's codification of tragedy. Limits of space do not permit a discussion of such modification in detail. But when, for example, Giraldi advocates invented rather than historical plots, and then claims that Aristotle also found unknown plots more pleasing, it becomes apparent that he is revising what Aristotle said to suit his own need.[22] Giraldi was the author of nine tragedies, and one of his contributions to the early development of the genre was to write tragedies with made-up plots. All but two of his tragedies had plots of his own invention. Perhaps his most significant innovation was to compose tragedies with happy endings. Six of the nine tragedies he wrote ended happily. Not surprisingly, he recommends tragedies 'a lieto fine' in his *Discorso*. While he acknowledges Aristotle's objection that plays with happy endings cater to the weakness and ignorance of the audience, he also argues that tragic plots with happy outcomes are especially marked by the recognitions prized by Aristotle for whom '. . . the most praiseworthy is that which brings about a change from bad to happy fortune. . . .'[23] What Aristotle had said when evaluating various kinds of recognitions (Chapter 16 of the *Poetics*) was that 'the best recognition is that which emerges from the events themselves, where the amazement and the surprise are caused by probable means, as in the *Oedipus* of Sophocles and the *Iphigenia* [1455a16]'. The inclusion of Euripides' *Iphigenia at Tauris* – a tragedy with a happy ending – as one of the examples suffices for Giraldi to adduce that Aristotle especially values recognitions that transform bad fortune into good.

Obviously Giraldi seeks to enlist Aristotle's support, even if it entails a partial reading of the *Poetics*, because by showing that prescriptions like feigned plots and happy endings agree with Aristotle's recommendations he is able to make both his innovative theory and practice of tragedy seem more normative. Aristotle's rules of tragedy may not be quite as capacious as Giraldi's rewriting of them suggests. Still, it is remarkable how he can accommodate Aristotle's precepts to the modern modifications of tragedy he proposes without distorting these precepts out of recognition. The *Poetics*, moreover, was the one theory that could so serve to authorize Giraldi's own guidelines for tragedy and comedy because it was the only ancient theory that offered genre-specific rules which transcended the norms of the one or two ancient master-texts advocated for each genre by the more conservative literary arbiters of Giraldi's time.

When such a conservative critic attacked Giraldi's tragedy, *Didone*, for not imitating *Oedipus tyrannus*, supposedly the model of tragedy privileged by Aristotle, Giraldi replied, in a letter dated 1543 to Duke Ercole II

[22] See G. B. Giraldi Cinzio, *Scritti critici*, ed. C. G. Crocetti (Milan: Marzorati, 1973), pp. 177–8.
[23] *Ibid.*, pp. 183–4.

of Ferrara, that this opponent was wrong in assuming that Aristotle's norms were derived from a single master text: 'As much as Aristotle esteemed the *Oedipus tyrannus*, he valued the other tragedies enough to take them into account as well when he formulated rules and laws for best composing tragedies'. Giraldi admits that his *Didone* differs from *Oedipus*, but is a legitimate instance of the genre no less than the tragedies of Euripides or of the Romans which also modified Sophoclean and then Greek tragic practice. Giraldi then maintains that Aristotle himself allows for modifications of the genre as it evolves according to changing tastes.[24] Aristotle's theory appeals to a modernist like Giraldi precisely because it does not advocate the servile imitation of *Oedipus tyrannus* but provides a definition of tragedy general and flexible enough to accommodate the modifications and innovations that are an inevitable part of historical change. What Giraldi maintains in his letter to Ercole is fully corroborated in his *Discorso* on comedies and tragedies where, within Aristotelian guidelines, he manages to inscribe his own modifications of tragedy as well as other new dramatic practice.

In the light of the limited Latin poetic canon set up by humanist educators, Aristotle's genre-specific but not text-specific rules seemed relatively capacious and liberating for those writers seeking to win legitimacy for various modern kinds of poetic practice. One finds, moreover, that the capaciousness and the elasticity of Aristotle's rules continued to be appreciated and exploited in the course of the major literary quarrels that erupt in Italy in the latter part of the sixteenth century. The quarrel about whether Ariosto's *Orlando furioso* was an epic or an inferior romance, the one about Dante's *Commedia*, the debate about the status of tragicomedy, all these disputes were, in one way or another, about whether modern poetic creations did or did not conform to what were perceived as Aristotelian requisites for legitimate poetry. Aristotle's authority was invoked by both sides in all of these debates. Just as bending and modifying Aristotle's dicta served to make room for modern writing, so a stricter more rigid reading of his rules could serve to exclude that writing. Because romantic and post-romantic biases have made us perceive neo-Aristotelian rules of art as designed to inhibit poetic innovation we have mistakenly emphasized the restrictive use and function of these rules. But what is remarkable, and needs to be reaffirmed, is how effectively modernists could enlist Aristotle to support their claims and to justify the opening up of generic canons. The kind of stretching of Aristotelian criteria briefly discussed in the case of Giraldi was to recur for the next hundred years. And not only were Aristotle's criteria for a genre stretched to make room

---

[24] See Weinberg (ed.), *Trattati di poetica*, vol. I, pp. 484–5. The entire 'Lettera sulla tragedia', as Weinberg calls Giraldi's letter in defence of his *Didone*, is to be found on pp. 470–86.

for innovations in that genre, but the generic system itself was stretched to make room for new genres. The durability of neo-Aristotelian poetics was intimately connected to the fact that its regulations, especially its rules for genres, allowed for innovative alteration and could be accommodated to evolving literary taste.

5

Horace in the sixteenth century: commentators into critics

Ann Moss

The first instinct of the humanist interested in formulating a theory of discourse was to go back (as for so much else) to an ancient prototype. As far as poetics was concerned, by far the most influential, as well as the most comprehensive, prototype was the *Ars poetica* of Horace, in which the humanists had an authoritative text on poetic composition to set beside the old and the newly discovered rhetorical treatises of Cicero. Although widely available in the late Middle Ages, the *Ars poetica* entered the age of print without much medieval impedimenta but with two sets of mainly explanatory annotations of respectable antiquity – one by Porphyrion from the third or fourth century, the other attributed to Acro and dating from the fifth century. These were frequently reprinted and they set a trend towards a prescriptive reading of Horace's poetics. In the fifteenth and sixteenth centuries commentaries proliferated. It was primarily in commentaries on texts that humanist scholars evolved, applied, and propagated the modes of reading which underlay the theory and practice of literary composition that they promoted so effectively. It follows that the commentaries they wrote on this, the very model of critical theory, are an integral part of the history of criticism, although the present survey cannot pretend to be more than a superficial sampling of this important material.

The first humanist commentary was published at Florence in 1482 and is the work of Cristoforo Landino (Christophorus Landinus) far better known as the author of the Neoplatonic interpretation of the *Aeneid* contained in his *Disputationes Camaldulenses* (?1480). The fact that Landino also published a grammatical and rhetorical commentary on the *Aeneid* (1483), a close critical and historical examination of Virgil's language, demonstrates how easy and normal it was for humanists of his generation to switch interpretative frames. His Horace commentary is, to a lesser extent, an example of critical syncretism. In his annotations to the text Landino mixes the intelligent, sober paraphrase of the grammarian with a wholesale rhetorical approach, appealing to Cicero's judgement that the poet is close kin to the orator, except that he operates under stricter metrical constraints, is freer to explore the potential of language, and writes, if anything, for a more sophisticated and better learned audience. Parallels between poetic composition and rhetorical technique which are implied in Horace are spelt out by Landino. He makes careful correlations between Horace's various recommendations and the rhetorical divisions of formal discourse into invention, disposition, and elocution. He associates Horatian decorum with traditional distinctions between high, middle, and low styles, with their appropriate subject-matter, vocabulary and figures. Like Cicero's orator, the poet draws on the arts of grammar and rhetoric for his words, and on philosophy for his substance. To this Ciceronian stress on erudition Landino adds the assumption that poetry is read, not listened to, and read at leisure, so the reader returns at will to re-read passages in his text. The purpose of this rereading is understanding, which Landino associates most readily with pleasure, and this in turn with the fiction proper to poets. On the question of fiction, there is, he says, a difference between the false [*falsum*], the empty [*vanum*], and the feigned [*fictum*]. The false is a mode of concealing something which did occur; the empty of talking about things which cannot occur; the feigned of talking about things which did not occur, but could have done. So the false and the feigned are devoid of truth, but they are plausible (*verisimile*); the empty is implausible. By things feigned we are delighted; by the false we are deceived; empty nonsense we despise. So it is clear that the matter proper to poets is fiction, for the aim of poetry is to delight. This account of poetic fiction occurs early in the commentary (on lines 7–8) and refers back to the definition of the poet Landino proposed in his preface rather than to his subsequent assimilation of the poet with the orator. The preface has strong Neoplatonic resonances: 'God creates from nothing. The poet, even if he does not present us with something got altogether from nothing, yet, under the inspiration of a divine fury, feigns things in finely fashioned verses, so that he seems to produce something sublime and worthy of deepest wonder by virtue of his own fiction-making and as it were, from nothing'.[1] It is precisely when the reader realizes that his first, naïve or literal reading was deceptive and that under this veil of fiction lie matters of the highest form of knowledge that he is imbued with pleasure. However, reading as allegorical interpretation is scarcely mentioned in the ensuing notes. It is perhaps significant of a change in interpretative feasibilities that the commentary of Landino, quite often reprinted, appears without its Neoplatonizing preface in a composite edition of Horace commentaries by the diligent and pragmatic German scholar, Georgius Fabricius (Basle, 1555).

That edition also includes the commentary by Iodocus Badius Ascensius (Josse Bade), which was first published at Paris in 1500 and may well have been the most frequently reprinted of all the commentaries on the *Ars poetica* in the sixteenth century. In utilitarian terms it has notable virtues.

---

[1] *Horatius cum quattuor commentariis* (Venice: B. Locatellus, 1494), fol. CLXV[v].

Firstly, Badius is explicitly prescriptive. He divides the work into twenty-six sections and at the end of each he interpolates a rule conveniently summarizing the main instructions for writing poetry contained in the section just annotated. Secondly, he is very comprehensive, and to illustrate key concepts he inserts long quotations from other sources, so that the commentary becomes a handy encyclopaedia of previous opinions. The fourth-century grammarians Diomedes and Donatus, together with the slightly later Priscian, had been the standard authorities on the poetic genres throughout the Middle Ages, and they reappear verbatim in Badius. For Diomedes, in the first half of the third book of his *Ars grammatica* (the remainder of that book is concerned with metrics), poetry may be narration of material feigned or true, in rhythm or in quantitative metre, written for profit and delight, and subscribing to one of three forms: (i) dramatic or 'mimetic', in which persons speak without intervention from the poet: tragedy, comedy, satyr-plays, mime, some of Virgil's eclogues; (ii) narrative or 'exegetic', in which the poet alone enunciates: sentences (Theognis), history (Hesiod), didactic poems (Lucretius, Virgil's *Georgics*); (iii) mixed forms, in which the poet speaks and introduces other speakers: heroic poems (Homer, Virgil's *Aeneid*), lyric (Horace, elegiasts). This apparently strange classification, which goes back to Plato's *Republic*, Book III, is one of various models which complicate subsequent attempts to categorize poetry by genres. Horace's own brief passage on metres and subjects appropriate to the different genres (lines 73–85) is supplemented by Badius to include contributions on drama from Diomedes and from Donatus, whose commentary on Terence was the main medieval authority in this particular field. On rhetorical elements in the *Ars poetica*, that is to say anything that can be related to invention, disposition, elocution, and characters of style, Badius refers on occasion to Quintilian, and to Cicero on almost everything. Badius takes every opportunity to build on to Horace's text a systematic poetics, structured according to categories which the grammarians thought proper to poetry, especially genre and metre, and according to principles of composition defined in rhetoric.

Badius's ability to make orderly patterns out of the sudden shifts of subject and tone in Horace's text was doubtless another reason for his commentary's success. Coherence and symmetry are strong points with Badius. He finds them displayed in God's creation and inherent in Horace's first injunction to the apprentice poet, and he imposes them on the conclusions he draws from the *Ars poetica*. So, on the matter of poetry (developing out of the one word 'materia' in line 38):

The matter is threefold: either altogether true, something which actually occurred, as in histories; or not true, but truth-like, something which could have occurred, such as the plots of comedies; or neither true nor truth-like, such as many poetic fables, for example, Virgil's ships changing to nymphs, and many of the metamorphoses in Ovid; yet these fables should be examined for some meaningful substance, either physical or historical or mystical.[2]

Badius here not only makes careful distinctions, but he insinuates a very medieval mode of allegorical interpretation into his definition of poetic fiction, while all the time referring to the authority of the *Rhetorica ad Herennium* (I.viii.13) on kinds of narrative. He continues with parallel series of threes: the three kinds of matter appropriate to the three kinds of style with their three characters, that is to say the elevated, involving gods, heroes and kings, the middle, primarily didactic, setting out instruction in morals, laws, and the liberal and mechanical arts, and, thirdly, the low, to be used for pastoral, comedy, Aesopic fables, and less sophisticated teaching. The rhetoric and poetic of the Middle Ages had systematized the three styles in just such a manner, and Badius, among others, transmits their distinctions at the formative period of Renaissance poetics, just when the new rhetorical manuals of the humanist classroom were tending to play down this particular medieval obsession. Badius is not always totally consistent, despite his love of system. In an earlier account of the matter of poetry (on the passage on poets and painters, lines 9–13) he declares that 'nothing may be introduced into poetic fiction which is not truth-like',[3] apparently disallowing poetic fable as he had previously defined it, but he then goes on to say that poets may introduce anything which does not contradict known historical fact or the philosophy and theology of the ancients. On such shifting foundations were future discussions of the status of poetic fiction to take place. On the other hand, the compulsion Badius has to draw conclusions points forward to many a future argument in poetry's defence, as when he says (elaborating Horace's neutral line 9) that poetry is superior to painting because its [rhetorical] colours do not fade, are immune to time and weather, and become more precious with age, as gold refined in fire. As far as other contested issues are concerned, on divine inspiration versus acquired technique (lines 295–7, 407–10) Badius supplies further quotations and examples of God-given genius (Plato, Virgil, Hesiod, Ennius) to compensate a little for Horace's ironies; on utility and pleasure (lines 333–4), he, like Horace, is even-handed.

A third relatively early humanist commentary takes us back to the less schematic approach of the Italians. Aulo Giano Parrasio (Ianus Parrhasius), wrote a commentary printed in Naples in 1531, and, like those of Landino and Badius, included sporadically in composite editions later in the century. Digressing quite frequently from strict annotation Parrasio touches more often than either of his predecessors on areas which were to become central to subsequent literary debate: the status of fiction, the morality of

---

[2] *Quint. Horatii Flacci de arte poetica opusculum aureum* (Paris: J. Petit, 1505), fol. VIII[r].
[3] *Ibid.*, fol. IIII[r].

literature, the problematics of literary imitation. His divagations connect but loosely to his text, but this in itself demonstrates how writing about the theory of poetic composition can at this time encompass issues often side-tracked by the more pragmatic prose rhetorics. Parrasio flatly refuses to imaginative artists the creative licence which Horace had conceded to them, provided they stopped short of total incongruity (lines 9–11). Parrasio proposes quite another sort of limitation on the fictions they invent, proscribing those which merely charm the ears, disparaging those which are a tissue of untruths, and commending only those which are based on a solid foundation of truth and attract the mind to images of virtue. By the latter sort he means fabulous narrations in which true and edifying meanings are veiled and can only be reached by a reading which interprets the fables allegorically. Even then, he rejects fables which employ base and monstrous material for allegorical purposes, and countenances only those which clothe sacred concepts in words of suitable dignity and images of suitable decorum. Of such are the poetry of Orpheus, the philosophy of Pythagoras, the hieroglyphs of the Egyptians, all of which conceal the deepest mysteries and arcane secrets of nature. In these the poet should immerse himself, submitting himself to the Socratic furies and taking care not to adulterate with any admixture of his own the fictions to which the furies inspire him, lest he 'couple serpents with birds' (after this long detour we have come back to Horace at line 13). Parrasio has incorporated at an early stage into the *Ars poetica* the concept of the allegorical truth of poetic fiction, not, like Badius, in its schematic, medieval form of physical, historical, moral, and allegorical distinctions, but, despite some Neoplatonic dressing-up, in a quite close paraphrase of Macrobius, *Commentarium in somnium Scipionis*, II. In this way Parrasio transmits a *locus classicus* for allegorical fiction-writing as an integral part of poetic theory.

Later in the commentary (on lines 408–11) Parrasio returns to poetic inspiration, in the context of Horace's conjunction of nature and art. Poetry, Parrasio comments, is an imitation of nature in the sense that ideas for artistic creation grow in us spontaneously and that any ability we have to conceive them and give them expression is a gift of nature. But this natural energy is not under our control and is weakened by deficiencies within us. It needs the reinforcement and direction it can get from well-tried artistic precepts, which we can substitute when natural inspiration fails us. When explaining the instruction contained in Horace's *Ars poetica*, Parrasio applies the same rhetorical categories as his predecessors, but with a marked emphasis on *elocutio* [style], by which he means 'the verbal expression of mental concepts'.[4] In his *excursus* on lines 24–31, where Horace alludes to the three levels of style, Parrasio takes his remarks on

---

[4] *Q. Horatii Flacci . . . omnia poemata* (Venice: J. M. Bonellus, 1562), fol. 126ʳ.

the characters of style and on faults to be avoided no further than Cicero and Quintilian. He is much more interested in the idea that style reveals the character and moral defects of the writer: 'more often than not it is true that as the style is, so is the life'.[5] He makes literary style a barometer of public as well as private morality. Virgil's fertile vein, abundance of resource, and good judgement reflect Rome at the height of her powers; Ovid's stylistic licence reflects her incipient decadence. However, it is style as an indicator of private morality that most concerns Parrasio and justifies the moral tone of his injunctions to the poet to cultivate the best in his character and in his writing. Parrasio here comes closer than either Landino or Badius to the root of the humanists' faith in the moral virtues of a literary culture. He is also much more voluble than they are on another, and closely related feature of the humanist project: literary imitation. The occasions Horace offers for elaborating on this were not taken up to any significant extent by the previous commentators, but Parrasio does so with enthusiasm. On lines 128–35, he talks about the good judgement needed to choose which author to imitate and what to imitate in him. Without models to work to, we cannot perfect what nature began in us. As latecomers we are all the more fortunate, for we can show our talent by rearranging what others have composed and giving it a new look, though we must add something of our own, or else, inevitably, we shall always lag behind. The special genius of the literary imitator is so to digest and reproduce what he has taken from his predecessors as to create something altogether different yet marked with recognizable traces of its origins.[6] Parrasio here, as in his previous assimilation of good morals and good style, owes much to Quintilian. But in an energetic peroration at the end of his commentary, Parrasio exhorts his young contemporaries to purge and prepare themselves for divine inspiration in language redolent with Neoplatonic enthusiasm, and affirms the superior moral values promoted by poetry with an altogether un-Horatian zeal and panache.

Read in the context of the commentaries of Landino, Badius, and Parrasio, with one or other of which it regularly appears up until the mid-1560s, the *Ars poetica* of Horace becomes a vehicle for the whole range of views on poetic theory available up to about 1530, as well as for ideas intrinsic to itself and merely reinforced by the commentaries, such as principles of coherence, appropriateness of moral characteristics depicted and of diction, normative features of the genres, and the relationship between poem and reader defined as the communication of instruction and pleasure. A commentary published by a German scholar at Strasburg in 1539 and reprinted there in 1545, the *Commentaria in artem poeticam Horatii* of Jodocus Willichius, confirms this encyclopaedic trend with

[5] *Ibid.*, fol. 126[v].   [6] *Ibid.*, fol. 136[v].

a 'prolegomena' devoted to various theories of poetic genre and with a wealth of erudite amplifications on the text. However, from the early 1540s to the mid-1550s there was a spate of new Italian commentaries whose main purpose was to relate the *Ars poetica* to the *Poetics* of Aristotle, a text which began to be a decisive influence on the course of literary criticism only after the influential Latin translation of 1536 and the major commentaries of Francesco Robortello, published at Florence in 1548, and of Vincenzo Maggi, which appeared at Venice in 1550. Both these editors in fact included an edition of Horace along with their Aristotle, thereby establishing a dual authority on poetic theory, and this will persist long after the Renaissance. These and other editions of the same period aim to make the two texts concord and this they achieve to their own satisfaction by aligning Horace section by section with parallels from Aristotle to prove that they are both working with the same set of ideas. Horace's insistence on coherence thus corresponds to Aristotle's description of plot; ethical decorum in Horace is the same as Aristotle's recommendation for the portrayal of characters in tragedy; Horace on truth and fiction parallels Aristotle on the necessary and the probable, and so on. The annotations open up the text of Horace to absorb Aristotle in much the same way as earlier commentaries had absorbed the medieval grammarians. The rhetorical framework, still firmly in place, also proves elastic, with Aristotle's constituents of tragedy sometimes reduced to plot and diction, and then immediately identified with the *res/verba* distinction so readily accommodated to traditional rhetorical analysis. Seen through Horace, Aristotle becomes instantly familiar and instantly accessible; seen under the name of Aristotle, the 'art of poetry' acquires a new gravity.

The *Poetica Horatiana* published at Venice in 1561 by Giovanni Battista Pigna is much more innovative. Pigna uses parallels from the *Poetics* to support his observations, but not as the organizing frame of his commentary. Organization is Pigna's strong point. He divides the text of the *Ars poetica* into eighty precepts which are collected at the end of his book and relate to the sections into which Pigna had split the text for annotation. The heads to these precepts are also arranged into a number of diagrammatic tables which divide and subdivide the argument of the whole *Ars poetica* and each of its constituent and related parts. The analysis is complex, but Pigna does draw clear lines of sense through Horace's text and makes of it a logically coherent exposition of theory and good practice. In thus discovering a rigorous methodology in the *Ars* (or, rather, imposing one on it) Pigna sets the tone for the conclusions he will derive from Horace concerning the province and properties of poetry, which he defines more strictly than most of his predecessors. Horace's injunction to follow paradigms of moral behaviour (lines 309–18) leads Pigna to circumscribe the scope of poetry. Its proper sphere is the moral, the imitation of human actions. If it touches on any other disciplines of enquiry, such as natural science or philosophy, it is only incidentally. Writers who versify science (Lucretius) are no poets at all. Aristotle's philosophy is too specialized and technical to be matter for poetry, and it lacks those heroic and religious elements to be found in Plato (demons, gods, mystical allegory, the immortality of the soul) which are more properly poetic, not, Pigna insists, because poetry is to be thought of as fiction veiling truth, but because these religious elements belong to the sphere of the probable, believed by everyone, and therefore have the status of things that could happen. It is precisely the poet's function to describe such things.[7]

Here we have both a rejection of the encyclopaedic attitude of the earlier humanists, for whom poetry encompassed every branch of knowledge, and also a downgrading of the theory which held that an allegorical relationship between fiction and truth was a necessary attribute of poetry. Their place is taken by Aristotelian concepts of probability and verisimilitude. Pigna returns to both points when he argues *in utramque partem* on the subject of poetry's utility and delight (lines 333–46). It is not the proper province of poetry to teach grammar, geography, politics, history, or theology. They should be learnt from specialist works of reference. The history to be found in poetry is mingled with fictions, and although this is proper to poetic discourse it makes for suspect history, which should be concerned with nothing but the truth. Poets may wrap the truths of philosophy in their fables, and properly so, for they give pleasure to those readers competent to recognize them. But this is no way for the ignorant to learn philosophy, for which they must go to the relevant technical treatises. Again, moral *sententiae*, adages, and maxims are the stuff of tragedy, but only as instances of the practical application of moral philosophy to probable circumstances; collections of moral commonplaces are a better source than plays for the principles of ethics.

Pigna is particularly dubious about the positive moral effects some would ascribe to poetry. It is the experience of history and the science of ethics that teach us what we ought to be; poetry tells us what we are.[8] Pigna is inclined to see the special purpose of poetry as the production of pleasure, while not denying the important contribution plays and public recitations have made in the more anarchic past to social cohesion and in the present to the private contentment of citizens in well-regulated states. The source of the pleasure peculiar to poetry is not in learning something new and useful, but in recognizing what we know already. This involves an interplay of truthlike reproduction with the memory of the onlooker or reader, so that what he has known, heard, or read in the past is reproduced

---

[7] *Ioan. Baptistae Pignae Poetica Horatiana* (Venice: V. Valgrisius, 1561), p. 72.
[8] *Ibid.*, pp. 75–6.

for him in the present, but in a form more beautiful and more perfect than his previous experience had shown him.[9]

Pigna's shift to a more specialized definition of literature is consistent with contemporary trends in the history of education and is reflected in commentaries on texts and in instruction manuals in the second half of the century. They too demonstrate how the proliferation of printed reference books had undercut the pretensions of poetry to encyclopaedic erudition, and there too we find hints of a perceived need to define the autonomy of the 'literary' and to stake its claims. They also latch on to the pedagogical usefulness of displaying information and argument in diagrammatic form, and they encourage the search for method, coherence, and clear divisions. A glimpse of the *Ars poetica* and the *Poetics* of Aristotle reduced to their lowest common denominator as a teaching text is provided by the *Commentarii in artem poeticam Horatii confecti ex scholiis Jo. Sturmii*, edited for Sturm's school at Strasburg (Strasburg, 1576).

The preface, which is by Sturm himself, states that all poetry is imitation, or *mimesis*, and that *mimesis* consists of six things, all of which are covered by Horace. Observe them well, and you will be an accomplished poet. The six things turn out to be Aristotle's essentials for tragedy: plot [*muthos* or *fabula*], which Sturm says may be about true things or about things that could happen, and this entails that the poet should choose his subject from Homer or from whichever writer he intends to imitate; character [*ethos*], under which Sturm conflates psychological characteristics appropriate to different ages and different kinds of human beings with the morally good or evil actions to which they give rise, and directs the poet to the character studies of Homer and Virgil; thought [*dianoia*], general ideas and opinions and their expression in speech, more especially in *sententiae* appropriate to the person speaking; diction [*lexis*], the kinds of verbal expression in which the three previous elements are to be imitated and enunciated; choruses, costumes, and stage-effects.[10] It will be seen that this simplistic version of Aristotle leans heavily towards literary imitation and Horatian decorum, and this indeed is the drift of the commentary. It interprets 'lecta res' in line 40 to mean both 'chosen' and 'already known', in the sense of knowing, from reading, how other authors have treated the matter and organized their exposition of it;[11] and it endorses what it takes to be Horace's discouragement of original subjects for plays (lines 125–30) defining 'original subjects' as plays on biblical themes.[12] If imitation stays too close to a model, it is servile, as Horace says (lines 131–5); but the commentary immediately counsels against straying too

[9] *Ibid.*, pp. 77–8.
[10] *Commentarii in artem poeticam Horatii confecti ex scholiis Io. Sturmii* (Strasburg: N. Wyriot, 1576), sig. Aii[r]–Aiii[r].
[11] *Ibid.*, sig. Bii[v]–Biii[r].   [12] *Ibid.*, sig. Dii[r].

far into untrodden territory.[13] There is, moreover, a more efficient way of perfecting one's style than by analysing the works of many authors. This is to collect vocabulary, arrange it in categories, and apply dialectical procedures of argument to the amplification of any subject with the vocabulary one has amassed.[14] This combination of stylistic *copia* with the formulae established by place-rhetoric for generating discourse is entirely typical of the method of composition taught in humanist schoolrooms in the last two-thirds of the century. The Strasburg commentary constructs a Horace who might have been taught there and learnt to make his points in due order by applying the processes of dialectical reasoning.

Another school edition, *Q. Horatii Flacci Ars poetica ad P. Rami Dialecticam et Rhetoricam resoluta* (1583), by a Dane, Andreas Kragius, reduces the *Ars* to a manageable eighteen precepts and sets out to prove that Horace's method of exposition differs in no way from that of Ramus, by analysing the text first according to the places of dialectic and then according to the figures of rhetoric. Horace had already been reconstructed, but rather more loosely, in the image of Ramus by the Spanish rhetorician, Francisco Sanchez de las Brozas (Sanctius). His *De auctoribus interpretandis sive de exercitatione praecepta* (written in 1556, reprinted in 1581 and 1591) starts ambitiously with a general theory of literary analysis, but soon narrows down its application to the *Ars poetica*. For Sanctius, analysis consists of 'unravelling' a text so as to reveal how it is put together out of the places of dialectical reasoning through which the subject-matter is drawn and by which propositions are argued. Sanctius traces places of argumentation through the *Ars poetica*, also applying Quintilian's definition of signifier and signified (the *verba/res* distinction of every humanist rhetoric) and making a nice concession to Spanish exuberance when he insists that painters and poets must, for example, depict Venus consistent with her familiar image, but may fill in the empty spaces round her at will with birds, flowers, trees, and running water.[15]

For a much more sophisticated critical edition of the *Ars poetica* we must go to France, to the edition of Horace's complete works by Denys Lambin, which was first published at Lyons in 1561 and then in a number of revised editions and reprintings. 'The best text and commentary before Bentley', as the modern commentator describes it, is a further example of that tendency to think of literature as a specialism which we noted in Pigna's commentary of the same year, but in the case of Lambin, that specialism is textual criticism in the strict sense, and the readers he has foremost in mind are not schoolboys practising verse compositions or even readers and writers of poetry, so much as his professional colleagues,

---

[13] *Ibid.*, sig. Diiii^v–Dv^r.   [14] *Ibid.*, sig. Fv+2^r.
[15] *Opera omnia*, 4 vols. (Geneva: Frères de Tournes, 1766), vol. II, p. 78.

like Henri Estienne, who was to write *Diatribae* (1575) against textual conjectures made by Lambin.

The judicious reading of the text of Horace is the business of Lambin in his general comments as well as in his discussion of manuscript variants. He elucidates Horace's pronouncements on poetry by very exact, very cogent paraphrase which makes fine distinctions of meaning, often in juxtaposition with parallels from other authors. Plato, Aristotle, and Cicero, in all their works which touch on poetry and rhetoric, provide Lambin with a context for Horace's views, but he does not wrest his author's meaning to fit theirs. This clear, intelligent, urbane exposition of the *Ars poetica* provides us with the unusual example of a humanist extending the responsibilities of literary scholarship as far as to promote the poetry of his own vernacular among the critically sophisticated, European readership which he would be expecting to reach with an edition of a major literary theorist. In editions after 1567, as an illustrative appendix to lines 141–2, Lambin quotes the first lines and a further projected passage from Ronsard's as yet unpublished *Franciade*, both in French and in Latin translation. The aim is to advertise abroad the achievements of France in 'good letters and liberal studies', and it is notable that Lambin the humanist perceives the fulfilment of the humanists' programme in France to be taking place in French literature, as well as in Latin contributions to scholarship like his own.

Do the commentaries on Horace's *Ars poetica* published during the sixteenth century make a distinctive contribution towards developing a discipline of literary criticism? As commentaries on an ancient text, their history mirrors the general evolution of commentary in that period, moving from the primarily explanatory mode of the grammarians' *enarratio* to the analytical and categorizing methodologies of later schoolmasters and the application of the specialist techniques of textual critics. Nevertheless, the subject-matter of the work perforce led its commentators to talk about poetry in general as well as this poem in particular. Even so, like their contemporaries, they were more interested in making poetry than in theorizing about it, and therefore in the pragmatics of prescription rather than in speculation about nature and effect. However, the traditional expectation of commentary was that it should not only explain and redeploy its text, but also contextualize it by bringing into play quotations from other writers. That is how the margins and appendices of editions of the *Ars poetica* became vehicles for transmitting the substance of quintessentially literary debates: on the related arts of discourse, rhetoric, and poetry; on the problematics of truth and fiction; on the ethical value of poetry, and, by implication, of all literature. The contributions of our commentators to these debates were rarely original, but it was they who set up the debates, and did so around the most widely read didactic work on literary composition.

6

Cicero and Quintilian

John O. Ward

What role did an increasingly comprehensive and critical reading of the rhetorical works of Cicero and Quintilian play in the development of Renaissance ideas about literary criticism? Of obvious initial interest is the insistence in the mature Cicero and in Quintilian that the trainee orator should, in the first place, read the poets, historians, and 'writers, or learned contributors to all good arts', and, in the second place (for the sake of practice), praise, interpret, and correct them, pointing out their failings and the aspects that required a critical response.[1] The influence of such prescriptions must be observed by the reader in other chapters of the present volume: here the interface between Renaissance students and the rhetorical works of Cicero and Quintilian alone can be sketched in, with some central attention to those passages in the new curriculum texts that can be expected to have assisted with a refinement and an enlargement of the contemporary view of the rhetorical functioning of language, and a sharper focus upon what distinguished rhetorical prose from poetry.

Of the major curriculum rhetorical texts inherited by the early fifteenth century from medieval usage, the most important were Cicero's *De inventione* and the approximately contemporary *Rhetorica ad Herennium*.[2] The former makes few references to language and even fewer to poetry, whilst the latter provides little specific analysis and instruction in prose style, despite being a 'complete' rhetorical *ars*. The 'mature' rhetorical works of Cicero, by contrast, and the much more comprehensive rhetorical textbook of the early imperial rhetor, M. Fabius Quintilianus, the *Institutio oratoria*, entered the teaching curriculum fully only in the fifteenth century. They provided extensive guidance on the subject of euphonious prose and the relative requirements of prose and verse, that is, the distinction between rhythm [*numeri, rhuthmoi*] and metre [*dimensio, metroi*] (rather than between pitch/accent, and quantity/duration), between *flexible* arrangements of syllable lengths, and *fixed* (metric, verse)

---

[1] Cicero, *De oratore* 1.43.158.
[2] J. O. Ward, 'Renaissance commentators on Ciceronian rhetoric', in *Renaissance eloquence: studies in the theory and practice of Renaissance rhetoric*, ed. J. J. Murphy (Berkeley, Los Angeles, London: University of California Press, 1983), pp. 126–73.

arrangements.[3] It is, arguably, attention to Quintilian's *Institutio oratoria* 9.4 [*compositio*] that distinguishes humanist from medieval prose practice. In fact, close study of classical prose practices (liberally infused with pre- paratory reading and imitation of classical poetry, itself a kind of display oratory but yet distinct enough) may well be classed as the major contribu- tion of the fifteenth-century rhetors to the subject of literary criticism. Quintilian's emphasis upon method (10.2.7 for example) and the whole profile and upbringing of the orator (Books I–II, XII, not unknown in the Middle Ages) were certainly refreshingly redolent of genuine classical prac- tice for those sufficiently keen to ponder upon them, but overwhelmingly, it seems, the parts of the rhetorical *œuvre* of Cicero and Quintilian brought newly into circulation in the fifteenth century extended the existing rhet- orical curriculum most significantly in the zone of *numerus oratorius*. To the greater currency of Cicero's mature rhetorical writings and of Quintilian's *Institutio* in the early Italian Renaissance, we must now turn.

Quintilian's *Institutio* is a special case. It is not that it was unknown in its entirety before Poggio Bracciolini's 'discovery' in 1416 of the complete text at St Gall;[4] it was rather a question of tastes and vocational demands that kept medieval rhetors away from the elaborate discussion of *elocutio* and method in *Institutio* Books VIII–XI.[5] The passages of Quintilian's text used in the Middle Ages did not illuminate the area of poetic style and lit- erary usage, being confined in the main to those parts of the *Institutio* that deal plainly enough with the technical details of courtroom oratory, and exercises/practices appropriate to it. Medieval rhetors used Quintilian to deepen their understanding of topics covered initially in the *Ad Herennium* and the *De inventione*; they did not generally use him to *extend* the cur- riculum. These tastes and demands were already changing by the turn of the fifteenth century: humanist attention to the complete Quintilian con- firmed a developing interest in close study of classical prose and poetic

[3] The standard treatments are E. Norden, *Die Antike Kunstprosa vom VI Jahrhundert v. Chr. bis in die Zeit der Renaissance*, 2 vols. (1909; reprint Darmstadt: Wissenschaftliche Buchgesellschaft, 1974), with G. Calboli, *Nota di Aggiornamento* (Padua: Salerno Editrice, 1986), and A. Primmer, *Cicero Numerosus: studien zum antiken Prosarhythmus* (Vienna: Öst. Ak. der Wiss. phil.-hist. Kl. Sitzungsb. 257, 1968); see also A. Scaglione, *The classical theory of composition from its origins to the present: a historical survey* (Chapel Hill: University of North Carolina Press, 1972), ch. 1, A. Leeman, *Orationis ratio: the stylistic theories and practice of the Roman orators, historians and philosophers*, 2 vols. (Amsterdam: Hakkert, 1963), vol. I, pp. 298ff, 308ff, and H. C. Gotoff, *Cicero's elegant style: an analysis of the Pro Archia* (Urbana: University of Illinois Press, 1979).
[4] L. D. Reynolds (ed.), *Texts and transmission: a survey of the Latin classics* (Oxford: Clarendon Press, 1983), pp. 332–4; R. Sabbadini, *Le scoperte dei codici latini e greci ne' secoli XIV e XV: nuove ricerche col riassunto filologico dei due volumi*, 2 vols. (Florence: Sansoni, 1905–14), vol. II, pp. 247–8; R. Sabbadini, *Storia e critica di testi latini*, 2nd edition (Padua: Antenore, 1971), ch. 7, pp. 283ff.
[5] Or, for that matter, from the reduced discussion of it in the fifth book of Martianus Capella's *De nuptiis mercurii et philologiae*.

style that is evident as early as Gasparino Barzizza's *De compositione*[6] and Guarino da Verona's 'trattatello' on the topic.[7] As late as the 1490s, however, *numerosa structura* was little known (according to Sabbadini) among men of learning, at best being preached rather than practised. George of Trebizond's *Rhetoricorum libri* v ('the first complete Rhetoric of the humanist movement', published at Venice in 1433–4) seems to have been something of a milestone, and its extensive discussion of euphonious prose style in the light of euphonious poetic style[8] includes the celebrated 'reworking' of some 'choppy, colliding phrases' from an epideictic speech by Guarino into 'smooth rolling periods', a transformation from careless and empty prose ['supina et futilis oratio'] in which nothing is put together with any power ['nihil fere viriliter colligatur'], into vibrant and flexible prose ['viva oratio et mobilis'], in which everything is uttered with forceful and compact economy ['expeditius omnia dicuntur et coacta atque comprehensa ita efferuntur'].[9]

The *De oratore*, *Orator*, and *Brutus* can lay a greater claim to being 'discoveries' of the fifteenth century (following the recovery of a complete manuscript of all three in the cathedral library of Lodi in 1421). While not, again, entirely unknown to the Middle Ages, their contents had little impact upon the medieval rhetorical curriculum. Yet these texts are overwhelmingly concerned with oratorical style, by way of the sort of nuanced discussion of euphonious prose rhythms that we have already encountered in Quintilian rather than by way of any mechanical description of figures. The *De optimo genere oratorum*, not clearly an authentic work of Cicero, and the *De partitione oratoria dialogus*, a severely technical work, also treat this topic relatively amply, and both enjoyed greater currency in the Renaissance than they did in the Middle Ages. Since the *Orator* is Cicero's last rhetorical work, and since by his own admission it contained

[6] AD 1420, dependent, it seems, upon Quintilian's *Institutio* and Martianus Capella's treatment of the subject: R. Sabbadini, *Il metodo degli umanisti* (Florence: Felice Le Monnier, 1920), p. 61.

[7] Dependent upon Martianus, Quintilian, and Cicero's *Orator* (and therefore written after AD 1422). According to his son, Guarino had in his teaching recommended 'the artifice of rhythm' for the practice of orators. B. Guarino, *De ordine docendi et studendi*, trans. in W. H. Woodward, *Vittorino da Feltre and other humanist educators* (1897; reprint New York: Bureau of Publications, Teachers College, Columbia University, Classics in Education no. 18, 1963), pp. 165, 177.

[8] Pages 370 to 526 (the end of the treatise) in the Lyons 1547 edition.

[9] John Monfasani, *George of Trebizond: a biography and a study of his rhetoric and logic* (Leiden: Brill, 1976), pp. 261–5; see also pp. 29–32, 262–99. For a fuller context, see J. Monfasani (ed.), *Collectanea Trapezuntiana: texts, documents, and bibliographies of George of Trebizond* (Binghamton: Medieval and Renaissance Texts and Studies/ Renaissance Society of America, 1984), pp. 360–411; R. Sabbadini, *La scuola e gli studi di Guarino Guarini Veronese* (Catania: F. Galati, 1896), pp. 73–5, 228–30; Scaglione, *The classical theory of composition*, pp. 135–7; M. Baxandall, *Giotto and the orators: humanist observers of painting in Italy and the discovery of pictorial composition 1350–1450* (Oxford: Clarendon Press, 1971), pp. 138–9.

the most extensive discussion to date of *numerosa oratio* in Roman criticism, we may suppose that the topic had become a passion of his.[10]

The chief consequence, then, for rhetorical and poetic studies, of renewed attention to the full text of Quintilian's *Institutio* and to Cicero's mature rhetorical works, was a deeper and enriched appreciation of the 'aural sweetening' and 'pleasure' provided by 'measured composition', the varied insertion [*diversa collocatio*] of metrical arrangements into classical prose [*numerus oratorius*, 'nombre oratoire', *numerositas*].[11] Here lay the criterion of artistic excellence, the benchmark for experiment in the vernacular, the measure of the distance travelled by the humanists from medieval (accentual) prose rhythms and stylistic norms. Here too lay the crucial distinguishing line between poetry and prose.

Turning from the classical texts themselves, to their commentators in the first phase of mature (Italian) philological humanism (the fifteenth and early sixteenth centuries), what response do we find to the insights contained in the mature rhetorical works of Cicero and the full text of Quintilian regarding the nature of oratorical and poetic linguistic effects and the importance of euphonious prose? Guarino da Verona, the most celebrated of the early humanist teachers, who taught the *Ad Herennium* continuously during the 1430s, 1440s, and 1450s at Ferrara, spent much time analysing *numerus oratorius* and *numerus poeticus*, as we learn from the witness of Battista, his son, and Janus Pannonius, his pupil. He required Virgil to be learnt by heart and, though he wrote little poetry himself, demanded the composition of Latin verse from his students. There are a few pages on euphonious prose composition in his short *Regule de ornatissimo et rhetorico dictamine Latino*, but the several versions of his *Ad Herennium* lectures pick up little of the topic. The influence of Virgil, however, is clear enough throughout these *Ad Herennium* lectures. It seems, in fact, that the study of rhetoric was simply part of a broader curriculum of which an adjacent major part took the form of close attention to classical, in particular, Virgilian, verse, with some use also of Terence, Lucan, Statius, and Ovid, and generalized poetic (mythological, legendary, Homeric) themes. Although he is more careful than the author of the *Ad*

---

[10] Reynolds (ed.), *Texts and transmission*, pp. 100ff, 111–12; Sabbadini, *Le scoperte*, vol. II, p. 209, *Storia*, pp. 77–108, and 'I codici delle opere rettoriche di Cicerone', *Rivista di filologia e d'istruzione classica* 16, 3–4 (1887), 97–120; M. Fumaroli, *L'âge de l'éloquence: rhétorique et 'res literaria' de la Renaissance au seuil de l'époque classique* (Geneva: Droz, 1980), pp. 47–56; P. S. Piacentini, 'La tradizione laudense di Cicerone ed un inesplorato manoscritto della Biblioteca Vaticana (Vat.lat.3237)', *Revue d'histoire des textes*, 11 for 1981 (1983), 123–46; Leeman, *Orationis ratio*, ch. 6, pp. 143ff, 155; Scaglione, *The classical theory of composition*, pp. 49ff, 85ff.

[11] Jacques-Louis d'Estrebay, *De electione et oratoria collocatione verborum libri duo* (Paris: Michel Vascosan, 1538), quoted in K. Meerhoff, *Rhétorique et poétique au XVIe siècle en France. Du Bellay, Ramus et les autres* (Leiden: Brill, 1986), p. 64 (compare also pp. 2, 6, 26, 331, 341–6).

Herennium to note the oratorical inapplicability of some examples provided, in general Guarino is content to clarify the *Ad Herennium*, rather
than to expand or even question its coverage or emphasis, nor is there
any evidence that he lectured seriously on any other of Cicero's rhetorical
works. Even in his treatment of the preface to *Ad Herennium* IV, where
strict adherence to the doctrine put forward by the author of the *Ad
Herennium* could have called into question the advisability of selecting
Cicero as a model for imitation (a practice advised by Guarino himself,
and fundamental to early Italian humanism), we find nothing but a patchy
paraphrase of the classical text itself. The teaching of Guarino's immediate predecessor Gasparino Barzizza, a studium lecturer in grammar
and rhetoric in the Milan–Pavia–Padua region, seems to have been overwhelmingly orientated towards oratory; poetic instruction figured only
as a component of his rhetorical and grammatical instruction.[12] Few of
Gasparino's pupils indulged much in poetry, but one who did (the minor
Paduan notary and schoolmaster Antonio Baratella), treated verse simply
as a form of highly ornamented functional display prose. Baratella, on his
own admission, wrote 48,165 verses, spread over thirteen works, and was
forever seeking employment as a court poet. He was (wrote Sabbadini), a
'meccanico della metrica'.

Guarino was clearly following established tradition in much of his
teaching, but his influence was, initially, considerable. His gloss on the
Ad Herennium, in a version not yet located in any manuscript, became,
anonymously, the first printed gloss on the *Ad Herennium*. Whether
the shortcomings of his gloss were those of the author or the editor, or
whether because fashions and standards were changing rapidly, Guarino's
gloss was soon replaced by others, notably by that of the Perugian humanist, Francesco Maturanzio.[13] In his comment on *Ad Herennium* 1.8.12
tertium genus orationis (an appropriate enough *locus*), Francesco recalls
Quintilian's approval of poetic exercises as a training for the orator: if
the pupil is trained in poetic narratives, he will be better at, more suited
to, and more conversant with the training for real-life narratives and
those pertaining to civil affairs. On the introduction to *Ad Herennium* IV,
however, both Francesco and his companion glossator Iodocus Badius
Ascensius (Josse Bade d'Aasche, an Italian-trained low-countryman who
taught and printed classical texts at Lyons and Paris), while content to
expound the arguments of the classical author and to accept the equivalence of poetry and rhetoric appropriate to the classical Peripatetic schools,
nevertheless consider that the existence of Cicero's speeches changed the

[12] See R. G. G. Mercer, *The teaching of Gasparino Barzizza with special reference to his
place in Paduan humanism* (London: Modern Humanities Research Association, 1979).
[13] See Guglielmo Zappacosta, *Francesco Maturanzio, umanista perugino* (Bergamo: Minerva
Italica, 1970).

situation: they are pre-eminently worthy of exemplary citation.[14] Such an approach certainly paved the way for the closer attention to Ciceronian theory and practice from which attention to *numerus oratorius* and to closer distinctions between poetry and oratorical prose arose, but, paradoxically perhaps, did not itself indulge in such attention.

Sophisticated attention to Roman prose rhythm was not therefore to be found in the established *Ad Herennium* glossing tradition. In the last quarter of the fifteenth century, however, the teachers of the *Ad Herennium* were jolted by a challenge from the Quintilian students to the effect that the revered *Rhetorica ad Herennium* may not have been an authentic work of Cicero. This challenge, despite the mayhem it caused initially, did not result in the abandonment of the *Ad Herennium* as a curriculum text. Indeed, the generation of commentators that succeeded the 'anonymous' Guarino da Verona is ample in its attention to the text, and, if the practice of Francesco Maturanzio is any indication, proficient in its composition of both verse and prose *orationes*. Francesco himself wrote a *De componendis versibus hexametro et pentametro opusculum*, 'a veritable and appropriate art of poetry in that age when poetry had been wrenched away from the hands of the grammarian'.[15] The early commentators on Quintilian, in fact, give little indication of the superiority of the *Institutio* over the *Ad Herennium* as a didactic curriculum rhetorical text. This is no more apparent than in the area of euphonious prose, an area in which the rival *Ad Herennium* had, as we have seen, offered so little real guidance.

Where they reach the books of the *Institutio* in question, the early commentators on Quintilian are, in the main, disappointing, producing little more than brief *argumenta*, paraphrases, cross-references, and discussions of textual variants.[16] Rafaello Regio, a controversial and quarrelsome lecturer in the Bergamo–Padua–Venice region, is perhaps the most accessible early commentator, and, since he launched the initial attack on the authorship of the *Ad Herennium* during the last decade of the fifteenth century, the most indicative.[17] Regio is content to discuss variant readings, to supply elementary definitions, explanatory information or references

---

[14] Badius, from fol. 104[r] in the 1531 Ioannes Crepin (Lyons) edition of the *Ad Herennium* with commentaries. This rare edition is housed in the Vatican, Bibl. Apost. Vat. Popag. III.151.

[15] Zappacosta, *Francesco Maturanzio*, p. 105; also pp. 95ff, 112ff, 127ff, 197ff (his *orationes* in praise of poetry), 259ff.

[16] See Ward, 'Renaissance commentators', pp. 158ff. Martinelli's discussion of Valla's important autograph glosses to the text does not mention prose rhythm (Lucia Cesarini Martinelli, 'Le postille di Lorenzo Valla all'*Institutio oratoria* di Quintiliano', in *Lorenzo Valla e l'umanesimo italiano*, ed. O. Besomi and M. Regoliosi (Padua: Antenore, 1986), pp. 21–50.

[17] There is a biography of Regio by M. J. C. Lowry in *Contemporaries of Erasmus: a biographical register of the Renaissance and Reformation*, ed. P. G. Bielenholz and T. B. Deutscher (Toronto: University of Toronto Press, 1985), vol. III, p. 134. The present study refers to the Venice 1493 'per Bonetum Locatellum' edition of his gloss.

to texts cited by Quintilian. Time and again, for example, he and his early associates pass up opportunities to comment on the relationship between oratorical and poetic language.

The *De oratore* glosses of Ognibene da Lonigo (Omnibonus Leonicenus) are typical of early work on the mature rhetorical works of Cicero.[18] In general content to paraphrase his text with minimal additional perspective or illustration, Ognibene here and there gives readers the benefit of his acquaintance with Quintilian. Thus, at a fascinating place, where Cicero proffers an account of the crucial no man's land between poetry and oratory (*De oratore* 3.44.173), he alludes to *Institutio* 9.1.22 and 9.4.122ff (where Quintilian cites *Orator* 66.221). Ognibene's summary definitions of the key terms here and his subsequent gloss *ad verba* are so preliminary as to enforce the conclusion that he aimed only to facilitate a reading of the Ciceronian text itself. The same impression can be gained from his comments on the again significant distinction between prose and verse at *De oratore* 3.48.184, or the intriguing comments on metaphor at 3.38.155ff, where, for example, the graphic poetic clause *tenebrae conduplicantur* (3.39.159) is glossed 'a veste sumitur' without any comment on what may be appropriate to poetry, what to oratory: 'whoever is desirous of grasping the art of structured discourse, should work over the *De oratore* with frequent reading, just as Scipio, seeking to acquire the arts of the commander, never let go the books of Xenophon' (again the adjuration to read the (classical) text itself).[19]

Jacques-Louis d'Estrebay's discussion of the passage from the *De oratore* in question (3.38.185) some years later well illustrates the maturing absorption of the sophisticated classical discussions of poetic discourse. Already approaching the nature of a textbook in itself, D'Estrebay's gloss provides a comprehensive schematic summary of Cicero's text, introducing a new terminological precision with additional material from (for example) Aristotle's *Rhetoric* III, *De arte poetica*, Quintilian's Book VIII (again extending a hint in Ognibene) and from a wider philological framework in general.[20] Thus, too, on *De oratore* 3.42.171 D'Estrebay gives many examples of harsh juxtaposition of words: the last syllable of one word and the first of the next should avoid 's' and 'x', 'x' and 'x', 's' and 'r', 'n' and 'p', 'l' and 'd' or 'a' and 'e', 'a' and 'o': without observance of this,

---

[18] Ognibene de' Bonissou Vicentino da Lanigo was a late fifteenth-century editor of (among other works) Cicero's *De officiis*, *Ad Herennium*, and *De inventione* and Quintilian's *Institutio*, and a follower of Vittorino da Feltre. For Barzizza's work on the *De oratore*, see Mercer, *The teaching*, pp. 77–9, 81, 92–3, 144 n.22, 153.

[19] Ognibene in the preface to his *De oratore* commentary in the Venice 1485 edition.

[20] The present study refers to the Paris 1557 and 1561 'apud Thomam Richardum' editions of D'Estrebay's gloss, the major gloss in the volume. For other commentators see Ward, 'Renaissance commentators', pp. 155–6. On D'Estrebay himself, the authoritative work is that of Meerhoff, *Rhétorique et poétique*.

'prose can be neither charming nor euphonious'. Full reference to Cicero's *Orator* is provided.

D'Estrebay's discussion reveals a passionate assimilation of Cicero's text. The transfer of modulation of voice and 'arrangement of words in periods' from poets to rhetors in antiquity at *De oratore* 3.44.174, already referred to, is extensively elaborated:

discourse [*oratio*] was originally crude [*rudis*] and ill-constructed [*inconditus*]; it later imitated verse and finally discovered rhythm [*numeri*]. For there is evidence that musicians were formerly poets, according to Quintilian in his chapter on music [quoted extensively, *Institutio* 1.10.9] from which we conclude that formerly musicians and poets held the position of philosophers. That Cicero says 'versum et cantum, verborum numerum et vocum modum' indicates a certain discrimination and difference between words. The 'verse' of the poets is the 'song' of the musicians, the rhythm [*numerus*] of the words lies in the placement of the feet, the rhythm [*modus*] of the voice lies in its inflection, which is varied in delivery. Verses and melodies [*cantus*] are joined in a song [*carmine*] which is sounded either from the mouth or a musical instrument [*organo musico*], as in the lyric [that is, played on a lute] and also in appropriate and elegant delivery. The *verborum numerus* and the *vocum modus* flow together in the production or delivery of a speech. *Vocum modum* he here calls *vocis moderatio*, *numerum verborum* he calls the *numerum conclusionis*, since it is primarily a matter of the *conclusio* or *periodus*. *Numerus oratorius* is said to have flowed from poetic metre.

At this point D'Estrebay begins to expand *De oratore* 3.44.175, the crucial distinction between poetry and oratory: there is a different rationale of composition for *negocia civilia* and 'poetry appropriate to banquets, the theatre, leisure time'. A verse [*versus*] is, for example, a hexameter, but *numerus* 'does not keep strictly to all the metrical feet, but is a matter of arrangement of syllables according to quantity or duration'. Comprehensive expansions of Cicero's terms and usages are then offered, and relatively judicious and original statements are provided in crucial areas:

for when the orator binds [*vinxit*, compare *Institutio* 9.4.19] a speech *modis et numeris* he does not simply adopt the practice of the poet [*continuat*] but relaxes it and frees it from the fixity of order ('liberat immutatione ordinis'), that is to say, he places [*collocat*] some metrical feet in his second sentence [*sententia*, *Institutio* 9.3.77], others in his third and so on; nor does he string out identical periods [*ambitus*, compare *Institutio* 9.4.22], but spreads some out in a more protracted manner [*diffundit porrectius*], completing others in moderate compass [*cursu modico perficit*] 'ita laxi et quasi liberi numeri videntur'. When I say *numeri*, those who are newcomers to this art speak of *pedes* so composed together that a speech might run with them aptly and properly [*decenter et apte*]. Which they may be and what the rules of composition are, I will discuss abundantly 'in libro de oratoria collocatione verborum et in commentario in Ciceronis oratorem'.

Despite occasional misinterpretations, D'Estrebay is quick to spot contradictions in his text, and, far more than any other commentator of his
day, is keen to see that every nicety of Cicero's views on oratorical rhythm
and its relationship with poetry is understood by his student/reader. Indeed,
his discussion is supremely Ciceronian. Thus, on *De oratore* 3.51.198 he
propounds poetry's greater concentration on sound than sense, echoing
Cicero *Orator* 19.68. His comments on the crucial discussion at *Orator*
19.66–8 are characteristic:[21] citing a *Ciceroniana sententia* in which
numerus is *suavis et iucundus*, he comments that:

> when Cicero sets up his rhythm, he does not count the feet, nor measure fixed
> intervals, nor link his feet in some predetermined order, nor does he set up a
> standard for almost religious adherence. What does he do then? He regulates his
> long and short syllables in such way that nothing is too drawn out or too rapid-
> fire, or too rough, or joltingly uneven, nor does he close before he reaches that
> point of discourse at which skilled ears judge a termination should be made.

Cicero's comments on the effect of an actual metrical poetic line in prose
(*Orator* 30.67) are eagerly expounded and explained, though never to the
exclusion of extraneous comments designed to elucidate the text.

D'Estrebay's gloss on Cicero's *De partitione oratoria dialogus* (a work
which his preface describes as being 'de numeris oratoriis et eloquendi
generibus'),[22] covers similar ground. Giorgio Valla too, a humanist commentator and teacher in the Milan–Pavia–Piacenza–Venice region, provides a sophisticated discussion of the topic, noting the particular aptness
of *numerus* in openings and closures from the practice of Livy, Sallust,
and Cicero. Citing Quintilian, Aristotle, and Cicero, Valla points out that
numerus oratorius spurns no *pedes*: it is the *pedum iuncturae* that must be
selected and rejected; detailed examples follow.[23]

Given the fact that D'Estrebay is everywhere mindful of the much fuller
discussion of oratorical rhythm in Quintilian's *Institutio* 9.4, why does he
not gloss the latter, and instead gloss always the mature works of Cicero?
The reason seems to have been in part an awareness that Quintilian's text
was of such size and pellucidity as to require only summaries, repeated
reading, and memorizing, rather than the massive glosses to which the
Ad Herennium was subjected. Quintilian's reign (without commentary)
as chief adviser on *numerus* had begun as early as 1420, with the work
of Gasparino Barzizza, and extended into the sixteenth century when the
proliferation of specialist treatises in rhetoric incorporated much from

---

[21] Pages xxxvii–xxxix of the Paris 1536 edition of D'Estrebay's gloss on the *Orator ad M.
  Brutum*.
[22] Lyons: Gryphius, 1538, *Partit. or* with the glosses of D'Estrebay and Giorgio Valla.
[23] Page 56 of the edition just cited. A wider range of commentaries, including that of
  D'Estrebay, is found in the Paris 1562 edition.

him but managed without the development of an extensive continuous gloss.[24] Cicero, on the other hand, was the great practitioner of oratory, as well as the great theorist. Renaissance rhetoric was, indeed, inaugurated, according to some, with Loschi's commentary in the late 1390s on eleven of Cicero's *orationes*.[25] In the preface to his gloss on the *De oratore*, D'Estrebay writes that the books of rhetoric to 'Quintus frater' (the *De oratore*) 'exceed everything handed down by Greeks or Latins on the art of discourse. All the written observations of all the rhetors taken together cannot be compared with this one work, in either depth, variety, elegance or any other praiseworthy feature.' An added recommendation was the fact that Cicero was not a tiro, but a senior, experienced, and respected member of the community. A final recommendation was the inadequacy of earlier glosses: Ognibene, says D'Estrebay, was an ignorant fraud and only he, D'Estrebay, is able to supply the long and arduous commentary on such a difficult, neglected, and crucial text as the *De oratore*!

The humanists had no monopoly in the Renaissance of ideas on poetry and rhetoric. Nor, among the humanists, can the few commentators noticed in the present chapter claim to represent in any balanced way the rich field of humanist discussion. Nevertheless, all humanists spent time at the coalface represented by the leading classical writings on rhetoric, poetics, and oratory. Among these latter, the mature rhetorical works of Cicero and Quintilian's *Institutio* represent a peak that has, in many senses, never been surpassed. Attention to them promoted among the glossators and their students the beginnings of a concern with classical (versus medieval) stylistic norms and paradigms, and within these, a developing feel for the theory and practice of prose rhythm, and a sharpened consciousness of the boundaries that needed to be observed to distinguish the field from that of poetry. There is evidence that humanist rhetorical commentators were already concerned with this area of interest before their commitment was enhanced (at the beginning of the century) by the 'rediscovery' of the appropriate Ciceronian texts, and (at the end of the century) by the alarming proposition that the *Ad Herennium*, which had previously governed their basic curriculum teaching in rhetoric, was perhaps not a work of Cicero. The precocity of a George of Trebizond or a Lorenzo Valla suggests that the commentators on Cicero and Quintilian lagged behind the rapidly proliferating practice of classical prose discourse in the fifteenth century, and it cannot be asserted unequivocally that the early commentators

[24] Adrien Turnèbe in his 1554 commentary on Quintilian makes the surprising and uncommon decision to give his views on the oratorical art in the form of extensive glosses on Quintilian (Fumaroli, *L'âge de l'éloquence*, pp. 462ff). On the sixteenth-century environment see T. Cave, *The cornucopian text: problems of writing in the French Renaissance* (Oxford: Clarendon Press, 1979).
[25] Monfasani, *George of Trebizond*, p. 265.

appreciated the highly controversial nature of Ciceronian prose theories.[26] Nevertheless, patchy though their work may at a distance of time seem, the Cicero and Quintilian commentators of the fifteenth and early six- teenth centuries participated in a reading and teaching programme that was to upgrade substantially the theory and practice of contemporary poetics.

[26] Leeman, *Orationis ratio*, ch. 6, esp. pp. 165–7; Scaglione *The classical theory of com- position*, ch. 1, esp. p. 51; Fumaroli, *L'âge de l'éloquence*, p. 458.

Poetics

7

Humanist classifications of poetry among the arts and sciences

William J. Kennedy

Humanist theory classified poetry among the arts and sciences in various and sometimes conflicting ways. A given classification affirms not only the priority of some genres, styles, modes, and topics over others, but also the values of a social class or order that poetry might address. Whether for a limited constitutional or patrician republic (Florence, Venice), for a partisan and privileged nobility (the courts of Naples, Urbino, and Ferrara in Italy, or of the Sidney and Leicester circles in England), for an emergently national monarchy (the kings of France or Spain), or for an urban bourgeoisie (Lyons, Barcelona, London), humanist theory formed a canon that defines what literature is or could be among the other arts. It classified poetry chiefly in relation to rhetoric, political philosophy, and the discourse of history.

Medieval grammarians ranked poetry among the natural and moral sciences, as did the Chartrian academician John of Salisbury in his *Metalogicon* (*c.* 1160) which associates poetry with *diacrisis*, 'vivid representation, graphic imagery', so that poetry 'would seem to image all the arts'.[1] Republican humanists of fifteenth-century Florence, however, associated poetry with rhetoric, serving as a practical means to stimulate the intelligence, inspire learning, and persuade to civic virtue. Cristoforo Landino's dialogue on the good life, *Disputationes Camaldulenses* (*c.* 1472), for example, interprets the *Aeneid* as the hero's journey to a Neoplatonic *summum bonum*.[2] Even though Landino allegorizes the poem in broad

---

[1] John of Salisbury, *Metalogicon*, trans. D. D. McGarry (Berkeley: University of California Press, 1955), pp. 66–7.
[2] Cristoforo Landino, *Disputationes Camaldulenses*, ed. P. Lohe (Florence: Sansoni, 1980), and *Scritti critici e teorici*, ed. R. Cardini, 2 vols. (Rome: Bulzoni, 1974). See Roberto Cardini, *La critica del Landino* (Florence: Sansoni, 1973); Craig Kallendorf, *In praise of Aeneas* (Hanover, NH: University Press of New England, 1989); and Deborah Parker, *Commentary and ideology: Dante in the Renaissance* (Durham, NC: Duke University Press, 1993).

abstractions, he grounds its figures of virtue and vice in a historical specificity unknown to medieval commentators. His later editions of Horace (1482) and Virgil (1487–8) complete the trajectory from medieval allegoresis to humanist philology by quoting from Greek sources, offering factual information from ancient historical writers, and corroborating interpretative inferences with close textual analysis. To promote Florentine culture, Landino applied similar techniques to vernacular texts, notably Dante's *Comedy* (1481) and Petrarch's *rime*.

In these endeavours, Landino tacitly adopted the methods of his Florentine rival, Angelo Poliziano. The latter gave classical literary study a discernible institutional push when he uncoupled it from the broad goals of civic humanism and entrusted it to the care of professional scholarship. His *Miscellanea* (1489), a collection of short, specialized treatises on textual recension and emendation, source study, and close exegesis, sets a new precedent for explicating poetry in the context of history, philosophy, and political oratory.[3]

North of Italy Desiderius Erasmus transferred the principles of humanist scholarship to the study of Scripture, and in the process challenged conventional academic categories in the 'republic of letters' with a more flexible notion of stylistic decorum than had earlier prevailed.[4] His interlocutors in *The godly feast* (1522) celebrate the heterogeneous styles of Scripture as the best of all literary models, conferring special honours upon Psalms, Proverbs, the Prophets, and the Gospels, and commending the eloquence of Plato, Plutarch, Virgil, Horace, and Cicero as useful supplements in secular literature.[5] Elsewhere Erasmus argues against narrow rules and rigid classifications. *The Ciceronian* (1527), an impassioned dialogue about stylistic imitation, urges writers to draw upon an assortment of literary models, adapting each to the particular topic and readership at hand: 'the Ciceronian idiom does not suit every cast of mind'.[6]

Guillaume Budé, jurist and royal secretary under Louis XII and Francis I and founder of the Collège des Lecteurs Royaux, gave a new name to the Erasmian science of literary study in *De philologia* (1532) by adopting

[3] *Angeli Politiani opera* (1553; facs. reprint Turin: Bottega d'Erasmo, 1970–1, ed. I. Maïer), 3 vols.; see Vittore Branca, *Poliziano e l'umanesimo della parola* (Turin: G. Einaudi, 1983).

[4] See *The antibarbarians* (1520), trans. M. M. Phillips, in *The collected works of Erasmus*, ed. C. R. Thompson *et al.*, 86 vols. (Toronto: University of Toronto Press, 1974–), vol. XXIII (1978), pp. 1–122, quoted from p. 42.

[5] *Colloquies*, trans. C. R. Thompson (Chicago: University of Chicago Press, 1965), pp. 46–78, where the Gospels are the 'most splendid possession' of all (p. 71).

[6] *The Ciceronian*, trans. B. I. Knott, in *Complete works*, vol. XXVIII (1986), pp. 337–448, quoted from p. 438; see Jacques Chomarat, *Grammaire et rhétorique chez Erasme*, 2 vols. (Paris: Les Belles Lettres, 1981), vol. I, pp. 399–450, 509–86; and vol. II, pp. 711–848.

the term 'philology' from Cicero's letters.[7] The study of sacred texts is *philologia prima*, and the study of all others (with Greek literature primary) constitutes *philologia secunda*, subordinate to the first. Replacing the earlier terms *grammaticus* and *rhetoricus*, which locate poetry in the domains of grammar and rhetoric, the term *philologus* designates a new scholarly office for students of *bonae litterae*.

Another Erasmian, Juan Luis Vives, born in Valencia as the son of a Jewish merchant who was later executed by the Spanish Inquisition, spent most of his adult life at Bruges, except for brief periods between 1523 and 1528 when he lectured at Oxford and served as preceptor for Mary Tudor and Queen Catherine of Aragon.[8] His *De disciplinis* (1532), a comprehensive treatise on educational reform, contests the inclusiveness of rhetorical genres (deliberative, judicial, and epideictic) for poetry and the principles of invention, arrangement, and elocution consequent upon them: 'they are mere practices that increase to infinity'.[9] What matters most is a pragmatics of expression, the discovery of individual forms appropriate to particular needs. In place of any conventional scheme for the arts and sciences emerges a plurality of 'disciplines' with variously overlapping categories and classifications.

Juan Huarte de San Juan, a learned physician in the impoverished Andalucian town of Baeza, adumbrated an early form of faculty psychology when he reclassified the disciplines in his *Examen de ingenios para las ciencias* (1575). According to Huarte, every power of the mind mirrors a different combination of humours, and each governs a particular art or science. Memory governs theology, cosmography, law, and the arts of language; understanding governs logic and natural and moral philosophy; imagination governs music, eloquence, and poetry, 'all the Arts and Sciences, which consist in figure, correspondencie, harmonie, and proportion'.[10] Though poets need the aid of memory, presumably to assist them in inventing appropriate topics, tropes, and figures, their work usually contravenes

---

[7] *De philologia* appears in *Opera omnia Gulielmi Budaei*, 4 vols. (1557; facs. reprint London: Gregg Press, 1966), vol. I, pp. 39–95. See also Guillaume Budé, *De philologia et de studio litterarum*, intro. A. Buck (Stuttgart: Friedrich Frommann, 1964); Marie-Madeleine de la Garanderie, *Christianisme et lettres profanes (1515–1535)* (Paris: Champion, 1976).

[8] To the latter Vives dedicated *De institutione feminae christianae* (1523) which notoriously attacks such 'pestiferous books' as the *Decameron*, *La Celestina*, medieval romances, and Poggio's satires. See Juan Luis Vives, *Opera omnia*, 8 vols. (1782–90; facs. reprint London: Gregg Press, 1964), vol. IV, p. 84; Spanish trans. *Obras completas*, ed. L. Riber, 2 vols. (Madrid: M. Aguilar, 1947–8), vol. I, p. 1003.

[9] Riber, 2.460; a shorter Latin version entitled *De tradendis disciplinis* discusses rhetoric in *Opera*, vol. VI, p. 356.

[10] Juan Huarte de San Juan, *Examen de ingenios para las ciencias*, ed. E. Torre (Madrid: Editora Nacional, 1976), p. 164; *The examination or triall of men's wits and dispositions*, trans. R. Carew (London: Adam Islip, 1594), p. 103.

logic and the systematic precepts of formal philosophy: 'eloquence and finenesse of speech cannot find place in men of great understanding'.[11] Poetry belongs to the category of *ingenium*, defined broadly as a power of discovering truth inductively and experientially, not through rational universals or predetermined classifications.

Drawing upon continental ideas, Tudor humanism related poetry to philosophy and history with strong social and political aims. *The governour* (1531) by Sir Thomas Elyot, a friend of More, Erasmus, and Vives, urges upon the ruling aristocracy an education in classical rhetoric, history, and philosophy, commending poetry as 'a mirror of man's life' that subsumes all these arts.[12] The *Arte of rhetorique* (1553) by Thomas Wilson iterates the debt of poetry to the natural and historical sciences, moral philosophy, and logic, but also avows its powerful role as an agent of society, persuading humankind 'to liue together in fellowship of life, to maintaine Cities, to deale truely, and willingly to obeye one an other'.[13] Likewise the anonymous *Arte of English poesie* (1589, by George Puttenham?) asserts that 'poets were the first priests, the first prophets, the first Legislators and politicians in the world'.[14] Poets in the present age no longer initiate policy but they help rulers and magistrates to govern by promulgating their ideas in a style 'briefer & more compendious, and easier to beare away and be retained in memorie'.[15]

Neoplatonic theories of poetry in sixteenth-century Italy also underscore poetry's political role, often gingerly since Plato had exiled the poets from his republic. The Ferrarese scholar Francesco Patrizi in his *Della poetica* (1586) brought Aristotle to the poets' defence by claiming that his *Poetics* constitutes the ninth book of his *Politics*. Just as the body politic strives for a 'consonance of harmony composed of contraries having different proportions among themselves', so the artist strives for harmonies that will promote civil justice.[16] Such a construction enhances the utility of Aristotle's *Poetics*, which had grown in prestige after its initial publication in 1508, its translations into Latin (1498, 1536) and Italian (1549), and Francesco Robortello's commentary in 1548. Throughout the sixteenth century Aristotle's formal distinctions penetrate other syntheses of Ciceronian rhetoric and Horatian poetics, conferring pride of place upon

---

[11] *Ibid.*, p. 179, trans. p. 120.
[12] Sir Thomas Elyot, *The book named the governor*, ed. S. E. Lehmberg (London: Dent, 1907), pp. 47–8.
[13] Thomas Wilson, *Arte of rhetorique* (1585; facs. reprint Oxford: Clarendon Press, 1909, ed. G. H. Mair), sig. Avii^r.
[14] George Puttenham (?), *The arte of English poesie*, ed. G. D. Willcock and A. Walker (Cambridge: Cambridge University Press, 1936), p. 6.
[15] *Ibid.*, p. 8.
[16] Francesco Patrizi da Cherso, *Della poetica*, ed. D. Aguzzi-Barbagli, 3 vols. (Florence: Istituto Nazionale di Studi sul Rinascimento, 1969–71), vol. II, p. 168.

intricate forms of lyric poetry in Bernardino Daniello's *La poetica* (1536) and Antonio Sebastiano Minturno's *De poeta* (1559) and *L'arte poetica* (1563–4).

Julius Caesar Scaliger, a polymath who claimed noble Veronese ancestry but settled in Agen France where he wrote philosophical and scientific treatises, brought Aristotelian ideas elaborately to bear upon Ciceronian and Horatian precepts in his *Poetices libri septem* (1561). This work classifies the language arts as necessary (logic, philosophy), useful (statecraft and political oratory), and pleasurable (narrative). The last divides into one species that records past truth (history) and another that invents fiction (poetry and drama).[17] A chapter on figurative language locates poetry between grammar and dialectics as an unnamed 'third science' that includes history and oratory, 'in whose common orbit public concerns are expressed through figures and rhetorical commonplaces'.[18] Hierarchies of topic and style classify genres from sublime hymns and odes to assorted epic and tragedy to base comedy and satire.

Lodovico Castelvetro in his translation of and commentary upon Aristotle's *Poetics* (1570) radically dissociated poetry from the other arts and sciences and defined it instead as an exceptional skill. Indeed, science counts for little in this classification, since poems should give pleasure rather than instruction. Nor does inspiration count since enlightenment may occur through derivative learning, while talent in versification and expression can improve through repeated practice. The poet is primarily a technician of poetry, a craft with its own rules about imitating the art of other poetry: 'imitation which is natural to me is one thing, and the imitation required by poetry is another'.[19] The pre-eminent genre is drama (necessarily so, as Castelvetro is following Aristotle), performed in public places for the common people, with tragedy reflecting the ideals of noble life and comedy the banalities of middle-class life.

Though drama had made its mark upon the ducal courts of northern Italy by the mid-sixteenth century, the preferred courtly form remained the elegant romance-epic epitomized by Ariosto's *Orlando furioso* whose multiple plots were defended most ably by Giovambattista Giraldi Cintio in his *Discorso intorno al comporre dei romanzi* (1554). The young Torquato Tasso endorsed this preference even while challenging it with the Aristotelian demand for unity in his *Discorsi dell'arte poetica*, drafted

---

[17] Julius Caesar Scaliger, *Poetices libri septem* (1561; facs. reprint Stuttgart: Frommann-Holzboog, 1987, ed. A. Buck), p. 1; partial translations in Frederick Morgan Padelford, *Select translations from Scaliger's 'Poetics'* (New York: Henry Holt, 1905), pp. 1–2.

[18] *Ibid.*, 1561 edn, p. 121.

[19] Lodovico Castelvetro, *Poetica d'Aristotele vulgarizzata e sposta*, ed. W. Romani, 2 vols. (Rome and Bari: Laterza, 1978–9), vol. I, p. 94; partial translation by Andrew Bongiorno, *Castelvetro on the art of poetry* (Binghamton: Medieval & Renaissance Texts & Studies, 1984), p. 43, with introduction, pp. xiii–xlviii.

in the 1560s when he was planning his epic *Gerusalemme liberata*.[20] Later Tasso tempered his romance impulses by contriving to express 'all the actions of political man', as he claimed in his *Allegoria del poema* (1575).[21] Eventually he balanced instruction and delight in his *Discorsi del poema eroico* (1594). This work classifies poetry with dialectic and logic in representing 'not the false but the probable' and especially 'the probable in so far as it is verisimilar' through demonstration, example, enthymeme, and even ambiguity.[22]

The humanists' classifications of poetry influenced the thinking of non-professional scholars and creative writers in several forms. Castiglione's interlocutors in *The book of the courtier* (1528) famously proclaim that, like music and painting, poetry is an art appropriate for exercise by the cultivated nobility and urban bourgeoisie.[23] Outside of Italy gentlemen amateurs like Sir Philip Sidney and Michel de Montaigne took this advice to heart. Sidney, an aspirant to knighthood in service to the crown, shared the sentiments of Elyot, Wilson, and Puttenham about the public role of poetry. *The defence of poesie* (composed ?1581) points out its legislating and historiographic functions amongst the Turks, Indians, Irish, and Welsh and it foregrounds the example of David as a poet-king whose Psalms inscribe history, prophecy, and divine law.[24] Poetry subsumes all the classifications of art and science as the poet 'goeth hand in hand with nature, not enclosed within the narrow warrant of her gifts, but freely ranging within the zodiac of his own wit'.[25]

Montaigne, whose family enjoyed its recently purchased nobility at Bordeaux, cites Castiglione with approval in his *Essays* (1580–8) while echoing an Erasmian resistance to classification.[26] The production of poetry, he claims in 'Divers evenemens de mesme conseil' ['Various outcomes of the same plan'] (I.xxiv), may be unconscious and unpremeditated, surpassing its author's conception and intent, so that an able reader may

---

[20] Torquato Tasso, *Prose*, ed. E. Mazzali (Milan: Riccardo Ricciardi, 1959), pp. 349–410; translation in Lawrence F. Rhu, *The genesis of Tasso's narrative theory* (Detroit: Wayne State University Press, 1993), pp. 99–154.

[21] Rhu, *The Genesis*, p. 157.

[22] Tasso, *Prose*, pp. 487–729, quoted on pp. 525–7; Torquato Tasso, *Discourses on the heroic poem*, trans. M. Cavalchini and I. Samuel (Oxford: Clarendon Press, 1973), pp. 29–30.

[23] Castiglione, *The book of the courtier*, part I, sections 46–9. Completed by 1516 and published by Aldo in 1528, *The book of the courtier* has been edited authoritatively by Bruno Maïer (Turin: UTET, 1955). See Paul O. Kristeller, 'The modern system of the arts', *Renaissance thought* II (New York: Harper & Row, 1965), pp. 163–227.

[24] *Miscellaneous prose of Sir Philip Sidney*, ed. K. Duncan-Jones and J. van Dorsten (Oxford: Clarendon Press, 1973), pp. 75–7.

[25] *Ibid.*, p. 78.

[26] *The complete essays of Montaigne*, trans. D. Frame (Stanford: Stanford University Press, 1957), I.xlviii (p. 213) and II.xvii (p. 480). For Montaigne's literary views see Glyn P. Norton, *Montaigne and the introspective mind* (The Hague: Mouton, 1975), pp. 170–84.

discover in it 'perfections beyond those that the author put in or perceived, and lends them richer meanings and aspects'.[27] It conforms to no narrow precepts except 'on a certain low level', as he argues in 'Du jeune Caton' (I.xxxvii): 'the good, supreme, divine poetry is above the rules and reason'.[28] Amongst ancients whom he lists in 'Des livres' (II.x), Montaigne prefers Virgil, Lucretius, Catullus, and Horace, and amongst moderns he names Boccaccio, Rabelais, and Johannes Secundus; in 'De la praesumption' (II.xvii) he adds Dorat, Beza, Buchanan, L'Hôpital, Montdoré, Turnèbe, Ronsard, and Du Bellay.[29] Everywhere he resists categorical definition. Critical commentary, symptomatic of the mind's 'natural infirmity', drives readers to seek out logical explanations and self-consistent interpretations, but 'it is more of a job to interpret the interpretations than to interpret the things, and there are more books about books than about any other subject: we do nothing but write glosses about each other' ('De l'experience', III.xiii).[30]

Another gentleman amateur, the impoverished *hidalgo* hero of *Don Quixote* (1605, 1615) by Miguel de Cervantes, expresses passionate views about literature (especially in 1.47, 2.3, 2.62), showing that Aristotelian categories had infiltrated popular discourse as he explains differences among genres – epic, lyric, tragic, comic – and the relationship of poetry to history, fact to fiction, and verisimilitude to universal truth. In an encounter with the wealthy *caballero* Don Diego de Miranda in 2.16, the hero defends poetry as a profoundly pleasurable pursuit that serves all the sciences and can be served, enriched, polished, and adorned by them in turn. The unimaginative Don Diego nonetheless clings to philistine literary tastes that favour soothing and familiar entertainment. He earns censure for disparaging poetry's usefulness when he berates his college-age son for majoring in literary studies rather than law. The boy too earns censure for preferring to read theory and criticism more than poetry itself. Don Diego and his son seem harbingers of classifications to come – a separation of poetry from practical affairs, the consignment of literature to an autonomous periphery, and a celebration of theory at the expense of texts. Who could have predicted such an outcome?

[27] *The complete essays*, p. 93.   [28] *Ibid.*, p. 171.   [29] *Ibid.*, p. 502.   [30] *Ibid.*, p. 818.

8

Theories of poetry: Latin writers

Ann Moss

The literary criticism of the first thirty years of the sixteenth century is best pursued in commentaries published in the margins of particular poetic texts and in the rambling miscellanies in which humanist scholars amassed the notes they made on their reading. Only belatedly did coherent theory begin to emerge from pedagogic practice. One of the earliest new works of the century devoted solely to the theoretical discussion of poetry was also destined to be the most successful. Girolamo Vida published his verse *De arte poetica* at Rome in 1527. The work is divided into three books by and large equivalent to the rhetorical distinctions of invention, disposition, and elocution. Its content derives from the key concepts of Horace, amplified by reference to rhetorical precepts, laced with a measure of Platonic enthusiasm, and expressed wherever possible in exemplary Virgilian language. The young poet is to peruse all nature, searching through a thousand shapes in which to embody thought, but, more often than not, it is the plenteous store of memory that comes to his aid, well stocked from the literary education advertised in Book I of Vida's poem (1.427–37). Vida's concern, and it is a concern which is altogether typical of the humanist literary theorist, is not with the reference poetic fiction makes to the realities of nature, but with the reference it makes to other literary texts. The art of poetry is the art of imitating the words of other poets rather than the art of imitating things, and Vida's model of artistic perfection and of poetic truth is Virgil.

One outcome of this preoccupation is the exploration at the beginning of Book II of the time peculiar to poetry, which is of a different order altogether from the time of history (II.51–159). The starting point of Vida's discussion is the Horatian distinction between the 'natural' chronology of history and the 'artistic' time-order proper to poetry, which starts at the midpoint of narrative and moves both backwards, in the memory of participants in the action, and forwards, in their anticipations, in prophecies, in signs and omens of things to come. Vida shows both how the writer carries simultaneously in his mind the past, present, and future contained within his work and how he manipulates the reader's sense of time and suspense, keeping him ever in reach of a discernible but continually deferred ending. Vida is at his most interesting when he thus investigates how the universe of poetry differs from commonly perceived nature. He does indeed insist that even at his most feigning the poet should not forfeit his credibility by diverting to the frankly implausible, but fictions adroitly blended with truth are the way to that embellishment and variation of nature, which is the joy of poetry (II.304–24, 339–46). What Vida does not seem to envisage is a mode of writing or of reading in which fiction functions as an allegorical expression of truth. This approach is quietly laid aside (II.316–19), and is replaced in Book III by the idea of the book as a universe of a thousand different forms and figures. Language mirrors nature best in its capacity to produce an infinite variety of dissimilar things (III.32–43).

It is the sheer pleasure of diversity that dominates the rhetorical repertory of figures and schemes in Vida's third book, together with a sense that language stretched to its fullest productive power is what we understand by poetry and can see exemplified in the language of the supreme poet, Virgil. The particular pleasure of poetic language is its capacity to effect multiple translations and transformations by metaphor, to appropriate a plurality of images and ideas by comparisons, to double its narrations by interpolating mythological stories and characters, and to contain all these different worlds in one space. It is primarily in its potential for amplification and variation through figures of speech that poetry is fictive and that poetry is pure pleasure, just as the ornamentation of elaborate architecture is pure pleasure (III.96–115). This enriched language, moreover, was once the language of the gods, and it is through poetry that we hear celestial harmonies (III.76–83). Towards the end of all three books Vida modulates into the Platonic language of inspiration, though not of Platonic allegory. It is the poetic idiom itself which has echoes of something divine, without any call to insist on its correspondence with the truth whether by making substitutions of things signified or by stressing its representational function.

Nevertheless, Vida does dwell at some length on two corollaries of the theory of divine inspiration, and thereby makes the poet himself, in both his public and his private *persona*, a vehicle through which to discuss the status and nature of literary production. At the end of Book I, which is mainly concerned with the education of the poet, we leave him in a rural retreat, set apart from civil and political life on a lofty Lucretian eminence (I.488–514). Vida shows little inclination to argue for the moral responsibilities of literature, by which some theorists (and all humanist teachers of good letters) claimed their place in society. He does, however, foreshadow something of the ambivalence and the introspection of other sixteenth-century poets, given to flaunting their self-proclaimed independence but not always comfortable in their isolation. The other consequence of accepting the paradigm of inspiration risks even greater exposure of the private self. In Book II Vida talks about natural inspiration as a gift, but a gift which may be withdrawn. The way to supplement the deficiencies of inspiration and to conjure the fickle god is to read poetry; the only way to harness the powers that possess the poet when the fit is on him is to apply critical rigour and restraint or to wait to recollect the heat of emotion in a rational tranquillity (II.395–454). Vida provides a model *persona* for later poets, who will introduce the problematics of the poet's divine but discontinuous *afflatus* into poetry reflecting on its own nature.

The *Naugerius* of Vida's fellow neo-Latin poet Girolamo Fracastoro may have been written round about 1540, but it was not published until the edition of his complete works at Venice in 1555. It never gained the colossal European reputation of Vida's *De arte poetica*, and indeed it supplies none of the formulae and precepts which assured to Vida's work a place in a market geared to expectations raised in school courses in rhetoric. Fracastoro's *Naugerius* is a prose dialogue which progressively refines ideas about the nature and purpose of poetry. Among definitions discarded at an early stage of the dialogue are mere entertainment (incompatible with the poet's sense of dedication and with the response one has to great poetry); the imparting of knowledge (the poet is not a specialist, but only borrows information from specialists); metrical form (a merely trivial distinction); teaching practical morality and natural history through the imitation or representation of people and things (not exclusive to the poet); exciting wonder, as Giovanni Pontano had written in his *Actius* towards the end of the fifteenth century, by shading truth with fictions and mythological inventions (true also of orators and historians). All these features are to be found in poetry. None of them gives to the poet a special function and purpose which belong to him and to nobody else.

Fracastoro eventually locates the defining characteristics of poetry in a concept of poetic language which owes much both to Aristotle and to Plato, but places much more emphasis on the style in which the poet treats his subject-matter than on the matter itself. Fracastoro approves of Aristotle's idea that the poet deals in universal truths (the kinds of things that could happen because they are probable and necessary) rather than in particular facts that have happened, but he turns from what is imitated to the language in which it is imitated. Unlike any other user of language, the poet has no aim other than to express universal ideas in the beautiful form appropriate to them and to pursue the beauty which characterizes the different kinds of poetic writing (the genres). Fracastoro is looking for an understanding of the aesthetic experience, rather than a philosophical definition of the relation of fiction to the real world of nature. The elements of beautiful speech are musicality, sonorities, metaphors, comparisons, digressions, arrangements of words, transitions, figures, all of which can give beauty even to a subject not beautiful in itself. All these combined can transport poet and reader into an ecstasy, which is not god-given, as Plato thought, but purely the effect of beautiful configurations of language. The invention proper to poets is verbal, and its purpose is to add beauty. To this end poets use fictions, but Fracastoro is careful not to invalidate the claims he makes for poetry by conceding that poets are liars. Beauty and falsehood are incompatible, because what is false is not only ugly, but has no existence. So evident falsehoods have no place in poetry. But the fictions poets use are capable of signifying true things, either by similarities in appearance or by allegorical interpretation (Fracastoro implies the physical, historical, and moral senses of the interpretative tradition), or because they were believed by the ancients, or because they are part of rhetorical amplifications which relate to the nature of the subject being represented.

The last part of the dialogue, in which Fracastoro argues that poetry is not only beautiful but useful, is predominantly Platonic. The poet is 'moved by real beauties' and reveals these to others in words, and in doing so he also records the true and the good. As in Vida, the idea of poetry as a particular kind of discourse is paramount, and the infrastructure of Fracastoro's beautiful poetic language, as he says in his conclusion, is to be found in the 'different elements of speech'. This keeps critical analysis within the rhetorical sphere of combinations of words, figures of speech, rhythm, composition, and the imitation of other poets, while at the same time Fracastoro differentiates the poetic from all other idioms of speech by its special dedication to beauty.

An even more ambitious dialogue, at least in terms of coverage, was Antonio Minturno's *De poeta* (1559). As the work proceeds, the dialogue form gets increasingly lost in *ex cathedra* prescriptions, as Minturno turns to the genres of poetry (epic in Book II, followed by books on tragedy, comedy, and lyric), and ends in Book VI with catalogues of examples of *sententiae*, figures, places of argument, and qualities of style. Before this shift into generic divisions and into rhetoric, Minturno has set out a wide range of theoretical positions in Book I, radiating from the proposition that poetry is primarily an art of imitation. As is not surprising at this date, the framework of the debate is Aristotelian, but the direction it takes has analogies with current syntheses of Aristotle and Horace. This is particularly true of the role Minturno gives to recognition. The pleasure and profit of artistic imitation lies in recognition of what is imitated, and such recognition presupposes knowledge. Minturno argues from this to the position that erudition is essential to poetry, a source of pleasure, profit, and admiration to the (suitably erudite) reader. Admiration in the sense of wonder and astonishment at the inexplicable, which Aristotle had thought peculiarly appropriate to epic, is for Minturno an effect proper for poetry, and if poets in pursuit of the marvellous describe things which cannot exist, Minturno will support them with Aristotle's preference for probable impossibilities over improbable possibilities. However, he normally understands imitation in the more familiar of its Aristotelian moulds, as imitation of human actions, not particular actions that are or were, but actions that we recognize as probable and necessary, and likely to be true. In this respect the language of the poets does not differ from the language of philosophers, who also infer universal truths from the observation of particulars. However, Minturno, in a way which will be common from now on, slips from the notion of 'like the truth' to 'like what ought to be', so that literature is vindicated in so far as it is a repertory of moral examples. Nevertheless, poets must not compromise their moral position by contradicting the truth, and it is therefore necessary to depict vices, but with a view to dissuade, so that a measure of exaggeration is not only allowed but encouraged. Reading involves a recognition of the moral qualities which have been knowledgeably and appropriately represented by the poet. The stress, however, is on what will persuade the reader to action, rather than on ingenious decipherment.

The other issue which stimulates most debate in the first volume of Minturno is the more characteristically Horatian question of whether poetry is primarily a product of art or of nature. Platonic inspiration breezes in and out, but Minturno is fundamentally convinced that poetry is an art form, that is to say, first, it has intelligible matter, coherent order and parts, and a method of treatment which can be rationally discussed, and, second, it is conducive to improvement in the quality of life. So the poet is best defined, in terms adapted from Quintilian by Pontano in his *Actius* and amplified with Aristotelian and Horatian overtones, as a good man skilled in speaking and in imitating, able to discourse in the best verse on any subject both fully and intelligently, able to represent all things which are susceptible to imitation in such a way as to excite wonder and to give pleasure and profit. In so far as a poem is a work of art it is the product of an ordered mind. With this further proof of the moral virtues of poetry, Minturno embarks on his elaborate demonstration of the art in terms of genres, divided and subdivided according to matter, means of performance, and appropriate diction.

In the field of literary criticism, the translation of dominance from Italy to France was first heralded by the publication of the *Poetices libri septem* of the Franco-Italian humanist, Julius Caesar Scaliger (1561). Scaliger, who died in 1558, could not have known the *De poeta* of Minturno, but he was thoroughly acquainted with the sort of arguments Minturno advanced for the moral responsibilities of literature, as he was with the whole range of critical approaches developed from various combinations of the Horatian, Aristotelian, Platonic, and rhetorical traditions. To these he added a vocabulary of technical terms inherited largely from the scholastics, which had not formed part of the rhetorical idiom of previous theorists but were in current use with university philosophers. Scaliger often affects a humanist's embarrassment with such 'jargon', but it is clear that his purpose, in which he largely succeeds, is to give a professional edge and stringency to the activity of literary criticism. Scaliger is not one for bland interchanges and syncretic mixes. It is significant that he does not use the dialogue form, and it is not for nothing that in the titles of two books of his *Poetice* we encounter the word 'criticus' for the first time in our review of Latin critical literature.

Scaliger's discussions of theoretical points are disseminated throughout the work, though they cluster at the beginning of the first four books: 'Historicus' (which includes poetic genres); 'Hyle' (metrics); 'Idea' (modes of verbal representation, including figures of speech); 'Parasceve' (characters of style). Perhaps the basic question to which Scaliger addresses himself is the division in poetic writing between *verba* and *res* [words and things]. This was a pedagogic simplification inherited from the rhetoricians, but recent discussion had emphasized and complicated it, pulling in one direction towards a theory of literature as self-referring, autonomous discourse, as in Fracastoro and even Vida, and in the other direction towards literature viewed as a transparent medium through which the things it is said to imitate, especially moral things, are clearly perceived. Scaliger, working from within the terminology imposed by the prestige of Aristotle's *Poetics*, accepts the basic idea that poetry is a form of imitation in which words stand as images for things, and he proceeds to enquire into the objects, means, and purposes of such imitation. Words denote things (persons, actions, and non-persons). Things are therefore the objects of verbal imitation and determine the range of signifiers brought into use to make plausible representations of things which do or did exist, or, and this is characteristic of poetry, of things without actual existence, but whose existence is accepted as feasible because they are represented in such a way that the reader recognizes them as possible or as necessary consequences of other things.

So far Scaliger operates mainly within the conceptual framework of verisimilitude. When he comes to the means of verisimilitude, or its matter and form, he comes to what he considers the stuff of poetry, that is to say, the choice and arrangement of words by which things are represented. Herein lies the conscious art of poetry, far superior to passively received inspiration, for in this art of verbal arrangement the poet establishes order, relationships, values, a 'second nature' of which he is the creator-god and lawgiver, which he can control at will until its completion, and from which he can eliminate the defects and deficiencies of that nature of which it is the more perfect mirror. Hence the critical attention Scaliger gives to the diction of poets, to figures of speech, to the collocation of words within a line or phrase, to the relationship of parts to the whole and to each other within a complete work, above all to rhythm and to metre, which is the arrangement of words peculiar to poetry, its very matter, which betokens harmony itself. However, Scaliger does not view the poetic universe as a totally autonomous and self-sufficient aesthetic construct.

In the first place, in so far as verbal signs denote things, they make reference to the real world, and they cease to function appropriately if they do not correspond adequately to the things they represent. Scaliger seems to go beyond Horatian decorum, implying that the choice and arrangement of words give form to things. Moreover, it is things they represent, not the author, who, though in control of his work, is effaced by his words. Second, and no less importantly, expression has an ulterior end, for nothing is made without a purpose, and the purpose of poetry is to generate right moral action or, in Horatian terms, to teach delightfully. In the last book of his work ('Epinomis', Chapter II) Scaliger even goes so far as to conclude that imitation is a totally inadequate definition of poetry, because all discourse is imitative (or fictive), as all words are images of things. But discourse which is artistically (or artificially) arranged carries conviction, imitating things in such a way as to turn our appetites to pursue the good and to shun the bad, not only in our reaction as readers but in our action as citizens. Even in the detail of a single line of poetry, and in his critical analyses, Scaliger comes right down to such detail, the purpose of artistically composed imitation is to 'make human life more ordered' ('Idea', Chapter I).

In the fifth book, 'Criticus', Scaliger abstracts passages in which different Greek and Latin poets treat similar subjects and makes close, evaluative comparisons between them. Comparable passages were frequently aligned in marginal commentaries on texts and were the very stuff of commonplace-books, but Scaliger was the first to make comparison a critical methodology. The criteria he applies in his evaluations are essentially the same as those of the humanist grammarians and rhetoricians: proprieties of vocabulary, felicities of sound and rhythmical combinations, qualities of style and diction, logical coherence, and evidence of an erudition which prevents mistakes and self-contradictions. When employed by earlier humanists, these categories of criticism were often very blunt instruments. In Scaliger they have an almost technical precision, because the vocabulary he employs, though still the same as that of his predecessors, has already been exhaustively defined in the earlier parts of his book.

Definition and order were certainly virtues Scaliger aimed to introduce into the nascent science of literary criticism, where they were in sore danger of being submerged in the tangled mass of ideas accumulated over years of enthusiastic synthesizing on the part of commentators and theorists. A similar longing for system underlies the *De poetica libri tres* published at Antwerp in 1579 by Giovanni Viperano who, amidst the moralizing concerns typical of the later sixteenth century, shows a penchant for sheer delight that one could sometimes wish in Scaliger. However, the delights of poetry were to become more and more the province of vernacular critics, while the systematic study of poetry in Latin was to be confined more and more to the schoolroom and lecture hall. The most influential systematizers of poetry in the last years of the century were the Jesuit pedagogues. Many of the ideas they propagated appear in the *Bibliotheca selecta* (1593) of Antonio Possevino which contains a much reprinted section 'De poesi et pictura ethnica, humana, et fabulosa collata cum vera, honesta, et sacra'. Possevino derives from his alignment of poetry with painting a strong sense of the power of language to activate the senses and the emotions by which reality is perceived. This gives an added verve to his references to the descriptive processes and 'colours' of rhetoric, and leads him to suggest that mere imitation of nature is a subservient posture for a poet, when the resources of language are there to be exploited for the extraordinary, the arresting, the far-fetched, the ingenious, and the recondite. It is precisely because their language is so extreme (to classically educated minds) that the Psalmist and other religious poets are so impressive. What is more, their poems do not depart from nature, for they tell the Truth.

The Jesuits' commitment to the criterion of Christian truth has radical implications for practical criticism. In the first place, it leads directly to censorship; in the second, it rehabilitates the late medieval mode of rigorously detailed allegorical interpretation as a way of saving ancient fictions for truth. However, such new departures do not really disturb the bland mixture of well-established critical commonplaces in what was destined probably to be the most influential of all sixteenth-century Latin theories of poetry. In one version or another the *Poeticae institutiones* (1594) of the Jesuit, Jakob Spanmüller (Iacobus Pontanus) was used by schools throughout Europe, so that every schoolboy knew that the proper definition of poetry was making [*facere*], contriving [*fingere*], or imitating [*imitari*], all three being synonyms; that the poet not only reproduced the forms of things that are, but generated, as if from nothing, new and wonderful likenesses of things which do not exist, but whose existence would not be impossible; that what was specific to poetry was this imitation or fiction-making and, less importantly, the use of metrical form; that no subject was outside the scope of poetry, but the subject in which it excelled was the imitation of the actions of human beings, represented for the instruction and pleasure of its readers; and that there was no source of poetic inspiration so potent as the studious and attentive reading of other poets.

9

Literary imitation in the sixteenth century: writers and readers, Latin and French

Ann Moss

Renaissance concepts of the relationship between artistically composed language and the true nature of things are usually bound almost inextricably with the presupposition that the genesis of literary composition lies in rhetoric and in the imitation of model authors. As Scaliger puts it (*Poetices libri septem*, v.x): 'We have a method of expressing the nature of things, for we imitate what our predecessors have said in exactly the same way as they imitated nature'. Even so, not all sixteenth-century concepts of literature entail literary imitation. It is, for example, virtually absent from writing which primarily invites an allegorical rather than a rhetorical reading. Allegorical interpretation may draw on other authors as repositories of information, but it is an essentially non-rhetorical mode in that it fundamentally depends on the reader's freedom to substitute one sign for another or one signified for another according to associative formulae which have nothing to do with concepts of style found in classical rhetoric. In rhetorically constituted discourse, meaning is derived from the choice and arrangement of words. In the sixteenth century the influence of classical rhetoric was paramount, and the lessons of humanist rhetoric were largely lessons in how to write like admired exemplars of literary expression in the ancient languages. The history of literary criticism in our period is therefore to a large extent a history of which models were recommended for imitation, of instructions as to how they were to be imitated, and of the side-effects of such prescriptions.

*

The close affiliation between the practice of literary imitation and the detailed criticism of passages of literary composition is evident well before Scaliger developed it into the critical method of his *Poetice*. To cite but one example from dozens, Etienne Dolet in his two treatises *De imitatione*

Ciceroniana (against Erasmus, Lyons, 1535, and against Floridus, Lyons, 1540) is clear about the stylistic virtues to be learnt from Cicero and incorporated into passages of original prose. They are first and foremost 'a splendid abundance of words', then a 'clever variety of aphorisms' and 'a pleasing arrangement of sounds and syllables'.[1] These virtues are to be acquired from an attentive reading of Cicero, an activity which is in itself a critical exercise aimed at discovering how Cicero's language achieves its effects, but which is put to a more stringent test when the reader is required to write like Cicero. The test is to produce a pastiche of Cicero's style without lifting whole phrases from the original, so that the new composition is totally Ciceronian, but not Cicero. All this involves the ability to make fine critical distinctions, both about the text studied and about the critic's own writing. The complementary procedures of analysis and genesis, which are crucial to the humanists' approach to rhetoric, are the progenitors of critically sophisticated readers and of highly self-conscious writers.

However, the programme of literary imitation, which the school-manuals take for granted and reduce to short and easily digestible precepts and examples, is highly problematic from several points of view. Dolet's Ciceronian tracts are contributions to a long-running debate about whether Cicero alone among prose-writers should be imitated, as a model of perfection which invalidates all others. The Ciceronian debate points up a fundamental dichotomy in the humanists' attitude to language. On the one hand, there is thought to be an invariable standard of perfection, be it Cicero or Virgil, which in theory is transposable by analysis and practice into modern writing, Latin or vernacular; on the other hand, the humanists were philologists, alert to changes in language, fully aware that the meaning of the Latin words they tracked through their authors was a product of their use, of their historical context, of their particular relationship to each other in any given text. The tensions between these two attitudes to language were implicit in the works of many a humanist. They had surfaced in disputes between defenders of Ciceronian stability and universality (Paolo Cortesi, Bembo, Christophe Longueil, Dolet) in one camp, and, in the other, those (Poliziano, Pico della Mirandola, Erasmus) who, whilst still advocates of literary imitation in principle, urged the claims of historical diversity and personal uniqueness and vested those interests in a free-ranging choice of models to imitate.

By the 1530s the exchanges between Poliziano and Cortesi, initiated in 1490, and between Gianfrancesco Pico and Bembo in 1512–13 had become exemplary texts in the debate, inserted, for example, in the *De elocutionis*

---

[1] Etienne Dolet, *De imitatione Ciceroniana adversus Floridum Sabinum* (Lyons: E. Dolet, 1540), pp. 10–16.

imitatione ac apparatu of Jacobus Omphalius, a work first printed in 1537 at Paris, again in 1555, and several times later in the sixteenth century. Omphalius himself raises most of the issues which dog the theory and practice of literary imitation all through the sixteenth century and follow it from Latin into the vernacular. Imitation, he claims, is not a prescription for servile copying or a licence to plagiarize, but a spur to emulation, as the imitator strives not only to reproduce the achievements of his forerunners, but to surpass them. There are implications for criticism here, as well as a challenge to new writers. An adequate reading of a composition written in the spirit of emulation must presuppose a knowledge of the original and the discrimination to say where the new work is better. At this point Omphalius comes up against an inhibiting feature of the humanists' programme of perfect Latinity reconstructed on universally applicable and immutable ancient models. If modern writers cannot, by definition, write better Latin than the Latin they are imitating or find better themes than the paradigms presented by ancient genres, then the only form of 'betterment' available to us lies in cosmetic ornament, 'so that what we have taken from others may appear better set off, better embellished in our own writing than in his from whom we have borrowed it, . . . so our aim should be not so much to demonstrate our capacity to imitate as to win praise by our skill in the artifice of ornamenting things'.[2] Here again, the criticism of contemporary writing is given a clear directive, and it is not towards any notion of 'original thought', but towards novelty and versatility in verbal ornamentation.

Another question with which Omphalius concerns himself is the relationship between model authors and the natural bent of the new writer, a relationship which becomes particularly problematic for the extreme Ciceronian position. As Poliziano says, arguing against the Ciceronians: 'You may accuse me of not expressing myself as Cicero would. So what? I am not Cicero. I am expressing myself.'[3] The anti-Ciceronians, like Poliziano, Gianfrancesco Pico, and Erasmus after them in his *Ciceronianus* of 1528, found their way to a compromise between literary imitation and native character by advocating the imitation of a multiplicity of authors. Erasmus suggests that if you seek out what is best in every author, and at the same time select what matches best with your own natural disposition, inwardly ruminate and thoroughly digest it, it will become truly your own, and not an alien affectation. So imitation, especially imitation of many authors, may be not only a training in judgement, but also a method of self-discovery. Reading becomes a way of defining and testing the self, and the literary critic, whom the humanists' interest in the historical context

---

[2] J. Omphalius, *De elocutionis imitatione ac apparatu* (Paris: G. Julianus, 1555), fol. 9^r.
[3] *Ibid.*, fol. 35^r–35^v.

of literary works had already turned towards literary history and the biography of authors, finds added incentive not only to seek out the man behind the style of the book on which he comments, but also to analyse his own personal reactions to it. However, the extreme Ciceronian argument, represented in the work of Omphalius by Cortesi, Bembo, and Omphalius himself, pulls equally strongly in another direction, subordinating personal idiosyncrasies (or, rather, educating them, as the humanists would claim) to a model of perfection. By this is meant not only perfection of style, but, because style is either a more or a less adequate representation of the truth about things and good style can be taught, perfection of moral virtue too, epitomized in the ideal rhetorician, 'a good man skilled in speaking'. Cicero and Virgil then become the supreme *exempla* of a universally valid concept of taste, which combines aesthetic judgement with moral poise, for 'speech', as Omphalius reminds us, 'is the mirror of the mind of man'.[4] The humanists' practice of literary imitation embraces widely divergent tendencies, culminating in the very different critical positions of a Montaigne and of a Scaliger, between which other sixteenth-century writers move, sometimes haphazardly, sometimes with a more conscious sense of the paradoxes and tensions involved.

The treatise by Omphalius is not an original work, but it is a good demonstration of the commonplaces of the sixteenth-century debate on literary imitation and of its origins in the humanists' practice of Latin prose and verse composition. The matter of the debate derives from the world of Latin literature, both from contemporary methods of teaching that literature, and, at a further remove, from ancient Roman theory which was itself preoccupied with constituting a national literature on Greek models. The debate transcends the linguistic boundaries of the vernaculars, whilst at the same imposing on them a model for literary theory which had been generated in a particular historical situation, but was now first and foremost relevant to the problems of writing in a dead language. The book by Omphalius shows this nicely, written, as it is, in Latin by a German rhetorician, published mainly in France, and incorporating texts representative of the ideas of Italian Latin humanists current since the last years of the fifteenth century. A similar review of the state of the question, published first in Italy in 1541, but later also in France, was the *De imitatione libri tres* of the Italian Bartolomeo Ricci. Ricci covers much of the same ground as Omphalius (indeed the two authors were to be brought together in a composite edition at Paris in 1579), but he attaches the terms of the debate more distinctly to the Horatian polarities of nature and art. Also, working, like all rhetoricians, from the point of view of the apprentice writer, he elaborates a concept of literary judgement which

---

[4] *Ibid.*, fol. 50ᵛ.

proposes an even closer amalgam of the moral and the aesthetic, starting, as it does, from self-assessment of one's 'nature' which is then supplemented and corrected by a training in critical discrimination and rhetorical technique, the aim of which is to reproduce standards of excellence found in ancient models of style.

In theory Omphalius is a Ciceronian and Ricci an eclectic in their choice of authors for imitation, but when they move from theory to method they both proceed by providing the reader with examples of phrases excerpted from Latin texts, whereby the new writer may learn to vary his expression of ideas and topics in a style consonant with models of good Latinity. The procedure is that of the humanist classroom, with its exercises in the variation and amplification of set themes, for which the most famous source of phraseology among many, many others was Erasmus's *De copia*. A strict Ciceronian could provide only phrases culled from Cicero, but most such instruments of resource range much more widely. This is particularly true of the commonplace-books in which the humanists' pupils were taught to collect quotations from the texts they studied, and which were carefully arranged in sections to illustrate ways of expressing general topics or of manipulating figures of speech. Here we have a method of literary imitation which is radically different from the careful reproduction or adaptation of an extended passage from a single text. The commonplace-book method juxtaposes words and phrases from diverse authors, leaving the new writer the freedom of arranging them at will to create a desired effect and of supplementing them with more and more stylistic variations on a given theme to produce that 'golden river with thoughts and words pouring out in rich abundance' in which Erasmus, at the beginning of *De copia*, saw the magnificence and splendour of artificially contrived speech. The widespread effect of the commonplace-book method of literary imitation may be inferred from the numerous humanist handbooks which recommend it and from the large number of printed commonplace-books, which attest its prevalence.

The juxtaposition of textual reminiscences favoured by the commonplace-book method of literary imitation raises certain questions for the critical reader in an even more acute form than does the extended reproduction of single models. These questions centre on recognition, which seems to have been as tangled a problem for contemporary critics as it is for modern readers of sixteenth-century poetry. Some humanist critics and rhetoricians imply that the aim of the imitator's art is to conceal his art, so carefully digesting, incorporating, transforming, and disguising his source-material that the reader is hard put to locate a precise model, while at the same time admiring a family likeness with all he judges to be best in literary style. The numerous printed phrase-books, notably the later editions of Ravisius Textor's famous dictionary of epithets, support this aim by listing Latin vocabulary and phrases of good pedigree, but without identifying the authors from whom they are taken. What the critical reader needs in order to pass an adequate judgement on writing derived from 'concealed' imitation is an educated sense of what constitutes literary style or poetic idiom. In addition, the adverse critic is entitled to pick on examples of flagrant plagiarism and condemn them as an offence against the first principles of this particular concept of the art of literary transformation. However, quotations or barely disguised borrowings from other authors, inserted without acknowledgement in a new composition, can also be viewed much more positively, as significant allusions, working intertextually to widen the scope of the new work, introduce complexities and ambiguities, and point up similarities and differences, stylistic, historical, even ideological. This mode of reading is dependent on recognition of the inserted text, and it was much promoted by the humanists' pupils' enforced memorizing of quotations (together with their attributions) collected in their commonplace-books. The practice of literary imitation makes both the function and the pleasure of recognition part of the critical reading of a literary work. What it does not provide is any formula for determining exactly what the status of textual recall may be in any given instance, whether it is merely an element in the genesis of the work, an unconscious reminiscence, an accidental coincidence of phraseology within a fairly circumscribed literary vocabulary, a marker for judging the skill with which an author has 'improved' on a previous text, or an agency for amplifying or perhaps undermining the sense of a passage.

All these functions are possible. Vida (*De arte poetica* (1527), III.185–266) recommends his young writer to adopt the matter, the diction, and the word order of ancient models, but his subsequent elaboration of the theme highlights the unresolved problems of reading a literature of imitation. On the one hand, he envisages a carefully contrived and dissimulative adaptation of the original text, which proceeds by stealth and 'deceives the reader'; and on the other, a flagrant flaunting of imitation, which has to be 'caught in the act' by the reader's recognition of the model passage before the new text can be adequately read, that is to say read as recasting, alluding to, or competing with the old. Vida himself draws attention to his own skill in applying the rhetorical scheme *allusio* (in its technical sense of a slight change made in a word to alter its meaning) to his imitation of ancient models: 'I am fond of playing with phrases of ancient authors ['antiquis alludere dictis'] and of using their selfsame words to express very different meanings . . . far be it from me to conceal my thefts and hide my plunder' (III.257–63). Indeed, Vida constantly illustrates theoretical topics in his poetics by imitations of Virgil which make their point only if the reader recognizes them as imitations. What literary imitation certainly did encourage was a search for literary antecedents for any text, and a belief that critical response is more or less sophisticated depending on the extent to which the reader shares the writer's literary culture.

*

Literary imitation, especially when it crossed linguistic boundaries into the vernacular, posed acute problems for the individual writer. Both as theorists and as vernacular poets, writers like Du Bellay and Ronsard were from the first stridently insistent in their claims to innovate, to 'travel an unknown path', yet they were well aware that the path they chose was well documented by their humanist forerunners in the field of literary imitation from whom they had learnt their lessons in the 'way of following Pindar and Horace' (see Ronsard's preface for the reader of his *Odes* of 1550).[5] Their whole programme for the creation of a 'new, no, rather, ancient poetry renewed', based on imitation of the ancients and of Italian poets (see Du Bellay's second preface to his *Olive*, 1550),[6] reproduced issues raised in the Ciceronian controversies of Latin humanists and was similarly beset with contradictions.

The tension between literary imitation and individual genius, already triggered in arguments among Latin humanists, was live for the new vernacular poets, with their sense of self further quickened by their sensitivity to the linguistic divide over which they had to translate their models for writing. Their earliest attempts to imprint their identity on their overall programme of literary imitation were learnt from humanist advocates of emulation, who urged new poets to 'better' the old by the versatility with which they complicated and embellished the copious verbal ornamentation in which they set ideas received from the tradition. Ronsard, in particular, also followed the lead of anti-Ciceronian humanists in their attempt to forge a compromise between literary imitation and native character by combining references to several authors in a single poem, thus securing for the new poet an independent editorial and directing role. However, it is true of both these solutions to the dilemma that the poet's own voice cannot properly be heard unless the reader recognizes the echoes set up by imitation in the poem, for without that recognition he cannot begin to detect traces of the poet's own intervention. Both ways lead to an implicit integrating and perhaps submerging of the new poet's voice in the harmonious, intertextual chorus of past masters.

Anxieties about the inhibiting effects of an overshadowing tradition seem to intensify as the poets mature, with Du Bellay in his *Regrets* of

---

[5] P. de Ronsard, *Œuvres complètes*, ed. P. Laumonier, I. Silver, and R. Lebègue, 20 vols. (Paris: M. Didier, 1914–75), vol. I, pp. 43–50.

[6] J. du Bellay, *Œuvres poétiques*, ed. H. Chamard, 6 vols. (Paris: M. Didier, 1908–31), vol. I, pp. 11–25.

1558 and Ronsard in his verse-epistles of the 1560s confronting their fear of failure, failure to find a place for themselves in the tradition, or, indeed, failure to write at all. Such anxieties were not ignored by the authors of humanist poetics, and, a characteristic paradox, echoes of Latin theorists can be heard in the most introspective ponderings of vernacular writers exploring the autobiographical mode. Certain paradigms recur. Neo-platonic theories of inspiration validate the poet's claim to experience and express his own particular poetic vision, but, as naturally and gratuitously as it is given, the vision may fade, and the poet sink into a debilitating depression, as Vida, for example, describes most graphically (*De arte poetica*, II.395–422). At such moments of intermission the inspiration may be artificially reactivated by reading and imitating ancient poets (II.423–44), but perhaps only to reproduce a pale image of the primal vision, just as Du Bellay in the *Regrets* attempts to compensate for the flight of the muses by the artifice of rhetorical patterning and Ronsard in his epistles of self-doubt conjures up the sacred fury by describing its effects in figured language. At another point, Vida, himself following Horace in the *Epistulae*, among others, sets the scene for the poet's style of life, pure from vice and innocent of crime, in a rural retreat, close to nature, immune from strife and free from care and worldly ambition (I.486–514). Once again, personal reference tends to coalesce with public common-place, but tensions are deliberately left in play. This is especially the case in Ronsard's poems, with their recurrent emphasis on what marks the difference between the poet and the norm, be it the moral strictures of his high calling to a poetic priesthood (as in the *Ode à Michel de L'Hôpital*)[7] or the alienating signs of sacred fury, which make the vulgar call him simply raving mad (as in the prologue to the *Hymne de l'automne*).[8]

Ronsard's later poetic practice, if not his abbreviated gestures towards poetic theory, frequently and somewhat unnervingly intrudes the personal subject into the intertextual web of allusion woven out of literary imitation. The discovery of an articulate self which this entails and affirms contributes towards his outspoken defence of artistic autonomy, often enunciated in terms of his personal freedom. This is at its most vehement in the historical circumstances of war and polemic which occasioned his letter to the reader at the head of his *Trois livres du recueil de nouvelles poésies* (1563).[9] Here, political polemic and literary criticism are closely enmeshed in a text where the Protestant enemies of Ronsard's personal and professional freedom are traduced, both because they have the fanatic's desire to compel and coerce, and because, as writers, they are bungling and unworthy imitators of Ronsard himself. In a proud reversal of the usual posture of

[7] Ronsard, *Œuvres complètes*, vol. III, pp. 118–63.
[8] *Ibid.*, vol. XII, pp. 46–50.   [9] *Ibid.*, vol. XII, pp. 3–24.

the vernacular humanist poet, Ronsard proclaims himself the model from which all draw. Yet, even where the paradigm of literary imitation provides the proof of his superiority as a poet, it is perceived to be a threat to him as an individual, as Ronsard attempts to shake himself free from the constraining images which his aping adversaries would foist upon him.

The self-assertiveness with which Ronsard replies in kind, but 'against the modesty of my nature', to Protestant attacks *ad hominem*, does not allay the anxiety of influence by which he is beset when he returns in 1569 to fable and fiction, themes which, he suggests, are more congenial to his nature and are certainly truer to his humanist's sense of where 'the subject of good poets' lies. It is precisely in his long retellings of ancient myths that Ronsard is apt to display most copiously the triumphs of the imitator's fertile act of re-creation, but also to hint at the fear of impotence which haunted those whose natural talents were nurtured under the shadow of superior models. Yet (and the paradox again is inescapable), if such hints are to be understood, these poems, above all others, demand a reader competent in the skills promoted by humanist literary criticism and its rhetoric of imitation. Sometimes quite directly the text of these poems recalls archetypes of myths and models of expression, but not solely for the reader's pleasure in recognition, nor solely in order that the new text may be recuperated for the literary canon. Just as significant are the differences to be sensed between prototype and imitation, the deviations and the contradictions creating interstices so that the poet's individual voice may be heard through the *personae*. Ronsard exploits and manipulates an increasing range of humanist methods of reading as the intervention of the personal subject becomes more insistent in his mythological poems from the late 1560s onwards. He not only works through commonplaces and textual reminiscence, but digresses into the interpretative mode of commentary, juxtaposing different and sometimes conflicting strategies for reading the myth he is narrating. One effect is that inserted patches of commentary almost (but never quite) decompose and on occasion even subvert his primary narration and its model texts by wayward amplification and highly personalized dissent.

For a more disconcertingly critical assay on the rhetorical orthodoxies of literary imitation we must turn to one of the most important critical readers of the sixteenth century, to Michel de Montaigne. The essay 'Des livres' (II.x), the greater part of which dates from the first edition of the *Essais* in 1580, starts with a bow to 'the writings of master-craftsmen' who speak better and 'with more authenticity' about things than Montaigne may do.[10] Set in clear opposition to them, the essays are described

---

[10] Michel de Montaigne, *The complete essays*, ed. and trans. M. A. Screech (London: Penguin, 1993), p. 457.

as 'assays of my natural abilities', fantasies, by means of which Montaigne endeavours to impart knowledge, not about things, but about himself, a kind of knowledge where 'my way of talking about things' counts more than the things themselves. We recognize components of the half-concealed infrastructure to the argument: the distinction between *res* and *verba* (things and words, matter and expression) familiar from rhetorical theory; the Horatian art/nature dichotomy; and the tension between canonical texts and the individual writer endemic in the rhetoric of literary imitation. At this point interpolations reworked in various editions of the essay subsequent to 1580 show that Montaigne himself, as reader of his own text, felt its inevitable slide towards the topic of intertextual writing. Montaigne claims that his borrowings, acknowledged and unacknowledged, are vehicles for saying what he cannot say so well himself, assisting the expression of his thoughts [*inventio*] with transplanted ways of developing them [quoted *loci*] and verbal enhancement [*elocutio*]. What he reserves for himself alone is composition [*dispositio*], for there the identity of the individual leaves its truest mark: 'I want people to see my natural ordinary stride, however much it wanders off the path'.[11]

Montaigne, rhetorical commentator on his own text, here takes us into the heart of his method of writing, richly intertextual, interlarded with unattributed quotations used both to suscitate and to amplify arguments, as much a product of literary imitation as any humanist's. His very insistence on himself, both as writer and as subject of writing, is the almost inevitable end-product of humanists' discussions about the possibility of rewriting the ancients in self-displaying texts. Montaigne writes as an informed participant in that critical debate, and into every one of its commonplaces he introduces his own idiosyncratic variation. His writing depends on memory, but he claims he has no memory. He both conceals and exposes his plagiarisms, and challenges his reader's good judgement to strip him of his borrowed feathers rather than bask in the pleasures of recognition. His particular inclination, like that of every humanist literary critic, leans towards poetry, from which he takes most of his interpolated Latin quotations, but he himself writes in prose. He oscillates between the living, unstable vernacular, in which he reveals his living, fluid self, and the Latin language, dead, but buried deep within him.[12]

Montaigne's writing is generated by his reading of 'the master-craftsmen' and by his reading of himself. Reading and writing are locked in the symbiotic relationship created by rhetorical lessons in the analysis and genesis of texts. In 'Des livres' ['Of books'] Montaigne begins by constituting himself as a writer set on transmitting knowledge about himself, rather than about things, and then constitutes himself as a reader with exactly the

---

[11] *Ibid.*, p. 459.   [12] See 'Du repentir', III.ii (*ibid.*, p. 914).

same purpose: when he studies books, he only looks for 'learning which deals with knowing myself'.[13] It is by means of this transition from writing to reading, with a common end in view, that Montaigne proceeds in this essay to a critical study of authors he has read. His overall judgement of them marks him as a humanist, with vernacular authors depreciated in favour of the ancients, with Boccaccio, Rabelais, and Heliodorus the only representatives of prose fiction (and read merely for pleasure), with Virgil as the paragon of poets, with moral philosophy (Terence, Plutarch, Seneca, Cicero) and history (especially Caesar) recommended as the best source of knowledge of 'man in general'. He employs the comparative method of contemporary historians of literature and the critical overview perfected by contemporary authors of *Praelectiones*. But among the array of approaches traditional with humanist expositors of texts he operates a significant shift of emphasis, disowning the exhaustive (and inexhaustible) pursuit of meaning [*interpretatio*] and the accumulated knowledge of things provided by explanatory annotation [*enarratio*], in order to focus on judgement [*iudicium*], the area of critical discourse where the language of humanist historians of literature had tended to be least probing. The judgement of Montaigne, the reader, is written out primarily in order to give us knowledge of Montaigne, the man, 'the measure of my sight not the measure of the thing'.[14] He notes, furthermore, that his judgement is not absolute, but changes over time, thus linking literary judgement into the temporality explored in Montaigne's autobiographical enterprise, something on which he expatiates further in 'Du jeune Caton' ['Of Cato the Younger'] (I.xxxvii).

At two crucial junctures Montaigne applies his judgement to literary imitation, firstly with respect to vernacular poetry, described in a cluster of comparisons which all stress its clownish aping of noble master-models.[15] Its Mannerist excesses are a cosmetic ornament, disguising an inability to use words to constitute thought and to 'signify more than they say', as Montaigne puts it when he amplifies this observation in 'Sur des vers de Virgile' ['On some verses of Virgil'] (III.v), an essay in which he goes so far as to hint that the instinct to imitate is a suicidal tendency.[16] Next in 'Des livres', emboldened by his self-granted licence to judge at variance to the norm, he finds even greater vacuity in Cicero himself, the paradigm of models for writing, whose rhetorical rigmaroles say nothing to 'me, who am only seeking to become more wise not more learned or more eloquent'.[17] In the case of wordy Cicero, and, even more pertinently, in the case of those writers who profess to get nearest to the grain of things, historians themselves, the good reader's judgement must undo the

---

[13] *Ibid.*, p. 459.   [14] *Ibid.*, p. 460.   [15] *Ibid.*, pp. 462–3.
[16] *Ibid.*, pp. 987, 990.   [17] *Ibid.*, p. 464.

fine weave of words in order to lay bare the historical truth, the raw, crude stuff of history, 'naked and unshaped' in all its diversity. And yet, the whole truth about the past is irrecoverable, or, at best, our knowledge of it 'very slack'. Words are the only real presence, and perhaps the only authentic subject is the writer, his mind and his personal judgement, about which Montaigne has such a 'particular curiosity'. The essay 'Des livres' ends by offering to his reader transcriptions of personal judgements Montaigne had made at particular moments of his life on the judgements of the historians he had read.

The elusive *res* of history may give place to critical judgement, but the *verba* of poetry are both more real and more refractory. The words and the fictions of the best poets, certain lines of Virgil, for example, activate in the reader a present intensity of life and feeling which life itself, either in the now or in its remembered past, cannot match. Judgement there falls short. There is no rule or reason whereby to judge such art, only the language of rapture and transport, the language of divine fury, to which Montaigne has recourse in a late addition to 'Du jeune Caton', commenting: 'Here is something of a marvel: we now have far more poets than judges and interpreters of poetry. It is far easier to write poetry than to appreciate it.'[18] Montaigne speaks for himself and for his age.

[18] *Ibid.*, p. 260.

10

Petrarchan poetics

William J. Kennedy

Credit for canonizing Petrarch's fourteenth-century *Rime sparse* usually goes to Pietro Bembo's *Prose della volgar lingua* (1525). Squeezing out of Petrarch's 200-year-old Siculo-Tuscan literary idiom the seeds of a factitious cultural heritage, Bembo promoted a style that spoke oddly to Italy's competing regional centres, much less to the emerging national literatures of monarchies outside of Italy. Yet Petrarchism became the dominant lyric style not only in Italy but throughout Europe. Divergent critical views of Petrarch inscribed in fifteenth- and sixteenth-century commentaries on the *Rime sparse* and *Trionfi* offer compelling evidence. They construct a narrative of multiple Petrarchs, heterogeneous versions of the *Rime e trionfi* conformable to opposing ideologies at different times and in different places.[1] In their light we may better understand Petrarch's place in a divided Italy, an imperial Spain, a monarchical France, and Protestant England.

The earliest Florentine biographies of Petrarch by Filippo Villani (1381), Pier Paolo Vergerio (1397), Leonardo Bruni (1436), and Giannozzo Manetti (1440s) reclaimed Petrarch's Florentine ancestry and depicted him as sympathetic to the republican spirit of civic humanism, but they offered few comments on his vernacular poetry.[2] Commentaries written under the auspices of despotic rulers in northern Italy a century later, however, read and interpreted the Italian verse on different horizons. Each supports claims sympathetic to the aristocratic, autocratic, and expansionist interests of Ghibelline monarchism or Venetian oligarchy, and each asserts a special relationship with the historical Petrarch who spent the longest period of his Italian residence in northern territories, first at Milan where he served

---

[1] For bibliographical information see Mary Fowler and Morris Bishop, *Catalogue of the Petrarch collection in the Cornell University Library*, 2nd edn (Millwood, NJ: Kraus-Thomson, 1974); on moralizing commentary see Thomas P. Roche, Jr., *Petrarch and the English sonnet sequences* (New York: AMS, 1989). A comprehensive survey is found in Gino Belloni, *Laura tra Petrarca e Bembo: studi sul commento umanistico-rinascimentale al 'Canzoniere'* (Padua: Antenore, 1992); and a detailed treatment in William J. Kennedy, *Authorizing Petrarch* (Ithaca: Cornell University Press, 1994).

[2] These texts are found in Angelo Solerti (ed.), *Le vite di Dante, Petrarca, e Boccaccio* (Milan: Francesco Vallardi, 1904–5); partial translations in D. Thompson and A. Nagel (ed.), *The three crowns of Florence* (New York: Harper & Row, 1972).

the Visconti (1353–61); then at Venice (1362–7); and finally in Padua and Arquà (1368–74) where Francesco da Carrara granted him an estate.

Antonio da Tempo, 'a judge in the city of Padua', and clearly not the more famous Antonio who composed an influential *De ritimis vulgaribus* in 1332, assembled the first full-scale commentary on the *Rime sparse* in the 1420s.[3] Addressing his work 'to Signor Alberto, of the noble Scaliger family of Verona' (sig. AVi^r), Antonio celebrated Petrarch's career as an exemplary public servant who advanced the cause of central government in northern Italy. Similar assumptions guided Francesco Filelfo, who served Filippo Maria Visconti in Milan. Accepting the duke's commission to annotate the text in the mid-1440s, Filelfo sees himself re-enacting his predecessor Petrarch's career at the Milanese court. Dedicated to 'your highness occupied in governing and a great many worthy affairs', but finished only as far as sonnet 136, his commentary would strengthen its patron's bid to rule wherever Petrarch's language is spoken – that is, throughout all northern Italy.[4] Within a generation Hieronimo Squarzafico completed the latter and published it along with his own at Venice in 1484.[5] Combined in one volume after 1503, the Antonio–Filelfo–Squarzafico commentaries with their view of Petrarch as a Ghibelline monarchist dominated the printing of the *Rime sparse* in twenty-two editions before 1522.

Pietro Bembo set out to change this view. Early in the century he supervised the first unannotated Aldine edition of Petrarch's *Cose volgari* (1501), claiming for his copytext the poet's own partially autographed final exemplar (Vat. Lat. 3195). A friend of Giuliano de' Medici and later secretary for two Medici popes, Leo X and Clement VII, Bembo fashioned his *Prose della volgar lingua* as a vigorous defence of Florentine cultural hegemony, certifying Petrarch's highly artificial literary language as an inescapable product of Florentine genius and promoting it as normative for all Italian poetry, a 'style that will be esteemed best and most beautiful by everyone'.[6] The composite nature of this style, cobbled together with bits of Provençal, Sicilian court usage, Latinisms, archaisms, and idiosyncratic neologisms, summons in Bembo's view a shared discourse of Medici cultural inheritance against contemporary factional strife. *Gravità* is its most important feature, whereby strategic clusters of what Bembo calls

---

[3] *Francisci Petrarcae . . . la uita & il comento supra li sonetti canzone & triumphi . . . composto & compilato per il doctissimo iurista misser Antonio da Tempo*, 2 vols. (Venice: Domenico Siliprando, 1477), sig. AVi^r. See Carlo Dionisotti, 'Fortuna del Petrarca nel "400" ', *Italia medioevale e umanistica* 17 (1974), 61–113.

[4] *Il comento deli sonetti et cançone del Petrarcha composto per messer Francesco Philelpho* (Bologna: Ugo Rugerius, 1476), sig. 2^v. See Ezio Raimondi, 'Francesco Filelfo interprete del Canzoniere', *Studi petrarcheschi* 3 (1950), 143–64.

[5] *Li canzoneti dello egregio poeta messer F. Petrarcha . . . io Hyeronimo gli ho exposti* (Venice: Piero Cremoneso, 1484).

[6] Pietro Bembo, *Prose e rime*, ed. C. Dionisotti, 2nd edn (Turin: Unione Typografico-Editrice Torinese, 1966), p. 176.

sharp 'masculine' sounds lend clear definition to otherwise cavernous and diffuse 'feminine' ones, 'an occult power, that, lingering in each word, moves one to assent to what one reads'.[7] Echoing Petrarch's sonnet 304, Bembo designates it a *stil canuto* ['mature style'].[8]

In 1525 Alessandro Vellutello offered a new paradigm for commentary in his edition of *Il Petrarcha*.[9] Vellutello's major contribution was to reorder the sequence of 'scattered' poems into a coherent narrative so as to square their implied story with known events in the author's life. Vellutello bases his authority on a careful reading of Petrarch's Latin correspondence and upon deductions from Petrarch's Latin and Italian poetry, but he also establishes his credentials as a student of social, political, religious, and amatory mores in Avignon and Vaucluse, and even as a cartographer of the surrounding region, for which he provides an extraordinary topographic relief map. Like a good ethnographer, he has visited the site and has conversed with its inhabitants. Their accounts yield startling results.

The first concerns Laura's identity. Parish records of Cabrières affirm that she could not have been the noble 'Laurette de Sade' who came of age in the 1360s, but was the unmarried daughter of an impoverished lord Henri Chiabau. Her meeting with Petrarch occurred not in the church of Santa Chiara at Avignon, as the poet had claimed, but rather on the flower-strewn plain of the Sorgue, where the inhabitants of Vaucluse and Cabrières make a pilgrimage each Good Friday. Vellutello's confidence that he has discovered the historical truth leads him to a tighter, more controlled chronology of the poet's love for Laura and its impact on his diplomatic career. To the two conventional sections, *in vita di Laura* and *in morte di Laura*, Vellutello adds a third section of non-amatory poetry that features the patriotic canzone 128, 'Italia mia', presents sonnets on the Babylonian captivity of the papacy at Avignon, and includes other poems that reflect political, polemical, and poetical issues.

Twenty-nine reprintings of Vellutello's edition made it the most widely circulated sixteenth-century text of the *Rime e trionfi*. Though other commentators restored the poems' conventional order, they devoted great care to answering or rebutting, modifying or revising Vellutello's conjectures. Among them were Sylvano da Venafro and Giovanni Andrea Gesualdo at Naples and Bernardino Daniello at Venice. Sylvano and Gesualdo both published their work in 1533, the former for a local audience, the latter for a wider readership. Under Spanish rule since 1503, the Naples of their era laboured to preserve its cultural identity with the rest of Italy. Sylvano displaces the Ghibelline emphases of Antonio da Tempo, Filelfo,

[7] *Ibid.*, p. 174.   [8] *Ibid.*, p. 168.
[9] *Le volgari opere del Petrarcha con la espositione di Alessandro Vellutello da Lucca* (Venice: Fratelli da Sabbio, 1525).

Squarzafico, and (in part) Vellutello when he focuses upon Petrarch's archetypal representations of love and well-bred amatory conduct: 'I write especially to please the ladies who might wish to understand more about matters that Petrarch writes of'.[10] Celebrating Petrarch's gallantry, piety, and Platonic detachment, Sylvano applauds the poet for expressing amatory sentiment in the decorous style of a Castiglionesque courtier.

Gesualdo's annotations submit this style to an exiguous rhetorical analysis. Under the mentorship of his kinsman Antonio Sebastiano Minturno, who later produced an influential dialogue on Greek and Latin poetic forms, *De poeta libri sex* (1559), with an application to Italian forms in *L'arte poetica* (1563–4), Gesualdo appears to be working through controversies about rhetoric and poetics aired at the Academy of Naples in his time.[11] He examines the literal and figurative discourse of each poem and he records debates about rival interpretations. He presents divergent opinions, offers reasons for each, and nudges his readers to interpret matters according to their own convictions. Unlike other glossators who propound a single strong thesis, Gesualdo offers many. The result is the longest, richest, and most studiously detailed commentary on Petrarch's *Rime e trionfi* in the sixteenth century, and one that was reprinted as the magisterial gloss on these texts in the 1554 and 1581 Basle editions of Petrarch's complete works.

Bernardino Daniello, a younger member of Bembo's Venetian circle, offered a competing rhetorical analysis with an accent on literary competence. In 1536 Daniello had published a synthesis of Ciceronian and Horatian precepts, *La poetica*, defining lyric poetry as a 'pittura parlante' that presents nuanced images of truth overlaid with figurative language.[12] In his commentary on the *Rime e trionfi* (1541) Daniello locates Petrarch in the context of other authors, both classical and contemporary, juxtaposing the poetry against sources, analogues, and later imitations. By reconstructing fragments from the classical past, Daniello shows how Petrarch collaborates with and rivals the greatest writers: 'I don't see any way in which our Petrarch is inferior to Theban Pindar or Venusian Horace'.[13] From these allusions, echoes, and literary cross-references,

---

[10] *Il Petrarca col commento di m. Syluano da Venaphro* (Naples: Antonio Iouino and Matthio Canzer, 1533), sig. +iiiiʳ.

[11] *Il Petrarcha colla spositione di misser Giovanni Andrea Gesualdo* (Venice: Fratelli da Sabbio, 1533); Antonio Sebastiano Minturno, *De poeta* (1559; facs. reprint Munich: W. Fink, 1970, ed. B. Fabian), and *L'arte poetica* (1564; facs. reprint Munich: W. Fink, 1971, ed. B. Fabian); for a partial translation see Allan Gilbert, *Literary criticism from Plato to Dryden* (Detroit: Wayne State University Press, 1962), pp. 274–303.

[12] *La poetica* (1536; facs. reprint Munich: W. Fink, 1968, ed. B. Fabian), p. 25.

[13] *Sonetti, canzoni, e triomphi di messer Francesco Petrarcha con la spositione di Bernardino Daniello da Lucca* (Venice: Giovannantonio de Nicolini da Sabbio, 1541), sig. *iiiʳ. See Ezio Raimondi, 'Bernardino Daniello e le varianti petrarcheschi', *Studi petrarcheschi* 5 (1952), 95–130.

Petrarch emerges as a contemporary of Virgil and Cicero, Horace and Ovid, Plato and Aristotle, Dante and Cino da Pistoia, and a prophet of Bembo and Ariosto, not only recapitulating Western literary discourse before his time, but also improving upon it and offering it as a model for subsequent Italian style.

Yet another kind of commentary reveals traces of Reformationist thought that mark Petrarch as a proto-Protestant critic of the Avignon papacy, scholastic logic, and incompetent scriptural study. In 1532 Fausto da Longiano dedicated his gloss on the *Rime sparse* to the Count of Modena who had encouraged Lutheran reform in that city.[14] Fausto interprets the text as a spiritual drama that unfolds amidst the courts of Europe where the Christian poet faces greed and corruption, baseness of every sort proffered by bishops and priests, popes and princes, *grandes dames* and whores, all while yearning for God's promise offered in the gospels and taught by Augustine. Practical, independent, and possessed of a deep faith in the divine word, Fausto's Petrarch shows the way for sixteenth-century courtiers to prosper in this world without losing their souls to unholy error.

In 1548 Antonio Brucioli dedicated his annotated edition of the *Rime sparse* to the daughter of Ercole II d'Este and Renée of France, who had harboured the heretical Clément Marot and Jean Calvin at Ferrara in the 1530s.[15] Like Fausto, Brucioli emphasizes courtly manners and a courtly style as the setting for Petrarch's moral action, and like Fausto he weighs Petrarch's judgement against scriptural quotations that apply to particular situations. Himself a translator of and commentator upon the Old and New Testaments, Brucioli presents the Bible as a major intertext, displacing earlier commentators' cross-references to classical literature and philosophy as an interpretative standard.

A third commentary with Reformist leanings was compiled by Lodovico Castelvetro, evidently in the 1540s before he left Italy for good. Retrieved from his papers and published posthumously by his nephew in 1582, the annotations emphasize as models for Petrarch's poetry the writings of the Greek and Roman ancients, but also passages from Psalms, Ecclesiastes, the Song of Songs, the New Testament, and the Church Fathers.[16] Castelvetro is every bit as capable a classical scholar as Gesualdo and Daniello, but more than them he knows the Bible and understands how it

---

[14] *Il Petrarcha col commento di M. Sebastiano Fausto da Longiano* (Venice: Francesco di Alessandro Bindoni, 1532).

[15] *Sonetti, canzoni, et triomphi di M. Francesco Petrarca con breue dichiaratione, & annotatione di Antonio Brucioli* (Venice: Alessandro Brucioli, 1548).

[16] *Le rime del Petrarca breuemente sposte per Lodouico Casteluetro* (Basle: Pietro de Sedabonis, 1582). See Ezio Raimondi, 'Gli scrupoli di un filologo: Ludovico Castelvetro e il Petrarca', *Studi petrarcheschi* 5 (1952), 131–210.

penetrates the *Rime sparse*. His focus upon verbal peculiarities, often as correctives to Bembo's linguistic speculations, may have proved irrelevant to a non-Italian audience, but the reach of his bolder conclusions about scriptural meaning and doctrinal associations surely attracted attention outside of Italy.

Such annotated editions brought Petrarch to a readership both inside and outside Italy, and to them one might add a vast array of other editions with shorter marginal glosses and interpretative aids. They include Paulus Manutius's explanatory notes printed in five Aldine editions after 1533, Francesco Alunno da Ferrara's *rimario* (1539), Francesco Sansovino's plagiarized observations (1546), Girolamo Ruscelli's elaborate concordance (1554), and Lodovico Dolce's lexical gloss (1560). Every regional centre in Italy, it might seem, tried to claim Petrarch for its own. But if the poet from Avignon and Vaucluse could be thought of as Milanese or Venetian or Neapolitan or Florentine, why not also as Provençal or French?

In 1533 coincidental with the marriage of the future Henri II to Catherine de' Medici, a union that prefigured the annexation to France of the power and prestige of Italy's most celebrated family, Maurice Scève announced that he had discovered the tomb of Petrarch's beloved Laura at the church of Santa Croce in Avignon. His discovery affirmed Laura's historical identity as Laurette de Sade against Vellutello's contentions, and it strengthened Petrarch's powerful hold over the French imagination. Its first published account occurs in a preface dated 25 August 1545, written by Jean de Tournes for his Lyons edition of the *Rime e trionfi*. In de Tournes' estimation, the event should 'quiet those commentators who every day overwork their brains in quest of Laura's identity'.[17]

The subsequent vogue of Petrarchism in France took many forms, as the chansons and sonnets of Scève's Lyonnais contemporaries Pernette du Guillet and Louise Labé would attest. Their feminine appropriation of Petrarch's rhetoric brings not just an inversion of the lover's and beloved's gendered qualities, but an entirely new critical and cultural imperative. Du Guillet's publisher writes that the poet's example should inspire her Lyonnais sisters 'to share in this great and immortal praise that the ladies of Italy have today earned for themselves and to such an extent that by their divine writings they tarnish the lustre of many learned males'.[18] This preface calls women to literary pursuits and it challenges French men as well as French women to outdo their Italian counterparts in learning and eloquence. Literary criticism turns into cultural criticism and political exhortation.

[17] *Il Petrarca* (Lyons: Jean de Tournes, 1545), sig. *3ʳ. See William J. Kennedy, 'The unbound turns of Maurice Scève', in *Creative imitation*, ed. D. Quint *et al.* (Binghamton: Medieval & Renaissance Texts & Studies, 1992), pp. 67–88.

[18] Pernette du Guillet, *Rymes*, ed. V. Graham (Geneva: Droz, 1968), pp. 3–4.

In Spain a no less explicit agenda guides the preface of Juan Boscán to his *Obras*, published in March 1543 at Barcelona. Assembled just before his death, this collection supplements Boscán's Petrarchan *sonetos* and *canciones* with others by Garcilaso de la Vega. In a prologue to his *libro segundo* the poet defends his Castilian imitations of Petrarch as augurs of a new literary standard for the international Spanish Empire. Affording the best model, Petrarch himself had followed models, including the Provençal Troubadours. Spanish poets can lay as much claim to anterior authority. Boscán, himself a bilingual Catalan- and Castilian-speaking member of Barcelona's upper-middle class, cites the Troubadour influence on Catalan poetry, and especially on the lyrics of Ausias March: 'From these Provençal poets came many excellent authors. Of them the most excellent was Ausias March.'[19] According to this logic, Petrarch's achievement was a historical accident. Any worthy descendant of the Troubadours, whether Spanish, French, or Italian, could have done likewise. In any event, the Iberians can now surpass Petrarch and elevate their language. As the future belongs to the kingdom of Castile, disenfranchised Italians may well envy Spain: 'It could be that before long the Italians might complain about seeing the excellence of their poetry transferred to Spain'.[20] The fame of Garcilaso as a noble courtier and military hero increased the prestige of his poetry even more than Boscán's, and by extension its value as a model for emergent Spanish literature, so that a few decades later it would merit its own canonizing commentaries by El Brocense (1574) and Fernando de Herrera (1580).

Social class and distinction likewise modified the development of Petrarchism amongst the nobility in France. At mid-century in Paris two factions of the latter were competing for power – the old aristocracy, and newer members who had risen from the bourgeoisie by virtue of industry, education, and public service. Many of the *rhétoriqueurs* came from humble ranks and they displayed their poetic skills as a way of advertising their verbal talent for hire to the crown. The older aristocracy reacted by devising its own programme for social and cultural advancement. Joachim du Bellay, a landless member of this aristocracy, summoned those of his class to regain their influence by pursuing an élite education in the classics. His *Deffence et illustration de la langue françoyse* (1549) argues that all languages have equal value, and that modern French can express wisdom and truth as well as ancient Greek and Latin or modern Spanish and Italian. Through exogamic marriage to classical and Italianate poetic forms, the French vernacular can increase, multiply, and enrich its own cultural patrimony: it is 'no vicious thing, but praiseworthy, to borrow

[19] Juan Boscán, *Las obras*, ed. W. I. Knapp (Madrid: Murillo, 1875), p. 171. See Ignacio Navarrete, *Orphans of Petrarch* (Berkeley: University of California Press, 1994).
[20] Boscán, *Las obras*, p. 172.

from a foreign tongue thoughts and words and appropriate them to our own'.[21] Du Bellay of course emphasizes creative imitation rather than mere translation, so that Petrarchan features of style, transposed into linguistic forms current at the French court, become or are made to become conveyors of social and political impulse, dynastic aspiration, and national ascendancy.

Criticism and appropriation of the lyric took a moralizing form in Protestant England. Sir Philip Sidney elaborated a poetic theory in *The defence of poesie* (composed ?1581) to show that Petrarch's model can best serve as a negative moral example. The *Defence* urges readers of poetry to put critical pressure upon the text's potential meanings, fleshing out partial explanations and correcting bad ones. Such readers may exert more power over a text than its author does. The poet allows an access to truth only because he 'nothing affirms, and therefore never lieth'.[22] The reader by contrast can always uncover a practical truth by refuting error, labouring to understand not 'what is or is not, but what should or should not be',[23] even when the text's author does not make the distinction. Petrarch's amatory poetry affords a perfect testing ground for this endeavour. Disciplined readers will recognize the 'wanton sinfulness and lustful love' inscribed in 'passionate sonnets' and will 'reprehend amorous conceits' dramatized there and elsewhere.[24] Rather than 'infect the fancy with unworthy objects', such poetry will train it to recognize error and resist abuse.[25]

The first critic of Sidney's sonnet sequence *Astrophil and Stella*, Thomas Nashe, honoured this advice in his commendatory epistle for its pirated edition of 1591. Upon a 'Sceane of Idiots' where Astrophil enters 'in pompe', Nashe describes the plot as one in which 'the tragicommody of loue is performed by starlight . . . The argument cruell chastitie, the Prologue hope, the Epilogue dispaire.'[26] A generation of sonneteers in late Elizabethan England allowed this criticism to inform its view of 'poore Petrarchs long deceased woes' (*Astrophil and Stella*, sonnet 15), turning criticism into poetic practice and poetic practice into art.

---

[21] Joachim du Bellay, *La deffence et illustration de la langue françoyse*, ed. H. Chamard (Paris: Didier, 1961), section 1.8, p. 17. For an English translation see *The defence and illustration of the French language*, trans. G. M. Turquet (London: J. M. Dent, 1939), p. 40. See Thomas M. Greene, *The light in Troy* (New Haven: Yale University Press, 1982), pp. 220–41; Margaret Ferguson, *Trials of desire* (New Haven: Yale University Press, 1983), pp. 18–53; and Glyn P. Norton, *The ideology and language of translation in Renaissance France and their humanist antecedents* (Geneva: Droz, 1984), pp. 290–302.

[22] *Miscellaneous prose of Sir Philip Sidney*, ed. K. Duncan-Jones and J. van Dorsten (Oxford: Clarendon Press, 1973), p. 102. See Roche, *Petrarch*, pp. 193–242.

[23] *Miscellaneous prose*, p. 102.

[24] *Ibid.*, p. 103.   [25] *Ibid.*, p. 104.

[26] *Syr P.S. his Astrophel and Stella* (1591; facs. reprint Menston: Scolar Press, 1970), sig. Aiii^r.

11

Translatio and translation in the Renaissance: from Italy to France

Valerie Worth-Stylianou

When, in 1345, Petrarch discovered at Verona a manuscript of Cicero's 'lost' works, the *Epistulae ad Atticum, ad Quintum fratrem* and *ad Brutum* (6–18), his excitement was immeasurable.[1] It was as though the access to this correspondence invited him to enjoy a new level of intimacy with the classical writer, and he expressed his delight in a letter addressed to Cicero himself. The event is an icon of Renaissance humanists' burning desire not only to retrieve the classical past, but also to initiate a dialogue with those whom they admired. The rediscovery of Greek and Latin manuscripts was a preliminary stage in the *translatio studiorum*, leading to the philologists' quests for the most accurately emended text, and thence to a process of commentary, as each scholar sought to interpret a work anew. The humanists of fourteenth- and fifteenth-century Italy vastly increased the corpus of classical texts available in the West: Petrarch and Poggio between them rediscovered approximately half of the works of Cicero which are now extant; Boccaccio found substantial parts of Tacitus at Monte Cassino; Salutati built up a private library in Florence of some 800 classical works, which he made available to others, and, by inviting the scholar Manuel Chrysoloras from Constantinople to teach Greek, gave added pace to humanists' energetic search for manuscripts from the East.[2] As new texts and new versions of familiar ones became available, translation soon occupied a significant place in the process of transmission, with scholars first rendering Greek texts into Latin, and, subsequently, Latin into the vernacular. In his comments in 1392 on a friend's revisions of a Latin version of the *Iliad*, Salutati was one of the earliest humanists to acknowledge the creative role of the translator, saying his restoration of the letter and the spirit of the source text required him to 'infuse a more pleasant texture'.[3] The issue was to lie at the heart of Renaissance thinking

[1] See R. Pfeiffer, *History of classical scholarship from 1300 to 1850* (Oxford: Clarendon Press, 1976), pp. 9–10.
[2] See R. R. Bolgar, *The classical heritage and its beneficiaries* (1954; reprint New York: Harper and Row, 1964); Pfeiffer, *History of classical scholarship*.
[3] See the analysis by G. P. Norton, *The ideology and language of translation in Renaissance France and their humanist antecedents* (Geneva: Droz, 1984), p. 37.

on not only translation but any imitation of the classics: how should the translator/imitator recapture the full vigour of the model? how far should his role be that of an interpreter of affective force as well as substance?

The first formal treatise on translation in the Renaissance, Leonardo Bruni's *De interpretatione recta* (*c.* 1426), also ascribed to the translator a creative role. Bruni accepted the necessity of a displacement of the source text, in order for it to be retrieved the more fully in the new idiom. He argued that the translator should bring to his task both a thorough philological scholarship and all the expressive powers of rhetoric. Only in this way could the translator convey the exact force [*vis*] the original author intended. Bruni's position laid a heavy burden on the translator, but exalted him to a lofty position. When taken up by translators of sacred texts, such a stance could be particularly controversial. Giannozzo Manetti's *De interpretatione recta* (embedded within his *Apologeticus* on translating the Psalter) proposed that the closest translation of Holy Scripture should aim at a reconstruction of the meaning, texture, and affective force of the original.[4] From such a viewpoint, the act of translation does not require a choice to prioritize *res* at the expense of *verba* or vice versa, but rather a commitment to retrieve and relocate both in the target language. It is a similar ideology which was to underlie Luther's hotly debated translation of Romans 3: 28 in his 1522 version of the New Testament: that man is justified 'allein durch den glauben' ['by faith alone'], for 'per fidem'. In his *Sendbrief vom Dolmetschen*, Luther defends his insertion of 'allein' as in keeping with the implied sense of St Paul and the usage of the German vernacular.[5] The specific case is obviously riddled with doctrinal implications, but Luther's statement of the translator's position is seminal in the creative autonomy and responsibility it accords to him, and is a logical development of the theoretical path trodden by Italian humanists of the preceding century.

It was in sixteenth-century France, however, that debates over translation were subsequently pursued with greatest vigour, for the transmission of classical texts prompted a searching enquiry into the status of all forms of imitative writing.[6] At first sight, it seems surprising that there is only one published work in France devoted solely to a theory of translation, namely Etienne Dolet's *La manière de bien traduire d'une langue en autre* (1540), and this is extremely short.[7] But we shall see that discourse on

---

[4] *Ibid.*, pp. 44–54.
[5] For a fuller discussion, see G. P. Norton, 'Literary translation in the continuum of Renaissance thought: a conceptual overview', in *Die literarische Übersetzung. Stand und Perspektiven ihrer Erforschung*, ed. H. Kittel and A. Frank (Berlin: Erich Schmidt, 1988), pp. 1–15.
[6] See T. Cave, *The cornucopian text: problems of writing in the French Renaissance* (Oxford: Clarendon Press, 1979).
[7] *La maniere de bien traduire d'une langue en aultre, d'avantaige de la punctuation de la langue françoyse, plus des accents d'ycelle* (Lyons: Etienne Dolet, 1540).

translation is usually embedded within broader discussions of rhetoric and poetics. Like Bruni, whom Dolet never names but had almost certainly read, the French humanist conceived of translation within the framework of rhetorical debates, and intended his treatise on translation to be one of nine parts of his ambitious (unfinished) *Orateur françoys*.[8]

Dolet describes five 'rules' which the ideal translator must follow: full comprehension of the source text; a perfect grasp of both languages; a refusal to be bound by word-for-word literal translation; a cautious avoidance of neologisms; and a respect for the harmony afforded by the 'observation des nombres oratoires' ['observation of the cadences of rhetoric'].[9] These precepts are calculated to produce a version which is at once faithful to the sense of the source text (the humanist's philological goal) and elegantly expressed in the target language (the rhetorical touchstone). The advice is general (only one concrete example is adduced), and far more open to debate and contradiction than Dolet's strident tone might suggest. In this, it should be contrasted with a little-known treatise by the English scholar Lawrence Humphrey, *Interpretatio linguarum* (1559), which provides the unique example of a Renaissance writer confident that a single, reductive method of translation can be described in detail. For Humphrey, as Norton has shown, each step of the translative process can be schematized into 'a Ramist-inspired *diagramma*',[10] which will provide a single 'solution' to the translator's task. Dolet, though, is not dealing in the *minutiae* of the translator's performance; his sights are set on the broader issue of validating a paraphrastic approach, which can subsume translation within the realm of imitation, freeing it from the constraints inherent in the 'literalist temper' of some other writers.[11]

Although Dolet does not explicitly name classical authorities, his rules echo key classical *loci* on the art of translation, and continue the debate initiated by the fifteenth-century Italian humanists,[12] in which remarks on translation by Cicero, Quintilian, and Horace are scrutinized, and Horace in particular made to lend weight alternately to both literalist and paraphrastic positions.[13] Horace's advice to the aspiring poet on the limits of slavish imitation ('nec verbo verbum curabis reddere fidus / interpres') ['if you do not seek to render word for word as a slavish translator'] (*Ars*

---

[8] G. P. Norton, 'Translation theory in Renaissance France: Etienne Dolet and the rhetorical tradition', *Renaissance and Reformation* 10 (1974), 1–13; and *The ideology and language of translation*, pp. 103–10, 203–17; and V. Worth, *Practising translation in Renaissance France: the example of Etienne Dolet* (Oxford: Clarendon Press, 1988), pp. 49–60.

[9] Dolet, *La maniere*, p. 13.

[10] Norton, *The ideology and language of translation*, p. 12.

[11] Norton, 'Translation theory', p. 33.

[12] See G. P. Norton, 'Humanist foundations of translation theory (1400–1450): a study in the dynamics of word', *Canadian review of comparative literature* 8, 2 (1981), 173–203.

[13] Norton analyses conflicting interpretations of these *loci* in *The ideology and language of translation*, pp. 57–110.

poetica 133) attracted conflicting glosses when lifted from its context and applied to translation. Cicero's *De optimo genere oratorum* is pressed into service by the paraphrastic camp since he claims to have translated the works of Aeschines and Demosthenes not 'as a translator, but as an orator' and instructs the orator 'it is not necessary to render word for word'[14] – this last injunction being closely paraphrased by Dolet's third precept. Located within a rhetorical construct, in accordance with classical tradition,[15] translation is envisaged by Dolet, as it had been by Bruni, as a work of crafted imitation, the vernacular version potentially capable of equalling its classical model. Given that Dolet had so ardently espoused the Ciceronian cause in the neo-Latin debate of the 1530s, his profession of faith in the power of *translatio* operating between languages, texts, and cultures is all the more striking.

Dolet's treatise was republished some ten times up until 1550–1; hereafter in France, theoretical remarks on translation come to occupy a new terrain. At the end of Part I of his *Deffence* Joachim du Bellay commends Dolet's projected *Orateur françoys*, but sweeps aside the needs of the aspiring orator, claiming that Dolet has already met these, so that he can now concentrate on the nascent poet.[16] Issues of translation are thus resited within the tradition of the *Ars poetica*. Both Dolet and Du Bellay share a vision of the French language as a vehicle of national glory, brought to its full potential in the working out of its relationship with its classical forebears; yet in the *Deffence* it is no longer a question of literalist versus paraphrastic approaches to translation, but rather of the identity of any imitative act of writing. Put at its simplest: should translation be accorded a place in the hallowed arena? Each of the three major poetic theorists of the mid-sixteenth century addresses the question. For Sebillet in 1548, the response was affirmative: 'translation is nothing other than imitation'.[17] Du Bellay was scarcely going to concede such an easy point to his rival, and the title of 1.5 of the *Deffence* throws down the gauntlet: 'That translations do not suffice to perfect the French language'. Translation is presented as an inferior form of imitation, incapable of bringing to the vernacular the prestige won by an original classical work. The practical value of translations is not contested, but they do not achieve that synthesis of imitation and original input which Du Bellay believed lay at the heart of great poetry. Writing in 1555, and free from the polemical rivalry of Sebillet and Du Bellay, Peletier du Mans steers a middle path,

[14] Cicero, *De optimo genere* v.14.
[15] Compare also Quintilian's remarks on the role of translation in the education of the orator, *Institutio oratoria* x.v.
[16] J. du Bellay, *La deffence et illustration de la langue françoyse* (Paris: A. l'Angelier, 1549), I.xii.
[17] T. Sebillet, *Art poétique françois* (Paris: G. Corrozet, 1548).

acknowledging that translation is a worthy form of imitation, yet hinting at the possibility that in practice human limitations and natural differences between languages (that is, the absence of complete synonymy) may stand in the way of the perfect version.[18] It is important to note the relative confidence Peletier now expresses in the powers of the vernacular, whereas in the preface to his own 1541 translation of Horace's *Ars poetica* he has asserted that the French language still required cultivation (not least through translation) to realize its potential. Perhaps it is indicative of the fact that translations and post-Pléiade vernacular poetry have both come to occupy recognized and respected terrains that by the time of Ronsard's *Abbregé de l'art poëtique* the question of the relationship between translation and other forms of imitation is not even raised, and in Vauquelin de la Fresnay's *Art poétique* the author moves quite easily from Horatian advice on imitation to his own positive estimation of recent French translations.[19]

These theoretical works distil the essential approaches to the transmission and translation of classical texts which are characteristic of Renaissance France. There exists alongside them a second, rich source: the prefaces of individual translations. Such texts must, of course, be treated with the reservation that they are always ultimately an apology for a single, completed performance of the translator. But in a period and nation which witnessed such a spectacular rise in the number of works translated and retranslated into the vernacular,[20] prefaces provide a series of fragmented moments of discourse. They are the more valuable in that so many of the translators of the Renaissance were also, at different times in their careers, men and women of letters, working within a literary context that embraced imitation as a major tool, and thus reflecting on the relationship between translation and other forms of writing.[21] Significantly, whereas many medieval versions of the classics remained anonymous, the majority of those published in Renaissance France blazon their translator's name.

---

[18] 'The truest form of Imitation is translation: the Translator binds himself not only to the Invention of someone else, but also to the Disposition: and even to the Elocution, as far as he can, and as far as the character of the target language allows.' J. Peletier du Mans, *L'Art poëtique* (Lyons: J. de Tournes et G. Gazeau, 1555; Paris: Belles Lettres, 1930; ed. A. Boulanger), p. 105.

[19] *Art poétique*, 1.949–98, in *Les diverses poésies du sieur de la Fresnaie, Vauquelin* (Caen: C. Macé, 1605).

[20] There is to date no exhaustive bibliography of sixteenth-century translations, but the surviving copies held in Paris libraries give some indication of the range and extent. See P. Chavy, *Traducteurs d'autrefois. Moyen Age et Renaissance. Dictionnaire des traducteurs et de la littérature traduite en ancien et moyen français (842–1600)*, 2 vols. (Paris and Geneva: Champion-Slatkine, 1988).

[21] For example, Clément Marot's version of Book I of Ovid's *Metamorphoses*; Du Bellay's renderings of parts of the *Aeneid*; Montaigne's filial labour of gallicizing Ramon Sibiuda's torpid *Theologia naturalis*.

Certain focal points of the theoretical expositions of Dolet, Sebillet, Du Bellay, and Peletier du Mans are echoed and amplified in many individual prefaces: in particular the balance between literalist and paraphrastic tendencies, the role of the translator as both interpreter and imitator, and the anxiety over the capacity of the vernacular to equal the riches of Latin or Greek. Like their medieval predecessors, Renaissance translators frequently affirm the moral utility of their text, but by the second half of the sixteenth century they may soften their stance in accordance with Horace's dictum 'omne tulit punctum, qui miscuit utile dulci' ['He has won every vote who has blended profit and pleasure'].[22] Typically, Amyot's preface to Plutarch's *Lives* asserts that the reading of history is 'that which best combines worthy pleasure [*honeste plaisir*] and profit [*utilité*]'.[23] Humanists are, equally, aware of the cultural treasures they are uncovering through their work of vulgarization,[24] and from the 1530s many prefaces use precisely the metaphor of recovering buried treasure to portray a consciousness of contributing to a public and collective literary heritage.[25] Yet the *translatio studiorum* is increasingly conceived as a heavy, potentially thankless task, a *topos* summed up by the formula 'travail sans gloire'.[26] Thus translators use their prefaces to defend the whole act of translation, and, by implication, their status as writers bound to close imitation. We could cite as an extreme example Du Bellay's double-edged claim in the preface to his version of part of the *Aeneid:* 'I have turned to retracing the steps of the classical writers, an exercise requiring tedious toil [*ennuyeux labeur*] rather than an inspired mind [*allegresse d'esprit*]'.[27] 'Labeur' may not betoken the inspiration of original compositions, but the term demands that the reader respect the translator's commitment and toils.

Implicit in 'labeur' is the translator's sound scholarship – or what Dolet, and before him Bruni, understood as the complete mastery of source and target languages. Herein lies the most crucial difference between medieval and Renaissance theories/practices of translation. Influenced by the philological impulse of the earlier humanists, sixteenth-century translators are almost universally concerned to demonstrate the fidelity and accuracy of their versions. The prose *remaniement* of Virgil, close to a romance, which appeared anonymously in 1483 was challenged in 1509 by the

---

[22] Horace, *Ars poetica* 343.

[23] *Les vies des hommes illustres grecs et romains, comparees l'une avec l'autre par Plutarque de Cherone* (Paris: Michel de Vascosan, 1559).

[24] The glosses/appendices to some translations resemble an encyclopaedia of classical culture. For example the translations of Cicero's *De amicitia* (1537) and *De legibus* and *Somnium Scipionis* (1541) by Jean Colin.

[25] See L. Guillerm, *Sujet de l'écriture et traduction autour de 1540* (Paris: Atelier National Reproduction des Thèses, 1988), p. 458.

[26] *Ibid.*, p. 371.   [27] *Deux livres de l'Eneide de Vergile* (Paris: F. Morel, 1561), p. 2.

posthumous publication of Octavien de Saint-Gelais's verse translation, composed with the intention 'to translate this book from its lofty, distinguished Latin word-for-word and as closely as possible'.[28] Similarly, the *Bible des poetes* (a popular prose translation of the *Metamorphoses*, accompanied by extensive moral and allegorical commentary), which had been inherited from the fifteenth century, was not republished with its allegorizations after 1531; in contrast, close verse translations of part or the whole of the *Metamorphoses* were published between 1532 and 1557 by Clément Marot, Barthélemy Aneau, and François Habert.[29] Were such translators therefore partisans of the 'literalist temper'? Not necessarily. Most translators concur on a fairly rigorous attention to the source text in its entirety and in all its detail: this is the grammatical definition of a philological or humanist approach, derived from fifteenth-century Italy. By 'word-for-word', Octavien simply meant that he had (usually) tried to give an account of every word of Virgil's text in his vernacular rendering. But it did *not* automatically follow that this would be achieved by word-for-word syntactic and lexical equivalence. Even in pedagogic manuals, where tabular presentation of Latin and French forms encourages the illusion of complete bilingual equivalence, authors must admit discrepancies in the comparative grammars of Latin and French.[30] In the same way, the appearance of some translations in a bilingual format *may* indicate a comparatively literal rendering,[31] but the unequal proportions of the Latin and the French cannot fail to strike the eye. True literalists, that is to say those seeking as close an approximation as possible to a prelapsarian linguistic convergence, are rare among theorists, rarer still as practitioners of the art. A striking exception is Aneau, who explains in the preface to his 1556 version of Book III of the *Metamorphoses*: 'Thus I have translated . . . these present substantives by French nouns as exactly and as closely as I have been able to, using interpretation, composition, equipollence and usurpation'.[32] Yet implicit is the recognition that strategies must be sought to bridge the undesirable gaps between the two linguistic systems. A similar point emerges in his preface to an earlier translation of Cicero, where he singles out the inferior (artificial) word-order of Latin as an element for the translator to reconstruct according to the (natural) criteria of French.[33]

---

[28] *Les Eneydes de Virgille* (Paris: A. Vérard, 1509), fol. Aii*ᵛ*.

[29] See A. Moss, *Ovid in Renaissance France* (London: The Warburg Institute, 1982), and G. Amielle, *Les traductions françaises des Métamorphoses d'Ovide* (Paris: Jean Touzot, 1989).

[30] See, for example, Robert Estienne *La manière de tourner en langue françoise les verbes actifz, passifz, gerundifz, supins et participes* (Paris: R. Estienne, 1532).

[31] For example, Louis des Masures's translation of the *Aeneid*, *L'Eneide de Virgile* (Lyons: Jan de Tournes, 1560).

[32] Preface to *Trois premiers livres de la Metamorphose* (Lyons: M. Bonhomme, 1556).

[33] Prefatory letter to Mellin de Saint-Gelais in *Oraison ou epistre de M. Tulle Ciceron a Octave* (Lyons: P. de Tours, 1542).

Outside school manuals, it is the paraphrastic position which gains strength in France from the 1530s, a movement surely allied to the surge of interest in classical rhetoric.[34] If strict equivalence between two languages is a near-impossible goal, the translator can offer in its stead a vernacular version, philologically sound, which aims to capture the energy, plenitude, and balance of the original through his creative skill. Thus translation is necessarily invested with the tensions of all other imitative writing, not least the ghostly presence of the original text.[35] In translating a speech of Cicero, Antoine Macault captures the dilemma with a striking comparison: his French version is to the source text what the written Latin text was to Cicero's original delivery of it: both recastings resemble their model, while relying on different strategies.[36] Yet, as so often, a cause for anxiety may be turned to the speaker's advantage. By emphasizing the impossibility of a word-for-word rendering, the translator is simultaneously drawing the readers' attention to his achievement, as he relocates the power of the model in its new French form. Some prefaces specifically allude to the challenge of conveying the style of the original in the vernacular, albeit by alternative (paraphrastic) strategies. Notable examples are those where a translator publishes together translations from two or three classical writers precisely to emphasize the individual stylistic identity of the texts. A 1554 translation by Papon of speeches of Cicero and Demosthenes posits a rhetorical competition between the greatest Latin and Greek orators[37] – conducted in the vernacular! Blaise de Vigenère's preface to his translations of Cicero, Caesar, and Tacitus, published together in 1575, underscores the contrast between the three styles, and shifts the emphasis from transmission of substance to that of style. Such a faith in the power of the vernacular to convey the essence of a classical text shows the strides translation theory and practice had made in France over three-quarters of a century.

One of the recurring *formulae* of translators from the 1530s onwards is their hope to make their classical subject 'speak French'. It is one of the many ironic twists of evolving literary tastes that the seventeenth century in general wished their Cicero or Homer not only to speak French, but to adopt the idiom of a contemporary *honnête homme*. Philological scruples

[34] Marginal notes to translations from *c.* 1540 increasingly highlight points of rhetorical interest, for example the translation of Cicero's first *Verrine oration* by Claude Chaudière in 1551.
[35] In the preface to his translation of the first *Verrine oration* Chaudière describes his French text as the mere 'shade' ['ombre'] of Cicero.
[36] Prefatory letter to Cardinal de Lorraine, in Antoine Macault's version of Cicero's *Pro Marcello* (Paris: A. Augereau, 1534).
[37] The translation is entitled *Rapport des deux princes d'eloquence, grecque, et latine, Demosthene et Cicero, à la traduction d'aucunes de leurs Philippicques* (Lyons: M. Roy et L. Pesnot, 1554).

of exactitude pale before the need to please (rather than instruct) a readership often overtly hostile to anything smacking of pedantry. Close translations become occasional exceptions to the general rule, and the only
defence of literal translation is, fittingly, couched in Latin[38] – a language
no self-respecting *honnête homme*, let alone *honnête femme*, would be seen
reading. Madame Dacier's much acclaimed (prose) translation of Homer
at the end of the seventeenth century is the more outstanding because it
does aim to make the original Homer recognizable to the reader, and its
translator is a woman with the distinction of a sound education in both
Greek and Latin. But, as Zuber has shown, the ethos of the *belles infidèles*
was dominant.[39] No longer were classical texts a *summum* demanding
all the powers of the vernacular to equal them; rather, they invited the
translator to improve upon them in the contemporary vernacular idiom.
Typical is the attitude of Perrot d'Ablancourt, whose translation of Lucian
in 1664 carries this defence of departing from the words, and even the
meaning of the original: 'Besides, just as in a beautiful face there is always
something one would wish were not there, so in the best authors there
are passages one must touch up or lighten, especially when these things
are done only to please . . . Thus I do not always bind myself to the words
or thoughts of this author, but remaining true to his aim I arrange things
in our way and our fashion.' A few sentences later he concedes: 'This
is not strictly translation. But this is better than translation.' The position
he adopts is radically at odds with the philological impulse which had
governed Italian and then French humanist attitudes to translation, and
he provides a very different answer to a familiar issue: how to define the
precise relationship between translation and imitation, and the relative
values accorded to each.

[38] On the work of Huet, Bishop of Avranches, see F. Hennebert, *Histoire des traductions
françaises d'auteurs grecs et latins, pendant le XVIe et le XVIIe siècles* (1861; reprint
Amsterdam: B. R. Grüner, 1968), pp. 178–9.
[39] Roger Zuber, *Les 'belles infidèles' et la formation du goût classique* (Paris: Armand Colin,
1969).

12

Invention

Ullrich Langer

In the European Renaissance the term *invention* has many senses, several of which inform poetic theory and literary criticism: a 'discovery', a 'finding', the 'faculty of discovery' but also the 'thing found'; something close to 'imagination', 'wit', and positively or pejoratively a 'technique' or 'artifice'. Dominating the concept of poetic invention is the meaning of *inventio* in (mainly Latin) rhetorical theory. The noun *inventio* corresponds to the verb *invenire* [to find, to discover, to come upon].[1] In rhetorical treatises, at the place of *invenire* we often find *reperire* [to find, to discover] or *excogitare* [to think of, to find by reflection]. The most lucid and accessible account of the process of 'finding' that informs rhetorical composition is given by Cicero, in his *De partitione oratoria* (especially 1.3–2.5). The orator derives his 'power' [*vis*] from two sources: first, his *res* (the 'things' of the speech: subject-matter, including both ideas and facts); second, his *verba* (the words chosen to convey subject-matter). The finding of subject-matter precedes the finding of words, and although *inventio* is sometimes loosely applied to both kinds of finding, generally *inventio* concerns only subject-matter, not words, which are the province of *elocutio* [eloquence].[2] In composing a speech the orator has in mind an aim, an intention (*quaestio*: either unlimited, in the sense of a general enquiry, or specific, a *causa*). In order to achieve this aim, the orator must find subject-matter that will both convince his audience (literally, produce faith, confidence, or belief, *fides*, in those he wishes to persuade) and move the audience's emotions. The sorts of 'things' that the orator finds are arguments [*argumenta*] which can be found in 'places' [*loci*]. An argument is a 'probable thing found' designed to produce confidence or belief

---

[1] In Aristotle's *Rhetoric* the concept of invention is less clearly delineated. Aristotle defines rhetoric as 'the faculty of discovering the possible means of persuasion in reference to any subject whatever' (1.2.1). 'Discover' translates here *theorein*, 'to look at', 'to contemplate'. Juan Luis Vives discusses the lack of discussion of methods of finding arguments in Aristotle's *Rhetoric*, claiming that the philosopher conceived of invention as belonging more to the area of dialectic (in his *De causis corruptarum artium* [1531], 4.2). See text in the *Opera omnia*, 8 vols. (1782–90; facs. reprint London: Gregg Press, 1964). All translations unless indicated otherwise are those of the present author.

[2] The distinction is made sometimes between *inventio* and *ornatus*, as in Julius Caesar Scaliger, *Poetices libri septem* (1561), 1.9. See edition of A. Buck (Stuttgart: F. Frommann-Holzboog, 1964).

in the audience. In other treatises Cicero varies the terms somewhat: invention is defined as the discovery of true or verisimilar subject-matter [*rerum verarum aut veri similium*] which renders the *causa* probable or plausible.[3] The classification of subject-matter chosen in order to convince and move an audience by rendering a *causa* plausible is the province of the art of 'topics' (from the Greek *topos*, a place). *Topica*, the 'art of discovery' [*ars inveniendi*], is to be distinguished from *dialectica*, the 'science of judging [validity]' [*scientia iudicandi*]. Taking his lead from Aristotle, Cicero deals with topics in the *De inventione* and the *Topica*. Although Cicero distinguishes them in the *Topica* (1.6–8), Quintilian points out in the *Institutio oratoria* (3.3.1–10) that in rhetorical theory invention and judgement are sometimes examined together.

A typical sixteenth-century condensed definition of invention can be found in Thomas Wilson, *The arte of rhetorique* (1553): 'The findyng out of apte matter, called otherwise Invencion, is a searchyng out of thynges true, or thynges likely, the whiche maie reasonably sette furth a matter, and make it appere probable'.[4] Wilson refers to the 'places of Logique' as the source of true subject-matter. In poetic invention the language is often similar. Torquato Tasso places greater emphasis on the excellence of the work itself, formed by the poet: the poet sets out to 'choose subject-matter [*materia*] such that it is apt to receive in it the more excellent form which the skill [*l'artificio*] of the poet will seek to introduce into it'.[5]

Invention, that is, finding of subject-matter, is generally but not always thought of as more important than the choice of words to adorn it.[6] Following Horace's dictum, 'words not unwillingly follow when the subject is provided' (*Ars poetica* 311), and Cicero's evaluation of invention as 'the most important [*princeps*] of all the parts [of rhetoric]' (*De inventione* 1.7.9), Renaissance theorists insist on the importance of invention in the process of poetic composition. Giason Denores in his 1553 commentary on the *Ars poetica* likens invention to the 'soul' of poetry. For Giovambattista Giraldi Cintio, the poem can be compared to a body, of which the subject-matter [*il soggetto*] is the bones which hold the flesh together. The choice of subject-matter, the first thing a poet considers, derives from invention (*Discorso . . . intorno al comporre dei romanzi*,

---

[3] See *De inventione* 1.7.9 and the Ciceronian *Ad Herennium* 1.2.3.
[4] *The arte of rhetorique* (1553; reprint Gainesville: Scholars' Facsimiles & Reprints, 1962; ed. R. H. Bowers), p. 18.
[5] *Discorsi dell'arte poetica e del poema eroico* (1587; reprint Bari: Laterza & Figli, 1964; ed. L. Poma), 'Discorso primo', p. 3.
[6] For some theorists invention is 'a mass of gold that does not shine' without ornament or elocution: Mario Equicola, *Libro de natura de amore*, 1525, cited in Bernard Weinberg, *A history of literary criticism in the Italian Renaissance*, 2 vols. (Chicago: University of Chicago Press, 1961), vol. 1, p. 95. See also, in the same vein, Aulo Giano Parrasio, *In Q. Horatii Flacci Artem poeticam commentaria* (Naples: B. Martirano, 1531), and Lodovico Dolce, *Osservationi nella volgar lingua* (Venice: G. G. De Ferrari, 1550).

1554). More hyperbolically, Alessandro Lionardi praises invention as constituting the beginning and foundation of the poetic composition because it derives from the noblest causes: 'first from quickness of wit [*ingegno*], a gift of Nature; then from having read, heard, and seen many things, and finally . . . from art, which shows us its decorum and aptness'.[7] Pierre de Ronsard likens invention to the 'mother of all things'; disposition (and by implication the other parts of rhetorical composition) follow invention as the shadow follows the body (*Abbregé de l'Art poëtique françois*, 1565).[8] For Lodovico Castelvetro the poet's 'essence consists in invention and without invention he is not a poet'.[9] For Sir Philip Sidney, the 'vigour of [the poet's] own invention' is the source of his superiority over philosophers, grammarians, and the like (*An apology for poetry*, 1595). Although Sidney's connection between invention and the creative imagination goes beyond the rhetorical sense of *inventio*, we do find in his formula an echo of Cicero's *vis oratoris*.

Even if the discussion of the concept and term 'invention' is limited to a rhetorical and poetic context, the links to other areas in Renaissance poetics are obvious. For invention of poetic subject-matter inevitably involves the related questions of imitation and 'creative' imagination. Departing somewhat from the analogy with the orator, the poet finds subjects that are contained in previous poets' books or historical material, or in nature, aided by his own 'wit' [*ingenium*] or by his 'fantasy'. He may find true matter or make up subject-matter on his own. Tasso says that 'subject-matter [*la materia*], which can still conveniently be called "argument", either is made up [*si finge*], and then it appears that the poet had a part not only in the choice, but also in the invention, or is taken from history'.[10]

Horace advised Latin poets to choose subject-matter that had already been treated by the Greeks, rather than 'present unknown and unsaid things' (*Ars poetica* 128–30), although he concedes that Latin poets have also done well when they chose native subject-matter (285–91). The generally agreed upon exclusion of entirely new, that is, unknown, subjects seems connected to the need to render subject-matter 'appropriate' to the audience which would fail to be persuaded and moved by material completely foreign to its cultural memory.[11] In the Renaissance, as well,

---

[7] *Dialogi . . . della inventione poetica* (Venice: Plinio Pietrasanta, 1554), pp. 10–11. Compare Juan Luis Vives: invention is not a matter of skill [*ars*] but of prudence; it arises from wit [*ingenium*], memory, judgement, and experience [*usus rerum*] (*De conscribendis epistolis* [1534], 'De inventione').

[8] In Francis Goyet (ed.), *Traités de poétique et de rhétorique de la Renaissance* (Paris: Librairie générale française, 1990), p. 472.

[9] *Poetica d'Aristotele vulgarizzata e sposta* (1570), ed. W. Romani, 2 vols. (Bari: Laterza, 1978–9), Part 3, section 7 (vol. I, p. 289).

[10] *Dell'arte poetica*, p. 4.

[11] See, for example, Alessandro Piccolomini, *Annotationi nel libro della Poetica d'Aristotile* (Venice: G. Guarisco, 1575), p. 152; cited in Weinberg, *A history of literary criticism*, vol. I, p. 549.

much discussion centres on the dialectic between native and non-native subject-matter, between ancient Greek and Latin subjects and those deriving from a more recent medieval or a mythic-archaic non-Roman past. Marco Girolamo Vida typically exhorts aspiring poets to 'learn your inventions from others'.[12] He then prescribes the poetic itinerary of invention: take subjects from the Achaeans and the Argive kingdoms, bring them to Latium, then carry the booty 'home'. The Virgilian epic journey is a model for the retrieval of worthy poetic subjects; however, each genre has its own sources of subject-matter. A convenient division is given in Bernardino Daniello, *La poetica* (1536): comic poets choose 'familiar and domestic operations', tragic poets choose deaths of great kings and the ruin of vast empires, heroic [epic] poets the most excelling deeds of emperors and those of other men magnanimous and valorous in arms, lyric poets the praises of Gods and of men, amorous worries of youth, games, banquets, celebrations, others choose tears, laments, miseries, others camps, woods, herds, flocks, cabins.[13]

The Renaissance poet also uses native subjects: old annals can provide the poet with verisimilar (but not necessarily true) arguments.[14] Romances and medieval poetry in general can be useful in training the poet's invention and judgement.[15] Guillaume des Autelz, criticizing the French Pléiade school's excessive imitation of Italian and Ancient models, praises the 'invention' of the *Romance of the rose* (*Replique ... aux furieuses defences de Louis Meigret*, 1551). There is an insistence in some quarters on Christian subjects (see Lorenzo Gambara, *Tractatio de perfectae poëseos ratione* (1576)), Tommaso Campanella, *Poetica* (composed *c.* 1596), and Vauquelin de La Fresnaye, *L'art poétique françois* (1605), and as a corollary we witness the composition of Christian epic poetry, such as Tasso's *Gerusalemme liberata* (1580) and Jean Chapelain's *La pucelle, ou la France délivrée* (1656). But Greek and Latin literature tends to constitute the most prestigious source of subject-matter. The finding of subject-matter in other poets is always perilously close to stealing, as is emphasized by Lodovico Castelvetro, who inveighs against the thefts perpetrated by writers such as Petrarch, Ariosto, Boccaccio, and even Virgil (*Poetica d'Aristotele*, 3.7). Virgil was also attacked by Sperone Speroni, in his *Discorsi sopra Virgilio* (composed 1563–4), as not having invented anything, because he borrows plot and arrangement from Homer. The distinction between imitation and mere translation serves to distinguish legitimate invention from theft, but in poetic practice it is less easy

---

[12] *De arte poetica*, ed. and trans. R. G. Williams (New York: Columbia University Press, 1976), line 751 in the version of 1517, line 542 in the version of 1527.
[13] See Weinberg, *A history of literary criticism*, vol. II, p. 723.
[14] See Pierre de Ronsard, in the 1587 preface to *La Franciade*, in *Œuvres complètes*, ed. P. Laumonier, R. Lebègue, G. Demerson, revised edn (Paris: Nizet, 1983), vol. XVI, p. 339.
[15] See Thomas Sebillet, *Art poétique françoys* (1548), in Goyet (ed.), *Traités de poétique*, p. 59.

to do so, since many poets had no qualms about literally translating previous poetry and integrating translated fragments into their own works.

Another source of subject-matter is 'nature', that is, more or less the world in its physical and spiritual aspects. Here the meaning of 'invention' becomes more 'the faculty of mimetic representation', 'imagination', and is derived, perhaps, from Greek sources, such as Aristotle's *Poetics* (especially 1448b5–23), and negatively, from Plato's *Republic* (10.600e–601b). Especially in the seventeenth century, under the influence of the Aristotelian poetics of Julius Caesar Scaliger, what may have been discussed under the rhetorical category of invention is sometimes displaced by a discussion of poetic 'fiction' and its construction by imitation.[16] The poet finds by means of his *wit, ingegno, génie, esprit,* his *fantasia,* or his *imagination* matter and forms that resemble nature, even if they are not to be found in nature. The poet constructs a sort of alternative but verisimilar world. The production of pleasure rivals 'persuasion' as the chief aim of invention. Even among the supposedly rationalistic critics of the seventeenth century, the insistence on reason and common sense does not detract from the seduction of the pleasurable, through deft 'invention': 'The secret is first of all to please and to touch: Invent *ressorts* [forces, means] that may bind me', says Nicolas Boileau to the aspiring poet in his *Art poétique* (1674).[17] The most hyperbolic description of invention as a pseudo-creative imagination before the seventeenth century is to be found in Sidney's *An apology for poetry*: 'Only the poet . . . lifted up with the vigor of his own invention, doth grow in effect another nature, in making things either better than nature bringeth forth, or quite anew, forms such as never were in nature, as the *Heroes, Demigods, Cyclops, Chimeras, Furies,* and such like; so as he goeth hand in hand with nature, not enclosed within the narrow warrant of her gifts, but freely ranging only within the zodiac of his own wit'.[18] Poetic invention allows, for Sidney, a mimetic perfecting of the real, a homage to divine creation. Similar tones can be found in Scaliger's *Poetices libri septem* (1561), when he discusses the difference between the historian and the poet (1.1), in George Puttenham's *Arte of English poesie* (1589, 1.1), and among late sixteenth-century Italian theorists, such as Lionardo Salviati, in his commentary on Aristotle's *Poetics* (composed 1576–86). A more tempered link between

---

[16] See, for example, Gerardus Joannes Vossius, *Poeticarum institutionum libri tres* (Amsterdam: L. Elzevir, 1647), 1.2, and his *De artis poeticae natura ac constitutione* (Amsterdam: L. Elzevir, 1647). We find a conventional discussion of *inventio,* however, in Vossius's *Commentariorum rhetoricorum sive oratoriarum institutionum* (Leiden: J. Maire, 1630), 1.2.

[17] In Boileau's *Œuvres complètes,* ed. A. Adam and F. Escal (Paris: Gallimard, 1966), p. 169, 3.25–6.

[18] *An apology for poetry,* ed. F. G. Robinson (Indianapolis, New York: Bobbs-Merrill, 1970), p. 14.

invention and imagination informs the poetics of his French predecessors. Thomas Sebillet emphasizes that 'the first point of invention is taken from the subtlety and perspicaciousness [*subtilité et sagacité*] of his wit [*esprit*]'.[19] According to the more expansive Ronsard, 'invention is nothing other than the good natural faculty of an imagination conceiving the ideas and forms of all things that can be imagined, celestial as well as terrestrial, animate or inanimate, in order to represent, describe, and imitate them' (*Abbregé de l'Art poëtique françois*).[20] Legitimate objects of invention are things that are, that can be, or that the Ancients considered to be true. Ronsard is more cautious than Sidney; he condemns 'fantastical and melancholy' invention (elsewhere he names Ariosto as one such inventor) as sick and monstrous. The French poet follows in this acerbic criticism a gentler Horace (*Ars poetica* 1–11), and humanist commentators on Horace, beginning with Cristoforo Landino (in his edition of Horace's *Opera*, 1482). The general consensus seems to be that nothing absolutely new can be invented, that is, 'conceived' or 'imagined', as 'all that is said has been said before' (a phrase from Terence oft cited).[21] However, while this is true of poetic subject-matter and of the distinct elements of a poem, this is not true of the whole of the composition.[22] Tasso claims that a poem is 'new' in which the treatment of the conflicts, the solutions, the episodes, is new, and the same cannot be said of a poem in which characters and argument are 'feigned', that is, made up by the poet, and the conflicts and their solutions are not new.[23] The degree of verisimilitude or truth of a poetic 'invention' continues to be a matter of debate throughout the sixteenth century, involving the distinction between the historian and the poet, and the responsibility of the modern poet to convey Christian truth.

In the seventeenth century we observe in some quarters an increased emphasis on the faculty of the *ingenium*, as the capacity to manipulate language in such a way that novel relationships are created between things of the world. This emphasis displaces the focus of invention from the finding of things, or subject-matter, to the finding of words, especially metaphors. Both Baltasar Gracián (*Agudeza y arte de ingenio*, 1642) and

[19] In Goyet (ed.), *Traités de poétique*, p. 58.

[20] In Goyet (ed.), *Traités de poétique*, p. 472. Ronsard's definition is well known to his successors: Pierre de Deimier imitates it in his *Académie de l'art poétique* (1610), as does Martin Opitz in the first major German vernacular poetics, his *Buch von der deutschen Poeterei* (1624).

[21] The strictures of rhetorical invention are left behind in some discussions of *fictio* (and its vernacular equivalents). See for example Giovanni Pietro Capriano: 'true poets must feign [*fingere*] their poetry out of nothing [*di nulla*]' (*Della vera poetica*, 1555, cited by Weinberg, *A history of literary criticism*, vol. II, p. 733).

[22] Lodovico Castelvetro, *Poetica d'Aristotele vulgarizzata e sposta*, 3.7.

[23] *Dell'arte poetica*, p. 5.

Emanuele Tesauro (*Il cannocchiale aristotelico*, 1670) are representatives of this shift.

Connected to both the mimetic and the rhetorical views of poetic invention, and partaking of the debates on newness and imitation, is an emphasis in Renaissance poetics on the invention (forming) of new words. Although in rhetorical theory this type of invention tends to be absorbed by the concept of eloquence, in the Renaissance the forming of new words took on an independent value, as an 'enrichment' of the vernacular. Both Horace (*Ars poetica* 48–53) and Cicero (*De finibus* 3.1.3) had allowed the use of new words to designate new things. The issue of the invention of words is relevant to the quarrels involving the appropriateness of strict imitation of Ciceronian Latin style in the early sixteenth century, but is discussed especially in defences of the vernacular. In Castiglione's *Libro del cortegiano* (1528) the 'forming' of new words, if they are derived from Latin, is encouraged (1.34).[24] Joachim du Bellay includes in his programme for the enrichment of the French language a chapter on the invention of words ['D'inventer des motz, & quelques autres choses que doit observer le poëte Francoys'].[25] These new words, however, should be formed by 'analogy' and by 'judgement of the ear'. Technical terms, vernacular equivalents of ancient proper nouns, and archaic vernacular words are among the possible choices. Rhetorical composition is here the model for lexical invention, which has become the vernacular poet's responsibility, and which participates in the nationalistic or generally political programme associated especially with epic poetry in the Renaissance.

The invention of subject-matter is, however, the foundation of the political ambitions of epic poetry. Virgil's *Aeneid* is a model for Renaissance poets, in part because his coming after Homer assured for imitation a vital role in his epic composition, in part because he produced an epic that flattered his patron Augustus with the notion of a Trojan lineage. Virgil's invention of the argument of the *Aeneid* is given as an example by Jacques Peletier du Mans, in his *Art poëtique* (1555). In his general definition, Peletier fully realizes the rhetorical-persuasive element already contained in Ciceronian invention: 'Invention is a strategy ['dessein'] deriving from rational imagination ['l'imagination de l'entendement'], in order to arrive at our goal'.[26] Virgil's epic was the product of such a strategy: 'Therefore

---

[24] The formation of words as an enrichment of the vernacular is a commonplace. See, for example, Juan de Valdés, *Diálogo de la lengua* (composed 1535; Madrid: Castalia, 1969; ed. J. M. Lope Blanch). On the inventions of words in poetic language, see López Pinciano, *Philosophía antigua poética* (Madrid: no pub., 1596), Epístola 6, and Vauquelin de la Fresnaye, *L'art poétique françois* (1605; Paris: Garnier, 1885; ed. G. Pellissier), 1.315–412.

[25] *La deffence et illustration de la langue françoyse* (1549), ed. H. Chamard (Paris: Didier, 1948), ch. 6.

[26] In Goyet (ed.), *Traités de poétique*, pp. 251–2.

Virgil undertook his *Aeneid*, desiring to render illustrious things Roman, and especially in order to celebrate the actions of Augustus. In order to arrive at this, he thought it necessary to make of Aeneas, founder of Roman royalty, a wise and war-like prince: that is his general and principal project of invention'.[27] Ronsard, in his own epic, followed the model indicated by Virgil and by his contemporary Peletier. He chose as subject-matter the (by then already doubtful) legend of the French kings' Trojan ancestry. This choice was guided by his *causa*, the pleasing of the king, Charles IX: 'Having an extreme desire to honour the French royal house, and especially Charles IX, my Prince, not only worthy of being praised by myself, but by the best writers in the world, because of his heroic and divine virtues, and whose hope promises no less to the French than the fortunate victories of his ancestor Charlemagne, as all those know who have the honour of personal knowledge of him, and at the same time desiring to render my own renown immortal: based on the common story, and on the old belief recorded in the Chronicles of France, I have not been able to find a better subject than this.'[28] In practical terms the invention of subject-matter is guided by the persuasion (a cynic would say, effective flattery) of the patron, and includes a glorification of the poet himself.

The fortunes of literary invention are determined in the Renaissance by at least two other factors. First, the treatment of invention as a part of dialectic, not of rhetoric, begins to influence vernacular rhetoric. Rudolph Agricola had already assigned invention to dialectic, in his *De inventione dialectica libri tres* (composed 1479, published 1523, 2.25). In Peter Ramus's vernacular *Dialectique* (1555), invention and disposition are incorporated into dialectic or logic, leaving rhetoric with elocution and delivery. Antoine Fouquelin's *Rhétorique françoise* (1555), a close imitation of Omer Talon's Latin *Rhetorica* (1548), reflects this impoverishment. Increasingly poetic invention will be severed from its roots, sometimes associated in the seventeenth century with the production of poetic tricks, conceits, and 'marvels', and finally transformed into something entirely unrelated, poetic 'creativity'. Concurrently, rhetoric will become mainly the art of embellishment, of tropes and figures, and lose the epistemological-mnemonic import that invention had always guaranteed to the orator and the poet.

Second, the term 'invention' has a strong parallel sense of empirical 'discovery', such as the discovery of printing, and even of poetry itself. Encyclopaedic catalogues of 'inventors' and inventions were printed, such as Polydore Vergil's *De rerum inventoribus* (complete edition 1521). Throughout the sixteenth and seventeenth centuries there was discussion

---

[27] *Ibid.*, p. 252.
[28] In Ronsard's 1572 preface to the *Franciade*, *Œuvres complètes*, vol. XVI, pp. 8–9.

of what 'invention' in this sense means, from Juan Luis Vives who speculates on the modalities of 'first invention' of the arts [*prima rerum inventio*] in his *De causis corruptarum artium* (1531, 1.1), to Sforza Pallavicino who analyses the joy of invention (*Del bene libri quattro*, 1644, 3.43). The hitherto relatively conservative rhetorical concept of invention became disconnected from the mediated communicative situation, and more attached to the will of the individual, who may be able to augment, by his 'own inventions', the learning of the Ancients.

13

Humanist education

Ann Moss

The ideals for education elaborated in rather piecemeal fashion in Italy during the course of the fifteenth century were promoted with astonishing efficiency throughout northern Europe in the early years of the sixteenth century, changing established habits of thought and transforming the language of nearly every discipline. Throughout the sixteenth century Latin literature (and, to a lesser extent, Greek literature) provided cultural, moral, and intellectual norms and, perhaps most important of all, a linguistic model, outside of which it became problematic, or at least eccentric, to operate. But it was no smooth takeover, nor yet complete. The humanists' programme was based on a dichotomy, insisting as it did that all education had to be transmitted in a foreign language. Moreover, it depended not only on the acquisition of Latin (that had always been true), but of a Latin, the 'good' classical Latin of the humanists, which had been the product of a historically distinct period in antiquity and could only be re-created by rigorous application of rules and the imitation of 'correct' authors. As the authors deemed correct were pagan authors, the bilingual situation of the educated élite was doubled by a bicultural situation in which Christian and pagan elements existed in an often uneasy symbiosis.

The century abounds in programmes for education, real or imagined, culminating in the rigorous organization of the Jesuits. But whether one looks at the rules of the Academy at Geneva (1559), the Lutheran programme of David Chytraeus (1564), the syllabus in force at the municipal school at Bordeaux (first published in 1583, well after its foundation), or the various states of the Jesuit *Ratio studiorum*, one is less struck by local or even confessional differences than by the overall homogeneity. Basic education throughout Europe was conducted through literary texts, and literature consisted primarily of the works of Cicero and a certain number of privileged Latin poets (Terence, Virgil, Ovid, Horace, Seneca, Martial) and some of the historians. Lists do differ, other poets come and go, but the solid core remains. What the schools have done by the end of the century is in effect to formulate the notion and the content of a literary canon.

The situation for Greek texts is similar, but less clear-cut, and all the indications are that as far as basic school education went, the study of Greek literature was often no more than a pious hope. What is totally missing from the canon (at least outside Italy) is vernacular literature. Not only does it remain marginal to every schoolboy's understanding of what literature is and how to read it, but the notion of a vernacular literary canon, and even the critical recognition of vernacular authors, seem to become feasible only when what is produced begins to approximate in style and genres to ancient models. Although the vernaculars of sixteenth-century Europe become so much more assertive in all sorts of fields, their inherently subversive threat to the cultural uniformity promoted by the humanists is countered by the cohesive force of a language shared by the educated élite. This was not just Latin, which was vulnerable, but the much more tenacious language of a common literary culture which transcended both national frontiers and confessional divides. The contents of the literary canon were crucial here, for, in a slightly paradoxical way, the fact that this canon was pagan protected the literary culture formed in Western Europe's schools against the destabilizing effects of religious schism. Editions, commentaries, and reference books moved freely, and the printing-press, which had originally enabled the rapid process of change in the school syllabus at the beginning of the century, was also to prove a means of standardizing the curriculum across Europe by encouraging the reproduction and marketing of standard texts and manuals of instruction. It is to such texts and manuals that one must look to gain a sense of how the literary canon was read and how such reading in turn fulfilled the claims of schools to teach their pupils good learning, good Latin, and good morals through the medium of good letters.

'In principle, knowledge as a whole seems to be of two kinds: of things and of words.' This is how Erasmus begins his *De ratione studii* (1512), and he goes on to demonstrate how both kinds of knowledge are to be derived from reading designated texts. But language is prior, 'grammar claims primacy of place', and indeed it is the grounding of all knowledge on the acquired ability to make careful critical distinctions about the use of words that characterizes humanist scholarship and humanist thinking in all spheres of its application. It was a mentality formed from the earliest years of schooling, going right back to the grammar class. The commentaries framing printed literary texts in editions contemporary with Erasmus are, among other things, etymological and analogical dictionaries. Any word of the text which is likely to be unfamiliar or is being used abnormally is provided with a Latin synonym and paraphrase, an indication of its literal and figurative uses, and an etymology where ancient sources provide one. And with increasing efficiency annotators throughout the sixteenth century search out quotations from the rest of an author's work and from other writers in order to illustrate cognate uses of a word, comparable figures of speech, and subtle differentiations in concept and expression. In sixteenth-century exegesis, the primary meaning of a text is derived by reintegrating the words from which it is composed into a reconstructed linguistic context. This is complicated by a certain ambivalence inherent in the attitude of many humanist scholars towards the context they so lovingly and painstakingly re-create. On the one hand, it is conceived as an ideal form of language, the correct Latinity they set themselves to inculcate into their pupils as a norm of verbal expression immune to the vicissitudes of time and place. But at the same time, they are intent on recovering and understanding the signifying habits of a particular historical period. In this they are inspired both by antiquarian zeal and by a desire to reactivate the authentic, and therefore historically conditioned voices of their authors. Reading then becomes an exercise in recognizing differences which enable one to respond with an appropriate historical sense to the vocabulary of the written products of a past and distant culture.

A knowledge of the 'things' of that culture was as essential as a knowledge of its language, and by 'things' were meant the contents of all branches of intellectual enquiry. For most pedagogues in the sixteenth century it was axiomatic that literature embraced the whole encyclopaedia of learning, some going as far as to claim that the elements of specialized disciplines such as philosophy and natural science were best absorbed through literature. The promoters of specialist subjects (and of the technical language that goes with them) were quick to defend their territory. The most spectacular episodes in this battle of the books were enacted on the common ground between literature and theology, where Erasmus and others followed Lorenzo Valla in applying to Scripture criteria of meaning evolved to elucidate pagan literary texts. The philologians threatened to undermine a doctrinal and institutional edifice based on readings of the Bible which they claimed were erroneous, using standards of proof derived from the historical and contextual method by now familiar to all lettered people from their elementary classes in Latin grammar. Powerful forces were mustered and religious loyalties invoked in order to resist or contain the incursions literary criticism had made into the precincts of theology. But perhaps the most decisive factor in the slow erosion of the overall grand design inherited from fifteenth-century humanism was the multiplication of printed works of reference which began to turn the tide irrevocably in the mid-years of the sixteenth century. Specialist reference books were published on aspects of the material culture of the ancient world, on mythology, on animals, and plants. While lip-service was still paid to the learning to be derived from literature and from poetry in particular, it had in fact become of secondary importance.

In the meantime the humanists' ambition to appropriate all spheres of intellectual enquiry had had interesting consequences. In late fifteenth-century Italy the marginal commentaries which massed information round literary texts began to take on a life of their own, as amorphous, uncoordinated volumes of *miscellanea*, notes on variant textual readings, odd gems of information quarried from recondite sources, parallel phrases from a plethora of authors, explanations of historical references, philosophical theories, and mythological allusions. These are the working-notebooks of the literary critics who commented on texts and expounded them in the classroom. Printing can catch such 'work in progress' and give it currency before it is refined into shape, coherence, and logical rigour. Sixteenth-century writers and readers revelled in these free-range ramblings, as can be seen from the proliferating volumes of *miscellanea, lectiones*, and *adversaria*. They are sometimes given a slightly more settled state when they are combined with another product generated by the humanist classroom, the colloquy, which in its embryonic form consists of model conversations to help boys in the grammar class to speak Latin, but in more sophisticated guise merges with the mature, urbane, learned, and essentially literary conversation of the Renaissance *convivium* or symposium. Textual criticism is to be found at its most trenchant in *miscellanea* and *adversaria*, and the literary theory of the Latin humanists as often as not in the conversation of guests at imaginary banquets. Such works retain traces of their marginal origins, looking in from the outside, talking round their centre, always open to expansion, amplifying at will, and commenting *ad rem*, but never bound to conclusions.

The humanists compensated in various ways for the gradual erosion of the authority on matters of fact previously accorded to fictive writing, and more especially to poetry. One response was to compete with the growing number of specialist reference works by stressing the specialism proper to literary scholarship: textual criticism. *Emendatio*, or text-correction, had been on the agenda of the grammarian since antiquity and had been part of the technical know-how of the humanist scholar and, more recently, of editorial advisers in the print-shops. But, despite the achievements of a Valla or a Politian, it is to the second half of the sixteenth century that we must look for the firm beginnings of a discipline of textual criticism, marked by the injection of some principles of rigour into the assessment of evidence and conjecture.

At a less technical level, commentaries from the last part of the sixteenth century on the canonical texts tend to dwell on aspects of literature which make it different from other branches of learning. The editions which Jakob Spanmüller (Iacobus Pontanus) produced for the Jesuit schools of Europe, and whose influence can be traced in Protestant schoolrooms too, illustrated the language of Latin poets with numerous parallels from other writers, Latin and Greek. The practice of accumulating quotations in this way seems to grow as the scientific authority invested in them declines. The ostensible aim is still, as it was in earlier commentaries, to refine the reader's own Latin, but the effect is also to introduce him into a communion of literary reference, to familiarize him with a cultural code which does not purvey information so much as reinforce a style of linguistic expression and allusion in which self-referring literariness is the predominant feature. As the focus of critical comment shifts towards verbal virtuosity, annotations draw ever more frequently on the resources of the science of speaking and writing, that is to say on rhetoric. Right from the beginning of the century, commentators had made it their business to excavate the rhetorical substructure of a text and name its parts. This type of analysis continued unabated, often in a short-hand form in the margins of school-texts, pointing up examples to be used to illustrate the principles of rhetorical theory taught in the classroom.

If grammar teaches the art of speaking (and writing) correctly, rhetoric teaches the art of speaking (and writing) with intelligence and polish, in such a way as to inspire conviction in the listener (or reader) by reasonable argument, to excite in him the desired emotional response, and to please his critical faculties with the felicities of a well-contrived style. Such aims are commonplace in sixteenth-century handbooks of rhetoric, and the recommended ways to achieve them remain virtually the same throughout the period and throughout the schools of Western Europe. The precepts contained in sixteenth-century school-manuals were ultimately derived from the rhetorical classics of antiquity, the works of Cicero, Quintilian, and the *Rhetorica ad Herennium*. From these they inherited the threefold division of rhetoric into forensic, deliberative, and demonstrative oratory. From their contemporary historical situation (but sanctioned by the approbation of authors like Seneca and Tacitus) some manuals acquired a bias towards imaginary occasions for persuasion and dissuasion and towards a descriptive, epideictic (or demonstrative) rhetoric soliciting praise or blame. Where such bias is present, the literary connotations of rhetoric are paramount. From classical models, too, the sixteenth-century manuals inherited the five essential elements in the composition and delivery of a speech: invention, disposition, elocution, memory, and pronunciation (including gesture), although the relative emphasis placed on these elements varied considerably and the last two were often omitted altogether.

Invention concerns the generation of discourse, and disposition the skill to order it appositely. In order to 'find' material appropriate to any theme, the learner was directed towards the 'places' of invention. A piece in praise of anything would run through the 'places' of epideictic rhetoric, which would supply arguments and amplifications generated from the subject's origin, its causes, its natural virtues, its acquired virtues, its past successes, present use and future purpose, its attendant circumstances, and so on. Schoolboys were expected to learn the places required for any type of subject and to recognize how they functioned and how they were ordered in literary passages set for study. They were similarly trained to recognize and reproduce the linguistic features catalogued under 'elocution', that is to say those ornamented and amplified turns of expression, more especially figures of thought and speech, which separate the language of poetry and oratory from the language of everyday use. The importance attached to figurative expression can be gauged not only by the space allotted to it in manuals of rhetoric, but from the plethora of printed handbooks devoted solely to schemes and tropes, illustrated with examples from prose and verse texts by approved Latin (more rarely Greek) authors. The formulation and manipulation of figures of rhetoric had been brought to a sophisticated perfection in classical languages, but they were just as feasible in the vernaculars, a point underlined in most handbooks of the later years of the century and not lost on the vernacular writers, none of whom was likely to have escaped the influence of the humanist classroom. The effect of their teachers' enthusiasm for displays of wit and erudition in stylish and ingenious verbal ornamentation was transferred directly from their practice-pieces in Latin to the vernacular works of their adulthood, and with it the concept of a literary language totally divorced from the naked prose and plain patterns of ordinary speech.

The rhetorical manuals had a dual purpose: to equip the student to recognize the fundamental principles involved in the intelligent and persuasive expression of ideas in words, and to give him the wherewithal to produce spoken and written compositions of his own. That new works were best invented by imitating the old was a principle scarcely ever seriously disputed by the overridingly influential schoolroom orthodoxy of the sixteenth century. What is discussed in numerous treatises is which authors are to be imitated and how. The wider issues raised by the question of which models to imitate are the stuff of the Ciceronian controversy, which provided the terms for a serious debate in which major humanist thinkers were engaged for a hundred years and more. The controversy got right to the crux of the humanist dilemma, setting the concept of language as an absolute and fixed norm of human communication against the concept of language as fluid, relative, and historically conditioned, setting pagan past against Christian present, ancient against modern, conservative limits against individual enterprise. However, echoes of the great debate reached the schoolrooms of Europe in a fairly attenuated form. The consensus of opinion there was that Cicero was far and away the best model for imitation, but not to the exclusion of others, particularly poets.

The problem of how to reproduce the best style of ancient models led to more divergent solutions, with direct bearing on the sort of critical awareness with which students were advised to approach their authors. The more thoroughgoing enthusiasts for Cicero tended to foster a particular intimacy with Cicero's vocabulary, the rhythms of his word-order and the way he arranged his material through the whole extent of a speech, essay, or letter. A more widespread training in composition was to set exercises in which the student was expected to show skill in working through the pertinent places of argument in order to generate compositions appropriate to different types of discourse. This approach to imitation is relatively free, though still bound to the vocabulary and phraseology employed by 'good authors'. It aims at variety rather than close pastiche. Material for varying set themes was provided by the student's commonplace-book, the notebook in which students were urged to list quotations from their reading under appropriate general headings. The commonplace-book suggests a method of reading as well as of writing, and it has implications for the critical attitudes readers brought to texts. With his commonplace-book in hand, the reader brought a series of pre-prepared headings: conceptual matrices into which he expected his reading-matter to fit. A further expectation was that all authors had the same material in common: they all contributed to the same book of commonplaces, which itself is the Book of Nature, in which nature is laid out as an intelligible text, whose language is the language of classical literature.

Schoolroom manuals of rhetoric, be they devoted to places, figures, commonplace-books, or all three, were aimed at the production of discourse. As far as prose composition was concerned, the three traditional genres of oratory (deliberative, forensic, epideictic) may have provided the ground-plan of most courses in rhetorical theory, but in practice the most likely forms in which pupils would exercise their skill in later life would be in delivering sermons and writing letters. At almost any school throughout the sixteenth century pupils took their first steps in prose composition by writing short letters on set themes. Letter-writing as taught by Erasmus and other earlier humanists was a protean form, ranging from the highly imaginative to the personal and familiar, a form whose virtues lay in clarity and brevity of expression, in a sensitive adjustment to the personality of the recipient, a 'low' style, but not uncultivated, one which reflected a versatile, well-furnished mind engaged in intelligent, urbane conversation. This is, of course, a highly sophisticated ideal, and one unlikely to be attained by the schoolboy, despite all the hints in his manuals. But rhetorical exercises were to be fertile in new mutations of old forms. Later in the century, Justus Lipsius presented his *Epistolarum selectarum centuria prima* (1586) as a psychological and moral portrait of himself: 'the style reveals the man'. Above all it reveals the man as critical reader, progressing, as he says in his *Institutio epistolarum* (1591), from the Ciceronian exercises of his boyhood, through Terence, Plautus, and the

Greek literature of his adolescence, to a style which is the taut, laconic, pungent, virile expression of the adult man, the style of Sallust, Seneca, and Tacitus.

Epistles were the earliest exercises for verse composition as well as for prose. Prose and poetry were perceived as virtually interchangeable. They were generated in the same way and were subject to the same procedures of analysis. However, verse composition was felt to have a particular contribution to make to a general training in style, and this called for certain discriminations. It sharpened the pupil's awareness of niceties of vocabulary (the differences between prose usage and poetic diction); it practised his ability to deploy figures of thought and speech (used more intensively in poetry); and it refined his sensitivity to sound combinations in Latin and Greek, and especially to the rhythms of Latin prose. Metrics belonged to the discipline of grammar, and instruction was to be had in the arid technicalities of treatises on versification. Judging by printed commentaries, the resources of metrical technique played a very subsidiary part in literary analysis. Similarly, the definition of poetic genres also belonged, if anywhere, to the elementary discipline of grammar, and we hardly ever find the concept of genre used as a critical tool in a running commentary on a poetic text. Genre would be dealt with in the teacher's introductory lecture or *praelectio* preceding his detailed exposition of what, more often than not, would be selected passages rather than whole books of poetry. School manuals on literary production tended to conform to a particular utilitarian pattern and that pattern was set by the traditional divisions of rhetoric. This did not really allow for more general discussions about the nature of literature, its relationship to truth, the place of inspiration and individual genius, or the social role of the imaginative writer, let alone the relation between sound and sense in poetry. Such issues were displaced into quite another theoretical genre, poetics, for which there certainly were ancient precedents and ancient models, but no obvious place in a school curriculum which still thought of the arts of language as grammar, rhetoric, and logic. It was the Jesuits, in the 1590s, who first began to publish school manuals on poetics, with detailed descriptions of the genres, in order to supply the needs of their classes in Humanities.

When it came to making evaluative judgements on the texts they analysed so exhaustively, the humanists used a vocabulary inherited from classical rhetoric. It slipped loosely between the aesthetic and the moral, and it is symptomatic of what was deeply problematic about their programme. Schools all advertised the training they offered in good Latin, good learning, and good Christian morals. Nevertheless, although the scope of good learning and the definition of good Latin are fairly evident in example and practice, the grounds for claims to good Christian morals are (and were) much less clearly perceptible. A naïve reading of many of

the works set for literary imitation is not likely to conclude that the correlation between good Latin and good morals is as obvious as so many
splendidly vague and viciously circular show-pieces of self-congratulatory
Renaissance rhetoric would have us believe. Although the more speculative and complex modes of medieval and Neoplatonist allegorical interpretation remained a lively force, they were not at the core of classroom
expositions of literary texts. As far as school reading was concerned, the
range of interpretative mechanisms most commonly brought into play was
very much controlled by the resources and demands of the rhetorical programme written into the curriculum. The shift to a rhetorical rather than
an allegorical strategy for moral reading can already be detected in Erasmus,
for whom the ethical content of pagan fable was a vital ingredient in
the nourishing blend of classical literature and Christian piety, the *pietas
litterata*, he never ceased to promote. According to Erasmus, in the *De
ratione studii*, the homosexual passion described in Virgil's second eclogue
is best read as an illustration of the truism that friendship can only exist
among similar people, and this commonplace may be divertingly amplified in the interests of plenitude of discourse (*copia*) with numerous
examples of fables illustrating good friendships between like-minded people, disastrous friendships between the ill-assorted. The subject-matter of
the eclogue is to be distributed under heads in the student's commonplace-
book, and the heads under which quotations were to be arranged in the
commonplace-book were, in the opinion of nearly all theorists, primarily
moral. Wherever the student wrote down quotations from Virgil's second
eclogue, we can be sure that they were mainly classified as moral matter,
not in the least bit neutral, but to be used as examples of moral behaviour
to be praised or, more likely in this case, to be blamed.

The underlying assumption that most of literature is to be classed as
epideictic rhetoric and, therefore, by definition, devoted to praise or censure, together with the mentality produced by the commonplace-book
and its morally based classification system, ensured that pupils trained to
read rhetorically would be programmed to read morally. The art of combining rhetoric and rectitude could be seen as integral to the range of
expertise which literary critics were beginning to claim as theirs alone,
and there was a sense in which this aspect of their expertise was useful
in the public domain. The establishment of the curricula of the northern
humanist schools in the last three-quarters of the century coincided with
the effects of the Reformation, which tended to consolidate institutes of
education and their syllabuses in much closer conformity with the interests of Church and State than had been the case in the more fluid period
of Italian humanism, before its spread into northern Europe. In Protestant
rhetorics, the Bible, often in the vernacular, is quoted at length to exemplify rhetorical precept and practice, in juxtaposition with classical texts.

'Correct' Bible-reading habits are formed in the young as they learn their lessons. Rhetoric can instil good religion as well as good morals. Catholics, similarly engaged in teaching good letters, good morals, and good religion, are rather more circuitous in their approach to the latter. Disinclined on religious grounds to use the Bible as a classroom manual, they exploit a copious rhetoric of examples, parallels, and comparisons, in which the pagan literature they teach is set side by side with Christian homily, Christian poetry, and Christian *exempla* of virtue and sanctity.

The rhetorical finesse learnt from a critical examination of literary texts could serve the dominant religious ideology. But more importantly, and more influentially, it could and did both educate and serve an élite governing class and its administrators. The training which a humanist education gave in judgement was exercised by sign-posting the heads of argument in any given passage and by allocating the matter of the passage to categories pre-established in a commonplace-book. On the one hand, it promised successful pupils an efficient technique for sorting their way through documents and through the mass of published material which the printing explosion had generated. On the other hand, the commonplace-book was a container in which the new was always absorbed and found a place; ideas were received and immediately matched to received ideas. Ideally, a humanist literary education offered an alliance of the efficient and the conservative eminently promotable to the political and financial managers of the school-system. Whatever its real merits in practical terms, it was undoubtedly attractive to the self-perpetuating class of gentlemen whom it nurtured and who in turn provided its pupils. It gave them a distinctive language and a range of cultural reference points, which, however dimly remembered in later life, were part of their formation and their bond as an élite. Moreover, the absence of any professional training in courses devoted primarily to good letters was in itself part of the equipment of a gentleman, the intelligent and versatile amateur, free from any trace of pedantry or jargon, who was to emerge in seventeenth-century France as the arbiter of European critical taste. He had in all probability been schooled by the Jesuits, who had adopted the humanists' curriculum, carefully trimming their texts and discouraging too much unprofitable enquiry.

14

Second rhetoric and
the *grands rhétoriqueurs*

Robert Griffin

Around the turn of the century literary historians bestowed the name 'Ecole des Grands Rhétoriqueurs' on an array of writers from the latter half of the fifteenth century through to the early reign of Francis I. Thereafter, they were viewed either as latecomers in a 'waning' Middle Ages or as precursors of more gifted 'schools' of Renaissance poets. As rewriting the past has progressed, a more robust reassessment has emerged for the aggregate works of humanists, artists, diplomats, mythologizing historians, and architects named Jean Meschinot (1422–91), Henri Baude (?1430–96), Jean Molinet (1435–1507), Destrées (?), Jean Robertet (?–?1502), Octavien de Saint-Gelais (1468–1502), Guillaume Cretin (?1472–1525), André de la Vigne (1470–1515), Pierre Gringore (1475–?1539), Jean Marot (?1463–1526), Jean Bouchet (1476–1557), Jean Parmentier (1494–1529), and Jean Lemaire de Belges (1473–1516) – with Petrarch, Eustache Deschamps, Christine de Pisan, and others on the margin.

Their improved rank in the evolution of Renaissance culture has stemmed from: discounting the polemic agenda of sixteenth-century *arts poétiques*; recognition of intertextual recollections as indices of artistic continuity; modern methodologies of decoding poetic language as a cultural artefact; and deeper conversance with the creative flair of this loose coterie which theatrically memorialized the liturgical festivals and official functions of the newly enriched bourgeoisie. They dramatized courtly gestures in the palaces of the powerful, ennobled the deeds of Burgundian dukes, the House of Austria, and embellished venturous policies of Louis XI and Charles VIII. No longer are these poets disparaged for the virtuosity of their rhyme *couronnée*, *rétrograde*, *léonine*, *équivoquée bilingue*, *double* or *triple*, *rauque*, *fratrisée*, *enchaînée*, *annexée*, and so on. While their muse neither flowed from nor led to a unified *art poétique*, criticism can now reconstruct cardinal points in the idiosyncratic art form of 'Second Rhetoric'. We are thus better placed to outline the medieval heritage of the so-called 'Grands Rhétoriqueurs' and to define their dynamic role both in shaping poetic form and in purveying ideals of form.

From the chronological extremes of Jacques Legrand's *L'Archiloge Sophie. Des rithmes et comment se doivent faire* (1405) until Gratien du Pont in 1539, treatises on versification were called variously *moderne rhétorique laie, arts de seconde rhétorique, rhétorique vulgaire et maternelle, rhétorique pour apprendre à rimer*, and *rhétorique métrifiée*.[1] Within this array, *vers* could denote a verse, a stanza, an entire section of a long poem, or merely paired end *rimes*, which in turn could indicate classifications of rhyme, such as internal rhyme or couplets; *stile* could refer to a particular *mode* of writing, to a class of versification, or to the poetic *form* generated by a rhyme scheme, as in Lemaire de Belges's *Couronne Margaritique*. Added complication comes from the sense of *poetrie*, an important adjunct to both prose and verse, which relied on biblical symbols and mythological figures to illustrate only a particular *colour* of rhetoric. Such fluid nomenclature invites the anachronism of judging a broad range of writers by aesthetic criteria of another age. A significant yet unheralded moment occurred in Clément Marot's *Complainte* 7 where *rethoriquer* is replaced by *poetiser* in the more modern sense, and where a perception of generational evolution emerges when the shade of his father visits his dreaming son and proceeds to loose cascades of 'Triste, transi, tout terny, tout tremblant' ['sorrowful, paralysed, completely dulled and shaking'] directly imitated from the early work of the older Guillaume Cretin.

A superior instance of embedding the eight parts of speech of Latin into French from the fourth-century authority, Aelius Donatus, is the poem 'Donet baillé à Loys' (1498). There Molinet addresses his wit to a presumed audience from the very real world, as a variation on the traditional assignment of classical rhetoric to teach, please, and move a hypothetical or real public; its poetic clauses comment on structures and precepts of all kinds for the transformation through rhyme of prosaic subjects.[2] The *rhétoriqueurs*, then, experimented with structural complications primarily as means of enhancing semantic and rhythmic possibilities of spoken language; separation of prose and verse is occasionally arguable and actually secondary to a primary concern for cultivating rhythmic cadences of speech which enhance structures of thought. According to Jacques Legrand, 'rhyme belongs in part to grammar and partly to rhetoric' as a means of stressing, directing, and thus defining linguistic relationships

---

[1] See Pierre Jodogne, 'Les "Rhétoriqueurs" et l'humanisme: problème d'histoire littéraire', in *Humanism in France*, ed. A. H. T. Levi (Manchester: Manchester University Press, 1970), p. 153; Eric Méchoulan, 'Les arts de rhétorique du XVᴱ siècle: la théorie, masque de la théorie?', in *Masques et déguisements dans la littérature médiévale*, ed. Marie-Louise Ollier (Paris: Vrin, 1988), p. 218; Paul Zumthor, *Le masque et la lumière* (Paris: Seuil, 1978), p. 206.

[2] Franco Simone, *Umanesimo, rinascimento, barocco in Francia* (Milan: Mursia, 1968), p. 190.

in a poem.[3] Hence, all components of a poetic line or an entire poem illuminate one another: 'euphony cannot be attained without diction, nor
diction without syllables, nor syllables without letters', as Molinet put it
in his *Art de rhétorique*.

At the height of the *rhétoriqueur* florescence, contemporary readers
summed up their art, as Rabelais did in lauding Jean Bouchet's eloquence
as a 'treasury of wisdom' for its *douceur et discipline* (1524). The identity
of eloquence with wisdom became a commonplace of the European
Renaissance from the time of Villon, as in Ficino's praise of grammar,
poetry, and rhetoric in the Golden Age for joining 'wisdom with eloquence, prudence with military art' (1492), and in Pico's 'lordship of concord'. The *discipline* in Rabelais's formulation means both erudition and
knowledge of the intrinsic constraints imposed by art forms.[4] Despite
appearances of rhyme divorced from reason, these forms are as inargu-
ably sanctioned as the social virtues preached at length by Meschinot in
the allegorical *Les lunettes des princes*.[5] In the brief compass of ballades,
they are as formally prescribed as the larger role of the *rhétoriqueurs* in
memorializing their social fabric by defining its place in history.

The sense of 'play' in their verbal alchemy is akin to the dance of
Wisdom before the mind's eye of God of Proverbs 8, who then creates the
world by circumscribing its forms. In the wake of Petrarch's *canzoniere*
and his Augustinian *Secretum*, Renaissance poetry continued obsessively
to probe the ambitious designs and fragmented meaning of post-Adamic
language, reconstructing the world by reordering creation, as intimated in
works like *Les lunettes des princes* or Cretin's Chant-Royal: 'L'altitonant
suprème plasmateur, / Monarche et chef en l'art d'architecture, / Avant
qu'il fut des siècles formateur / Fist ung pourtraict de nouvelle structure,
/ Pour repparer l'offense et forfaicture / Du père Adam' ['The heavenly
creator, King and master architect, prior to shaping the course of centuries,
portrayed a new structure, in order to repair the offence and forfeit of
father Adam']; man and God are unified in the Virgin's 'Temple construict
par divin artifice . . . De droict compas et juste quadrature' ['Temple built
by divine workmanship . . . according to weight, shape and measure'].[6]

---

[3] Legrand in M. E. Langlois (ed.), *Recueil d'arts de seconde rhétorique* (Paris: Imprimerie
   nationale, 1902), pp. xi–xii.

[4] This recalls Regnaud le Queux's *Instructif de la Second Rhétorique* in the anthology *Jardin
   de plaisance et fleur de rhetorique* (1501; facs. reprint Paris: F. Didot, 1910–25), 2 vols.,
   with its *locus classicus* of eloquence subsumed under wisdom: 'de sapience on ordonne /
   Sa loquence en fait de practique / Ou d'estude' ('eloquence is grounded by wisdom in
   theory and in practice', my trans.).

[5] *Les lunettes des princes* is available in C. Martineau – Genieys's edition (Geneva: Droz, 1972).

[6] In the *Jardin de plaisance* the world is created by wisdom in tandem with love. Compare
   Langlois, *Recueil*, Traité II, p. 40. Throughout *rhétoriqueur* poetry and the tractates of
   Second Rhetoric we find mention of sacralized letters infused into human understanding
   by the muse of grace.

Thus did amorphous notions intersect: rhyme, rhythm, metre, the *poesis* of *ruach Adonai* in Genesis 1, and the creative measuring of infinite Wisdom in Proverbs. Opening on to a subsequent section, the incomplete segment of Petrarchan *terza rima* in Lemaire de Belges's *La concorde des deux langages* mirrors at once the dance of the three Graces unfolding on to the world at court and the creative 2 : 1 Pythagorean ratio which dominates the entire work.

Dynamic counterpoise to formal limits arises naturally from the variety of rhymes proposed by manuals of Second Rhetoric and from the resulting structural rhythm of thought as the concomitant of poetic voice. Thus does Georges Chastellain cite Virgil and Cicero in his *Epître* 14, proclaiming: 'User me faut de verbal sapience . . . Tulle en escript par forme delitieuse; / Où clarté a, n'est jamais diseteuse . . . J'ay en parler rhetorical saveur' ['I must use verbal wisdom . . . Cicero employs it through delightful form; his clarity is never verbose . . . my speech is flavoured with rhetoric']. The *douceur* which Rabelais praised in this freedom is found in the treatment of religion, politics, morals, culture, special events, and in the Puys competitions on fixed themes, where alliances were formed as skills were honed. The Puys-Notre Dame, for instance, developed from the *académies dévotes* of Caen, Dieppe, and especially Rouen, which became crucibles for refining taste. Renaissance valuation of *copia rerum ac verborum* originated partly from extremes such as Meschinot's thirty-two ways of reading the joys and pains of the Virgin and Destrées's comparable explanation in 'La Vie de Sainte Catherine' (1501): 'The Virgin's name appears here four times: at the outset, in chiasmus, and at the end . . . prayerful praise which is interwoven so that it can be read forward, backward, and from all sides'. Although Legrand sensed that the alexandrine represented a natural metric limit, at the other extreme is an anonymous *Art de rhétorique* which by its infinite regress tests limits of meaning by reducing verse to a single phoneme.[7]

Against the background of the Puys competitions and under the aegis of the liberal arts, Eustache Deschamps had viewed the metrical arrangement of words as: a 'natural' music derived from the Boethian *Consolation of philosophy*; independent from lyric poetry and 'artificial' instrumental

---

[7] 'L'art de rhétoricque pour rimer en plusieurs sortes de rime', in *Recueil de poésies françaises des xve et xvie siècles*, ed. A. Montaiglon (Paris: Jannet, 1861), vol. III, p. 125. At the end of the fifteenth century Jehan Thenaud used the eulogistic term 'puys de sapience' which 'polit la langue et enrichit son possesseur' ['font of wisdom . . . which polishes language and enriches its possessor', my trans.], cited by Marc-René Jung in 'Poetria', *Vox Romanica* 30 (1971), p. 63; compare Parmentier's Chant-Royal presented for *puys* competition in 1518, where Mary is praised as 'Sapience infinie, / Qui nostre routte en sa charte compasse' ['infinite Wisdom, / Who charts the road we travel', my trans.]. She is the interstice between 'saincte Théologie' ['sacred Theology'] and 'subtille Astrologie' ['subtle Astrology'] in a firmament that is proportionate and concordant.

music; and overall more concerned with form than content.[8] In the prosopo-
poeia of Guillaume Machaut, the ultimate *trouvère* and Deschamps's
preceptor, we glimpse the implications of natural music: 'Je, Nature, par
qui tout est formé' (see John 1: 3). Nature comes to the poet as an Annun-
ciation to bestow 'Sens, Rhétorique, Musique'. Here again, earlier critics
erred in reducing Lemaire's insightful 'rhetoric and music are the same
thing' to mere equation of poetic affect with music.[9] Judging from Molinet's
nuanced summary ('Plain rhetoric is a kind of music called rhythm . . .
Music is heavenly resonance, the voice of angels, the joy of paradise, hope
in the air, the Church's organ, the song of birds, the re-creation of sad and
desolate hearts, the punishment which drives out devils') it is clear that the
rhétoriqueurs strove for polyphonic proportion of all kinds. In Franchino
Gafori's *Theorica musice* (1496), this harmonic spectrum includes music,
speech, and a panspiritual inspiration which links the poetic muse to
rhythm, to tones of the natural dodeciad scale, stations of the zodiac,
serial patterns, expressive forms, and to the concordant melos of spheres,
the pulse beat of the universe, and fountainhead of all creation. Indeed, in
his *Epître à Georges Chastellain*, Jean Robertet assigns this harmonic as
an overall function of Second Rhetoric: 'Embellissant tout autre humain
ouvrage / Par élégant et haute réthorique, / Moins ressemblant humaine
qu'angélique' ['Embellishing all other human works, through elegant and
noble rhetoric, which seems more angelic than human']. This momentary
link posited with the transcendent goes to the heart of the creative transformation of Second Rhetoric, suggesting not only its affinity with early
Renaissance music theory but also its patent kinship with late medieval
painting. Johan Huizinga generalized tellingly on how fifteenth-century
art renders the outward appearance of things, yet, recalling the spatio-
temporal precepts of wholeness, harmony, and radiance laid down by
Aquinas, 'preserves its mystery for all time to come'.[10] The triune Thomist criteria adapt to the peculiarly visual and auditive qualities of *rhétoriqueur* poetics. The *hortus conclusus* of the rondeau, for instance,
often embroiders on the theme of the Virgin as both the biomorphic
Temple of Solomon and the feminized figuration of the world created
by God's compass. This poetic form (to paraphrase Aquinas) creates an
enclosed hermetic field of self-defined rhymes and self-defining, impractical

---

[8] *Art de dictier*, in *Œuvres complètes*, ed. G. Raynaud (Paris: F. Didot, 1891), vol. VII, 'De
Musique', pp. 269–70; Roger Dragonetti demonstrated that Deschamps's view on 'La
poésie, ceste musique naturele', derives from Boethius, in *Mélanges R. Guiette. Fin du
Moyen Age et Renaissance* (Antwerp: Nederlandse Boekhandel, 1961), p. 62.

[9] *Œuvres complètes de Jean Lemaire de Belges* (1882–91; reprint Geneva: Slatkine, 1971),
vol. III, p. 197.

[10] Zumthor has argued that emblematic poetry aspires to physical representation, in *Le
masque et la lumière*, p. 214. Compare Huizinga, *The waning of the Middle Ages* (New
York: Doubleday, 1954), pp. 267, 276.

relationships, where everything within the frame is regarded organically. Synthesis of perception is followed by analysis of apprehension [*consonantia*]: a complex, divisible, separable, harmonious sum of its parts. The rhythm of its structure is apprehended as self-bounded and self-contained, part joining part within its prescribed limits, against an immeasurable background of transcendent space and time.

As for painting, few examples demonstrate better than that of Jan van Eyck how Huizinga's observation also captures the comparable miniaturism of *rhétoriqueur* poetry: as van Eyck invented painting, Second Rhetoric too formularized essential aspects of modern poetry. In van Eyck's 'Betrothal of the Arnolfini' (1434) a simple corner of the real world suddenly appears affixed on a panel as if by magic. Like a Molinet or Lemaire de Belges, the ornamental miniaturist is both absent and a witness to the moment, testifying to the event as a notary might be asked to declare that he had been present at a similar solemn act. And like an emblematic conceit, we read 'Johannes de eyck fuit hic' above the small convex mirror on the recessed wall. The reflecting surface distorts the realistic foreground subject, the encoded image of the painter-witness, and the invisible yet omnivoyant eye of God which is redundantly symbolized in the rosary and single candle burning in the elaborate chandelier. The symmetrical grouping is composed with the stillness and rigid, symbol-laden ceremony of the Mass. The instant when the *claritas* of the aesthetic image is luminously grasped by the mind which has been arrested by its wholeness and fascinated by its harmony is the silent stasis of aesthetic pleasure. The universe of the painting is expressed through an abundance of rich particulars which all document, transform, and eternalize this self-sufficient microtext which profoundly influenced Velasquez, Courbet, and Manet. As in the Mass, then, memorial transfiguration is the essential function of Second Rhetoric.[11] While a work like Octavien de Saint-Gelais's *Séjour d'honneur* (published 1519) can be read as a manual of living well, the moral precepts of courtliness in Jean Marot's *Doctrinal des princesses* (1520) make it a more typical *rhétoriqueur* opus, as in Chastellain's 'Beauté, vertu conjoint emprès leur forme' ['Beauty and virtue blended through their forms'].

---

[11] While the programmatic introduction to Molinet's edition of the *Roman de la rose* equates the muse with divine grace, his metaphors of choice view transformation as a naturalized role of the flowers of rhetoric.

15

The rhetoric of presence: art, literature, and illusion

François Rigolot

Fascination with the idea of illusionist representation pervades the history of Renaissance culture. Great artists were generally convinced that they had been endowed with a power to instil a supernatural degree of life into their artefacts. The Pygmalion fantasy can be seen as emblematic of this faith in the illusionist qualities of art. The famous Greek myth exemplifies the belief in the power of art to *give life* rather than to represent it. In Ovid's version of the story Pygmalion is a sculptor who falls in love with the statue he has fashioned, and the gods answer his prayers by turning the cold marble into living flesh (*Metamorphoses*, x). This myth naturally captivated the imagination of many artists and writers from Donatello to Michel de Montaigne and William Shakespeare. The triumph of representational skill is traditionally associated with the power of art to arouse passions. This was still common theoretical currency in the Renaissance.

The painter could so subdue the minds of men that they would fall in love with a painting that did not represent a real woman. In his *Treatise on painting* Leonardo tells the following anecdote: 'I made a religious painting which was bought by one who so loved it that he wanted to remove the sacred representations so as to be able to kiss it without suspicion. Finally his conscience prevailed over his sighs and lust, but he had to remove the picture from his house.'[1] If for today's critics illusionist virtuosity is suspect at best as a criterion of artistic worth, it was indeed highly praised by classical authority. Pliny's well-known account of the evolution of painting had a long-standing impact on the criteria used through the centuries to assess the quality of visual art. In Chapter xxxv of his *Natural history* Pliny tells us that painting began with tracing an outline round a man's shadow (v), using a single colour ('monochrome'), then discovered light and shade, and the contrast of colours (xi), climaxing with the masterpieces of Apelles, so lifelike that 'they challenged Nature herself' (xxxvi). In other words, the very progress of the *techne* showed an evolution from badly representational flat pictures to polychrome lifelike images which had the power to deceive the spectator.

---

[1] *Treatise on painting*, ed. A. P. McMahon (Princeton: Princeton University Press, 1956), no. 33.

In his *Theologia Platonica* Marsilio Ficino ecstatically recalls Pliny's most famous examples of illusionary artfulness: ravenous birds preying over Zeuxis's painted grapes, excited dogs barking at Apelles' horse and hound scenes, lascivious men ogling Praxiteles' marble statue of Venus (XIII.3). To Ficino and his Neoplatonic disciples this was tangible proof of the power of art to deceive the viewers and rouse their passions. Plato had raised the ethical issue about Homer's representations in the *Republic*. If the artist's chief aim was to instruct, one way to safeguard his reputation was to read his works *allegorically*. By introducing discrete allegorical interpretations of their works, Renaissance painters and poets could therefore sidestep the moral objections of their critics, finding an identity in which moral worth and aesthetic freedom could be simultaneously established by an ability to produce lifelike illusions.

The pervasiveness of the 'rhetoric of presence' in the Renaissance is mirrored in the numerous rhetorical terms used by theorists for the representation of reality. In his Latin treatise on poetics (1561), which summarizes two centuries of humanist ideas, Julius Caesar Scaliger devotes chapters to a number of roughly synonymous terms like *demonstratio, descriptio, effictio, enargeia, claritas, perspicuitas*, and so on (*Poetices libri septem*, III.24 and I.1). But the word *enargeia* is probably the most widely used to describe the Renaissance attempt to display the world under the guise of language.

In his *Rhetoric* Aristotle remarked that 'often Homer, by making use of metaphor, speaks of inanimate things *as if they were animate*' and he added that 'it is to *creating actuality* ['energeian poiein'] that his popularity is due' (III, XI.3). The word *energeia*, for Aristotle, refers to the paradox of producing a powerful lifelike effect through words. In Roman times, a strange etymological confusion took place, as the two Greek paronyms *energeia* and *enargeia* were semantically conflated. *Energeia* was usually translated into Latin as *actio* [activity, actuality, power], and *enargeia* as *illustratio* or *evidentia* [visuality, vividness]. In classical and Renaissance poetic theory the two meanings tended to combine, as if the artistic power [energy] to represent reality had necessarily to be linked with sight, the 'noble sense', which is associated with light and creativity.

In Cicero's *Orator*, the writer's ability to describe inanimate things as if they were animate is expressed in visual, iconic terms. And in his discussion of the use of *pathos* in conjunction with *ethos*, Quintilian shows that eloquence derives its force from the orator's ability to create a 'verbal vision', by which the mind imagines things with such vividness that they seem to be present in front of the beholder's eyes ('quae non tam dicere videtur quam ostendere', *Institutio oratoria* VI.2).[2] During the Renaissance,

---

[2] See also IV.2.63; IV.2.123; VI.2.29–31; VIII.3.70, and IX.2.40. On the appearance of these issues in the context of Italian Renaissance poetics, see Glyn P. Norton's remarks on the *romanzo* in the present volume (pp. 332–3).

the interest for artistic 'energy' was reinforced by the widespread doctrine of *ut pictura poesis* and the exemplary discourse of classical authors, such as Pliny and Plutarch, on pictorial representation.

Leon Battista Alberti's crucial concept of *istoria* derives from the idea that a truly effective narrative should be able to trigger the beholder's emotions. In his treatise *Della pittura* (*c.* 1435), he writes: 'The *istoria* which merits both praise and admiration will be so agreeably and pleasantly attractive that it will capture the eye of whatever learned or unlearned person is looking at it, and will move his soul'.[3] By depicting appropriate movements of the body, the painter will arouse the desired emotions in the spectator. Affective realism is the key to a rhetorically successful art work. From Alberti to Montaigne the case of Timantes of Cyprus fascinated the humanist imagination. Unable to represent Agamemnon's grief at Iphigenia's immolation, the Greek painter preferred to drape the father's face and 'let his most bitter distress be imagined, even though it was not seen'.[4]

In his *Deffence et illustration de la langue françoyse* (1549) Joachim du Bellay makes fun of bad translators who lack 'ceste *energie* [meaning both *energeia* and *enargeia*] . . . comme un peintre peut representer l'ame avecques le cors de celuy qu'il entreprent tyrer après le naturel' ['this energy . . . as a painter is able to depict the soul through the body of the one he undertakes to represent in his natural form'].[5] The pictorial analogy brings body and soul together to give them life; and the portrayed subject regains the 'exquisite truth' of Nature itself. The metaphor of the painter appears infinitely desirable to a writer whose ultimate goal is *hypotyposis*, that is in Peacham's words, a 'description so vivid that it seemeth rather paynted in tables than expressed in wordes'. In the same vein, Edmund Spenser claims that the pictures of *The shepheardes calender* (1579) are 'so singularly set forth, and portrayed, as if Michel Angelo were there, he could nor amende the best, nor reprehende the worst'.[6]

In classical rhetoric the art of verbal description was known as *ekphrasis* in Greek. Although the term was used rather loosely at first, it gradually acquired a more technical meaning, namely the literary description of a work of art. In the second half of the Quattrocento Homer came to be regarded as the source of all ekphrastic knowledge. In his *Oratio in expositione Homeri* Angelo Poliziano praised the bard for the visionary

---

[3] *On painting*, trans. J. R. Spencer (New Haven: Yale University Press, 1966), p. 75.

[4] Alberti, *On painting*, p. 78. See Montaigne, *The complete essays*, trans. D. M. Frame (Stanford: Stanford University Press, 1965), Book I, chapter II, pp. 6–7.

[5] *La deffence et illustration de la langue françoyse*, ed. H. Chamard (Paris: Didier, 1948), pp. 40–1. See also Chamard's commentary on the word 'énergie', pp. 35–6, n. 5.

[6] *Poetical works*, ed. J. C. Smith and E. de Sélincourt (Oxford: Clarendon Press, 1912), p. 612.

character of his *mimesis*.[7] In spite (or perhaps because) of his blindness Homer was able to place human things in front of our eyes ('ante oculos constituit'). His description of Achilles' shield could be considered as the prototype of all ekphrastic scenes. As Hephaistos's masterpiece plays a crucial role in the *Iliad*'s structure, it offers a vivid recapitulation of the main events of the Trojan story and gives a new *insight* into the great cycles of human life. Nothing could be more important to the Florentine Neoplatonic circles of Cosimo de' Medici.

Later, in the sixteenth-century humanist reader's mind another exemplary work of art loomed just as large: Aeneas's own shield in the *Aeneid* (Book VIII). J. C. Scaliger's eulogy of Virgil's vivid description and Montaigne's enthusiastic comments on this scene are well known. The essayist was particularly enthralled by Virgil's ability to capture Venus's charming beauty as she turns to Vulcan to beg arms for her son: 'Poetry reproduces an indefinable mood that is more amorous than love itself. Venus is not so beautiful all naked, alive and panting, as she is here in Virgil.'[8] This is perhaps the best concrete example of *enargeia* ever given by Renaissance writers. Virgil's *mimesis*, as Montaigne's gloss testifies, has indeed reached climactic proportions. Like Pygmalion's statue, the poet's Venus commands a potentially ravishing 'presence', because its fictional unreality is felt to be more real than life itself.

Following Homer's model, Virgil describes Aeneas's shield as an 'indescribable text' ['non enarrabile textum', VIII.625]. On this living symbol of imperialist power the major scenes of future Roman history are lavishly displayed in the most vivid detail. Motion and speech animate this unreal work of art – so unreal, indeed, that it represents a future, which is *past* and therefore well known to Virgil's humanist readers, but which has not yet unfolded for Aeneas, and is therefore incomprehensible to him. As a naïve reader, Aeneas appears marvelling at the artful scenes but unable to make sense out of them. Virgil's clever, self-conscious use of *enargeia* points to the centrality of illusionism in the rhetorical process of Renaissance artistic, literary, as well as historical discourse.

At the same time, many Renaissance writers found material for *ekphrasis* in dreams, portents, and the marvels of Nature generally. In sixteenth-century visions, strange mythological statues move about with mysterious animation. To quote George Chapman's *Ovid's banquet of sense* (1595): 'To these dead forms, came living beauties essence / Able to make them startle with her presence'.[9] Yet, enthusiasm for illusionist representations became disturbing as the Reformation developed. This very same *enargeia*

[7] Angelo Poliziano, *Opera omnia* (Lyons: Gryphius, 1546), vol. III, p. 63.
[8] Montaigne, *Essays*, Book III, chapter V, p. 645.
[9] *Poems of George Chapman*, ed. P. Bartlett (New York: Modern Language Association of America; London: Oxford University Press, 1941), p. 54.

was to prompt the destruction of art, as a radical remedy against a major source of idolatry. Actually the moral, political or metaphysical implications of Plato's condemnation of art were never entirely brushed aside. The implication that the painter's subject is a lie, because twice or thrice removed from reality (that is, from the realm of Ideal Forms), remained central to the humanist theory of imitative representation. Iconoclasm was, perhaps, one of the most extreme historical manifestations of the repressed fascination with the mimetic power of art.

The Renaissance compulsion for a 'rhetoric of presence' was perhaps best illustrated by Erasmus's *De duplici copia verborum et rerum* (1513). In this textbook on the 'abundance of words and ideas' the prodigal image of cornucopia is used to characterize the productiveness of literary discourse. Expanding upon Cicero's and Quintilian's recipes for variations of all kinds (the very exemplification of *copia*), the Dutch humanist developed a theory of his own, in which the rhetorical expansion of language became both a celebration of verbal inventiveness and a warning against the treacherous use of words to seduce and deceive. Proliferation belongs to nature, and it can be a sign of health as well as a disease. Thus the recurrent image of the horn of plenty can send misleading signs as it reinforces the feeling that language is the inescapable mediator of human experience.

Erasmus's concern with the ostensible presence of things in language is reflected in his famous definition of *enargeia*: 'Ea [*enargeia*] utemur quoties . . . rem non simpliciter exponemus, sed ceu coloribus expressam in tabula spectandam proponemus, ut nos depinxisse, non narrasse, lector spectasse, non legisse videatur'[10] ['We use *enargeia* whenever . . . we do not explain a thing simply, but display it to be looked at as if it were expressed in colour in a picture, so that it may seem that we have painted, not narrated, and that the reader has seen, not read'[11]]. To be effective great literary descriptions must possess the power – *enargeia* – to set before the reader the very object or scene being described. Yet, in the process of producing enthralment or astonishment, this power may exceed the limits of verisimilitude. As a result, the very *energy* which achieves lifelike vividness may paradoxically solicit the reader's disbelief. The writer's desire to make his object breathe, move, and speak is somehow undermined by the duplicitous connection between the 'real' and the 'imaginary'. *Res*, after all, may simply be the deceptive result of artistic skill, actual *verba* masquerading as *res*, a 'simulacrum' of the real essence of things. Appearances often fail to communicate the disguised, oblique message which lies under the surface of things. In John L. Austin's parlance,

---

[10] *Opera omnia*, 9 vols. (Basle: Froben, 1540), vol. I, p. 66.
[11] Text translated by Terence Cave, in '*Enargeia*: Erasmus and the rhetoric of presence in the sixteenth century', *L'esprit créateur* 16, 4 (Winter 1976), p. 7.

the *enargeia* may be nothing more than a particular 'illocutionary mode': a way of *doing* something else in the act of *using words*.

In the face of the duplicitous nature of human language and its uncertain capacity to represent the world, Erasmus reaffirmed his fundamental belief in the transformative power of the Word of God. The analogy between human and divine eloquence was of crucial importance to him. In Reformation times, this claim to transcendent truth was shared by contemporary Evangelical thinkers like Calvin, Lefèvre d'Etaples or Melanchthon. They were convinced that only the *Logos* of the Holy Scriptures could redeem and save humankind ['Verbum Dei sufficit'].[12] The highest form of *enargeia* was, then, to be found in the Gospel of God, which could restore and revitalize the nature of things and bring truth not only before our eyes [*ante oculos*] but within our hearts [*in pectora*]. With the rediscovery of Longinus's *On the Sublime* such a 'Rhetorik der Affecte' was to reach its highest point. Yet, no matter how vibrant these logocentric pleas may have been, they were constantly challenged by the actual literary practice of contemporary writers, who pointed to the darker side of rhetoric in their endless search for meaning.

To be sure, fascination with hermetic and oracular language was pervasive among humanists who hoped to combine elements of Christianity, Neoplatonism, and Judaism to lead their readers, through the intricate maze of multiple beliefs, to the 'evidence' of eternal unity. The compulsive vividness of esoteric symbolism was much praised by Christian Caballists. Giovanni Pico della Mirandola and Jean Bodin tapped the 'enargic' resources of the so-called *prisca theologia*, a storehouse of pre-Christian mythological writings, to establish a historical continuum between classical antiquity and the Judeo-Christian Revelation. Practising poetry also meant borrowing frequently from 'mythographies', vast repertories of pagan tales, such as Ovid's *Metamorphoses*, with many allegorical and moral significations. Through the vivid rendition of selected *fabulae* the poet would attempt to reveal profound and universal truths, and mimetically invite his readers to recognize hidden values with a higher significance [*altior sensus*].

Seen in this light, Renaissance Neoplatonic poetry had much closer affinities to philosophy, indeed to theology, than to rhetoric. It aspired to be knowledge of the 'real', that which goes beyond appearances, to seize the profound meaning of things and bring it vividly in front of the reader's eyes. In some extreme cases the search for a 'higher meaning' was accompanied by almost alchemistic experiments with language. In the works of

---

[12] Lefèvre d'Etaples, *Commentarii initiatorii in Quatuor Evangelia (1522). The prefatory epistles of Jacques Lefèvre d'Etaples and related texts*, ed. E. F. Rice (New York: Columbia University Press, 1972), p. 435.

Burgundian *rhétoriqueurs* and Flemish *rederijkers* words themselves became seductive fictions concealing the mysteries of an arcane reality. Music and painting were used as powerful metaphors for the representation of reality. Great poets were those who, through appropriate techniques, succeeded in striking the eye or the ear with stupendous clarity. In their compositions language came to possess qualities that were not only sonorous (syllables as musical notes) but also visual (words as the brush strokes of a painter). Such experimentation was, perhaps, most manifest in the literature of emblems (Andrea Alciato), figurative dreams (Francesco Colonna), rebuses (Jean Marot), and tapestries (Enrique de Villena), which contributed to the revival of the classical and medieval tradition of *technopaegnia* and *carmina figurata*.

In an age that saw the introduction of the printing-press, oral reciting was also used as a powerful metaphor to convey a sense of linguistic immediacy. François Rabelais and William Shakespeare used a wealth of popular, 'oral' material to recapture the living forces connoted by the carnivalesque spirit and make them the vehicle of a new, utopian order, based on perpetual, 'comic' self-renewal. Bakhtin was right to emphasize the significance of folk culture for the proper understanding of Rabelais's narratives. But the humanistic tradition of literary banquets is just as relevant.[13] In Erasmus's *Colloquia* the carefree ambience of Plato's *Symposium* combines with the serious narrative of the Gospels' Last Supper. Literary conviviality operates as an archetypal ekphrastic device that forcefully contributes to 'energize' fiction and engage the reader in the rhetorical illusion of a vitalistic experience. The deceitful trappings of *enargeia* are fully at work in the works of Ariosto, Ronsard, Spenser, and others, who vainly tried to regain the plenitude of lost origins through what Glyn Norton has aptly called the epic language of 'palpability'.[14]

A good picture, says Robert Burton, is a 'falsa veritas'.[15] But a false truth is not necessarily a lie. By freeing up the latent powers of pictorial representation, Renaissance literary theory remained deeply indebted to its classical origins. But, as the sixteenth century proceeded, the logocentric optimism of early humanism often yielded to a more problematic questioning of the epistemological nature of 'eye-ravishing art'. Beyond Erasmus's copious mode of celebration [*festivitas*], in which words are filled with the very plenitude of things, loomed the humanist's fear of the fallacy of language and the indeterminacy of meaning.

---

[13] See Michel Jeanneret, *A feast of words: banquets and table talk in the Renaissance*, trans. J. Whiteley and E. Hughes (Chicago: University of Chicago Press, 1991).

[14] 'Rabelais and the epic of palpability: *enargeia* and history (*Cinquiesme Livre*: 38–40)', *Symposium* 33 (Summer 1979), 171–85.

[15] *The anatomy of melancholy* (Oxford: John Lichfield and James Short for Henry Cripps, 1624), p. 233.

16

The paradoxical sisterhood:
'ut pictura poesis'

Christopher Braider

The doctrine *ut pictura poesis* ('as is' or 'as in painting, so is' or 'so in poetry') lies at the heart of Renaissance aesthetics, the central theme and presiding dogma of the theory and practice of painting and poetry alike. Accompanied by the 'witty antithesis' attributed by Pliny (*De gloria Atheniensium* 3.347a) to Simonides of Chios, the chiastic *poesia tacens, pictura loquens* ('painting is mute poetry, poetry a talking picture'), Horace's defining tag (*Ars poetica* 361) appears in virtually every treatise on art or poetry from the early Renaissance to the close of the Enlightenment. Now explicitly in the rehearsal of the Horatian and Simonidean watchwords, the ubiquitous 'comparisons' or 'parallels' of poetry and painting, or the recurrent *paragone* debating the relative value or 'precedence' of the Sister Arts, now implicitly in the perennial references to poetry not merely as Aristotelian 'imitation', but as painting, limning, drawing, sketching, colouring, depicting, or portraying, *ut pictura* is the universal presumption of all writers on poetry and poetics. It offers thus a key to understanding both what poetry was thought essentially to be and aim for and the place it occupied as the dominant mode of high cultural expression.

Yet despite the crucial role it played in Western aesthetics from the mid-fifteenth century down to Gotthold Ephraim Lessing's *Laokoon* of 1766, finally rejecting the doctrine on the basis of a critical reassessment of the formal 'boundaries' defining the irreducible differences between the so-called Sisters, the theory's actual content is surprisingly meagre. There was on one hand the set of commonplaces drawn from a scattering of ancient authorities and *loci classici*: the passages on imitation, plot, and the relationship between poetry and history in Aristotle's *Poetics*; Horace's *Ars poetica*, source for both the *ut pictura* trope and the related doctrine *dulce et utile* (333ff) demanding the combining of 'instruction' with 'delight'; Lucian's characterization of Homer as a 'great painter' at *Eikones* 8; Cicero's *De inventione*, *Orator ad Brutum*, and *De oratore*, and Quintilian's *Institutio oratoria*, grounding the verbal emulation of visual art in rhetoric; and a handful of tirelessly recycled *exempla* gathered in Pliny's *Historia naturalis* or Plutarch's *Moralia* and *Life of Alexander* from the legends surrounding the ancient Greek painters,

especially Zeuxis and Apelles. These classical sources were then supplemented by modern authorities drawn from the extensive if still remarkably homogeneous body of contemporary theoretical writings devoted
to the topic, the most cited representatives being: Leon Battista Alberti's
De pictura (1435), the first systematic Western treatise on the theory
and practice of visual art; Julius Caesar Scaliger's *Poetices libri septem*
(1561) and Lodovico Castelvetro's *Poetica d'Aristotele* (1570), establishing Aristotle as the central reference for all subsequent discussion of aesthetic representation; Lodovico Dolce's *Aretino* (1577); Giovanni Paolo
Lomazzo's *Trattato* (1584); Torquato Tasso's *Discorsi dell'arte poetica*
(1587); Sir Philip Sidney's *An apology for poetry* (1595); Charles Alphonse
Dufresnoy's *De arte graphica* (1667); André Félibien's *Entretiens* (1666–
85) and *Conférences de l'Académie royale* (1669), containing Charles
Le Brun's famous lecture on Poussin's *Israelites gathering manna in the
wilderness*; Giovanni Pietro Bellori's *Vite* (1672), offering, alongside
critical lives of the canonically foremost modern artists, a sampling of
remarks by Poussin, with Leonardo one of the few painters accorded an
authoritative voice; John Dryden's *Parallel between painting and poetry*
(1695); Roger de Piles's *Abrégé de la vie des peintres* (1699) and *Cours
de peinture par principes* (1708); and Jean-Baptiste Du Bos's *Réflexions
critiques* (1719).

The core of the doctrine emerging from these sources is easily summarized. All art aims at 'imitation', by which was meant not only the 'imitation of nature', but also (and chiefly) that of what Rensselaer Lee[1] aptly
calls 'significant human action', the noble 'histories' set forth in Holy
Scripture and heroic verse ancient and modern. The most immediately
persuasive and forceful (if not necessarily the most uplifting) form of
imitation is painting. For unlike poets who, depicting actor, scene, and deed
through words, are limited to using conventional verbal signs standing
for, but thereby also displacing, the things they represent, painters deploy
the 'natural signs' constituted by the images of things themselves. It is to
this that painting owes its *enargeia*: its capacity to realize the rhetorical
ideal of creating an overwhelming sense of direct physical presence carrying both the matter and the inner meaning of the actions it portrays into
the spectator's very soul. Whence the special relevance of stories like that
of Zeuxis's grapes: a picture so lifelike birds descended to pick at the
depicted fruit. Whence too the surprising way in which the Ficinian Neoplatonist, Lomazzo, champion of the poetic Idea as the ultimate type and
source of aesthetic representation, asserts (2.1) how, beholding paintings
where the expressive movements of the characters are described in a

---

[1] Rensselaer Lee, *'Ut pictura poesis': the humanist theory of painting* (New York: Norton,
1967), pp. 9–23.

'natural' or 'lifelike' manner ('con moti al naturale ritratti'), spectators are compelled to reproduce the corresponding urges and emotions, smiling with those who smile, thinking or marvelling with those who think or marvel, desiring the beautiful women presented in admirable nudes or hungering for the foods they see painted figures eat, and even growing drowsy before the images of people fast asleep. Thus poets should so far as possible replicate painting, aiming to produce in words the sense of vivid dramatic presence painters achieve in the expressive mirroring of heroic deeds: the more readily so given that, as Aristotle (*Poetics* 1448a) reminds us, human beings take pleasure in representations for their own sake, regardless of what they portray, thereby combining instruction with delight in precisely the way Horace mandates. Endowed with the special gift of engendering the illusion of immediate reality and giving pleasure in the very means by which it informs and edifies, painting resumes all of the properties humanist poetics and rhetoric most prized.

Nevertheless, simple as the central ideas behind *ut pictura* may be, the cultural evolution it indexes proves highly complex. One sign of this complexity is the curious overdetermination at work in the treatment of the authorizing Horatian tag. As cited by Renaissance theorists, the crucial phrase is the product of a pronounced misreading, a 'creative misprision'. This misprision was favoured by a corrupt punctuation of Horace's text tying the key verb *erit* ['will be'] to the initial phrase *ut pictura poesis* rather than to the actual subject of the main clause. This yields, in place of Horace's careful comment that *it will sometimes happen*, in poetry as in painting, that one work is best viewed close to and another from a distance, the general stricture, 'ut pictura poesis erit': it *will be*, always and essentially, in poetry as in painting. But even allowing for the enabling mispunctuation, Horace's phrase can only mean what Renaissance writers made it mean when wrested from its proper context. Beyond whatever Horace may or may not have intended, there was what the Renaissance *desired* from his text: the authority for a universal theory of poetry and art based on values and goals quite foreign to anything the Augustan poet might have conceived for himself.

But a still more telling sign of the overdetermining forces shaping *ut pictura* aesthetics is the fact that, despite being couched in terms of poetry's debt to the example of painting, the doctrine had at bottom less to do with painting than with a highly rhetorical ideal of *poetry* and the literary aims and interests of which poetry was the pre-eminent expression.

The tradition's fundamental literary bias is already inscribed in its proximate origins in early humanists' reverence for the ancient past and the methods used to recover the lost legacy of classical languages and letters. As Michael Baxandall points out, the doctrine arises in the first instance as the fruit of a largely formal exercise: an almost accidental by-product of the at once philologically naïve and comically literal reproduction of comparisons and *ekphrases* met with in Aristotle, Horace, Cicero, and Quintilian or the texts assembled in the great primer of classical Greek, the Greek Anthology, with a view less to conning their actual critical content than to enabling imitators to master the intricacies of classical periodic prose.[2] At this level, *ut pictura* emerges as a central preoccupation simply because it was found so to be in ancient literature and because, taken as a set theme for oratorical discourse, it provided a topic rich in opportunities for deploying the hypotactic rhetorical structures of comparison and contrast, simile and antithesis, basic elements for elaborate Ciceronian periods. The initially purely formal imitation of ancient texts both in the reconstructed original and in humanist emulation revived the canons and tastes dictating the metaphors ancient writers used to analyse literary and visual works of art and the analogies these metaphors encouraged them to draw.

The preponderance of this rhetorical model is also reflected, as Baxandall notes, in the fundamental categories of humanist art theory itself.[3] Thus alongside the evidence of the value placed on *enargeia*, a value deriving from the persuasive force associated with the figure of *hypotyposis* in the forensic or deliberative rhetoric of Cicero and Quintilian, there is the testimony of what, even more perhaps than the projective geometry of one-point or direct linear perspective, stands as Alberti's central discovery, namely, *composition*: a principle informing the analysis and interpretation of visual art to this day. Understood as the process by which a painter's basic conception, the instigating 'invention' determining the choice of *istoria* or narrative subject the painting is to represent and the manner in which it is to represent it, comes to assume expressive visual form, Albertian composition is directly borrowed from the parsing of Ciceronian periods. Just as a hypotactic sentence is constructed out of clauses composed of phrases in turn framed by the individual words that form the medium of oration, so the painterly *istoria* is constructed out of 'bodies' (representing the dramatic actors) composed of 'members' (the diversely arranged parts of the actors' bodies) built up from the 'planes' or colour patches that constitute the stuff in which painters work. Moreover, painting as a whole was analysed into three 'parts' modelled precisely on the three traditional 'parts' of rhetoric: *inventio*, the moment of conception and the working up of material, *dispositio*, providing an effective outline and arrangement, and *elocutio*, finding the most affecting and persuasive terms by which the whole may be given detailed verbal expression.

---

[2] Michael Baxandall, *Giotto and the orators: humanist observers of painting in Italy and the discovery of pictorial composition, 1350–1450* (Oxford: Clarendon Press, 1971), see ch. 1.

[3] *Ibid.*, pp. 121–39.

Thus, in the Albertian version, mediated by *compositione*, a process over-lapping the moment of conception and that of formal disposition, the instigating *inventione* leads first to the *circonscriptione* by which its formal expression is sketched out and then to the *receptione di lumi*, the play of colour, reflectivity, and light-and-dark by which the figures described in the moment of *circonscriptione* take on living, expressive contour and substance. And in later versions, dating, for instance, from Dolce, *inventione* gives rise to *disegno*, the defining 'line' or 'design' brought to final perfection through *colorito*, expressive, life-giving colour and light.

But the clearest sign both of *ut pictura*'s fundamentally literary tenor and of the poetic idealization with which this underlying literariness was confederate is the transvaluation operated by and within the authorizing *ut pictura* trope itself. It is important to bear in mind in any attempt to assess *ut pictura*'s significance that, in enjoining poets to imitate painterly example, the theory inspired a practice that went quite the other way. 'As painting, so poetry' ultimately implied the reverse, 'as poetry, so painting', and it is to this reversal that we owe the most salient and far-reaching features of *ut pictura* aesthetics.

The first and most obvious of these, attested by Alberti's insistence on the *istoria* as being the painter's 'greatest work', is the unanimity with which the 'highest' form of painting was taken to be 'history' painting: painting devoted to visualizing tales drawn from the repository of Holy Scripture, classical letters and myth, and modern epic poetry. Nor are the 'histories' involved chosen primarily for their intrinsic visual interest, important as this may be, but rather for their 'moral' qualities: the exem-plary character of the heroic virtues they portray, virtues it is painters' task to translate into vivid and convincing visual form. While painters gravitate towards subjects that also contain visual interest, striving to find or 'invent' the most satisfying as well as striking and faithful visual expression they can, the ultimate aim remains to put beholders in mind of the virtuous examples 'history' records: great and noble deeds illustrating the signal human virtues it is art's business to teach by lending them a presence and expressive charm capable of persuading us to replicate them in our own lives. Even though painting became a model on the strength of its persuasive dramatic presence and a related realism the envy of poets, the ends this persuasive realism served remained fundamentally poetic.

Conversely, for all poetry was taken to be a form of painting, the best poets (Homer, Virgil, Dante, Ariosto, Tasso, Shakespeare) being conven-tionally portrayed as the best 'painters' too, the sort of painting writers had in mind was sharply and narrowly defined by goals of poetry's mak-ing. This is what enabled Sidney, a Protestant idealist anxious about the inherent 'idolatrousness' of visual representation, to claim that poetry is essentially 'an art of imitation, for so Aristotle termeth it in his word *mimesis*, that is to say a representing, counterfeiting, or figuring forth – to speak metaphorically, a speaking picture',[4] while nevertheless wholly repressing any mention of painting as such. It also explains how Piles, in other respects one of the most perspicuous exponents of the nature and powers of visual art *per se*, came to assert not only that 'the Poet's principal aim is to imitate the mores and actions of men: Painting has the same object',[5] but that the disposition or design adopted in achieving this goal conforms to formal criteria derived from dramatic poetry rather than properties intrinsic to painting itself, calling on painters to view the canvas 'as a stage on which each figure plays its role'.[6] Painterly *disegno* becomes the direct visual counterpart of the Aristotelian unities of action, place and – as attested by the neoclassical practices of Poussin and Le Brun, creating what Norman Bryson styles 'legible bodies' bound by the discipline of expressive narrative exposition – even time.[7]

One result of the poetic idealization to which this subjected painting was a system of stylistic norms and canonic procedures tellingly at odds with the supporting pictorial rhetoric, and in particular the claim that that in which poetry most resembles her Sister is their common effort to present what Sidney calls a 'perfect picture' of the 'particular truth of things'[8] – a picture deemed perfect first of all for its 'truth to nature'. Thus a major impetus behind the desire to remake poetry in painting's image, reproducing in verbal form the effects the new techniques of pictorial naturalism placed at painters' disposal, came from the general notion of both verbal and visual art as 'imitation of nature': a notion linked with the humanist emphasis on the scale and shape of human experience reflected in the emergence of Vitruvian Man as the decisive measure of all things. But it is already remarkable how the essentially *architectural* ideal espoused here actively remakes the nature it claims mirror-like to imitate. When Giorgio Vasari, prototype of modern art history as Alberti is of modern art criticism, lauds Giotto for being the first post-classical artist to paint 'after nature', this praise has to be set beside what Vasari presents, in the opening chapters of his *Vite* (1568),[9] as the self-evident bond between Giottesque naturalism and the rationalization of architectural space imposing a lucid order on the barbaric clutter and lack of unified vision or plan characterizing building before the Quattrocento. The aim is then not

---

[4] Sir Philip Sidney, *An apology for poetry*, ed. G. Shepherd (Manchester: Manchester University Press; New York: Barnes and Noble, 1973), p. 101.

[5] Roger de Piles, *Cours de peinture par principes* (Paris: J. Estienne, 1708), p. 452.

[6] Roger de Piles, *Abrégé de la vie des peintres* (Paris: F. Muguet, 1699), p. 43.

[7] Norman Bryson, *Word and image: French painting of the Ancien Regime* (Cambridge: Cambridge University Press, 1981), pp. 29–57.

[8] Sidney, *An apology for poetry*, ed. G. Shepherd, p. 107.

[9] See the edition of M. Sonino, K. Clark, and Gaston du C. de Vere, 3 vols. (New York: Abrams, 1979).

simply to portray things *as they are*, but, after the manner of architects refashioning the social and physical world of Renaissance Italy, to portray them as they *should* be: the naturalism that originally inspired the pursuit of painterly example becomes a rhetorical device designed to enlist assent to an ideal far removed from the ordinary experience painting appears to mimic.

The curious duplicity of perspective and intent this suggests is further registered in the ambiguities shaping the notion of the 'imitation of nature' itself. For both terms, 'imitation' and 'nature', are subject to revealing equivocation. When poets and painters are said to 'imitate nature', the nature meant is, first and last, nature as portrayed in great poetry and art. The point, as Piles forcefully puts it in the 'Portrait of the ideal artist' prefacing his collection of the lives of real ones, is not to learn to imitate nature *directly*, but instead to begin by imitating her as selected and 'rectified' in the noblest works of the past.[10] For all the Renaissance propounds the view of imitation as the sort of illusionistic replication typified by the tale of Zeuxis's grapes, it also ceaselessly rehearses the parallel story of how the legendary Greek proceeded when commissioned to paint the portrait of Helen. Faced with the task of portraying not merely the most beautiful woman who ever lived, but the very Image and Type of womanly Beauty itself, Zeuxis did not (as the story of the grapes might suggest) choose the most beautiful woman he could find, but a number of different women, selecting each one's best feature (this one's eyes and another's throat; here the nose, there the figure) in order to compose from the collected parts the closest possible approximation of Helen's finally ideal, and therefore inimitable, loveliness. And for work of this sort, being as it is so wholly a product of art rather than of nature *per se*, only the already existing patrimony of artistic creation can serve as a model.

What is at issue in the imitation of nature is thus rarely (if ever) the world of empirical experience only fully claimed for active exploration and representation in the northern seventeenth century of Baconian science and the 'descriptive' art of the Dutch Golden Age. Whether viewed, as in Scaliger or Dolce, from an Aristotelian perspective as a 'form' abstracted or deduced from (without however being at all reducible to) empirical observation, or viewed, as most spectacularly and influentially in Lomazzo, as a Platonic Idea from which the empirical itself is ultimately seen to derive, the 'nature' poets and painters imitate is finally a product of imaginative 'invention', something at once discovered and created beyond and even in defiance of natural experience. Whence, in seventeenth-century France, the neoclassical Academy's conception of 'la belle nature' in contradistinction to nature itself, or Piles's authoritative

---

[10] De Piles, *Abrégé*, p. 17.

insistence that the truly great painter shuns what he calls the 'poverty of ordinary nature' (*Abrégé* 222) in order to imitate her, not in her 'particular products', deemed invariably 'defective', but in her 'principle' or 'intention' (21–2). For it is only at the level of her 'intention', as *natura naturans* rather than *natura naturata*, that nature can be said to be 'perfect' and therefore worthy of imitation.

Besides, as Lee (citing Irving Babbitt) reminds us, *ut pictura*'s true concern was never really physical or external nature at all, but rather 'human nature, and human nature not as it is, but, in Aristotle's phrase, as it ought to be, "raised . . . above all that is local and accidental, purged of all that is abnormal and eccentric, so as to be in the highest sense representative" '.[11] What was ultimately at stake in *ut pictura* was then the promotion and, as the early modern period progressed towards its culmination (or catastrophe) in the advent of the modern itself at the close of the Enlightenment, the *defence* of a certain poetic idealism variously reflected in the values of 'decorum', noble 'expressiveness', and the overarching 'rule of art' governing not only pictorial naturalism, but the baser appetites with which, for all the Renaissance prized it, painting remained identified in the post-Tridentine south as much as the Reformation north. Which is why *ut pictura* came to an end when it did. By the close of the eighteenth century, the deliberately anti-poetic version of realism associated with the rise of the novel had taken hold. Accordingly, the idealism of which *ut pictura* had been the bearer had shifted ground, turning towards what Lessing, Kant, and the Romantics show to be the non-visual, otherworldly realm of the Sublime.

---

[11] Lee, '*Ut pictura poesis*', p. 9.

17

Conceptions of style

Debora Shuger

Before the late seventeenth century, the language of criticism develops within the rhetorical tradition. Renaissance discussions of style accordingly centre on prose, a focus reflecting the cultural priority of the humanist paideia over vernacular poetry throughout the period.[1] The fullest and most important of such discussions occur in the great scholarly neo-Latin rhetorics, although these subsequently inform vernacular rhetoric, as well as poetics, music theory, and art criticism. Because stylistic concepts evolve within the pan-European culture of neo-Latin humanism, it seems possible to sketch a general outline of Renaissance stylistics; yet because the cultural and political functions of these rhetorical categories shift from country to country, such an overview needs to be supplemented by consideration of specific national contexts. This chapter will therefore examine the dominant trends in Renaissance stylistics but also their divergent ideological exfoliation in France and England.

Renaissance terminology for stylistic analysis draws upon four principal categories, all borrowed from classical rhetoric. Style may be described in terms of (1) the *genera dicendi* – the Roman categories of low/plain, middle, and grand style (or their Greek equivalents);[2] (2) its classical prototypes; for example, a style may be labelled as Senecan, Tacitean, or Ciceronian; (3) its characteristic features, especially syntactic; Renaissance rhetorics thus classify styles as periodic, curt, copious, laconic, pointed, loose; and (4) the related distinction between Attic (brief), Asiatic (copious), and Rhodian (intermediate) styles. These categories are not exclusive; one may describe an author as using an Asiatic middle style or pointed Senecan brevity. Nor are they unambiguous. In Renaissance (as in classical) rhetoric, for example, the plain style includes an informal conversational manner, the type of speech characteristic of 'low' persons, the unartistic plainness of logical/scholastic argument, and a graceful cultivated urbanity. Montaigne, Mistress Quickly, Aquinas, and Dryden are all in one sense or another plain stylists.

[1] Marc Fumaroli, *L'âge de l'éloquence: rhétorique et 'res literaria' de la Renaissance au seuil de l'époque classique* (Geneva: Droz, 1980), pp. 19–30.
[2] While Renaissance poetics tend to relate the *genera* to social distinctions (the grand style for kings, the low style for commoners), the rhetorics prefer to analyse the *genera* in terms of their functions: teaching, delighting, moving.

The significance of these categories does not lie in their descriptive precision; they are crucial because Renaissance theorists use these terms to relate the formal characteristics of discourse to larger cultural issues. Renaissance rhetorics, that is, employ stylistic categories to articulate the political, philosophical, and theological implications of lexical or syntactic patternings. Modern scholarship on Renaissance rhetoric, in turn, dates from the recognition that the sixteenth- and seventeenth-century rhetorical controversies are charged with ideological valence: that changes in what appears to be a formalist aesthetic in fact adumbrate the central tensions in Renaissance intellectual and political history.

From their original publication between 1914 and 1929 up to the 1980s, Morris Croll's essays on Renaissance anti-Ciceronianism provided the basic model for virtually all Anglo-American scholarship on Renaissance style.[3] Yoking an impressive grasp of neo-Latin rhetorical theory with a firm sense of the cultural resonances of style, Croll developed a historical paradigm at once elegant and erudite centring on the opposition between Ciceronian and what he called 'Attic' stylistic ideals.

For Croll, Ciceronianism, with its commitment to a single authoritative model, embodied the conservative formalism of the Age of Orthodoxy.[4] Stressing words over matter, Ciceronianism encouraged an ornamental and oral style structured by the musical cadences of the period and by the elaborate aural play of the sophistic figures of sound. Such a style is, Croll argued, fundamentally *rhetorical* both in its appeal to the sub-rational pleasures of the ear and emotions and in its reliance on cultural commonplaces. While perfectly suited to persuade an unlettered auditory, it offered nothing to an 'intellect intent upon the discovery of reality'.[5]

Politian and Erasmus inaugurated the anti-Ciceronian reaction, but a fully developed alternative stylistic model only emerged in the last quarter of the sixteenth century. Between 1567 and 1590, two leading continental scholars, Marc-Antoine Muret and Justus Lipsius, worked out a new conception of style, whose origins were philosophic rather than rhetorical. This style, which Croll identified with the Attic plain style, substitutes Silver Latin models for Cicero. More important, it substitutes the figures of thought – aphorism, antithesis, paradox, sententiae – for the rhetorical figures of sound and replaces Cicero's musical periods with a briefer and less elaborate syntactic structure.[6] These formal changes in turn reflect a radically different understanding of discourse. The anti-Ciceronians aimed at expressivity rather than formal beauty; the 'brevities, suppressions, and

---

[3] These essays were posthumously collected in *'Attic' and Baroque prose style: essays by Morris Croll*, ed. J. M. Patrick and R. O. Evans with J. M. Wallace (Princeton: Princeton University Press, 1966).
[4] Croll, *'Attic' and Baroque*, pp. 110, 120.   [5] *Ibid.*, pp. 54–6, 59–60.
[6] *Ibid.*, pp. 18–21, 54, 87–9.

contortions' of late Renaissance atticism attempt to capture the thought processes of 'the free individual self who should be the ultimate judge of the opinions of all the sects and schools'.[7] Yet, while allied to the plain style by its philosophic intentions, such prose also strives for the sombre magnificence and spiritual intensity characteristic of Baroque art. The combination of these potentially antithetic aims creates a style of allusive, dense brevity and expressive contortion able to articulate the 'secret experiences of arduous and solitary minds', the disillusion of the modern intellectual under the absolutist regimes of the seventeenth century. The history of prose style in the late Renaissance thus narrates the transition from the Ciceronian formalism of an oral, ritualized, and traditional culture to a style capable of expressing the libertine, sceptical, individualist, and rationalistic impulses that define modern consciousness.[8]

For most of the twentieth century, scholarship on Renaissance rhetoric has worked within Croll's model, focusing on the rise of modern prose,[9] on the anti-Ciceronian plain style,[10] and on the opposition between rhetoric and philosophy.[11] Disagreement has largely centred on whether science, Protestantism, Ramism, or utilitarianism (or any combination thereof) played a more decisive role in the evolution of modern prose than Croll's anti-Ciceronian savants,[12] while Richard Lanham gave the whole argument a deconstructivist twist by defending the aesthetic playfulness of 'Ciceronian' rhetorical ornament against the logocentric plain style.[13]

The first major revision of the Crollian model, however, comes with Marc Fumaroli's immense and immensely learned history of French

[7] *Ibid.*, pp. 86, 181.   [8] *Ibid.*, pp. 8–11, 62–4, 79, 95, 110, 194–5, 201.

[9] Robert Adolph, *The rise of modern prose style* (Cambridge, MA: M.I.T. Press, 1968); R. F. Jones, 'Science and English prose style in the third quarter of the seventeenth century', in *The seventeenth century: studies in the history of English thought and literature from Bacon to Pope* (Stanford: Stanford University Press, 1951), pp. 75–110; George Williamson, *The Senecan amble: prose form from Bacon to Collier* (Chicago: University of Chicago Press, 1951).

[10] Wesley Trimpi, *Ben Jonson's poems: a study of the plain style* (Stanford: Stanford University Press, 1962); Williamson, *Senecan amble*.

[11] Samuel Ijsseling, *Rhetoric and philosophy in conflict: an historical survey*, trans. P. Dunphy (The Hague: M. Nijhoff, 1976); Richard Lanham, *The motives of eloquence: literary rhetoric in the Renaissance* (New Haven: Yale University Press, 1976); Stanley Fish, *Self-consuming artifacts: the experience of seventeenth-century literature* (Berkeley: University of California Press, 1972); Jerrold Seigel, *Rhetoric and philosophy in Renaissance humanism: the union of eloquence and wisdom, Petrarch to Valla* (Princeton: Princeton University Press, 1968).

[12] Adolph, *The rise*, p. 115; R. F. Jones, 'The moral sense of simplicity', in *Studies in honor of Frederick W. Shipley*, Washington University Studies, new series 14 (1942), pp. 265–88; Perry Miller, *The New England mind: the seventeenth century* (New York: Macmillan, 1939), pp. 327–58; Walter Ong, *Ramus, method, and the decay of dialogue: from the art of discourse to the art of reason* (Cambridge, MA: Harvard University Press, 1958).

[13] See Richard Lanham, *The motives of eloquence: literary rhetoric in the Renaissance* (New Haven: Yale University Press, 1976).

Renaissance rhetoric, *L'âge de l'éloquence*, published in 1980.[14] Fumaroli abandons Croll's Hegelian account of the gradual triumph of the modern *Geist*, instead viewing Renaissance stylistic controversies in terms of French *political* history: the simultaneous emergence of a centralized nation-state and French classicism out of the institutional and ideological struggles between the court, the magistrates, and the post-Tridentine church.[15] Fumaroli, unlike Croll, recognizes the crucial change separating classical from Renaissance rhetorical theory: Renaissance societies were monarchies; they lacked anything equivalent to the ancient forum and senate that could serve as a venue for significant public oratory.[16] Except for an abortive attempt during the political crises of the 1590s to revive the Ciceronian grand style, French secular rhetoric thus stressed the plain-style genres of written prose by which alone power could be negotiated in monarchic regimes.[17] The central debates in Renaissance rhetoric do not oppose an anti-Ciceronian plain style to the ornate and passionate full-ness of Cicero's speeches but to what Fumaroli calls 'Ciceronian atticism' – the style of Cicero's familiar epistles and philosophical dialogues, a style characterized by elegance, lucidity, and propriety rather than by the acoustic and emotional devices of popular oratory.[18] The heart of Fumaroli's argument lies in his claim that these stylistic alternatives arti-culate the fundamental socio-political divisions within French élite culture.

Such divisions distinguish both the anti-Ciceronians and Ciceronians into two main groups. The first type of anti-Ciceronianism, which closely resembles Croll's Attic style, borrows from early imperial rhetoric to express the solitary consciousness of the melancholy '*grande âme*', dis-dainful of courtly delicacies and empty compliment. Abandoning the now-hollow modes of civic eloquence, intellectuals like Lipsius carved out styles capable of expressing their sense of heroic selfhood and contemplat-ive inwardness – styles characterized by brevity, wit, archaism, innuendo, paradox, and suggestive density.[19]

---

[14] For an English summary, see Fumaroli's 'Rhetoric, politics, and society: from Italian Ciceronianism to French classicism', in *Renaissance eloquence: studies in the theory and practice of Renaissance rhetoric*, ed. J. J. Murphy (Berkeley: University of California Press, 1983), pp. 253–73.

[15] Fumaroli, *L'âge de l'éloquence*, pp. 197, 432, 498, 667.

[16] Fumaroli, 'Rhetoric', p. 258; similar observations can be found in Nicholas Caussin, *De eloquentia sacra et humana, libri XVI* (1619), 3rd edn (Paris: Joh. Mauritus, 1630), p. 759; Johann-Henricus Ursinus, *Ecclesiastes, sive de sacris concionibus libri tres* (Frankfurt: Hermsdorffius, 1659), preface; Jacques Davy du Perron, *Avant-Discours de rhétorique ou traitté de l'éloquence*, in *Les diverses œuvres de l'illustrissime Cardinal Du Perron* (Paris: A. Estienne, 1622), p. 759.

[17] Fumaroli, *L'âge de l'éloquence*, pp. 492–503, 513, 570.

[18] *Ibid.*, pp. 54, 227; see also Adolph, *The rise*, pp. 141–3.

[19] Fumaroli, *L'âge de l'éloquence*, pp. 59–60, 82–3, 90, 127–34, 153–60, 173, 677; see also Juan Luis Vives, *De ratione dicendi* (1533), *Joannis Ludovici Vivis Valentini opera omnia*, 8 vols. (Valencia: B. Montfort, 1782–90), vol. II, p. 178; Justus Lipsius, *Epistolica*

This version of anti-Ciceronianism took deeper root in Spain than France, where a second type of anti-Ciceronianism predominated, especially among the *aristocratie de Robe* – the élite circle of Gallican magistrates, advocates, and humanist scholars. This magisterial anti-Ciceronianism abjures expressivity as well as ornament; severely impersonal, it relies on a 'rhetoric of citations' – the incorporation of untranslated swatches of classical and patristic material – to convey its sense of the unity of truth, its commitment to the timeless authority of ancient wisdom, its humanistic primitivism. Montaigne borrowed his style from this rhetoric of citations while at the same time recasting it into a subjective and sceptical mould.[20]

The rhetoric of citations seems peculiar to the northern European *respublica litterarum*; a radically different stylistic ideal developed in sixteenth-century Italy. Based on Cicero's non-oratorical writings, this style has both a courtly and humanistic lineage. The first type of Ciceronian atticism becomes the normative style of the Italian courts; graceful, sweet, and yet simple, it evinces the *sprezzatura* and *negligentia diligens* of Castiglione's courtier.[21] But a more philosophic and erudite Ciceronianism developed alongside this aulic version. Thus in Bembo an aesthetic Platonism tinged with Paduan naturalism exfoliates into an ideal of stylistic beauty and purity – a *secular* aesthetic that implicitly divorces the beautiful artefact from either moral or spiritual obligations. So Etienne Dolet, one of the few sixteenth-century French Ciceronians, argues against both classical and Christian orthodoxy that the true orator need not be a good man but just one who speaks ornately and sweetly.[22] Both Bembo and Dolet reject any notion of stylistic individualism or expressivity; eloquence strives towards Beauty, not the revelation of personality.[23] Melanchthon's Protestant Ciceronianism has a less Platonic flavour; his Cicero serves as the model for a lucid philosophic prose, whose beauty results from the perfect adaptation of form to function.[24] But both Italian

---

institutio (Frankfurt: J. Wechel and P. Fischer, 1591), pp. 17–23. The *Epistolica institutio* is available in the recent edition of R. V. Young and M. T. Hester, *Principles of letter-writing: a bilingual text of Justi Lipsii Epistolica institutio* (Carbondale: Southern Illinois University Press, 1996).

[20] Fumaroli, *L'âge de l'éloquence*, pp. 431–2, 439, 444–5, 468, 473, 488–9, 551, 566, 663–5, 681.

[21] *Ibid.*, pp. 80–1, 88–9.

[22] Etienne Dolet, *L'Erasmianus sive Ciceronianus* (1535), ed. E. V. Telle (Geneva: Droz, 1974), p. 107.

[23] Fumaroli, *L'âge de l'éloquence*, pp. 111, 116–23, 174.

[24] Philip Melanchthon, *Elementorum rhetorices libri duo* (1531), *Opera quae supersunt omnia*, ed. C. G. Bretschneider, 28 vols. (1834–60; New York: Johnson Reprint Corp., 1963), vol. XIII, pp. 421, 459–61, 501; 'Reply of Philip Melanchthon in behalf of Ermolao', trans. Quirinus Breen, in Quirinus Breen, *Christianity and humanism: studies in the history of ideas*, ed. N. P. Ross (Grand Rapids: Eerdmans, 1968), pp. 55–61.

and northern Ciceronians stressed the written, plain-style virtues of naturalness, polish, beauty, and clarity; they advocated an Attic, not oratorical,
Ciceronianism.[25]

Scaliger's Virgilian *Poetices libri septem* (1561) fuses humanist Ciceronianism to an Augustan aesthetic that identifies artistic maturity with the
flowering of a fully developed civilization – and hence not with the pris-
tine simplicity of Homeric or republican antiquity. Classic art – correct,
regular, polished – thus becomes the achievement of a centralized court
culture.[26] In the seventeenth century, this Augustan Ciceronianism becomes the basis of French classicism. Under Louis XIV aulic and humanist Ciceronianism combine to form a new national-monarchic style that
symbolized Richelieu's union of the two aristocracies of sword and pen
into a single élite dependent on the crown. Urbane, correct, natural,
dignified, this new style marks the triumph of vernacular 'polite literature'
and monarchic art over both the flowery mannerisms of French Jesuit
preaching and the erudite severity of the Gallican rhetoric of citations
– the triumph of secular court culture over Tridentine internationalism
and the *respublica litterarum*, of *belles-lettres* over *lectio divina* and *bonae
litterae*. Fumaroli's study, which covers approximately the same time
period as Croll's, thus reverses its conclusions; at least in France, poetics
and rhetoric move *towards* Ciceronianism, although this term has a
different meaning in Fumaroli than it does for Croll.

The only form of significant popular oratory in the Renaissance was
ecclesiastical; if Cicero and Demosthenes were to return from the dead,
as Ramus put it, they would become preachers.[27] The religious conflicts
of the post-Reformation period sparked an unprecedented interest in
questions of biblical rhetoric and sacred oratory: the sixteenth century
produced about seventy sacred rhetorics, the seventeenth over a hundred.
English vernacular rhetorics give a misleading picture of Renaissance
homiletic theory. Often markedly puritan, they generally adopt the
medieval sermon manuals' puritanical distrust of deliberate art.[28] The
scholarly neo-Latin rhetorics, both Catholic and Protestant, are less
austere. Beginning with Erasmus's *Ecclesiastes* (1535), these texts draw
on the full resources of classical theory in order to discover the linguistic

[25] Fumaroli, *L'âge de l'éloquence*, pp. 460, 601–3, 612–18, 666; Dolet, *L'Erasmianus*,
pp. 42–3, 50, 58, 69, 83–5, 95; see also Peter Ramus, *Ciceronianus* (Paris: A. Wechel,
1557), pp. 19, 99, 120–4; Vives, *De ratione*, pp. 137, 143, 152.
[26] Fumaroli, *L'âge de l'éloquence*, pp. 452–4, 575, 666.   [27] Ramus, *Ciceronianus*, p. 61.
[28] Debora Shuger, *Sacred rhetoric: the Christian grand style in the English Renaissance*
(Princeton: Princeton University Press, 1988), pp. 50–4, 69–71, 93–5, 100, 108–9;
Adolph, *The rise*, pp. 78–130, 191–4; Jones, 'The moral sense', and 'The attack on
pulpit eloquence in the Restoration: an episode in the development of the neo-classical
standard for prose', in *The seventeenth century: studies in the history of English thought
and literature from Bacon to Pope* (Stanford: Stanford University Press, 1951), pp. 111–42.

forms capable of expressing God's grandeur and eliciting spiritual desire. They therefore generally locate preaching (and biblical eloquence) in the *genus grande* – the style of passionate oratory on the most serious and important subjects.

But they do not, in general, advocate a *Ciceronian* grand style. Rather, the two principal factors in the development of the late Renaissance Christian grand style are, first, the assimilation of Hellenistic rhetorical theory, especially the works of Demetrius, Hermogenes, and Longinus;[29] and second, what may be called the 'theorization' of rhetoric – the attempt to ground a sacred aesthetic on epistemic, psychological, and theological premises.[30] The rhetorics most deeply influenced by Hellenistic sources describe the sacred grand style as fraught with mystic solemnity, numinous darkness, and sublime exaltation. Other sacred rhetorics combine Roman rhetorical theory with Augustine's psychology of the will and an Aristotelian epistemology to create a stylistic ideal at once vividly theatrical and powerfully expressive.[31]

The result is often strikingly unclassical (or at least un-neoclassical). Matthias Flacius Illyricus's *Clavis Scripturae Sacrae*,[32] emphasizes the pregnant obscurity, harsh asymmetry, figural richness, vivid theatricality, and mysterious solemnity of biblical rhetoric (which he locates in the *genus grande*). The *Clavis*, which draws heavily on Demetrius and Hermogenes, is explicitly anti-Ciceronian, stressing brevity over *copia*, difficult suggestiveness over harmonious lucidity, asymmetry over periodicity, the numinous over the natural.

But Flacius's massive study slightly *antedates* Muret and Lipsius's conversion to anti-Ciceronianism. This near-simultaneous emergence of biblical and neo-Stoic anti-Ciceronianism points to a crucial and unremarked link between rhetorical 'modernism' and what Barbara Lewalski has

---

[29] Shuger, *Sacred rhetoric*, pp. 154–92; see also John Monfasani, *George of Trebizond: a biography and a study of his rhetoric and logic* (Leiden: Brill, 1976); Annabel Patterson, *Hermogenes and the Renaissance: seven ideas of style* (Princeton: Princeton University Press, 1970).

[30] Shuger, *Sacred rhetoric*, pp. 193–240; Ruth Wallerstein, *Studies in seventeenth-century poetic* (Madison: University of Wisconsin Press, 1950), pp. 14–81; Louis Martz, *The poetry of meditation: a study in English religious literature of the seventeenth century* (New Haven: Yale University Press, 1954); Klaus Dockhorn, 'Rhetorica movet: protestantischer Humanismus und karolingische Renaissance', in *Rhetorik: Beiträge zu ihrer Geschichte in Deutschland vom 16.–20. Jahrhundert*, ed. H. Schanze (Frankfurt: Athenaion, 1974), pp. 17–42; Barbara Kiefer Lewalski, *Protestant poetics and the seventeenth-century religious lyric* (Princeton: Princeton University Press, 1979); John O'Malley, *Praise and blame in Renaissance Rome: rhetoric, doctrine, and reform in the sacred orators of the papal court*, c. 1450–1521 (Durham, NC: Duke University Press, 1979).

[31] See Fumaroli, *L'âge de l'éloquence*, pp. 147–9, 258–74; Shuger, *Sacred rhetoric*, pp. 194–240.

[32] First published in 1562 and regularly thereafter until 1719, the work was widely available in England; see Shuger, *Sacred rhetoric*, pp. 113–17.

termed 'Protestant poetics'.[33] The similarities between sacred and secular anti-Ciceronianism reflect the pervasive impact of late antique spirituality – whether Stoic, Neoplatonic, or Christian – on Renaissance cultural forms, the same spirituality suffusing the late antique rhetorics. This lineage helps explain the fundamentally religious cast of many English anti-Ciceronians (most notably Andrewes, Donne, and Browne), as well as the pervasive seventeenth-century English emphasis on the affective/ expressive ends of language over its cognitive or aesthetic aims – an emphasis characteristic of both Stoic and Augustinian rhetorical theory.[34] The complex intertwining of rationalist and mystical tendencies in anti-Ciceronian rhetorical theory may likewise elucidate the curious fusion of Tacitean realism and Catholic devotion in writers like More, Lipsius, and Muret, or the equally unfamiliar mixtures of libertinism and spirituality that one finds in Nashe, Donne, Chapman, Greville, Burton – and Erasmus. The rhetorical tradition registers and explicates the unfamiliar interpenetration of sacred and secular impulses characteristic of early modern culture.

*

Over the course of the seventeenth century, English stylistic trends follow the same trajectory that Fumaroli observes in French prose. Thus George Williamson's *The Senecan amble* documents both the explosion of anti-Ciceronian styles under the Stuarts and their gradual displacement by a 'polite' Ciceronian plain style during the second half of the century. The parallel evolution of English and continental stylistics results, at least in part, from the widespread use of continental rhetorics in the English schools. Even a rather elementary textbook like Thomas Farnaby's *Index rhetoricus* (1625) draws on Alsted, Caussin, Chytraeus, Erasmus, Hyperius, Keckermann, Soarez, D'Estrebay, Sturm, Trebizond, and Vossius, as well as the full range of classical authorities. Tutors at Oxford and Cambridge regularly assigned Caussin's *De eloquentia sacra et humana*, Vossius's *Commentariorum rhetoricorum*, and Keckermann's *Systema rhetoricae* to their undergraduates.[35]

However, except for Thomas Wilson's *Arte of rhetorique*, the English themselves produced nothing comparable to these massively erudite continental treatises, partly because England long lacked a scholarly press willing to publish Latin tomes the size of a major metropolitan phone

---

[33] See Barbara K. Lewalski, *Protestant poetics and the seventeenth-century religious lyric* (Princeton: Princeton University Press, 1979).

[34] Fumaroli, *L'âge de l'éloquence*, pp. 59–62, 153–8; Shuger, *Sacred rhetoric*, pp. 227–40. See, for example, James Howell, *Familiar letters or epistolae Ho-Elianae*, 3 vols. (London: Dent, 1903), vol. I, pp. 14, 254; Samuel Clarke, *A collection of the lives of ten eminent divines* (London: W. Miller, 1662), p. 427; Izaak Walton, *The lives*, intro. G. Saintsbury (London: Oxford University Press, 1927), pp. 49, 75.

[35] Shuger, *Sacred rhetoric*, pp. 110–17.

directory, partly because many English rhetorics, following Ramus, restrict *elocutio* to the enumeration of tropes and schemes, dropping consideration of style *per se*.

Yet abundant, if fragmentary, evidence suggests that early modern Englishmen understood style as politically significant form – the crucial premise of both classical and continental rhetoric. Thus Puttenham's rhetorical *Arte of English poesie* (1589) interprets late sixteenth-century aulic style as both mirroring and enacting 'the exercise of power and privilege' in the Elizabethan court.[36] A similar paradigm can be discerned in Richard Flecknoe's 1653 account of Tudor-Stuart rhetorical fashions:

> That of Queen *Elizabeths* dayes, *flaunting* and *pufted* like her *Apparell*: That of King *Jame's*, *Regis ad exemplum*, inclining much to the *Learned* and *Erudite*, as (if you observe it) in the late Kings dayes, the *Queen* having a mayne *ascendancy* and *predominance* in the Court, the *French style* with the Courtyers was chiefly in *vogue* and Fashion.[37]

Regis ad exemplum is one way to look at it. A century earlier, a different stylistic politics surfaces in Wilson's *Arte of rhetorique*, which advocates a single 'classless' style as the linguistic corollary of English national self-consciousness:

> Do we not speake, because we would have other to understand us, or is not the tongue geven for this ende, that one might know what another meaneth? . . . Therefore, either we must make a difference of Englishe, and saie some is learned Englishe, and other some is rude Englishe, or the one is courte talke, the other is countrey speache, or els we must of necessitee, banishe al suche affected Rhetorique, and use altogether one maner of language.[38]

This feeling for style as the expression of national and class identity surfaces in unexpected quarters: in, for example, the late sixteenth-century debates over English versification, which describe quantitative metrics in terms of Roman law absolutism, while associating rhyme with the 'gothic', common law valorization of immemorial custom. Both Sidney's Arcadian rhetoric and *The Faerie Queene*'s 'gothic' archaisms seem to insinuate a defence of aristocratic privilege against the encroachments of centralized monarchy, whose official style – the humanist style of Cecil and Elizabeth – was conspicuously brief, plain, and sententious.[39]

---

[36] Frank Whigham, *Ambition and privilege: the social tropes of Elizabethan courtesy theory* (Berkeley: University of California Press, 1984), p. 30.

[37] Richard Flecknoe, *Miscellania* (London: T. R., 1653), p. 77.

[38] Thomas Wilson, *Arte of rhetorique* (1553), ed. T. Derrick, The Renaissance Imagination 1 (New York: Garland, 1982), p. 329.

[39] Richard Helgerson, *Forms of nationhood: the Elizabethan writing of England* (Chicago: University of Chicago Press, 1992), pp. 21–62; Mary Thomas Crane, *Framing authority: sayings, self, and society in sixteenth-century England* (Princeton: Princeton University Press, 1993), pp. 116–21, 130–5.

As these examples indicate, English stylistic canons and controversies, like their French equivalents, adumbrate the socio-political tensions attendant upon the emergence of the early modern nation-state. But Fumaroli's account of the politics of style in Renaissance France cannot be transposed *simpliciter* into an English context. The continued use of law French among English jurists inhibited the development of a 'common law' style comparable to the anti-Ciceronianism cultivated by Gallican magistrates. English anti-Ciceronianism, in fact, often had aulic rather than *érudit* associations, as Joseph Hall's comparison of Senecan brevity to portrait miniatures implies. King James's preference for 'plaine, honest, naturall, comelie, cleane, short, and sentencious' language likewise points to fundamental divergences between English and continental political styles. In Catholic Europe, Ciceronianism implied absolutist ideology and religious orthodoxy.[40] In England, Ciceronianism had no official standing outside the classroom. Hooker and Milton, the two great English Ciceronians, would probably have neither received nor accepted membership in Richelieu's Académie Française. However much England borrowed from continental rhetorics, when these texts migrated across the Channel, they did not necessarily retain their original ideological valences. Hence Richard Holdsworth, from 1637 to 1643 the Master of Emmanuel College, Cambridge – a fiercely Puritan institution – regularly assigned Caussin's Jesuit rhetoric to his undergraduates; the 'English Seneca', Joseph Hall, was a royalist bishop; and Milton, England's Virgil, a republican Independent.

As these examples suggest, English stylistic theories during the Renaissance do not manifest a clear official/oppositional dichotomy; indeed, the distinguishing feature of English rhetorical practice during this period may be the absence of a recognized official or orthodox stylistic norm. Hence in England the relation between style and ideology appears far more provisional and fluid than on the Continent. English writers sharing a single political interest draw on vastly different rhetorical models. Thus, for instance, Spenser's neo-gothic romance, Sidney's Arcadian rhetoric, and Haywood's Tacitean history of Henry IV articulate the aristocratic Protestant values of the Leicester–Essex circle. Conversely, the same stylistic allegiance may serve opposing political ideologies: of the two editions of Longinus printed in seventeenth-century England, one was the work of a royalist, the other of a Cromwellian.[41] Both stylistic thought and

---

[40] Williamson, *Senecan amble*, pp. 192n, 194.
[41] Annabel Patterson, *Reading between the lines* (Madison: University of Wisconsin Press, 1993), pp. 258–9. On the passage of English Taciteanism from a courtly to an oppositional/subversive mode, see Malcolm Smuts, 'Court-centered politics and the uses of Roman historians, c. 1590–1630', in *Culture and politics in early Stuart England*, ed. K. Sharpe and P. Lake (Stanford: Stanford University Press, 1993), pp. 21–43.

practice in Renaissance England thus resist diachronic schematization. The history of Tudor/Stuart style might rather be configured as a series of micro-narratives tracing the fluctuating, experimental, and often unexpected alignments between English socio-political groupings and the dominant rhetorical categories of the European Renaissance.

18

Sir Philip Sidney's *An apology for poetry*

Wesley Trimpi

This treatment of Sir Philip Sidney's *An apology for poetry* supports the views that his humanistic defence of literature [*poesis*] is, in its broadest interpretation, Ciceronian; that his conception of the poetic 'image' derives from the scholastic analysis of Christian psychology; and that his most pervasive literary debts are to Aristotle and Horace. It emphasizes, in addition, the importance of Aristotle's *Rhetoric* in Sidney's analysis of poetic subject-matter in relation to the *materiae* of the other arts and sciences; and, on the basis of sources untraced until now, shows that, by rejecting Neoplatonic attitudes towards poetry, his argument is more consistent than previously recognized.[1]

Since poetry has fallen from 'the highest estimation of learning' to be 'the laughing-stock of children', Sidney proposes to bring four 'available proofs' to its defence (96.2–4). For ease of reference, we shall refer to these proofs as (1) by antiquity, (2) by etymology, (3) by 'kinds', and (4) by purpose. Each of the last three arises reasonably out of its preceding proof, and, as will be apparent, overlaps to some degree with each of the other proofs. Taken together these constitute Sidney's central argument and form, even before their subsequent recapitulation and amplification, just under half of the treatise as a whole (96.8–115.34).

The first proof is primarily introductory and argues for the pre-eminence of poetry on the basis of its antiquity. In most cultures the earliest, and often the most distinguished, writings have been in verse, and this has

---

[1] Sidney's treatise exists in two forms: *The defence of poesie* printed by William Ponsonby in London in 1595 and *An apologie for poetrie* printed by Henry Olney in London in the same year. The *Defence* is included in A. Feuillerat's *The complete works of Sir Philip Sidney*, 4 vols. (Cambridge: Cambridge University Press, 1912–26), vol. III, pp. 3–46; the *Apologie*, in G. G. Smith's *Elizabethan critical essays*, 2 vols. (Oxford: Oxford University Press, 1904), vol. I, pp. 148–207 (with valuable notes) and has been re-edited by Geoffrey Shepherd in *An apology for poetry or the defence of poesy* (London: Nelson, 1965) with some textual conflation. Shepherd's treatment of Sidney in his introduction and notes is consistently well informed and sensibly balanced; his edition is cited, by page and line, in the text. In addition to Shepherd, the reader should consult K. Eden, *Poetic and legal fiction in the Aristotelian tradition* (Princeton: Princeton University Press, 1986), pp. 143–7, 157–75. Further commentary may be found in the editions of J. A. van Dorsten (Oxford: Oxford University Press, 1966) and F. G. Robinson (Indianapolis: Bobbs-Merrill, 1970).

even been true (anticipating the fourth proof) of historians and philosophers. This is true even of the prose of Plato, since his dialogues 'feigneth
many honest burgesses of Athens', and poetically describe 'the circumstances of their meetings, as the well ordering of a banquet, the delicacy of
a walk, with interlacing mere tales, as Gyges' Ring, and others, which
who knoweth not to be flowers of poetry did never walk into Apollo's
garden' (97.14–20; cf. 128.8–130.10). Among philosophers, Plato,
along with Boethius (114.19–24), has the greatest gift for fiction and therefore suffers less from eristic abstractions than the 'moral philosophers'
whom Sidney later caricatures in scholastic dress.

The second proof begins the main steps in the logical argument, and
Sidney takes the etymologies for 'poet' as his point of departure. The
Latin term for 'poets', *vates*, means diviners, oracles, or prophets, whose
words include, not only the *sortes Virgilianae* about the future and the
carmina against present evils, but also David's 'notable *prosopopeias*' in
the 'heavenly poesy' of the psalms which make us see 'God coming in His
majesty' (98.20–99.21). Yet, as corroborated by the third proof of 'kinds',
even psalmistry must be set aside to make room for the activity from
which the Greeks derive the name 'poet' itself, *poiein* or 'to make'. Sidney
characterizes the activity of 'a maker' principally 'by marking the scope'
of the other arts and sciences, each of which has the given 'works of
Nature for his principal object'. While each other art and science is committed to treat its 'proposed matter' assigned to it by Nature, 'only the
poet, disdaining to be tied to any such subjection . . . within the narrow
warrant of her gifts', ranges 'within the zodiac of his own wit'. Nature has
'never set forth the earth in so rich tapestry as divers poets have done';
while 'her world is brazen, the poets only deliver a golden' (99.33–100.33).
Turning from natural settings to human beings, Nature has never produced,
as private virtues, 'so true a lover as Theagenes, so constant a friend
as Pylades, so valiant a man as Orlando', or, among public virtues, 'so
right a prince as Xenophon's Cyrus', or, as a combination of public and
private virtues (like those possessed by Spenser's King Arthur) 'so excellent a man every way as Virgil's Aeneas'. Nor should the fact that these
literary portraits are not 'essential' (that is, products of nature), but
exist 'in imitation or fiction' (that is, as products of art), be of concern.
'For any understanding knoweth the skill of the artificer standeth in
that *Idea* or fore-conceit of the work, and not in the work itself' – as it
would if the work *were* a product of Nature, having God as its ultimate
'maker' who 'makes' by creating and, hence, whose 'skill' stands directly
'in [the existence of] the work itself'. 'And that the poet hath that *Idea* is
manifest, by delivering them forth in such excellency as he hath imagined
them.' Such delivery is nevertheless 'substantial', since while Nature might
produce one particularly excellent Cyrus, Xenophon, if we understand

his 'making' aright, has bestowed 'a Cyrus upon the world [in order] to make many Cyruses' of those princes who can imitate him (100.34–101.13).

These famous expressions of the second proof are echoed later in the recapitulation of the four proofs (120.12–36) and in answering the charge that poets are liars (123.28–124.27). In the second of these, the answer is that the poet 'nothing affirms, and therefore never lieth'. Only the arts and disciplines with a specialized body of knowledge to learn and communicate can fall into error and mislead. 'The poet never maketh any circles about your imagination, to conjure you to believe for true what he writes.' While reading 'in History looking for truth, they go away full fraught with falsehood, so in Poesy looking but for fiction, they shall use the narration but as an imaginative ground-plot of a profitable invention' (see n. 15). In the recapitulation, Sidney briefly summarizes the argument of the second proof in his most incisive definition of *poiein*: 'Whereas other arts retain themselves within their subject, and receive, as it were, their being from it, the poet only bringeth his own stuff, and doth not learn a conceit out of a matter, but maketh matter for a conceit' (120.19–22). With all these passages in mind, brief comments on two issues of the second proof will facilitate discussion of proofs three and four.

The first issue concerns the distinction between the products of art and the products of nature: 'the skill of the artificer standeth in that *Idea* or fore-conceit of the work, and not in the work itself' (101.3–4). That the artist must first have a conception of his work in his mind before he can execute it (as opposed to the 'spontaneous' production of nature or of God) and that this conception, being prior, is somehow more noteworthy than its production, could be Platonic, Aristotelian, Stoic (Senecan), Ciceronian, Boethian, Thomistic, as well as Neoplatonic.[2] In the light of Sidney's general disapproval of the Neoplatonic analysis of mimetic representation, the recent tendency to associate his phrasing with the Neoplatonic speculation about the arts and even with its reflection in the Mannerist theory of painting seems less than persuasive. Two interrelated sources, one 'psychological' and the other 'literary', seem preferable. The first is Seneca's *Epistulae* 58.19–21 combined with *Ep.* 65.7, works we can be fairly sure Sidney knew because of his use of *Ep.* 88 (104.19–25nn). In *Ep.* 58 Seneca equates the word *idea* with the *exemplar* to be imitated and explicitly says that the *idea* is not only outside the work but prior to it, that is, a 'fore-conceit'. In *Ep.* 65, he says both the *idea* and the

---

[2] E. Panofsky's famous study of 1929, *Idea: a concept in art theory*, trans. J. Peake (Columbia, SC: University of South Carolina Press, 1968), gives examples of nearly all of these possibilities, and his description of the pictorial meanings of 'Idea' in the High Renaissance is closer to Sidney's than those in the Mannerist period.

exemplar may not only be outside the mind for the artist to contemplate (as implied in *Ep.* 58), but they may also be conceptions which he has already established in his mind.[3]

This quasi-psychological use of *exemplar* as *idea* combines easily with two Horatian passages, *Ars poetica* 309–18 and *Epistles* 1.2.1–31, both important to Sidney. In turning from natural settings to describe his fictionalized portraits of public and private human virtues (discussed above), Sidney sees each of these as first being an 'Idea or fore-conceit' and exemplifies it, ultimately, in Xenophon's portrait of Cyrus. So, in his first passage, Horace, depicting similar public and private virtues, recommends to the learned imitator to look to the exemplar of life and customs and draw thence particular living voices ['respicere exemplar vitae morumque iubebo / doctum imitatorem et vivas hinc ducere voces', 317–18]. Horace introduces his virtues to be portrayed by observing that the organizing principle and source of writing well is 'wisdom' [*sapere*, as distinct from knowledge of the specialized sciences]. As Sidney also points out (97.10–20), Horace says that the Socratic pages can show forth this 'wisdom' in the characters they portray whose qualities are your general subject [*rem*], and, once this subject has been 'foreseen', its expression in words [*verba*] will willingly follow ['Scribendi recte sapere est et principium et fons. / rem tibi Socraticae poterunt ostendere chartae, / verbaque provisam rem non invita sequentur', 309–11]. Sidney could easily render *ostendere* by 'to figure forth' and associate his 'notable images of virtues' (103.29) with *rem*, such as the exemplary description of Aeneas, to 'be worn in the tablet of your memory', which he later substitutes for the detailed *exemplar Ulixen* in Horace's second passage (*Ep.* 1.2.1–31). Sidney's substitution is clearly intentional, since he quotes Horace's own line (*Epistles* 1.2.4) to make the point that his portrait of Aeneas, quite as much as that of Horace's Ulysses, will surpass Chrysippus and Crantor in the teaching of *virtus* and *sapientia* (119.30–120.5). Furthermore, since the poet 'doth not learn a conceit out of a matter, but maketh matter for a conceit', his initial conception of the *exemplar* to be imitated, preceding its expression, is clearly an 'Idea or fore-conceit', a *provisam rem*.

The further issue concerning the second proof is Sidney's possible debt to the ancient ideal of rhetoric as established by Plato, Aristotle, and Isocrates and later restated by Cicero. When Sidney marks the limited 'scope' of the specialized arts and sciences, he includes 'the rhetorician and logician' among the specialists. These, he says, 'considering what in

---

[3] For the Renaissance confusion of the heuristic purpose of *paradeigma* in philosophy [*exemplar*] with the exemplary purpose of *paradeigma* in rhetoric [*exemplum*], see W. Trimpi, *Muses of one mind* (Princeton: Princeton University Press, 1983), App. A. For the literary application of technical terms borrowed from rhetorical, philosophical, or mathematical discourse in this essay, see the index of topics in *Muses of one mind*.

Nature will soonest prove and persuade, thereon give artificial rules, which still are compassed within the circle of a question according to the proposed matter' (100.12–15). The 'question' here can be of two kinds: the 'indefinite' question or *thesis* of the logician who, uncommitted to any particular situation, may argue it from either side, and the 'definite' question or *hypothesis* of the rhetorician who seeks an 'action' or judgement on an individual case. Neither of these arts in their ideal ancient formulation, however, were to be confined to a 'proposed matter' but, drawing upon both generic and specific questions, could be applied freely to any material, real arguments (of the lecture-hall or courtroom) or fictional arguments (of the library or the stage). In fact, Aristotle returns several times to this distinction in the second introductory chapter of his *Rhetoric* (1.2.1, 1.2.7, 1.2.20–2), and Cicero often repeats it (*De oratore* 2.2.5 *et al.*).

Unlike other arts like medicine, geometry, or arithmetic, each of which 'can instruct or persuade about its own particular subject-matter', rhetoric observes, Aristotle insists, 'the means of persuasion on almost any subject presented to us', not on any special class of subjects (1). The kind of rhetorical argument [enthymeme], moreover, which 'really belongs to rhetoric' is that based on general lines of enquiry [*topoi*, commonplaces]. This kind is universal and can 'apply equally to questions of right conduct, natural science, [and] politics', while the other kind, based on special lines of enquiry, can 'apply only to particular groups or classes of things'. Failure to recognize this 'important distinction', which 'has been wholly overlooked by almost everybody', has caused speakers to ignore the fact 'that the more correctly they handle their particular subject the further they are getting away from pure rhetoric'; the better, that is, they select 'propositions suitable for special Lines of Argument', the closer they come to setting up a distinctly separate science (20–1).[4]

Aristotle extends this freedom of the arts of discourse from a specific subject-matter to poetry in the *Poetics* (9) by distinguishing it from the 'given' materials of history in a passage which Sidney carefully paraphrases (109.19–34). That Sidney also had direct knowledge of these distinctions, which echo through his last three proofs, from the *Rhetoric* becomes probable in the light of a remark made by John Hoskins about the treatise: '*Sr Phillip Sidney*, betrayed his knowledge in this booke of *Aristotle* to me, before euer I knewe that hee had translated any pte of it, for I found the 2 first bookes englished by him in the handes of the noble

---

[4] *Aristotle: Rhetoric and Poetics*, trans. W. R. Roberts and I. Bywater (New York: Random House, 1954). On this 'important distinction' [*megiste diaphora*], see the comments of W. M. A. Grimaldi with respect to the references to Cicero below. *Aristotle, Rhetoric I: a commentary* (New York: Fordham University Press, 1980), pp. 71–2.

studious *Henry Wotton*'.[5] If we assume that Sidney would have translated from a Latin version of the *Rhetoric*, it seems harder to explain this testimony away than to accept it. As Shepherd points out (143–4) Edward Wotton, with whom the *Apology* opens, was half-brother to Henry and spent the winter of 1574–5 with Sidney at the court of Maximilian II in Vienna. He was, furthermore, 'a beneficiary under Sidney's will and a pall-bearer at his funeral'. That Sidney drew on Aristotle's comments on 'pure rhetoric' to emphasize poetry's unique freedom from Nature, is further suggested, as we shall see, by the Ciceronian background of Sidney's fourth proof. As Cicero insists that the ideal orator negotiate between generic and specific issues – similar to Aristotle's general and special lines of enquiry – so Sidney insists that the poet combine in his *imago* the philosopher's abstract proposition [*thesis*] and the historian's particular case [*hypothesis*].

The third proof of 'kinds' emerges logically out of the derivation of 'poetry' from *poiein* to indicate its definitive activity as that of 'making' and is introduced by a description of how that activity is to be realized. Poetry 'is an art of imitation, for so Aristotle termeth it in his word *mimesis*, that is to say, a representing, counterfeiting, or figuring forth – to speak metaphorically, a speaking picture – with this end, to teach and delight' (101.33–6).[6] There have been, Sidney immediately continues, 'three several kinds' of poetry. These 'kinds', as we learn from the ultimate source of this distinction in Proclus's *Commentary on the Republic* (*Dissertation* VI, Lib. 2, Chs. v–vii) are not literary 'genres' nor themes (subjects) appropriate to specific genres *per se*. They are, rather, the expression of three different types or 'levels' of psychic activity [*energeia*] corresponding to three different conditions [*hexis, habitus*, dispositions] of the soul. In the Neoplatonic speculation, these activities and conditions of the soul (which different 'kinds' of poetry express) are categorized according to the four levels of intelligibility sketched in Plato's metaphor of the Divided Line (*Republic* 509D–511E) in which the two levels above the Line contain intelligible entities [*to noeton*], the two below visible entities [*to horaton*].

Above the Line, the 'highest' kind of poetry will express in hymn and allegory the noetic intuition of primary causes and the life of the gods;

---

[5] 'The direccõns for speech and style', in *The life, letters and writings of John Hoskyns*, ed. L. B. Osborn (New Haven: Yale University Press, 1937), p. 155. Hoskins lived from 1566 to 1638, and Osborn dates the *Direccõns* between 1598 and 1603, choosing 1599 as most likely.

[6] For Aristotle, not only has metaphor a heuristic function (*Rhetoric* 3.10.1–3) but *mimesis* itself (*Rhetoric* 1.11.21–4; *Poetics* 4.1–5, 9.1–4). Sidney could have derived the association of imitation with both learning and pleasure from *Poetics* 4.1–5 (to which he refers at 114.5–8) or *Rhetoric* 1.11.21–4 or have conflated Aristotle with Horace (*Ars poetica* 333–4, 343–4).

the second kind of poetry will express, in philosophical exposition, the dianoetic life of the reason in its pursuit of knowledge through the human sciences. The third kind of poetry treats all the objects below the Line: in the third category it represents the actual objects of our experience, both animate and inanimate, which form the material of belief [*pistis*] or opinion [*doxa*] with as much accuracy as appearances permit [*eikastikos*]; in the lowest category it represents images [*eikones*], the objects of conjecture [*eikasia*], such as shadows [*skias*] and reflections [*phantasmata*] on water and textured surfaces, with little or no concern for verisimilitude [*phantastikos*]. In the Proclean speculation, only the third kind of poetry, since it 'imitates' the objects of sensation below the Line, is mimetic and, especially in its lowest form, is justifiably excluded by Plato from the Republic. In developing his conception of the 'right poet', Sidney invokes this Neoplatonic hierarchy in order to reject it, a rejection in accord with his later refusal to see 'divine' inspiration, as adapted (without Plato's irony) from the *Ion*, as necessary to the poet (130.2–10) or Platonic philosophy in its most abstract, that is, mathematical, guise (114.35–115.6). In fact, Sidney would agree with his historian that virtue should not be learnt 'in the dangerless Academy of Plato' (105.34), for virtue, as Sidney says of poetry (which best teaches it), 'is the companion of the camps', while 'the quiddity of *ens* and *prima materia* will hardly agree with a corslet' (127.6–9).[7]

Corresponding to Proclus's first (noetic) poet are Sidney's poets who 'imitate the inconceivable excellencies of God'. Such are David, Solomon, Moses, and Deborah, and 'though in a full wrong divinity', Orpheus, Amphion, and 'Homer in his Hymns' (101.38–102.8). Corresponding to Proclus's second [dianoetic] poet are Sidney's poets 'that deal with matters philosophical: either moral . . . or natural . . . or astronomical . . . or historical': all of whom offer 'the sweet food of sweetly uttered knowledge' (102.14–20). But because the second kind of poet – and Shepherd rightly believes the first kind as well (30) – 'is wrapped within the fold of the proposed subject, and takes not the course of his own invention', Sidney proceeds 'to the third, indeed right poets'. Like Proclus, he sees his third

---

[7] For the Neoplatonic reconstruction of classical literary theory, see Trimpi, *Muses of one mind*, Part 2, especially ch. 8, with special attention to Proclus on pp. 200–19. For Proclus in the Renaissance, see P. O. Kristeller, 'Proclus as a reader of Plato and Plotinus, and his influence in the Middle Ages and in the Renaissance', *Colloques internationaux du C.N.R.S*: 'Proclus – lecteur et interprète des anciens' (Paris: Editions du CNRS, 1987). For the transcription of a Latin epitome of Proclus's treatment of poetic 'kinds' by Gesner, see W. Trimpi, 'Konrad Gesner and Neoplatonic poetics', in *Magister regis: studies in honor of Robert Earl Kaske*, ed. A. Groos (New York: Fordham University Press, 1986), pp. 261–72, where Proclus is suggested as the ultimate source of Sidney's distinctions (n. 9). For his immediate sources, see below.

'kind' of poet as mimetic, but, rejecting the Neoplatonic analysis, he returns to an Aristotelian conception of *mimesis*. Borrowing 'nothing of what is, hath been, or shall be', the mimetic poet ranges 'with learned discretion, into the divine consideration of what may be and should be'. Unlike the 'meaner sort of painters', who, bound to nature like the historian, 'counterfeit only such faces as are set before them', he is like the painter, 'who having no law but wit' does not paint 'Lucretia whom he never saw, but painteth the outward beauty of such a virtue'.[8] Properly called 'makers', these poets 'make to imitate, and imitate both to delight and teach: and delight to move men to take that goodness in hand, which without delight they would fly as from a stranger, and teach, to make them know that goodness whereunto they are moved' – the objective 'to which ever any learning was directed' (102.21–103.8). Since Sidney uses the Proclean analysis to argue, through its rejection, for the ethical power of *mimesis* – from which his fourth proof directly arises – his possible immediate sources should be briefly mentioned.

Sidney might have known a Latin translation of the *Commentary on the Republic* itself, or some epitome of it such as Gesner's (see n. 7), perhaps appended to an edition of Plato with or without attribution to Proclus. With Proclus still unidentified, however, scholars have most often seen a parallel between Sidney's treatment of 'kinds' and an incomplete division of 'kinds' of poetry, solely according to subject-matter, in Scaliger's *Poetices libri septem* (1561) I.2. There are some similarities, to be sure, in the representatives of the first two 'kinds', but Sidney considers subject-matter primarily with respect to its free adaptability to mimetic representation, and Scaliger does not even mention a mimetic 'kind' at all.[9] Short of his direct knowledge of Proclus's commentary, the best evidence we have of Sidney's knowledge of Proclus's distinctions, whether or not he knew their provenance, is from Minturno's *De poeta* (1559), a compendium which Sidney used. Though Minturno does not mention Proclus by name either, there can be no doubt that he is drawing upon his commentary or some redaction of it on pp. 53–6.[10] Whatever his immediate

---

[8] The fact that the 'outward' expression of the face revealed character, while exploited by the Mannerists in art as Shepherd points out (102.30n), derives from an ancient ethical/ psychological commonplace: see Cicero, *Laws* 1.26–7; Ovid, 'facies animo dignaque parque' (*Fasti* 2.758), from which the figures in Shakespeare's tapestry: 'The face of either ciphered either's heart' (*Rape of Lucrece*, 1396).

[9] A. C. Hamilton correctly points out the differences between Sidney and Scaliger, but, not knowing the ultimate source of the views that Sidney is rejecting, he wrongly stresses his affinity with the Neoplatonic attitude towards imitation. 'Sidney's idea of the "right poet"', *Comparative literature* 9 (1957), 51–9.

[10] See especially the list of the four Homeric singers, associated by Proclus with the four levels of Plato's Divided Line (*Dissertation* VI.2.vii), on p. 55. In addition to Scaliger, G. G. Smith notes Minturno's division of 'kinds' of poets as parallel to Sidney's but without reference to its origin.

source, Sidney had at his disposal the specifically Neoplatonic attack upon *mimesis* to which he is responding in his third and fourth proofs.

His fourth proof is an expanded analysis of the moral efficacy of the third (mimetic) 'kind' of poetry. Christian and humanistic, it combines its arguments into a synthesis remarkably similar to the portrait of the ideal orator which Cicero derives from Plato, Aristotle, and Isocrates. Sidney begins by returning once again to the same specialized arts and sciences and applies to them the broadly diffused Platonic/Aristotelian distinction between the productive and prudential faculties (Plato, *Protagoras* 318B–23; Aristotle, *Nicomachean ethics* 6.4–5; Seneca, *Epistulae* 88; St Thomas, *Summa theologica* 1.2. qu. 21. art. 2 and qu. 57 art. 3 and 5).[11] Those who have assumed human felicity to lie in the acquisition of knowledge and its application in the productive arts and sciences must soon realize that the astronomer 'looking to the stars might fall into a ditch, that the enquiring philosopher might be blind in himself, and the mathematician might draw forth a straight line with a crooked heart'. From this experience they will recognize that all these disciplines 'are but serving sciences, which, as they have each a private end in themselves, so yet are they all directed to the highest end of the mistress-knowledge, by the Greeks called *architectonike*, which stands (as I think) in the knowledge of a man's self, in the ethic and politic consideration, with the end of well-doing and not of well-knowing only'. Indeed, 'the ending end of all earthly learning being virtuous action, those skills, that most serve to bring forth that, have a most just title to be princes over all the rest' (104.10–37). To show that poetry most deserves this title, Sidney begins his famous comparison between the poet and his two most conspicuous rivals as teachers of moral virtue, the moral philosopher and the historian.[12]

Sidney's ironic portraits of the moral philosopher, very much in scholastic dress, and the historian are shrewd vignettes, not just of professional types, but of intellectual habits, which anticipate certain details in Bacon's

---

[11] See *Muses of one mind*, App. B.
[12] History here takes the place of rhetoric in its ancient debate with philosophy, since history, like rhetoric, deals with the particular case, the 'definite question' of Cicero (see Antonio Sebastiano Minturno, *De poeta* (1559; reprint Munich: W. Fink, 1970), p. 123). It is sometimes assumed that Sidney's famous comparison is a commonplace borrowed from Italian criticism. A careful perusal of B. Weinberg's *A history of literary criticism in the Italian Renaissance*, 2 vols. (Chicago: University of Chicago Press, 1961), however, will show that Italian critics *either* find poetry superior to philosophy (because its lessons are more pleasing, varied, and apprehensible), *or* poetry superior to history (because it reveals the universal). Only selections from the unpublished lectures of Bartolomeo Maranta (1563–4) make *both* points in some relation to one another at the same place in the text (vol. I, p. 487). Despite other similarities to Sidney, it is most unlikely that Maranta was known to him. If Shepherd is right that 'Sidney is adapting "Amiot to the Readers" on history' in North's *Plutarch* (171), Sidney nevertheless transfers Amyot's emphasis on the historian's power to move to the poet.

critique of false scientific methods.[13] The philosophers 'casting largesse as they go of definitions, divisions, and distinctions, with a scornful interrogative do soberly ask whether it be possible to find any path so ready to lead a man to virtue as that which teacheth what virtue is'. The historian responds that the philosopher, 'teacheth a disputative virtue' which thrives 'in the dangerless Academy of Plato', while he teaches an active virtue, at home on the battlefield, and through innumerable instances conveys 'the experience of many ages', story by story. In sum, 'the philosopher therefore and the historian are they which would win the goal, the one by precept, the other by example. But both, not having both, do both halt.' Standing 'so upon the abstract and general', the philosopher expresses his 'bare rule' harshly and obscurely in 'thorny argument', while 'the historian, wanting the precept, is so tied, not to what should be but to what is, to the particular truth of things and not to the general reason of things, that his example draweth no necessary consequence' (105.8–107.8).

Now the poet 'coupleth the general notion with the particular example', and what the philosopher says 'should be done, he giveth a perfect picture of it in some one by whom he presupposeth it was done'. This exemplary picture is an 'image of that whereof the philosopher bestoweth but a wordish description, which doth neither strike, pierce, nor possess the sight of the soul', and consequently his 'infallible grounds of wisdom' must 'lie dark before the imaginative and judging power, if they be not illuminated or figured forth by the speaking picture of poesy' (107.9–34). The historian, on the other hand, claims to bring you abundant 'images of true matters', rather than 'such as fantastically or falsely may be suggested to have been done'. Sidney first answers him in Aristotle's words from the *Poetics* (9), that since the poetic image 'dealeth with *katholou*', or 'the universal consideration', and history 'with *kathekaston*, the particular', poetry is '*philosophoteron* and *spoudaioteron*, that is to say, it is more philosophical and more studiously serious than history' (109.21–7). He then adds that were a person to act in a certain way simply on the basis of something's having already occurred, it would be 'as if he should argue, because it rained yesterday, therefore it should rain to-day'. Such an action might appear reasonable 'to a gross conceit; but if he [one better informed] know an example only informs a conjectured likelihood, and so go by reason', the poet will appear to surpass the historian to the extent that he can 'frame his example to that which is most reasonable', whereas 'the historian in his bare *was*' must often permit 'fortune to overrule the

---

[13] Bacon's empirical ant resembles Sidney's historian, his scholastic spider Sidney's moral philosopher, and his wide-foraging and productive bee Sidney's poet (*Novum organum*, 1.95). The bee was, coincidentally, an ancient symbol for the poet, its honey for poetry. See also Shepherd's citations of Bacon (170, 179).

best wisdom'. He must 'tell events whereof he can yield no cause; or, if he do, it must be poetical' (110.18–32). Sidney borrows 'conjectured likelihood' from the legal *status conjecturalis* which concerns the question *an sit* (did such and such a thing happen?) which is the principal question that the historian, confined 'in his bare *was*', would address.[14]

Sidney brings his argument to its climax by invoking the Christian emphasis upon the will. Even if we were to grant that the 'methodical proceeding' of the philosopher might possibly instruct more completely, no one would 'compare the philosopher in moving with the poet', nor refuse to admit 'that moving is of a higher degree than teaching'. For no one can be taught unless he be 'moved with desire to be taught', and the aim of all instruction in morality is 'that it moveth one to do that which it doth teach' – for, 'as Aristotle saith, it is not *gnosis* but *praxis* must be the fruit' (112.25–36). Not only is Sidney's Aristotelian ethical doctrine here thoroughly Thomistic, but his account of the moral function of the 'image' comes right out of medieval faculty psychology.

First for Sidney, the exemplary *imago* has the power to overcome the limits of philosophy by rendering its truth visible to 'the sight of the soul' (107.16), and this palpability has a far greater and more immediate effect upon moving the emotions than abstract conceptions do (compare Thomas Aquinas, *Summa theologica* 1. qu. 1 art. 9). The poetic image, or the confluence of *imagines* in a fictional narrative, may also overcome the ethical limits of history through the poet's power to reveal the 'universal' by choosing exemplary figures and thereby supplying causes for effects in the 'imaginative ground-plot' of his 'profitable invention'.[15] By means of the poetic image, that is, philosophy becomes apprehensible, history comprehensible – a combination strikingly anticipated by Dante (*Paradiso* 17.136–42). But, second, the 'image' itself already carried a moral valence for the Middle Ages through the doctrine of 'intention' upon which the Christian emblematic tradition rests. The 'image' of a wolf on the page or in the mind carried with it its inherent ethical quality (*intentio*) of 'wolfishness', and the emotions generated by that 'image' would resemble

---

[14] See *Muses of one mind*, pp. 345, 353–61. Whatever the value of its curiously obtuse precision, Sir William Temple's Ramist 'analysis' of the *Apology* is closer to this explanation of 'conjectured likelihood' than to Shepherd's (73–5, 178): see *William Temple's analysis of Sir Philip Sidney's 'Apology for poetry'*, ed. and trans. J. Webster (Binghamton: State University of New York Press, 1984), pp. 106–9. (For Ramus and Sidney, see Shepherd, 32–5.)

[15] The 'universal', Aristotle says, is precious because it reveals the cause, *Posterior analytics* 88a5. The 'ground-plot' corresponds to the 'dramatic hypothesis' [*hupothesis*], the argument of the play, as Aristotle writes, which the poet 'should first simplify and reduce to a universal form [*ektithesthai katholou*], before proceeding to lengthen it out by the insertion of episodes' (*Poetics* 17.3). See *Muses of one mind*, ch. 2 on 'The hypothesis of literary discourse', esp. pp. 50–8, for the tradition of Sidney's terms, particularly of 'presupposeth' at 107.11 [= *prae* + *supponere* = *hupotithemi*].

those aroused by the actual presence of a wolf. This 'moralization' of
the image becomes most effective in the combined *intentiones* revealed in
the manifold motivations and actions of fictional characters in epic and
drama. In fact, it is through our recognition of such *intentiones* that the
events themselves become *exemplares*.[16] In his defence of literature, therefore, Sidney concentrates on the longer narrative genres in verse or prose
which offer the plasticity of space and time to develop his *imagines*. While
often acute and historically important, his remarks on the shorter poetic
genres are scattered and unsystematic, and do not attempt to show how
the lyric might fulfil, in its own way, the ethical and psychological functions of his 'mimetic' portraits.[17]

[16] For understanding Sidney's *Apology*, the best account of this medieval tradition of faculty
psychology and its sources in antiquity is in F. A. Yates, *The art of memory* (Chicago:
University of Chicago Press, 1966), chs. I–IV. See also K. Eden, *Poetic and legal fiction*
(see n. 1), pp. 143–7, and M. Carruthers, *The book of memory* (Cambridge: Cambridge
University Press, 1990), pp. 53–4, 68–9, 149, 183. For Sidney on poetry and 'the art of
memory', *Apology*, 122.

[17] Sidney's most extended example of practical criticism deals directly with this plasticity
of space and time in his analysis of contemporary dramatic plots and characters
(133.37–137.23, esp. 134.38–135.29). If one includes stylistic faults afflicting longer
forms as well, his comments on the shorter genres (including the psalms) occur at
99.6–21, 101.37–108.13, 115.23–6, 116.1–117.7, 118.19–119.11, 125.2–23, 133.22–
36, 137.24–139.24. He repeats some of his advice in *Astrophil and Stella*: see esp. sonnets
1, 3, 6, 15, 28, 45, 74.

19

Aristotle, Horace, and Longinus: the conception of reader response

Nicholas Cronk

The rhetorical complexion of literary criticism in the sixteenth and seventeenth centuries focuses attention on the poet as 'maker' of the text rather than on the reader (listener) as 'maker of sense' of the text. To talk, as Horace does, of the poet's aim is to presuppose an author-centred approach: readers are dismissed in the *Ars poetica* with the throwaway remark that the old prefer profit while the young pursue pleasure.[1] In the last third of the seventeenth century, at the high point of French neoclassicism, concern for clarity was paramount and seemed to place the reader in a wholly passive role: the Cartesian Bernard Lamy wrote in *De l'art de parler* (1675) that in order to attain a gentle and clear style, 'one should leave nothing to the reader to guess'.[2] It would be misleading however to take at face value this apparent neglect of the reader. Theorists of poetry and rhetoric have always been concerned with the affective impact of language, and literary critics of the Renaissance and seventeenth century give voice to the issue of reader-response by building on the rhetorical inheritance of Horace, Aristotle, and, increasingly in the seventeenth century, Longinus.

Horace's *Epistula ad Pisones*, known usually as the *Ars poetica*, remained a dynamic presence in the literary criticism of the Renaissance and seventeenth century, though it had been familiar since the Middle Ages. Dolce's Italian version appeared in 1535, Jacques Peletier du Mans's French translation in 1545 was first published anonymously in 1541, and the first English version, by Archdeacon Drant, appeared in 1567. Boileau's *Art poétique* (1674), a poem of 1100 lines, contains over one hundred lines lifted directly from Horace's *Ars poetica* (plus another hundred lines borrowed from other poems of Horace). The part of Horace's poem which generated most debate is the description of the poet's aims as being to instruct and delight; here is the passage, in the translation of Ben Jonson (1640):

---

[1] D. A. Russell and M. Winterbottom (ed.), *Ancient literary criticism: the principal texts in new translations* (Oxford: Clarendon Press, 1972), p. 288 (Horace, *Ars poetica* 341–2). Unless noted otherwise, all translations are those of the present author.

[2] B. Lamy, *De l'art de parler* (Paris: A. Pralard, 1675), p. 212.

Poets would either profit, or delight,
Or mixing sweet, and fit, teach life the right . . .
The *Poems* void of profit, our grave men
Cast out by voyces; want they pleasure, then
Our Gallants give them none, but passe them by:
But he hath every suffrage, can apply
Sweet mix'd with sowre, to his Reader, so
As doctrine, and delight together go.[3]

This notion of the dual aim of poetry recurs again and again in the period: Julius Caesar Scaliger, whose long Latin treatise *Poetices libri septem* (1561) was hugely influential in France, claims that 'Indeed the poet teaches, he does not merely delight';[4] Sidney, in his *Apology for poetry* (1595), writes that 'Poesy therefore is an art of imitation . . . with this end, to teach and delight'.[5] Constantly repeated by the poets of the Renaissance, the doctrine came in time to be applied beyond the genres of poetry and tragedy. When Molière speaks of 'the duty of comedy being to correct men while entertaining them',[6] he is using Horace to defend, and to dignify, a genre which had been held in low esteem; similarly, French novelists throughout the seventeenth century use the Horatian dictum both to defend their emergent genre and to provide the starting point for an enquiry into the functions and aims of the novel as a genre.[7] The idea, though commonly discussed, does not become commonplace. La Mesnardière prefaces his *Poétique* (1639) with a lengthy 'Discours' in which he defends the utility of poetry against the view of Castelvetro that the aim of poetry was purely one of pleasure. The Horatian dictum is pivotal to the French neoclassical idea of art's moral function: the phrase 'one should instruct and please' is incorporated by La Fontaine into one of his *Fables*.[8]

If the writer's purpose is limited to instruction and delight, then the reader's role might seem somewhat passive. But in order to instruct and delight readers, it is necessary also to move them – as Sidney remarks:

And that moving is of a higher degree than teaching, it may by this appear, that it is well nigh the cause and the effect of teaching. For who will be taught, if he

---

[3] *Horace, his art of poetrie*, trans. Ben Jonson, in his *Works*, vol. VIII, ed. C. H. Herford and P. and E. Simpson (Oxford: Clarendon Press, 1947), pp. 327, 329 (*Ars poetica* 333–4, 341–4).

[4] Quoted by René Bray, *La formation de la doctrine classique en France* (Paris: Hachette, 1927), p. 64.

[5] Sir Philip Sidney, *An apology for poetry*, ed. G. Shepherd (Manchester: Manchester University Press, 1973), p. 101.

[6] *Tartuffe*, 'Premier placet' (1664).

[7] See G. J. Mallinson, 'Fiction, morality, and the reader: reflections on the classical formula *plaire et instruire*', *Continuum* 1 (1989), 203–28.

[8] La Fontaine, *Fables*, VI, 2, 'Le Lion et le chasseur'.

be not moved with desire to be taught? and what so much good doth that teaching bring forth (I speak still of moral doctrine) as that it moveth one to do that which it doth teach?[9]

Horace's dictum encourages consideration of the affective impact of literature all the more readily as the threefold aim of instructing, delighting, and moving is a distinction well familiar from ancient rhetoric, where it was usually allied to the three styles, 'low', 'middle', and 'high' respectively.

The most prominent formulation of literature's power to move is the idea of *catharsis* expounded in Aristotle's *Poetics*: 'A tragedy is a *mimesis* of a high, complete action . . . effecting through pity and fear the *catharsis* of such emotions'.[10] Unavailable before the end of the fifteenth century, and not widely known before the middle of the sixteenth, the impact of this text on Renaissance literary criticism was enormous and unprecedented. Giorgio Valla's translation into Latin appeared in 1498, and the Greek text was published for the first time in Venice by Aldus in 1508. The first vernacular translation, by Bernardo Segni into Italian, was published in 1549; but there were no French or English translations until over a century later. The fame of the work was established by a series of major Latin commentaries, notably those of Francesco Robortello (1548), Bartolomeo Lombardi and Vincenzo Maggi (1550), Pietro Vettori (1560), and Antonio Riccoboni (1585); Lodovico Castelvetro (1570) and Alessandro Piccolomini (1575) also wrote important commentaries in Italian.

The *Poetics* were invariably interpreted within the existing moralistic framework of literary-critical thought deriving from Horace, and already by the mid-sixteenth century there had occurred what has been called a 'fusion' of Horatian and Aristotelian criticism.[11] Robortello and Maggi both wrote commentaries on Horace's *Ars poetica* complementary to, and published together with, their commentaries on Aristotle; and a century later, Dryden, in his *Essay of dramatick poesie* (1668), can speak of Horace's *Ars poetica* as 'an excellent Comment' on Aristotle's *Poetics*.[12]

The precise meaning of *catharsis*, discussed with tantalizing brevity in the *Poetics*, was the subject of wide debate in the Italian Renaissance: Paolo Beni, who published a commentary on the *Poetics* in 1613, claimed to know at least a dozen different interpretations of Aristotle's definition of tragedy.[13] A moralistic interpretation of *catharsis* provided a useful

---

[9]   Sidney, *Apology for poetry*, ed. Shepherd, p. 112.
[10] Russell and Winterbottom (ed.), *Ancient literary criticism*, p. 97 (*Poetics* 1449b24–8).
[11] See Marvin T. Herrick, *The fusion of Horatian and Aristotelian criticism, 1531–1555* (Urbana: University of Illinois Press, 1946).
[12] John Dryden, *An essay of dramatick poesie*, in *Works*, ed. S. H. Monk (Berkeley: University of California Press, 1971), vol. XVII, p. 17.
[13] Italian Renaissance debate concerning *catharsis* is described in B. Hathaway, *The age of criticism: the late Renaissance in Italy* (Ithaca: Cornell University Press, 1962), pp. 205–300.

counterbalance to the idea (familiar from Plato's *Republic*) that the arts
which excite emotions are harmful; but explaining the moral mechanism
of purgation did not prove easy. Antonio Sebastiano Minturno (*De poeta*,
1559) gave a quasi-medical account, according to which the arousal of
pity and terror purifies us of the disorder engendered by violent passions
and teaches us to avoid the misfortunes that would cause a repetition of
such unpleasant emotions; others, like Castelvetro, were less literal-minded
in their explanations of the process of purgation. The debate, confused
though it was, had the effect of concentrating attention on the emotional
impact of (in the first instance) tragedy; thus when Sidney speaks of
tragedy 'stirring the affects of admiration and commiseration',[14] he is
clearly indebted to Aristotle, even though he inverts the order of Aristotle's pity and terror, and even though he turns fear into *admiration*.
Seventeenth-century critics mostly repeated one or other of their Renaissance predecessors, though French practitioners of tragedy continued to
ponder Aristotle's definition. Pierre Corneille recounts the utilitarian view
of tragedy according to which the spectacle of the evil effects of passion in
another causes us to 'purge' that emotion in ourselves and avoid similar
calamity – but adds disarmingly that he doubts if this has ever actually
worked in practice.[15] Racine, perhaps taking the hint from Corneille, distances himself from the habitual moralistic interpretation of *catharsis*,
noting that tragedy 'by exciting pity and terror, purges *and moderates* these
types of passion. So by arousing these passions, it removes from them
everything which is excessive and corrupt and returns them to a moderate
and reasonable state' [my emphasis].[16] There was also an attempt to broa-
den the notion of *catharsis* by applying it to comedy: Riccoboni elaborates
this idea in his treatise on comedy (1579, revised 1585); and Molière's
declared aim of 'correcting' his audience while entertaining them adds to
the echo of Horace an allusion to Aristotelian *catharsis*.[17]

The notion of *catharsis* was a powerful tool for exploring a certain
form of emotional impact, but its use was confined to the discussion of
audience response in the theatre; to describe the impact on the reader of
written texts, critics had to search elsewhere. The Platonic idea of poetic
fury, as derived from the *Phaedrus* and the *Ion*, was well known to the
Renaissance; and although the more rationalist critics were deeply suspicious of the concept, its influence shaped even French neoclassical

---

[14] Sidney, *Apology for poetry*, ed. Shepherd, p. 118.
[15] P. Corneille, *Second discours*, in *Writings on the theatre*, ed. H. T. Barnwell (Oxford:
Blackwell, 1965), pp. 28–38.
[16] J. Racine, *Principes de la tragédie*, ed. E. Vinaver (Manchester and Paris: Nizet, 1951),
pp. 11–12.
[17] See W. D. Howarth, 'La notion de la catharsis dans la comédie française classique', *Revue
des sciences humaines* 152 (1973), 521–39.

criticism.[18] The idea of divine fury concerns in the first instance the poet's act of creation, but it could equally well be used also to account for reader-response: if the poet was inspired, then so too would be the reader. Here is how, in the 1680s, the French author Louis Thomassin presents the argument of Plato's *Ion*:

Divine fury, with which not only poets must be animated but also those who read their works with profit, is like a celestial spirit which ravishes them and transports them outside of themselves, so that the readers or listeners, just as much as the poets, are connected to this divine spirit, like several iron rings holding together and hanging from a magnet.[19]

Further support for the idea of the reader's inspiration could be found in Longinus, whose treatise became widely known only in the course of the seventeenth century: the first published translations appeared in Italian in 1639, in English (*Of the height of eloquence*) in 1652, and in French, by no less a critic than Boileau, in 1674. It was not difficult to incorporate certain of Longinus's ideas into the existing amalgam of Aristotelian and Horatian thinking concerning reader-response:

Grandeur produces ecstasy rather than persuasion in the hearer; and the combination of wonder and astonishment always proves superior to the merely persuasive and pleasant. This is because persuasion is on the whole something we can control, whereas amazement and wonder exert invincible power and force and get the better of every hearer.[20]

Longinus could be quoted in circumstances where Plato could not, and Longinus's treatise exercised a powerful influence on seventeenth-century thinking about the emotive power of literature.

The critical thought of Boileau, often considered (misleadingly) as the *summa* of French neoclassicism, shows how these various (and on the surface opposing) influences were assimilated into a more or less coherent body of thought. The *Art poétique* is, as we have seen, suffused with the influence of Horace. Yet the poem also bears the mark of Neoplatonism;[21] and this cannot be fully disentangled from the influence of Longinus: the *Art poétique* was first published together with Boileau's translation of Longinus, the *Traité du Sublime*, in 1674, the two works clearly conceived

---

[18] See J. Brody, 'Platonisme et classicisme', in *French classicism: a critical miscellany*, ed. J. Brody (Englewood Cliffs: Prentice-Hall, 1966), pp. 186–207; and N. Cronk, 'Une poétique platonicienne à l'époque classique: le *De furore poetico* de Pierre Petit (1683)', *Dix-septième siècle* 37 (1985), 99–102.

[19] Louis Thomassin, *La méthode d'étudier et d'enseigner chrétiennement et solidement les lettres humaines . . . : De l'étude des poètes*, 3 vols. (Paris: Muguet, 1681–2), vol. I, p. 103.

[20] Russell and Winterbottom (ed.), *Ancient literary criticism*, p. 462 (*On Sublimity* 1.4).

[21] See D. C. Potts, '"Une carrière épineuse": Neoplatonism and the poet's vocation in Boileau's *Art poétique*', *French studies* 47 (1993), 20–32.

of as complementary – there was no edition in Boileau's lifetime of the *Art poétique* which did not include the *Traité du Sublime*. His literary criticism provides a striking example of how, at the end of the seventeenth century, the various critical traditions deriving from Horace, Aristotle, Plato, and Longinus came increasingly to coalesce.

Although a system of literary criticism grounded on rhetoric necessarily fosters a view of the reader as the object of the text's affective impact, the modern notion of the reader's active engagement with the text is not entirely absent. French neoclassical discussion of taste, for example, reveals a fine awareness of 'reader-competence'. The notion of a 'difficult' text which challenges the reader – like Barthes's *texte scriptible* – is familiar to all Neoplatonists. It followed from the Neoplatonist notion of imitation that the poet must necessarily employ hermetic language in order to convey, and to protect, his divinely inspired vision; this concern with allegorical and symbolic discourse has a major impact on Renaissance poetic theory, for example that of the Pléiade.[22] Even in the rationalist climate of French neoclassicism, hermetic writing found a legitimate outlet in the emblem and in apparently innocuous salon genres like the *énigme* and the *métamorphose*, both of which provided pretexts for the abbé Cotin to broach theoretical discussion of the nature of poetic difficulty.[23] Emotive impact and poetic difficulty come together in Longinus, when he writes that 'real sublimity *contains much food for reflection*, is difficult or rather impossible to resist, and makes a strong and ineffaceable impression on the memory' [my emphasis]:[24] both these aspects of reader-response inform the literary criticism of the early modern period.

[22] See D. P. Walker, 'Esoteric symbolism', in *Music, spirit and language in the Renaissance*, ed. P. Gouk (London: Variorum Reprints, 1985), ch. 15 ('Esoteric symbolism') [the work is unpaginated; pp. 218–32 in original printing, 1975].
[23] See N. Cronk, 'The enigma of French classicism: a Platonic current in seventeenth-century poetic theory', *French studies* 40 (1986), 269–86.
[24] Russell and Winterbottom (ed.), *Ancient literary criticism*, p. 467 (*On Sublimity* 7.3).

20

Italian epic theory

Daniel Javitch

The surge of Italian theorizing about epic that began in the mid-sixteenth century was part of a general effort to systematize poetic discourse by classifying and defining it according to its various genres. Aristotle's *Poetics* acquired unprecedented value in the second half of the sixteenth century precisely because its method and orientation suited the need to define poetry in terms of its genres and of their differences. The Greek text was made to spawn a much more systematic theory of genres than Aristotle had intended.[1] Late Cinquecento theorization of comedy makes this amplification of the *Poetics* particularly apparent since Aristotle left no substantive definition of comedy, or if he did, as was promised at the beginning of Chapter 6, it was subsequently lost. The lacking discussion of comedy did not prevent commentators from erecting what they imagined would be an Aristotelian theory of comedy. Indeed, it encouraged such projections, beginning with Francesco Robortello's 'Explicatio' on the art of comedy appended to his commentary on the *Poetics* (1548), and Giovan Giorgio Trissino's discussion of comedy in the *Sesta divisione della Poetica* (composed *c.* 1549) which follows what is, for the most part, an Italian paraphrase of Aristotle's *Poetics*. Eventually these reconstructions become independent attempts to codify comedy, for example Antonio Riccoboni's *De re comica* (1579). What was proclaimed to be Aristotle's codification of epic was, in a similar way, what sixteenth-century interpreters projected on the basis of Aristotle's brief discussion. Whereas Aristotle said next to nothing about comedy, he did devote two brief chapters (23 and 24) of the *Poetics* to epic, but without considering epic's distinctive attributes in any detail. Cinquecento theories of epic developed by filling out this scanty profile, and by conflating Aristotle's comments with what were perceived to be similar precepts in Horace's *Ars poetica*. Again, what began as slight amplification of Aristotle's pronouncements on epic in Trissino's last division of his *Poetica* became

[1] See D. Javitch, 'The assimilation of Aristotle's *Poetics* in sixteenth-century Italy', in the present volume (pp. 53–65).

extensive discussions of the genre within treatises on poetry, or independent treatises on the genre, for example, Torquato Tasso's later *Discorsi del poema eroico* (1594).

The first part of this essay will summarize the norms prescribed for epic in this *trattatistica* using, aside from Trissino's and Tasso's codifications, the following sources: Antonio Sebastiano Minturno's *L'arte poetica* (1564), Tasso's earlier *Discorsi dell'arte poetica* (originally composed between 1562 and 1565), Camillo Pellegrino's *Il Carrafa o vero della epica poesia* (1584) and Giason Denores's *Poetica* (1588). Such a digest does not mean to suggest that these norms became fixed or even widely accepted. The second half of this essay will show that these prescriptions were actually contested, stretched, and redefined as it became evident that they were designed to exclude chivalric romance from the canon of heroic poetry. Still, there was sufficient agreement about the formal and thematic requisites of the genre among various neo-Aristotelian codifiers to allow for the following synopsis.

One of the reasons sixteenth-century codifications of epic theory seem so derivative of Aristotle is because they usually organize themselves (Tasso's is an exception) around the four qualitative parts according to which Aristotle had analysed tragedy: plot; *ethos* or characterization; thought; and diction. Moreover, the tendency, warranted by Aristotle's claims about the similarities between tragedy and epic, was to transfer to epic the norms that the Greek philosopher had defined more fully for tragedy. Thus, in terms of plot, the plot of epic was to consist of a single unified main action with a beginning, middle, and end. Aristotle's recommendation that the plot be single and integrated was often reinforced by Horace's similar demand that it be 'simplex . . . et unum' (*Ars poetica* 23). Horace's other precepts on integrating the parts into a unified whole were conflated with Aristotle's similar demands at the end of Chapter 8. Also Horace's praise of Homer for his artistic selection of material, and for his hurrying into the midst of the story (*Ars poetica* 136–52) was corroborated by Chapter 23 of the *Poetics* (1459a30–6) where Aristotle points out that Homer did not deal with the entire Trojan War, but singled out one section of the whole story. Sixteenth-century commentators invoked the example of the *Aeneid* even more frequently than the *Odyssey* when arguing for the desirability of starting *in medias res* or for the advantages of organizing the narrative according to an *ordo obliquus* rather than a chronological *ordo naturalis*. Continuity as well as unity were called for. The main action could be suspended to make room for episodes, but these had to serve the main plot and not jeopardize its integrity in any way.

As for its subject, epic dealt with the memorable action of one or more illustrious individuals, a known event recorded in history rather than a made-up story. Aristotle had not stipulated that the subject of the epic plot be historical, but he had pointed out in Chapter 9 (1451b15) that tragic poets stick to names of men whose existence has been attested because the possible is persuasive, and what has occurred is evidently possible. When Tasso proposes in the first of his *Discorsi dell'arte poetica* that the epic poem must be founded on the authority of history, elaborating upon Aristotle's reasoning in Chapter 9, he explains that a historical subject-matter serves to lend epic greater verisimilitude adding that 'it is not verisimilar that an illustrious action, such as those in an heroic poem, would not have been written down and passed on to the memory of posterity with the help of history'.[2]

Epic protagonists were to be the same illustrious or highly placed ones that were to be found in tragedy. Thus the norms of characterization prescribed by Aristotle for tragedy (in chapter 15) were transferred to epic, contaminated by Horatian prescriptions on decorum of character. Sixteenth-century epic theorists called for exemplary behaviour in epic protagonists, a criterion not discussed by Aristotle. Thus the latter's primary requirement that the character be good [*khrestos*] was taken to mean that he or she be not simply a person of quality but a paragon of virtue. Actually, Aristotle made no distinction between tragic and epic protagonists. It became apparent, however, that the virtuous heroes that the theorists called for in epic differed from the middlingly good characters Aristotle recommended for tragedy, but it was not till Tasso defined the heroic poem that this un-Aristotelian distinction was clearly formulated.[3] The exemplarity of epic characters was meant to serve the epideictic and moral function that the Renaissance usually ascribed heroic poetry. Aristotle, of course, never attributed such a didactic function to poetry.

The scanty remarks in the *Poetics* on the formal properties of epic invited elaboration, especially the size, the magnitude of epic. Aristotle had acknowledged at the end of Chapter 17 (1455b15) that ancillary episodes were permissible in epic, and that they contributed to the *magnitudo* and variety which distinguished it from tragedy. This, along with his praise of Homer's use of amplifying digression (for example, the catalogue of ships in *Iliad* 2), and the recognition that the epic poet can narrate events that occur simultaneously in different places (Chapter 24, 1459b23–31), served to authorize the inclusion of episodes as a means of achieving the characteristic 'ampiezza' ['breadth'] of epic. Yet the impulse to digress from the main action or to amplify it with ancillary episodes had to be strictly disciplined: such accretions were sanctioned as long as the

---

[2] The translation used of Tasso's early *Discorsi* is by Lawrence Rhu in *The genesis of Tasso's narrative theory: English translations of the early poetics and a comparative study of their significance* (Detroit: Wayne State University Press, 1993), p. 100. For the original see Torquato Tasso, *Prose*, ed. E. Mazzali (Milan: Ricciardi, 1959), p. 351.

[3] See Tasso, *Prose*, p. 360.

episodes were probable and necessary (though what that meant was itself debated among the theorists), and related to, or were subordinate to, the main action, and did not lead to separate ends.[4] The integration of episode to main plot was the principal consideration. The stricter theorists argued that the *Iliad* or the *Aeneid* had to serve as exemplars of such integration since no episode could be removed from either of those poems without deforming or doing notable harm to them. In general, the amplifying function of episodes received a good deal more attention and definition than in the *Poetics*, as well as exemplification from post-Aristotelian practice, especially Virgil's.[5]

The greater duration of the epic action, which also distinguished it from that of tragedy, remained, on the whole, unspecified, although Minturno, for one, did propose a year as the limit. What was generally required was that the size of the poem or rather of the action that it embodied be such that, from beginning to end, it could be easily remembered or apprehended by the reader or audience. 'That poem is suitably large', Tasso maintains, 'in which the memory does not darken or fail but, taking the whole in at once, can consider how one thing connects with another and depends on a third and how the parts are in proportion to themselves and to the whole.'[6]

Aristotle's insistence on the need for tragic imitations to be probable and credible was reiterated by the Cinquecento theorists of epic, both in their discussion of plot development and of characterization. However, Aristotle's recognition that epic had more room for the marvellous and the irrational (1460a13: 'what is improbable, from which amazement arises most, is more admissible in epic . . .') allowed for some loosening of the constraints of verisimilitude imposed on tragedy. How far therefore the epic poet could strain the credibility of his audience, what were the impossible probabilities that Aristotle preferred to possible improbabilities (1460a26), were issues that were discussed more extensively.

Similarly Aristotle's passing acknowledgement of epic's greater capacity to provoke wonder encouraged some codifiers to consider epic's peculiar emotional effects, and to recognize that these differed from the pity and fear Aristotle demanded from tragedy. For example, in his early *Discorsi* Tasso correctly observed that, contrary to the claims of orthodox commentators, epic and tragedy did not have similar ends.

It is manifestly clear that the same effects do not proceed from tragedy and epic. Tragic actions arouse terror and pity . . . Epics, however, did not originate to

---

[4] On the need to control the diversity produced by episodes, see Tasso's discussion in the third of his *Discorsi del poema eroico*, in *Prose*, pp. 597–600.

[5] J. C. Scaliger, who considered Homer inferior to Virgil, singled out the Camilla episode in the *Aeneid* as a model example of the way episode should be integrated to plot. See *Poetices libri septem* (1561; reprint Stuttgart: Frommann-Holzboog, 1987), p. 144.

[6] Rhu, *Genesis*, p. 117; Tasso, *Prose*, p. 371.

move either terror or pity, nor was this condition required in them as necessary. Therefore, if we call the actions of tragedy and epic equally illustrious, their illustriousness is of different natures . . . Heroic illustriousness . . . is based on undertakings of exalted martial valor and on deeds of courtesy, generosity, piety, and religion. Such actions, appropriate for epic, in no way suit tragedy.[7]

While other codifiers shared Tasso's claim that the 'maraviglia' particular to epic was generated, as Giason Denores would put it, by 'any virtuous feat that surpassed the ordinary capacity of great men', Tasso was the first to discuss extensively how epic wonder should be produced. For example, the miraculous was another traditional source of the marvellous, but if wonder was produced by divine or supernatural interventions, Tasso argued that these had to conform to Christian beliefs to be credible.[8] The marvellous did not only reside in the poem's subject-matter, but could also be achieved by the artistry of its form, by its stylistic features, by its *verba*.[9]

Italian codifiers had to find a vernacular equivalent for the Greek hexameter, the metre of ancient epic which Aristotle considered one of the few features to distinguish it from tragedy (epic's mode of enunciation, its size, and duration were the others). Trissino proposed the 'endecasillabo sciolto', considering that *ottava rima* and other rhyme schemes were inadequate for epic's gravity. However, most contemporaries (except for Denores) disagreed with Trissino's critique of *ottava rima* and accepted this rhymed verse as the most appropriate for heroic narrative. 'We can see today', writes Alessandro Piccolomini in his 1575 commentary on the *Poetics*, 'that, despite the efforts of learned men and good poets to prescribe either *terza rima*, in Dante's manner, or the unrhymed hendecasyllable, [as the metre] for the vernacular epic poem, *ottava rima* has nonetheless clearly prevailed'.[10]

The codification of epic that emerges in the middle of the Cinquecento did not simply consist of disembodied formulations and rules. Theorizing about genres in the sixteenth century was almost always related to contemporary poetic practice, or, to be more precise, to disputes about that practice. Thus Trissino's prescription of the unrhymed *endecasillabo* brings to mind his own vernacular epic written in this verse, the *Italia liberata dai goti* (1547–8). Some twenty years in the making, Trissino's poem was the first to be deliberately modelled on Homer's example, and

---

[7] Rhu, *Genesis*, pp. 107–8; Tasso, *Prose*, pp. 359–60.
[8] See Tasso, *Prose*, pp. 355 and 538.
[9] For example, Trissino (see B. Weinberg (ed.), *Trattati di poetica e retorica del Cinquecento* (Bari: Laterza, 1970), vol. II, pp. 48–50) and Denores single out extended similes as sources of 'maraviglia' in epic.
[10] Alessandro Piccolomini, *Annotationi . . . nel libro della Poetica d'Aristotele* (Venice: G. Guarisco, 1575), pp. 383–4.

made to conform to Aristotle's prescriptions. It turned out to be a resounding failure. On the other hand, Ariosto's *Orlando furioso*, a chivalric romance which did not observe neoclassical principles, had become by the mid-century the most popular poem of modern times. Between 1540 and 1570 it was reprinted about ninety times, and by the 1560s more editions of the *Furioso* were being reissued than Petrarch's already canonical *Canzoniere*. Thanks to the promotional efforts of its Venetian publishers, it was also being acclaimed as the heretofore missing classic of Italian narrative poetry, the modern equivalent of the great epics of antiquity.

Theorizing about epic in the second half of the sixteenth century could not ignore the tremendous success and reputation of the *Furioso*, nor, for that matter, the failure of Trissino's neoclassical epic.[11] It so happened that the *Orlando furioso* enjoyed its greatest success and was being proclaimed the new heroic poem of the age between the 1540s and the 1570s, the same period during which Aristotle's *Poetics* was being assimilated and conflated with Horace's *Ars poetica* to shape the rules of epic outlined above. This conjunction could not fail to provoke controversy given that critics perceived that Ariosto's poem flouted what were understood to be Aristotle's prescriptions for epic. The new classicists were quick to point out Ariosto's transgressions and to deny the *Furioso* the heroic status it was being accorded.

One cannot help being struck by how the development of epic theory is related to the disparagement of chivalric romance that builds up in the middle decades of the century. Indeed, the norms of epic previously summarized are initially formulated in attacks against *Orlando furioso* that begin to appear just before 1550. These first attacks against Ariosto's best-seller, which we only know about at second hand, might be said to define epic by negation, dwelling as they do on the failure of the *Furioso* to observe the epic requisites set down by Aristotle.[12]

This tendency to define epic poetry by using the deficiencies of the *Furioso* and other *romanzi* as counter-examples recurs in most of the theorizing about epic produced in the second half of the sixteenth century. But before examining the literary politics that underlie the codification of epic it should be noted that the attacks the new Aristotelians mounted against the *Furioso* prompted Giovambattista Giraldi Cintio to write his *Discorso intorno al comporre dei romanzi*, and Giovanni Battista

---

[11] Contrasting Trissino's failure with Ariosto's enormous success, Tasso writes 'Trissino, on the other hand, who proposed to imitate the poems of Homer devoutly . . . is mentioned by few, read by fewer, esteemed by almost no one, voiceless in the theater of the world and dead to human eyes'. Rhu, *The genesis*, pp. 117–18; Tasso, *Prose*, p. 372.

[12] For an important account of this earliest neo-Aristotelian criticism of the *Furioso* see Giovanni Battista Pigna's 1548 letter to Giovambattista Giraldi Cintio, reprinted in G. B. Giraldi, *Scritti critici*, ed. C. G. Crocetti (Milan: Marzorati, 1973), pp. 246–7.

Pigna to write *I romanzi*, the first theorizations of the chivalric romance. Giraldi's response, the 1554 *Discorso*, was the first attempt to formulate a theory of the chivalric romance as a genre quite distinct from ancient epic. Giraldi proposed that the *romanzo* could not be judged according to ancient epic norms because it was a more modern kind of poetry and observed different formal laws. Giraldi's historicizing of poetic norms was perhaps his most lasting contribution to sixteenth-century theory. Challenging the orthodox classicist view that Aristotle's (and for that matter Horace's) poetic principles, being the product of natural reason, were unchanging and held for all poetic composition, Giraldi argued that such composition changes as customs and tastes themselves change over time. If, in the present age, 'romanzatori' compose their works according to different poetic norms from those advocated by Horace and Aristotle it is because these norms conform better to modern taste than the anachronistic ones of ancient epic. The main features of romance that Giraldi sought to justify were its multiplicity of plots, and of protagonists, and the relative discontinuity and other peculiar narrative aspects such multiplicity necessitated. According to Giraldi the copiousness and *varietà* produced by the many plots and protagonists of chivalric romance were particularly cherished by modern audiences.

   Giovanni Battista Pigna's *I romanzi*, the other pioneering codification of the romance, was also conceived as a rebuttal to the neo-Aristotelian attack against the *Furioso*. Like Giraldi, Pigna asserted that the romances were composed according to some principles that differed from ancient epic. He distinguished the multiple plot structures and the feigned subject-matter of the *romanzo* from the historical matter and single plot of classical epic. However, Pigna sought to show that as the genre evolved into its superior Italian phase (culminating with the *Furioso*), it eventually embodied most of Aristotle's criteria for epic poetry. In so far as the romance is an imitation of heroic actions and deals with matter that is exemplary, marvellous yet verisimilar, it is like classical epic. Pigna was much more prone than Giraldi to make the *romanzo* conform to Aristotle's *Poetics*. 'In speaking of romances', he claims at one point, 'Aristotle has been our guide although he never spoke of them'.[13] Giraldi's original effort to give the *romanzo* a separate generic identity was fiercely contested during the next thirty-five years. The new Aristotelians had to refute his claims because to recognize the chivalric romance as a new genre was to deny a fundamental premise of the neoclassicists: that poetic art has universal and unchanging norms. If Aristotle, they maintained, did not

---

[13] *I romanzi di M. Giovan Battista Pigna* (Venice: V. Valgrisi, 1554), p. 65. For a more general discussion of the *romanzo* in the context of Italian Renaissance prose fiction and poetics, see the essay of Glyn P. Norton in the present volume (pp. 328–36).

include the *romanzo* in his generic system, then it simply was not legitimate poetry. Thus, when Antonio Sebastiano Minturno distinguishes
the lowly and flawed *romanzo* from the higher and proper kind of poetry
that is epic, he refuses to grant this inferior form of writing the dignity of a
separate generic identity. In the first book of his *Arte poetica* (1564) where
this critique of the *romanzo* is to be found, we see the recurrence of a phenomenon already apparent in Pigna's account of the first neo-Aristotelian
attacks against Ariosto, namely that epic needs to be contrasted to its
transgressive opposite, the romance, in order to be fully defined. But more
than that, in Minturno's *Arte poetica* it becomes evident that an inherent
function of epic theory is not simply to castigate the *romanzo*, but to
exclude it as non-poetic.

For Minturno the *romanzo* – Ariosto's included – does not observe
rules of its own, but consists rather of transgressions of various unchanging artistic principles which define heroic poetry, for example unity of
action, narrative coherence, and continuity. It should be understood that
by including the *Furioso* in his condemnation of the *romanzo* Minturno
not only sought to refute Giraldi's legitimation of the modern genre, but
also to refute the more numerous champions of the *Furioso* who, like
Pigna, tried to affiliate it to Homer's and Virgil's epics and to argue that
it conformed to Aristotle's prescriptions for epic narrative. By the 1560s
Aristotle's *Poetics* had become more widely known and more authoritative, a development which enabled Minturno to make it more evident
than it had been a decade earlier that Ariosto's poem simply did not
observe the formal norms Aristotle had established for epic, efforts to find
such a congruence notwithstanding.

The most important contribution to epic theory in this period was
Tasso's *Discorsi dell'arte poetica*, only published in 1587 but originally
composed between 1562 and 1565, about the same time that Minturno's
treatise appeared. Tasso shared Minturno's perception that the romance
was a defective kind of poetic composition, and his codification of epic
was also impelled by a critique of the *romanzo*. In his second 'discorso'
this critique takes the form of refuting Giraldi's legitimation of the chivalric
romance on the grounds that it is different from traditional epic poetry.
According to Tasso, the confusing multiplicity, the excessive length, the
absence of beginnings and ends, the discontinuity of both Boiardo's and
Ariosto's romances are not, *pace* Giraldi, formal features of the *romanzo*
as an independent genre. They are structural flaws inherent in episodic
narratives that refuse to observe classical, that is proper, norms of unity
and continuity. As readily as he recognized the success of *Orlando furioso*,
Tasso's theory aimed to point out how badly Ariosto put together
his poem, and, by implication, how artistically superior would be the
epic that conformed to the norms he set forth, namely his own heroic

Gerusalemme liberata. Minturno's and Tasso's view that the modern romance is a defective and transgressive kind of heroic composition was reiterated by neo-Aristotelians for the next two decades. By the time, however, that Camillo Pellegrino reasserts this view in his 1584 dialogue *Il Carrafa o vero della epica poesia*, the lowly and vulgar *romanzo* is given a more specific profile. *Il Carrafa* was the first published work that championed Tasso's *Gerusalemme liberata* and claimed that, in comparison to Ariosto's *Furioso*, Tasso's work was a far superior epic poem. Debate over the relative merits of the two works began almost immediately after the original publication of Tasso's poem in 1581, but it was Pellegrino who first brought together the various claims made about the superiority of the *Liberata* as an epic. By clearly championing Tasso over Ariosto he sparked off a critical debate between the *Ariostisti* and the *Tassisti* that lasted until the end of the century.[14]

Pellegrino argued that Ariosto chose to write a popular *romanzo* instead of an epic, and given the inferiority of that type of writing, he could not have hoped to achieve Tasso's degree of honour in epic poetry. But as he distinguishes the romance from epic to establish its inferiority he singles out the following features: its imitation of many actions, and of many protagonists, including wicked and immoral ones; its completely false stories; its lack of gravity; its unconnected digressions and, in general, its confusing lack of unity. These features are all deemed defective, but they begin to constitute a generic definition nonetheless. Quite unlike Giraldi's definition of romance which aimed to affirm the legitimacy of the modern counterpart of epic, Pellegrino's definition aims to show every way the *romanzo* fails to conform to the perennial norms of epic formulated by Aristotle. We have seen that this kind of criticism had been levelled at chivalric romance for over three decades. But rather than merely objecting about the failure of the *romanzo* to satisfy epic norms, Pellegrino now has Tasso's poem to invoke as proof that these norms can be admirably fulfilled in modern Italian poetry.

Pellegrino's opponents were quick to perceive that by categorizing Ariosto as a mere *romanzatore* in comparison to a true epic poet like Tasso, Pellegrino was trying to disqualify *Orlando furioso* as heroic poetry, and they fought back. Pellegrino's main opponent in this debate was Lionardo Salviati. His response, in defence of Ariosto, was published anonymously in several tracts beginning with the *Difesa dell'Orlando furioso. Contra 'l dialogo dell'epica poesia di Camillo Pellegrino* (1584) and culminating in the *Infarinato secondo . . . risposta al libro intitolato*

---

[14] For a survey of this prolonged debate see Bernard Weinberg, *A history of literary criticism in the Italian Renaissance*, 2 vols. (Chicago: University of Chicago Press, 1961), vol. II, pp. 991–1073.

Replica di Camillo Pellegrino (1588). Salviati realized that the debate about the merits of Ariosto's *romanzo* centred around the issue of whether it was a different kind of poem from the epic defined by Aristotle, and embodied in Homer's and Virgil's practice. His strategy was to marshal every possible argument to show that there was no such difference.[15] He first maintains that to differentiate the *romanzo* and the epic poem, as Pellegrino has done, is to defy Aristotle's principles. Salviati is committed to these rational principles; he simply does not believe that his opponent has understood Aristotle, and he refutes him by reinterpreting the *Poetics* in a way that will support his case. In this instance he proceeds to challenge Pellegrino's generic distinction by pointing out that, according to Aristotle (Salviati is referring to *Poetics* 1448a24), it is the different subject, the different means, and the different manner or mode that serve to distinguish different poetic genres. Applying these three criteria to the romance and the epic, he maintains that both imitate the actions of illustrious persons, both use verse to do so, and both are narrative in their manner or mode. Both are therefore generically identical.[16] To further challenge Pellegrino's claim that, unlike the matter of epic, the matter of romance includes unworthy deeds enacted by morally dubious characters, Salviati reminds his opponent that Homer similarly includes vile individuals along with higher-ranking protagonists. Actually, one of Salviati's most original strategies is to assimilate Ariosto's *romanzo* to the canonical epics of antiquity by showing that most of the so-called imperfections of the *Orlando furioso* are also recognizable features of Homer's and Virgil's heroic poems. Thus against the charge that the *romanzo* lacks the unity, both formal and thematic, that characterizes epic poetry, Salviati quite effectively demonstrates that the ancient epics possess within their unified plots much the same sort of multiplicity castigated in the *Furioso*.[17]

Salviati also refutes the charge that Ariosto violated the Aristotelian demand for unity by arguing that Aristotle had a different standard of unity for epic than he did for dramatic poetry. He even provides a graphic illustration of the almond-shaped structure of a properly designed epic plot, filled out in the middle by the breadth and variety of material called for by Aristotle.[18] According to Salviati such amplitude is the 'virtù

---

[15] For a fuller account of Salviati's defence of the *Furioso*, see D. Javitch, *Proclaiming a classic: the canonization of 'Orlando furioso'* (Princeton: Princeton University Press, 1991), pp. 112–22.

[16] Using the same 'Aristotelian' reasoning as Salviati, Tasso had previously challenged the generic differentiation of epic and romance in the second of his *Discorsi dell'arte poetica* (*Prose*, p. 377), but in order to criticize Boiardo's and Ariosto's artistic deficiencies.

[17] Francesco Patrizi had already made the same argument about the multiplicity of Homer's poems in his *Parere . . . in difesa dell'Ariosto*, appended with other texts to Tasso's *Apologia in difesa della sua Gerusalemme liberata* (Ferrara: G. C. Cagnacini, 1585).

[18] Lionardo Salviati, *Lo 'nfarinato secondo* (Florence: A. Padovani, 1588), p. 73.

propria' of the heroic poem, whereas the thinness of the single plot desirable in the tragedy is a flaw in epic. The *Furioso*, he then demonstrates, is constructed according to the precepts of plot unity that he has derived from Aristotle. Nor does Salviati have to distort Aristotle out of recognition to make his case. It is precisely because Aristotle's observations about epic's characteristic amplitude (*Poetics* 59b23–31) could be used to justify Ariosto's narrative practice that a debate could take place. This review of the debate about what constituted heroic poetry makes apparent how unfixed the boundaries of epic remained despite the efforts to establish its formal and semantic properties. Both theorists and poets were aware that there were more than merely theoretical disagreements involved in the definition of this and, for that matter, any genre. Important and pragmatic issues of exclusion and inclusion were at stake bearing not only on the status of one new poetic composition, but on the legitimacy of modern poetry generally. Conservative critics realized that genre theory, while pretending to offer a universal definition of a given genre, had to place definite limits on the body of texts and features it considered to arrive at that definition. They exploited such inherent selectivity in genre theory to exclude texts they sought to degrade or to disqualify. This is particularly evident in Pellegrino's definition of epic poetry in *Il Carrafa*, a definition aimed to disqualify *Orlando furioso* as epic. Pellegrino's effort to exclude Ariosto's poem would have not been so necessary had the poem not already acquired epic status thanks to the promotional efforts of Ariosto's champions. But the very status it had achieved posed a threat to the rigid neoclassical idea of epic that Pellegrino and his colleagues wanted to institute. Lionardo Salviati fought back because he immediately realized that what was at stake was the formation of the canon of texts that would be called epic, and he wanted to prevent that canon from being so closed. To challenge Pellegrino he had to redefine his opponent's criteria of epic in such a way that they would again accommodate *Orlando furioso*. He managed to do so while still grounding these criteria on Homeric and Virgilian precedents, and on what he argued was a superior reading of Aristotle's *Poetics*. Ultimately then the debate between Pellegrino and Salviati not only revealed the exclusive potential of neo-Aristotelian genre theory, but also its capacity to be stretched according to the demands of an evolving literary canon.

21

The lyric

Roland Greene

Within the loose system of literary genres that existed in the passage from the Middle Ages to the Renaissance, lyric has an especially problematic trajectory. For one thing, lyric is always – even today – the most fugitive of genres when it comes to a theory of its identity. And for another, the period in question is probably the starting point of the modern idea of lyric productions as short, intense, and exquisite redactions of impassioned speech – a notion that is much further developed in the Romantic period, but has recognizable beginnings in the early Renaissance. One consequence of this latter view is that lyric theory comes to seem almost a contradiction in terms: where it is assumed that speech can be idealized into poetry and poetry naturalized into speech, a poetics of lyric like those of epic or drama can seem beside the point. Moreover, the disparity between the available terms of lyric theory and the actual productions of the genre becomes arrestingly evident in this period. In many ways the most acute poetics of the early modern lyric is written out in poems themselves, such as Garcilaso de la Vega's *Egloga tercera* (written *c.* 1526, published 1543) and Edmund Spenser's *Shepheardes calender* (1579), where poets and their audiences often find the common ground for genre-orientated conversation they otherwise lack. Hence the emergence of lyric in this period – its separation from the other genres, its theory and practice – must be sought in many untoward places, and witnessed alongside other events.

At the beginning of the early modern period, one finds an incommensurability between what is then labelled as lyric and what we now call by that name: the technical term as received from classical Greek and the ill-defined corpus of brief, subjective writing in verse are approaching one another, but are not yet fully joined. During the sixteenth century the descriptive term and the discursive reality come to accommodate each other fairly well, although the account of how they do so remains to be written. In this essay, a few touchstones of the process will have to suffice: the developing notion of lyric as a kind of writing much concerned with materiality; the genre's compact with subjectivity; and the role of lyric in society, which depends on reconciling materiality, subjectivity, and other features in a specifically modern programme for the genre.

The view of lyric as a minor type of poetry, defined by external factors
and not implicated in emergent modern issues such as subjectivity, runs
through the fourteenth and fifteenth centuries; it is a commonplace of
these periods that lyric theory, as such, is only intermittently separable
from rhetorical theory, and that would-be critics and theorists have to
make an explicit case for lyric's non-identity with rhetoric until about
1600.[1] A late treatment of lyric as minor and theoretically unexciting can
be found in Julius Caesar Scaliger's Aristotelian *Poetices libri septem*
(1561). The table of contents of Scaliger's Book 1, concerning the history
of poetry, begins with chapters on such matters as 'the indispensability of
language' and 'the origin of poetry, its causes, effects, form, and material',
and then allots chapters to particular kinds of poems such as pastoral
(Chapter 4) and comedy and tragedy (Chapter 5). Well down the list come
Chapters 44 ('lyric poetry'), 45 ('hymns'), 46 ('dithyrambs'), and 50
('funeral and marriage songs, elegies, etc.').[2]

What is lyric here? Scaliger thinks of lyric as a loose category of sung
poetry including odes, idylls, paeans, and other celebratory compositions.
About a decade later, the English theorist Roger Ascham claims greater
import for lyric among the *genera dicendi* (literally, 'genres of speaking').
For Ascham and many others in this period, writing itself is divided into
the four categories of poetic, historical, philosophical, and oratorical,
while the first of these, the *genus poeticum*, consists of comic, tragic, epic,
and melic poetry.[3] Though the place of 'melic' or lyric poetry in Ascham's
scheme goes somewhat unelaborated, the increasing consequence of the
genre is unmistakable: it has moved up to claim everything in poetry not
already under comedy, tragedy, or epic. And another ten years later, Sir
Philip Sidney asks those who would disparage poetry, 'is it the Lyric that
most displeaseth, who with his tuned lyre and well-accorded voice, giveth
praise, the reward of virtue, to virtuous acts; who gives moral precepts,
and natural problems; who sometimes raiseth up his voice to the height of

---

[1] Charles Sears Baldwin, *Renaissance literary theory and practice*, ed. D. L. Clark (New
York: Columbia University Press, 1939); Bernard Weinberg, *A history of literary criticism
in the Italian Renaissance*, 2 vols. (Chicago: University of Chicago Press, 1961), vol. I,
pp. 1–37; François Rigolot, *Le texte de la Renaissance: des rhétoriqueurs à Montaigne*
(Geneva: Droz, 1982), pp. 25–40. Paul Zumthor, *Towards a medieval poetics*, trans.
P. Bennett (Minneapolis: University of Minnesota Press, 1992), gives an especially useful
account of medieval lyric that complicates some of the summary observations in the
present essay.

[2] Julius Caesar Scaliger, *Poetices libri septem* (1561; facs. reprint Stuttgart: Friedrich
Frommann, 1964), ed. A. Buck, p. aiiii2'; *Select translations from Scaliger's Poetics*, trans.
F. M. Padelford (New York: Henry Holt, 1905), pp. ix–x. Compare Lodovico Castelvetro's
remarks on Aristotle's neglect of epideictic and lyric poetry in *Poetica d'Aristotele
vulgarizzata et sposta* (Vienna, 1570), ed. B. Fabian (Munich: W. Fink, 1968), p. 42'; trans.
A. Bongiorno (Binghamton: Medieval and Renaissance Texts and Studies, 1984), p. 49.

[3] Roger Ascham, *The scholemaster* (London, 1570), in *Elizabethan critical essays*, ed.
G. G. Smith, 2 vols. (Oxford: Clarendon Press, 1904), vol. I, p. 23.

the heavens, in singing the lauds of the immortal God?'[4] How is European poetics conducted through the views expressed in these three statements by Scaliger, Ascham, and Sidney – the first of which, decidedly old fashioned for its time, assumes the marginality of lyric, while the others claim ever more ambitious and socially indispensable purposes for it? What are the underlying issues on which these positions depend? A few observations may be made and hypotheses advanced.

Poetic artifice, as Veronica Forrest-Thomson conceives it in a landmark study of twentieth-century poetry, is the property compounded from 'the rhythmic, phonetic, verbal, and logical devices which make poetry different from prose'.[5] One important subset of artifice is materiality, or the physical reality of poetry as sounds and letters. In early modern poetics, the artifice of lyric, especially material artifice, is one of the properties treated as definitive of the genre at large and used to foreground lyric from other instances of poetry in general. Lyric, it might be extrapolated from a developing Renaissance consensus, is the kind of poetry in which material considerations, from simple rhymes to elaborate technopaegnia or graphic patterns, are nearly always recognizable and immediate. Materiality can be for lyric what a common national or political culture can be for epic, and what the social experience of the theatre can be for drama, namely a horizon that organizes individual responses into a collective reception, and allows the genre its distinctive stamp as a literary kind. Hence in the period of the late Middle Ages through to the Renaissance, one sees poets and theorists coming to propose (not always explicitly) that the essence of lyric can be described as coextensive with its physical forms – for instance, the ballad, the canzone, and most of all, the sonnet. The Cistercian monk Juan Caramuel de Lobkowitz plots this conviction almost to the point of absurdity in his *Metametrica* (1663), a voluminous collection of rhyme-words, metrical and aural demonstrations, and permutational schemes that enable a reader with no inspiration whatever to fashion a poem out of available building-blocks.[6] Forms that might seem shop-worn to a modern reader are still freshly material for Renaissance audiences, and speak to the artificial purposes of the genre in ways that may strike us today as overly, even superstitiously, formalist.[7]

---

[4] Sir Philip Sidney, *A defence of poetry*, in *Miscellaneous prose of Sir Philip Sidney*, ed. K. Duncan-Jones and J. van Dorsten (Oxford: Clarendon Press, 1973), p. 97.

[5] Veronica Forrest-Thomson, *Poetic artifice* (Manchester: Manchester University Press, 1978), p. ix.

[6] Juan Caramuel de Lobkowitz, *Primus calamus ob oculos ponens metametricam* (Rome: F. Falconius, 1663).

[7] See, for example, María José Vega Ramos, *El secreto artificio: qualitas sonorum, maronolatría y tradición pontaniana en la poética del Renacimiento* (Madrid: Consejo Superior de Investigaciones Científicas, Universidad de Extremadura, 1992), on theories of sound properties in early modern poetry. I am grateful to Julian Weiss for bringing this book to my attention.

Something of a transition can be seen by starting with a fourteenth-century treatise by Giovanni Boccaccio, where an extensive defence of 'poetry' involves little effort to differentiate what we call lyric from the other kinds of fiction that Boccaccio includes under his single rubric. Poetry in this general sense is 'a sort of fervid and exquisite invention, with fervid expression, in speech or writing, of that which the mind has invented', he writes. It 'adorns the whole composition with unusual inter-weaving of words and thoughts; and thus it veils truth in a [fictional and fit covering]'.[8] Boccaccio's definition is scarcely prepared to allow for artifice or materiality outside the context of adornment, as an actual condition of representation or a kind of knowledge in itself. Implicitly lyric is kept within strict limits, and assimilated to the other genres by means of an all-purpose description.

By the middle of the fifteenth century, however, notions of lyric poetics are very much in process; and in his *Proemio e carta* (written *c.* 1445–9), one of the decisive texts for the modernization of Spanish letters, the Marquis of Santillana argues in these terms for the value of *poesía*:

And what sort of thing is poetry – which in our vernacular we call the gay science – but a fashioning of useful things, covered or veiled with a beautiful covering, composed, distinguished, and scanned by a certain count, weight, and measure? . . . And who doubts that as the green leaves in springtime garnish and accompany the naked trees, the sweet voices and beautiful sounds adorn and accompany every rhyme, every metre, every verse, of whatever art, weight, and measure?[9]

In Santillana's first formulation here, the unusual term *fingimiento* ('fashioning' or 'making') replaces the more standard *ficción*:[10] compare Dante's 'rhetorical fiction composed in music' ['fictio rethorica musicaque poita'][11] and Boccaccio's 'fictional and fit covering' ['uelamento fabuloso atque decenti']. In the second formulation, the determined attention to sounds and rhythms in the figure of the leaves suggests that the covering might be believed almost as interesting as what it covers; that the fashioning of a poem depends perhaps as much on the capacity to dispose sounds

[8] Giovanni Boccaccio, *Genealogiae*, ed. S. Orgel (New York: Garland, 1976), p. 104[r]; *On poetry: being the preface and the fourteenth and fifteenth books of Boccaccio's Genealogia deorum gentilium*, trans. C. G. Osgood, 2nd edn (Indianapolis: Bobbs-Merrill, 1956), p. 39, translation modified as indicated.
[9] Marqués de Santillana, 'Proemio e carta', *Obras completas*, ed. A. Gómez Moreno and M. P. A. M. Kerkhof (Barcelona: Planeta, 1988), pp. 439, 447.
[10] Julian Weiss, *The poet's art: literary theory in Castile c. 1400–60* (Oxford: Society for the Study of Mediaeval Languages and Literature, 1990), p. 191.
[11] Dante Alighieri, *De vulgari eloquentia*, ed. P. V. Mengaldo (Padua: Antenore, 1968), p. 39; *De vulgari eloquentia, Dante's book of exile*, trans. M. Shapiro (Lincoln, NB: University of Nebraska Press, 1990), p. 74.

and forms as it does on, again, fictive invention (versus the protocol of Boccaccio's poetic process). Santillana's conceit of leaves on trees is a telling one. He appears to be about to pose the familiar dichotomy of outer 'concrete material' and inner 'ideas' – in which, by long tradition in medieval poetics, the latter have the upper hand[12] – when he veers off to portray 'sounds' that cover 'rhymes' and 'metres': a poetics, it seems, of sheer materiality, where nothing qualifies as substance beneath the artifice. In reality, because Santillana has already articulated the stock contrast between 'useful things' and 'beautiful covering', his audience will probably read the same terms in this second iteration in spite of the some-what unexpected words that he actually writes. All the same, Santillana gestures towards a fuller conception of lyric artifice than has existed to this point, and anticipates the arguments and experiments of the next two centuries.

Between Boccaccio's and Santillana's dicta, of course, something important has happened: the emergence of Petrarchism across national borders as a renovative force in European poetics. From the standpoint of the present essay, the mode of lyric writing based on the example of Francesco Petrarca carries a unique weight in the early modern period. It instantiates a set of expectations about lyric – for instance, that to rethink the genre is to reinvent various lyric forms, and that modern lyric involves a fresh charter between meaning and artifice, opening manifold new ways for a poem to operate as a fiction. Aristotle's *Rhetoric* and *Poetics*, though they have little to say about lyric poetry as such, become increasingly visible between the mid-fifteenth and the mid-sixteenth centuries, owing especially to the commentary by Francesco Robortello of 1548 and the Italian translation of Bernardo Segni the next year; Horace's *Ars poetica* had been in circulation during the Middle Ages, and met Aristotle in the Renaissance as an anachronistic precursor and its counterweight in a mutual critique. However they differ in the import they attach to the mimetic and rhetorical purposes of poetry, as Bernard Weinberg shows, Aristotle and Horace alike authorize the early modern conviction that form and meaning can be – must be – adjusted to one another, that they are adaptable by genre and within genres. The rise of an artifice-orientated lyric poetics can be seen where Giovanni Giorgio Trissino, best known as a poet of epic and drama and an Aristotelian theorist, inveighs against rhyme in received fashion in about 1550, only to make an exception for lyric in a specifically early modern way: 'in the choruses of tragedies and comedies and in poems whose matter is love or praise, where sweetness and attractiveness are especially desirable, rhymes with their rules are not

---

[12] D. W. Robertson, Jr., *A preface to Chaucer* (Princeton: Princeton University Press, 1962), p. 16.

to be given up, but ought to be received and adopted as principal causes of this attractiveness and sweetness'.[13]

English literary theory of the same moment is limited by a view that can seem imperceptive to modern readers but that tells us much about how materiality was seen as both a problem and the defining feature of the lyric genre. As Derek Attridge has shown, until late in the sixteenth century there was no reliable distinction in practice between the words *rhythm* and *rhyme*, but both interchangeably referred to a complex of material effects – accentual rhythms as well as 'the falling out of verses together in one like sounde'[14] – that were understood as opposed to quantitative verse. One of the qualities that marked *rithme* (where the two modern meanings are joined in a single English word *c.* 1560) for denigration, Attridge proposes, was that its effects could actually be recognized by all readers, while quantity based on classical models became increasingly difficult to perceive as native metres grew more prominent. Here then is an instance of materiality based in the physical facts of the English language set against an idealized, non-material prosody. Eventually the two terms are distinguished from one another because of the volume of emergent lyric writing after about 1580, including Petrarchan poetry, that demonstrates a fresh adjustment of form and meaning which supersedes that of classical quantity.

Most of all, the newly invented or revived lyric forms in this period – such as the canzone, the sestina, and the sonnet – manifestly entail the bringing together of history, subjectivity, and poetic artifice.[15] Each form, in other words, embodies a characteristic attitude towards the representation of historical and social events, a set of conventions for accommodating the individual standpoint, and a material realization that adjusts both history and subjectivity to one another and makes their relation seem

---

[13] Giovan Giorgio Trissino, *Poetica* (Venice: A. Arrivabene, 1562), translated in A. H. Gilbert (ed.), *Literary criticism: Plato to Dryden* (Detroit: Wayne State University Press, 1962), p. 214. Most of Trissino's *Poetica* was published in 1529, but the last sections (Parts V and VI) including that on rhyme seem to have been written about 1549, and were published in 1562. According to Weinberg (*A history of literary criticism*, vol. II, p. 1155), the title pages of some copies bear the date 1563, but seem otherwise indistinguishable from the 1562 edition.

[14] William Webbe, *Discourse of English poetrie* (London: no pub., 1586), in *Elizabethan critical essays*, ed. Smith, vol. I, p. 267, quoted in Derek Attridge, *Well-weighed syllables: Elizabethan verse in classical metres* (Cambridge: Cambridge University Press, 1974), p. 95.

[15] On the sonnet, among many other treatments, see Ernest Hatch Wilkins, 'The invention of the sonnet', in *The invention of the sonnet and other studies in Italian literature* (Rome: Edizioni di Storia e Letteratura, 1959), pp. 11–39, and François Rigolot, 'Qu'est-ce qu'un sonnet? Perspectives sur les origines d'une forme poétique', *Revue d'histoire littéraire de la France* 84 (1984), 3–18; on the canzone, Wilkins, 'The canzone and the minnesong', in *Invention of the sonnet*, pp. 41–50; on the sestina, Marianne Shapiro, *Hieroglyph of time: the Petrarchan sestina* (Minneapolis: University of Minnesota Press, 1980).

inevitable. The sonnet works for Renaissance audiences because it organizes a vivid stand-off between the world and the self in a short and highly reproducible poetic integer; the breaks in sense and feeling that invariably run through sonnets (chiefly between the eighth and ninth lines) evidence the shifts in this uneasy but durable balance, where the world interrupts the self and vice versa. Accordingly, the early modern sonnet becomes the semi-official vehicle of contemporaneous lyric, and both commentary and theory respond to it as a given. 'I esteem a sonnet by Petrarch more highly than all the romances', writes Antonio Minturno in 1564, highlighting the form's fictional ambitions ('all the romances' refers to narrative fiction) within 'a' single, delicately wrought material circumscription.[16] Richard Tottel introduces his landmark collection *Songes and sonettes* or *Tottel's miscellany* (1557), a modernizing force in English poetry, with a similar tribute: 'That to haue wel written in verse, yea & in small parcelles, deserueth great praise, the workes of diuers Latines, Italians, and other, doe proue sufficiently'. He goes on to argue that the lyrics of Thomas Wyatt and the Earl of Surrey, some adapted out of Petrarch but many more representing the particular amatory complaints of various personae, have national reach, adding to the store of English eloquence and honouring 'the Englishe tong'.[17] Such announcements appear in most of the European literatures around mid-century, and the Italianate sonnet is often professed as the key to a new era.

Much of the appeal of sonnet sequences in this period has to do with their minute recalibrations of the single sonnet's equilibrium of inner and outer worlds, without finally allowing one to dominate the other. Moreover, the sonnet has it both ways in an age that sees the rise of both individualism and national literary cultures: each sonnet seems a uniquely personal event or artefact – and its speaker often declares the singularity of his or her experience – and yet the multiplication of the form by the tens, hundreds, and thousands reveals it as a widely held template, a fictional genre as well as an index of cultural modernity. The sonnet enables European cultures – and others, as we continue to learn[18] – to share a technology of ideation and feeling, to convey and receive first-person fictions, to think through a common medium, all the while professing the particular identity of each society, poet, and speaker.

Therefore lyric comes to have a complex relation to the early modern debate over the nature and value of fiction. Productions such as the sonnet

---

[16] Antonio Minturno, *L'arte poetica* (Venice: G. A. Valvassori, 1564), translated in Gilbert (ed.), *Literary criticism*, p. 276.
[17] *Tottel's Miscellany (1557–1587)*, ed. H. E. Rollins, rev. edn, 2 vols. (Cambridge, MA: Harvard University Press, 1965), vol. i, p. 2.
[18] For example, *Flores de varia poesía* (1577) is a European-inspired lyric anthology compiled in Mexico City. The modern edition is by Margarita Peña (Mexico City: Secretaría de Educación Pública, 1987).

sequence witness how single integers 'become' fictional in their accumulation, and show thereby the untenability, where lyric is concerned, of vivid distinctions between true and untrue, original and received, first-person and collective. A poem that appears to hold to a particular construction of these values – say, a typical love sonnet seen as what it claims to be, a unique, confessional speech from the heart – turns out, in the context of almost a hundred redactions, to seem more artificial and culturally grounded than it does alone, its first-person voice a kind of screen for shared thoughts and emotions. If absorption is the property that allows uncritical identification with a lyric speaker, making his or her thoughts and feelings seem the reader's own,[19] such a work of many integers will often remain absorptive but in a more sophisticated way than any single one: the humanist illusion of a unique commerce between two individual consciousnesses through the medium of the text falls away, to be replaced by the equally humanist recognition that a successful poem will often speak of its individuality while depending on its intertextuality. (Some types of collective lyric, such as psalmody, have doctrinal reasons to remain absorptive in an anti-fictional fashion: thus psalters by accomplished writers of lyric fiction, such as Sir Philip Sidney's unfinished one, can make compelling examples of the tensions in early modern poetics.[20]) Moreover, one's idea of the poet himself may shift over one hundred sonnets, from a confessionally minded original to an arranger of received materials to – finally, as the series becomes fully circumstantiated – something akin to a writer of fiction with a complete franchise for invention and development.

Is a given sonnet then more or less 'true'? Most Renaissance theorists would aver that it maintains a claim on truth, but exchanges a lower for a higher standard, achieving the mediated but powerful truth of fiction, such as epic or tragedy. Pierre de Ronsard, one of the leading figures in the French poetic movement known as the Pléiade, may have something like this in mind in a famous dictum in the *Abbregé de l'Art poëtique françois* (1565): 'while the aim of the orator is to persuade, that of the poet is to imitate, to invent, and to represent those things that are, or can be, verisimilar'.[21] What Ronsard appears to cast around for is perhaps a formula for describing the peculiar purchase on 'things' found not only in poetry overall but in state-of-the-art, late-century European lyric such as

---

[19] Charles Bernstein, *A poetics* (Cambridge, MA: Harvard University Press, 1992), pp. 9–89.
[20] Roland Greene, 'Sir Philip Sidney's Psalms, the sixteenth-century psalter, and the nature of lyric', *Studies in English literature 1500–1900* 30 (1990), 19–33, and Rivkah Zim, *English metrical psalms: poetry as praise and prayer, 1535–1601* (Cambridge: Cambridge University Press, 1987).
[21] Pierre de Ronsard, *Abbregé de l'art poëtique françois*, in *Œuvres complètes*, ed. P. Laumonier, I. Silver, and R. Lebègue, 20 vols. (Paris: M. Didier, 1914–75), vol. XIV, p. 13.

he writes: an imitation of a single utterance gives way to another and then another, and as they store up particularity and variety, these lyric fictions – most concerning love, such as Ronsard's *Les amours* (1552 and 1553) and *Sonnets pour Hélène* (1578), but others dealing with worldly affairs, such as Joachim du Bellay's *Les regrets* (1558) – come to seem less like mere 'songs and sonnets' and more like feats of outright invention and representation. If poetry in general is thought to start from seemingly direct expression, double back to take in received models, and irrupt into the poet's invention of a virtual nature ('more natural invention than artificial or superstitious imitation'),[22] as Ronsard, Du Bellay, and many others believe,[23] then lyric achieves this elevated standard by means of its graduated approach to fictional world-making – and not only in the sonnet sequence, but in the sestina, the ode (Pindaric and otherwise), the *stance*, and many other dynamic forms and collocations. Through its most artificed and ambitious productions, then, lyric eventually meets up with the other types of poetic fiction, such as epic, and shares to an extent in their developing early modern poetics.

If lyric is often defined in this period by the intersection of its material and representational properties, one convention in which they commonly meet is the depiction of the human subject. Between the loosely defined purposes of medieval lyric – a generic formation that exists almost outside literary theory of the time – and the strong charter given to lyric under Romanticism, something significant occurs. During the Renaissance the genre becomes, in effect, a widely acknowledged vehicle for both representing and rethinking many of the questions about subjectivity that become current in the age of humanism. How do human beings construct reality out of their particular experiences? What is the value of an individual consciousness, of one person's experience? How may consciousness – as a complex of thought, emotion, and belief – be portrayed in a discursive medium? Questions such as these are under discussion throughout the early modern period, in a variety of intellectual settings such as history, philosophy, and law. But after the example of Petrarch's *Canzoniere*, lyric poetry comes to be seen as perhaps the most readily available fictional space in which they can be dramatized and explored. The interpenetration of consciousnesses within and without the poem is remarked by George Puttenham in *The arte of English poesie* (written 1579, published 1589) in a famous passage on love poetry, where he rehearses the collapse of the divide between poetic and empirical subjects and the fashioning of thought and feeling through a process of absorption

---

[22] Joachim du Bellay, preface to the second edition of *L'Olive* (Paris, 1550), in *Œuvres poétiques*, ed. D. Aris and F. Joukovsky, 2 vols. (Paris: Classiques Garnier, 1993), vol. I, p. 11.
[23] Pierre de Ronsard, 'Au lecteur' (1550), in *Œuvres complètes*, vol. I, pp. 43–50.

mediated by 'formes'.[24] Such a notion partly accounts for the disjunction between Scaliger and Sidney above: while the former thinks of lyric as an almost miscellaneous category, answerable chiefly to its classical character of poetry sung to a lyre, Sidney's contemporaries have witnessed the development of a generic mission that is more unified but also double-edged. The party line offered to 'poet-haters' and the general public is that the moral element of lyric superintends all the others – sensual, ideological, and so forth – perceived to be in play; that properly disposed, lyric makes brave warriors and good citizens. But it is equally clear late in the century that lyric renders visible and problematic the questions of selfhood and individuality that are erupting everywhere in the culture.

In an influential argument, Joel Fineman proposed that what we call early modern lyric originated out of conventions of epideixis or praise – recall Sidney's 'lyre and well-accorded voice [that] giveth praise, the reward of virtue, to virtuous acts' – because as it constructs an object of celebration, lyric praise establishes 'a kind of grammar of poetic presence that controls the way the poet can articulate himself. The rhetorical nature of praise, the self-conscious logic of its panegyricizing logos, renders certain subjective postures rhetorically convenient to the praising poet . . . The poet's praise of "thee" will regularly turn out to be a praise of "me"'.[25] Moreover, early modern epideixis as Fineman describes it includes an idealized view of the relation between the physicality of the poetic object and that of the poem itself: pre-existent images, essences, and 'ideas' are 'materialized in the poetry of praise. They are present as things or artifacts the very physicality of which is thematically exploited, explicitly remarked, as though through this physicality it were possible to instantiate the rhetorical logic of an idealizing poetics based on the effective force, the "actuality", of likeness.'[26] Fineman's account thus maps one widely accepted Renaissance mode of relation between the physical world and the artificial or material poem: the poem replaces the world of actuality and contingency with another, virtual one, and a powerful cultural consensus keeps the audience from treating the outcome as distortion or omission. In fact, each realized poem reinforces the interlocking understandings of artifice, *mimesis*, and poetic consciousness, and the entire enterprise gains momentum from each lyric integer.

As Fineman would have it, this treaty between persons and materials within and without the poem holds its force in European poetics until Shakespeare's *Sonnets* (written 1590s, published 1609). With the *Sonnets*,

---

[24] George Puttenham, *The arte of English poesie*, ed. G. D. Willcock and A. Walker (Cambridge: Cambridge University Press, 1936), p. 45.

[25] Joel Fineman, *Shakespeare's perjured eye: the invention of poetic subjectivity in the sonnets* (Berkeley and Los Angeles: University of California Press, 1986), pp. 7, 9.

[26] *Ibid.*, p. 12.

226 of 786 Poetics: Literary forms

he argues, this idealized notion of representational language is replaced by
'a different account that characterizes language as something corruptingly
linguistic rather than something ideally specular, as something dupli-
citously verbal as opposed to something singly visual'.[27] He insists that
the *Sonnets* recapitulate, examine, and finally overthrow this received
poetics, which will come to seem hopelessly outdated around the turn of
the seventeenth century. The consequence for poetic subjectivity is that
where prior subjects have been constructed in the successful correspondence of essences, things, and persons, Shakespeare's speaker is estranged
from this convention even as he observes its remnants in his poems:
'because they are a discourse of the tongue rather than of the eye, because
they are "linguistic", Shakespeare's verbal words are, in comparison to an
imago, essentially or ontologically at odds with what they speak about' –
including their own voice or person. 'The subject of Shakespeare's sonnets
experiences himself *as* his difference from himself.'[28] Thus a new instance
of lyric subjectivity is established, according to Fineman, and the *Sonnets*
become the avatar of a general event in the history of consciousness.

What are the uses of the foregoing sketch, centred as it is on a single
work of the later sixteenth century, for a more wide-ranging account of
lyric theory in the early modern period? One needs to detach Fineman's
argument from the text to which it emphatically joins itself, and retell the
unsettling of lyric subjectivity through many more examples over a larger
time-line. The revision he describes begins much earlier, with Petrarch
himself: John Freccero and Giuseppe Mazzotta have shown how Petrarch's
own poetics is informed by what Fineman calls a 'perjured eye', or a consciousness of the difference between what is seen and what is articulated,
a sense that 'language bears an essential otherness to the desire that generates it'.[29] Notwithstanding Fineman's insistence that Petrarchism is
informed by a visionary, epideictic poetics, that movement belongs near
the beginning of the run of literary and cultural history that he ascribes to
the *Sonnets*. Petrarchism in the sense he means it – an idealist poetics of
likeness – never existed; instead of being embodied in a historical moment
and later lost, such a poetics was probably always unavailable, and an
explicit sense of the built-in inadequacies of language and form recurs in
literary theory from the troubadours on. Santillana's statement quoted
above hints at the suspicion that lyric is sheer language, with nothing
beneath its 'beautiful covering'. Santillana's contemporary Ausias March,
nearly two hundred years older than Shakespeare, seems to indicate the

---

[27] *Ibid.*, p. 15.   [28] *Ibid.*, pp. 15, 25.
[29] Giuseppe Mazzotta, 'The Canzoniere and the language of the self', *Studies in philology*
75 (1978), 294, rpt. in *The worlds of Petrarch* (Durham, NC: Duke University Press,
1993), p. 78.

exhaustion of an epideictic tradition and the corresponding need to establish his own subjectivity in the space that separates him from his object: 'We are all crude in our ability to express / what a fair and honest body deserves'.[30] March's distance from a living epideictic tradition is, if anything, greater than that of many continental contemporaries because he writes in Catalan, where his poetic effects seem doubly estranged from his models.

Golden Age Spanish lyric, as a number of recent critics have noted, is marked by a growing sense of language as not only the constitutive medium of lyric but its problem, tempting poets and readers with the prospect of 'the union of language and concept which will transcend both terms and embody a primal, linguistic plenitude' but ultimately frustrating them as it invariably calls attention to itself.[31] On similarly close examination, the same could certainly be said for English, French, Italian, Portuguese, and other early modern poetries. Everywhere in this period the lyric poet, even more than other literary artists, is the agent of society who manages to gesture towards univocation while he shows the physicality and indeterminacy of actual language in operation, keeping a cultural myth alive at the same time that he demonstrates its untenability in the early modern world.[32] And it is often in the balance of these forces that lyric poets display linked subjectivities under construction: the borders between world and self (for instance as evidenced by the grammatical features called deictics), and between these representations and the poem as an objective artefact (as shown by figurative language and other examples of artifice), will vary from one poet to another – in fact might be said to allow each poet to ratify his or her distinctive identity – and are often under discussion in this period (for instance, in Puttenham's elaborate *Arte* and Lope de Vega's elegant 'Introducción a la justa poética' (1620)) as a leading symptom of lyric individuality.

It is in this interest that Fernando de Herrera, in his commentary on the poetry of Garcilaso de la Vega (1580), lingers over the usage of 'traslación' or metaphor, and in so doing affirms to his audience that the strategic deployment of 'otherness' goes to constitute both the poem's persona and the reader's own consciousness – two subjectivities meeting across the verbal divide of the lyric, and built (or rebuilt) there in mutual relation: 'He who hears them is carried by cogitation and thought to other parts, but he does not go, or travel by road, because the entire translation,

[30] Ausias March, *Obra poética completa*, ed. R. Ferreres, 2 vols. (Madrid: Castalia, 1979), vol. I, pp. 210–12.
[31] Paul Julian Smith, 'The rhetoric of presence in poets and critics of Golden Age lyric: Garcilaso, Herrera, Góngora', *Modern language notes* 100 (1985), 223–46.
[32] Malcolm K. Read, 'Language and the body in Francisco de Quevedo', *Modern language notes* 99 (1984), 235–55.

which is found with some reason, is approached through the senses themselves, largely the eyes, the sharpest faculty.'[33] Starting inauspiciously
from a standard observation about the contrast between 'proper' and
'alien' words, the passage excerpted here makes one of the most comprehensive claims for lyric in the Renaissance: that its workmanship, its
strategies of representation, and its characteristic first-person stance come
together to enact a virtual travel of the mind, and to build a subject out
of what he or she is not – an identity out of difference and plurality. In
'moving' meanings we adjust both the self within the poem and the one
without, and nothing remains the same in the poet, the reader, and by
extension the larger society to which they belong. Fineman's Shakespearean voice at odds with itself and its objects is already acknowledged
here; so is the plurivocal world outside the poem, often believed to be
exclusive to the other genres. Herrera – actually addressing Garcilaso's
second sonnet here, and thus responding to a poetics that extends back
through Santillana to Petrarch – recuperates the early modern lyric project as constructive, differentiated, and of its time.

Early modern lyric artifice is finally not simply a property but a problem, a witness to the difficulties of representation; lyric subjectivity is
not an achieved portrait but an occasion for reflection on subjecthood at
large; and lyric fiction, always an oxymoron in action, tends to call into
question the very terms by which it is received and understood, and acts
as a force for the critical renewal of its genre. Largely on account of social
and cultural exigencies we are now beginning to recover, and in spite of
the fluidity of terminology and the fugitiveness of early modern literary
theory, the Renaissance sees a long-running – and for succeeding centuries, a formative – discussion of lyric and its contexts.

---

[33] Antonio Gallego Morell (ed.), *Garcilaso de la Vega y sus comentaristas*, 2nd edn (Madrid:
Gredos, 1972), pp. 318–19, my translation. See the remarks by Mary Gaylord (née) Ran-
del, 'Proper language and language as property: the personal poetics of Lope's *Rimas*',
Modern language notes 101 (1988), 228–9.

22

Renaissance theatre and the theory of tragedy

Timothy J. Reiss

To deal briefly and justly with tragedy from the fifteenth to the seventeenth century in Europe is not easy. In wit and fecundity of critical debate, variety and brilliance of practice, and unusual abundance of both, these years are exceptional in the record of any artistic production. One might think tragedy so rare an occurrence – fifth-century Athens, Renaissance Europe, Enlightenment Germany, Russia, and Scandinavia – as to be a narrow endeavour, easy to epitomize. Renaissance tragedy, however, was so fundamental to the establishment of vernaculars, the development of literature, the making of national theatres, to political, religious, educational, and epistemological debate, indeed, to the 'passage to modernity', as to make its study central to any understanding of modern Western culture. In tragedy, humanists found a tie with a striking grandeur of the ancients. To imitate it seemed a way to grasp their most solemn thoughts and inhabit their deepest emotions. It was an art form old but unfamiliar; it offered a kind of acid test for claims of renewal. Those who suggested tragedy to be familiar and local provoked vehement debate.

Explaining tragedy to the reader of his French translation of *Electra* in 1537, the French scholar and diplomat, Lazare de Baïf, called it 'a morality composed of great calamities, murders, and adversities inflicted on noble and excellent personages'.[1] In 1548 Thomas Sebillet averred that 'French morality in a way substitutes for Greek and Latin tragedy, especially in that it treats serious and princely deeds. And if the French had agreed that morality were always to end in grief and unhappiness, morality would be tragedy.' Like tragedy morality provided 'narrations of illustrious, magnanimous, and virtuous deeds, either true, or at least probable [*vraysemblables*]. For the rest, we take it according to the shaping of our customs and life [*à l'information de nos mœurs et vie*], not bothering about the grief or joy of the ending.'[2]

---

[1] Lazare de Baïf, *Tragedie de Sophocles, intitulee, Electra . . . traduicte . . . en rythme françoyse* [?1529] (Paris: Etienne Rosset, 1537). All translations are the author's, unless otherwise indicated.

[2] Thomas Sebillet, *Art poétique françoys* (1548), ed. F. Gaiffe (Paris: Cornély, 1910), pp. 161–2.

Typically asserting novelty and rupture, Joachim du Bellay crossly denied Baïf's and Sebillet's claim in 1549, protesting that the 'ancient dignity' of comedy and tragedy had 'been usurped' by farce and morality. Poets should work first, 'to embellish [the] language'.[3] Replying a year later, Barthélemy Aneau wrote that while he knew no French verse comedy, he did know 'some tragedies, and good ones . . . Farce and morality usurp nothing from them . . . but are quite different poems.' Siding with Du Bellay in 1555, Jacques Peletier dismissed 'moralities and suchlike plays' as comedy, whose 'true form' also did not exist in French.[4] Jean de la Taille summed up the quarrel in 1572, spurning not just 'farces and moralities', but tragedies like Théodore de Bèze's 1550 *Abraham sacrifiant* and Louis des Masures's 1563 Protestant trilogy on David, *Tragédies saintes*, as 'cold and unworthy of the name of tragedy', with 'neither sense nor reason', often made of 'ridiculous words [mixed] with badinage'.[5] These plays, he wrote, did not follow the rules of Aristotle and Horace, adopt the three unities, deal with great, imperfect secular personages, or end in catastrophe.

Had he known them, he could have included English works like Thomas Preston's *Cambises* (c. 1562–4), far less regular than those named, combining history, farce, and allegory in its Herodotan tale of the fall of a great prince at the top of his pride; or *Gismond of Salerne* (1567–8), moralizing a bloody story from Boccaccio with matter from Seneca and Lodovico Dolce and such roles as Megaera and Cupid. He could have mocked a 1563 'tragedy of *Nabuco Donosor*' seen at Plasencia in Spain's Extremadura.[6] He might have scorned Juan de Mal Lara's *Tragedia de San Hermenegildo*. Played in Seville in 1570, its five acts put allegorical with historical and legendary figures and tragedy with comedy.[7] He might even have cut a Cretan *Abraham*, based on Luigi Groto's *Lo Isach* (itself printed in 1586 but put on about 1558).[8] La Taille and Aneau had in mind dramas of this sort.

The century's early decades had seen many mixed 'tragedies' on religious and other themes. There were experiments all over Europe, and

[3] Joachim du Bellay, *La deffence et illustration de la langue françoyse*, ed. H. Chamard (Paris: Didier, 1970), pp. 125–6.
[4] [Barthélemy Aneau], *Le Quintil Horatian sur la defence & illustration de la langue Françoyse . . .* [Following Sebillet], *Art poétique françoys* (1555; reprint Geneva: Slatkine, 1972), sig. 106[v]. Jacques Peletier du Mans, *L'art poëtique* (1555; reprint Geneva: Slatkine, 1971), p. 71.
[5] Jean de La Taille, 'De l'art de la tragédie', in *Saül le furieux; la famine, ou les Gabéonites: tragédies*, ed. E. Forsyth (Paris: Didier, 1968), pp. 4, 8.
[6] Hugo Albert Rennert, *The Spanish stage in the time of Lope de Vega* (1909; reprint New York: Dover, 1963), p. 23.
[7] Alfredo Hermenegildo, *La tragedia en el Renacimiento español* (Barcelona: Planeta, 1973), pp. 97–104. The play had thirty-two speaking parts.
[8] Margaret Alexiou, 'Reappropriating Greek sacrifice: *homo necans* or *ándropos thusiáxon?*' *Journal of modern Greek studies* 8 (1990), 97–123.

older forms of moralizing theatre in classical garb were often named 'tragedy'. Moralities from biblical or other sources were common. The Franco-Italian Quintinianus Stoa's *Theandrothanatos* (a Passion) and *Theocrisis* (a Last Judgement), printed in 1515 (the first alone in 1508), had great success. Nicolas Barthélemy's 1529 *Christus Xylonicus* (Christ defeating hell by the Cross), titled *tragoedia* in editions after 1536, was very popular.[9] Perhaps more important were the Protestant dramas of the Low Countries and German lands, admired across northern Europe (casting La Taille's bile in the year of the Saint Bartholomew's massacre in unappealing light).

In Switzerland during these early years, Johann Kolross, Sixt Birck, Pamphilus Gengenbach, Niklas Manuel, and others were writing German-language classicizing moralities. Zwingli's Zurich successor Heinrich Bullinger wrote a *Lucretia* around 1526. Printed in 1533, it was among other things a defence of republicanism. Two years later Paul Rebhun's better-known *Susanna* used acts, scenes, and a 'Senecan' style. It portrayed hierarchical authority, trust in a Catholic God as bulwark against tyranny, and submission of women. It was a tragedy with a 'happy' ending. In 1532 Birck also wrote a *Susanna*: this Swiss drama condemning the elders, mounting another strong defence of republican government. In Latin in 1537 it was titled *comedia tragica*. (Tibortio Sacco's 1524 Italian *Sosanna* was a '*Tragedia*'.) The German Thomas Naogeorgus's *Pammachius* (1538), *Hamanus* (1543), and others, the Dutch Willem Gnapheus's *Acolastus* (1529: the prodigal son) and Cornelius Crocus's 1536 *Joseph*, won European recognition, with many editions. *Pammachius* was a vast allegorical morality on the Antichrist aimed at Catholic–Protestant strife. The last two were 'comic' moralities, justifying Peletier's criticism. These and others had wide popular circulation.

This is catalogue enough to suggest that for two-thirds of the sixteenth century authors of tragedies and their theory disputed issues of continuity and tradition, discontinuity and originality, antiquity and modernity, vernaculars and Latin, ethics and genre, religion and politics. It matters that these dramas coincided with *Everyman*, best known of moralities. Played in the late 1400s, it had four editions between 1508 and 1537. Whether it or the Flemish *Elckerlyc* (written *c.* 1470, printed 1495) translated the other is still argued. Latinized as *Homulus* by C. Sterck of Maastricht, it was printed in Cologne in 1536 by Jasper von Gennep, who issued his own German translation the same year. A 1539 classicized version, *Hecastus*, by the Dutch Georgius Macropedius (Georg van Langveldt),

[9] Plays on the harrowing of hell, with its archetypal theme of Good vs. Evil, were popular from at least the thirteenth century across Europe: see the important introduction by Irena R. Makaryk (trans. and ed.), *About the harrowing of hell (Slovo o zbureniu pekla): a seventeenth-century Ukrainian play in its European context* (Ottawa: Dovehouse, 1989), pp. 97–142.

had six German translations. In 1540 Naogeorgus did a *Mercator* on the
same theme (German in 1541). *Acolastus* itself, put into German in 1534
and into English by John Palsgrave in 1540, was an Everyman type morality. Throughout the century Italy kept its loved *sacre rappresentazioni*,
Spain its *farsas*, France its *moralités*.[10] All suited well enough Baïf's,
Sebillet's, and their opponents' claims.

All this is important. For it is still too often asserted that Renaissance
humanists, especially Italian, remade tragedy and its theory from their
discovery of the Greek tragedians and Aristotle's *Poetics*. Such was hardly
the case. Giorgio Valla indeed published a full Latin *Poetics* in 1498, and
the Aldine press a Greek text in 1508. But tragedy was known throughout the Middle Ages from Horace's *Ars poetica*, Seneca's plays, the
Terentian commentaries of fourth-century grammarians Aelius Donatus
and Diomedes, and, from the thirteenth century, Hermann the German's
1256 Latin translation of Averroes' Arabic gloss on Aristotle. The tie
to morality recalled in the sixteenth century signals both this continuity
and the great breadth of the tradition in question: from Poland to Spain,
from England to Crete, from the German lands to Italy. Fifteenth-century
rediscoveries built on this continuity, which thus needs tracing. How
one then explains the flowering of tragedy in the sixteenth century will
be resolved in the second half of this chapter.

Gustave Lanson named Seneca's tragedies 'the operating manual' for
sixteenth-century humanist tragedy (a still common view).[11] They surely
were for the earliest post-Ancient tragedy of all: Albertino Mussato's
Latin *Ecerinis* (1314) relating the fall of the tyrant Ezzelino da Romano
(1194–1259). The play has five acts, a small cast, chorus of Paduans, and
a boastful cruel protagonist. Mussato's tragedy was really a moral allegory
on Tyranny. Around 1390 Antonio Loschi wrote an *Achilles*, and about 1429
Gregorio Correr a *Progne*. Seven other mixed Senecan plays appeared in
Italy from 1377 to 1500. In 1394 a royal Valencian audience saw *L'hom
enamorat y la fembra satisfeta*, a 'tragedy' by Mosén Domingo Mascó,
counsellor to King Juan I.

If tragedies were not continuous from Seneca's first century to the
Christian fourteenth, the idea of tragedy was – one familiar and normative

---

[10] Spanish terms are confusing. For most of the sixteenth century *autos* meant biblical,
legendary, or martyrological dramas. *Farsas* designated plays on moral-allegorical subjects (and farces). It may be that later *comedias divinas* perhaps came from the first, *autos*
from the last: Rennert, *Spanish stage*, p. 7, n. 2; Hermenegildo, *Tragedia*, pp. 129–30.
In Poland, Jan Jurkowski published a mixed morality in 1604, *A tragedy of the Polish
Scilurus*. Thomas Heywood still thought 'Tragedy, History, . . . Morall' wholly entangled:
An apology for actors (London: Nicholas Okes, 1612), sig. F4'. As late as 1634 a German
morality, *Tragoedia von Tugenden und Lastern*, was performed in Copenhagen for Christian IV's celebration of his son's wedding.

[11] Gustave Lanson, 'L'idée de la tragédie en France avant Jodelle', *RHL* 11, 4 (Oct.–Dec.
1904), p. 547.

for the Renaissance. Horace had distinguished comedy and tragedy, defined stylistic propriety (suited to genre, but within a play to rank, emotion, character, fortune, occupation, age, sex, and place of origin), explained how tragedies must adopt known stories or be consistent in fictive ones, and praised action over narration, save where decorum forbade performance of atrocious or fantastic acts. An author should beware of using a *deus ex machina*, and not put more than three speakers on stage at once. He wanted five acts and an integrated chorus whose aim was not only to divide the acts, but to embrace an ethics of goodness, temperance, justice, lawfulness, amity, and peace. He gave a 'history' of satyr play and tragedy from Thespis to Aeschylus to Old Comedy. A dramatist should know life to draw character and event aright. Poets, he wrote, 'Aut prodesse volunt aut delectare . . . / aut simul et iucunda et idonea dicere vitae' ['wish to benefit or to please . . . / or to speak matter at once pleasing and useful to life', *Ars poetica* 333–4]. Such a poet was both born and made.

Possibly even more important for the Middle Ages were the two grammarians. In Book III of his *Ars grammatica*, Diomedes had compared tragedy and comedy. The one offered 'heroic fortune in adversity', the other showed 'private and civil fortune without peril to life'. As this dealt with the private, so that treated 'of palaces and public places'. Tragedy introduced 'great men, leaders, and kings', recorded 'lamentations, exiles, and murders', and 'frequently and almost always' drew 'sorrowful conclusions to joyful affairs and the recognition, for the worse, of children and former events'.[12]

Unlike Diomedes, Donatus had edited Terence, with an essay and glosses on the plays. He defined New Comedy as 'pertain[ing] with its common argument rather generally to all those who experience average fortune, and at the same time offer[ing] spectators less bitterness and much pleasure: elegant in argument, appropriate in custom, useful in maxim, agreeable in wit, apt in metre' ['concinna argumento, consuetudine congrua, utilis sententiis, grata salibus, apta metro'].[13] Parts of this definition could, of course, apply equally well to tragedy, and several times the text praises Terence for not sliding into the tragic (as Plautus sometimes did). For the differences between the two are very great:

In comedy, people's fortunes are average, dangers and threats few, the ends of actions joyous. In tragedy, all is the opposite: persons are great, terrors vast, endings deadly. The first starts in turbulence, but ends in calm. In tragedy things

---

[12] Edwin W. Robbins, *Dramatic characterization in printed commentaries on Terence 1473–1600* (Urbana: University of Illinois Press, 1951), p. 7.
[13] Aelius Donatus, 'De tragoedia et comoedia', in *Publii Terentii Carthaginiensis Afri Comoediae sex . . .*, ed. J. A. Giles (London: Jacobi Bohn, 1807), pp. xvii–xviii (Evanthius). The text was a composite by Evanthius (also fourth-century) and Donatus, but thought wholly the latter's until the seventeenth century.

are done in the contrary order. Where in tragedy is expressed the idea that life is to be fled, in comedy it is eagerly to be seized. Finally, every comedy is drawn from fictive arguments, tragedy is often drawn from historical belief [*ab historica fide*].[14]

Through the Middle Ages Diomedes's and Donatus's views on tragedy were standard. In the seventh century, Isidore of Seville, citing Horace on the origins of the name, praised tragedians who 'excelled in plotting plays made in the image of truth' ['excellentes in argumentis fabularum ad veritatis imaginem fictis']. He added that 'comic writers relate actions of private people; tragedians, rather, public events and histories of princes. Also, the plots of the tragedians are taken from grievous things; those of the comics from joyful ones.' Returning to the subject later, he wrote that tragedies 'sing the ancient actions and deeds of infamous princes in mournful verse while people watch'. Comedies 'sing the acts of private people in verse or gesture, and express in their plots the debaucheries of maidens and loves of harlots'.[15]

Isidore clearly had performance in mind, but usually the now often pejorative idea of tragedy did not. Matthew of Vendôme's *Ars versificatoria* (*c.* 1175) made Tragoedia one of the Muses attendant [*pedissequas*] on Philosophia – an ugly one: 'shrieking her various loud moans amongst the group, she "throws out bombast and sesquipedelian words", and supported by buskined feet, severe appearance, menacing brow, she thunders her various prognostications with customary ferocity.' Matthew's 'pedissequas', 'sesquipedalia', and 'pedibus coturnatis' were surely ironic, and his just earlier reference to Boethius's *Consolation of philosophy* to present Philosophia recalls that her first action at the start of that work was angrily to cast out all the poetic Muses. Horace's quoted line, 'projicit ampullas et sexquipedalia verba' (*Ars poetica* 97), signals a derogation from the grand style that Geoffrey of Vinsauf observed in his almost contemporaneous (early thirteenth-century) *Documentum*.[16]

In Toledo in 1256 Hermann the German put into Latin Averroes' gloss on Aristotle's *Poetics*. Among the Spanish-Arabic scholar's major points were that poetry was an aspect of logic, a rhetoric that persuaded by moving the imagination, with a purpose entirely ethical. Poetry was praise [*laudatio*] or blame [*vituperatio*], teaching virtue, discouraging vice.

---

[14] Donatus, 'De tragoedia et comoedia', p. xix (also Evanthius).

[15] *Isidori Hispalensis Episcopi Etymologiarum sive originum libri* xx, ed. W. M. Lindsay, 2 vols. (1911; reprint Oxford: Clarendon Press, 1989), Bks. VIII.vii.5–6; XVIII.xlv–xlvi.

[16] Matthew of Vendôme, *Ars versificatoria*, in E. Faral, *Les arts poétiques du xiie et du xiiie siècle: recherches et documents sur la technique littéraire du moyen âge* (1924; reprint Paris: Champion, 1962), pp. 107–93, here, p. 153; Geoffrey of Vinsauf, *Documentum sive de modo et arte dictandi et versificandi* (*Instruction in the method and art of speaking and versifying*), trans. and intro. R. P. Parr (Milwaukee: Marquette University Press, 1968), p. 88.

Tragedy was characteristic of the first, since it portrayed people better than they are, comedy typified the second. They persuaded by *imagines* depicting the truth of reality so as to move the audience (one recalls Isidore's *imago veritatis* or even Sebillet's later *information* [Lat. *informatio*], which spoke directly to the 'shaping' a morality gave to familiar habit). Such images do this in good part because they are *credible*, they fit the *belief* of the audience, its *credulitas*, and conform to 'typical characteristics' [*consuetudo*] – one is now reminded of Evanthius's *consuetudo* and *fides*, as well as Sebillet's *information des mœurs*: nor may it be indifferent that the story Averroes found best suited to tragedy was that of Abraham and Isaac.[17]

For Hermann and Averroes none of this concerned performance. Aristotle's spectacle became *consideratio*, 'argument or proof of what is correct belief or correct behaviour', misplaced in poetry (not, unlike Aristotle's spectacle, in its *analysis*) because this 'does not consist in arguments or in philosophical speculation', but 'operates by the use of a representational mode of speech'.[18] Representations, images, shapings of reality, move an audience by grief, pity, and fear to understand virtue and vice, and to desire the former. While this is not what we now think of as 'Aristotle', these arguments brought new sophistication to the minimalist idea of tragedy inherited from Horace and the grammarians. At the same time, Hermann's translation clearly fits Horatian, Diomedean, and Donatian views. Indeed, their conceptual apparatus, set in didactic rhetoric and ethics, no doubt had much to do with Hermann's choice of terms. He added a theory of reception and representation resting on a concept of *imagines*, of 'shaping fantasies', of imagination 'informing' general truths with 'a local habitation and a name' (and vice versa) moving reader and listener to feel and grasp the general through the particular.[19]

Even the non-dramatic argument was usual. Dante saw in tragedy and comedy 'a certain kind of poetical narration', echoing the same writers: the oppositions of style, the matters of dignity, status, emotions, and sphere of action.[20] In the same years, the Dominican Nicholas Trevet (*d. c.* 1334)

[17] These are from the first part of Hermann's widely known text, matching Aristotle's first six chapters, 1447a–1450b: A. J. Minnis and A. B. Scott, with D. Wallace (ed.), *Medieval literary theory and criticism c.1100–c.1375: The commentary tradition* (Oxford: Clarendon Press, 1988), pp. 289–96. The Abraham example matches Aristotle's praise of *Cresphontes*, *Iphigenia*, and *Helle* in 1454a (ch. 14).

[18] Minnis and Scott (ed.), *Medieval literary theory*, p. 296.

[19] *A midsummer night's dream* (V.1.5–17) is used, like Sebillet and *Abraham* plays, to signal that these concepts and arguments will be absorbed by later ideas of literary and dramatic representation, production, and reception. (Aristotle's *plot* also depicted universal action in particular representation.)

[20] Dante Alighieri, 'Epistle to Can Grande della Scala: extract', in Minnis and Scott (ed.), *Medieval literary theory*, pp. 458–69, here, p. 459. The *De vulgari eloquentia* (2.4.7) expressed the same view.

glossed Seneca's tragedies, emphasizing their ethical intent, their imaging of the truth (quoting Isidore), their being 'sorrowful verses on the misfortunes of great men'. His idea of performance was confused, but his gloss had 'wide diffusion throughout Italy'.[21] Chaucer, too, held such views: 'Tragedie is to seyn a certeyn storie, / As olde bookes maken us memorie, / Of hym that stood in greet prosperitee, / And is yfallen out of heigh degree / Into myserie, and endeth wrecchedly' ('The Prologue of the Monk's Tale', lines 1973–7).

A century after Dante and Trevet and shortly after Chaucer, between 1420 and 1440, Firmin le Ver, Carthusian prior of Saint-Honoré-lès-Abbeville, defined Tragedia in his Latin lexicon (again versus comedy) quite according to Horace, Seneca, the grammarians, and Hermann. It was 'a mournful song [*carmen luctuosum*] that begins happily and ends in sorrow'. 'TRAGEDIA has to do with most inhuman things: as one killing a father (*Oedipus*) or mother (*Orestes*), or eating a son (*Thyestes*) ... TRAGEDICUS', he ended, means 'mournful, deadly. *No French equivalent*'.[22] The acerbic tone recalls Matthew of Vendôme. The final remark signals the relative distance of the idea. Yet the idea remained the same. So it did when Lorenzo Valla contemporaneously ascribed it to Cicero and Quintilian, to the effect that tragedies always concerned 'sad and terrible things'.[23]

These remarks coincided in date with the Senecan tragedies of Loschi and Correr, as with Leonardo Dati's 1442 *Hiempsal*, as much morality as tragedy, using not just Seneca's style and Sallust's characters, but Strife, Treachery, Envy, Want, Theft, and Rapine. Such a play returns us to the moralities. Their tie to the ethical didacticism of the Latins, as well as to claims about misery and sorrow, however Christianized (but not in Dati), is now apparent. Indeed, a few years later (mid-1470s), 'l'Infortuné' wrote a 'Fleur de rethoricque' which contrasted '*moralitates*' with '*comediis*'. The author drew on tradition. Allegory ['parabolee maniere'] must be succinct and clear ['Sans superfluite actainte / En expliquant fort la matiere'], language noble ['De belles collocutions'], in high style ['De belles demonstracions / Rethoriques ornacions'], and sown with *sententiae* ['auctorisees / Par deues diffinicions / Affin que mieulx soient prisees'].

---

[21] Nicholas Trevet, 'Commentary on Seneca's tragedies: extracts', in Minnis and Scott (ed.), *Medieval literary theory*, pp. 340–60, here, pp. 342, 344, 346. The last citation is from Antonio Stäuble, 'L'idea della tragedia nell'umanismo', in *La rinascita della tragedia nell' Italia dell'umanismo. Atti del IV convegno di studio Viterbo Giugno 1979* (Viterbo: Sorbini, 1980), p. 53, who examines Trevet's views and Mussato's similar ones in his *Vita di Seneca*, pp. 48–54.

[22] Latin text in Lanson, 'L'idée de la tragédie', p. 542, n. 2.

[23] Lorenzo Valla, *In errores Antonii Raudensis adnotationes* (1444), quoted by Bernard Weinberg, *A history of literary criticism in the Italian Renaissance*, 2 vols. (Chicago: University of Chicago Press, 1961), vol. 1, p. 86.

Vice is to be condemned, virtue praised. This was opposed to the humour of comedy. L'Infortuné urged that people talk and act according to rank, occupation, and age: this of 'mysteries, chronicles, romances, and histories', but the counsel shared its chapter with morality, and surely applied to it as well.[24]

Morality here was not the same as tragedy, whose name, Le Ver had said, was not yet in French. But it was compared with comedy, defined in didactic terms from Horace and Averroes, given devices from Seneca. Prefacing his much reprinted *Terence* a decade later, Iodocus Badius Ascensius (Josse Bade) could explain tragedy only by citing Horace, Donatus, and Diomedes. Tragedy and its theory was firstly a continuation. Valla may have issued his *Poetics* in 1498, but when his notes on the text appeared in the posthumous 1501 *De expetendis ac fugiendis rebus opus*, while naming *muthos* [plot] as the soul of poetry, he left vague whether *fabula* (that is, *muthos*) or Horatian style mattered more. Silent on *mimesis* and *catharsis*, Valla wrote that the 'aim of tragedy is to produce or reproduce tears and lamentations', 'and so is named undoer of life' ['ob hoc vitae solutrix dicta']. 'Tragedy's end dissolves life, that of comedy reaffirms it.'[25] This was Latin and medieval, not Greek; echoing Badius, it quoted Evanthius. Valla's Aristotle had small effect even on him, it seems.

Forty years on, in 1536, Alessandro Pazzi made a better translation. But only in 1548 did Francesco Robortello's exegesis, *In librum Aristotelis De arte poetica explicationes*, begin to place Aristotle in the critical mainstream: by addition not replacement. Roman and Averroist strands remained foundational, because their didacticism fitted humanist pedagogical concern for a civic and moral rhetoric, because they had always or for centuries been integral to the idea of tragedy, and because for many years humanists had been questioning Aristotle's authority in other areas of knowledge. They did so, too, because Latin Seneca was available in myriad editions from 1484 on.

However, writers were meanwhile finding the Greek tragedians. This discovery had a far more immediately momentous and influential effect on actual practice (and so theory). Aldus printed a Greek Sophocles in 1502, Euripides (minus *Electra*) in 1503, Aeschylus (less *Choephoroe*) in 1518. Erasmus published Latin translations of Euripides's *Iphigenia in Aulis* and *Hecuba* in 1506. From then on translations into Latin and

---

[24] L'Infortuné, *Le jardin de plaisance et fleur de rethorique*, ed. E. Droz and A. Piaget, 2 vols. (Paris: Firmin-Didot, 1910; Champion, 1925), vol. 1 [facsimile of *c.* 1501 edition], sig. cii^{r-v}.

[25] E. N. Tigerstedt, 'Observations on the reception of the Aristotelian *Poetics* in the West', *Studies in the Renaissance* 15 (New York: Renaissance Society of America, 1968), pp. 17–19.

the vernaculars came apace, most of the latter in the 1530s and 1540s – although few of Aeschylus.

In 1515 Giovan Giorgio Trissino used the other two as models for his *Sofonisba*, founding tragedy on a love theme, observing unities of time and action, and writing in the *versi sciolti* [blank verse] that would become normal in Italian tragic dialogue. He used Greek divisions and choruses, but since the tragedy had a prologue and four episodes, it effectively had five acts. Renowned and often reprinted, the play was not staged before 1562, although a French 'version' by Mellin de Saint-Gelais was played to Catherine de' Medici and Henri II in 1554 and 1556. Also about 1515, Giovanni Rucellai wrote a *Rosmunda* based on *Antigone*, printed in 1525. This rediscovery and reworking of the Greeks prepared the way for the impact of Pazzi (himself a major translator into Latin and Italian of Sophocles and Euripides) and Robortello. Elsewhere, interest in the composition of 'tragedies' was also vigorous. To the many already mentioned, one may add the 1502 publication in Spain of Vasco Díaz Tanco's tragedies – the earliest collection. As in so many lands, classicizing tragedy was in Spain from the earliest years of the sixteenth century.

This Spanish drama was 'created and written almost exclusively by *conversos*'.[26] Tragedy was formative in making new ways of thought and action (through linguistic and rhetorical changes, pedagogical device, religious, political, and ethical dispute). So the central role of this marginal group is noteworthy – the more so as Reformers in Switzerland and the Low Countries did likewise. Not accidentally did Luther (in *Table talk*) assert theatre's primary educational role. Later in the century, Philip Melanchthon added that next to the Bible, tragedies should be a schoolchild's breviary.[27] Johannes Sturm put this view to work in his Strasburg academy, and Jesuits across Europe made tragedy (and comedy) a main pedagogical tool: in line with clichéd Horatian, Ciceronian, and Averroist didactic maxim, let it be recorded.[28]

Early on then Reformers in the north and *conversos* in Spain found tragedy particularly suited to novel aspirations. Perhaps a like impulse initially led Italians away from Seneca's familiar tragedies towards unknown Greeks and reworkings of the morality form, using tales from new

---

[26] Hermenegildo, *Tragedia*, p. 19.

[27] A German *Hecuba* was played in the Wittenberg circle as early as 1525. Melanchthon lectured on Euripides. In the same group, Vitus Winsemius made a full Latin Sophocles (Frankfurt, 1546; 2nd edn 1549): Richard Alewyn, *Vorbarocker Klassizismus und griechische Tragödie: Analyse der 'Antigone' Übersetzung des Martin Opitz* (1926; reprint Darmstadt: Wissenschaftliche Buchgesellschaft, 1962), p. 9. Neogeorgus did another Latin Sophocles in 1558.

[28] The most famous Jesuit tragedy was Jacob Bidermann's *Cenodoxus*, first played in Augsburg in 1602. A sort of Faustian Everyman, Cenodoxus finally admits his just damnation. By the mid-1500s use of theatre was written into the statutes of some English schools.

sources, but retaining allegory, popular verse forms, and the old mixture of styles. Issues never differed much even if a 'tragedy' like Sacco's *Sosanna* was concerned with an ethical 'theology' rather than the northerners' political one. As Du Bellay was to do, Italian theorists urged tragedy as a means to renew the vernacular (as Horace had in the *Ars poetica*). Swiss, German, Dutch, Spanish, and French writers readily took their plays from one language to another. All argued that tragedy was the best way to give their languages the semantic and stylistic power of Greek and Latin. The prefatory poems addressed in the 1560s–80s by a cast of major humanist writers to Robert Garnier (the greatest French humanist tragedian) laud him for making French equal the languages of antiquity. Thomas Heywood insisted that English had thus been made 'a most perfect and composed language'. Often tragedies were *about* language and its effort to express new understanding of the world and human relations.[29] By the same token, they gave access to new ethical and political realities.

Seneca's tragedies had always been taken to interpret Horatian didacticism in political and ethical terms. Guidance about vice and virtue was achieved as much by their *sententiae*, their maxims, as by the fall into misery they represented. Tragedy's utility lay both in its performance of persons whose character and actions could be linked to the spectators' experience of life and in moral and political aphorisms (which editions often listed). That tragedy taught princes and magistrates to rule was a Renaissance cliché. Norton's and Sackville's 1561 *Gorboduc* was lauded for its portrayal of characters' brutal and heedless manoeuvres, its rant, and maxim: 'full of stately speeches, and wel sounding phrases, clyming to the height of *Seneca* his style, and as full of notable morallitie, which it doth most delightfully teach, and so obtaine the very ende of *Poesie*'.[30] A commentary on ethical behaviour, it warned Elizabeth of the disastrous results of uncertain succession (via the Theban myth). The most unusual, but most interesting and thorough, work on tragedy's civic role was Giason Denores's 1586 *Discorso*, concluding that tragedy (like comedy and epic) aimed at political *utilità*. It began similarly, claiming tragedy and the rest were 'for public benefit and utility, to which, by reason and the maxims of the wise, must be directed all arts and professions of humans who live in a civilized way [*accostumatamente*] in cities'.[31]

---

[29] Timothy J. Reiss, *Tragedy and truth* (New Haven: Yale University Press, 1990), pp. 2–5, 40–77, and *passim*. Heywood's comment is in *Apology*, sig. F3'.

[30] Sir Philip Sidney, *The defence of poesie* (1595), in *Prose works*, ed. A. Feuillerat, 4 vols. (1912; reprint Cambridge: Cambridge University Press, 1968), vol. III, p. 38. The play was 'defectuous in the circumstaunces', since 'faultie in both place and time' – so unfit as a model.

[31] Giason Denores, *Discorso intorno a . . . la comedia, la tragedia et il poema eroico . . .*, in *Trattati di poetica e retorica del Cinquecento*, ed. B. Weinberg, 4 vols. (Bari: Laterza, 1970–4), vol. III, pp. 418, 375. Writing his 'Reden van de waerdicheyt der poesie'

The Roman tragedian's major mid-century pupil, Giovambattista
Giraldi Cintio of Ferrara, agreed that tragedy's chief purpose was to draw
lessons from grave and decorous imitation of royal, public actions, showing how only reason could defeat vice. More generally, he wrote in 1543,
'tragedy, whether it has a joyful or an unhappy end, with pity and horror
purges minds of vice and leads them into virtuous habits' ['gl'induce a
buoni costumi'].³² The pity, fear, and wonder (a third effect added a bit
later, notably by Robortello and then standard) felt by the audience had
a similar didactic purpose for Cintio and most mid-century writers. One
may see in these *buoni costumi* Hermann's *consuetudo* and Sebillet's
mœurs (others' *mores*), even Denores's *accostumatamente*: Averroist
reading of Aristotle's *ethos*, character. New however was Cintio's purgation, Aristotle's *catharsis*.

The injection of 'purgation' into the theoretical debate added a new
dimension. The spectator became integral to tragedy's medium, not just
recipient of its messages. Senecan tragedy, like morality, persuaded by
rhetorical device and trope: the poet as orator (often being called so).
Even in Averroes, the poet's shaping images aimed to make their recipient
understand them as corresponding to known and rational belief. In its
varied interpretations, purgation made the tragic spectator's emotional
and 'psychological' reaction an element in tragedy's construction and
dramatic functioning. They thus became essential to the idea of dramatic
imitation itself. Indeed, Julius Caesar Scaliger's flat denial of the utility
of the notion of purgation in 1561 ['praeterea *katharsis* vox neutiquam
cuivis materiae servit': 'furthermore, the word *katharsis* is in no way of
service to anything of the matter'] may be taken as counterproof. For
Scaliger, despite constant reference to Aristotle, was holding a familiar
claim: the basis [*sita*] of poetry was imitation [*imitatio*], but only as means
to teaching pleasurably [*docendi cum delectatione*]. 'The poet above all
teaches, and does not simply please, as some once thought.'³³

The notion of *catharsis*, as Scaliger's bluntness suggests, was not easy to
cope with: it deeply involved the spectator in the very 'imitation' performance achieved. Scaliger insisted that theatre and its poetry, like rhetoric,

---

['Lecture on the value of poetry'] in Holland in 1510–15, Pieter Corneliszoon Hooft
argued not only poetry's general utility ('to found cities, to create laws'), but its particular role of fighting for freedom from tyranny during the Dutch Revolt: Maria
A. Schenkeveld, *Dutch literature in the age of Rembrandt: themes and ideas* (Amsterdam:
J. Benjamins, 1991), pp. 57–8, 69.

³² Giovambattista Giraldi Cintio, 'Discorso over lettera ... intorno al comporre delle
comedie e delle tragedie ...', in *Scritti critici*, ed. C. G. Crocetti (Milan: Marzorati,
1973), p. 176. Cintio argued later that invented plot and happy end were best, no doubt
because while his bloody Senecan *Orbecche* of 1541 had success and influence, the 1543
Didone and *Cleopatra* did not. His next six tragedies were all *di lieto fin*.

³³ Julius Caesar Scaliger, *Poetices libri septem*, facs. edn, intro. A. Buck (Stuttgart and Bad
Cannstatt: Frommann Holzboog, 1987), pp. 12ᵃ (I.vi), 1ᵇ (I.1).

had persuasion as an end. Imitation was drama's means. It persuaded to knowledge, *scientia*, 'truly and simply' defined as 'a habit of mind [*habitus animi*] conclusively founded on a necessary or a loose idea' (p. 2ᵃ: I.i). *Habitus* is akin to older ideas of belief (*fides* or *credulitas*), and fits Scaliger's insistence on a didacticism owing more to tradition than to Aristotle. This spirit ruled his later 'definition' of tragedy, whose *res* are: 'great, abominable, orders of kings, slaughters, despair, self-hangings, exiles, bereavements, parricides, incests, conflagrations, battles, puttings out of eyes, weepings, wailings, deep laments, funerals, eulogies, dirges'. Action is important only as it shows and teaches 'character', *affectus*, again, here, not dissimilar to 'habit of mind' (pp. 144ᵇ: III.xcvi; 348ᵃ: VII.I.iii). In 1570 Lodovico Castelvetro fought these claims more or less systematically: tragedy was for pleasure (although he added endless qualifications), character was revealed only through the centrality of action. *Catharsis* was of major importance.

Interpretations were abundant. Among the earliest was Antonio Sebastiano Minturno's in his 1559 *De poeta*. Following Aristotle's use of the term elsewhere, he understood *catharsis* as analogous to medical purging, arguing that by such violent emotions as pity and fear tragedy ejects these and all others: ambition, lust, anger, avarice, pride, fury, and 'unbridled desire'.[34] Like Piero Vettori in his 1560 *Commentarii* on the *Poetics*, Castelvetro saw *catharsis* as Aristotle's answer 'to his master Plato'. Pity and fear are not ejected – and surely not other passions – but frequent experience arms us 'against [the] weaknesses' they are. No longer worrying about them makes 'the pusillanimous magnanimous, the timorous brave, and the compassionate severe'. Regarding characters it works by the spectator's emulation, regarding events (action) it works partly by losing fear of things that we see not to affect us and partly by repeated reduction of worry.[35]

These two conceptions remained equally influential. In 1586 Lorenzo Giacomini expounded Minturno's view on tragic purgation to the Accademia degli Alterati: affective sympathy caused the passion represented to arouse and eject the same passion in the spectator. Denores held that tragedies aimed 'via pleasure to purge [the spectators] of the most important passions of the soul [*affetti dell'animo*] and direct them to a good life, the imitation of virtuous people, and the conserving of good commonwealths [*alla conservazion delle buone republiche*]'.[36] Here Denores

---

[34] Weinberg, *A history of literary criticism*, vol. II, p. 739.

[35] Lodovico Castelvetro, *On the art of poetry: an abridged translation of 'Poetica d'Aristotele vulgarizzata e sposta'*, ed. and trans. A. Bongiorno (Binghamton: Medieval and Renaissance Texts and Studies, 1984), pp. 55–7.

[36] Lorenzo Giacomini, *De la purgazione de la tragedia*, in Weinberg (ed.), *Trattati di poetica*, vol. III, pp. 347–71. See esp. pp. 354–5; Denores, *Discorso*, vol. III, p. 411.

brought his concern for civic utility to Minturno's view of purgation, adding Castelvetro's idea that reducing passion lets reason rule. Sir Philip Sidney proposed a like view, saying that tragedy, 'by sturring the affects of *Admiration* and *Comiseration*, teacheth the uncertaintie of this world' and the limits of power. Setting aside fear, Sidney thought tragedy enlivened some passions for moral and political ends by calming others, as did Denores.[37]

By 1611, enlarging on Castelvetro, recalling the Aristotle–Plato dispute, and absorbing the medical analogy, Daniel Heinsius argued that the aim of purgation was to alleviate the passions with the express goal of letting reason rule.[38] The view embodied years of Stoic argument already seen in Castelvetro, Denores, and Sidney. The 'father of German poetry', Martin Opitz, pursued it in 1625 in the preface to his translation of Seneca's *Trojan women*: watching suffering and evil, we learn steadfastness [*Beständigkeit*] and to withstand misfortune rationally.[39] By the century's turn, then, the two interpretations were consolidated. Clearly bound in pedagogical tradition, 'purgation' had brought to the actual *functioning* of tragedy a theory of the spectator's emotions, passions, states of mind, and of the events and actions one might expect to ensue once they were changed in certain ways.

This explains many other arguments about the ideal composition and making of tragedies. When Castelvetro argued with Aristotle and against Scaliger that plot, 'the representation of human actions', was the foundation of tragedy, and 'necessarily draws to itself character and thought', he was working towards something rather new about character. Firstly, people's 'virtues and vices' are revealed in action, which alone, *pace* Scaliger, causes 'the reversal from happiness to misery'. So plot is the end of tragedy, and character suited to it, not the reverse. An agent's moral qualities are shown through plot. Not these qualities but plotted reversal and recognition move the spectator.[40] Character inheres in action. It is not, as Scaliger argued, its cause or effect. Secondly, this 'product' of performed action has to be staged so as to affect the spectator.

In a famous passage in *Hamlet*, the prince advised his players how they were to act: 'suit the action to the word, the word to the action', 'hold as t'were the mirror up to nature', and certainly not prate like those actors he has seen 'who have so strutted and bellowed that I have thought some of Nature's journeyman had made men, and not made them well, they

---

[37] Sidney, *Defence*, vol. III, p. 23. In *Compendio della poesia tragicomica* (Venice: G. B. Ciotti, 1601), Battista Guarini argued alike.
[38] Daniel Heinsius, *On plot in tragedy*, trans. P. R. Sellin and J. J. McManmon, ed. P. R. Sellin (Northridge: San Fernando Valley State College, 1971), pp. 11–14.
[39] Alewyn, *Vorbarocker Klassizismus*, pp. 6–8.
[40] Castelvetro, *Art of poetry*, pp. 58–9, 64–72.

imitated humanity so abominably' (III.ii). The actors were not to identify with character. Proper performance involved absorption in action, not the strutting of an agent. 'Passion', Hamlet confirmed, was to be mouthed and gestured with 'a temperance that may give it smoothness'. It, too, must not impede the action. Hamlet might never say just what is mirrored nor how the mirroring works, but many others would do so. In 1631, Jean Ogier de Gombauld wrote that authors who limited time of action to twelve hours – a demand first made by Castelvetro – 'have not so much thought to represent a past thing, as to act as if it were present; as if their characters were real Hercules, Thrasos, or Amintas'. Something past is just that: a *thing*. A writer must bring it to the *present*, make action a *presence*, characters real.[41]

In 1656, the abbé d'Aubignac clarified what this meant: 'I well know that theatre is a sort of illusion, but the spectators must be deceived in such a way that they do not imagine themselves to be so, even though they may know it. While you are deceiving them, their mind [*esprit*] must not know it; only when they reflect on it.' In 1674 René Rapin added that a tragedy is 'agréable' only when the spectator 'becomes sensitive to everything shown to him ['qu'on luy représente'], when he enters all the different feelings of the actors, when he is involved in ['qu'il s'intéresse dans'] their adventures, when he fears and hopes, when he grieves and rejoices with them'.[42] By this second half of the seventeenth century such claims were clichés no less in England than in France. What they asked was the *spectator*'s identification and empathy – not an actor's. The player becomes a reflecting *surface*, Hamlet's mirror, who performs for the spectator those actions by and into which that audience is to feel and be moved. But it does not feel the emotions of 'a wrathful hero, a daring adventurer, or a wise man', or the 'moral nature of each', as Castelvetro criticized Scaliger for 'gabbling'.[43] Rather was it moved by the *general* nature of passion and morality as they derived from action.

What we have then is less 'affects' [*affectus*] particular to one individual than *costumi*, *mœurs*, *consuetudines* shared by all. The character with whom the spectator identifies embodies customary characteristics. This explains a devaluing of Seneca. Roger Ascham wrote that, '[i]n Tragedies . . . the *Grecians*, *Sophocles* and *Euripides* far ouer match our *Seneca*, in *Latin*, namely in *oikonomía et Decoro*, although Senecaes elocution and

---

41 Jean Ogier de Gombauld, *L'Amaranthe, pastorale* (Paris: François Pomeray, Anthoine de Sommaville, & André Soubron, 1631), Préface.

42 François Hédelin, abbé d'Aubignac, *Pratique du théâtre*, ed. P. Martino (Algiers: Carbonel; Paris: Champion, 1927), p. 210; René Rapin, *Réflexions sur la poétique d'Aristote, et sur les ouvrages des poètes anciens et modernes* (Paris: F. Muguet, 1674), p. 19.

43 Castelvetro, *Art of poetry*, p. 67.

verse be verie commendable for his tyme'.[44] Right and decorous organization of subject thus mattered more than sparkling dialogue and maxim.
Later theorists argued that words might obstruct action and spectators'
identification. In 1692 Thomas Rymer accused Shakespeare of having too
often impeded action with words, 'a sort of heavy baggage, that were better out of the way, at the push of Action'.[45] In the 1670s Nicolas Boileau
and the rest would be saying nothing else.

Such identification, such internalizing of emotion, came from the
debate about *catharsis* and its conclusions. In its pursuit, other new
(sometimes old) demands were made. While on 'character', one of these is
of special interest: Aristotle's *hamartia*. Because purgation had an ethical
goal, it was natural that *hamartia* would come to mean an ethical failure
for which the protagonist bore responsibility. Exemplary were figures of
overweening pride such as Tamburlaine or Faustus, but the indecisiveness
of a Hamlet, the passion of an Antony, the ambition of a Caesar all fit
the mould. Such a moral flaw generalized specific moral attributes, but
also led towards a psychologizing of character matching the spectator's
ability to identify: with a person whose likeness to oneself one increasingly
recognized.

Verbal rant and artificiality were not the only impediments. Many
thought the chorus blocked action and its presence was much debated. It
was defended on grounds that it gave moral issues their clearest statements and that its music created specific emotional effects in the auditor.[46]
Gradually, though, the tragic followed the comic chorus to oblivion,
and for much the same reason: it distracted the spectator from the action.
Similarly, Castelvetro argued for those three unities to which we saw
La Taille refer just two years later. Following Aristotle, he wrote that a
plot must be whole (pp. 73–80) and have a certain magnitude (pp. 80–7).
That magnitude means it must be confined to twelve hours, because this
is readily within the span of the spectator's memory (p. 83). It must treat
a single action (pp. 84, 242). It must also, Castelvetro added, occur in a
single place: 'tragedy is confined not only to a single city, village, field, etc.,
but as much of any of them as can be seen by the eyes of a single person'

[44] Roger Ascham, *The scholemaster* (1570), in *The English works*, ed. W. A. Wright (Cam-
bridge: Cambridge University Press, 1904), p. 276. The work was written *c.* 1563. The
Greeks had always countered Seneca. Their spread is emphasized by Jan Kochanowski's
(1530–84) vernacular Euripidean *Dismissal of the Greek envoys*, played before Stefan
Batory at Jazdów near Warsaw in 1578. *Oedipus tyrannus* inaugurated Andrea Palladio's
Teatro Olimpico in 1585.

[45] Thomas Rymer, 'A short view of tragedy', in *The critical works*, ed. C. A. Zimansky (New
Haven: Yale University Press, 1956), p. 86.

[46] See, for example, Giovanni Bardi, 'Discourse addressed to Giulio Caccini, called the
Roman, on ancient music and good singing', in *The Florentine camerata: documentary
studies and translations*, ed. Claude V. Palisca (New Haven: Yale University Press, 1989),
p. 109.

(p. 242). Many later writers would explain that these limitations avoided making the spectator's memory and imagination impede empathy.

For that reason, many argued later that time and place should ideally match those of performance and stage. Although French and Italian tragedy went further in this direction than English, Dutch, or Spanish, such demands were increasingly made. Pierre Corneille may not always have held to such restrictions in practice, but he did in his three *Discours* of 1660: telling how he had obeyed them or why he had been justified in ignoring them. Contrariwise, Lope de Vega's 1609 *Arte nuevo de hacer comedias en este tiempo* largely denied these strictures (save for unity of action), and indeed the moral scheme advanced even in English tragedy (certainly by the seventeenth century's end) was never accepted in the Spanish, which portrayed in its tragedies' protagonists ambiguity of human action and ambivalence of ignorance and knowledge. This made a very different theatre, countering notions of spectatorial *identification*.[47]

While Spanish tragedy did not use action to the same ends, it urged its importance no less. The centrality of action as the motor of purgation was why Cintio argued that *suspense* made tragedies most moving. Thus he thought less-known, even fictive, plots to be 'more pleasing and more effective' than known ones. They were effective in assuring that 'the spectators remain suspended between horror and pity until the end'. Suspense must not depend on an auditor's bafflement, but on skilful plotting: the spectator 'sees himself led towards the end, but stays doubtful as to the outcome'.[48] A like emphasis on action is also why so many repeated Scaliger's almost parodic list of tragedy's woes. During the late sixteenth-century *Theaterstreit* in England John Northbrooke, Stephen Gosson, Philip Stubbes, Thomas Nashe, and later William Prynne (*Histriomastrix*, 1633) typically repeated it in some form. Maybe most famous (or infamous, for those seeing him as just naïve) was Opitz, for whom tragedy dealt 'with princes's desires [*willen*], killings, despair, infanticides and parricides, conflagrations, incests, wars and revolt, laments, howling, sighing, and suchlike'. He repeated Scaliger's list. Walter Benjamin sought to 'rehabilitate' Opitz by arguing he was founding the *Trauerspiel*, the 'mourning play' taken as opposed to *Tragödie*.[49] The argument cannot be made for Opitz historically (if not philosophically): couched in normative terms, his list repeated common claims about the importance for everyone of tragic *action* ('mourning', too, had its common place).

---

[47] Alice Craven, 'Staging consciousness: baroque characterization and the case of Calderón', unpublished Ph.D. thesis, New York University (1992).

[48] Cintio, 'Discorso', pp. 178, 184.

[49] Martin Opitz, *Buch von der deutschen Poeterey*, in *Aristarchus sive De contemptu linguae teutonicae und Buch von der deutschen Poeterey*, ed. G. Witkowski (Leipzig: Veit, 1888), pp. 119–207, here, p. 154 (from ch. 5); Walter Benjamin, *The origin of German tragic drama*, trans. J. Osborne (London: NLB, 1977), p. 62.

Except for the Spanish case, it is fair to say that all this was at least theoretically in place by the first decades of the seventeenth century. Across Europe tragedies were written according to them: England and France were most productive, but Holland was not far behind (notably with Joost van den Vondel), while Italy and Germany, 'even' Crete, Poland, Sweden, and elsewhere had greater or lesser activity. Spain became special in another way: by mid-century all its great tragic authors but Calderón had died or ceased writing – indeed, so had most of its minor ones.

From these developments, with their accent on psychological consistency, ethical responsibility, political duty, and dramatic concentration and symmetry, writers of the early decades of the seventeenth century created a tragedy showing a confidence in human power and authority absent from their humanist predecessors, even when they used the same subjects. A new sense of 'psychological' characterization and individual responsibility and a wholly new emphasis on relations between such individuals marked the change. The importance of language as such was almost wholly subdued, and tragedy's political concerns became internal to the drama (Grecian not Senecan, we might say) rather than an element of tragedy's broader social role, as it had been when aphoristic reflection was the principal form they took. Tragedy did now indeed 'teach' through emotional identification.

Critics and writers like Dominique Bouhours and Boileau, Rapin, Rymer, and John Dennis claimed to believe that these results could be achieved by those 'Rules of Aristotle' which were 'nothing but Nature and Good Sense reduc'd to a Method'. But John Dryden still gave an essentially Horatian/Donatian definition of tragedy, as 'a just and lively image of human nature, representing its passions and humours, and the changes of fortune to which it is subject; for the delight and instruction of mankind'.[50] Shakespeare might be reinvented according to the rules of reason, but Dryden would echo Sebillet's distinction of ancient formulae and modern *mœurs*, who himself was picking up on Cintio's adjustment of Aristotle's *'regole'* to the *'costumi de' tempi nostri'*: tragedy should follow the Ancients' rules, 'those things only excepted which religion, customs of countries, idioms of language, etc., have altered in the super-structures'.[51] 'Aristotle' was a shorthand for the arguments that had developed. The term bespoke novelty in tradition. The seventeenth century

---

[50] The quotation is from Dennis's *Impartial critick* (1693). A general appraisal is in Timothy J. Reiss, *The meaning of literature* (Ithaca: Cornell University Press, 1992), pp. 161–9 and ff. The Dryden quotation is from his 1668 *Essay of dramatic poesy*, in his *Selected criticism*, ed. J. Kinsley and G. Parfitt (Oxford: Clarendon Press, 1970), p. 25.

[51] For this 'invention' of Shakespeare, see Reiss, *Meaning*, esp. pp. 238–9, 247–62, and *Tragedy and truth*, pp. 204–18, 292–7. For the rest: Cintio, 'Lettera sulla tragedia [1543]', in Weinberg (ed.), *Trattati di poetica*, vol. I, pp. 469–86, here, p. 485; Dryden, *The grounds of criticism in tragedy* (1679), in *Selected criticism*, p. 165.

saw change in socio-political context more than in *critical* and *theoretical* grounds. Literary work related differently to state government and authority. New theoretical themes and ethical goals, critical objectives and political claims were assuredly refined and developed throughout the century, but they remained essentially true to the theoretical arguments elaborated in the previous century.

23

Elizabethan theatrical genres and literary theory

George K. Hunter

The practice of Elizabethan drama cannot easily be brought into focus for us by the statements of Renaissance literary criticism. Literary criticism in the period was, of course, tied to the humanist project of recuperating a classical literary and cultural order (revered as an aspect of a classical social order that had shown its power by dominating the known world and leaving Latin as the natural medium for all serious discourse). The vernacular drama of Shakespeare and his fellows was, however, a commercial and pragmatic enterprise, dependent not on the precepts of authority but on the willingness of a heterogeneous contemporary audience to take delight in what they were shown. Moreover, the taste of Elizabeth's court (unlike that of the Italian princes) did not contradict in essentials that of the common people who found entertainment in the popular playhouses, and this makes it possible to speak of a homogeneous taste in English drama, to be set against the theorizing of the Continent. There were, of course, aristocrats in tune with the demands of current literary criticism, who sought to return drama to a strictly classical form (as did Fulke Greville,[1] Sir William Alexander,[2] Lady Elizabeth Cary[3] and the Countess of Pembroke[4]); but the purposes of these people did not point towards performance, since that would be (as Greville remarks) 'to write for them against whom so many good and great spirits have already written'.[5] And in the universities students not only performed Latin comedies but wrote close imitations of them (modified by innovations

---

[1] *Poems and dramas of Fulke Greville*, ed. G. Bullough, 2 vols. (Edinburgh: Oliver and Boyd, 1939).
[2] William Alexander, Earl of Stirling, *The monarchic tragedies* (1604), in *The poetical works*, ed. L. E. Kastner and H. B. Charlton, 2 vols. (Manchester: Manchester University Press, 1921).
[3] Lady Elizabeth Cary, *The tragedy of Mariam, the fair queen of Jewry*, ed. B. Weller and M. Ferguson (Berkeley: University of California Press, 1994).
[4] Mary Herbert, Countess of Pembroke, *The tragedie of Antonie* (translated from Garnier) (London: W. Ponsonby, 1595).
[5] Fulke Greville, *The life of the renowned Sir Philip Sidney*, ed. N. Smith (Oxford: Clarendon Press, 1907), p. 224.

found in Italian plays and *novelle*, especially those that enlarged the roles of women).[6]

These, however, were specialized and protected enclaves. In the popular arena, as in Elizabeth's court, plays were in competition with fencing matches, acrobatic displays, fireworks, bear-baiting, and they could stay in competition because, in dealing with narrative content, the authors chose to emphasize separate moments of surprise, wonder, passion, and excitement rather than the closely articulated sequence of action that critical theory endorsed. In such a context the supposedly vulgar interest in novelty and variety was the prime quality that dramatists had to cultivate.

The principal interest of home-grown literary criticism in the England of this period was in the moral status of literature.[7] Could it be argued that literature improved the virtue of those who were affected by it? Of all genres, performed drama was the most difficult to defend in such terms, for not only was acting itself subject to religious objections but commercial performance was thought to encourage the worst attitudes of the worst classes in the country. John Marston in his pageant play, *Histriomastix*, probably written for an Inns-of-Court 'revel', defines these as 'the common sort of thick-skinned auditors', and speaks of the authors as those who, 'all applauded and puffed up with pride / Swell in conceit, and load the stage with stuff / Raked from the rotten embers of stale jests; / Which basest lines best please the vulgar sense'.[8]

The stark contrast set up between a classic drama (like Greville's), designed to make readers *think*, and a performed drama aiming to raise excitement, conceals, however, the clear fact that popular dramatists did learn to practise an art or *techne*, and one that at some points attaches to debates and theories prevalent in the Italian academies.[9] Grammar school education regularly included the study of Terence's plays, and the annotations that pedagogues had accumulated over the previous century brought a weight of supplementary critical comment with a diffused presence throughout the culture.[10] Donatus's definition of comedy (or Cicero's, as was usually said) as 'imitatio vitae, speculum consuetudinis, imago

[6] See F. S. Boas, *University drama in the Tudor age* (Oxford: Clarendon Press, 1914), and Alan Nelson, *Early Cambridge theatres: college, university, and town stages, 1464–1720* (Cambridge: Cambridge University Press, 1994).
[7] See *Elizabethan critical essays*, ed. G. G. Smith, 2 vols. (Oxford: Clarendon Press, 1904).
[8] *The plays of John Marston*, ed. H. H. Wood, 3 vols. (Edinburgh: Oliver and Boyd, 1939), vol. III, pp. 273–4.
[9] See Joel Spingarn, *A history of literary criticism in the Renaissance* (New York: Columbia University Press, 1925) and Bernard Weinberg, *A history of literary criticism in the Italian Renaissance*, 2 vols. (Chicago: University of Chicago Press, 1961).
[10] See T. W. Baldwin, *William Shakspere's small Latine and lesse Greeke* (Urbana: University of Illinois Press, 1944) and *Shakspere's five-act structure* (Urbana: University of Illinois Press, 1947).

veritatis' ['an imitation of life, a reflection of daily habit, an image of truth'] seems to have been known to every literate person, and no doubt played a part in tempering the native taste for romantic and chivalric adventures (with the usual paraphernalia of enchanters and hermits, impenetrable forests, and a king's daughter in disguise). This was a mode that paid little regard to the antithesis between tragedy and comedy, and the early theatrical repertory treated even classical themes in these terms. Such 'interludes' as *A new tragical comedy of Apius and Virginia, wherein is lively expressed a rare example of the virtue of chastity* (1564),[11] or *A lamentable tragedy mixed full of pleasant mirth, containing the life of Cambyses, king of Persia* (1561),[12] offer 'tragical' stories ('tragedy' meaning 'the falls of princes') ending in the establishment of an over-arching moral viewpoint, but without giving the audience any sense of a unifying vision established by genre. These plays belong, of course, to the infancy of English drama. Along with the establishment of permanent companies and purpose-built playhouses comes an awareness that generic titles imply separate structures of meaning.

The acceptance of this idea (so that the Shakespeare First Folio presents his plays as 'Comedies, Histories and Tragedies') has a continuous effect on the developed popular drama, but more as a dialectic than a law of exclusion. Several plays of the nineties use the idea of genre to highlight the arbitrariness of the viewpoint the dramatist contrives. Thus the anonymous *A warning for fair women*[13] begins with an Induction in which Comedy, History, and Tragedy contend for possession of the stage. The material of the play raises a genuine question, since the story being told is specific and true (and so 'historical'), is concerned with characters of low station and commonplace behaviour (and so belongs to Comedy), but presents overpowering passion and violent action (murder) and therefore is a 'Tragedy'. The distinction at issue does not appear, however, as one of form but of rhetorical focus. Tragedy (who wins the power to dominate the stage) 'must have passions that must move the soul / Make the heart heave and throb within the bosom', and asks us to view Comedy (and History) as 'slight and childish', designed only 'to tickle shallow unjudicious ears'.

The language used in this dispute illuminates many of the ways in which English deployment of the classical genres subverts neoclassical assumptions. The story told in *A warning for fair women* depends for its

---

[11] *Apius and Virginia* (1559/67) ed. R. B. McKerrow (London: for Malone Society by C. Whittingham & Co., 1911).

[12] Thomas Preston, *Cambyses* (1560–1), in Joseph Q. Adams, *Chief pre-Shakespearean dramas* (Boston, New York [etc.]: Houghton Mifflin, 1924).

[13] Anon., *A warning for fair women* (1598/9), ed. C. D. Cannon (The Hague: Mouton, 1975).

effect on its local familiarity, the comic inconsequence of the way things happen; its *imitatio vitae, speculum consuetudinis, imago veritatis* allows these terms to have an immediate social reference to the daily life of the audience. So the highly charged language of suffering [*pathos*] attached to the hero isolates him and denies his passion any generalizing power. *A warning for fair women* is an extreme case, but placing violent tragic emotions amid the reductive realism of a network of personal relations is common enough throughout the repertory. The best-known of all heroes, Hamlet, can be used to make this very point. The tragic *pathos* of his soliloquies isolates him from an external world that is allowed to be 'more real' (in the sense of 'more like life'). Unlike any classical or neoclassical hero, on his way to his appointment with death Hamlet must enter this world, joke with gravediggers and tease Osric. The tragic is part of a dialectic that keeps the claims of individual agony and of a 'more serious' [*spoudaioteros*] action always flanked by a memory that real life is composed of ordinariness. 'Mingling kings and clowns' (in Sidney's words)[14] is regarded by the critics as merely a solecism, since in order to achieve literature's moral-social purpose *decorum* should ensure that each character stays within his fixed social station. But though *Hamlet* begins with a representation of kings as kingly, ambassadors as ambassadorial, counsellors giving counsel, and fathers giving advice, the process of the play progressively undermines these decorous rigidities. And in such terms *King Lear* must also be judged as a highly indecorous play. For here the king's madness, unlike that of Ajax or Heracles or Pentheus, turns him into a fool in a company of fools, so that his high seriousness must be detached from its social or religious trappings and repositioned as a depth of inner resource that carries him through a random and disarticulated world, yet still 'every inch a king'. The Greco-Roman protagonists who suffer destruction of the worlds they thought they could control – Hercules Furens, Medea, Thyestes, Pentheus, Oedipus – can blame gods or mythic history for their misfortunes; the existence of these powers defines the meaning of what has happened. But the psychological focus of Elizabethan drama leaves us with human nature as the only source of power. This produces a number of formal consequences. The restricted number of actors in classical tragedy cannot provide the variety of human pressures to which the Elizabethan hero must respond, the variety of dilemmas his nature requires him to answer. The unities of time and place are likewise, given these priorities, liable to be regarded as mere impediments in the way of an achieved tragic vision in which the internal dimension of experience renders insignificant the external markers of continuity and coherence.

---

[14] *An apology for poetry*, ed. G. Shepherd (Manchester: Manchester University Press, 1973), p. 135.

The models critics found in Roman and Italian comedy raised fewer
formal difficulties than those that classical tragedy posed for English playwrights, but more obvious moral difficulties for the social guardians of the
time. Comedy could only be defended, it would seem, as a kind of anti-
toxin [showing] 'the filthiness of evil' as a means to teach 'the beauty of
virtue' (as Sidney puts it).[15] Sidney also tells us that comedy shows 'the
common errors of our life, which [the author] representeth in the most
ridiculous and scornful sort that may be',[16] so that comedy and satire
become twins. The recurrent subject-matter of comedies being the socially
disruptive passion of love, their actions dismay critics; they are condemned as favouring the spontaneity of youth over the wisdom of age and
as privileging the immorality of servants (Roger Ascham thought that 'ye
shall find . . . almost in every comedy no unthrifty young man that is not
brought thereunto by the subtle enticement of some lewd servant').[17] The
Christian Terence of humanist schoolmasters was designed to evade this
difficulty, to keep the excellence of classical comic form, while substi-
tuting the Prodigal Son parable for the love-adventures of the Roman
adulescens.[18] But the understanding of dramatic structure thus procured
could not be confined to moralized narrative. The formal pattern of pro-
tasis, epitasis, catastasis (Scaliger's addition), and catastrophe derived its
popularity from its capacity to hold together the much more complex and
diversified action that Elizabethan audiences evidently wished to see, in
plays involving differentiated and overlapping groups, where moral views
were as diversified as social roles. It is worth noticing that when Elizabethan dramatists domesticated classical-style comedies they tended to
double the plots. When Jonson imitated Plautus in *The case is altered* or
Shakespeare copied Ariosto in *The taming of the shrew*, both displayed
one plot in the cross-lights provided by another. The counterpoint of
modes of behaviour (taming versus wooing) opens the logic of each plot
to a variety of alternative judgements. And this was only one of the ways
in which *ethos* was allowed to emancipate *muthos*. In a play like *Love's
labour's lost*, for example, we see characters poised between open alternatives, and becoming freely human by the process of making choices
(the process by which *ethos* is manifested, according to Aristotle).[19] The
rephrasing of intrigue as psychological development allows plot to move
through its neoclassical phases without the restrictive presence of an
external manipulator.

---

[15] *Ibid.*, p. 117.   [16] *Ibid.*
[17] *The schoolmaster* (1570), cited in E. K. Chambers, *The Elizabethan stage*, 4 vols.
(Oxford: Clarendon Press, 1923), vol. IV, p. 191.
[18] Such as the *Rebelles* (1535) and *Asotus* (1537) of Macropedius, the *Acolastus* (1529) of
Gnaephius, the *Studentes* (1549) of Stymmelius.
[19] *Poetics* 1450.b 9ff., 1454.a.15ff.

The Elizabethan stage (in court as well as in town) found Comedy to be more to the taste of its patrons than Tragedy; but Tragedy appeared to the age, as to all ages, the more impressive genre. For critics, of course, the fact that Aristotle had dealt with this genre was a prime cause of attention; and the obscurity of the *Poetics* allowed interpretations and counter-interpretations to flourish everywhere. The Aristotelian comment that Englishmen found most germane to their own priorities was that which distinguished tragedy from comedy in terms of noble [*spoudaios*] versus ignoble [*phaulos*] actions.[20] The definition of these terms is, of course, capable of endless reinterpretation. Is the distinction a moral one (good versus bad), or do the words have a social meaning? Renaissance commentators had few doubts; the idea that tragedy was separated from comedy by the gulf between rulers and ruled was a standard assumption. But the religious and political situation of England in the period gave the issue a special colouring. Henry VIII and his Protestant propagandists had used drama to defame Roman Catholic doctrine and the democratic drama of Elizabeth's reign was continually attracted (in spite of censorship) to politically sensitive questions. The 'falls of princes' that English tragedies inherited from the *contemptus mundi* stories of the Middle Ages could no longer be, under these circumstances, mere representations of arbitrary Fortune or even (as in contemporary Italian court tragedy) the consequence of the private passions of rulers, but rather had to be the object of political judgement.

The explicit reason Sidney gives for praising Sackville and Norton's *Gorboduc* is stylistic, and his description of its purpose is moral. Yet, remembering his earlier description of 'high and excellent tragedy' as one that 'maketh kings fear to be tyrants and tyrants manifest their tyrannical humours',[21] we are bound to suspect that this play struck him because it offered advice to the Queen. The idea that tragedy has its dignity because it deals with political situations[22] is no doubt connected to the idea that it is by its nature suitable for an audience of kings. In Kyd's *The Spanish tragedy*, when Hieronimo, the hero, offers a play to the Spanish court (intending to turn the fictional action into a literal bloodbath) he is invited to put on a comedy. He scoffs at the idea: 'Fie, comedies are fit for common wits: / But to present a kingly troop withal, / Give me a stately-written tragedy; / *Tragoedia Cothurnata*, fitting kings, / Containing matter, and not common things'.[23] Weight and substance ('matter') no doubt takes us

---

[20] *Poetics* 1448a. [21] *An apology for poetry*, p. 117.

[22] Thomas Lodge in his *Defence of poetry, musick, and stage plays* (1579) tells us that Greek tragic writers not only dealt with 'the miserable fal of haples princes' but also that they led to 'the reuinous decay of many countryes'. *Elizabethan critical essays*, ed. G. G. Smith, 2 vols. (Oxford: Clarendon Press, 1904), vol. I, p. 80.

[23] In *The works of Thomas Kyd*, ed. F. S. Boas (Oxford: Clarendon Press, 1901), IV.ii, pp. 155–60.

some way towards *spoudaios* (in the sense of 'serious'), but the context in which Kyd makes the point defines its seriousness as attached not only to the fate of the hero but to that of the whole political organization.

The view of tragedy that the Renaissance inherited from Aristotle (even when given a simpler and more prescriptive moral structure by association with Horace's *Ars poetica*)[24] offered a psychological explanation of tragedy through the mysterious doctrine of *hamartia*. But Elizabethan dramatists could hardly incorporate that doctrine inside the structures they wished to compose. Sidney makes a moral rather than a psychological point out of it, saying that tragedy 'stirring admiration and commiseration, teacheth the uncertainty of this world' (making kings fear to be tyrants).[25] Milton (in his preface to *Samson agonistes*) comes close to Aristotle, but only, of course, in respect of an ending made calm and passion-free by God's understood approval. Between these two, it is the habit of English performed tragedy to resolve personal *pathos* by political reconciliation. Violent passions, in destroying individuals, break the social bonds that hold them together. After death, it is the state that must be reconstituted, with a soothing promise of better times to come. Thus in *Macbeth*, once 'the tyrant' is killed, the new king can promise a new political system: 'My thanes and kinsmen, / Henceforth be earls, the first that ever Scotland / In such an honour named . . .'.[26] Similarly, *Titus Andronicus* ends not with the passionate self-justification of the hero or even with the punishment of the villain but with a comforting intention: '. . . afterwards, to order well the state, / That like events may ne'er it ruinate'.[27]

The bias of the English dramatic imagination towards the political can no doubt be held responsible for the interest audiences (and so dramatists) displayed in a genre standing somewhere between tragedy and comedy, and justified by a process different from that found in either of those. I refer here to the history play.[28] Thomas Rymer, castigating Elizabethan tragic drama for its failure to match up to continental critical requirements, thought that 'the tragedies of the last age' were defective in that, like history plays, they were concerned with 'particulars' rather than the grandeurs of generality.[29] In this, as elsewhere in his critique, Rymer is

[24] See Marvin T. Herrick, *The fusion of Horatian and Aristotelian criticism 1531–1555* (Urbana: University of Illinois Press, 1948).

[25] *An apology for poetry*, pp. 117–18.   [26] v.viii.62–4.

[27] These final lines, omitted in the first Quarto but printed in Quartos 2 and 3 and in the Folio, are often placed in the footnotes in modern editions. But whether Shakespeare wrote them or not, the company seems to have allowed them as an entirely appropriate form of ending for the play.

[28] See Irving Ribner, *The English history play in the age of Shakespeare* (New York: Barnes & Noble, 1965).

[29] *The critical works of Thomas Rymer*, ed. C. A. Zimansky (New Haven: Yale University Press, 1956), pp. 22–3, 62, 182.

drawing on the *Poetics*.[30] Aristotle finds poetry more noble and more philosophic than history because it deals not with what men do but with what they ought to do (being the kinds of persons they are).[31] The history play cannot aspire to this kind of general truth [*to katholou*]. But the English history play had no such aspiration. Even Sidney[32] deserts Aristotle on this issue – influenced, it would seem, by Amyot's preface to his translation of Plutarch's *Lives* – and makes philosophy and history equally necessary as preparatives for poetry, noting 'how much the wisest senators and princes have been directed by the credit of history'.[33] And even Calvin approves of an art that represents things 'which the eyes are capable of seeing' and 'histories and events'.[34] The first appreciation we hear of English history's theatrical presence points to its role as a source of local pride: Its virtue (says Thomas Nashe) is that it provides a mirror 'wherein our forefathers' valiant acts . . . are revived, and they themselves raised from the grave of oblivion and brought to plead their aged honours in open presence'.[35] And it can only make this effect because it seems to deny art in order to assert truth. Of course this is not the whole story. Shakespeare's history plays, the central documents in any treatment of the genre, offer a more complicated relationship between past and present, but still invite the audience to see themselves as the inheritors of the struggles depicted on the stage, whether in the dynastic process that led to the emergence of the Tudor hegemony, or in the religious disputes that (as in *King John*) justified the creation of a national church.

The Elizabethan history play belongs to a particular moment in the national life of a particular country. By 1625 the particular circumstances that favoured its existence had disappeared and so the genre withered. There was no comparable European movement and no theoretical justification to give it a larger identity. The power of Shakespeare's representations is, presumably, the main reason why we still think of such plays as occupying a significant space on the generic map.

The other 'new' genre on the Elizabethan stage takes us in a different direction. Tragicomedy[36] was allowed by the theorists to have an ancient model in the *Amphytruo* of Plautus, since gods appeared in that play, but

[30] In the same period Samuel Butler spoofs this attitude in his 'Upon Critics who judge of modern plays precisely by the rules of the Ancients', speaking of those who 'Reduce all tragedy by rules of art, / Back to its antique theatre, a cart, / And make them henceforth keep the beaten roads / Of reverend Choruses and Episodes'. *Satires and miscellaneous poetry and prose*, ed. R. Lamar (Cambridge: Cambridge University Press, 1928).
[31] 51b. 3ff.   [32] *An apology for poetry*, pp. 105–6.
[33] *Ibid.*, p. 106.   [34] *Institutes of the Christian religion*, I.ii.12.
[35] *The works of Thomas Nashe*, ed. R. B. McKerrow, 5 vols. (Oxford: Blackwell, 1966), vol. I, p. 212.
[36] See F. H. Ristine, *English tragicomedy, its origin and history* (New York: Columbia University Press, 1910), and Marvin T. Herrick, *Tragicomedy; its origin and development in Italy, France, and England* (Urbana: University of Illinois Press, 1955).

only to secure human happiness in love. The instance did not do much to
rescue the reputation of the early Tudor plays described above and stig-
matized by Sidney as 'mongrel tragicomedies . . . match[ing] hornpipes
and funerals'.[37] By process of time, however, a developing English taste for
refinement in drama made some audiences willing to accept Italian
instruction in a form in which comic and tragic impulses could be harmonized. Guarini's *Il pastor fido*[38] could not achieve its innovations
without engaging in a critical war and producing a theoretical defence (the
Compendio della poesia tragicomica),[39] but clearly the play answered a
need felt by the sophisticated tastes of the early seventeenth century. The
genre emerged, as Guarini's title tells us, as an extension of the courtly
mode of pastoral poetry. Pastoral lovers, naïve and innocent, could easily be
seen as subject to the oppressions of fate. Lacking any capacity for heroic
resistance (and so for tragic action), they had to rely on quasi-Christian
resignation and purity of mind to secure a happy ending. Guarini's subtle
mixture of pastoral poetry, Christian sentiment, and the structure of the
Oedipus rex persuaded the cognoscenti of Europe to see in its seamless
poetic texture a delicate evocation of their own lives under the benign
oversight of increasingly absolute monarchs.

The genre made its first appearance on the English stage in Fletcher's
The faithful shepherdess (1608).[40] It was damned by its audience, but survived as a much lauded printed text, accompanied by a preface rehearsing
the Guarinian argument. But the survival of that argument on the English
popular stage depended on considerable attenuation of the original form.
Shakespeare's *The winter's tale* (1610) can be called 'a pastoral tragicomedy' (like *Il pastor fido*), and is probably in some sense a response to
Fletcher's play, but it draws its strength from older forms of romance, as
found already in its source, Greene's *Pandosto* (1588).[41] The cunning
interweaving of the plots in Guarini's play, so that apprehension and hope
are continually blended together, is turned into an episodic, stop-and-start
sequence, carried by a melange of styles (alternating base realism and
exalted idealism), and a plot movement that constantly invokes time and
constantly defies it. Place, no less than time, is handled with what can
only be called a confident indifference, and the turn to happiness at the
end requires us to rejoice in the artfulness of its own improbability.

---

[37] *An apology for poetry*, pp. 135–6.
[38] Venice: G. B. Bonfadino, 1590. Colophon date is 1590; actual date appears to have been
     December 1589.
[39] Venice: G. B. Ciotti, 1601.
[40] John Fletcher, *The faithful shepherdess*, in *Elizabethan and Stuart plays*, ed.
     C. R. Baskervill, V. B. Heltzel, and A. H. Nethercot (New York: Henry Holt & Co.,
     c. 1934).
[41] Robert Greene, *Pandosto*, in Alexander B. Grosart, *Life and complete works in prose and
     verse of Robert Greene*, 15 vols. (London and Aylesbury: privately printed, 1881–6).

Shakespeare, it would seem, is catering to a heterogeneous audience, with something for every taste, where Guarini is devising the most refined expression of a single taste.

Ben Jonson was the only Englishman in this period who was both a major contributor to the theatrical repertory and also a scholar well enough versed in classical and neoclassical criticism to act out both the tensions between the two roles and the conditions of compromise between them. If his 'Apology for *Bartholomew fair*', constructed as a dialogue between himself and John Donne and intended as an introduction to his translation of the *Ars poetica*, had survived the fire in his library, we would probably have a more adequate sense of the argument between his literary practice and his critical ideals. What we are left with are a series of ad hoc excerpts and reported opinions. It is clear that Jonson was ill at ease with the theatrical profession that gave him his income. His preface to *Sejanus* bewails the fact that it is not 'needful or almost possible in these our times, and to such auditors as commonly are presented, to observe the old state and splendour of dramatic poems with any preservation of popular delight'. The 'state and splendour' were probably tied in Jonson's mind to a didactic purpose that would 'steer the souls of men as with a rudder'.[42] His evaluation of his own work was far enough from theatrical common sense to allow him to believe that *Catiline* was his masterpiece, largely, it seems, because he could show the speechifying Cicero as the hero of the action.

In his critical pronouncements Jonson goes along with the purest of Aristotelian dogmas (as mediated by Heinsius's *De tragoediae constitutione*):[43] 'The fable is called the imitation of one entire and perfect action, whose parts are so joined and knit together as nothing in the structure can be changed or taken away without impairing or troubling the whole . . . to be let grow until the necessity ask a conclusion, [provided that] it exceed not the compass of one day.'[44] And this he seems to hold as equally true for comedy as for tragedy. An analysis of Jonson's own dramatic structures (both comic and tragic) makes it clear, however, that he, like others who genuflect before the unities of place and time, takes avoidance of explicit breaches of the rules to be sufficient fulfilment of them. *Volpone*, he tells us, 'presents quick comedy refined / As best critics have designed. / The laws of time, place, person he observeth'; but when we look at the actual performance we see that the laws are fulfilled by sleight

---

[42] Ben Jonson, *The staple of news*, Prologue for the Stage, 23–4, in *Ben Jonson*, ed. C. H. Herford and P. and E. Simpson, 11 vols. (Oxford: Clarendon Press, 1925–52), vol. VI.

[43] Daniel Heinsius, *De tragoediae constitutione* (1611; reprint Hildesheim and New York: Olms, 1976) and Daniel Heinsius, *On plot in tragedy*, trans. P. R. Sellin and J. J. McManmon (Northridge, CA: San Fernando State College, 1971).

[44] *Timber: or discoveries*, in *Ben Jonson*, ed. Herford and Simpson, vol. VIII, pp. 645, 647.

of hand rather than structural integrity. The multitude of scenes (nineteen in all), the speed of shift from one place to another, allows an idea of simultaneity that common sense would deny. The whole is held together less by an 'entire and perfect structure' than by a panic that compresses the explosive individuality of the characters and induces every member of the large cast to get caught in the toils of one another's projects. The complexity and richness of these superimpositions, the continual busyness of detail, the variety of clashing rhetorics mark these plays as the product of an Elizabethan (one might even say a Gothic) imagination, however neoclassical the terms in which they have to be defended.

24

Defining comedy in the seventeenth century: moral sense and theatrical sensibility

G. J. Mallinson

In the seventeenth century, comedy is a genre in search of an identity. Its association with traditions of popular entertainment and the absence of coherent classical principles give it lower prestige than tragedy or epic, and writers set out during this period to articulate criteria which will define and enhance its literary value. Much early criticism concentrates on form. In France, writers of pastoral stress the value of a new regular and non-tragic drama in the Italian mode, and prefaces often focus on questions of structure applicable to both tragedy and comedy.[1] Ben Jonson's comments in his *Discoveries*,[2] themselves much influenced by Daniel Heinsius and Julius Caesar Scaliger, draw attention to features common to both genres, and the same outlook informs Pierre Corneille's first *Discours*[3] where he applies to comedy some of the principles outlined in Aristotle's *Poetics*. Corneille's theoretical analysis is complemented by a series of critical readings (*Examens*) of his own early comedies which often single out deficiencies in construction or subject their specifically comic features to strict formal scrutiny. Such structural approaches imply that comedy is worthy of serious consideration, but do little to distinguish it from other genres. Terminology is often imprecise, and at the beginning of the century in France the term *comédie* may be used to designate any kind of play from farce to tragicomedy. Most comedies claim to represent life as it is, unlike tragedy with its historical plots, but there can be great variety among the texts produced. In his preface to *La veuve* (1634),[4] Corneille defines the genre as a reflection of the tastes of his (increasingly refined) audience ['La comédie n'est qu'un portrait de nos actions et de nos discours']. The resultant text is an essentially pastoral form of comedy founded on amorous intrigue. In his terms he echoes Jonson's

---

[1] Compare Jean Mairet, preface to *Sylvanire* (Paris: F. Targa, 1631); Charles Vion Dalibray, *L'Aminte du Tasse* (Paris: P. Rocolet, 1632).
[2] Ben Jonson, *Timber, or discoveries made upon men and matter*, first published in *The works of Benjamin Jonson* (London: R. Meighen, 1640), vol. II.
[3] Pierre Corneille, *Discours de l'utilité et des parties du poème dramatique*, in *Le théâtre de P. Corneille* (Paris: A. Courbé & G. de Luyne, 1660), vol. I.
[4] Pierre Corneille, *La veuve* (Paris: F. Targa, 1634).

insistence on 'deedes, and language, such as men doe use'[5] but the English
dramatist uses such principles as the theoretical basis of a more satirical
form of comedy, consciously removed from the model of Shakespearean
pastoral.

These differences in practice beneath similarities of critical language are
related to quite radical divergences of opinion about the aim of comedy in
both England and France. Some argue that the genre should have a morally
corrective force. In England, Jonson holds a rigorously classical view, re-
stating the aim 'to profit and delight';[6] he sees the comic writer as a social
critic, and comedy as a place where 'the time's deformity (is) Anatomiz'd
in every nerve and sinew'.[7] These views are repeated later in the century
where they underlie many essentially moral readings of contemporary
comedy. Thomas Shadwell, in his preface to *The sullen lovers* (1670),[8]
praises Jonson and rejects the modern literary taste for 'bawdy and profaneness', a view strengthened in his preface to *The humorists* (1671)[9]
where he sees the duty of comic writers 'to render their Figures of Vice and
Folly so ugly and detestable, to make people hate and despise them . . .'.
At the end of this period, Jeremy Collier, in his *Short view of the immorality and profaneness of the English stage* (1698),[10] offers a moral critique
of plays by John Dryden, Sir John Vanbrugh and others. But there are
alternative views. At the turn of the century, John Lyly had stressed the
pleasure to be derived from his work,[11] implicitly putting a moral aim into
the background, and this attitude is reflected later among the defenders
of Restoration comedy. Dryden views the manners of his age in a much
less satirical spirit than had Jonson, and in his important preface to *An
evening's love* (1671)[12] he defends the plot against charges of immorality;
he sketches out a new conception of comedy, no longer the critical analysis
of humours as exemplified in the work of Jonson but rather a theatrical
celebration of wit. He argues that 'the first end of comedy is delight, and
instruction only the second', a view echoed by William Congreve in his
Prologue to *The way of the world* (1700):[13] 'To please, this time, has been
his sole pretence; He'll not instruct, lest it should give offence'.

The same debate is found in France. In the early decades of the century,
many dramatists assume or explicitly stress the value of comedy as a

[5] Ben Jonson, Prologue to *Every man in his humour* (London: W. Barre, 1601).
[6] Prologue to *Epicoene, or the silent woman*, in *Works* (London: W. Stansby, 1616).
[7] Introduction to *Every man out of his humour* (London: W. Holme, 1600).
[8] Thomas Shadwell, *The sullen lovers, or the impertinents* (London: H. Herringman, 1670).
[9] Thomas Shadwell, *The humorists* (London: H. Herringman, 1671).
[10] Jeremy Collier, *A short view of the immorality and profaneness of the English stage* (London: S. Keble, 1698).
[11] Prologue to *Sapho and Phao* (London: T. Cadman, 1584).
[12] John Dryden, *An evening's love, or the mock astrologer* (London: H. Herringman, 1671).
[13] William Congreve, *The way of the world* (London: J. Tonson, 1700).

source of pleasure, and no moral purpose is implied in the many comedies of love, intrigue, and misunderstanding written in the 1630s and 1640s. Corneille is one of the most articulate defenders of this view, making the point in his preface to *La suivante* (1637)[14] and in *L'illusion comique* (1639)[15] embodying it in the form of a comedy which glorifies the theatre's right to provide entertainment rather than moral instruction. His later comedy, *Le menteur* (1644), which places a liar at the centre of a comedy of intrigue, arouses specific critical debate on this subject. Although accused of setting a dishonourable example, Corneille will not fix his play in a moral strait-jacket, insisting that the hero's lies are tricks [*friponneries*] rather than flaws, and suggesting that the theatrical world he inhabits is a world apart with its own conventions and values. In his later preface 'Au lecteur' to *Le menteur* of 1648,[16] he suggests that the principles by which we should judge a comedy are different from those of the theoretical or moral purist; aesthetic appreciation and not moral rectitude is the mark of good judgement. It is no surprise to him that his more 'correct' sequel, *La suite du Menteur* (1645), written to placate his critics, is less successful as a play: the hero may have lost his moral *défauts*, but this has entailed the loss of theatrical *agréments*.[17] This distinction marks a decisive moment in the criticism of comedy. The argument will be heard again in England at the end of the century in Robert Wolseley's eloquent preface to Rochester's *Valentinian* (1685)[18] in which he defends the reputation of its author and argues for aesthetic and not just moral criticism of literature.

It is with the works of Molière that debate about the nature of comedy and the criteria for judging it is most frequently engendered. In the preface to his early *Précieuses ridicules* (1659)[19] he adopts the language of the classical satirist in the Jonsonian mould, seeing his function to mock the *vicieuses imitations* of all that is good. Later, though, this traditional conception is subjected to scrutiny as he extends the range of his subject-matter to particularly sensitive areas. In his preface to *Tartuffe* (1669),[20] a comedy banned for its presentation of religious hypocrisy, Molière argues that ridicule, the principal weapon of the satirist, is a more powerful deterrent than menace; his *satire*, consequently, is more effective than solemn moralizing. Such an argument skilfully counters the critical attacks of such as Pierre Nicole in his *Traité de la comédie* (1667) which

[14] Pierre Corneille, *La suivante* (Paris: F. Targa, 1637).
[15] Pierre Corneille, *L'illusion comique* (Paris: F. Targa, 1639).
[16] *Œuvres de Corneille* (Paris: A. Courbé, 1648), vol. II.
[17] Pierre Corneille, *La suite du Menteur* (Paris: A. de Sommaville & A. Courbé, 1645).
[18] Robert Wolseley, preface to Rochester's *Valentinian* (London: T. Goodwin, 1685).
[19] Molière (Jean-Baptiste Poquelin), *Les précieuses ridicules* (Paris: C. Barbin, 1659).
[20] Molière (Jean-Baptiste Poquelin), *Le tartuffe, ou l'imposteur* (Paris: J. Ribou, 1669).

separate comedy from moral values, but it also implies a crucially different conception of the audience and of the dramatist's relationship with his
public. Critics who argue that comedy may corrupt posit an impression-
able audience; Molière, though, argues that contemporary spectators are
not misled by his play, not only because they have sturdy moral standards
but also because they know how to appreciate the nature of his comedy.

Debate about the moral function of comedy inevitably raises another
question about the criteria for judging its value: should they be theoretical
or theatrical? There is a tension throughout the century, in both England
and France, between theorists and dramatists. In his *Critique de l'Ecole
des femmes* (1663)[21] Molière suggests that the true value of a comedy
is to be determined not by the extent to which it obeys rules, but by
its impact in the theatre ['l'effet qu'elle fait sur nous']; he wrests critical
authority from the theorist, caricatured as the unsuccessful practitioner,
and invests it in the successful dramatist. In England, Dryden favours 'the
judgment of an artificer in his own art', a point subsequently repeated by
contemporaries who resist the influence of French classical rules. Critics
like Thomas Rymer may staunchly defend them, but dramatists are less
enthusiastic, and John Dennis in his *A plot and no plot* (1697)[22] notes inci-
sively that '. . . regularity in a Comedy signifies little without Diversion'.

This sensitivity to the importance of 'diversion' [*divertissement*] is
reflected, too, in the attention paid to the text in performance. Critics hostile to the genre suggest that performance in the theatre gives to a comedy
an impression of value which cannot survive scrutiny as literary text,[23]
and Dryden argues in his Dedication to *The Spanish fryar* (1681)[24] that
the 'more lasting and the nobler design' is to please the reader rather than
the audience. Molière, though, argues from the opposite standpoint. In
his preface to *Les précieuses ridicules* he laments that the printed text cannot reproduce the physical gestures or modulations of voice which are an
essential part of the play, a point taken up again in his preface to *L'amour
médecin* (1666). His own acclaimed skill as a mime and comic actor
inspires some more theatrical analysis of his work, and leads to a broader
exploration of what constitutes comedy. In his comments on *Sganarelle,
ou le cocu imaginaire* (1660),[25] for instance, Neufvillenaine gives a
detailed account of the play, blending narration of plot with a discussion
of its representation on stage and a clear attempt to analyse the actor's art.

---

[21] Molière (Jean-Baptiste Poquelin), *La critique de l'Ecole des femmes* (Paris: E. Loyson, 1663).
[22] John Dennis, *A plot and no plot* (London: R. Parker, 1697).
[23] Compare Gabriel Guéret's comments on Tartuffe in his *Promenade de Saint-Cloud* (1669), ed. G. Monval (Paris: Librairie des Bibliophiles, 1888), p. 49.
[24] John Dryden, *The Spanish fryar* (London: R. & J. Tonson, 1681).
[25] Molière (Jean-Baptiste Poquelin), *Sganarelle, ou le cocu imaginaire* (Paris: J. Ribou, 1660).

Such writing is an important early example of critical resistance to the reduction of comedy to a purely *literary* genre, divorced from its roots in the theatre.

A related problem for those seeking to define comedy is the role of laughter and, by extension, the validity of a hierarchy within comic writing as a whole. Already in England this problem had been addressed by Lyly who sought a more refined form of comedy, intended 'to breed soft smiling, not loud laughing'.[26] For some French writers in the early decades of the century, however, it is the arousal of laughter which defines their work as *comedy*[27] and Corneille proudly asserts that his first comedy *Mélite* succeeded in making his audience laugh without recourse to farce. Later on, though, he and others move away from this view. Some of Corneille's most innovative critical thinking comes in his *Dédicace* to *Don Sanche d'Aragon* (1650)[28] in which he argues that comedy is defined first and foremost by the nature of its action and not even by status of characters; laughter is considered an optional concession to popular taste. This is a view expressed, too, by Jonson who, in his *Discoveries*, follows Sidney's and Heinsius's misreading of Aristotle and denies a place to laughter.

It is with Molière, though, that we see a sustained defence both of laughter and, more generally, of a non-hierarchical conception of the genre. Like Corneille and other French dramatists of the 1630s, he seeks to define a specific identity for comedy, and like many, he argues that theatrical pleasure is the principal aim of the dramatist. But unlike most of his predecessors, he situates laughter at the base of his vision. What had formerly been seen as the mark of comedy's lowly status, is seen now in terms of a unique challenge ['une étrange entreprise'] to the dramatist's skills, the more so in Molière's case as he seeks to entertain audiences from both town and court. To arouse laughter in these circumstances requires a skilful refinement of traditional comic methods. Furthermore he vigorously defends the equal status of all forms of comedy, both popular and more literary. In his critical writings as well as in his works themselves, he does more than anyone to diversify the notion of the genre, and he develops in quite sophisticated ways a close correlation between different modes of comic expression, suggesting that techniques common to farce can be used to achieve far-reaching analysis of character or social manners. In his *Critique de l'Ecole des femmes*, written to defend a comedy criticized for gratuitous, low humour, he defends the representation of his hero Arnolphe's joy at the sexual naïveté of his intended wife, when she

---

[26] Preface to *Sapho and Phao*.

[27] Compare Discret, *Alizon* (Paris: J. Guignard, 1637); Paul Scarron, *Jodelet ou le maître valet* (Paris: T. Quinet, 1645).

[28] Pierre Corneille, *Don Sanche d'Aragon* (Paris: A. Courbé, 1650).

had asked him whether babies are conceived through the ear. Fearful that
he may be cuckolded, Arnolphe is both amused and reassured by such
innocence. Molière argues that the incident has an immediate comic effect
at the level of linguistic wit ['un bon mot'], but that it also reveals the
nature of his hero's character ['une chose qui caractérise l'homme']. This
is a fine example of the subtlety of Molière's comic practice, which brings
together pleasure and insight, but it reflects also his critical confidence, as
he uncovers, analyses, and justifies his method. This kind of analysis will
be picked up and echoed by some later commentators on the plays. In his
Lettre sur le Misanthrope (1667)[29] Jean Donneau de Visé singles out for
praise the comedy's capacity for arousing both laughter and reflection,
and in his *Epitaphe de Molière* (1673) La Fontaine sees in him a unique
blend of Plautus and Terence, two dramatists frequently invoked to articulate criticism of comedy at this time and to exemplify the low and
the high.

Discussion of individual plays in the course of the seventeenth century
raises many important issues relating both to the nature of comedy and to
a methodology for its evaluation: the contrasting claims of moral and
hedonist approaches to the genre, the conflicting authorities of the dramatist and the theorist, a growing sensitivity to the essential value of performance. What is striking, though, is the very varied nature of the comedies
produced over this period, both in England and France, a variety which
in part reflects the inevitable evolution of tastes but which also underlines the diversity of literary traditions from which comedy springs. Not
surprisingly, therefore, it proves impossible to establish any theoretical
model. Those who attempt to do so tend to isolate or distort. This is most
striking in later readings of Molière which often reduce his work to those
plays which can be identified with the classical principle of moral instruction. Boileau's explicit rejection of the farcical *Fourberies de Scapin* and
his preference for the more refined (and by implication more authentic)
comedy *Le misanthrope* exemplifies a critical approach which is widely
adopted; Molière is characterized as the castigator of human folly and it
is in this capacity that he is judged. Indeed, the move to develop aesthetic,
theatrical criteria for the evaluation of comedy, apparent in debates about
individual plays throughout the century, is never wholly sustained. This
is doubtless due in part to the constant mistrust of the theatre by the
Church, as made evident again in Bossuet's *Maximes et réflexions sur la
comédie* (1694).[30] Such criticism gives further impetus to readings from
an essentially moral perspective, and determines the nature of much writing both of and about comedy in the following century.

---

[29] Molière (Jean-Baptiste Poquelin), *Le misanthrope* (Paris: J. Ribou, 1667).
[30] Jacques Bénigne Bossuet, *Maximes et réflexions sur la comédie* (Paris: J. Anisson, 1694).

25

Dialogue and discussion in the Renaissance

David Marsh

The present survey traces the theory and practice of dialogue from the fifteenth to the seventeenth century, the two centuries when the form most flourished in Western European letters.[1] During this period, the theorists of dialogue, who were often also its practitioners, conceived of their enquiry as engaging the broadest issues of language and social behaviour. The study of the *genre* is at once critical and historical, since writers of dialogue develop their ideas both within an intellectual exchange and within a larger social context. Recent studies have accordingly examined Renaissance dialogue either in its formal aspect (as literary structure and the articulation of argument) or in its referential aspect (as a mirror of society and a record of language).[2]

The humanist dialogue arose in Italy around 1400, contemporary with the revival of Greek studies and with new styles in the visual arts. Generally a learned composition written in Latin, the dialogue of this initial period reflects the new philosophical freedom and eclecticism which were fostered by the rise of mercantile communes and by the weakening of papal authority through schism. Appropriately, the favoured model is the Roman orator Cicero, whose dialogues depict the leisurely philosophizing of learned optimates. While providing arguments on opposite sides of a question [*in utramque partem*], Cicero leaves his debates unresolved and hence implicitly open for the reader to decide.[3]

Although no Quattrocento writers of dialogue formulate explicit theories of the *genre*, their choices of theme and structure imply a critical awareness of specific goals in reviving classical forms. The pioneer in the field was Leonardo Bruni, an early translator of Plato and Aristotle and

---

[1] The classic study of the dialogue is that of Rudolf Hirzel, *Der Dialog: Ein literarhistorischer Versuch*, 2 vols. (1895; reprint Hildesheim: Georg Ohms, 1963).

[2] On the formal aspect of dialogue, see Jon R. Snyder, *Writing the scene of speaking: theories of dialogue in the late Renaissance* (Stanford: Stanford University Press, 1989). On the social aspect, see Raffaelle Girardi, *La società del dialogo: retorica e ideologia nella letteratura conviviale del Cinquecento* (Bari: Adriatica Editrice, 1989) and Virginia Cox, *The Renaissance dialogue: literary dialogue in its social and political contexts, Castiglione to Galileo* (Cambridge: Cambridge University Press, 1992).

[3] On the Quattrocento revival of classical dialogue, see Francesco Tateo, *Tradizione e realtà nell'umanesimo italiano* (Bari: Dedalo Libri, 1967); and David Marsh, *The Quattrocento dialogue: classical tradition and humanist innovation* (Cambridge, MA: Harvard University Press, 1980).

later chancellor of Florence. His *Dialogi ad Petrum Histrum* (1401–6) depicts prominent Florentines arguing for and against the greatness of Dante, Petrarch, and Boccaccio. The work at once established the Renaissance adoption of Cicero as a model for discussion and diction, both of which are implicit in Bruni's emphasis on *disputatio* as a polite exchange of views rather than a scholastic debate.[4] A second humanist to follow Cicero was the papal secretary Poggio Bracciolini, who composed various dialogues portraying his Roman and Florentine friends, as well as a collection of (often scurrilous) *Facetiae*, which he described as the conversational diversion of learned men.[5]

The humanists were seldom as highborn or wealthy as Cicero's optimates; and the 'modern' issues of nobility and economy lent themselves quite naturally to the Ciceronian model of contrasting debates *in utramque partem*.[6] In their Latin prose, moreover, Quattrocento humanists were aware that they could seldom rival Ciceronian eloquence. While borrowing Cicero's philosophical terminology, they generally sought to write in a colloquial rather than oratorical style. Issues of language were not limited to points of Latinity alone. The 'universal man' Leon Battista Alberti composed an Italian dialogue in four books titled *Della famiglia*; and in the preface to his third book he argues that the vernacular can rival the classical languages in treating important subjects.[7]

The later fifteenth century witnessed the diffusion of Italian humanism through new schools, libraries, and presses. Emerging centres of power now offered patronage to prestigious scholars, whose informal circles were often known as 'academies'.[8] Under Cosimo and Lorenzo de' Medici, Florence was host to a group of Platonists led by Marsilio Ficino.[9] After the restoration of the papacy to Rome in the 1430s, the resident curia and newly founded Vatican library offered considerable attraction to career humanists.[10] Naples was home to the circle of Giovanni Pontano,

---

[4] English translation in Gordon Griffiths, James Hankins, and David Thompson (ed.), *The humanism of Leonardo Bruni: selected texts* (Binghamton: State University of New York Press, 1987), pp. 63–84. See also Riccardo Fubini, 'All'uscita dalla scolastica medievale: Salutati, Bruni, e i "Dialogi ad Petrum Histrum"', *Archivio storico italiano* 150 (1992), 1065–103, esp. 1081–4.

[5] See the collected essays in *Poggio Bracciolini 1380–1980 nel VI centenario della nascita* (Florence: Sansoni, 1982).

[6] See Albert Rabil, Jr., *Knowledge, goodness, and power: the debate over nobility among Quattrocento humanists* (Binghamton: State University of New York Press, 1991).

[7] Marsh, *Quattrocento dialogue*, pp. 78–99.

[8] See Vincenzo De Caprio, 'I cenacoli umanistici', in *Letteratura italiana. I. Il letterato e le istituzioni*, ed. Alberto Asor Rosa (Turin: Giulio Einaudi, 1982), pp. 799–822; and Amedeo Quondam, 'L'Accademia', in *ibid.*, pp. 823–98.

[9] See James Hankins, 'The myth of the Platonic academy of Florence', *Renaissance quarterly* 44 (1991), 429–75.

[10] See Anthony Grafton (ed.), *Rome reborn: the Vatican library and Renaissance culture* (Washington, DC: Library of Congress, 1993).

which survives today in the Accademia Pontaniana.[11] By 1500 the advent of printing and the rise of courtly society in Italy were accelerating the codification of two literary languages: Ciceronian Latin and Tuscan Italian. An extreme clash between oral and print cultures occurred in Venice around 1500, when the great printer Aldo Manuzio assembled his own *sodalitas* of humanist editors and required them to speak in classical Greek.[12] But the prestige of the new learning made it extremely adaptable to new social contexts, and such rigid purism was rare. Even after 1500, when dialogues mirrored a shift to court society by admitting both women and the vernacular, they generally retained the Ciceronian model.[13] The most important alternative tradition to the Ciceronian model was furnished by the second-century Greek satirist Lucian, whose humorous dialogues mock the received learning of ancient philosophy and mythology. Scholars have always found satire amenable to recreation as well as reprehension; and as one of the first Greek authors studied by Renaissance humanists, Lucian soon attracted numerous translators and imitators.[14] During the Quattrocento, Lucian's influence is prominent in witty Latin dialogues by Alberti and Pontano.[15] In the sixteenth century, Lucian was most popular north of the Alps, where he was translated and imitated by writers of the stature of Erasmus and Thomas More.[16] In France, although Lucian's reputation for irreverence soon made his name a catchword for heterodoxy, 'Lucianisme' is a prominent feature of satirical writers like François Rabelais and Bonaventure Des Périers.[17] And even though two Lucianic works were eventually placed on the Index, Lucian enjoyed continued, if restricted, popularity and influence in sixteenth-century Spain and Italy.[18] Yet while the moral import of his satire was often lauded, Lucian generally received short shrift from sixteenth-century theorists like Sigonio and Speroni, who were loath to justify laughter as elevating or edifying.[19]

[11] On Pontano, see Carol Kidwell, *Pontano: poet and prime minister* (London: Duckworth, 1991).

[12] De Caprio, 'I cenacoli umanistici', p. 815.   [13] Cox, *Renaissance dialogue*, pp. 12–17.

[14] See David Marsh, *Lucian and the Latins: humor and humanism in the early Renaissance* (Ann Arbor: University of Michigan Press, 1998).

[15] Keith Sidwell, 'Lucian in the Italian Quattrocento', unpublished Ph.D. thesis, University of Cambridge (1975); Emilio Mattioli, *Luciano e l'umanesimo* (Naples: Istituto per gli studi storici, 1980).

[16] Craig R. Thompson, *The translations of Lucian by Erasmus and St. Thomas More* (Ithaca/Binghamton: The Vail-Ballou Press, 1940).

[17] Charles-Albert Mayer, *Lucien de Samosate et la Renaissance française* (Geneva: Slatkine, 1984); Christiane Lauvergnat-Gagnière, *Lucien de Samosate et le lucianisme en France au xvie siècle: athéisme et polémique* (Geneva: Librairie Droz, 1988).

[18] Michael O. Zappala, *Lucian of Samosata in the two Hesperias: an essay in literary and cultural translation* (Potomac: Scripta Humanistica, 1990).

[19] On Sigonio, see Cox, *Renaissance dialogue*, pp. 26–9; and Snyder, *Writing the scene*, pp. 34, 84–6. On Speroni, Cox, *ibid.*, p. 75.

In Italy, the vernacular dialogue of Ciceronian stamp flourished most during the first half of the sixteenth century, although most writers tended to use the form in an overtly didactic way.[20] The most influential dialogue of the early sixteenth century was Baldesar Castiglione's *Il cortegiano*.[21] Formally, Castiglione continued the ascendancy of Ciceronian models, especially *De oratore*, but his dialogue changed sixteenth-century ideas about social conversation and comportment. The interlocutors of *The courtier* both espouse and embody the refinement of the new court culture and of a Tuscan *koinē* as its linguistic medium. Castiglione's idealized portrait of the courtier – who combines the dialogic skills of learning, wit, and manners with aristocratic prowess and nonchalance – was immensely popular and influential. In the sixteenth century, the book was translated into English, French, Spanish, German, Polish, and Hungarian. In 1574, Stefano Guazzo published an Italian dialogue titled *La civil conversazione* which, by transforming Castiglione's graceful courtier into a learned gentleman, enjoyed similar popularity and diffusion throughout Europe.[22]

While courtly dialogue in Italy emphasized the social aspects of human interactions, the later sixteenth century produced a number of theoretical treatises which interpreted dialogue as the representation of philosophical discourse.[23] The codification of standards for dialogue writing was fostered by two movements of ideological retrenchment: the academic rediscovery of Aristotle's *Rhetoric* and *Poetics* initiated by Francesco Robortello, and the strictures of the Counter-Reformation promulgated by the Council of Trent (1545–63). Of the four major Italian theorists of dialogue who wrote between 1562 and 1585, all were connected with Padua, the centre of academic Aristotelianism; and all (with one exception) fell under the cloud of the Roman Inquisition. The exception was Carlo Sigonio, a professor at Modena whose brief Latin treatise *De dialogo* attempts to reconcile Plato and Aristotle: he conceives of dialogue as the representation of a cognitive enquiry (Aristotelian *mimesis*) which often contains elements of Platonic myth-making.[24] Sigonio's treatise enjoyed considerable fortune, and his ideas were generally accepted, with some modifications, by later theorists. Less fortunate personally was the classical scholar Lodovico Castelvetro, whose Italian commentary on

[20] Cox, *Renaissance dialogue*, pp. 63–9.
[21] *Ibid.*, pp. 47–60. For a modern edition of Castiglione, see *Il libro del cortegiano*, 2nd edn, ed. B. Maier (Turin: U.T.E.T., 1964).
[22] Stefano Guazzo, *La civil conversazione*, ed. A. Quondam, 2 vols. (Modena: Franco Cosimo Panini, 1993). See also Girardi, *La società del dialogo*, pp. 65–79; Giorgio Patrizi (ed.), *Stefano Guazzo e la 'Civil conversazione'* (Rome: Bulzoni, 1990); and Cox, *Renaissance dialogue*, pp. 24–5.
[23] Snyder, *Writing the scene*, and Cox, *Renaissance dialogue*, esp. pp. 61–83.
[24] On Sigonio, see William M⁰Cuaig, *Carlo Sigonio: the changing world of the late Renaissance* (Princeton: Princeton University Press, 1988), esp. pp. 50–3 on *De dialogo*.

Aristotle's *Poetics*, written in 1567 after he had fled Italy charged with heresy, contains several *obiter dicta* on the nature of dialogue.[25]

The other two theorists of dialogue were Italian poets who had become friends at the University of Padua. The ageing polygraph Sperone Speroni, accused of immorality for his vernacular dialogues on love, felt compelled to appear before the Holy Office in Rome in 1574, and wrote an *Apologia* defending his works as 'comedies' in which certain licentious passages can be justified philosophically as having heuristic value.[26] His younger contemporary, the poet Torquato Tasso, also wrote several Italian dialogues before composing his 1585 treatise, *Discorso dell'arte del dialogo*, which follows Sigonio in defining dialogue as the imitation of a discussion.[27]

In general, all of these figures endorsed Sigonio's notion of a central speaker [*princeps sermonis*] as essential to the didactic function of dialogue: the heuristic value of discussion had been supplanted by the need for clear exposition of Aristotelian systems or religious verities. Despite the continued practice of disputation in higher instruction, universities like Padua seem to have discouraged dialogues written in the classical manner. Beyond the Alps, Petrus Ramus and his disciples, by applying Aristotelian logic to all branches of knowledge, caused the 'decay of dialogue' posited by Walter Ong, who observes tersely that 'the Ramist arts are monologue arts'.[28] When the dialogue maintained its vitality, it often assailed Aristotelian certitudes, as in Galileo's *Dialogo dei massimi sistemi* (1632), a work which provoked a far-reaching reaction against dialogue in Italy.

Indeed, except for Galileo, seventeenth-century Italy produced no revitalization of the dialogue; and theorists assigned the *genre* to the realm of didacticism. In his *Del dialogo* of 1628, the Neapolitan patrician Giambattista Manso follows the Sigonian tradition of endorsing the (Platonic) didacticism of an authoritative speaker.[29] The career of the

[25] Snyder, *Writing the scene*, pp. 134–46.
[26] On Speroni, see Jean-Louis Fournel, *Les dialogues de Sperone Speroni: libertés de la parole et règles de l'écriture* (Marburg: Hitzeroth Verlag, 1990); Snyder, *Writing the scene*, pp. 87–133; and Cox, *Renaissance dialogue*, pp. 70–83.
[27] Snyder, *Writing the scene*, pp. 146–80. See the critical edition of Tasso's work by Guido Baldassari, 'Il discorso tassiano "Dell'arte del dialogo"', *Rassegna della litteratura italiana* 75 (1971), 93–119. For a modern translation and edition of the *Discorso*, see C. Lord and D. Trafton (ed.) *Tasso's 'Dialogues': a selection, with the 'Discourse on the art of dialogue'* (Berkeley, Los Angeles, London: University of California Press, 1982), pp. 15–41.
[28] Walter J. Ong, *Ramus, method, and the decay of dialogue* (Cambridge, MA: Harvard University Press, 1958), p. 187. Compare Cox, *Renaissance dialogue*, pp. 103–4: 'The new concept of a formal logic autonomous from disputation and teaching would not find a clear formulation before Descartes and the Port-Royalists, but, long before them, Ramist logic, while still eminently "communicative", bore unmistakable traces of the rift which was to come'.
[29] Giambattista Manso, *Del dialogo* (Venice: Deuchino, 1628); Snyder, *Writing the scene*, pp. 185–97; Cox, *Renaissance dialogue*, p. 67.

theorist, Pietro Sforza Pallavicino, is symptomatic of the times. Forced to leave Rome in 1632 as a result of his sympathies with Galileo, Pallavicino joined the Jesuit order in 1637, and returned to the Collegio Romano as a professor of philosophy. There he penned a number of conservative and orthodox works, including a *Trattato dello stile e del dialogo* (1646), in which he endorses a neo-Aristotelian ideal of dialogue as a pleasant form of instruction.[30]

Since dialogue was now serving the ideals of Counter-Reformation education, it is no wonder that it was again silenced, as it had been by Augustine more than a millennium earlier. Jesuit educators now insisted that a spiritual authority supervise any form of 'Ciceronian' debate. And for its didactic style Pallavicino lauded Augustine's *Contra academicos*, the very dialogue which had condemned the rhetorical freedom and philosophical eclecticism of ancient dialogue as incompatible with Christian faith.[31]

French readers too apparently favoured didactic reading, and preferred the discourse and treatise to the less direct vehicle of dialogue. In 1658, Paul Pellisson-Fontanier could write that, although dialogue had once been highly esteemed by the leisurely Greeks and Italians, the impatient French could no longer abide the form.[32] But in the end, it was an intellectual revolution, rather than Gallic petulance, which caused the decline of dialogue.

The purported superiority of French literary culture soon inspired a revival of dialogue across the Channel. In 1663, one Samuel Sorbière published a disparaging account of English customs and theatre. In reply, John Dryden composed his *Essay of dramatic poesy*, a dialogue printed in 1668, in which four interlocutors examine the validity of the Aristotelian unities of French tragedy. Combining wit and good manners, Dryden's dialogue suggests that, whereas the French unities constrict poetic invention, the greatness of English poets like Shakespeare transcends any rules. The age of the Sublime was approaching.

---

[30] Pietro Sforza Pallavicino, *Trattato dello stile e del dialogo* (Rome: Eredi del Corbelletti, 1628); Snyder, *Writing the scene*, pp. 197–213; and Cox, *Renaissance dialogue*, pp. 79–81.

[31] Marsh, *Quattrocento dialogue*, pp. 42–3; Cox, *Renaissance dialogue*, pp. 68, 78.

[32] Quoted by Le Guern, 'Sur le genre du dialogue', in *L'automne de la Renaissance*, ed. Jean Lafond and André Stegmann (Paris: J. Vrin, 1981), p. 145.

26

The essay as criticism

Floyd Gray

Before Michel de Montaigne and Francis Bacon used the word to designate their respective works (unlike in all but a few details), the essay began to take form in the epistolary writings of Cicero and Seneca, Plutarch's *Moralia*, the compilations of *sententiae*, *exempla*, and *lectiones* of late antiquity and their humanist counterparts. Montaigne gave the title *Essais* to his 1580 volume as an appropriate designation for a work in which a variety of seemingly unrelated historical and moral examples culled from his readings are pondered and compared, apparently in desultory fashion, for their relative value, thereby conjugating etymologically the *exagium* of essay and the *krinein* of criticism.[1] Similarly, the 'fragments of my conceites'[2] that Bacon published in 1597 under the title *Essays* are a selection of adages and aphorisms from his many commonplace-books, carefully contrived to convey practical precepts in a methodical and convincing manner. In 'Of studies', he aptly summarizes his underlying strategy: 'Read not to contradict and confute; nor to believe and take for granted; nor to find talk and discourse; but to weigh and consider',[3] recalling Montaigne's deliberative practice and anticipating Charles-Augustin Sainte-Beuve's definition of a critic as simply a person who knows how to read and who shows others how to read.

Born of *otium*, Montaigne's *Essais* represent originally his attempt to capture and tame the chimeras and fantastic monsters which idleness and leisure generated in his mind. Progressively, however, he perceives disorder as natural order, and discursive inconclusiveness as a prerequisite to the immediate reproduction of the reality of his thought and self. In opposition to those who sought definitions and conclusions, Montaigne was increasingly concerned with comparisons and differences, viewing the essay finally as a record of diverse occurrences, irresolute and contradictory ideas: 'I am unable to stabilize my subject', he writes, 'it staggers confusedly along with a natural drunkenness'.[4] It is precisely this apprehension

---

[1] Latin *exagium*, a weighing; Greek *krinein*, to separate, discern, discriminate.
[2] As he calls them in the dedicatory letter to his brother Anthony. See *The works of Francis Bacon*, ed. J. Spedding, R. L. Ellis, and D. D. Heath (New York: Hurd and Houghton, 1869), vol. XII, p. 289.
[3] Bacon, *Works*, p. 252.
[4] *The essays of Michel de Montaigne*, trans. and ed. with an introduction and notes by M. A. Screech (London: Penguin, 1991), p. 907.

of the unpredictable and indefinite which informs the fundamental vocation of the essay as criticism and eventually as genre.

Literary historians have long attempted to write the prehistory of the
essay, to locate its origin in recognized forms, to define and categorize it
as genre. Bacon pointed the way with his remark that the word is late but
the thing ancient, undoubtedly taking his clue from Montaigne in concluding that Seneca's *Epistles to Lucilius*, if one marks them well, are but
essays.[5] Pierre Villey was the first to examine systematically the literary
context from which the essay that Montaigne embodied ultimately evolved,
and to qualify it as the gradual personalization of an impersonal form.[6]
Others have confirmed a predilection for the *ordo neglectus* in the art
and literature of the time and have described the essay as developing out
of the letter, the dialogue, and collections of miscellanea. It has been
suggested that Renaissance rhetoric ultimately constitutes the literary
matrix of these heterogeneous texts and that they eventually acquire an
autonomous status through the addition of autocommentary: the *locus
communis* becomes the medium of writers who, no longer satisfied with
merely copying, meditate as well on the material they collect and imprint
it with their own, usually moralizing, interpretation.[7]

Generally speaking, reading in the Renaissance was concerned essentially with the acquisition of inscribed knowledge, and criticism, concurrently, with philology and rhetoric, that is to say its accurate and orderly
transmission. Montaigne is unique in his age in considering books – his
own as well as those of others – as objects of diversion: 'If anyone says to
me that to use the Muses as mere playthings and pastimes is to debase
them, then he does not know as I do the value of pleasure, plaything or
pastime'.[8] His privileging of pleasure and propensity for ludic indifference
are reflected in a kind of reading, more practical than theoretical, which
marks the beginnings of eudemonic or 'voluptuous' criticism in France,[9]
and a kind of relaxed and undogmatic writing that was to become a new
literary genre.

In assimilating his encyclopaedic readings into an intellectual configuration, Montaigne's writing experience is in itself an outstanding
example of implied critical discourse. Moreover, his expressed commentary

---

[5] See Francis Bacon, *Essays*, with annotations by R. Whately (Boston: Life and Shepard, 1868),
   p. xxxvii. Montaigne's reference however is to Lucilius, the Latin poet, 'who committed
   to paper his deeds and thoughts and portrayed himself as he knew himself to be' (p. 719).
[6] Pierre Villey, *Les sources et l'évolution des 'Essais' de Montaigne*, 2 vols. (Paris: Hachette,
   1908).
[7] The *Adages* of Erasmus afford numerous examples of authorial intervention and interpretation.
[8] Montaigne, *Essays*, p. 934.
[9] See Albert Thibaudet, *Physiologie de la critique* (Paris: Nouvelle Revue Critique, 1930),
   p. 156. Alfred Glauser calls Montaigne the creator of French literary criticism. See his
   Montaigne paradoxal (Paris: Nizet, 1972), p. 67.

no longer serves merely to confirm moral intent; on the contrary, stressing disparities, proselytizing accepted ideas and traditional opinions, it brings into focus the criterion of authority. Prompted by quotations or embedded in appropriated texts, Montaigne's *marginalia* increasingly move to the fore and finally prevail. What emerges, however, is less an autobiography than the peculiar dynamics of an indeterminate and questioning reader. From its relatively humble origin, the essay becomes in Montaigne's hands a complex, highly individual confrontation with the accumulated literary, cultural, ethical past and present. Bacon notwithstanding, the word was not new, in English or in French,[10] nor the thing ancient, except perhaps in its superficial conformity with the conventions of familiar epistolary or dialogic writing.

In any event, Montaigne was convinced both of the originality of his enterprise and consubstantiality with his book, resolutely placing it and himself outside of and in opposition to the sphere of preconceived models and genres. From the very beginning, his collection of aphorisms, quotations, examples is distinguished by the clash of conflicting points of view, reproducing thereby the discriminating movement of the critical mind, but without any of its prescriptive, restrictive, or meliorating tendencies. *Dubito* for him is as much a necessary condition of thinking and writing as *cogito* was for Descartes. If by genre one means a form or a norm to which a number of examples can be made to comply, then the *Essais* are a form unto themselves, a genre *sui generis*, which explains Montaigne's constant preoccupation with their specificity and idiosyncrasies. It is less by its 'formlessness' than its multiplicity of forms that the essay generates the genre of which it was to become a precursor. The essay is not art, but nature – Montaigne's nature. Without him, it is a vain chrysalis, an empty, imitable shell.

Reading and reflections on writing are major concerns of the *Essais*, and Montaigne is aware of the limits of both. Suspicious of allegorical hermeneutics, he raises the question of authorial intention: 'Is it possible that Homer really wanted to say all that people have made him say?'[11] On the other hand, he realizes that if writing is interpretation, reading is a form of rewriting and that texts tend consequently to engender multiple meanings: 'A competent reader can often find in another man's writings perfections other than those which the author knows that he put there, and can endow them with richer senses and meanings'.[12] His comments on questions of imitation, invention, imagination, style, the use and abuse of rhetoric and rhetorical figures, are shaped both by the concept

[10] The *Dictionnaire historique de la langue française* (Paris: Dictionnaires le Robert, 1992) dates the word from 1140; the *OED* gives examples from the fourteenth and fifteenth centuries.
[11] Montaigne, *Essays*, p. 662. [12] *Ibid.*, p. 144.

of classical taste and an appreciation of the subtleties of various stylistic techniques. Inasmuch as he sees a correlation between what an author is and writes, his remarks inevitably take into account, long before Sainte-Beuve or Hippolyte Taine, the biographical factor. His knowledge extends to most Greek and all of Latin literature (whether in the original or in translation), including neo-Latin writings. In addition, he was familiar with, but appreciated in varying degrees, contemporary Italian and French authors.

'Des livres' provides a crucial paradigm of his reading habits and literary taste. Even if he allows himself to be guided by chance – 'If one book wearies me I take up another, applying myself to it only during those hours when I begin to be gripped by boredom at doing nothing'[13] – he invariably takes a position, states an opinion, expresses his preferences. Since his perspective is essentially that of a critic of himself as reader, interested in measuring his ability to discern as well as qualifying the degree of his pleasure, he tends to proceed by hierarchies and comparisons. What distinguishes his classifications from those of his contemporaries is that they are based on personal criteria rather than on the authority of tradition or convention. Thus his reasons for disliking Cicero's moral treatises are aesthetic rather than philosophical. He finds his way of writing, and every other similar way, affected and boring, because his prefaces, definitions, partitions, etymologies needlessly consume the greater part of his work. He prefers the directness and sharpness of Plutarch, Tacitus, and Seneca, contending that neither grammatical distinctions nor an ingenious conjecture of words and argumentations can compensate for a lack of substance and solid reason.

He accords little space in his text to authors he finds merely diverting: Boccaccio, Rabelais, Johannes Secundus; the fact that he simply names them, without any comment whatsoever, is already a kind of condemnation. The momentary amusement others afforded, the furtive pleasure he took in reading them during his childhood, become negative values in his later evaluation, coloured as it is by age and distance: 'this aged heavy soul of mine can no longer be tickled by good old Ovid (let alone Ariosto): his flowing style and his invention, which once enraptured me, now barely have the power of holding my attention'.[14]

When it is a question of books which give him real pleasure, Montaigne has no difficulty, despite his inherent irresolution, finding ways (1) to formulate judgements – elsewhere usually hesitant and qualified – which are surprisingly clear and definitive: '. . . it has always seemed to me that in poetry Virgil, Lucretius, Catullus, and Horace rank highest by far – especially Virgil in his *Georgics*, which I reckon to be the most perfect

---

[13] *Ibid.*, p. 459.   [14] *Ibid.*, p. 460.

achievement in poetry . . .'; 'And in the *Aeneid* the fifth book seems to me the most perfect'; (2) to wish for even more perfection in his favourite author: 'there are passages in the *Aeneid* in which Virgil, if he had been able, would have given a touch of the comb'; (3) to perceive the kind of profit he can derive from another kind of writer: 'I also love Lucan . . . not so much for his style as for his own worth and for the truth of his opinions and judgements'; (4) to describe the sources of his reading pleasure: 'As for that good poet Terence – the grace and delight of the Latin tongue – I find him wonderful at vividly depicting the emotions of the soul and the modes of our behaviour'; (5) to conclude that he has no taste for the *Axiochus* because it is too weak for a book attributed to Plato.[15]

Comparison engenders criticism, and the more Montaigne examines writers he likes, the more his text expands and the more his judgement confirms and affirms itself. Parallels between Plutarch and Seneca, Pliny the Younger and Cicero, Democritus and Heraclitus, Seneca and Tacitus, provide compelling examples of literary analysis motivated and structured by the play of similarities and dissimilarities. Maintaining that an author's style is what reveals or conceals the man, he admires Socrates for refusing the figures and fictions of the supplication Lysias had put in writing for him and for defending himself with truth and sincerity, the natural ornaments of his speech.[16]

Fundamentally impressionistic and anti-rhetorical, Montaigne's criticism tends to translate itself into dynamic metaphors founded on the opposition between art and nature. He contrasts the measured, regular, graceful progression which his reading of the ancients taught him to consider ideal – *et vera incessu patuit dea* – with the disjointed, tense, 'comic' movement he associates with himself and his book. This distinction leads him to prefer the 'even smoothness' of Catullus to the 'sharp goads' of Martial; the lofty and sustained flight of Lucretius and Virgil to the fluttering and hopping of Ariosto or the fantastic hyperboles of Spanish and Petrarchan conceits; to condemn contemporary writers of comedy who need three or four plots from Terence or Plautus to make one of their own, or who pile up in a single play five or six stories from Boccaccio.[17] Finally, it allows him to admire the solemn effectiveness of medieval church music and architecture or the sublime conjunction of popular and learned poetry.

Generally speaking, poetry provides him with more pleasure than prose, and he finds himself diversely affected by a variety of forms, not so much higher or lower as different in colour: first a gay and ingenious fluency; then a keen and lofty subtlety; finally a mature and constant power: Ovid, Lucan, Virgil.[18] Comparing the lines of five Latin poets in praise of Cato and appreciating each for its distinct qualities, he concludes, in terms

[15] *Ibid.*, pp. 460–1.   [16] *Ibid.*, p. 1194.   [17] *Ibid.*, p. 461.   [18] *Ibid.*, p. 260.

reminiscent of Plato's *Symposium* and *Ion*, that the beauty of 'divine' poetry is infinite, its power magnetic, and its essence above reason and rules: 'It does not exercise our judgement, it ravishes it and enraptures it'.[19] Whereas prose by definition [*prorsa oratio*] proceeds rectilinearly and signifies directly, verse [*versus*] implies inflection, language turning back on to itself, words suggesting more than they actually state, stimulating the play of memory and imagination. The same criteria of fullness and evocativeness appertain, but poetry is enhanced by the addition of sensual attraction and brings into play elements of taste and experience.

Ruminating on a passage from Lucretius and conflating it with one from Virgil, Montaigne is struck by the plenitude of poetic language: 'the sense discovers and begets the words, which cease to be breath but flesh and blood. They signify more than they say.'[20] His comments on Virgil and Lucretius can be compared, for their intrinsic and seminal value, to the texts themselves. Here we discover the literary critic as he will be represented later by Sainte-Beuve and Albert Thibaudet, who, by his mimetic gift, speaks of literature in an equivalent language, for whom words have body, therefore weight and palpable substance, who is essentially creative in his criticism. His admiration for Virgil and poets in general encourages him to privilege writing over experience, to consider letters superior to life. Animals may have language, but they have no literature, and it is this awareness of the role of letters in the shaping of life and our idea of life that is one of Montaigne's most perceptive contributions to criticism. He finds that poetry not only expresses love to the point of giving it life, but that it surpasses love itself: 'the powers and values of that god are found more alive and animated in poetry than in their proper essence', adding this statement which may appear somewhat paradoxical at first, but which translates nevertheless a literary truth: 'Venus is never as beautiful stark naked, quick and panting, as she is here in Virgil'.[21] Flesh may age and die, but poetry subsists forever in all its original radiance and energy.

Despite superficial similarities, such as titles, quotations, and classical allusions, there is next to nothing of Montaigne in Bacon. The essence is gone, only the bare structure remains. With Bacon, the essay becomes a genre, and criticism a manner or a method of considering abstract questions and problems, none of which is properly literary. Whereas Montaigne multiplies and develops, Bacon selects and condenses. In the *Essays*, as in much of his work, he deconstructs the record of the past, in an attempt to isolate the truth hidden in human experience and example. Instead of reducing a subject to its basic principles however, his insistent accumulation of contradictory *sententiae* and propositions makes it

[19] *Ibid.*   [20] *Ibid.*, p. 987.   [21] *Ibid.*, p. 958.

appear more subtle and complex. Contrary to Montaigne, he does not talk about himself, and what little he reveals appears dimly in the interstices of his text. What characterizes his essays is their objectivity, but behind their lapidary stillness we come to sense the presence of a man anxiously focused on the contradictions and convolutions of the human mind. The *Essays* are fragmented and taut, more compelling for their incisiveness than their breadth. Bacon's meditations leave little to the imagination, as though he meant his words to be definitive. But concise statements are not necessarily conclusive or memorable, even when presented with all the persuasive subtlety of his rhetorical art.

Whereas Bacon affirms, Montaigne knew how to doubt, and criticism was first of all the science of doubt, the reaction of the *kritikoi* against the *grammatikoi*.[22] In Montaigne, ancient and humanist criticism becomes 'essayism', comprising the tangential interpretation of traditional literary texts together with a comparative evaluation of universal manners, customs, prejudices, and beliefs. Empirical rather than theoretical, without the constraints of rhetoric and philology, the essay is concerned with style and sensibility, leisure and pleasure, judgement and taste rather than with rules and techniques. Montaigne's book is the source of a certain kind of criticism in France, the prototype of countless *Lundis*, *Approximations*, *Réflexions*, *Prétextes*.[23] Finally, as language dealing reflexively with language, the 'weighing' of the essay is the activity of criticism itself.

[22] See Dirk M. Schenkeveld, 'Oi kritikoi in Philodemus', *Mnemosyne* 21 (1968), 178–9.
[23] Successively, works by Sainte-Beuve, Charles Du Bos, Thibaudet, and Gide.

27

The genres of epigram and emblem

Daniel Russell

While the word 'epigram' entered the French language at the end of the fourteenth century, it remained rare until the sixteenth, and the earliest citations of the word in the *Oxford English Dictionary* all date from the sixteenth century. Likewise, the term did not become common in German until the sixteenth and seventeenth centuries. The modern epigram does seem in some respects to be truly an invention of the Renaissance. And like the other truly Renaissance genres, the emblem and the essay, it is a genre whose development was directed to some extent by its etymology as it was assembled from a combination of classical models and medieval subliterary gnomic traditions. The word meant 'inscription' in the classical languages, and Renaissance epigrams too were often meant to serve as literal or figurative inscriptions for real or putative monuments or works of art.

Naturally, the epigram was not an entirely new form. In Germany the Baroque epigram was in some respects closer to the medieval *Spruch* than to the classical epigram. In French poetry, short-form verse, ending with a proverb or a famous line of poetry, was common in the later Middle Ages following the example of Eustache Deschamps, and these short forms were even discussed in some detail in the arts of *seconde rhétorique*. Since late antiquity, gnomic sayings had been stretched into distichs or other combinations of rhyming verse for mnemotechnic considerations, in ways that often turned them into epigrams in all but name. Like the ancient epigrams, these short poems provided *tituli*, or captions and inscriptions, for mosaics, tapestries, and stained glass windows. In some cases they were ekphrastic condensations of Bible lore, following a tradition that dated back to Prudence and other early Christian writers, and are often reminiscent of the quatrains attached to Holbein's *Historiarum Veteris Testamenti Icones* (1538).

But the Renaissance poets deliberately chose other models for the epigram, including, especially, Martial, but also the epigrams of the Greek Anthology and Catullus, following a Renaissance tendency to modernize medieval forms by reshaping them along the lines of, and often with explicit reference to, ancient works and genres. With the progressive rediscovery of Greek and Roman culture, Renaissance poets turned to these models to breathe new life into short-form verse. In practice this meant that poets chose new poetic pretexts and tried to write votive, triumphal, or mortuary inscriptions, such as Clément Marot's epitaphs, where this model was combined with the pointed satire of Martial's much appreciated epigrams.[1] Or their inspiration was more self-consciously humanist and recalled votive epigrams of the Greek Anthology as in Geoffroy Tory's *Aediloquium ceu disticha . . . & epitapha septem* (1530).

In the middle years of the sixteenth century the vogue of the neo-Latin epigram spawned what was to become a truly new Renaissance 'genre', the emblem. Emblems began as a collection of illustrated epigrams, composed by Andrea Alciato, the Milanese jurist, and first published in Augsburg by Heinrich Steyner in 1531. Some 40 per cent of the texts for these 'emblems' were Alciato's Latin translations of epigrams from the Greek Anthology, many of which he had already published in the anthologies edited by Soter and Cornarius in the late 1520s, while others may be seen to be imitations and variations of Anthology-like material. The origin of the emblem reminds one of the origin of the essay: both forms were born as a collection of pieces modelled on, but slightly different from, earlier works of much the same sort as the model for Michel de Montaigne's *Essays* may be found in the collections of anecdotes, loosely known as *Silvae* or *Diverses leçons*, by such writers as Pedro de Mexia and Antoine du Verdier, both of whom worked in ways sometimes parallel to those of the emblematists. In each case, the title of the collection provided, through its etymology, and through its use to characterize a collection of modified versions of a standard form, the seed from which an entire genre was to grow. The *emblema* was a piece of decorative inlaid work, as in a mosaic or intarsia, or a detachable ornamental appliqué, especially for gold or silver tableware. The word was not common in medieval Latin, and did not emerge in the European vernaculars before the first translations of Alciato's work. Still, the emblem too had close ties to late medieval antecedents, and most especially to the illustrated proverbs,[2] a relationship that betrays yet another link between emblem and epigram.

What is often called the canonical form of the emblem consists of the tripartite structure that characterizes the early Parisian editions of Alciato's work. The outlines of a genre began to emerge when the Paris publisher Christian Wechel established a distinctive paginal format for Alciato's emblems that French humanists such as Guillaume de La Perrière and Gilles Corrozet, and their publisher Denys Janot, adapted for

---

[1] For an idea of the French understanding of the epigram in the middle of the sixteenth century, see Thomas Sebillet, *Art poétique françois*, ed. F. Gaiffe, new edition by Francis Goyet (Paris: Nizet, 1988), pp. 102–14.

[2] See Grace Frank and Dorothy Minor (ed.), *Proverbes en rime* (Baltimore: The Johns Hopkins University Press, 1937).

works they began to characterize generically as emblems. That structure consists of a title that sometimes takes the form of a proverb or maxim, a picture and a short verse text that explains the relationship between title and picture, a relationship that is almost always less than self-evident to the observer who does not possess some sort of specialized knowledge, knowledge that will be conveyed by the epigrammatic text. In Alciato's emblem *Paupertatem summis ingenijs obesse, ne prouehantur* ['Poverty hinders the greatest talents from advancing'], we see a young man, or boy, with one arm weighted down by a stone, while the other is lifted by wings towards heaven. The wings are his talent, the epigram tells us, and the stone represents poverty, thus indicating that: 'By virtue of my talent I could have flown through lofty citadels, / were it not that hateful poverty held me down'.[3]

While this structure dominates the discussion of the emblem form, or the emblem as genre, it is far from telling the whole story. Indeed, the emblems were often published without pictures, even from the earliest days of the phenomenon, and in the edition of his complete works, whose production Alciato oversaw shortly before his death, the emblems are not illustrated. Nevertheless, some real or imagined combination of picture and text quickly became the norm, and the notion of genre, as concerns the emblem, is consequently complicated by the combination of texts with pictures, as well as the use of texts in an often subordinate capacity to comment on those pictures as the epigrams of the Greek Anthology often did for ancient monuments and works of art. The concentration on an image tended to deflect attention away from the form the text would take; indeed, the emblem never did develop a fixed textual form that was deemed necessary to its generic integrity. As a result, the texts of emblems tended to range widely in length, and an emblem might contain a number of different kinds of texts in prose and in verse. Emblem texts, consequently, spread in all directions, and Henry Hawkins's *Partheneia sacra* (1633), for example, has a complicated nine-part structure with seven textual components explaining and moralizing two pictorial elements labelled 'The devise' and 'The emblem'. Attached to 'The emblem' there is a twelve-line verse text called 'The poesie', that qualifies as the epigram. The other components are short prose texts called 'The character', 'The morals', 'The essay', 'The discourse', 'The theories', and 'The apostrophe'. It has recently been shown that all of the 'Essays' are translated directly from the Jesuit Etienne Binet's *Essay des merveilles de nature*, thus rendering at least one of Hawkins's titles generically insignificant.[4] But such

---

[3] English translation from the University of Toronto Press edition of the emblems: *Andreas Alciatus. The Latin works. The emblems in translation*, ed. P. M. Daly, V. W. Callahan, and S. Cuttler, 2 vols. (Toronto: University of Toronto Press, 1985), p. 121.

[4] Etienne Binet, *Essay des merveilles de nature* (Rouen: R. de Beaurais & J. Osmont, 1621).

borrowings do highlight the heterogeneous and mosaic-like quality of the emblem text, and they also blur the lines between what is the emblem and what is commentary upon the emblem, or even an independent development upon the emblem, which, for its part, may be understood to remain a discrete, tripartite entity within a larger composition.

Throughout the sixteenth century the texts of emblems tended to conform to the formal norms of the epigram; that is, they tended to range from four to twelve lines of verse, although some, like the *Epigrammata* of Camerarius, still did take the form of a distich, which certain writers on poetics had recently begun to bar from epigrams. While there was much attention in the early years to the epigrammatic brevity in the emblem text, and while theorists continued to pay lip-service to this ideal well into the seventeenth century, emblem texts became less epigrammatic as the epigram came to be defined less and less by its role as a virtual or real inscription. As the point and wit of Martial's epigrams increasingly became the standard for the genre, the epigram became less important as a model for the emblem text.

In the seventeenth century, as the emblem text became longer and more formally heterogeneous, its role also changed, and its centrality became greater, at least in most of the religious and didactic emblem books. The texts of Gabriel Rollenhagen's *Nucleus emblematum selectissimorum* (1611–13) were distichs in Latin and quatrains in their French version, and served mainly as moralizing inscriptions for the pictured signs or scenes, but when George Wither took up the Crispin de Passe plates for these emblems twenty years later (*A collection of emblemes*, 1635), to make them into what he called 'better' emblems, his texts ran to thirty lines each. Only by an incredible stretch of the imagination could these texts be called inscriptions. Here, and elsewhere in the seventeenth century, the text tended to supersede the picture, as the image came increasingly to be little more than the starting point for the rhetorical development of a theme as was often done in Jesuit sermons through the first two-thirds of the seventeenth century.

The epigram was not immune to the pressures for such expansion either. Sometimes sonnets functioned like epigrams, especially in satirical ones of the kind we find in Joachim du Bellay's *Regrets* (1558), and by the early years of the seventeenth century it was possible to speak of a sonnet-epigram. Perhaps the pointed structuring of the epigram also influenced the form of Shakespeare's sonnets with their ending in a pointed couplet. Likewise, Bacon modulated the essay form by incorporating such features of the epigram as pithy sayings and the brisk phrasing; Owen Felltham (*Resolves: divine, morall, politicall*, 1628) pushed this trend towards hyperbolic concision and the more pointed expression of aphorism, while Donne extended the epigram to revive the paradox or 'problem'. So while features of the epigram were used to modulate other genres, the seventeenth-century epigram itself could also be modulated to recall a variety of other genres from the epic, to the georgic, to the elegy.[5] As Scaliger had observed with no more than a modicum of exaggeration, 'There are as many kinds of epigrams as there are things'.[6]

The question then remains of what provides the generic adhesive that holds diverse epigrammatic compositions together in a generic pool. Aside from the continuing requirement of brevity, the generic specificity of the epigram shifted in the early seventeenth century as the epigram tended to be seen mainly as the vehicle for conceits and points, following Baltasar Gracián and other theoreticians of the Baroque style. As it did so, it became more cleverly cerebral and drifted away from the concerns and shapes of the emblem in the strict sense. It was then that Martial came back into almost exclusive favour as a model and tended to replace the Anthology epigrams that had formed the principal influence until at least the middle years of the sixteenth century, around the time of the creation of emblems.

In the seventeenth century, as 'wit' or *argutia* became increasingly fashionable, the epigram became the prime vehicle for the expression of Baroque conceits, and its constitution influenced all kinds of rhetorical expression. While it is common to associate epigrammatic wit with satire, it could also be turned to the needs of religious expression when the intention was to inspire awe or astonishment. Richard Crashaw composed pious Latin epigrams early in his career, possibly as part of a scholastic exercise, but the best of these seventeenth-century religious epigrams were the highly cerebral works of the Scottish neo-Latin poet, John Owen, who exercised a considerable influence in Germany.

Taking his cue from Gracián, Pierre Laurens notes the importance of contingency in the construction of the most successful and awe-inspiring conceits.[7] That is, the striking and extraordinary event was prized in its individuality above the general, just as the device or *impresa*, the other emblematic form composed of only a short motto and simple symbolic figure, with its insistence on particular qualities or individual ideas, was considered to be superior to, and nobler than, the emblem with its dedication to the expression of the universal.

What then binds together inscription-epigrams like the ones in the Greek Anthology and the pointed ones in the tradition of Martial into

---

[5] Alastair Fowler, *Kinds of literature: an introduction to the theory of genres and modes* (Cambridge, MA: Harvard University Press, 1982), pp. 195–202.
[6] 'Epigrammata autem genera tot sunt, quot rerum.' J. C. Scaliger, *Poetices libri septem*, 3rd edn (Lyons: P. Santandreanus, 1586), p. 431.
[7] *L'abeille dans l'ambre: célébration de l'épigramme* (Paris: Les Belles Lettres, 1989), pp. 356–61.

a single genre? G. E. Lessing addressed this question interestingly in his essay 'Zerstreute Anmerkungen über das Epigram'[8] where he observes that the inscription on a monument is designed to satisfy the viewer's curiosity about the monument and does so through an informative description. A higher form of the epigram, according to Lessing, is not attached to any actual physical object, but the first part of such an epigram fulfils the monument's function by elaborating a verbal symbol with its attendant mystery in such a way as to excite a curiosity to be satisfied in the last part of the epigram which explains that mystery.[9] For Lessing only the subtler second kind of epigram was really literature. Likewise, the early emblem sometimes combined the two types of epigram, as, for example, in those of La Perrière in his *Morosophie* of 1553, where the first two lines of the French quatrain describe the picture, while the last two explain it and draw a moral lesson. This model was taken up by early French Baroque poets like Guillaume de Salluste du Bartas later in the century to be used more as Lessing would have it in the pure, literary epigram that does not take any external picture or monument as its support. But in the quatrains inserted into his *Sepmaine* – the way Fowler (pp. 197–8) shows epigrams, or epigrammatic elements, to have been inserted into works in other longer poetic genres – the second part of what is usually a quatrain-like grouping draws a moral from the image described in the first two lines, but there is never any hint of a conceit; wit was not in Du Bartas's arsenal, nor is there any indication that he wished it to be; these are purely emblematic images.

In short, the epigram and emblem remained more intrinsically related than is usually noticed, and the ongoing similarities can help understand both genres better. After all, in German an epigram is a *Sinngedicht*, while an emblem is often called a *Sinnbild*. These two terms suggest similar compositions in which the stress in expressing meaning moves from the text in the epigram to the picture in the emblem. But whatever the emphasis, the point of an epigram always remained incarnate, and anchored in the particular, just as the emblem remained attached to a physical picture or object, even when it was pretending to the most abstract generality. And as Lessing reminds us, the epigram is equally bipartite in its attention to a particular image.[10] It is not surprising, then, that the two forms began to lose their centrality in European culture at about the same time, in the closing years of the seventeenth century, when Edward Philips was able to call the epigram, that epitome of the pointedness and wit so characteristic of the early seventeenth century, simply 'the fag end of poetry'.[11]

---

[8] G. E. Lessing, *Werke*, 8 vols. (Munich: C. Hanser, 1970–9), vol. V (1973), pp. 420–529.
[9] Compare R. K. Angress, *The early German epigram: a study in Baroque poetry* (Lexington: University of Kentucky Press, 1971), p. 20.
[10] Lessing, *Werke*, vol. V, pp. 421ff.   [11] Cited by Fowler, *Kinds of literature*, p. 217.

28

Humour and satire in the Renaissance

Anne Lake Prescott

Although medieval Europe, like all cultures, enjoyed wit and satire, Renaissance humanists and others had a specific interest in classical views of the risible and in definably classical genres. The interest, however, was seldom expressed with much subtlety even by major critics. When Sir Philip Sidney, for example, briefly mentions the 'bitter but wholesome Iambic, who rubs the galled mind' and the gentler 'Satyr' who 'sportingly never leaveth till he make a man laugh at folly', or when Joachim du Bellay advises the French to give up inept native forms and imitate such poets as Horace in 'modestement' taxing the age's vice, the limitations of Renaissance genre theory are clear.[1] Renaissance scholars and writers thought about the history of satire and the nature and function of humour, but thanks in part to a tendency to prize the moral and didactic with just a nod or two at the recreative, their speculations – even those of the great Isaac Casaubon – lagged behind the imaginative complexity of actual practice.[2] A certain unease in Renaissance commentary on satire and humour can also be explained by the need, when following the ancients, to adapt classical genres and styles to a culture with dukes and kings, not senators and emperors, to new media and new means of censorship, and to a religion that urges us to love our enemies, not to humiliate them into suicide as, it was said, the ancient satirist Archilochus had done when he invented the iambic. Those who imitated ancient humour are therefore often careful to say that laughter repairs the hard-working body and spirit, that an acid-dipped pen can serve as a doctor's scalpel, that fools and villains need a good rhetorical drubbing, that one may bite back at detractors, or that those who wince at satire are probably guilty of something.[3]

[1] *The defence of poetry*, in *Miscellaneous prose of Sir Philip Sidney*, ed. K. Duncan-Jones and J. van Dorsten (Oxford: Oxford University Press, 1973), p. 95; Joachim du Bellay, *La deffence et illustration de la langue françoyse* [1549], ed. H. Chamard (Paris: Didier, 1948), pp. 118–19.

[2] For Causabon, too, the 'soul' of satire is 'the persecution of vice and exhortation to virtue, to the achieving of which ends it uses humor and jesting like a weapon'. P. E. Medine (trans.), 'Isaac Casaubon's *Prolegomena* [1605] to the *Satires* of Persius', *English literary Renaissance* 6 (1976), p. 288.

[3] Robert C. Elliott's *Power of satire: magic, ritual, and art* (Princeton: Princeton University Press, 1960) thinks this discomfort arises from satire's source in cursing and magic. This

Efforts to revive classical satire also share a concern for self-promotion and public performance, a fascination with voice and its modulations, and an interest in the physiology and psychology of laughter. The ambiguity inherent in the risible, ran the largely Aristotelian theory set out by such authorities as Laurent Joubert, causes organic (often cardiac) flutter: we feel delight but also shock in noting something unexpected or even ugly. Without delight there is no humour, but delight alone is not funny. As our hearts, for example, alternately constrict and swell with sorrow and joy, the pericardium pulls on our diaphragms and we say, 'Ho, ho, ho'.[4] In moderation, this is salubrious. Indeed, some Renaissance jests cite humour's curative effects: in one, a man dying of a blocked intestine prays for salvation and when his fool scoffs that God will hardly grant him Heaven after denying him 'so small a matter as a fart', the invalid laughs until his innards loosen and he recovers.[5]

The Renaissance found in classical writers two major if incompatible models or theories concerning witty speech, one stressing what is suavely urbane, the other looking to a tradition of the rough and unruly. Both require sharpness and flexibility, a capacity for the quick turns that Aristotle said characterized wit, but the first model is associated chiefly with sophisticated jesting or Horatian irony, whereas the second suits complaint, Juvenalian vitriol, or the less festive modes of saturnalian subversion. The first, especially as described in classical works on rhetoric and oratory, is more likely to win friends at court or on a jury, the second to destroy or cure vice with caustic ridicule. Whatever Renaissance authors' willingness to mix tones and styles and thus to merge these two models, the persona of a courtier telling a good story to his duke or Thomas More expressing mild dismay at his own Utopia differs markedly from that of Aretino imagining prostitutes' conversations, Rabelais's Panurge drowning a merchant's sheep, or John Marston raving with savage indignation.

Renaissance jestbooks are not always nowadays recognized as a classical imitation, although many are in crisp neo-Latin and touch on such

and other studies not cited here are listed in Marjorie Donker and George Muldrow, *Dictionary of literary-rhetorical conventions of the English Renaissance* (Westport, CT: Greenwood Press, 1982); Angela J. Wheeler, *English verse satire from Donne to Dryden: imitation of classical models* (Heidelberg: Carl Winter, 1992); and Dustin Griffin, *Satire: a critical reintroduction* (Lexington: University Press of Kentucky, 1994), who examines the role of provocation, enquiry, play, and pleasure in classical and early modern satire.

[4] Marvin T. Herrick, *Comic theory in the sixteenth century* (Urbana: University of Illinois Press, 1964), ch. 3; and Laurent Joubert, *Traité du ris* (1579), edited and translated as *Treatise on laughter* by Gregory de Rocher (University, AL: Alabama University Press, 1990). Sidney, however, while admitting that delight and laughter 'may go well together', says delight 'hath a joy in it' but laughter 'hath only a scornful tickling' (*Defence*, p. 115).

[5] See Thomas Nash, 'Philopolites', *Miscellanea, or a fourefold way to a happie life* (London: J. Dawson, 1639), sig. Nn3ʳ. Joubert (pp. 127–8) describes patients cured by monkeys' japes.

philosophically fraught topics as logical paradox or the shiftiness of words and perspective. Even vernacular collections like the Italian humanist Lodovico Carbone's *Cento trenta novelle o facetie* (?1469–71), *A hundred mery talys* (1526), compiled by Thomas More's brother-in-law, John Rastell, or *Tales and quick answers* (c. 1532) took many jokes from ancient or modern Latin authors such as Cicero, Macrobius, Valerius Maximus, Poggio Bracciolini, and Erasmus.[6] The early Renaissance therefore had no doubt that collecting jokes (*facetiae*, that is, not fables, allegories, *exempla*, epigrams, apothegms, or short stories, despite much generic overlap) was a humanist endeavour. Collectors could cite the precedents of, for example, Cicero's *De oratore* (87–90) and Quintilian's *Institutio oratoria* (VI.3), which have sections on the political or forensic usefulness of joking. Macrobius's late classical *Saturnalia* associates jokes with festive dining (compare Erasmus's colloquy, *Convivium fabulosum*) and Aulus Gellius fills his *Attic nights* with funny anecdotes. Cicero even alludes to a jestbook by J. Caesar Vopiscus and Quintilian describes a now lost collection of Cicero's own sometimes risqué jokes. Early modern jestbooks, then, may have ended as popular chapbooks like the witless if likable *Dobsons drie bobbes* (1607), but they began as part of a rhetorically orientated attention to strategically facetious discourse and in their way belong with other examples of Renaissance *imitatio*. This stress is even clearer in vernacular books on social performance. Thus Castiglione devotes a section of *The courtier* (1528) on the art and taxonomy of the jest and Thomas Wilson's *Arte of rhetorique* (1553) spends many pages (like Castiglione's, much indebted to Cicero) on how to refresh the 'dulnesse of mannes nature' with the 'swete delite' of funny stories.[7]

The rhetorical and psychosomatic power of witty jests, able so easily to slide from productive merriment to cruel mockery, led some to condemn their use by Christians. Wilson says, not without relish, that a 'nippynge taunte' can 'abashe a righte worthy man, and make hym at his wittes ende, through the sodein quip and unloked frumpe'.[8] But Psalm 1 reprimands those who 'sit in the seat of the scorner', and St Paul forbids 'foolish talking' and 'jesting [*eutrapelia*], which are things not comelie' (Ephesians 5:4). The translators of the 1560 Geneva Bible claim that 'jesting' means merely what is 'vaine' or 'may hurt your neighbour; for

---

[6] Barbara Bowen, 'Renaissance collections of *facetiae*, 1344–1490: a new listing', *Renaissance quarterly* 39 (1986), 1–15; 'Renaissance collections of *facetiae*, 1499–1528', *Renaissance quarterly* 39 (1986), 263–75. P. M. Zall, *A hundred merry tales* and *A nest of ninnies* (Lincoln, NB: University of Nebraska Press, 1963, 1970), reprints a number of English jestbooks.

[7] Ed. Thomas Derrick (New York and London: Garland, 1982), p. 274. The margins of a 1510 manual for cardinals by Paolo Cortesi note the rhetorical categories of the jokes he includes; see Barbara Bowen (ed.), *One hundred Renaissance jokes* (Birmingham, AL: Summa, 1988), p. 49.

[8] Wilson, *Arte of rhetorique*, p. 275.

otherwise there be divers examples in the Scriptures of pleasant talke, which is also godlie'. Nevertheless, the derisive tendency of much religious polemic, together with the political effectiveness of witty backbiting, lent credibility to those who disapproved. When William Tyndale called Thomas More 'Master Mock', he meant that More's hostile jesting disqualified him as a Christian authority.[9] Even Shakespeare, who jested well and often, shows in *Love's labour's lost* and *Much ado about nothing* how wit can deny charity or fend off love. Consequently, those who write about or collect jests often condemn slander and vulgarity, even while attacking the solemn-minded for social inadequacy. The preface to Poggio's jestbook (1470), for example, both asserts the author's good intentions and warns that he cannot please the stupid or 'rustic'. The defence recalls the insistence of Quintilian and others that the *facetus* person is urbane, literate, civilized.

The Renaissance also saw a revival of non-dramatic classical satire. Not all satirical or humorous work looked back to the Greeks and Romans, of course. Erasmus's Christian folly, the anti-episcopal impudence of Martin Marprelate's polemics, William Baldwin's straight-faced play with marginal exclamations in *Beware the cat*, and Thomas Nash's play with typefaces, estates satire like John Skelton's *Colin Clout* or George Gascoigne's *Steel glas*, censor-evading 'nonsense' like Clément Marot's *coq à l'âne* epistles, beast fables like Spenser's *Mother Hubberds tale*, and the mock letters that caricature obscurantism and the *ars dictaminis* in *The letters of obscure men* by Ulrich von Hutten and others owe much to medieval precedent or recent material and cultural circumstance. Parodists, too, often preyed on fellow moderns, like Du Bellay laughing at Petrarch ('J'ay oublié l'art de Petrarquizer'), while macaronics that disconcertingly mix ancient and modern tongues assume both the death of Latin for the general population and its afterlife among the educated.

Some forms, though, required a reader to look over the writer's shoulder to classical models: formal verse satire, its short cousin the epigram, Menippean satire, and semi-Menippean genres such as Lucianic dialogues (Louise Labé's *Débat de Folie et d'Amour* is one example), or paradoxes like Erasmus's *Praise of folly* and other exercises in rhyparography of the sort collected in Caspar Dornavius's huge *Amphitheatrum* (1619).[10]

---

[9] More called Tyndale himself the mocker; for the exchange, see Thomas More, *The answer to a poisoned book*, ed. S. Foley and C. H. Miller (New Haven: Yale University Press, 1985), p. 8 and note.

[10] Lucian is revived also in satirical voyages like those in Rabelais or Joseph Hall's *Mundus alter et idem* (1605) and in such visions of the underworld as Caelius Curio's *Pasquillus ecstaticus* (translated in ?1566 as *Pasquine in a traunce*), John Donne's *Ignatius his conclave*, or lampoons printed during Britain's civil war. Makers of paradox often claim to follow Erasmus in reviving an ancient genre exemplified by Ovid's *Nux* or the pseudo-Virgilian *Culex*.

Verse satire found its chief models in Horace, Persius, and Juvenal, although many agreed that Lucilius, whose work survives in fragments, had established Roman satire (the innumerable Renaissance Latin and vernacular epigrams often imitate Martial and, to a lesser extent, the Greek Anthology). Critical thought about the genre, though, was hampered by an old etymological error, for many mistakenly traced 'satyre' back to the 'satyr' plays of archaic Greek drama. Chapter 13 of George Puttenham's *Arte of English poesie*, for example, tells how early satirists disguised themselves as 'gods of the woods, whom they called Satyres or Silvanes', reciting 'verses of rebuke'. Puttenham would have liked the imaginary stage designs of Sebastiano Serlio, who sets comedy and tragedy in cities but satire in a leafy forest hamlet.[11] Because satyrs are rustic, naughty, and oversexed, resembling goats from the waist down, it seemed reasonable to allow satire its capers and grins; no wonder the frontispiece to George Wither's 1620 *Workes* shows 'Satyr' ('Vices Executioner') as a hirsute creature with tail, whip, and erect animal penis.[12] Isaac Casaubon's *De satyrica graecorum poesi et romanorum satira* proved that 'satire' is more probably from *satura*, meaning 'full, stuffed', like a *lanx satura* or dish filled with varied foods.[13] It took time, though, for critics and poets to accept this perhaps unwelcome correction.

Roman satirists offered a variety of styles to imitate: 'Juvenal burns, Persius taunts, and Horace smiles', said the scholar and critic J. C. Scaliger.[14] English formal verse satire in the Roman manner begins with Thomas Wyatt's intelligent naturalizations of Horace, but late Elizabethans, notably Thomas Lodge, Joseph Hall, John Marston, Everard Guilpin, and John Donne, found Juvenal's vituperative indignation or Persius's moral intensity more engaging. So they roughed up their metre and tone to suit both their preference for angry insult and satire's imagined source in unkempt irreverence.[15] Even when he adapts passages in Horace's *Sermones* 1.9 for his own fourth satire, Donne avoids Horatian

---

[11] Marie-Madeleine Martinet, 'Espace satyrique et distance satirique', in *La satire au temps de la Renaissance*, ed. M. T. Jones-Davies (Paris: Touzot, 1986), pp. 223–31. Puttenham's views were widespread and may be found in, for instance, William Webbe's *A discourse of English poetrie* (1586) in G. Gregory Smith (ed.) *Elizabethan critical essays*, 2 vols. (1904; reprint Oxford and New York: Oxford University Press, 1971), vol. I, and in John Harington's preface to his translation of Ariosto's *Orlando furioso* (1591), edited by R. McNulty (Oxford: Clarendon Press, 1972).

[12] George Wither, *The workes* (London: J. Beale for T. Walkley, 1620).

[13] Isaac Casaubon, *De satyrica Graecorum poesi, & Romanorum satira* (Paris: A. & H. Drouart, 1605), Bk. II, ch. 4.

[14] *Poetices libri septem* (1561), IV.98: 'Juvenalis ardet, instat apertè, jugulat. Persius insultat. Horatius irridet'. A. Buck (ed.), Stuttgart: F. Frommann-Holzboog, 1964.

[15] Donne's fourth satire, for example, has a deliberately bumpy start: 'Well; I may now receive and die; My sinne / Indeed is great, but I have beene in / A Purgatorie, such as fear'd hell is / A recreation, and scant map of this'.

urbanitas, and Joseph Hall's *Virgidemiae* v.iii thinks 'Satyre should be like the Porcupine, / That shoots sharpe quils out in each angry line'.[16]

Doubtless one reason for such a flashy show of temper is the satirists' social context. Unlike the courtier Wyatt (who nevertheless courageously criticized Henry VIII), many Elizabethan and Jacobean satirists wrote as citified young men on the loose, still marginal professionally and socially, and more interested for the moment in making a splash or literary experiment than in pleasing the sensible or powerful. The persona adopted by English verse satirists can appear pathological, spitting out lines that claim the moral high ground yet seem uncharitably furious, sex-obsessed, xenophobic, misogynist, and terrified or contemptuous of Catholics, Puritans, 'sodomites', courtiers, and subversives. It is unlikely that the authors themselves were crazed with outrage; Hall was to become a bishop and Donne the Dean of St Paul's. There must be something beyond personality or etymological misunderstanding to account for the incoherencies and hyperboles. Perhaps it was a combination of youthful swagger, the economic distress of the late 1590s, *fin-de-siècle* disillusion, and anti-Petrarchan or anti-Spenserian reaction.[17]

At its best (which probably means Donne), Elizabethan satire implicitly explores the unstable mentality behind its claims to cure society's ills. It is at its subtlest in probing with some nervousness the nature of language, the verbal enormities committed by social misfits, and the government's power to muzzle those who bark. Such satire gives the sense of operating at the margin of the morally, socially, or politically permissible. In June of 1599 the authorities decided that the line had been crossed: a proclamation ordered satires by Marston, Guilpin, Hall, and others to be burned and forbade any further printing of 'Satyres or Epigrams'.[18] During the next reign satirical poetry continued to be published, as did translations of the Romans and versified political or social humour, yet, despite titles like Wither's *Abuses stript, and whipt* (1613), the energy went out of satire in the Juvenalian or Persian manner. It did not desert prose, however, especially the sort of prose called 'Varronian' or 'Menippean'.

Menippean satire, the few critics who described it agreed, was invented by Menippus, the third-century BC Cynic who figures often in the dialogues

---

[16] Joseph Hall, *Virgidemiae* (London: T. Creede for R. Dexter, 1597–9), sig. F3*v*.

[17] Some satirists boast of shunning love poetry, like Everard Guilpin rejecting 'whimpring Sonnets, puling Elegies' for 'Tearmes of quick Camphire & Salt-peeter phrases' (*Skialetheia* (1958; facs. reprint London: Oxford University Press, 1931), sigs. B8*r*, C3*r*), or John Marston (*The scourge of villainie*; 1599; facs. reprint Edinburgh: Edinburgh University Press, 1966) sig. E6*v*) refusing to 'lisp' out 'melting poesie' aimed at 'some female soule'. Marston rightly says his lines suited 'the swaggering humor of these times' ('Certain satyres', sig. C1*v*).

[18] The proclamation is reprinted in Joseph Hall, *Poems*, ed. A. Davenport (Liverpool: Liverpool University Press, 1949), pp. 293–4.

of Lucian, and was revived in Roman times by Varro. Pierre Pithou's preface to the *Satyre Ménippée* (1594) can thus claim a long genealogy: 'As concerning the adjective *Menippized*, it is not new or unusuall, for it is more then sixteene hundred yeares agoe, that Varro called by Quintillian, and by S. Augustine, the most skilfull amongst the Romanes, made Satyres of this name also'; Macrobius attached Menippus's name to it because that philosopher had 'made the like before him, al ful of salted jestings, and poudred merie conceits of good words, to make men to laugh, and to discover the vicious men of his time'. Similar satires were made by Lucian, Petronius, Apuleius, 'and in our age that good fellow Rabelaiz, who hath passed all other men in contradicting others, and pleasant conceits'. Pithou complains that Rabelais has many 'salt and biting words' fit only for the tavern, but in fact one reason for Menippean satire's popularity in the Renaissance was the opportunity it provided for just such laxness, for what has been called its 'ease of composition, its permissive organizational principles, its capacities for display and digression, . . . its tradition of facile caricature, and its breadth of possibilities for impersonation'.[19]

Menippean satire is, then, a *lanx satura* piled high with discourse. Often that may be its main point or attraction. Thomas Nash's *Lenten stuffe* (1599), for example, is not about much of anything except the ability of Tom Nash to put more words on the plate as he turns a discussion of fish into verbal Carnival. So, too, Sir John Harington's *Metamorphosis of Ajax* (1596) postpones its promised description of the water closet until nearly the end of the text, a teasingly loquacious delay and release that is the text's subtlest scatological joke. Often genial, such satires can nevertheless be pointed, like Petronius's *Satyricon* laughing at Roman society or Seneca's *Apocolocyntosis* imagining the postmortem 'pumpkinification' of the emperor Claudius; Henri Estienne's Menippean *Apologie pour Hérodote* is sharply anti-Catholic, and the pamphlets fired back and forth between Martin Marprelate and his opponents are Menippean polemics.

After the Renaissance, the dishevelled satyr-dances of Hall, Marston, and Donne give way to the disciplined couplets of Dryden and Pope. Menippean satire, too, had a brilliant future with writers like Swift and Sterne. Renaissance critics often misconceived the history of satire and

---

[19] I quote the English translation by T. W. W[ilcox?]: *A pleasant satyre or poesie: wherein is discoursed the Catholicon of Spayne* (London: by widow Orwin for T. Man, 1595), sig. BB1. The definitive edition of the *Satyre Ménippée* is that of 1594 (facs. reprint Geneva: Slatkine, 1971). For the French original of passages quoted here, see the edition by Ch. Marcilly (Paris: Garnier, ?1882) pp. 330–1. Eugene Kirk, *Menippean satire: an annotated catalogue of texts and criticism* (New York and London: Garland Press, 1980), p. xiii. Scott Blanchard, *Scholars' bedlam: Menippean satire in the Renaissance* (Lewisburg: Bucknell University Press, 1995) adds the pleasure taken by the learned in erudite mockery of scholarly pretension.

Renaissance writers could similarly mistake the nature of what they imitated. In their hands genres or styles often refused to know their place or retain their identity. This blurring of distinctions, though, gave Renaissance wit its freedom and vitality, its continuing power to disturb and amuse.

Theories of prose fiction

29

Theories of prose fiction in England: 1558–1700

Paul Salzman

There is a significant methodological problem which has to be addressed before any 'history' of critical ideas about prose fiction in England in the sixteenth and seventeenth centuries can proceed. During the period in question, no writer saw works like Philip Sidney's *Arcadia* (1590), Thomas Nashe's *Unfortunate traveller* (1594), Margaret Cavendish's *Blazing world* (1666) or William Congreve's *Incognita* (1692) as belonging to the same genre. Therefore, when we consider issues such as debates over appropriate style in prose fiction, or controversies about characterization in romance, it is important to remember that such issues never extended to any conception of a genre constructed by the twentieth century in response to the modern obsession with the novel.

Notions of the novel and its origins cast a cloud over considerations of both the nature of prose fiction in the period preceding the eighteenth century and theoretical ideas from the earlier period which might in some way have anticipated the work of Defoe, Richardson, and Fielding. A considerable body of recent theoretical writing has revisited and refocused the thesis of Ian Watt's influential *Rise of the novel*.[1] The work of Lennard Davis, Michael McKeon, J. Paul Hunter, and Robert Mayer has changed our ideas of the novel's prehistory, but all these writers look *back* at the earlier period in order to understand more clearly the developmental model proposed initially by Watt, projecting a form of teleological determinism which hampers any chance of looking at pre-eighteenth-century fiction from within its own concerns.[2] (Exactly the same problem occurs in A. J. Tieje's work on early prose fiction, despite his greater focus on actual works of fiction from the sixteenth and seventeenth centuries.[3]) In

---

[1] Ian Watt, *The rise of the novel: Studies in Defoe, Richardson, and Fielding* (Berkeley: University of California Press, 1957).

[2] See Lennard J. Davis, *Factual fictions* (New York: Columbia University Press, 1983); Michael McKeon, *The origins of the English novel 1600–1740* (Baltimore: The Johns Hopkins University Press, 1987); J. Paul Hunter, *Before novels: the cultural contexts of eighteenth-century English fiction* (New York: Norton, 1990); Robert Mayer, *History and the early English novel* (Cambridge: Cambridge University Press, 1997).

[3] See especially A. J. Tieje, 'The expressed aim of the long prose fiction from 1579 to 1640', *Journal of English and Germanic Philology* 11 (1912), 402–32.

this consideration of the 'criticism' of prose fiction from 1558 to 1700, I have endeavoured to recapture the issues present within the period itself by specifying as far as possible which genres give rise to specific critical concerns, but to some degree the heuristic construction of prose fiction as a category reveals the difficulty of moving away from the developmental model brought about by the modern valorization of the novel form.

This is particularly evident in relation to Elizabethan fiction, where virtually all criticism is located in only two places: prefaces to individual works, and within Sir Philip Sidney's *An apology for poetry*. Before Sidney wrote, the most interesting discussion of prose fiction and its effects occurs in relation to the short story as translated and adapted from European writers (Boccaccio, Bandello, Belleforest, Marguerite de Navarre) by William Painter in *The palace of pleasure* (1566), Geoffrey Fenton's *Tragical discourses* (1567), and George Pettie's *Petite palace of Pettie his pleasure* (1576) – Pettie adapted classical rather than European stories. Painter sees what he calls 'histories' as possessing a moral purpose – he says they are intended to 'render good examples, the best to be followed, and the worst to be auoyded' – but they are also offered as vivid entertainment: they are 'depainted in liuelye colours'.[4] Geoffrey Fenton is more concerned to stress the moral purpose of such fictions: 'I wishe that as in wryting thies tragicall affaires I have founde the faulte of mine owne life, that also the reste of the younglings of our countrey in reding my indevor, may breake the slepe of their large follye'.[5] Both these writers' concern to stress the moral efficacy of these stories may be seen in the context of Roger Ascham's criticism, in *The scholemaster* (1570), of 'fonde bookes, of late translated out of Italian into English, sold in every shop in London, commended by honest titles the soner to corrupt honest manners'.[6] Ascham probably had Painter in mind when he made his famous remark that 'ten Morte Arthures do not the tenth part so much harm as one of these books made in Italie and translated in England'.[7] While this – not uncommon – moral criticism provoked a defence of the morality of such stories, it also needs to be seen in relation to Painter's admission of their power, a power which, even in Painter's dedicatory remarks, seems to overwhelm any didactic aim: 'In these Histories be depainted in liuelye colours, the vglie shapes of insolencye and pride, the deformed figures of incontinencie and rape, the cruell aspects of spoyle, breach of order, treason, ill lucke and ouerthrow of States and other

---

[4] William Painter, *The palace of pleasure*, ed. J. Jacobs, 3 vols. (London: David Nutt, 1890), vol. I, p. 5.
[5] Geoffrey Fenton [translation of Matteo Bandello], *Certain tragicall discourses*, ed. R. L. Douglas, 2 vols. (London: David Nutt, 1898), vol. II, p. 313.
[6] In *Elizabethan critical essays*, ed. G. G. Smith (London: Oxford University Press, 1959), vol. I, p. 2.
[7] *Ibid.*, p. 4.

persons. Wherein also be intermixed, pleasaunte discourses, merie talke, sportinge practises deceitfull devices, and nipping tauntes, to exhilarate your honor's minde'.[8] In contrast to Painter and Fenton, Pettie seems less concerned with didacticism, and writes in a tone of courtly *sprezzatura*, often satirizing the heavy moral tone of his predecessors: 'I dare not compare this woorke with the former Pallaces of Pleasure, because comparisons are odious, and because they containe Histories, translated out of grave authors & learned writers: and this containeth discourses, devised by a greene youthfull capacitie, and reported in a manner *ex tempore*'.[9]

The relationship between a purported didactic intention and Pettie's suggestion that the aim of fiction is simply 'to pleasure you' is of course worked out in all forms of criticism throughout this period of literary history, but, in relation to prose fiction, most notably so in Philip Sidney's theory, in *An apology for poetry*, and in his practice in *The Arcadia*. In his *Apology*, Sidney is at pains to include prose fiction in his definition of poetry: 'there have been many most excellent poets that never versified', citing Xenophon and 'Heliodorus in his sugared invention of that picture of love in Theagenes and Chariclea; and yet both of these wrote in prose: which I speak to show that it is not rhyming and versing that maketh a poet' (p. 81).[10] For Sidney, it is 'delightful teaching' which makes for poetry, 'that feigning notable images of virtues, vices, or what else' (p. 81). Sidney's account of poetry's advantages over both history and philosophy depends upon the idea that poetry, by presenting a 'speaking picture' (p. 86), will move the reader. The poet 'doth not only show the way, but giveth so sweet a prospect into the way, as will entice any man to enter into it' (p. 92). In a statement that once again points to the power of prose fiction, Sidney famously stresses the power of narrative over its hearers: 'with a tale forsooth he cometh unto you, with a tale which holdeth children from play, and old men from the chimney corner' (p. 92). Prose fiction's vivid narratives will move those to virtue who would be left indifferent by the teachings of philosophy. It is this stress on the didactic possibilities of prose fiction that leads to Sidney's grudging praise for the chivalric romance: 'Truly, I have known men that even with reading *Amadis de Gaule* (which God knoweth wanteth much of a perfect poesy) have found their hearts moved to the exercise of courtesy, liberality, and especially courage' (p. 92).

Many of Sidney's remarks in the *Apology* that relate to prose fiction could be seen as justification for his practice in *The Arcadia*, most notably

[8] Painter, *The palace of pleasure*, vol. I, p. 5.
[9] George Pettie, *A petite pallace of Pettie his pleasure*, ed. H. Hartman (New York: Oxford University Press, 1938), p. 4.
[10] Page references are to *Miscellaneous prose of Sir Philip Sidney*, ed. K. Duncan-Jones and J. van Dorsten (Oxford: Clarendon Press, 1973).

his interest in writers who have 'mingled matters heroical and pastoral' (p. 94). It is, however, important to note that *The Arcadia* does not always follow these didactic rules for fiction: to take just one example, Sidney's heroes are hardly examples of unadulterated virtue. However, writers who followed Sidney in any consideration of the purpose of prose fiction tend to mingle together the prescriptions of the *Apology* and the exemplary model of *The Arcadia*. Thus Francis Meres wrote, in *Palladis tamia* (1598): 'As Xenophon . . . and as Heliodorus . . . so Sir Philip Sidney writ his immortal poem, *The Countess of Pembrooke's Arcadia* in Prose; and yet our rarest poet'.[11] In *Pierces supererogation* (1593), Gabriel Harvey praises *The Arcadia* in terms which recall earlier story collections, now superseded by Sidney's work: 'Will you needes haue a written Pallace of Pleasure, or rather a printed Court of Honour? Read the Countesse of Pembrookes Arcadia, a gallant Legendary, full of pleasurable accidents and proffitable discourses'.[12] Writers imitated and adapted *The Arcadia* for over a century and what we might call a theory of Arcadian fiction was expressed in prefaces and treatises, mostly in fairly brief remarks about Sidney's style or remarks that echo the ideals of *An apology for poetry* and see them as perforce carried out in *The Arcadia*. For example, Sir William Alexander wrote a bridging passage to fill the gap between the old and revised versions of *The Arcadia* and also praised Sidney's example in his critical treatise, *Anacrisis* (1634), stating that *The Arcadia* is 'the most excellent Work that . . . hath been written in any Language . . . affording many exquisite Types of Perfection for both the Sexes'.[13]

As well as the didactic purpose taken from *An apology* and attributed to *The Arcadia*, many comments about Sidney and about prose fiction in general in this period address issues of style. This can partly be related to the influence of John Lyly's *Euphues: the anatomy of wit* (1578) on prose style in general. Euphuism had its admirers and its detractors during its strongest period of influence, which lasted for about a decade. Thus, to take two representative examples, while William Webbe praised Lyly in *A discourse of English poetrie* (1586), 'as he which hath stept one step further therein than any either before or since he first began the wyttie discourse of his Euphues', by 1602, Thomas Campion, in *Obseruations in the art of English poesie*, criticized 'that absurd following of the letter amongst our English so much of late affected, but now hist out of Paules Churchyard'.[14] The interest in prose fiction as an exemplar of prose style is also apparent in relation to *The Arcadia*, which attracted the praise of many for its style, and was a feature of two significant rhetorical handbooks:

---

[11] *Elizabethan critical essays*, ed. Smith, vol. II, pp. 315–16.   [12] *Ibid.*, p. 282.
[13] *Critical essays of the seventeenth century*, 3 vols., ed. J. E. Spingarn (Bloomington: Indiana University Press, 1963), vol. I, p. 187.
[14] *Elizabethan critical essays*, ed. Smith, vol. I, p. 256; vol. II, p. 330.

Abraham Fraunce's *Arcadian rhetoric* (1588) and John Hoskins's *Directions for speech and style* (c. 1600). Hoskins in particular takes the great majority of his numerous illustrations of rhetorical tropes from *The Arcadia*, turning it into a virtual style manual. The issue of an appropriate style and discussions of the didactic purpose of fiction point to the importance of works like *Euphues* and *The Arcadia* as models for appropriate discourse and behaviour. Some recent work on Elizabethan fiction has raised the important question of the intended audience for this fiction.

This question, perhaps, is generated by a number of references in prefaces and within the fiction itself to women readers. These have been interpreted by Caroline Lucas as an indication of a specific increase in female readership in general in this period and a corresponding interest on the part of fiction writers in attracting that audience.[15] Accordingly, in *Euphues and his England* (1580), the sequel to *Euphues*, Lyly has a preface addressed 'To the Ladies and Gentlewoemen of England', in which he states that 'Euphues had rather lye shut in a ladyes casket, then open in a Schollers studie'.[16] A much more complex and, I believe, convincing account of this phenomenon is Lorna Hutson's.[17] Hutson sees the fiction examined here thus far as being implicated in a crisis in the nature of friendship between men under the advent of humanism in England. Hutson sees, not an address to women in works such as *Euphues*, so much as indication of 'the importance of women as signs of credit between men' (p. 7). Hutson reads the fiction of the 1560s and 1570s as 'the formal and thematic expression of concern about the pervasive textualization of the signs of masculine honour, and of the signs of credit and trust between men' (p. 88). Thus, even if there may have been a female readership of some size for this fiction, 'its preoccupation with lengthy speeches of courtship made to women, rather than lengthy descriptions of combats between men, may have less to do with the anticipated pleasure of women readers than with the displacement of masculine agency from prowess to persuasion' (p. 89).

An increasing number of women were engaged in the production of prose fiction in the seventeenth century and I will discuss some of their statements about its nature below. In the sixteenth century, however, we really only have the figure of Margaret Tyler, who translated part of a chivalric romance, Diego Ortúñez de Calahorra's *Mirror of princely deeds and knighthood* (1578). In a preface which has recently received a

[15] Caroline Lucas, *Writing for women: the example of woman as reader in Elizabethan romance* (Milton Keynes: Open University Press, 1989).

[16] *The complete works of John Lyly*, ed. R. W. Bond, 3 vols. (Oxford: Clarendon Press, 1902), vol. II, p. 9.

[17] Lorna Hutson, *The usurer's daughter: male friendship and fictions of women in sixteenth-century England* (London: Routledge, 1994); further references in parentheses.

good deal of attention from scholars interested in tracing early modern women's writing, Tyler acknowledges that the story may be 'more man-like than becometh my sex' (p. 19),[18] but states that chivalric deeds may be recounted by women as well as men: 'it may be borne withal not only in you men which yourselves are fighters, but in us women to whom the benefit in equal part appertaineth of your victories' (p. 20). Tyler forth-rightly states that 'it is all one for a woman to pen a story as for a man to address his story to a woman' (p. 23). This argument is, of course, not exclusively directed to the penning of fiction. All Tyler says about the genre she translates is that it offers 'the just reward of malice and cowardice, with the good speed of honesty and courage', but its main purpose is 'rather . . . to beguile time than to breed matter of sad learning' (p. 23).

In the seventeenth century, the major change in theories of prose fiction occurred through discussions of the political implications of the romance form. Sidney's friend Fulke Greville offered an interpretation of *The Arcadia* as an exemplar of political morality; he saw the narrative as a demon-stration of the dangers of abandoning right rule: 'when sovereign princes, to play with their own visions, will put off public action, which is the splendour of majesty' (p. 10).[19] Greville saw Sidney's heroes as 'effemin-ate princes' and claimed that Sidney's intent 'was to turn the barren philo-sophy precepts into pregnant images of life' (p. 10). For Greville, Sidney's romance was unrelentingly didactic (clearly in accord with Greville's own view of life): 'I know his purpose was to limn out such exact pictures of every posture in the mind that any man, being forced in the strains of this life to pass through any straits or latitudes of good or ill fortune, might (as in a glass) see how to set a good countenance upon all the discountenances of adversity, and a stay upon the exorbitant smilings of chance' (p. 11).

A major influence on the explicit reorientation of romance in a political direction was John Barclay's *Argenis*, first published in Paris in 1621. *Argenis* was written in Latin, but soon found three English translators, including Ben Jonson, whose version was, alas, lost in the infamous fire of November 1623. *Argenis* is a political allegory which uses the romance form to explore (in disguise) a series of political and historical events. Barclay presents a theory of this form of fiction through the voice of his alter ego in *Argenis*: the writer Nicopompus. When some of the charac-ters engage in a debate over the role of the writer in relation to political propaganda, Nicopompus outlines a theory of a fictional genre which will allow for detailed political commentary and social critique under the disguise of romance. He 'will compile some stately Fable, in manner of a

---

[18] References are to *Women writers in Renaissance England*, ed. R. Martin (London: Long-man, 1997).
[19] References are to *The prose works of Fulke Greville, Lord Brooke*, ed. J. Gouws (Oxford: Clarendon Press, 1986).

History' which, like Argenis itself, may be related 'to the truth of any late or present passage of State'.[20] This is both a description of *Argenis* itself and a prescription for a romance genre which will offer a serious and detailed examination of history as the background to current 'passages of state'.

In England, this notion of the purpose of fiction was taken up during the Civil War by a series of royalist romances, and theorized in some detail in the preface to Sir Percy Herbert's *Princess Cloria* (1661). Herbert's romance is modelled on *Argenis* and the preface reiterates many of Barclay's views on the efficacy of this genre. Whoever wrote the preface draws attention to the Civil War as an event which has what might be called literary repercussions, in so far as a mode needed to be found (at least by royalists) which could encompass the contingencies of historical change within a framework which provided some reassurance of a heroic outcome: 'the groundwork for a Romance was excellent, and the rather since by no other way almost could the multiplicity of strange actions of the times be expressed, that exceeded all belief and went beyond every example in the doing' (p. 212).[21] The preface also underlines the fact that such a work will offer some historical veracity despite the requisite mixture of 'several sorts of invention and fancies' (p. 214).

As Nigel Smith has pointed out, 'Romance was seen to be a political form by members of both sides in the political conflict' of the Civil War.[22] This does not mean that romance was only seen in political terms during this period. The other major theorizing of romance occurred through the fashion for French heroic romance in England in the 1650s and early 1660s. Not only the romances themselves, but the quite elaborate critical material about the form was rapidly made available to English readers. For example, within a romance like Madeleine de Scudéry's *Clélie*, characters discuss the nature of the conventions behind the notion of *vraisemblance* and the use of history.[23] Such ideas are elaborated in the preface to *Ibrahim* (trans. 1653). At a later date, Pierre-Daniel Huet's account of the form was quickly translated, indicating an interest in heroic romance still evident in the 1670s. It is worth noting that Huet stresses the non-political side of the heroic romance: 'romances . . . have Love for their principal Theme, and meddle not with War and Politicks but by accident'.[24]

[20] John Barclay, *Barclay his Argenis*, trans. K. Long (London: Seile, 1625), p. 109.
[21] References are to *An anthology of seventeenth-century fiction*, ed. P. Salzman (Oxford: World's Classics, 1991).
[22] Nigel Smith, *Literature and revolution in England 1640–1660* (New Haven and London: Yale University Press, 1994), p. 236.
[23] See *Clelia*, trans. G. Havers, 5 vols. (London: for H. Moseley and T. Dring, 1655–61), IV.2, p. 201.
[24] Pierre-Daniel Huet, *A treatise of romances and their originals* (London: R. Battersby, for S. Heyrick, 1672), p. 6.

This can be seen in the interesting series of comments made on the French romances by Dorothy Osborne in the course of her letters to William Temple. She recommends her favourites to him and stresses particularly the character studies (portraits) that formed part of the genre: 'I sent you a part of Cyrus [that is, Scudéry's *Artamène; ou, le Grand Cyrus*] last week where you will meet with one Doralize . . . the whole story is very good but her humor makes the best part of it'.[25]

The interest in characterization in fiction runs through various strands of seventeenth-century commentary, particularly in relation to the interest in the character as a form in its own right. John Hoskins addresses this issue in relation to Sidney's *Arcadia*, claiming to see the influence of Theophrastus on Sidney's characterization and noting the nature of a large range of characters in Sidney's romance.[26]

However, as testimony to the strength of interest in the political potential of the romance form, the main example of an English romance in the French heroic genre, Roger Boyle's *Parthenissa* (1651–1656/1669), has a keen interest in the political dimension of the form. In the preface to the first part, Boyle explains how, when in France, he realized that a knowledge of the heroic romance was essential and the genre turned him into a 'Freind to readeing' (p. 7).[27] Boyle's main concern is to detail the historical sources used for the romance and to attest to its truth value: 'This contayning much of Truth 'tis like Ore in which the Refyner will have Drosse, and Mettle, and indeede almost the best Histtorians, differ herein, not in the Quallity, but the Quantity; at least as to the causes & retayles of Wars, sometimes even in the very events' (p. 10).

After the Restoration, another French form was much translated and imitated in England: the *nouvelle*. Again, comments on this form are rather perfunctory and are to be found scattered amongst prefaces. There is considerable continuity of interest in the issue of verisimilitude in fiction, though this takes a variety of forms. Aphra Behn prefaces virtually all her fiction with asseverations of truthfulness. A good example is Behn's statement in the dedication to Henry Pain of *The fair jilt* (1688) that the work: 'has but this merit to recommend it, that it is truth: truth, which you so much admire. But 'tis a truth that entertains you with so many accidents diverting and moving that they will need both a patron and an assertor in this incredulous world. For however it may be imagined that poetry (my talent) has so greatly the ascendant over me, that all I write must pass for fiction, I now desire to have it understood that this is

[25] Dorothy Osborne, *Letters to Sir William Temple*, ed. K. Parker (London: Penguin, 1987), pp. 145–6.
[26] John Hoskins, *Directions for speech and style*, ed. H. H. Hudson (Princeton: Princeton University Press, 1935), p. 41.
[27] References are to Roger Boyle, *Parthenissa* (London: no pub., 1651).

reality, and matter of fact, and acted in this our latter age'.[28] *Oroonoko*
(1688) begins in a similar vein: 'I do not pretend, in giving you the history
of this royal slave, to entertain my reader with the adventures of a feigned
hero . . . nor in relating the truth, design to adorn it with any accidents,
but such as arrived in earnest to him'.[29] Fidelity to some historical 'truth'
is generally seen in these prefaces as proof of the seriousness of what
might otherwise be a discredited genre.

An interesting exception is offered by Margaret Cavendish, who prefaces
her utopian *Blazing world* (1666) with a defence of fancy: 'fictions are an
issue of man's fancy, framed in his own mind according as he pleases,
without regard to whether the thing he fancies be really existent without his mind or not'.[30] While Cavendish states that her work of fiction
(appended to a philosophical disquisition) will serve only 'to delight the
reader with variety', involving, as it does, the creation of 'a world of my
own', she too stresses that the fancy that powers such works of recreation
must be linked to a more serious framework: 'lest my fancy should stray
too much, I chose such a fiction as would be agreeable to the subject I
treated of in the former parts'.[31] In a particularly interesting preface to her
collection of stories in prose and verse, *Natures pictures drawn by fancies
pencil to the life* (1656), Cavendish roundly condemns the romance form,
particularly eschewing its amorous bent, but at the same time echoes the
moral defence of the romance as a form which will cultivate virtue: 'my
endeavour is to express the sweetness of Vertue, and the Graces . . . I hope
this work of mine will rather quench Amorous passions, than inflame
them'.[32] In the preface, one senses the continuing power of the romance
form to overwhelm the reader, leading to comic notions of resistance on
Cavendish's part. Accordingly, Cavendish proposes narratives which will
counteract the romance's propagation of dangerous, 'amorous passions'.
The stress on a moral purpose (or series of purposes) therefore registers
some apprehension that romance needs to be resisted, especially by female
readers.

Virtually at the end of the period under consideration here, William
Congreve offered a succinct and typically witty summing up of the whole
debate over the appropriate form for prose fiction in the preface to
Incognita (1692). Congreve offers a subtly loaded contrast between the
romance and the novel, which in some ways echoes Cavendish's reserva-
tions about the excessive affect produced by the romance:

[28] Aphra Behn, *Oroonoko and other works*, ed. P. Salzman (Oxford: World's Classics,
   1994), p. 74.
[29] *Ibid.*, p. 6.   [30] *An anthology of seventeenth-century fiction*, ed. Salzman, p. 252.
[31] *Ibid.*
[32] Margaret Cavendish, *Natures pictures drawn by fancies pencil to the life* (London: for
   J. Martin and J. Allestrye, 1656), pp. 13–14.

Romances are generally composed of the constant loves and invincible courages
of heroes, heroines, kings and queens, mortals of the first rank, and so forth;
where lofty language, miraculous contingencies and impossible performances
elevate and surprise the reader into a giddy delight, which leaves him flat upon
the ground whenever he gives off, and vexes him to think how he has suffered
himself to be pleased and transported, concerned and afflicted, at the several
passages which he has read, viz., these knights' success to their damsels'
misfortunes and such like, when he is forced to be very well convinced that
'tis all a lie.   (p. 474)[33]

When Congreve moves on to define the novel, he claims for it a greater
verisimilitude, but, given the way in which he has described the reader's
response to romance, this verisimilitude is in the service of ironic distance
rather than involvement and identification: 'Novels are of a more familiar
nature; come near us, and represent to us intrigues in practice; delight us
with accidents and odd events, but not such as are wholly unusual or
unprecedented – such which, not being so distant from our belief, bring
also the pleasure nearer us. Romances give more of wonder, novels more
delight' (p. 474).

Finally, Congreve draws a parallel with drama: 'there is something of
equality in the proportion which they bear in reference to one another
with that between comedy and tragedy' (p. 474). This is seen as a
significant pointer to a narrative method which will model itself upon
dramatic form: 'Since all traditions must indisputably give place to the
drama, and since there is no possibility of giving that life to the writing
or repetition of a story which it has in the action, I resolved in another
beauty to imitate dramatic writing, namely in the design, contexture and
result of the plot. I have not observed it before in a novel' (p. 474).

Thus Congreve offers a 'unity of contrivance' to match drama's unity of
action. The resultant novel of intrigue is far less original than Congreve
claims, but the contrast between novel and romance, set out so vividly
in his preface, remained a feature of theories of fiction throughout the
following century, being echoed, for example, in Clara Reeve's *Progress
of romance* (1785).

---

[33] References are to *An anthology of seventeenth-century fiction*, ed. Salzman.

30

Theories of prose fiction in sixteenth-century France

Glyn P. Norton

By the time Marguerite de Navarre had completed most of the *Heptaméron* (1540–5), French Renaissance prose fiction was already very much a porous literary artefact. The fluidity of the form itself – its resistance to definition or reduction to structural uniformity – was fully advertised in the ranging nomenclature by which shorter prose fiction was known to its French readers: *devis, récit, conte, histoire*, and *nouvelle*. Largely immune to differentiation, these terms, despite occasional attempts by modern critics to identify taxonomic distinctions, were used almost interchangeably to designate a literary form whose structure, content, and style were rooted not only in the home-grown literary culture of medieval France (the *fabliau*, profane and largely devoid of moral appeal, and the *exemplum*, didactic and prescriptive), but in the more crafted aesthetic format of Italian prose fiction, notably Boccaccio's *Decameron*, where artistic effect seemed frequently to marginalize, if not eclipse, a humanist policy of moral earnestness and *sovrasenso*. Of special relevance is the fact that unlike Italy and its early Renaissance experimentation (especially in the *Decameron*) with metrical cadence [*cursus*] in artistic prose, there is little indication that French prose fiction writers of the fifteenth and sixteenth centuries were able fully to bridge the gap between poetics and the *dictamen prosaicum*. Theories of prose fiction and the kinds of technical distinctions that one might expect in related critical settings thus found themselves, as will become clear, largely excluded from the poetic arts of writers such as Sebillet, Du Bellay, Peletier du Mans, and Ronsard.

When Laurent de Premierfait composed the first French translation of the *Decameron* (1411–14; first printed in 1485), however, his earlier translation (1400) of Boccaccio's high-minded Latin treatise, *De casibus*, on the fortunes of noble men (what Aldo Scaglione terms an 'anti-Decameron' because of its moralistic, non-escapist qualities)[1] had already confirmed for the French audience the moral authority of Boccaccio's mature Latin works, namely *De casibus, De claris mulieribus*, and the

---

[1] Aldo Scaglione, *Nature and love in the late middle ages* (Berkeley and Los Angeles: University of California Press, 1963), p. 118.

Genealogia deorum gentilium. In a series of seminal articles (1907–9) Henri Hauvette established that French readings of the *Decameron* were shaped in large part by the even more popular moralistic appeal contained in the humanist's Latin *œuvre*[2] – an appeal ratified in Boccaccio's carefully phrased embrace of fiction's loftier moral purpose in the *Genealogia*: 'Fiction is a form of discourse, which, under guise of invention, illustrates or proves an idea; and, as its superficial aspect is removed, the meaning of the author is clear. If, then, sense is revealed from under the veil of fiction, the composition is not idle nonsense.'[3]

Laurent de Premierfait's principal contribution to the critical assessment of French Renaissance prose fiction lay in the way he adapted its most authoritative Italian source, the *Decameron*, to fit a cosmic moral structure in which narrative becomes an adumbration of mankind's post-lapsarian condition. Thus, developments in shorter French prose fiction from the mid-fifteenth to the mid-sixteenth century gave rise to a critical context increasingly focused away from the escapist strategy of the Boccaccian frame and on the issues of narrative truth, its ratification in the empirical context of daily life, and its link to the as yet fledgling topic of verisimilitude. These trends are recorded by the anonymous author of the first collection of French *nouvelles*, the *Cent nouvelles nouvelles* (completed *c.* 1462; first printed by Vérard in 1486) and in Philippe de Vigneulles of Metz's own similarly titled *Cent nouvelles nouvelles* (composed *c.* 1515; unpublished until 1972).

During the 1530s and 1540s, these early French attempts to define shorter prose fiction through its consonance with the reader's inventory of present experience and its transcription of believable events [*nouvelles*] served to fragment the environments and thereby classes of subject-matter and style under which storytellers and compilers appealed to their imagined readership. At this moment, narrative prose became what Gabriel Pérouse has termed 'a magma ready for every kind of metamorphosis'.[4] There were no literary moulds able to contain this generic magma because each production was predicated on its own freshly generated format and its particularities of audience. Those same issues of novelty, fictional accreditation, historical veracity, and the chivalric narrative past embedded in the mock seriousness of François Rabelais's prologues to *Pantagruel* (1532) and *Gargantua* (1534) were also played out in a variety of other critical settings encompassing works both of shorter and longer fiction.

---

[2] Henri Hauvette, 'Les plus anciennes traductions françaises de Boccace', *Bulletin italien* 7 (1907), 281–313; 8 (1908), 1–17, 189–211, 285–311; 9 (1909), 1–26, 193–211.

[3] Giovanni Boccaccio, *Boccaccio on poetry*, trans. and ed. C. Osgood (Princeton: Princeton University Press, 1930), p. 48.

[4] Gabriel-A. Pérouse, *Nouvelles françaises du XVIe siècle: images de la vie et du temps* (Geneva: Droz, 1977), p. 7. All translations, unless indicated otherwise, are those of the present author.

Noteworthy among the former are Nicolas de Troyes's *Grand parangon des nouvelles nouvelles* (1536), La Motte Roulant's *Les fascetieux devitz des cent nouvelles nouvelles* (1549), Claude de Taillemont's *Discours des champs faëz à l'honneur et exaltation de l'amour et des dames* (1553), Bonaventure des Périer's *Nouvelles récréations et joyeux devis* (1558), and Henri Estienne's *Apologie pour Hérodote* (1566).

In terms of longer prose fiction, several literary events during the 1530s and 1540s served to initiate an assessment of the *roman* which, despite the topic's wholesale exclusion from the formal poetic arts, would nonetheless carry the critical momentum well into the seventeenth century. These events were significant for the way they expanded on issues already addressed in earlier appraisals of Boccaccio, adapting them to those more defensive postures that the smug challenges of French humanism seemed to thrust on apologists of novelistic fiction. With the publication of the early French novel, *Jehan de Paris* (1533) and Jeanne Flore's *Decameron*-inspired *Comptes amoureux* (c. 1530–5), the stock components of the journey-novel, described later on by Jacques Peletier du Mans in the *Art poëtique* (1555) as an assemblage of 'chivalric adventures, loves, journeys, enchantments, combats, and other similar things',[5] invest these more cohesive works with an ontological value based in an itinerary of moral progression. Where the *nouvelle* transcribed life through discrete, anecdotal events constituted as the residue of recent memory, the *roman* tended to embrace the totality of an organic cycle reflecting more a pattern of purposeful symbolic movement than the fragmented vision of a near past.

It is this sense of ontological coherence that served more than any other factor to reshape the French Renaissance interpretation of Boccaccio's *Decameron*. Sparked no doubt in part by the Neoplatonist revival, the equation between fable and life recalled the long tradition of abstract landscapes and its dialectic of wilderness, pleasance, and itinerant movement enshrined as fixtures of courtly romance. Revived interest in such travel symbolism and its unique Renaissance entanglement with the issue of Fortune and its inconstancy were recorded by Gilles Corrozet in the Prologue ('Aux Viateurs et Pelerins de ce monde') to his translation of Cebes of Thebes's *Tabula* (1543).[6] The timing of this preface was not unpropitious, occurring as it did two years before Emilio Ferretti's liminary epistle to Marguerite de Navarre in Antoine Le Maçon's translation of the *Decameron* (1545). Ferretti's remarks (in Italian) offer the most astute critical humanist review of the *Decameron* available to the French

---

[5] Jacques Peletier du Mans, *L'art poëtique*, ed. A. Boulanger (Paris: Les Belles Lettres), II.8, pp. 78–9.
[6] *Le tableau de Cebes*, trans. G. Corrozet (Paris: D. Janot, 1543), sig. II^r–IIII^r.

audience of the mid-sixteenth century. As an Italianist and humanist legist
at the Valois court, he tries to harmonize the interpretative extremes, on
the one hand, tying the ornamental function of Boccaccio's frame story to
the quasi-poetic strategy of a 'poet in prose' ['poeta in prosa'],[7] on the
other, reaffirming the deeply rooted theme of Boccaccian moral earnestness as a way of reminding the reader of the *cornice*'s conformity to a
religio-moral *gradus* moving from a lower order of *somma noia* [the
'extreme ennui' of historical truth] to a higher order of pleasure [*somma
diletto*] (sig. ã iijʳ). Tellingly, Ferretti alerts his French reader to the risks
of Boccaccian *cursus* and its clausulae that finish almost always in verbs,
'against the law of nature, and the cleansed pens of today' (sig. ã iijᵛ). The
Boccaccio who had judged himself in the *Decameron* to be 'so light'
['sí lieve'] earns in Ferretti's sustained humanist reappraisal the kind of
totalizing reassessment that places the work within a comprehensive theory
of narrative: a craft of stylistic proportion embracing the admixture of
tragic, comic, and elegiac styles, the Horatian Peripatetic compromise
of the pleasurable and the useful [*dilettare/giocare*], and the fortuitous
action of unstable Fortune and its accidents ['la instabilità de la fortuna, e
de gli accidenti suoi . . .', sig. ã iijʳ].

It was probably this resonant critical justification that served more than
any other factor to induce Marguerite de Navarre one year later to frame
her own collection of tales in a unifying structure of itinerant movement
steeped in an atmosphere of abstraction and moral portent. Her frame
thus never allows her reader to drift very far from the topicality of historical and topographical truth, supporting her vow to imitate Boccaccio
save only in her commitment 'not to write any tale [*nouvelle*] that was not
a truthful story [*véritable histoire*]'.[8] Ferretti's trifling allusion to the flaw
of poetic *cursus* in the *Decameron* – the blemish 'against the law of nature
and the cleansed pens of today' – has assumed a larger significance in
Marguerite's mind as she appears to draw a distinction between *nouvelle*
and *véritable histoire*, the former associated with Boccaccio's more inventive project and its escape into open-ended fiction, the latter with levels
of truth and historical accreditation. The practical result of this policy is
Marguerite de Navarre's explicit truncation of the very *topos* most associated with Boccaccio's poetic escapism, namely the *locus amœnus* and

[7] *Le Decameron de Messire Iehan Bocace Florentin*, trans. A. Le Maçon (Paris: E. Roffet,
1545), sig. ã iijʳ [further references are to this edition]. For a full discussion of the letter, see
Glyn P. Norton, 'The Emilio Ferretti letter: a critical preface for Marguerite de Navarre',
Journal of Medieval and Renaissance studies 4 (1974), 287–300.
[8] Marguerite de Navarre, *The Heptaméron*, trans. P. A. Chilton (Harmondsworth: Penguin
Books, 1984), p. 68. My translation highlights Marguerite's juxtaposition of *nouvelle* and
histoire. For a more complete analysis of the *Heptaméron* prologue see Glyn P. Norton,
'Narrative function in the *Heptaméron* frame-story', *La nouvelle française à la Renaissance*, ed. L. Sozzi and V.-L. Saulnier (Geneva and Paris: Slatkine, 1981), pp. 435–47.

its descriptive opulence: 'At midday [the storytellers] all went back as arranged to the meadow, which was looking so beautiful and fair that it would take a Boccaccio to describe it as it really was. Enough for us to say that a more beautiful meadow there never was seen'.[9] It is difficult not to note here the underlying conundrum of the narrator excluding, in the name of truth, a strategy of depiction and falsification admittedly empowered to make truth palpable, 'to describe [the meadow] as it really was' ['le dépaindre à la vérité']. While Ferretti's humanist breadth had sought to harmonize the disparity between poetic prose and a symbolic itinerary of religio-moral ascent, Marguerite de Navarre's prologue seems predicated on two distinct but irreconcilable views of narrative truth, the one based on the expulsion of humanist rhetorical poetics, the other on the conviction that such economy loses in descriptive authenticity what it gains in the pure contemplation of adventure, piety, and symbolic progression.

The prologue to the *Heptaméron* signalled, in a way, the predominant critical trend in novelistic fiction for the second half of the sixteenth century. Less concerned with defining longer fiction as the scriptural imprint of imagination or *phantasia*, attention gradually shifted towards problematizing the way such fiction reflected the multiple levels on which truth could engage reader belief. This shift had the predictable effect of making it less easy to discuss the topic of prose fiction without also bringing into the picture the overlapping prerogatives of historical methodology and the genre of history.

Two of the period's most prominent literary voices, Jacques Amyot in his version of Heliodorus (1547) and Etienne Jodelle in his preface to Claude Colet's version of *Palladine of England* (1555), were among the first to address the challenge of bringing prose fiction into the mainstream of literary endeavour through its alignment with the higher disciplines of poetry and history.[10] Amyot's view of prose fiction, indebted to his rereading of Horace and Strabo, had all the hallmarks of a mythohistoric project – a structure defined by its conflation of historical truth [*historiale vérité*], with a residual pleasure derived from the inventive 'novelty of curious and wondrous things' ['la nouvelleté des choses estranges et pleines de merveilles', sig. Aii^v] and the affective structuring of these features in a rhetorical format that elicits the reader's pleasurable response from the linear

---

[9]   Marguerite de Navarre, *The Heptameron*, trans. P. A. Chilton, p. 69.
[10]   References are to Heliodorus, *L'histoire æthiopicque, traitant des amours de Theagenes et Chariclea*, trans. J. Amyot (Paris: B. Groulleau, 1547); and *L'histoire Palladienne*, trans. C. Colet (Paris: J. Dallier, 1555). For a general discussion of Amyot's Prologue and its contribution to a definition of the French Renaissance novel, see A. Maynor Hardee, 'Towards a definition of the French Renaissance novel', *Studies in the Renaissance* 15 (1968), 25–38.

flow and arrangement of its mythohistoric parts (sig. Aii"). Fittingly, it
is a member of the Pléiade, Etienne Jodelle, who later contributed to
the further humanist dignification of fiction by disavowing publicly his
former distaste for such writing. Like Amyot, his humanist contemporary,
Jodelle seems bent on legitimizing the novelistic craft by claiming it as
a species of historiographic composition, referring to it as 'cette façon
d'historier' ['this manner of writing history', sig. ã ii"].

By the early 1550s critical assessments of the *roman* had shifted to
the prefatory texts of the century's most successful and quintessential
romance, the *Amadis de Gaule*. At a time when humanists like Angelo
Poliziano, rediscovering the ancient topos of *fides historiae*, were busy
declaiming 'the wonderful faith of history reborn', theoreticians of prose
fiction were beginning to lean more and more on the characteristics of
history as a way of fortifying the case for the novel and, over the long
term, even venturing to reverse the relative prestige of the two crafts.[11] In
his prefaces to Books X (1552) and XI (1560) of the *Amadis* romance,[12]
Jacques Gohorry, a doctor known for his interest in occultism, centres his
critical remarks on the capacity of fable to overlay the inner coherence
of life ['l'institution de la vie et des meurs', Book X, sig. ã iii'] and, ultimately, to claim the high ground of truth over history's frequent reliance
on shaky eyewitness accounts (Book XI, 'Préface aux lecteurs'). With G.
Aubert's prefatory 'Discours' (1556) to his translation of Book XII (1560),
the issues are further sharpened when the translator tries to account for
the dearth of contemporary historical chronicle relative to the abundance
of narrative fiction (viz. novels). The reason adduced by Aubert has to do
with the intrinsic nature of the *roman* and its totalizing structure reaching
out to embrace qualities of discourse and exemplary acts in a way that
allows the reader to 'contemplate, as on a universal stage, the varied shifts
of fortune, the stirrings of world events, the inconstancy of human affairs
... things depicted much better in an invented narration than in a true
story [*une histoire véritable*]'.[13]

In the prefaces to Jacques Gohorry's translation of Book XIII of the
Amadis series (1571), the alliance of prose fiction with the increasingly
politicized role attributed to rhetorical poetics in the climate of civil strife
which, by 1571, was consuming French society seemed to authorize
fiction's claims as a literary palliative. Against this panorama of sectarian
intolerance, the palace academies created by Charles IX and Henri III

---

[11] Angelo Poliziano, *Opera omnia* (Basle: N. Episcopius, 1553), p. 621.
[12] References are to Jacques Gohorry (trans.), 'A ... Marguerite de France', *Le dixiesme livre d'Amadis de Gaule* (Paris: V. Sertenas, 1552); Jacques Gohorry (trans.), 'Préface aux lecteurs', *L'onziesme livre d'Amadis de Gaule* (Paris: E. Groulleau, 1560).
[13] G. Aubert (trans.), 'Discours ... au lecteur', *Le douziesme livre d'Amadis de Gaule* (Paris: J. Longis and R. le Mangnier, 1560), sig. ã iiij".

became the generative centres of a moderating, irenic spirit forged around the arts of poetry, music, and eloquence. Rhetoric in particular was thought to play a crucial role in this agenda of conciliation because it dealt in the affective mechanisms of persuasion and pleasurable appeal.[14] In the context of these cultural developments, Jacques Gohorry's prefaces to Book XIII of the *Amadis* constituted not only a striking critical advance over the tendency of theorists to avoid some of the larger structural issues in longer prose fiction, but also a reaffirmation of Emilio Ferretti's early stand on its poetico-moral value. In his prefatory epistle to Catherine de Clermont, Gohorry made what may well be the first French Renaissance attempt to justify and explain novelistic structure through explicit connection with the technical organization of eloquence, in this case Cicero's remarks on *narratio* in the *De partitione oratoria* (ix.31–2). His discussion thus marked an abrupt reversal of Marguerite de Navarre's earlier resistance to the rhetorical challenges of her frame story.

Concluding his epistle with 'a demonstration of the art of rhetoric, consisting in the composition or construction of novels and believable only to those who contemplate closely their entire architecture', Gohorry prescribes for the 'Romanceur' those precepts exclusive to oratorical performance and, more pointedly, to that part of the speech having to do with the statement of facts [*narratio*] in a way that induces charm [*suavitas*; *délectation*] and belief through verisimilitude [*probabilitas*; *les choses vraysemblables*].[15] Questions of style ('ornate, concise, flowing'), sequence of subject ('chronological order'), descriptions of place, the progression, cause, and distinction of actions, the creation of a 'more pleasurable narration' through the introduction of 'new things or things unseen or unheard' to which he adds the qualities of 'admiration, suspense, unexpected issues, intermixture of emotions, dialogues between people, grief, rage, fear, joy, and desire' (sig. ã iij^v) are laid out almost verbatim from what is generally considered Cicero's most purely scientific rhetorical work (the *De partitione oratoria*). The one rhetorical anachronism in this otherwise slavishly Ciceronian theoretical prop is Gohorry's curious use of 'floride' ['ornate'], a term of Quintilianesque extraction used to denote the third kind of style [*floridus* or *anthēron*] whose main purpose, like that of poetry, is to charm [*delectare*] or conciliate [*conciliare*] (*Institutio oratoria*, XII.x.58–9). It is not inconceivable, therefore, that

[14] On these aspects of eloquence at the Valois court, see Glyn P. Norton, 'Amyot et la rhétorique: la revalorisation du pouvoir dans le *Projet de l'éloquence royale*', in *Fortunes de Jacques Amyot*, ed. M. Balard (Paris: Nizet, 1986), pp. 191–205.

[15] J. Gohorry (trans.), 'Epistre à . . . Caterine de Clermont, Contesse de Rects', *Le trezieme livre d'Amadis de Gaule* (Paris: L. Breyer, 1571), sig. ã iij^{r-v}. [Further references are to this edition]. The synonymy of the terms *probabilis* and *verisimilis* in Ciceronian terminology is confirmed in the reference to 'narratio verisimilis' in the *De oratore* (II.xix.80).

the appearance of 'floride' in the setting of a statement on the affective potential of narrative fiction served not only to make an associative link with Quintilian's more fulsome enquiry into the mechanisms of audience appeal, but to establish the kinship of the term with a policy of concili-ation and a unity of thought and feeling. This is as close, perhaps, as Gohorry came to claiming the stuff of fiction, its repository of ancestral myths and chivalric adventures, as a conduit back to a purer mytho-historic harmony embodying what he clearly felt was the moderating cultural policy of 'nostre tres excellent Roy Charles neufieme, amateur de poesie, de musique, d'histoire, et de la chasse' (sig. ã iij^r). In his adjoining 'Préface aux lecteurs', the translator widens the breach between the 'croniqueurs' whose fabricated accounts have come to demean the value of historical narrative and the romancers whose higher mission transforms them into 'imitators of poetry, itself founded . . . on fiction enclosing the secrets of profound learning' (sig. ẽ^v).

Gohorry's prefaces to Book XIII of the *Amadis de Gaule* vied with those of Ferretti and Amyot for their status as the most compelling critical appraisals of prose fiction in the French Renaissance. Collectively, these texts honoured a level of truth resident in novelistic fiction that was poetically, rhetorically, and morally resonant and, therefore, viewed as superior to the ideologically suspect claims to objectivity advanced by historians. As a consequence, by the close of the sixteenth century, critical evaluations of prose fiction appeared targeted on an upward trajectory of prestige and respectability in inverse proportion to the downward slide of history into the theoretical Pyrrhonism that was to mark its course into the seventeenth century. Against this backdrop of growing cynicism in his-toriographic theory, the critical trend towards forging an alliance between prose fiction and poetry and, in the specific case of the *Amadis* prefaces, towards ever more shrill denunciations (in the bookseller's preface to Book XIX [1582] history has become 'this monstrous Proteus'!)[16] is solid evidence that the Boccaccian aesthetic with its embrace of ontology and rhetoric, moral earnestness and ornamental prose, had settled into the mainstream of critical assessments of prose fiction.

With the publication of Book XXII of the *Amadis* (1615), the anonym-ous 'Préface au lecteur' followed this trend to its absolute conclusion by situating prose fiction in the kind of amalgam hinted at earlier on in Gohorry's preface to Book XIII. The integral purpose of this courtly *roman-fleuve* was thought to rest on a total conciliating experience, harmonizing the claims of poetry, rhetoric, prose, music, and Moral and Natural Philosophy and channelling them into an act of irenic pacification

---

[16] Gabriel Chappuys (trans.), *Le dixneuvfiesme livre d'Amadis de Gaule* (Lyons: J. Beraud, 1582), sig. *3^v. The remark is probably that of Beraud, the bookseller.

against the 'piteuses nouvelles' of contemporary armed conflict.[17] Fittingly, on the threshold of the 'Age of Eloquence', this final stage in the French *Amadis* project was marked by a literary strategy that sought to equalize the respective prerogatives of poetry and prose as companion arts and to do so in such a way that the question of truth and its connection with history was all but muted by the need to probe the potential of language to change men's hearts: 'Along with reason, God gave us eloquence [*oraison*], and with understanding, discourse [*parole*]. It is thus true that poets induce great delight in our mind through the copiousness, cadence, and effective harmony of their verse, but prose and speech that is free and unimpeded ['prose et discours libre et non contraint'] is equally pleasurable given the fact that it contains wondrous things no less rare than those of the loftiest poetry' (n.p.). What was *nouvelle* in a climate of national strife and conflict was no longer the engaging narratives of recent memory, but the bleak accounts of national upheaval now denounced as the disquietingly new and alienating. The comforting face of ancestral myth peering from the pages of the *Amadis* romance contained the vision of a serene, pre-classical France whose values and cultural images would emerge in the seventeenth century to shape the art of conversation ['discours libre et non contraint'] and replay the harmony of a mythohistoric past in new works of prose fiction.

---

[17] 'Préface au lecteur', *Le vingt et deuxiesme livre d'Amadis de Gaule* (Paris: G. Robinot, 1615), sig. ẽ ij^v. The author of the preface is unidentified as is the translator.

Seventeenth-century theories of the novel in France: writing and reading the truth

G. J. Mallinson

The seventeenth century sees widespread consideration of the theory and practice of fiction. During this period, prefaces to novels become the location not just of praise but of more extended analysis, and novels themselves begin to incorporate reflection on their own workings. Similarly, a body of critical writing takes shape, manifested in different forms: reviews of individual texts, satirical commentaries or theoretical essays on the genre as a whole. This critical activity, though, is largely centred on France. In England, writers like Dorothy Osborne may reflect in letters on French heroic romance, but there is very little independent analysis or theorizing. Discussion about the novel is almost invariably second-hand, as is seen in the large number of translations and adaptations of French texts.

A current of hostility to novels and novelists is apparent throughout the century. Some, like Pierre Nicole,[1] condemn fiction out of hand, branding the novelist a brazen murderer [empoisonneur public]. In rather less vituperative manner, Langlois[2] gives expression to many widely voiced criticisms of imaginative literature, and on more than one occasion Jean-Pierre Camus and Charles Sorel attack writers of fiction both past and present.[3] Novels are dismissed on the grounds that they consist largely of time-wasting fantasy [resveries], or, conversely, that they are morally corrupting, appealing through their tales of amorous adventure to man's physical nature. Langlois likens the novel reader to Narcissus, lured by illusion into empty, dangerous imaginings, and Sorel's Berger extravagant (1628) follows the tradition of Cervantes' Don Quixote, mocking a hero whose confusion of fiction and reality is the sign of madness. However, such criticism is not unequivocal. Langlois's text is divided into two parts, the first an unsparing attack on the novel, but the second an equally energetic defence; and both Sorel and Camus, in spite of their antagonism, are

[1] Pierre Nicole, Les imaginaires, ou lettres sur l'hérésie imaginaire (Liège: A. Beyers, 1667).
[2] Fr. Langlois, Le tombeau des romans, où il est discouru i) contre les romans ii) pour les romans (Paris: C. Morlot, 1626).
[3] Compare Jean-Pierre Camus, Dilude to Petronille (Lyons: J. Gaudion, 1626); Charles Sorel, Le berger extravagant, 3 vols. (Paris: T. du Bray, 1628); De la connoissance des bons livres (Paris: A. Pralard, 1671).

themselves prolific novelists. Such writers may see novels as worthless, but they see potential value in the novel and many attempt to create a more valid and valuable formula for the genre.

It is on the double ground of realism and moral effect that debates about fiction will most frequently be engaged. What unites most analysts is the view that a novel should embody truth, thereby providing pleasure and profit for the reader. Opinions diverge, though, over the nature of this ambition and how it should best be achieved. In the first half of the century particularly, many argue that the novelist should represent moral truth, designed to enlighten and correct; novels are evaluated according to this criterion, only deemed to have fulfilled their purpose if they present the reader with models to follow and others to avoid, rewarding virtue and punishing vice. In his *Dilude* to *Petronille* (1626) Camus contrasts his own works, characterized by their qualities of radiant truth [*lumière*, *vérité*] with other fiction marked by its misleading falsehood [*ténèbres*, *mensonge*]; and Langlois praises John Barclay's *Argénis* for being 'véritable' in spite of its being an invented tale. This critical attitude is given systematic expression later in the century in two important theoretical texts: Georges de Scudéry's preface to *Ibrahim* (1641)[4] which introduces and formalizes the Golden Age of heroic romance and Pierre-Daniel Huet's *Traité sur l'origine des romans* (1670)[5] which codifies the principles at a time when they were already beginning to go out of fashion. These principles are echoed in England, where Sir Philip Sidney's *Arcadia* (1590) is praised for its capacity to provide moral enlightenment.[6] From here it is but a short step to a conception of fiction as the essential guide to life; far from providing a culpable and damaging diversion from moral reflection, it is seen as a central part of education. Jean Desmarets de Saint-Sorlin argues in his preface to *Rosane* (1639)[7] that his work offers valuable lessons for the reader, and the same point is made later by Madeleine de Scudéry, who stresses the wide-ranging moral and social benefits which the novel might provide.[8] The image of the novelist as irresponsible visionary and *rêveur* is thus robustly rebuffed.

Such critics clearly distinguish, though, between the truth of fiction and the truth of everyday experience. Although many novelists may claim that their novels have a historical setting, they do not aim to give the reader history, warts and all. Desmarets adopts a classical principle in defence of his *Rosane* which had recently been wielded against Pierre Corneille's *Le*

4 Georges de Scudéry, *Ibrahim, ou l'illustre Bassa*, 4 vols. (Paris: A. de Sommaville, 1641).
5 Pierre-Daniel Huet, *Traité de l'origine des romans*; preface to Madame de La Fayette, *Zayde* (Paris: C. Barbin, 1670).
6 Compare Sir William Alexander, *Anacrisis, or a censure of some poets ancient and modern* (1634); first published in W. Drummond, *Works* (Edinburgh: J. Watson, 1711).
7 Jean Desmarets de Saint-Sorlin, preface to *Rosane* (Paris: H. le Gras, 1639).
8 Madeleine de Scudéry, *Clélie, histoire romaine* (Paris: A. Courbé, 1657–62).

Cid (1637). History, he argues, is made up of untamed and irregular incident [*extravagance*], unlike his fiction which is shaped by principles of order and propriety [*raison* and *bienséance*]; history may give us particular truth [*le vrai*], but fiction gives us a more general, moral truth [*le vraisemblable*]. Similarly, François Le Métel de Boisrobert defends his *Histoire indienne* (1629)[9] by adapting Aristotle's distinction between history and poetry, seeing in fiction a process of moral embellishment which represents reality as it should be, not as it is; and Madeleine de Scudéry implicitly adopts the same approach in her transformation of distant historical settings to suit modern and more refined tastes. This is a theory of fiction which underlies several generations of novels characterized by their idealized characters – courageous warriors, respectful lovers, chaste heroines – operating in a world where virtue reigns supreme; it would be associated with the term *roman*.

This attitude, expressed in different ways throughout much of the century, is the target for attack from various quarters, however. Some critics question such principles on aesthetic grounds. Madeleine de Scudéry is mocked by Boileau[10] for her edulcoration of history, not because he favours untreated truths in fiction, but because he considers it fundamentally absurd to claim as historical heroes with modern *précieux* concerns. Others ridicule the tireless representation of moral perfection. Sorel[11] ironically suggests that the heroic self-control of lovers in novels is pure fantasy, and Gabriel Guéret[12] transposes his own disbelief as reader to the hero of one such novel (Scudéry's *Cyrus*), simply unable to accept as true the multiple, miraculous escapes of his beloved Mandane from her abductors. The charmed, ordered world of such fiction is seen to be an illusion which deceives nobody, and critics strip away from this theory the veneer of moral idealism, appealing to the reader's common sense and experiences. Since such novels do not reflect the way we are, they are judged to have no value, and novels born of this principle are dismissed with the same kind of scorn as earlier novels like the *Amadis*. Charles Sorel, in a celebrated pun, sees such heroes as worthless cyphers ['ces héros n'estoient que des Zéros'][13] and François Hédelin, abbé d'Aubignac, while accepting the moral ambitions behind the theory, argues that the resultant fiction is simply unreadable.[14]

[9] François le Métel de Boisrobert, *Histoire indienne d'Anaxandre et d'Orazie*, 5 vols. (Paris: F. Pomeray, 1629).
[10] Nicolas Boileau-Despréaux, *Dialogue des héros de roman*, in *Œuvres* (Paris: E. Billiot, 1713).
[11] Charles Sorel, *Remarques sur les XIIII livres du Berger extravagant* (Paris: T. du Bray, 1628).
[12] Gabriel Guéret, *La promenade de Saint-Cloud* (Paris: T. Jolly, 1669).
[13] Charles Sorel, *De la connoissance des bons livres* (Paris: A. Pralard, 1671).
[14] François Hédelin, abbé d'Aubignac, *Conjectures académiques*, ouvrage posthume (Paris: F. Fournier, 1715).

In a more creative mode, comic novelists set out to develop an alternative conception of the genre and argue positively for modern settings and
less unrelievedly heroic action. André Mareschal and Sorel in the early
decades of the century[15] argue in different ways that the value of their
texts and of the genre as a whole lies in its ability to reflect reality as it is
experienced and recognized by the reader; they are followed later by Paul
Scarron who praises the Spanish *novela* for bringing moral lessons closer
to home,[16] and Antoine Furetière who attempts to situate the novel in an
everyday world systematically shorn of all heroic trappings.[17] The same
trend is seen in England when William Congreve praises those novels
'such which not being so distant from our belief bring also the pleasure
nearer us' in the preface to his delicately ironical *Incognita* (1692).[18] Such
writers, like the theorists of heroic novels, attempt to justify and validate
their approach by appropriating the vocabulary of truth, relegating all
other fiction to the valueless realm of the unreal. Sorel, in his *Bibliothèque
françoise* (1664),[19] suggests that comic novels come closer to reality ['le
genre vray-semblable'], while heroic texts are dismissed as mere products
of the imagination [*fiction*]. And in his *Connaissance des bons livres*
(1671) he contrasts the 'tableaux naturels' of comic fiction with those
'aventures chimériques' of heroic novels, which show us a misleading
vision of human capability. This critical debate clearly opposes two registers, the heroic and the comic, but it is an opposition of means rather than
of aims. Comic novelists like their heroic counterparts often lay claim to
a general truth, asserting that their novels are not just *romans à clef* with
one specific satirical target[20] but that they have a broader significance.
And both, significantly, use similar metaphors to suggest that their texts
give a recognizable picture of the world – in his comic *Roman satyrique*
(1624) Jean de Lannel likens the novel to a mirror in which the reader
might see and rectify his faults,[21] an image taken up by Scudéry in her
heroic romance *Clélie* (1657–62).

It is clear that many theorists and practitioners claim for themselves a
central ground, far from the imaginative excesses of the *roman*, conceived
as being full of implausibly heroic incidents, but far too from the empty
banality or mere parody of some comic fiction. It is on this ground that
there develops in the middle of the century another strain of critical

---

[15] Compare André Mareschal, preface to *La Chrysolite, ou le secret des romans* (Paris:
T. du Bray, 1627); C. Sorel, *Polyandre* (Paris: A. Courbé, 1648).
[16] Paul Scarron, *Le romant comique* (Paris: T. Quinet, 1651).
[17] Antoine Furetière, *Le roman bourgeois* (Paris: L. Billaine, 1666).
[18] William Congreve, *Incognita, or love and duty reconcil'd* (London: P. Buck, 1692).
[19] Charles Sorel, *La bibliothèque françoise* (Paris: Compagnie des Libraires du Palais,
1664).
[20] Compare Charles Sorel, preface to *Polyandre*.
[21] Jean de Lannel, preface to *Le romant satyrique* (Paris: T. du Bray, 1624).

thinking which seeks to define the form and content of the novel in a new way, and which raises other theoretical issues. In an important interlude embedded in his *Nouvelles françoises* (1657), Jean Regnault de Segrais[22] reconceives the opposition of heroic and comic fiction by making a different, crucial distinction between two kinds of fictional approach: the first which he classifies *roman* is determined by considerations of moral propriety [*bienséance*] and structured by the 'imagination', while the second, termed *nouvelle*, is more truthful and modelled more closely on history. Sorel follows a similar path in his *Bibliothèque françoise*, seeing in this theory of the *nouvelle* the embodiment of *vraisemblance*, and more closely comparable, he argues, to 'histoires véritables'. A little later, in a wide-ranging theoretical essay, Du Plaisir[23] takes over and develops the critical stance already adopted by comic novelists, contrasting the idealizing excesses [*prodiges*] of the *roman* with the more sober realism [*peintures naturelles*] of the *nouvelle*. He defines this approach to fiction not so much in terms of what most closely corresponds to life, but of what most obviously distinguishes it from outmoded traditions of the *roman*, and he identifies those features of both structure and content no longer to be accommodated in the *nouvelle*: the traditional opening *in medias res* which the novel had taken over from classical epic is to be rejected in favour of a simpler chronological (and historical) narrative form, subject-matter is to be less remote and characters less idealized. Fiction is no longer distinguished from and raised above history; it seeks to emulate it. The novelist is the one who plumbs what Du Plaisir calls the abyss [*abîme*] of human nature and conveys this to the reader; he is not obliged to fit facts into a proper form, to 'adoucir'. It is in the context of such thinking that Bernard le Bovier de Fontenelle praises Catherine Bernard's *Eléonor d'Yvrée* for its sensitive analysis of human feelings in a letter first published in *Le Mercure* of September 1687, and in Mlle de La Force's account of her *Histoire secrète de Henri IV* (1695)[24] she explicitly moves away from the traditional ideas of fictional representation, claiming to show the reader nature as it is ['telle qu'elle est'] in all its frailty and irregularity [*foiblesse* and *bizarrerie*], terms which had earlier been so resolutely dismissed. In England, interestingly, at about the same time, Aphra Behn makes similar distinctions between her texts and mere products of the imagination, writing in the Dedication to *The lucky mistake* (1685) that the story 'has more of reality than fiction'.[25] This new body of critical

[22] Jean-Regnault de Segrais, *Les nouvelles françoises* (Paris: A. de Sommaville, 1657).
[23] Du Plaisir, *Sentiments sur les lettres et sur l'histoire avec des scrupules sur le style* (Paris: C. Blageart, 1683).
[24] Charlotte-Rose de Caumont de La Force, *Histoire secrète de Henri IV* (Paris: S. Bernard, 1695).
[25] Aphra Behn, *The lucky mistake* (London: R. Bentley, 1689).

ideas takes shape alongside the very traditional theorizing of René Rapin,[26] and it is some time too before texts catch up with it. Segrais recognizes that modern settings inevitably arouse expectations in the reader of a particularly comic action, and even when writers avoid this trap, they frequently struggle to produce something essentially different. At the end of the century, the abbé de Villiers remarks with some irony that the *histoire secrète*, a form of fictional writing which may claim to adopt such principles, bears more than a passing resemblance to the *roman*.[27]

The *nouvelles* of the Comtesse de Lafayette go further than any in the period to embody some of these ideas, and they inspire some of the century's most important critical thinking both about the nature of the fitting subject for fiction, and about how it should be represented. It is in the contrasting critical approaches of two readers to *La Princesse de Clèves* (1678), Jean-Baptiste-Henri de Valincour and the abbé de Charnes,[28] that we find not only an insight into this new conception of the novel but also into a methodology of reading. Valincour finds fault with the text because it portrays weakness of character, criticizing the hero, Nemours, on moral grounds because he behaves in an unchivalrous and unseemly way. In his response to this analysis, though, Charnes argues that the reader should judge not according to moral criteria, but according to experience: if the character represented faithfully reflects human nature as it is recognized to be, then it is well done and should be appreciated as such. It is significant that Charnes uses the term 'vraysemblable' to describe this 'truthfulness', ridding it of the essentially moral connotations which had surrounded it in earlier phases of the debate. Like critics before him, Charnes makes a fundamental distinction between novel and history, idealization and reality, but unlike Desmarets he situates the true novelist in the realm of the historian, who should not present a misleading or idealized view. In addition, though, he raises more specific questions of critical method. He suggests that Valincour's reading is a *mis-reading*; the distinction between the 'héros romanesque' and the 'héros d'histoire' must be seized if one is to understand the text.

This debate about the nature of fiction is clearly not just about how novels should be written, but also about how they should be read. Many critics argue that in order to have value novels should signify, and it is on these grounds that they may give privilege to their own texts, taking over metaphors of skilfully seasoned foods or of sugared pills to suggest the beneficial substance and significance of their work, made palatable

---

[26] René Rapin, *Réflexions sur la poétique de ce temps* (Paris: F. Muguet, 1675).
[27] Pierre de Villiers, *Entetiens sur les contes de fées* (Paris: J. Collombat, 1699).
[28] Jean-Baptiste Henri de Valincour, *Lettres à Mme la Marquise *** sur le sujet de la Princesse de Clèves* (Paris: S. Mabre-Cramoisy, 1678); Abbé de Charnes, *Conversations sur la critique de la 'Princesse de Clèves'* (Paris: C. Barbin, 1679).

by their artistic skills.[29] Such images raise, though, the problem of how
meaning is conveyed to the reader. In the course of the century, critics
question the validity or appropriateness of digestion as an implied or
explicit analogy of the reading process, recognizing that to read is a less
passive and potentially less predictable act. A number of critics acknowledge that texts may be read differently from the way they were originally
conceived.[30] Camus notes ruefully that although a novelist may intend to
promote good by representing the moral downfall of a wicked character,
vice often appeals far more to the reader than pictures of virtue; in his
preface to *Aristandre* (1624) he refers to such morally problematical
moments, describing them significantly as 'ticklish' [*chatouilleux*].[31] Fifty
years later Valincour will go further and suggest that what might be
intended in *La Princesse de Clèves* as the representation of the heroine's
ideal moral courage when faced with a dilemma, may not be so easily
replicated in the reader: controlling one's literary imagination is rather
more straightforward than controlling one's feelings. At another level,
there is widespread suspicion of allegorical readings, both in principle and
in particular cases. Sorel is very scathing on this subject, arguing in *Le
berger extravagant* that one can read into a text whatever one wishes,
and the same argument is voiced at the end of the century both by De
Villiers (*Entretiens sur les contes de fées* (1699)), who admits to being
tired of 'perpétuelles allégories', and by D'Aubignac in his *Conjectures
académiques*. From here it is but a short step to questioning the possibility
of actually writing a novel which might conform to the ideal picture so
easily painted in theory of a text which has a controllable and morally
beneficial effect on the reader. In *Clélie* Herminius accepts that the theory
of pleasurable but substantial fiction is desirable, but wonders about the
practice. And later in the century De Villiers argues that a novel which
faithfully represents human weakness as well as strength, but which is
not, nevertheless, corrupting, would probably be quite unreadable; in
retrospect he sees that this was the fate of Camus. To be both realistic and
moral is an impossible formula, and yet it is for failing on one or other of
these counts that so much criticism of the novel takes issue with the texts.
For others, though, this debate leads to a conception of the reader who
approaches a novel from a less morally vulnerable standpoint, who is
less the passive recipient of a text and more an active participant in it. At
various times in the course of the century, novelists suggest that the meaning

[29] Compare Camus, *Dilude to Petronille* (1632); Desmarets de Saint-Sorlin, preface to
Rosane (1639); Mareschal, preface to *La Chrysolite, ou le secret des romans* (1634);
Sorel, preface to the *Histoire comique de Francion* (1623); Furetière, preface to *Le
roman bourgeois* (1666).
[30] Compare Charles Sorel, *Remarques*; Huet, *Traité*.
[31] Jean-Pierre Camus, *Aristandre* (Lyons: J. Gaudion, 1624).

of their work can only be arrived at with care and implicitly identify two categories of reader – those who remain at the surface, and those who understand its deeper significance. Langlois characterizes the reading process as a delightful search for meaning and in his very important preface to *Chrysolite* (1627), aptly subtitled *Le secret des romans*, Mareschal develops the notion of a second reading which will reveal the true sense of a text; he addresses his novel to enlightened readers ['les meilleurs esprits & les plus clairs-voyans'], alone capable of achieving this. Sorel adopts a similar attitude, albeit more aggressively, in his prefaces to *Francion* (1623–33), suggesting that only a few 'esprits assez sains' ['suitably sound minds'] will be able to understand the text as it is intended. Such criticism implies a reader/novelist relationship which is not that of pupil/teacher, but one closer to that of equals. The novel now is not intended just to entertain or to instruct, but to encourage an intellectual bond; the ideal critic is not the one who simply enjoys, but the one who understands.

At one level, then, the attempt to formalize the genre of the novel in the seventeenth century leads from a theory of idealized heroic fiction in the first half of the period to one which seeks a more truthful representation of life as it is in the second half. However, to see the debate in these simple chronological terms is to oversimplify its nature. Throughout the century, writers of comic fiction offer different alternatives to the heroic model even before the principles themselves lose favour; and even in the second half of the century, the same aim to combine pleasure with truth continues to underlie the thinking, albeit in a different context. Beneath these principles, though, is a growing awareness of the crucial if problematical relationship which exists between text and reader. Doubts about the novelist's ability both to embody truth in his text, and to convey it adequately, spill over into the next century.

32

Theories of prose fiction and poetics in Italy: *novella* and *romanzo* (1525–1596)

Glyn P. Norton with Marga Cottino-Jones

Narrative fiction in Italy was already strongly rooted in the heritage of Boccaccio and his successors by the time Pietro Bembo's *Prose della volgar lingua* appeared in 1525, having earned a conspicuous place within the prevailing literary tastes and social codes of the day. In Book II of Castiglione's *The courtier*, Federico Fregoso describes the practice of 'long and continuous discourse' ['ragionar lungo e continuato'] by certain men who 'so gracefully and entertainingly narrate ['con tanto bona grazia e così piacevolmente narrano'] . . . , that with gestures and words they put it before our eyes and almost bring us to touch it with our hand'.[1] Fregoso's homage to the gift of narration is striking not only for its social ratification of a broad literary trend, but for the way it frames this gift within qualities of presentation that give a subtle nod to the concept of *enargeia* and the rhetoric of presence discussed by François Rigolot elsewhere in the present volume. Strongly reminiscent of Leon Battista Alberti's remarks on *istoria* in the *Della pittura* (*c*. 1435), Fregoso's statement sanctions the practice of narration as a social event vested with its own aesthetic and rhetorical justification. The reach of this activity extends even into such paraliterary forms as letters and treatises (political, theoretical/descriptive, moral/philosophical) where fictional narratives are frequently embedded as diversions in a larger 'scientific' project (for example, the letters of Pietro Aretino and Giambattista Marino, Aretino's *Ragionamenti* and *Carte parlanti*, and Alessandro Piccolomini's *La Raffaella*). The socio-aesthetic emergence of storytelling helps to account for the Cinquecento's commitment to the genres of *novella* and *romanzo* both as literary activities and, more to the point, as objects of literary-critical scrutiny.

The *novella*

The *novella* is, of course, not an invention of the late Italian Renaissance; rather its roots reach further back into such early pre-*Decameron*

---

[1] Baldesar Castiglione, *Il libro del cortegiano*, ed. A. Quondam (Milan: Garzanti, 1981), p. 183; *The book of the courtier*, trans. C. S. Singleton (Garden City: Anchor Books, 1959), p. 141.

works as the *Libro dei sette savi* and the *Cento novelle antiche* (both late thirteenth-century). With Boccaccio's *Decameron* (1350s), however, the *novella* is incorporated into a literary masterpiece of great aesthetic scope, contained within a structural frame [*cornice*] and apportioned over a chronological timetable [*giornate*]. To varying degrees, the *novella* collections that follow in the wake of the *Decameron* are cognisant of their literary archetype, but it is with the publication of Bembo's *Prose* that Boccaccio's masterpiece passes into the literary-critical awareness of the Cinquecento. Stocked with examples from the *Decameron*, the *Prose* singles out Boccaccio's work for its attention to the way prose – its dissimilarity from verse notwithstanding – can emulate prosodic cadence and thus elicit feeling merely from an accented syllable placed penultimately in the sentence.[2] Expectations to the contrary, however, Bembo's canonization of the *Decameron* as the model for artistic prose was succeeded by only a loose-knit body of critical discussion on Boccaccio's work and, in more general terms, on the *novella*. Rather than initiate broader literary approaches to the *Decameron*, Bembo's analysis of prosodic technique and diction in Boccaccio's work seems (with the notable exception of Giovambattista Giraldi Cintio's *Discorso* on the romance (Venice: G. Giolito De Ferrari, 1554) and Daniele Barbaro's *Della eloquenza* (Venice: V. Valgrisio, 1557)) to have sparked only more humdrum (albeit influential) lexicographic treatments such as Francesco Alunno's *Le ricchezze della lingua volgare . . . sopra il Boccaccio* (Venice: Aldus, 1551) and Girolamo Ruscelli's *Vocabolario generale di tutte le voci usate dal Boccaccio* (Venice: G. Griffio, 1552), published as Part II of his translation of Boccaccio's tales.

Nonetheless, the record, while sporadic, is instructive. One of the earliest and, perhaps, least-known sixteenth-century critical appraisals of the *Decameron* is the prefatory letter (in Italian) contained in Antoine Le Maçon's French translation of Boccaccio's work (1545) and composed by Emilo Ferretti, a well-known Italian expatriate, legist, and 'homme de lettres' at the Valois court.[3] The principal merit of this text is its recognition of Boccaccio's narrative masterpiece as a poetic achievement. Such recognition places Ferretti squarely within Bembo's critical camp and seems

[2] *Prose della volgar lingua*, ed. C. Dionisotti (Turin: Unione Tipografico-Editrice Torinese, 1966), Book II: xv, pp. 162–3. Bembo cites as an example the way the *Proemio*'s opening sentence heightens the reader's sense of *gravità* through placement of an accented penultimate syllable in the word *affliti*: 'Umana cosa è l'avere compassione agli afflitti' ['it is a human quality to have compassion for those who suffer'].

[3] For biographical information on Ferretti and his contributions to Franco-Italian cultural exchange during the period, see Glyn P. Norton, 'Emilio Ferretti and the Valois court: a biographical clarification', *Studi Francesi* 76 (1982), 76–9. On Ferretti's literary-critical contribution, see Norton's essay on French Renaissance prose fiction in the present section (pp. 305–13).

to have sufficient resonance that it will be echoed only three years or so later by Giovan Giorgio Trissino when he cites the *Decameron* as a poem whose moral *gradus* (hence, literary unity) makes it analogous to Dante's *Commedia.*[4] Ferretti's discovery in the *Decameron* of a fully developed stylistic and poetic scheme (tragic, comic, and elegiac) echoes the same division of poetic styles in Dante's *De vulgari eloquentia* (II.iv.5–6). This early 'poetic' reading of the *Decameron* – promoted in a Franco-Italian setting – thus appears to point the way to the work's subsequent exposure as a target of transcultural literary-critical attention and debate. And while there ensues no systematic 'quarrel' over Boccaccio on a scale comparable to that over Dante, the Roville publication (Lyons, 1557) of Luca Antonio Ridolfi's *Ragionamento sopra alcuni luoghi del Cento novelle del Decameron* highlights a dialogue between an Italian (Alessandro degli Uberti) and a Frenchman (Claude d'Herberé) on instances of linguistic misuse in certain of Boccaccio's tales. Missing in this work, however, is the deeper poetic vision of Ferretti and Trissino. Instead, critical attention is narrowly focused on an inventory of objections which catalogue the *Decameron*'s departure from linguistic norms.

This approach is recalled and, to a degree, repeated around 1567 in an exchange of letters between Lodovico Castelvetro and Francesco Giuntini, the latter having produced an edition of the *Decameron* in 1557 (also at Lyons by Roville). Castelvetro records his side of the discussion – a rejoinder to Ridolfi's earlier position – in the *Lettera del dubioso academico*, reprinted in the 1727 edition of Castelvetro as a fragment titled *Alcuni difetti commessi da Giovanni Boccaccio nel Decamerone.*[5] While addressing in his letter a number of religio-ethical 'faults' [*difetti*] committed by Boccaccio, Castelvetro suggests that these weaknesses undermine the rhetorical power of the *cornice* 'to make the plague more fraught with misery, and to arouse greater compassion in the readers' minds'.[6] Gone here is the progressive tone of Bembo's secular commentary on the infusion of *gravità* within Boccaccian prosodic arrangement. Throughout the letter, Castelvetro repeatedly calls his reader back into an atmosphere of *religious* gravity through a conflation of 'textual error' with 'sin' recorded in the sustained repetition of the corresponding verb and noun forms *peccare/peccato* to describe Boccaccio's 'transgressions'. In this

---

[4] Trissino, *La quinta e la sesta divisione della poetica* (c. 1549), in *Trattati di poetica e retorica del Cinquecento*, ed. B. Weinberg, 4 vols. (Bari: Laterza, 1970), vol. II, pp. 11 and 18.

[5] Lodovico Castelvetro, *Opere varie critiche* (1727; reprint Munich: W. Fink, 1969), pp. 108–11. The fragments relating to Ridolfi (pp. 114–20) refer, it would appear, to the 1560 Roville edition in which the discussion contained in the 1557 printing is expanded to encompass also Petrarch and Dante.

[6] 'per fare la pistolenza piena di maggior miseria, e muovere compassion maggiore ne gli animi de' Lettori. . . .' *Ibid.*, p. 109.

post-Tridentine environment (and more pointedly, only three years or so after the Tridentine Index), Castelvetro's corrective suggests that the more chilling winds of the Counter-Reformation have already begun to blow across commentary on the *Decameron*. This trend will follow its natural course towards an 'official' *Decameron* in 1573 (by Vincenzo Borghini), its title fully advertising its censorial origins, *Il Decameron . . . ricorretto in Roma et emendato secondo l'ordine del sacro Concilio di Trento*.

The only organized discussion of the *novella* to have come down from the sixteenth century is Francesco Bonciani's lecture to the Accademia degli Alterati in 1574: *Lezione sopra il comporre delle novelle [Lesson on how to compose 'novelle']*.[7] There is nothing to suggest that this text is a response to any specific literary-critical precedents. However, its single-minded focus on the comic dimension of the *novella* and notions of the 'ridiculous' appears to tie it not only to strong interest in the comic short story by Bonciani's contemporary Tuscan *novellieri* (notably, Grazzini, Frontini, and Firenzuola), but also to two earlier Latin treatises (Francesco Robortello's *Explicatio de salibus* (1548) and Vincenzo Maggi's *De ridiculis* (1550)) in which the *novella* is compared with such shorter comic prose forms as mottoes and witty jokes. An equally plausible scenario – though overlooked by Bernard Weinberg – is the possible tie of Bonciani's lecture to a cluster of half-remembered issues from remarks delivered to the Alterati three years or so earlier by Baccio Neroni. One of the propositions that Neroni is called on to defend (though counter to Aristotelian views) addresses the necessity of verse as an ingredient of poetry. This leads him to certain peripheral topics in which he ascribes to prose only the *comic* low style and its 'familiar and ordinary speech', launches a defence of verse by association with the prosodic apparatus of ancient periodic style (the *dictamen prosaicum*), and refuses to classify Boccaccio as a poet.[8] Neroni's *Lezioni*, with tenuous Aristotelian support, would thus appear to seal in advance the terms of Bonciani's proposal by leaving him only a 'comic' option for the *novella*, associating it with the low style, and seeming to pre-empt any claims for the strong prosodic tradition behind narrative prose. Boccaccio, though singled out by Bonciani as the archetypal model for novelistic composition, is effectively silenced as a corroborating voice on behalf of poetic diction in the *novella*.

Bonciani's work springs few surprises and seems puzzlingly muted in its strategy. He constructs his theoretical enquiry into the *novella* along Aristotelian lines and turns throughout to the *Decameron* for textual

---

[7] The text is available in B. Weinberg (ed.), *Trattati di poetica e retorica del Cinquecento* (Bari: La Terza, 1972), vol. III, pp. 135–73. All page references are to this edition.

[8] Neroni, *Tre lezioni sulla poetica* (*c.* 1571), in Weinberg (ed.), *Trattati di poetica*, vol. II, pp. 624–8. The work exists only in manuscript form, its authorship attributed to Neroni by Weinberg.

support. As Emilio Ferretti had already attempted to do, Bonciani seeks to reconcile the ethical and aesthetic dimensions of prose narrative, though departing from his predecessor in a key way by refusing to recognize it as a species of poetics. In this, his remarks seem to emerge from Neroni's earlier hard-line agenda on the autonomy of verse and prose. The *novella* cannot, therefore, be the work of a 'poeta in prosa', as Ferretti describes Boccaccio, but rather uses 'discourse [*orazione*] which is uncadenced [*sciolta*] and in prose . . . whereas poems always adopt verse'.[9] While Ferretti ascribed to narrative prose (in its Boccaccian form) the full range of tragic, comic, and elegiac styles, Bonciani is unequivocal in his exclusion of the *novella* from the prerogatives of tragedy and epic with their aspiration to 'loftiness of speech' [*grandezza del favellare*]. Instead, he sees such prose as governed by certain aesthetic constraints which establish a linkage between the social standing of the characters, their actions, and the discourse through which these realities are expressed: 'since *novelle* are in prose and contain actions performed by ordinary people [*persone ordinarie*] who appear ridiculous, it is clearly not fitting that they [*novelle*] use that same loftiness of speech that tragedy and epic would use' (p. 164). Earlier on, he makes it clear that narrative prose entails a kind of abrupt socio-aesthetic triage which filters out the two extremes (the great because their station is above derision and the poor because they merit only our compassion) in order to showcase the loutish masses – those of coarse temperament [*di grossa pasta*] – who inhabit the vast middle ground of the low-born (p. 162).

Bonciani's remarks on the *novella* (echoing Neroni's more general assertions) are shaped largely by his Aristotelian reading of what constitutes poetry. Finding in the interpretative history of the *Poetics* that Aristotle's use of *logos* is limited exclusively to verse, Bonciani implies that the *novella*, because it is prose, can thus never be an instance of *logos* (pp. 139, 144). Bernard Weinberg has called attention to the way Bonciani's text appears to settle on a clear line of argument only after telescoping and dichotomizing its way – sometimes hesitatingly so – from the broad considerations of Aristotelian verse theory to an extremely narrow definition of the *novella*'s main elements.[10] As the author moves from more encompassing poetic issues, he addresses Aristotle's distinction of 'object', 'manner', and 'means' as a way of describing how the *novella* differs from other genres. The category of 'object' deals with human actions and, for Bonciani, the level on which short stories represent these actions is that of everyday experience ['come tutto il dì si veggiono', p. 139], its ethical

---

[9] Weinberg (ed.), *Trattati di poetica*, vol. III, p. 143. For a more complete discussion of Bonciani's text, see Weinberg, *A history of literary criticism in the Italian Renaissance*, 2 vols. (Chicago: University of Chicago Press, 1961), vol. I, pp. 538–41.

[10] See Weinberg, *A history of literary criticism*, vol. I, pp. 539 and 540.

alternatives split between virtue and vice, but 'not in their supreme degree in a single person' ['in niuno in così supremo grado si ritruovano', p. 139]. A further generic parting of the ways occurs when he decides to restrict his discussion to comic tales as settings of the ridiculous, especially those that feature men 'of coarse temperament' – once again, the low-born middle. Within this middle caste, Bonciani singles out those gripped by a limited madness – something more akin to half-wittedness [*scemo*] – yet whose actions are 'thoroughly out of balance' ['al tutto fuor di squadra', p. 162]. The goal is to induce laughter and to do this the writer must invent characters whose dominant trait is cleverness [*ingegno*] and thus capable of evoking the marvellous [*maraviglia*].

Bonciani's concern with the affective mechanism of *maraviglia* as an ingredient of narrative technique places him, despite the strict exclusion of higher poetic genres from his discussion, in the company of such theoreticians as Bartolomeo Maranta who, in the *Lucullianae quaestiones* (1564), had described the 'marvellous' actions of tragic and epic plot as those which are 'unheard of, new, and completely unexpected'.[11] Thus, as the reader is drawn into a posture of admiration – the chief aim of *maraviglia* – Bonciani's comic fool achieves authenticity through his power to make the reader wonder at his wit, to allow him to experience a new range of human potential (p. 163). Not surprisingly in light of similar links by Maranta in the above work and by Tasso in his *Discorsi del poema heroico* (composed 1575–80; printed 1594), Bonciani ties *maraviglia* explicitly to the concept of verisimilitude [*verosimiglianza*], ascribing to the *novella* levels of plausibility unattainable in tragedy and comedy where action cannot be extended beyond the artificial twenty-four-hour frame. The *novella* thus imitates the scale of life itself, unbounded in magnitude.

As for the other Aristotelian subcategories of 'manner' and 'means', Bonciani calls for a 'mixed' narrative ('manner') interspersed with monologues and dialogues by the characters themselves (pp. 142–4), thereby enhancing the rhetorical dimension of the story. Furthermore, since the *novella* falls outside the conventional metrics of imitation addressed by the *Poetics*, its adoption of prose constitutes an additional and wholly separate mode of 'means', leaving unaccounted for (indeed, Neroni has already seen to that) the well-known Boccaccian practice of *cursus* and rhythmic end-cadence. The modes of plot (nine in number, with examples of each from the *Decameron*), the tenets of decorum and verisimilitude, and the correlation of the plain style [ἰσχνός] with the characters' social station all lead up to the topic of structural organization with its tripartite breakdown into *prologue* (presenting the setting and characters), *knotting*

---

[11] '. . . inaudita, ac nova, & praeter expectationem.' Bartolomeo Maranta, *Lucullianarum quaestionum libri quinque* (Basle: no pub., 1564), p. 89.

[*scompiglio*] which embroils the characters in complicated actions, and *unknotting* [*sviluppo*] which resolves those complexities and opens the way for the conclusion (pp. 164–5).

The only surprise here (or perhaps not, in the wake of Baccio Neroni's earlier *Lezioni*) is the fact that the ancient theory of *dictamen prosaicum* – artistic prose – plays no role in Bonciani's remarks. One is correspondingly puzzled by the failure of Bembo's *Prose della volgar lingua* to leave any imprint on the treatise when, in fact, it could have provided its author with the tools and authority to undertake a full poetic rehabilitation of the *novella* as an art form. Emilio Ferretti's allusion to the 'poeta in prosa', Trissino's homage to Boccaccio's prose-poems, and Daniele Barbaro's adoption of the *Decameron* as a text on rhetorical poetics, prove that the Renaissance had not completely forgotten that poetry and prose had always overlapped. We are indebted in no small way to the 'grands rhétoriqueurs' and, later on, to Pietro Bembo for keeping the flame burning. As early as the thirteenth century, in fact, John of Garland in his *Poetria* listed among his four 'modern' *prose* styles (distinguished by their cadences) the vague category of 'poets who write in prose' ['quo stylo utuntur vates prosayce scribentes'].[12] Bonciani's separation of prose narrative from the habitat of poetry seems, therefore, to clash with a theoretical tradition that had worked its way even into the stylistic features of Boccaccio's great prose masterpiece. For Bonciani, never the twain shall meet in the *novella* and his treatise tends to enshrine that position already framed in broader terms three years earlier by his colleague, Neroni. His *Lezione sopra il comporre delle novelle* is virtually the last word – indeed, the only systematic one – on this topic to come down to us from a Renaissance thinker, but the fact that it existed only in manuscript until the eighteenth century limited its range of possible influence largely to the assembled worthies of the Alterati.

The *romanzo*

Any investigation of the critical material surrounding the Italian Renaissance *romanzo* is at once caught on the horns of a dilemma as it strives to account for the gap between theory and practice. This dilemma is embedded in a kind of generic riddle: can the *romanzo* still be a *romanzo* when it is in prose? Tradition and literary practice say that it can if the genre's Boccaccian ancestry is any guide, its origins located in what is frequently referred to as 'the first great example of the European novel', Boccaccio's

---

[12] Cited in Ernst Robert Curtius, *European literature and the Latin Middle Ages*, trans. W. Trask (New York and Evanston: Harper Torchbooks, 1963), p. 151, n. 14.

Filocolo (1336–8) and in his *Fiammetta*, together with their verse counterparts, the *Filostrato* and the *Teseida*. Its literary momentum as a prose
genre continues in the late Quattrocento with Sannazaro's *Arcadia* (albeit
mixed with verse) and Caviceo's *Libro del peregrino*, though flagging
discernibly in the Cinquecento before its resurgence in the following
century.[13] Tellingly, it is in the Cinquecento when the textual record is so
sparse – limited largely to Lodovico Corfino's *Istoria di Phileto veronese*
(1497/8–1556; attributed) and Nicolò Franco's *Philena* (1547) – that
theoretical interest in the genre strongly asserts itself, albeit largely under
the stimulus of the critical reception of Ariosto and Tasso.

This anomaly (hence, dilemma) appears even more pronounced if
one considers the fact that when Cinquecento theorists write about the
romanzo they customarily have in mind the genre in its poetic rather than
its prose form. One notable exception is Sperone Speroni whose anti-
Ariosto fragment, *De' romanzi* (*c.* 1585), denies that the *Orlando furioso*
is a romance at all and contends, moreover, that the genre denotes only
prose works in French or Spanish.[14] Again, one suspects, as with the
novella, that it is the Cinquecento's general unwillingness (Bembo's *Prose*
notwithstanding) to reaffirm the viability of the *dictamen prosaicum*, at
least in the domain of narrative prose fiction, which redirects critical attitudes towards the *romanzo* as poetry rather than prose romance in the
tradition of Boccaccio's *Filocolo*.

With narrative prose effectively exiled – at least in the august circle of
the Alterati – from the environment of poetic achievement, literary critics
are free to canonize the *romanzo* as an entirely new (and non-prose) category of poetry suited to a new literary age – 'this new kind of heroic
poetry', as Giulio Guastavini will call it in his *Risposta all'infarinato
academico della Crusca* (1588).[15] To the extent, however, that the *romanzo*
still retains features which transcend the limits of versification – subject-
matter, character, plot/action – it cannot be disqualified from the present
discussion if only because it is firmly tied to a prose tradition that will
emerge with redoubled energy in the seventeenth century. Thus, the claims
of theorists to the contrary, the *romanzo* would, indeed, appear to keep

---

[13] For an overview of the Renaissance prose *romanzo*, see *The Cambridge history of Italian
literature*, ed. P. Brand and L. Pertile (Cambridge: Cambridge University Press, 1996),
pp. 231–2.

[14] *De' romanzi* was first published in Speroni's *Opere* (Venice: D. Occhi, 1740), vol. v,
pp. 521–8. I use the date proposed by Weinberg, *A history of literary criticism*, vol. ii,
p. 1023. Daniel Javitch suggests that it was written shortly after publication of Bernardo
Tasso's *Amadigi* (1560): *Proclaiming a classic: the canonization of 'Orlando furioso'*
(Princeton: Princeton University Press, 1991), p. 93.

[15] '. . . questa nuova maniera di poesia Eroica. . . .' (Bergamo: C. Ventura, 1588), p. 9". For
further discussion of the *romanzo* in the context of Italian Renaissance epic, see Daniel
Javitch's essay in the present volume (pp. 210–15).

its principal generic trappings even when it crosses over into prose. Of course, this does not preclude the opponents of the period's prototypical verse *romanzo* – the *Orlando furioso* – from trying to bring down the entire edifice by raising the more destabilizing query: is Ariosto's work really a poem? And while the present essay will not seek to address the ancient topic of verse's relationship to prose, it is crucial to our grasp of the critical issues surrounding the *romanzo* not to forget that Dante, in the *De vulgari eloquentia* (II.I.), while distinguishing between verse and prose as species of writing, also adopts an authoritative position that would go largely unchallenged for generations to follow: that poetry has primacy over prose and that prose, taking its imitative cue from poetic models, has the power to emulate poetics.[16] In other words, the canonization of Boccaccio as a prose writer whose work reflects his poetic gifts places Bembo, Ferretti, Trissino and others directly within the ambit of Dante's stand and weakens correspondingly the argument of the *romanzo* apologists who, by and large, tend to discount any options for prose in the composition of this genre. Not surprisingly, it also pits them against such hard-liners as Alessandro Vellutello who, in an epistolary preface to the readers of Agostino Ricchi's *I tre tiranni* (1533), argues categorically that prose, limited in its possibilities either to historical narrative or oration, can never hope to reproduce the fictional fables [*finte favole*] of the poets.[17]

1554 is 'the year of the comet', as it were, for the critical history of the *romanzo* – a narrow chronological window through which we glimpse a richly illuminating set of insights into the genre. In this year, several literary events centred on the romance set off a decisive critical debate: an epistolary exchange between Giraldi Cintio and Giovanni Battista Pigna, both defenders of Ariosto, Pigna's *I romanzi*, and Giraldi's *Discorso intorno al comporre dei romanzi* [*Discourse on the composition of romances*]. Many of the basic issues in what is to be part of a spirited and contentious 'quarrel' over Ariosto and Tasso lasting until the end of the century are thrashed out in the letters of Pigna and Giraldi: a defence of the *Furioso*'s perceived structural disorder and digressive action, its social mix of the high- and the low-born, and its descriptive opulence. The letters thus set the stage for the writers' full-scale theoretical treatment of romance in their respective treatises; henceforth, it would be impossible to disentangle the doctrine of *romanzo* from the critical history of Ariosto's poem (though the latter is not directly our present concern).

---

[16] '. . . because what is set out in poetry serves as a model for those who write prose, and not the other way about – which would seem to confer a certain primacy [on poetry]. . . .' Dante, *De vulgari eloquentia*, ed. and trans. S. Botterill (Cambridge: Cambridge University Press, 1996), p. 47.

[17] Agostino Ricchi, *Comedia . . . intittolata I tre tiranni* (Venice: Bernardino di Vitali, 1533), sig. Aij[v].

In his *I romanzi*, Giovanni Battista Pigna focuses his attention mainly on questions of plot and affect. Realizing that in order to define 'this new kind of heroic poetry' he must establish its divergence from the epic, he defines epic structure as built around the single action of one man, its subject-matter based on 'truth' and on characters of high birth. Romances, on the other hand, combine truth and falsehood and 'devote themselves to several deeds of many men, but . . . they concern especially one man who should be celebrated above all others'.[18] That 'one man' – 'un perfetto cavagliere' – embodies the chivalric code, his actions, digressive and interrupted though they may be, plotted along a narrative trajectory that is nonetheless unified in its parts and episodes. The chief aim of this structure is to bring pleasure and wonder [*maraviglia*] to the reader (listener) through its sheer multiplicity and diversity. Such multiplicity, patterned on the rhythm of life itself ['il tenore della vita humana'], unites epistemological goals ['il voler sapere'] with the shifting fortunes [*mutamenti*] of joy and sadness, the latter emotion tied to the value of compassionate response and pathos [*pietà*; *misericordia*].[19] These considerations lead directly into a highly telling remark that brings us back once again to the world of Boccaccio, the storyteller. Pathetic pleasure, Pigna asserts, is rooted in the fact that 'it is a human quality to have compassion on those who suffer'. This unattributed reference to the opening lines of the *Proemio* to the *Decameron* – 'Umana cosa è aver compassione degli afflitti' – takes its power, as we have seen in our earlier look at Bembo's *Prose* and the *novella*, from the way it harmonizes prosodic patterns (the penultimate accented syllable) with emotional impact [*gravità*].[20] The stuff of romance is thus very much about an appeal to the movement of the heart – 'il moto del cuore', as Pigna calls it – arising from rhetorical artistry and thus not unreminiscent of Quintilian's celebrated remarks on *pectus* [feeling] and *vis mentis* ['force of imagination'] in Book x (vii.15). Pigna's discussion of affective purpose in the romance constitutes the main theoretical bridge between *I romanzi* and Giraldi Cintio's *Discorso* of the same year.

In his effort to prove an Aristotelian bond between the *Poetics* and the *Discorso intorno al comporre dei romanzi*, Bernard Weinberg gives short shrift to issues having only an incidental connection to Aristotle's treatise, yet which otherwise enrich and amplify our grasp of the critical tradition from which Giraldi's work appears to have emerged. Thus, beyond

---

[18] Cited and translated by Weinberg, *A history of literary criticism*, vol. 1, pp. 445–6.
[19] *Ibid.*, p. 446.
[20] On the use of binary, antithetically related pairs in Boccaccio's *Proemio*, in particular the correlation of *afflitti* with *compassione/piacere*, see Robert Hollander's collection of his essays, *Boccaccio's Dante and the shaping force of satire* (Ann Arbor: The University of Michigan Press, 1997), pp. 96–7.

Aristotle, the frame of reference within which the *Discorso* defines the *romanzo* is that both of Boccaccio and, once again, of Bembo's *Prose*. Speaking of a section that takes up more than half his entire work – that on diction and prosodic technique – Giraldi observes that 'for this part of my discourse I have reread [Bembo's] *Prose* for his precepts . . .'.[21] And while his reacquaintance with the *Prose* no doubt helps account for his emulation of Boccaccio, he also cites (pp. 64, 76) the decisive role played by Francesco Alunno's *Ricchezze* in shaping his appreciation of Boccaccian diction.

The theoretical foundation of the first part behind him with its justification of digressive action, plot unity amidst multiplicity, and fabulous subject-matter, Giraldi is free to embark on a review of how the language of *romanzo*, in light of what Boccaccio (and other Tuscan writers) have taught him, aspires to poetic vitality. This is a part of Giraldi's work that is markedly more Quintilianesque than it is Aristotelian. In a passage which, at first blush, seems to undercut his own strategy, he calls on the writer of romance to 'strive so that the ordering and composition of his verses be such that his stanzas seem one piece of prose . . . as to the order and ease of the discourse' (p. 122). In this ostensible erasure of the gap between poetry and prose, one has the sense that there is a homage to spoken style and its requisite display of facility and art in the guise of nature lurking beneath the surface ready to break through. In this, we are not far away, it would seem, from the illuminating conversion described in Quintilian's Book x, with its metamorphosis of the orator from a creature of technical wizardry into one of *hexis* [ease of speech; facility] and *phantasia* (x.vii.1–18) [visualization; imagination]. In what could well be read as a précis of Quintilian's text on imagination and simultaneity of concept and utterance, Giraldi, in the crowning statement of the second part, couches his remarks on the diction of romance, as Alberti and Castiglione had done before him, in the rhetoric of presentation:

It also seems to me that the words can be so significant and so apt in revealing the thoughts as to be impressed on the reader's mind with such efficacy and vehemence that one feels their force and is moved to participate in the emotions under the veil of words in the poet's verses. This is the *Enargeia*, which does not reside in the minute . . . but in putting the thing clearly and effectively before the reader's eyes and in the hearer's ears, assuming that this is done artfully with appropriate words . . . which are, as it were, born together with the thing.

(p. 135)

As a type of narrative, no less than Alberti's *istoria* and Castiglione's 'long and continuous discourse', the *romanzo*, for Giraldi Cintio, draws the

[21] *Giraldi Cinthio on romances*, trans. and ed. H. L. Snuggs (Lexington: University of Kentucky Press, 1968), p. 75. All references to the *Discorso* are to Snuggs's edition and to his translation.

reader into an experience that is all-consuming and whose measure of achievement lies both in the quality of pleasure induced and the resonance of diction expressed. Giraldi's latent Quintilianism – the consonance between feeling and poetic incarnation – is one of the reader's last impressions as he leaves the *Discorso*: 'The things we have stated . . . will give life to the work, moving the emotions and putting actions and manners in the reader's view, just as if he should see them with his eyes' (pp. 154–5). Three years later, these same issues will help shape Giraldi's theory of epic when, in a letter to Bernardo Tasso, he connects the Greek concept (albeit this time in its conflated form, *energia*) with the Latin equivalent, *evidenza* (from *evidentia*, vividness).[22] Ideas about the vitality of the poetic text and its link to the Greek paronyms, *enargeia/energeia*, will find their way into the works of other Italian Renaissance theorists. The ultimate irony in this theoretical progression, however, will be reached when Camillo Pellegrino's *Carrafa* (1584) pairs the Greek term for 'vividness' and its connotation of verbal profusion with a state beyond the reach of language – Ariosto's poetic diction with its '*je-ne-sais-quoi* of hidden *energia* which compels you to read it'.[23]

The fact that Giovambattista Giraldi Cintio sees fit to situate his theory of romance in a specific prosodic apparatus suggests that conditions are now ripe (though it will take more than thirty years until full germination) for the genre's eventual canonization in a 'new poetics'. Much of the critical fuss over the *romanzo* between 1554 and the publication of Giuseppe Malatesta's strongly anti-Aristotelian *Della nuova poesia* (1589) and its sequel, *Della poesia romanzesca* (1596), is a series of variations on the themes formalized early on in the Pigna/Giraldi exchange, with dissonant notes sounded from time to time by the defenders of Torquato Tasso's *Gerusalemme liberata* (1581). Malatesta's two works thus enter the picture towards the close of a vigorous critical dialogue over the respective merits of Ariosto and Tasso and at a time when literary doctrine was beginning to reflect a more temporizing view of art, culture, and society.

In order to define a new poetic system – the 'poesia romanzesca' – Malatesta is obliged to canonize the circumstances in which aesthetic innovation takes place and to do so he must discredit the notion of fixed laws of poetics, such as those represented by the ancient poetic arts. In his *Della nuova poesia, overo delle difese del Furioso, Dialogo* (1589),

---

[22] *Lettera a Bernardo Tasso sulla poesia epica* (1557), in *Trattati di poetica*, ed. Weinberg, vol. II, pp. 469–70.

[23] '. . . in ogni sua parte ha non so che di occulta energia che ti sforza a leggerlo.' *Il Carrafa* (1584), in *Trattati di poetica*, ed. Weinberg, vol. III, p. 333. Compare Francesco Bonciani, *Lezione della prosopopea* (1578), in *Trattati di poetica*, ed. Weinberg, vol. III, p. 251 (on Aristotelian *energeia* / metaphor of action); and Giovan Pietro Capriano's *Della vera poetica* (1555), in *Trattati di poetica*, ed. Weinberg, vol. II, p. 320 (on the power of expression and 'energia' through metrical technique).

he advances the principle of nature to refute the Aristotelian belief in immutable poetic laws. Accordingly, the 'principles of the arts founded on the laws of nature' find themselves subject to the transforming stress of the world around us, what he calls 'cosi incostanti, & mutabili' ['inconstant and changeable things'].[24] Just as it had done for Malatesta's contemporary, Michel de Montaigne, environment in all its variety determines a correspondingly mutating subject-matter and thus, for the reader, an enhancement of pleasure within the unfolding present (Montaigne's 'plaisirs présents', as he calls them (III.xiii)).[25] The more Malatesta's law of poetic variety distances itself from the immovable Aristotelian object, the more it affirms pleasure and taste as qualities of response to the multiplicity of the narrative itself; a romance like the *Furioso* is good simply because its plot reflects the unstable rhythm of human experience. A new and true poetic art, such as that embodied by the *Furioso*, bears the imprint of the times in which it evolves, 'that mutation which, as an art, it was necessary that it should find' (p. 106).

In his 1596 sequel to the preceding work, *Della poesia romanzesca*, Malatesta drafts an unapologetic manifesto on this 'new' literary form. Having fully rejected the orthodoxy of ancient poetics, he now seems to be navigating in the same general waters as Giraldi Cintio, yet extending Giraldi's view of prosodically induced pleasure to the broader issue of the *romanzo*'s structural variety. Again, we find ourselves much closer here to a *rhetorical* siting of romance theory than we do to any ancient poetic canon and are reminded of Quintilian's similar call for variety in Book XII (x.69–71) in which he calls on the Orator to 'use all the styles [high, low, middle] as necessary . . . altering much to suit persons, places, and times. . . . He will not everywhere be the same.'[26] As with Quintilian's Orator, the circumstantial frame is everything for Malatesta and his 'new' poetics of romance. Drawn from qualities within the *empeiria*, the aesthetic dimension (and with it, the pleasure) of the romance are derived from three sources: the senses, custom, and nature. Once poetic strategy is conditioned by temporization, laws can no longer be invoked in its behalf, giving way instead to a new kind of intellectual, artistic, and sensory status – Montaigne would term his 'present pleasures' 'intellectuellement sensibles, sensiblement intellectuels'[27] – based on a shifting narrative perspective.

---

[24] *Della nuova poesia overo delle difese del Furioso, Dialogo* (Verona: Sebastiano dalle Donne, 1589), pp. 85–6. All page references are to this edition.
[25] *Les Essais de Michel de Montaigne*, ed. P. Villey and V.-L. Saulnier (Paris: Presses Universitaires de France, 1965), p. 1107.
[26] Cited in *Ancient literary criticism*, ed. D. A. Russell and M. Winterbottom (Oxford: Clarendon Press, 1972), p. 415.
[27] *Les Essais*, ed. Villey and Saulnier, p. 1107.

For Malatesta, the correlation between a context of experimentation [*empeiria*] and textual 'performance', ties the art of romance, much like that of the Orator, to a process of deregulation in which all the arts 'that are discovered for our delight always keep adapting themselves to usage, and the best rule that they have is to have no better rule than this'.[28] As a consequence, 'we concede . . . to poetry what cannot be denied it as an art and as an art of this kind, I mean mutation [*la mutatione*] and variation [*le variatione*]'.[29] Much as Boccaccio's *cornice* was seen by his late Renaissance interpreters as a schema of human life, so Giuseppe Malatesta sees the *romanzo* as the microcosm of the changing universe we inhabit as readers: 'it seems that the romance, imitating in this the most wonderful effects of her who is the mistress of all artificers – I mean Nature – has striven to bring it about that human spirits should wonder at seeing in a poem, almost as in a little world, many divers things (unlike one another) concur in producing so well disposed and ordered a whole'.[30] In a telling bit of humanist fancy, Malatesta imagines an Aristotle redux who, upon returning from the afterlife, would feel compelled to construct an entirely new poetic art of romance – a sequel to the *Poetics* – from the texts which best exemplify the genre.

Theories of the *romanzo* share with those of the *novella* a need to relate their respective genre to an image of human experience that is richly symbolic. The *novella* posits a relationship between *maraviglia* and the scale on which narrative prose strives to imitate life. As described by Francesco Bonciani, everything in the *novella* thus expresses a bond between the text's diction and structure and its power to represent human action, albeit at its lowest common denominator, the comic fool. Within the theory of *romanzo*, a new poetic code is introduced that breaks openly with the generic tradition of the epic. The elements that define this new code – those of diction, structure, and character – are thus imagined to mirror an ongoing process of change. When Giovanni Battista Pigna speaks of the *mutamenti* of joy and sadness embedded in the inconstancy of human life, he seems to anticipate Malatesta's more thoroughgoing enquiry into *mutatione* as a way of describing how the romance miniaturizes poetically a certain vision of the world. And when Giraldi Cintio reflects at length on the modalities of diction and feeling, he likewise paves the way for Malatesta's culminating statements on pleasure as a response to the narrative's essential diversity. Against the backdrop of Montaigne's philosophical and aesthetic mutability, Malatesta's remarks on the 'new poetics

[28] *Della poesia romanzesca overo delle difese del Furioso, ragionamento secondo . . . delle difese del Furioso ragionamento terzo* (Rome: G. Faciotto, 1596), pp. 10–11. Cited and translated by Weinberg, *A history*, vol. II, pp. 1061–2.
[29] *Ibid.*, p. 21. Cited and translated by Weinberg, *A history*, vol. II, p. 1062.
[30] *Ibid.*, p. 247. Cited and translated by Weinberg, *A history*, vol. II, p. 1062.

of romance' help transform the concept of the narrative hero into that of a protagonist who can only move forward, facing the irreversibility of his own acts. This new kind of poetic hero no longer measures himself against a static code of behaviour, but rather responds to the tests thrown up in the course of life's cycle of uncertainty. But illuminating as they are, these are critical concepts that await a mind capable of bringing them greater philosophical depth and validation. In his *El héroe* (1637), Baltasar Gracián would eventually rise to this challenge by linking the notion of heroic self-determination to the shaping forces of courtly environment – their circumstance and manner – and through them, to that semblance of infinity through which the hero engages with the inconstancy that surrounds him.[31]

---

[31] On the semblance of infinity in Gracián, see *El héroe*, in *Obras completas*, ed. A. Del Hoyo (Madrid: Aguilar, 1960), p. 8.

Contexts of criticism:
metropolitan culture and
socio-literary environments

33

Criticism and the metropolis:
Tudor-Stuart London

Lawrence Manley

Literary culture in Tudor-Stuart London was dominated by no single institution such as the Florentine chancery, the Roman curia, the Parisian academies, the University of Leiden, or the language societies of the German imperial cities. It was a product, rather, of the many intersecting influences that helped to make London the second-largest European metropolis by the later seventeenth century. As the seat of the court, London was frequented by the English ruling class and by nobility, scholars, and diplomats from throughout Europe. The centre of a commercial empire with outposts in the major cities of Europe and the Mediterranean, London was also home to a wealthy and socially mobile merchant class receptive to learning and religious reform. The legal proceedings of Parliament and the other chief courts of the realm, as well as the educational and social activities of the Inns of Court, drew Englishmen from throughout the realm into an orbit where eloquence was at a premium. As the main conduit for government revenue and the transfer of landed wealth, seventeenth-century London became home to the marriage market, social season, and leisure and luxury industries that attracted an urbanizing gentry for whom investment in culture was among the least expensive forms of conspicuous consumption.[1] In keeping, then, with its political and economic pre-eminence, Tudor-Stuart London exercised a dominant influence on literary culture throughout the realm. The 1557 act incorporating the Company of Stationers of London and giving them authority over printing throughout England restricted the printing of books to London and the two presses at Oxford and Cambridge. Just as the political order of 'the noble and faithful city of London and other civil places of England' was held up as an example to the 'rude countries' of the remoter provinces,[2]

---

[1] F. J. Fisher, 'London as a centre of conspicuous consumption in the sixteenth and seventeenth centuries', in *Essays in economic history*, ed. E. M. Carus-Wilson, 2 vols. (New York: St Martin's Press, 1962), vol. II, pp. 197–207; R. Malcolm Smuts, *Court culture and the origins of a royalist tradition* (Philadelphia: University of Pennsylvania Press, 1987), ch. 3.

[2] *A lamentation in which is showed what ruin and destruction cometh of seditious rebellion* (1536), in David Berkowitz (ed.), *Humanist scholarship and public order* (Washington: Folger Shakespeare Library, 1984), p. 97.

so 'the vsuall speach of the Court and that of London and the shires lying
about London within lx. myles, and not much aboue' became the nation's
theoretically accepted linguistic norm.[3] As the 'Epitome or Breviary of
all Britain', abounding in 'excellent and choice wits', and attracting a
mobile population 'by birth for the most part a mixture of all the
countries' of the realm,[4] London embodied, in its diversifying patterns of
social exchange and combination, the discursive potential of the emerging nation.[5]

In England, the humanist revival of classical letters took firm root in
London, among a generation whose members were (like Thomas More,
John Colet, and Thomas Lupset) born into London's citizen class or (like
William Grocyn, Thomas Linacre, and William Lily) active in the city's
leading institutions. Their presence in the city led Erasmus to declare that
'there is no land on earth which, even over its whole extent, has brought
me so many friends, or such true, scholarly, helpful, and distinguished
ones, graced by every kind of good quality, as the single city of London'.[6]
The visible embodiment of the humanist movement was the new grammar
school at St Paul's, founded *c.* 1512 by John Colet to inculcate 'good
maners, and literature' for 'the erudicyon and profyt of chyldren my coun-
tre men Londoners specyally'.[7] In seeking to enable students 'to prosper in
good life and in good literature',[8] the statutes and curriculum of the new
St Paul's placed a novel insistence on the pursuit of letters as a legitimate
lay activity and a basis for the active life of citizenship. While 'Cristen
autors' were recommended to 'encrease . . . worshippinge of God . . . and
good Cristen life and manners', Colet's curriculum of 'good literature
bothe Laten and Greeke' simultaneously refuted the stigma of idolatry

---

[3] John Hart, *A methode . . . to read English* (1570), in Bror Danielsson (ed.), *John Hart's
works on English orthography and pronunciation*, Stockholm Studies in English 5 (1955),
p. 234; George Puttenham, *The arte of English poesie*, ed. G. D. Willcock and A. Walker
(Cambridge: Cambridge University Press, 1936), pp. 144–5.

[4] William Camden, *Britannia* (London: R. Newberry, 1586), *Britain, or a chorographicall
description*, trans. P. Holland (London: G. Bishop and J. Norton, 1610), pp. 421,
435; 'Apologie for the cittie of London', anon., in John Stow, *A survey of London*, ed.
C. L. Kingsford, 2 vols. (1908; reprint Oxford: Clarendon Press, 1971), vol. II, p. 207.

[5] Lawrence Manley, *Literature and culture in early modern London* (Cambridge: Cambridge University Press, 1995).

[6] Ep. 195, in *The correspondence of Erasmus*, trans. R. A. B. Mynors and D. F. S. Thomson,
in *The collected works of Erasmus* (Toronto: University of Toronto Press, 1974–), vol. II,
p. 199; compare Ep. 118, in vol. I, pp. 235–6.

[7] 'The Statutes of Saint Paul's School', in Nicholas Carlisle, *A concise description of the
endowed grammar schools in England and Wales*, 2 vols. (London: Baldwin, Cradock,
and Joy, 1818), vol. II, p. 71; Colet, *Aeditio* (1527; facs. reprint Menston: Scolar Press,
1971), n.p. See also Joan Simon, *Education and society in Tudor England* (Cambridge:
Cambridge University Press, 1966), pp. 73–80; and Kenneth Charleton, *Education in
Renaissance England* (London: Routledge & Kegan Paul, 1965), ch. 4.

[8] *The collected works of Erasmus*, vol. VIII, p. 237.

that attached to pagan authors and extolled them as the antidote to the barbarism of 'the later blind world'.[9]

The method of Colet's curriculum, humanist *imitatio*, entailed a number of important literary-critical corollaries: the creation of a canon of model ancient authors to exemplify literary excellence; the development, as a prelude to composition, of techniques of rhetorical as well as grammatical analysis; a pedagogical cultivation of the vernacular which, by enhancing its flexibility and normative status, was to produce an 'establyshed mariage, betwene the two tonges'[10] of Latin and English as equally legitimate literary media. As the basis for the 'Royal Grammar' officially promulgated by Henry VIII (1542) and later sovereigns (Edward VI, 1547; Elizabeth I, 1559), the school texts of Colet and Lily became the staple of English literary education into the later seventeenth century. Supplemented by an expanding body of rhetorical handbooks, model colloquies, phrase books, and dictionaries which reflected a heavy emphasis on style, the humanist curriculum promoted an aesthetic of facility, copiousness, and variety that prevailed throughout Europe but that, as the number of popular handbooks, compilations, and dictionaries suggests, found a particular resonance in the copious and variegated society of Renaissance London.[11]

Colet's ideal of public education based on merit received wide support among Cromwellian reformers such as Starkey, Marshall, and Morrison, and it was soon adapted, by humanists like Sir Thomas Elyot and Roger Ascham, to the traditional 'priuate brynging vp of youth in Ientlemen and Noble mens houses'. The treatises of Elyot and Ascham represented an important early step in the process by which the feudal habits and chivalric values of the landholding class were gradually replaced by participation in a national 'community of honors' mediated by a common system of letters.[12] Ascham was, with Sir John Cheke, Sir Thomas Smith, Thomas Wilson, and others, among a generation of Cambridge scholars who, together with their Cambridge students William Cecil, Walter Mildmay, and Francis Walsingham, came to dominate the inner circle of the Tudor regime into the later Elizabethan reign. The prosaic pragmatism of these scholars asserted itself in a number of ways: in their adaptation of classically inspired eloquence to public affairs and 'to the sense and vnderstanding of the

---

[9] Carlisle, *Endowed grammar schools*, pp. 76–7.

[10] *Ioannis Palsgravi Londoniensis, ecphrasis Anglica in comoediam Acolasti*, ed. P. L. Carver (Oxford: Early English Text Society, 1937), p. 9.

[11] Louis B. Wright, *Middle-class culture in Elizabethan England* (Chapel Hill: University of North Carolina Press, 1935), chs. 5, 10.

[12] Ascham, *The scholemaster* (1570), in *English works*, ed. W. A. Wright (Cambridge: Cambridge University Press, 1904), pp. 171, 205–7; Sir Thomas Elyot, *The book named the governor* (1530), ed. S. E. Lehmberg (London: Dent; New York: Dutton, 1962), pp. 12–15, 28, 40–6; Mervyn James, *Society, politics, and culture: studies in early modern England* (Cambridge: Cambridge University Press, 1986), p. 328.

common people';[13] in a concern for intellectual discipline and rhetorical effectiveness that produced such fledged Aristotelian-Ciceronian logics and rhetorics as Wilson's *Rule of reason* (1551) and *Arte of rhetorique* (1553) and Lever's *Art of reason* (1573); and in a sharply critical attitude towards the velleities of vernacular verse and fiction.[14]

Responding, in part, to the political domination of this older generation, a younger generation of Elizabethan courtiers developed the idea of vernacular poetry as the amateur pursuit 'of Ladies and young Gentlewomen, or idle Courtiers . . . for their priuate recreation'.[15] Governed by ideals of calculated artlessness and facility that derived from Castiglione's *Book of the courtier* (trans. 1561), and opposed both to the sobrieties of 'scholarly affectation' and to the 'base . . . seruile' exigencies of commercial publication, the theory of poetry at court was marked especially by hostility towards the many varieties of bourgeois and popular literature. The litany of literary offences included a host of popular forms: the 'vncountable rabble of ryming ballad-makers';[16] the 'old Romances of historicall times, made purposely for the common people';[17] 'the gross deuises and vnlearned Pamphlets' that crowded the London bookstalls;[18] the 'mungrell' improbabilities of the popular stage;[19] and the polyglossal patterns of commerce and vernacular culture that made 'our English tonge a gallimaufray and hodgepodge'.[20] The courtly defence of poets as the ornament to 'Kinges and Princes, great and famous men' thus extended in new ideological terms a mid-Tudor policy that had classified popular players and ballad sellers among the species of vagabonds and masterless men.[21]

The courtly attack on vernacular forms of authorship was reinforced by a preaching clergy that made London the 'very Arke of the presence of

---

[13] Thomas Wilson, *The three orations of Demosthenes* (London: H. Denham, 1570), sig. j.; compare Ascham, *The scholemaster*, p. 298.

[14] See, for example, Ascham, *The scholemaster*, p. 290.

[15] Puttenham, *The arte of English poesie*, p. 158. See Richard Helgerson, *Self-crowned laureates: Spenser, Jonson, Milton, and the literary system* (Berkeley: University of California Press, 1983), pp. 25–35, and Daniel Javitch, *Poetry and courtliness in Renaissance England* (Princeton: Princeton University Press, 1978).

[16] William Webbe, *A discourse of English poetrie* (1586), in G. Gregory Smith (ed.), *Elizabethan critical essays*, 2 vols. (1904; reprint Oxford University Press, 1971), vol. I, p. 246.

[17] Puttenham, *The Arte of English poesie*, p. 83.

[18] Webbe, *Discourse*, in Smith (ed.), *Elizabethan critical essays*, vol. I, p. 246; compare Ascham, *The scholemaster*, p. 290.

[19] Sir Philip Sidney, *An apologie for poetrie* (1595), in Smith (ed.), *Elizabethan critical essays*, vol. I, p. 199; compare George Whetstone, *Dedication to Promos and Cassandra* (1578), in Smith (ed.), *Elizabethan critical essays*, vol. I, p. 59.

[20] *Epistle dedicatory to The shepheardes calendar* (1579), in Smith (ed.), *Elizabethan critical essays*, vol. I, p. 130.

[21] Proclamation enforcing statutes against vagabonds, 28 April 1551, in Paul C. Hughes and James F. Larkin (ed.), *Tudor royal proclamations*, 3 vols. (New Haven: Yale University Press, 1964–9), vol. I, p. 517.

God, above all other places of this land'.[22] Extreme scripturalism, dictating that all words 'not out of the mouth of the Lord' (Jer. 23: 16) were 'consecrated to idolatry', helped to fuel a clerical attack directed at all genres of imaginative literature, including 'our songs and sonnets, our Palaces of Pleasure, our unchaste fables and tragedies and such like sorceries'.[23] Hostility to the popular stage arose in part from a concern, shared with the City of London authorities, about threats to social and moral order emanating from the theatres' heteroglot ambience; but it was also supported by an animus against all popular writing on social and moral questions, which, in so far as it violated the discursive monopoly held by the alliance of ministry and magistracy, was regarded as the unauthorized discourse of men without calling.

The formal *apologiae* in which writers like Sidney and Lodge replied to the clerical campaign were supplemented by responses from the theatrical world itself – by Thomas Heywood's defence of playing as an 'ornament to the city',[24] by Shakespeare's celebratory uses of popular recreations and pastimes, by Jonson's ridicule (in *Bartholomew Fair*, for example) of the puritanical literalism that confounded fiction and reality. Between 1560 and 1642, when well over fifty million visits were made to London playhouses, the English drama achieved a level and quality unprecedented since antiquity. The stage was a source both of dramatic theory, explicit and implicit, and of new forms of historical and sociological insight influential in the history of literary criticism. In a repertory that included more than a hundred comedies set in London, for example, consciousness of the many ways in which 'the Citty is a Commodie'[25] became a fertile source of comic theories, including those of Jonson. More broadly, and in keeping with the variety of acting companies, repertories, and clienteles in the London theatre world, a wealth of prologues, epilogues, and inductions-in-the-theatre addressed a heterogeneous audience well versed in the nuances of genre and style.

Alongside the theatre, London produced a generation of serio-comic pamphleteers (including Robert Greene, Thomas Nashe, and Thomas

---

[22] Thomas Jackson, *The conuerts happines* (London: J. Windet for C. Knight, 1609), p. 30.
[23] Stephen Gosson, *Plays confuted in five actions* (1582), in Arthur Kinney, *Markets of bawdrie: the dramatic criticism of Stephen Gosson*, Salzburg studies in English literature 4 (1972), p. 151; Edward Dering, *Briefe and necessary instruction needeful to be known of all householders* (London?, 1572), sig. Aiii'. See Jonas Barish, *The antitheatrical prejudice* (Berkeley: University of California Press, 1981), ch. 4, and Russell Fraser, *The war against poetry* (Princeton: Princeton University Press, 1970).
[24] *An apology for actors* (1612), in O. B. Hardison, Jr. (ed.), *English literary criticism: the Renascence* (Englewood Cliffs, NJ: Prentice-Hall, 1963), p. 226.
[25] Edward Sharpham, *The Fleire* (1607), 2.1.124–34, in Christopher Gordon Petter, *A critical old spelling edition of the works of Edward Sharpham* (New York: Garland, 1986), p. 265.

Dekker) whose immersion in the city's burgeoning *demi-monde* and
market-place of print led to new claims for literary professionalism and
for the moral legitimation of authorship by commercial motives and by
personal, mundane experience.[26] Writing, in John Danby's phrase, 'down'
Fortune's Hill to an emerging heteroglot urban audience, the pamphleteers parlayed their status as unpatronized, estateless, and degraded
urbanites into a new form of literary celebrity, revealing what it meant, in
Dekker's wonderful phrase, 'to be a man in Print'.[27]

The pace by which Greene was rumoured to 'haue yarkt vp a Pamphlet
in a day & a night' reflected both a new consciousness of the urban tempo
that creates 'news' and a new sensitivity to market-place conditions
that left writers 'euery hour hammering out one piece or other out of this
rusty Iron age'.[28] Important differences separate this latter image from
Milton's portrait of revolutionary London as a 'mansion house of liberty'
and 'shoppe of warre' with 'anvils and hammers waking, to fashion out
the plates and instruments of armed justice in the defence of beleaguer'd
Truth'. But in Thomas Goodwin's concept of the city as 'the greatest
mart for truth in this last age', as in Milton's celebration of Londoners
'disputing, reasoning, reading, inventing, discoursing . . . musing, searching, revolving new notions and ideas',[29] there is a fundamentally similar
recognition of the ways in which discursive possibilities were created
and sustained by the city's dynamic environment. The desire to exploit
these possibilities gave rise to a variety of utopian schemes to formalize
London's status as the nation's intellectual capital – from the mid-Tudor
proposals of Sir Nicholas Bacon and Humphrey Gilbert, to the polite
academies of the Caroline age, to the Commonwealth plans of Samuel
Hartlib, to the Restoration establishment of the Royal Society in London,
the greatest of all 'former, or present seats of Empire'.[30]

London's status as intellectual capital was enhanced by the Inns of
Court, those 'noblest nurses of humanity and liberty' by virtue of whose
presence (according to Sir George Buc) 'London may not onely challenge
iustly the name and stile of an Universitie, but also a chiefe place in the

[26] Edwin H. Miller, *The professional writer in Elizabethan England* (Cambridge, MA: Harvard University Press, 1959); Phoebe Sheavyn, *The literary professional in the Elizabethan age*, ed. J. W. Saunders, 2nd edn (New York: Barnes and Noble, 1967).
[27] *Poets on fortune's hill* (London: Faber and Faber, 1952), p. 45. Thomas Dekker, *The non-dramatic works*, ed. A. B. Grosart, 5 vols. (London: Huth Library, 1884–6), vol. I, p. 78.
[28] Thomas Nashe, in R. B. McKerrow (ed.), *The works of Thomas Nashe*, 5 vols. (1904; reprint Oxford: Basil Blackwell, 1966), vol. I, p. 287; Dekker, *Non-dramatic works*, vol. III, p. 178.
[29] Thomas Goodwin, *Works*, ed. J. C. Miller, 12 vols. (Edinburgh: James Nichol, 1861), vol. IV, p. 313; Milton, *Areopagitica* (1644), in *The complete prose works*, ed. D. M. Wolfe, 8 vols. (New Haven: Yale University Press, 1953–82), vol. II, pp. 553–7.
[30] Thomas Sprat, *History of the Royal Society*, ed. J. I. Cope and H. Whitmore Jones (1959; reprint St Louis: Washington University Press, 1966), pp. 86–8.

Catalogue of Vniuersities'.[31] The Inns were not only a centre of legal
education but also served as fashionable residences and finishing schools
for young gentlemen, who were encouraged by the Gray's Inn Revels for
1594-5 to 'frequent the Theatre, and such like places of Experience; and
resort to the better sort of Ord'naries for Conference, where they may
. . . become accomplished with Civil Conversations'.[32] The agonistic
practices of the Inns, with their moots and boltings, were a stimulus to the
contemporary fashion for 'quips and sentences . . . and paper bullets' and
to explorations of the contingency of utterance in such practical handbooks as Abraham Fraunce's *Lawiers logike* (1588) and John Hoskins'
Directions for speech and style (*c.* 1599). The Inns' worldly and competitive atmosphere was a factor in the development of the curt Senecan style,
compressed form, and critical spirit of Bacon's precedent-setting *Essays*
(1597), and perhaps as well in his pragmatic and highly influential dismissal of poetry as 'fained history'.[33]

The most important contribution of the Inns to theory and criticism,
however, was through the imitation of classical verse satire by such residents as John Donne, John Marston, and Everard Guilpin. The Inns of
Court satirists cultivated a neoclassical genrism that, by discriminating
both the modes of ancient satire and its differences from other kinds,
established satire as an alternative means of laureateship and a medium of
literary as well as social criticism. Along with the 'Sense, shortnesse, and
salt'[34] of the epigram and the 'accurate and quick description'[35] of the
newly created prose character, the 'snaphaunce quick distinction'[36] of
verse satire marked the advent of an urbane consciousness and manner
opposed to the idealism and hyperbolic eroticism of courtly genres.

Such classically inspired urbanity was reinforced by the development
of a fashionable 'Town' society in the West End of Jacobean and Early
Caroline London.[37] Drawing the social spheres of country, court, and city

[31] Jonson, Dedication to *Every man out of his humour*, in *The complete plays*, ed.
G. A. Wilkes, 4 vols. (Oxford: Clarendon Press, 1981), vol. I, p. 279; Sir George Buc,
'A Discourse, or Treatise of the third universitie of England', *The annales, or generall
chronicle of England, begun first by maister Iohn Stow, and after him continued . . . by
Edmund Howes* (London: T. Adams, 1615), p. 984.

[32] *Gesta Grayorum*, ed. D. Bland (Liverpool: Liverpool University Press, 1968), p. 41. See
also Philip J. Finkelpearl, *John Marston of the Middle Temple* (Cambridge, MA: Harvard
University Press, 1969).

[33] *The advancement of learning*, Bk. II, in J. E. Spingarn (ed.), *Critical essays of the seventeenth century*, 3 vols. (1908-9; reprint Bloomington: Indiana University Press, 1957),
vol. I, pp. 5-6.

[34] *Paroemiographia* (1659), in *Lexicon tetraglotton* (London: J. G. for S. Thomson, 1660),
unpaginated preface.

[35] John Stephens, *Satyricall essayes characters and others* (London: N. Okes, 1615), t.p.

[36] John Marston, *The scourge of villanie* (1598), in *The poems*, ed. A. Davenport (Liverpool:
Liverpool University Press, 1961), p. 122.

[37] Martin Butler, *Theatre and crisis, 1632-1642* (Cambridge: Cambridge University Press,
1984), p. 141.

together for business and pleasure, the confluence of urbanizing gentry with gentrifying city in 'the Town' made London the 'inn-general of the gentry and nobility of this nation', the place 'Where the refined spirits of our Ile / Ingenious discourse communicate'.[38] As the *locus* of widened possibilities for social and intellectual exchange, the 'Town' became a literary domain that transcended the separately encoded *decora* of 'Country', 'Court', and 'City' outlined by Puttenham and formalized in the generic theory of Thomas Hobbes.[39] Its status was enhanced by the creation of an 'Augustan idea', anticipated, for example, in the cultural analogies of Jonson's *Poetaster* (1601) and reinforced by royal edicts and policies equating London with imperial Rome.[40] Its chief hallmarks were an urbane manner of beholding the self and the world and the cultivation of classically inspired genres, including epigram, elegy, epistle, ode, and essay, as media of social and literary criticism. In discovering 'ways to be more intimate and informal'[41] in a metropolitan setting of increasing complexity and grandeur, the urbane social mode inaugurated by Ben Jonson and his many imitators worked out a cosmopolitan 'way of life' by moving inwardly and selectively towards the privatized domains of self, friends, distinctive place, and occasion. Drawing heavily on the example of Horace, and mediated by such Stoic and Epicurean ideals as *apatheia* (or freedom from passion) and *ataraxia* (or imperturbability), and *oikeosis* (or reasonable like-mindedness), new modulations of epistle, elegy, ode, and critical prose were adapted to the discriminating choices demanded by the burgeoning pace and scale of metropolitan life.[42] Jonson's recognition that 'Variety is incredible; and therefore we must search' prompted both his Senecan critical motto – *tanquam explorator* – and his poetic and critical attempts to 'find the best', to 'extract, and choose the best of all . . . known'.[43]

[38] Thomas Fuller, quoted in Lawrence Stone, 'The residential development of the West End of London in the seventeenth century', in *After the Reformation: essays in honor of J. H. Hexter*, ed. Barbara C. Malament (Philadelphia: University of Pennsylvania Press, 1980), p. 388; Dudley North, 'Metropolis', in *A forest promiscuous of several seasons productions* (London: D. Pakeman, 1659), p. 17.

[39] Puttenham, *The Arte of English poesie*, p. 284; Hobbes, 'Answer to Sir William Davenant's preface before *Gondibert* (1650)', in Spingarn (ed.), *Critical essays*, vol. II, pp. 54–6.

[40] Proclamation for buildings, 16 June 1615, in Paul C. Hughes and James F. Larkin (ed.), *Stuart royal proclamations* (Oxford: Clarendon Press, 1973–), vol. I, p. 346; see also Howard Erskine-Hill, *The Augustan idea in English literature* (London: Edward Arnold, 1983).

[41] Alastair Fowler, *Kinds of literature: an introduction to the theory of genres and kinds* (Cambridge, MA: Harvard University Press, 1982), pp. 195–202.

[42] Katharine Eisamen Maus, *Ben Jonson and the Roman frame of mind* (Princeton: Princeton University Press, 1984), ch. 5.

[43] *Discoveries*, lines 833–6; 'Epistle. To Katherine, Lady D'Aubigny', lines 17–20; 'To William Roe', line 3, in *The complete poems*, ed. G. Parfitt (New Haven: Yale University Press, 1975), pp. 395, 114, 84.

By the early seventeenth century, London had become, according to Edmund Waterhouse, 'a Collection and digest of all men and things, to all ends and accomplishments of life'.[44] In its anthologizing impulse, the social mode shared (with such new metropolitan phenomena as pleasure gardens, exclusive and enclosed squares, clubs, salons, private indoor theatres, private collecting, and a rudimentary museum culture) in a process of appropriation by interiorization. In the many poems they wrote on gardens, houses, paintings, music, and collections, the poets and critics who followed Jonson's example were searching for what Harold Toliver has called ways to 'showcase reality'.[45]

In so far as it promoted 'differentiation, refinement, and the enrichment' of the person,[46] the critical search for distinction contributed to the social stratification of taste. This stratification was effected not only by the casual and incidental criticism of such works as Henry Peacham's *Complete gentleman* (1622), Drayton's 'Epistle to Henry Reynolds' (1627), and the many 'sessions of the poets' pieces by writers from Suckling to Wither, but also by a wave of anthologizing that, beginning during the Civil War, produced some forty anthologies in as many years. Typically professing to be collected by 'persons of Quality' and addressing themselves to 'the refined'st Witts of the Age', the new anthologies gathered, alongside poets in the social mode from Jonson and the Beaumonts to Waller and Sedley, a variety of polite phrase-lists, exemplary letters, games, puzzles, rebuses, and codebooks whose aim was to encode sophistication and selectivity.

As with the rationalization of other societal resources at the Restoration – of language, education, and markets – the anthologized dissemination of a generalized *vers de société* made literature a public institution which contained 'within itself the principle of its own continuation'.[47] The national literature did not become homogeneous, but it was marked increasingly by an interiorientation of urbane *decora* and a levelling confluence between polite and popular urban modes. London's was thus a metropolitan influence in which forces ancient and modern, classical and continental, polite and popular, activist and scholarly – opposed in theory – were merged in critical, as in creative, practice. Its importance as an environment of literary criticism is reflected in the fact that John Dryden, the 'father of English criticism', was neither a courtier nor a scholar, but a metropolite.

---

[44] Edward Waterhouse, *The gentleman's monitor* (T. R. for R. Royston, 1665), p. 295.
[45] *Lyric provinces in the Renaissance* (Columbus: Ohio State University Press, 1985), p. 100.
[46] 'The metropolis and mental life', in *Classic essays on the culture of cities*, ed. Richard Sennett (Englewood Cliffs, NJ: Prentice-Hall, 1969), p. 57.
[47] Pierre Bourdieu, *Outline of a theory of practice*, trans. R. Nice (Cambridge: Cambridge University Press, 1977), p. 189.

34

Criticism in the city: Lyons and Paris

Timothy Hampton

The development of French poetry and criticism in the sixteenth century cannot be understood without reference to the growth and transformation of two great urban centres, Lyons and Paris. Although there was much exchange between the cities, with figures headquartered in Paris active in Lyons and vice versa, these cities offer contrasting images of the relationship between criticism and its social and institutional milieu. Indeed, the mere presence of Lyons as a cultural centre rivalling Paris is one of the features that sets the Renaissance apart from other moments in French cultural history, for it complicates the relationship of centre and margin, capital and province, that has tended to dominate French cultural life since the early seventeenth century. Lyons was the port of entry through which the Renaissance came to France. Not only did its location, virtually on the Italian border, make it the point of exchange for all contact with the peninsula to the south, but Lyons underwent a rapid process of transformation during the late fifteenth and early sixteenth centuries that made it a city of international importance. From the early 1400s Lyons had been famous for its commercial fairs. These events, which attracted merchants from all over Europe, were initially held twice a year for six days. Then, by decree of Charles VII in 1444, a third fair was added, and all of them were extended to twenty days each. The crown's aim in promoting Lyons was to establish the city as the mercantile crossroads of Europe, thereby turning her rival and neighbour Geneva into a backwater. Thus, for a sizeable portion of each year Lyons became a hotbed of all types of economic activity. The fairs brought with them mercantile exchanges, helped on by a special royal dispensation facilitating currency traffic and use of the recently invented letter of exchange. They also furthered cultural exchange, as literate burghers from all parts of Europe brought their goods to market. The international atmosphere of the fairs lent the city a cosmopolitanism unknown elsewhere in France.[1]

---

[1] On the cosmopolitanism of Lyons see Robert Gascon, *Grand commerce et vie urbaine au XVIe siècle* (Paris: Presses Universitaires de France, 1971); Natalie Zemon Davis, *Society and culture in early modern France* (Stanford: Stanford University Press, 1975); Lucien Romier, 'Lyons and cosmopolitanism at the beginning of the French Renaissance', in *French humanism, 1470–1600*, ed. W. L. Gundersheimer (London: Macmillan, 1969), pp. 90–109; and James B. Wadsworth, *Lyons 1473–1503: the beginnings of cosmopolitanism* (Cambridge, MA: Mediaeval Academy of America, 1962).

If one were to look for a single object that embodied the ferment stimulated by the development of the fairs, that object would be the printed book. Beginning in the 1470s Lyons developed into one of the centres of the European book trade. Peasants from the surrounding countryside soon migrated to the city to seek employment in the workshops of such famous printers as Jean de Tournes and Sebastian Gryphius – creating urban overcrowding and eventual civil unrest. Lyonnais printers turned out everything from annotated editions of the classics to popular chapbooks. The presence of the presses meant that Lyonnais intellectuals had easy access to virtually all of Italian Renaissance literature, as well as to the innumerable commentaries on classical texts that were being produced by humanist intellectuals throughout Europe.[2]

Accompanying the expansion of the fairs and the growth of printing was the rise of Lyons as perhaps the major European banking centre. This development had important social and cultural consequences beyond its obvious economic significance, for the central position that the city came to occupy in a developing pan-European mercantile system attracted wealthy and educated foreigners. Most important in this cosmopolitan population was the sizeable colony of Italian financiers, representing virtually every major city and banking family in Italy. With them came the literary and artistic fruits of the Italian Renaissance, which soon attracted the attention of the local élite.

The influence of this international community on the taste and style of a local intelligentsia is important in understanding the cultural development of the city. For Lyons, unlike virtually every other cultural centre in the sixteenth century, had no university. Its sole noteworthy educational institution was the Collège de la Trinité, which was briefly headed by the humanist scholar Barthélemy Aneau. Cultural life had always, of course, been strongly influenced by the presence of the Church, but that institution was thrown into crisis during the first decades of the sixteenth century. There was no other sizeable public institution to fill the void opened during that crisis. The lack of a university meant that the intellectual life of the city was largely in the hands of aristocrats, wealthy bourgeois such as the poet Maurice Scève, and professionals like the doctors Symphorien Champier and François Rabelais. To these were added members of the printing trade, like the controversial philosopher Etienne Dolet. The spread into France of the new intellectual and artistic doctrines fostered by Italian humanism thus met neither resistance from an entrenched intellectual clan nor the controlling presence of a single ruler or patron. It was neither in court nor in cloister that the Lyonnais Renaissance was forged, but in

---

[2] For the development of printing in Lyons, see Lucien Febvre and Henri-Jean Martin, *The coming of the book*, trans. D. Gerard (London: New Left Books, 1976).

such locations as the hillside house of the jurist Pierre Sala, where leading intellectuals gathered regularly.

Criticism in Lyons is linked both to the intellectual coterie, an institution which prefigures the salon culture of the seventeenth century, and to a strong sense of civic identity. The presence of a cosmopolitan reading public in Lyons means that poetry and criticism tend to be defined in terms reflecting an emerging civic society, instead of an ecclesiastical community or a court. Relationships between individual and collectivity are thus often mediated by images of small groups of initiates, rather than by references to official institutions. Moreover, this relative independence produces a paradox often seen in work by Lyonnais thinkers. One finds a simultaneous stress on the importance of community and on the power of the individual to seek self-definition apart from community. This contradiction might be seen most clearly in the bourgeois poet Louise Labé, who evokes and praises a community of women readers, only to use that imaginary community as a foil against which to define an unconventional personality. Similarly, when, in 1547, Jean de Tournes published an edition of Petrarch's works, he included a letter written by himself in Italian to the poet Maurice Scève. This epistle recalled how the young Scève, then just beginning his career, achieved fame for 'discovering' the tomb of Petrarch's Laura in Avignon. The re-creation of that event by De Tournes suggests that both he and Scève sensed the power of the printed book to create a reputation and construct a particular image of the intellectual. For while the 'discovery' of the tomb took place in 1533, the letter appeared at a moment when Scève, who had withdrawn from public life to work on his masterpiece *Délie*, was returning to take charge of preparations for Henri II's entry into Lyons. De Tournes reinforces Scève's portrayal of himself as a solitary figure. Just as Scève spent his early days like Petrarch, contemplating ruins (in a beautifully ironic touch, contemplating Petrarch's ruins), so does he return from the solitude in which he has been singing of his absent lady. However real Scève's retirement from public life, De Tournes's letter casts his return in a mythical context, creating the poet as the French Petrarch and Lyons as the Gallic answer to Florence.

The examples of Scève and Labé suggest that, in a context lacking strong official institutions, renown must be produced or managed against the backdrop of an imaginary community. Yet the very presence of the printing trade meant that works by Lyonnais writers not only circulated among the small groups of friends whom they so consistently evoked, but reached a wider public as well. For particularly strong-willed individuals, like the unconventional polemicist Dolet, this wider public provided an audience as important as the community of 'Dames Lïonnoizes' was for Labé. Yet for others it was the source of uneasiness. And in these cases the coterie or literary fraternity could be evoked as an imaginary space within which anxiety about printing might be subsumed. The lyric poet Clément Marot, whose work influenced virtually every Lyonnais writer of the day, prefaced Dolet's 1538 edition of his poetry with a letter to the printer thanking him for putting together an edition following the poet's specifications. Some printers, laments Marot, have stuffed collections of his poems with works by other writers, among them heretics, thereby harming his good name and endangering his person. Now, thanks to Dolet, says Marot, booksellers will sell, not a loose collection of pages, but a real book. This letter, by a poet largely dependent on royal pensions, reflects both the power and powerlessness of the author in a mercantile society. For it depicts a producer trying to control the handling of his product as it enters an uncertain new market. Yet at the same time Marot's gesture of thanks recalls a much more traditional patronage system, in which the benefactor is praised for helping the poet bring forth his works. Marot links himself and Dolet in a relationship that suggests at once the professional *confrérie*, the band of friends and, possibly, even the Protestant congregation – with which Marot and Dolet, like many Lyonnais intellectuals, were involved.[3]

The work of these Lyonnais thinkers reflects the tensions that traverse a society in which such official cultural institutions as the court and the university play a minor role. A somewhat different situation pertained in Paris. Here intellectual life circulated between a series of strong institutions which were often at odds with each other, and every critic was faced with the difficult problem of negotiating between political and religious forms of authority. The seat of traditional intellectual power was the Sorbonne, with its influential Faculty of Theology. Here, in the medieval scholastic tradition, men of the Church lectured on theology and dialectic to students from all over Europe. If the printing trade in Lyons was at the forefront of the circulation of new ideas, Parisian printers found themselves under the eye of university censors, who feared the new invention and even succeeded at one point, in 1534, in forcing the king to issue a proclamation outlawing it. The increasing rigidity of the Sorbonne towards new intellectual currents led to attacks, not only on philosophers like Dolet and Erasmus, but even on such writers of fiction as Rabelais himself. Because it was basically a college of theology, the Sorbonne operated under the authority of the Church and took its orders from the pope. Its relationship to the Crown had often been that of an adversary. Tension between the two institutions increased during the 1520s, when Francis I developed an interest in humanist thought and the court, located in the newly renovated Louvre and at nearby Fontainebleau, began to attract

---

[3] Marot's preface is in his *Œuvres poétiques*, ed. G. Defaux, 2 vols. (Paris: Garnier, 1990), vol. 1, pp. 9–11. On the religious context, see J. H. M. Salmon, *Society in crisis: France in the sixteenth century* (London: Benn, 1975), and Davis, *Society and culture*, chs. 1–3.

brilliant artists and writers from all over Europe. In 1517, at the urging
of his secretary, the Hellenist Guillaume Budé, Francis began work on a
school for the study of ancient languages. This support for the institution
that would become the Collège de France was an attempt to imitate Italian
precedents such as the Florentine Academy. But the school was also, with
its course of free and public lectures, a response to a void in cultural life
left by an increasingly conservative Sorbonne.[4]

However, from within the university itself there arose new structures
that would shape the great cultural projects marking the middle years of
the century. These new institutions were the *collèges*, which had originated
in the fifteenth century, as charitable organizations for poor students. The
collèges soon began to offer their own courses, frequently taken in conjunction with the regular university curriculum. It was in the *collèges* that
the new doctrines of humanism and Protestantism found many of their
most fervent advocates – and some of their most energetic enemies: the
philologist Lefèvre d'Etaples taught at the Collège du Cardinal-Lemoine;
both Calvin and Erasmus received their formation at the Collège de
Lisieux; on the faculty of the Collège de Navarre one could find the great
orientalist Guillaume Postel, as well as the man who would later teach
Montaigne in Bordeaux, George Buchanan; among the students was
Ignatius Loyola.

It was in this context, where small pedagogical circles were beginning
to constitute themselves as challenges to the official organ of pedagogy,
that there was formed the most influential intellectual group of the middle
years of the century, the group known as the Pléiade, which took shape
around the teaching of Jean Dorat, at the Collège de Coqueret. Dorat
taught Greek to Ronsard, who spent five years at Coqueret, as well as
to Jean-Antoine de Baïf. And his instruction included discussions held at
the house of Baïf's father, Lazare, a former diplomat, who seems to have
turned his residence into a kind of mini-academy for the promotion of
poetry and music. Ronsard owned a house nearby, as did Jean Galland,
a friend of Ronsard and principal of the Collège de Boncourt. To this
complex of buildings were attracted many of the most talented young
writers of the day.[5] The doctrines of the Pléiade, with their programme
to renovate French letters by a return to classical models, were thus
developed in a pedagogical institution, but in a context marginal to the
official university establishment. Indeed, this marginality is even geographical; Baïf's villa was located at the edge of old Paris, near the city moat.
In this setting were forged many of the ideas that would later emerge in

---

[4] For the full history of this project see Abel Lefranc, *Histoire du Collège de France* (Paris:
Hachette, 1898).
[5] On the origins of the Pléiade see Frances A. Yates, *The French academies of the sixteenth
century* (London: Routledge & Kegan Paul, 1988), ch. 2.

such major critical treatises as Ronsard's *Abbregé de l'Art poëtique françois* (1565) and Joachim du Bellay's *Deffence et illustration de la langue françoyse* (1549).

Yet if the Lyonnais context produced intellectual currents linked to the rise of printing and the development of a civic intelligentsia, Parisian intellectuals were caught between the twin institutions of the court and the university. The university's connections to an increasingly intolerant papacy made it resistant to change. Indeed, probably the most brilliant thinker of his generation, the philosopher Peter Ramus, met with derision and repression when he tried to refute the conventional understanding of Aristotle taught in the Faculty of Theology. Instead, the members of the Pléiade, who were mostly from the petty nobility, linked their fortunes to the court, and to the game of political favour. Rather than flirting with the new ideas preached by the Reformation movement, as had many of their Lyonnais counterparts, they remained within the ambit of Catholic orthodoxy and focused on a vast, royally sanctioned project to renew French thought.

This close connection between royal power, Catholic orthodoxy, and cultural criticism means that, though the Pléiade must surely be understood as the first of the innumerable avant-garde movements in French cultural history, its rise to cultural dominance coincides with a general reaction against the spread of the very types of intellectual and religious heterodoxy that flourished in the Lyonnais context of the 1530s and 1540s. It also accounts for the way in which the critics of the Pléiade define their own authority. Such Lyons writers as Labé, in the dedication to her *Poésies* (1555), Dolet, in his many prefaces, and Aneau, in the *Quintil Horatian* (1550) that he wrote to answer Du Bellay's *Deffence*, make it clear that they are speaking within a specific civic context *to* a developing reading public which may be either Lyonnais or French. Ronsard and Du Bellay, by contrast, claim to speak *for* France. Their project is to establish themselves as the spokesmen for French culture. As such, they must construct a mythical France which can authorize their project. Because they are allied with a courtly culture that embodies the state, they are able to claim authority to speak – whether they are actually at court or not. Thus even Du Bellay, whose courtly successes were relatively modest, draws his literary authority from his absence, from the way he constructs his life in Rome as both a mythical poetic exile and a service to the king. Contrast this with Marot's writings during his exile in Ferrara, in which the king, as personal patron, is praised, whereas 'France' is associated with the 'ingrate' judges who drove Marot out. For Marot 'France' is a group of specific people. For Du Bellay it is a myth.[6]

---

[6] See Marot's *Epistres*, ed. C. A. Mayer (London: The Athlone Press, 1958), pp. 194–207.

Thus one may draw a general contrast between a Lyonnais context defined by a secular civic culture and a Parisian setting marked by the presence of crown and university. By the last years of the century, however, this cultural geography had been transformed. The wars between Protestants and Catholics that broke out in the 1560s tore the political and social fabric of France apart. And the fragile balance between contexts, institutions, and critics that had shaped both the Lyonnais flowering and the Pléiade was upset. The political collapse engulfed the intellectual contexts that had produced French critical thought, sometimes in very direct ways. By the late 1530s, an increasingly impatient crown began to crack down on intellectuals suspected of heresy. The controversial Dolet was burned on the Place Maubert in Paris. This scenario of execution would be repeated twenty-five years later when criticism fell prey, not to royal decree, but to mob violence. By 1571 the splendid court that had authorized the work of the Pléiade had fallen into confusion and decadence, and ideological rigidity polarized the intellectual community. Ronsard allied himself with the ultra-Catholic Queen Mother, Catherine de' Medici, and even sanctioned violence against his Protestant countrymen. When attempts by moderate forces at court to mediate between warring factions broke down, the people of Paris took power into their hands. In the St Bartholomew's Day Massacre, the great Ramus, adversary of the Sorbonne, was murdered in his rooms by a mob, decapitated, and thrown into the Seine.[7] No longer a mere backdrop or context for criticism, the city itself rose up to destroy the critic.

---

[7] On Ramus, see the definitive study by Walter Ong, *Ramus, method and the decay of dialogue* (Cambridge, MA: Harvard University Press, 1958).

35

Culture, imperialism, and humanist criticism in the Italian city-states

Diana Robin

The new criticism that emerged at the end of the fourteenth century in Italy had its roots in the movement to revive classical studies known as humanism. The humanists, however, sowed the seeds of an ambiguous legacy; they wrote critical essays on liberty, the ideal state, and the quest for the good, but they also produced propaganda for their states that ignored injustice at home and rationalized – in the name of peace and security – a policy of terror and aggression abroad. But this humanism – whatever its long-term force – could not have flourished either in its civic or more contemplative forms without the innovations of Petrarch. He was the first to couch modern concerns in the classical Latin of Cicero and Livy. Embracing civic, literary, philosophical, and religious themes, his writings include criticism in the form of letters, a Latin epic poem after Virgil's *Aeneid*, and lyric poetry in Italian.[1]

There was a gulf nevertheless between the fifteenth-century humanists and Petrarch. They had access to a tradition Petrarch never knew: the Greek philosophers, orators, historians, tragedians, and poets. After the invention of the printing-press, the humanists of the later fifteenth century had at their disposal a variety and volume of classical and modern texts that would have amazed Petrarch: the new technology of movable type allowed more books to be produced in the last fifty years of the fifteenth century than all the scribes in Europe had written prior to that time.

Other features distinguish this first century of humanism from the periods before and after it: the dominance of Latin over the vernacular as the lingua franca of serious criticism; the enormous mobility of leading writers of the period, who moved typically between cities and courts; the related importance (for a mobile literary culture) of the epistolary genre as the essential medium of expression for the humanists; the rise of a number of distinct and different regional humanisms in the Italian city-states, each with its own local character; and lastly, yet most importantly, the disdain inherent in the ideology of Renaissance humanism for social justice. When the humanists espoused the themes of liberty and the dignity of man, they

[1] Petrarch, *Rerum familiarium libri I-VIII*, trans. A. S. Bernardo (Albany: State University of New York Press, 1975).

355

spoke only for and to a small enclave of the adult male citizenry – men
highly educated and born to wealth and privilege.[2]

*

Among the leading Renaissance city-states in Italy, Florence was the first
to promote the revival of Greek studies and to foster a humanism that was
primarily civic in its orientation. Beginning with Coluccio Salutati, a
succession of Florentine chancellors stressed the importance of education
in training citizens for active roles in government. Interdisciplinary studies
in the classics – the languages, literature, history, and philosophy of
Greece and Rome – were the essentials of such an education.

Salutati, born to uneducated parents, studied law at the university in
Bologna and served as a secretary at the papal court in Rome before coming to the chancellorship of Florence, an office he held until his death in
1406.[3] His career and close association with members of the Florentine
ruling class exemplify the alliance between lower-class men with a university education and men of property that typified humanist patronage in
the Italian cities. Salutati's republicanism was Roman and Ciceronian: he
assumed that affairs of state were best managed by an élite class of men
whose wealth and birth entitled them to govern. Though his voluminous
collection of Latin letters included treatises on liberty, the role of the good
citizen, freedom of the will, and the primacy of the active life over the contemplative one, he never considered popular government a viable alternative to oligarchy.

Politics and literary studies went hand in hand for the humanists.
Though Salutati never mastered Greek himself, the generation of humanist chancellors who followed him were well-read in both Latin and Greek
literature. The subsequent chancellor of Florence, Leonardo Bruni,
together with Cosimo de' Medici and Palla Strozzi, the two wealthiest
merchants in the city in the 1430s, were instrumental in bringing a
succession of noted Hellenists to the university in Florence. Among these
outsiders two Italians, Francesco Filelfo and Giovanni Aurispa, brought
back from Constantinople the first large-scale collections of the canonical
authors of ancient Greece – Homer, Sappho, Thucydides, Aeschylus,
Sophocles, Euripides, and Plato – all virtually unknown in Europe at that
time even in translation.[4]

During this first period of the flourishing of Greek studies in Florence,
Palla Strozzi, Cosimo de' Medici, Niccolò Niccoli and other wealthy

[2] Lauro Martines, *Power and imagination* (New York: Vintage Books, 1979), pp. 191–217.
[3] On the intellectual and biographical background of Salutati, see Ronald G. Witt, *Hercules
at the crossroads: the life, works, and thought of Coluccio Salutati* (Durham, NC: Duke
University Press, 1983).
[4] N. G. Wilson, *From Byzantium to Italy: Greek studies in the Italian Renaissance* (Baltimore:
The Johns Hopkins University Press, 1992), pp. 25–7.

merchants and bankers in the city bought up the extensive collections of rare Greek codices that now constitute the core manuscript holdings of the Laurentian Library in Florence. At the same time, unknown Latin works were still being rediscovered. Scouring libraries in France, Germany, and Switzerland, the Florentine chancellor Poggio Bracciolini discovered such lost works as Lucretius's *De rerum natura*, the first complete manuscript of Quintilian's *Institutio oratoria*, and several lost orations of Cicero.

During his chancellorship, Bruni translated works of Plato, Aristotle, Xenophon, and Plutarch. He also composed two other works, which were to serve as models for a kind of proto-nationalistic rhetoric: the *History of the Florentine people* and the *Panegyric to the city of Florence*.[5] Both works served as patterns for the kind of propaganda works that humanists in other cities were later commissioned to write. The Florentine historians Matteo Palmieri, Giannozzo Manetti, and the chancellors Benedetto Ascolti and Bartolomeo Scala carried on the tradition of civic humanism fostered by Bruni and Salutati, while Leon Battista Alberti, the most versatile of the Florentine humanists, wrote essays and criticism on architecture, painting, the family, all of which had a strong civic component.

In the later fifteenth century, as power became more consolidated in the hands of a small group of patrician families, civic concerns receded among the humanists, and a more literary and philosophical criticism took its place in Florence. The Neoplatonists who gathered around Lorenzo de' Medici – men such as Donato Acciaiuoli, Cristoforo Landino, Marsilio Ficino, and Pico della Mirandola – represented the vanguard of this new criticism. At the centre of this group was Ficino, whose translations of the complete works of Plato would revolutionize philosophical studies in the later fifteenth century. Angelo Poliziano, another member of the Laurentian circle and certainly the most original philologist of his generation, has been called the founder of modern textual criticism and literary analysis.[6] Towards the close of the century, the writings of the Florentine historians Niccolò Machiavelli and Francesco Guicciardini reveal disillusionment with both the new philosophical studies and the constraints of criticism under humanist patronage.

*

In 1404–6, Venice incorporated the cities of Padua, Vicenza, and Verona under her rule, a move that signalled not only the founding of her *terra firma* empire but also the articulation of expansionist aims that were

[5] Text in Benjamin G. Kohl (trans. and ed.) and R. G. Witt (ed.), *The earthly republic: Italian humanists on government and society* (Philadelphia: University of Pennsylvania Press, 1978), pp. 121–75.

[6] Anthony Grafton, *Joseph Scaliger: a study in the history of classical scholarship* (Oxford: Clarendon Press, 1983), pp. 9–44; Angelo Poliziano, *Opera omnia*, ed. I. Maier, 3 vols. (Turin: Bottega d'Erasmo, 1971).

cultural as well as military. The writings of the Venetian humanists were to provide an ideology that represented Venice's foreign and domestic policies as both rational and just to the rest of Italy and Europe. Like the Florentines, the Venetians subsidized histories – such as those of Francesco Contarini, Antonio Donato, Bernardo Giustiniani, and others – that glorified the state and its policies.

The first Greek scholars and teachers in Venice, as in Florence, were outsiders like Guarino da Veronese and Filelfo, who were sent to Constantinople as envoys of the patriciate to master the Greek language and to buy Greek books. Their sponsors were Venetian nobles – men such as Francesco Barbaro, Leonardo Giustiniani, and Marco Lippomano – whose wealth came from trade with the East and land holdings outside the sea-locked city of Venice.

While Guarino and Filelfo were expected to indoctrinate a new generation of Venetians in Greek philosophy, the studies in Plato and Neoplatonism so assiduously cultivated in Florence never took root in Venice. Medieval traditions grounded in Aristotle, Averroes, Aquinas, Scotus, and Ockham prevailed in Venice and at the University of Padua.[7] Influenced more by Aristotle's moral philosophy and the scholastics than by Cicero and Sallust, the Venetian humanist Giovanni Caldiera stressed the analogy between religious and élitist republican values in his trilogy, *On virtue*, *On economics*, and *On politics*.[8] For Caldiera, there was one God, one doge, and one paterfamilias; a citizen's loyalty to the state began with his *pietas* towards God and his family. The Venetian nobleman Lauro Quirini, writing on the question of political leadership and social class disagreed with the Florentine humanists who argued that men of low birth could aspire to government office if they had sufficient learning. He defended the Venetian oligarchy in his treatise *On nobility* by arguing that patricians alone were qualified to serve the state, and that nobility could only be acquired by heredity, not by education. Other works with a strong moral orientation, such as Francesco Barbaro's *On wifely duties*, celebrated a culture unapologetically patriarchal, misogynistic, and insular.[9]

Venetian conservatism continued to prevail throughout the second half of the fifteenth and the beginning of the sixteenth centuries – a conservatism reflected in the humanist programmes of the three public schools in Venice (the two *scuole di San Marco* and the Rialto school) and in the new printing-presses. The arrival of the Greek scholar, editor, and printer

---

[7] Paul Oskar Kristeller, *Renaissance thought: the classic, scholastic, and humanistic strains* (New York: Harper Torchbooks, 1961), pp. 24–69.
[8] Margaret L. King, *Venetian humanism in an age of patrician dominance* (Princeton: Princeton University Press, 1985), pp. 98–157; on Caldiera see pp. 101–3; on Quirini, pp. 119–23.
[9] Text in Kohl and Witt (ed.), *The earthly republic*, pp. 179–228.

Aldus Manutius in Venice in the 1490s strengthened Venice's position as the centre of the publishing industry in Italy, while the Aldine press abetted the humanist programme of canonizing a select group of texts from the ancient world. Attracting humanists from all over Italy to his workshop, Aldus initiated the practice of printing larger and cheaper editions of books. The rise of printing in Venice was accompanied by the advancement – led by Ermolao Barbaro the Younger, Girolamo Donato, Marcantonio Sabellico, and Aldus himself – of a new scientific approach to textual criticism that placed emphasis on philological and grammatical expertise over the civic concerns of an earlier generation of humanists.

Venice and the cities of the Veneto also witnessed the rise to prominence of three women humanists in the fifteenth century, Isotta Nogarola of Verona, Laura Cereta of Brescia, and the Venetian scholar, Cassandra Fedele, each of whom left published collections of letters and other writings in Latin.[10] Both Cereta's and Fedele's letters present a persona that is self-consciously female and one that differs radically from the male humanist model. Only Cereta, however, Italy's first feminist writer, addresses her epistolary criticism to the problems of women as a class.

*

In Milan, institutional support for literature and the arts was centred in the ducal court in the fifteenth century. Here Milan differed from Florence and Venice, where the sources of humanist patronage were more varied and diffuse. Financial support for the university at Pavia, for literature and the arts, and the dispensation of diplomatic and chancellery appointments (posts entirely occupied by humanist writers) all depended on the good-will of the duke.

Economically, Milan resembled the oligarchical republics of Venice and Florence more than it did other monarchies in Renaissance Italy. While Milan continued to be a centre for the manufacture of clothing and arms throughout the fifteenth century, nonetheless the duchy remained dependent on revenues raised from the taxation of the client cities it controlled.[11]

While four successive lords of Milan had proved, by the middle of the century, that they could equal or surpass the power of Florence and Venice in war, culturally Milan still stood in the shadow of those two cities. The university at Pavia lacked the standing of the great medieval universities

[10] For relevant texts, see Margaret L. King and Albert Rabil, Jr. (ed.), *Her immaculate hand: selected works by and about the women humanists of Quattrocento Italy* (Binghamton: State University of New York Press, 1983); Albert Rabil, Jr., *Laura Cereta: Quattrocento humanist* (Binghamton: State University of New York Press, 1981).

[11] Francesco Cognasso, 'Il ducato visconteo e la reppublica ambrosiana', in *Storia di Milano*, ed. G. Martini, 16 vols. (Milan: Fondazione Treccani degli Alfieri, 1953–66), vol. VI, pp. 387–448.

of Bologna and Padua, while its faculty lacked the political clout of the Florentine professors. The most famous of the Greek refugee scholars – Johannes Argyropulos, Demetrius Castrenus, Demetrius Chalcondylas, Callistus, Gaza, and Constantine Lascaris – all taught briefly in Milan and Pavia, but moved on after a year or two to Florence, Rome, or Naples.[12]

By the opening of the fifteenth century, such luminaries as the Byzantine ambassador to Italy, Manuel Chysoloras, and Gasparino Barzizza, who taught Filelfo, Panormita, and Alberti at Padua, had already been active in Milan. In the 1430s, however, the Duke of Milan, Filippo Maria Visconti, gave humanism its first real impetus. Though privately Visconti professed a preference for vernacular over Latin literature, he was expected as lord of Milan to retain Latin-speaking orators who could act as foreign envoys, write letters and policy statements, and compose speeches, poems, and *novelle* to be read at court in that language. Other well-known scholars active at the Visconti court in the 1420s and 1430s included Giovanni Lamola and Flavio Biondo, who left Milan for Florence, and Antonio Beccadelli (Panormita), Bartolomeo Facio, and Lorenzo Valla, all three of whom eventually left Milan for the court of King Alfonso in Naples.

When Milan went to war with Florence in 1397–1402, the humanists in those cities waged an ideological battle over the ideal form of government. Antonio Loschi defended monarchy as the perfect state, while the Florentine chancellor Salutati praised republican government and the ideal of *libertas*. The debate was revived in the late 1420s when the two imperial city-states each fought to gain hegemony for itself over the city of Lucca. In his *Encomium of the city of Florence*, Leonardo Bruni put forward claims that made the élitist republic in Florence sound like a socialist utopia, while Pier Candido Decembrio in his *Panegyric for the city of Milan* praised monarchy as the best of all forms of government.[13] But republican ideals – not of Cicero's republic but of the medieval communes – were still alive in mid-fifteenth-century Milan. In 1447, a coalition of Milanese noblemen and city guildsmen replaced the Visconti monarchy with a popular republican government.[14]

The dominant figure in Milan's cultural scene in the last half of the fifteenth century, Francesco Filelfo, a professor of literature educated in Constantinople and Padua, had taught at Florence, Venice, and Bologna before coming to the Visconti court.[15] After arriving in Milan in 1440, he

[12] See Eugenio Garin, 'La cultura milanese nella metà del xv secolo', in *Storia di Milano*, ed. Martini, vol. vi, pp. 545–608.
[13] See Hans Baron, *The crisis of the early Italian Renaissance* (Princeton: Princeton University Press, 1966), pp. 69–70.
[14] On the republic's critics, see Diana Robin, *Filelfo in Milan: writings 1451–1477* (Princeton: Princeton University Press, 1991), pp. 85–103.
[15] See Garin, 'La cultura milanese', in *Storia di Milano*, ed. Martini, vol. vi, pp. 545–608; Robin, *Filelfo in Milan*, pp. 3–10, 82–110.

served four successive Milanese dukes as court poet and orator. Well known throughout Italy for his Greek scholarship and the major collection of Greek poems he wrote, he brought a succession of distinguished Byzantine professors of Greek to Milan. His Latin letters contain essays critical of the abuses perpetrated against civilian populations during the Milanese wars of succession, the corruption that existed under the two years of popular republican rule in Milan, and the imperialist agenda of both superpowers, Milan and Venice.

Political commentary and criticism as well as propaganda proved to be a major industry among the Milanese humanists. Pier Candido Decembrio, Giovanni Simonetta, the Piacenzan Antonio di Ripalta, and later Bernardino Corio all produced profiles of the Sforza dukes, their military campaigns, and their times.

*

Two other regional centres of humanism – Rome and Naples – must be considered separately for their different castings of the classical revival in Italy. Compared to the thriving cities of the north, Rome and Naples were still economic backwaters in the fifteenth century. While the established industries early on in fifteenth-century Rome were jewellery making, innkeeping, and international banking, it was not until the 1470s that mining and manufacture of iron, the production of silk, and printing were introduced by King Ferrante to the vast rural kingdom of Naples.[16]

Roman humanism differed from that of other cities because of the pervasive influence of the papacy in its cultural affairs. In Rome, humanism evolved as a constant reweaving of the ideologies of ancient Rome as *caput mundi* and empire, of papal rule, and of Thomist theology.[17] Fifteenth-century Rome was not, however, a cultural monolith in the sense that humanist Naples was. Although the papal court was the hub of cultural production in humanist Rome, there were also other centres of intellectual activity: principally, the patronage-dispensing *familiae* or households of cardinals, diplomats, and bankers residing in the city, the informal learned 'academies' of *amici*, the university, and influential presses such as that of Pannartz and Sweynheym.

Humanism came a little later to Rome than to the cities of the north. The first of the humanist popes, Nicholas V, assembled one of the most important libraries of classical texts in Europe; he commissioned translations

---

[16] Jerry Bentley, *Politics and culture in Renaissance Naples* (Princeton: Princeton University Press, 1987), p. 27.

[17] Charles Stinger, *The Renaissance in Rome* (Bloomington: Indiana University Press, 1985), pp. 1–13; John D'Amico, 'Humanism in Rome', in *Renaissance humanism, foundations, forms, and legacy*, ed. A. Rabil, Jr., 3 vols. (Philadelphia: University of Pennsylvania Press, 1988), vol. 1, pp. 264–95.

of the ancient Greek authors, and he brought some of the most distinguished scholars, critics, and poets in Italy to Rome. The next two popes,
Calixtus III and Pius II, were preoccupied with the planning of a military
mission to liberate Constantinople from Turkish rule; neither contributed
materially to the work of the humanists. After Pius II's death, Paul II made
open war on one of the most prominent humanist academies of the period,
that of Pomponio Leto, arresting and ordering the torture of members of
Leto's circle whom he charged with promoting republicanism, Platonism,
and sodomy in the Vatican state. The last two popes to distinguish the papal
throne before the sack of Rome in 1527, Julius II and Leo X, brought to
the papal court men thought to be among the best Latin stylists in Italy.

Among the prominent intellectual *familiae* and academies in Rome, the
circle of Greek refugee scholars, philosophers, and theologians around the
Byzantine exile, Cardinal Bessarion, included Theodore Gaza, Andronicus
Callistus, Domizio Calderini, Niccolò Perotti, and George of Trebizond.
Influenced by Ficino and the Florentine academy, their writings and debates
during the 1450s–1470s show an increasing interest in synthesizing the
thought of Plato and Aristotle with the Christian theologians.[18] Other
Roman academies prominent at the end of the century such as those of
Paolo Cortesi and Johann Goritz focused their efforts on the cultivation
of Latin eloquence, an activity some Roman humanists found politically
safer than the study of Greek philosophy.

Humanism in Naples differed from northern Italian humanism because
of the dominance of the king in every aspect of Neapolitan culture. There
were no educational or political institutions – no public or independent
schools, libraries, universities, no senate, or council – and no significant
aristocratic patronage that existed outside the ducal court.

The chief figures of Neapolitan humanism included writers and scholars
who came to Naples from the metropolitan cities of the north: Giannozzo
Manetti from Florence; Lorenzo Valla and Antonio Beccadelli (Panormita)
who both had worked in Milan; and the Greek emigré scholars Theodore
Gaza, George of Trebizond, and Constantine Lascaris, who had taught in
such cities as Venice, Milan, and Rome before coming south. The self-image
fostered by the first Aragonese king of Naples, Alfonso, and his humanist
propagandists was more like that of a provincial condottiere-prince than
that of the head of one of the leading city-states in Italy. Alfonso com-
manded his own troops in battle, and encamped with his court writers
at his side.

While criticism languished under the absolute despotism of the Aragonese
kings, the Neapolitan humanists wrote lyric poetry. Two long-lived humanist

---

[18] John Monfasani, *George of Trebizond. a biography and a study of his rhetoric and logic*
      (Leiden: Brill, 1976).

academies flourished at the court of Naples: the first presided over by Panormita, and the second by Giovanni Pontano. Departing from the Latin satires and critical essays of the Quattrocento humanists in the north, Pontano's fellow academicians Il Chariteo and Sannazaro wrote vernacular eclogues in the style of Virgil while he himself composed piscatorial and pastoral poems in Latin.

*

But Naples was the exception. Throughout the rest of Italy the critical essay, replacing in the fifteenth century the exegetical, line-by-line commentary of prior centuries, was – whether framed as a letter, an oration, a dialogue, or a poem – an essential feature of Renaissance humanism. Sometimes this new criticism focused simply on the solving of a textual crux, or on a question of form, style or influence. More often than not, however, the humanist scholar of literature, the textual critic, the excavator of lost classical texts was also politically engaged, whether he or she posed as a poet, historian, philosopher, or a dispassionate critic of culture and society.

36

German-speaking centres and institutions

James A. Parente, Jr.

The production of literature in early modern Germany was conditioned by the complex socio-political organization of the Holy Roman Empire. In contrast to other Western European lands, the Empire lacked a vibrant literary capital, similar to Paris, London, or Madrid, that functioned as a centre of learning, a gathering place for aspiring intellectuals, and a mass market for the consumption of their works. Book publication was scattered throughout the Empire from major printers in Frankfurt, Leipzig, and Strasburg to smaller presses at individual courts. Literary criticism was similarly dispersed, and only a few works, such as Martin Opitz's *Buch von der deutschen Poeterey* (1624), attained an influence that transcended the boundaries of an imperial city or territory. The flowering of poetological speculation at a particular place and time was most often determined by the presence of a single energetic person, or an unusually productive group of poets, but their influence frequently remained limited to their immediate environment and ended with their deaths.

Literary criticism in the Empire was generally produced in two places: the courts, both secular and ecclesiastical, and the cities, at municipal grammar schools, gymnasia, and universities or at private gatherings of poets in literary societies. Occasionally, the courts were the prime sponsors of the schools, as was the case in Heidelberg where the Count of the Palatinate appointed the first humanist lecturers in the 1450s, or in late sixteenth-century Munich where the ruling Wittelsbach family financed the ambitious Counter-Reformation programme at the Jesuit gymnasium. Writing about literature was carried out by the functionaries of these courts or schools, whose primary duties lay elsewhere, in education, law, theology, local government, and, less frequently, medicine and natural science. Despite these professional differences, most authors had received the same educational background in Renaissance humanism. They were well versed in Greco-Roman letters, ancient rhetoric and its Renaissance adaptations, and in Renaissance notions of literature and poetic composition. They wrote proficiently in Latin and German, and often in other European languages. And they shared the desire to demonstrate German poetic talent by emulating the ancients, and in the seventeenth century, by establishing German as a literary language equal in expressiveness and elegance to other Western European vernaculars.

Renaissance notions of literature first appeared north of the Alps in the early fifteenth century when humanist-schooled Italian scholars, chiefly clerics and lawyers, were chosen by northern princes for university positions and administrative offices at court. The most famous of these Italian guests was Enea Silvio Piccolomini, the future Pius II, who as imperial secretary (1443–5) to Emperor Friedrich III, promoted the study of antiquity and impressed his contemporaries with his unencumbered Latin style. By the 1450s, German humanists who had been trained in Italy, such as the poet Petrus Luder, the lawyer Albrecht von Eyb, and the physician Heinrich Steinhöwel, spread Renaissance ideas about antiquity and literary composition in their lectures (Luder) and German translations of Greco-Roman and recent Italian writers. Vienna, the imperial capital, and the leading cities of several secular and ecclesiastical principalities (Cologne, Heidelberg, Tübingen, Strasburg, Basle, Leipzig, Wittenberg, Nuremberg, Augsburg, Ingolstadt) became gathering places for these new scholars, who were engaged as secretaries, librarians, tutors, ambassadors, councillors, orators, historians, physicians, or municipal functionaries. Besides their official duties, many early humanists, such as Conrad Celtes and Johannes Cuspinianus at the court of Emperor Maximilian I (ruled 1493–1519), lectured on ancient writers at the local university and composed poetry that glorified the ruling authorities. In recognition of their accomplishments, the Holy Roman Emperor followed the ancient tradition of designating the loyal poet a 'poeta laureatus', crowning him with a wreath of laurel and granting him special privileges and a stipend. This power was soon transferred to local territorial princes, and shortly thereafter, most humanist centres possessed their own poet laureates, or had profited from such a personage's sojourn in their community.

Many humanist poets in the late fifteenth century also gathered in informal groups (*collegium*; *contubernium*; *sodalitas*) to discuss the recovery of the Greco-Roman past, edit and publish the works of the ancients or medieval German imitators of antiquity (for example, Hrotsvitha von Gandersheim), and create poetic works that gave evidence of antiquity's afterlife in northern Europe. Occasionally the members of a poetic circle collaborated on an edition or a literary composition, but they chiefly abetted their colleagues' ambitions by criticizing their writings, or by seeing their works through the press. The earliest officially established literary sodality, the *Sodalitas litteraria per Germaniam* (or *Sodalitas Rhenana*), was headed by Johann von Dahlberg, the Bishop of Worms and chancellor of the University of Heidelberg, who fostered the dream of Conrad Celtes to create a German equivalent of the Italian *accademia*, similar to Marsilio Ficino's in Florence or to Pomponio Leto's in Rome. Similar groups were established in Vienna and Cracow, where humanists had been meeting since the 1450s, and with less pomp in Cologne, Erfurt (the circle of Mutianus

Rufus), Augsburg, Nuremberg, and Strasburg, and still more modestly, in
Olmütz (Olomouc) and Linz. There is only scant evidence of what trans-
pired at sodality meetings, whose members rarely met but communicated
through an extensive correspondence. In 1497, at a gathering of the Rhenish
sodality at the house of Johann von Dahlberg, for example, a Latin drama
by Johannes Reuchlin was performed with much success by students at
the university. But the correspondence of many humanists reveals a more
sanguine, and perhaps even a more accurate, picture: after the official
poetry recitations and critiques, the sodality meetings often degenerated
into drinking parties, in the tradition of the 'turba philosophorum',
populated by boisterous musicians and prostitutes.

With the onset of the Reformation, the literary circles that still continued to meet, disintegrated. The constitution of these organizations
had been rather tenuous – only the *sodalitas Rhenana* appears to have
established a unified programme and code of behaviour, though this
document is lost – and the internecine controversies that broke out over
the value of Hebrew in the 1510s and of Luther in the 1520s hastened
the collapse. Subsequent literary-critical discussions were confined to the
scholarly activities of Protestant and Catholic educators. Many of Philipp
Melanchthon's theories of literature appeared in his editions and translations (Greek into Latin) of an author's works for his students in Wittenberg, or in his correspondence with other humanists, such as Joachim
Camerarius, who were engaged in similar editorial activities. Joachim
Vadianus [Watt], the author of the earliest comprehensive poetics in the
Empire (*De poetica et carminis ratione liber*, 1518) composed his work
while lecturing on the subject in Vienna; and the Greek specialist, Jacob
Micyllus [Moltzer], published his important metrical text, *De re metrica*
(1539), while revising the curriculum at the gymnasium in Frankfurt for
Lutheran students. The absence of a central institution to which all these
scholars belonged meant that literary discussions took place through correspondence. In the Empire, more than any other European land, humanists fostered the utopian vision of a *respublica litteraria* to compensate for
their geographical isolation. There were, of course, specific periods in particular places in which intellectual life in the sixteenth century seemed unusually lively: Wittenberg in the 1520s and 1530s around Melanchthon;
the Strasburg gymnasium in the 1580s and 1590s with an extensive
humanist programme in rhetoric, poetry, and history; and Heidelberg
in the 1590s and early 1600s where poets such as Paul Melissus Schede
and Julius Wilhelm Zincgref attempted to introduce the poetic reforms of
the Pléiade into Latin and German verse. With the exception of the compendious poetics of Georg Fabricius [Goldschmied] (*De re poetica*, 1565),
rector of the Fürstenschule at Meißen, and of Jacob Pontanus [Jacob Span-
müller] (*Poeticarum institutionum libri tres*, 1594), a Jesuit priest and

gymnasium director in Augsburg, few literary-theoretical works between 1550 and 1600 were ever published, and little literary-critical discussion took place.

In the early seventeenth century, writing about poetry outside the confines of educational institutions once again occurred. In 1617, the establishment of *Die Fruchtbringende Gesellschaft* (FG), the first of the many so-called language societies (*Sprachgesellschaften*) of the Baroque period, by Prince Ludwig von Anhalt-Köthen, reawakened interest in the potentiality of German as a literary language and the need for the creation of an (albeit late) Renaissance literature similar to recent developments in France, Italy, the Netherlands, Spain, and, to a lesser extent, England. Ludwig, a member of the Accademia della Crusca, had been impressed by that organization's purification of the Italian language from linguistic barbarisms, and its progress towards an ideal vernacular literary speech. Eager to introduce similar principles to the Empire, he, along with a small circle of noble relatives and acquaintances, founded the FG. As its name intimated, the society was devoted to pruning the German language so that its poets would produce the finest fruits. Ludwig and his followers hoped to achieve this goal in two ways. First, they attempted to create a unified German language, free from ambiguous regionalisms and archaisms, and a standardized German grammar as fundaments of elegant writing. As customary elsewhere in Europe, the normative language was deemed a vernacular speech informed by Greco-Roman rhetoric; poetological norms were similarly derived from Greco-Roman literary practice. Secondly, they attempted to enrich the literary vocabulary of German by compiling lists of *Stammwörter*, which were of ancient origins – extending, so they believed, to the time of Adam – and, by nature, accurate and logical expressions of meaning. With this base, they planned to enrich the German language, to expand its *copia verborum*, through new combinations of these *Stämme*, based on their study and translation of Greco-Roman, and, more significantly, recent Renaissance works. Thanks to these efforts, the stylistic modes of expression of ancient genres (for example, pastoral, epic) were greatly expanded, and reworkings of newer literary forms (for example, the novel) appeared in German. Ludwig himself translated Petrarch's *Trionfi*, and fellow members Diederich von dem Werder and Tobias Hübner translated extensively from sixteenth-century French and Italian literature (for example, Ariosto, Du Bartas, Tasso).

In addition to its linguistic functions, the FG was established to nurture the preservation of German virtue. Correct social deportment and a righteous character were regarded as essential qualities for all scholars of German and for German poets. Such ethical requirements recalled the Greco-Roman insistence on the orator's (and, in the Renaissance, the poet's) exemplary character, but also appealed to the aristocratic ideal of the *gentilhomme*, embraced by Ludwig and his noble companions.

The ties between the members were further enhanced by their adoption of society names (for example, 'Der Nährende' for Prince Ludwig), the assumption of a device, usually drawn from nature (for example, a particular plant, flower, or tree), and a verse saying that corresponded to the member's character. Ludwig also strove for the elimination of class boundaries between the various members, not only between the learned bourgeoisie and the aristocrats, but between the greater and lesser nobility, and for the smoothing of religious differences (there were few clerics in the group). But such grand egalitarian designs remained utopian fantasies, especially after Ludwig's death in 1650. Despite the intentions of its founders, the FG gradually functioned more as an élite club for aristocrats who were more gentlemen than scholars, rather than as an institutional leader of poetic reform.

Other language societies evolved in the first half of the seventeenth century with similar linguistic, literary, and ethical intentions. Three of these played a major role in the development of German literature and criticism: the *Deutschgesinnete Genossenschaft* (1642/3; DG); the *Pegnesischer Blumenorden* (1644; PBO); and the *Elbschwanenorden* (1658; ESO). In contrast to the FG, the membership in these societies was primarily bourgeoisie, though some patricians and landed nobility were included. Each of these groups emphasized a different approach to the revitalization of German language and literature. The DG, which was based in Hamburg, reflected the linguistic interests of its founder, the prolific, idiosyncratic poet Philipp von Zesen. Zesen was a tireless student of German etymology and orthography, and in his enthusiasm to eradicate all foreign elements from the vernacular, he invented German equivalents for many words with non-Germanic origins. For example, the German word for window, *Fenster*, which was derived from the Latin *fenestra*, was now replaced by Zesen's 'tage-leuchter'. Zesen composed several poetological works explicating his theories, and he introduced his reforms into his poetry, his numerous translations of seventeenth-century French novels, and his own original prose works. Although his orthographic programme found few imitators, his extensive prose writings considerably advanced the development of the novel in German.

Zesen regarded his society as an heir to earlier associations of Germanic poets, the late medieval meistersingers and the Dutch chambers of rhetoric (*Rederijkers*), where correct usage had been strictly enforced. In contrast, the patrician Georg Philipp Harsdörffer and his co-founder, Johann Klaj, the initiators of the PBO, sought to re-create the pastoral idyll of antiquity in contemporary Nuremberg. More than any other language society, the PBO produced an extensive corpus of literature and literary criticism that reflected the cosmopolitan taste of its members and contributed to the development of many innovative poetic forms. The founding document of the PBO was a pastoral novel in which Harsdörffer and his followers, bearing names from Sir Philip Sidney's *Arcadia*, experimented with different metres, the onomatopoeic range of German in their new, so-called *Klinggedichte*, and the boundaries between words and images (*Bildgedichte*). These innovative activities continued in Harsdörffer's *Frauenzimmer Gesprächspiele*, which contained original poems, translations, especially from French and Italian lyric and prose, an early German-language libretto, and elegant conversations on contemporary music, poetry, politics, and intellectual life. Johann Klaj, the other founding member, explored the traditional distinctions between genres with his *Redeoratorien* that combined music, lyrical verse, and grandiose visual images. And Harsdörffer's successor, Sigmund von Birken, not only composed a new voluminous poetics (*Teutsche Rede-bind- und Dicht-kunst*, 1679), but also contributed to the development of the pastoral and German novel theory.

The achievements of the other main seventeenth-century language society, the ESO, founded in the north German town of Wedel by the Lutheran pastor-poet Johann Rist, were more modest. Rist's circle typified the small private gatherings of writers that took place throughout the Empire during the seventeenth century, which, like the sodalities of the late 1400s, served as workshops for poetic composition and publication. In contrast to the other main societies, the membership in Rist's group was composed mostly of pastors, and as a consequence concentrated on composing poems for musical accompaniment and hymns. Similarly parochial ambitions were also shared by the poets' circle around Simon Dach and Heinrich Albert in Königsberg, the so-called *Kürbishütte* group, where the poets met in Albert's garden to inscribe some of their verses on pumpkins, symbols of the transitoriness of the world. Other literary societies arose in Strasburg: *Die aufrichtige Tannengesellschaft* (founded 1633; dissolved in 1658), which followed the FG's attempt to purify German; and the intimate *Poetisches Kleeblatt*, founded in 1671, whose name reflected the size of its initial membership (3). Many of these organizations disappeared in the late seventeenth century with the death of the founder, or after two or three successive leaders, but the idea of a literary society for the mutual criticism of its members' poetic writings continued into the 1700s. The last groups that met primarily for literary purposes were the *Teutschschreibende Gesellschaft*, active in Hamburg between 1715 and 1717, whose founders, the poet B. H. Brockes and the philologist Michael Richey, encouraged debate on literary theory and poetic composition; and Johann Christoph Gottsched's *Deutsche Gesellschaft* (re-established in 1727) that became a platform for the neoclassical poetological ideas of his

Versuch einer critischen Dichtkunst vor die Deutschen (1730). Among these male-dominated societies (only the DG and PBO had female members), the short-lived Académie des Loyales (1617–25), founded by Anna von Anhalt-Bernburg, the sister-in-law of Ludwig von Anhalt-Köthen, remained exceptional for its exclusively female membership (all noblewomen), its dedication to the translation of French and Italian Renaissance literature, and its disregard for original German-language composition.

In addition to these language societies and poets' circles, writing about literature continued at universities and gymnasia throughout the Empire. Augustus Buchner, whose *Anleitung zur deutschen Poeterey* was published posthumously in 1663, taught at Wittenberg University; Daniel Morhof (*Unterricht von der Teutschen Sprache und Poesie*, 1682) was professor of rhetoric and poetry at the newly founded (1665) university in Kiel; and the neoclassical Francophile, Christian Thomasius, lectured at Leipzig and Halle. These university professors not only presented their own theories, but also promoted the poetological ideas of works composed outside of academic circles. The most widely read of all Baroque poetics, for example, Martin Opitz's *Buch von der deutschen Poeterey* (1624), written while Opitz was serving the Silesian Duke of Liegnitz, was critiqued, expanded, and disseminated by, among others, Buchner and Andreas Tscherning. The lectures and published works of these academicians also influenced the poetological ideas of many language-society members such as G. P. Harsdörffer and Sigmund von Birken. With the demise of these societies in the early eighteenth century, literary-critical ideas became increasingly confined to lecture halls and only attained a broader audience through their appearance in monthly or weekly journals to which many academics contributed.

37

Courts and patronage

Michael Schoenfeldt

Although not often linked to the issue of literary criticism, patronage, as the dominant social relationship in Renaissance Europe, inevitably affected the processes of literary judgement. Before and amid the emergence of a market economy of literary relations, most writers depended upon the support and/or the goodwill of the rich and powerful. 'Since both poets and critics were closely connected with the ruling aristocracies, either by birth or by the system of patronage', remarks Vernon Hall in one of the few works to consider the social dimensions of literary criticism, 'their definition [of poetry] was in aristocratic terms'. The Renaissance, Hall argues, founds its literary categories on the grounds of social rather than aesthetic discrimination.[1] Almost every work of literature produced in the Renaissance bore some mark of the hierarchical organization of the society in which it was produced. Through an elaborate system of reward, patrons sustained certain genres, styles, and authors; at the same time, they actively discouraged others by means of sanctions that ranged from simple stinginess to active censorship and corporal punishment. Because they emphasize the ways that political forces impinge on the very aesthetic values that purport to transcend the grimy world of politics, recent developments in criticism – particularly American new historicism and British cultural materialism – have prepared us to attend anew to the relationship between structures of political power and the practices of literary criticism in the Renaissance.

A central problem in Renaissance literary criticism – the establishment of the vernacular as a legitimate medium for literary utterance – is itself in part a function of the effect of courtly power on aesthetic choice. In France, Joachim du Bellay, author of the *La deffence et illustration de la langue françoyse* (1549), openly appealed to nationalistic sentiment, making it the patriotic duty of every writer to use vernacular French. In England, a series of writers including Sir Philip Sidney and Edmund Spenser attempted to make the vernacular the equivalent of classical languages by deliberately imitating classical metres in English verse in

---

[1] *Renaissance literary criticism: a study of its social content* (New York: Columbia University Press, 1945), p. 231.

order to produce what Spenser calls the 'kingdom of our own language'.[2] Likewise, the Renaissance taxonomy of the genres located aesthetics in a classificatory organization that paralleled in many ways the social and political hierarchy. The resulting emphasis on the aesthetic value of decorum – making certain kinds of speech appropriate to certain genres – enforced the fusion of criteria that were at once social and aesthetic. Moreover, the Renaissance placement of epic as the highest genre was in part a response to the pressure that courts could exert upon aesthetic judgement, since epic was the genre most fully concerned with the founding of empires. The widespread ambition to compose an epic issued from the desire to do for one's own country what Virgil had done for Augustan Rome – to establish a national mythology.[3]

As a result of the wealth and influence which they by definition possess, courts proved to be particularly active sites of practical literary criticism. The great Renaissance courts set the styles that were imitated all over the kingdom, and that supplied the standard for other European realms. Throughout the period a continual and dynamic interplay emerges between the aesthetics of courtly behaviour and the fashions of literary taste. Baldesar Castiglione's *Il libro del cortegiano* (1528), the most popular guide to courtly conduct in the period, subordinated the composition of poetry to the larger goal of winning the prince's favour in order to lead him to virtue. But as Daniel Javitch asserts, the model of court conduct Castiglione's work puts forward shares many features with literary aesthetics.[4] Life at court, and literature produced at court, required the exploitation of opportunities for irony, ambiguity, paradox, and equivocation. Indeed, not only did Castiglione's work affect the processes of literary judgement but George Puttenham's *Arte of English poesie* (1589), a work professing to be a guide to poetic composition, proved to be a virtual conduct book for courtiers. Puttenham argues tellingly that 'beau semblant' – the art of honest dissimulation – is 'the chiefe profession as well of Courting as of poesie'.[5] Relatedly, the unique trait that Castiglione

[2] See Derek Attridge, *Well-weighed syllables: Elizabethan verse in classical metres* (London: Cambridge University Press, 1974), and the discussion of the nationalistic goals of such aesthetic experimentation in Richard Helgerson, *Forms of nationhood: the Elizabethan writing of England* (Chicago: University of Chicago Press, 1992). The first work in this vein was Dante's *De vulgari eloquentia*.

[3] In France, the most famous product of this desire was probably Pierre de Ronsard's *La Franciade* (1572); in England, it was Edmund Spenser's *The Faerie Queene* (1590; 1596), which glorified England's courtly present by staging that present in terms of its feudal past.

[4] *Poetry and courtliness in Renaissance England* (Princeton: Princeton University Press, 1978). In *Ambition and privilege: the social tropes of Elizabethan courtesy theory* (Berkeley: University of California Press, 1984), Frank Whigham argues further for the rhetoricity of courtly identity, asserting that courtesy literature 'articulate[s] a sophisticated rhetoric, indeed an epistemology, of personal social identity', p. xi.

[5] *The arte of English poesie*, ed. G. D. Willcock and A. Walker (Cambridge: Cambridge University Press, 1936), p. 158.

bestows upon his ideal courtier – *sprezzatura*, an artificial spontaneity, or a studied nonchalance which allowed one to contrive naturalness – emerges from the cusp of aesthetics and behaviour. Castiglione's emphasis upon the aristocratic avoidance of laboured affectation had an immense impact on subsequent aesthetics, and their place in society, discouraging members of the nobility from printing their literary works, and encouraging an aesthetic whereby the finest work of art is produced by a labour which it at once conceals and discloses.[6]

Castiglione offers, moreover, profound insight into the ways that the pressures of courtly existence produce an aesthetic of secrecy in writing. The writer is not only to disguise the artifice that produces the literary artefact but also to blend opacity and clarity in the language from which the artefact is constructed: 'if the words which a writer uses have in them a little, I will not say difficulty, but subtlety that is hidden . . . they do give a certain greater authority to the writing and cause the reader to proceed with more restraint and concentration, to reflect more, and to enjoy the talent and the doctrine of the writer'. The cultivated hermeticism Castiglione describes at once protects the writer from the charge of dealing too explicitly with current affairs and generates a social bond of coterie experience with knowing readers.[7] Likewise, the Renaissance courtly penchant for pastoral derived not from an anthropological fascination with the speech of actual shepherds but rather from the capacity of the form to address matters of state under the veil of apparently simple figures.[8] To read such a genre well is to comprehend the covert political *negotium* lurking within the pastoral *otium*.

Literary criticism is further influenced by the pressures of patronage in the fact that so much of the literary criticism of the period is executed in prefatory material, deliberately interwoven with deferential addresses to the powerful, whose favour a writer hopes to earn or sustain. Dedication after dedication declares the patron of the work to be at once its inspiration, its best reader, its protector, and (if necessary) its censor. Annabel Patterson makes a compelling claim for the intimate connection between courtly politics and literary aesthetics, arguing that the historical pressures of censorship paradoxically produced what the twentieth century

---

[6] See J. W. Saunders, 'The stigma of print: a note on the social bases of Tudor poetry', *Essays in criticism* 1 (1951), 139–64.

[7] *The book of the courtier*, trans. C. S. Singleton (Garden City: Anchor Books, 1959), p. 49. On the tactical deployment of secrecy, see Lois Potter, *Secret rites and secret writing: royalist literature 1641–1660* (Cambridge: Cambridge University Press, 1989), and Richard Rambuss, *Spenser's secret career* (Cambridge: Cambridge University Press, 1993).

[8] See the influential articles by Louis Montrose: ' "Eliza, queene of shepheardes," and the pastoral of power', *English literary Renaissance* 10 (1980), 153–82, and 'Of gentlemen and shepherds: the politics of Elizabethan pastoral form', *English literary history* 50 (1983), 415–59.

came to think of as the unhistorical realm of 'the literary' by encouraging an aesthetic of the encoded message that demanded the close reading so valued by the new criticism. Political necessity thus produced an esoteric style that subsequent readers elevated to an aesthetic principle. But court censorship, Richard Burt reminds us, frequently involved a relationship of collaboration rather than repression between writer and censor. Burt argues that we should imagine censorship itself as a particularly inter-ventionist mode of practical literary criticism, a practice that generates the frequently productive parameters of literary utterance.[9]

Despite such potential complicities between the production and the censorship of literature, literary criticism often arises in the period from the need to justify the very existence of imaginative literature to those figures of power who would censor or outlaw it. Since Plato banished poetry from his Republic, the utility of poetry to the state was in a per-petual state of interrogation. Among the attractions of didactic literary theory was the fact that such justification was comparatively easy.[10] But among the demerits of such theory was that it necessarily shared so much common ground with the detractors of poetry, since both apologists and attackers emphasized poetry's capacity to move its audience. The apolo-gists of course stressed that poetry could move to virtue, but the detractors could reply that vice was an equally likely goal. Sir Philip Sidney, courtier and author of the finest English critical essay of the sixteenth century, *An apology for poetry* (written 1581–3), conceded that literature was not innocent of the world. All he could argue was that it could make the world better, not worse. The post-Romantic notion of a disinterested aesthetic realm was blissfully unavailable to Renaissance literary theor-ists. Literature expresses moral doctrine forcefully, Sidney argues, and makes it more plausible, thus making its readers better people. If those readers are also princes or advisers, thus making the writer a kind of courtier, this is all to the good.

'The end' of poetry, argues the influential Franco-Italian critic Julius Caesar Scaliger, 'is the giving of instruction in pleasurable form, for poetry teaches, and does not simply amuse, as some used to think'.[11] As such, poetry is an important extension of the humanist goal of bettering the world through education. 'Since literature was considered to be both educative and disciplinary', argues Hall, 'the task of the poet and the

[9] Annabel Patterson, *Censorship and interpretation: the conditions of reading and writing in early modern England* (Madison: University of Wisconsin Press, 1984); Richard Burt, *Licensed by authority: Ben Jonson and the discourses of censorship* (Ithaca: Cornell University Press, 1993).

[10] See Robert L. Montgomery, *The reader's eye: studies in didactic literary theory from Dante to Tasso* (Berkeley: University of California Press, 1979).

[11] F. M. Padelford, *Select translations from Scaliger's 'Poetics'* (New York: Henry Holt, 1905), p. 2.

critic was no less than the remolding of society'.[12] The Renaissance defence of poetry – based on its capacity to teach, to please, and to move – entailed traits necessary for thriving at court. As a result, poetry is frequently portrayed as a sugar-coated pill, a therapeutic if potentially bitter nugget wrapped in the delights of literary artifice. The close relationship between teaching and delighting that had been a central thrust of literary criticism at least since Horace demands that the issue of literary performance migrate within the parameters of courtly conduct. Much of the literary criticism in the Renaissance emerges in the fertile territory shared by political oratory and courtly behaviour.[13]

As a result of the various pressures that figures of power could exert upon writers, styles and genres blossomed and faded, subject to the taste of a prince or patron as well as to the ever-changing vagaries of court fashion. In England, John Hoskins describes the flexibility such stylistic shifts imposed upon aspiring courtiers: 'we study according to the predominancy of courtly inclinations . . . I have used and outworn six several styles since I was first Fellow of New College, and am yet able to bear the fashion of [the] writing company'.[14] Probably the most famous Renaissance patron of the arts, Lorenzo de' Medici, was himself a poet, and supported some of the most eminent writers, philosophers, and scholars of his time. A truly seminal figure in the emergence of Renaissance humanism, Lorenzo subsidized in part Marsilio Ficino's translation of the works of Plato into Latin, and thus made possible the vogue of Neoplatonism which swept Renaissance Europe, and in which Lorenzo's own poetry participated. Lorenzo was, moreover, a notably generous sponsor of Politian, the finest Greek scholar and textual editor in Italy at that time. Further north, Francis I of France created royal readerships in Hebrew, Greek, Latin, and mathematics, in what was to become the Collège de France, and founded a royal library whose contents he helped to publish. Philip IV of Spain, advised by the Count of Olivares, the king's favourite and principal minister, inaugurated the Golden Age of Spain by bringing to court such luminaries as Lope de Vega, Quevedo, Antonio de Mendoza, and Calderón de la Barca to sing the praises of the young king. In the England of Elizabeth I, love poetry thrived, as the metaphorics of amorous verse reflected the dynamics of suit, service, and recompense characteristic of a patronage society under a female monarch.[15] Throughout Europe,

[12] Hall, *Renaissance literary criticism*, p. 14.
[13] Indeed, G. K. Hunter argues that the submission of humanist ideals to the demands of courtly taste encouraged the growth of imaginative literature in Elizabethan England (*John Lyly, the humanist as courtier* (Cambridge, MA: Harvard University Press, 1962)).
[14] *Directions for speech and style* (c. 1599), ed. H. H. Hudson (Princeton: Princeton University Press, 1935), p. 39.
[15] Arthur Marotti, ' "Love is not love": Elizabethan sonnet sequences and the social order', *English literary history* 49 (1982), 396–428.

Renaissance courts had a powerful and direct impact on the literary tastes of the times.

The effect of the court upon literary fashion can be registered in the way that the change in monarchs in England from Elizabeth to James I precipitated a change in the predominant literary genre from Petrarchan lyrics to works of theology, philosophy, and history. James I, whose tastes varied widely from those of his predecessor, imagined himself as the English Solomon, and rewarded those writers whose works most effectively appealed to this self-image. The monarch thus played a major role in creating a socio-literary environment where some of the finest religious poetry ever written – the *Holy sonnets* and divine hymns of John Donne and *The temple* of George Herbert – was able to flourish. One can also measure the trajectory of this change in monarchs in the literary career of a courtier such as Sir Walter Ralegh. Showing great courtly dexterity, Ralegh strategically moves from the courtly performance of erotic supplication to Elizabeth in *A book of the ocean to Cynthia* (probably written in 1592, but not published until 1870) to his *History of the world* (1614), a work of courtly advice dedicated to Prince Henry, the heir to the English throne.[16]

One of the most successful poets at negotiating the patronage network under James and subsequently under his son Charles I was Ben Jonson, a figure so immersed in this network that Robert C. Evans has termed him a 'patronage poet'.[17] A confirmed classicist and a leading literary critic, Jonson demanded that poetry instruct and delight. Stylistically, he favoured verse that required clarity, directness, and economy, and criticized many of his contemporaries for their adherence to other aesthetic standards. Jonson inaugurated a mode of neoclassical verse, at once cool and graceful, polished and detached, that would become the primary model for cavalier poetry – the verse written by loyal followers of Charles I – and that would reach its apotheosis in the carefully balanced couplets of John Dryden and Alexander Pope.

Like Jonson a court poet and a powerful critic, Dryden was instrumental in developing this new courtly aesthetic. His *Essay of dramatick poesy* (1668) elevated rationalism, restraint, and the curtailment of free imagination to the pinnacle of aesthetic value, and made popular a new style based not on secrecy but rather on clarity. Along with Nicolas Boileau in France – whose *L'art poétique* was published in 1674 – Dryden offers a clear set of rules for the regulation of writing, including the notorious three unities of dramatic composition. In so doing, he inaugurates the

[16] Leonard Tennenhouse, 'Sir Walter Ralegh and the literature of clientage', in *Patronage in the Renaissance*, ed. G. F. Lytle and S. Orgel (Princeton: Princeton University Press, 1981), pp. 235–58.
[17] *Ben Jonson and the poetics of patronage* (Lewisburg: Bucknell University Press, 1989).

neoclassical privileging of reason and balance that was to dominate eighteenth-century aesthetics.

In contrast, Milton's *Paradise lost* (1667 in ten books; 1674 in twelve), in many ways the last work of the Renaissance, at least in England, deliberately repudiates the courtly rules that Dryden's literary and critical practice elevates. As a committed defender of the regicides and a member of Oliver Cromwell's revolutionary government, Milton rejects the contemporary courtly fashion of rhymed couplets in favour of blank verse. Terming rhyme 'the invention of a barbarous age, to set off wretched matter, and lame metre', Milton argues that rhyme arrests meaning in a way analogous to the processes by which monarchs suppress their subjects. For Milton, true poets are the enemies of monarchs, not their courtiers. In *Paradise lost*, moreover, Milton allows the fallen angels, particularly Belial and Satan, to represent the epitome of the courtly aesthetic of flexibility, irony, and persuasiveness this essay has sketched. In so doing, Milton, a poet whose social and political vision opposed the network of courts and patronage, shatters the fragile link between rhetoric and ethics that Renaissance literary criticism had attempted to establish. Writing an epic but repudiating the nationalism that had attracted Spenser and Ronsard among others to the genre, Milton undoes the connection drawn since Castiglione between courtly conduct and literary aesthetics.

Despite their immense differences in politics and aesthetics, Milton and Dryden together helped to disperse the influence of a centralized court on literature, the one by rejecting the court entirely, the other by cultivating sponsors among figures whose resources had little to do with the court. 'No longer dependent exclusively upon the court and its ramifications', argues J. W. Saunders, Augustan poetry 'flourished in every library of every country home, wherever it might be in the wide countryside, for the squire needed the poets to assert his cultured civilizedness'.[18] As individual patronage was supplanted by corporate sponsorship, frequently through the innovation of subscription editions, the country squire replaced the monarch and the courtly patron as the principal arbiter of taste, and the primary dispenser of largesse.

---

[18] 'The social situation of seventeenth-century poetry', in *Metaphysical poetry*, ed. M. Bradbury (Bloomington: Indiana University Press, 1970), p. 23.

38

Rooms of their own: Literary salons in seventeenth-century France

Joan DeJean

The literary salon is among the few truly original institutions in the history of French culture. The literary assemblies first noted in sixteenth-century France were naturally not without precedent – notably in sixteenth-century Italy. However, no other country ever produced a *tradition* of such gatherings. For, whereas most European nations at one time or another knew some degree of salon activity – salons were particularly prevalent throughout Europe in the eighteenth century – only in France did salons flourish without interruption for nearly two centuries. During that time, a veritable culture developed in the salons. The influence of that culture was so powerful that at certain periods – particularly in the late seventeenth and the early eighteenth centuries – French culture seemed almost synonymous with salon culture. An important aspect of salon culture's influence can be noted in the definition of literary criticism as it was first practised on a large scale in France.

In France the salon tradition really began around 1610, when the Italian-born marquise de Rambouillet, having deemed the French court insufficiently sophisticated, decided to establish an alternate court in her townhouse near the Louvre. The Revolution of 1789 brought the salon tradition to an abrupt end, just as it terminated so many other institutions that had flourished under the *ancien régime*. The salon did resurface in the nineteenth century. Once the tradition had been broken, however, the new assemblies recovered neither the flavour nor the prestige of their precursors.

While the true tradition was still alive, the salons were not yet referred to by that name – 'salon' designated only the formal reception rooms in which assemblies were generally held in the eighteenth century rather than the gatherings themselves. During the first decades of their existence, the assemblies took place in more intimate settings. In this respect as in so many others, the marquise de Rambouillet's influence was decisive. Rather than in any more public space, she received her guests in an inner sanctum to which one gained access only by traversing the formal salons. This was the marquise's bedchamber, referred to by all simply as *la chambre bleue*. There, she seated her guests in the space between the bed and the wall, known as a *ruelle*, while she herself remained in bed. Not all early salons were organized around the *ruelle*, but all did maintain an atmosphere of informality. And thus the first salons were designated by familiar, casual terms – for instance, 'the Saturday' referred to the weekly gathering at Madeleine de Scudéry's home in the Marais.

The early salons were intimate gatherings. Contemporary accounts, such as the numerous descriptions that have come down to us of meetings in *la chambre bleue*, show that, even if over time the composition of a circle was naturally subject to change, at any given moment each salon remained remarkably stable. This meant that members could be certain week after week of the range of opinions that would be voiced in any discussion. This stability explains the first important role played by the salons in the history of literary criticism. Members gathered on a regular basis to exchange ideas in wide-ranging, free-wheeling discussions. In the process, they developed a collective taste, a taste that later proved enormously influential when these fledgling writers came of age and became the most important figures of the French Classical age. At the same time, members used the salons to come of age as writers, by trying out their works on each other. In the early 1640s, for example, Pierre Corneille read *Polyeucte* (published 1643) to the *habitués* of *la chambre bleue* and fought with them over Christian tragedy's future in France. (They thought, correctly, that it was a lost cause.) Some twenty years later, the Comtesse de Lafayette who became known as the inventor of the modern novel circulated drafts of her early works (*La Princesse de Montpensier*, 1662; *Zayde*, 1669) among the members of her circle to generate their opinions for discussion.

Thus in the early decades of the salon, members in effect initiated the first large-scale practice of literary criticism in France. Granted, this critical practice was almost exclusively informal, leaving virtually no written trace. However, it trained all the major literary figures of the nation that was on its way to a century of domination over the European intellectual scene to think as literary critics. That training had a resounding impact on the unfolding of the French Classical age.

Its most evident impact can be measured by the proliferation of formal (published) literary criticism – it even could be argued that this proliferation actually signified the birth of a tradition of literary criticism in France. Prior to the salon era, whereas most textual commentary was devoted exclusively to Greek and Latin literature, occasional critics had begun to recognize the existence of a French literary tradition. Antoine Fouquelin's *La rhétorique française* (1555), for instance, included, in addition to the examples from ancient poets that were the standard references in his day, examples of each rhetorical figure taken from contemporary French poets.

Until the reign of Louis XIV, however, such attempts at codifying French production were the exception rather than the rule. Then, throughout the second half of the seventeenth century, attempts at drawing up the history of French literature suddenly became frequent. Some of them – notably the *Recueil des plus belles pièces des poètes français depuis Villon jusqu'à M. de Benserade* (1692), a collection attributed to either Marie-Catherine d'Aulnoy or Bernard Le Bovier de Fontenelle – make an attempt at a comprehensive overview. Others elect a far more limited scope. Witness the example of Claude de Vertron's *La nouvelle Pandore, ou les femmes illustres du siècle de Louis le Grand* (1698), which considers only the accomplishments of recent women of letters.

As the title of Vertron's volume indicates, the initial impetus to write the history of French literature was inspired by the creation of the first notion of periodization: the early historians of the French tradition promoted the use of the term 'the century of Louis XIV' as a concept defining the literary production of the seventeenth century (or at least that part of the century that followed the inception of the salon tradition) as indissociable from the Sun King's reign. In addition, the first French literary histories would also have been inconceivable without the salon tradition. The miniature courts in the salons fostered the impression that there was a French literary tradition – the simple fact that virtually all the major contemporary writers were meeting together on a regular basis must surely have made this an inevitable conclusion. Finally, the style of this early literary criticism was massively influenced by the forms developed in and from salon debate.

Most notable is the tendency of much early criticism to reproduce in written format the atmosphere of the often heated exchange of ideas that characterized salon gatherings. An important part of the seventeenth-century critical production that can be related to salon culture takes the form of interrelated attack and defence. One of a pair of tracts or volumes takes apart a work – for example, a play by Molière or Racine – exposing thereby all the new work's alleged defects. The companion text responds point by point, claiming that the defects are in reality innovations so radical that the other critic had not been able to appreciate them. So closely do these works reproduce the salon format that they often take the form of critical dialogues: several characters with opposing views on literary issues gather together, as if in a salon, to debate the merits of each position.

The format of these paired critical exchanges demonstrates that the so-called quarrels that proliferated around innovative works of seventeenth-century literature – the quarrel of *L'école des femmes* (1662), the quarrel of *La Princesse de Clèves* (1678) – were closely related to the debates central to salon culture. Indeed, there is evidence to suggest that, on occasion at least (for example, in the case of the quarrel over *La Princesse de Clèves*), both sides of the dispute were generated from within the same salon circle, as if reflecting the desire to make public the complexity of these discussions. The proliferation of such critical writing proves that the activity of seventeenth-century literary salons had convinced a generation of writers that the critical analysis of literary texts was an essential intellectual endeavour.

The salons played a major role in generating new literary forms. An experiment would be announced and a model proposed: members would then compose their own examples and bring them in to be exchanged, discussed, and revised. It was thus that, in the late 1650s, a passion for verbal portraits was launched from the salon of the duchesse de Montpensier (known as la Grande Mademoiselle). The experimentation in her salon, in which members composed both self-portraits and the portraits of other members, culminated in two volumes, the 1659 *Recueil des portraits et éloges* and the 1663 *La galerie des portraits de Mademoiselle de Montpensier*. It was also responsible for the widespread use of portraits in contemporary literature, notably in the early novel, where the portrait was among the principal techniques for the exploration of individual psychology. And the portrait resurfaces in contemporary criticism, for instance, in Charles Perrault's two-volume *Les hommes illustres qui ont paru en France pendant ce siècle* (1696–1700), which takes the form of a series of portraits.

Of all the generic innovations imagined in the salons, the one, perhaps, with the greatest long-term impact on the French tradition was a new kind of public letter, letters created more as literary artefacts than as private documents. These witty, highly stylized missives – which first circulated among salon *habitués* and subsequently were often published – initially became popular in the marquise de Rambouillet's salon. Her salon's unofficial bard, Vincent Voiture, originated an epistolary model that remained in fashion for the remainder of the *ancien régime*. Experimentation with epistolarity in the salons influenced both the development of actual correspondences such as the marquise de Sévigné's (after having made her début in *la chambre bleue*, Sévigné frequented salons nearly all her life) and the beginnings of epistolary fiction. In addition, numerous early works of textual analysis, such as the volume written in defence of Lafayette's novel, J.-B. de Valincour's *Lettres à Madame la marquise *** sur le sujet de 'La Princesse de Clèves'* (1678), show the influence of epistolary models developed in the salons.

For literature and literary criticism alike, however, by far the most important innovation generated by the salon tradition was not merely a form, but a style, what became known as the conversational style. (It was often referred to as 'l'esprit de la conversation'.) The intimate atmosphere of seventeenth-century salons fostered the notion that each meeting was an extended conversation. In the salons, members became adept in the practice of what became known as 'the art of conversation'. With the

salons' proliferation, the cultivation of the conversational art became a
way of life for France's cultural élite. In the seventeenth century, conversation attained the status of a fine art, one in which all cultivated French
men and women tried to excel. And, in an era in which conversational
brilliance was considered a mark of genius, pedantry was all but banished
from the literary scene.

In such an age, literary criticism functioned, as at perhaps no other time
in its history, primarily as a discourse shared by cultivated, non-professional
readers, rather than as doctrine promulgated by professional scholars.
This critical practice – referred to either as 'worldly' [*mondain*] criticism
or simply as salon criticism – is presented as a conversation among equals,
a conversation in which opposing points of view are freely exchanged and
one in which no absolute authority figure controls access to truth. In view
of this self-presentation, it is hardly surprising to note that salon criticism
gave a view of seventeenth-century literature that is both far more open to
diversity and far less hierarchical than the vision that has come down to
twentieth-century readers from the great tradition of literary history in
France, that of the nineteenth century. According to this view of contemporary literary production, all genres receive recognition. We thus find the
genre traditionally presented as the century's crowning glory, neoclassical
tragedy, placed on equal footing, for example, with a genre that subsequent, more traditional literary history chose to ignore for as long as
possible, the novel. (The novel was only fully recognized by French
literary history in the late nineteenth and early twentieth centuries.) Contemporary production is considered in its full diversity, with the goal of
understanding generic differences and innovations, rather than making
value judgements. In this conversation among equals, literary criticism
was assigned the task of keeping an informed public aware of changes on
the literary scene; readers were expected to come to their own conclusions.

Worldly criticism's vision of contemporary literature continued to be
promoted as long as the salon tradition survived. Then it was suppressed,
and the disorderly record of literary variety that it provided disappeared.
A number of literary values went into decline along with 'la critique
mondaine'. The most notable demise was that of the art of conversation.
It was not that conversational brilliance suddenly ceased to be valued
in France. No longer, however, was the conversational style commonly
accepted, as was generally the case during the Golden Age of the salons,
as the essence of the French style.

Perhaps the most significant transformation in the literary landscape
related to the demise of salon criticism concerned the importance attributed to women of letters. The seventeenth-century literary salon was
among the rare institutions in the history of the republic of letters that
functioned as a female preserve. Salons were always presided over by

women. For nearly two centuries, the movement responsible for the creation of the art considered quintessentially French remained under female control. Salon criticism faithfully reflected that reality. Accordingly, its volumes paid tribute to women's writing with a seriousness that subsequently vanished from criticism and that has reappeared only in recent decades. Women writers were represented in them in numbers unheard of since a more conventional literary history effaced the record of an extraordinary female participation in the republic of letters.

The disappearance of salon criticism and its alternate vision also impoverished our sense of the history of literature and of literary criticism in other ways. Twentieth-century theorists might be surprised to learn that current attempts to distinguish between the essence and the construction of femininity in literary and critical discourse have precedent in debates aired some three hundred years ago. Virtually all the major male writers of the late seventeenth and the early eighteenth centuries were salon *habitués* during the formative years of their careers. In their journals and their critical works, many of them recorded what appears to have been a commonly held contemporary belief. The most innovative modern writing, they tell us repeatedly, would be achieved if writers were able to live up to a theoretical dream that is once again haunting today's modernity, that is, if writers were able to produce a style in which twentieth-century readers will recognize a precursor of the concept Hélène Cixous terms *écriture féminine*. The most innovative modern writing, male writers from Perrault to Montesquieu to Marivaux believed, would be created by writers, male and female, who had learned how to think as women.

Finally, an appreciation of salon culture is of particular interest for a history of literary criticism, a domain in which female participation has been notoriously limited. When the full role of the seventeenth-century literary salon ceased to be recognized, an important memory was lost, that of perhaps the most influential contribution ever made by women to the production of commentary on literary texts. For, even if the women of the salons for the most part did not actually compose literary criticism – Marguerite Buffet and Marie-Jeanne L'Héritier were notable exceptions – they created an atmosphere in which diverse forms of critical activity became a central preoccupation of their nation's social élite. At no other time in the history of French culture has literary criticism been so thoroughly integrated into the daily life, not only of those we would describe in our modern vocabulary as intellectuals, but also of all cultivated men and women. This may well stand as the most significant contribution ever made by women to the tradition of literary criticism.

* See also Elizabeth Guild's 'Women as *auctores* in early modern Europe' in the present volume (pp. 426–32).

39

Renaissance printing and the book trade

George Hoffmann

No single image, perhaps, better captures the elusive relationship that printing bore to Renaissance literary criticism than the frontispiece of Guillaume Budé's *De studio literarum recte ac commode instituendo* (1532). Beneath the title, Josse Bade, the renowned Parisian printer of Budé and Erasmus, inserted a woodcut of a printer pulling hard on a press bar, flanked by an inker knocking up the balls on one side, and on the other, two typesetters busy composing.[1] Although it seems to suggest a particular correlation between the best-known Parisian shop of the time and the latest manifesto of France's most celebrated humanist, the image proves to be merely Bade's ordinary device, and a somewhat formulaic one at that. Budé's book in turn registers little awareness of the new medium through which it was destined to pass, and his silence points to the curious fact that while print culture and a new literary consciousness seem to have developed in parallel, they often did so in relative ignorance of each other.

This unwitting indifference could cut both ways. Etienne Pasquier, one of the most perceptive casual critics of contemporary French writers, had little that was perceptive to say about printing except to note with irony that 'the inventor of artillery was a monk, and of printing a knight'.[2] Notwithstanding the remarkable blind spot that many contemporaries experienced with regard to the 'print revolution', modern scholars have been tempted to find in the invention of printing a key to any number of pivotal changes in Renaissance intellectual life. Two classic studies on the

---

[1] Philippe Renouard, *Bibliographie des impressions et des œuvres de Josse Badius Ascensius*, 3 vols. (1908; New York: B. Franklin, 1967), vol. I, pp. 42–7; vol. II, pp. 239–40; see also *Imprimeurs et libraires parisiens du XVIe siècle*, vol. II (Paris: Service des travaux historiques de la ville de Paris, 1969), pp. 20 and 268. Guillaume Budé, *De philologia; de studio litterarum: Faksimile-Neudruck der Ausgabe von Paris 1532*, ed. A. Buck (Stuttgart and Bad Cannstatt: F. Frommann, 1964). On Budé, and this treatise in particular, see Marie-Madeleine de La Garanderie, *Christianisme et lettres profanes: essai sur l'humanisme français (1515–1535) et sur la pensée de Guillaume Budé* (Paris: Champion, 1995), pp. 311–44.

[2] 'l'inventeur de l'Artillerie, fut un Moine, et de l'Imprimerie un Chevalier', *Recherches de la France*, ed. M.-M. Fragonard and F. Roudaut *et al.*, 3 vols. (Paris: Champion, 1996), vol. II, p. 969.

spread of printing have led the way for most subsequent commentators, Lucien Febvre and Henri-Jean Martin's *L'apparition du livre* and Elizabeth Eisenstein's *The printing press as an agent of change*.[3] Nearly every student has now become familiar with the basic theses expounded in these works, namely that the increased circulation and accessibility of mass-produced books helped spur religious reform, the rise of science, and the development of vernacular literatures. Indisputable as this may be, a quantitative approach does not explain the qualitative changes that print culture effected in the literary-critical practice of the Renaissance.

It is tempting to locate such changes in printed books' physical appearance. Extending McLuhan's thesis on the transformative power of media, Walter Ong proposed some years ago that printed works opened up a potential for visual presentation that led to the rise of new binary and arborescent methods of organizing rhetoric.[4] Although rhetorical categories came closest to constituting what might be termed a critical vocabulary for both writers and commentators in the Renaissance, Ramus's proposed reforms in fact had relatively little impact upon the practice of literary commentary. Ong's underlying assumptions concerning print's 'visual' revolution prove disputable: Charles de Bovelles's and Jacques Lefèvre d'Etaples's experimentation with arborescent figures, for example, owes far less to printing innovations than to a rich medieval tradition illustrated by Honorius d'Autun's twelfth-century *Clavis physicae*, Ramon Lull's fourteenth-century *Ars magna* or Gregor Reisch's 1496 *Margarita philosophica*.

As for the appearance of new page layouts for bilingual editions, printing the *Complutensian polyglot* from 1514 to 1517 certainly created a larger impact than if it had remained in manuscript form, yet nothing in principle would have prevented Garcia Jiménez de Cisneros from having the parallel columns of Hebrew, Greek, and Latin text copied by hand instead of using the presses of Arnão Guillen de Brocar in Alcalá. If anything, the relative difficulty of imposing typeset of marginalia and arrays of gloss such as found in medieval manuscripts would have encouraged the development of free-standing critical writing, already exemplified by Angelo Poliziano in the 1489 *Miscellanea*. The tendency to simplify production by aligning the typographic presentation of a text and its commentary bestowed upon the latter a new central role on the page, as

---

[3] Elizabeth Eisenstein, *The printing press as an agent of change* (Cambridge: Cambridge University Press, 1979); Lucien Febvre and Henri-Jean Martin, *L'apparition du livre* (1958; reprint Paris: Albin Michel, 1971). A more recent sampling of views can be found in the *Histoire de l'édition française: le livre conquérant, du moyen âge au milieu du XVIIe siècle*, ed. R. Chartier and H.-J. Martin (Paris: Promodis, 1982).

[4] *Ramus: method, and the decay of dialogue* (1958; Cambridge MA: Harvard University Press, 1983), pp. 75–91.

in Marc-Antoine Muret's and Rémy Belleau's commentaries of Ronsard's poetry in 1553 and 1560.[5]

A much-neglected contribution that printers made to the world of Renaissance letters concerns the increased availability of novel kinds of school texts, a phenomenon well illustrated by Thomas Brumen of Paris, three-quarters of whose production consisted of interfoliated and double-spaced quarto editions in which the student copied the translation between lines and their teacher's literary and grammatical commentaries in the margins and extra leaves.[6] Contemporary observers did not fail to appreciate this 'invention':

> These books contained everything that one read in school classes, in its order, whether it be taken from Cicero, Virgil, rhetoric, or any other author; and when the professors translated either into French or another Latin version, the pupils glossed between the printed lines; in the same manner, the annotations dictated by the professors were copied by the pupils on blank pages that had been inserted for this purpose between the printed ones, whereas before, the pupils had copied their own texts at a great inconvenience.[7]

Surviving copies, mutilated by heavy use and rendered nearly illegible by tightly packed notes, tell one much about teachers' new insistence upon paying close attention to textual detail and, at the same time, about the growing independence of commentary with respect to the text itself.

A less dramatic but equally profound influence that the mechanics of printing exerted upon early modern literary criticism concerns textual editing. During the Renaissance, as now, literary study began with, and depended upon, the establishment of accurate texts. But in spite of eliciting some genuine enthusiasm, printing aroused much suspicion in early institutional and intellectual milieux, particularly regarding the facile editing and abridgements it seemed to foster. Observers were justified in suspecting that the pace of work and the rush to finish before rivals' editions reached the market encouraged hastily edited and poorly proofread works that tended to be based upon little, if any, scholarship. Mechanical reproduction may have held the promise of increased

---

[5] Marc-Antoine Muret, *Commentaires au premier livre des 'Amours' de Ronsard* (Geneva: Droz, 1985), and Rémy Belleau, *Commentaire au second livre des 'Amours' de Ronsard* (Geneva: Droz, 1986).

[6] Philippe Renouard, *Imprimeurs et libraires parisiens du XVIᵉ siècle: fascicule Brumen*, ed. E. Queval and G. Guilleminot (Paris: Bibliothèque Nationale, 1984), p. 34.

[7] Author's translation. Jean de Gaufreteau, *Chronique bordeloise*, ed. J. Delpit, 2 vols. (Bordeaux: G. Gounouilhou, 1876–8), vol. I, p. 209, quoted by Louis Desgraves, *Dictionnaire des imprimeurs, libraires et relieurs de Bordeaux et de la Gironde (XVᵉ–XVIIIᵉ)* (Baden-Baden: V. Koerner, 1995), pp. 203–4. See Glyn P. Norton, *The ideology and language of translation in Renaissance France and their humanist antecedents* (Geneva: Droz, 1984), pp. 140–2.

standardization of texts, but this would be received as a welcome development only in so far as what was standardized in fact proved to be accurate. Add to this the fact that once finished, printers often discarded the original they had used – destroying for future generations precious manuscript evidence – and one can understand why many scholars might have concluded that the potential threat posed by printing outweighed its advantages. It seems possible that the new preoccupation with philology and manuscript collation arose at least partially out of concern over the extremely poor quality of editions beginning to circulate in ever greater numbers.

Into the breach that threatened to divide humanists from printers stepped Aldo Manuzio (Aldus Manutius), a grammarian connected to the circle of Pico from 1482 to 1484, and more significantly, to Poliziano, who was laying the groundwork for modern textual criticism. Although he hardly took full advantage of Poliziano's innovations, he understood the need for exercising greater care in selecting a copy text and emending readings upon conjecture alone. Responsible for 126 editions between 1494 and his death in 1515, the most famous of which is the exquisite *Hypnerotomachia Poliphili*, Aldus introduced Greek founts to Venice and specialized in octavo editions of Latin authors with press runs occasionally higher than two thousand, an astounding figure for the time. Although he devoted himself primarily to Greek and Latin editions, he printed Pietro Bembo's editions of Petrarch's *Canzoniere* in 1501 and Dante's *Commedia* in 1502, landmarks on the way towards recognition of vernacular literature.

Aldus has often reaped praise due others: his father-in-law and publisher, Andrea Torresani, and the aristocratic patron, Pierfrancesco Barbarigo, owned a controlling interest in his shop and successfully managed his business at a time when stiff competition was flushing out rival printers – by 1500, Venice alone counted 150 presses. It was a gifted type-cutter, Francesco Griffo, who surmounted the technical problems associated with designing Greek founts which included all the necessary diacritics by introducing vertical kerning in order to avoid multiplying to excess the number of types.[8] Yet no one can deny that Aldus played a crucial historical role in breaking down resistance to the new medium of print. Erasmus, who did not hesitate to condemn printers 'who try to save every penny, do not use a corrector, but give us contaminated, mutilated, lacerated, and generally bad texts', addressed Aldus as a peer and friend, 'if you find an obvious mistake anywhere, for I am human, you have my permission to alter it at your discretion: by doing so you will act the part

[8] Martin Lowry, *The world of Aldus Manutius: business and scholarship in Renaissance Venice* (Oxford: Blackwell, 1979), pp. 82–6.

of a friend . . . there is no responsibility that I would not now venture to entrust to my dear Aldus'.[9]

Aldus's overly meticulous nature, which might have continued to be a handicap had he remained primarily a scholar, served him splendidly in his role as editor and proofreader. Although his editions fall far short of modern scholarly standards,[10] his achievement is altogether another matter when measured against that of printers in his day. Careful attention to textual detail became his trademark, embodied by the form of a dolphin and an anchor entwined, which inspired Erasmus to write his famous commentary on the adage, *Festina lente*, 'hasten slowly'. 'Aldus, making haste slowly', declared Erasmus admiringly, 'has acquired as much gold as he had reputation, and richly deserves both'.[11] If the nimble dolphin could stand for printing's accelerated means of reproduction, the anchor recalled the scholar's patience. It was as if Aldus calculated by his very person to counter the notion that printing was a speeded-up (and consequently debased) medium for textual transmission.

Printing in fact boasted one undeniable advantage over manuscripts: if one proofread early enough, one could reset type, whereas a scribe enjoyed fewer options with regard to a pen stroke already indelibly committed to the page. In other words, although the initial typesetting could easily prove inferior to scribal work, movable type afforded the opportunity to achieve a level of correction unattainable even in the best scriptorium. To some extent, the spirit of perfectibility could extend into re-editions; hence not only did Aldus contribute to the longest-running editorial project of the period, printing in 1508 the edition of the *Adagia* that secured Erasmus's fame, but he also revised his own 1493 Latin grammar in 1501, 1508, and 1514.

The future of this enterprise, however, lay across the Alps. Guillaume Fichet and Johann Heylin had arranged for Paris's first press to operate in the Sorbonne's library in 1470, a time when Germany and Italy already counted more than thirty fully-fledged print shops. But it was Josse Bade (Ascensius) who truly imported the formula of the printer-scholar to Paris after working nearly seven years as a corrector for printers in Lyons – portal to France for Italian novelties. Author of a number of commentaries, Bade produced 720 editions between 1503 and the time of his death

[9] *The correspondence of Erasmus*, trans. R. A. B. Mynors and D. F. S. Thomson, ed. W. K. Ferguson, *The collected works of Erasmus*, vols. I–XI (Toronto: University of Toronto Press, 1974–), vol. II, 1975, p. 136; see also his *Adagia*, 1520 edition, sig. ā2ʳ, 1523 edition, sig. 2x6ᵛ. Rudolf Hirsch quotes early printers and Erasmus's criticism of rivals who poorly corrected their editions, *Printing, selling and reading, 1450–1550* (Wiesbaden: O. Harrassowitz, 1967), pp. 45–8.

[10] Lowry, *The world of Aldus*, pp. 224–56.

[11] *Adages*, trans. and annotated by R. A. B. Mynors, in *The collected works of Erasmus* (Toronto: University of Toronto Press, 1991), vol. XXXIII, Part II.i.1, 15.

in 1535. During his first four years of operation, he employed Beatus
Rhenanus as corrector and this, coupled with his own extensive experience, probably did much to found his presses' reputation.[12] He worked
hard to disseminate Erasmus's writings in France, yet after 1526 he sided
with the Parisian theological faculty and Noël Béda in their split with
Erasmus and Jacques Lefèvre d'Etaples.

Aldus and Bade had both worked as scholars before they became
printers, but such credentials were not common among their colleagues.
Peter Schoeffer in Mainz, Johann Mentelin in Strasburg, Anton Koberger
in Nuremberg, Christopher Froschauer of Zurich, Erhard Ratdolt in Augsburg, and Ulrich Zell of Cologne would all have identified themselves as
artisans, rather, or as businessmen. Another of their kind, William Caxton
(?1422–91), embodies the uniqueness of England's trajectory through
early print culture. A professional merchant and inspired amateur scholar
who learned the basics of printing from Johann Veldener in Cologne,
Caxton pursued publication in English at a time when vernacular languages still had not fully asserted themselves in print and in proportions
(perhaps 75 per cent of his total output) unmatched by any other European printer. His *Morte d'Arthur* remains a model both of English usage
and of enlightened editing.[13] After the incorporation of the Company of
Stationers in 1557 (which meant that the English were the only printers in
Europe to retain a guild-like structure), printing in England was restricted
to London and the presses of Oxford and Cambridge. Both university
presses had begun as modest projects by German immigrants (in 1478 and
1519 respectively) only to quickly fail until the schools revived the idea
several decades later. Typically lagging behind continental practices by a
generation or more, and unable to claim a single one of the great humanist
editions to their credit, English printers nevertheless sustained one of the
most vibrant national literatures.

Johann Froben in Basle illustrates another approach, distinct from that
of Caxton, of Bade, and of Aldus. Possessing no pretension to scholarship,
professional or otherwise, detracted little from the quality of Froben's editions, of which he produced more than five hundred between 1491 and his
death in 1527; by 1517, he even became Erasmus's preferred printer, to
Aldus's and Bade's dismay. Like Aldus, Froben relied upon a partner to
handle the business side of operations (first Johann Petri, then Wolfgang
Lachner); but unlike his Venetian counterpart, he was both more interested

---

[12] Renouard, *Bibliographie des impressions*, vol. i, p. 55, *Imprimeurs et libraires parisiens*,
vol. ii, p. 14. John F. D'Amico, *Theory and practice in Renaissance textual criticism:
Beatus Rhenanus, between conjecture and history* (Berkeley: University of California
Press, 1988), pp. 45–7.
[13] N. F. Blake, *Caxton and his world* (New York: London House and Maxwell, 1969),
pp. 101–24.

and versed in the technical aspects of printing.[14] With a limited knowledge of Latin, and none of Greek, Froben relied for proofreading and
textual advice upon the proven skills of Beatus Rhenanus and Konrad
Pellikan, and he gave Erasmus free rein over his proofs in his ground-
breaking edition of Jerome in 1516. A rare eyewitness account reveals
Froben largely unconcerned with proofreading;[15] that Froben's reputation
for accuracy was equal to, if not higher than, that of Aldus and Bade
should raise some doubts about how central and how sustained was the
importance of the printer-scholar for the humanists' enterprise.

Aldus, Bade, and Froben were all nearly forty or older at the turn of
the century; although some constants of the book trade would endure,
their experience already little resembled that of the newer generation of
printers. By the end of Bade's life, printed books had become a familiar
feature in most educated people's lives, and publishers no longer needed
to combat scepticism about the potential of print itself – the work of Aldus
and Froben has effectively proven that printed works could be both
elegant and accurate. Controversy had now turned to the uses of print, and
it is no accident that the last of the great Renaissance scholar-printers,
the Estiennes, became embroiled in religious disputes to the point that
they had to flee Paris for Geneva.

Robert Estienne (?1503–59), a lexicographer and renowned biblical scholar, heir by marriage to Bade's presses and by birth to Henri I
Estienne's established reputation as a printer, upheld such exacting standards that his editions remained standard references centuries afterwards.
He introduced innovations such as verse numbering still in practice today,
and for his 1550 edition of the Greek New Testament, he collated no
fewer than fifteen manuscripts – demonstrating just how far the quality of
printed editions had come in the hundred years since Gutenberg's forty-
two-line Bible.[16] Henri II Estienne (1531–98) carried on the pioneering
lexicographical work that his father had begun in the *Thesaurus linguae
latinae* of 1531 and the Latin–French and French–Latin dictionaries of
1538 and 1539–40, with his own monumental *Thesaurus linguae graecae*
in 1572–3, which nearly bankrupted the family.[17] Arguably, no reference

[14] Josef Benzing, *Die Buchdrucker des 16. und 17. Jahrhunderts im deutschen Sprachgebiet*,
    2nd edn (Wiesbaden: O. Harrassowitz, 1982), p. 32; Karl Brandler, 'Johannes Frobenius:
    "Ein Fürst des Buchdrucker" des 16. Jahrhunderts in Basel', *Fuldaer Geschichtsblätter*
    36 (1960), 135–48.
[15] Johan Gerritsen, 'Printing at Froben's: an eye-witness account', *Studies in bibliography*
    44 (1991), 149–50.
[16] See Elizabeth Armstrong, *Robert Estienne, royal printer: an historical study of the elder
    Stephanus*, 2nd edn (Appleford, England: Courtenay studies in Reformation theology,
    1986).
[17] See Fred Schreiber, *The Estiennes: an annotated catalogue of 300 highlights of their
    various presses* (New York: E. K. Schreiber, 1982); *Henri Estienne*, Cahiers V.-L. Saulnier,
    5 (Paris: Ecole normale supérieure de jeunes filles, 1988).

tool benefited more from re-editions than dictionaries, and Robert Estienne had already expanded his French–Latin dictionary in 1549, followed by Théodore Thierry's revision in 1564 and Jean Nicot's in 1573 and again in 1606. Meanwhile, the art and science of textual editing, as developed by Poliziano and Pier Vettori and put into practice by printers like Aldus and Bade, would attain its greatest realization in France's Joseph Scaliger,[18] but a new model for publishing was developing in the Netherlands that would shortly direct the book trade away from the humanists' textual concerns.

Modern methods of organization and inventive partnerships explain the huge volume of Christophe Plantin's production in Antwerp and Leiden, where he published over 2000 titles from 1555 until his death in 1589. He championed the use of copperplate engraving in order to attain a higher quality of illustration at a time when most printers still relied upon the simpler woodcut.[19] Although Plantin's catalogue still boasted prestigious humanist editions (subsidized by a lucrative liturgical mono-poly in Spain), the Elzevier family in Leiden committed itself fully to bargain pocket editions.[20] The format had been pioneered by Aldus more than a century earlier, but now there were no philological aspirations; while Aldus had laboured to raise printing to a level of scholarly respect-ability, Bonaventura (1583–1652) and Abraham I (1592–1652) capitalized upon the new confidence invested in print to bring books to the barely literate.

Although the new medium of print had exerted its most tangible influ-ence not upon exegesis but upon textual criticism, this latter had played a central role in the world of Renaissance letters. At first, the impact printing made had been a negative one, drawing more attention to textual criticism as a reaction to the dubious quality of the editions it put into circulation in ever greater numbers. But the tendency towards stand-ardization that it introduced, coupled with the potential that it opened for multiple stages of correction, allowed the most dedicated scholars to realize the humanist dream of restoring *bonae literae*.

---

[18] See Anthony Grafton, *Joseph Scaliger: a study in the history of classical scholarship* (Oxford: Clarendon Press, 1983).

[19] See Leon Voët, *The golden compasses: a history and evaluation of the printing and publishing activities of the Officina Plantiniana at Antwerp*, 2 vols. (Amsterdam: Van Gendt, 1969).

[20] See David W. Davies, *The world of the Elseviers, 1580–1712* (1908; reprint The Hague: Nijhoff, 1954).

Voices of dissent

Voices of dissent

40

The Ciceronian controversy

John Monfasani

The Ciceronian controversy in the Renaissance was primarily a battle over Latin because only Latin authors could in a strict sense imitate Cicero. That is why even though the Ciceronians and their critics quarrelled over style, the deepest fault-line separating the two sides was not an issue of style, but of language. As Horace observed (*Ars poetica* 71–2) – and Renaissance theorists universally acknowledged – language constantly changes and it is *usus* [current usage] that determines the *norma loquendi* [linguistic standard]. But Latin in the Renaissance was a dead language. It had long lost its community of native speakers and could only be learned at school from books. Consequently, underlying the Renaissance debates over Ciceronianism lay the question of what properly constituted *usus* for a dead language.

One might argue that Latin was really not a dead language since it had remained in use throughout the Middle Ages. However, medieval Latin, for all its differences with classical Latin, was no more dead or alive than the neoclassical Latin of the humanists. It too was a language without a native-speaking community, learned from books, and generally immune to the evolution experienced by the living, vernacular tongues.[1]

Petrarch, the first great humanist, grasped the difference between the Latin of his own time and that of antiquity. But his ideas on the history of Latin were fuzzy. He idolized Cicero as the supreme embodiment of classical Latin eloquence. Yet his own Latin was still burdened with medievalisms and smacked more of Seneca than of Cicero. Moreover, not clearly distinguishing between stylistic imitation and linguistic imitation, he rejected the exclusive imitation of Cicero and encouraged instead an eclectic approach towards the imitation of the classics.

By the beginning of the fifteenth century, however, humanists had a different perspective. They criticized Petrarch's Latin as insufficiently classical. More importantly, they were predominantly Ciceronians. Whether they actually achieved their goal or not, they sought to model their Latin after Cicero's. They had drawn the consequences of two fundamental Petrarchan premises: first, that classical Latin was true Latin; and, second,

---

[1] See J. Ijsewijn, 'Le latin des humanistes français: évolution et étude comparative', in *L'humanisme français au début de la Renaissance* (Paris: Vrin, 1973), p. 340.

that Cicero represented the pinnacle of classical Latin prose. If classical Latin had reached a high point in Cicero, then it would be foolish for those reviving classical eloquence to imitate anyone other than the best classical author or, at the very least, to imitate classical authors indiscriminately.

In his *De sermone Latino et modis Latine loquendi*, written about 1507 and first printed in 1514, the Roman curial official Adriano Castellesi gave exact expression to this evolutionary understanding of Latin. He divided classical Latin into four periods, the third of which was the *tempus perfectum*, the age of Cicero, while the others were in one way or another 'imperfect'. Castellesi's main target was the Apuleians, that is, admirers of the second-century author Apuleius whose style featured archaic words and artificial constructions. But Castellesi's underlying principle was more profound. It undercut all linguistic eclecticism, including that of the most illustrious eclectic of the previous generation, Angelo Poliziano.[2]

In about 1488, in a letter to the young humanist Paolo Cortesi, Poliziano had started the Renaissance controversy by attacking the Ciceronians as apish slaves. He had argued that since Latin was a dead language, there was no current usage to bind him and he was free to employ any word or phrase he found among the classical authors. For him no one moment in antiquity was normative. But Castellesi showed that if one defined proper Latin as classical Latin, then eclecticism produced improper Latin since it cohered with no period of classical Latin. The effect would be the same if one were to write English combining the peculiarities of authors from Chaucer to Hemingway. Consequently, if Cicero's age was the classical age of Latin *par excellence*, then neoclassical Latin must cohere with Cicero's Latin.

Poliziano's main argument, however, against Ciceronianism rested not on eclecticism, but on the individuality of an author. He could not apishly imitate Cicero, he explained, because his task as a writer was to express himself: *non sum Cicero; me exprimo*. Gianfrancesco Pico della Mirandola voiced an analogous notion in an exchange on the question of imitation with Pietro Bembo in 1512. Pico argued that we each have our innate, individualistic idea of beauty and it is to this idea that our style must conform.

However, as Paolo Cortesi put it in responding to Poliziano, it is all well and good to talk about one's own individualistic style; but in respect to antique Latin we are in the position of pilgrims in a foreign land. Classical Latin is alien territory to us. We need a guide in a world which is not our own.

---

[2] See G. W. Pigman, III, 'Versions of imitation in the Renaissance', *Renaissance quarterly* 33 (1980), p. 6.

The clearest expression of this approach is Giulio Camillo Delminio's *Della imitazione* written about 1530 in response to Erasmus's *Ciceronianus*.[3] Significantly, as we shall see, Delminio wrote his treatise in Italian. Since Latin is not spoken any more in the way that French is spoken, but is shut up in books, and since the written form of its perfect age [*perfetto secolo*] is available in these books, what right has he, a foreigner, Delminio asked, to mix the language of the perfect age with that of other times and other languages and to substitute his linguistic judgement for that of Cicero's? Would not the French laugh at me, a foreigner, if I got it into my head to start coining new French vocabulary?

Delminio's reference to spoken French raises the last major consideration affecting the thinking of the Ciceronians, namely, the connection between written and spoken classical Latin. The humanists began to face this issue early in the fifteenth century.[4] Leonardo Bruni denied that the common folk spoke Latin. He believed that the educated spoke Latin and the populace a vernacular. Lorenzo Valla seems to have agreed, even though he strangely insisted that the Italian dialect of contemporary Rome was also Latin. Other humanists, however, rejected the theory of classical bilingualism and argued that the educated and uneducated both spoke Latin, the difference being one of degree in the propriety and complexity of their speech. They were right.

Neither side of this debate constituted a coherent block in their attitude towards the vernacular. But of those who insisted upon classical monolingualism, the Ciceronian Francesco Filelfo gave a significant historical reason for writing occasionally in the vernacular.[5] He used the vernacular, he explained, for low and familiar matters. He could not speak nor, for that matter, write authentic antique colloquial Latin. So he used Tuscan instead. Filelfo's historical insight was correct. We have lost the ordinary speech of the Latins, both the Vulgar Latin of the common people and the educated colloquial Latin of the elite. The Latin of Plautus's and Terence's plays is a literary construct and not a replication of ordinary Latin speech.[6]

Pietro Bembo, the leading Ciceronian theorist of the early sixteenth century, followed up the implications of Filelfo's logic. On the one hand, he cultivated literary Italian – indeed, he played a major role in regularizing it – and, on the other, he avoided speaking Latin. Consistent with that practice, he argued at the start of his *Prose della volgar lingua* (published in 1525) that just as the Romans had two languages, their native Latin

[3] See G. W. Pigman, III, 'Imitation and the Renaissance sense of the past: the reception of Erasmus' *Ciceronianus*', *Journal of Medieval and Renaissance studies* 9 (1979), pp. 169–71.
[4] See A. Mazzocco, *Linguistic theories in Dante and the humanists* (Leiden: Brill, 1993).
[5] F. Tateo, 'Francesco Filelfo tra latino e volgare', in *Francesco Filelfo nel quinto centenario della morte* (Padua: Antenore, 1986), pp. 64–5.
[6] L. R. Palmer, *The Latin language* (London: Faber & Faber, 1954), pp. 80–94.

and the Greek they learned in school, so too Italians had two languages: Italian, which was 'proper, natural, and domestic', and Latin, which was 'foreign and unnatural', taken from books, and used only exceptionally. On top of that, it was impossible to recover Latin's colloquial classical form.

Many humanists disagreed with Bembo about Italian as a literary language. Some even tried to speak Latin *Cicerone*, that is, as Cicero would have spoken it. But most Ciceronians seem to have conceded Bembo's point that Italian was the only viable colloquial language the Italians had. When Erasmus pilloried the Italian Ciceronians for their reluctance to speak Latin, his chief opponent, Etienne Dolet, acknowledged the fact.[7] Other contemporaries also noted the Ciceronians' reticence in colloquial Latin. The Ciceronians' desertion of colloquial Latin influenced Italian humanists as a whole. In a manual of 1517 on colloquial Latin, the German humanist Petrus Mosellanus complained about the wretched speech [*sermo immundus*] to which Italians were reduced when forced to speak colloquial Latin. In the second half of the century at Rome, when Marc-Antoine Muret forsook Ciceronianism, he specifically condemned the debilitating effect that Ciceronianism had on spoken Latin in Italy. In contrast, Erasmus first wrote his *Colloquia* precisely to promote facility in Latin conversation, which he believed could be made properly classical. Other humanists wrote manuals of Latin conversation in the course of the sixteenth century, but not one was an Italian Ciceronian. Ciceronianism had consequences for how one viewed the vernacular, but, contrary to common belief, in the case of many Ciceronians it meant embracing the vernacular as the ordinary language of discourse and also as a literary language.

Pietro Bembo is especially interesting in this regard. He sought to justify the use of Italian as a literary language and to establish the Tuscan classics of the Trecento as the standard of that language. He treated the relationship of Italian to Latin as analogous to the classical relationship of Latin to Greek, that is, the latter was the low-status maternal tongue and the former the high-status foreign language learned in school. As the Latins elevated their language of everyday discourse into a comprehensive literary language, so too, Bembo contended, ought the Italians. The outcome of such a programme would of course be the eventual supplantation of Latin by Italian as the standard literary and scientific language of Italians. The advance of the vernaculars did eventually cause the demise of Latin as the language of learning and literature. But in the early sixteenth century Latin still held its privileged position. Therefore Bembo was quite

---

[7] Etienne Dolet, *L'Erasmianus sive Ciceronianus d'Etienne Dolet (1521)*, ed. E. V. Telle (Geneva: Droz, 1974), pp. 94–5.

consistent in his linguistic and literary theory when he argued for Ciceronian imitation in Latin. Cicero and Virgil provided for him the same literary standard in Latin that Petrarch and Boccaccio did in Italian.

Ciceronians from Bembo and Delminio in the first half of the sixteenth
century to Paolo Manuzio in the middle of the century to Paolo Beni in the
early seventeenth century wrote extensively in Italian. Beni, like Bembo,
even became involved in a major controversy concerning literary Italian.
Collectively, the Ciceronians were not linguistic dinosaurs or absurd
pedants. Indeed, in some respects, they were the avant-garde.

When Erasmus published the *Ciceronianus* in 1528, he did not know
Bembo's *Prose della volgar lingua* nor his letter of 1512 on Ciceronian
imitation to Gianfrancesco Pico della Mirandola. Nonetheless, Erasmus's
dialogue remained the definitive answer to Bembo and the Ciceronians
for the rest of the Renaissance. Erasmus's Latin was distinctly non-
Ciceronian. He explained his linguistic theory in the *De duplici copia*:
since Latin no longer had a community of native speakers, its norm was
the written monuments of modern learned men [*eruditi*] and the classical
authors they favoured.[8] Erasmus did not specify who were the modern
eruditi, but he certainly did not include the medieval scholastics among
them though theoretically he should have.

Erasmus first encountered Ciceronians in his visit to Italy in 1506–9.
He poked fun at them in his edition of St Jerome of 1516. But matters
first came to a head only in the 1520s, when he began to receive news from
Italy and Spain that the Ciceronians were criticizing his Latin. Worse, they
greatly preferred his recently deceased young compatriot, the Ciceronian
Christophe Longueil. By early 1526 Erasmus was complaining about the
appearance in Italy of a wicked sect, the *Ciceroniani*, who were causing as
much evil in Italy as the Lutherans were in Germany. The *Ciceroniani* were,
he insisted, purveyors of paganism. Furthermore, he wrote, Christophe
Longueil had come to no good because of his Ciceronianism.[9] In the
Ciceronianus, he caricatured Longueil as Nosoponus, the obsessive
pedant whom Bulephorus, Erasmus's persona in the dialogue, cures of
the disease of Ciceronianism. The Ciceronians as a whole he branded
paganizing perverters of Christianity. In addition, as imitators of Cicero
they were not only stupidly apish, but also insanely anachronistic, trying
to express in the vocabulary of first-century BC pagan Rome the radically
different material and spiritual conditions of sixteenth-century Christian
Europe. In a masterful survey of Latin literature, meant to show that no
one was ever a true Ciceronian except Cicero, Erasmus was able to get

---

[8] *De duplici copia verborum ac rerum commentarii duo*, ed. B. I. Knott, in Erasmus, *Opera
omnia*, vol. I.6 (Amsterdam: North Holland Pub. Co., 1988), p. 42, lines 321–6.
[9] Erasmus, *Opus epistolarum*, ed. P. S. Allen *et al.*, 12 vols. (Oxford: Clarendon Press,
1906–58), vol. V, pp. 514–21; vol. VI, pp. 143–6, 356, 395.

in a few more digs at his rivals, the most malicious of which was the belittling of Guillaume Budé's Latin by putting it on a par with that of the Parisian printer Josse Bade.

The *Ciceronianus* was a polemical *tour de force*; but even when it was right, it was frequently beside the point. For instance, it is true that only Cicero can be Cicero. But the goal of the Ciceronians was not to remake themselves into someone else. Rather it was to assimilate the language and style of Cicero in order to express themselves in the best possible form in a language which was not their own.

More fundamentally, Erasmus's three main arguments fail. Two are red herrings. The pedantry which supposedly prevented Ciceronians from writing more than a few lines a night simply was not true. The Ciceronians wrote a great deal and with vigour and alacrity. No less false was the charge of paganism. Erasmus became absolutely paranoiac about this. Even in a letter written a month before he died, he was still railing against Ciceronianism as the work of Satan. But the charge was nonsense. All known Ciceronians were Christian believers, including the poets and scholars of the supposedly pagan Roman Academy. Where Erasmus saw paganism, we should see differences of literary sensibility. Moreover, the sort of paganizing Good Friday sermon which Erasmus said he once heard in Rome delivered before the pope was, in fact, an extraordinarily rare occurrence, if it even happened at all.[10] Erasmus's third argument, that the Latin of the Ciceronians violated historical decorum, is true. But it works equally well against Erasmus's own Latin. All classical Latin was anachronistic in the Renaissance. Furthermore, as Etienne Dolet pointed out in rebuttal, Longueil's Roman orations, filled with references to non-existent *patres conscripti* [assembled senators], *Senatus*, *tribuum suffragia* [votes of the Roman tribes], and so on, were exactly what Longueil's audience expected.[11] It was, as Dolet put it, the *usus loquendi*, the convention for such speeches in Renaissance Rome. If one spoke of Christian things to the uneducated, then any Latin would be out of place; and if one spoke to the educated, then they would easily understand and appreciate the speaker's Ciceronian diction. That, Dolet could have said, would be the *usus* of the *eruditi*, which Erasmus himself had acknowledged in the *De duplici copia*.

Erasmus's *Ciceronianus* stirred up a hornet's nest of opposition, the history of which would take us far beyond the bounds of the present discussion. But two points are worth making. First, though Ciceronianism had its opponents in the sixteenth century, the best known of whom was Peter

[10] J. W. O'Malley, *Praise and blame in Renaissance Rome: rhetoric, doctrine, and reform in the sacred orators of the papal court, c. 1450–1521* (Durham, NC: Duke University Press, 1979).

[11] Dolet, *L'Erasmianus*, pp. 27–34, 177–81.

Ramus, the evidence is overwhelming that Ciceronianism continued to thrive in the Renaissance. The sheer number of Ciceronian editions, commentaries, epitomes, lexica, citations in manuals, prescriptions in curricula, and treatises on imitation prove that Cicero and, to a lesser extent, Ciceronianism dominated Latin and rhetorical instruction.[12] Second, the battle over Ciceronianism in the Renaissance was not between those who wished to maintain Latin as a living idiom against those who wished to mummify Latin in its classical state. Rather it was a battle over two different visions of neoclassical Latin. Both sides were classicizing reactionaries. The fight was over what constituted proper classical Latin. The Ciceronians of the Renaissance were enormously diverse in temperament, convictions, and even style (compare, for instance, George of Trebizond, Paolo Cortesi, Pietro Bembo, and Mario Nizolio). Their opponents were also diverse, but generally more receptive to the neologisms needed to maintain the applicability of Latin to contemporary society.

Since the Renaissance, the opponents of Ciceronianism have won out among neo-Latinists. On the other hand, since the Renaissance Latin has virtually disappeared as the medium of educated discourse. The Ciceronians did not cause this change, but some, such as Pietro Bembo, correctly foresaw and welcomed it.

[12] For instance, see *Index Aureliensis: catalogus librorum sedecimo saeculo impressorum* (Baden-Baden: V. Koerner, 1989), vol. I.8, pp. 11–333.

41

Reorganizing the encyclopaedia: Vives and Ramus on Aristotle and the scholastics

Martin Elsky

In *Ideology and utopia* (1936), the sociologist Karl Mannheim regarded the breakup of the medieval Church as the historical condition of the emergence of a new professional class, the intelligentsia, which served the emerging political structures of early modern Europe. That class, of which Juan Luis Vives and Peter Ramus were among the most influential members, was to a great extent encompassed by thinkers that have come to be known as Renaissance humanists, whose principal intellectual impact was to replace the philosophically orientated logical arts of late medieval scholasticism with literary arts dominated by rhetoric. Both Vives and Ramus played a major role in this transformation. To use Peter Sharratt's phrase, their goal was to reorganize the encyclopaedia of the arts.[1] Their lingering appeal to Aristotle on a host of matters notwithstanding, both considered themselves to be engaged in an advance guard intellectual reformation of great proportions that to some extent depended on an assault against Aristotle, the authority of the academic and intellectual establishment of the late Middle Ages – an Aristotle understood in the particular way he was institutionalized by scholastic thinkers. This contest of ideas took place within academic institutions; the stakes were intellectual influence on the newly emerging social and political formations.

Juan Luis Vives's own early education was firmly within this scholastic mould. As he became exposed to humanistic attitudes, he reacted strongly against the dominion of logic over language, an early indication that language teaching and language theory were to become the centre of gravity of his thought. His first full attack on scholasticism came in 1519 when he wrote *In pseudodialecticos* [*Against the false dialecticians*] in the form of a letter attempting to convince a friend to take up humanistic studies.[2]

In this work Vives argues that scholastic philosophic language is completely artificial and useless for anything other than logical disputation.

[1] Peter Sharratt, 'Recent work on Peter Ramus (1970–1986)', *Rhetorica* 5 (1987), p. 7.
[2] For Louvain as the specific context of Vives's early writing, see Lisa Jardine, *Erasmus, man of letters: the construction of charisma in print* (Princeton: Princeton University Press, 1993), pp. 14–23; and Josef Ijsewijn, 'J. L. Vives in 1512–1517: a reconsideration of evidence', *Humanistica Lovaniensia* 26 (1977), 83–100.

It is not a *sermo*; it is spoken by nobody, and therefore it has no real existence. As a metalanguage that aspires to the condition of a *verbum universalis et rationalis*, it undermines the very basis of language in history and actual speech. Vives's linguistic goal was to revive Latin as a *sermo*, a natural language; he thus identified *consuetudo* [usage] as the sole norm of all language. By usage he meant the conventions historically established in acts of communication, conventions that could be learned not through deductive rules designed to structure truth statements – propositions – in a culturally neutral language suitable for philosophy, but in the diction, grammar, and syntax of great authors, the very norms that the scholastics tried to eliminate from truth statements.

Like many humanists of his generation, Vives made his pronouncements about language as an educator, and as such his articulation of a fundamental philological concept contributed to the complete transformation of language pedagogy and to the founding of a new educational institution (the grammar school) – in short, to the reorientation of the entire *ratio studii* towards reading authors rather than constructing propositions. That true language is based on the conventions of speech as used in civic society is perhaps the central idea behind Vives's proposal for changing the entire course of studies in *De tradendis disciplinis* [*On education*] (1531). The most important structural feature of his revised curriculum is the privileged position of grammar and rhetoric in the lower and higher divisions of the curriculum respectively. The ascendancy of logic over the language arts was thus formally renounced.

The ethical purpose of Vives's language-based curriculum was to teach '*prudentia*' (sometimes translated as 'practical wisdom'), or knowledge of the necessities of life, as opposed to philosophy in the technical scholastic sense. Though he retains some Aristotelian notions of truth, Vives holds Aristotle himself responsible for scholastic disputes about topics of useless complexity. He further extends his criticisms to Aristotle in *De causis corruptarum artium* [*On the causes of the corruption of the arts*] (1531) and in *De Aristotelis operibus censura* [*On judging the works of Aristotle*] (1538). He depicts even those Aristotelian works closest to his own interests as obscurantist, abstract, and speculative, and therefore useless in the world of human affairs.

His philosophical response to this obscurantism is a curriculum based on probable truth, as opposed to the certitude claimed by scholastic logic. The ultimate goal of this curricular project was, after learning correct language through imitation of ancient authors, the persuasive social and psychological use of language. Vives turns to the informal logic of humanist dialectic for the rules of persuasive argument based on probable truth; rhetoric in turn teaches how to produce a desired effect by coordinating the place and time of expression with the subject-matter at hand and with the personality of the audience, all considerations barred in scholastic logic but epitomized by 'prudence'. That many of these ideas could have been found in Aristotle's works on rhetoric, dialectic, ethics, and politics reveals how exclusively Aristotle had become associated with abstract thought perplexingly expressed. The importance of Aristotle as the philosopher of civic virtue in the *polis* was all but lost to scholastic and humanist alike.

The language programme of *De tradendis disciplinis* is the intellectual foundation for a culture with new practical and political concerns, furthered by a new professional agenda. While promoting his moral and intellectual interests, Vives's curriculum also fulfils the practical needs of an expanding state administration in early modern Europe; Vives translates his language-based curriculum and its offer of 'prudence' into concrete professional aims: management of state affairs. Those who go no further than the language skills of the lower curriculum are suitable for the lower positions in public administration; those who master the higher rhetorical disciplines are suitable to govern states, to be judges as well as theologians (persuasive preachers rather than expositors of metaphysical quiddities). Vives thus places into practice, in the most concrete way, his antischolastic view of language as the *instrumentum societatis hominum*.

Vives's antischolasticism finds further expression in his treatment of history as the perfect expression of rhetoric because it leads to the highest form of prudence: the ability to conjecture about the future based on the past. Historical narrative replaces the scholastic's logical proposition as the truth-genre. Narrative emerges as the formal encoding of probabilistic knowledge, hence the importance of history for statecraft, the ultimate embodiment of humanist 'prudence' and the perfect vehicle of Vives's combined intellectual and professional programme. Ironically, Vives could have found a similar theory of narrative in Aristotle's *Poetics*. He stops short, however, of endorsing a theory of fictional narrative; with few exceptions, Vives remained largely hostile to poetry and imaginative literature.

If literary authors – historians and orators, that is, but not poets – are the repository of cultural authority, then classical Latin is the ideal language of that authority. Here too Vives's linguistic theory is the vehicle of a larger concern, in this case the ambitious political programme of Spanish Catholicism. Writing at the dawn of the Reformation, he urges that humanist Latin and all it implies replace scholastic Aristotelianism as the universal linguistic and intellectual framework of Christian unity within a Christian empire (ironic in light of Vives's Jewish background). Unlike the twentieth-century revival of rhetoric as an instrument of cultural debate in response to the erosion of common values, Vives's humanistic rhetoric is motivated by a drive to a uniform society ultimately responsive to religious authority.[3]

Under the influence of the humanist Johannes Sturm at the University of Paris, Pierre de la Ramée [Petrus Ramus] articulated his newly adopted humanism, like Vives, in contention with the scholastic Aristotelianism of his own education. A contested tradition has it that Ramus unsuccessfully defended an anti-Aristotelian Master of Arts thesis in 1536; no doubt, however, surrounds the anti-Aristotelianism of his 1543 publication of three works, each reflecting his academic lectures: *The structure of dialectic* [*Dialecticae partitiones*], *Training in dialectic* [*Dialecticae institutiones*] and *Remarks on Aristotle* [*Aristotelicae animadversiones*]. (Because Ramus's articulation of his ideas was related to ongoing academic lectures, these and other works went through many revisions depending on his classroom practice at any given time. Scholars are therefore sensitive to special emphases in particular editions of the same work.) The publication of these works led to vehement criticism at least in part because they were received as attacks on the university establishment. Ramus defined the aim of his humanist educational reform, the union of philosophy and eloquence, against Aristotle and his influence. He saw himself as re-establishing this union, long abandoned in the scholastic dark ages, by furthering the work begun by Rudolph Agricola in his *De inventione dialectica* (1480). Alternately blaming Aristotle himself and his scholastic followers for the corruption of learning, Ramus repeated the charge that Aristotelian logic has no utility for anything other than obscurantist disputation. He adopts a deliberately controversialist attitude, dressed in an irreverent, sarcastic, even contemptuous tone towards Aristotle. In addition to his technical critique of Aristotelian logic, for example his doctrine of syllogism, Ramus charges Aristotle with a chaos of predicates, a laborious complexity of categories, an unsystematic approach to the topics of rhetoric, and altogether an over-elaborate exposition of logical and dialectical subjects.

Consequently, the utility of Aristotle's logic was drastically diminished. Logic, Ramus insisted, must be directed towards making learning useful for something outside the university, namely civic virtue, and to do so, it must be made an instrument for such literary arts as history, rhetoric, and oratory, after the model of Cicero and Quintilian (though, paradoxically, Ramus often attacks Cicero and Quintilian as followers of Aristotle). For this purpose, in characteristic humanist fashion, Ramus replaced logic with dialectic, and turned to the work of Agricola, long favoured by

---

[3] For the inability of humanism to critique itself and the society from which it emerges, in contrast to Machiavelli's concept of the function of dialectic in a republican polity, see Victoria Kahn, 'Habermas, Machiavelli, and the critique of ideology', *Publications of the modern language association of America* 105 (1990), 464–76.

humanists for rendering dialectic an instrument of the literary arts. He was particularly attracted to Agricola's division of dialectic into invention (the construction of the fundamental underlying structure of an argument that can be reduced to a *locus communis*, or a commonplace) and judgement (or the progressive steps in an argument). Whereas Agricola expounded the technique of invention, Ramus took it upon himself to develop the art of judgement. He thus goes further than most humanists by devising a method of his own to replace the abhorred Aristotelian logic.

Ramus's revised dialectic resulted in several original and long-range influential contributions. In what is still the most comprehensive treatment of Ramus's thought, Walter Ong has argued that the greatest significance of Ramus's dialectic was its transformation of oral (or perhaps more accurately, manuscript) culture to print culture.[4] In addition, in rationalizing and streamlining the curriculum, he insisted that each art should have its own special function which should not be duplicated by any other. Accordingly, and with momentous consequence, some scholars feel, he restricted dialectic to invention and judgement, and rhetoric to the ornaments of language, including elocution, diction, tropes, and figures. For Ramus, dialectic, not rhetoric, thus emerged as the most important art to replace the Aristotelian logical legacy.

Another far-reaching Ramist innovation stemming from his anti-scholastic reforms was his insistence on the unity of knowledge. Because discourse and reason are one, he argued, the same dialectical method should be applied to all disciplines. He thus breaks down the distinction between probable and demonstrable truth, between logic and dialectic. Philosophical and rhetorical discourse collapse into each other, as dialectic becomes the underlying intellectual architecture of all the disciplines. (For Ramus, dialectic serves as a method to read as well as produce texts.) In this way, he provided a simplified and effective method, the *unica doctrinae instituendae methodus*, to construct arguments in every subject or discipline – indeed, to structure the totality of knowledge. In this triumph of pedagogy, literary works, like those of Cicero and Virgil, provide the model discourse.

Ramus's use of poems and orations to reveal the dialectical argument underlying all discourse was double-edged, however. It posed as much potential to weaken essential humanist concerns as it did to advance them. Poems and orations may perfectly well illustrate the efficient Ramist breakdown of discourse into a structured argument progressing in steps (dialectic) and its stylistic and figurative ornaments (rhetoric), but the separation of invention and judgement from rhetoric had the effect of

---

[4] Walter J. Ong, *Ramus, method, and the decay of dialogue* (Cambridge, MA: Harvard University Press, 1958). For the visualizing technique of the Ramist dichotomizing method, see pp. 200–2.

reducing literary language – especially poetic language – to the inessential decoration of an argument rather than the indispensable vehicle of truth and insight.[5] From this viewpoint, instead of uniting philosophy and eloquence, Ramus divorced them, as Sharratt argues:[6] the high degree of rhetorical ornament in humanistic arts may in fact inevitably reveal their low intellectual level. In this sense, Ramist analysis verges on insinuating that rhetorical ornament may actually attenuate the underlying logic of a literary work. The rhetorical ornament of literary discourse may be little more than an effective means of teaching audiences of low abilities, including schoolchildren. Though Ramus was actually ridiculed for his attraction to the soft literary arts instead of the exactitude of hard logic, the ultimate implications of his reforms do not necessarily bolster the claims of literary discourse. In the end, Ramus may have helped to foster the production of two discourses, one for a learned, one for a popular audience, a practice followed by Bacon in his division between unornamented truth for the initiated and ornamented for the uninitiated. Ramus's reform of dialectic may have been steeped in the humanism of its day, but its emphasis on method and its reduction of all discourse to an underlying structured argument were to take the art of discourse in the direction of scientism.

From the pedagogical and social perspective, Anthony Grafton and Lisa Jardine claim, the greatest success of Ramus's anti-scholastic recourse to one single method was that it made the arts available to students of many intellectual levels.[7] Ramism, that is, targets those same students that Vives acknowledged as the beneficiary of the lower division of the curriculum, those who were headed to be lower-level civic officials, instead of those interested in the rigours of true scholarship, the responsibility of rule, or the high ideals of civic humanism – that is, according to Grafton and Jardine, the children of the mercantile class. (It is, however, well to remember that the Ramist John Milton belonged to this class.) They thus charge Ramus with sophism in the worse sense – debasing the intellectual level of the arts to the level of practical skills purveyed for the improvement of social position, as, they claim, is evident in the careers of two late sixteenth-century Ramist teachers, Claude Mignault and Gabriel Harvey. However far-reaching Ramus's reforms, his importance is still

---

[5] See Thomas O. Sloan, 'The crossing of rhetoric and poetry in the English Renaissance', in *The rhetoric of Renaissance poetry from Wyatt to Milton*, ed. T. O. Sloan and R. B. Waddington (Berkeley: University of California Press, 1974), pp. 212–43.

[6] Peter Sharratt, 'Peter Ramus and the reform of the university: the divorce of philosophy and eloquence', in *French Renaissance studies, 1540–70: humanism and the encyclopaedia*, ed. P. Sharratt (Edinburgh: Edinburgh University Press, 1976), pp. 4–20.

[7] Anthony Grafton and Lisa Jardine, *From humanism to the humanities: education and the liberal arts in fifteenth- and sixteenth-century Europe* (Cambridge, MA: Harvard University Press, 1986), pp. 161–209.

granted only grudgingly because he continues to be charged with popularizing and intellectual shallowness. However, there have been attempts
to reverse many of these negative evaluations of Ramus and his effect on
poetry, especially his role in creating a specifically Protestant spirituality
in dialectic and poetry.[8]

The post-scholastic reforms of Vives and Ramus thus belong to the histories of philosophy, of literary criticism, and of socio-political institutions, and students in such fields are likely to evaluate these thinkers in
different ways. The challenge posed by Vives and Ramus to the medieval
Aristotelian legacy in their disciplinary reorientation towards the language arts had considerable influence on literature in the broad sense,
especially prose genres like history and oratory. However, because they
were themselves either hostile (like Vives) or insensitive (like Ramus) to
imaginative literature, it was left to others to apply their ideas to the writing and study of poetry in the early modern period. Ironically, it was, at
least in part, to the Aristotle of the *Poetics* that such an influential writer
as Sir Philip Sidney, for example, turned to articulate a rhetorical concept
of poetic fiction.

---

[8] See Rosemond Tuve, *Elizabethan and metaphysical imagery* (Chicago: University of
Chicago Press, 1947); and Tamara A. Goeglein, 'Utterances of the Protestant soul in the
Faerie Queene: the allegory of holiness and the humanist discourse of reason', *Criticism*
36 (1994), 1–19.

42

The rise of the vernaculars

Richard Waswo

Robert Burton's complaint in 1621 that he could find no publisher willing to print his mammoth book in Latin marks the achievement of a kind of revolution during the sixteenth century.[1] As the result of a conscious campaign and numerous polemics, first developed in Italy, then continued in France, the results of which were simply transferred to England, the major vernacular languages of Western Europe had by that date effectively dislodged the monopoly held by Latin on all forms of serious, written or printed, enquiry. When, just a century earlier, intellectuals or scholars wished to address the widest audience of their peers, there was no choice about the language: Erasmus's *Moriae encomium* [*Praise of folly*] (1511), More's *Utopia* (1516), Polydore Vergil's *Anglicae historiae libri* XXVI (1534). But in 1614, Sir Walter Ralegh offered a far larger historical project to this wider public as *The history of the world*. In the same year, Professor Edward Brerewood published an equally ambitious project (on the very subject of vernacular languages and their relation to Latin): *Enquiries touching the diversity of languages, and religions through the . . . world*. And perhaps the most ambitious of all projects had earlier appeared in Sir Francis Bacon's *The advancement of learning* (1605). Both Brerewood's and Bacon's texts were subsequently translated *into* Latin – a sign of both the lost dominance and continued prestige of the ancient lingua franca.

The general history of this displacement has long been known,[2] and its causes not far to seek: the rise of nation-states and consciously cultivated national literatures, the explosion of literacy made possible by print and mandated by Protestantism. The rise of vernaculars fits seamlessly into the story of our progressive modernity; it seldom detains us. But just what kind of, and how significant a, phenomenon this is might give us pause. The most stimulating thinker on the subject invites us to consider it in

---

[1] *The anatomy of melancholy*, ed. F. Dell and P. Jordan-Smith (New York: Farrar and Rinehart, 1927), pp. 23–4.
[2] The standard accounts are: Bruno Migliorini, *Storia della lingua italiana*, 3rd edn (Florence: Sansoni, 1961); Ferdinand Brunot, *Histoire de la langue française*, vol. II (Paris: Armand Colin, 1906); Richard Foster Jones, *The triumph of the English language* (Stanford: Stanford University Press, 1953).

global terms; speaking of the use of all learned languages (including Latin, classical Chinese and Arabic, rabbinical Hebrew), he says:

The fact that at a crucial stage in its development the most advanced thought of mankind in widely separated parts of the globe has been worked out in linguistic economies far removed from the hearth and from the entire world of infancy would seem to deserve far more attention than it has received, if only because it has received almost no attention whatsoever.[3]

Father Ong goes on to specify among the common features of learned, 'masculine', languages that all are second acquisitions, after a spoken mother tongue; learned by writing, 'controlled by script'; all-male.[4] Let us pause to imagine what this meant for someone growing up in Europe between roughly AD 500 and 1600. If you wished, from whatever rare accident of birth or experience, to acquire conceptual (as opposed to operational) knowledge of anything; if you had the least curiosity about the life of the mind or even the least ambition for such advancement as the ability to write might procure – you were probably a boy. And certainly you could pursue such curiosity or ambition only by first learning another language than the one you naturally spoke, another which itself was spoken only in the formal institutions (educational, religious, governmental) of your society, not in the everyday world of its material transactions. Whatever the subject that might have tempted your curiosity, from botany to versification, access to it was possible only in Latin. You, of course, would not have complained about this; that was just how it was. If you found the Latin too tough or boring, you dropped out; if not, you went ahead and took your place in one of the cultural bureaucracies where all members understood perfectly that 'culture' was what came from somewhere else, was conducted, transmitted, and administered in the language that you had so painstakingly learned, that separated you from *hoi polloi* out there in the streets and gave you a status and income (maybe just a little) better than theirs. If you rose to some managerial level in your bureaucracy, you would have a Latin epitaph to announce this superior status to posterity.

Apart from the psychosexual schizophrenia in this situation – its identification of 'mother' tongues and 'father' gods, its gendered split between material and 'cultural' worlds – is the somewhat more obvious sociocultural hierarchy that it imposes. What, and what alone, counts as learning, constitutes the objects of serious study, is what had already been written about in Latin (or, belatedly, in ancient Greek or Hebrew). Since

---

[3] Walter J. Ong, *Interfaces of the word: studies in the evolution of consciousness and culture* (Ithaca: Cornell University Press, 1977), p. 28.
[4] See also his penetrating analysis of 'Latin language study as a Renaissance puberty rite', in *Rhetoric, romance, and technology* (Ithaca: Cornell University Press, 1971), pp. 113–41.

all of contemporary life was perforce excluded from this body of writing, it did not count. Nor did this matter much while all of Western history was regarded as the same Augustinian moment in time: that downward slide from the Resurrection to the Second Coming, during which, in the Middle Ages, ancient people are depicted in art and fiction wearing the clothes, inhabiting the spaces, and having the manners of contemporary, transalpine Europeans. Only when the earlier generations of Renaissance humanists began to see the past as different from the present, thus invent-ing a modern sense of history, did the exclusion of the present as an object of knowledge begin to matter, or even begin to be felt. For when every-thing knowable was seen as contemporary, there was no exclusion. When everything stopped being contemporary, the costumes in paintings became antique; Gothic architecture was scorned and replaced by clas-sical models; medieval Latin was ridiculed by lovers of Ciceronian style; spatial perspective was adopted as an equivalent to the new temporal perspective of someone now looking far back at a distant world – that is, the Renaissance occurred.

And only after it occurred could the monopoly of Latin be perceived and consciously resisted. The process and motivation of the resistance clearly show it to be a form of cultural decolonization, an attack on a for-eign domination, and on an implicit concept of 'culture' that assumes it to be the sole property of a (spatial or temporal) metropolitan elite. The grounds of the attack were furnished, willy-nilly, by those who wished to constitute themselves as this élite: the Latin humanists of the fifteenth cen-tury. For it was they who discovered history in the different usages of clas-sical and medieval Latin, and who conceived of linguistic change in terms of the organic metaphor of growth, maturity, and decline. Flavio Biondo found different levels of usage within classical Latin; Leonardo Bruni and Leon Battista Alberti generalized the biological metaphor to include all languages as being potentially subject to a 'natural' cycle of flourishing and decay.[5] Alberti has also the distinction of producing (before 1472) the first known grammar of any modern language.[6] The production of gram-mars for vernaculars would become a key tactic in the campaigns of the next century, an essential demonstration that present, spoken tongues were not the unregulatable chaos they had long been thought, but could be reduced to the same kind of rules as Latin and Greek. This was the

[5] See Cecil Grayson, *A Renaissance controversy: Latin or Italian?* (Oxford: Clarendon Press, 1960); Riccardo Fubini, 'La coscienza del Latino negli umanisti', *Studi medievali*, series 3,2 (1961), 505–50; Hans Wilhelm Klein, *Latein und Volgare in Italien* (Munich: M. Hueber, 1957).

[6] *La prima grammatica della lingua volgare*, ed. C. Grayson (Bologna: Commissione per i testi di lingua, 1964). Grayson's attribution of authorship is confirmed, and the whole field surveyed, by W. Keith Percival, 'Grammatical tradition and the rise of the vernaculars', *Current trends in linguistics* 13 (1975), 231–75.

strategy of assimilating vernaculars to the canons of description inherited
from the classical world; it would develop during the sixteenth century
into a more aggressive strategy of competition with the ancient languages:
from showing that vulgar tongues could do all that Latin could do to
showing that they could do more or better.[7]

The idea, however, that made such strategies possible, was that of the
speech community, which grew out of the Latin humanist perception
that language is a socio-historical product whose 'rules do not fall from
heaven' but are inferences from communal use at any given time.[8] This
idea, derived from Quintilian, was developed most radically and explicitly in the work of Lorenzo Valla (q.v., II.I.a; v.4.bi). It was the basis of
his widely influential descriptive account of classical Latin, *Elegantiae*, and
of his new language-based philosophy, *Dialecticae disputationes*. Though
Valla himself regarded Latin as innately and incontestably superior to
vernaculars,[9] the semantic and epistemological importance he and other
humanists gave to linguistic usage could not be confined to the language
that most people heard only from the pulpit and the podium. The fifteenth-
century élite had promoted a new way of seeing all languages that would
undermine in the next century the privilege they ascribed to one.[10]

The undermining was carried on first in Italy, in a series of published
dialogues (1525–70) whose central importance is that they legitimized
vernacular languages and the forms of present life they incarnated as
objects of knowledge, worthy of serious attention.[11] By so doing, they
redefined 'culture' as something that all speakers might have, inclusive in
principle, though still pretty exclusive in practice. For the vernaculars
in question were those that already possessed, and were rapidly being
encouraged to augment, a prestigious body of written literature. The cultural decolonization of the modern occident from the domination of Latin
was, after all, only beginning. One beginning was to draw what soon
became a classificatory distinction between 'living' and 'dead' languages,

---

[7] These strategies and metaphors are analysed in some detail by Richard Waswo, *Language and meaning in the Renaissance* (Princeton: Princeton University Press, 1987), ch. 4.

[8] Lorenzo Valla, *Ars grammatica*, ed. P. Casciano (Milan: A. Mondadori, 1990), line 181: 'De celo quoniam non lapsa est norma loquendi'.

[9] His views on the subject are analysed by Hanna-Barbara Gerl, *Rhetorik als Philosophie: Lorenzo Valla* (Munich: W. Fink, 1974), pp. 231–50.

[10] This process, suggested long ago by Hans Baron, *The crisis of the early Italian Renaissance*, 2 vols. (Princeton: Princeton University Press, 1955), vol. I, pp. 308–12, is described in detail by Carlo Dionisotti, *Gli umanisti e il volgare fra Quattro e Cinquecento* (Florence: F. le Monnier, 1968), and extended and modified by Sarah Stever Gravelle, 'The Latin–vernacular question and humanist theory of language and culture', *Journal of the history of ideas* 49 (1988), 367–86.

[11] Useful surveys of these debates are Robert A. Hall, Jr., *The Italian Questione della Lingua: an interpretative essay* (Chapel Hill: University of North Carolina Press, 1942), and Maurizio Vitale, *La questione della lingua* (Palermo: Palumbo, 1967), pp. 22–63.

a distinction first made by Pietro Bembo, advocating the literary cultivation of a form (semi-archaic Tuscan) of Italian whose value is that of present communication: 'one must say that whoever writes in Latin now is writing for the dead rather than for the living'.[12] Dante, of course, would have agreed; this was precisely why he defended at length his use of the vernacular to explain his vernacular poems to his contemporaries.[13] Dante had also written a treatise advocating precisely the standardization of a literary idiom for all Italy;[14] but he wrote it in Latin, and it remained virtually unknown for over two centuries – until 1529, when Giovanni Giorgio Trissino repeated its argument in his dialogue, *Il castellano*. For until then, after the humanist revaluation of the importance of the speech community, there was no context in which naturally spoken languages could be taken seriously.

By far the most sophisticated, well-balanced and wide-ranging of all the polemics in the campaign to liberate vernaculars was Sperone Speroni's *Dialogo delle lingue* (1542). The disputants here illustrate the various interests in and functions of language that are at stake in qualifying actual, present life as 'culture': classical scholarship and vernacular *belles-lettres*, to be sure, but also empirical science and urban courtly society. The disputes they have – about accepting the linguistic usages of the past as a limit on present practice, about the inefficiency of access to scientific knowledge if contained only in ancient tongues, about the possibility of translating such knowledge, about the expressive power of native vs. learned languages, about whether all languages are equal or unequal in value, different or identical in function – virtually set the agenda for the quarrel between the ancients and moderns that would continue into the eighteenth century.[15] What is more, Speroni dramatizes all these oppositions in a way that makes clear their sterility as oppositions, that shows no party to the quarrel to have a monopoly on the truth, that honours, in sum, the multiple functions of language in the newly historicized and expanded notion of what counts as culture.

One such function, which will make spoken vernaculars superior to Latin for subsequent polemicists, is that of the emotional power and cognitive accuracy with which we can express thoughts in the language we learn 'della bocca' (as Speroni's Courtier puts it), as opposed to the one we

---

[12] *Prose della volgar lingua nella quale si ragiona della volgar lingua* (Venice: G. Tacuino, 1525), fol. 18ᵛ: 'Che quale hora Latinamente scrive, a morti si debba dire che egli scriva piu che a vivi'.

[13] *Il convivio* (1.5–10), ed. G. Busnelli and G. Vandelli, 2 vols. (Florence: F. Le Monnier, 1968), vol. I, pp. 33–60.

[14] *De vulgari eloquentia*, trans. A. G. F. Howell, in *Latin works of Dante* (London: Temple Classics, 1904).

[15] As Hans Baron observed: 'The *querelle* of the Ancients and Moderns as a problem for Renaissance scholarship', *Journal of the history of ideas* 20 (1959), 3–22.

learn in school. This point gets heavy emphasis in the selection of (often verbatim) borrowings from Speroni that make the argument in Joachim du Bellay's *Deffence et illustration de la langue françoyse* (1549), the text which started the vernacular bandwagon rolling in France.[16] The programme of the Pléiade was (that of Speroni's Courtier) to advocate as a literary, written vernacular the spoken idiom of gentlefolk – a programme that was both advocated and practised in the England of Dryden and Congreve. Far from excluding the imitation of the classics, it coexisted with it, indeed implemented it in a way designed to secure an immediacy of communication with a contemporary audience. But perhaps the more interesting (because less studied) dimension of the new legitimacy of vernacular culture is the political.

The humanists all had a vivid sense that the development of a language was not just organic by itself, but was organically (and ideally) connected to the power of its speech community in the world. Largely from Livy, they pictured the greatness and virtue of the Roman Empire as culminating in the Golden Age of its literature, at the summit of its Republic. This vision inspired Bruni and Alberti to hope for a similar literary/political flourishing for the Florentine Republic. But in the next century the same vision, sorely tried by the civil wars and foreign occupations of several of the great city-states, suggested that degeneracy and conquest had pre-empted any such achievement. Speroni's most conservative character claims the Italians deserve the chaos of unimprovable dialects they speak. France, however, was not only unconquered, but expanding, and her widening dominion was to be accompanied by the assiduous production of literature written in the language that came most naturally from the mouth. Just whose mouth one speaks with becomes a resonant metaphor in Jacques Peletier's enthusiastic extensions of what Du Bellay borrowed from Speroni. Urging the poet to write from his own experience (and not just to reproduce what he has read in books), Peletier threatens: 'Otherwise . . . nothing will be said of him except that he speaks with the mouth of another, by rote and in debt'. Earlier, castigating the reproduction in French of classical themes and styles, Peletier sees it as self-chosen bondage: 'We keep our own tongue in slavery ourselves; we show ourselves foreigners in our own country. What sort of nation are we, to speak perpetually with the mouth of another?'[17]

What is being presented here as a kind of liberation depends precisely on the humanist discovery that a language is a form of life, that it constitutes

---

[16] The plunderings of Speroni were demonstrated by Pierre Villey, *Les sources italiennes de la 'Deffense et illustration de la langue françoise' de Joachim du Bellay* (Paris: H. Champion, 1908).

[17] *L'Art poëtique* (1555), ed. A. Boulanger (Paris: Les Belles Lettres, 1930), pp. 221, 114 [my trans.].

a world and our experience of it, and is coextensive with culture itself. Peletier's wish to be free of ancient domination is echoed in various ways in other polemics. Claudio Tolomei, in *Il Cesano* (1555), attacks the old assumption that all (Romance) vernaculars are but 'corruptions' of Latin, urging that no language ever exists in a 'pure' state, that all are subject to influence and change and hence of equal potential value. Benedetto Varchi's *L'Hercolano* (1570) claims at length that the literary value of his own vernacular literature is in fact higher than that of Latin or Greek. The cultural legitimation of mother tongues is thus usually confined (and will be more so in seventeenth-century neoclassicism) to the written speech of a political and literary élite. But the principle that language is culture recognizes no class boundaries, and was occasionally applied even to legitimize the speech of the illiterate. The most radical such applications deny, in their invention of descriptive linguistics, the very (prescriptive) idea of grammatical correctness. Charles de Bovelles maintains, in *Liber de differentia vulgarium linguarum*, that there are no such things as faults in any native tongue whatsoever, that vernaculars are ungovernable, and ridicules the efforts of his contemporaries – by citing endless local variations in speech – to reduce them to rules. Joseph Webbe, summarizing for his countrymen much of the continental debates and scholarship on the matter, from Valla to Montaigne, makes the same flat denial: 'whatsoever is in use, is neither inconvenient, nor a Soloecism'.[18]

Montaigne, of course, created in his vernacular a new literary genre with a new subject, and was a connoisseur of the culture he found in native speech, often opposing it to more learned pretensions and limitations. He avoids no expressions 'that are used in the streets of France; those who would combat usage with grammar make fools of themselves'; and he offers as examples of linguistic competence those innocent of any acquaintance with grammar or rhetoric, a 'lackey, or a fishwife of the Petit Pont', who 'will talk your ear off, if you like, and will perhaps stumble as little over the rules of their language as the best master of arts in France'.[19] Montaigne accepts and affirms vernaculars in their ever-changing vitality, regarding even the fate of his own, correctly, as dependent both on the merits of its users and the power of the speech community to which they belong: 'It is for the good and useful writings to nail it to themselves, and its credit will go as go the fortunes of our state'.[20]

To have learned to speak with one's own mouth means to value that speech as both an object of knowledge and the embodiment of a culture

---

[18] *An appeale to truth, in the controversy betweene art & use; about the best and most expedient course in languages* (London: G. Latham, 1622), p. 36.
[19] *The complete essays*, trans. D. M. Frame (Stanford: Stanford University Press, 1958), pp. 667 (III.5), 125 (I.26).
[20] *Ibid.*, p. 751 (III.9).

worth having. It is to declare that the materials and processes of daily life are as fully 'cultural' as the ruined monuments and dead languages of the ancient world. It is to overthrow the internalized domination of a foreign community, to decolonize the mind. Western Europe began thus to decolonize itself from antiquity during the sixteenth century, at just the moment when it also began to colonize the rest of the world. This historical irony is manifest in the identical campaign for the legitimation and liberation of vernaculars being waged today by some African writers. In English, the most tireless and articulate of these is Ngugi wa Thiong'o, who stopped writing novels in English in 1977 to start producing fiction, poetry, and drama in his mother tongue, Gikuyu. As a polemicist, Ngugi continues to insist that the only real African literature must be written in African languages – for all the same reasons that sixteenth-century Italians, Frenchmen, and Englishmen advocated and practised enriching their own mother tongues. Ngugi aims to overcome the condition of 'colonial alienation', which he defines as: 'an active (or passive) identification with that which is most external to one's environment. It starts with a deliberate disassociation of the language of conceptualization, of thinking, of formal education, of mental development, from the language of daily interaction in the home and in the community. . . .'[21] What Ngugi is describing as the effect of modern imperialism is the legacy of the ancient, the condition of occidental culture itself during the millennium between the collapse of the old empire and the formation of the new, and global, one.

The fortunes of European nation-states were considerably enhanced by the conscious legitimation and cultivation of their native tongues and literatures, as Montaigne suggested, and as the author of the first published grammar of a modern vernacular (Alberti's was not printed until this century) well knew. Dedicating his work to Queen Isabella of Spain in 1492, Antonio de Nebrija explains to her the utility of the project: that since Her Majesty has subdued many 'barbarous cities and nations of strange tongues', his grammar will facilitate their understanding of 'our language' and the laws which the conqueror imposes on the conquered, just as Latin grammars did for Latin.[22] And so it went. Western Europe decolonized itself culturally from ancient Rome only to imitate it; it contested the model only by becoming it, by imposing on others the cultural alienation it had so long known.

[21] *Decolonising the mind: the politics of language in African literature* (London/Nairobi: James Currey/Heinemann, 1986), p. 28.
[22] *Gramática castellana*, ed. P. Galindo Romeo and L. Ortiz Muñoz (Madrid: Junta del Centenario, 1946), p. 11.

43

Ancients and Moderns: France

Terence Cave

Histories of literature are inclined to treat the Quarrel of the Ancients and Moderns as a rather parochial dispute among French *lettrés* of the late seventeenth and early eighteenth century, echoed in England in the 'Battle of the Books'. The personal quarrels and rivalries of that period are however better seen as the local idiom in which long-standing cultural issues were articulated; the apparently surprising virulence it engendered is no doubt an indication that a critical moment had been reached, a moment whose significance is clearer from our own historical vantage point.

The designation of a group of 'ancient' texts or writers, whether as bearers of authority or as models, is a widespread cultural phenomenon. Although it necessarily implies a reader or writer whose position in a present moment is defined contrastively with these Ancients,[1] the further step of coining designations for the group of 'new' writers is an important one. That step was already taken in antiquity: in Alexandria, the moderns were called *neoteroi*; Latin writers – among them Cicero – used the Greek word or translated it as *novi* (or *neoterici*), although it is important to note that these terms were not used to mark out distinct periods of cultural history.[2] The word *modernus* – 'one of the last legacies of late Latin to the modern world', as Curtius puts it – did not appear until the sixth century.

The antithesis was recast in different ways during the Middle Ages: not only the pagan authors of the past, but Christian texts also (the Bible, the Church Fathers) were called *veteres*; the terms *moderni* and *neoterici* came to be applied to theologians such as Aquinas, or in another context to the nominalist grammarians and logicians. With the rise of humanist learning in Italy, then in northern Europe, new kinds of opposition begin to take shape. The humanists are by definition partisans of the *antiqui*, attempting to consign the logic and neo-barbaric Latin of the scholastics

---

[1] The capitalized form 'the Ancients' is used here to designate the writers of a past age (usually classical antiquity); the 'ancients' (lower case) are the writers (the opponents of the 'moderns') who insist on the superiority of the Ancients.
[2] See Ernst Robert Curtius, *European literature and the Latin Middle Ages*, trans. W. R. Trask (London and Henley: Routledge & Kegan Paul, 1979), p. 251. Curtius summarizes the history of the ancients–moderns opposition (pp. 251–5); ch. 14 (pp. 247–72) as a whole ('Classicism') should be consulted for the history of the terms 'classic', 'classicism', etc.

to a 'middle age'; on the other hand, a debate between Coluccio Salutati and other humanists, recorded in the form of a dialogue by Leonardo Bruni (1401–6), already anticipates the seventeenth-century quarrel in that it turns on the merits of Dante, Petrarch, and Boccaccio as a modern canon, equal or even superior to the Ancients.[3]

The positioning of the 'new' writer in relation to ancient models was from the outset acknowledged to be problematic. Petrarch was himself already deeply enmeshed in the politics and ethics of 'imitation',[4] and the Ciceronian debates of the fifteenth and sixteenth centuries turned the problem into a virulent controversy, one which again foreshadows the *querelles* of the neoclassical period.[5] Both sides accepted the value of ancient *auctores* as founts of wisdom and as models for form and style; but the Ciceronians' exclusive emphasis on Cicero as a model for prose (or Virgil for poetry) was by definition conservative and entailed a suspicion of creative freedom or innovation, whereas the anti-Ciceronians stressed the need for new forms and styles to meet the needs of a culturally different age. To this extent, the anti-Ciceronians were proto-moderns, although they did not characterize themselves as *moderni*. Erasmus's dialogue *Ciceronianus* (1528) provides a rich repertory of their arguments. A detailed knowledge of the ancient corpus is to be transformed by a process of fragmentation and individual selection into a storehouse of materials; the present-day writer's own experience and imagination will then re-shape them into the expression of that writer's personal and cultural identity. This theory of imitation, by placing its focus in the present and in a distinctively individual consciousness, anticipates many important developments in early modern culture; it is also linked in Renaissance education theory with the practical uses of classical learning as a repertory of models for diplomacy, administration, governance, and the conduct of war. That such debates were by no means limited to questions of academic politics is demonstrated by the ways in which the defence of vernacular writing shifts the ground. The quarrel in Salutati's circle is only one episode in a long-running debate over the uses of the Italian language; in the *Concorde des deux langaiges* of the French poet Jean Lemaire de Belges (1511), the cultural achievements of France appear in rivalry with those of Italy, represented primarily by Dante and Petrarch. It is no accident that Lemaire was also a polemist who defended an early form of non-schismatic Gallicanism.

[3] See Hans Baron, *The crisis of the early Italian Renaissance*, 2 vols. (Princeton: Princeton University Press, 1966), pp. 225–69, 332–53.
[4] See Thomas M. Greene, *The light in Troy: imitation and discovery in Renaissance poetry* (New Haven and London: Yale University Press, 1982), pp. 81–146.
[5] See Greene, *Light in Troy*, pp. 171–96. See also Ann Moss, 'Literary imitation in the sixteenth century: writers and readers, Latin and French' in the present volume (pp. 107–18).

A strong nationalistic emphasis is also apparent in the writing of mid-sixteenth-century French poets. In his *Deffence et illustration de la langue françoyse* (1549), Joachim du Bellay points out that the Ancients wrote in their own vernacular; modern writers of Latin are vainly attempting to piece together fragments of a ruined building. He rehearses the anti-Ciceronian arguments in favour of eclectic and innovative imitation, applying them now to the vernacular. At the same time, he rejects the native tradition of French poetry as unworthy of imitation, encouraging poets to revert to the consecrated models of antiquity (together with Petrarch).[6] He also imagines a time in the future when the French language will forge its own forms of eloquence and become capable of independently expressing the whole range of human knowledge.[7]

Du Bellay is a typical vernacular humanist of the sixteenth century, upholding the ancients but formulating a poetics which affords ample opportunities for new departures. He adopts the cyclical schema of the *translatio studiorum*, and his mental habits are dominated by metaphors of natural growth and decline, together with agricultural procedures (planting, grafting) that suggest the symbiosis of nature and culture.

Du Bellay's Italian contemporaries, despite their individual differences of emphasis, achieved a similar balance in their revival of Aristotelian poetics. The humanist philosophers of Padua had set out to reclaim Aristotelian thought as a whole from the scholastics; the interpretation and dissemination of the *Poetics* turned out to be the most spectacularly successful element in their programme. By the late sixteenth century, Aristotelian poetics had become both a new source of ancient authority and a matrix for the reading of genres and forms unknown in antiquity, as is apparent from the 1550s onwards in the debates over the nature and status of the romance.[8]

Montaigne holds a critical position in the history of attitudes to antiquity. He is a late humanist, thoroughly familiar with the Latin canon and with major Greek authors such as Plutarch, but also with Italian and French writers; in 'On books' (II.10) as elsewhere in the *Essais*, his reading preferences appear as characteristically eclectic and personal. Similarly, his chapter on education (I.26) relativizes the canon by placing the value of education not in the materials required but in the formation of the individual judgement. In his own writing, he carries the principle of free imitation to the point of no return: he quotes, cites, borrows

---

[6] Joachim du Bellay, *La deffence et illustration de la langue françoyse*, ed. H. Chamard (Paris: Didier, 1948), pp. 107–26.

[7] *Ibid.*, pp. 58–83. The first book of the *Deffence* is concerned throughout with the positioning of French language and culture in relation to classical antiquity.

[8] See Daniel Javitch, 'The assimilation of Aristotle's *Poetics* in sixteenth-century Italy' in the present volume (pp. 53–65).

endlessly from every conceivable source, but always in order to expand the consciousness of the first-person writer whose mobile 'portrait' he claims to elaborate. That his title – here meaning something like 'soundings' – was later to become the name of a genre is highly instructive: in Montaigne, the essay-form is already a proto-modern practice of writing which allows the author to avoid resembling an *auctor*, to remain mobile, mutable, outside any hierarchy of genres.

At the same time, it is important to read the *Essais* in relation to earlier and later examples of the Renaissance miscellany – Erasmus's *Adages*, and English equivalents like Bacon's *Essays*, Robert Burton's *Anatomy of melancholy*, and Thomas Browne's *Pseudodoxia epidemica*. Such works often seem difficult of access for the modern reader because they draw liberally on the bric-a-brac of a literary culture which is now largely defunct; they nonetheless played a critical role in mediating between a world dominated by the notion of written authority and another world in which economic, political, and technological changes were beginning to take effect. Erasmus, Montaigne, and the English humanists wrote for an age in which books were coming to be regarded, not as privileged objects composing an ideal library (such as the one in Montaigne's famous tower), but as disposable commodities, rapidly disseminated and put to many different uses, often unpredictable ones.

The paradigmatic instance of Montaigne's proto-modern versatility is his experimental transcription of Pyrrhonist arguments in the 'Apologie de Raimond Sebond' (II.12). He could not have foreseen that, by inserting these arguments into a vernacular text which was to become a best-seller, he transformed a disconcerting set of Greek paradoxes into one of the most powerful intellectual weapons of the early modern world. Sextus Empiricus, an obscure ancient *auctor*, became within a few generations the source of arguments which could be used against authorities of all kinds. If Montaigne had remained ignorant of Pyrrhonism, he might still have been a cultural relativist; but it is clear that this strand in his epistemology was what, for seventeenth-century readers, gave the sharp edge to his reflections.

We are speaking here, then, of a precise historical moment, of the very fault-line which defines our retrospective conception of the 'early modern'. Montaigne was in many ways a conservative; his scepticism reinforced his belief that human understanding of the natural world was inherently limited; his empiricism was personal and practical, leading to no conception of scientific progress. Indeed, he clearly belongs to an *episteme* in which there was no separation between the 'arts' and the 'sciences': both were textual and depended heavily on the notion of textual authority.

It was not long, however, before strands which in the *Essais* are still interwoven were to be progressively separated. Descartes used Pyrrhonism

as a tactical weapon to create the *tabula rasa* on which a new philosophy and a new science were to be constructed: the Ancients are deprived
at a stroke of their authority, and the storehouse of wisdom they were
supposed to have bequeathed is now read as an accumulation of errors
and mutually invalidating opinions.[9] Descartes is not interested in the
humanist concept of eloquence, and the consequence is a sharp dividing
line between philosophy (which for Descartes includes science) and what
we now call literature. Pascal disagreed with Descartes on almost every
fundamental point, but he too made a critical distinction between two
kinds of knowledge. In the *Préface sur le traité du vide* (?1651), he argues
that textual authority is absolute in fields where the truth is established
once and for all and therefore cannot be improved on: history, geography,
letters, and above all theology. In mathematics and empirical science,
by contrast, authority is valueless; here, human thought is capable of
indefinite linear progress.[10] Hence Pascal is an ancient in some domains, a
modern in others. As we move into the period where these labels begin to
be rallying cries, suggesting crude polarization, it is important to see that
such careful distinctions are available.

By the time Pascal wrote his preface, French poets and dramatists were
already beginning to establish positions along the lines of an ancients–
moderns divide. In the preface to his second play *Clitandre* (1632),
Corneille pays homage to the Ancients while arguing that, since the arts
and sciences are subject to perpetual development, modern writers should
have the freedom to transgress ancient precept.[11] As the theatre became an
increasingly popular form of entertainment at all levels of society, writers
and critics began to draw on the corpus of Aristotelian poetics in order
to establish norms for dramatic composition. Corneille's own dramatic
achievement would have been unthinkable without this critical activity,
but his writings on the theatre over the next twenty-five years make it
clear that he reserved the right to depart from even the most hallowed
Aristotelian principles. That this is more than a literary issue is evident
from the fact that the Académie Française, founded in the mid-1630s,
began to legislate not only on matters of linguistic correctness but also
on the supposed 'rules' governing drama, with Aristotle as the ultimate
authority. The enormous success of Corneille's *Le Cid* in 1637 provoked
the first of a more or less continuous series of literary quarrels, and here
it is striking that it was Richelieu, the king's minister, who invited the

---

[9] In addition to Descartes's classic move towards the *cogito* in the *Discours de la méthode*,
Part 4, see *Les passions de l'âme*, ed. G. Rodis-Lewis (Paris: Vrin, 1966), Part I, article 1,
pp. 65–6.
[10] Blaise Pascal, *Œuvres complètes*, ed. L. Lafuma (Paris: Seuil, 1963), pp. 230–2.
[11] Pierre Corneille, *Writings on the theatre*, ed. H. T. Barnwell (Oxford: Blackwell, 1965),
pp. 174–5.

Académie to pronounce on Corneille's play. An increasingly authoritarian royal power thus invokes the authority of the Ancients in order to control a potentially disturbing form of social entertainment (although, as we shall see, the Académie was not always on the side of the Ancients).

It was in these years, too, that salon life, dominated by intelligent and resourceful women like the marquise de Rambouillet, began to make a major contribution to French culture. The prevailing taste of the salons inclined towards the 'modern' genre of heroic romance, which was in many ways the narrative counterpart to Corneille's heroic tragedies and tragicomedies (see for example the lengthy mid-century romances of Madeleine de Scudéry); salon conversation turned on topics such as the ethics of love, but also on the education and (relative) emancipation of women, and eventually also the scientific advances of the day. The literature of this period is predominantly optimistic in tone, presupposing a belief in human capacities in both the moral and the intellectual sphere.

The salons helped to ensure the survival of such 'modernist' ideas into the second half of the seventeenth century, but now against much sharper opposition.[12] The cultural fashions determined by court society underwent a major shift in the 1650s as a result of the defeat of the old aristocracy in the Fronde and the subsequent assumption by Louis XIV of absolute rule (1661). The mood of an aristocratic society deprived of real power and held virtually captive at court was nourished by another source: Jansenist notions of radical human incapacity, propagated by secular circles sympathetic to Jansenism, and not least by Pascal, began to gain a wide currency as a focus of imaginative writing. La Rochefoucauld, Molière, La Fontaine, and Racine all drew in their different ways on a psychological and ethical pessimism that proved peculiarly appropriate for a society caught in a rigid hierarchy and subjected to the principle that power is all-important. This is one of the great moments of French literature; but it is also a moment of retreat, when reverence for the Ancients becomes a shibboleth, a token perhaps of security.

La Fontaine, Racine, La Bruyère, and above all Boileau proclaimed a normative view of literary composition for which the Ancients provided a paradigm: as La Bruyère put it, 'Everything has already been said; we come too late'.[13] Yet the briefest comparison with Renaissance humanist attitudes to antiquity shows how much has changed. The use of the vernacular is now taken for granted; in place of the high-flown eloquence of Ciceronian oratory, or the eclectic, allusive style of the anti-Ciceronian, the ideal has become a refined and economical language capable of many nuances but never pretentious – the language of the 'honnêtes gens de

[12] See A. H. T. Levi, '*La Princesse de Clèves* and the *Querelle des anciens et des modernes*', *Journal of European studies* 10 (1980), 62–70.
[13] La Bruyère, *Les caractères*, ed. R. Garapon (Paris: Garnier, 1962), p. 67.

cour'. Boileau's commentaries (1694) on the treatise *On the Sublime* attributed to Longinus (which Boileau had translated into French in 1674) clarified Longinus's distinction between grandiloquence and the true Sublime, which may be present in the simplest utterance as a virtually inexplicable power to astonish and move – the 'je ne sais quoi' that is the mark of authentic linguistic mastery.[14] Homer and the Bible equally afford examples of this quality; the late seventeenth-century ancients sought to emulate their divine simplicity while adapting them to the taste and manners of seventeenth-century court society. Boileau's *Art poétique*, La Fontaine's *Fables*, La Bruyère's *Caractères*, Racine's tragedies, are all 'imitations' of ancient models in a sense that Erasmus or Du Bellay might have recognized but could never have foreseen. The proto-moderns of the Renaissance are paradoxically, then, the forerunners of the neoclassical ancients.

In the heyday of Louis XIV's reign, the ancients were in the ascendant, creating a new canon which has since become a defining feature of the French cultural and national identity. Yet the proliferation of rival salons and cenacles favoured the survival of a vigorous countercurrent. Corneille remained active until 1674, and his dramatic achievement was now cited by the moderns as a benchmark; in a work published in 1670, Desmarets de Saint-Sorlin upheld the superiority of modern poets and novelists and argued that women's taste was to be preferred to that of scholars and pedants; and Cartesian ideas and new scientific conceptions were by now being widely discussed in polite society. Women continued to play a prominent role: they claimed the right to be educated in every branch of learning, including the new science, and even demanded freedom from the patriarchal and sexual oppression of marriage. These issues, and the conflicts they gave rise to, are already reflected in a highly nuanced way in several of Molière's comedies; Boileau's tenth *Satire* (1694) gives a cruder portrait of the so-called 'précieuses ridicules'.[15]

Desmarets de Saint-Sorlin's intervention, and Boileau's counter-attack in his *Art poétique*, marks the beginning of an explicit 'querelle des anciens et des modernes'. In the 1670s, the moderns were already well represented in the Académie Française; full-scale conflict broke out in 1687, when Charles Perrault read his pro-moderns poem *Le siècle de Louis le Grand* in the Académie. In 1688 he published the first of his dialogues entitled *Parallèle des anciens et des modernes* (others appeared up to 1697), and in 1694 he wrote an *Apologie des femmes* to counter Boileau's satire. Boileau continued to champion the Ancients, principally

[14] See John Logan, 'Longinus and the Sublime' in the present volume (pp. 529–39); also Jules Brody, *Boileau and Longinus* (Geneva: Droz, 1958).
[15] Boileau, *Œuvres complètes*, ed. A. Adam and F. Escal (Paris: Gallimard, 1966), pp. 73–4.

through his *Réflexions sur Longin*, until an uneasy reconciliation was brought about in 1694.

In France, the quarrel was to break out again and continue into the new century, with Madame Dacier as defender of the Ancients and Houdar de La Motte as her adversary.[16] In England, where Saint-Evremond spent many years in exile, producing literary essays in defence of Corneille and other moderns, the French quarrel was prolonged in the 1690s by writers such as Sir William Temple, William Wotton, and Richard Bentley; Swift was to enlist on the side of the Ancients in *The battle of the books*.[17] Reverberations were felt as far afield as Greece.[18]

Fontenelle's *Digression sur les anciens et les modernes* (1688) provides an economical and incisive glimpse of the kind of argument the moderns had at their disposal and of the style they cultivated. Like Pascal in the *Préface* mentioned above,[19] Fontenelle takes a commonplace conception of history and turns it on its head. Nature was not more vigorous in antiquity, nor were the Ancients supermen. The potentialities of human nature remain the same, so that, with the passage of time, it is to be expected that human knowledge will gradually increase except during periods of war and political instability such as the Middle Ages. It might seem, Fontenelle further argues, that the expansion of knowledge would be limited by the inability of the mind to cope with excessive amounts of material; but the increase in volume has been accompanied by a parallel understanding of method, which enables the mass of new materials to be controlled and organized.

When one compares such arguments with, say, those of Du Bellay, a major shift of perspective becomes clear. Du Bellay had also claimed that nature is potentially equally fertile in all periods, but had remained within the paradigm of the natural cycle of productivity and decline: we may perhaps seek to outdo the Ancients, but this will not be a phase in an indefinite linear process, only another cultural monument which later ages will set beside the achievement of Greece and Rome. Fontenelle, by

---

[16] For the eighteenth-century continuation of the quarrel, see Jonathan Lamb, 'The sublime' (ch. 17) in *The Cambridge history of literary criticism*, vol. IV, *The eighteenth century*, ed. H. B. Nisbet and C. Rawson (Cambridge: Cambridge University Press, 1997), pp. 394–416.

[17] For a detailed account of the quarrel in England, see Joseph M. Levine, *The battle of the books: history and literature in the Augustan Age* (Ithaca and London: Cornell University Press, 1991). See also Joshua Scodel, 'Seventeenth-century English literary criticism: classical values, English texts and contexts' in the present volume (pp. 543–54).

[18] See Paschalis M. Kitromilides, *The Enlightenment as social criticism* (Princeton: Princeton University Press, 1992), pp. 133–42. Kitromilides shows that the Western European conception of Greek antiquity was an important factor in the evolution of the Greek sense of identity in modern times.

[19] Pascal brilliantly reverses the view that the ancients are old and therefore wise and experienced (*Préface*, p. 232, col. 1).

contrast, draws on the Cartesian emphasis on method in order to posit a continuing and progressively cumulative achievement in all domains. Fontenelle's cultural relativism has its limits – he thinks it unlikely that the peoples of the 'torrid' or the 'glacial' zones will ever be able to take part in this triumphal progression; but his crisp, witty style has a bite which makes short work of muddled and convention-bound thinking.[20] In the *Digression* one can already perceive the way of thinking and writing which will become in the eighteenth century the model for Enlightenment ideals and for the whole ensuing tradition of liberal humanism.

In this sense, it may seem evident that the moderns won the battle. In the eighteenth century, antiquity will continue to provide models for tragedy and the epic, but posterity will assign these neoclassical continuations a relatively minor place in the European canon. Yet we have seen that the supporters of the Ancients, in France at least, had already bequeathed a canon which in itself proved the supreme capacity of modern writers, and it is hard to imagine that the moderns could have succeeded, in the literary sphere at least, without that demonstration. Furthermore, the prestige of 'classical' education will ensure the survival of a significant part of the ancients' view, together with a canon that serves as a marker of social and cultural identity.

Major issues, then, are carried by this debate: the idea of progress, the nature and purposes of education, the cultural position of women, the way in which canon formation becomes engaged in social and political issues and in the construction of a national identity. But the shifting terms and constantly drawn boundaries of the debate also suggest that there is no crude and simple equivalence between a programme of consecrated reading and political authority. Canons have always shown themselves to be open to reinterpretation, to renewal from within as well as extension beyond prescribed limits. Even La Bruyère, a hard-line ancient, is capable of seeing the court of Louis XIV, not as the centre of the universe, but as a strange place somewhere on the map thousands of miles from where the Hurons live.[21] Likewise, it will be evident to anyone who reads this debate that the modern is not the positive term in an ancients–moderns antithesis, but rather a vantage-point which shifts with the viewer.

* For an account of the Quarrel of Ancients and Moderns in England and Italy in the present volume, see respectively the chapters of Joshua Scodel, 'Seventeenth-century English literary criticism: classical values, English texts and contexts' (pp. 543–54) and Marga Cottino-Jones, 'Literary critical developments in sixteenth- and seventeenth-century Italy' (pp. 566–76).

---

[20] Fontenelle, *Entretiens sur la pluralité des mondes; Digression sur les anciens et les modernes*, ed. R. Shackleton (Oxford: Clarendon Press, 1955), pp. 161–73.
[21] *Caractères*, pp. 244–5 ('De la cour', 74).

44

Women as *auctores* in early modern Europe

Elizabeth Guild

The *querelle des femmes* was a pan-European but primarily French textual phenomenon. Although its successive attacks on, and defences of,
women represent a rhetorical controversy between men about women, it
was nonetheless one of the significant sites of gender debate in pre- and
early modern Europe. The *querelle* survived sporadically in Europe for
four centuries, but was not responsible for the changes in cultural and
material settings and conditions necessary for women to become authors
and publish their work. It tended, rather, to be symptomatic of factors for
inertia and change beyond its bounds, or else functioned parallel to developments for and by women elsewhere: in England, for instance, women did
not begin to counter misogynist attacks until comparatively late (Jane
Anger, *Her protection for women*, 1589),[1] and their challenges tend not to
range beyond the internal authority, rules, and rhetoric of the *querelle*.

Its earliest feminist contribution, Christine de Pisan's *Livre de la cité des
dames* (1405), initiated a mode of feminist literary criticism in the form
of diagnosis and critique of the pathology of representations of women
in the Western textual tradition, most immediately the *Roman de la rose*.
This diagnostic criticism challenged textual manifestations of masculine
authority over women, exposing it as rooted in ideology rather than
Nature and Reason as men claimed; as such, it was one of the founding
conditions for women's writing other than ventriloquistic of the masculine tradition. However, its function was to serve broader challenges to
misogyny rather than as specifically textual criticism. What it demonstrated was the need for women writers to find ways of establishing their
place in relation to an exclusively masculine literary tradition, questioning
its authority and criteria, as a necessary condition of possibility of their
writing; for to be recognized as an author [*auctor*] required a cultural
authority [*auctoritas*] that all but exceptional women lacked. Women
writers of the period other than contributors to the debate were also
aware of a significant element of gender politics in the contests over the

[1] Jane Anger, *Her protection for women* (1589), ed. S. G. O'Malley, in *The early modern
Englishwoman: a facsimile of essential works, 'Defences of women'*, Part I, *Printed writ-
ings, 1500–1640*, ed. B. Travistsky and P. Cullen, *et al.*, 10 vols. (Aldershot: Scolar Press;
Brookfield, VT: Ashgate, 1996–), vol. IV [unpaginated].

nature and scope of literature engaged by literary critics, particularly at moments when the authority of tradition was challenged by advocates of reform and of less exclusory definitions of the field of letters. However, in practice, women's critical discourse developed neither in the context of the *querelle* nor within the conventional territory of literary criticism. This was, not least, because both discourses remained embedded in the rhetorical and conceptual models that had to be unsettled before women's authority to write would be admitted.

By the end of the seventeenth century in France, literary criticism was playing a decisive part in circumscribing the institution of 'French literature', an emergent and profoundly contested field. Critics had previously been mainly concerned with classical texts, and their authoritative and conservative practice was rooted in learned humanist culture marked by the same qualities: and by its almost exclusive masculinity. Critical authority relied on gender, in that gender gave access to formal education, hence knowledge of Greek, Latin, rhetoric, and the highly codified interpretative and critical practices developed by humanist scholars and their successors. Most women writers in pre- and early modern Europe lacked the right, authority, and formation necessary to engage in this discourse, and traditionalists played deaf to signs of learning in women or attacked them as pedantry.[2] Even when socio-cultural conditions changed to the extent that aristocratic women (and more rarely bourgeoises) could satisfy their desire for learning and culture, their writing was constrained by powerful prohibitions and inhibitions: the ideological equation between silence and chastity, which condoned sexual slander as a masculine mode of criticism of women's writing; masculine denial of women's reason, or else contempt for it; the injunction that women not display their knowledge and, by implication, base any claim to authority on it. This cultural climate ruled women out of critical discourse with its authoritative display of knowledge; rare exceptions include the Quattrocento Italian Isotta Nogarola, and in France, Marie de Gournay or, later, Anne Dacier, a Greek scholar and translator, whose translations such as *Les poésies d'Anacréon et de Sapho* (1681) included textual criticism and commentary. But Dacier's literary criticism was not feminist; Nogarola was subjected to attacks on her sexual honour, and Gournay's forays into literary criticism earned her pain and contempt.

In early modern European culture textual production was almost exclusively masculine; almost any literary writing by a woman had to negotiate inherited, authoritative rhetoric, aesthetics, and representational codes,

---

[2] See L. Timmermans, *L'accès des femmes à la culture (1598–1715)* (Paris: Champion, 1993), and E. Berriot-Salvador, *Les femmes dans la société française de la Renaissance* (Geneva: Droz, 1990).

and thus may be interpreted as a sort of critical reinscription of the elements of the tradition. In Italy writers such as Tullia d'Aragona, Veronica Franca, Veronica Gambara, and Gaspara Stampa; in England, such as Isabella Whitney, Mary Wroth, and Aphra Behn; and in France, Louise Labé, Pernette du Guillet, and the Dames des Roches implicitly questioned prevailing aesthetic and conceptual criteria in their reorientations of the conventions of love lyric, exchanging the place of silent object for writing subject.[3] However, this is an indirect mode and not the primary aspect of the writing. The minority of women whose writing did include literary criticism (and French women take the lead in this respect) tended to elaborate different sites and discourses for it, such as Hélisenne de Crenne's and Louise Labé's prefaces to their work, and the former's letters, in which she argued for creative autonomy as a woman's legitimate freedom from masculine authority; and Madeleine de Scudéry included literary criticism (such as a discussion of sixteenth-century French poetry) in her *Conversations nouvelles* (1684), whose form reflects the status and authority of conversation within salon culture. Women's refashioning of the novel was a product of the same culture; their innovative prose implied critique of traditional modes of representation and, in the case of the Comtesse de Lafayette's work, questioned literary *vraisemblance* [plausibility] and with it, the mimetic function of prose narrative. Masculine aesthetic, psychological and ethical norms are challenged by her representation of female protagonists, and the reader's expectations directly invoked and unsettled as the functions and limits of what was considered 'natural', 'plausible', or even representable are exposed in works such as *La Princesse de Clèves*, *La Comtesse de Tende*, and *La Princesse de Montpensier*. Such critical reorientations rely on two of the key recognitions of the *querelle*: firstly, that what was at issue was not sex but gender, and that representations of women, like their cultural construction (gender), were open to change; secondly, that women's relation to human reason should be contested and recognized as not inferior to men's, and thus the authority of their challenging and innovative literary representations and aesthetics acknowledged.

These women's writings reveal their awareness that linguistic and literary contestations incorporated debates over gender, and that the vicissitudes of women's writing reflected those within the larger debates over the nature of human reason. However, neither landmark feminist arguments within the *querelle des femmes* tradition for the equality of women's reason such as those made by Marie de Gournay in the 1620s, nor Cartesianism's reconceptualization of human reason as ungendered,

[3] See A. R. Jones, *The currency of Eros: women's love lyric in Europe, 1540–1620* (Bloomington: Indiana University Press, 1990).

nor salon culture with its promotion of women's cultural authority and judgement, secured a basis for women's thinking and writing being granted authority equal to men's. By the late seventeenth century, women's writing and informal critical authority were increasingly marginalized: along with the *Modernes*, with whose ethos their writing tended to be associated, they lost the broader *querelle* over the nature and cultural function of French literature to the *Anciens*.[4]

The lack of place (other than marginalized) for women in the field of letters confirmed a founding concern of Christine de Pisan's text: the need for a different community for women, enabling their autonomy and creativity. This anticipated both the cultural and material factors enabling women's writing, and a recurring theme of women's critical practice, namely the need to establish a feminine audience so as, not least, to defend and sustain the place of women's writing. Chief proponents included Hélisenne de Crenne and Louise Labé (writing in the mid-sixteenth century), the Venetians Moderata Fonte and Lucrezia Marinella (publishing in 1600 and 1601), and in England, the poets Katherine Philips and Jane Barker (publishing in 1664 and 1688). Although Philips and, possibly, Barker, established such a coterie, and Labé participated in mixed humanist coteries in Lyons, and although there were trans-European networks of correspondents, English women writers were isolated and scattered, and only in France with the development of literary salons did such communities emerge. In Italy women had access to humanist academies and to university education, but this did not produce many women writers and literary critics: powerful cultural inhibitors such as masculine authority and marriage still silenced them.

In France in the seventeenth century, as in England later, one of the most significant factors in women's coming to writing and gaining substantial cultural influence was the worldly culture of the salons led by women. Their social interaction with leading male writers initiated reforms of established literary genres such as the novel and developed new ones such as the portrait and epistolary literature. Conversation gained prestige as an art in which women were particularly adept, and involved literary critical discussion in which women's judgement and taste were paramount. Conversation profoundly influenced the style of the novel. Marguerite Buffet's *Les éloges des illustres savantes tant anciennes que modernes* (published with *Nouvelles observations sur la langue françoise*, 1668) attests this. Brilliant conversation is defined as literary and exemplary; thus her celebration of her contemporaries includes those whose conversation was regarded as illustrious. This records women whose skills

[4] See T. J. Reiss, *The meaning of literature* (Ithaca and London: Cornell University Press, 1992).

would otherwise leave no trace, and extends the scope of literary criticism. Collective tastes formed, and discussion was deemed to be between cultural equals, producing in turn less hierarchical and more liberal critical opinions than were to be found elsewhere. New critical terms and criteria developed that could not simply be assimilated back into traditional debates and codes. However, such innovations were paradoxically a vulnerability of this work: notions of spontaneous, natural responses and sensibilities were marginalized by masculine opponents as inferior (identified with *nature*) to their masculine *culture*. Nonetheless, temporarily, here women could be agents rather than merely consumers; their conversational literary criticism was important in this respect, as the hinge between consumption (reading) and production (writing). None of these developments can, strictly speaking, be said to belong in the *querelle des femmes* tradition; and yet all reflect women's quarrels with masculine culture as articulated there. However, women secured neither a place nor authority as writers and critics through salon culture: towards the end of the century, authoritative conservatives such as Boileau had effectively marginalized women writers, who became hostages in the wider critical quarrel between the *Anciens* and *Modernes*. Even Cartesianism's promotion of women's reason was not powerful enough to combat the weight of tradition harnessed in Boileau's attacks (*Les héros de roman*, 1674), primarily on Madeleine de Scudéry, who replied with one of her '*Conversations*', *De la médisance* (1684). Here issues of gender met those of power, authority, and aesthetics: for Boileau, the novel threatened to open up literary culture to an undesirably wide public, and Scudéry's 'crime' was to be both a woman and a novelist.

Scudéry is a rare figure in this three-hundred-year period. She was a highly successful, prolific writer, who wrote literary criticism and included it in her novels: for instance in conversations which are performances of worldly critical discussions, in her female characters' comments and endless storytelling designed to incite the reader to interpret and play literary critic, and indirectly in terms of representations of women that challenged traditional gender aesthetics. However, she had predecessors and contemporaries who produced literary criticism in a variety of modes.

Madeleine and Catherine des Roches were the only women writers to figure in Scudéry's history of the poetry of their time. Their Poitiers salon and the Lyons coteries open to women are the only French collectivities to produce poetry and forms of challenging feminist criticism in the sixteenth century. There were no comparable developments in Britain, and in Italy publishing women authors tended to be less polemical, with the exception of Laura Terracina's critique of Ariosto's representation of women (*Discorso sopra il principio di tutti i canti d'Orlando furioso*, 1555) and Lucrezia Marinelli's criticism of misogyny in poetry and challenge to the defences of women by Tasso and Speroni (*Le nobiltà, et eccelienze delle donne: et i diffetti, e mancamenti de gli huomini*, 1600). Madeleine des Roches promoted authorship as fundamental to women's subject-hood: she conceptualized creative writing as an act of self-construction – incompatible with marriage. Her daughter (who did not marry) articulated the relationship between cultural and domestic labour in her poetry: she expressed a creative fusion between pen and spindle (her spindle makes poetry), avoiding misogynist critique of neglect of feminine duty and of learning as defeminization (reason being a masculine attribute). Here creative writing combined with (mediatory) gender and literary criticism. For profound challenges to prevailing masculine authority, and for literary criticism which conceptualized writing in terms of selfhood and change, we must look to Labé and Crenne, who claimed autonomy for women's creative expression. Both invoked a necessary community of women readers to sustain their work; Labé went further than Crenne in urging that her readers become not only educated but also writers, arguing that writing enabled women to exchange their position as objects in masculine culture for subject status. Labé's argument extends the terms of the *querelle* through subtle manipulation of its rhetoric and in urging women to write: to be cultural agents as well as consumers.

An important shift in the history of reading is inscribed in terms which reflect the *querelle* in Marguerite de Navarre's *L'Heptaméron* (published posthumously, 1558/59): her women protagonists lead a critique of inherited modes of textual interpretation, questioning masculine authority and reason, and exposing masculine interpretation as self-serving and violent.

The only other French woman writer whose literary criticism survives is Marie de Gournay, the first editor of Montaigne's *Essais* (1595). Her position illustrates that there was no simple correspondence between feminist critical practice and either reformist literary ideals or the *querelle*: her two feminist polemics, which shifted the terms of the *querelle*, neither responded to nor generated other texts. In the earlier of the two, *Egalité des hommes et des femmes* (1622), her defence of women is conceptually radical in its argument for difference and equality rather than the traditional hierarchical opposition, but is nonetheless vulnerable in that Gournay appeals to the oldest authority, God, to legitimate and protect her case. This appeal to authority may be a residue of the humanist training that enabled and disabled her as a writer, in broader terms. It made of her a defender of the later sixteenth-century poets against new linguistic and aesthetic doctrines. Her learning authorized her critical position, but a learned woman defending the past was doubly vulnerable to rejection and mockery. The other vulnerability of her position, despite her defence of poetry involving such feminist strategies as reinscribing traditionally feminine images of poetry and languages so that a link between gender and creativity became conceptually significant rather than a pretty *topos*, was her attachment to the old logic of resemblance and reliance on analogy, which may be read as confining her thinking to an epistemological past.[5]

On the other hand, her recognition of the role of gender in creativity anticipated a later feminist critique of Cartesianism, with its promotion of disembodied rationality and thereby neglect of gender. The influence of Cartesianism on salon women is difficult to assess. Although a Cartesian ascetic embodiment benefited some women who remained unmarried to think, talk, and write freely, critique of Cartesian reason prevailed. *Préciosité* is the feature of salon culture that bore more directly on women's literary criticism; not surprisingly, given its roots in linguistic critique. The most evident *précieuse* influence was on the novel, particularly Scudéry's and Lafayette's; and it was in the thematic, stylistic, aesthetic, and conceptual reforms to the genre, particularly in terms of the representation of women, that the most lively literary criticism – new writing as critique of the traditions of the genre and, by implication, broader cultural critique – emerged. We may consider this a mode of literary criticism these women writers made particularly their own, leaving the traditional struggles over authority of interpretation to men.

The issues contested in the *querelle des femmes* preceded and outlasted its debates, without, however, decisively influencing women's innovative writing practices. As women gained authority as writers they also engaged in critical quarrels; and although masculine authorities tended to triumph, women's considerable critical influence particularly in French salon culture is now being acknowledged, thanks to revisionist literary history and criticism, led again by women.

* See also Joan DeJean, 'Rooms of their own: literary salons in seventeenth-century France' in the present volume (pp. 378–83).

[5] See C. Bauschatz, 'Marie de Gournay's gendered images for language and poetry', *Journal of medieval and Renaissance studies* 25, 3 (Fall 1995), 489–500.

Structures of thought

45

Renaissance Neoplatonism

Michael J. B. Allen

Renaissance Neoplatonism was the creation of the fifteenth-century Florentines Marsilio Ficino and Giovanni Pico della Mirandola and had a profound and far-reaching impact on the cultural as well as the intellectual and religious life of Europe for well over two centuries. It contributed a *forma mentis* that transcended disciplinary and national boundaries without necessarily coming into direct conflict with other contemporary mind-sets, those we associate with Aristotelianism, Protestantism, Ramism, neo-scholasticism, Hermeticism, Copernicanism, Tridentism, and so forth. Literature and its interpretation only played an ancillary role in what was at heart a philosophico-theological movement anchored in the concerns of medieval Catholicism but inspired by the attractive example of Plato's newly discovered dialogues on the one hand and by the dauntingly technical commentaries of the Neoplatonists on the other. But it did mean that the Platonic dialogue, with its dramatic shifts from interrogation to exposition to myth to fable to quotation to dialectical division in various sequences and combinations, was set up not so much as the literary but as the hermeneutical model; and that Plato's style, with its lucidity, suppleness, and figurative and ironic variety, became acknowledged as a way of doing philosophy that was in marked contrast to the wrangling of the schools and to the analytic systematizing of Aristotle. Plato became not only the great alternative to the Stagirite as a philosopher but a more profound and compelling alternative to Cicero as a model rhetorician.

One of the obvious issues the Platonic dialogue poses is that of genre. Ancient doxologists, such as Diogenes Laertius in his *Lives of the philosophers* 3.49–51, 58–61, had divided up the dialogues rather crudely under such heads as 'political', 'ethical', 'logical', 'physical', and 'obstetrical'; but this could not satisfy those who were impressed by the dramatic unity of many of Plato's masterpieces and by the complexity and variety that subsisted in that unity. The Florentine Neoplatonists accordingly turned to their predecessors among the ancient Neoplatonists for authority in establishing a view of the Platonic dialogue as unified by an overriding theme, a *skopos*, but at the same time as accommodating a variety of concerns. The monistic orientation of their metaphysics conditioned this holistic approach to the forms and structures of Plato's writings, yet it sprang too from a deeply held conviction that Plato the rhetorician had understood the human psyche, its addiction to pleasure and its search for transcendence; that he was a magus who could enchant with his spells, a poet who had been inspired by the nine Muses and their leader Apollo (etymologized as the Not-of-Many) to inspire others.

The theme of inspiration was necessarily primary, given Socrates's account in the *Phaedrus* 244A–245C of the four divine madnesses of poetry, prophecy, priesthood, and love, and given the serious challenge the *Ion* presented to a Neoplatonist. Ficino analysed both texts at various times – the myth of the charioteer in the *Phaedrus*, for example, with its score or so of memorable images is constantly invoked throughout his and Pico's works and supplies them with a number of standard terms and phrases. But he used them to generate not a poetics so much as an 'ecstatics', a theory of inspiration that is not peculiarly literary but which nonetheless stems from the rhapsodic experience of Ion as a reciter of Homer's poetry. Even if we do not accede to Socrates's line of argument in the *Ion*, we tend to see this little colloquy nowadays as an essentially comic portrait of a naïve rhapsode, an actor with no real grasp of what he is doing. In his introduction to the dialogue for his great 1484 Latin translation of the collected works of Plato, Ficino saw it otherwise: as a major statement on the descent of divine madness into a human being who becomes a medium for a god's voice, a trumpet for the divine. In the process he addresses, not the epistemological question Socrates keeps asking – What does Ion know as he recites and afterwards? – but rather the psychological question – What does it feel like to be a medium of poetry? Is it an experience of total possession and loss of self or does one discover another and higher self which becomes creatively involved in, or changed by, the poem and its rendering? Should we examine the post-rhapsodic Ion Socratically on what he knows about the technicalities of Homer's acquaintance with the skills of chariot-driving, concocting posset remedies, or fishing with leads (537A–538D), three of Homer's themes? Or should we give him the coveted gold crown for his narrative evocation of Achilles springing upon Hector, for his empathic weeping at the sorrows of Andromache, Hecuba, or Priam (535B), for the 'force' of his acting?

Plato had introduced the image of the magnet to us somewhat ironically, but it was Ficino who teased out the logical consequences: that the god or gods inspired the poet with a divine madness which he in turn transmitted to the rhapsode reciting his poetry, who then transmitted it to his auditors. The result was a 'chain' of inspiration that descended from the divine but was all of a piece, enabling the ordinary listener to come into touch with the originary god. In this concatenation, the poem is merely one of the links, a carrier of the magnetic force which flows through it and on to the rhapsode and then to his audience, uniting it both with the

Muses, the source of all poetic activity, and with Apollo as the unitary god beyond them. The characteristics of the poem, and certainly the features that prompt a formalistic analysis, are irrelevant to the principal issue: that to hear the poem is merely to step on the first rung on the long ladder of inner ascent. Certainly, the kinds of questions that Aristotle's *Poetics* invites are not germane. Ficino is generating rather an audience response theory that assumes that all auditors will ultimately respond in the same way to contact with the power of the divine; and it is a theory – initially at least – of passivity: the more passive the rhapsode, the better he may serve as a medium. This is to look at it perhaps too negatively, for Ficino's assumptions are predicated on the authority that Christianity has traditionally accorded virginity, humility, foolishness for Christ's sake, submission to the divine Will, patience even unto death. The paradoxes with which its otherworldliness invests the pleasures of this world necessarily transform the Socratic Ion into a holy fool, a patient expounder of the epics, even as they enmesh Socrates himself in an intricate web of ironies not of his own making.

However, neither the *Iliad* nor the *Odyssey* is the kind of poem that Ficino has in mind in adumbrating his theory of Platonic ecstatics, even though Plato, like any cultured Greek, had frequently quoted from them. The proper medium of divine inspiration is the divine hymn that Plato had lauded in his *Republic* and *Laws*, and one of which the *Phaedo* 60D declares Socrates had himself composed in prison in honour of Apollo. It was best exemplified for Ficino, however, in the collection of Orphic hymns which the Renaissance supposed of immense antiquity, but which we now view as a compilation of the third or fourth century AD. Plato had quoted from various *Orphica* known to him and the later Neoplatonists from the collection of hymns; and this in itself invested the Orphic poem with Platonic authority. Moreover, Ficino and Pico had inherited from Proclus and others a conception of a line of six ancient theologians, the *prisci theologi*, stemming from the poet-priest Zoroaster and the Egyptian magus Hermes Trismegistus and culminating in Plato. Third in the succession was Orpheus who had charmed the beasts and descended into the underworld, but more importantly had sung hymns to all the gods to the accompaniment of ritual fumigations of incense, myrrh, saffron, and other odoriferous substances.

The hymns consist almost exclusively of ritual invocations of a deity's names and attributes, of a list of *aretai*, the good deeds associated with its power, and of an exultatory recognition of the extent of this power in the cosmos and of man's indebtedness to its gifts. Given Orpheus's traditional association with a lyre – the subject of considerable debate among Renaissance lutanists and musicologists as to its stringing and tuning – Ficino supposed that the hymns were sung or chanted in a perfect wedding of words and chords, of the quantities that words have in Greek and Latin and of the notes and intervals of the lost musical scales of antiquity. Moreover, Ficino possessed what he called an Orphic lyre, with a picture of Orpheus enchanting the beasts painted on it; and his rapturous performances of Orphic-Platonic hymns to that lyre became musical events in Florentine patrician circles, and notably with the Medici.

That the Orphic hymns could possess such authority in a Christian community, however secular and enlightened, was due almost entirely to the fact that, although they were thoroughly polytheistic in sentiment and Ficino himself had not publicized his translations for fear that they would promote a new demonolatry (as he writes in a letter to a close friend), they were prefaced by a famous monotheistic palinode. This served, not to invalidate the eighty-six subsequent hymns, but to characterize them as veils of images and attributes investing the unimaginable divine. Orpheus became the gentiles' counterpart to David, his hymns their psalms, his Thracian lyre the harp of the Lord. In striking Orphic chords and intoning Platonic hymns, Ficino was therefore recalling in part at least the biblical singer, extending the canon of the psalter and reaffirming the ideal wedding of poetry and music in the act of worship. The impact of this revived Ficinian Orphism or 'Ionism' on Renaissance lyric and particularly on Ronsard and the Pléiade should not be underemphasized. It would be interesting to explore its impact both on Renaissance psalmody, given that rendering the psalms into verse became a penitential exercise for Protestants, and on the attempts by poets such as Sidney and Campion to revive the classical metres and to wed them to music.

Renaissance poets and critics became preoccupied, however, not by the ideal of the divine hymn – even Sir Philip Sidney sets it aside in his *Apology for poetry* in order to discuss 'right' poetry instead – but by the interpretative challenges of the classical, and particularly the Roman, epic and its imitations. In Italy this preoccupation was complicated, moreover, by the presence of the *Divine comedy*. Nurtured on both Virgil and Dante, the Italian Platonists generated a hermeneutic that was indebted alike to medieval allegoresis, religious and secular, and to the ancient allegorizing of Homer and Virgil. In this they were not striving to be original – the adventures of Landino's Aeneas for instance are predictably those of a soul on the Platonic quest – but the authority of these two great poems and the universal acceptance of their high seriousness did force them to confront Plato's expulsion of the poets from his ideal republic. While Sidney and others, enamoured of Plato's own powers as a poetic writer, might later explain this expulsion away, Ficino in particular felt compelled to explore the arguments behind Plato's attack on poetry and to confront its repudiation of Homer and Hesiod. Here, obviously, the model of Ion did not pertain.

The two great originary Greek poets had erred in two major respects: they had both attributed human passions and failings to the immortal gods, anthropomorphizing them in our own frail image as creatures of anger, jealousy, fear, and desire; and they had articulated a false theogony that had the primal gods emerging from chaos and then copulating together in the manner of humans to produce subsequent generations. In the second error they thus aligned themselves with those natural philosophers (physicists and cosmologists) who denied the sovereignty of providence and the primacy of beauty and order in the generation of the world. Ironically, in the Neoplatonic reading of the *Symposium* Plato had discussed the 'chaos' of longing that is the condition of each hypostasis in the ontological hierarchy before it is actualized by the One and the Good, thus incorporating the Hesiodic notion into his metaphysics. Still, it was not the same as positing Chaos as the primal state, a move that effectively linked the poets with the atheists and Epicureans of later polemics. On this foundation of false metaphysics and theology, it was almost inevitable that the poets should build an edifice of false ethics, re-creating as the primal psychological condition the chaos of passion from which the ordering virtues of temperance, justice, courage, and prudence could never emerge. In short, the poets had promoted an upside-down view of the world which, since it lacked the fundamental insights of true philosophy, lacked too the grounds of an authentic piety.

Nevertheless, the philosopher could listen to their siren songs with impunity and even ultimately with profit, because he could interpret all for the best by reference to the One and the Good, and not to Chaos, as the beginning and end of all things. The rightmindedness, the virtue, and the subtlety of the interpreter (and not now of a rhapsode like Ion) became the new key to the validity of poetry in the Platonic republic. We must banish the popular poets from the city, writes Ficino, but not from the state. Far from the callow throng of the city's susceptible and suggestible youths, the poets can do no harm. To the contrary, they can be safely and profitably heard as it were in exile by the philosophers, since they can reinterpret their mysteries *more Platonico*, and turn their stories [*mythoi*] to the cause of the Good. Thus the intention of the interpreter not that of the poet determines what is good or bad poetry in the sense of what can and cannot serve virtue. Not only can the interpreter pierce through the veils of allegory and imagery to gaze on the eternal truths, he can validate the poets' errors by reinterpreting their figures in the light of Plotinian metaphysics. Hermes, not Apollo or the Muses, becomes the presiding deity of poetry because he is the deity of its reception. The chain of magnetic force that linked Ion to the bard has been replaced by the caducean staff that dispels in the intelligent and pious auditor the clouds, however golden, of misconceit.

Even so, the 'ancient enmity', the 'old quarrel' between philosophy and poetry, as the *Republic* 10.607BC puts it, remained a bitter one, more particularly in that the comic poets had played a role in the condemnation of Socrates on the grounds, hypocritically given their own irreligiousness, of impiety: blood was on their hands. Obviously, this was not true of the dead poets: Socrates had himself declared that from boyhood he had been possessed by 'a certain love and reverence for Homer' (*Republic* 10.595B) and that he would willingly die ten times to meet 'Orpheus and Musaeus, Hesiod and Homer' (*Apology* 41A); and throughout his life, as with any educated Athenian, Homer had been constantly on his lips as the creative genius of Greek, the generator of its ornaments and flowers. We thus have a profoundly fissured sense of poetry and poets in the Neoplatonic tradition that derived heterogeneously from Socrates's personal reverence for Homer and yet the role of the comic poets in his trial and condemnation; and from Plato's moral and political strictures and yet the witness of his myths of divine frenzy and of his own soaring flights.

A controversy simmered too between the poets and the philosophers over the nature of the Platonic Forms and our apprehension of them. If artists' pictorial imitations of physical objects had been condemned in the *Republic* 10.596A ff. as being at three removes from reality, the verbal imitations of poets were less easily dismissed. Plotinus had spoken to the beauty and truth of pure colours and abstract shapes and promoted the theory that the artist was imitating the ideal Forms of objects rather than confining himself to a necessarily faulty reproduction of what was already a faulty artefact or object in nature. In this regard he appears to be the first Platonist to provide on Platonic grounds, and despite Plato himself, a non-mimetic defence of art. But an epic poet imitates not so much static objects like the shield of Achilles as the deeds of men, the unfolding in time of the virtues of Odysseus, Cyrus, or Aeneas. Plato's metaphysics is essentialist and timeless and regards all temporal phenomena at best as participating in essence, at worst as illusory. But the Neoplatonists, in focusing on Soul as the third hypostasis and basing themselves on the argument on self-motion in the *Phaedrus* 245C–246A, underscored the necessarily temporal nature of all that exists in and through movement, corporeal or rational (that is, of discursive reasoning). If the angelic intelligence [*mens*] is the faculty in traditional psychology of intuitive perception, by contrast the human reason [*ratio*] must wheel from premises to conclusions, must circle in the *circus maximus* of ratiocination round the analysis of an Idea that only the *mens* can contemplate directly. Even so, this circling, beginning as the gradatory movement of logic or analysis, approaches in ever tighter and tighter circles to the angelic stasis of intuition. For the end of thought is the enforming power of an Idea.

In so far as the great poets are able to speak to the shaping power of Ideas, they re-enact the circling with which we approach the Ideas ever more closely in the process of reasoning. Hence their poems can serve our soul-chariots, the vehicles by which we ascend to the outermost convex rim of the intellectual heaven thence to contemplate afar what the *Phaedrus* 247A calls the 'blessed spectacles' of intelligible reality. Again we are closer to the divine hymns of Orpheus and David than to the complex surface of an epic narrative however hermetically allegorized. Indeed, it would be fair to say that Neoplatonism, for all the encouragement it accorded in antiquity and the Renaissance to the bolder displacements of allegoresis, was nonetheless anchored in the world of the divine lyric, of the incantation and the laud; and thus to the state of rapture that song induced in the singer and listener alike, each bound to the other and to the god, enthusiasts in the original meaning of the word. That enthusiasm, *furor* or *mania* defines Neoplatonism's engagement with poetry, and thus with the poet not the poem, accounts for the centrality of passages from the *Ion* and the *Phaedrus* rather than those from the *Republic* and *Laws* in the Renaissance's re-engagement with Neoplatonism. They not only define the nature of the new Platonic poetics, they also redefine Plato's banishment of the poets, amongst whom were two of the most venerable mentors of the Greeks, the source of their *paideia*.

In the Cinquecento Aristotelian poetics was revived by Italian academicians, as Bernard Weinberg has amply documented,[1] and occasioned a major shift of perspective: from the state of the poet to the shape and genre of the poem; from the nature of inspiration to the labour of the file; from the unveiling of metaphysical truths to the establishing of proper canons for plotting, characterization, and style; from the elusive music of inward ascent to the determination of matters of diction and metre. The confusion that ensued even in the most gifted minds in choosing between these two competing, if not diametrically opposite poetics, is evident in the case of Sidney's *Apology*, but must have been general. However, while a new generation turned with curiosity to Aristotle's ideas on the poem as an object of study and analysis, still it remained fascinated by the Platonic emphasis on the poet as god-possessed subject. These twin foci, indeed, continued to determine the nature of critical debate through the Enlightenment until the situation was transformed by the Romantics and their revolutionary theory concerning the 'esemplastic' powers of what had always been a subordinate and easily deluded faculty, the imagination.

---

[1] B. Weinberg, *A history of literary criticism in the Italian Renaissance*, 2 vols. (Chicago: University of Chicago Press, 1961).

46

Cosmography and poetics

Fernand Hallyn

Cosmography or the description of the constitution of the world, comprising astronomy as well as geography, is related to poetics either by analogy (poems being taken as metaphors of the cosmos, the object of cosmography) or by exposition (in poetry aiming partially or totally at practising the writing of cosmography). Both relations will be considered here, as well as some effects of the scientific revolution on them. Since it is, of course, impossible to be exhaustive, only some of the most representative texts will be mentioned and broad characteristics will be highlighted, rather than specific differences.

The analogy between *cosmos* and *logos*, establishing unity and harmonious variety as the basic rules of classical rhetoric and poetics, is already present in Plato.[1] Augustine develops this analogy in a variety of influential texts.[2] Among the other ancient sources, Macrobius, who stressed the similarity between Virgil's poetry and God's Creation (*Saturnales* v.1.19–20), is one of the most important. In the early Renaissance, the theme reappears in many prescriptions for artistic variety, also inspired by the Byzantine tradition following Hermogenes and 'imported' into Italy by George of Trebizond.[3] Angelo Poliziano, for example, developed in detail the Macrobian comparison between Virgil's work and God's Creation in his 'Manto' (1482, lines 351–67), where the vivid descriptions of the poet's text are said to mirror the most 'variegated species' [*discors facies*] of the beauty of the world.[4] Many Renaissance authors claimed a similar beauty for their works.[5] The theme of poetry as an analogue of

---

[1] L. Brisson, 'Le discours comme univers et l'univers comme discours. Platon et ses interprètes néo-platoniciens', in *Le texte et ses représentations* (Paris: Presses de l'Ecole Normale Supérieure, 1987), pp. 121–8. Unless otherwise indicated, the translations in the present chapter are those of the author.

[2] M.-S. Rostvig, 'Ars aeterna: Renaissance poetics and theories of divine creation', *Mosaic* 3 (1969–70), 40–61.

[3] See M. Baxandall, *Giotto and the orators: humanist observers of painting in Italy and the discovery of pictorial composition, 1350–1450* (Oxford: Clarendon Press, 1971).

[4] See Angelo Poliziano, 'Manto' (Florence: Miscominus, 1482). A facsimile reprint of the 1482 Latin text is available in Perrine Galand's French translation of Poliziano's 'Les silves' (Paris: Les Belles Lettres, 1987), pp. 132–71.

[5] See P. Galand-Hallyn, 'Discours-nature et naturel du style chez Politien et Ronsard', in *Les yeux de l'éloquence: poétiques humanistes de l'évidence* (Caen: Paradigme, 1994), ch. III, p. 7.

the world because of its 'energetic' descriptions and the *concordia discors* of their variety is repeated by Vida (*De arte poetica*, III.64–75), Ronsard ('*Elégie à Des Masures*', 1–13), Vauquelin de La Fresnaye (*Art poétique*, III.659–75), Tasso (*Discorsi del poema eroico*), and others.[6] It is applied by George Chapman to Homer's description of Achilles' shield, by Arthur Golding to Ovid's description of the Sun's palace,[7] and so on.

Outside of those qualitative aspects, poetry was also considered as a mirror of quantitative relations between the parts of the world. The analogy of prosody and celestial harmony, present in Cicero (*De oratore* III.45) and Augustine (*De musica*, VI), was developed by Cristoforo Landino in his commentary on Dante, where he insists on the analogy between poetry and God's Creation according to number, measure, and weight (*Wisdom*, XI.20): the feet of a verse obey rules of number, the difference between long and short syllables rules of measure, and the weight of a poem is constituted by meaning and emotion.[8] Many others, from Polydore Vergil to Marvell, develop the same theme, often adding Plato and Pythagoras to the biblical reference.[9] The poetics of quantitative harmony are not limited to prosody, but could be applied also to the work as a whole, whose structure had then to embody the Pythagorean or Platonic formulas for the harmony of the universe.[10]

If the poem is a mirror of the variety of the cosmos and formally dominated by a similar musical harmony, the poet can be thought of as being analogous to God. In the 'Proemio' to his commentary on Dante, Landino expands on this:

And the Greeks said that poet comes from that word piin [*sic*]: which is a middle term between 'to create', which is appropriate to God when from nothing he brings something forth into being, and 'to make', which is said of men in every art when they compose something out of matter and form. This is why, although the fiction of the poet is not completely made out of nothing, yet it departs from making and comes very close to creating.[11]

Although defending the analogy on the grounds of etymology, Landino also insists on the inferiority of the poet by comparison with the Christian

---

[6] See Girolamo Vida, *De arte poetica*, ed. R. G. Williams (New York: Columbia University Press, 1976); Pierre de Ronsard's 'Elegie a Louis des Masures', in *Ronsard II: odes, hymns and other poems*, ed. G. Castor and T. Cave, 2 vols. (Manchester: Manchester University Press, 1977), vol. II, pp. 128–31; Vauquelin de La Fresnaye, *L'art poétique*, ed. G. Pelissier (Paris: Garnier, 1885); Torquato Tasso, *Discorsi dell'arte poetica e del poema eroico*, ed. L. Poma (Bari: Laterza, 1964).

[7] Compare S. K. Heninger, Jr., *Touches of sweet harmony: Pythagorean cosmology and Renaissance poetics* (San Marino, CA: Huntington Library, 1974), pp. 380–1.

[8] See E. N. Tigerstedt, 'The poet as creator: origins of a metaphor', *Comparative literature studies* 5 (1968), p. 458.

[9] Heninger, *Touches of sweet harmony*, pp. 382–5.

[10] Rostvig, 'Ars aeterna', p. 70.

[11] Text cited in Tigerstedt and translated by the present author, 'The poet as creator', p. 458.

God. Unlike God, the poet does not really create *ex nihilo*. Since he combines and transforms already extant materials, he might seem closer to the
demiourgos of the *Timaeus*. But, although it is generally admitted during
the Renaissance that the poet does not create out of nothing, he nevertheless often appears to rival God or functions as a vehicle through which
divine Creation reaches a perfection which it does not have in itself. In this
way, certain influential writers of the sixteenth century minimalize or seek
to compensate for the poet's original inferiority.

For Julius Caesar Scaliger, the creations of art are superior to those of
nature. This thesis, developed in the framework of a Mannerist theory of
ideas,[12] is based on the Aristotelian notion of *mimesis* and the difference
between poetry and history. The world of the poem realizes far better the
laws according to which it functions. It is free from the hazards which
form obstacles between an idea and its realization (*Poetices libri septem*,
III.25).[13] The poet creates an *altera natura* superior to Nature: 'since poetry
gives an appearance to what does not exist, and a better appearance to
what exists, it gives the impression of creating the things themselves, like
another God. . . .'[14] Scaliger also considers prosody in a similar way: in
the world, musical harmony is only realized on the global level of planet-
ary motion, but not in the detailed structure of its sublunar region; only
poetry realizes a rigorous harmony [*numerosa concordia*], maintained in
every syllable of every verse.[15]

Moreover, Sir Philip Sidney in *An apology for poetry* asserts that the
poet 'doth grow in effect another nature'. The richness and beauty of
poetry surpass the variety of the world: 'Nature never set forth the earth
in so rich Tapistry as diverse poets have done, neither with so pleasant
rivers, fruitful trees, sweet-smelling flowers, nor whatsoever else may
make the too much loved earth more lovely. Her world is brazen, the
Poets only deliver a golden.' This superiority of poetry can only be
explained by the fact that the author does not simply combine from materials which exist in the world, but creates, like God, from 'ideas', inner,
freely conceived representations. In Sidney's words, the poet is 'not
enclosed within the narrow warrant of [nature's] gifts, but freely ranging
within the Zodiack of his owne wit'.[16] The poet is endowed with his own
inner world, complete in itself, surrounded by its own firmament.

---

[12] Compare E. Panofsky, *Idea: a concept in art theory* (New York: Harper & Row, 1968).
[13] Scaliger, *Poetices libri septem*, ed. A. Buck (1561; facs. reprint Stuttgart and Bad
    Cannstatt: F. Frommann, 1964), Book III, ch. 25, p. 113.
[14] *Ibid.*, Book I, ch. 1, p. 1.
[15] See C. Balavoine, 'La *Poétique* de J.-C. Scaliger: pour une mimésis de l'imaginaire', in
    La statue et l'empreinte: la poétique de Scaliger (Paris: Vrin, 1986), pp. 107–29; see
    esp. p. 115.
[16] *The defence of poesie*, ed. J. A. van Dorsten (London: Oxford University Press, 1966),
    pp. 23–4.

During the Renaissance, cosmography was often considered to be part of the encyclopaedic knowledge necessary to excel in the highest poetic genres. The knowledge of arts and sciences was seen as a source of invention in general, with a capacity to help the poet generate adequate descriptions and comparisons. But cosmography also played an important role as a specific subject-matter in so-called 'scientific poetry'. It even gave birth to a genre termed *poésie naturelle* by Guillaume Colletet: 'Natural poetry is one that treats thoroughly the things of Nature, as well the Celestial bodies as the sublunary and elementary bodies'.[17]

The introduction of scientific subject-matter in poetry was also subject to criticism. Aristotle had already stated that Homer and Empedocles had nothing in common, except the fact that both wrote in verse; Empedocles deserves to be called a 'naturalist' rather than a 'poet' (*Poetics*, 1.47b). As a consequence, sixteenth-century critics of scientific and cosmographic poetry generally follow Aristotelian lines.

Commenting on Aristotle's judgement on Empedocles in his *Annotationi nel libro della Poetica d'Aristotele*,[18] Alessandro Piccolomini warns that poets should not introduce into their comparisons and descriptions elements 'hidden in the depths of the arts and the sciences', because these passages will not be understood by most readers and also, more importantly, because there is an absence of 'imitation' in such a procedure. Scientific matters lack two fundamental qualities demanded by the Aristotelian notion of *mimesis*. They do not readily lend themselves to action, but rather to descriptive developments. And no transposition into better or worse is possible since, for the poet, science falls within the domain of objective truth. Accordingly, for Piccolomini, one should admit that Homer and Virgil are greater poets than Lucretius and Dante.

In England, Sidney also takes an Aristotelian stand on the subject. Speaking of poems which 'deal with matters philosophical', he remembers the *Poetics*' opposition between Homer and Empedocles when he writes that verse is 'but an ornament and no cause to Poetrie, since there have bene many most excellent Poets that never versified, and now swarme many versefiers that need never answere to the name of Poets'.[19] The writer who transmits knowledge through verse is 'wrapped within the fold of the proposed subject, and takes not the course of his own invention'. Lack of 'invention' implies lack of 'imitation' in the Aristotelian sense. And the phrase, 'wrapped within the fold of the proposed subject', is undoubtedly meant to be contrasted with the idea of 'freely ranging

---

[17] G. Colletet, *Traité de la poésie morale et sententieuse*, in *L'art poétique* (Paris: A. de Sommaville and L. Chamhoudry, 1658), p. 38.
[18] Alessandro Piccolomini, *Poetica d'Aristotele* (Venice: G. Guariseo, 1575), p. 36.
[19] Sidney, *The defence of poesie*, p. 26.

within the Zodiack of his owne wit', by which Sidney characterizes, as we
have seen, the truly creative poet.

Certainly, the use of scientific material could sometimes be defended
within the Aristotelian theory of poetry as *mimesis*. Servius, commenting
on Virgil's *Georgics*, already noted that the poetic exposition of knowledge implies the use of a fictional teacher–student relationship.[20] Similar
arguments were advanced to defend Dante, who had been accused by
Bembo and others of having introduced too much 'philosophy' in his
Divina commedia. Alessandro Rinuccini, in manuscript notes attributed
to him (*c.* 1587), stresses that philosophy is the appropriate subject-
matter for a dialogue between the learned protagonists of Dante's fiction;
in this way, scientific themes contribute to the verisimilitude of imitation:

> Those who blame him for treating the sciences in an overrefined way do not see
> that he goes according to verisimilitude; for two private persons like himself and
> Vergil could better employ themselves in contemplations than might heroes who
> are responsible for the governing of others; and the place and the time and the
> occasion, as he brings these about by degrees, required them to do so. In a word,
> he imitates a man who wishes to learn.[21]

But the use of these scientific subjects was also justified on purely theoretical grounds. There was another definition of poetry, based not on the
use of fiction, but on metre, proposed in antiquity by Plato (*Phaedrus*
258d) and others. If poetry is defined only by its metrical form, then it
becomes possible for the poet to write about all subjects, irrespective of
whether or not they are cast in a fictional mode. Before 1406, Coluccio
Salutati, in his unfinished *De laboribus Herculis* (1.4), had already declared that most of the genres of discourse [*artes sermocinales*] have
their own subject-matter and their restricted finality; they complete one
another without crossing the other's boundaries: a grammarian does not
compete with a rhetorician. Only poetics is not subject to this kind of distributive limitation. Having no subject-matter of its own, able to address
all subjects, poetry brings the other genres of discourse to perfection.
Thus, although only one form of discourse amongst others, poetry can
substitute for all of them: 'Now, the subject-matter of poetry is not something determined . . . but it is universal and widely open. . . .'[22]

Of all the possible scientific subjects, cosmography ranks among the
highest and the most appropriate to the poet. Indeed, Pontus de Tyard

---

[20] Compare B. Effe, *Dichtung und Lehre: Untersuchungen zur Typologie des antiken
Lehrgedichts* (Munich: Beck, 1977), p. 21.

[21] Alessandro Rinuccini [attributed notes], MS Ashburnham 562 of the Biblioteca Lauren-
ziana, cited and translated by B. Weinberg, *A history of literary criticism in the Italian
Renaissance*, 2 vols. (Chicago: University of Chicago Press, 1961), vol. II, p. 886.

[22] C. Salutati, *De laboribus Herculis*, ed. B. L. Ullman, 2 vols. (Zurich: Thesaurus Mundi,
1951), vol. I, p. 18.

writes in his *Le premier curieux* (1557): 'Since . . . man could not wish nor receive a greater good than the real knowledge of things, I esteem happy and desirable the condition of a man who spends his life with the sciences . . . man is born to contemplate the world'.[23] Science, and especially the consideration of the world-order, is not an affair for specialists alone. It concerns the humanity of man and, as such, ought to engage the interest and meditation of all humankind. The poet, according to Jacques Peletier du Mans, is best able to fulfil this calling; cosmographic poetry is not only justified, but exalted: 'There is no beauty in Nature's universe, / There is no secret in Science's diversity, / Of which, through Verses full of grave pleasantness, / For all the spokesman should not be the Poet'.[24] Cosmographic poetry is thus endowed with a dual role (*docere/placere*), able, on the one hand, to teach the ignorant to see the natural wonders of the universe, on the other, to offer the learned an object of study best suited to occupying their leisure time [*otium*].

How, then, are cosmological metaphors and cosmographic poetry affected by the scientific revolution? Cosmological metaphors depend on a world-view in which correspondences and analogies play a fundamental role; they continue to be used, even beyond the seventeenth century, not only by Enlightenment and Romantic poets, but also by rationalist critics like Marmontel. Indeed, cosmographic poetry continues to be written until well into the nineteenth century. What interests us here, however, is that there exists also, from the early seventeenth century on, an awareness of a new relationship between science and literature. The 'new science',[25] with its distrust of 'ordinary' language, its insistence on mathematical and experimental methods, tends to separate itself from poetry. Man no longer appears as a privileged creature, the contemplator for whose admiration the world has been made. John Donne's celebrated lines in his *First anniversary*, where he regrets the destruction of the traditional cosmos by the 'new Philosophy', are among the most explicit signs of a crisis in this relationship. The clearest manifestation of a transformation is probably the development of a poetics of wit [*ingegno, ingenio, esprit*]. One such example revealing its ambiguous relationship to the 'new science' in the oxymoron of its title is Emmanuele Tesauro's *Il cannocchiale Aristotelico* [*The Aristotelian perspective glass*, 1655].

Tesauro speaks in an ambiguous way about the telescope. To be sure, he sees in it a transcendence of natural human perception, opening a new area of scientific discovery. But he is more interested in the technology of the marvellous than in the progress of science. For him, the meaning of the

---

[23] *Le premier curieux*, ed. J. C. Lapp (Ithaca: Cornell University Press, 1950), p. 1.
[24] *Œuvres poétiques* (Paris: R. Coulombel, 1581), p. 72.
[25] See the following chapter of Ann Blair in the present volume, 'Natural philosophy and the "new science" '.

telescope is not Promethean: its praise occurs in a section of the work which proposes to admire human wit as a form of optical illusion; the telescope itself becomes primarily the object of tropological *tours de force*, suggesting an instrument of magic rather than of science: it is presented as 'wings of glass', which permit one to 'cross the seas without sails' and to 'fly to the heaven quick as lightning'.[26]

This displacement from the sphere of knowledge to pure pleasure also characterizes Tesauro's treatment of tropes, the main subject of the *Cannocchiale*. 'Ingenious' tropes are not called on to reveal truth. The only aim of metaphors such as those applied to the telescope is to be admired for themselves: 'And the marvellous comes forth from . . . the fact that the soul of the listener, subdued by the novelty, considers the sharpness of the representing mind and the unexpected image of the represented object'.[27] The ingenious mind contemplates its own acuity [*acutezza*] in the unexpected metaphor. But, contrary to Narcissus, it is never dominated by that image. Its metaphors are conscious inventions, entirely dominated by a technical mastery for which a treatise like the *Cannocchiale* provides detailed methodological instruction.[28]

The ingenious metaphor has no cosmological or cosmographical reference. It is scarcely more than ornament, mere cosmetics. But these cosmetics have at least a double significance. First, the longing for ornament is precisely what distinguishes man from all other creatures: 'To men alone, not to the animals nor to the angels, did Nature give a certain nausea of everyday objects . . .'[29] Through its metaphors, the ingenious mind transforms the ordinary, normative world of speech into a world of contemplative wonder through which man realizes his uniqueness. But the ancient etymological play on *cosmetics* and *cosmos* should not be forgotten. Taking up the traditional analogy between the author and the Creator, Tesauro argues that, precisely because ingenious tropology does not claim to have any referential bearing, it comes closest to a creation *ex nihilo*: 'So, it is not without reason that ingenious men are called divine. Since, just as God produces what is from what is not, in the same way wit produces beings from non-beings: it makes the lion become a Man, and the eagle a town.'[30] But such an affirmation in a rhetoric excluding truth as well as verisimilitude may be read rather as just another cosmetic mask than as a real glorification.

---

[26] E. Tesauro, *Il cannocchiale Aristotelico* (Venice: Milocho, 1682), p. 55 [1670; facs. reprint Bad Homburg: Gehlen, 1968, ed. A. Buck].
[27] *Ibid.*, pp. 164–5.
[28] See F. Hallyn, 'Port-Royal et Tesauro: signe, figure, sujet', *Baroque* 9–10 (1980), 76–86.
[29] Tesauro, *Il cannocchiale*, p. 74.   [30] *Ibid.*, p. 51.

47

Natural philosophy and the 'new science'

Ann Blair

The studies by Marjorie Hope Nicolson, and others, of the impact of the 'new science' on seventeenth-century English literature assumed an unproblematic demarcation between science and literature. Since the 1950s this notion has been challenged, both by new trends in 'literature and science' (from cyberspace to the rhetoric of science) and by recent historical scholarship. In particular, as this brief sketch will suggest, the historical complexity of the relations between natural philosophy and literature in the early modern period belies not only the traditional assumption of a separate science which 'influences' literature, but also the more recent intimations that science simply *is* literature. In the Renaissance proper (say, until 1630) the methods, goals, and individuals involved in the two clusters of disciplines overlapped in a number of ways. During the seventeenth century new developments in both science and literary criticism tended, sometimes self-consciously, to define the two fields as separate and even opposed. Although one can see in these trends the foundations for our modern sense of a gulf between science and literature, at the time such a gap was not so readily apparent.

Carrying on an ancient tradition, natural philosophy in the Renaissance searched for certain, causal knowledge about nature primarily through the interpretation of and commentary on authoritative texts. Bookish methods promised more exciting results than ever once they could be applied beyond the writings of Aristotle and his scholastic commentators, already central to the medieval curriculum. Thanks to humanism, a vast number of newly discovered ancient works about nature became available: late antique commentaries on Aristotle (for example, Philoponus, Simplicius, and Alexander of Aphrodisias); accounts of pre-Socratic, Epicurean and Stoic, hermetic and Neoplatonic cosmologies and philosophies; and new works and better versions of old ones by still canonical figures, like Aristotle, Ptolemy, and Galen.[1] Until roughly the mid-seventeenth century the main practice of natural philosophy was to emend and interpret, compile and sort, reconcile and imitate such disparate texts.[2]

[1] See Anthony Grafton, *New worlds, ancient texts: the power of tradition and the shock of discovery* (Cambridge, MA: Harvard University Press, 1992).
[2] See Ann Blair, Anthony Grafton, Owen Hannaway, and Lynn Joy, 'Reassessing humanism and science', *Journal of the history of ideas* 53 (1992), 535–84, and the works cited there.

In the universities, natural philosophy (one of the four branches of philosophy, alongside logic, metaphysics, and ethics) consisted in the explication of and commentary on canonical texts, starting with Aristotle's *Physics* on the principles of nature (space, time, motion and the like), and advancing to more specialized works on meteorology, psychology or theoretical medicine. The academic boom of the late sixteenth and early seventeenth centuries produced countless theses, professorial treatises, and textbooks on these topics.[3] For broader, non-specialist audiences authors located outside the university (often doctors, lawyers or clerics) compiled and debated the nature and causes of myriad natural (and in some cases mechanical) 'facts' garnered from the wide range of available books, ancient and modern. Although these different kinds of works might include direct observations, second-hand reports and local lore alongside information derived from books, this traditional kind of natural philosophy created new knowledge primarily through the compilation, criticism, and explication of texts.

At the same time, before 1630, a handful of works introduced the emphases identified with 'modern science': notably new claims for the applicability of mathematics to the physical world, and for the relevance of empirical observation and practical applications to natural knowledge. Although scientific by modern standards, these new concerns, too, grew in part out of the humanist methods of textual recovery and imitation. Thus current scholarship agrees with Kepler when he complained that Copernicus, in launching an astronomical revolution, 'had imitated Ptolemy rather than nature'.[4] Similarly, in rejecting the traditional division of labour between the learned doctors and the menials who performed dissections, Andreas Vesalius invoked the methodological precepts of his ancient model Galen.[5] For Niccolò Tartaglia, an autodidact employed as military engineer to the Duke of Urbino, Euclid's *Elements*, newly available in the vernacular, provided the format and ideal for his attempt to mathematize and lend higher status to ballistics.[6] Whether mathematical, empirical or social, the scientific innovations of the sixteenth century drew from ancient texts a rich supply of models, methods, data, and theories.

Although founded on the imitation of ancient models and the manipulation of textual sources, Renaissance natural philosophy did not generate any theories of literary practices specific to its goals. In this sense it did

[3] Charles B. Schmitt, 'The rise of the philosophical textbook', in *The Cambridge history of Renaissance philosophy*, ed. C. B. Schmitt, Q. Skinner, E. Kessler, and J. Kraye (Cambridge: Cambridge University Press, 1988), pp. 792–804.
[4] Noel Swerdlow and Otto Neugebauer, *Mathematical astronomy in Copernicus' De revolutionibus*, 2 vols. (New York: Springer-Verlag, 1984), vol. I, p. 32.
[5] Andreas Vesalius, *Epitome*, trans. L. R. Lind (New York: Macmillan, 1949), preface.
[6] Niccolò Tartaglia, *Nova scientia*, in *Mechanics in sixteenth-century Italy*, ed. S. Drake and I. E. Drabkin (Madison: University of Wisconsin Press, 1969).

not directly contribute to the formulation of literary-critical precepts. The suggestive metaphor of reading the 'book of nature', as a companion volume to the Bible, for example, did not entail a particular interpretative method. Drawn from both biblical and ancient sources (notably St Paul, Lucretius, and the Stoics), the metaphor is a commonplace used to support contradictory attitudes towards natural philosophy. At one extreme, for example, Galileo finds that the 'book of nature' is written in the language of mathematics, which speaks more clearly than the language of Scripture; at the other, the Protestant scientific poet Du Bartas, following Luther, believes that the 'book of nature' can only be read through the glasses of faith.[7]

Instead of developing a literary method specific to their subject, natural philosophers drew from the humanist education and ambient culture shared by the educated élite. Natural philosophers did not form a separate professional group and received little formal specialized education outside medical faculties or London's new Gresham College for mathematical practitioners. Even mathematicians, whose methods and topics had been clearly delineated since antiquity, were also trained as humanists. Thus, although each author is primarily identified with one field or the other, Renaissance 'literature' and 'science' overlap in a number of canonical figures. Almost every philosophical author had occasion to compose literary exercises of some kind, especially poems, in academic gatherings or early salons, in the front matter to books, or in commemoration of political or academic ceremonies.[8] Galileo left two comedies and a few neo-Latin poems in manuscript and published a critique of Tasso's style. Championing the classical simplicity and order of Ariosto, Galileo attacked the *Gerusalemme liberata* for its excessively intricate syntax and amplifications, its distortions of Tuscan vocabulary, and for the lack of psychological coherence of its characters; while Galileo participated in this way in a general turn against Mannerism in the years 1590–1615, he too shunned classical Latin in favour of an Italian style that tended towards polemical excess and a personal tone in an effort to reach out to a broader audience.[9] Kepler composed a 'Dream' imitated from Lucian

---

[7] *Discoveries and opinions of Galileo*, trans. S. Drake (New York: Doubleday, 1957), p. 196 ('Letter to the Grand Duchess Christina'), pp. 237–8 (*The Assayer*); Jan Miernowski, *Dialectique et connaissance dans la Sepmaine de Du Bartas* (Geneva: Droz, 1992), ch. 10. More generally, Hans Blumenberg, *Die Lesbarkeit der Welt* (Frankfurt: Suhrkamp, 1981).

[8] See for example, on the poems of Tycho Brahe interspersed in his prose works, Peter Zeeberg, 'Science versus secular life: a central theme in the Latin poems of Tycho Brahe', *Acta conventus neo-Latini Torontonensis*, ed. A. Dalzell, C. Fantazzi, and R. J. Schoeck (Binghamton: Medieval and Renaissance texts and studies, 1991), pp. 831–8.

[9] Erwin Panofsky, *Galileo as a critic of the arts* (The Hague: M. Nijhoff, 1954); Leonardo Olschki, 'Galileo's literary formation', in *Galileo, man of science*, ed. E. McMullin (New York: Basic Books, 1967), pp. 140–59.

and Plutarch, in which he imagines the earth as seen from the moon, and a serio-comic paradox on the snowflake as a new year's gift to a courtly patron. Even in a technical work like the *Mysterium cosmographicum* (1596), in which he develops his theory that the planets are nested between the perfect solids, Kepler displays a sophisticated authorial self-consciousness when he describes the difficulties of matching the data to his theory in the first edition and, in a later edition of 1620, adds a thorough critique of his earlier work in long, probing footnotes. Conversely, some figures central to Renaissance literary criticism were also active in natural philosophy: notably Girolamo Fracastoro (medicine), Francesco Patrizi (anti-Aristotelian natural philosophy), and Jacques Peletier du Mans (arithmetic).

Even while 'doing science', natural philosophers contributed to the development of literary languages, forms, and metaphors. Galileo's *Dialogue concerning the two chief world systems* (1632), for example, is considered a landmark in the development of Italian as a vernacular, as is Bacon's *Advancement of learning* (1605) for English; yet both authors also composed other works in Latin. Natural philosophy was involved both in the early emergence of the vernaculars and in the late persistence of Latin. Latin continued to be used into the eighteenth century for works addressed to a specialist or academic audience, most famously Newton's *Principia* (1687) or Linnaeus's *Systema naturae* (1735). But already in the sixteenth century, artisans with little or no Latin literacy (in fields ranging from surgery to engineering and pottery) successfully laid claim to greater respectability as authors of technical treatises which offered an improved mastery of nature (Paré, Tartaglia, the English mathematical practitioners). Some self-consciously used the vernacular to challenge established academic and intellectual hierarchies, attacking, for example, the priority of theory over practice (Palissy), or of ancient learning over theosophic wisdom (Paracelsus). These calls for the vernacular to free natural philosophy from the narrow ranks of those indebted only to classical learning were also echoed by literary figures like John Rastell (*c.* 1510) and Sperone Speroni (1547).[10] Natural historians were also among the first to introduce the vernacular, both in nomenclatures and in the composition of treatises (for example, by Guillaume Rondelet, Pierre Belon, Leonhard Fuchs); the difficulty of identifying local vernacular terms for plant and animal species with the ancient ones was well known since the fifteenth-century controversies concerning the translation of Pliny's *Natural history* and remained of the utmost importance in trying to follow accurately

---

[10] Leonardo Olschki, *Geschichte der neusprachlichen wissenschaftlichen Literatur*, 3 vols. (Vaduz: Kraus Reprint, 1965), vol. II, pp. 166–9; [John Rastell], *The nature of the four elements*, ed. J. S. Farmer (New York: AMS Press, 1970), sig. A ij^{r-v}; Sperone Speroni, *Dialogo delle lingue*, in *I dialoghi* (Venice: Aldus, 1542) ff. 103^v–28^r.

ancient medical recipes.[11] At the same time, increasing numbers of translations from the Latin of ancient and Renaissance natural philosophy contributed to the development of a vernacular vocabulary on scientific topics. But the authors involved complained about the difficulty of their task, and debates over the proper use of borrowings from Latin and other languages, versus innovative coinings, or colloquialisms from local dialects, continued long into the seventeenth century.[12] Indeed Thomas Sprat's famous call in 1667 for a 'plain and simple' style, which R. F. Jones saw as the origin of a new 'utilitarian' and anti-rhetorical prose, is, after many years of debate, increasingly interpreted as a reaction not against rhetoric itself, but against the crabbed Latinisms in the English prose of contemporary scholars. Particularly in the translation of scientific works, neologisms were frequently coined on Latin models, so that some English books even included glossaries explaining the new words; John Evelyn and John Wilkins were among those who, like Sprat, called for an end to the excessive use of Latinisms and of words having several meanings. Robert Boyle too complained about the ambiguity of chemical language in particular.[13]

Natural philosophers also helped to develop new literary forms: the utopia (Bacon, Campanella), the cosmic voyage (Kepler, Huygens), the debate (Bruno), the essay and the aphorism (Bacon).[14] Metaphors of theatres, books, and jokes of nature pepper their writings.[15] A more conventional form especially widespread during the Renaissance, the dialogue, surfaces in many kinds of natural philosophical works, from technical

[11] Charles Nauert, 'Humanists, scientists and Pliny: changing approaches to a classical author', *American historical review* 84 (1979), 72–85.

[12] Francis F. Johnson, 'Latin versus English: the sixteenth-century debate over scientific terminology', *Studies in philology* 41 (1944), 109–35; Ann Blair, 'La persistance du latin comme langue de science à la fin de la Renaissance', in *Sciences et langues en Europe*, ed. R. Chartier and P. Corsi (Paris: Centre Alexandre Koyré, 1996), pp. 21–42.

[13] See the influential analysis of Thomas Sprat's *History of the Royal Society* (1667) in Richard Foster Jones, *Ancients and moderns: a study of the rise of the scientific movement in seventeenth-century England* (1936; New York: Dover, 1982), pp. 221–36. For a current assessment, see Brian Vickers, 'The Royal Society and English prose style: a reassessment', in *Rhetoric and the pursuit of truth: language change in the seventeenth and eighteenth centuries* (Los Angeles: William Andrews Clark Memorial Library, 1985), pp. 3–76, and the literature cited there.

[14] Rosalie Colie, *The resources of kind: genre-theory in the Renaissance*, ed. B. Lewalski (Berkeley: University of California Press, 1973), pp. 89–90. Colie no doubt has in mind: Francis Bacon, *New Atlantis* (1624; published 1627) and Tommaso Campanella, *The city of the sun* (c. 1602); Kepler's 'Somnium' composed in 1609 and circulated in manuscript in his lifetime (as discussed in James S. Romm, 'Lucian and Plutarch as sources for Kepler's "Somnium"', *Classical and modern literature* 9 (1989), 97–107), and Christiaan Huygens, *Cosmotheoros*, published posthumously in 1698, which, however, does not develop the idea of a lunar voyage as explicitly; Giordano Bruno, *The Ash Wednesday supper* (1584); and Francis Bacon, *Essays* (1597–1625), and the aphorisms of the *Novum organum* (1620).

[15] Paula Findlen, 'Jokes of nature and jokes of knowledge: the playfulness of scientific discourse in early modern Europe', *Renaissance quarterly* 43 (1990), 292–331.

treatises of medicine or astronomy (Jean Fernel's *De abditis rerum causis*, 1550, Kepler's *Epitome*, 1618–21) to the simple questions and answers of textbooks for beginners, in encyclopaedic compilations (Jean Bodin's *Universae naturae theatrum*, 1596) and natural theologies (Lambert Daneau, *Physica christiana*, 1597). The didactic dialogue could be used to powerful effect, as Galileo discovered when his *Dialogue* of 1632 engaged rhetoric in the battle between the cosmologies with such success that it was condemned.[16]

Finally, the Renaissance was the heyday of a phenomenon which has often puzzled modern sensibilities, that loosely termed 'scientific poetry'. Throughout Renaissance Europe, newly recovered examples and reports of ancient Greek and Latin poetry about nature (for example, Manilius, Virgil, Hesiod, Columella, Oppian, Nicander, Xenophanes, Lucretius) spawned imitators: among them, George Buchanan, *Sphaera* and Du Monin, *Uranologie* (1585 and 1583, astronomy); Giovanni Pontano, *Urania* (1480, astrology and meteorology); Girolamo Fracastoro, *Syphilis* (1530); Augurelli, *Chrysopoeia* (alchemy, 1518); Marco Vida, *Bombyx* (on the silkworm, 1527).[17] These largely didactic poets were motivated by practical goals, to facilitate memorization of useful knowledge, or to display their virtuosity in this most difficult form of imitation. In the wake of the work of the Pléiade in the 1550s and 1560s French poets envisioned themselves as learned and inspired guides to a Christianized and often Neoplatonized universe. They perceived deeper links between the poet and the natural philosopher – for example, in a shared demonic inspiration (Ronsard, *Hymnes*, 1553, 1556), or in the recondite understanding of secret wisdom (Maurice Scève, *Microcosme*, 1562; Guy Le Fèvre de La Boderie, *Encyclie*, 1571; or the alchemical poets Joseph du Chesne, *Grand miroir du monde*, 1587; or Clovis Hesteau de Nuysement, *Table d'Hermès*, among other poems composed 1620–4). The heavens especially were valued as a suitably exalted topic for poetry which would sing the praises of God the divine creator[18] (J.-A. de Baïf, *Météores*, 1567; Jean-Edouard du Monin, *Uranologie*, 1583, among others).

Whether didactic or lyric in orientation, these poets pursued a goal common to both poetry and natural philosophy: to ally the *utile* with the *dulce*. In a close parallel to the hackneyed Horatian tag about the purpose

---

[16] See, most recently, Jean Dietz Moss, *Novelties in the heavens: rhetoric and science in the Copernican controversy* (Chicago: University of Chicago Press, 1993), and the literature cited there.

[17] Paul van Tieghem, *La littérature latine de la Renaissance: étude d'histoire littéraire européenne* (Geneva: Slatkine, 1966), pp. 132–6; James R. Naiden, *The Sphera of George Buchanan* (Philadelphia: privately published, 1952), pp. 5–17.

[18] Albert-Marie Schmidt, *La poésie scientifique en France au seizième siècle* (Paris: Albin Michel, 1938); Isabelle Pantin, *La poésie du ciel en France dans la seconde moitié du seizième siècle* (Geneva: Droz, 1995).

of poetry, natural philosophy was routinely praised in the Renaissance for both teaching the wisdom and providence of God, and delighting the reader with the varied detail of natural description (*docere et delectare*).[19] Through most of this period the scientific knowledge contained in such poetry rested on traditional knowledge transmitted from ancient sources and available in the most basic pedagogical manuals; descriptions of the heavens by the poets of late sixteenth-century France, for example, bear no traces of the knowledge or concerns current among astronomers at the time.[20] For that reason, poetry has served as a useful gauge of the penetration of the new scientific ideas to a broader public and of the conceptual transformations that occurred in that process. For example, many astronomers objected to Copernicanism, but never on the grounds that it displaced humans from their noble place at the centre of the universe; on the contrary, the Aristotelian objection was that the earth was too crass and unworthy a body to share in the perfect motions of the heavenly bodies. But poets like John Donne, perceiving the end of a number of long-traditional notions, expressed dismay and uncertainty at a world changing its centrepoint, at the 'breaking of circles' – feelings which the natural philosophers never voiced.[21]

As the Renaissance developed a new poetics, inspired by Aristotle's rediscovered work on the subject, over time literary theory worked to exclude natural philosophy written in verse from the purview of poetry. While some critics, like Patrizi, Fracastoro, and J. C. Scaliger, still favoured scientific poetry, the strict Aristotelians like Speroni, Varchi, Vettori, and Minturno condemned it.[22] By the early seventeenth century, in France, the classical rules laid out by Malherbe sealed the oblivion of the poets of the preceding generation. In England, however, scientific poetry generally aroused less criticism. Even Sidney, one of its strongest opponents, wavered in his condemnation, praising for example its venerability.[23] A flow of original works (most notably, Abraham Cowley's *Liber plantarum*, 1673), of scientific passages in longer poems (Milton), of editions of classical works, and of translations of Renaissance poems continued throughout the seventeenth century. Encouraged by various members of the Royal Society at the end of the century, English nature

[19] Ann Blair, *The theater of nature: Jean Bodin and Renaissance science* (Princeton: Princeton University Press, 1997), chs. 1, 5, pp. 33, 160.

[20] Pantin, *La poésie du ciel*, pp. 435–94.

[21] Marjorie Hope Nicolson, *The breaking of the circle: studies in the effect of the 'new science' upon seventeenth-century poetry* (Evanston, IL: Northwestern University Press, 1950).

[22] Robert Schuler, 'Francis Bacon and scientific poetry', *Transactions of the American philosophical society*, 82, 2 (1992), 7.

[23] Robert Schuler, 'Theory and criticism of the scientific poem in Elizabethan England', *English literary Renaissance* 15 (1985), 6–7.

poetry culminated in a flowering of georgic, descriptive, and natural theological poetry praising the glories of divine creation which lasted well past
1700.[24] Throughout this progressive shift in poetic topics away from natural philosophy and towards the description of nature or of husbandry,
one work continuously exercised critics on account of both its philosophy
and its poetry: once rediscovered in 1417, Lucretius's *De rerum natura*
was endlessly reviled for its Epicureanism, praised for its poetry, and imitated for its descriptions of nature.[25] By the end of the eighteenth century,
however, the nature poem was eclipsed by the lyric poem and nature
books in prose, partly under the renewed attacks of literary theorists.[26]

From the mid-seventeenth century on, the 'new science', too, contributed in various ways to a progressive separation between science and
literature, although the legacy of Renaissance interrelations continued
later than the programmatic statements of various 'new scientists' would
indicate. Francis Bacon and René Descartes, both posthumously hailed as
leaders into new (and quite different) kinds of natural philosophy, agreed
at least in proclaiming the utter uselessness of traditional bookish methods
of acquiring knowledge. Although historians have noted in their work
some unacknowledged debts to earlier methods and texts,[27] these statements were effective in first spreading the notion, now commonplace, that
science is antithetical to literature. To free themselves from the 'idols'
which Bacon associated with received language, some projectors devised
new, symbolic languages that would match reality.[28] But the 'language'
which the new science successfully developed was mathematics: Isaac
Newton's *Principia* (1687), despite being immediately lionized, soon removed the study of physics beyond the ken of the educated non-specialist.
Although the life sciences still remained accessible to the lettered élite
through the eighteenth century, Newton effectively drove a wedge into the
kind of vast research programme which he himself had undertaken, of
tracing divine activity through alchemical, historical, and biblical learning

---

[24] Dwight Durling, *Georgic tradition in English poetry* (Port Washington, NY: Kennikat
Press, 1964), pp. 3–32; Anthony Low, *The georgic revolution* (Princeton: Princeton
University Press, 1985), pp. 117–54.
[25] Simone Fraisse, *Une conquête du rationalisme: l'influence de Lucrèce en France au
seizième siècle* (Paris: Nizet, 1962); Wolfgang Bernard Fleischmann, *Lucretius and English literature 1680–1740* (Paris: Nizet, 1964).
[26] Durling, *Georgic tradition*, p. 217.
[27] Paolo Rossi, *Francis Bacon: from magic to science*, trans. S. Rabinovitch (London:
Routledge & Kegan Paul, 1968); Roger Ariew, 'Descartes and scholasticism: the intellectual background to Descartes' thought', in *Descartes: the Cambridge companion*, ed.
John Cottingham (Cambridge: Cambridge University Press, 1992), pp. 58–90; more
generally, Tom Sorell (ed.), *The rise of modern philosophy: the tension between the new
and traditional philosophies from Machiavelli to Leibniz* (Oxford: Clarendon Press, 1993).
[28] For example, John Wilkins, *Essay towards a real character, and a philosophical language*
(Menston, Yorkshire: Scolar Press, 1968).

as well as mathematical physics.[29] The foundation of the Royal Society (1662) and of the Académie Royale des Sciences (1666) also laid the foundations for the specialization of science, although for a time the Royal Society included not only the famous players in the development of the mechanical philosophy (like Boyle and Hooke), but also figures associated primarily with aesthetic and antiquarian pursuits (like Evelyn, Dryden, Wren, Aubrey or Cowley).

'Literature' and 'science' had only begun by the end of this period to form distinct conceptual worlds; neither was 'literary criticism' clearly defined. The impact of scientific developments on literary criticism has more to do with a shared context than with a specific theoretical legacy. The Scientific Revolution contributed to the general trend of the 'moderns' to reject ancient authority and rely on rational rules. While during the sixteenth century the renewal of scientific disciplines was still largely based on the imitation of the ancients and on methods of textual compilation and commentary, by the end of the seventeenth century the traditional scientific authorities (except perhaps Hippocrates) had been replaced with new systems of explanation and description supported variously by rational speculation, mathematical laws, empirical observation, and experimental testing. In evolving towards this 'modern' outcome, scientific practice, both traditional and innovative, was nonetheless noticeably shaped by the literary concerns central to a humanist education. Thus literary goals, forms, methods, and justifications can be detected in most natural philosophical works of this period.

---

[29] Betty Jo Dobbs, *The Janus faces of genius: the role of alchemy in Newton's thought* (Cambridge: Cambridge University Press, 1991).

48

Stoicism and Epicureanism: philosophical revival and literary repercussions

Jill Kraye

Interest in Stoicism and Epicureanism was rekindled in the early modern era as a result of the intensive study, on the part of humanists, of ancient texts, some of which were works of high literary as well as philosophical merit. For this reason, even though neither of these classical philosophical systems was centrally concerned with literary criticism, their revival had important repercussions on the interpretation of literature and on matters of style.

Stoicism

The main tenets of Stoicism were well known to scholars of the Middle Ages and early Renaissance, above all through the philosophical writings of Seneca. In the 1580s, however, Stoic philosophy began to become much more fashionable – a trend which lasted until the 1660s – due principally to the efforts of the Flemish humanist Justus Lipsius. From his immensely popular *De constantia* (1584) to his authoritative edition of Seneca (1605), Lipsius presented a comprehensive and attractive account of Stoicism.[1] He saw his mission as both philosophical and literary. On a philosophical level, Lipsius wanted to convince his contemporaries that Stoicism was the philosophy best suited to their needs; he did this by emphasizing the similarities, rather than the differences, between Stoicism and Christianity, and by presenting the often criticized Stoic doctrine of emotionlessness as a feasible and rational response to the political turbulence of the times. In literary terms, Lipsius wanted to reverse the judgement of earlier humanists such as Erasmus, who admired the moral content of Seneca's writings but who, like many ancient critics, regarded his writing as, at times, flat and prone to enigmatic obscurity.[2] Lipsius's

---

[1] Justus Lipsius, *De constantia* (Antwerp: Plantin, 1584); Seneca, *Opera*, ed. J. Lipsius (Antwerp: Plantin and J. Moretus, 1605).

[2] Erasmus, *Opus epistolarum*, ed. P. S. Allen *et al.*, 12 vols. (Oxford: Clarendon Press, 1906–58), vol. VIII, pp. 25–41. On Seneca's stylistic failings Erasmus cites Quintilian, 10.1.125–9; Aulus Gellius 12.2; and Suetonius, *Caligula* 53 (whose critical comment, 'sand without lime', Erasmus also discussed in *Adagia*, 2.3.57).

aim was to rehabilitate the terse, pointed, and epigrammatic Silver Age Latin of Seneca and Tacitus (whom he edited in 1575) as an alternative to the florid oratorical periods of Ciceronianism, which he considered to be enervated and bloodless.[3]

The revival of Stoic philosophy was thus closely associated with the promotion of a distinctive prose style, in which the studied brevity of Seneca replaced the ornate abundance of Cicero.[4] According to his English translator, Arthur Golding, Seneca's sentences were 'short, quick, and full of matter; his wordes, sharpe, pithie and unaffected; his whole order of writyng grave, deepe, and severe; fitted altogether to the reforming of mennes myndes, and not the delyghting of their eares'.[5] The former slave turned philosopher, Epictetus, the most important Greek source for Stoic moral doctrines, was likewise considered to have written in a 'lively, concise, sharp and bitting manner, which touches, pierces and penetrates to the bottom of the hardest hearts; the purpose of his writings was not to delight but to be beneficial'.[6] Even writers who were not specially well disposed towards Stoic philosophy expressed approval of Seneca's statement that 'elaborate elegance is not a manly apparel' (*Letters* 115, 2–3):[7] it was cited by Michel de Montaigne to express his distaste for empty Ciceronian eloquence, and by Robert Burton, who claimed to be 'seeking with Seneca, *quid scribam, non quemadmodum*, rather what, than how to write'.[8]

The chief spokesman of Stoicism in Spain, Francisco de Quevedo, not only drew on arguments from Lipsius to suggest a biblical origin for Stoic philosophy, he also strove to bring into Spanish the extreme concision, deliberate abruptness, and predilection for asyndeton that Lipsius had made fashionable in Latin.[9] Another vernacular author influenced by Lipsian ideas was Bishop Joseph Hall, who earned the nickname 'our English Seneca' as much for his prose style, with its aphoristic pithiness and witty antitheses, as for his adherence to Stoic philosophy, whose doctrines he adopted in a highly selective manner.[10]

---

[3] Justus Lipsius, *Opera omnia*, 4 vols. (Wessel: A. Hoogenhuysen, 1675), vol. II, p. 971.

[4] There was classical precedent for the notion of a Stoic style: see Diogenes Laertius, *Lives of the philosophers* (7.59), who describes its characteristics as 'lucidity, conciseness, appropriateness, distinction'. This passage is taken over verbatim in Thomas Stanley, *The history of philosophy*, 2nd edn (London: Thomas Bassett, 1687), p. 436.

[5] Seneca, *The woorke*, trans. A. Golding (London: John Day, 1578), sig. *2ᵛ.

[6] Epictetus, *Les propos*, trans. Jean Goulu de Sainct François (Paris: Iean de Heuqueville, 1609), sig. ã6ʳ.

[7] Seneca, *Ad Lucilium epistulae morales*, trans. R. M. Gummere, 3 vols. (Cambridge, MA: Harvard University Press, 1953–71), vol. III, p. 20.

[8] Michel de Montaigne, *The complete essays*, trans. M. A. Screech (London: Penguin, 1987), p. 282 (1.40: 'Reflections upon Cicero'). Robert Burton, *The anatomy of melancholy*, ed. T. C. Faulkner *et al.* (Oxford: Clarendon Press, 1989–), vol. I, pp. 17–18.

[9] Francisco de Quevedo, *Obras completas*, ed. L. Astrana Marín, 2 vols. (Madrid: Aguilar, 1945–60).

[10] J. Hall, *The works*, 10 vols. (Oxford: P. Wynter, 1863).

The prose style associated with Lipsian Stoicism was not without its severe critics: both the Latin and vernacular versions were charged with obscurity and harshness. The humanist Daniel Heinsius, delivering the funeral oration for Joseph Scaliger, Lipsius's successor at the University of Leiden, complained that the 'lean and jejune speech, juiceless and meagre, broken by some short phrases and plays on words, or by abrupt clauses' adopted by those who attempted to imitate the inimitable Lipsius, 'occasioned nausea and disgust'.[11] Thomas Powell, in his English translation of a Stoic treatise by the Bolognese scholar Virgilio Malvezzi, described the style 'as right Laconick, strict and succinct; so farre, that his brevity doth sometimes cloud his sense, and makes each period a Riddle to some capacities'.[12] And François de La Mothe le Vayer, in his *Considérations sur l'éloquence françoise de ce temps* (1638),[13] maintained that the 'stile coupé' of Malvezzi and Quevedo, with its exaggerated brevity and spasmodic rhythm, resembled the speech of an asthmatic.

The reawakened interest in Stoic philosophy also had implications for the interpretation of literary texts. Since the Middle Ages, Seneca's philosophical works had been separately transmitted from his tragedies and were often regarded as the product of two different authors. This division continued in the age of printing: both Erasmus and Lipsius included only the prose works in their editions of Seneca. In his earlier *Animadversiones* (1588) Lipsius had argued that, of the plays, only the *Medea* was written by the philosopher, attributing the others to at least three different authors. On the other hand, his friend Martin Antoine Del Rio, a Spanish Jesuit, believed that all the plays except the *Octavia* were not only written by Seneca but also reflected the same Stoic doctrines that were expressed in the treatises and letters. Rejecting Lipsius's strenuous efforts to demonstrate that Stoicism was fundamentally compatible with Christianity, Del Rio went out of his way, in the *Syntagma tragoediae Latinae* (1593-4), an anthology of Latin tragedy for use in Jesuit colleges, to identify and condemn the pernicious Stoic tenets which he found lurking within the plays 'like a scorpion hiding under foliage',[14] such as the corporeal nature of God and the insistence on self-reliance which removed any need for divine assistance. Del Rio's Stoic reading of Seneca's tragedies, though not his hostility to Stoicism, rapidly gained influential adherents and established itself as the standard interpretation of the plays until our own century.[15]

[11] *Autobiography of Joseph Scaliger*, trans. G. W. Robinson (Cambridge, MA: Harvard University Press, 1927), p. 83.

[12] V. Malvezzi, *Stoa triumphans*, trans. T. Powell (London: J. G., 1651), sig. B2ʳ.

[13] François de La Mothe le Vayer, *Considérations sur l'éloquence françoise de ce temps* (1638), in *Œuvres* (Paris: A. Courbet, 1662), p. 449.

[14] Martin Anton del Rio, *Syntagma tragoediae Latinae* (1593-4; Paris: P. Billaine, 1619-20), sig. ē2ʳ.

[15] R. Mayer, 'Personata Stoa: Neostoicism and Senecan tragedy', *Journal of the Warburg and Courtauld Institutes* 57 (1994), 151-74.

In relation to the study of poetry, the Stoic revival had an impact on the way in which early modern critics read the Roman satirists, especially Persius. Isaac Casaubon, in his enormously learned edition of Persius (*Satirarum liber*, 1605), constantly pointed out parallels between the *Satires* and the writings of Seneca, Epictetus, and the Emperor Marcus Aurelius. Casaubon, moreover, rated Persius above Horace and Juvenal on the ground that he was more consistently committed than his rivals to Stoic philosophy, which he expressed with such precision and learning that 'he props up the Stoa better even than Zeno', the founder of the sect, or Zeno's disciple Chrysippus.[16]

Casaubon's judgement was challenged in 1692 by John Dryden, in 'A discourse concerning the original and progress of satire', the preface to his translations of Persius and Juvenal. Ranking Persius well below Horace and Juvenal, Dryden described his verse as 'scabrous, and hobbling', and criticized him for his obscurity, which resulted from the 'brevity of his style, and crowding of his figures'. Persius could not therefore 'be allowed to stand in competition either with Juvenal or Horace', who shared the palm between them, since judged in relation to 'profit and delight, the two ends of poetry in general', Horace was the more profitable, and Juvenal the more delightful. Nevertheless, feeling himself 'obliged to give Persius his undoubted due', Dryden grudgingly admitted that, compared to 'his two competitors', he was more instructive in moral philosophy and stuck more closely to the teachings of Stoicism, 'the most noble, most generous, most beneficial to human kind, amongst all the sects, who have given us rules of ethics'.[17]

Epicureanism

It was not until the middle of the seventeenth century that Epicureanism had its philosophical revival. Up to that point, Epicurus's denial of divine providence and of the immortality of the soul, his atomistic physics and his belief that pleasure was the highest good ensured that hostility to his philosophy, on religious, scientific and moral grounds, remained the norm.

Because Epicurus's philosophy was held in low repute, the *De rerum natura* of his greatest Latin disciple, Lucretius, failed to gain the enthusiastic critical approval that its merits as a masterpiece of Latin poetry warranted. Although the poem was rediscovered in 1417, first printed *c.* 1473 and widely read by humanists, its controversial subject-matter discouraged the composition of commentaries. Not until 1504 was an exposition published: *In Lucretium paraphrasis*, by the minor Florentine philosopher

---

[16] Persius, *Satirarum liber*, ed. I. Casaubon (Paris: Drouart, 1605), sig. ã4ʳ; compare Cicero, *Academica* 2.24.75.

[17] *Essays of John Dryden*, ed. W. P. Ker (Oxford: Clarendon Press, 1900), pp. 69–96.

Raffaele Franceschi, who covered only the first three books and left literary considerations aside, concentrating exclusively on explaining the philosophical doctrines of the poem.

A full-scale, systematic commentary on *De rerum natura* was finally produced in 1511, by the Bolognese humanist Giovan Battista Pio. An enthusiast of rare and archaic Latinity, Pio devoted considerable attention to lexicographical issues; but he also made an effort to make the poem more palatable to a Christian audience.[18] By contrast, the French humanist Denys Lambin left no doubt in his erudite commentary on *De rerum natura* (1563–4) that he regarded the Epicurean philosophy expounded by Lucretius as reprehensible from a religious and moral point of view and absurd from a scientific one.[19] What interested him was Lucretius's poetic style and the purity of his Latin, which he regretted had been put to the service of such disreputable ideas. In a similar vein, Isaac Casaubon described Lucretius as an 'author of the best Latinity', while denouncing his view of the soul as 'quite mad'.[20] For Francis Bacon, he was the 'Poet, that beautified the Sect, that was otherwise inferiour to the rest'.[21]

Lambin's major contribution to *De rerum natura* was philological, establishing a text which would remain standard until the nineteenth century; but his dedication of the commentary to Book II to Pierre de Ronsard indicates that one of his aims was to encourage the poets of his own day to study Lucretius's technique and language. Ronsard and the rest of the Pléiade, sharing the general disdain for the doctrines espoused by Lucretius, were inspired by the mythological set pieces, such as the invocation to Venus (1.1–43) and the description of Cybele (2.598–645), rather than the philosophical passages. The few Epicurean themes to be found in their poetry were limited to commonplaces such as *carpe diem*, which more often derived from the eclectic Horace (*Odes* 1.11) than from the dogmatic Lucretius. Abraham Cowley clearly associated this topos with Epicureanism: the lines 'Today is Ours; what do we fear? / Today is Ours; we have it here' come in a poem entitled 'The Epicure' (1656); but his source, far from being a work of Epicurean ethics, was the *Anacreontea*, delightfully frivolous Greek verses about wine and love, 'translated paraphrastically' by Cowley. In 'The Garden' (1667), dedicated to John Evelyn, who in 1656 had published an English version of Book I of *De*

---

[18] Giovan Battista Pio (ed.), *In Carum Lucretium poeta commentarii* (Bologna: H. de Benedictis, 1511).

[19] Denys Lambin (ed.), *De rerum natura libri sex* (Paris and Lyons: G. and P. G. Roville, 1563–4).

[20] W. B. Fleischmann, 'Lucretius Carum, Titus', in *Catalogus translationum et commentariorum*, ed. P. O. Kristeller *et al.* (Washington, DC: Catholic University of America, 1960–), vol. II, pp. 349–65, at 352–3.

[21] F. Bacon, 'Of truth', in *The essayes or counsels, civill and morall*, ed. M. Kiernan (Cambridge, MA: Harvard University Press, 1985), p. 8.

rerum natura, Cowley presented a more accurate and positive account of the sect: 'Whoever a true Epicure would be, / May there find cheap and virtuous luxurie'.[22]

Lucretius had greater success as a model for Renaissance authors attempting to compose scientific didactic poetry.[23] But the problems which dogged the reception of Epicureanism were evident here too: while Lucretius's metre and diction were imitated, the philosophical and religious views he expounded were either ignored or rebutted. The Protestant martyr Aonio Paleario, in his *De animorum immortalitate* (1536), used poetic techniques he had learned from Lucretius to compose a pious refutation of the Epicurean denial of immortality and divine providence.[24] The only scientific poet bold enough to employ Lucretian hexameters and language to support genuinely Lucretian ideas (atomism and the existence of an infinite number of worlds) was Giordano Bruno, whose heretical beliefs led to his being burned at the stake by the Church in 1600.

The fact that *De rerum natura* was mostly about science led Girolamo Frachetta, in his *Breve spositione di tutta l'opera di Lucretio* (1589), to deny that it could be classified as poetry: 'it is not the metre which constitutes a poem', he maintained, 'but the subject-matter'; therefore Aristotle (*Poetics*, 1447b18–19) had rightly called Empedocles a 'scientist' [*physiologos*] rather than a poet, and the same was true of Lucretius.[25] The comparison of Lucretius with Empedocles had already been made by Aldus Manutius in the preface to his 1500 edition of the poem. Unlike Frachetta, Aldus praised Lucretius for having imitated the pre-Socratic practice of expressing philosophical doctrines 'in elegant and learned verse'.[26]

The key figure in the scholarly reconstruction and re-evaluation of Epicureanism was the French scholar and priest Pierre Gassendi. Using humanist methods, Gassendi (*Animadversiones*, 1649; *Syntagma philosophicum*, 1658) analysed the ancient sources of Epicureanism, above all Book x of Diogenes Laertius's *Lives of the philosophers* (*Animadversiones*), containing texts by Epicurus and a sympathetic biography of him, and Lucretius's *De rerum natura*. Wanting to replace Aristotelianism with a classical philosophy better suited to the new mechanistic science being

[22] *The works of Mr. Abraham Cowley*, 9th edn (London: H. Herringman, 1700), p. 29 ('The Epicure') and pp. 105–9, at 107 ('The garden').

[23] F. Joukovsky, 'L'épicurisme poétique au XVIᵉ siècle', in *Association Guillaume Budé: actes du VIIIᵉ congrès* (Paris: Les Belles Lettres, 1969), pp. 639–74; C. Goddard, 'Lucretius and Lucretian science in the works of Fracastoro', *Res publica litterarum* 16 (1993), 185–92.

[24] Aonio Paleario, *De animorum immortalitate libri III* (Lyons: S. Gryphius, 1536).

[25] Girolamo Frachetta, *Breve spositione di tutta l'opera di Lucretio* (Venice: P. Paganini, 1589), p. 2.

[26] *Aldo Manuzio editore: dediche, prefazioni, note ai testi*, ed. G. Orlandi, 2 vols. (Milan: il Polifilo, 1975), vol. I, pp. 33–4. The point that Lucretius had been an imitator and admirer of Empedocles was also made by Pietro Crinito in chapter 19 of his *De poetis Latinis* (Florence: P. Junta, 1504).

developed by Galileo, Descartes, and Hobbes, but feeling strongly the need to defuse the criticisms which had always hindered Christians from adopting the system, he introduced modifications – often drastic ones – which brought Epicureanism into line with the truths of the faith.

By doing so, Gassendi laid the foundation for a revival of interest in Epicureanism, particularly in France and England, in the second half of the seventeenth century. Lucretius benefited from the greater acceptance now accorded to his master Epicurus. Jacques Parrain, in his French translation of *De rerum natura* (1682), asked whether there was any pagan philosopher whose views were not in large measure repugnant to Christianity: Plato's dialogues, after all, were filled with lasciviousness, while Aristotle had held that the world was not created by God.[27] William Temple (who identified the ethical ideals of Epicurus's Garden with the innocent pleasures of English gardening) wondered why Lucretius's account of the gods' lack of concern for human affairs 'should be thought more impious than that given by Homer', who portrayed them as 'perpetually busie in all the worst or meanest actions of men'.[28] But the old tradition of intolerance did not die out. Thomas Creech, who produced the first complete English translation of the poem in 1682, supplied his version with detailed notes attacking the 'absurd principles' and 'absurd opinions' espoused by Lucretius, though he was prepared to praise the poet's 'excellent discourses against the fear of Death, his severe dehortations from Covetousness, Ambition and fond Love'.[29]

Apart from Lucretius's Epicureanism, another issue which provoked critical debate was the poetic propriety of the erotic passages at the end of Book IV of *De rerum natura*. Creech felt it necessary to leave them out; while Michel du Fay, in his Delphin edition (1680), had placed these verses in an appendix, refusing to provide a translation or notes because he judged them unsuitable for the 'modest and chaste reader'.[30] Pierre Bayle, on the other hand, regarded Lucretius's frank description of 'certain things which concern generation' as no more objectionable than a medical discussion. In the article on 'Lucrèce' in his *Dictionnaire historique et critique* (1697), Bayle maintained that there was nothing in the poem which indicated that the author was debauched.[31] There was, he said, a big difference between poets such as Catullus and Ovid who revelled in lewd language and those, like Lucretius, who were obliged to make

[27] *Les œuvres de Lucrece*, trans. J. Parrain (Paris: T. Guillain, 1682), sig. *10ʳ.
[28] Sir William Temple, *The works*, 2 vols. (London: J. Round, 1731), vol. I, pp. 170–90, at 174.
[29] Lucretius, *His six books 'De natura rerum'*, trans. T. Creech (Oxford: A. Stephens, 1682), pp. 8–9, sig. b4ᵛ.
[30] Michel du Fay (ed.), *De rerum natura libri sex* (Paris: F. Leonard, 1680), p. 362.
[31] Pierre Bayle, *Dictionnaire historique et critique* (Rotterdam: R. Leers, 1697).

use of obscene words in order to explain natural processes. Dryden, defending his decision to translate the offending passage, along with four other selections from the poem, into 'luscious English' in his *Sylvae* (1685), compared Lucretius's account, like Bayle, to that of a physician. The strength of *De rerum natura*, in Dryden's eyes, was that Lucretius 'had chosen a Subject naturally crabbed' and 'adorn'd it with Poetical descriptions, and Precepts of Morality', preparing the way for Virgil's *Georgics*. Its weakness consisted not so much in the poet's supposed obscenity or his Epicurean views on the mortality of the soul, which he dismissed as 'so absurd, that I cannot if I wou'd believe them', but rather in the regrettable fact that Lucretius had 'aim'd more to instruct in his Systeme of Nature, than to delight . . . In short, he was so much an Atheist, that he sometimes forgot to be a Poet.'[31]

[31] J. Dryden, *The works*, ed. E. Miner (Berkeley: University of California Press, 1956–), vol. III, pp. 9–13.

49

Calvinism and post-Tridentine developments

Catharine Randall

Born in Noyon, France in 1509, John Calvin left his homeland due to religious persecution exercised by Francis I on Evangelical and Reformed believers at the time of the *Affaire des placards* (1534). Marguerite de Navarre, sister of Francis I and a devout Evangelical with close connections to Jacques Lefèvre d'Etaples, Guillaume Briçonnet, and the Cercle de Meaux, was a friend of and patron to many Calvinists, among them the poet Clément Marot who provided the first Protestant translation of the Psalms into French (1543), and Calvin himself. Calvin was influenced by, and in turn influenced, French Evangelicals. By 1541, the date of the publication of his *Institution de la religion chrestienne*, Calvin had established himself in Geneva and had begun his attempt to reconfigure Geneva as a Protestant anti-Rome.

Calvinist literature develops in Switzerland and France. It can be said to be a godfather to later Puritan literature in Scotland and England, notably in John Bunyan's *Grace abounding to the chief of sinners* (1666), with its depiction of the sinful self as literary creator or in the Calvinist pessimism of Jacobean tragedy. Calvinist literature also demonstrates some affiliations with Evangelical literary production, most notably Bonaventure des Périers's *Cymbalum mundi* (1537),[1] an allegorical satire on religious persecution, some of the religious-flavoured tales of Marguerite de Navarre's *L'Heptaméron*, and the religious satire found in Rabelais's *Quart livre* (1548).

Calvinist literature is primarily informed by theology. It is grounded in a paradox. The Calvinist injunction was to ignore the self so that the self would not hinder the focus on God. However, the Calvinist tradition of individual spiritual examination of conscience (in contrast to the mediated system of priestly confession in Catholicism) gave rise to an intense anxiety about the self, and a constant surveillance of it. That ultimately resulted in literary expression of that self's concerns and world-view. Increasingly, the Calvinist confessional perspective informed the content of the written work. In time, many post-Tridentine Calvinist authors tended more in the direction of fiction or, at least, para-theological

---

[1] Bonaventure des Périers, *Cymbalum mundi* (1537), ed. P. Nurse (Manchester: Manchester University Press, 1958).

works, rather than in that of strict scriptural exposition or exegesis. Thus, Théodore de Bèze's collection of emblems about witnesses to the Protestant cause, *Icones, ou vrais pourtraicts des hommes illustres* (1580), in many instances does not address religious issues, but rather matters taken from everyday life which he then leaves unilluminated by an explicitly religious perspective. This is a surprising development, given that the Renaissance conceived of fiction as *fingere*, 'lying', an assumption further intensified by the Calvinist emphasis on truthful saying and the conjunction of *verbum* with *res*. The great Calvinist epic and prose-writer, Agrippa d'Aubigné, exemplifies this shift during his career. After a youthful, secular publication of poetry influenced by Petrarchism and entitled *Le printemps* (1571) he then sought to write careful expositions of the Psalms, and sought in his writing to avoid 'artifice'. But by the era in which he began to write *Les tragiques* (1577), he had determined that the evils of his century required a totally different style, one in which verve and unrestrained despair, malice, animosity or reproach could be given free rein. Such a change in tone necessitated the intervention of the authorial self, thereby preparing the way for more fictional inventiveness and liberties taken with history – as is the case with his highly personal and partisan *Histoire universelle* – by Calvinist writers. He articulates his clarion call for a new *style engagé* in the preface to *Les tragiques*: 'If anyone should reproach me that my impassioned verses / are built on nothing but murder and blood, / That one can only read in them fury, massacre and rage / Horror, poison, treachery and carnage, / I answer him: Friend, these words with which you take exception / Are the raw vocabulary of a new art I undertake to devise . . . / This century, different in its mores, demands a different style'.[2] This more personal and inventive approach to writing resulted in such texts as that penned by Béroalde de Verville, also a Calvinist, in the highly eclectic, apparently disorganized and anecdotal, but actually quite subversive work *Le moyen de parvenir*.[3] Published in 1610, De Verville's text, a book which, in his words, 'unbooks itself' ['le livre se dé-livre'], advocates a playfulness and even a salaciousness that would have been unthinkable to the first generation of Calvinist writers. He moves out of the troubled climate of his times, using that as a rationalization for a free, licentious, unanchored conception of fiction.

Calvin's writing was ecclesiological and theological on the whole; representative of his concerns are the *Institution de la religion chrestienne* (1541 in French translation) and the *Catéchisme* (1542). However, his

---

[2] Agrippa d'Aubigné, *Œuvres*, ed. H. Weber, J. Bailbé, and M. Soulié (Paris: Gallimard, 1969), 'Princes', lines 59–77.

[3] Béroalde de Verville, *Le moyen de parvenir*, ed. I. Zinger (Nice: University of Nice, 1988), p. 15.

eloquence and satirical style, as evident in some of his more explicitly polemical works, such as the *Traité des reliques* (1543) or *Des scandales* (1550), convey a more literary tenor. *Des scandales* is particularly important in this regard, as it is in this tract that Calvin explicitly contrasts the *stylus rudis* of Scripture with the flowery rhetoric of the Pléiade poets much in vogue at the time; Calvin exalts and seeks to imitate the former. Calvin uses two metaphors in the *Institutes* – stuttering speech and eyeglasses – to describe the relationship – and the chasm – between God's significance and human sense. He says that God babbles, as does an infant, when he speaks to us, because we are yet infants in our ability to understand Scripture. Calvin says that God provides us with spectacles to help us better view his Will for us. This process, called accommodationism, demonstrates that, at best, we may hope to learn and to imitate the style of the Scriptures; certainly we could never rival or surpass it. Like Paul in 1 Corinthians 1, Calvin instructs, one who preaches – or writes – well of the gospel will not employ eloquence in any way that might distract from the appropriate focus on God's Word. Calvin's preface to Clément Marot's translations of the Psalms is a particularly important document in the development of Calvinist literary theory; in it, Calvin lists the steps necessary for all writers to take so that their word may conform to that of God. In some respects, this programme does not differ radically from contemporary concerns of humanist scholars for accuracy and fidelity in translation, but Calvin's persistent exalting of Scripture as the template for good writing is unique. Calvin's eagerness to jettison the self is manifested in his sermons; he rarely uses the first-person singular pronoun. And in a letter giving advice to Jacques de Bourgogne, Calvin advises him to subordinate everything to God – and this includes one's writing style: one should abandon all, even annihilate one's own heart and desires, and write in accordance with God's Will and Word. This is precisely what Calvin himself claims to have done in penning the *Institutes*: he has revealed the underlying architecture of God's Word, not his own. His aim is not to devise a theological system, but rather to display the meaning of Scripture. Appropriately, his style is influenced by legalistic circles of the day; having trained as a humanist and a lawyer, Calvin now resorts to the clearest, most logical and accurate verbalizations available to him. Employing a highly persuasive rhetoric of proselytization, Calvin enjoins his audiences to repulse the world, in all of its aspects: 'I do intend to think on the difficult straits in which you find yourself . . . if you think of worldly considerations that could hold you back; but you need instead to reach a *firm* conviction, in order to repulse *anything* that might try to counteract it', he writes in a letter to Monsieur de Falais in 1543.[4] Calvin's

---

[4] Jean Calvin, *Lettres à Monsieur et Madame Falais* (1543), ed. F. Bonali-Fiquet (Geneva: Droz, 1991), Letter I, p. 37.

continuators develop this vein, and are literary creators within this confessional perspective. Necessarily, to the extent that they progressively deviate from Calvin's mandates and venture into the realm of fiction or – as with D'Aubigné's *Les avantures du Baron de Faeneste* – occasional downright obscenity, they stand in some tension *vis-à-vis* their mentor. They are able to find some licence for literary development in Calvin's extensive body of exegetical and expository writing on all the books of the Bible (with the exception of the Song of Songs; Calvin rejected this book as allegorical, a literary system he felt fostered deception and misrepresentation), in that exposition is a much more liberal, quotidian-focused, mode than line-by-line exegesis.

In general, a Calvinist literary paradigm may be established in which word is always given primacy over image (even in the case of emblem books), in which Scripture is the prototype for writing and writing seeks to illuminate Scripture. At the same time this writing betrays a fault-line: the words of the self seek to praise the Creator but also attest to a problematic relation to the divine Word in that human expression is marked by the Fall. It is essential that the concept of 'Calvinist aesthetics', for years taken by scholars to be an oxymoron, be recognized as a real and operative factor in the construction of the theological arguments that these texts express. Calvinism is marked by a vexed, but productive tension regarding its intermingling of theological and literary concerns.

Calvinist literary contributions were invariably generically mixed, and encompass such genres as travel literature, martyrologies, political/theological polemic, biblical meditations, epic poetry, emblem books, prose fiction, and autobiography.

Jean de Léry, a Huguenot pastor and voyager to the New World, wrote of his encounter in 1556 in Brazil with savages who did not know the Lord. In *Histoire d'un voyage* (1578), he struggled with how to situate such radical otherness within the framework of his religious perspective. Léry's travel writing, always situated in a theological grid, is a literary reaction to and departure from the purported travel narratives of the Catholic writer, André Thevet, author of *Cosmographie du Levant* (1554) and *Cosmographie universelle* (1575), among other works. Thevet's claims to have visited these countries proved false, and Léry therefore advanced the corrective of stipulating truth claims for one's narrative. Thus, the authorial self, so problematic because marked by sin in Calvinist theology, paradoxically became the guarantor of authenticity in the text.

Jean Crespin, head of a Protestant printing house, wrote the most extensive and widely read Calvinist martyrological compendium, entitled *Histoire des martyrs* (1564). This *Histoire* was influenced by the Anglican writer and priest John Foxe's later *Acts and monuments* (popularly known as the *Book of the martyrs*, 1563). However, Crespin's collection also differed from its model, thereby delineating a uniquely Calvinist method for the compilation and elaboration of martyrological narrative. Crespin included virtually all available documentation of the circumstances of a martyr's trial, final speech, and execution. Crespin invited readers who had been eyewitnesses to these events to send in documentation for inclusion in future editions. He thus innovated by creating a participatory body of Protestant readers who assisted in the construction of confessional illustration. Crespin also reacted against the Catholic genre of hagiography (as represented by Jacobus Voragine, for instance, in his *Légende dorée* (12th c.) and as continued in some degree by Foxe with, for instance, his *exemplum*-like portrait of Luther) by refusing to offer a portrait-like life of the saint; instead, he required his readers to reconstitute the confessor through reference to their spoken and written words.

Philippe Du Plessis-Mornay, political figure and theorist, was one of the most influential Calvinists in the French kingdom during the period of the Catholic League and right after the Wars of Religion. An intimate of Henri IV, Mornay was the representative of the Calvinist churches at the Mantes Assembly and the Saumur Assembly, at which he lobbied for, and obtained, significant concessions for Huguenot worship. He also wrote political polemic of a very high calibre. Among his most noted works are *Vindiciae contra tyrannos* (1581; translated under the title *De la puissance légitime du prince sur le peuple et du peuple sur le prince*), which he is generally believed to have co-authored with the tyrannomach, or regicide theorist, François Hotman. In addition, he wrote extensive *Mémoires* (1624–5). His wife, Charlotte de Mornay, an equally ardent Calvinist, wrote her own *Mémoires*. These form a diptych with her husband's writing although, as is the case for most Calvinist women writers, Madame de Mornay really did not speak much about herself but rather recounted her husband's exploits.

Pierre Viret, the Swiss Reformed theologian, was the author of several spicy, rhetorically deft polemical tracts, including his *Dialogue du désordre* (1545). The *Dialogue* establishes ordinary life as an appropriate arena from which images and comparisons may be drawn to enhance one's writing. This position conforms to orthodox Calvinism in that it upholds the experience of the self (however flawed) against the experience of the Church: what Catholicism calls the authority of tradition (an alternate source of authority distrusted and denied by Calvinists). The *Dialogue* is also important for Reformed stylistics in that it establishes the genre of dialogue, wherein a true back-and-forth is developed between varying perspectives both didactically and dramatically. This seems an appropriate medium for the communication of Reformed concepts consonant with the dialectical method of reasoning exercised in the development and elucidation of Reformed theology.

Henri Estienne, scion of the renowned family of Calvinist printers, wrote political polemic as well as works that take up characteristically Renaissance/humanist issues such as the nature and signifying capacity of language and the written word. His *Apologie pour Hérodote* (1566) is a case in point. It contains, in addition, frequent attacks on Catholic distortions of worship, and so also fits under the rubric of polemical literature.

Théodore de Bèze, Calvin's successor in Geneva, wrote a history of the Reformed church in several volumes (*Histoire ecclésiastique des églises réformées*, 1580). He also composed an emblem book entitled *Vrais pourtraicts des hommes illustres* (1581), in which, as is also the case for one of the few Calvinist women writers, Georgette de Montenay, author of a Protestant emblem book, he relies on an abstract representational system (often composed of geometrical figures) rather than on realistic landscapes or elaborate images, in order to obviate too-extensive privileging of image over word. Taking up a similar theme, Bèze authored a *Vie de Calvin* (1564) which conformed to the new, peculiarly Protestant form of martyrological narrative as described under Crespin. He also wrote meditations. His *Chrestiennes méditations* (1581), for example, is remarkable for its Baroque quality of self-representation; accordingly, Bèze uses Scripture as the point of departure for an extravagant series of meditations on the nature of the self and the world.

Théodore Agrippa d'Aubigné, contemporary and schoolmate of Bèze, authored an immense body of Calvinist literature. His *Les tragiques* (1616), an enormous epic poem in seven books, is perhaps the best known. Generally studied as a document detailing Huguenot persecution during the Wars of Religion (1562–94), it is also valuable as a literary document. D'Aubigné attempts to craft a persuasive and militant prose style suited to the Protestant experience. Like Bèze, who in the prologue to his scriptural play *Abraham sacrifiant* (1550) rejected his former humanist writing style in favour of the plain style of Scripture, D'Aubigné is self-conscious about his distinction as a Calvinist writer. In fact, he engaged in a vitriolic polemic campaign against the Catholic writer Ronsard. Ronsard's response is the *Discours des misères de ce temps* (1562) and *Continuation du Discours* (1533). D'Aubigné's task is to use human expression to convey appropriately the majesty of the unsurpassable divine Word. Ironically, despite the frequent disclaimers of personal merit characteristic of the relentlessly anti-Arminian Calvinists, he ends up by writing extensively about himself. His *Avantures du baron de Faeneste* (1630), for example, are a thinly fictionalized portrait of a Huguenot nobleman (Enay) who is disgusted by the deceptive use of words and reliance on appearances at court as epitomized by his Catholic interlocutor (Faeneste). (The names are Greek and refer, respectively, to True Being and False Semblance.)

D'Aubigné's *Sa vie à ses enfants* (date unknown, published posthumously in 1729) is an important, perhaps unprecedented, self-vaunting auto-biography by a Calvinist writer. By providing a personal perspective into larger historical and religious questions, it complements his third-person narrative of church history contained in his several-volume study entitled *Histoire universelle* (1626). D'Aubigné's *Méditations sur les psaumes* (1627) also contains instances of autobiographical asides within the framework of biblical exposition, such as the Psalm in which he departs from the text he is explicating in order to lament the death of his wife, Suzanne de Lézay.

Guillaume Salluste Du Bartas, soldier, poet and diplomat, friend of Henri IV, was widely read on the Continent and in England, where he much influenced the Puritan poet John Milton. He had a very close relationship with James VI of Scotland, whose play *La Lépante du roi d'Ecosse* he translated, while the king translated Du Bartas's *Uranie*. Du Bartas's encyclopaedic epic poem, *La sepmaine* (1578; *La seconde sepmaine*, 1584), portrayed the seven days of Creation and attempted to describe all aspects of the world in relation to the divine plan for the created order. Unlike Catholics, who felt that they could read in the world God's book, Du Bartas, as a good Calvinist, insisted that the world contained traces of the Word, but that, due to its sinful nature, complete legibility of such signs was no longer possible. Only Scripture could provide the necessary knowledge about the world. Simon Goulart, successor to De Bèze as pastor in Geneva, annotated Du Bartas's *La sepmaine* (1581). Some of his annotations substantially revised his predecessor. Consistent with the post-Tridentine emphasis on incarnational imagery, he incorporated more images, for example, in an attempt to appeal to a broader readership. Du Bartas also wrote religious drama, most notably the play *La Judit* (1574) in which he rewrote the biblical story of Judith's murder of the pagan tyrant Holofernes. He reshaped it as an explicitly Calvinist drama in which God's divine Word instructs this devout woman in her task (Du Bartas whimsically and proleptically shows Judit reading her [Christian!] Bible before going out to do the deed).[5]

Other Calvinist theatre was created by Jean de la Taille in his play *Saül le furieux* (1572). Calvinist theatre is generally derived from Old Testament stories. It differs from Catholic religious plays in that it seeks to elucidate the protagonist's reaction to his personal relationship with his God. However, *Saül le furieux* is an interesting case. It is demonstrably much influenced by classical theatrical interpretation of the biblical story (such as that of Seneca's *Hercules furens*), but La Taille, apprehensive that more

---

[5] For an overview of the Calvinist attitude towards theatre, see Gerard Jonker, *Le protest-antisme et le théâtre de langue française au XVIᵉ siècle* (The Hague: Wolters, 1939).

doctrinaire Calvinists would criticize such reliance, denied those sources. His work thus attests to a certain unease on the part of the Calvinist literary creator with the theological framework within which he creates, as well as to the deployment of subterfuge to try to counter constraints on aesthetic expression. *Saül le furieux* is also a valuable document in that it shows the content of the Wars of Religion inflecting the playwright's exposition of the biblical context.

Probably the most important piece of Calvinist play writing was the *Abraham sacrifiant* (1550) of Théodore de Bèze (see *supra*), because it provided a model for how Calvinists could write theatrical work. In his preface to the play, Bèze explicitly rejected any sort of profane writing or fictitious development. Theatre, as with all Calvinist prose, was to derive *only* from Scripture; essentially, Calvinist theatre was to be biblical paraphrase. Robert Garnier's plays, accordingly, demonstrate a thorough conversance with Old Testament texts, and display, in *Les Juifves,* thematically, a Calvinist condemnation of idolatry in ancient Israel. In *Saül le furieux* we find a near point-by-point transliteration of the David and Saul story. A similar slavish following of Old Testament texts is evident in Antoine de Montchrestien's *Aman* and *David.* Louis des Masures's *Tragédies sainctes* (1566), composed of the trilogy of *David combattant, David triomphant* and *David fugitif* retells the biblical narrative through paraphrase and word-by-word borrowings. In addition, many minor morality plays satirizing the Catholic Church were written by several Calvinist playwrights during the period 1523–89. Calvinism had a major influence on theatre on the Continent; predestination, in particular, accorded well with a tragic view of human nature.[6]

Bernard Palissy was a potter, ceramicist, architect, and ardent Calvinist who eventually died as the result of imprisonment and persecution for his faith. He wrote an unusual book titled *La recepte véritable* (1563). This work was a multifaceted book in which Palissy meditated in a proto-geological sense on fossils he found, strata of soil he observed, and on the nature of creation. In the *Recepte*, he also developed in literary fashion parables (especially the favourite Protestant parable, that of the talents), and described, through an elaborate dramatization of Psalm 104, the actual establishment of the Reformed church at Saintes, of which he was a member. In this, he conforms to the Calvinist model of deriving licence for dramatic textual development from a scriptural source. In addition, Palissy devised blueprints for an idealized garden reminiscent of the Garden of Eden. His garden, however, differed in that it situated the reader within a series of garden niches inscribed with scriptural tags. This created a sort of emblem structure comprised of divine text, Palissy's

---

[6] See Dennis Klinck's study 'Calvinism and Jacobean tragedy', *Genre* 11 (1976), 333–58.

text and its structures, and the image of the reader reading himself into both Scripture and *Recepte*.

Calvinist poetry is represented not only by Agrippa d'Aubigné, but also by poets such as Jean Chassignet and Jean de Sponde (*Méditations*, 1588), a Calvinist who later recanted his Protestant faith. The development of a specifically Calvinist writing style is heavily influenced by the versions of the Psalms that proliferated during the 1550s and 1560s, notably the Psalm paraphrases by Clément Marot (1543 and the 1562 definitive text) and Olivetan's Bibles (1535 and 1540). Stylistically, the Calvinist idiom is typified by reliance on antithetical pairs to structure the poem. Such a structure is consonant with Calvinist dialectics, in which dichotomies are yoked to portray the disjunction, yet interrelationship, between heaven and earth, man and God.

In post-Tridentine Calvinist literature, it can be seen that literature is at the service of theology, yet not wholly subordinate to it or even, as has been the customary interpretation, obviated by it. Thus, despite the Calvinist theological system's negative view of literary self-expression, a very rich body of such literature does, indeed, exist. Calvin, who finds as early as Augustine an emphasis on the existence of a biblical rhetoric, uses humanist techniques of analysis augmented by the metaphysical focus provided by the Reformed faith. In his study of Calvinist rhetoric, Olivier Millet demonstrates that, once converted (*c.* 1530), Calvin's style changed quickly, intentionally, and irrevocably. Millet asserts that, for Calvin, the problem of a biblical rhetoric has three parts.[7] Theologically, Calvin must seek to understand how the immutable truth of God's Word can be understood and read in its human transcription (the doctrine of biblical inerrancy); apologetically, he must defend a biblical style against the humanist or pagan standard against which it stands; and as a Christian exegetical writer he must seek exactly to understand how each figure of rhetoric is used in the Bible, the better to communicate it to the hearers. By the 1550s, in a time of intense religious strife, Calvinist followers find a need for a more elastic interpretation of the breadth provided by these mandates, adding their personal perspective in order to make their arguments more compelling to a readership not necessarily composed entirely of fellow believers, and employing fiction as a weapon of persuasion to lure in a potentially hostile reader and convert him to the cause. In both cases, the Bible provides not only a model, but also absolute authority; simply, in the case of later Calvinist writers, this authority is, in some measure, delegated to themselves as literary co-creators.

[7] Olivier Millet, *Calvin et la dynamique de la parole: étude de rhétorique réformée* (Geneva: Slatkine, 1992), p. 231.

50

Port-Royal and Jansenism

Richard Parish

The terms 'Port-Royal' and 'Jansenism' serve in different ways as metonyms for the (originally theological) ethos of Augustinian pessimism which dominated a significant part of French thought and writing in the later part of the seventeenth century. Port-Royal was the name of two convents: one in the Vallée de Chevreuse, near Paris (Port-Royal-des-Champs), now in ruins; and the other in the city (Port-Royal-de-Paris), currently a hospital. The communities associated with the two sites were, first, an order of Cistercian nuns, reformed by Angélique Arnauld, who had become abbess in 1602, and of which Jean Duvergier de Hauranne, abbé de Saint-Cyran and student contemporary of Jansen, became spiritual director in 1634, following the nuns' move to Paris in 1625–6. Secondly, a group of laymen, the so-called 'solitaires' or 'Messieurs de Port-Royal', who occupied the rural convent from 1637, and who founded in the vicinity a series of respected schools ('les petites écoles'), whose most celebrated pupil was Jean Racine. The term 'Jansenism' stems from the name of the bishop of Ypres, Cornelius (gallicized Corneille) Jansen, whose seminal (posthumously published) work, the *Augustinus* (1640), provided the principal theological point of reference for the movement. Neither term is fully definitional or comprehensive; but both have to some extent become interchangeable shorthands.

Taken first at a theological level, the current of Augustinian pessimism was a phenomenon associated with the Catholic (or Counter-) Reformation which, in its various (and on occasion conflicting) manifestations, replied to or, in this case, arguably reflected the Protestant Reformation of the previous century. It was in the wake of the Council of Trent (1545–63), and in reaction to a perceived shift in Roman orthodoxy towards an unwarranted emphasis on free will, that the more strident forms of pessimism came to the surface. The primary articulation of the neo-Pelagian position was furnished by Molina's *De concordia* (1588), and the group empirically most closely identified with the ethical implications of such a tendency was the Society of Jesus, founded in 1540. Jansenism was throughout anxious to distance itself from accusations of crypto-Calvinism levelled by its opponents, and indeed insisted on its obedience to the Holy See and on its eucharistic orthodoxy; however it repeatedly suffered both condemnation by the papacy and persecution by the French monarchy. Finally, after nearly a century of vicissitudes, its doctrines were condemned by the Bull *Unigenitus*, promulgated by Clement XI in 1713. Thematically the broadly theological manifestations involved an emphasis on the Fall, and on the wretched condition of postlapsarian man; a resultant concentration on the primacy of grace over free will in matters of salvation; a stress on the dynamic nature of conversion; and the practice of a rigorously austere lifestyle.

Its relationship to literary milieux appears to stem from a (superficially paradoxical) coincidence between membership of the salons and sympathizers with its tenets, a phenomenon explicable at least in part by their common aristocratic origins and (in one interpretation) by the potential afforded by religious heterodoxy for the expression of political dissent in an absolutist regime. Certain key writings further underscore this shared filiation: the stress in Pascal's *Lettres provinciales* (1656–7) on the accessibility of theological issues to laymen and, even more crucially, to laywomen (in the (probably fictive) reply to the second letter); the references to gambling, hunting, and other aristocratic pastimes, as well as the appeal made to the ethos of *honnêteté* in the *Pensées*; and the application of a pessimistic world-view to social concerns in La Rochefoucauld's *Maximes* (1665).

Turning to more specifically textual questions, it is clear that the base text of the theological aspects of the movement should be considered as Jansen's *Augustinus*; and yet, in another sense, it is significant more as a point of symbolism and of conflict than as a source of reference or authority. The seminal figure of the mid-seventeenth century upon whom such issues are more precisely focused is the writer and controversialist Antoine Arnauld (brother of Angélique, and known as *Le Grand Arnauld*). His treatise *De la fréquente communion* (opposing the laxist use of this practice) was published in 1643, and constituted a defence of rigorist teaching on penitential and sacramental matters. However, the major episode to involve Arnauld was the condemnation by Innocent X in the Bull *Cum occasione* (1653) of five statements ('les cinq propositions') drawn, or allegedly drawn, from the *Augustinus*, four as heretical, one as false. The ensuing (and complex) dispute as to whether the propositions were, on the one hand, heretical (the 'question de droit') and, on the other, as to whether they were to be found verbatim in the *Augustinus* (the 'question de fait') resulted in the censure of Arnauld in 1656 following the publication of his *Seconde lettre à un duc et pair*, and initiated the polemical exchanges of which Pascal's *Lettres provinciales* are the major contemporary document.

Blaise Pascal, whose reputation as a scientist preceded his notoriety as a polemicist, *moraliste*, rhetorician, and, above all, Christian apologist, composed during 1656 and 1657 a series of seventeen complete letters and an (unfinished) eighteenth one. The *Provinciales* are primarily remarkable for the triumph of *haute vulgarisation* that they represent. They open with a quartet of letters defending Arnauld, written by a fictive investigatory epistoler ('Louis de Montalte') to his friend in the provinces, the 'ami provincial', whence the title. The tone is characteristically that of the 'honnête homme', the enlightened social being in search of intellectual (here theological) elucidation; the form of investigation is at first dialogic; and the appeal made evolves from an emphasis on common sense to one on orthodoxy. Then, as the substantive issues concerning Arnauld are progressively dismissed, there emerges a fierce attack on the Society of Jesus, on the grounds of penitential laxism, in the second series of letters (five to ten). This is the work's most skilful comic moment, deploying hyperbole and *reductio ad adsurdum* against the backdrop of the mounting indignation of Montalte. The pivotal eleventh letter then defends the use of mockery [*raillerie*] in theological dispute, claiming simply to answer scandal by ridicule. The remaining letters adopt an overtly polemical (and biblical) accent, abandoning the disingenuous persona, and concluding on a reassertion of Arnauld's innocence, now addressed directly by the (necessarily still anonymous) author to the king's Jesuit confessor, Annat. The letters elicited a series of replies from their Jesuit casualties, although these never achieved the same degree of impact, hampered as they are by defensiveness and (fatal in a polemical context) by nuance. The *Provinciales* afford a striking example of the transition from the populist and apparently ephemeral subject-matter of their opening to the reassertion of the fundamentals of (pessimistic) Christian theology in their conclusion; and their gradual shift from an ironic tone to an impassioned one mirrors that evolution. In their polarized insistence on a dualistic Christian paradigm (Fall, Redemption) and in their denial of any compromise with the values of the world (despite, paradoxically, their *mondain* appeal), they anticipate, or in some areas overlap with, the interplay of 'misère' and 'grandeur' in the *Pensées*.

The most celebrated work to be associated with Port-Royal is also by Pascal, and is universally known as the *Pensées*. It is the central text of the movement to the extent that it combines the theological ethos of Jansenism with the scientific, *mondain*, and above all rhetorical preoccupations of its writer. At the same time, the text as we have it is in other respects a bewildering puzzle. The unfinished notes for a Christian apologia have undergone much editorial attention and critical analysis; but the one feature of the eventual form which appears to remain certain is that the project was bipartite, moving from an initial and hyperbolically immanent exploration of the human condition perceived in broadly pessimistic terms ('Misère de l'homme sans Dieu', 'Wretchedness of man without

God') to an exploration of and remedy for (what subsequently emerges as) postlapsarian anguish.

Humankind's dilemma is portrayed in terms which pre-emptively necessitate an explanation which takes account of a first nature from which it has departed; and biblical evidence reinforces the historicity of such an interpretation. Imagery is used to reinforce this argument, most notably the image of man as a 'roi dépossédé' ['disinherited king'] deprived of what had formerly been his rightful status, as is demonstrated by his very awareness of deprivation. The doctrine of the Fall, however unappealing and even unjust it may appear, is nevertheless, in Pascal's thinking, less of a paradox than the bewildered self-perception of man in its absence. Inevitably, given the need to moderate the arrogance of man's reason that the apologist perceives, the emphasis is most insistently placed on his frailty and mortality. The inevitable sense of a deeply pessimistic outlook is further enhanced by the work's incompleteness, offering as it does no positive correlative to the negative anthropology and, subsequently, theology of its fragments. The outlines of the project suggest that it would have been fiercely anti-deistic, and in addition would have placed great emphasis on the sole ultimate efficacity of supernatural conviction ['inspiration'] in the business of salvation. Some aspects of Pascal's apologetic system are subsequently taken up by Jean de La Bruyère in his *Caractères* (1688–94), although this later work has little theological coherence; and parts of his *moraliste* concerns by Pierre Nicole in his *Essais de morale* (1671 onwards).

Formally, it appears likely that the apology would have contained certain of the rhetorical devices deployed in the *Lettres provinciales*, notably dialogue and epistolary form, and that its fragmentation, whilst clearly to some degree the result of contingency, may well point to at least a non-linear mode of argument as being the most likely medium of persuasion in a putative finished version. Several fragments also explicitly address themselves to questions of style and rhetoric. From these it appears that the persona of the apologist would have been at pains to appeal to the rhetorical criterion of *ethos*, and to present himself as an 'honnête homme' rather than a theologian or a mathematician. He further stresses his awareness of the fact that certain of his arguments will have been used previously, but emphasizes that 'the arrangement of the material is new', and seeks a style that will be at once naturalistic and memorable.* It is, however, evident that such writing will be the result of a self-concealing rhetoric, since perfect clarity and simplicity of style, it elsewhere emerges, was the unique privilege of Christ.

Three further writings by Pascal, usually grouped under the broader heading of *Opuscules*, should be mentioned. The first is the *Ecrits sur la grâce* (*c.* 1657–8; first published 1779), an (unfinished) attempt, first, to classify the tenets of what is perceived as orthodoxy, and described as the view of the 'disciples de Saint Augustin', and to distinguish it from the teaching of Calvinists on the one hand and Molinists on the other; and, secondly, to account for the chronology of the fall from grace in individuals, a process described (in a particularly tortuous sequence) as a mutual separation from God, or a 'double délaissement'. The ultimate causation for such an event is inevitably left mysterious, and deemed to emanate from 'un jugement juste, quoique caché' ['a just, yet hidden judgement'] by God. Secondly, we should note the treatise *De l'esprit géométrique et de l'art de persuader* (composed no later than 1657–8), in which the apologist shows himself aware of the need to develop the 'art d'agréer' ['art of pleasing'] alongside the 'art de convaincre' ['art of convincing']; and, whilst recognizing the superiority of the geometric method in those areas where it may pertinently be deployed, he contrasts with it a subtler but more efficacious means of persuasion. Finally, we possess the transcript by Nicolas Fontaine of a conversation held between Pascal and Issac Le Maître de Saci at Port-Royal (early in 1655?), and usually referred to as the *Entretien avec Monsieur de Saci* (first published in 1728). This shows Pascal deploying a dialectical mode of argument in the establishment of the truth of the Christian gospel, in distinction to the more direct approach of his interlocutor.

A further category of Port-Royal writing is constituted by the collaborative efforts of certain of the 'solitaires' in the production of two theoretical treatises. The *Grammaire générale et raisonnée* (*Grammaire de Port-Royal*) of 1660 resulted from a collaboration between Arnauld and Claude Lancelot. It substitutes a logical, analytical approach for the more usage-based view of grammar which had formerly prevailed, and its stated aim is to lead its readers 'to accomplish through learning what others accomplish . . . through habit'. Two years later in 1662, there appeared *La logique ou l'art de penser* (*Logique de Port-Royal*) by Arnauld and Nicole, a work strongly imbued with and crucial in the dissemination of Cartesian methodology. It consists of two prefatory 'discours' and four parts, devoted respectively to the mental acts of 'concevoir' ['conceiving'], 'juger' ['discerning'], 'raisonner' ['reasoning'], and 'ordonner' ['organizing']. The second discourse, which preceded the second edition, is devoted to replies to objections, and it is here that the authors stress that their purpose in including a discussion of rhetoric is in order to discourage over-exuberance: 'The mind provides no shortage of thoughts, usage generates expressions; and the figures and flowers of speech are only too abundant. Therefore, virtually everything depends on avoiding certain inappropriate kinds of writing and speaking, and, above all, an artificial, rhetorical style formed by false and overstated ideas and by over-wrought figures, which is the greatest of all imperfections' (a hyperbole incidentally).

The first part deals *inter alia* with the relationship between ideas and things as expressed through signs, univocal and equivocal terms, and the risk of confusion incurred when 'we attend more to words than to things' (I.xi – although such confusion may be obviated by the careful and appropriate use of definition). The place for a 'style figuré' ['figurative style'] is nonetheless conceded, notably among the Church Fathers, in order to 'produce in the soul the feelings of reverence and love that one must have towards Christian truths' (I.xiv). The final chapter (I.xv) is entitled: 'Des idées que l'esprit ajoute à celles qui sont précisément signifiées par les mots' ['Of ideas through which the mind supplements those whose meaning is expressed exactly by words'], and its purpose is glossed in the second discourse: 'in revealing the nature of figurative style, [the chapter] explains simultaneously how that style is used and shows the correct rule for discriminating between good and bad figures'. In point of fact it is largely concerned with the difference between 'ideas evoked and those whose meaning is made explicitly manifest' by the deictic pronoun 'hoc' ['ceci'] in particular with regard to an erroneous (that is, Protestant) understanding of the words of eucharistic consecration. The second part is principally composed of grammatical analysis. We might however pause at II.xiv, 'Des propositions où l'on donne aux signes le nom des choses' ['Of propositions in which one confers on signs the names of things'], in which attention is first given to the distinction between those propositions 'which would be absurd if one conferred on the signs the name of the things signified' and those which would not; and to the assertion that 'the simple and obvious incompatibility of the terms is not sufficient reason to lead the mind to a symbolic meaning', in certain specified circumstances of which the addressee is made aware. Biblical evidence is then adduced, returning again in the last example to the words of consecration.

The third part deals in turn with syllogisms, *loci*, and sophisms, and here two chapters stand out. The first, III.xvii, deals with *loci argumentorum* and is deemed apt in the second discourse to 'serve to reduce the superabundance of commonplace thoughts'. The tenor of this chapter is thus to prioritize natural argument, emanating from the subject itself, over and above formal *loci*, and its thesis is compressed into a résumé of St Augustine to the effect that eloquent people 'practise rules because they are eloquent; but do not use them in order to become eloquent'. Conversely, 'nothing makes a mind more barren in thoughts that are exact and sound than this pernicious profusion of banalities'. The conclusion, however, concedes the desirability of 'une teinture générale' ['a nodding acquaintance'] with such *loci*, and the next chapter (III.xviii) indeed illustrates the *loci* of grammar, logic, and metaphysics. Finally the last and longest chapter of this part (III.xx) is devoted to '[les] mauvais raisonnements que l'on commet dans la vie civile, et dans les discours ordinaires' ['the defective arguments advanced in everyday life and in ordinary discourse']. The second discourse claims for it that, 'by showing how never to accept as beautiful that which is false, [the chapter] presents incidentally one of the critical rules of true rhetoric, and one which can, more than any other, train the mind in a manner of writing that is simple, natural, and judicious'; and, in a negative paraphrase of the *captatio benevolentiae*, underlines 'the care that one must take not to arouse the rancour of those to whom one is speaking'. More fully, the first part is concerned with 'the sophisms of self-pride, self-interest, and passion', and their power to convince against 'the acuity of truth and the force of reasoning'. After stressing thereby the subjective element in assent to any given proposition, it goes on to expose the consequences thereof, given that 'the human mind is not only prone to self-love, but also naturally jealous, envious, and cunning with respect to others'. One development of this concerns the undesirability of talking of oneself, illustrated positively with reference to the diffidence shown by Pascal in this respect, claiming as he did 'that Christian piety nullifies the human self and that human civility conceals and restrains it', and negatively in terms of Montaigne. (It might however be mentioned *en passant* that certain of the 'solitaires' left memoirs.) The second part moves on to '[les] faux raisonnements qui naissent des objets mêmes' ['the false arguments that emanate from objects themselves'], and initially considers the dangers of judging by an exterior characterized by 'a certain inflated and grandiose eloquence'. On the other hand the more widespread recognition of the axiom that only the true is beautiful would remove both futile ornament and erroneous thought, and although 'it is true that this precision makes style more plain and less inflated . . . it also makes it sharper, more sober, clearer, and more worthy of an *honnête homme*'.

Moving now away from the stricter adherents of Jansenism, we should draw attention to two writers who share a good deal of the world-view of a Pascal, and yet who are in different ways more distant from the precise ethos of Port-Royal. First, the dramatic corpus of Jean Racine, whose nine mature tragedies, written between 1667 and 1677, culminate in *Phèdre*. In this play, as in its immediate predecessor *Iphigénie*, Racine introduces an important supernatural dimension into his writing. The gods of *Iphigénie* are portrayed as vindictive and capricious, taunting Agamemnon to sacrifice his daughter in order to launch his becalmed fleet. The fact that Racine resolves the dilemma of the innocent Iphigénie's sacrifice by introducing a substitute figure (Eriphile), whom he depicts as morally less pure than the eponymous heroine, in no way detracts from the sense of an unanswerable governing order, whose humiliation of humankind serves rather to enhance the dignity of the latter's suffering. *Phèdre* takes this supernatural dimension one stage further, by making the heroine the descendent of the gods, and by associating her punishment with her guilty, because incestuous, passion for Hippolyte. Here we may see the possibility of a reading of the play's story as a mythological expression of a kind of Christian pessimism. First, Phèdre is guilty not because of what she has done (existence), but because of what she is (essence), and has furthermore inherited her guilty status; it is easy to see the affinity between such a condition and the Christian doctrine of original sin. Secondly, she compares her guilty self with the (as she believes) innocent and divinely favoured couple of Hippolyte and Aricie, thereby attracting a parallel with a doctrine of the predestination of the elect and of the condemned. She is, in this reading, a Christian figure from whom grace has been withheld. (This analogy may appear to break down in the face of Hippolyte's destruction by Neptune; but equally the category of those who are denied the grace to persevere is admitted in Pascal's *Ecrits sur la grâce*.) Finally, Phèdre's 'gloire' in this play is expressed by her yearning for a lost state of innocence, and a profound awareness of her unworthiness. Here again, a parallel with the Pascalian consciousness of the loss of a prelapsarian state comes easily to mind. In his two final tragedies, Racine turned to the Bible, and to the Old Testament, for his subjects, and in the later of these, *Athalie* (1691), seeks to effect the difficult marriage of a tragic and a biblical story. Athalie is, at the tragic level, the victim of Jehovah and of his earthly servants; despite her ruthlessness, her portrayal is not entirely dark, and is considerably alleviated morally by the explicit prediction within the text of the degradation of Joas, whose coronation concludes the play, and whose survival (as a successor of Moses and David) is in turn the criterion of the Christian redemption, equally foretold in prophecies within the text. Read from the biblical angle, however, its tragic status is diminished precisely by that redemptive promise, and the Racinian supernatural, omnipotent but anarchic in the pagan plays, is portrayed in its Judeo-Christian form as endowed with a telos, making sense of intervening suffering and doubt by the ultimate certainty of a Saviour.

The second work which, on one reading, is associated with the spirit of Port-Royal is the collection of *sententiae* known as the *Maximes* (1666) of the duc de La Rochefoucauld. Unlike the *Pensées* of Pascal, the work of La Rochefoucauld is a finished work, a thematically non-sequential series of finely honed phrases, based around the examination of humankind's motivation, and discerning the role of fortune, physiology, and above all self-deception in even, or particularly, its most apparently virtuous actions. The degree to which it is cognate with Augustinianism is, however, problematic, since virtually all the evidence to support such a view is extrinsic. In a contemporary letter (to Thomas Esprit), La Rochefoucauld presents the justification for his work as the portrayal of the falsity of pagan virtue, and the need for human nature to be corrected by Christianity; and, in the preface to the fifth edition, the view is reiterated that the *Maximes* only attend to humankind in its fallen state, with the rider that their bleak analysis is inapplicable to the elect. A more objective reading of the work leaves in no doubt the degree of coincidence between the *moraliste* pessimism of La Rochefoucauld and the tragic vision of Pascal's godless interlocutor; and yet the tone is radically different, lacking as it does any transcendent reference (maxims dealing with God were rigorously suppressed), and any sense of despair faced with the laying bare of multiple and often unflattering motives. What rather emerges is an appeal for lucidity, and a recognition of the potential for objectively beneficial effects to emanate from what would traditionally be regarded as vicious causes. In its subject-matter, it may well constitute a preparation for a pessimistic version of Christian belief; in its emphasis it is too consistently secular for such a purpose to be tenable.

In conclusion, it is important to consider to what extent Augustinian pessimism can be said to have had any more direct literary critical manifestations, bearing in mind the forbidden status that dramatic and novelistic fiction held in the Jansenist ethos; and recognizing elsewhere the universal subservience of what we would consider as literary (that is, rhetorical or stylistic) questions to a higher (that is, moral or theological) purpose. In one area, that of theatrical performance, the emphasis, predictably, is entirely negative. As Nicole writes in his *Traité de la comédie* (1667), the theatre is not only a frivolous (and thus irreligious) distraction, but is dangerous by virtue of its representation, and thus promotion of the passions of hatred, anger, ambition, revenge and above all love in both actors and spectators (a criticism which he further extends to the reading of novels). Such a view is later explicitly addressed in Racine's defensive preface to *Phèdre,* in which he stresses that 'vice is depicted everywhere [in the play] in colours which both reveal and revile its monstrosity', hoping thereby to reconcile tragedy with 'a multitude of people celebrated for their piety and learning, who have condemned it in recent times'. Secondly, Pascal gives some attention in a brief series of fragments to the question of 'beauté poétique'. On the one hand, he concedes that 'one does not know what constitutes that pleasure which is the object of poetry' any more than one knows the 'natural model that one must imitate'. On the other, he recognizes the existence of such a model and, in a diatribe against jargon, invites a comparison with the likely aesthetic assessment of a person or house constructed on similar principles to a bad sonnet. The ideal is once again exemplified by 'les gens universels' ['universal beings'], who transcend such categories, who 'do not require a label and who see hardly any difference between the poetic craft and that of an embroiderer'.

Less narrowly, it could be argued that two further features are discernible. The first is, perhaps, best described as an attitude of mind, which may simplistically be designated tragic. The particular emphasis on humankind's postlapsarian dilemma is easily consonant with the kind of anguished questioning of human purpose attributed by Pascal to the unbeliever confronting the hidden God, the 'Dieu caché' of Isaiah; and coinciding with the tragic statements of Agamemnon or Phèdre as they address bewilderment or damnation. The specific theological reinforcement of a tonality drawn, in the case of the *moraliste* from humanist scepticism, in that of the dramatist from tragic myth, unites the two major literary manifestations of the pessimistic tendency. Secondly, we may appeal to an attitude towards language. Fallen discourse is symptomatic of the postlapsarian state: the loss of perfect communication is a further concomitant of original sin, and, whereas the rigorous tenets of linguistic theory to emanate from Port-Royal seek to remedy this, we are at the same time confronted with the need rhetorically to compensate for it. The appeal to rhetoric is thus overt in Pascal's *Art de persuader*; and indirectness of discourse is manifested by formal fragmentation in the *moralistes* (*Pensées*, *Maximes*), and by ambiguity of utterance in the dramatic texts.

The recurrence of the concept of paradox in what has preceded is not simply a convenient way of reconciling apparent inconsistency. Port-Royal/Jansenism appeals to the world as a starting point for a rejection of the world; it condemns the theatre, yet nurtures one of France's most universally acclaimed dramatic writers; it begins from a transcendent imperative, yet informs an ethos which, in certain manifestations, is strikingly secular; it offers systematic treatises on grammar and logic, yet gives rise to writing which is remarkable for the polysemic and the suprarational. Part of this is the result of a confusion between the narrow, theological sense of the term and a broader, more inexact usage. But partly it is also an appropriate amplification of the central tension between aspiration and pragmatism which is, in turn, the inevitable concomitant of an emphasis on the postlapsarian dimension to Christian theology.

* All translations in the present essay were undertaken collaboratively by the author and editor.

Neoclassical issues: beauty, judgement, persuasion, polemics

51

Combative criticism: Jonson, Milton, and classical literary criticism in England

Colin Burrow

English literary criticism between 1580 and 1670 is often regarded as the poor relation of Europe. The classicizing remarks of many English critics in the period might seem on the face of it to justify this opinion. In 1591 Sir John Harington, in his defence of Ariosto's *Orlando furioso*, claimed that neoclassical critics 'would have an heroicall Poem (as well as a Tragedie) to be full of *Peripeteia*, which I interpret an agnition of some unlooked for fortune either good or bad, and a sudden change thereof: of this what store there be the reader shall quickly find'.[1] Aristotle does argue that *anagnorisis* (Harington's 'agnition') and *peripeteia* ('reversal of fortune') should ideally coincide (*Poetics* 1452a), but he would balk at Harington's conflation of the two into a composite which can be liberally sprinkled over any heroic poem. Edmund Spenser also shows a weak grasp on neoclassical principles and vocabulary in his Letter to Ralegh, appended to *The Faerie Queene* (1590). He shows some awareness of Horace's recommendation that a heroic poem should not begin 'ab ovo' (*Ars poetica* 147): 'a Poet thrusteth into the middest, . . . and there recoursing to the thinges forepast, and diuining of thinges to come, maketh a pleasing analysis of all'.[2] But his critical remarks are belied by his practice: *The Faerie Queene* does not begin in the middle of a single action in anything like the sense that Spenser, or Horace, claimed it should. In the same period George Puttenham presented his *Arte of English poesie* (published 1589) in the form of a rhetorical manual, which minimizes the importance of narrative structure in favour of the schemes and tropes of rhetoric. The criticism of Aristotle and Horace was slow to naturalize in England.

The chief reason why classical criticism had such relatively shallow roots in England was that vernacular critics in the 1590s confronted an acute shortage of words in which to praise literature, let alone analyse its form. It was not just technical vocabulary – such as 'peripeteia', which Harington brought into English – which was lacking; rather there was no

---

[1] G. Gregory Smith (ed.), *Elizabethan critical essays*, 2 vols. (Oxford: Oxford University Press, 1904), vol. II, p. 216.

[2] *The Faerie Queene*, ed. A. C. Hamilton (London and New York: Longman, 1977), p. 738.

stable language in which to praise literature, let alone describe the intricacies of literary structure. The word 'literature' is not used to mean 'writing of value' in England before the eighteenth century. 'Imagination' in the late sixteenth century tends to mean the passive faculty that recombines sense impressions, and so generates dreams and delusive composites such as the mythical chimera (part lion, part goat, part snake), and by 'the later seventeenth century it is often opposed to terms of praise such as 'wit' and 'judgement'. Both Puttenham and Sir Philip Sidney attempt to give 'imagination' a positive sense, as a capacity to render an idealized image of the world, but both revert to the traditional, pejorative sense, within a paragraph.[3] In the critical vocabulary of late sixteenth-century England 'poet' could be used as a synonym of the highly uncomplimentary 'fantastic', and the word could be spat out as an insult.[4] The first task of an English critic was to create a language in which to defend poetry.

His or her second task was *self*-defence. In the competitive literary market-place of late sixteenth-century London critics such as Thomas Nashe and William Webbe were more concerned to create a canon of named, great writers, than to debate, say, the merits of single or double catastrophes. Rival writers – who are presented in Elizabethan satire and criticism as a nameless horde of ink-spilling incompetents – haunt late Elizabethan poets, poets who themselves were unsure of the value of their own occupation. Other writers are consequently represented as 'plagiaries' (a word which enters the language in the 1590s), or 'rhymesters'. Only the few deserve to be called 'poet' in the new, elevated sense which Elizabethan critics attempted to impose on the word.

In this environment a peculiarly English form of 'combative' classicism developed, less theoretically rigorous, but arguably more energetic, than its European equivalents. Fragments of classical vocabulary and precept were adopted as weapons in the battle to distinguish true poet from false rhymester. Sir Philip Sidney turns in the final section of his *Apology for poetry* (composed c. 1579, printed 1595) from his idealizing description of the poet 'freely ranging onely within the Zodiack of his owne wit', to a survey of contemporary English writing habits. He attacks an anonymous mass of contemporary dramatists for failing to limit the action of their plays to a single place and to the timespan of a single day, in accordance with '*Aristotles* precept and common reason'.[5] Sidney's onslaught marks

---

[3] Smith (ed.), *Essays*, vol. I, p. 157; vol. II, pp. 19–20. See William Rossky, 'Imagination in the English Renaissance: psychology and poetic', *Studies in the Renaissance* 5 (1958), 49–73.

[4] Smith (ed.), *Essays*, vol. II, p. 19; *Ben Jonson* [Works], ed. C. H. Herford and P. and E. Simpson, 11 vols. (Oxford: Clarendon Press, 1925–52), vol. VIII, p. 572. Henceforth *Jonson*.

[5] Smith (ed.), *Essays*, vol. I, pp. 156, 197. See O. B. Hardison, 'The two voices of Sidney's *Apology for poetry*', in *Sidney in retrospect: selections from English Literary Renaissance*, ed. A. F. Kinney (Amherst, MA: University of Massachusetts Press, 1988), pp. 45–61.

the emergence of a prescriptive concern with formal unity (although the word was not used in this sense until the 1660s) in English criticism. It also, more crucially, initiates a line of criticism in which a concern with classical precept was used to distinguish the true poet-critic from incompetent and nameless rivals.

In this respect Ben Jonson is Sidney's greatest heir. Jonson's reputation as the man who 'gave a new and increased prestige to the rules formulated by the Italians'[6] stems chiefly from his collection of prose observations, *Timber, or discoveries*, and from his punishingly close translation of Horace's *Ars poetica*. Both of these were published posthumously, however, in 1640. For Jonson's immediate contemporaries his critical achievements must have seemed patchy: he promised, but did not deliver, a translation of Horace, and a commentary on it (which does not survive), possibly in the form of a dialogue with Donne. He also boasted of a treatise on rhyme, which was never printed.[7] Drummond of Hawthornden recorded the uncharitable remarks which Jonson had made about his contemporaries (for example, 'that Don[n]e for not keeping of accent deserved hanging. That Shaksperr wanted Art')[8] in the course of extremely one-sided conversations. The remarks are those of a poet who came of age in the 1590s, for whom classical theory remained secondary to self-assertion. In his early play *Poetaster* (1601) Jonson presented a thinly veiled image of himself in the character of Horace, whose position as a satirical arbiter of taste is used to pour scorn on Jonson's rival playwrights Marston and Dekker. Classical criticism enables Jonson to voice his sense of superiority.

Many of Jonson's plays have prologues modelled on Terence, which offer precepts of composition, and berate his contemporaries for failing to adhere to them. His earliest critical remarks are influenced by the elevated defence of poetry presented in the first section of Sidney's *Apology*. By around 1605, however, he gravitates towards the more formal concerns of the final section of Sidney's treatise. In the original version of *Every man in his humour* (1601) Lorenzo junior defends the art of poetry in the most rarefied tones of Sidney, as shining, 'Blessed, aeternal, and most true divine' (v.iii.317). Jonson added a prologue to the revised version of the play (printed 1616) which shows the development of his critical thought. In it he prescribes formal rules for dramatic construction, and attacks contemporary playwrights for violating the unities of time and place. They 'Fight over *Yorke*, and *Lancasters* long jarres: / And in the tyring-house bring wounds, to scarres' (11–12). *Volpone* (1607) takes this tendency further, and proclaims Jonson's observation of 'the lawes of time, place, persons'.[9]

---

[6] J. E. Spingarn (ed.), *Critical essays of the seventeenth century*, 3 vols. (Oxford: Oxford University Press, 1908–9), vol. I, p. ix.

[7] Preface to *Sejanus* (1605), *Jonson*, vol. IV, p. 350; vol. I, p. 132; vol. I, p. 134.

[8] *Jonson*, vol. I, p. 133.

[9] *Jonson*, vol. V, p. 24.

Through the early years of the seventeenth century Jonson presents the
laws of dramatic form in an increasingly favourable light.

Jonson's *Timber, or discoveries* is a miscellany of prose observations
(some of which must date from after 1612, others after 1629) which
chiefly derive from a *mélange* of writers including Quintilian, Seneca,
Vives, and Heinsius. Jonson always adapts his originals, and often heightens
their imagery, so that metaphors of growth, and of combat (as one would
expect of a man who boasted that he once had disarmed Marston of
his pistol) spring out of his translations. He follows Juan Luis Vives
(whose works he possessed) in arguing that ancient literature should
not provide an exclusive prescriptive framework for the modern. Earlier
writers 'open'd the gates and made the way, that went before us; but
as Guides, not commanders'.[10] Barbed with metaphors of combat, this
develops an interest that dates from Jonson's earliest sorties into classical
criticism. In his attitudes to classical prescription he was what might be
termed a 'soft conventionalist'. That is, he held that the prescriptions of
past criticism can assist a writer in so far as they are expressions of naturally intuited truths, but in so far as they are simply received conventions
they could be changed in response to subsequent natural intuitions, or to
subsequent changes in customs.[11] Jonson first expressed this position in
Every man out of his humour (1600). Dismissing the requirement for
a chorus, and that 'the whole Argument fall within compasse of a dayes
business' as 'too nice observations', Cordatus (who is himself part of
a chorus) says that his author has followed 'Plautus and the rest', who
'augmented it [drama] with all liberty, according to the elegancie and
disposition of those times, wherein they wrote. I see not then, but we
should enjoy the same licence, or free power, to illustrate and heighten our
invention as they did' (Induction, 237–70). Samuel Daniel in *A defence
of rhyme* (1603) had opposed the importation of classical quantitative
metres into England on similar grounds: to impose foreign conventions
on native customs was a kind of tyranny analogous to the overturning of
the convention-based Common Law, since it would involve overriding
both native customs and the natural intuitions of native writers. Daniel
vigorously stated the soft conventionalist's faith in natural intuition:
'Me thinkes we should not so soone yeeld our consents captive to the author-
itie of Antiquitie . . . We are the children of nature as well as they.'[12]

Throughout his career, Jonson directed the whitest heat of his animosity at those who failed to absorb the substance of past writers into

---

[10] *Ibid.*, vol. VIII, p. 567. See Richard S. Peterson, *Imitation and praise in the poems of Ben Jonson* (New Haven and London: Yale University Press, 1981), pp. 4–13.

[11] See Lawrence Manley, *Convention: 1500–1700* (Cambridge, MA: Harvard University Press, 1980), pp. 188–95.

[12] Smith (ed.), *Essays*, vol. II, pp. 366–7.

themselves, and who consequently either produced the undisciplined outpourings of nature, or regurgitated the overeaten relics of another's wit. He often colours this topic with metaphors of digestion, and can often also invoke the more gruesome forms of *in*digestion to attack those who fail to assimilate their reading. Montaigne is accused of presenting matter which is 'raw, and undigested', and at the end of *Poetaster* Crispinus is made to vomit out his barbarous polysyllabic words.[13] Eating (a subject always dear to Jonson) is never far from his mind when discussing poetry – the Cook in *Neptune's triumph* (1624) even claims that poetry and cookery were invented on the same day. Jonson instinctively identifies language with personal substance ('Language most shewes a man: speake that I may see thee'),[14] and links the absorption of past writing with the formation of solid personal identity. Only by absorbing past example can writers 'stand of themselves, and worke with their owne strength',[15] emerge from the crowd of rivals which surrounds them, and produce a living re-creation of past writing.

A 'living' re-creation of past literature is, however, a surprising ideal to be entertained by one who holds that each age is circumscribed by its own customs: if the *mores* of ancient Rome and those of Jacobean London differ immeasurably, how can the earlier world ever be revived in the later? Dryden was to recognize this problem, and came to advocate a form of translation which answers the hypothetical question, how would a given writer compose 'had he lived in our age, and in our country'?[16] Jonson produced no such theoretical formulation of how to accommodate ancient customs to modern. But his critical writings (and indeed his poems) make vigorous use of biological metaphors – of life, birth, and digestion – to bridge the gap between past and present. In 'To Penshurst' Martial's country maids become ripe for marriage, in a landscape which teems with life and which longs to be eaten; in 'Drink to me only with your eyes' a dead rose culled from Philostratus '*grows*, and smells, I swear, / Not of itself, but thee' after it has been sniffed by his mistress.[17] Jonson's theoretical remarks on the practice of imitation also deploy biological metaphors to suggest a relationship of consubstantiality between an author in the past and one in the present. He follows Seneca and Quintilian, for whom the imitation of past authors assisted the formation of the personal lexis, style, and character of a potential orator, in describing how a modern writer builds his own substance from ancient writing. He defines *imitatio* in typically gustatory terms: 'to bee able to convert the

---

[13] *Jonson*, vol. VIII, p. 586.   [14] *Ibid.*, p. 625.   [15] *Ibid.*, p. 615.
[16] *Essays of John Dryden*, ed. W. P. Ker, 2 vols. (Oxford: Clarendon Press, 1900), vol. I, p. 239. Compare vol. I, p. 252; vol. II, pp. 113–14.
[17] 'To Penshurst', ll. 51–6; compare Martial III.xlviii.33–40. 'Song To Celia', ll. 15–16; compare Philostratus, Epistles 2 and 46.

substance, or Riches of an other *Poet*, to his owne use. To make choise of one excellent man above the rest, and so to follow him, till he grow very *Hee*: or, so like him, as the Copie may be mistaken for the Principall. Not, as a Creature, that swallowes, what it takes in, crude, raw, or indigested; but that feedes with an appetite, and hath a Stomacke to concoct, divide, and turne all to nourishment.'[18] The thought here derives ultimately from Seneca's requirement in Epistle 84 that an imitator assimilate earlier writing as bees do honey; but it is the live heart of Jonson's own poetics, and makes him a theorist to whom the revitalizing metaphor of 'Renaissance' is singularly appropriate. He is eager to believe that past literature can be absorbed into the living substance of contemporaneity, even though he cannot provide a theoretical formulation of how that might come about.

For Jonson, however, it is always only one lone poet, perhaps assisted by a patroness, who revives past literary excellence. As a result of his conviction that the vulgar stubbornly refuse to absorb the customs of the past, and fail to appreciate the classic poet, Jonson can appear to use classical precedent only to ensure that he stands out in strong and solitary opposition to his age. Imitators, he claims, can produce something like their prototype, 'which hath an Authority above their owne'.[19] That phrase suggests that even Jonson's later thought is at least in part designed to weld the authority of ancient writers on to his own in order to distinguish him from the mass of rhymesters. What his criticism lacks is any theory of how classically derived fictions could influence and benefit a wide, national audience.

In this respect he differs markedly from John Milton, whose criticism, scattered through poems and prose treatises written during the most changeful forty years of English history, 1630–70, has all the energy and changefulness of its period. At Cambridge in the late 1620s, when still under the influence of Jonson, Milton wrote *Prolusions* which create soaring fantasies of the poet's influence. Poetry 'raises aloft the soul smothered by the dust of earth and sets it among the mansions of heaven'.[20] Throughout the 1630s and 1640s he presents a poet (for which read himself) as an elevated, solitary creature 'with his garland and singing robes about him'.[21] Milton's criticism, however, like that of Sidney and Jonson, takes heat and energy from adversity. In the *Apology for Smectymnuus* (1643) his description of the poet as one who 'ought him selfe to bee a true Poem, that is, a composition, and patterne of the best and honourablest

---

[18] *Jonson*, vol. VIII, p. 638.   [19] *Ibid.*, p. 616.
[20] *Complete prose works*, ed. D. M. Wolfe *et al.*, 8 vols. (New Haven: Yale University Press, 1953–82), vol. I, p. 243. Henceforth *CPW*.
[21] *CPW*, vol. I, p. 808; *Elegia sexta* 53–60, *Epitaphium Damonis* 162–78; *L'allegro* 130–44; *Il penseroso* 109–20. All references to *Poems*, ed. J. Carey and A. Fowler (Harlow: Longman, 1968).

things'[22] is a modification of Quintilian's belief that the ideal orator should be a model of purity and sagacity. Milton's defence of the poet was prompted, however, by vicious attacks on his character by Joseph Hall, a veteran of the satirical infighting of the 1590s in which Jonson had played so great a part. Milton is another embattled classic, a poet whose image of himself as a man of singular and isolating wisdom depends upon his opposition to enemies, rival poets, and poetasters.

The chief unifying theme of Milton's critical writings is his identification of the poet and the orator: a poet 'ought him selfe to bee a true Poem', as the orator, for Cicero and Quintilian, ought to be 'a good man skilled in speaking'.[23] He shares this identification of the poet and good man with Ben Jonson, who asserted in the Epistle attached to *Volpone* that none can be 'the good Poet, without first being a good man'.[24] Milton's orator-poet would be anathema to Jonson, however. From his anti-prelatical tracts of the 1640s onwards, Milton attempts to unite Cicero's ideal orator, who participates in the management of the state by using his virtuous eloquence to persuade his audience to virtue, with the figure of a prophet, who speaks divinely inspired words to an audience which should ideally consist of the godly. Where Jonson's ideal poet can feign a commonwealth, Milton's would help govern and rejuvenate one.[25]

Milton was as much a master of the schemes and tropes of rhetoric as Jonson, but a recurrent feature of his criticism is to make that training appear to be an irrelevance. He claims that since love of truth is the sole criterion of eloquence, the orator, though versed in the regimen of classical rhetoric, can discard 'those Rules which best Rhetoricians have giv'n'. The words of a lover of truth 'like so many nimble and airy servitors trip about him at command, and in well order'd files, as he would wish, fall aptly into their own places'.[26] Words become a squadron of marching Ariels, bedecked with muskets for the wars of truth, which without any formal disposition transmit the zeal of the speaker to the listener. This is potentially the most radical poetic adopted by any English Renaissance writer, since, in theory, it could exclude all formal decorum in favour of zealous expression. The significant element in speech or writing is the virtue of a speaker and its effect on an audience, not the formal rules which might ensure that an utterance had such an effect.

Milton's most substantial piece of literary criticism in the 1640s, the proem to *The reason of church government* (1642), Book II, is a digression from an attack on prelatical church government. It shows the paradox of

---

[22] *CPW*, vol. I, p. 890.
[23] Quintilian, *Institutio* I, proem 9; XII.i.   [24] *Jonson*, vol. V, p. 17.
[25] *Ibid.*, vol. VIII, p. 595; compare Quintilian, *Institutio* I, proem 10: an orator can 'guide a state by his counsels'.
[26] *CPW*, vol. I, p. 949.

his early criticism: in order to advocate a poetics which goes beyond regulatory formalism he has first to invoke that formalism. He proceeds at first through territory well trodden by sixteenth-century Italian critics as the poet deliberates over whether in writing epic 'the rules of *Aristotle* herein are strictly to be kept, or nature to be followed'[27] – that is, whether neoclassical prescriptions for the form of epic be adopted, or the freer structures of Ariosto's romance. When he goes on to consider the figure of the poet, the full purpose of the digression in the context of his attack on prelatical church government becomes clear. He sketches a poetic in which both prose (in which he claims only to have the use 'of my left hand')[28] *and* verse are subordinated to the ultimate end of a godly poet-orator: to transform the nation. 'These abilities, wheresoever they be found, are the inspired guift of God, rarely bestow'd, but yet to some (though most abuse) in every Nation: and are of power beside the office of a pulpit, to imbreed and cherish in a great people the seeds of vertu and publick civility, to allay the perturbations of the mind and set the affections in right tune.'[29]

Even here, at the centre of Milton's poetics of Reformation, there are traces of what might be called a godly Quintilianism, and of Aristotelianism. Many Renaissance commentators, including Daniel Heinsius, believed that Aristotle meant by 'catharsis' the due regulation of passions to their proper objects and occasions – to 'set the affections in right tune'.[30] Milton advocates a similar ethical function for poetry, but also presents the poet as one who praises God, and sings 'the deeds and triumphs of just and pious Nations doing valiantly through faith against the enemies of Christ'. Surrounded by the traditional adversaries of the English classic poet – 'libidinous and ignorant poetasters', and 'the trencher fury of a riming parasite'[31] – Milton creates a religious transformation of that classic poet, one concerned with 'instructing and bettering the Nation at all opportunities'. *Of education* (1644) advances a similar argument: that the goal of literary training is active participation in both civic and religious life in Parliament and pulpit. Familiarity with classical poetics has as its final end the transformation of Church and state by a body of godly orators.

Through the 1650s royalist critics came to recognize both the power and danger of godly rhetoric. Thomas Hobbes in *Behemoth* (1679) blamed the Civil War in part on the reading of classical rhetoricians – including

---

[27] *Ibid.*, p. 813.
[28] *Ibid.*, p. 808. John Hall is described as 'not altogether left-handed in Prose', *Horae Vacivae* (London: E. G. for J. Rothwell, 1646), fol. A7ʳ.
[29] *CPW*, vol. I, pp. 816–17.
[30] Aristotle, *Poetics* 1449b; compare *Politics* 1341b; Daniel Heinsius, *De tragoediae constitutione* (Leiden: J. Balduinus, 1611), p. 30. See n. 45 below.
[31] *CPW*, vol. I, pp. 818, 820, 819.

Cicero – who express hostility to kings.[32] Sir William Davenant, in his preface to *Gondibert* (1651) (which was addressed to and answered by Hobbes), argued that poetry should ideally unify and harmonize a nation. He directed vehement scorn at those who claimed divine inspiration (they 'should not assume such saucy familiarity with a true God'), and described orators as 'so much more unapt for governing, as they are more fit for Sedition'.[33] Milton's poetics of the 1640s have a powerful political edge, which his opponents in the next decade felt, and attempted to blunt.

Milton's early poetics depend for their success on a particular moment in English history. To unite the roles of Ciceronian orator and inspired prophet depends on the extraordinary receptiveness of a godly national audience. Orators exhort and persuade in the forum; prophets traditionally cry in the wilderness. Milton's later criticism is determined by the breakdown of this unstable fusion of roles.[34] In 1660 he published *The readie and easy way to establish a free commonwealth*, a desperate address to an audience which had become so deaf to his godly rhetoric that they were contemplating the restoration of Charles II. His peroration is spoken by a rhetorician alienated from his audience: 'Thus much I should perhaps have said though I were sure I should have spoken only to trees and stones; and had none to cry to, but with the Prophet, O *earth, earth, earth!* to tell the very soil it self, what her perverse inhabitants are deaf to'.[35] Milton had always been fascinated by the solitary death of Orpheus, torn apart by Thracian women, rather than by the poet's mythical ability to civilize by song.[36] In *The readie and easie way* he presents himself as an Orpheus with a broken lyre, for whom stones and trees no longer dance to the music of godly civility, but obstinately remain trees and stones. The orator-poet of the godly commonwealth becomes a Jeremiah (22: 29) crying in the wilderness.

The poetics implicit in Milton's late masterpiece, *Paradise lost* (1667), stem from and dramatize this isolation of poet from audience. In deliberate contrast to the conversational and conciliationist style in which Dryden voices his Restoration criticism, Milton presents himself as a lone voice of inspired zeal, hoping his poem will 'fit audience find, though few', and fearing the dismemberment of Orpheus, by 'Bacchus and his revellers'.[37] The poem is full of quiet points of resistance to its age.

[32] *English works*, ed. Sir William Molesworth, 11 vols. (London: John Bohn, 1839–45), vol. VI, p. 168; vol. III, pp. 18–29.
[33] *Gondibert*, ed. D. F. Gladish (Oxford: Clarendon Press, 1971), pp. 38, 22, 19.
[34] See Irene Samuel, 'The development of Milton's poetics', *Publications of the modern language association of America* 92 (1977), 231–40.
[35] *CPW*, vol. VII, pp. 462–3.
[36] 'Lycidas', 58–63; *Paradise lost* VII.32–8; compare Puttenham, in Smith (ed.), *Essays*, vol. II, pp. 6–7.
[37] *Paradise lost* VII.31, 33.

Prefixed to the fourth and subsequent issues (1668) is a note on 'The
Verse', which attacks rhyme as 'the Invention of a barbarous Age', and
defends the poet's choice of blank verse as 'an example set, the first in *English*, of ancient liberty recovered to Heroic Poem from the troublesom and
modern bondage of Rimeing'.[38] This is the last growl of Milton's extreme
anti-conventionalism. His assertion that unrhymed verse marks a return
to 'ancient liberty' indicates his radical hostility to any inherited institution – including at times even the Common Law – which conflicts with the
continuing demands of reformation. For him not to rhyme is to cast a
wistful glance back towards both the versification and the true republican
liberty of Rome.

Paradise lost is so deliberately at odds with the poetic forms and theories of Restoration England that it had less influence on Milton's immediate contemporaries than on his successors. Recent critics have detected
signs that Milton anticipated the interests of Addison, Burke, and Dennis
by writing with Longinus's theories of the Sublime in mind.[39] Longinus
(whom Milton cites in *Of education*) was translated in 1652 into rhapsod-
ical English by John Hall (a regicide, and almost the only contemporary
admirer of *Areopagitica*). Hall's preface presents *Peri hupsous* as a manual
of rhetoric for advocates of liberty in an age of print. For Milton in the
1660s the claim by the philosopher in the final section of Longinus's treatise
that '*Democracie* is the best *Nurse* of high Spirits'[40] would have a particular resonance, as would his quotation of the great creative word 'Let there
be light' as an instance of the religious Sublime (9.9). Milton frequently
attached the epithet 'sublime' to poetry, as did his friend Andrew Marvell
in his dedicatory poem on *Paradise lost*. The soaring poet described in
the prologues to Milton's epic seeks the heights advocated by Longinus,
and fears the fall – crashing down from the stars with Bellerophon (VII.12–
20) – which *Peri hupsous* confesses to be the chief danger of aspiring so
high (33.2).

Paradise lost also probes many of the theoretical problems of earlier
English criticism. Satan plays a major part in this aspect of the poem. In
Book IV, disguised as a toad, he inspires Eve with a dream of eating the
forbidden fruit, and of falling. Adam believes the dream to be the product
of a passive form of 'imagination', which has simply recombined the sense
impressions of the human couple's earlier conversations about the Tree
of knowledge. Yet even Adam recognizes that Eve's dream contains 'addition strange', a transgression and a fall which she has never experienced

[38] *CPW*, vol. VIII, p. 14. See John M. Steadman, *The walls of paradise: essays on Milton's
poetics* (Baton Rouge and London: Louisiana State University Press, 1985), pp. 131–42.
[39] Annabel Patterson, *Reading between the lines* (London: Routledge, 1993), pp. 256–72.
[40] *Peri hupsous, or Dionysius Longinus of the heights of eloquence* (London: Roger Daniel
for Francis Eaglesfield, 1652), p. 78.

(v.95–116). Satan turns the imagination into an active, but deadly, force which contributes to the fall of man. Satan was to become a central figure in the creative aesthetics of Romantic poets, partly because through him Milton attempted to explore and extend the range of Renaissance thought about the imagination.[41] For writers in the English empiricist tradition, such as Bacon and Hobbes, imagination presents a danger of misrepresenting reality; in Milton's godly poetics it presents the danger of proudly claiming one's own creativity, rather than seeing oneself as a recipient of divine influence. Satan also enacts a deadly parody of the process of re-creative imitation which had been at the heart of Jonson's criticism. In Book II Milton's devil encounters his daughter Sin (648–870). She is part woman and part snake, and has obvious affiliations with both the classical Scylla, and Spenser's monstrous snake-woman Errour. Although she is a self-evidently imitative offshoot of earlier writing, Sin claims Satan as her 'author' (II.864), and breeds from their incestuous union both Death and a generation of hellhounds. This allegorical episode explores some of the longest-standing problems of English Renaissance criticism: imitation becomes at once a creative, life-giving process (as Jonson had regarded it), and a deadly inbreeding of an author divorced from God with his own creations. The episode of Satan's encounter with Sin and Death was also to become definitional of the Sublime in the early eighteenth century: Death's 'shape . . . that shape had none' became the principal example of the obscure Sublime for Edmund Burke.[42] The pseudo-creative poetics of the episode, in which a derivative figure, Sin, claims Satan as her creator, also have strong affiliations with one of Longinus's own criteria of the Sublime: it should be so powerful that anyone reading it will believe that he himself wrote it. As Hall put it, 'naturally our souls are so enflamed by true *heights* that they generally *elevate* themselves, and in a *transport* of *joy* and *wonder* own and father those great things that are presented to them, as if themselves had produced them'.[43] Satan is just such a sublime surrogate artist in his relations with Sin and Death. Milton's late works develop the combative posture of the English classical critic into an extreme form: the lone prophet pushes neoclassical criticism towards the sublime irregularity which was to become a central criterion of literary value in the work of later English critics such as John Dennis.

Milton's last critical remarks in the preface to *Samson agonistes* (1671), however, seem to mark a return to classically regulated formalism. 'Tragedy', claims the preface, is 'said by *Aristotle* to be of power by raising pity and

---

[41] John Guillory, *Poetic authority: Spenser, Milton and literary history* (New York: Columbia University Press, 1983).

[42] *Paradise lost* II.666–7; *A philosophical enquiry into the origin of our ideas of the Sublime and beautiful*, ed. J. T. Boulton, 2nd edn (Oxford: Blackwell, 1987), p. 59.

[43] Hall, *Peri hupsous*, p. 11; Longinus 7.2.

fear, or terror, to purge the mind of those and such like passions, that is
to temper and reduce them to just measure with a kind of delight, stirred
up by reading or seeing those passions well imitated'. Milton goes on to
offer a homeopathic definition of *catharsis*: 'so in Physic things of melan-
cholic hue and quality are used against melancholy'.[44] There has been
extensive debate as to the precise sources of these remarks. Guarini and
Minturno had both put forward a homeopathic model of *catharsis*. Daniel
Heinsius's *De tragoediae constitutione* (1611) argues that like passions
purge like, and also advances the view that *catharsis* regulates emotions to
their proper objects and occasions.[45] The sources of Milton's Aristotelian
observations are, however, less significant than the fact that he associates
himself at this very late stage in his career with the vocabulary of neoclassicism. No statement in the corpus of Milton's writings is so categorical
about the value of 'ancient rule'. Although Milton appears to have adapted
his defence of *Samson* to the growing tide of Restoration neoclassicism,
it is nonetheless in keeping with his progressive isolation from his audience: instead of assuming, as he had done in the 1640s, that love of truth
is a sufficient condition for moving and persuading, he recognizes in his
final years that a carefully unified structure, which appears impeccably
to conform with classical precedent, can assist the rhetorical and moral
effect of fiction. But the moral and religious end of literature remains
Milton's chief concern to the last. As in *The reason of church government*,
the object of tragedy in the preface to *Samson* is 'to set the affections in
right tune'. The central section of the preface cites Paraeus's view that
the Book of Revelation is a holy tragedy (which again recalls *The reason
of church government*),[46] and invokes Gregory of Nazianzen's *Christus
patiens* 'to vindicate Tragedy from the small esteem, or rather infamy,
which in the account of many it undergoes at this day with other common
Interludes'.[47] The preface to *Samson agonistes* retains the central features
of English classicism in its Miltonic dress: the holy poet uses a classicizing
vocabulary to distinguish himself from those who are guilty of 'introducing trivial and vulgar persons, which by all judicious hath been counted
absurd' into a dramatic form which is properly august and sacred. Milton's
zealous hostility to the Restoration stage (for which, he remarks, *Samson*

[44] *CPW*, vol. VIII, p. 133.
[45] Paul R. Sellin, 'Sources of Milton's catharsis: a reconsideration', *Journal of English
and Germanic philology* 60 (1961), 712–30, and his 'Milton and Heinsius: theoretical
homogeneity' in *Medieval epic to the 'epic theatre' of Brecht: essays in comparative
literature*, ed. R. P. Amato and J. M. Spalek, University of Southern California studies in
comparative literature 1 (Los Angeles: University of California Press, 1968), pp. 125–34.
Compare Martin Mueller, 'Sixteenth-century Italian criticism and Milton's theory of
catharsis', *Studies in English literature* 6 (1966), 139–50; Steadman, *Walls of paradise*,
pp. 69–107.
[46] *CPW*, vol. I, p. 815.   [47] *Ibid.*, vol. VIII, p. 135.

'never was intended')[48] seems worlds away from Jonson's vilifications of rival poets; but the stance of an English classic poet, preserving his ideals against a threatening multitude of poetasters, underlies the work of both writers – and it was, *mutatis mutandis*, to become a central element in the self-images of Dryden, Pope, and Swift in the later manifestations of English classicism.

[48] *Ibid.*, p. 136.

52

The rhetorical ideal in France

Hugh M. Davidson

In seventeenth-century France the evolution of rhetoric and the ideal based on it are, at first, strongly influenced by earlier developments in Italian humanism and by Jesuit theories and pedagogy. But it is important to note that interest in the *ars bene dicendi* comes to a head in a clearly visible way and takes on peculiar force in the fourth decade of the century, with the founding in 1635 of the French Academy. External conditions were favourable for a new cultural initiative: after the religious wars of the sixteenth century, France was entering a period of pacification, of relative prosperity, of movement towards political unity. It was also a period marked by the emergence of educated and active élites – in the magistrature, in the clergy, in certain elements of the aristocracy, especially those associated with the court. A design, national in scope and centred on the king as a strong monarch – not yet *le roi soleil*, but Louis XIV was on his way – was being promoted by Richelieu and others. As a newly created source of intellectual and literary guidance, the Academy soon defined its mission in a way that not only fitted perfectly into the national programme, but also promoted actively what we are calling here the rhetorical ideal. By the instruments of its fourfold project – which called for the creation of a Dictionary and a Grammar, to be followed by treatises on Rhetoric and Poetics – the Academy sought to make possible a culture based on *éloquence*.

To understand this coincidence of politics and rhetoric and to appreciate it as a historical force, we may wish to recall a part of Cicero's legacy that must surely have attracted the attention of these French planners. Two of his theses may be noted: (1) that the power of speech and of communicating rational thought is *the* distinctive mark of humanity, and it is natural to want to perfect that power and to use it well; and (2) that the progress of civil society – not to mention its very existence – depends on a work of communication and persuasion; for without it, how will human beings be brought together and led to apply what they know in common action? Eloquence is essentially human and it is supremely useful: those two values help us to understand the commitment willingly made by many theorists and writers of the seventeenth century in France.

Incidentally, it is well to keep in mind the distinction between rhetoric and eloquence. To Cicero and to the more careful seventeenth-century theorists eloquence is much less the product of rhetoric than a level of practice and a degree of achievement that furnish the materials on which a supporting art and its rules may be based.

The Academy fell far short of realizing its ambitious programme. The first edition of its dictionary appeared almost sixty years later, in 1694. It did not produce a grammar or treatises on rhetoric and poetics. Still, its plan was so symptomatic of a generally held set of assumptions that one can see in retrospect that much of the work was carried out in an effective if not very orderly way by various individuals: as, for example, by Claude Favre de Vaugelas in his *Remarques sur la langue française*, by René Bary and Le Sieur Le Gras and others in their rhetorical treatises, by Dominique Bouhours, René Rapin in their discussions of prose and poetry, by Nicolas Boileau, Molière, Pierre Corneille, and Jean Racine in their critical reflections and prefaces. Nor is it fanciful to say that two influential productions of the Port-Royalists expressed a negative reaction to the aims and claims of those who expected so much of rhetoric and its possibilities. Antoine Arnauld and Pierre Nicole had their programme, which, with the collaboration of Claude Lancelot, they did bring to completion, with the publication of the *Grammaire générale* (1660; Arnauld and Lancelot) and their *Logique* or *Art de penser* (1662; Arnauld and Nicole). The Port-Royalists undertook no rhetoric or poetic, two significant and not accidental omissions, on which we shall comment later.

What took place was something like a rhetoricizing of the whole of the literary landscape. This is so because of the way in which that landscape was conceived and made intelligible. The usual line of thought is that prose and the art that guides it are fundamental, primary; then poetic expression comes into view as being in many ways a *prolongement*. It continues the process of refinement and ornamentation already begun in order to achieve eloquence in prose, adding to it all the possibilities available in versification, broadly understood, and in the free use of figures.

In extended treatments it was necessary to subdivide the two main headings. The domain of prose included forensic discourse (*éloquence du barreau*) and preaching (*éloquence de la chaire*); and one sees occasional references to something like deliberative rhetoric, which is appropriate, for example, in the *cabinet du prince* (there being few or no uses in a monarchy for the kind of eloquence specifically intended for public assemblies). Some of its functions and tropes are taken over by the *éloquence de la chaire*, since it treats of future matters in this world and the next, and of what should be done in the former as a preparation for the latter. The discourses of history and philosophy fall, of course, under the heading of prose. They may be treated according to rhetorical principles when

those are slightly generalized; and this fashion is well illustrated by Rapin
in his series of observations and comparisons, as we shall see. Under the
heading of poetry, the subdivisions may be made according to general
classes such as dramatic, lyric, and narrative, but the level of analysis is
more often that – as in the *Art poétique* of Boileau – of the many attempts
to define the various poetic genres, from epic to epigram.

*

In French drama of the seventeenth century we can see readily the consequences of the decision to analyse and discuss literature in the rhetorical
mode. The documents are at hand, containing fully worked-out critical
positions: François d'Aubignac's *Pratique du théâtre* (begun in 1640,
finally published in 1657) and Corneille's three *Discours sur le poème
dramatique* (appearing in 1660 as introductions to the three volumes of
his collected works).

D'Aubignac's treatise is in fact a *Rhétorique du théâtre*. He accepts the
context for literary expression set by the Academy: dramatic poetry is
called to assume a role in strengthening the monarchy and in furthering its
purposes. He does not hesitate to refer to the theatre as an *école de vertu*.
(Racine was to use the same phrase later when, near the end of his career,
he turned to writing plays based on biblical subjects.) For D'Aubignac
drama is essentially a matter of language. The main happenings on the
stage are speeches, and they must be eloquent. The characters in a play are
attempting to move, instruct, influence, persuade one another; each one is
an orator, and it is his or her purpose to excel in these verbal interactions
with partners and interlocutors.

In passing, let us note that the rhetorical framework is much more pervasive than what might be suggested by those lines. D'Aubignac's theory
as a whole lays for us the basis for a series of revealing analogies. If we
reflect for a moment (and keep in mind the sort of arguments that classical dramatists often put in prefaces as they publish their plays), we realize
that the situation on the stage is, in a real sense, duplicated in the theatre
itself. There the poet is the original speaker; his play is what he has to say
and to present. He sets it before the audience to produce an effect and
to achieve a favourable verdict: 'We who work for the public . . .' writes
Racine in the *dédicace* of *Andromaque*. One can even go further. The
basic situation appears once again, now in real life, as the spectators leave
the theatre to take up their usual concerns and activities. In society they
are agents with determinate characters and values, presenting words and
gestures to fellow men and women, with the aims of communicating,
pleasing, moving, and persuading in those interactions. It becomes possible thus for us to understand certain moral implications of the rhetorical
ideal – to grasp, for example, the close links between it and the aristocratic

code of *bienséance* and *honnêteté*, of doing and saying what is appropriate to times, places, and persons. Indeed, the fact that the king interests himself in sponsoring the theatre suggests a final analogy. As D'Aubignac sees it, a prince may, as a matter of political prudence, provide for his subjects *divertissements* that convey officially recognized values, and, by their quality, reflect the dignity of his crown.

Whereas in his treatise D'Aubignac assumes the part of official theoretician for the perfecting of drama in France, Corneille writes in his prefaces and in the three *Discours* with the aim of defending and rationalizing his own dramatic practice. Rather than stress the political and moral uses of the theatre, he is inclined to emphasize the pleasure experienced by his audiences at the performances of his plays. But he balances ingeniously his position, arguing that one cannot please if utility of the moral sort is absent, but neither can one please if one neglects the rules of dramatic composition.

Corneille has, in fact, a clearer understanding than D'Aubignac of the nature of poetics. D'Aubignac subordinates poetics to rhetoric totally, but Corneille is more discriminating. He shows, at least by moments, a real sense of the Aristotelian point of view, according to which rhetoric is related to only one of the constituent parts of a tragedy – 'thought' – and that part must be treated so as to fit with other parts into an effective dramatic whole. In other ways he contrasts interestingly with D'Aubignac. D'Aubignac argues unceasingly for *la vraisemblance* – which he locates between the *le vrai* and *le possible*, both of those being unsuitable in the theatre – as the chief criterion of what is to be presented in a dramatic work, if it is to be accepted by the spectators. Corneille, who had been criticized by learned critics as being guilty of improbabilities in his plots, holds that *vraisemblance* is sometimes but not always relevant as a requirement. Its presence or absence is not decisive in judging the value of a dramatic work.

However, despite these and other differences, it is plain that, as literary critics, D'Aubignac and Corneille belong to the same family of minds. In their judgements and theorizing there are many signs of an initial decision to reflect on the theatre in a context that is set by rhetoric and its typical conditions. But their positions do give us a useful sense of the intrafamilial diversity possible within the shared basic framework.

*

With Boileau and his *Art poétique* (1674) the discussion of literature in the spirit of rhetoric continues, broadening from drama to a survey of the whole spectrum of poetry. The main topics come from the traditional list of operations performed by orators: invention, disposition, elocution, memory, delivery. In the context of poetry, the last two may be set aside, but the first three are the source of a distinction *sine qua non* in Boileau's thinking – the familiar pair of *res* and *verba*, content and expression. This analytical device guides the argument of the first *chant* of his poem, where he gives poets general advice on matters of thought and composition; and it underlies the whole treatment of genres found in the next two *chants*. They present his views first on minor genres – like elegies, odes, sonnets, epigrams, for example – and then on the major genres – epic, tragedy, comedy. In defining and classifying he proceeds by specifying the parallel notions of content and expression to the requirements of the various poetic kinds. Often he finds himself led to a *dédoublement* of the two basic terms: he must point out not only beauties but also possible faults, since poets may fall into errors of judgement in both phases of composition. In treating a particular genre Boileau may spend more time and space on one of the two topics than the other. They are always closely linked, however, and to comment on one is to have in mind and to comment on the other.

Boileau's way of dealing with the history of French poetry and of genres is influenced by rhetorical theory. In this perspective his focus is on poets conceived as inventors and, when successful, models. His little narratives turn, as one might foresee, on changes in content and expression. After trials and errors, certain poets make the right decisions in those matters. For example, 'Enfin Malherbe vint' ['At last Malherbe came']: at last he came, after the errors of Ronsard, to the rescue of French poetic expression in general. The same thing may occur in the history of a genre, where, for example, tragedy owes much to the happy inventions of Aeschylus and Sophocles. Such solutions of poetic problems serve to perfect literary forms and to guide later poets. And the process of definition does not come to a halt at some *point de perfection*. Other poets may come on the scene and innovate further in exemplary ways, since the rules for genres come from practice, just as the principles of rhetoric come from actual eloquence.

What are we to think of the destination of poetic works, of the audiences to whom they are directed? What about the character of the experience caused in them by the works? Once more, in Boileau's mind, there emerge the elements of a rhetorical transaction. Poets offer their work to audiences; and in the *Art poétique* those audiences are present in several guises. One notes (1) the speaker, the *je* in the poem, who is both theorist and critic; (2) the collective juries formed by spectators and readers; (3) more privately, the severe friend-critic needed by every poet, to whom he should willingly submit his verses; (4) Louis XIV, saluted by Boileau as the perfect judge and patron. Without attempting to recover, from Boileau's indications, anything like a full account of aesthetic experience, we may at least mention what he sees happening in all these audiences as they make up their minds regarding poems: activities involving *les yeux*, *l'oreille*, *le cœur*, *l'esprit*, and taking place on a special level of seeing, hearing, feeling, and knowing.

Complex reactions of this kind complete the transaction passing (1) from the poet (2) through the work (3) to the audience (4) for a specific aim. Here it is possible to appreciate the distinctive strength and vitality of this critical framework. It encourages Boileau and his contemporaries to discuss poetry in four sets of terms fitted to four different factors; however, those sets are bound together necessarily by relations of analogy and causality; as a result, in considering any one of the four factors – poet, poem, audience, aim – he and we may easily see implications for the other three. The possibilities in this framework underlie the particular balance achieved in the *Art poétique*. Their interrelations explain, also, how Boileau, as he goes along, can make quick changes of focus from one factor to another without loss of coherence. Such shifts in the centre of attention are common in the *Ars poetica* of Horace; no doubt Boileau intended to profit by the example.

When Boileau published in 1674 his *Art poétique*, he included in the same volume his translation of the treatise of Longinus's *On the Sublime*. This fact involves us in a fascinating juxtaposition. The argument presented by Longinus is based on premises differing in important ways from those of Boileau in his poem, and it is a delicate matter to determine exactly what he made of the treatise of Longinus. In translating it he seems to have been sensitive particularly to matters having to do with the effect of sublime writing on the audience: that would be consistent with the audience-centred position that he sets forth in his *Art poétique*.

On several points the art of Longinus seems unorthodox when placed in the perspective we have been exploring. Everything along the line of the rhetorical transaction is redefined and a new balance is struck, this time in favour of the writer or poet rather than the public. Instead of being patrons and judges, their part is to be caught in the current of the writer's inspiration, and to be raised, by moments at least, to the level of great souls and their unique kind of thought, feeling, and expression. This modification of the rhetorical ideal, emphasizing genius and exalted experience, supplied arguments for both sides in the Quarrel of the Ancients and the Moderns during the last two decades of the seventeenth century. Partisans of the Moderns could stress the primacy of genius over art, and more particularly over art based dogmatically on imitation of the Ancients; and partisans of the Ancients could argue, as Boileau does, that sublimity and its effects are not dated, as is attested by the fact that the excellence of the Ancients has been recognized by many generations of readers.

*

The critical works of the Jesuit father René Rapin were much appreciated when they appeared and then on into the early years of the next century. They treat poetry in a context much broader than that of Boileau. Collected in two volumes in 1684, they give us a relatively systematic view of *belles-lettres* – the phrase comes often from his pen – as a whole. The first volume contains *Comparaisons* of some Ancients, the pairs being Demosthenes and Cicero, Homer and Virgil, Thucydides and Livy, Plato and Aristotle. In the second volume he set out his *Réflexions* on eloquence, poetics, history, and philosophy, including therewith – again in his words – a judgement of the authors who had distinguished themselves in those four parts of literary expression.

Rapin has in mind not closely argued discourse, but an easily followed discussion of examples and principles. Although he makes regular use of the familiar distinction between nature and art, he likes to emphasize, like Longinus, the importance of natural gifts and genius. With Boileau, he continues the trend away from the erudite and didactic tone adopted regularly by D'Aubignac and sometimes by Corneille. He attaches great importance to judgements of appropriateness, as in the matching of content and expression, those two essential aspects of eloquence. In fact, *bienséance* is the supreme criterion for him; critical judgement draws on it everywhere, as it moves from the smallest details to the most general aspects of composition. This single-mindedness reminds us of D'Aubignac: indeed, in seventeenth-century criticism *bienséance* and *vraisemblance* often seem to be two sides of the same coin, recalling by turns moral and cognitive values, always within a perspective that is basically rhetorical.

However, Rapin does introduce some achievements and possibilities only hinted at in what we have seen so far. Out of eloquence, poetry, history, and philosophy he makes something like a quadrivium that is conceived along rhetorical lines. The categories that he applies to oratory – such as content and style, the intentions of the author, the character of the audience, considerations of time and place – pass readily into every one of the main divisions of his subject.

Poets have as their principal aim to please, though they must also be useful (Rapin is a great admirer of Horace). On the other hand, historians aim first for truth and instruction, as they go about – obviously a new application of the *res/verba* distinction – treating their broad subject-matter, which will be expressed in narrations, in portraits and character studies, and occasionally in set speeches. But they are not excused from giving pleasure: in their truth-telling they must take care not to let their presentations become tedious.

Rapin develops a similar line of thought when he takes up philosophy. He conceives of it in effect as a compendium of opinions and maxims that have been held and promoted by the members of the seven principal *sectes*. He sees his readers as distinguishing, judging, and selecting among all these views what is acceptable in the light of the best ['la plus belle'] of all philosophies, which is *savoir vivre*. This he defines, in an obvious extension of a leading rhetorical principle, as adapting oneself reasonably and freely to times, persons, and affairs at hand. Philosophical matters will not be treated technically: one will follow the example of Cicero, who always writes on such topics 'en homme de qualité'. Rapin achieves in his two volumes a little *summa*, reviewing effectively for his audience the contents of a general literary culture.

*

For several decades rhetoric had enjoyed the status of an architectonic art, assuming the task of defining, relating, teaching, and practising all of the genres of verbal expression (with side-effects and influences in the fine arts as well). However, in the 1680s it became increasingly plausible to argue that rhetoric had definite limits, that its claims to universal relevance could be challenged. As a matter of fact, we in turn, on reading Rapin's work, have the impression that a narrowing has taken place. Although it is broad in scope, his programme seems to address the interests of a particular class. He does not have a clear view of the earlier charter of rhetoric, when as a discipline it offered solutions to the situation and problems of the French nation as a whole.

Bernard Le Bovier de Fontenelle's *Digression sur les anciens et les modernes* (1688) gives a good indication of what is happening to the rhetorical ideal. Taking the side of the Moderns, he notes an important difference between the situation of the sciences and that of the arts. In the latter progress is limited – since the arts allegedly reach their point of perfection at a relatively early time – whereas in the physical, mathematical, and medical sciences, no limit is in sight. This is Fontenelle's first demotion of the arts.

The second is even more serious. He bases his argument on a distributive approach to the arts and sciences, assigning them in their diversity to particular faculties of the mind. Instead of associating eloquence and poetry with reason, as Boileau and others regularly did, he considers them to be essentially products of the imagination. Generally speaking, imagination did not enjoy a good press in seventeenth-century France; as a faculty it awakened suspicions, because it tended to substitute its fictions for true conceptions of the world around us. And that is just what Fontenelle wishes to stress: eloquence and poetry must be recognized as lacking in serious cognitive content, and therefore as irrelevant to scientific knowledge or theorizing. He reduces their role in practical life as well. In a monarchical regime such as that in France he thinks that eloquence has much less to do than it had in the great assemblies of antiquity; as for poetry, he simply says provocatively that it has never been of much use.

Charles Perrault in the four volumes of his *Parallèle des anciens et des modernes* (1688–97) carries this process of revision one step further. He works out in considerable detail a system of *belles-lettres* and *beaux arts*, in which eloquence and poetry are associated in their defining aspects with music, painting, sculpture, and architecture. In place of the leading role it formerly had, rhetoric takes on, in Perrault's scheme, the status of one among many arts, some literary, some plastic, some musical. And in turn, the proper territory of that ensemble is to be distinguished from the domains of logic, morals, metaphysics, and spectacularly success-ful modern sciences like mathematics, physics, astronomy, navigation, geography.

Indeed, as early as 1637, in the first section of the *Discours de la méthode*, René Descartes had somewhat respectfully but quite definitely dismissed poetics and rhetoric as being unnecessary arts. If one had the proper natural gifts, according to him, pleasing poems and convincing speeches would come without need for help from poetics or rhetoric. Twenty-five years later Arnauld and Nicole of Port-Royal continued this line of thought with their *Art de penser*, the concluding section of which introduced and extended the theme of intellectual method in a way reminiscent of Descartes. It is significant that, although Arnauld and Lancelot produced also an influential treatise of general grammar, that work lays the foundation not for a rhetoric but for the logic of Arnauld and Nicole. In the latter work logic and geometry, when suitably generalized, could take over the functions once assumed by the discipline of com-munication and persuasion. Blaise Pascal, in the fragmentary text that we know as 'De l'esprit géométrique', went so far as to lay the ground-work for an *art de persuader* that is explicitly an *art de démontrer*. In the *Provinciales* (1656–7) he made brilliant use of those principles as he attacked, on behalf of his Jansenist friends, the definitions, propositions, and arguments of the Jesuits.

There was, however, a second line of innovation in opposition to the rhetorical ideal, one essentially different from the projects of Port-Royal and Pascal. The developing sciences were highly technical; and if they were to gain wide acceptance, they had to learn what we have come to call *vulgarisation*. Descartes had shown one path to follow in his *Discours*, but Fontenelle turned out to be a master of this rhetorical mode. Curiously enough, he found a precedent and an example in Cicero, who appears in this new context not as the theoretician of universal eloquence but as the intermediary who managed to make the subtleties of Greek philo-sophy accessible to educated Roman readers. Fontenelle's *Entretiens sur la pluralité des mondes* (1686), of strict Cartesian inspiration but intended for a general audience, and his later series of *Eloges* of distinguished scientists – partly biographical and partly expository – are thus variations on the Ciceronian formula, though worked out in terms of seventeenth-century science rather than of philosophy. The *Entretiens*, by the way, were to lead directly to a remarkable work of rebuttal in the same popularizing genre – Voltaire's *Eléments de la philosophie newtonienne* (1738).

*

Actually, in a survey such as this we must take account of still another intellectual current that challenges the expansive rhetorical ideal with which we began. This movement is made up of thinkers concerned with religion and with theology. Pascal, again, and Jacques Bénigne Bossuet illustrate in their apologetic and didactic works what happens to rhetoric and, incidentally, to the discussion of literature, when they are placed in a strict Augustinian perspective. For them truth is not circumstantial, not dependent on *vraisemblance* and *bienséance*, nor yet a matter of scientific investigation and proof, but something found in the specific order of faith, where souls are engaged in a movement inward and upward in search of their author and end.

Although both Pascal and Bossuet must solve problems of persuasion and conversion and belief, any rhetoric that seeks to be independent and universally applicable cannot give satisfactory guidance. An art of persuasion must be for them – as, indeed, it was for the Cartesians – secondary, subordinate; but, setting aside the Cartesian solution, it seeks here its principles not in geometry but in Scripture and sacred theology. Recast and taken up into an integrative dialectic, rhetoric has a limited role to play in conveying religious truth to hearers and readers.

Once more, Pascal innovates. Although traces of his art of persuasion based on geometry may be found in the *Pensées*, he asserts there the primacy of the *ordre du cœur*, a discursive order that he sees in the Bible and in the works of Augustine. To paraphrase his view: this new procedure is essentially *digressive*; in Pascal's practice it starts from paradoxes found in Nature, human nature, and the Bible; however, the end, the *unifying end* of the discourse, is always kept in view. And there one must say that the proximate end is not really persuasion but a receptive attitude, while the ultimate and ever-present end is God, since the whole process is designed to prepare the reader for receiving gifts of faith and grace.

Bossuet is less anti-Ciceronian than Pascal; and he arrives at an adjustment of traditional rhetorical discipline that meets his requirements. His emphasis on divinely inspired truth makes invention in the usual sense unnecessary, and in fact a human intrusion to be avoided; his concentration on reaching the moral conscience of his hearers precludes any attempts to please their ears or to cause idle stirrings of their imaginations. He wants nothing to interfere with the process of absorbing the truth. Taking up an argument from Augustine, he does make a place for eloquence: instead of being a matter of artifice it arises out of the wisdom being communicated, it comes *à la suite de la sagesse*. Wisdom marches in front, followed by eloquence as a servant, as someone present but not summoned, *etiam non vocatam*.

*

To be complete, a treatment of the rhetorical ideal in France would have to deal with the discipline in at least four contexts: (1) in the changing scene of cultural life; (2) in the minds and habits of writers and artists; (3) in a formal analysis, designed to make explicit fruitful ambiguities of subject-matter and method; and (4) in an ensemble, more or less encyclopaedic, of arts and sciences. This essay has touched on matters in all four of those, but has treated mainly topics related to the second and the third. It has sought to suggest the actions and interactions of at least three families of minds: the convinced proponents of the rhetorical ideal, the enthusiastic promoters of the new sciences, and those for whom what counts above all is faith, grace, and religious commitment. As it was worked out in intrafamilial variations and interfamilial confrontations, rhetoric became involved in a complicated process, sometimes being rejected outright but more usually undergoing adaptations to new circumstances or assimilations to other intellectual techniques. In those vicissitudes, the basic discipline and the ideal growing out of it proved to be extraordinarily productive and provocative in France in the seventeenth century.

53

Cartesian aesthetics

Timothy J. Reiss

The title of this chapter may appear doubly anachronistic. On the one hand, the word *aesthetics* was first used by Alexander Gottlieb Baumgarten only in 1735. On the other, the philosophy of beauty and taste that it came to designate relates to a 'system of the arts' (literature, music, sculpture, architecture, painting centrally – with theatre and dance) that itself has been held not to have been established until well into the eighteenth century.[1] No doubt the elements, theory, and practice that constituted the system developed over many years. But it is not evident that they owe anything very specific to 'Cartesianism' – let alone to René Descartes – and terms like 'Cartesian aesthetics' have mostly meant vague ideas about the adoption of certain concepts as source of inspiration and artistic guide. The intention of this chapter is quite different. First, it will show that sixteenth-century debates in what were once the sciences of the quadrivium raised most of the issues basic to what we now call aesthetics. Second, it will show that Descartes picked up these issues, giving them large place in his work: whence they became typical of debate about art in his time. So it will propose, thirdly, that the meaning of later aesthetic argument is seen more clearly through this Cartesian lens. In the eighteenth century Descartes's greatest impact may well have been in aesthetics. He 'was not a man of letters', wrote Edward Gibbon in 1761, 'but literature is under deep obligation to him'.[2]

Descartes's first ordered work was his 1618 *Compendium musicae*, as much about art as about science or philosophy. After finishing his liberal arts, he turned first to law in his search for a well-grounded knowledge, then to music and the mathematics in which its study was based. They were in fact perfect bridges from letters to the 'marvellous science' whose discovery he foresaw in winter 1619. For by the late sixteenth century, music and its theory sat in the midst of the arts and sciences. Still principal among mathematical sciences, from the fifteenth-century rediscovery

---

[1] For this last, see Paul Oskar Kristeller, 'The modern system of the arts', in *Renaissance thought II: papers on humanism and the arts* (New York: Harper & Row, 1965), pp. 163–227.

[2] Edward Gibbon, *Essay on the study of literature* [1761], in *The miscellaneous works of Edward Gibbon*, ed. John, Lord Sheffield (London: Blake, 1837), p. 633.

of many ancient writers on music, it had accumulated other questions. Primary were the effort to understand the nature of Greek music and elaborate a mathematics enabling a rational comprehension of modes, harmony, pitch, tunings, and the rest. Beyond these, three more were of essential interest.

Ancient writers were unanimous that music had manipulatable effects on its hearers. Although sixteenth-century writers agreed that modern music gave no evidence of such miraculous effects as those claimed for ancient music (even as they endlessly reiterated them), they were obsessed with finding, mathematically if possible, how music affected its hearers. The affecting was not casual. It involved the motion of the soul's passions, related to humours and temperaments. So the obsession was tied to debates about *catharsis* and imitation. They wondered what it meant to call music mimetic, what 'representation' was in question. Lastly, linking these issues, they fought over the relation between words and music. By century's end most agreed that music should affect its public by capturing mood, temper, rhythm, and meaning of the verse it set. Claudio Monteverdi became celebrated for his achievement in this regard.

If music affected its hearers in some comprehensible way, and if the relations called notes, tuning, pitch, and rhythm could be expressed mathematically, did this not mean that the affecting was not just rational, but quantifiable? There was no disjunction, *pace* most commentators, in Descartes's starting a mathematical treatise on music theory by saying: 'Finis, vt delectet, variosque in nobis moveat affectus' ['its aim is to please, and to move in us divers affections/passions']. This will prove a new version of Horatian *delectare* and *prodesse*. Nor was it odd that he went on to write of sympathetic vibrations and arousal of passions, of senses and their pleasure, and of proportionality between object and related sense.[3] These were familiar – as Descartes emphasized by echoing a well-known comment on art at the start of his science: 'Since art came from nature, it would rightly be held to have done nothing if it neither moved nature nor gave pleasure' ['nisi naturam moveat ac delectet'].[4] Cicero spoke of eloquence, but generalized the issue. Descartes knowingly set his *Compendium* between 'art' and 'science'.

Music remained embedded in advancing mathematical sciences. From technical and practical calculation, abstracted and generalized, a demonstrative logic would come. As practice and tool for organizing thought and knowledge, mathematics were ever more foundational. In 1492, Franchino

---

[3] René Descartes, *Compendium musicae*, in *Œuvres*, ed. C. Adam and P. Tannery, 2nd edn, 11 vols. (Paris: Vrin/CNRS, 1974–86), vol. x, pp. 89–92.

[4] Marcus Tullius Cicero, *De oratore*, ed. and trans. E. W. Sutton, completed H. Rackham, 2 vols. (1942; reprint Cambridge, MA: Harvard University Press; London: Heinemann, 1967–8), vol. II, p. 156 (III.1.197: author's trans.).

Gaffurio devoted over half his hugely influential *Theorica musice* to numerical debate, on the old ground of universal harmony being ruled by numerical ratios.[5] His 1496 *Practica musice* gave new ground. The second and fourth books treated mensural music and rhythmic notation. Book II's first chapter analysed poetic metre and rhythm: both 'poets and musicians' assign time values and give them symbols.[6] Rhythm, he quoted Aristides Quintilianus, 'consists of times in space', and must be understood as 'measured composition grasped not by metrical theory but by the number of syllables as judged by the ear . . . Rhythm, indeed, seems quite similar to metre. Yet it cannot exist by itself without metre. For metre is theory with measure, rhythm is measure without theory.'[7]

Gaffurio's expansion of familiar theory of rhythmic notation was in some ways novel: metrics as both theoretical and practical; rhythm as rational measure *and* its understanding. Still newer was his extension of the rules of proportion. Traditionally these were limited to pitch and consonance. Gaffurio applied them to rhythmic measurement and notation: 'We propose a double understanding of musical proportion: first in disposition of sound by consonant intervals (which is matter for the theorist), second in temporal quantity of those same sounds by numbers of notation: which is thought an active or practical question.'[8] He elaborated especially on proportions of musical rhythm, without ignoring those of pitch, essential as they were thought to be to relations between music (and poetry) and human passions. Familiar from antiquity, the idea was becoming central to the search for a rational aesthetics.

In his *Theorica*, Gaffurio clearly expressed the old idea that musical training was needed 'for moderating the motions of the soul under rule and reason' ['sub regula rationeque']. Only 'motions of the soul ['motus animi'] . . . that agree with reason belong to the right harmony of life' ['qui rationi conveniunt ad rectam uitae pertinent harmoniam'].[9] Like others, Gaffurio showed especially in his 1518 *De harmonia musicorum instrumentum opus* (written by 1500) how music harmonized the soul by exact mathematical proportions; the 'emanations' or vibrations striking the senses and through them the mind marking that relation of mind and body. A field opened to be exploited through the century.

In 1529 Lodovico Fogliano tied calculus to sense perception in another way, defining consonance less by ratio than hearing. It 'is a mingling of

[5] Franchino Gaffurio, *Theorica musice*, intro. G. Vecchi (1492; facs. reprint Bologna: Forni, 1969), fols. [cvi^v]-di^r (II.6).
[6] Franchino Gaffurio, *Practica musice*, intro. G. Vecchi (1496; facs. reprint Bologna: Forni, 1972), fol. aai^r (II.1).
[7] *Ibid.*, fol. aaii^r (II.1).
[8] *Practica*, fol. [eevi^v] (IV.1). Ann E. Moyer, *Musica scientia: musical scholarship in the Italian Renaissance* (Ithaca: Cornell University Press, 1992), pp. 75–8.
[9] *Theorica*, fol. a[v]^r (I.1).

two sounds distant by height and depth pleasing to the ears; and dissonance, the contrary of consonance, is the mingling of two sounds distant by height and depth displeasing to the ears'.[10] Sound was generated by motion of air. Neither air, nor body, nor motion, it was, rather, an affective quality existing as such only in and for the ear: *passibilis qualitas* – able to touch a *passionem*. Gaffurio had discussed sound's nature at length in the *Theorica*, leaving the issue in doubt but agreeing that sense and reason were judges of its effect. He found reason superior: 'Just as ear is affected by sounds or eye by sight, so mind's judgement is affected by numbers or continuous quantity'.[11] Forty years on, Fogliano insisted on primacy of sense experience and yet returned to numerical ratios and Euclidian geometry. Sound was *not* number, but its motion and rational effect might be described *by* number.

Girolamo Cardano also held music's effect on the emotions to depend not on proportion but on how we *perceive* proportion. 'It is sufficiently clear from our discussions of beauty', he wrote in the 1574 *De musica*, 'that the simplest proportion is the most pleasing to the ears'.[12] In his 1559 *De subtilitate*, he opined:

every sense especially enjoys things which are recognized; those recognized things are called consonance when heard, beauty when seen. So, what is beauty? A thing perfectly recognized; for we cannot love things which are not recognized. Vision perceives those things that stand in simple proportions: duple, triple, quadruple, sesquialtera, sesquitertia . . . Certainly there is delight in recognition, sadness in non-recognition. Further, things are not recognized when they are imperfect and obscure; they are boundless, confused, and indeterminate. Those things are boundless that cannot be known; therefore the imperfect cannot delight, nor be beautiful. Thus, whatever is commensurate is beautiful, and wont to delight.[13]

All depends on perception, on *knowing* and *how* one knows. Nor did Cardano by chance use as his standard of beauty simple musical proportions: octave (2:1), octave and a fifth (3:1), double octave (4:1), fifth (3:2) and fourth (4:3). Taking Fogliano's views with Cardano's, one could hope to describe such perception of proportions mathematically. Since proportions might be experimentally measured in the air's motion, and since the given perception *is* Fogliano's *passibilis qualitas*, one might expect a

[10] Lodovico Fogliano, *Musica theorica* (1529; reprint New York: Broude, 1969), fol. xv[r] (Sect. II.2). Moyer, *Musica scientia*, p. 144, and Claude V. Palisca, *Humanism in Italian Renaissance musical thought* (New Haven: Yale University Press, 1985), pp. 20–1.

[11] Gaffurio, *Theorica*, fol. c[v][v] (II.4).

[12] Hieronymus Cardanus, *On music*, in *Writings on music*, ed. and trans. C. A. Miller (n.p.: American Institute of Musicology, 1973), p. 73 (ch. 1).

[13] Quoted and trans., Moyer, *Musica scientia*, pp. 161–2.

measure of emotive effect, of that proportionality between object and affected sense to which Descartes would refer. Clearly, too, the *perceiver* was increasingly important for understanding how a work of art might mean and have beauty. Here some mention must be made of another area of artistic concern where like conclusions had been reached.

Before music, painting faced like pressures. Slow development of perspective effects throughout the thirteenth and fourteenth centuries, in Cimabue, Giotto, the Lorenzettis, and Filippo Brunelleschi's early fifteenth-century experiments, peaked in Leon Battista Alberti's *De pictura* (c. 1435). It gave mathematical and geometrical rules of perspective. Alberti also argued that not size but 'historia' most 'satisfied the intellect'. *Historia* named a pleasing ordering of planes rendering bodies and their relations to express story and emotion. The best *historia* 'captivates the eye of the learned or unlearned spectator with delight and motion of the soul' ['cum voluptate et animi motu']. It must have abundance and variety, yet such simplicity and clarity as tragic and comic poets achieve with their few characters. When those painted show 'motion of the soul ['animi motum'], then will *historia* move spectators' souls ['animos deinde spectantium movebit historia'] . . . These motions of soul are known from motions of body.'[14]

Geometrical perspective rules were specifically bound to the goal of moving the soul's passions: those 'motions of the soul, that the learned call affections, like anger, grief, joy, fear, desire, and others of the sort'. Painters will learn these from experience and by associating with 'poets and orators'.[15] They express these passions in perspective painting whose *historia* conforms to the rules of pleasing beauty noted more precisely elsewhere as: 'a form of sympathy and consonance of the parts within a body, according to definite number, outline and position, as dictated by *concinnitas*, the absolute and fundamental rule of Nature'.[16] One can hardly miss how similar the definition is to Cardano's – or how perspective gave priority to the fixed place of the *observer*'s eye as music theory eventually emphasized the listener's role.

Alberti's work was followed by Leonardo's and by Piero della Francesca's *De prospectiva pingendi* (1470–80), which specified the spectator's eye as first element in perspective. Piero wrote two geometry

[14] Leon Battista Alberti, *On painting and sculpture: the Latin texts of 'De pictura' and 'De statua'*, ed. with trans., intro., and notes by C. Grayson (London: Phaidon, 1972), pp. 72, 78, 80. The more exact translation is confirmed by Alberti's 1436 Italian text: *Della pittura*, ed. L. Mallè (Florence: Sansoni, 1950).
[15] Alberti, *On painting*, pp. 82 ('motus . . . animorum, quos docti affectiones noncupant, ut ira, dolor, gaudium, timor, desiderium et eiusmodi'), 94.
[16] Leon Battista Alberti, *On the art of building in ten books*, trans. J. Rykwert, N. Leach, and R. Tavernor (Cambridge, MA and London: MIT Press, 1988), p. 303 (IX.v).

treatises widely influential due to their unacknowledged inclusion in two works by Luca Pacioli. Pacioli introduced Alberti's and Piero's perspective work to Albrecht Dürer – who published his own in 1525.[17] The title page of Pacioli's mathematical work, the *Divina proportione*, dedicated it to 'students of philosophy, perspective, painting, sculpture, architecture, music, and other mathematical matters'. Pacioli also contributed to the mathematics of music. These connections clearly matter. Painting and music were now held to have mathematically analysable effects on spectator and listener. Pietro Bembo implied that the effects of poetry might be treated similarly: its *gravità* and *piacevolezza* [pleasingness] depended on 'il suono, il numero, la variazione' ['sound, number, variation'].[18] By the late fifteenth century, even more by the 1540s, these arguments would inevitably be linked to Aristotelian *mimesis* and *catharsis*.

No less than painting or poetry, music achieved its effect by imitation. Already in 1489 Marsilio Ficino urged one to 'remember that song is a most powerful imitator of all things. It imitates the intentions and passions of the soul as well as words; it represents also people's physical gestures, motions, and actions as well as their characters [*mores*] and imitates all these and acts them out so forcibly that it immediately provokes both the singer and the audience to imitate and act out the same things'.[19] Cardano drew from the *Poetics* the kinds of *mimesis* of 'artistic music' – 'manner [*modus*], sense [*sensus*], and sound [*sonus*]' – the last two corresponding to Aristotle's object and medium. He added music's 'expiative and purgative force' by its arousal of 'strong emotions' and passions ('humility and pride, excitement and calm, joy and sorrow, and cruelty and tenderness').[20] Discussion of imitation easily shaded into that of *catharsis*.

Arguments about *what* was being imitated and *how* merged with those about effect. Music, art, and poetry moved by affecting the passions. Music, Louis Le Caron wrote, 'educates manners, softens anger, calms irritations, and tempers ill-ordered passions'. It has the 'virtue of tempering and tuning *les afections de l'ame*'. The 'wondrous effects of music' are such, added Pontus de Tyard, that 'passions are moved and calmed by its sweet ravishments'. Music 'tunes the affections, passions and corporeal and intellectual powers one with another, and does for the Soul's dissonances what purgation or correction of superfluous humours does for the

[17] Albrecht Dürer, *The painter's manual*, trans. with comm. by W. L. Strauss (New York: Abaris, 1977).
[18] Pietro Bembo, *Prose della volgar lingua* [1525], in *Prose e rima*, ed. C. Dionisotti (Turin: Unione Tipografico-Editrice Torinese, 1966), p. 146.
[19] Marsilio Ficino, *Three books on life [De triplici vita]*, ed. and trans. C. V. Kaske and J. R. Clark (Binghamton: Medieval and Renaissance Texts and Studies, 1989), pp. 358–9 (III.xxi).
[20] Cardanus, *On music*, pp. 142 (ch. 36), 102 (ch. 18), 150 (ch. 39).

restitution of health'.[21] Like everyone, Le Caron and Tyard emphasized that number and measure attained these effects, no less in poetic rhythm and metre than in musical rhythm and harmony.

Mimesis had been retuned by these debates as expressive relation between artist, artwork, and recipient. Effects were achieved because the well-ordered work 'imitated' consonances of the soul. What was expressed and gave pleasure was sympathetic vibration of the soul's passions. In a way, *mimesis* became less important. What was imitated might be actions and feelings, but just as they *moved* similar effects in the receiver. The tempering of which so many spoke did not simply *have*, but *was* a moral effect. *Prodesse* and *delectare* coincided. To say that art's goal was to please presupposed both beneficent effect and ruled order making such pleasing and effect possible. The tuning of the soul thus accorded with all the claims of (mathematical) reason.

Reason and emotion met, regarding music, in Gioseffo Zarlino, whose *Istitutioni harmoniche* (1558) had vast impact: including on Descartes. Averring music's rationality, he asserted that emotional effect (Fogliano's *passibilis qualitas?*) was achieved by a mixture of harmony, metre, and companion text. Emphasizing music's 'certezza' and 'primo grado di verità' (from its place in mathematical science), he also urged that music's centrality came from its rational accord with human and natural harmonies: 'for nature consists in such proportion and temperament that every like joys in like and desires it'. Music's purpose is 'to give pleasure and delight to hearing', simply to perfect that sense, as sight is perfected when it perceives 'a beautiful and proportionate thing' ['vna cosa bella & proportionata']. Music may seek first to please, but that aim is inseparable from its rational rule, which 'disposes the soul to virtue and rules its passions' ['dispone l'animo alla virtù, & regola le sue passioni']. It 'accustoms [the soul] to rejoice and grieve virtuously, disposing it to virtuous habits'.[22]

Objects are pleasing [*grati*] and smooth [*suavi*] to the proper sense [*propio sentimento*] as they are proportionate [*proportionati*] to it. Just so, 'musical science . . . treats sounds and tones [*voci*] which are the proper objects of hearing. It analyses only the harmony [*concento*] . . . born from pitches [*chorde*] and tones [*voci*], and considers nothing else at all.'[23] Whether or not Zarlino was playing on *propio* and *proportionati*, he was assuredly connecting proportionality of object to sense with the internal mathematico-musical proportions his treatise examined at length. Descartes

[21] Louis Le Caron, *Les dialogues*, ed. J. A. Buhlmann and D. Gilman (Geneva: Droz, 1986), pp. 255 ('Valton', Dialogue III), 278 ('Ronsard', Dialogue IV); Pontus de Tyard, *Solitaire second*, ed. C. M. Yandell (Geneva: Droz, 1980), pp. 171, 238. Author's translations.
[22] Gioseffo Zarlino, *Le istitutioni harmoniche* (1558; reprint New York: Broude, 1965), pp. 4 (I.1), 8 (I.3).
[23] *Ibid.*, p. 278 (III.71).

took up these two proportionalities in the guiding Praenotanda opening his treatise: 'the object in which difference of parts is least is more easily perceived by a sense' . . . 'we say that parts of a whole object differ less among themselves according as the proportion between them is greater'.[24] His treatise analysed the latter as they concern rhythm and consonance. But he also always insisted on 'proportionality' between a sense and its proper object.

'All the senses', he wrote, 'are capable of some pleasure [*delectatio*].' 'For this pleasure a certain proportion [*proportio quaedam*] is needed of the object with the sense in question. It follows, for instance, that the crashing of muskets or of thunder seems unfit for music, since it evidently damages the ears just as the excessive brightness of the sun looked at directly damages the eyes.' He drew this example from Zarlino, who had followed his remark about objects being *grati* and *suavi* to the *propio sentimento* with the contrary case: that of 'our eye, damaged by looking at the sun, because such an object is not proportionate to it'.[25] Descartes added in his third Praenotandum that 'an object must be such as to fall on the sense with neither too much difficulty nor confusedly'. It is better that 'lines' of an object be more 'equal' than overly complex. Simplicity and clarity of visible line applied no less to musical organization of sound: arithmetical rather than geometrical proportions, because the differences are everywhere equal and tire the senses less.[26]

Zarlino singled out Fogliano as alone having truly understood and analysed musical proportions.[27] Like him, he urged that the rational, mathematically analysable relationship enabling music to affect humours and move passions was so by virtue of proportional relations *within* the object (sound) and of similarly 'proportional' relations *between* object and sense (ear). These proportionalities made music pleasing, an imitation (of nature and the passions), and able to affect the recipient. As Salomon de Caus put it in 1615: 'Music is a science by which is made a disposition of low and high notes, "*proportionables*" among themselves and separated by just intervals, by which sense and reason are satisfied'.[28] Music as a mathematically orientated science was validated by its satisfaction of sense and reason. Contrariwise, the reason for such satisfaction was the mathematical order embedding it. Descartes's *Compendium* did not originate this rationalist claim, but embodied and focused it, enabling his later work to generalize it.

---

[24] Descartes, *Compendium*, in *Œuvres*, ed. Adam and Tannery, vol. x, p. 91 (Praenotanda 4 and 5).
[25] *Ibid.* (Praenotanda 1 and 2); Zarlino, *Istitutioni*, p. 278.
[26] *Ibid.* (Praenotanda 6).   [27] Zarlino, *Istitutioni*, p. 279.
[28] Salomon de Caus, *Institution harmonique, divisee en deux parties* (Frankfurt: J. Norton, 1615), fol. 2^v.

As we recall that Descartes, like Zarlino, Cardano, and others, made it a first point to emphasize that the objective of music – art – was to please, we must also recall that that pleasure was both rational and moral. It retuned the passions. The well-tempered soul would act in accord with prudence, justice, temperance, and wisdom. Descartes was equally taken by these antique virtues. That is no doubt why he, like Alberti, referred first to the effects achieved by 'authors of elegies and tragedies', and why like contemporaries he insisted that 'proportionality' eased reception and effect of art. Thus, musical beat is indicated by bars so that

> we can more easily perceive all the parts of a composition and be pleased by the 'proportions' that must be in them. Such proportion is used so very often in the parts of a composition to help our *apprehension* in such a way that when we hear the end, we remember at that very time what was at the beginning and in the rest of the composition.

This occurs because *nostra imaginatio* easily combines the simple successive proportions marked by bars.[29]

Likewise, tones between consonances make the passage between such consonances easier on the listener, for too great a disproportion 'would tire auditors and singers'.[30] This need to ease the recipient's internalizing of the artwork explains Jean Mairet's and others' demand that theatre not strain the imagination and memory by jumping spatial and temporal barriers or by not using the three rules of unity.[31] It explains John Denham's requirement, as he apostrophized the Thames, that form not obstruct thought: 'O could I flow like thee, and make thy stream / My great example, as it is my theme! / Though deep, yet clear, though gentle, yet not dull, / Strong without rage, without ore-flowing full.' Depth with clarity, variety without confusion, interest with pleasure – so many familiar themes. He wrote these lines in 1655. Forty years later John Dryden, dedicating the *Aeneid*, made them a 'test of poetic insight'.[32] The need not to impede emotional effect by overworking memory and imagination explains Dominique Bouhours's belief in clarity and 'transparency' of language ('Fine [*beau*] language resembles pure, clean water without taste') and like views held by almost all.[33] Such transparency, simplicity, clarity, and regularity had laws as exact as those of geometry.

Its aim, Boileau's colleague, René Rapin pointed out in 1674, was to 'shake the soul with such natural and such human motions [that] all the

---

[29] *Compendium*, *Œuvres*, ed. Adam and Tannery, vol. X, pp. 89, 93–4.
[30] *Ibid.*, pp. 112, 115.
[31] Jean Mairet, preface to *Sylvanire*, ed. R. Otto (Bamberg: Buchner, 1890), pp. 16–17.
[32] Sir John Denham, *The poetical works*, ed. T. H. Banks, 2nd edn (New Haven: Yale University Press, 1969), pp. 77, 54.
[33] Dominique Bouhours, *Les entretiens d'Ariste et d'Eugène* [1671], ed. F. Brunot (Paris: A. Colin, 1962), pp. 37, 34.

impressions it receives please it'.[34] Descartes said little else. A slow beat rouses 'slow' passions – 'languor, sadness, fear, pride, and such' – a fast beat such passions as joy. 'A more precise treatise on the matter', he added, 'depends on an exquisite knowledge of the motions of the soul', on which he was not yet ready to expand, although knowledge of them was wholly necessary fully to understand and produce musical effects.[35] Insisting, too, that the simpler the melody the greater the effect, he again echoed the view of many before him.

He drew exactly on this to analyse Jean-Louis Guez de Balzac's letters in 1628. 'Purity of language', he wrote, is like 'health in the human body'. Language is 'more excellent as it leaves no impression on the senses'. The beauty of such writing is 'in the harmony and temper of the whole' ['in omnium tali consensu & temperamento']. He spoke of elegance and variety, of 'dignity' of phrase and match between thought and form, of its origin 'in zeal for truth and wealth of common sense' ['ex zelo veritatis & sensûs abundantiâ'].[36] In letters to Marin Mersenne from November 1629 into early 1630, Descartes returned to music – and language. Both, he thought, could satisfy the demand that they be universal, both held the possibility of an emotive and imaginative response according to specifiable rule. These were the years when he was writing the *Regulae* and beginning the *Géométrie*. These letters seem to express doubts: taste is individual and cannot be gauged; consonances have no qualities commensurable with the passions; the beautiful may have no common measure since it depends on individual taste, itself related to particular experience and memory.[37]

All this may seem diametrically opposed to the *Compendium* and the letter on Balzac. It shows, rather, a deepening of the debate. The comprehension of beauty is indeterminable for any individual: although we may *call* 'the most beautiful' what pleases most people. This is not radically subjectivist (as some have suggested), but part of the effort to adjust rule and passion, particular experience and universal humanity. For general rules are no good unless they enable 'one's understanding to show the will the choice it must make'.[38] Such rules bridge understanding and action, imagination and practice. They will be extremely simple, and will show us how and why (*modus* and *ratio*) a given object is 'measurable'.[39] The impress of earlier work remains clear. Indeed, the *Regulae* and later the

---

[34] René Rapin, *Réflexions sur la poétique d'Aristote, et sur les ouvrages des poètes anciens et modernes* (Paris: François Muguet, 1674), pp. 173–4.

[35] *Compendium, Œuvres*, ed. Adam and Tannery, vol. x, pp. 95, 111.

[36] René Descartes, *Œuvres*, ed. Adam and Tannery, vol. i, pp. 7–9.

[37] *Ibid.*, vol. i, pp. 76–80 (20 November 1629); pp. 86, 96 (18 December 1629); pp. 106–9 (January 1630); pp. 126–7 (4 March 1630); pp. 132–5 (18 March 1630).

[38] *Ibid.*, vol. x, p. 361 (Regula i). For 'the most beautiful', see *Œuvres*, vol. i, p. 133.

[39] *Ibid.*, vol. x, p. 447 (Regula xiv).

Passions de l'âme, whatever their particular goals, responded to this early search to balance rule against experience, to explain the effects of art, to understand how aesthetic pleasure operates, and what it is that we may call the beautiful.

These issues and debates have been thought predominant only much later. But the sixteenth-century hope for a quantification of *mimesis* and *catharsis* clearly gave later aesthetic enquiry its root and branches. Endless seventeenth- and eighteenth-century writers called for artistic rules as trustworthy as Euclid's *Geometry*, to understand art's pleasing purpose: the rules of aesthetic pleasure matched general human emotional possibility. In 1741, Yves-Marie André noted how 'essential beauty' depended on a 'natural geometry' of symmetry, order, regularity, and proportion, the whole demanding 'unity', but characterized by 'brilliance' and 'diversity'. It works on the 'order of ideas in our minds', and 'feelings in our hearts' (read 'souls').[40] This was not aberrant. It returns us to Gibbon and universal Enlightenment claim.

[40] Yves-Marie André, *Essai sur le beau*, in *Œuvres philosophiques*, ed. V. Cousin (1843; reprint Geneva: Slatkine, 1969), pp. 5–6, 29.

54

Principles of judgement: probability, decorum, taste, and the *je ne sais quoi*

Michael Moriarty

The notion of *vraisemblance* [probability], which is in some sense the keystone of French neoclassical poetics, has both a technical content, indicating to the poet how to secure the audience's engagement with the text, and a more ideological content, referring to the social and moral ideas in virtue of which the work will be judged. It is the latter sense that is dealt with here.

The link between the notion of *vraisemblance*, as a criterion of artistic validity, and ethical judgements appears in Georges de Scudéry's statement, apropos of Corneille's *Le Cid*, that, although the historical original of Chimène did in fact marry the Cid, 'it is not probable that an honourable maiden should marry her father's murderer'.[1] He is here using the term 'vraisemblable' to denote the realm of general truth (as distinct from particular historical truth), which Aristotle identifies as the object of poetry.[2] The Académie Française agreed with this: the poet's task is to purify his material of the dross of historical contingency, in keeping with 'the universal idea of things':[3] he is to consider what is proper for a young woman in general rather than what Chimène actually did, and because her behaviour belies 'the moral propriety ['la bienséance des mœurs'] of a young woman presented at first as virtuous', it offends *vraisemblance*.[4] (This looks like an accusation of inconsistency rather than impropriety. But the Académie's term for inconsistency is 'inégalité'.[5]) In other words, the question, for these critics, is not whether Corneille has *made* Chimène's behaviour credible: it is intrinsically incredible.

The Académie's pronouncement in its *Sentiments [. . .] sur la tragicomédie du Cid* exhibits the intimate link between the neoclassical concept of *vraisemblance* and that of *bienséance* [decorum]: what it is *probable* a character will do is what is *appropriate* for him or her.[6]

[1] Georges de Scudéry, *Observations sur 'Le Cid'*, in *La querelle du Cid: pièces et pamphlets*, ed. Armand Gasté (Paris: H. Walter, 1898), p. 76.

[2] Aristotle, *Poetics* IX.1–5 (1451a–1451b), in *Aristotle, 'The poetics', 'Longinus', 'On the Sublime', Demetrius, 'On style'*, ed. W. H. Fyfe and W. R. Roberts (Cambridge, MA: Harvard University Press; London: Heinemann, 1927).

[3] Gasté (ed.), *La querelle du Cid* p. 366.   [4] *Ibid.*, p. 365.   [5] *Ibid.*, pp. 372, 390.

[6] Gérard Genette, 'Vraisemblance et motivation', in *Figures II* (Paris: Seuil, 1969), pp. 71–99 (see esp. pp. 71–4).

The link is stressed also by Hippolyte-Jules Pilet de La Mesnardière in his *Poëtique* of 1640. He distinguishes 'ordinary probability' and 'rare probability'. The former is based on the qualities, natural or accidental, manifested in people's habitual actions. The latter covers what sometimes happens against expectation: say, the defeat of a skilful warrior by one less skilful. The former is preferable.[7] He links 'ordinary probability' with Aristotle's concept of 'appropriateness' in characterization (*Poetics* xv.4 (1454a)). Characters should be represented with the qualities that go with their age, passions, current situation, rank, nation, and gender. National and gender traits are listed by La Mesnardière in considerable detail. Unless the action of the play imperatively requires it, a woman should not be depicted as brave, or learned, or a servant as judicious.[8]

The question, then, is how what is probable, and/or fitting, is determined. We have seen already that the term 'probable' is often used to designate what is generally true. But it is also used by seventeenth-century theorists in the sense of what is generally accepted. Thus, in René Rapin's concise formula, 'the probable is all that conforms to public opinion'.[9] It is not easy to see how this is to be reconciled with the former view, which Rapin also holds.[10] Thus Rapin undercuts the ideal of characterization based on nature, on the carefully observed movements of the human heart, by stating that since the human heart is profoundly mysterious, one should attempt to 'speak of character in accordance with public opinion'.[11] What this means is that the notion of *vraisemblance* can exercise a pragmatic function of ideological censorship in confirming 'public opinion', or even a set of stereotypes equated with public opinion, reinforcing on the imaginary level the power-relationships of everyday life.[12] The requirement that women should be represented as vain, timid, and flighty[13] is a case in point. There is a literary agenda here, to condemn the Italian epic (Ariosto and Tasso) for its faulty representation of gender (of women as immodest or as heroic),[14] and, more broadly, to censor the

---

[7] Hippolyte-Jules Pilet de La Mesnardière, *La poëtique* (1640; reprint Geneva: Slatkine Reprints, 1972), pp. 35–40. Compare Aristotle, *Poetics* xxv.29 (1461b).

[8] La Mesnardière, *Poëtique*, pp. 119–38. Compare Jean Chapelain, *Opuscules critiques*, ed. A. C. Hunter (Paris: Droz, 1936), p. 130; Pierre Corneille, 'Discours du poème dramatique', in *Œuvres complètes*, ed. G. Couton, 3 vols. (Paris: Gallimard, 1980–7), vol. III, p. 131; René Rapin, *Réflexions sur la poétique de ce temps*, ed. E. T. Dubois (Geneva: Droz, 1970), p. 44.

[9] Rapin, *Réflexions*, ed. Dubois p. 39; compare François Hédelin, abbé d'Aubignac, *La pratique du théâtre*, ed. P. Martino (Algiers: Carbonel; Paris: Edouard Champion, 1927), p. 76.

[10] Rapin, *Réflexions*, ed. Dubois, p. 41. On these discrepancies, see Aron Kibédi Varga, 'La vraisemblance: problèmes de terminologie, problèmes de poétique', in *Critique et création littéraires en France au XVIIᵉ siècle* (Paris: Editions du CNRS, 1977), pp. 325–32.

[11] Rapin, *Réflexions*, ed. Dubois, pp. 43–4.

[12] See Aron Kibédi Varga, *Les poétiques du classicisme* (Paris: Aux Amateurs de Livres, 1990), p. 40; compare Genette, 'Vraisemblance et motivation', p. 73.

[13] Rapin, *Réflexions*, ed. Dubois, p. 42.   [14] *Ibid.*, p. 43.

Baroque delight in the unexpected which the image of the female hero serves to gratify.[15] But one should not ignore the extra-literary effect of such representations. In fact, the theoretical interest of the concepts of *vraisemblance* and *bienséance* lies partly in the way in which literature and life can interpenetrate within them.

For *bienséance* can also denote 'decency' or 'propriety' as determined by the audience's sensibilities. Corneille uses the term when he observes that his audience would find a representation of incestuous passion revolting.[16] And the useful distinction is sometimes drawn between this latter kind of 'external' *bienséance* and the former 'internal' kind (conformity between a character's actions and his or her 'nature').[17] But to the extent that this latter kind is viewed as determined by public opinion, the distinction tends to collapse, and what is fitting in the sense of conforming to the nature of a character is often difficult to distinguish from what is fitting in the sense of conforming to the audience's morality.

Sometimes, in a third sense, the term *bienséance* seems to refer to the overall coherence of a representation, as when Nicolas Perrot d'Ablancourt states that 'the mixture of the serious and the ridiculous has something monstrous about it which infringes *bienséance*'.[18] Likewise, it is invoked by Jean-Louis Guez de Balzac in his critique of Daniel Heinsius's *Herodes infanticida*, to condemn the inclusion of pagan elements (the Furies) in a story from sacred history.[19]

Judgements of *bienséance*, then, sometimes appeal purely to extra-literary moral or social criteria, sometimes are subtly combined with literary judgements. Jean-Baptiste-Henri de Valincour remarks that the reader's pleasure in *La Princesse de Clèves* is spoiled by the thought that the hero, the duc de Nemours, has behaved in a way unsuited 'not just to the great nobleman he is, but to any private gentleman'.[20] What counts here is that the perceived infringement of ethical assumptions about nobility violates what Valincour asserts is a generic requirement of the historical novella: that the reader should be attached to the principal characters.[21]

---

[15] See Ian Maclean, *Woman triumphant: feminism in French literature, 1610–52* (Oxford: Clarendon Press, 1977), pp. 64–87.

[16] Corneille, *Rodogune*, 'Appian Alexandrin', in *Œuvres complètes*, vol. II, p. 196; and compare p. 202.

[17] René Bray, *La formation de la doctrine classique en France*, new edn (Paris: Nizet, 1961), p. 216.

[18] Nicolas Perrot d'Ablancourt, *Lettres et préfaces critiques*, ed. R. Zuber (Paris: Didier, 1972), p. 215.

[19] Jean-Louis Guez de Balzac, *Œuvres*, 2 vols. (Paris: Thomas Jolly and Louis Billaine, 1665), vol. II, pp. 534–8.

[20] Jean-Baptiste-Henri du Trousset de Valincour, *Lettres à Madame la Marquise *** sur le sujet de 'La Princesse de Clèves'*, ed. A. Cazes (Paris: Bossard, 1925), p. 203.

[21] *Ibid.*, pp. 225–6.

Bienséance is not always seen as determined by public opinion. Certain writers reject public opinion as a criterion, and invoke instead a minority 'good taste'. We find the term coming into play in the 1630s: Guez de Balzac helped to give it currency.[22] But it receives fullest attention after around 1660.

Taste is usually distinguished from the operations of the reason, although the findings of taste are often held to be in accordance with the dictates of the reason.[23] Thus Antoine Gombaud, chevalier de Méré, distinguishes two kinds of *justesse* (rightness, right judgement): one deals with matters of taste and sentiment, the other with logical relationships.[24] The domain where these faculties are authoritative is the *bienséances*, but they also regulate all kinds of pleasure ['agréments'].[25] But if this is so they should apply to literature as well, as an aspect of social life, rather than an autonomous field, with its own distinctive norms. And indeed taste, for Méré, is a faculty that pertains to the ideal figure of the *honnête homme*, defined by him as one who would be the perfect courtier in the perfect court.[26] By stressing the role of training and discipline in the formation of taste, Méré ties the quality closely to the needs and values of polite society.[27] *Honnêteté*, moreover, is universal, and overrides any knowledge pertaining to a particular field. Thus, the vision of literature conveyed in this discourse of taste is in direct conflict with that put forward by the professional men of letters, the rule-givers, encountered elsewhere: 'Those who are strongly attached to the rules have little in the way of taste',[28] writes Méré; and elsewhere, 'You should follow rules and methods only in so far as they are approved by good taste'.[29] Hence the unvarying tendency, not only in Méré, but in writers like Charles de Saint-Evremond whose conception of taste is also linked to the ideal of the *honnête homme*, to dismiss scholars as pedants, and to affirm instead a distinctive judgement of questions of language and literature in keeping with *honnêteté*. Though Méré admires Homer,[30] he condemns Virgil as ignorant of the *bienséances* that govern 'the commerce of the world'. The man of taste judges a piece of writing in keeping with his own response to it: he will not admire Virgil simply because 'the learned [Julius Caesar] Scaliger' does so, because ultimately one has to judge the critic too by one's private feeling.[31]

[22] Guez de Balzac, *Œuvres*, vol. II, p. 369.
[23] Antoine Gombaud, chevalier de Méré, *Œuvres complètes*, ed. C.-H. Boudhors, 3 vols. (Paris: Fernand Roches, 1930), vol. II, p. 129; Dominique Bouhours, *La manière de bien penser dans les ouvrages d'esprit*, new edn (1715; reprint Brighton: University of Sussex Library, 1971), pp. 516–17.
[24] Méré, *Œuvres complètes*, vol. I, pp. 96–7.
[25] Méré, *Lettres*, 2 vols. (Paris: Denis Thierry and Claude Barbin, 1682), vol. I, p. 218.
[26] Méré, *Œuvres complètes*, vol. III, p. 78.   [27] *Ibid.*, vol. I, p. 44; vol. III, pp. 98–9.
[28] Méré, *Lettres*, vol. I, p. 138.   [29] *Ibid.*, vol. I, p. 217.
[30] *Ibid.*, vol. I, p. 94.   [31] *Ibid.*, vol. I, pp. 133–6.

Méré constantly stresses the rarity and distinctiveness of good taste, as of *honnêteté*.[32]

In Saint-Evremond, what is basically the same structure of feeling is juxtaposed with a far greater interest in literature and history. His letter to Corneille on the latter's *Sophonisbe* shows a profound understanding of the playwright's political and historical world-view, his sense of the otherness of antiquity ('the good taste of antiquity', as Saint-Evremond puts it):[33] this leads him to propound the need for a new aesthetic to allow for the changes in belief and customs since the ancient world (which implicitly denies the claim of the rule-governed critic to authority based on timeless standards derived from antiquity).[34]

The conception of judgements of taste as indemonstrable is linked to the notion of the *je ne sais quoi*. The use of the term in France has been traced to the influence of Longinus on humanist rhetoric from about 1550: it is used in the *Apologie de monsieur de Balzac* (1627), with reference to its Italian origin.[35] However, the term (like 'taste') has to be seen as the object of competing discourses: in the mouth of Méré, it serves for instance to register judgements of social incongruity (the pretensions of a scholar to *honnêteté*);[36] Nicolas Boileau uses it to denote the particular quality of a literary work that satisfies 'the general taste of mankind', a quality he interprets as the expression of an idea that everyone must have had, in a form that seizes their attention.[37] (Here, the taste in question is universal, not the prerogative of a few.) The extensive discussion in Dominique Bouhours's *Entretiens d'Ariste et d'Eugène* (1671), emphasizing, on the other hand, the omnipresence of the *je ne sais quoi* – in nature, art, and even divine grace – seems aimed at preserving mystery as a means to sustaining the ideal of harmonious conversation.

As a critic, Bouhours belongs chronologically and in spirit to René Bray's third phase of classicism, after 1660, concerned with establishing correct taste rather than formulating rules.[38] In *La manière de bien penser dans les ouvrages d'esprit* (1687) he links good taste to a classical poetics, based on Latin and Greek models against Spanish and Italian, an aesthetic of naturalness, though leaving room for the sublime conception, against the bold Baroque conceit. To that extent, Bouhours is echoing the *Réflexions*

---

[32] *Ibid.*, vol. II, p. 522; *Œuvres complètes*, vol. II, p. 91.

[33] The correspondence is in Corneille, *Œuvres complètes*, vol. III, pp. 725–7.

[34] Charles Marguetel de Saint-Denis, seigneur de Saint-Evremond, *Œuvres en prose*, ed. R. Ternois, 4 vols. (Paris: Didier, 1962–9), vol. III, p. 348.

[35] Balzac, *Œuvres*, vol. II, p. 133 (the sequence of page numbers restarts after p. 717: the number here refers to the second sequence).

[36] Méré, *Œuvres complètes*, vol. I, p. 30.

[37] Nicolas Boileau-Despréaux, Préface, in *Œuvres complètes*, ed. C. Adam and F. Escal (Paris: Gallimard, 1966), p. 1.

[38] Bray, *La formation*, p. 364.

sur la poétique de ce temps of his fellow Jesuit René Rapin (1675): but Rapin seems, over and above this, to be developing a different agenda, implicitly condemning the purist aesthetics of the mid-century, geared to polite society, and embodied in the writings of Vincent Voiture and Jean-François Sarasin, for the resultant sacrifice of grandeur of thought and style.[39] In the end, no poetry is worth writing but that which, like Homer and Virgil, goes straight to the heart.[40] The structure of feeling here has strong affinities with Boileau's: the same distrust of an exclusive *mondain* aesthetics; the same insistence that the highest kind of utterance (what Boileau calls 'the Sublime') is characterized as a *force* that 'sweeps away, ravishes, transports' the reader;[41] the same insistence that this force is supremely realized in the great writing of antiquity. Taste is now defined by Boileau as the quality that has enabled generations of human beings to appreciate that force: and to be unable to feel it is the strongest proof of lack of taste.[42] In other words, the criterion of good taste is located no longer in the subject (the kind of person who holds the taste in question) but the object of the taste, the time-honoured work of art that serves as a touchstone of the individual's discernment.

The pressure shaping this account of taste, which Boileau put forward most fully in *Réflexions sur Longin* (first published 1694), now comes, not so much from a struggle for hegemony within the literary field between professional men of letters and *honnêtes gens*, as from a quarrel among men of letters, between partisans of the Ancients and the Moderns. Already in 1684, the sense of the Ancients as under pressure from modern prejudice had caused Anne Le Fèvre, the future Mme Dacier, to argue that a narcissistic absorption in one's own point of view, which she defines as the essence of bad taste, was characteristic of the contemporary age as a whole, blinding it to any merits that did not reflect its own standards. This leads her to formulate, in one of the most interesting analyses of the period, a conception of taste in terms of a relationship of harmony or dissonance between the mind, the object, and objective reason, the function of which is to discredit spontaneous response as a reliable guide to value.[43]

The modernist position may be seen as adapting the social-axiological taxonomy that we find in Méré or Saint-Evremond (people of taste/pedants/the ignorant populace) from its original object, the intercourse of polite society, to scientific and artistic progress. In Charles Perrault's *Parallèle des anciens et des modernes*, first published 1688–92, a version of culture is developed that opposes bigoted partisans of antiquity to

[39] Rapin, *Réflexions*, ed. Dubois, pp. 54–5.   [40] *Ibid.*, pp. 68–70.
[41] Boileau, *Œuvres complètes*, p. 338.   [42] *Ibid.*, pp. 524–5.
[43] Anne Le Fèvre, *Le Plutus et les nuées d'Aristophane: comédies grecques traduites en françois* (Paris: Denis Thierry and Claude Barbin, 1684), Préface.

men of real expertise and talent (who by implication are aware of or even promoting this progress): 'taste' enables a third category, the interested amateur, to adjudicate between them.[44]

On the Ancients' side, however, the affirmation of the enduring validity of classical models went with a certain suspicion of contemporary social and moral trends. In Jean de La Bruyère's *Les caractères*, as in the Boileau–Perrault controversy, we find specifically literary judgements combining with, and perhaps even helping to shape, a whole network of polarized ideological attitudes: about luxury, about the status of women, about the direction of French society, compared to an idealized primitive past.[45] Beneath the seventeenth-century literary controversy, we can hear rumblings of later quarrels between Voltaire and Rousseau. By the mid-eighteenth century these could be formulated in explicitly moral, social, and economic terms, although, after all, Rousseau's challenge to the dominant values of French society began with a discourse about the sciences and the arts. But it may well be that the literary discourses and controversies of the seventeenth century helped to engender the sphere of public opinion that made such later conflicts possible.

---

[44] Charles Perrault, *Paralelle des anciens et des modernes en ce qui regarde les arts et les sciences*, 2nd edn, 4 vols. (Paris: Veuve Coignard and Jean-Baptiste Coignard, 1692–6), vol. II, Préface, p. vi.

[45] On La Bruyère's attitude to the Ancients, see *Les caractères ou les mœurs de ce siècle*, in *Œuvres complètes*, ed. J. Benda (Paris: Gallimard, 1951), 'Des ouvrages de l'esprit', 15 (p. 68); 'De la société et de la conversation', 75 (pp. 172–3).

55

Longinus and the Sublime

John Logan

Boileau published his *Œuvres diverses* in 1674, when he was thirty-eight. The volume comprises revised versions of poems already published as well as works seeing print for the first time. The most substantial of the newly published works, a translation of Longinus, is also the only one specifically named in the title: *Œuvres diverses du Sieur D*** avec le traité du Sublime ou du merveilleux dans le discours traduit du grec de Longin.*[1] An introductory text, 'To the Reader', accounts for the presence of the translation: 'I originally made this Translation to instruct myself rather than with the intention of giving it to the Public. But I believed that people would not be offended to find it here following the [*Art poétique*], with which this Treatise has some relation, and in which I have even inserted several precepts that are taken from it.'[2] The modesty of this statement finds an echo in the 'Préface' to the translation itself (pp. 333–40). There, after presenting a brief anecdotal sketch of its presumed author, Cassius Longinus, Boileau says that the treatise manifests its author's qualities: 'His sentiments have something about them that marks not only a sublime mind, but a soul that is far above the ordinary'. He therefore has no regrets about the time – 'some of my evenings' – he has spent translating such an excellent work, especially since he is in a position to say with confidence that 'it has hitherto been understood only by a very small number of scholars' (p. 336).

That their number should be small is unsurprising. Not much more than half of the Greek text survives in the best manuscript; the lacunae alone must have discouraged many prospective editors and translators. What remains, once it was printed, must have struck most of its Renaissance readers – for whom Aristotle, Horace, and Quintilian represented responsible literary criticism – as highly idiosyncratic and unorthodox at best, subversive and incomprehensible at worst. Its utter disregard of ordinary distinctions must have made more than one Renaissance reader quite uneasy. Little wonder, then, that the story Boileau confidently summarizes should be one of fits and starts, occasional moments of enthusiasm

---

[1] The first edition, in-quarto, was printed for Denys Thierry.
[2] See Boileau, *Œuvres complètes*, ed. F. Escal (Paris: Gallimard, 1966), p. 856. Unless otherwise noted, all translations are by the present author.

followed by long silences, confusion as to authority (starting with the author of the treatise itself), lack of interest on the part of educated but unscholarly readers, and conflicting views of the treatise on the part of scholars.

Bibliographical evidence unearthed by Bernard Weinberg and Jules Brody tells the story in detail.[3] Most of the conclusions to which the evidence points must remain provisional, but one seems certain: until Boileau's translation was published, Longinus remained virtually unknown to all but a handful of scholars and writers, most of whom were interested in the treatise chiefly for its great philological treasure, the ode by Sappho that is preserved in it and in it alone. Michel de Montaigne, the one writer who, before Boileau, seems to have fully understood the principles that inform the treatise, neither mentions it nor names the author to whom it is conventionally attributed.

'Muret', Boileau goes on to say, 'was the first who undertook to translate [Longinus] into Latin, at the request of Manuzio; but he did not complete this work' (p. 336). Marc-Antoine Muret mentions this translation himself in his edition of Catullus, first published by Manuzio in 1554.[4] Commenting upon Catullus 51, 'Ille mi par esse', Muret writes:

And now, at this juncture, it gives me great pleasure to earn the especial gratitude of all those who are captivated by enthusiasm for antiquity and by the charm of tender, voluptuous poetry. For when, at the instance of that same man who urged me to write this commentary (I refer to Paulus Manutius, a man of remarkable learning and singular virtue), I was beginning to translate into Latin the treatise of Dionysius Longinus, Περὶ ὕψους, On the Sublime, which has never before been published, so that this outstanding Greek work should be published simultaneously with a Latin translation by me, I discovered in it indeed not only many things of sufficient merit to warrant the book itself being eagerly awaited by all cultured people, but also a most enchanting ode by the poetess Sappho, of which Catullus has translated the greater part in these lines which have just been quoted above.[5]

Several points in this part of Muret's commentary require attention. First, and most important, the treatise had, in fact, already been edited by Francesco Robortello, whose interest in literary criticism presumably – if somewhat paradoxically – led him to Longinus in 1554 as it had to

[3] Bernard Weinberg, 'Translations and commentaries of Longinus, On the Sublime, to 1600: a bibliography', Modern philology 47 (February 1950), 145–51; Jules Brody, Boileau and Longinus (Geneva: Droz, 1958).

[4] Catullus, et in eum commentarius M. Antonii Mureti (Venice: Paulus Manutius, 1554). For a reproduction of the pages on which Muret's commentary appears, see François Rigolot, 'Louise Labé et la redécouverte de Sappho', Nouvelle revue du seizième siècle 1 (1983), pp. 28–9.

[5] Page 57ʳ⁻ᵛ. The translation is Mary Morrison's; see her 'Henri Estienne and Sappho', Bibliothèque d'humanisme et Renaissance 24 (1962), 389–90.

Aristotle earlier, and whose edition had been printed in Basle a few weeks before Muret's Catullus was printed in Venice. Furthermore, Muret's translation has never been found. Finally, his discovery of Sappho's ode in the text of *On the Sublime* may well have been anticipated by Henri Estienne;[6] it was, as we shall see in a moment, certainly anticipated and abetted by Franciscus Portus. But there can be no doubt that Muret, a poet as well as a gifted literary critic,[7] was the first to find inspiration in Longinus for a comparison that goes well beyond the needs of philology: 'Now who is there', he asks, 'at least amongst those who have some feeling for literature and culture, who will not derive the keenest pleasure from comparing side by side the verses of a woman who far excelled all other poets in human history in this genre, and those of the most voluptuous of all the Latin poets?'[8]

Muret's commentary concludes with a discussion of the woeful state in which the poem was found (presumably in the manuscript Manuzio was to base his edition on) before a learned philologist cleaned it up. In giving credit where it is due, Muret inadvertently muddles still further the question of who first discovered the ode of Sappho (and hence that of who first discovered the text in which it is preserved):

This ode, however, because it was corrupt in several places and the lines themselves confused and jumbled together, had been emended and correctly divided before the book came into my hands by a man who has an excellent knowledge of both Latin and Greek, Franciscus Portus, the same who has made a great number of very happy emendations in many of the best Latin and Greek writers, especially Aeschylus – texts which up to now have been circulated in a corrupt state in all the printed editions. I was therefore anxious not to deprive him of the praise he deserves. But now I think there is no one who is not impatient to listen to the tenth Muse.[9]

And the ode follows, so that readers can not only listen to Sappho but perform the comparative exercise alluded to earlier in the commentary – an exercise that requires them only to turn one leaf back if they do not know the Catullan text by heart.

As Mary Morrison observes, 'It is with a real sense of occasion and emotion that Muret triumphantly liberates this imprisoned masterpiece and sends it vibrating out into the Renaissance air to start the second phase of its existence'.[10] That is certainly true, but Muret's role as liberator invites scrutiny. Perhaps among the 'many things of sufficient merit'

---

[6] Morrison, 'Henri Estienne and Sappho', p. 389, and Rigolot, 'Louise Labé', pp. 19–31, esp. pp. 27–31.

[7] Julia Haig Gaisser, *Catullus and his Renaissance readers* (Oxford: Clarendon Press, 1993), p. 159.

[8] Muret, p. 57[r–v]; Morrison, 'Henri Estienne and Sappho', p. 390.

[9] Muret, p. 57[v]; Morrison, p. 390.   [10] Morrison, 'Henri Estienne and Sappho', p. 390.

he found in Longinus was the principle, examined in Chapter 22, of inversion or suspense, exemplified by Demosthenes and Thucydides. By telling his reader first about his discovery of the ode, then about the textual problems associated with it, then, rather circumstantially, about the emender, Muret creates a drama so compelling that when he finally releases the poem from its long captivity, the details of his coming to know the text, of his authority for passing it on, almost cease to matter. It takes a determined reader to wonder about the context in which Muret found the poem, to wonder what was his purpose, not only in quoting it as he does and where he does, but in surrounding it with an ample commentary of his own. A more determined reader might well wonder why Muret makes no reference to Catullus 64 at this point nor to Sappho and Longinus in his commentary on line 61 of that poem.

Franciscus Portus's contribution to the text of Longinus, which may have begun as early as 1530–5,[11] does not end with his emendations of the ode. In 1569–70, his edition of Longinus appears in a volume that includes texts by two other 'most outstanding masters of the art of rhetoric', as the title calls them, Aphthonius and Hermogenes. Portus is the first editor to divide the *Peri hupsous* into chapters. As far as subsequent editions of Longinus are concerned, Portus's is authoritative at least until the end of the seventeenth century and, for all practical purposes, it might as well be the *princeps*.[12]

Between Francesco Robortello's *princeps* and Portus's edition, which was the third and last Greek edition to be published in the sixteenth century – and the last to be published for more than sixty years – appeared the first extant Latin translation, by Domenico Pizzimenti (1566), dedicated to Aldo Manuzio, the son of Paolo. Another Latin translation, by Pietro Pagano, appeared in 1572. Neither translation seems to have been known at all before both were reprinted in 1644. In his preface to the *Traité du Sublime*, Boileau refers to both translations as 'so shapeless and rough that it would do their authors too much honour to name them' (p. 336).

All told, then, the sixteenth-century bibliographical evidence suggests that the *Peri hupsous* was rediscovered only to be generally neglected, at least as a work of literary criticism. A comparison with Aristotle's *Poetics* is telling: between 1554 and 1600, for instance, the Greek text was printed no fewer than seventeen times; translations into Latin (eleven accompanying the Greek text) appeared some twenty-six times; translations into Italian were printed five times. Even without the additional weight of commentaries, printed thirteen times, and scores of allusions to the *Poetics*

[11] See Pierre Costil, *André Dudith, humaniste hongrois, 1533–1589: sa vie, son œuvre et ses manuscrits grecs* (Paris: Les Belles Lettres, 1935), p. 282, n. 5.
[12] See Brody, *Boileau and Longinus*, p. 10.

in other texts, this imposing record gives a good sense of what was considered an important text, at least as far as literary criticism or theory was concerned, in the Renaissance. An even more striking example is the *Ars poetica* of Horace, which, between 1555 and 1599, was printed at least thirty-six times.[13] In comparison with these giants, Longinus casts almost no shadow at all.

In sixteenth-century Italy, the little attention Longinus did attract was mainly in learned circles. The *Peri hupsous* was known, of course, to Paolo Manuzio, who, in addition to editing it, may have been inspired by it to compose his *Discorso intorno all'ufficio dell'oratore* (printed in 1556).[14] We may assume that it was known to Miguel da Silva, the Portuguese humanist and cardinal to whom Castiglione dedicated *Il cortegiano* in 1528 and to whom Manuzio dedicated his edition of Longinus in 1555, the year before Da Silva died. It was known, as we have seen, to Portus and Muret; but Portus became a Calvinist under the influence of Renée de France in Ferrara, had to leave the city in 1554, and ended up as a professor of Greek in Geneva, where his edition was printed.[15] It is likely that these early associations with heterodoxy not only contributed to the rather dismal fortunes of *On the Sublime* in Catholic Europe during the Counter-Reformation but made the treatise more appealing than it might have been otherwise to a later group of Augustinian dissidents, the Jansenists and their supporters, among whom Boileau figured prominently. The commentary Portus produced, perhaps shortly after the publication of his edition, 'the only full-scale sixteenth-century commentary on Longinus now extant',[16] remained unpublished until the eighteenth century. As for Muret, who was burnt in effigy at the stake in Toulouse for being a sodomite and a Huguenot,[17] the only explicit reference to Longinus in his works seems to be in his commentary on Catullus 51. Since that text remains unchanged from 1554 to 1562, and since no sign of his Latin translation has surfaced, it may be conjectured that his interest in the treatise did not extend beyond the ode by Sappho that Catullus imitated.[18]

[13] Information based on catalogue records for the Robert W. Patterson, Class of 1876, Collection of Horace in the Rare Books and Special Collections Department of the Princeton University Library.

[14] See Marc Fumaroli, *L'âge de l'éloquence: rhétorique et 'res literaria' de la Renaissance au seuil de l'époque classique* (Geneva: Droz, 1980), pp. 165–7.

[15] See Costil, *André Dudith, humaniste hongrois*, p. 282, n. 1, and Bernard Weinberg, 'ps. Longinus, Dionysius Cassius', in *Catalogus translationum et commentariorum: mediaeval and Renaissance Latin translations and commentaries*, 7 vols. (Washington, DC: The Catholic University of America Press, 1960–), vol. II (1971), p. 198.

[16] Weinberg, 'Translations and commentaries of Longinus', p. 149.

[17] The second charge seems less founded than the first. See Charles Dejob, *Marc-Antoine Muret: un professeur français en Italie* (Paris: Thorin, 1881), p. 56.

[18] A possible allusion to Longinus occurs in an oration Muret gave in 1572 on Cicero. See Fumaroli, *L'âge de l'éloquence*, p. 170, n. 256 and p. 178, n. 271.

In his *Carmina nouem illustrium feminarum*, printed at Antwerp in 1568, Fulvio Orsini not only reproduces the Greek text of the ode by Sappho (p. 9) but quotes, in his own commentary (pp. 283–4), part of the analysis that follows the poem in the *Peri hupsous*. Orsini seems thus to be the first to extract a critical judgement from the treatise and reinscribe it, in the original Greek, in a text that is not an edition of the treatise. The passage he quotes is of considerable critical perspicacity: 'For instance, Sappho everywhere chooses the emotions that attend delirious passion from its accompaniments in actual life. Wherein does she demonstrate her supreme excellence? In the skill with which she selects and binds together the most striking and vehement circumstances of passion.'[19] Orsini's interest in the *Peri hupsous* is likely to have led him to translate it and introduce it to scholars and artists (including Michelangelo) in Rome whose patrons were members of the Farnese family.[20]

The treatise was certainly known to Muret's student, Francesco Benci,[21] as it was to Francesco Patrizi da Cherso, who corresponded with Orsini and who mentions Longinus some twenty times in his *Della poetica*. Patrizi is the first to refer to Longinus in the vernacular, calling him 'Dionigi Longino' early in the first *deca* (1586) of his work.[22] In the second *deca*, also printed in 1586, 'Longino' is named again and the verb 'ikonographei' (10.6, on Homer) is quoted and translated (vol. II, p. 64). Twelve references occur in the third *deca* alone, the *Deca ammirabile*; but this part of the *Poetica* remained unpublished until 1969. Patrizi's interest in the treatise reflects his often unconventional and unorthodox attitudes towards poetry, which he believes is inseparable from the marvellous [the *mirabile*],[23] by which he means something very much like what Longinus describes in 1.4: 'The effect of elevated language upon an audience is not persuasion but transport. At every time and in every way imposing speech, with the spell it throws over us, prevails over that which aims at persuasion and gratification.'[24]

---

[19] *Longinus On the Sublime: the Greek text edited after the Paris manuscript*, ed. W. Rhys Roberts (1899; 2nd edn 1907; rpt. Cambridge: Cambridge University Press, 1935), p. 69.

[20] See Gustavo Costa, 'The Latin translations of Longinus's Περὶ Ὕψους in Renaissance Italy', in *Acta conventus neo-latini bononiensis = Proceedings of the fourth international congress of neo-Latin studies, Bologna 26 August to 1 September 1979*, ed. R. J. Schoeck (Binghamton: Medieval & Renaissance Texts & Studies, 1985), pp. 224–33, esp. pp. 228–30.

[21] Fumaroli, *L'âge de l'éloquence*, pp. 177–8.

[22] See Francesco Patrizi da Cherso, *Della poetica*, ed. D. Aguzzi-Barbagli, 3 vols. (Florence: Istituto Nazionale di studi sul Rinascimento, 1969–71), vol. I, p. 44.

[23] Bernard Weinberg, *A history of literary criticism in the Italian Renaissance*, 2 vols. (1961; rpt. Chicago: University of Chicago Press, 1974), vol. II, p. 785.

[24] *On the Sublime*, ed. Roberts, p. 43. Patrizi quotes this passage in full and in part in *La deca ammirabile* (vol. II, p. 265; compare pp. 304 and 325); see also vol. III, pp. 367 and 387–8.

In France, Longinus seems to have attracted little attention before the seventeenth century. Henri Estienne must have known the treatise, but no edition of it came from his presses – in fact, it was not until 1663 that the Greek text, edited by Tannegui Lefebvre, a Huguenot, was printed in France.[25] Estienne seems to have been principally interested in it for the text of Sappho's ode, which he included in his second edition of Anacreon (1556)[26] and in his *Carminum poetarum nouem* (1560). The great philologist Denys Lambin refers to Longinus in an oration he delivered in 1571; a copy of Robortello's edition of Longinus bearing Lambin's name and his manuscript notes is preserved in the Bibliothèque Nationale.[27] Jacques Amyot must have consulted a manuscript or a printed edition of Longinus for the text of Sappho's ode, which is recited at an important moment in Plutarch's *Amatorius* (763a) but not preserved in any manuscript of the text. In Amyot's translation, the ode appears in its proper place.[28]

Montaigne, who handsomely acknowledges his debts to Amyot's Plutarch, never mentions Longinus; but three passages in the *Essais* echo the distinction Longinus makes in 1.4 between pleasure and transport or ecstasy.[29] In the earliest passage, printed in 1580, Montaigne says: 'What I see produced by these rich and great souls of the past, I find way beyond the furthest stretch of my imagination. Their works do not only satisfy and fill me, but astonish me and transfix me with admiration' (pp. 482–3).[30] In a passage printed for the first time in 1588, he says of Lucretius and Virgil, 'This is not a soft and merely inoffensive eloquence: it is sinewy and solid; it does not so much please as fill and ravish: and it ravishes the strongest minds the most' (p. 665).[31]

The most extensive and important of the three passages was not printed until after Montaigne's death. The essay 'Of Cato the younger', in its first form (1580–8), concludes with these words: '[Cato] was truly a model chosen by nature to show how far human constancy could go. But I am not equipped to treat this rich subject here. I want only to make

[25] *Dionysii Longini philosophi et rhetoris περὶ ὕψους libellus, cum notis, emendationibus, & praefatione Tanaquilli Fabri* (Saumur: Ioannes Lenerius, 1663).

[26] See Robert Aulotte, 'Sur quelques traductions d'une ode de Sappho au XVIᵉ siècle', *Lettres d'humanité* (December 1958), 108–9, and Morrison, 'Henri Estienne and Sappho', p. 388.

[27] See Dorothy Gabe Coleman, 'Montaigne and Longinus', *Bibliothèque d'humanisme et Renaissance* 47 (1985), p. 407.

[28] *Les œuvres morales & meslees de Plutarque*, 2 vols. (Paris: M. Vascosan, 1572), vol. II, p. 608ʳ⁻ᵛ.

[29] The discussion of Montaigne that follows is based in part on J. L. Logan, 'Montaigne et Longin: une nouvelle hypothèse', *Revue d'histoire littéraire de la France* 83 (1983), 355–70.

[30] II.17, 'De la præsumption' ['Of presumption']. *The complete essays of Montaigne*, trans. D. M. Frame (1958; reprint Stanford: Stanford University Press, 1975), pp. 482–3. The present author has slightly modified Frame's translation here and below.

[31] III.5, 'Sur des vers de Virgile' ['On some verses of Virgil'], p. 665.

the lines of five Latin poets in praise of Cato contend together.' And five
quotations (from Martial, Manilius, Lucan, Horace, and Virgil) follow,
with scarcely any commentary, except for the sentence that precedes
the last: 'And the master of the choir, after displaying in his painting
the names of the greatest Romans, ends in this way: "Cato giving them
their laws".'[32] Some time between the publication of the 1588 edition of
the *Essais* and his death, Montaigne made significant modifications in this
essay. One addition provides an extensive introduction to the combat
among quotations, which he says is 'both in Cato's interest, and, incidentally, in their own':

Now a well-educated youngster should find the first two languid compared with
the others, the third lustier, but overcome by the extravagance of its own power.
He should think that there would be room for one or two more degrees of
inventiveness before coming to the fourth, at the sight of which he will clasp his
hands in admiration. At the last one – which is first by quite a space, a space our
youth will swear no human mind can fill – he will be stunned and speechless.

(p. 171)

The expression 'he will be stunned and speechless' – 'il s'estonnera, il se
transira' – not only reaches back to 'Of presumption' but leads directly
to a rich meditation on the mysteries of poetry and criticism: 'Here is a
wonder: we have many more poets than judges and interpreters of poetry.
It is easier to create it than to understand it. On a certain low level it can
be judged by precepts and by art. But the good, supreme, divine poetry
is above the rules and reason. Whoever discerns its beauty with a firm,
sedate gaze does not see it, any more than he sees the splendour of a
lightning flash. It does not persuade our judgement, it ravishes and over-
whelms it' (p. 171).

The 'lightning flash' is another echo of Longinus, who uses it in 1.4 to
describe the effect of the Sublime and in 12.4 to characterize Demosthenes. Most Longinian of all, though, is the principle that informs
Montaigne's giving the greatest praise to the last and, one might say, least
obviously poetic of his five quotations. To understand the principle, we
have only to consider the context of the quotation: the description in
the *Aeneid* (8.663–9) of the shield of Aeneas. After a rather bombastic
description of the abodes of hell and of Catiline's punishment, a line
appears that is strikingly different both from those that precede it and
from the highly figured description of the sea that follows it. The line is
'secretosque pios, his dantem iura Catonem' ['and separated (from the
wicked), the good, Cato giving them their laws'] and Montaigne quotes
and praises its second hemistich precisely because of its astonishing

[32] II.37, 'Du jeune Caton' ['Of Cato the younger'], pp. 171–2. In the 1588 edition, 'choir'
(*chœur*) becomes 'heart' (*cœur*).

simplicity. Standing in sharp contrast to the wicked Catiline, the just and their lawgiver are isolated spatially, grammatically, and, above all, rhetorically.[33] The difference between this verse and those that frame it in Virgil is as stunning as the difference between the first four quotations on Cato in Montaigne's essay and the fifth, a difference Montaigne draws attention to by quoting not the whole line but a fragment of it: four simple words.

The line of the *Aeneid* from which Montaigne quotes has, in fact, the same kind of poetic perfection that Longinus praises in 9.9: 'Similarly, the legislator of the Jews, no ordinary man, having formed and expressed a worthy conception of the might of the Godhead, writes at the very beginning of his Laws, "God said" – what? "Let there be light, and there was light; let there be land, and there was land".'[34] Virgil depicts the just and *their* lawgiver with the same power, the same simplicity. His line, like a thunderbolt, scatters everything before it and shows his powers at a single stroke.

Montaigne's understanding of Longinus is not only unique in his century; it remains unequalled and unsurpassed until the appearance of the *Dissertation sur la Joconde* almost seventy years into the next.[35] To be sure, many allusions to *On the Sublime* occur in works of seventeenth-century French and Italian writers printed before 1674,[36] but most of them punctuate discussions of the sublime or grand style and do not reflect, for instance, any comprehension of – or sustained interest in – the Sublime as a force that can make the simplest words as powerful as a bolt of lightning, that can astound and ravish reader and critic alike. One interesting exception is La Fontaine, who, in *Les amours de Psyché et de Cupidon* (1669), has his character Ariste not only mention Longinus by name but paraphrase *Peri hupsous* 1.4 in a dialogue concerning comedy and tragedy.[37] A different kind of exception is to be found in Racine's angry paraphrase of *Peri hupsous* 14.2 in the preface to *Britannicus* (1670). New editions and Latin translations of the treatise are scarcely more numerous in the seventeenth century than in the sixteenth century, and they are printed, with few exceptions, in Protestant countries. Gabriel de Petra, who taught Greek in Lausanne, had his Greek–Latin edition

---

[33] Only one other verse in Virgil begins with a form of 'secretus' ('secreti', *Aeneid* 6.443), but it does not stand on its own as *Aeneid* 8.670 does.

[34] *On the Sublime*, ed. Roberts, p. 65.

[35] On the authorship of the *Dissertation*, see Brody, *Boileau and Longinus*, p. 31, n. 1, and pp. 110–13, and Boileau, *Œuvres complètes*, pp. 1063–4.

[36] See Brody, *Boileau and Longinus*, pp. 13–18; Fumaroli, *L'âge de l'éloquence*, *passim*, esp. pp. 277, 335, 348, 549, n. 301, 577 n. 354, 581, 650 n. 541, 682–3; and Fumaroli, 'Rhétorique d'école et rhétorique adulte: remarques sur la réception européenne du traité "Du Sublime" au XVIᵉ et au XVIIᵉ siècle', *Revue d'histoire littéraire de la France* 86 (1986), 33–51.

[37] La Fontaine, *Œuvres diverses*, ed. P. Clarac (Paris: Gallimard, 1958), p. 184. See also Brody, *Boileau and Longinus*, pp. 29–31.

printed in 1612 by Jean II de Tournes, a Huguenot who fled Lyons in 1585 for Geneva. The Anglican Gerard Langbaine (1609–58/9) produced an edition, heavily but silently indebted to Petra's, that was printed in Oxford by William Webb (1636, 1638, and 1650); and Jacob Tollius's edition was printed in Utrecht in 1694. As noted earlier, the Huguenot scholar Tannegui Lefebvre is responsible for the first French edition of Longinus, which was printed in Saumur in 1663. Pizzimenti's Latin translation was reprinted twice in Venice (Salicata, 1643 and 1644). It was also reprinted, along with Pagano's Latin translation and Petra's Greek text, in Carolus Manolesius's edition (Bologna: Sumptibus HH. Evangelistae Ducciae, 1644). A French translation was done *c.* 1645, perhaps by Mazarin, but it remained unknown until Bernard Weinberg published it in 1962.[38] The only vernacular translations published before Boileau's are Niccolò Pinelli's (Padua, 1639), which seems to have left almost no trace, and John Hall's (London, 1652), which seems to have passed mostly unnoticed in its own time.[39]

Jean-Louis Guez de Balzac, who probably knew Longinus as early as 1627,[40] represents an intriguing special case. He alludes obliquely to the Longinian comparison of Cicero and Demosthenes in 1631;[41] refers in a letter of 1641 to a discourse he has composed on the *Peri hupsous* that he will soon send to Chapelain;[42] and uses the Greek title of the treatise sometime after 1645 to mock a learned man, perhaps Joseph Scaliger or his pedantic father.[43] Shortly thereafter, in the preface to *Socrate chrétien*, Balzac once again takes up the comparison of Cicero and Demosthenes;[44] towards the end of the book, however, he mentions the praise Longinus gives to Moses and the 'fiat lux' of Genesis only to reduce the matter to one of style and to reject it as unworthy of a Christian: 'This sublimity of style is not the object of my passion today. I have a higher sublimity in mind' (p. 273).

Boileau's reaction to this statement might have taken two forms. First, with the encouragement of his brother Gilles, or Guillaume Lamoignon, or perhaps Olivier Patru, he might have consulted 'la Critique payenne' ['the pagan criticism'] to which Balzac alludes. In Longinus, Boileau would have discovered an astute critic whom Balzac was ill advised to dismiss.

[38] See Bernard Weinberg, 'Une traduction française du *Sublime* de Longin vers 1645', *Modern philology* 59 (1962), 159–201.

[39] See Weinberg, 'Une traduction française', pp. 176–81 and Brody, *Boileau and Longinus*, p. 11.

[40] In the *Apologie pour monsieur de Balzac* (1627; reprint Saint-Etienne, 1977), Longinus 1.4 is paraphrased (pp. 73–4) and reference is made to 'le Sophiste Longin' (p. 75).

[41] *Les œuvres de monsieur de Balzac*, 2 vols. (Paris: Thomas Jolly, 1665), vol. I, p. 324.

[42] *Œuvres*, vol. I, p. 847. The date printed, 1644, is almost certainly wrong.

[43] Balzac, *Entretiens*, ed. B. Beugnot, 2 vols. (Paris: Didier, 1972), vol. I, p. 107.

[44] *Socrate chrestien* (Paris: Augustin Courbé, 1652), fol. E8ʳ.

Then, yielding to an irresistible temptation, Boileau would have taken Balzac's aspiration to a 'higher sublimity' as an invitation to ruin him with a quick parody. In fact, Boileau's parodic response could easily have taken the form – and be the source – of an astonishing moment in the 1674 'Préface' to the *Traité du Sublime*. To illustrate the difference between the Sublime as Longinus understands it and the sublime or grandiloquent style to which Balzac, among others, mistakenly reduces it, Boileau transforms the 'fiat lux' into 'The supreme Arbiter of nature with a single word formed the light' – an amplification that is uncannily reminiscent of Balzac at his most orotund and makes him pay dearly for his sanctimonious dismissal of Longinus as a critic. As Boileau goes on to say of his parody, 'That is in the sublime style, but it is nevertheless not Sublime, because there is nothing very marvellous in it, nothing one couldn't easily come up with. But, *God said: Let there be light; and there was light.* This extraordinary turn of phrase, which so well marks the obedience of the Creature to the orders of the Creator, is truly sublime, and has something of the divine about it' (*Œuvres diverses*, p. 338). This crucial distinction mattered deeply to Boileau; it is developed in subsequent versions of the preface to the *Traité du Sublime* and is the object of sustained analysis in the tenth of his *Réflexions critiques*, composed after 1710 and published posthumously. In this late work, it is interesting to note, the parody of the 'fiat lux' reappears, more outrageously bloated than ever (compare p. 555).

Whether or not Boileau turned to the *Peri hupsous* because Balzac had misunderstood and finally rejected it, his own predilections and preoccupations led him, perhaps as early as 1664, to a full-scale engagement with Longinus. The brilliant translation he published ten years later made that engagement public but by no means marked its end. In rescuing Longinus from almost complete oblivion, Boileau put an end to a long story of neglect. In continuing to explore the mysteries of the Sublime until his death, he radically transformed the purview of literary criticism.[45]

[45] It is a pleasure to thank Jan Logan, François Rigolot, John Considine, Alexander Ulanov, Charles Fineman, and John Keaney for their invaluable encouragement and assistance. For eighteenth-century views of the Sublime, see Jonathan Lamb's essay in *The Cambridge history of literary criticism*, ed. C. Rawson and H. B. Nisbet, vol. IV, *The eighteenth century* (Cambridge: Cambridge University Press, 1997), pp. 394–416.

A survey of national developments

56

Seventeenth-century English literary criticism: classical values, English texts and contexts

Joshua Scodel

Seventeenth-century English critics applied classically derived conceptions of the writer's aims, natural endowments, and artistic method to English literature. A flexible neoclassicism not only shaped poet-critics like Jonson and Dryden but also accommodated to the canon authors who did not fit a rigid classical paradigm, such as Chaucer, Shakespeare, Donne, and Milton. Throughout this century of intense socio-political conflict and change, classical norms, adapted to English developments, acquired a range of new cultural meanings.

The early seventeenth-century poet-critic Ben Jonson draws mainly upon Roman sources: the rhetoricians, Seneca, and particularly Horace, upon whom Jonson based his cultural role and his belief that the critic must be an excellent poet himself. Like Horace (*Ars poetica* 333–46), Jonson argues poetry should combine pleasure and utility by teaching with delight. Like the pseudo-Ciceronian *Ad Herennium* (1.2.3), Jonson claims 'naturall wit' or talent, a writer's primary qualification, must be shaped by 'exercise', imitation and study (of classical models), and 'art' (knowledge of rules for effective expression). As Quintilian advises (*Institutio oratoria* 10.3.5-6), one must temper vigorous 'invention', the discovery of interesting material, with strong judgement regarding material's suitability; after giving invention free reign, one must judiciously revise.[1]

Just as Roman authors sought to surpass Greek models, English authors must emulate the classics. Neither ignoring nor slavishly following ancient precedents, the good writer transforms them. Jonson stresses that classicism itself demands independence by echoing Seneca's claim that the 'Ancients' are 'Guides, not Commanders'. Adapting a Roman boast that orators of Cicero's time equalled those of 'insolent' Greece, Jonson praises English Renaissance orators, culminating in Francis Bacon, for equalling or surpassing 'insolent *Greece*, or haughty *Rome*'.[2]

Jonson applies classical criteria to Shakespeare.[3] His *Discoveries* criticizes Shakespeare's falling short of classical norms by not tempering his

---

[1] C. H. Herford and Percy and Evelyn Simpson (ed.), *Ben Jonson*, 11 vols. (Oxford: Clarendon Press, 1925–52), vol. v, pp. 23, 164; vol. VIII, pp. 615–16, 636–9, 642.
[2] *Jonson*, vol. VIII, pp. 567, 585–6, 591, 638.   [3] *Ibid.*, pp. 390–2, 583–4.

'excellent *Phantsie*' with revisions. Jonson's elegy on Shakespeare hails his superiority to ancient dramatists despite 'small *Latine*, and lesse *Greeke*' (line 31). Shakespeare is 'Soule of the Age!' (line 17) and 'not of an age, but for all time!' (line 43): as the profoundest voice of his times, he became a time-transcending English classic. Yet Jonson self-consciously appropriates '*My*' (lines 19, 56) Shakespeare to imagine an ideal classicizer tempering 'Nature' with 'Art' (lines 47–64). Jonson's proclamation that to write well one must, like Shakespeare, revise at the '*Muses* anvile' (line 61) echoes Horace's urging that the poet find a critic who will bid him return faulty lines to the 'anvil' (*Ars poetica* 441). Thus while praising the deceased, Jonson hints that his own Horatian classicism might have perfected Shakespeare's writings.

Jonson presents his own works as both classical and innovative in classically sanctioned ways. Major predecessors emphasized poetry's transcendence of mundane reality: Philip Sidney celebrated poetry's 'golden' world of paragons, while Bacon noted poetry's gratification of our desire for 'Acts . . . Greater' than reality.[4] Jonson, by contrast, follows Horace (*Ars poetica* 338), arguing that poetic fictions should be verisimilar representations of social life. In favourite genres like comedy and epigram, Jonson shows formal indebtedness to ancient models but diverges from them in depicting the contemporary world. While praising *Volpone*'s adherence to classical formal laws, Jonson claims *The alchemist* exemplifies English comedy's unsurpassed 'mirth', which derives from England's distinctive 'humors' (comic temperaments). Jonson also uses the classical emphasis on literary pleasure to justify deviations from ancient practice. Drama should provide 'what . . . the People . . . desire' (as Jonson renders *Ars poetica* 153). Invoking Horace, Jonson defends *Sejanus*'s lack of chorus by noting that not all ancient conventions retain 'popular delight'.[5]

Yet Jonson also worries about pandering to degraded tastes by pleasing without teaching. Excoriating both the 'sordid multitude' and ignorant gentlemen, Jonson, a self-made man, embraces the Roman theme that merit (not lineage) determines 'true nobility'. He often addresses a moral-intellectual élite who appreciate classical values and seek didactic 'profit' as well as pleasure from literature.[6]

'Learned' Jonson, as he was called, decisively influenced subsequent criticism. Tributes, which poured out upon his death in 1637, generally used his own criteria to praise him. William Cartwright's claim that

---

[4] G. Gregory Smith (ed.), *Elizabethan critical essays*, 2 vols. (Oxford: Oxford University Press, 1904), vol. I, pp. 156–7; J. E. Spingarn (ed.), *Critical essays of the seventeenth century*, 3 vols. (Oxford: Clarendon Press, 1907), vol. I, p. 6.

[5] *Jonson*, vol. IV, p. 350; vol. V, pp. 24, 164, 294; vol. VIII, pp. 315, 587.

[6] *Jonson*, vol. III, p. 435; vol. IV, pp. 43, 131; vol. VIII, p. 583; compare Seneca, *Epistle* 44; Juvenal, *Satire* 8.

'Classick' Jonson 'rob[bed]' and 'improv'd' the ancients is typical.[7] Jonson's example also encouraged his followers, the 'Sons of Ben', to emulate the classics directly. Their verse criticism espouses a wider range of classical values than his. While Jonson eulogized Shakespeare only by transforming him, his successors found in Horace's praise of Pindar (*Ode* 4.2) a model for the judicious, rule-and-precedent bound poet's appreciation of the daring poet who transcends conventions. Horace begins by declaring Pindar's 'immense', 'bold', 'lawless' style as inimitable as a flooding river's natural force; yet the onward rush of Horace's five-stanza sentence praising Pindar wittily demonstrates Horace's imitative art by capturing the Greek poet's grand style (lines 1–24). Horace then proceeds in his usual style to describe his own modest, laboured, artful vein, thus affirming the distinctive value of both poetic manners (lines 27–32). In a panegyric elegy that provides the most insightful contemporary appreciation of John Donne, the Jonsonian Thomas Carew adopts this Horatian model.[8] While Jonson reportedly criticized Donne's rough metre and obscurity,[9] Carew praises Donne's rejection of 'Pedantique' classicism (line 25) and suggests Donne's harsh metre and violent conceits reveal a 'Giant phansie . . . too stout' (line 52) for conventional language. Carew imitates Donne's rugged metre and paradoxes while denying he can write an elegy worthy of Donne. Glorifying Donne's 'fresh invention' (line 28), Carew's imitation paradoxically underscores his Horatian distance from Donne's anti-classical originality.

In response to new socio-political conditions, however, Carew modifies the Horatian stance. While Horace describes Pindar as 'lawless', Carew praises Donne's 'strict lawes' (line 61) and 'just raigne' (line 64) as 'a King, that rul'd as hee thought fit / The universall Monarchy of wit' (lines 95–6). Donne resembles God, whom the English Church's 'Homily against Disobedience' calls the 'universal monarch'. The homily claims earthly monarchs, appointed by and resembling God, must be obeyed.[10] Carew suggests an analogy between Donne and Charles I as godlike rulers deserving obedience. Protests against Charles's absolutist pretensions, which fed the king's 1629 decision to dispense with Parliament, focused upon his alleged belief he could rule as he pleased, while his defenders argued that his absolute rule allowed him to rule only as was fitting, under God. Writing during Charles's suspension of Parliament, Carew enlists Donne in defence of the king by describing a monarch whose absolute but not arbitrary power over his poetic kingdom corresponds to Carew's vision of Charles I's rule over England.

---

[7] *Jonson*, vol. XI, pp. 457–8.
[8] Thomas Carew, *Poems*, ed. R. Dunlap (Oxford: Clarendon Press, 1949), pp. 71–4.
[9] *Jonson*, vol. I, pp. 133, 138.
[10] *Certain sermons or homilies* (Oxford: Oxford University Press, 1840), pp. 492–3.

Edmund Waller adapts Horace's paradigm to praise John Evelyn's Lucretius translation (1656).[11] Translating – making the classics English – was a major seventeenth-century patriotic endeavour. Waller expresses imperialist joy: Evelyn conquered Lucretius's 'fort' (line 37). While Jonson criticized Lucretius's 'rough' archaic style as contrary to Horatian norms,[12] Waller, a Jonsonian famous for 'smooth' verse, eulogizes England's poetic acquisition by recalling Horace's Pindar and Carew's Donne: Lucretius's 'boundless', 'free' wit 'boldly' (lines 13, 15, 19) proclaims unconventional views; his style reflects a 'vast . . . argument' for which Latin was 'too narrow' (lines 21, 25). Writing during the Interregnum following Charles I's execution, Waller stresses 'bold' poetry's subversive possibilities by associating free-thinking Lucretius, whose 'Democratical' cosmos obeys 'No Monarch' (lines 4, 6), with rebellious Englishmen, who had abolished their monarchy.

Andrew Marvell's 1674 verse panegyric on John Milton's *Paradise lost* simultaneously adapts Horace's model and imitates Jonson to defend a poet daring in poetry and politics.[13] Marvell, the greatest Son of Ben, confronts a poet who combined pagan epic and Scripture in a highly original synthesis. Marvell's first ten lines evoking the 'bold' poet's 'vast design' – the Christian cosmos and all sacred history – measure Milton's ambition against Marvell's modest Horatianism. While the periodic sentence, enjambments, varied caesurae, and diction imitate Milton, Marvell's use of rhyme pointedly distinguishes him from the blank-verse epic poet. The final ten lines apologize for Marvell's rhymes and declare Milton's 'sublime' work transcends this 'fashion'. In his preface to *Paradise lost* (1667), written during (and against) the Restoration, Milton gave political resonance to his classicizing rejection of rhyme by eschewing the 'modern bondage of Riming' for 'ancient liberty', the poetic analogue of his support for Parliament and Charles I's execution.[14] Though Marvell prudently leaves politics implicit, his praise of Milton's rejecting rhyme commends the poet's uncompromising stances, political and poetic. Marvell's admission to initial 'misdoubting' (line 6) fear that Milton had tainted Christianity with classical myth in revenge for his blindness hints at Milton's bitterness over the Restoration, since *Paradise lost* associates Milton's blindness and political isolation (7.26–8). By recalling Jonson's opening expression of apprehensive 'doubt' (line 4) in his commendatory

---

[11] Edmund Waller, *Poems*, ed. G. T. Drury (London: Lawrence and Bullen, 1893), pp. 149–50, 326–7.

[12] *Jonson*, vol. VIII, p. 622.

[13] Andrew Marvell, *Complete poems*, ed. E. S. Donno (Harmondsworth: Penguin, 1972), pp. 192–3.

[14] John Milton, *Complete poems and major prose*, ed. M. Hughes (New York: Odyssey, 1957), p. 210.

verses upon a translation of the Roman poet Lucan,[15] Marvell obliquely compares Milton to Lucan, who defiantly composed a republican epic under Nero. But Marvell's praise of the 'majesty' that 'reign[s]' throughout the epic (line 31) wittily implies Milton transcended anger by creating his own godly poetic kingdom.

Despite greater knowledge of classical (especially Greek) and Renaissance poetics and greater intellectual independence than previous English poet-critics, Milton's own views on the poet's training and purpose recall Jonson. Believing himself born a poet, Milton complemented 'nature' with 'study'. Combining pleasure and utility, Milton's ideal poet elicits 'virtue' by making truth 'pleasant'. But the Jonsonians were predominantly secular. Ambitious to write Christian poetry in high genres whose classical exemplars treated pagan myth, Milton focused on the relationship, central to Renaissance Italian poetics, between classical and Christian values. Drawing on the widespread conception of the Bible as generic compendium, Milton argues for Scriptural analogues to major classical genres. Both true religion and the mastery of classical 'decorum' and generic 'laws' will help Milton rival the greatest classical and Renaissance poets. While the Jonsonians generally accepted Horace's association of inspiration with 'mad', undisciplined poetry (*Ars poetica* 453–76), Milton declares poetry a divinely inspired 'gift' requiring prayer as well as discipline. Like Torquato Tasso, in *Paradise lost* Milton asks for inspiration from the Christian deity rather than a pagan Muse.[16]

Milton also diverges from the Jonsonians in venerating England's two most generically ambitious poets, Chaucer and Edmund Spenser, as a native, 'Protestant' epic line rivalling the classics. (Like many English Protestants, Milton deemed Chaucer 'proto-Protestant' for denunciations of the medieval clergy and Church in both authentic and apocryphal works.[17]) Spenser imitated Chaucer as the English Virgil and the 'well of English undefyled'. Following Roman insistence on staying close to contemporary usage (Horace, *Ars poetica* 46–72; Quintilian, *Institutio oratoria* 1.6.3), Jonson condemned imitation of Chaucer and Spenser's archaizing style. By contrast, Milton's 'Manso' (1639) hails Spenser and Chaucer as the models of English poetic achievement. Jonson argues that poetry surpasses philosophy in didactic power; in Milton's *Areopagitica* (1644), Spenser, 'a better teacher than Scotus or Aquinas', exemplifies this superiority.[18]

---

[15] *Jonson*, vol. VIII, p. 395.   [16] Milton, *Poems*, pp. 84, 667–71.

[17] Caroline F. E. Spurgeon, *Five-hundred years of Chaucer criticism and allusion (1357–1900)*, Part 1 (Oxford: Oxford University Press, 1914), pp. 104–6, 112–13, 122–5, 151–3, 173–4, 220–1.

[18] Milton, *Poems*, pp. 128, 728–9; Edmund Spenser, *Poetical works*, ed. J. C. Smith and E. de Sélincourt (London: Oxford University Press, 1970), pp. 222, 424–6, 442–3 (*The Faerie Queene*, 4.2.32; *The shepheardes calender*, February, June); *Jonson*, vol. VIII, pp. 618, 636.

Yet like the Sons of Ben, Milton recognizes the greatness of poets different from himself. In one of the earliest positive acknowledgements of Shakespeare's 'natural' writing, Milton's 'On Shakespeare' (1630) claims that the dramatist's 'easy numbers' shame 'slow-endeavoring art' (lines 9–10). Conscious of laboriously nurturing his own talent, Milton abases himself before Shakespeare like Horace before Pindar. In *L'allegro* and *Il penseroso* (*c.* 1637), Milton sympathetically explores contrasting poetic temperaments (youthful, lighthearted versus experienced, grave) even though *Penseroso*, envisioning Milton's poetic maturation, gets the final word. While the *Penseroso* poet wishes to write Chaucerian-Spenserian poetry with rich allegorical and spiritual resonances – 'Where more is meant than meets the ear' (line 120) – *L'allegro* celebrates both 'nature' and classical 'art' by pairing 'fancy's child' Shakespeare with 'learned' Jonson (lines 132–4).[19]

L'allegro and *Il penseroso* patriotically celebrate native poetry's diversity, and Milton's 1640s prose polemics posit a reciprocal relationship between poetic and national greatness. Promoting the Puritan 'reformation', Milton imagines writing 'high strains' praising England's Providential guidance and a great work, like classical and Italian epics, instructing 'a great people'. In the 1650s he compares his prose defences of the king's execution and the Interregnum regime to an epic celebrating his countrymen. Although distinguishing (like Jonson) between an intellectual-moral élite and the 'vulgar' of all classes, Milton the polemicist enthusiastically imagines his poetry instructing 'all'. After the Restoration, however, Milton invokes classical norms to critique an erring England. *Paradise lost* addresses the 'fit . . . though few' (7.31). Like his defence of blank verse, Milton's preface to *Samson agonistes* challenges English readers' literary values with classical norms, suggesting that only those who understand ancient tragedy and Aristotelian *catharsis* can evaluate Milton's play. Milton condemns tragicomedy – defended by Jonson and recently celebrated in John Dryden's *Essay of dramatic poesy* (1668) as expressing the English genius for 'variety' – for deviating from ancient practice.[20]

Milton's Puritan classicism may be compared with William Davenant's Royalist classicism in the 1650 preface to his epic *Gondibert*. Writing during (and against) the Interregnum, Davenant praises epic for mirroring and shaping a courtly élite, whom it glorifies and instructs in governance. Identifying English social divisions with Aristotle's distinction between

---

[19] Milton, *Poems*, pp. 63–4, 68–76.

[20] Milton, *Complete prose works, volume 1 (1624–1642)*, ed. D. M. Wolfe (New Haven: Yale University Press, 1953), pp. 471–3, 616, 898; *Poems*, pp. 346, 549–50, 669–70, 838; *Jonson*, vol. VII, pp. 9–10; John Dryden, *Of dramatic poesy and other critical essays*, ed. G. Watson, 2 vols. (London: J. M. Dent, 1962), vol. I, pp. 58–9. For further discussion of Jonson's and Milton's differing sense of audience, see also Colin Burrow's essay in the present volume, pp. 492–6.

the few receptive to moral persuasion and the many requiring punishment (*Nicomachean ethics* 10.9.9–10), Davenant declares epic should not address common people, who respond only to 'punishment'. Like other Royalists who link poetic 'inspiration' with refractory Puritan 'enthusiasm', Davenant rejects inspiration in favour of Horatian sources of authority: talent, learning, and discerning critics. In reaction against imaginative excess, Davenant diminishes the poet's cultural authority. Presenting the philosopher Hobbes as his best critic, he claims that philosophical judgement must regulate poets' 'wilde' thoughts and thus diminish their resemblance to the rebellious commoners, whom Davenant compares to 'Wilde beasts'. The philosopher, rather than the poet himself, is now responsible for judiciously tempering poetic fancy.

Ambivalence about poetic power generates contradictions in Davenant's classicism. While preventing poets from surpassing predecessors, imitation, like philosophy, checks poetic 'excesses'. Following Aristotle, Davenant generalizes that all goodness avoids extremes. Yet to re-establish courtly rule requires grand ambition rather than mere goodness, in politics and poetry. Condemning excessive ambition, Davenant nevertheless notes that 'good men' display 'too little appetite' for greatness and power. Aspiring to poetic greatness and didactic force, Davenant precariously lauds his own deviations from classical models.[21]

After the Restoration, critics felt a profound rupture between the present and the 'last age' of stable, monarchical culture. Many considered literary reform guided by criticism necessary to promote England's internal order and external power. The simultaneous rise of 'Empire and Poesy' (to quote the Earl of Roscommon) was cliché. The neoclassical criticism of Louis XIV's powerful France provided a model for emulation. While familiar themes continued – balancing pleasure and instruction, 'nature' and 'art', 'fancy' and 'judgement' – more extended discussions of rules and evaluative analyses of the stylistic decorum, verisimilitude, and morality of texts emerged. Figures like Thomas Rymer, who were critics more than creative writers, exemplified the growing split, evident in Davenant, between poetic 'fancy' and critical 'judgement'.

Yet critics' authority never went unchallenged. Robert Howard and William Temple championed poetic freedom against critical rules. Defending herself as a female playwright, Aphra Behn denied that 'musty rules' and the classical 'learning' reserved for males were necessary for successful drama. Samuel Butler protested that poets, not 'Pedants & Philosophers', judge poetry best. Like Jonson, Dryden, the period's greatest critic, modelled himself on the 'most instructive' poet-critic, Horace. Dryden claimed

---

[21] William Davenant, *Gondibert*, ed. D. F. Gladish (Oxford: Clarendon Press, 1971), pp. 7–9, 12–14, 18, 22–5.

poets were the 'most proper' but not the only legitimate critics; critics' judgements helped keep poetic 'fancy' within correct 'bounds', but self-appointed 'censors' were too arrogant.[22]

Rymer, the most rigid proponent of Aristotelian rules as codified by French critics, lambasted Elizabethan drama for deviating from the formal unities (of place, time, and action) as well as the verisimilitude, decorum, and 'poetic justice' supposedly present in classical plays. While generally granting that classical literature and criticism embodied some permanent, fundamental norms, opponents defended literary variety. John Dennis contended literature must adapt to divergent religions and customs. Dryden found Rymer's norms overly 'circumscribed'; conventions must be appropriate to an age and nation's 'dispositions'.[23]

Dryden's 1668 *Essay* defends English drama's deviations from classical and French rules. With speeches by proponents of classical, French neoclassical, Elizabethan, and Dryden's own rhymed drama, the work examines how different dramatic forms please or instruct in diverse cultures before giving England's defenders the last word. Modern drama has virtues lacking in classical, such as pathetic love-scenes, which social norms kept ancient dramatists from depicting. French drama's moral seriousness and unities nicely counterbalance the French people's 'airy and gay temper'. By contrast, English drama's unsurpassed comedies and pleasing variety of action and character suit a 'more sullen people' who seek to be 'diverted'. Discharging the first English salvo in the 'quarrel between Ancients and Moderns' that engaged both English and French intellectuals through the early eighteenth century, Temple proclaimed in 1690 the general superiority of classical literature and culture to modern. He agreed with Dryden, however, concerning modern English comedy's pre-eminence. Like Jonson, Temple ascribed its greatness to the nation's distinctive 'humours', which Temple influentially linked to English liberty and free-spiritedness.[24]

While Rymer dismissed the changing tastes of the 'unthinking vulgar' in favour of the transhistorical norms of 'men of sense', Dryden attempted

---

[22] Spingarn (ed.), *Essays*, vol. II, pp. 106–7, 280, 307; vol. III, p. 84; Aphra Behn, *Works*, ed. J. Todd, 7 vols. (Columbus: Ohio State University Press, 1992–6), vol. v, *The plays, 1671–7* (1996), pp. 162–3; Dryden, *Dramatic poesy*, vol. I, pp. 108–9, 173, 225; vol. II, pp. 30–1.

[23] Thomas Rymer, *Critical works*, ed. C. A. Zimansky (New Haven: Yale University Press, 1956), pp. 17–76, 82–176; John Dennis, *Critical works*, ed. E. N. Hooker, 2 vols. (Baltimore: The Johns Hopkins University Press, 1939–43), vol. I, pp. 11–12; Dryden, *Dramatic poesy*, vol. I, pp. 212–19; vol. II, p. 195.

[24] Dryden, *Dramatic poesy*, vol. I, pp. 41–3, 60; Spingarn (ed.), *Essays*, vol. III, pp. 32–72, 91–107. On the eighteenth-century continuation of the 'Quarrel of Ancients and Moderns', see Douglas Lane Patey, 'Ancients and moderns', in *The Cambridge history of literary criticism*, ed. C. Rawson and H. B. Nisbet, vol. IV (Cambridge: Cambridge University Press, 1997), pp. 32–71.

to mediate between contemporary and permanent values. While claiming that he must please contemporary audiences to succeed as a writer, Dryden criticized excessive accommodations to transient 'popular' taste. Great works, however diverse, please the 'learned', 'judicious', and 'all ages'.[25]

Norms of correctness and refinement shaped the widespread view of English literary progress from medieval and/or Elizabethan 'natural' incorrectness to Restoration refinement. Dryden describes verse style's growth from Elizabethan infancy to Restoration maturity. Rymer and Dryden note Waller's refinement of prosody; Dennis claims Dryden finished what Waller began.[26] Dryden identifies his view of literary progress with Horatian classicism. Horace attacked those who venerated older writers for age alone (*Epistle* 2.1.18–89) and claimed his predecessor Lucilius would have corrected his rough style had he lived in Horace's polished times (*Satire* 1.10.68–71). The *Essay* invokes Horace to defend Elizabethan deviations from classical precedent, but Dryden later cites the 'great refiner' Horace to justify Restoration criticism and correction of Elizabethan crudities. Dryden even projects on to Horace notions of literary progress derived from the Baconian tradition's (anti-classical) view that 'one age learning from another, the last . . . know[s] more . . . than the former'.[27]

Yet like many contemporaries, Dryden also worried that his Renaissance predecessors were superior in fundamentals. His influential treatments of Jonson and Shakespeare, which did much to reverse their relative standing, suggest that the learned, classical poet was inferior to the 'natural' genius. While respecting Jonson as English neoclassicism's founder, Dryden believed that he and his age could excel in classical correctness. Dryden claims Jonson wrote the most 'correct' plays of his day and had 'fewer failings' than others. He examines with admiring detail how *Epicoene*'s plot combines classical correctness with English variety. Yet Dryden also claims Jonson had little 'fancy' and, despite his judiciousness, suffered from his age's 'errors'. Shakespeare, by contrast, presented a stiffer challenge. Though his uneven, 'careless' style displays 'fancy' beyond 'the bounds of judgement' and his implausible plots (rightly attacked by Rymer) smack of an unrefined age, without learning or labour, Shakespeare emerges as the 'most comprehensive' of modern and 'perhaps' all poets, displaying profound knowledge of humanity through matchless depictions of character. 'Divine' Shakespeare 'in a manner . . . left no praise' for successors.

[25]   Rymer, *Critical works*, pp. 20, 62; Dryden, *Dramatic poesy*, vol. I, pp. 116, 145–7, 200, 276–7; vol. II, p. 162.
[26]   Rymer, *Critical works*, p. 127; Dryden, *Dramatic poesy*, vol. I, pp. 7, 171–2; vol. II, p. 281; Dennis, *Works*, vol. I, p. 14.
[27]   Dryden, *Dramatic poesy*, vol. I, pp. 23, 170, 177, 188; compare Francis Bacon, *The new organon*, ed. F. H. Anderson (New York: Macmillan, 1960), pp. 80–1.

In confrontation with him, Restoration correctness appears not as un-ambiguous progress but as a survival strategy; as Dryden's *Essay* suggests, given their predecessors, Restoration dramatists must 'attempt some other way'.[28]

Dryden's defence of Shakespeare (against Rymer) as a 'genius' despite his 'faults' recalls Horace's advice to forgive great writers' small faults (*Ars poetica* 347–60) and Longinus's *On the Sublime*, which declared the faulty 'sublime' writer's superiority to the faultless but mediocre (32.8–36.4). Though Longinus had been translated into English in 1652, his major influence upon criticism dated from Boileau's 1674 French translation. Longinus provided Dryden and his contemporaries classical authority for exalting literary qualities besides correctness. Already in 1670 Dryden proposes poets should be 'bold' rather than 'over-care[ful]'; by 1677 he couples Horace and Longinus to defend erring 'sublime genius'.[29]

As Dryden on Shakespeare attests, praise of 'sublime' incorrectness could be as patriotic as the pursuit of correctness; a much echoed Waller line proclaimed English verse 'Bold and sublime, but negligently dressed'.[30] Hence a cult of Milton burgeoned. Admiring but ambivalent, Dryden himself treats Milton as both a 'sublime' classic above carping and an incorrect author needing revision. Dryden's preface to his operatic adaptation of *Paradise lost* praises it as one of England's 'most sublime' poems and defends Miltonic 'boldness'. Nevertheless Nathaniel Lee captures Dryden's corrective intent by praising Dryden's 'refin[ing]' in 'softest Language' what Milton 'roughly' rendered in 'hard spun thought'. Elsewhere Dryden celebrates Miltonic 'sublimity' but criticizes 'flat' passages, 'harsh' metre, 'antiquated' diction (contrary to Horatian precept), and deviations from classical epic. Echoing Jonson's claim to have loved Shakespeare 'this side Idolatry', Dryden declares uncritical praise of Milton 'idolatry'. Yet in the 1690s 'idolatrous' critics hail Milton the 'sublime' national treasure: Joseph Addison's 'Account of the greatest English poets' is typical in placing 'Bold, and sublime' Milton 'above the critick's nicer laws'. In 1695 Dennis declares English verse 'bold and sublime' before comparing Milton to sublime Pindar; in 1704 he claims Milton's 'daring Genius' honoured England with an epic whose 'irregular[ity]' transcends ancient rules.[31]

Longinus notes the view that sublimity depends upon political freedom (section 44). English contrasts between sublimity and correctness had socio-political resonance, since the former was associated with the English

[28] Dryden, *Dramatic poesy*, vol. I, pp. 67, 69–76, 85, 92, 148, 173, 231, 246, 252–3, 257.
[29] *Ibid.*, vol. I, pp. 143, 197; vol. II, p. 178.   [30] Waller, *Poems*, p. 214.
[31] Dryden, *Dramatic poesy*, vol. I, pp. 196, 199; vol. II, pp. 32, 84; *Jonson*, vol. VIII, p. 584; John T. Shawcross (ed.), *Milton: the critical heritage* (London: Routledge & Kegan Paul, 1970), pp. 83, 105; compare pp. 107, 114; Dennis, *Works*, vol. I, pp. 43–4, 333–4.

subject's liberty, the latter with both the English and the absolutist French court. Critics ascribed the refinement of Restoration English literature to increasing court influence. Dryden argues earlier English playwrights were 'unpolished' because they had little exposure at court; Robert Wolsely declares the Earl of Rochester's court residence helped him 'reform' an early seventeenth-century drama. Yet courtliness also stifles free expression and bold sublimity. In his final years as a Jacobite outcast from William III's court, Dryden compares verse licences derived from English predecessors to the Magna Carta. He contrasts Juvenal's 'zealous' attacks on tyranny with the 'Court slave' Horace's 'servile' satires and English 'sublimity' with French 'servil[ity]' towards classical rules. Dryden presents courtly France's writers as even less free than Augustan Rome's: Virgil's 'honest' advice to Augustus in the *Aeneid* proves a 'courtier' need not be a 'knave', but French critics, cowering under an 'arbitrary master', 'durst' not notice. While the Jacobite patriot Dryden decries French critics' enslavement, the Whig Temple attacks them as 'Arbitrary Rulers', apes of their tyrant.[32]

With political resonances always close at hand, critics contrast native tradition's complex, unrestrained dramatic plots, stylistic vigour, and daring turns of thought with French correctness. A major late seventeenth-century critical and artistic project was, however, to temper English or Elizabethan vigour with French or Restoration correctness and thereby properly blend order with liberty (like England's idealized 'balanced' constitution). Richard Flecknoe advocated drama 'neither too plain' (like the French) 'nor too confus'd' (like the Elizabethan); in Dryden's *Essay*, even the Elizabethan drama's defender advised a 'mean' between French deficiencies and Elizabethan excesses. Contrasting Elizabethan drama's rude power with Restoration 'skill' but lack of 'genius', Dryden praised William Congreve in a 1694 poetic address for tempering Elizabethan 'strength' and 'bold[ness]' with Restoration 'grace' and judgement so that 'The present age of wit obscures the past' (lines 2, 12–13, 19, 57).[33] The praise expressed more hope for English culture, however, than conviction about Congreve.

The discussion of English poetry in Dryden's *Preface to his Fables* (1700), a collection of translations, offers final expression of his broad sympathies and his sense that English literature must harmonize its diverse virtues. Exalting native tradition, Dryden claims that Chaucer rivals classical epic and deserves, like Homer and Virgil, his nation's veneration. Recalling

[32] Dryden, *Dramatic poesy*, vol. I, pp. 181–2; vol. II, pp. 132, 161–2, 247; John Dryden, *Essays*, ed. W. P. Ker, 2 vols. (Oxford: Clarendon Press, 1900), vol. II, pp. 174, 179; Spingarn (ed.), *Essays*, vol. III, pp. 2–3, 84.
[33] Spingarn (ed.), *Essays*, vol. I, p. xcviii; vol. II, pp. 93, 298; Rymer, *Critical writings*, p. 80; Dryden, *Dramatic poesy*, vol. I, pp. 56, 63; vol. II, pp. 161–2, 169–72, 238, 247.

his treatment of Shakespeare, Dryden declares Chaucer stylistically and metrically crude but endowed with a 'comprehensive nature' that could depict 'the whole English nation in his age'. Dryden's appreciation of Chaucer's mimetic genius is as innovative as his praise of Shakespeare's.

Dryden surveys English poetry in terms of different 'linea[ges]', contrasting the epic line of Chaucer, Spenser, and Milton with a 'correct' line from Edward Fairfax to Waller. Through translation Dryden positions himself as these two traditions' unifying heir: just as Spenser claims Chaucer's soul was 'transfused' into his own, so Dryden calls his own Chaucerian translations a 'transfusion'; yet Dryden 'polishe[s]' and 'correct[s]' Chaucer. Seeking to blend diverse English traditions, Dryden indeed blurs distinctions between original and imitative, rough and correct. Dryden aligns himself as an imitative poet with both Chaucer and English verse generally in claiming that Chaucer's 'refine[ment]' of Italian materials shows how English 'genius' 'improve[s] an invention' rather than 'invent[s]'. Allowing that he and his own times have not attained perfection, Dryden modestly hopes that his own work will survive long enough to 'deserve correction' in turn. More interestingly, he tempers the progressivist norm of refinement itself with a more relativistic conception of literary change: expanding Horace's comments on linguistic instability (*Ars poetica* 70–2), he offers his modernizing of Chaucer as a response to the linguistic and cultural changes by which all poetry, however great, becomes 'obsolete', 'obscure' and in need of revitalizing 'transfusion'.[34]

Criticism from Jonson to Dryden reveals an increasingly confident and diversified recognition of English literature's greatness. While Jonson condemns deviations from classical norms in order to found an English classical line, Dryden uses classical criteria to criticize, refine, and finally harmonize diverse traditions in order to construct an English canon rivalling the classics. Dryden's judicious but generous range of appreciation provides a model for the best subsequent criticism of English literature.

---

[34] Dryden, *Dramatic poesy*, vol. II, pp. 270–1, 277–91.

57

French criticism in the seventeenth century

Michael Moriarty

Seventeenth-century French criticism has generally, and with some reason, been seen as the imposition of a set of doctrines: adherence to 'the rules'; the imitation of selected and generalized Nature and of the ancients, according to the criteria of probability [*vraisemblance*] and decorum [*bienséance*]; the combination of pleasure and instruction; the separation and hierarchy of genres; the dramatic unities. The affirmation of these requirements began in the 1620s, and gathered momentum in the following decade. By around 1660 the neoclassical system was well in place, although it has been argued that its elaboration was only definitively accomplished in the eighteenth century. The content of these doctrines is explicated elsewhere in this volume; the emphasis here is on the significance they assume in the context of the social relationships of seventeenth-century French literature. This is explored via the objects, the implied public, the channels, and the agents, of critical discourse.

'Criticism' in late Renaissance France was potentially encyclopaedic in scope: its aim was, through the exegesis of profane and sacred texts, from antiquity and the early Christian era, to make the truths they contained available to the contemporary world. The focus of seventeenth-century criticism is narrower and more concentrated. Its object is a more selective range of texts, what contemporaries often referred to as *belles-lettres*. Poetry, including theatre, prose fiction (of a romance or a realistic type), letters, and fragmentary works of moral or social reflection (but also history) appear central, works of science, philosophy, theology marginal or absent. The tendency was to preserve, of the humanist critic's activity, only that part which dealt with the linguistic and literary qualities of the text; the concern was more with identifying legitimate sources of textual pleasure than with the text as a source of truth. Hence a specifically literary criticism took shape; and its growth can be seen as both reflecting and contributing to the emergence in the seventeenth century of literature as a relatively autonomous field, a distinct sphere of production and consumption with its specific institutions, and within which specific knowledges, values, and norms were being elaborated.[1] But we are dealing with

---

[1] On the history and structure of the literary profession in seventeenth-century France, see Alain Viala, *Naissance de l'écrivain: sociologie de la littérature à l'âge classique* (Paris: Editions de Minuit, 1985), to which what follows is much indebted.

tendencies rather than established states of affairs. Thus although the use of the word *critique* in connection with the judgement of the merit of an author or work is well attested in the 1630s, Antoine Furetière's dictionary of 1690 still associates it with the broader critical activity of 'les Scaligers, les Casaubons, les Lipses, les Erasmes, les Turnèbes'.[2] Moreover, literary criticism continued to be conceived (like rhetoric) as a guide to production as well as consumption: indeed, poetics and rhetoric were still closely bound up in this period, and the notion of oral eloquence affected attitudes to writing. The medium of most of this new criticism was the vernacular, itself reflecting the turn away from Renaissance humanism and towards a national audience, albeit a broader one than the humanist republic of letters. Towards the end of the seventeenth century, however, a kind of revival of the Renaissance philosophy of criticism took place, in the philological and historical scholarship of a Bayle, geared once again to intervention in religious and philosophical controversy.

Seventeenth-century criticism expanded its intended readership from scholars to a broader public which in some sense it helped to create. This shift of orientation, and the proximity of the critical activity to the practice of literature, is clear from the genres of critical discourse: much of the most significant criticism of the period was conveyed not in systematic dissertations (François Hédelin, abbé d'Aubignac's *Pratique du théâtre* being a notable exception) or commentaries on Aristotle but in prefaces to or critiques of individual literary works: a single readership, for literature and for criticism, was thus postulated. This broader public was dominated by the aristocratic strata of the court and the salons, and extended downwards to the middle bourgeoisie. Within it, women played both a practical and a symbolic role of importance. As holders or frequenters of salons, they could enable a writer to translate his cultural capital into social recognition: they embodied a model of discernment without scholarship that served to legitimate male aristocrats also. The critical ideology of this public was geared to pleasure, and to principles of evaluation such as 'taste', rather than the more formal criteria adduced by scholars. Works (such as those of Sorel and Du Plaisir listed below) were produced whose explicit goal was to furnish this broader public with a basic literary competence: significantly, they often juxtapose discourse on literature with advice on conversation, letter-writing, and correct language.

The periodical press that developed especially in the second half of the century provided a new channel for discourse about literature addressed to a non-scholarly social élite. Such publications, again, indicate a vision

---

[2] See Jean Jehasse, 'Les sens et emplois du mot "critique" au XVIIe siècle', in *Guez de Balzac et le génie romain* (Saint-Etienne: Publications de l'Université de Saint-Etienne, 1978), pp. 497–513.

of literature and of culture by the contexts into which they insert literary discourse: Jean Donneau de Visé's *Mercure galant* included reports on recent plays and novels alongside military, diplomatic, and society news, illustrated fashion reports, poems, songs, and puzzles. It invited readers to contribute their views on the behaviour of the heroine of *La Princesse de Clèves*, or, simultaneously, on the origin of beauty spots: many respondents dealt with both. The *Journal des savants* of the same year (1678), reporting chiefly on publications in science, philosophy, ecclesiastical and secular history, and medicine, also lists a treatise on poetics: it is as if we are dealing with two quite alien socio-cultural worlds.

The range of texts and genres covered by critical discourse was modified by tendencies in literary consumption. For instance, most scholars held that epic was the premier genre, and the criticism of the epic is of great theoretical importance; but, partly because of the failure of seventeenth-century poets to produce an epic of really convincing success, it was theatre that generated the most significant critical discourse. This is less to do with deference to Aristotle's placing tragedy above epic than with the fact that when methodical criticism in French began to take off in the 1630s, it had to come to terms with an ever-expanding corpus of contemporary dramatic texts, and with the established tastes of a theatre-going public. The relative breadth and heterogeneity of this public provided a new potential audience for literary criticism, but also inflected critical thinking, and the fascination of neoclassical dramatic criticism consists largely in its attempt to reconcile theoretical allegiance to Aristotle and his commentators with the *de facto* norms of the contemporary theatre. As to other forms, prose romance, popular more with the broad public than with scholars, was assimilated by its defenders to epic, and branded by its detractors, such as Boileau, as a perverted pastoral, a travesty of the heroic mode. Charles Sorel acknowledges the emergence of a new form of prose fiction by devoting a chapter of the *Bibliothèque française* (1664) to 'le roman vray-semblable', but the new genre receives what is held to be its first systematic examination in Du Plaisir's *Sentiments sur les lettres et sur l'histoire* (1683).

The influence of criticism on public taste was largely mediated through its influence on authors, to whom much seventeenth-century criticism was implicitly or explicitly addressed. If tragedians came to observe the unities of time and place this was probably less to do with a 'refinement' in public taste than with the need to validate one's status with fellow literary-professionals committed to upholding these standards. For it was very risky for a dramatist to count on success with his public and to flout altogether the opinions of the professional men of letters, as Pierre Corneille found out during the controversy over his tragicomedy *Le Cid*: the literature market was simply, until the mid-nineteenth century, too little developed to enable a writer to live respectably from his pen, independently of the recognition of the institutions, such as academies, in which writers organized themselves.

Which brings us to the critics. We may distinguish the criticism of the professional man of letters, whose social identity is bound up with his writing, from that of the amateur whose social position is quite independent of his or her writing. For the latter, discourse on literature is subjected to extra-literary norms and agendas, such as the social ethic of *honnêteté*. François de La Mothe-Fénelon's *Dialogues sur l'éloquence* (composed *c.* 1680) address a central problem in late seventeenth-century criticism, the relationship of precepts to the Sublime, but the norms applied are those of the pulpit.[3] The professionals on the other hand make much of their possession of a body of specifically literary knowledge necessary for valid judgement or production, which is part of their self-definition as a profession.

Those like Jean Chapelain and the abbé d'Aubignac, who swayed the fortunes of criticism in seventeenth-century France belonged, significantly, to the group that did most to shape the literary profession: those whom Alain Viala has termed the *nouveaux doctes*, men of letters generally of bourgeois background, who abandoned the encyclopaedic culture of earlier generations of humanists, and confined their erudition to the domain of language, rhetoric, and poetics, through which they could make contact with a broader élite public. In general, they combined critical and literary writing, attempting to create the taste by which their works might be enjoyed, though Chapelain's epic *La pucelle* and D'Aubignac's tragedies were not notably successful. It is important to recognize that, in the early seventeenth century, literature was not a profession held in high esteem among courtiers: Chapelain complained that they treated 'poet' as synonymous with 'buffoon' and 'parasite'.[4] In seeking to establish themselves on a good footing with the dominant class, the *nouveaux doctes* were committed to elaborating a new image of the man of letters. In part, this involved internalizing the standards of polite society: thus Paul Pellisson-Fontanier's eulogy of Jean-François Sarasin couples the defence of literature for entertainment with praise of Sarasin's ease, rare for a man of letters, in polite society. But it also involved developing the idea of the 'rules', standards, derived in principle from the ancients, which it is the role of the man of letters to maintain, in order to offer polite society a kind of pleasure that befits its dignity. Thus when Sarasin himself writes as a dramatic critic, he closely links his discussion to Aristotle's *Poetics*, so

---

[3] François de Salignac de La Mothe-Fénelon, *Œuvres*, vol. i, ed. J. Le Brun (Paris: Gallimard, 1983), pp. 8–10. On *honnêteté* see ch. 54, pp. 525–6.
[4] Jean Chapelain, letter to Mlle de Gournay, 10 December 1632, in *Opuscules critiques*, ed. A. C. Hunter (Paris: Droz, 1936), p. 371.

signalling his solidarity with professional men of letters. Perhaps the perfect expression of the ideal of the new literary profession and its relationship with the dominant social groups comes in the preface to Racine's *Bérénice* (1671), where he invites his audience to trust their own pleasure in the work, and leave it to the professionals to concern themselves with the rules that have enabled the pleasure to be produced. The writer's role is here subordinate, but indispensable: he supplies his audience with a pleasure the source of which is outside their knowledge, and the relationship between them is one of euphoric complementarity. Where the writer is sufficiently confident of his standing with the public he will go beyond Racine's claim that the rules are designed to please, and assert that to please is itself the rule, and that the spectator's own responses, about which he or she cannot be mistaken, are a sufficient index of quality: we find this approach in Molière's *Critique de l'Ecole des femmes* and La Fontaine's preface to the *Fables*. The self-affirmation of the profession as such, and of the autonomy of the literary field, is on the contrary strongest where a critic insists that pleasure that does not conform to rule is invalid. Thus D'Aubignac argues that spontaneous judgement of a category like *vraisemblance* is prone to error: experience and study of theatre are essential; one must know the rules in order to judge.[5] For Chapelain too, good sense is not enough: the public should familiarize itself with the rules, as a set of 'invariable precepts and dogmas of eternal truth', bringing together a host of discrete observations such as no one person could have discovered in many lifetimes.[6] The rules are a quasi-impersonal wisdom of which Aristotle, Horace, and so forth, are the mouthpieces; and one of the key critical discourses of the period was similarly, in form at least, impersonal (though drawn up by Chapelain): the *Sentiments* formulated by the Académie Française, under pressure from its founder Cardinal Richelieu, aimed at settling the controversy on Corneille's tragicomedy *Le Cid* (1637).[7]

In the wake of the success of *Le Cid*, Corneille published a poem, the *Excuse à Ariste*, in which he represented his success as the fruit of sheer merit, operating independently of patrons and networks of supporters (with the thinly veiled implication that his fellow authors could not say the same). This appeared as a shocking violation of professional solidarities, and prompted his fellow playwrights Jean de Mairet and Georges de Scudéry into bitter ripostes. In the resulting pamphlet war the critical debate of preceding years came to a head in a clash of theoretical arguments

[5] François Hédelin, abbé d'Aubignac, *La pratique du théâtre*, ed. P. Martino (Algiers: Carbonel; Paris: Edouard Champion, 1927), pp. 79–82.
[6] Chapelain, *Opuscules critiques*, p. 297.
[7] Documents relating to the quarrel may be found in Armand Gasté (ed.), *La querelle du Cid: pièces et pamphlets* (Paris: H. Welter, 1898).

(often juxtaposed with personal abuse so violent that Richelieu eventually ordered an end to the controversy) in which a conflict of visions of literature was at stake.

The most important attack on Corneille, Scudéry's *Observations sur le Cid* (1637),[8] focused largely on his infringements of the dramatic rules: *vraisemblance*, the unities, and *bienséance*. But in the 1630s these norms were only in the process of being imposed in theory and practice. Of his first play, *Mélite*, performed in 1629–30, Corneille later wrote that it did not conform to the rules because when he wrote it he had never heard of them.[9] Already, however, in 1628, François Ogier had felt obliged to defend his friend Jean de Schélandre's tragicomedy *Tyr et Sidon* in a preface attacking blind submission to ancient practice and theory.[10] He criticizes the unity of time (then usually known as the 'règle des vingt-quatre heures'), and the resort to messengers rather than direct representation; defying classical notions of purity of genre, he defends the invention of tragicomedy (not just tragedy with a happy ending but tragedy with comic elements) by urging its fidelity to the mixture of joy and suffering in human life (Dr Johnson was to say as much for Shakespeare). Chapelain's *Lettre sur la règle des vingt-quatre heures*[11] defending the rule, dates from 1630; in the following year Corneille's future enemy Mairet published the tragicomic pastoral *La Silvanire*, the first French play to conform fully to the unities, prefaced with an important critical discourse justifying them as a necessary aid to the spectator's imagination.

Ogier's arguments had involved a certain cultural relativism. Ideals of female beauty differ from one nation to another: the same is true of the spiritual beauties of poetry.[12] Ancient drama is too leisurely for the impatience of the French. The ancient methods were devised for a different time, place, and people (he cites the religious significance of Greek tragedy), and should be selectively adapted to contemporary practice.[13] Such arguments, anticipating those of the Moderns in the quarrel with the Ancients, were taken up by the anonymous author of the anti-Scudéry *Discours à Cliton*: there is always scope for innovation in arts and science, deference to the authority of the Greeks, Latins, and Italians is a betrayal of French poetic sovereignty.[14] In the preface to *La Silvanire* (1631), however, Mairet had admitted his debt to the Italian pastoral, whose merits,

[8] Gasté (ed.), *La querelle du Cid*, pp. 71–111.
[9] Pierre Corneille, 'Examen de *Mélite*', in *Œuvres complètes*, ed. G. Couton, 3 vols. (Paris: Gallimard, 1980–7), vol. I, p. 5.
[10] François Ogier, *Tyr et Sidon*, Préface, in Jean de Schélandre, *Tyr et Sidon*, ed. J. W. Barker (Paris: Nizet, 1974), pp. 150–61.
[11] Chapelain, *Opuscules critiques*, pp. 113–26.
[12] *Tyr et Sidon*, Préface, ed. J. W. Barker, p. 157.   [13] *Ibid.*, pp. 155, 158.
[14] *Discours à Cliton*, in Gasté (ed.), *La querelle du Cid*, pp. 241–82 (see pp. 251, 259–60).

however, he ascribed to rigorous adherence to ancient rules.[15] This seems
to suggest that, by going to the source, French writing could attain universal values, while escaping indebtedness to other modern literatures.

Corneille's reply to Scudéry (*Lettre apologétique*, 1637),[16] did not rise
to this level of generality: the fact that the play had given pleasure, to the
court and to Richelieu, is urged as sufficient proof of its merit. Jean-Louis
Guez de Balzac took the same line when Scudéry tried to enlist his support. Balzac enjoyed immense prestige as the creator of a powerful image
of the man of letters as one who reconciles the fruits of study with those
of polite society; respectful of the ancients, but contemptuous of contemporary humanism. Now, he urged that to have pleased a whole kingdom
was a greater achievement than to produce a play conforming to the rules;
nature is superior to art and knowing the art of pleasing is worth less than
being able to please without art.[17]

Scudéry's reply helps to reveal something further of the ideological
investment in the notion of rule. To make the people's pleasure the goal of
the drama is to reduce the poet to the status of an acrobat or a fiddler. The
people can appreciate nothing in the theatre but superficial display.[18] Likewise, La Mesnardière insists that the people can derive neither profit nor
pleasure from tragedy: clowns and acrobats are all they can appreciate.[19]
What this implies is that the experience of pleasure in conscious conformity to the rules and the assimilation of the didactic content of the
play (the requirement that drama should instruct as well as please) serve
to distinguish the superior mind from the 'people'. The same structure of
feeling is in Chapelain. Theatre was instituted principally for utility rather
than pleasure, so pleasure is not an adequate yardstick of merit: besides,
there are true and false pleasures. The former are based on *vraisemblance*
and appeal to 'minds born to politeness and civility': as for the rabble's
opinion, it is of no concern to the poet.[20] Public approval is valid only
when confirmed by experts,[21] and to trust one's own response as an indicator of merit is to risk resembling the populace.[22] The rules, then, con-
secrate the work as the product of an art: they remove it from the authority
of the populace, but equally their existence obliges the members of the
social élite to defer in their judgement to the masters of the art, if they are

[15] Jean de Mairet, *La Silvanire*, Préface, in *Théâtre du XVIIᵉ siècle*, ed. J. Schérer, J. Truchet,
and A. Blanc, 3 vols. (Paris: Gallimard, 1975–92), vol. I, p. 479.
[16] *Œuvres complètes*, vol. I, pp. 800–3.
[17] The exchange is in Gasté (ed.), *La querelle du Cid*, pp. 452–6.
[18] Gasté (ed.), *La querelle du Cid*, pp. 457–63.
[19] Hippolyte-Jules Pilet de La Mesnardière, *La poëtique* (1640; reprint Geneva: Slatkine,
1972), pp. P–R.
[20] Chapelain, *Opuscules critiques*, pp. 123–5.
[21] *Sentiments de l'Académie Française sur la tragicomedie du Cid*, in Gasté (ed.) *La querelle
du Cid*, p. 360.
[22] Chapelain, *Opuscules critiques*, p. 195.

to judge of literature in keeping with their social superiority. The rules serve therefore to legitimate the poet's status as a purveyor of pleasure to the public of the dominant groups, but not dependent on them.

The criticism of *Le Cid* seems, to us, to ignore the extraordinary richness of the psychological, ethical, and political content of the play. But the issues it focuses on are central to the definition of literature and the literary profession. Take the unities. Without the unities, as Chapelain had earlier argued, no *vraisemblance*; without *vraisemblance*, the audience cannot believe; without their belief, no instruction.[23] Thus the capacity of the poet to instruct the public at large, one of his key claims to dignity, lapses if the unities are not observed. More generally, what the Académie sees as some of Corneille's most serious errors (the choice of subject, the handling of the dénouement, the cramming of an excessive number of actions into a twenty-four-hour period)[24] come under the heading of 'plot' as defined by Aristotle: the arrangement of the actions.[25] They thus affect not only the essence of tragedy, but what is most central to poetics as such. For psychology (both the depiction and the arousal of the passions, which the Académie singles out as a virtue of *Le Cid*) is not intrinsically part of the domain of poetics: it also belongs to rhetoric.[26] To emphasize plot, and by extension poetics, thus helps the new generation of men of letters to establish a specific identity among the learned. It is thus more central to the definition of the new literary profession.

But *Le Cid* was judged also by the rules of *vraisemblance* and *bienséance*, artistic canons permeable to extra-poetic criteria. For Scudéry the fact that the heroine Chimène is still prepared to love the hero Rodrigue after he has killed her father, and to let him realize the fact, authorizes terms like 'shameless', 'monster', 'prostitute'.[27] In milder language, the Académie agreed;[28] whereas another anonymous polemicist, claiming to champion the ladies, defends Chimène's love as a spiritual attachment, nobler than the merely natural relationship of kinship, and asserts her right to resist sacrificing it to external interests.[29] The literary text is here caught up in very general contemporary arguments about the position of women, reinforced by a transposition of its ethical thesis into literary terms: both Chimène and Corneille are divinely inspired, and not subject

---

[23] *Ibid.*, pp. 115–17.   [24] Gasté (ed.), *La querelle du Cid*, pp. 365–70.
[25] Aristotle, *Poetics* VI.8–19 (1450a), in *Aristotle, 'The Poetics', Longinus, 'On the Sublime', Demetrius, 'On style'*, ed. W. H. Fyfe and W. R. Roberts, LCL (Cambridge, MA: Harvard University Press; London: Heinemann, 1927).
[26] Aron Kibédi Varga (ed.), *Les poétiques du classicisme* (Paris: Aux Amateurs de Livres, 1990), p. 15, n. 23; the passions are, of course, treated at length by Aristotle in the second book of the *Rhetoric*. See also Corneille, 'Discours du poème dramatique', in *Œuvres complètes*, vol. III, p. 123.
[27] Gasté (ed.), *La querelle du Cid*, pp. 80, 82, 94.
[28] *Ibid.*, pp. 372–5.   [29] *Ibid.*, pp. 466–81, esp. 470–1.

to merely human standards. (Significantly, Mairet was prepared to concede, contemptuously, that the play had the favour of women as well as of the people.[30])

It is difficult to see how the judgement of the Académie, overall unfavourable to Corneille, could have been otherwise without the *raison d'être* of the whole institution being undermined. He did not himself go along with the arguments of some of his supporters: to do so would have been to marginalize himself altogether in the world of a triumphant neoclassicism. Writing in 1648, he thus denounced the idea of a French non-Aristotelian dramaturgy; he claimed that the fundamental precepts of Aristotle were timelessly and universally valid, and he defended *Le Cid* as owing its success to conformity with Aristotle's conception of the tragic hero.[31] This had not prevented him in 1647 from attacking a central tenet of the neoclassical orthodoxy by arguing that the subject-matter of a tragedy should not conform to *vraisemblance*, because the kind of conflict that creates powerful tragedy involves overriding normal ties of kinship or friendship.[32] It is not surprising that ten years later he was repeatedly criticized in the abbé d'Aubignac's *La pratique du théâtre*, a summa of neoclassical dramaturgy. The spirit of D'Aubignac's work testifies to the extent to which the neoclassical codes had established themselves: he implies that nothing need be added to the theoretical debates as such, and often omits or skims over key theoretical issues: his interest is in the actual dramatic mechanisms by which the playwright is to achieve his goal.[33] His strictures if anything encouraged Corneille to continue to take an independent and productive critical line. The edition of his works he published in 1660 included three critical discourses, one on the dramatic poem in general, one on tragedy, and one on the unities, with references predominantly to his own works, and also a set of retrospective critiques ['examens'] of each of his plays to date.[34] To point to the ways in which his theoretical argumentation meshes with the validation of his own dramaturgy is not to detract from his quality as one of the finest critics of the period, and the most original; indeed, to miss the connection would be to misunderstand the constant dialectic he sets up between the development of theory and the experience of theatre. He uses Aristotle flexibly and resourcefully, enlisting his support when he can, arguing against him when he cannot. By enunciating new 'rules',[35] he implies that theatrical experience and the example of a modern writer can rank authoritatively

---

[30] *Ibid.*, p. 295.   [31] Corneille, 'Avertissement', *Œuvres complètes*, vol. I, pp. 695–6.
[32] *Ibid.*, vol. II, *Héraclius*, 'Au lecteur', p. 357.
[33] D'Aubignac, *Pratique du théâtre*, ed. P. Martino, pp. 21–3.
[34] References to Corneille's *Trois discours sur le poème dramatique* are to *Œuvres complètes*, vol. III, pp. 117–90.
[35] Corneille, *Œuvres complètes*, vol. III, pp. 136, 176.

alongside the ancient oracles. Heretically, he asserts that the aim of poetry is pleasure, to which utility is secondary;[36] that we can discover forms and procedures unknown to antiquity;[37] that wonderment ['admiration'] at a character's virtue can purge the passions perhaps more effectively than pity and terror;[38] and that, *pace* Aristotle, the hero of a tragedy may be perfectly virtuous.[39]

Despite attacks from a few independent spirits like Sorel, sceptical as to the necessity or utility of the unities,[40] neoclassical orthodoxy remained the dominant aesthetic until well into the succeeding century. But the superb ease with which Nicolas Boileau-Despréaux's *Art poétique* (1674) sums up its tenets may obscure some subtle shifts in the vision of literature he propounds. To affirm that poetry is a divine gift, and, moreover, that what is not excellent is worthless, promotes an image of the author more reminiscent of pre-classical, Renaissance, models and quite contrary to Chapelain's claim that a good knowledge of theory will ensure successful practice, even without an exceptional talent.[41]

Criticism of new genres was pushing into new territory. Jean-Baptiste-Henri de Valincour's *Lettres* on *La Princesse de Clèves* (1678) deplore the faults in the plot, with due attention to neoclassical standards: but he lays great stress on the power of the psychological analysis; the depiction of the passions so that the reader can recognize them from his or her own experience; and the power of the text to create an almost hallucinatory presence of the action.[42] These themes can in fact be paralleled in Boileau, especially bearing in mind Longinus's discussion of 'images' (vivid mental pictures), but the point is that the recognition-effect alluded to here is self-verifying (I know 'this is just how I felt'). The reader's experience no longer needs to be checked against a body of rules safeguarded by a literary profession, and the possibility of a reader-centred aesthetic takes shape. In Du Plaisir's more generalizing *Sentiments sur les lettres et sur l'histoire* (1683), where the heroic romance, which could at least claim a doubtful classical ancestry in the epic, is rejected in favour of the short narrative dealing with 'the ordinary course of nature', there is a similar emphasis on the reader's capacity to identify with the story, and on the work of style in bringing out complexities of psychology.[43] The depiction

---

[36] *Ibid.*, vol. III, pp. 117–19.   [37] *Ibid.*, vol. III, Agesilas, 'Au lecteur', p. 564.

[38] *Ibid.*, vol. II, 'Examen de *Nicomède*', p. 653.   [39] *Ibid.*, vol. III, p. 147.

[40] Charles Sorel, *De la connoissance des bons livres ou examen de plusieurs auteurs*, ed. L. Moretti Cenerini (Rome: Bulzoni, 1974), pp. 192–7.

[41] Compare Boileau, *L'art poétique*, I.1–6 and IV.29–40, and Chapelain, *La pucelle*, Livres I–XII, Préface, in *Opuscules critiques*, p. 259.

[42] Jean-Baptiste-Henri du Trousset de Valincour, *Lettres à Madame la Marquise *** sur le sujet de 'La Princesse de Clèves'*, ed. A. Cazes (Paris: Bossard, 1925), pp. 159, 187, 169.

[43] Du Plaisir, *Sentiments sur les lettres et sur l'histoire, avec des scrupules sur le style*, ed. P. Hourcade (Geneva: Droz, 1975), pp. 50, 52.

of the passions had been recognized as a value in the neoclassicism of the first half of the century: what is arguably new is its proclaimed centrality. Moreover, when like Corneille, Du Plaisir accepts that the central action may be improbable, thus offering the author an opportunity to display his skill by justifying in context what seems incredible in itself (pp. 47–8), he is in effect promoting the author by distancing him from norms shared with the profession and the public. Here too he comes into conflict with the neoclassical orthodoxy.

Late seventeenth-century criticism, as René Bray pointed out long ago, consists more of arguments about taste than of discourse about rules. But arguments over taste in the late seventeenth century – as discussed above in the chapter devoted to that topic – are bound up with crucial cultural and even ideological divisions.[44]

---

[44] See Michael Moriarty, 'Principles of judgement, probability, decorum, taste, and the *je ne sais quoi*' in the present volume (pp. 522–8).

58

Literary-critical developments in sixteenth- and seventeenth-century Italy

Marga Cottino-Jones

Critical speculation about the arts and, more particularly, about literature attained a level of high sophistication in sixteenth- and seventeenth-century Italy, as social and economic growth within a dozen or so city-states gave rise to concurrent intellectual flowering, focused around self-conscious movements. The most influential of these movements was humanism, and more specifically two types of humanism: *civic humanism*, with its philosophy of *vita activa-politica* [active-political life] by which literature and civic life were drawn together in clear opposition to the ideals of scholarly withdrawal encouraged by Platonism; and *vernacular humanism*, with its defence of the vernacular against Latin as well as of the Moderns against the Ancients, 'encouraging the moderns to seek to rival antiquity in their vernacular languages and literatures'.[1] After imitating the Ancients, philosophers and poets dared to surpass them: the generation of Marsilio Ficino was succeeded by that of Pico della Mirandola and Poliziano.

While Florence could justifiably lay claim to being the cradle of civic humanism, it was in Venice that the largely theoretical dimension of Florentine speculation on the role of the city-state matured into what became a way of life envied by Western intellectuals everywhere. The Venetian aristocracy's focus on civil and commercial activity that had stunted letters during the thirteenth and fourteenth centuries, made it, by the fifteenth and sixteenth centuries, Europe's best-educated ruling class. Even if the philological production of the Florentine *studium*, with the rise of commercial printing, dominated the Quattrocento by the century's close, Venice emerged as the hub of European cultural endeavours. Typical among these was the printing house of Aldo Manuzio (*c.* 1450–1515) whose Hellenophile Accademia Aldina drew upon the philological acumen of Erasmus, Pietro Bembo, and others to place critical editions of

[1] H. Baron, *The crisis of the early Italian Renaissance* (Princeton: Princeton University Press, 1966), p. 461. See also R. Weiss, 'Italian humanism in Western Europe', in *Italian Renaissance studies*, ed. E. F. Jacobs (London: Faber and Faber, 1960), and P. Burke, *Culture and society in Renaissance Italy (1420–1540)* (London: Batsford, 1973).

Greek as well as Latin texts into wide circulation, and – of signal novelty – 'classics' of another stripe, epitomized by Bembo's edition of Petrarch (1501) set in Aldus's newly cut, slanting, compressed humanistic type, thereafter known as *Italic*.

Critical thought and discourse in sixteenth- and seventeenth-century Italy were thus shaped by the literary and cultural concerns formulated by the humanists, or by the reactions their programmes elicited in the various dynamic, competing urban centres of Italian cultural life.[2] The most conspicuous issues debated throughout these two centuries revolved around two arguments: (1) the *questione della lingua* (the polemics about language) which affirmed or denied linguistic models, norms, and the authorial canon; and (2) debates on Aristotle's *Poetics*, treating genres, unities, proprieties, and decorum among levels of style.

*

To demonstrate that Florentine possessed a logical structure no less coherent than that of Latin, Leon Battista Alberti set in writing before 1454 the unpublished *Regole della lingua fiorentina*, thus establishing for the first time a form of codification for a vernacular language that seemed poised to challenge the literary supremacy of Latin. But the decisive champion of Florentine was Pietro Bembo, the Venetian arbiter of Cinquecento taste, whose *Prose della volgar lingua* (1525) defined the 'questione della lingua' in terms of the two most important problems debated during the period: the literary use of the vernacular over Latin and the specific territorial qualifications that such a vernacular should have in order to gain national recognition.[3] The first problem did not seem to be taken very seriously by Bembo or his followers, who easily accepted the primacy of the vernacular over Latin, given the high number of important vernacular texts produced from the fourteenth century on. As to the kind of vernacular to be used as the national literary language, Bembo strongly believed that none presently in use as a living language could meet the requirements. Consequently he opted for an exclusively literary solution by proposing to find this ideal language in the Florentine vernacular of

[2] C. Vasoli, 'L'estetica dell'umanesimo e del Rinascimento', in *Momenti e problemi di storia dell'estetica*, 2 vols. (Milan: Marzorati, 1959), vol. I, pp. 325–433; F. Tateo, *Retorica e poetica fra Medioevo e Rinascimento* (Bari: Adriatica, 1960); and A. Battistini and E. Raimondi, 'Retoriche e poetiche dominanti', in *Letteratura italiana*, ed. A. Asor Rosa, 9 vols. (Turin: Einaudi, 1984), vol. III, pp. 5–339, esp. pp. 44–82.
[3] W. Moretti and R. Barilli, 'La letteratura e la lingua, le poetiche e la critica d'arte', in *La letteratura italiana, storia e testi*, ed. C. Muscetta, 9 vols. (Bari: Laterza, 1973), vol. IV: 2, pp. 487–571, esp. pp. 492–7. See also B. Migliorini, 'La questione della lingua', in *Questioni e correnti di storia letteraria*, ed. A. Momigliano (Milan: Marzorati, 1949), pp. 1–75; and C. Dionisotti, *Gli umanisti e il volgare fra Quattro e Cinquecento* (Florence: F. Le Monnier, 1968).

Petrarch and Boccaccio, two of the most renowned Italian writers who lived and wrote in the fourteenth century. This solution, denying the validity of a currently spoken language, set as an ideal goal the linguistic perfection of two fourteenth-century Florentine literary models destined to become respectively the undisputed masters of poetic and prose language throughout the sixteenth and seventeenth centuries.

Bembo's solution met with serious opposition and resistance within and beyond Florence. According to Vincenzo Colli, called Il Calmeta, in his *Trattato della volgar poesia* in nine books – a text which, though now lost, was widely discussed by Bembo and Castelvetro – the ideal literary language was the courtly language [*lingua cortigiana*] spoken at the Roman court. Several other solutions were proposed mostly in reaction to Bembo's thesis, among which the best-known are those of Castiglione and Trissino. In the dedicatory letter to the second edition of his *Cortegiano* (1527), the Mantuan diplomat openly stated his opposition to the supporters of an archaic language and claimed his right and that of his fellow writers to adopt a contemporary language currently in use in the noble courts of the most prominent cities of Italy. Giangiorgio Trissino, on the other hand, adopting Dante's linguistic proposals formulated in the *De vulgari eloquentia*, debated Bembo's thesis both in his *Epistola de le lettere nuovamente aggiunte ne la lingua Italiana* (1524) and in the dialogue *Il castellano* (composed in 1528 and published in 1529), on the basis that Petrarch's and Boccaccio's language did not correspond to the Florentine or Tuscan idiom at all, but rather, represented a *volgare illustre*, an ideal superior vernacular that represented the Italian language nationally at its best.

This thesis of a national vernacular (neither Florentine nor Tuscan) was attacked by several Tuscan writers, including Lodovico Martelli in his *Risposta alla Epistola del Trissino* (1524), Claudio Tolomei in his dialogue *Il Cesano* (written in 1527–8 and published in 1555), and later, Benedetto Varchi in his *Hercolano* (completed in 1564 and published posthumously in 1570). The best known among the defenders of the national adoption of the Florentine vernacular, however, was Niccolò Machiavelli who discussed his solution at length in his *Discorso ovvero Dialogo, in cui si esamina se la lingua in cui scrissero Dante Boccaccio e il Petrarca si debba chiamare Italiana, toscana o fiorentina* (probably written in 1514 and published only in 1730 as an appendix to Benedetto Varchi's *Hercolano*). In the first part of the *Discorso*, Machiavelli strongly endorses the Florentine vernacular as the literary language of Italy and challenges Dante's linguistic theories in a *volgare illustre* by having him, as a character in the work, admit that the language he used in the *Divine comedy* coincided on all levels of style, even the lowest, with the Florentine vernacular. The second part relates the levels of style to literary genres and arraigns Bembo's dismissal of base realism in a forceful defence of vernacular comedy. Machiavelli's advocacy of a vigorous plebeian vernacular was revived in the seventeenth century by Bernardo Davanzati in his letters and in his translations from the classics and by Michelangelo Buonarroti il Giovane (the painter's nephew) who delighted in rustic comedy.

Bembo's thesis eventually prevailed and, with the publication of his *Prose*, achieved special authority in Florence, notably through Lionardo Salviati who recorded his ideas concerning philology and grammar in the *Avvertimenti della lingua sopra 'l Decameron* (published in two volumes in Florence in 1584 and 1586). Here he shared Bembo's advocacy of a fourteenth-century literary language as a linguistic ideal to be imitated by the modern writers in pursuit of linguistic perfection. At Salviati's death, the Accademia della Crusca (founded in 1582) carried on his project to compile a dictionary of the Italian language, publishing it in Venice in 1612 under the title *Vocabolario degli Accademici della Crusca*. Its goal was to preserve the Italian language at its highest point of development, namely in the literary language of fourteenth-century Florentine writers and, among the moderns, of those who imitated Petrarch and Boccaccio. Though not greeted with unqualified approval, the publication of the *Vocabolario*, with subsequent editions in 1623, 1691, and 1729–38, represented an important achievement for the 'questione della lingua' which – until the time of Manzoni – would henceforth centre around the claims of competing linguistic systems, the one based in archaic classical Florentine (as canonized by the *Crusca*), the other in the contemporary vernacular, two different yet equally rhetorical responses to the problem.

The question of literary models was a direct outgrowth of the polemics raised by the 'questione della lingua'.[4] Once more, it was Bembo who legitimized the classical theory of imitation and of literary models, establishing Petrarch and Boccaccio as the canonized *auctores* and respectively models of imitation in poetry and prose. For Bembo, Petrarch's verse set the norm for lyric discourse and marked the neutralization of all linguistic tension and asperity in a superior harmony of form and sounds. His readings of the poet's works are full of critical insight particularly on lyric technique and his use of metrics and phonetics.

Bembo's admiration for Petrarch was widely shared throughout Italy and it was Lodovico Castelvetro in particular who became the main catalyst for the immense prestige that the poet's work enjoyed both in Italy and abroad. His commentary on the *Canzoniere* (1582) is based on the rigorous application of philology and on a painstaking investigation of

---

[4] M. Aurigemma, 'La teoria dei modelli e i trattati d'amore', in *Letteratura italiana, storia e testi*, vol. IV: 1, pp. 327–69.

classical sources, initiating in its wake a trend of critical commentary that set a standard for the scholarly interpretation of earlier poetic texts.[5]

In a more critical vein, Bembo's admiration for Petrarch was matched by open criticism of Dante, the other great fourteenth-century Italian poet whose poetic language was deemed too harsh, overtly realistic, and lacking in elegance and harmony.[6] Bembo's judgement remained largely unassailed throughout the sixteenth and seventeenth centuries, although several critics opposed such criticism in the name of a more balanced assessment of Dante's poetry. Among these, the most influential was Iacopo Mazzoni, who, in his *Discorso in difesa del divino poeta Dante* (1573), examined the *Divine comedy* from the standpoint of its rhetorical virtuosity, the richness of its poetic language, and its abundance of classical reference. Vincenzo Borghini, one of the most important and rigorous editors of his time, also evinced a perceptive grasp of Dante's poetry, calling attention to its underlying tragic inspiration. By mid-century the Florentine Academy promoted public readings of Dante's poem held by well-known *literati* such as Benedetto Varchi and Giambattista Gelli. Among the commentaries to emerge from this critical resurgence, the most compelling were those of Alessandro Vellutello, Bernardino Daniello, and Lodovico Castelvetro. Eventually, the Accademia della Crusca identified the convergence of two defensive postures, the one centred on Dante, the other on the Florentine vernacular. As a consequence, the *Divine comedy* emerged, together with Petrarch's *Canzoniere* and Boccaccio's *Decameron*, as one of the main lexical sources for the Academy's *Vocabolario*. The seventeenth-century interest in Dante, however, remained on the whole desultory as demonstrated by the very few (only three and, at that, philologically inept) editions of his poem.

While Petrarch's fortunes continued to flourish into the next century, Boccaccio's found themselves shaped by unfolding religious and political events in Italy, especially during the period of the Counter-Reformation. While in the fifteenth century Boccaccio's Latin works had been greatly admired in Italian humanist circles, at the beginning of the sixteenth century it was his work in the vernacular, especially the *Decameron*, that attracted the attention of scholars and public alike and was elevated, after the publication of Bembo's *Prose*, to an exemplary model for Italian prose.[7] By the middle of the century, however, the Counter-Reformation spirit censured the openly irreverent and licentious representation of life

[5] D. Della Terza, '*Imitatio*: theory and practice: the example of Bembo the poet', *Yearbook of Italian studies* 1 (1971), 321–5.

[6] F. Maggini, 'La critica dantesca dal '300 ai nostri giorni', in *Questioni e correnti di storia letteraria*, pp. 123–66.

[7] A. Chiari, 'La fortuna del Boccaccio', in *Questioni e correnti di storia letteraria*, pp. 275–348.

depicted in the *Decameron* and took steps to limit the work's influence in Italian culture and society. The outcome was Vincenzo Borghini's 1573 expurgated edition of the *Decameron . . . ricorretto in Roma et emendato secondo l'ordine del Sacro Concilio di Trento*. In this climate of censure and orthodoxy, Boccaccio's texts were slowly marginalized and his recognition left to the more receptive embrace of foreign readers and imitators. Indeed, Paolo Beni's *L'anticrusca*, published in Padua in 1612 as a rebuttal to the *Vocabolario degli Accademici della Crusca*, turned out to be not only an anti-Boccaccio pamphlet but a defence of the Moderns against the Ancients, thus inaugurating the well-known *querelle* that would last more than a century both in Italy and abroad.

In fact, the signs of the *querelle* had already begun to emerge in late sixteenth-century literary disputes over the question of whether modern writers need continue to emulate their loftier Greek and Roman models or whether the latter had been surpassed by the Moderns as exemplary authorities in the use of language and style. The cultivation of individual 'genius' (in our sense first used in Cellini's autobiography), as expressed in a distinctive manner [*maniera*], placed imitation under greater critical scrutiny. By the end of the sixteenth century, a new generation of thinkers and practitioners, whose sense of emulation towards the past was a direct legacy of the early humanists, started to challenge the supreme exemplarity of the Ancients, while assigning an increasingly ascendant role to the Moderns. This shift was due in part to the growth of scientific enquiry and with it a transformation of man's sense of place in the cosmos. No less than scientific and moral speculation, literary achievement was often shaped by the impact of empirical discoveries, astronomic as well as geographic, that revealed a world quite different from what the Ancients had believed it to be. Furthermore, such revolutionary inventions as printing and firearms (the technology of print and war) became catalysts for a widening gulf between the modern and the classical worlds.

It was this self-conscious new spirit that inspired Tommaso Campanella (1568–1639) to praise modern times over the past, claiming that more notable history had been made in the last 400 years than in the foregoing 4000, and that more books had been written in the last 100 years than in the foregoing 5000. It was a similar conviction that triggered Alessandro Tassoni's vitriolic attack on the most revered *-isms* of his time; namely, Petrarchism, Aristotelianism, and classicism.[8] Having been the victim of

---

8   In his *Considerazioni di A. Tassoni sopra le 'Rime' del Petrarca con confronto dei luoghi dei poeti antichi di varie lingue* (Modena: G. Cassiani, 1609; probably composed as early as 1602 on the author's return from Spain), Tassoni sought to call attention to Petrarch's indebtedness to the Provençal poets and at the same time deride his imitators and their tactics. These *Considerazioni* triggered a heated polemic between Aristotelians and anti-Aristotelians involving prominent academicians, among them Cesare Cremonini from the University of Padua, one of the most influential Aristotelians of the period.

more than his share of persecution as a man of letters, Secondo Lancellotti (1583–1643), in his *Farfalloni degli antichi istorici notati* (1636), did not hesitate to undermine the taboo of the classics' infallibility by reciting the mistakes and incongruities found in several canonical classical authors. Even Emanuele Tesauro (1592–1695), one of the most representative literary theorists of the period, shared his century's admiration for the Moderns, impugning the 'fusty old curiosities' [*anticaglie*] he claimed to find even in Dante, while exalting the superiority of novel, inventive, and ingenious contemporary usage.

If any word was more often used than *ingegno* in the century, it was *nuovo* – the manifest result of genius. The poet-philosopher Campanella initiated this trend by invoking the Muses to assist him in creating a 'canzone novella', while the scientist Galileo composed the dialogues of the 'scienza nuova', and the poet-rhetorician Gabriello Chiabrera (1552–1638) declared that he wanted to discover 'nuovi mondi', just as his fellow Savonese, Colombo, had done. Of Dante, Chiabrera admired his daring specificity ['arditezza ... del particolareggiare'] and in his own *œuvre* sought 'to venture and to experiment'. Even the more restrained Fulvio Tesi (1593–1646) was acclaimed for his 'novità dello stile'. Artists practising the most diverse arts experimented with new genres,[9] invented new techniques, and discovered new ways to express artistic refinement that they proclaimed *nuova*, while remaining largely indifferent to the legacy of the classical past.

Modernità, embodying *novità* and *ingegno*, thus became a concept highly favoured in early seventeenth-century Italy. In his *Pensieri* (1608–27), Tassoni examined several ways in which the Moderns had proved their superiority over the Ancients, either by improving the latter's works through a more refined use of language and style, by exceeding the literary output of classical writers, or by reflecting in their modern works the spiritual enlightenment provided by the Christian religion. This view was echoed by Lancellotti in his treatise *L'oggidí ovvero il mondo non peggiore né più calamitoso del passato* (1622; second part in 1636) where he derides those who lament the inferiority of the present to the past. Giambattista Marino, himself the most famous poet of the century, openly defended his own poem, the *Adone*, in terms highly favourable to contemporary poetry (Letters to Achillini and Bruni).[10]

---

[9] One of these new genres was the mock-heroic poem. On the one hand, while this genre continues the early Renaissance comic experimentation with parodic deformation of literary élitist forms illustrated by Pulci's *Morgante* and Berni's *Rifacimento*, on the other, it seems to relate more closely to the intention to call into question traditional models and rules and to arraign classical models in favour of a lighter, less ponderous approach to poetry.

[10] Giambattista Marino, *Epistolario: seguito da lettere di altre scrittori del Seicento*, ed. A. Borzelli and F. Nicolini, 2 vols. (Bari: Laterza, 1911–12), vol. 1 (1911), pp. 259–60.

Indeed, the polemic over Marino's *Adone* and, through it, over the epic genre, added another page to the 'Querelle des Anciens et des Modernes', as it set contemporary epic poets against the classical literary past and earlier Italian models. For Alessandro Tassoni, in his *Varietà di pensieri di A. Tassoni, divisa in IX parti* (1612), both Ariosto and Tasso were seen as epic poets superior to the ancients: 'those two paramount champions of our time, whom present-day envy may well shake and torment, and yet it will not prevent them from becoming in the future the most distinguished and glorious poets who ever lived'.[11] Nicola Villani, in his *Ragionamenti dell'accademico Aldeano sopra la poesia giocosa de' Greci, de' Latini e de' Toscani* (1634), defends Marino and his *Adone*, asserting that contemporary poets have more to offer than either the Greeks and Romans or the Tuscans 'in so far as concerns poetic discourse, the use of language, rhyme and rhythm'.[12] In this view, modern Italian writers came to be regarded as better poets than their Tuscan predecessors, a stand already recorded in Paolo Beni's *L'anticrusca* (1612) as well as in his *Cavalcanti* (1614), where he extends his polemic by affirming Tasso's superiority over Boccaccio. By repudiating Boccaccio in order to defend Tasso, Beni draws attention backhandedly not only to the regulatory power of the Accademia della Crusca, founded on principles of emulation and on a conservative homage to authority, but to its active policy of canonizing the Ancients in a century fascinated with the audacious and the unexpected, with the Moderns as agents of the *nuovo*.

*

The first sixteenth-century treatises on poetics were for the most part inspired by Platonic and humanist thought, as were Bembo's works, together with much of the speculation on love and beauty so fashionable in the early Renaissance. Indeed, the principle of authority attributed to the great classical thinkers and their latter-day humanist epigones earned them a commanding presence in Renaissance and Baroque poetics. Nonetheless, the traditional homage paid to the *auctores* was not enough to check the combative dialogues that would break out simultaneously over the main function of poetry. These debates focused on whether to imitate, to please [*delectare*], or to teach [*docere*]. What made this argumentative strategy so appealing to contemporary minds was the fact – often overlooked by Italian critics – that such critical reflection did not take as its sole aim the elaboration of a purely theoretical system, but dealt quite concretely with poetry as a craft.

---

[11] See Tassoni, 'Pensieri diversi', in *Prose politiche e morali*, ed. G. Rossi (Bari: Laterza, 1930), vol. I, x, ch. xiv, p. 318.

[12] See Villani, 'Rime piacevoli', in *Ragionamenti dell'accademico Aldeano sopra la poesia giocosa de' Greci, de' Latini e de' Toscani* (Venice: Pinelli, 1634), p. 81.

The growing influence of Aristotle's *Poetics*, even in the early sixteenth century, attested to a new interest in 'the practical function of artistic representation'.[13] Indeed, according to its etymology, poetics always referred to a collection of principles, rules, and guidelines on 'how to make poetry'. At least two centuries of Western literary tradition, as demonstrated by the great national literatures of France, England, and Spain, drew heavily on the monolith of Italian critical codification, even if the practical results in Italy itself were scarcely impressive.

The ascendancy of Aristotle's *Poetics* in Italy was already underway by the fifteenth century. The treatise was first translated by Giorgio Valla in 1498, and the 1508 Aldine edition of the Greek text was followed by a second Latin translation by Alessandro de' Pazzi in 1536. The first Italian edition was then published in 1549 by Bernardo Segni. Many commentaries were written in Italian as well as in Latin. The most important of the latter were written by Francesco Robortello, Bartolomeo Lombardi, Vincenzo Maggi, Pietro Vettori, and Antonio Riccoboni, and of the former by Castelvetro, Piccolomini, and Salviati. This timely rediscovery of the *Poetics* coincided with the urge to codify literary experience. The lessons derived from Aristotle's treatise dealt with the process of building a system of rules for artistic representation and with the genres that appealed most to literary audiences.[14]

Thus two aesthetic trends, based respectively in the Platonic and Aristotelian traditions – and sometimes combining both – helped shape sixteenth- and seventeenth-century concepts of poetry. The Platonic influence is particularly visible in a group of important treatises that underline the importance of poetics as the first of the formal arts and establish its rigorous adherence to the three levels of style – high, medium, low – derived from the Horatian tradition of *decorum*.[15] This notion, while contextualizing several different earlier traditions, would help provide the momentum for later seventeenth-century discussions of *wit* or *concettismo*.

The most representative treatise of this trend was Bernardino Daniello's dialogue *Della poetica* (1536) which extolled poetics as the supreme legislator of the arts and sciences. For Daniello the foundation of poetic discourse was the Ciceronian triad of *inventio*, *dispositio*, and *elocutio*,

---

[13] Vasoli, 'Estetica', p. 377. For a more detailed enquiry into Italy's reception of Aristotle's *Poetics*, see Daniel Javitch's essay in the present volume, 'The assimilation of Aristotle's *Poetics* in sixteenth-century Italy' (pp. 53–65). Javitch highlights, in particular, the view that the sixteenth-century interest in the *Poetics* was related to the period's parallel experimentation with generic classification and the way it tended to read into the work a more comprehensive genre system than was warranted.

[14] See Vasoli, 'Estetica', pp. 376–400; Battistini and Raimondi, 'Retoriche e poetiche dominanti', pp. 86–91; and C. Dionisotti, *Geografia e storia della letteratura italiana* (Turin: Einaudi, 1977).

[15] See M. T. Herrick, *The fusion of Horatian and Aristotelian literary criticism, 1531–1555* (Urbana: University of Illinois Press, 1946).

though its overall goal was based on the Horatian Peripatetic compromise of utility and pleasure [*docere/delectare*]. While Daniello does not deal specifically with the concept of imitation, several other treatises equally concerned with poetics did so, especially in venerating the great *auctores* of the past. Imitation represented, therefore, the ideal of speaking well [*bene dicere*], as the style and examples proposed by the great *auctores* became the most important resources in the technical training of modern authors. The most authoritative among these treatises were Giulio Camillo Delminio's *Della imitazione* (*c.* 1530), Bartolomeo Ricci's *De imitatione* (1541), and Girolamo Fracastoro's dialogue *Naugerius sive de poetica* (1555).[16]

The critical debate over imitation led naturally to critical discussions about genres, particularly under the influence of Aristotle's theories. According to the *Poetics* the preferred genres were the tragic and the epic. The privileging of these genres led to a growing interest in their codification along with a parallel concern for moral and psychological issues, based on the criteria of *verisimilitude* and *credibility* and on the use of specific, highly sophisticated poetic devices. Other discussions addressed the distinction between the chivalric poem or 'romanzo' and the heroic poem, and the definition of tragedy. The most significant work in this area was done by Giovanni Giorgio Trissino, Sperone Speroni, Giovambattista Giraldi Cintio, and Torquato Tasso. Trissino, one of the most influential Aristotelians of his time, expounded his views on the tragic in the preface to his tragedy *Sofonisba* (1529) and elaborated on the *Poetics* in his commentary in two parts, *Le prime quattro divisioni della poetica* (1529) and *La quinta e la sesta divisione della poetica* (1562). In contrast, Sperone Speroni and Giovambattista Giraldi Cintio were both considered champions of 'modernism' because of their polemical stand against the principle of authority and their unrestrained questioning of established Aristotelian norms and regulations. Speroni directed his critical attention to the category of *elocutio*, which addresses both the criteria for embellishing poetic discourse and its power to elicit pleasure and emotion. He applied his poetic views, founded on the marvellous [*meraviglia*] and the pleasurable [*diletto*], to his tragedy *Canace* (intended for performance in 1542), a play which provoked ferocious critical reaction from the Aristotelian camp.[17] Giraldi Cintio's main contribution to this critical debate is his celebrated *Discorsi intorno al comporre de i romanzi delle commedie e delle tragedie* (1554) in which he strongly defended the writing of 'romanzi' as a typically modern poetic genre. If the 'romanzi' went unmentioned by the old

---

[16] See F. Ulivi, *L'imitazione nella poetica del Rinascimento* (Milan: Marzorati, 1959).
[17] On this specific point see Bernard Weinberg, *A history of literary criticism in the Italian Renaissance*, 2 vols. (Chicago: University of Chicago Press, 1961), vol. ii, pp. 917–18.

poetics, Aristotle's included, it was simply because they were unknown in those times. Giraldi was also very much in favour of an author's relative autonomy in adhering to established poetic codes. Torquato Tasso likewise took part in the debate over literary genres with his *Discorsi dell'arte poetica*, read for the first time in the Ferrara Academy around 1570, and in the *Discorsi del poema eroico* (1594), where he worked out a distinction between the tragic and the epic in terms of style, topics, inspiration, and goals.[18]

Both Giraldi Cintio and Tasso represent a need to combine the respect for a tradition of poetic rules and exemplary classifications with the belief in the uniqueness of the individual poetic experience. Tasso's *meraviglioso* [marvellous] prepares for Marino's poetics of the *meraviglia*, which, together with *concettismo*, was the poetics that best expressed in both its positive and negative aspects all the contradictions of the Baroque age.[19] In that period, an awareness of language and attention to technical innovation and visual effect, and consequently to the sensual, the emotional and the spectacular, dominated all forms of art and innovatively combined Aristotelian and Platonic influences, while strongly underlining the affective goal of artistic creation [*delectare*]. At the same time, the Counter-Reformation spirit maintained a strong hold on the didactic treatises of the times and their strict adherence to the primacy of *docere*. Daniello Bordello's *L'uomo di lettere difeso ed emendato* (1645), Matteo Peregrini's *Delle acutezze* (1639), and Emanuele Tesauro's *Il cannochiale aristotelico* (1654) provide the best examples of seventeenth-century theoretical writing, combining the didactic tendencies of the Counter-Reformation with the elaborate style based on the poetics of *meraviglia* and *concettismo*.[20]

Finally, Lodovico Castelvetro's contribution to the history of poetics needs to be acknowledged, particularly for his 1570 *Poetica d'Aristotele vulgarizzata et sposta*. Castelvetro reconsiders the humanistic dualism between history and poetry, *verisimilitude* and the *real*, underscoring its ontological split and chronological segmentation (first, you have the things represented (history), and only afterwards their representation (poetry)). According to Castelvetro, poetry's goal is thus *delectare* rather than *docere*, but *delectare* with a strong cognitive qualification, as it develops out of the recognition of how perfectly the representation of the

---

[18] G. Baldassarri, 'L'apologia del Tasso e *la maniera platonica*', in *Letteratura e critica: Saggi in onore di Natalino Sapegno* (Rome: Bulzoni, 1977), vol. IV, pp. 223–51.

[19] See F. Croce, 'Le poetiche del Barocco in Italia', in *Momenti e problemi*, vol. I, pp. 547–75.

[20] C. Varese, 'Teatro, prosa, poesia', in *Storia della letteratura italiana*, ed. E. Cecchi and N. Sapegno, 8 vols. (Milan: Garzanti, 1967), vol. V, pp. 521–928, esp. pp. 740–52; F. Croce, 'Critica e trattatistica del Barocco', in *Storia della letteratura italiana*, vol. V, pp. 473–518, esp. pp. 495–6 and 500–6.

real was achieved, rather than out of the exceptionality of the poetic form. The cognitive essence of the pleasure of poetry is seen by Castelvetro in net conflict with the more vatic view of poetry as emotional transcendence, the so-called Platonic divine *furor* which Castelvetro lucidly refutes as the fabrication of poets for gaining favour among their public.

Castelvetro's polemic stand against the Platonic *furor* was shared by other important Aristotelians of the time such as Alessandro Piccolomini and Lionardo Salviati. A counter-position emerged, however, in the late Renaissance and early Baroque period, authorizing the more charismatic Platonic position and signalling the approach of a 'new era'. The exponents of this trend, from Giordano Bruno to Campanella and even partly to Galileo, were, in fact, the most authoritative representatives of the 'new science'. For them, poetry as a way to truth draws on an emotional experience closely related to the tradition of the Sublime. Bruno's *Degli eroici furori* (1585) stands as one of the most uncompromising anti-Aristotelian manifestos of the times especially in the way it calls into question binding rules and precepts, as 'poems are not born from rules . . . but rather rules from poems'.[21] This declaration was later echoed by Marino, the renowned Baroque poet, in his own assertion that 'the real rule . . . is to know how to break the rules at the right time and place . . .' (Letter to Girolamo Preti).

The cycle of critical speculation derived from the humanist fascination with the classics, and later articulated around a systematic codification of rules inspired by Aristotle's *Poetics*, seems to wane by the seventeenth century with a call for abandonment of the codification itself. And yet the influence of the argumentative strategy so typical of these centuries continued generating new energy at the level both of poetic and scientific discourse, especially in light of man's new ontological position in the cosmos and the drift away from anthropocentrism. It is not surprising that Giambattista Vico, the great Italian thinker who closes this era and opens the age of Enlightenment, was both a poet and a philosopher, thus bearing witness to the importance of the legacy left by these two highly combative centuries, particularly in the field of poetics and the corresponding speculative discourse on poetry.

[21] G. Bruno, 'Degli eroici furori', in *Dialoghi italiani* (Florence: Sansoni, 1958), p. 959.

59
Cultural commentary in seventeenth-century Spain: literary theory and textual practice

Marina Brownlee

Seventeenth-century Spain (alternately referred to as part of the 'Golden Age', as the Baroque, or, more recently, as 'Early Modern Spain') was, like our own post-modern era, analytical, self-reflexive, and sceptical, a period as committed to cultural commentary and even indictment – in spite of the repressive ethos of the Counter-Reformation. As a result of the inevitable controversies which ensued, this period, like today's post-modernism, stages an ongoing interrogation of categories in a variety of ways that are visible both in the literature and art being produced at that time and in the provocative theorizing to which they gave rise.

In terms of literary production, both periods likewise concern them-selves very centrally with the power and constraints of *mimesis*. Like post-modernism, the Baroque is the cultural expression of a society bent on critically appraising the myths of the preceding era which viewed itself as paradigmatically 'modern'. Both movements undermine a humanist vision – be it that of Erasmian humanism or secular humanism. Both like-wise overtly discredit utopic cultural structures – be they imperial or Marxist. In other words, both demythologize – that is what the crisis of legitimacy is all about. The Baroque like post-modernism is much more form-conscious than the age that preceded it, and to which it is responding. The existence of these two movements, in addition, was first perceived in the plastic arts and only thereafter in literature. Both exploit the same literary figures: antithesis, oxymoron, paradox, catachresis, hyperbole, and example.

In recent years, these cultural affinities have led to a fundamental rethinking of the hitherto prevailing and distorted view that Golden Age literary production is a largely homogeneous extension of the state and its official discourses. On the one hand, seventeenth-century Spain was painfully aware of its decline in power and cohesiveness both at home and abroad. The events of 1492, the Reconquest followed – paradoxically – by the Conquest, would have long-term negative effects of which Spain's finest writers were keenly aware. The racial purification concluded in January of that year, after a struggle of seven hundred years, was rendered rather insignificant by comparison with the multiracial legacy

578

of Columbus's discovery in October of the same year. The politics of blood purity would pose tremendous problems for centuries, and its role as one of the major 'systems of exclusion', to use Michel Foucault's term, is elaborately borne out by the history and literature of the time.[1]

The complexity of this period and its literary representation cannot be overemphasized. María de Zayas, for example, would lament the passing of the Golden Age represented by the Catholic kings, from the perspective of the decaying seventeenth-century society in which she lived in a very particular sense, namely, from the perspective of gender relations: 'In other times, especially those of King Ferdinand . . . it was not necessary to take men by force, or in chains, as is necessary today (to the unhappiness and misfortune of our Catholic king); in his day, men would give up their fortunes and themselves: the father to defend his daughter; the brother to defend his sister; the husband to defend his wife; and the suitor his lady'.[2] In addition, as we now realize after having shed the positivistic legacy of nineteenth-century literary history, seventeenth-century Spanish literature – far from serving as a mouthpiece of the state – often criticizes its most revered values. If we consider, for example, the revenge tragedies of Lope de Vega we see that they are not, by any means, predictable and unproblematic celebrations of matrimonial ethics as defined by Church and state. *El castigo sin venganza* bears eloquent testimony to this fact. Likewise, Calderón's *Vida es sueño* cannot be read as a straightforward illustration of the Counter-Reformation's emphasis on asceticism and the vanity of earthly things. It is, to an equal if not greater degree, a staging of the conflict between individual subjectivity and absolutism, as represented by Segismundo and his father, King Basilio. Calderón, in effect, dramatizes the crisis of legitimation that results from a society that finds itself unwilling to accept blindly the belief that authority and absolute control are inherently good.

Such representation of subjectivity points towards the new appreciation of the individual human subject, which is the hallmark of the modern era. And, indeed, the ideological complexities of this seminal period have, after a lengthy and detrimental identification of it as 'Baroque' (with all of the negative associations that this period term entails), finally, and quite appropriately, given way to its identification as Early Modern Spain.

The one feature of this period which differs from subjectivity as conceived by much of post-modernism is that the post-modern subject is too often construed as an overdetermined function of ideology. (Freudian, Marxist, and Althuserian notions of subjectivity are totalizing models

---

[1] See 'The subject and power', *Critical inquiry* 8 (1982), 777–95.
[2] *Novelas amorosas y ejemplares*, ed. A. de Amezúa (Madrid: Aldus, 1948), p. 455. My translation.

which are often enlisted in this kind of criticism.) We should avoid such simple equations in the study of Early Modern Spanish literature, for although the Counter-Reformation mentality produced a considerable number of like-minded literary texts, it also provoked the writing of innumerable texts that resisted its dictates. Cultural formation, as we now realize, is not something which can be prescribed, imposed, and implemented. Rather it is a phenomenon which emerges as a consequence but also frequently in spite of numerous external factors – political, economic, religious, and so on. Early Modern Spain offers dramatic testimony to this fact – to the intricate nature of culture and its literary representation. Because Calderón wrote *autos sacramentales* which by definition dramatized the Eucharist in terms of personalized theological abstractions, we should not assume that he represented an uncritical portrayal of official discourses. Witness, for example, *El alcalde de Zalamea*, considered by many to be Calderón's masterpiece, a play that glorifies a commoner who defies the social abuses of a higher class. In other words we must avoid the time-worn assumption that a given author represents a single discursive position. Needless to say, not only can one individual author constitute multiple, and even contradictory subject positions, but authors writing at the same moment may vary greatly in axiological terms. We have only to recall the radically different continuation of a model text like *Don Quijote* I by Cervantes in his Part II, and by Avellaneda or, in terms of gender, of Zayas' *novelas* and those of Mariana de Carvajal. The question then arises, should we look for points of contact or for differences in mapping out seventeenth-century trends in Spanish literature and literary theory? The remarks that follow attempt to suggest both.

If we consider theatrical production from the period, we find that it was both enormous – 'the largest combined body of dramatic literature from a single historical period'[3] – and enormously controversial. At the root of the controversy was the collective disdain of aestheticians and moralists alike for the new three-act *comedia* invented by Lope de Vega (a disapproval which they extended to novelistic prose fiction as well). The *comedia*, like the *novelas* and novels being written at the time, were considered of dubious merit both in moral and aesthetic terms, an attitude which stemmed primarily from the fact that these literary forms lacked antique paradigms.

In his playfully conceived *Arte nuevo de hacer comedias* (1609), written after he had composed many plays, and in part as a defence of his *comedia nueva* against its neoclassical detractors, Lope advocates such practices as the mixed form, that is, insertion of comic relief in serious,

---

[3] Henryk Ziomek, *A history of Spanish Golden Age drama* (Lexington: University of Kentucky Press, 1984), p. 247.

even tragic plays: 'By combining tragedy and comedy, / Terrence and Seneca, although it may be / like another Minotaur for Pasiphae, / they will make (the play) at times grave, at others ridiculous, / because such variety is enjoyable'.[4] The genius of Lope's theatrical production (by his own account roughly 1500 plays) was that he streamlined the classical five-act play into three acts, created realistic character types who expressed themselves in vivid dialogue and poetic diction unencumbered by rhetorical excess, and he also knew how to address social issues of his day. The result was a theatre of immediacy which rendered the stately drama on the model of Cervantes' well-wrought *Numancia* largely obsolete, thereby also making impossible Cervantes' youthful ambition to make his career as a dramatist.

The new theatre was criticized by such theorists as Suárez de Figueroa, Cascales, López Pinciano, and Torres Rámila for its disregard of Aristotelian theory of the three unities. Yet one of the ironies of this criticism is that such critics interpreted Aristotle's adherence to the three unities of time, space, and action erroneously, according to Renaissance Italian misinterpreters of the *Poetics*. Echoing the disapproval of the *antiguos* (the conservative neo-Aristotelians) and their misinformed backreading, the priest in 1.48 of *Don Quijote* (1605) laments as follows:

What could be more ridiculous than to paint us a valiant old man and a young coward, an eloquent servant, a statesmanlike page, a king as a porter, and a princess a scullery-maid? And they pay no more regard to the place or the time in which their action is supposed to occur. I have seen a play whose first act opened in Europe, its second in Asia, and its third ended in Africa. And if there had been four acts, the fourth no doubt would have finished up in America; and so it would have been played in all four quarters of the globe.[5]

In 1617 Torres Rámila published *La spongia*, 'the sponge used to erase or clean up . . . Lope's entire opus'.[6] According to Entrambasaguas, this work (no longer extant) represents a systematic critique that judges the major works of the 'Monster of Nature' according to neo-Aristotelian principles. Despite such adverse criticism, however, it was clear that Lope's theatrical innovation was a brilliantly versatile form with an immediate appeal for its audience, a medium capable of treating the most compelling issues of the day: for example, religion, gender relations, colonialism, and so on. One of the most outspoken and humorous defences of Lope's new form is offered by Tirso de Molina when he argues

[4] *Arte nuevo de hacer comedias en este tiempo*, ed. J. de José Prades (Madrid: Clásicos Hispánicos, 1971), lines 174–8.
[5] *The adventures of Don Quixote*, trans. J. M. Cohen (Harmondsworth: Penguin, 1950), pp. 248–9.
[6] Joaquín de Entrambasaguas y Peña, *Una guerra literaria del siglo de oro. Lope de Vega y los preceptistas* (Madrid: Tipografía de Archivos, 1932), p. 113.

in his *novela* collection *Los cigarrales de Toledo* that 'Because God was the first tailor who dressed our first parents, is that a justification for our wearing animal skins as they did, and for our condemning suits?'[7]

The *vulgo* [masses] alluded to by both Cervantes and Lope, among others, became, in seventeenth-century Spain, an influential consumer sector. With the advent of the *corral* [public playhouse][8] they had, for the first time of any consequence, easy access to the theatre. It was this *vulgo*, moreover, which was denigrated by conservative critics of Lope as the group which tolerated his unorthodox innovations, thereby allowing them to gain currency. In writing of this group, E. C. Riley aptly observes that 'to the Golden Age writer the *vulgo* was rather what the *bourgeois* was to that of the nineteenth century, a class distinction with a general imputation of philistinism'.[9]

The uniqueness of Lope's career is suggested by Pérez de Montalbán, who indicates that at the age of five Lope translated Claudius Claudianus's *De raptu Proserpinae* from Latin into Spanish. He wrote in all existing literary genres, secular and sacred, treating such diverse subjects in his theatre as Ovidian mythology, history and legend, current events, honour plays, cloak and dagger plays, plays based on Italian *novelle*, pastoral plays, and plays based on popular literature, especially ballads [*romances*]. Lope's sensitivity to cultural controversy is exemplified in his depiction of social tensions between classes in such works as *Peribáñez* and *Fuenteovejuna*, and his interest in exposing, for example, the perils of arranged marriages (especially from the female perspective) can be seen in a number of his *comedias de costumbres* [plays of manners].

Criticism of aristocratic society and the exposition of theological issues characterize the intellectual project of Lope's illustrious successor, Tirso de Molina, who vies (along with Vélez de Guevara) as the second most prolific playwright after Lope. The play by Tirso that has received the greatest amount of commentary, *El burlador de Sevilla y convidado de piedra* (1616–30), was written during a time of social and political disorder. This *comedia* focuses on the libertinism of the protagonist, Don Juan Tenorio, who assumes that he will, no doubt, have sufficient time to ask God's forgiveness for his profligacy. Hence, his repeated remark: '!Qué largo me lo fiáis!' ['What a long time you (God) grant me!']. This figure, along with Hamlet, Faust, and Don Quijote, is considered to be one of

---

[7] *Cigarrales de Toledo*, ed. V. Said Armesto (Madrid: Biblioteca Renacimiento, 1913), p. 127.

[8] See Bruce W. Wardropper's introduction to *Siglos de oro: Barroco*, ed. B. W. Wardropper, et al., *Historia y crítica de la literatura española* 3 (Barcelona: Crítica, 1983), p. 24 and, for a different view, José Antonio Maravall, *Culture of the Baroque: analysis of a historical structure*, trans. T. Cochran (Minneapolis: University of Minnesota Press, 1986), p. 102.

[9] E. C. Riley, *Cervantes' theory of the novel* (Oxford: Clarendon Press, 1962), p. 109.

the great myths of modern subjectivity. The issue of free will – subjective desire and its implications within the social order, an especially controversial topic at the time when Tirso wrote – is the central focus of the work.

Of all the plays written in the Spanish language with a pan-European diffusion, the most famous is Calderón's philosophical drama, *La vida es sueño* (1631–5), written, among other reasons, as a cautionary example for the Spanish monarchy. Set in Poland, the other defender of Christendom against the Turks, this allegory exposes the ephemeral meaning of earthly power and the relationship of determinism to free will. Like *El burlador*, this play focuses with equal intensity on subjectivity – the degree to which an individual is able to determine his own destiny, and the relationship of his subjective desires to the body politic. In its title *La vida es sueño* reflects the seventeenth-century's fascination with paradox, with the juxtaposition of contradictory values in the relentless search for phenomenological truth. Also Baroque in its conception is the play's carefully related secondary plotting, and play-within-a-play artifice, as is its interest in cross-dressing as a way of interrogating issues of gender and sexuality. The magisterial use of rhetorical figures conveys powerfully the implications of self-imposed human bondage – literal and metaphorical – indicating also the method by which one may attain liberty from the proper exercise of free will.

Indeed, an obsession with rhetoric and its relationship to appearance and reality, that is, epistemology and its implications for human subjectivity, is at the centre of all seventeenth-century literary expression. And, in the field of poetry, it is the literary currents of *culteranismo* and *conceptismo* which constitute the two most important developments. The first literary movement, *culteranismo*, corresponds to a poetry of extreme artifice resulting from the use of deliberate semantic difficulty, Latinate syntax and vocabulary, and a taste for classical allusion. Within this literary environment, the most characteristic figure is hyperbaton – the displacement of parts of speech from their normative position. Those poets who engaged in this type of writing were clearly élitist, writing for a cultivated reader who could appreciate the obscurity in language, syntax, and allusion – the opposite of the *vulgo*, the undiscriminating masses, who were charged by disapproving theoreticians with allowing unorthodox, hence, in their estimation, bad literature to become accepted as legitimate.

Luis de Góngora y Argote (1561–1627) is the poet who developed this celebration of verbal artifice to perfection – or in the estimation of his unappreciative critics – to excess. His two *Soledades* (1613) and the *Fábula de Polifemo y Galatea* (1613) (a retelling of Ovid's *Acis and Galatea* (*Metamorphoses* XIII)) offer a wealth of superlative examples of what came to be known somewhat pejoratively as *culteranismo* (a calque on *luteranismo*, Lutheranism).[10] Among his supporters was Díaz de Ribas, who in 1624 begins his *Discursos apologéticos por el estilo del Polifemo y Soledades* as follows: 'Novelty produces unfamiliarity and contradiction. The style of Don Luis de Góngora in these works (although it conforms to the example of the poets of antiquity and their rules) seems new to our age, which is not used to the magnificence and heroism which poetry requires.'[11]

Those who disapproved of this new poetry wrote with equal vehemence. The celebrated historian and literary critic, Francisco de Cascales, provides a well-known example in his attack on Góngora, the *Cartas philológicas* (1638): 'It is clear that a writer seeks to teach, entertain and move the emotions of the reader, and that obscurity prevents him from achieving these three goals. But, how can a reader be taught if he doesn't understand the text? How can something incomprehensible please? How can a reader's spirit be moved if he is left hungry after multiple readings?'[12] We see that here too the emphasis is on subjectivity, that of the individual reader in his actualization of a given text, and that of the artist figure and his extraordinary verbal prowess as creator. Another of his detractors, Juan de Jáuregui, provides one of the most pointed attacks against Góngora in his *Discurso poético contra el hablar culto y oscuro* and the *Antídoto contra 'Las soledades'* (both written in 1624). Collard identifies the violent passions provoked by Góngora's poetry – both for and against it – as, in large measure, the catalyst for 'a new vocation, even profession, that of the literary critic, whose function is defined on the basis of the controversy over Lope and Góngora'.[13] Indeed, every major city in Spain during the sixteenth and seventeenth centuries could boast at least one *academia* – a gathering place where writers and critics would discuss in great detail every aspect of the production and reception of literature (its implications and impact). Madrid, Seville, and Valencia were centres for many such institutions. Smaller cities were also involved in this ongoing critical debate, and there were even such *tertulias* for the study of Spanish literature in Italy. The study of these literary academies is interesting both in and of itself and because it reveals the considerable degree of complexity at issue in the use that writers made of *conceptismo* and *culteranismo*. In describing these two literary environments, for example, it becomes clear both from the nature of the more nuanced academic

[10] Andrée Collard, *Nueva poesía: conceptismo, culteranismo en la crítica española* (Madrid: Castalia, 1967), p. 15.
[11] Cited in *Documentos gongorinos*, ed. E. Joiner Gates (Mexico: Colegio de México, 1961), p. 35.
[12] *Cartas philológicas*, ed. J. García Soriano, 3 vols. (Madrid: Clásicos Castellanos, 1930), vol. I, p. 195.
[13] Collard, *Nueva poesía*, p. 2. My translation.

debates (and from textual analysis of the works themselves) that we are not dealing with two hermetic phenomena which are each found in an unadulterated form. The personal animosity of Quevedo and Góngora – recorded in numerous vituperative allusions to one another – has, for a long time – and quite anachronistically – been construed as an extension of these two literary movements. Yet the two currents, far from being antithetical, are often found to be operative and mutually reinforcing within the same text. For all of his condemnation of Góngora's rhetorical excesses, Lope exploits *culteranismo* very willingly and to great advantage. Likewise, Góngora clearly relies on the *concepto* even in the *Soledad primera*, for example: 'The maidens paused beneath the vaults of shade / In the fresh painted glade'[14] where 'al fresco' refers both to the verdant nature of the trees being evoked, and to a method of artistic production, the fresco.

Baltasar Gracián's *Agudeza y arte de ingenio* (1642) offers a testimony to the fascination with rhetoric in his theoretical compendium of literary conceits [*conceptos*], while serving additionally as a companion to his ambitious Christianized *Odyssey*, *El criticón* (1651–7). For Gracián, *agudeza* refers to the artful use of unexpected analogy (a term derived from the Italian Mannerist Pellegrini's *Agutezze*). He offers a broad (somewhat ambiguous) definition of *concepto* as: 'an act of understanding which uncovers the relationship between concepts'.[15] As a result, the *concepto* is used to refer both to *agudeza* [keenness of wit] and to a particular kind of metaphor – one which exploits disparity in the terms of the comparison. Moreover, for Gracián it is not simply a useful form of poetic embellishment. It is, rather, a heuristic tool, fundamental on both aesthetic and ethical grounds. In the first of his sixty-three *discursos* on the subject he affirms that: 'understanding without wit or concept is sun without light, without rays'. Hence, the conceit is an integral component of the reader's understanding, a pedagogical resource of great value. Indeed, Gracián's anatomy of conceits discloses his overriding interest in this rhetorical figure as being its didactic potential, its ability to communicate ethical truth: 'the need for conceits is as evident for prose as it is for verse. Where would St Augustine be without their subtlety and St Ambrose without their weightiness? . . . Truths are forbidden merchandise; the harbours of scandal and disappointment; as a result, they must disguise themselves so that reason may enter, she who esteems them so highly.' The conceit, then, is a vehicle for moral reflection, for the construction of the

[14] *The solitudes of Don Luis de Góngora*, trans. E. M. Wilson (Cambridge: Cambridge University Press, 1965), lines 594–5.
[15] *Agudeza y arte de ingenio*, ed. E. Correa Calderón, 2 vols. (Madrid: Castalia, 1969), vol. I, pp. 50, 51.

'prudent man' [*discreto*] which lies at the heart of Gracián's philosophico-literary project throughout his works, and which, in turn, is an 'essential component of the modern subject's vision of itself as "in control" '.[16]

The mental agility implicit in the *concepto* finds some of its most powerful expression in the prose and poetry of Francisco de Quevedo y Villegas (1580–1645). Quevedo's masterful exploitation of the conceit is evident in his five *Sueños* (apocalyptic 'visions' that indict the vice and hypocrisy prevalent during the decadent period in which he lived). These texts were written between 1606 and 1622, yet, because the censors did not approve of them, they did not appear until 1627. His picaresque novel *Historia de la vida del Buscón, llamado don Pablos*, was written between 1603 and 1608; however, it remained unpublished until 1626 (because like the *Sueños* it too failed at first to receive approval from the national board of censors).

The *Buscón* is essential to any study of seventeenth-century Spanish prose because of its unparalleled exploitation of *conceptismo*. This text has been identified by some as the epitome of the picaresque novel, by others as anti-picaresque, the text which definitively caricatures the genre. This pseudo-autobiographical form that explores human subjectivity not as it pertains to the world of the nobility, as detailed by the *comedia*, or of the lyric court poet, but of the social outsider – the thief, the prostitute, the murderer. 'Picaresque' is the adjectival form of 'pícaro', a noun of uncertain etymology, which first appeared in 1525. Akin to the English term 'delinquent', the figure of the picaro represented an innovation in Western literary representation – the expansion of possibilities whereby the underclass and its existence became, for the first time, the primary focus of the text. Debate continues as to the parameters of the Spanish picaresque tradition that continued unabated in Spain until the publication of *Estebanillo González* in 1646. The genre is defined by some according to thematic concerns, others by the autobiographical form. The slipperiness involved in defining this genre is evident by the ongoing debate as to whether Lazarillo de Tormes or Guzmán de Alfarache is the first picaresque, and by the disparity evident in the number and titles various critics attribute to it. Whereas the form made its first appearance in the mid-sixteenth century with *Lazarillo de Tormes* (1554), the picaresque genre did not gain currency until the end of the century, with the publication of Mateo Alemán's *Guzmán de Alfarache* (1599, 1602). This text is one of the most frequently edited works of the seventeenth century, with eighteen Spanish editions as well as translations into Dutch, German, Italian, Latin, and the English translation of the influential James

---

[16] Anthony J. Cascardi, 'The subject of control', in *Culture and control in Counter-Reformation Spain*, ed. A. J. Cruz and M. E. Perry, *Hispanic issues* 7 (1992), p. 250.

Mabbe. The tremendous appeal of the picaresque derives from its status as literature of immediacy, literature which rejects, indeed parodies, the mythic paradigms of romance, presenting instead man's pessimistic and alienated relationship to his environment.

The fascination with the picaresque has been attributed to the tremendous social, political, and economic upheaval that Spain experienced in the sixteenth and seventeenth centuries. Yet roughly the same conditions were operative in the rest of Europe until 1600. As a result, America Castro advanced the theory that these texts were spawned primarily from the discontent felt by the *conversos* (from the anonymous *Lazarillo* author to Mateo Alemán), a form that was later exploited by Christian writers (chief among them Quevedo in his *Buscón*).[17] Equally controversial to the *Lazarillo* with respect to its place in the evolution of the picaresque, Quevedo's text is viewed by some as the zenith of the genre, by others as a deconstruction of it – a text which rewrites incidents from *Lazarillo* and *Guzmán* in the form of blatant and stylized caricature.

Whether or not Castro's *converso* theory is the impulse for the creation of this literature of disorder, what can be said with certainty is that it became an object of fascination. In 1605, for example, a masked ball took place in Madrid in which the participants dressed as picaros. It became a source of entertainment to read these texts from such diverse perspectives as voyeuristic curiosity in lawlessness, a taste for social satire, or for the satisfaction derived by spiritually inclined readers who follow the tracks of a sinner who repents of his or her waywardness.

This literature thematizes the technique of perspectivism, of novelistic discourse whereby the instability of language, of referentiality between sign and signified, mirrors man's chaotic perception of the cosmos. Representation of a disordered reality is also at the root of Gracián's ambitious allegorical project, his philosophical novel entitled *El criticón* (published between 1650 and 1657). Relying upon a dialogic tension between reason (represented by the mature man of the world, Critilo) and instinct (advocated by the youthful and innocent Andrenio), Gracián generates a universe full of conflicting perceptions, an exposé of earthly appearances that portrays the philosophy of disillusion as the most satisfying approach to an inescapably deceptive material world – 'ir muriendo cada día' ['dying on a daily basis'].

This text has rightly been termed a Christianized Homer to the degree that its protagonist, like Ulysses, begins to live the most significant part of his life after Critilo has been shipwrecked, at which point he – in the company of the 'noble savage'Andrenio – travels throughout the world. The

---

[17] Americo Castro, *La realidad historica de España* (Mexico: Editorial Porrua, 1954), p. 514.

importance of the work is not confined to the allegorical peregrination, however, for it is fashioned from an original gallery of *conceptos*. Illustrative of Gracián's imaginative expression of concepts is, for example, his explanation of 'diphthongs': 'diptongo es un hombre con voz de mujer, y una mujer que habla como hombre . . . Diptongo es un niño de setenta años, y uno sin camisa crujiendo seda' (III.iv) ['a diphthong is a man with a woman's voice and a woman who speaks like a man . . . A diphthong is a seventy-year-old child and one who goes shirtless while rustling silk'].

The metacritical issue of literature's ability to represent 'reality', that is, its mimetic potential, is nowhere more visible than in the so-called neo-Aristotelian controversy carried out during the seventeenth century in Spain. The rediscovery and translation during the Renaissance of Aristotle's *Poetics* led to a close scrutiny of the texts being written in terms of the Aristotelian precepts. Imaginative literature's moral and aesthetic impact – especially its dangerous potential – was the focus of the discussion. Like the objections discussed above in the domain of the *comedia*, *libros de caballerías* [romances of chivalry] and *novelas* were criticized for the same reasons, namely for their transgressions of verisimilitude in space, time, and character decorum.

Authors not only inserted remarks reflecting their views of the neo-Aristotelian *preceptos*, they transformed them into literature. Among the rich production of *novela corta* in the seventeenth century, Lope de Vega's *Novelas a Marcia Leonarda* (1621, 1624) stand out in this regard, offering metacritical remarks so voluminous in number that, like *Tristram Shandy*, the space they occupy outnumbers the narrative itself. Temporal verisimilitude is violated in a bold and witty manner by Lope in one of these *novelas* by presenting the Reconquest (celebrated on 6 January 1492) as postdating Columbus's discovery of the New World (12 October 1492), and even more flippantly, by presenting himself as having participated in the time-frame of those events. Cervantes' *Novelas ejemplares* (1613) defy the theoreticians' precepts even more blatantly. Indeed, the collection's very title daringly challenges the critical presupposition that novels and *novelas* are incapable of exemplarity. Audacious proof of this revisionist attitude to the form comes most dramatically in the last tale of the collection, *El coloquio de los perros*: literary theory is debated by two dogs who have miraculously attained the gift of speech, indeed, even the capacity for incisive philosophical debate. Cervantes turns the theoreticians' obsession with the question of which kinds of literature are able to represent reality adequately on its head. He offers us instead a critique of the nature of reality itself, thereby gesturing towards the impoverished nature of the critics' perspectives.

The most sustained treatment of critico-theoretical issues of seventeenth-century Spain is found in *Don Quijote* (Part I – 1605 and Part II – 1615).

From the very first moments of the work – the prologue to Part I which functions, in fact, like an anti-prologue – we find a dense orchestration of metaliterary issues. The burlesque sonnets that precede it (for instance, from the Cid's horse in praise of Don Quijote's Rocinante) set the tone for the tongue-in-cheek treatment of literary theory and practice that is the hallmark of Cervantes' writing. This lighthearted interrogation of the laudatory prefatory sonnet tradition illustrates the playful approach to literary criticism inscribed on so many pages of the work. Yet, Cervantes is equally capable of exploiting literary convention in very serious terms – for instance, the literary depiction of religious conversion – to point up its existential reductionism, as with Zoraida and her father in the Captive's tale (I.39–41). While the *Quijote* has been interpreted by some as the ultimate romance of chivalry, by others as the text that definitively destroyed the genre's authority, it is, paradoxically, both. Cervantes saw through the veil of romance to its existential root, its universal appeal. In spite of all the novelistic cynicism of the picaresque and of the age in which he lived, Cervantes understood the enduring appeal of the world of romance – its perennial appeal to the subjective order of reality. In his choice of an old man for the hero of his masterpiece, he was not simply parodying the paradigmatically virile youth of chivalric romance, or the universal phenomenon of ageing with all its inherent complexities. In addition to these functions, Don Quijote figures the defeated heroism of the Spanish empire, its nostalgic yearning for past glory.

Cultural commentary is also at the centre of Cervantes' *Trabajos de Persiles y Sigismunda* (1617), a posthumously published work which has led to a great deal of debate and speculation. This text was highly prized by Cervantes, as, for example, the prologue to his *Novelas ejemplares* attests, claiming that the *Persiles* 'dares to compete with Heliodorus'.[18] To claim such a competition was an audacious gesture, given the prestige enjoyed by Heliodorus's *Ætheopica* (fourth century AD), considered by the Renaissance which rediscovered it in 1526 to be the venerable ancient model for long prose fiction – for the writing of the kind of 'purified romance' the Canon of Toledo advocates (echoing Tasso) when he remarks that 'the epic may be written in prose as well as in verse' (I.47, p. 426). Whereas the *Persiles*, with its Greek romance mixture of adventure and amorous intrigue, including such exotic details as lycanthropy and witches with flying carpets, appealed to its seventeenth-century reading public, later centuries, particularly the twentieth, have found it difficult to account not only for such fantastic details, but even more for the idealizing nature of this text, its largely predictable character portrayal and

---

[18] *Novelas ejemplares*, ed. J. Bautista Avalle-Arce, 3 vols. (Madrid: Castalia, *c*. 1982), vol. I, p. 65.

optimistic axis of *amor–patria–religión*, after the existential complexities and psychological probing that characterize the *Quijote* which thematizes epistemology. As Alban Forcione puts it, '[Cervantes'] greatest writings are preoccupied with the difficulty of ascertaining truth'.[19] The *Persiles*, however, conforms to the literary project of the *Quijote* in that it too offers not only a compelling narrative, but also a metaliterary meditation on narratology and on cultural identity as well. In the case of the *Persiles*, the issue of cultural pluralism and the need to reconceive the radically altered category of *lo bárbaro* (which now included not only the Jew and the gypsy, but also the *criollo*, the *mestizo*, and the *indiano*) reflect broader currents at work in Spanish society. It was this new multiracial and multiethnic reality that posed such a tremendous challenge to Early Modern Spain. Throughout the century, subjectivity and 'Spanishness' itself, like literary production and theory, were unstable categories in the process of being rethought.

---

[19] 'Afterword: exemplarity, modernity, and the discriminating games of reading', in *Cervantes' exemplary novels and the adventure of writing*, ed. M. Nerlich and N. Spadaccini (Minneapolis: Prisma Institute, 1989), p. 339.

60

The German-speaking countries

Peter Skrine

The vitality of intellectual life in the German-speaking lands of the Holy Roman Empire during the late fifteenth and early sixteenth centuries is reflected in the contribution made by German scholars and writers to humanism and, more particularly, to Renaissance poetics. Even before the new invention of printing became established, access to high-quality Latin texts ranging from antiquity to the early Renaissance had been made easier by the anthology compiled by Albrecht von Eyb and entitled *Margarita poetica* (Strasburg, 1459; first printed Nuremberg, 1472). This influential compendium reinforced the conviction that careful reading of texts with a view to imitation was an essential element of education and intellectual improvement, an approach which was to be sustained throughout the long period under discussion here. *De arte versificandi* (1511) by Ulrich von Hutten advocated similar principles, this time in the context of a manual of poetry based on the accepted assumption that the study of good models is an essential part of the poet's training. As a humanist, Hutten also emphasizes the need for wide-ranging knowledge on the poet's part, a requirement already put forward in even more ambitious terms by Germany's greatest humanist writer, Conrad Celtis, in his *Ars versificandi et carminum* (c. 1486), a manual which offers sound guidance by an expert practitioner of neo-Latin verse who was convinced that between them *ars*, *usus*, and *imitatio* provided the basic essentials for creative success. Thus the close relationship between reading, study, and creativity became firmly established as an essential feature of literary theory and practice in Germany for a long time to come. The humanist poet Eobanus Hessus brought the Greek language and the Greek literary tradition into the discussion in a treatise entitled *Scribendorum versuum maxime compendiosa ratio* (1526) published when he was appointed teacher of poetics at the Nuremberg gymnasium or grammar-school recently founded by Philipp Melanchthon, the scholar-reformer who saw to it that in Germany high standards of scholarship and education became an integral part of the Lutheran Reformation. But the most ambitious of all Germany's contributions to the Renaissance debate on poetry, poetics, and the study and analysis of literature was *De poetica et carminis ratione* (1518) by the Swiss humanist Vadianus or Joachim von Watt. This comprehensive work provided a survey of German and European literature from antiquity to the present – and with due regard for the medieval, the popular, and the vernacular – which was to remain unparalleled in Germany until the appearance of Daniel Georg Morhof's *Unterricht von der Teutschen Sprache und Poesie*, published some 160 years later in 1682.

The establishment of the new concept of literature in terms both of poetics and of a practical strategy for the renewal of literary studies and literary activity in Germany arose from the pedagogic background of the gymnasium or (Latin) grammar-school. During the period from the Reformation to the Enlightenment this meant primarily, though not exclusively, the Lutheran system of secondary and also to some extent of tertiary education pioneered by Melanchthon, who announced his programme as early as 1518 in his inaugural lecture as professor of Hebrew and Greek at the University of Wittenberg, *De corrigendis adolescentiae studiis*, and in the two works which followed it: *De rhetorica* (1519) and *Compendiaria dialecticis ratio* (1520), both frequently reprinted, and both laying emphasis on *inventio* and on exact and methodical expository technique. An educational system so firmly based on the trivium (and quadrivium) encouraged the retention until well into the eighteenth century of a division of language-related study into the three parallel and interrelated elements of grammar, rhetoric, and logic, and this tripartite conception remained the dominant feature of the German approach to literary activity and to literature for at least the next 200 years. Educated minds were conditioned by it from an early age, for it was central to the educational system of Protestant Germany, which was itself soon complemented by a renewal of educational standards and methods in those areas of the Holy Roman Empire which remained under the aegis of the Roman Catholic Church or returned to it during the Counter-Reformation. Moreover the rationale of the trivium had (or appeared to have) the weight of classical antiquity behind it. The humanists' respect for the authority of the classics is an abiding feature of the history of literary education in Germany and conditioned the evolution of a concept of German literature during a period when the classical authors dominated the school curriculum and Latin continued to be the medium of teaching at grammar-school, university, and Jesuit college. Indeed, Latin remained the predominant language of serious theology even in a church which had embraced the vernacular as part of its rejection of Rome; it continued to be the medium of academic study until it began to give way to German around the turn of the eighteenth century: not until then did the number of books published in German start to exceed the number in Latin.

The diglossia of the German educated minority had a profound and far-reaching effect on the evolution of an intrinsically German concept of literature and literary criticism. Throughout the sixteenth and seventeenth centuries it is true to say that a more sophisticated level of discourse obtains in Latin publications on the subject, such as *De re metrica* (1539) by Jacobus Micyllus, the headmaster of the Frankfurt grammar-school; German treatments of it are for the most part less intellectually demanding and often amount to little more than vulgarizations. Throughout the sixteenth century, works written in German were mainly if not exclusively populist: the popular genres thrived, though most did not conform to the classical categories: satire, however, provided common ground. Sometimes vernacular works were written by 'literate' authors who also used Latin, such as Ulrich von Hutten, Sixt Birck, and Luther himself; sometimes they were written by authors with little or no Latin, such as Jörg Wickram and Hans Sachs. But no serious attempt was made to include vernacular works within an overall concept of literature or to relate them explicitly to the classical generic categories. Satire, in which the sixteenth century in Germany was exceptionally rich, is a case in point: it provided common ground, but its Latin and vernacular exponents and their works coexisted for the most part in separate compartments.

The concept of a vernacular literature was, however, gaining acceptance among the educated upper and middle classes especially in the Protestant areas of Germany, a trend perceived most clearly by the writer and theorist who was to become the dominant literary figure of the seventeenth century: Martin Opitz. Often referred to as the 'father of German poetry', Opitz wrote in both Latin and German throughout his life, but while still a pupil at the grammar-school of Beuthen he composed a Latin oration which proclaimed the pre-eminence of the German vernacular. *Aristarchus sive de contemptu linguae teutonicae* (1617) argues the case for a concept of literature specifically German in character and based on the antiquity and intrinsic nobility of the German language and its potential parity with the other accepted literary vernaculars of modern Europe: 'There is no reason why our language, too, should not emerge from obscurity . . . this fine, tender yet robust language which has come down to us over the years, uncontaminated and undiluted. You must learn to love it, to work on perfecting it, and to show yourselves to be men in it.' The note struck here was new, though it had been anticipated elsewhere, as in France by Joachim du Bellay. *Aristarchus* was deliberately intended as an essay in positive criticism, as is suggested by its title (an allusion to Aristarchus of Samothrace, the type of the constructive critic, as opposed to Zoilus, the destructive critic), and it may be seen as marking the decisive point at which the classicizing tradition of humanism converged with the modernist trend already evident in the Renaissance literary cultures of most other major European countries.

Opitz followed his essay with a more explicit treatise, *Buch von der deutschen Poeterey* (1624), which soon established itself as the authoritative

German work on literature, a reputation it was to retain until the appearance in 1730 of Johann Christoph Gottsched's *Versuch einer kritischen Dichtkunst vor die Deutschen*. Introduced by a general survey on the lines of *Aristarchus*, its subsections focus on the skills needed by a would-be poet: inspiration is of the essence, but for Opitz, as for Celtis a century before him, it is not enough, and should be complemented by proper appreciation of the processes of composition and of the aptness of poetic forms as vehicles for particular topics and modes of expression. This leads the author to define and illustrate the literary genres known to him and in so doing to take some initial and hesitant steps into the as yet untouched field of specifically German literary criticism as he compares and contrasts instances of good and bad practice especially in the field of lyric poetry. His choice of German examples as opposed to foreign models was extremely limited, however, since none conformed exactly to his own new understanding of the relationship between language, prosody, and scansion. This was the price exacted for the Opitzian 'breakthrough'. Despite his obvious love of his own language and his respect for Germany's noble past (he was even aware of the medieval German literary heritage), Opitz effectively discarded the continuing tradition of vernacular literature and in so doing seriously delayed the development of a school of practical criticism commensurate with those of France, Italy, or England. Instead he argued that new works should be created which respected the rules and prescriptions laid down in his treatise: many of these works he provided himself in the genres of tragedy, prose narrative, epic poetry, and in the various lyric forms he advocated, such as the sonnet. Many were translations or adaptations of admired models ranging from Sophocles and Seneca to Ronsard, Barclay, and Sidney.

In the wake of Opitz's enthusiastic yet prescriptive encouragement, a considerable number of other books set out to instruct their readers on how to write. Their emphasis was mainly on verse, and from the critical point of view they have their importance because, simplistic and prescriptive though they generally were, they trained generations of German speakers and readers to appreciate the distinctive virtues of form and style and helped to establish a recognized and widely accepted norm for written literary German, an expressive medium which in many parts of the German-speaking lands was almost as artificial as Latin, since it often diverged very considerably from the grammar, syntax, and lexis of spoken dialect. In the strictly literary domain, Opitz's treatise therefore had a function analogous to that of Luther's Bible translation in the general sphere of the spoken and written language. With it the notions of correctness, aptness, and decorum, familiar to all readers of neo-Latin poetics, finally made their appearance in German critical discourse, though in cultural circumstances and a linguistic context which differed in important

respects from those pertaining elsewhere. The analogy with the Netherlands is close (and Opitz, a great admirer of the work and ideas of Daniel
Heinsius, was well aware of it); obvious, too, are the differences from
France, where theoretical arguments loomed large and the Bible played
little part in the emergence of modern literature, and from England, where
Bible translation and literary creativity coincided closely, and theories of
language and literature were of relatively subordinate importance.

Opitz's pioneering work was followed by a sequence of manuals on the
art or, rather, the craft of literary composition in verse and prose. Philipp
von Zesen's *Deutscher Helicon* (1640), written at the age of twenty,
and *Von der Kunst hochdeutsche Verse und Lieder zu machen* (1642) by
Johann Peter Titz transmitted to a wider public the views of their highly
respected mentor, Augustus Buchner, which were then posthumously published as his *Anleitung zur Deutschen Poeterey* (1665), a compendium of
German poetics which amplified Opitz with considerable originality and
frequent reference to Julius Caesar Scaliger, and was based on lectures
which had already influenced the many poets and writers who were
his pupils. Buchner and Zesen concentrated on verse; Johann Matthäus
Meyfart turned to prose. In Coburg in 1634 Meyfart published a *Teutsche
Rhetorica* to set alongside his Latin manual on the subject, *Mellificium
oratorium* (1628–37); in it he concentrates on questions of style with
emphasis on rhythmical and tonal effects and on the importance of the
underlying syntactic structure.

A very different approach designed for a primarily female readership
is exemplified by the *Frauenzimmer-Gesprächspiele* (1641–9) by the
Nuremberg author Georg Philipp Harsdörffer, a set of model conversations between six representative persons of both sexes on a wide variety of
topics of general interest including the art of writing, which probably both
reflects and encouraged a conscious improvement in standards of social
and literary intercourse without which criticism in the accepted sense
does not easily flourish. Indeed, the work contains passages which may be
regarded as the first German manifestations of literary criticism proper.
Harsdörffer followed the *Gesprächspiele* with his notorious *Poetischer
Trichter* or 'Poetic funnel' (1647–53), which sets out to help its readers to
acquire the skills of poetic composition which, in its author's view, should
be based on syntactic and rhetorical structures since 'rhetoric is to poetry
what walking is to dancing'.

Harsdörffer's colleague Sigmund von Birken also contributed a manual
of poetry to the growing number in German: his *Teutsche Rede-bind- und
Dichtkunst* (1679) adopts a more sophisticated and abstract approach to
the century's concern with generic distinctions. A different social grouping is addressed in the *Poetische Tafeln, oder Gründliche Anweisung zur
Teutschen Verskunst* (1667), largely the work of Martin Kempe though

published under the name of Georg Neumark, the secretary general of the Fruchtbringende Gesellschaft, Germany's most illustrious learned society in the seventeenth century, and one primarily concerned with the cultivation and promotion of the German language. Kempe's remarkably wide frame of references indicates the broad cultural horizons of learned and aristocratic circles in Germany at the time.

On a less ambitious plane, works such as *Der Deutsche Poet* (1664) and *Der Deutsche Redner* (1666) by Balthasar Kindermann provided a receptive and growing readership with pretensions to public speaking and the writing of occasional verse with guidelines on how to do so. *Der Deutsche Poet* is rich in definitions and examples drawn from recent and contemporary authors which reveal the period's own conception of its poetry – often at variance with modern critical assessments – and clearly indicate that a literary canon was being formed. It also illustrates the growing importance of the literary expert as a transmitter of useful up-to-date guidance to readers intent on practising the art of literary composition; indeed, the primary function of the literary critic or his equivalent and precursor in seventeenth-century Germany was to provide practical advice to the widening social spectrum of would-be practitioners of occasional verse – such as poems for birthdays, weddings, and funerals – in countless larger and small regional urban centres throughout the many states that composed the Germany of the period. These groupings were drawn principally from the professional middle class and lower aristocracy who were benefiting from the revival of trade after the Thirty Years War and from the development and expansion of education, the legal system, and the civil services of the cities and states which made up the Empire. This role was to continue well into the eighteenth century, during which it was gradually superseded by that of the literary critic as purveyor of sensible and informed opinions about new publications and the literature of the past.

As the seventeenth century progresses, an intermediate critical function also becomes increasingly discernible, namely an emphasis on the value of reading *per se*. Authors write in order to instruct, edify, and improve; the reader reads to inform himself. Thus the potential influence of reading-matter on the individual moves to the centre of discussion, and becomes a major concern of authors whose prefaces consequently begin to display a marked tendency to provide a moral justification for their work. 'Readership' is scarcely defined as yet; but potential readers are directly addressed by authors aware of the need to prepare and condition their audience. Their occasional allusions to the work of other writers may be seen as a first step towards a new understanding of literary criticism as we have come to know it. But the literary critic as such does not make his appearance until the advent of the medium which needed him and could provide him with scope to display his judgement: the critical journal or review. The first journals of this type in Germany were Otto Mencke's *Acta eruditorum* (1682: it ran for a hundred years) and the *Monatsgespräche* issued from 1688 to 1690 by the philosopher Christian Thomasius, one of the chief precursors of the German Enlightenment, with the main objective of providing reviews of new books grouped according to kind and subject-matter. However, it was not until the 1730s that journals, periodicals, and reviews established themselves as an integral part of the German literary scene, the most influential early example being the *Beyträge zur critischen Historie der deutschen Sprache, Poesie und Beredsamkeit* edited in Leipzig from 1732 to 1744 by the authoritative literary pundit Johann Christoph Gottsched. The tripartite conception made explicit in its title, with its division into language, poetry, and rhetoric, harks back to Opitz. Yet its appearance is a clear indicator of the steady rise in the production of literary works (including fiction), which in the seventeenth century has been estimated as a mere 5 per cent of total book production; this in turn points to the growth of an educated readership capable of making the publication of a regular review financially viable.

Book production had fallen off in Germany during the Thirty Years War and was slow to regain momentum, a factor which undoubtedly affected the relatively slow development of literary criticism. Literary publishing was slow and sparse (the situation in law and theology was very different) and one gains the impression that the response of readers was slower still. This was largely the reason why the handbook of poetry persisted as the vehicle for what critical writing there was: in its pages passing reference could be made to works which the author might assume his readers had read if only because he had read them himself. Thus Albrecht Christian Rotth, the deputy headmaster of the gymnasium at Halle, recalls in his *Vollständige Deutsche Poesie* (1688) how eagerly he had responded in younger years to the compendious novel *Herkules und Valiska* by Andreas Heinrich Buchholtz (1659): 'the author of *Herkules* seeks to inject the fear of the Lord through his writings. And indeed he is not unsuccessful in doing so, as witness the fact that when I myself read it in younger years, it was frequently not without the arousal of feelings of religious devotion and often not without tears' (Chapter 7). Here the critical comment, such as it is, is still essentially retrospective: the effect of the work is recorded rather than postulated.

Poetry and drama were covered more or less adequately by the handbooks: in Germany there was an almost total absence of the critical prefaces to published plays which formed such an important part in the development of literary criticism in seventeenth-century France. But it was the rise of the novel as a popular and relatively new genre which did most to stimulate active criticism in the more modern sense. Rotth was one of the first to discuss the genre at length, and in doing so he cites specific titles to support his view that the primary aim of the genre is to provide credible examples of, for instance, life at court, or true virtue. Significantly he counters his welcome to the novel for its informative role by voicing misgivings as the possibly pernicious effects of fiction especially on the susceptible young reader, a view he shares and may have borrowed from Pierre-Daniel Huet's *Traité de l'origine des romans* (1670), translated into German in 1682 and into Latin the year after. That this was a widely held preoccupation is shown by the Swiss writer Gotthard Heidegger, whose *Mythoscopia Romantica oder Discours von den so benannten Romans* (1698) is based on the discussions of contemporary literary topics by his circle of acquaintances in St Gallen in the 1690s. The whole question of fiction and its aesthetic and moral value was addressed with greater subtlety by Birken when he expounded his distinction between 'Geschichts-Gedichte' and 'Gedichts-Geschichte', the one founded on fact, the other a credible invention, thus inaugurating Germany's long-lasting critical preoccupation with the notion and nature of realism in literary art.

A decisive shift of critical emphasis is discernible in the approach of a number of writers in the later seventeenth century, notably Daniel Georg Morhof in his impressive *Unterricht von der teutschen Sprache und Poesie* (1682) and Erdmann Neumeister in his *De poetis Germanicis huius seculi praecipuis dissertatio compendiaria* (1695), an ambitious survey of the century's literary achievements which displays critical insight and acumen in its presentation of what by now had become an accepted canon, even if it differs almost totally from the received canon of today. Morhof, by contrast, may be regarded as the inaugurator of the critical approach to the history of literature, as opposed to the chronological or alphabetical surveys favoured by contemporaries such as his pupil Neumeister. Again, the tripartite structure is evident: Morhof commences his *Unterricht* by examining the origins and history of the German language and the evolution of German poetry and surveying the other literatures of Europe, and only then turns his attention in Part III to German poetry itself. Thanks to the example of models such as John Dryden and René Rapin, to both of whom he owes a good deal, and to some first-hand knowledge of the Netherlands and England, Morhof, the most distinguished scholar of his day at the University of Kiel, manages to raise the level of critical discussion in his comparisons between German literature and the other main European literatures: their influence also enables him to give qualified approval to the 'new' genre of the novel, and especially to those by contemporaries such as Christian Weise, which have the merit of delighting and instructing their readers. It was indeed in the prefaces to contemporary German novels of the 'low' satirical and picaresque kind by authors such as Johann Beer and Weise that definite attempts were being made at the time to engage in critical analysis of the new genre, its aims and its appeal, and to create a critical framework by means of references to other works of the same kind.

The incipient change of critical direction thus heralded was confirmed at the turn of the century by the epigrammatist Christian Wernicke in the preface to his revised collection of *Uberschriffte* (1701 and 1704). Not only does Wernicke praise simplicity and recommend the abandonment of the stylistic excesses of the 'Baroque' writers who had come to dominate the German literary canon: he also praises the contemporary literature of France, observing that it was able to reach its present perfection largely because the publication of a good French book is always promptly followed by a so-called 'critique', the effect of which is that readers' minds are opened and authors are kept within due bounds. Thus the basis was laid for two of the main trends which permeate German literary criticism in the next century.

61

The Low Countries

Theo Hermans

In its broad outline and intellectual context, the history of literary theory and criticism in the Low Countries during the sixteenth and seventeenth centuries is not radically different from that of other parts of Europe. The fundamental presuppositions concerning the nature and function of serious literature, the division into genres, and, as Renaissance ideas strike root, the role of ancient models, are found here as elsewhere. The historical progression, too, shows a familiar pattern, as a high-prestige humanist culture spills over into vernacular writing, the willingness to imitate sources in other languages is followed by the emancipation of vernacular literature, and eventually the classical models make room for a post-Renaissance neoclassicism.

By and large, the number of writings on poetic or dramatic theory in the Low Countries during the Renaissance remained remarkably small (as was also the case with respect to art theory), and practical criticism was virtually absent until the 1670s. Nevertheless, the theorizing that took place shows a number of distinctive features. In mapping these it will be convenient to distinguish four successive periods. The first, from approximately 1470 to 1550, sees the dominance of the poetics of the so-called Chambers of Rhetoric. The second, from about 1550 to 1600, is marked by the absorption of new genres and ideas deriving from France and from the humanist republic of letters. The third, which runs from c. 1600 until c. 1670, shows the flowering of a self-conscious vernacular culture and the gradual waning of humanism as an innovative force. The fourth, which takes us into the eighteenth century, brings the adoption of French neoclassicism as the new literary model.

In the course of the second half of the fifteenth century, as the printed book entered the Low Countries and an interest in humanism began to manifest itself, a new form of literary organization, the so-called 'Chambers of Rhetoric', became established in most parts of the territory. Set up during the period of Burgundian rule on the model of the 'puys' which were active in northern France, the Chambers were closely linked with local élites, and with the powerful urban patriciates in particular. They quickly grew into the most important literary institutions in the Low Countries, and dominated vernacular literary production throughout the sixteenth century. The first handbooks of poetics and rhetoric in Dutch were written in these circles.

The poetic forms practised by the Chambers were similar to those of the French 'rhétoriqueurs'. In formulating the moral ideals and practical norms of behaviour of an élite, the formal sophistication which their poems and plays exhibited served both an artistic end and a strategy of social differentiation. This explains not only the Rhetoricians' preference for intricate versification and complex allegory, but also the nature of their views about poetics, which concentrated on those aspects of verse technique known in France as *seconde rhétorique*. Their poems in praise of rhetoric described the art not in terms of classical persuasive rhetoric but as a gift from the Holy Ghost, suggesting both a religious context and a readiness to appreciate formal elaboration and the musical qualities of verse. At the same time, rhetoric, equated with elocution, was also called a craft, something which is learned.

The poetics of the Chambers was summed up in the *Conste van Rhetorike* [*Art of rhetoric*] by Matthijs de Castelein, a manual in verse written in the late 1540s and published posthumously in 1555. It acknowledged a debt to Jean Molinet's *Art de rhétorique* (1493) and codified a large number of poetic forms, including some extremely elaborate ones, such as the 'chessboard', eight times eight verses which can be read in thirty-eight different ways. Although various passages occur in which Cicero, Quintilian, and Horace are invoked, De Castelein's interest restricted itself to aspects of elocution, reducing classical poetic forms to those practised by the Chambers.

While the work produced in the Chambers often contained classical references, their sources were rarely known at first hand, as early humanism here developed largely separately from vernacular culture. If humanism was late in coming to the Low Countries, this was partly because the main university, at Louvain (founded 1425), remained a bastion of scholasticism. A chair in poetics was established in the Faculty of Law there in 1477 but had little effect. More important was the setting up of a number of Latin schools in the late fifteenth century. They included the one at Deventer which had Alexander Hegius as its rector and was the first school north of the Alps to teach Greek.

Foremost among the early Dutch humanists was Rudolph Agricola, who was trained in Italy. His main work *De inventione dialectica*, written in 1479 and published in 1515, stressed the close relationship between dialectic and rhetoric, the importance of *inventio* and the pragmatic and moral thrust of the entire argumentative system. His oration 'In praise of philosophy', delivered in Ferrara in 1476, likewise privileged the three trivium subjects together (grammar, dialectic, rhetoric) as the key to all other scientific and ethical pursuits. In the next generation of humanists

Erasmus built on the interest in poetry and classical studies at the Latin schools of Gouda and Deventer, and quickly rose to international prominence. Suffice it here to mention, in the age of Erasmus, the influential grammatical works of Johannes Despauterius, which included an *Ars versificatoria* (1510) and treatises on genres (*De carminum generibus*, 1511) and figures of style (*De figuris*, 1519).

The second half of the sixteenth century, although a period of religious persecution, political upheaval, and military conflict, saw closer contacts between humanist and vernacular literature. In the northern Netherlands the new university of Leiden, founded in 1575, became the main seat of humanist learning.

Humanist culture generally continued the Erasmian tradition of biblical and especially philological studies, with Justus Lipsius as its most illustrious representative. His edition of Tacitus (1574), which set new standards in text editing, made him turn away from Ciceronianism to a more compact and elliptical expression, but did not lead to theoretical reflection on the issue of style. In the same way the northern humanist Janus Dousa, who was in touch with prominent French humanists as well as with the vernacular writers of Holland, showed himself to be acutely aware of matters of poetics but did not publish anything of substance on the topic. Latin school drama, on the other hand, informed the *Syntagma tragoediae Latinae* (1593) by the Antwerp Jesuit Martin Antoine Del Rio. Its first part, on tragedy, confirmed the growing interest in Seneca as a model, even though it also argued that subjects taken from history rather than mythology were the most suitable to provide the necessary moral instruction.

The new departures in vernacular writing date from around the middle of the century, as innovative poetic forms were introduced from France and a sustained effort to translate Ancient and contemporary humanist literature into Dutch got under way. The more progressive Chambers of Rhetoric usually acted as the main channel. In the 1550s the Antwerp rhetorician Cornelis van Ghistele was the first to translate a series of classical plays, including the *Antigone* of Sophocles (1556, from the Latin), which, however, he interpreted entirely in moralizing and didactic terms. The preface to the translation (1566) by Marcus Antonius Gillis of the *Emblemata* of Johannes Sambucus, on the other hand, went to considerable lengths to explain to the reader the exact nature of a genre that was new to Dutch letters. The first Dutch textbook on classical rhetoric was Jan van Mussem's *Rhetorica, dye edele const van welsegghene* [*Rhetoric, the noble art of eloquence*] of 1553, a slight book probably intended for school use, which consisted for the most part of passages culled from Cicero, Quintilian, and the *Rhetorica ad Herennium*, with examples borrowed from Erasmus. In the introduction Van Mussem disparaged the

'Rhetoricians' in the Chambers who reduced rhetoric to mere verse technique and rhyme.

Similar critical and polemical noises directed at the traditional Chambers were heard in programmatic statements by innovative vernacular poets from the 1560s onwards. The various pronouncements also show the coexistence of two rather different conceptions of poetry. They may be referred to as a 'rhetorical' versus an 'inspirational' view of poetry.

The 'inspirational' view, which was ultimately indebted to the Platonic tradition of the Italian academies via the intermediary of French Pléiade circles, combined poetry as creation and as *mimesis*. In imitating the world as created by the deity, the poet performed a creative, semi-divine act. The creative impulse found its embodiment in elocution, versification, and style, and consequently poetry was conceived as fundamentally different from rhetoric in the argumentative, Ciceronian sense. This conception, and the sharp distinction between poetry and rhetoric, was enunciated, for example, by Lucas de Heere in the dedication of his *Hof en boomgaert der poësien* [*Garden and orchard of poetry*] (1565), the first Dutch-language collection to employ metrical verse and to feature sonnets and other Renaissance forms. In the northern Netherlands it was defended in robustly polemical tones by Jan van Hout, in an oration delivered at Leiden University around 1576 and in the satirical preface (1578) to his – now lost – translation of George Buchanan's *Franciscanus*.

The 'rhetorical' line of thought, more closely aligned with the tradition of Christian humanism, was particularly strong in and around the Amsterdam Chamber of Rhetoric *De Eglentier* [*The eglantine*]. Its members shared with figures like D. V. Coornhert an interest in moral philosophy. For them, as for the humanists, rhetoric was the vehicle of critical reason which would lead to truth and virtue. The basis of this view was the Ciceronian notion of eloquence as 'wisdom speaking well' [*copiose loquens sapientia*]. Poetry therefore *was* rhetoric, and argumentative in its essence. The poem's formal beauty should support the argumentation, otherwise it would be hollow and unfocused.

In his poems and plays Coornhert declared himself to be concerned with 'truth', in contrast to the verbal ostentation and 'poetic' – that is, fictional – fabrications produced by the traditional rhetoricians. Poems in praise of rhetoric written from the 1560s onwards by leading Eglentier members like H. L. Spiegel, Roemer Visscher, and Egbert Meynertsz emphasized the argumentative aspect of poetry in the context of Christian and ethical enlightenment. Not surprisingly perhaps, these circles also produced, in the 1580s, the first set of trivium handbooks in Dutch, publishing in quick succession the *Twe-spraack vande Nederduitsche letterkunst* [*Dialogue on Dutch grammar*] (1584), *Ruygh-bewerp vande redenkaveling* [*Outline of dialectics*] (1585), and *Rederijck-kunst* [*Art of*

Rhetoric] (1587). H. L. Spiegel is generally credited with having authored them.

The 'inspirational' and the 'rhetorical' tendencies came together in the early seventeenth century, when in the newly created Dutch Republic vernacular writing along classical lines grew in self-confidence and esteem, the traditional Chambers of Rhetoric lost impetus, and the forms of literary writing practised in the Latin schools left their imprint on literature written in Dutch.

Although the latter half of the sixteenth century had seen a sizeable dramatic production, theoretical reflection had largely been restricted to prefaces and dedications. This was to change after 1600, when drama rather than poetry became the focus of critical attention. A key figure in this development was Daniel Heinsius, whose influence as a creative writer and especially as a theoretician was widespread and profound. Heinsius's early views on poetry and drama were formulated in the dedication of his play *Auriacus sive Libertas saucia* [*Orange, or wounded freedom*] (1602), in his inaugural oration at Leiden *De poetis et eorum interpretibus* [*On poets and their interpreters*] (1603), and in his essays on Hesiod (1603). They revealed a strongly 'inspirational', Platonic conceptualization in which the creative aspect is emphasized to the point of placing *ingenium* above *ars*, and poetry above reason. The Hesiod Prolegomena, however, already began to show more interest in questions of structure and in the function of poetry as moral instruction, allowing Heinsius to describe drama in rhetorical-didactic terms. His closeness to J. C. Scaliger's views on tragedy at this stage is evident, for example, from the similarity between the dramatic outline of the Ceyx and Alcyone story (from Ovid's *Metamorphoses*) in Scaliger's *Poetics* of 1561 (Book III ch. 97) and Heinsius's outline of a possible Pandora play in his 1603 treatise on Hesiod. But whereas Scaliger regarded Seneca as the supreme model (as did, in the Low Countries, Lipsius, Dousa, Scriverius, and others), Heinsius even then expressed a preference for the Greeks.

The change to a structural, Aristotelian conception of drama became fully evident in the treatise which followed Heinsius's edition of the *Poetics* of Artistotle (1610) and which was first published as *De tragica constitutione* (1611) and then in 1643 as *De tragoediae constitutione*. Here Heinsius described the nature and function of tragedy in fully Aristotelian terms. Tragedy is an imitation of human action in which the plot serves the overall aim of a therapeutic, ethical, and aesthetic effect on the audience, for whom *catharsis* brings about a harmony of the emotions. Since the plot is moved forward through action to its calamitous dénouement, character is subordinate to action.

In later years Hugo Grotius added his comments on tragedy in the Prolegomena to his Latin translation (1630) of Euripides' *Phoenissae*, largely agreeing with Heinsius but disputing the need for an unhappy ending. In the same vein Gerard Vossius, whose *Oratoriae institutiones* of 1606 had been instrumental in bringing Heinsius to a more structural view of drama, published his *Poeticae institutiones* in 1647, continuing the Aristotelian interpretation begun by Heinsius and offering a comprehensive codification. He included a number of topics which Heinsius had left aside, such as the role of the chorus, and agreed with Grotius that tragedy should portray 'serious actions' without necessarily having an unhappy ending. With Vossius's thorough compilations the Dutch humanist contribution to literary theory was virtually over.

Dutch-language culture meanwhile had developed a strong classicizing tendency, which after a vigorous start eventually lived on in its pure form in the work of only one writer. The link with the humanist world was strong, as is evident, for example, from the praise heaped on Heinsius and Grotius in the 'Oration concerning the excellence of poetry' which P. C. Hooft delivered in Amsterdam some time between 1610 and 1615 and which constitutes the most extensive vernacular statement on poetry in the early seventeenth century. It also showed in the eagerness with which Dutch playwrights responded to Heinsius's call, in the preface to his *Auriacus*, to take up patriotic themes. They did so with particular attention to the purity of their native language, conscious that they were building a national culture in a newly independent state.

Hooft was, with Samuel Coster and G. A. Bredero, among the prime movers behind the establishment of the forward-looking Dutch Academy [*Nederduytsche Academie*] in Amsterdam in 1617. But Bredero died a year later, and in the 1620s Coster fell silent and Hooft turned from poetry and plays to historiography. It was left to the prolific Joost van den Vondel to continue the classical tradition. This he did in impressive fashion, befriending Grotius and Vossius in his quest for literary guidance. While Grotius regarded Seneca's *Troades* as the 'Queen of tragedies', Vondel translated it into Dutch (1626). In the 1630s he discarded the Senecan style, and with his translation of Sophocles' *Electra* (1639) began to move towards a Greek conception of tragedy, expounding his ideas on the genre in the prefaces of his numerous plays. By the mid-century Vondel was the most prominent writer and literary theoretician in the Netherlands. He translated Horace's *Ars poetica* as an exercise (published 1654), and in the Horatian advice of his *Aenleidinge ter Nederduitsche dichtkunste* [*Introduction to Dutch poetry*] of 1650 he urged poets to speak in 'divine cadences and the language of the Gods'. His most important statement on drama was the preface to *Jeptha* (1659), a play designed as a model tragedy on Aristotelian principles. The preface offered a detailed discussion of every aspect of the Aristotelian conception of tragedy as interpreted by humanist scholarship, with reference to Heinsius, Vossius, and many others.

On the Amsterdam stage, however, Vondel's later classical plays proved notably less successful than the more entertaining non-classical plays. This latter tendency, which had much in common with English and Spanish drama, had found a theoretical defence earlier in the century in Theodore Rodenburgh's *Eglentiers borst-wering* [*The eglantine's rampart*] of 1619. It borrowed liberally from Sidney's *Defence of poesie* (1595) and Thomas Wilson's *Arte of rhetorique* (1553), and referred approvingly to Lope de Vega's *Arte nuevo de hacer comedias* [*New art of writing plays*] (1609). Another defence of these 'novelistic' plays with their eventful plots and spectacular staging came in the preface to the *Medea* (1667) of Jan Vos. He argued for the primacy of visual depiction and for an artistic expression derived from 'nature' and 'experience', denouncing the classical authorities on the grounds that, just as in philosophy the Ancients had been overtaken by modern thinkers, so in art too they had lost their pre-eminence. The popular success of plays in this style would lead to a neoclassical counter-offensive in the 1670s.

After the mid-century the formative role of humanist poetics had ended and France gained prominence as the new cultural model. In the Netherlands the society Nil Volentibus Arduum [Nothing is hard for those who try], set up in 1669 and closely associated with the Amsterdam theatre, became the carrier of the aesthetic ideals of French classicism.

In trying to overcome what they saw as the defective stagecraft of Vondel's classicism and the artistic and moral excesses of the non-classical line, the 'Nil' members found their theoretical mainstay in the combination of Aristotle and Corneille. Their main theoretician was Andries Pels, who offered practical guidelines in his adaptation of Horace's *Ars poetica* (1677) and in his *Gebruik en misbruik des tooneels* [*Use and abuse of the theatre*] (1681). The Society held regular meetings to discuss theoretical issues, including relatively new topics such as verisimilitude, decorum ['bienséance'], and the theory of the passions. Their collective manual *Naauwkeurig onderwys in de tooneelpoëzy* [*Accurate instruction in dramatic poetry*], written c. 1670–1 but not published until 1765, contained the most comprehensive poetics of the age and displayed detailed knowledge of ancient and contemporary theory. With their penchant for polemic, to which they gave free rein in prefaces and replies to opponents, they also introduced a new and original form of 'applied' criticism which consisted of rewriting existing plays, both original works and translations, adapting them to the proper 'rules' and frequently adding sharply worded prefaces detailing the original's 'errors' and their own 'corrections'. In doing so, they took Dutch theatre into the Age of Reason and determined its course until well into the eighteenth century.

Bibliography

Reading and interpretation: theories of language, exegesis, Evangelism, commentary

Primary sources and texts

Aristotle, *Poetics* with the *Tractatus coislinianus*, reconstruction of *Poetics II*, and the fragments of the *On poets*, trans. R. Janko, Indianapolis: Hackett, 1987.

Poetics, ed. and trans. S. Halliwell, LCL, Cambridge, MA: Harvard University Press, 1994.

Bacon, Francis, *The advancement of learning*, ed. G. W. Kitchin, London: Dent, 1915.

Francis Bacon, ed. B. Vickers, The Oxford Authors, Oxford and New York: Oxford University Press, 1996.

The works of Francis Bacon, ed. J. Spedding, R. L. Ellis, and D. D. Heath, London: Longmans, 1857–74, 14 vols. [Facs. reprint Stuttgart and Bad Cannstatt: Frommann Holzboog, 1989].

Bade, Josse [Iodocus Badius Ascensius], *Quinti Horatii Flacci de arte poetica opusculum ab Ascensio familiariter expositum*, Paris: T. Kerver, 1500.

Rhetorica Marci Tullii Ciceronis cum commento M.T.C. Rhetoricorum libri quatuor, Lyons: J. Crepin, 1531 [Vatican Library Bibl. Apost. Vat. Popag. III.151; contains Bade's commentary on the *Ad Herennium*].

Biblia complutense, 6 vols., Alcalá: Arnão Guillen de Brocar, 1514–17.

Boccaccio, Giovanni, *Genealogie deorum gentilium libri*, ed. V. Romano, Bari: Scrittori d'Italia 200–1, 1951, 2 vols. [Preface, Books 14–15 trans. and ed. C. G. Osgood, Princeton: Princeton University Press, 1930].

Brink, C. O. *Horace on poetry: the 'Ars poetica'*, Cambridge: Cambridge University Press, 1971.

Castelvetro, Lodovico, *Poetica d'Aristotele vulgarizzata e sposta*, ed. W. Romani, Bari: Laterza, 1978–9, 2 vols.

Erasmus, Desiderius, *Ausgewählte Werke*, ed. H. and A. Holborn, Munich: C. H. Beck, 1964.

Ecclesiastes sive concionator evangelicus (1535), in *Opera omnia emendatiora et auctiora*, ed. J. LeClerc, vol. v, Leiden: Petrus Vander Aa, 1703–6, 10 tomes in 11 vols.

The handbook of the Christian soldier (Enchiridion militis christiani), in *The collected works of Erasmus*, ed. J. W. O'Malley, vol. LXVI, Toronto: University of Toronto Press, 1988, pp. 1–127.

Opera omnia emendatiora et auctiora, ed. J. LeClerc, Leiden: Petrus Vander Aa, 1703–6, 10 tomes in 11 vols.

Opera omnia, Amsterdam: North-Holland Pub. Co., 1971– .

Opus epistolarum, ed. P. S. Allen, *et al.*, Oxford: Clarendon Press, 1906–58, 12 vols.

Estrebay, Jacques-Louis d', *M. Tullii Ciceronis De oratore ad Quintem fratrem dialogi tres*, Paris: M. Vascosan, 1540.

Giraldi Cintio, Giovambattista, *Lettera sulla tragedia* (1543), in *Trattati di poetica e retorica del '500*, ed. B. Weinberg, Bari: Laterza, 1970, vol. I, pp. 469–86.

Scritti critici, ed. C. G. Crocetti, Milan: Marzorati, 1973.

Kragius, Andreas, *Q. Horatii Ars poetica ad P. Rami Dialecticam et Rhetoricam resoluta*, Basle: S. Henricpetrus, n. d. (Preface dated 1583).

Lambin, Denys [Dionysius Lambinus], *Q. Horatius Flaccus . . . opera D. Lambini emendatus*, Lyons: J. de Tournes, 1561.

Landino, Cristoforo [Christophorus Landinus], *Opera Horatii cum commentario Christophori Landini*, Florence: A. Miscominus, 1482.

Luther, Martin, *D. Martin Luthers Werke*, Weimar: H. Bohlau, 1883– , 58 vols.

Luthers Werke in Auswahl, ed. O. Clemen, Berlin: Walter de Gruyter, 1960, 6 vols.

Maggi, Vincenzo, and Lombardi, Bartolomeo, *In Aristotelis librum De poetica communes explanationes*; 1550; reprint Munich: W. Fink, 1964.

Monfasani, John (ed.), *Collectanea Trapezuntiana: texts, documents, and bibliographies of George of Trebizond*, Binghamton: Medieval and Renaissance Texts and Studies/Renaissance Society of America, 1984.

Montaigne, Michel de, *The complete works of Montaigne: Essays, Travel Journal, Letters*, trans. D. M. Frame, Stanford: Stanford University Press, 1967.

Essais, ed. P. Villey and V.-L. Saulnier, Paris: Presses Universitaires de France, 1965 (see esp. bk. I, 25; I, 26; III, 5; III, 13).

Ognibene da Lonigo [Omnibonus Leonicenus], *In Marci Tullii oratorem . . . commentarium*, Venice: A. Torresanus and B. de Blavis, 1485.

Ovide moralisé en prose (texte du quinzième siècle), ed. C. de Boer, Amsterdam: North-Holland Pub. Co., 1954.

Parrasio, Aulo Giano [Aulus Janus Parrhasius], *Q. Horatii Flacci Ars poetica, cum trium doctissimorum commentariis A. Jani Parrhasii, Acronis, Porphyrionis*, Paris: R. Estienne, 1533. First (posthumous) edition of Parrasio, Naples: B. Martirano, 1531.

Pigna, Giovanni Battista, *Ioan. Baptistae Pignae Poetica Horatiana*, Venice: V. Valgrisius, 1561.

Poliziano, Angelo, *La commedia antica e l' 'Andria' di Terenzio*, ed. R. L. Roselli, Florence: Sansoni, 1973.

Rabelais, François, *Œuvres complètes*, ed. J. Boulenger, Paris: Gallimard, 1959 (see esp. *Gargantua*, Prologue; *Third* and *Fourth Books*).

Regio, Rafaello [Raphael Regius], *Quintilianus cum commento*, Venice: B. Locatellus, 1493.

Riccoboni, Antonio, *De re comica*, published with Riccoboni's commentary and translation of Aristotle's *Rhetoric*, Venice: P. Meiettus, 1579, pp. 431–57 [Work actually appeared in 1585].

Robortello, Francesco, *In librum Aristotelis De arte poetica explicationes*, Florence: L. Torrentinus, 1548 [Reprint Munich: W. Fink, 1968.].
Explicationes de satyra, de epigrammate, de comoedia, de elegia (1548), in *Trattati di poetica e retorica del Cinquecento*, ed. B. Weinberg, Bari: Laterza, 1970, vol. I, pp. 495–537.
Sanchez de las Brozas, Francisco [Franciscus Sanctius], *De auctoribus interpretandis sive de exercitatione praecepta* (composed 1556), in *Opera omnia*, 4 vols., Geneva: Frères de Tournes, 1766, vol. II, pp. 75–96.
Scaliger, Julius Caesar, *Poetices libri septem*; 1561; facs. reprint Stuttgart and Bad Cannstatt: Frommann-Holzboog, 1987, ed. A. Buck.
Sturm, Johannes [Ioannes Sturmius], *Commentarii in artem poeticam Horatii confecti ex scholiis Io. Sturmii. Nunc primum editi, opera et studio Ioannis Lobarti Borussi*, Strasburg: N. Wyriot, 1576.
Trissino, Giovanni Giorgio, *La quinta e la sesta divisione della Poetica* (c. 1549), in *Trattati di poetica e retorica del Cinquecento*, ed. B. Weinberg, Bari: Laterza, 1970, vol. II, pp. 7–90.
Turnèbe, Adrien, *In M. Fabii Quintiliani de Institutione oratoria libros XII . . . commentarii*, Paris: T. Richardus, 1554.
Valla, Lorenzo, *Collatio Novi Testamenti*, ed. A. Perosa, Florence: Sansoni, 1970.
Opera Omnia; 1540; facs. reprint Turin: Bottega d'Erasmo, 1962, 2 vols.
Repastinatio dialectice et philosophie, ed. G. Zippel, Padua: Antenore, 1982, 2 vols.
The treatise of Lorenzo Valla on the Donation of Constantine, trans. C. B. Coleman, New Haven: Yale University Press, 1922.
Wilkins, John, *An essay towards a real character and a philosophical language*, London: S. Gellibrand and J. Martin, 1668.
Weinberg, Bernard (ed.), *Trattati di poetica e retorica del Cinquecento*, Bari: Laterza, 1970–4, 4 vols.
Willichius, Lodocus, *Commentaria in artem poeticam Horatii*, Strasburg: C. Mylius, 1539.

Secondary sources

Aguzzi-Barbagli, Danilo, 'Humanism and poetics', in *Renaissance humanism, foundations, forms and legacy*, ed. A. Rabil, Jr., 3 vols., Philadelphia: University of Pennsylvania Press, 1988, vol. III, pp. 85–169 [see esp. pp. 103–7 on Horace].
Azibert, Mireille, *Horace, Cicéron, et la rhétorique au XVIᵉ siècle*, Pau: Marrimpouey, 1972.
Bédouelle, Guy, *Lefèvre d'Etaples et l'intelligence des Ecritures*, Geneva: Droz, 1976.
Bentley, Jerry H. *Humanists and holy writ: New Testament scholarship in the Renaissance*, Princeton: Princeton University Press, 1983.
Boyle, Marjorie O'Rourke, 'The chimera and the spirit: Luther's grammar of the will', in *The Martin Luther quincentennial*, ed. G. Dünnhaupt, Detroit: Wayne State University Press for *Michigan Germanic studies*, 1985, pp. 17–31.

Erasmus on language and method in theology, Toronto: University of Toronto Press, 1971.

Rhetoric and reform: Erasmus' civil dispute with Luther, Cambridge, MA: Harvard University Press, 1983.

Branca, Vittore, *Poliziano e l'umanesimo della parola*, Turin: G. Einaudi, 1983.

The Cambridge history of Renaissance philosophy, ed. C. B. Schmitt, *et al.*, Cambridge: Cambridge University Press, 1988.

Camporeale, Salvatore I. 'Lorenzo Valla, "Repastinatio, liber primus": retorica e linguaggio', in *Lorenzo Valla e l'umanesimo italiano*, ed. O. Besomi and M. Regoliosi, Padua: Antenore, 1986, pp. 217–39.

Lorenzo Valla: umanesimo e teologia, Florence: Istituto Palazzo Strozzi, 1972.

Cave, Terence, *The cornucopian text: problems of writing in the French Renaissance*, Oxford: Clarendon Press, 1979.

Eden, Kathy, *Poetic and legal fiction in the Aristotelian tradition*, Princeton: Princeton University Press, 1986.

Elsky, Martin, *Authorizing words: speech, writing, and print in the English Renaissance*, Ithaca and London: Cornell University Press, 1989.

Feyerabend, Paul, *Against method*, London: New Left Books, 1976.

Garcia Berrio, Antonio, *Formacion de la teoria literaria moderna: la topica horaciana en Europa*, Madrid: CUPSA, 1977–80, 2 vols.

Gawthrop, Richard, and Strauss, Gerald, 'Protestantism and literacy in early modern Germany', *Past and present* 104 (1984), 31–55.

Gerl, Hanna-Barbara, *Rhetorik als Philosophie: Lorenzo Valla*, Munich: W. Fink, 1974.

Grafton, Anthony, *Joseph Scaliger: a study in the history of classical scholarship*, Oxford: Clarendon Press; New York: Oxford University Press, 1983–93, 2 vols.

Hathaway, Baxter, *The age of criticism: the late Renaissance in Italy*, Ithaca: Cornell University Press, 1962.

Marvels and commonplaces: Renaissance literary criticism, New York: Random House, 1968.

Herrick, Marvin T. *Comic theory in the sixteenth century*, Urbana: University of Illinois Press, 1950.

The fusion of Horatian and Aristotelian literary criticism 1531–1555, Urbana: University of Illinois Press, 1946.

Kelley, Donald R. *Foundations of modern historical scholarship: language, law, and history in the French Renaissance*, New York: Columbia University Press, 1970.

Kerrigan, William, and Braden, Gordon, *The idea of the Renaissance*, Baltimore: The Johns Hopkins University Press, 1989.

Knowlson, James, *Universal language schemes in England and France 1600–1800*, Toronto: University of Toronto Press, 1975.

Kretzmann, Norman, 'History of semantics', in *The encyclopaedia of philosophy*, ed. P. Edwards, vol. VII, New York: Macmillan & The Free Press, 1967, pp. 358–406.

Kuhn, Thomas S. *The structure of scientific revolutions*, 2nd edn, Chicago: University of Chicago Press, 1970.

Lebègue, Raymond, 'Horace en France pendant la Renaissance', *Humanisme et Renaissance* 3 (1936), 141–64, 289–308, 384–419.

Lubac, Henri de, *Exégèse médiévale: les quatre sens de l'Ecriture*, Paris: Aubier, 1959–64, 4 vols.

Marmier, Jean, *Horace en France au XVIIᵉ siècle*, Paris: Presses Universitaires de France, 1962.

Martinelli, L. C. 'Le postille di Lorenzo Valla all'*Institutio oratoria* di Quintiliano', in *Lorenzo Valla e l'umanesimo italiano*, ed. O. Besomi and M. Regoliosi, Parma, Atti del convegno internazionale di studi umanistici, 1984, Padua: Antenore, 1986, pp. 21–50.

Mathieu-Castellani, Gisèle, and Plaisance, Michel (ed.), *Les commentaires et la naissance de la critique littéraire. France/Italie (XIVᵉ–XVIᵉ siècles)*, Paris: Aux Amateurs de Livres, 1990.

Meerhoff, K. *Rhétorique et poétique au XVIᵉ siècle en France. Du Bellay, Ramus et les autres*, Leiden: Brill, 1986.

Minnis, A. J. and Scott, A. B. *Medieval literary theory and criticism c. 1100– c. 1375: the commentary-tradition*, Oxford: Clarendon Press; New York: Oxford University Press, 1988.

Monfasani, John, *George of Trebizond: a biography and a study of his rhetoric and logic*, Leiden: Brill, 1976.

Moss, Ann, *Poetry and fable: studies in mythological narrative in sixteenth-century France*, Cambridge: Cambridge University Press, 1984.

Norden, E. *Die Antike Kunstprosa vom VI Jahrhundert v.Chr. bis in die Zeit der Renaissance*; 1909; reprint Darmstadt: Wissenschaftliche Buchgesellschaft, 1974, with G. Calboli, *Nota di Aggiornamento*, Padua: Salerno Editrice, 1986, 2 vols.

Padley, G. A. *Grammatical theory in Western Europe, 1500–1700: the Latin tradition*, Cambridge and New York: Cambridge University Press, 1976.

Patterson, Lee and Nichols, Stephen G. (ed.), *Commentary as cultural artifact*, The south Atlantic quarterly 91, 4 (1992).

Rosenmeyer, Thomas, 'Ancient genre theory: a mirage', *Yearbook of comparative and general literature* 34 (1985), 79.

Rummel, Erika, *Erasmus' annotations on the New Testament: from philologist to theologian*, Toronto: University of Toronto Press, 1986.

Sabbadini, R. *Il metodo degli umanisti*, Florence: F. le Monnier, 1920.

   Le scoperte dei codici latini e greci ne' secoli XIV e XV: nuove ricerche col riassunto filologico dei due volumi, Florence: Sansoni, 1905–14, 2 vols.

   La scuola e gli studi di Guarino Guarini Veronese, Catania: F. Galati, 1896.

   Storia e critica di testi latini, 2nd edn, Padua: Antenore, 1971.

Scaglione, A. *The classical theory of composition from its origins to the present: a historical survey*, Chapel Hill: University of North Carolina Press, 1972.

Seznec, Jean, *The survival of the pagan gods: the mythological tradition and its place in Renaissance humanism and art*, New York: Harper Torchbooks, 1961.

Showermann, G. *Horace and his influence*, Boston: Marshall Jones, 1922.

Spingarn, J. E. *A history of literary criticism in the Renaissance*, New York: Harbinger Books, 1963.

Stemplinger, Eduard, *Horaz im Urteil der Jahrhunderts*, Leipzig: Dieterich, 1921.

Tate, J. 'Horace and the moral function of poetry', *Classical quarterly* 22 (1928), 65–72.

Tigerstedt, E. N. 'Observations on the reception of Aristotle's *Poetics* in the Latin West', *Studies in the Renaissance* 15 (1968), 7–24.

Trimpi, Wesley, 'The meaning of Horace's "Ut pictura poesis"', *The Journal of the Warburg and Courtauld institutes* 36 (1973), 1–34.

Turolla, Enzo, 'Aristotele e le "Poetiche" del Cinquecento', *Dizionario critico della letteratura italiana*, ed. V. Branca, Turin: Unione Tipografico-Editrice Torinese, 1974, pp. 133–9.

Villey, Pierre, *Les sources italiennes de la 'Deffense et illustration de la langue françoise' de Joachim du Bellay*, Paris: Champion, 1908.

Waswo, Richard, *Language and meaning in the Renaissance*, Princeton: Princeton University Press, 1987.

Weinberg, Bernard, *A history of literary criticism in the Italian Renaissance*, Chicago: University of Chicago Press, 1961, 2 vols. [See esp. vol. 1, pp. 71–249 on readings of Aristotle and Horace].

Wittgenstein, Ludwig, *Tractatus logico-philosophicus*, London: Kegan Paul, Trench, Trubner, 1933.

Zumthor, Paul, *Babel, ou, l'inachèvement*, Paris: Seuil, 1997.

POETICS

Humanist classifications

Primary sources and texts

Bembo, Pietro, *Prose della volgar lingua, Gli asolani, Rime*, ed. C. Dionisotti, 2nd edn, Turin: Unione Tipografico-Editrice Torinese, 1966.

Budé, Guillaume, *Opera omnia Gulielmi Budaei*; 1557; facs. reprint London: Gregg Press, 1966, 4 vols.

Castelvetro, Lodovico, *Castelvetro on the art of poetry: an abridged translation of 'Poetica d'Aristotele vulgarizzata e sposta'*, trans. A. Bongiorno, Binghamton: Medieval and Renaissance texts and studies, 1984.

Poetica d'Aristotele vulgarizzata e sposta, ed. W. Romani, Bari: Laterza, 1978–9, 2 vols.

Daniello, Bernardino, *La poetica*; 1536; facs. reprint Munich: W. Fink, 1968, ed. B. Fabian.

Du Bellay, Joachim, *La deffence et illustration de la langue françoyse*, ed. H. Chamard, Paris: Didier, 1948.

The defence and illustration of the French language, trans. G. M. Turquet, London: J. M. Dent, 1939.

Elyot, Sir Thomas, *The book named the governor*, ed. S. E. Lehmberg, London: Dent, 1908–9.

Erasmus, Desiderius, *The collected works of Erasmus*, ed. C. R. Thompson, *et al.*, Toronto: University of Toronto Press, 1974– , 86 vols.

Fracastoro, Girolamo, *Naugerius, sive de poetica dialogus*, trans. R. Kelso, Urbana: University of Illinois Press, 1924.

Huarte de San Juan, Juan, *Examen de ingenios para las ciencias*, ed. E. Torre, Madrid: Editora Nacional, 1976.
The examination or triall of men's wits and dispositions, trans. R. Carew, London: Adam Islip, 1594.
Landino, Cristoforo [Christophorus Landinus], *Disputationes camaldulenses*, ed. P. Lohe, Florence: Sansoni, 1980.
Scritti critici e teorici, ed. R. Cardini, Rome: Bulzoni, 1974, 2 vols.
Minturno, Antonio Sebastiano, *L'arte poetica*; 1564; facs. reprint Munich: W. Fink, 1971, ed. B. Fabian.
De poeta; 1559; facs. reprint Munich: W. Fink, 1970, ed. B. Fabian.
Patrizi [da Cherso], Francesco, *Della poetica*, ed. D. Aguzzi-Barbagli, Florence: Istituto Nazionale di studi sul Rinascimento, 1969, 3 vols.
Poliziano, Angelo, *Angeli Politiani opera*; 1553; facs. reprint Turin: Bottega d'Erasmo, 1970–1, ed. I. Maïer, 3 vols.
Possevino, Antonio, *Bibliotheca selecta de ratione studiorum*, Rome, Vatican, 1593.
Puttenham, George (?), *The arte of English poesie* (1589), ed. G. D. Willcock and A. Walker, Cambridge: Cambridge University Press, 1936.
Scaliger, Julius Caesar, *Poetices libri septem*; 1561; facs. reprint Stuttgart and Bad Cannstatt: Frommann-Holzboog, 1987, ed. A. Buck.
Select translations from Scaliger's 'Poetics', trans. F. M. Padelford, New York: Henry Holt, 1905.
Sidney, Sir Philip, *Miscellaneous prose of Sir Philip Sidney*, ed. K. Duncan-Jones and J. van Dorsten, Oxford: Clarendon Press, 1973.
Spanmüller, Jakob [Iacobus Pontanus], *Poeticarum institutionum libri* III, Ingolstadt: A. Sartorius, 1594.
Tasso, Torquato, *Discourses on the heroic poem*, trans. M. Cavalchini and I. Samuel, Oxford: Clarendon Press, 1973.
Prose, ed. E. Mazzali, Milan: R. Ricciardi, 1959.
Vida, Girolamo, *De arte poetica*, ed. and trans. R. G. Williams, New York: Columbia University Press, 1976.
Viperano, Giovanni, *De poetica libri tres*, trans. P. Rollinson, Greenwood, SC: Koberger, 1987.
Vives, Juan Luis, *Opera omnia*; 1782–90, ed. G. Mayans; facs. reprint London: Gregg Press, 1964, 8 vols.
Weinberg, Bernard (ed.), *Trattati di poetica e retorica del Cinquecento*, Bari: Laterza, 1970–4, 4 vols.
Wilson, Thomas, *Arte of rhetorique* (1553), ed. T. Derrick, The Renaissance imagination 1, New York: Garland, 1982.

Secondary sources

Aguzzi Barbagli, Danilo, 'Humanism and poetics', in *Renaissance humanism: foundations, forms and legacy*, ed. A. Rabil, Jr., 3 vols., Philadelphia: University of Pennsylvania Press, 1988, vol. III, pp. 85–169.
Balavoine, C. and Laurens, P. (ed.), *La statue et l'empreinte: la poétique de Scaliger*, Paris: Vrin, 1986.

Branca, Vittore, *Poliziano e l'umanesimo della parola*, Turin: Einaudi, 1983.

Cardini, Roberto, *La critica del Landino*, Florence: Sansoni, 1973.

Chomarat, Jacques, *Grammaire et rhétorique chez Erasme*, Paris: Les Belles Lettres, 1981, 2 vols.

Dionisotti, C. *Geografia e storia della letteratura italiana*, Turin: Einaudi, 1977.

Ferraro, R. M. *Giudizi critici e criteri estetici nei 'Poetices libri septem' (1561) di Giulio Cesare Scaligero rispetto alla teoria letteraria del Rinascimento*, Chapel Hill: University of North Carolina Press, 1971.

Greene, Thomas M. *The light in Troy: imitation and discovery in Renaissance poetry*, New Haven and London: Yale University Press, 1982.

Kristeller, Paul O. 'The modern system of the arts', *Renaissance thought* II, New York: Harper & Row, 1965, pp. 163–227.

La Garanderie, Marie-Madeleine de, *Christianisme et lettres profanes (1515– 1535)*, Paris: Champion, 1976.

Parker, Deborah, *Commentary and ideology: Dante in the Renaissance*, Durham, NC: Duke University Press, 1993.

Rhu, Lawrence, *The genesis of Tasso's narrative theory: English translations of the early poetics and a comparative study of their significance*, Detroit: Wayne State University Press, 1993.

Weinberg, Bernard, *A history of literary criticism in the Italian Renaissance*, Chicago: University of Chicago Press, 1961, 2 vols.

The rediscovery and transmission of materials: imitation, translation, invention, Petrarchan poetics

Primary sources and texts

Boileau-Despréaux, Nicolas, *L'art poétique*, in *Œuvres complètes*, ed. A. Adam and F. Escal, Paris: Gallimard, 1966.

Bruni, Leonardo, *De interpretatione recta*, in *Leonardo Bruni Aretino Humanistisch-Philosophische Schriften*, ed. H. Baron; reprint Wiesbaden: M. Sandig, 1969.

Castelvetro, Lodovico, *Poetica d'Aristotele vulgarizzata e sposta*, ed. W. Romani, Bari: Laterza, 1978–9, 2 vols.

Dolet, Etienne, *De imitatione Ciceroniana adversus Floridum Sabinum*, Lyons: E. Dolet, 1540.

Dialogus De imitatione Ciceroniana adversus Desiderium Erasmum Roteroda-mum, pro Christophoro Longolio; 1535; facs. reprint Geneva: Droz, 1974.

La manière de bien traduire d'une langue en autre; 1540; reprint Paris: J. Tastu for Téchener, 1830.

Du Bellay, Joachim, *La deffence et illustration de la langue françoyse*, ed. H. Chamard, Paris: Didier, 1948.

Erasmus, Desiderius, *Dialogus Ciceronianus*, ed. P. Mesnard, in Erasmus, *Opera omnia*, vol. I, 2, Amsterdam: North-Holland Pub. Co., 1971, pp. 581–710.

Gesualdo, Giovanni Andrea, *Il Petrarcha colla spositione di misser Giovanni Andrea Gesualdo*, Venice: Fratelli da Sabbio, 1533.

Gilbert, Allan, *Literary criticism from Plato to Dryden*, Detroit: Wayne State University Press, 1962.

Huet, Pierre-Daniel, *De interpretatione libri duo*, The Hague: A. Leers, 1683.

Humphrey, Lawrence, *Interpretatio linguarum: seu de ratione convertendi et explicandi autores tam sacros quam prophanos*, Basle: H. Frobenius and N. Episcopius, 1559.

Luther, Martin, *Sendbrief vom Dolmetschen*, ed. K. Bischoff, Tübingen: M. Niemeyer, 1965.

Manetti, Giannozzo, *De interpretatione recta*, in *Apologeticus (Adversus suae novae Psalterii traductionis obtrectatores apologetici libri v)*, Vatican Library Pal. lat. 41.

Omphalius, Jacobus, *De elocutionis imitatione ac apparatu . . . Io. Francisci Pici Mirandulae ad Petrum Bembum et Petri Bembi ad Io. Franciscum Picum Mirandulam de imitatione epistolae duae*, Paris: G. Julianus, 1555. First edition of Omphalius, *De elocutionis imitatione*, Paris: S. de Colines, 1537.

Opitz, Martin, *Buch von der deutschen Poeterey*, ed. C. Sommer, Stuttgart: Reclam, 1970.

Peletier du Mans, Jacques, *L'art poëtique*, ed. A. Boulanger, Paris: Les Belles Lettres, 1930.

Ricci, Bartolomeo, *De imitatione libri tres*, Venice: sons of Aldus, 1545. First published 1541.

Ronsard, Pierre de, prefaces to *La Franciade*, in *Œuvres complètes*, ed. P. Laumonier, R. Lebègue, and G. Demerson, rev. edn, vol. xvi, Paris: Nizet, 1983.

Scaliger, Julius Caesar, *Poetices libri septem*; 1561; facs. reprint Stuttgart and Bad Cannstatt: Frommann-Holzboog, 1987, ed. A. Buck.

Sebillet, Thomas, *Art poétique françoys*, ed. F. Gaiffe, Paris: Droz, 1932. [New edn by F. Goyet, Paris: Nizet, 1988.]

Sidney, Sir Philip, *An apology for poetry*, ed. G. Shepherd, Manchester: Manchester University Press; New York: Barnes and Noble, 1973.

Miscellaneous prose of Sir Philip Sidney, ed. K. Duncan-Jones and J. van Dorsten, Oxford: Clarendon Press, 1973.

Solerti, Angelo (ed.), *Le vite di Dante, Petrarca, e Boccaccio*, Milan: Francesco Vallardi, 1904–5.

Tasso, Torquato, *Discorsi dell'arte poetica e del poema eroico*, ed. L. Poma, Bari: Laterza, 1964.

Thompson, David, and Nagel, Alan (ed.), *The three crowns of Florence*, New York: Harper & Row, 1972.

Traités de poétique et de rhétorique de la Renaissance, ed. F. Goyet, Paris: Librairie générale française, 1990.

Vauquelin de la Fresnaye, Jean, *L'art poétique*, ed. G. Pelissier, Paris: Garnier, 1885.

Vellutello, Alessandro, *Le volgari opere del Petrarcha con la espositione di Alessandro Vellutello da Lucca*, Venice: Fratelli da Sabbio, 1525.

Vida, Girolamo, *De arte poetica*, ed. and trans. R. G. Williams, New York: Columbia University Press, 1976.

Vives, Juan Luis, *De conscribendis epistolis*, ed. C. Fantazzi, Leiden: Brill, 1989.

Wilson, Thomas, *Arte of rhetorique* (1553), ed. T. Derrick, The Renaissance imagination 1, New York: Garland, 1982.

Secondary sources

Amielle, G. *Les traductions françaises des Métamorphoses d'Ovide*, Paris: J. Touzot, 1989.

Amos, Flora, *Early theories of translation*, New York: Octagon Books, 1921.

Aulotte, Robert, *Amyot et Plutarque: la tradition des 'Moralia' au XVIe siècle*, Geneva: Droz, 1965.

Beardsley, Theodore, 'Hispano-classical translations printed between 1482 and 1699: a study of the prologues and a critical bibliography', unpublished Ph.D. thesis, University of Pennsylvania, 1961.

Belloni, Gino, *Laura tra Petrarca e Bembo: studi sul commento umanistico-rinascimentale al 'Canzoniere'*, Padua: Antenore, 1992.

Birkenmajer, Alexander, 'Der Streit des Alonso von Cartagena mit Leonardo Bruni Aretino', *Beiträge zur Geschichte der Philosophie des Mittelalters*, 20 (1922), 129–210.

Bolgar, R. R. *The classical heritage and its beneficiaries from the Carolingian Age to the end of the Renaissance*; 1954; reprint New York: Harper & Row, 1964.

Brucker, Charles (ed.), *Traduction et adaptation en France à la fin du Moyen Age et à la Renaissance: actes du colloque organisé par l'Université de Nancy II, 23–25 mars 1995*, Paris: H. Champion, 1997.

Buck, August, Heitmann, Klaus, and Mettmann, Walter (ed.), *Dichtungslehren der Romania aus der Zeit der Renaissance und des Barock*, Frankfurt: Athenäum, 1972.

Castor, Grahame, *Pléiade poetics: a study in sixteenth-century thought and terminology*, Cambridge: Cambridge University Press, 1964.

Cave, Terence, *The cornucopian text: problems of writing in the French Renaissance*, Oxford: Clarendon Press, 1979.

Chavy, Paul, *Traducteurs d'autrefois. Moyen Age et Renaissance. Dictionnaire des traducteurs et de la littérature traduite en ancien et moyen français (842–1600)*, Paris and Geneva: Champion-Slatkine, 1988, 2 vols.

Coleman, D. G. *The Gallo-Roman muse: aspects of Roman literary tradition in sixteenth-century France*, Cambridge: Cambridge University Press, 1979.

Conley, Carey H. *The first English translators of the classics*, New Haven: Yale University Press, 1927.

Dionisotti, Carlo, 'Fortuna del Petrarca nel "400"', *Italia medioevale e umanistica* 17 (1974), 61–113.

Fowler, Mary, and Bishop, Morris, *Catalogue of the Petrarch collection in the Cornell University Library*, 2nd edn, Millwood, NJ: Kraus-Thomson, 1974.

Gardini, Nicola, *Le umane parole: imitazione nella lirica europea del Rinascimento, da Bembo a Ben Jonson*, Milan: Mondadori, 1997.

Greene, Thomas M. *The light in Troy: imitation and discovery in Renaissance poetry*, New Haven and London: Yale University Press, 1982.

Guillerm, Luce, *Sujet de l'écriture et traduction autour de 1540*, Paris: Atelier National Reproduction des Thèses, 1988.

Hulubei, A. 'Virgile en France au XVIe siècle', *Revue du seizième siècle* 18 (1931), 1–77.

Kennedy, William J. *Authorizing Petrarch*, Ithaca: Cornell University Press, 1994.

Kibédi Varga, Aron, *Rhétorique et littérature: études de structures classiques*, Paris: Didier, 1970.

Kushner, Eva, and Chavy, Paul (ed.), *Translation in the Renaissance*, special issue, *Canadian review of comparative literature*, 8, 2, Spring 1981.

Larwill, Paul H. *La théorie de la traduction au début de la Renaissance*, Munich: Wolf, 1934.

Lathrop, Henry, *Translation from the classics into English from Caxton to Chapman (1477–1620)*, Madison: University of Wisconsin Press, 1933.

Matthiessen, Francis O. *Translation: an Elizabethan art*, Cambridge, MA: Harvard University Press, 1931.

Meerhoff, K. *Rhétorique et poétique au XVIᵉ siècle en France. Du Bellay, Ramus et les autres*, Leiden: Brill, 1986.

Moss, Ann, *Ovid in Renaissance France: a survey of the Latin editions of Ovid and commentaries printed in France before 1600*, London: The Warburg Institute, 1982.

Poetry and fable: studies in mythological narrative in sixteenth-century France, Cambridge: Cambridge University Press, 1984.

Norton, Glyn P. *The ideology and language of translation in Renaissance France and their humanist antecedents*, Geneva: Droz, 1984.

Patterson, Warner F. *Three centuries of French poetic theory: a critical history of the chief arts of poetry in France (1328–1630)*, Ann Arbor: University of Michigan Press, 1935, 2 vols.

Petris, Alfonso, 'Le teorie umanistiche del tradurre e l' "Apologeticus" di Giannozzo Manetti', *Bibliothèque d'humanisme et Renaissance* 37 (1975), 15–32.

Pigman, G. W., III, 'Neo-Latin imitation of the Latin classics', in *Latin Poetry and the classical tradition*, ed. P. Godman and O. Murray, Oxford: Clarendon Press, 1990, pp. 199–210.

Quint, David, Ferguson, Margaret W., Pigman III, G. W., and Rebhorn, Wayne A. (ed.), *Creative imitation: new essays on Renaissance literature in honor of Thomas M. Greene*, Binghamton: Medieval and Renaissance texts and studies, 1992.

Rener, Frederick M. *'Interpretatio': language and translation from Cicero to Tytler*, Amsterdam and Atlanta: Rodopi, 1989.

Roche, Thomas P., Jr. *Petrarch and the English sonnet sequences*, New York: AMS, 1989.

Rummel, Erika, *Erasmus as a translator of the classics*, Toronto, Buffalo, London: University of Toronto Press, 1985.

Sabbadini, Remigio, 'Del tradurre i classici antichi in Italia', *Atene e Roma* 3 (1900), 202–17.

Il metodo degli umanisti, Florence: Le Monnier, 1922.

Schwarz, Werner, 'The theory of translation in 16th-century Germany', *Modern language review* 40 (1945), 289–99.

'Translation into German in the 15th century', *Modern language review* 39 (1944), 368–73.

Steiner, Thomas R. *English translation theory 1650–1800*, Assen: Van Gorcum, 1975.

Weinberg, Bernard, *A history of literary criticism in the Italian Renaissance*, Chicago: University of Chicago Press, 1961, 2 vols.
Workman, Samuel, *Fifteenth-century translation as an influence on English prose*, Princeton: Princeton University Press, 1940.
Zuber, Roger, *Les 'belles infidèles' et la formation du goût classique*, Paris: A. Colin, 1969.

Rhetorical poetics: humanist education

Primary sources and texts

Brinsley, J. *Ludus literarius*; 1612; facs. reprint Menston: Scolar Press, 1968.
Chytraeus, D. *De ratione discendi, et ordine studiorum in singulis artibus recte instituendis*, Wittenberg: no pub., 1564.
Erasmus, D. *On the method of study [De ratione studii ac legendi interpretandique auctores]*, ed. and trans. B. McGregor, in *The collected works of Erasmus*, vol. XXIV, Toronto, Buffalo, and London: University of Toronto Press, 1978.
Garin, E. *Il pensiero pedagogico dell'umanesimo*, Florence: S. Giuntine, 1958.
Ratio atque institutio studiorum Societatis Iesu, Rome: Jesuit College, 1606. First definitive edition in 1599.
Richer, E. *Obstetrix animorum, hoc est brevis et expedita ratio docendi, studendi, conversandi*, Paris: Drouart, 1600.
Sturm, J. *De literarum ludis recte aperiendis*, Strasburg: W. Rihelius, 1538.
Verepaeus, S. *Institutionum scholasticarum libri tres*, Antwerp: J. Bellerus, 1573.

Secondary sources

Baldwin, T. W. *William Shakspere's small Latine and lesse Greeke*, Urbana: University of Illinois Press, 1944, 2 vols.
Bolgar, R. R. *The classical heritage and its beneficiaries from the Carolingian Age to the end of the Renaissance*; 1954; reprint New York: Harper & Row, 1964.
Chomarat, Jacques, *Grammaire et rhétorique chez Erasme*, Paris: Les Belles Lettres, 1981, 2 vols.
Dainville, F. de, *La naissance de l'humanisme moderne*; 1940; reprint Geneva: Slatkine, 1969.
Grafton, Anthony, and Jardine, Lisa, *From humanism to the humanities: education and the liberal arts in fifteenth- and sixteenth-century Europe*, Cambridge, MA: Harvard University Press, 1986.
Grendler, P. F. 'Education in the Renaissance and Reformation', *Renaissance quarterly* 43 (1990), 774–824.
  Schooling in Renaissance Italy: literacy and learning, 1300–1600, Baltimore: The Johns Hopkins University Press, 1989.
Howell, W. S. *Logic and rhetoric in England*; 1956; reprint New York: Russell and Russell, 1961.
Huppert, G. *Public schools in Renaissance France*, Urbana and Chicago: University of Illinois Press, 1984.

Ong, Walter J. *Ramus, method, and the decay of dialogue: from the art of discourse to the art of reason*; 1958; reprint New York: Octagon, 1974.

Overfield, J. H. *Humanism and scholasticism in late medieval Germany*, Princeton: Princeton University Press, 1985.

Porteau, P. *Montaigne et la vie pédagogique de son temps*, Paris: Droz, 1935.

Scaglione, Aldo, *The liberal arts and the Jesuit college system*, Amsterdam and Philadelphia: J. Benjamins, 1986.

Skinner, Quentin, *Reason and rhetoric in the philosophy of Hobbes*, Cambridge and New York: Cambridge University Press, 1996.

Strauss, G. *Luther's house of learning: indoctrination of the young in the German Reformation*, Baltimore and London: The Johns Hopkins University Press, 1978.

Vasoli, Cesare, *La dialettica e la retorica dell'umanesimo: 'invenzione' e 'metodo' nella cultura del XV e XVI secolo*, Milan: Feltrinelli, 1968.

Vickers, Brian, *In defence of rhetoric*, Oxford: Clarendon Press, 1988.

Rhetorical poetics: second rhetoric and the 'grands rhétoriqueurs'

Primary sources and texts

Anthologie des grands rhétoriqueurs, ed. P. Zumthor, Paris: Union générale d'éditions, 1978.

Le jardin de plaisance et fleur de rethorique; 1501; facs. reprint Paris: Firmin-Didot, 1910.

Recueil d'arts de seconde rhétorique, ed. E. Langlois; 1902; reprint Geneva, Slatkine, 1974.

Recueil de poésies françoises des XVe et XVIe siècles, ed. A. de Courde de Montaiglon and J. de Rothschild, Paris: Jannet, 1855–78, 13 vols.

Secondary sources

Brown, Cynthia Jane, *The shaping of history and poetry in late medieval France: propaganda and artistic expression in the works of the 'rhétoriqueurs'*, Birmingham, AL: Summa, 1985.

Doutrepont, Georges, *La littérature française à la cour des ducs de Bourgogne*, Paris: Champion, 1909.

Les grands rhétoriqueurs, Actes du Ve Colloque international sur le moyen français, 1985, Milan: Vita e pensiero, 1985.

Grands rhétoriqueurs, Cahiers V.-L. Saulnier, 14, Paris: Presses de l'Ecole Normale Supérieure, 1997.

Huizinga, Johan, *The waning of the Middle Ages: a study of the forms of life, thought and art in France and the Netherlands in the XIVth and XVth centuries*, New York: Doubleday, 1954.

Jodogne, Pierre, 'Les "rhétoriqueurs" et l'humanisme: problèmes d'histoire littéraire', in *Humanism in France at the end of the Middle Ages and in the early Renaissance*, ed. A. H. T. Levi, Manchester: Manchester University Press, 1970, pp. 150–75.

Joukovsky-Micha, Françoise, 'L'héritage médiéval', in *La gloire dans la poésie française*, Geneva: Droz, 1969, pp. 101–46.

Patterson, Warner F. *Three centuries of French poetic theory: a critical history of the chief arts of poetry in France (1328–1630)*, Ann Arbor: University of Michigan Press, 1935, 2 vols.

Rigolot, François, *Le texte de la Renaissance: des rhétoriqueurs à Montaigne*, Geneva: Droz, 1982.

Simone, Franco, 'La scuola dei rhétoriqueurs', in *Umanesimo, rinascimento, barocco in Francia*, Milan: Mursia, 1968, pp. 169–201.

Zumthor, Paul, *Le masque et la lumière*, Paris: Seuil, 1978.

Rhetorical poetics: the rhetoric of presence

Primary sources and texts

Alberti, Leon Battista, *On painting*, trans. J. R. Spencer, New Haven: Yale University Press, 1966.

Burton, Robert, *The anatomy of melancholy*, Oxford: J. Lichfield and J. Short for H. Cripps, 1624. [ed. F. Dell and P. Jordan-Smith, New York: Farrar and Rinehart, 1927].

Du Bellay, Joachim, *La deffence et illustration de la langue françoyse*, ed. H. Chamard, Paris: Didier, 1948.

Erasmus, Desiderius, *Opera omnia*, Basle: Froben, 1540, 9 vols.

Ficino, Marsilio, *Theologia Platonica sive de immortalitate animorum*, ed. and trans. R. Marcel, Paris: Les Belles Lettres, 1964–70, 3 vols.

Leonardo da Vinci, *Treatise on painting*, ed. A. P. McMahon, Princeton: Princeton University Press, 1956.

Montaigne, Michel de, *The complete works of Montaigne: Essays, Travel Journal, Letters*, trans. D. M. Frame, Stanford: Stanford University Press, 1967.

Poliziano, Angelo, *Opera omnia*, Lyons: Gryphius, 1546.

Scaliger, Julius Caesar, *Poetices libri septem*; 1561; facs. reprint Stuttgart and Bad Cannstatt: Frommann-Holzboog, 1987, ed. A. Buck.

Spenser, Edmund, *The shepheardes calender*, in *Poetical works*, ed. J. C. Smith and E. de Sélincourt, Oxford: Clarendon Press, 1912.

Secondary sources

Bergmann, Emilie L. *Art inscribed: essays on ekphrasis in Spanish Golden Age poetry*, Cambridge, MA: Harvard University Press, 1979.

Cave, Terence, '*Enargeia*: Erasmus and the rhetoric of presence in the sixteenth century', *L'esprit créateur* 16, 4 (Winter 1976), 5–19.

Galand-Hallyn, Perrine, *Le reflet des fleurs: description et métalangage poétique d'Homère à la Renaissance*, Geneva: Droz, 1994.

Gent, Lucy, *Picture and poetry 1560–1620: relations between literature and the visual arts in the English Renaissance*, Leamington Spa: J. Hall, 1981.

Gombrich, Ernst Hans, *Art and illusion*, Princeton: Princeton University Press, 1961.

Hagstrum, Jean H. *The sister arts: the tradition of literary pictorialism and English poetry from Dryden to Gray*, Chicago: University of Chicago Press, 1958.

Krieger, Murray, *Ekphrasis: the illusion of the natural sign*, Baltimore: The Johns Hopkins University Press, 1992.

Lausberg, Heinrich, *Handbuch der literarischen Rhetorik*, Munich: M. Hüber, 1960.

Ong, Walter J. *The presence of the word*, New Haven: Yale University Press, 1967.

Panofsky, Erwin, *Idea: a concept in art theory*, trans. J. Peake, Columbia, SC: University of South Carolina Press, 1968.

Plett, H. F. *Rhetorik der Affekte. Englische Wirkungsästhetik im Zeitalter der Renaissance*, Tübingen: M. Niemeyer, 1975.

Wind, Edgar, *Pagan mysteries in the Renaissance*, rev. edn, New York: Norton, 1968.

Rhetorical poetics: the paradoxical sisterhood, 'ut pictura poesis'

Primary sources and texts

Alberti, Leon Battista, *On painting and sculpture: the Latin texts of 'De pictura' and 'De statua'*, ed. with trans., intro., and notes by C. Grayson, London: Phaidon, 1972.

Bellori, Giovanni Pietro, *Le vite de' pittori, scultori et architetti moderni*, Rome: Per il success. al Mascardi, 1672.

Dolce, Lodovico, L'Aretino. *Dialogo della pittura*, Lanciano: Carabba, 1913.

Dryden, John, *Parallel between painting and poetry*, London: Printed by J. Hepinstall for W. Rogers, 1695. Published as Preface to Dryden's translation of Dufresnoy's *De arte graphica*.

Du Bos, Abbé [Jean-Baptiste], *Réflexions critiques sur la poésie et sur la peinture*, préface D. Désirat, Paris: Ecole nationale supérieure des beaux-arts, 1993.

Dufresnoy, Charles-Alphonse, *The art of painting by C. A. Du Fresnoy, with remarks ... by Mr. Dryden ...*, London: Printed by J. Hepinstall for W. Rogers, 1695. Translated by Dryden and published with his *Parallel between painting and poetry*.

Félibien, André, sieur des Avaux et de Javercy, *Entretiens sur les vies et sur les ouvrages des plus excellens peintres anciens et modemes*, Paris: P. Le Petit, 1666–88.

Conférences de l'Académie royale de peinture et de sculpture. Pendant l'année 1667, Paris: F. Léonard, 1669.

Lomazzo, Giovanni Paolo, *Trattato dell'arte della pittura, scoltura et architettura*, Milan: Paolo Gottardo Pontio, 1584.

Piles, Roger de, *Abrégé de la vie des peintres*, Paris: F. Muguet, 1699.

Cours de peinture par principes, Paris: J. Estienne, 1708.

Sidney, Sir Philip, *An apology for poetry*, ed. G. Shepherd, Manchester: Manchester University Press; New York: Barnes and Noble, 1973.

Tasso, Torquato, *Discorsi dell'arte poetica et del poema eroico*, ed. L. Poma, Bari: Laterza, 1964.

Secondary sources

Baxandall, Michael, *Giotto and the orators: humanist observers of painting in Italy and the discovery of pictorial composition, 1350–1450*, Oxford: Clarendon Press, 1971.

Braider, Christopher, *Refiguring the real: picture and modernity in word and image, 1400–1700*, Princeton: Princeton University Press, 1993.

Bryson, Norman, *Word and image: French painting of the Ancien Régime*, Cambridge: Cambridge University Press, 1981.

Hagstrum, Jean, *The sister arts: the tradition of literary pictorialism and English poetry from Dryden to Gray*, Chicago: University of Chicago Press, 1958.

Hulse, Clark, *The rule of art: literature and painting in the Renaissance*, Chicago: University of Chicago Press, 1990.

Lee, Rensselaer, *'Ut pictura poesis': the humanistic theory of painting*, New York: Norton, 1967.

Mitchell, W. J. T. *Iconology: image, text, ideology*, Chicago: University of Chicago Press, 1986.

Panofsky, Erwin, *Idea: a concept in art history*, trans. J. Peake, Columbia, SC: University of South Carolina Press, 1968.

Spencer, John R. ' "Ut rhetorica pictura": a study in Quattrocento theory of painting', *The Journal of the Warburg and Courtauld institutes* 20 (1957), 26–44.

Rhetorical poetics: conceptions of style

Primary sources and texts

Cresolles, Louis de, *Theatrum veterum rhetorum, oratorum, et declamatorum . . . libri v*, Paris: S. Cramoisy, 1620.

Dolet, Etienne, *L'Erasmianus sive Ciceronianus d'Etienne Dolet (1535)*, ed. E. V. Telle, Geneva: Droz, 1974.

Du Vair, Guillaume, *De l'éloquence françoise et pourquoy elle est demeurée si basse*; 1594; ed. R. Radouant, 1907; reprint Geneva: Slatkine, 1970.

Erasmus, Desiderius, *Dialogus cui titulus, Ciceronianus, sive, de optimo genere dicendi*, ed. A. H. T. Levi and trans. B. I. Knott, in *The collected works of Erasmus*, vol. XXVIII, Toronto: University of Toronto Press, 1986.

Flacius Illyricus, Matthias, *Clavis Scripturae Sacrae, seu de sermone sacrarum literarum, in duas partes divisae* (1562), Leipzig: J. J. Erythropilius, 1695.

George of Trebizond, *Rhetoricorum libri v*, Venice: Vindelinus de Spira, c. 1472.

Granada, Luis de, *Ecclesiasticae rhetoricae, sive, de ratione concionandi, libri sex*, Lisbon: A. Riberius, 1576.

Keckermann, Bartholomew, *Rhetoricae ecclesiasticae, sive artis formandi et habendi conciones sacras* [1600], in *Opera omnia quae extant*, vol. II, Geneva: P. Aubertus, 1614, 2 vols.

Systema rhetoricae, Hanover: G. Antonius, 1608.

Lipsius, Justus, *Epistolica institutio*, Frankfurt: J. Wéchel and P. Fischer, 1591.

Principles of letter-writing: a bilingual text of Justi Lipsii Epistolica institutio, ed. R. V. Young and M. T. Hester, Carbondale: Southern Illinois University Press, 1996.

Melanchthon, Philipp, *Elementorum rhetorices libri duo* [1531], in *Opera quae supersunt omnia*, ed. C. G. Bretschneider, vol. XIII, Brunswick and Halle: C. A. Schwetschke, 1834–60, 28 vols.

Ramus, Petrus, *Ciceronianus*, Paris: A. Wéchel, 1557.

Soarez, Cyprian, *De arte rhetorica libri tres, ex Aristotele, Cicerone, et Quinctiliano praecipue deprompti*, Cologne: Cholinus, 1557.

Vossius, Gerardus, *Commentariorum rhetoricorum, sive oratoriaium [sic] institutionum, libri* VI, 3rd edn, Leiden: I. Maire, 1630.

Wilson, Thomas, *Arte of rhetorique* (1553), ed. T. Derrick, The Renaissance imagination 1, New York: Garland, 1982.

Secondary sources

Adolph, Robert, *The rise of modern prose style*, Cambridge, MA: M.I.T. Press, 1968.

Clément, Michèle, *Une poétique de crise: poètes baroques et mystiques (1570–1660)*, Paris: Champion, 1996.

Croll, Morris, *'Attic' and Baroque prose style: essays by Morris Croll*, ed. J. M. Patrick and R. O. Evans with J. M. Wallace, Princeton: Princeton University Press, 1966.

Fumaroli, Marc, *L'âge de l'éloquence: rhétorique et 'res literaria' de la Renaissance au seuil de l'époque classique*, Geneva: Droz, 1980.

Jones, Richard F. *The seventeenth century: studies in the history of English thought and literature from Bacon to Pope*, Stanford: Stanford University Press, 1951.

Lewalski, Barbara K. *Protestant poetics and the seventeenth-century religious lyric*, Princeton: Princeton University Press, 1979.

Meerhoff, Kees, *Rhétorique et poétique en France au XVIᵉ siècle: Du Bellay, Ramus et les autres*, Leiden: Brill, 1985.

Murphy, James J. (ed.), *Renaissance eloquence: studies in the theory and practice of Renaissance rhetoric*, Berkeley: University of California Press, 1983.

Shuger, Debora, *Sacred rhetoric: the Christian grand style in the English Renaissance*, Princeton: Princeton University Press, 1988.

Williamson, George, *The Senecan amble: prose form from Bacon to Collier*, Chicago: University of Chicago Press, 1951.

Rhetorical poetics: Sir Philip Sidney's *An apology for poetry*

Primary sources and texts

Aristotle, *Aristotle: rhetoric and poetics*, trans. W. R. Roberts and I. Bywater, New York: Random House, 1954.

Greville, Sir Fulke, *Life of Sir Philip Sidney*, Oxford: Clarendon Press, 1907.

Hoskins, John, 'The direccōns for speech and style', *The life, letters and writings of John Hoskyns*, ed. L. B. Osborn, New Haven: Yale University Press, 1937.

Minturno, Antonio Sebastiano, *De poeta*; 1559; reprint Munich: W. Fink, 1970.

Sidney, Sir Philip, *An apology for poetry or the defence of poesy*, ed. G. Shepherd, London: Nelson, 1965.

An apologie for poetrie, in *Elizabethan critical essays*, ed. G. G. Smith, 2 vols., Oxford: Oxford University Press, 1904, vol. I, pp. 148–207.

Temple, Sir William, *William Temple's analysis of Sir Philip Sidney's 'Apology for poetry'*, ed. and trans. J. Webster, Binghamton: State University of New York Press, 1984.

Secondary sources

Eden, Kathy, *Poetic and legal fiction in the Aristotelian tradition*, Princeton: Princeton University Press, 1986.

Kristeller, Paul O. 'Proclus as a reader of Plato and Plotinus, and his influence in the Middle Ages and in the Renaissance', *Colloques internationaux du CNRS*: 'Proclus – lecteur et interprète des anciens', Paris: Editions du CNRS., 1987.

Panofsky, Erwin, *Idea: a concept in art theory*, trans. J. Peake, Columbia, SC: University of South Carolina Press, 1968.

Robinson, Forrest G. *The shape of things known: Sidney's 'Apology' in its philosophical tradition*, Cambridge, MA: Harvard University Press, 1972.

Trimpi, Wesley, 'Konrad Gesner and Neoplatonic poetics', *Magister regis: studies in honor of Robert Earl Kaske*, ed. A. Groos, New York: Fordham University Press, 1986, pp. 261–72.

Muses of one mind: the literary analysis of experience and its continuity, Princeton: Princeton University Press, 1983.

Weinberg, Bernard, *A history of literary criticism in the Italian Renaissance*, Chicago: University of Chicago Press, 1961, 2 vols.

Yates, Francis A. *The art of memory*, Chicago: University of Chicago Press, 1966.

Rhetorical poetics: concepts of reader response

Primary sources and texts

Boileau-Despréaux, Nicolas, *Art poétique* and *Traité du Sublime*, in *Œuvres diverses*, ed. F. Escal, Paris: Gallimard, 1966.

Corneille, Pierre, *Writings on the theatre*, ed. H. T. Barnwell, Oxford: Blackwell, 1965.

Dryden, John, *An essay of dramatick poesie*, in *Works*, ed. S. H. Monk, vol. XVII, Berkeley: University of California Press, 1971.

Kibédi Varga, Aron, *Les poétiques du classicisme*, Paris: Aux Amateurs de Livres, 1990.

La Mesnardière, Jules de, *La poétique*; 1640; reprint Geneva: Slatkine, 1972.

Lamy, Bernard, *De l'art de parler*, Paris: A. Pralard, 1675.

Racine, Jean, *Principes de la tragédie*, ed. E. Vinaver, Manchester and Paris: Nizet, 1951.

Russell, D. A. and Winterbottom, M. (ed.), *Ancient literary criticism: the principal texts in new translations*, Oxford: Clarendon Press, 1972.

Sidney, Sir Philip, *An apology for poetry*, ed. G. Shepherd, Manchester: Manchester University Press, 1973.

Weinberg, Bernard (ed.), *Critical prefaces of the French Renaissance*; 1950; reprint New York: AMS, 1970.
A history of literary criticism in the Italian Renaissance, Chicago: University of Chicago Press, 1961, 2 vols.

Secondary sources

Bray, René, *La formation de la doctrine classique en France*, Paris: Hachette, 1927.
Brody, Jules, 'Platonisme et classicisme', in *French classicism: a critical miscellany*, ed. J. Brody, Englewood Cliffs: Prentice-Hall, 1966, pp. 186–207.
Castor, Grahame, *Pléiade poetics*, Cambridge: Cambridge University Press, 1964.
Cronk, Nicholas, 'The enigma of French classicism: a Platonic current in seventeenth-century poetic theory', *French studies* 40 (1986), 269–86.
'Une poétique platonicienne à l'époque classique: le *De furore poetico* de Pierre Petit (1683)', *Dix-septième siècle* 37 (1985), 99–102.
Hathaway, Baxter, *The age of criticism: the late Renaissance in Italy*, Ithaca: Cornell University Press, 1962.
Marvels and commonplaces: Renaissance literary criticism, New York: Random House, 1968.
Herrick, Marvin T. *The fusion of Horatian and Aristotelian criticism, 1531–1555*, Urbana: University of Illinios Press, 1946.
Howarth, W. D. 'La notion de la catharsis dans la comédie française classique', *Revue des sciences humaines* 152 (1973), 521–39.
Mallinson, G. J. 'Fiction, morality, and the reader: reflections on the classical formula *plaire et instruire*', *Continuum* 1 (1989), 203–28.
Potts, D. C. ' "Une carrière épineuse": Neoplatonism and the poet's vocation in Boileau's *Art poétique*', *French studies* 47 (1993), 20–32.
Walker, D. P. 'Esoteric symbolism', in *Music, spirit and language in the Renaissance*, ed. P. Gouk, London: Variorum Reprints, 1985, ch. 15. [Work is unpaginated; pp. 218–32 in original printing, 1975].

Literary forms: Italian epic theory

Primary sources and texts

Denores, Giason, *Poetica di Iason Denores. nella qual . . . si tratta secondo l'opinione d'Arist. della tragedia, del poema heroico, & della comedia*, Padua: P. Meietto, 1588.
Giraldi Cintio, Giovambattista, *Scritti critici*, ed. C. G. Crocetti, Milan: Marzorati, 1973.
Minturno, Antonio, *L'arte poetica del Sig. Antonio Minturno*, Venice: G. A. Valvassori, 1564.
Pellegrino, Camillo, *Il Carrafa, o vero della epica poesia* (1584), in *Trattati di poetica e retorica del Cinquecento*, ed. B. Weinberg, Bari: Laterza, 1972, vol. III, pp. 311–44.
Pigna, Giovanni Battista, *I romanzi di M. Giouan Battista Pigna*, Venice: V. Valgrisi, 1554.

Salviati, Lionardo, *Difesa dell'Orlando furioso contra'l Dialogo dell'epica poesia di Cammillo Pellegrino*, Florence: D. Manzani, 1584.

Lo 'nfarinato secondo ovvero dello 'nfarinato accademico della Crusca, risposta al libro intitolato Replica di Camillo Pellegrino ec, Florence: A. Padovani, 1588.

Tasso, Torquato, *Apologia del S. Torquato Tasso in difesa della sua Gierusalemme liberata, a gli Accademici della Crusca, con le accuse, & difese dell'Orlando furioso dell'Ariosto*, Ferrara: G. Vasalini, 1586.

Discorsi dell'arte poetica e del poema eroico, ed. L. Poma, Bari: Laterza, 1964.

Discourses on the heroic poem, trans. M. Cavalchini and I. Samuel, Oxford: Clarendon Press, 1973.

Prose, ed. E. Mazzali, Milan: Riccardo Ricciardi, 1959.

Trissino, Giovanni Giorgio, *La quinta e la sesta divisione della Poetica* (c. 1549), in *Trattati di poetica e retorica del Cinquecento*, ed. B. Weinberg, Bari: Laterza, 1970, vol. II, pp. 7–90.

Weinberg, Bernard (ed.), *Trattati di poetica e retorica del Cinquecento*, Bari: Laterza, 1970–4, 4 vols.

Secondary sources

Baldassarri, Guido, 'Introduzione ai *Discorsi dell'arte poetica* del Tasso', *Studi tassiani* 26 (1977), 5–38.

Borsetto, Luciana, 'In che maniera di verso? normalizzazione e sperimentazione nella scrittura dell'epica', in *Il furto di Prometeo: imitazione, scrittura, riscrittura nel Rinascimento*, Alexandria: Orso, 1990.

Forcione, Alban, *Cervantes, Aristotle, and the 'Persiles'*, Princeton: Princeton University Press, 1970.

Javitch, Daniel, 'The emergence of poetic genre theory in the sixteenth century', *Modern language quarterly* 59 (1998), 139–69.

Proclaiming a classic: the canonization of 'Orlando furioso', Princeton: Princeton University Press, 1991.

Rhu, Lawrence, *The genesis of Tasso's narrative theory: English translations of the early poetics and a comparative study of their significance*, Detroit: Wayne State University Press, 1993.

Vasoli, Cesare, 'Francesco Patrizi e il dibattito sul poema epico', in *Ritterepik der Renaissance*, ed. K. W. Hempfer, Stuttgart: Steiner, 1989.

Weinberg, Bernard, *A history of literary criticism in the Italian Renaissance*, Chicago: University of Chicago Press, 1961, 2 vols.

Literary forms: the lyric

Primary sources and texts

Boccaccio, Giovanni, *Genealogiae*, ed. S. Orgel, New York: Garland, 1976. [Translation of Preface and Books 14–15, trans. C. G. Osgood, 2nd edn, Indianapolis: Bobbs-Merrill, 1956].

Du Bellay, Joachim, *L'Olive*, in *Œuvres poétiques*, ed. D. Aris and F. Joukovsky, Paris: Classiques Garnier, 1993, 2 vols. [See especially Preface to the second edition of *L'Olive*].

Gilbert, A. H. (ed.), *Literary criticism: Plato to Dryden*, Detroit: Wayne State University Press, 1962.

March, Ausias, *Obra poetica completa*, ed. R. Ferreres, Madrid: Castalia, 1979, 2 vols.

Minturno, Antonio, *L'arte poetica*, Venice: G. Valvassori, 1564.

Puttenham, George (?), *The arte of English poesie*, ed. G. D. Willcock and A. Walker, Cambridge: Cambridge University Press, 1936.

Ronsard, Pierre de, *Abbregé de l'art poëtique françois*, in *Œuvres complètes*, ed. P. Laumonier, I. Silver, R. Lebègue, Paris: M. Didier, 1914–75, 20 vols.

Santillana, Iñigo López de Mendoza, marqués de, 'Proemio e carta', in *Obras completas*, ed. A. Gómez Moreno and M. P. A. M. Kerkhof, Barcelona: Planeta, 1988, pp. 437–54.

Scaliger, Julius Caesar, *Poetices libri septem*, ed. A. Buck, Stuttgart and Bad Cannstatt: F. Frommann-Holzboog, 1987.

Sidney, Philip Sir, *A defence of poetry*, in *Miscellaneous prose of Sir Philip Sidney*, ed. K. Duncan-Jones and J. van Dorsten, Oxford: Clarendon Press, 1973.

Trissino, Giovanni Giorgio, *La quinta e la sesta divisione della Poetica*, in *Trattati di poetica e retorica del Cinquecento*, ed. B. Weinberg, Bari: Laterza, 1970, vol. II, pp. 7–90.

Webbe, William, *Discourse of English poetrie* (1586), in *Elizabethan critical essays*, ed. G. G. Smith, Oxford: Clarendon Press, 1904, 2 vols.

Secondary sources

Castor, Grahame, *Pléiade poetics: a study in sixteenth-century thought and terminology*, Cambridge: Cambridge University Press, 1964.

Fenoaltea, Doranne and Rubin, David Lee (ed.), *The ladder of high design: structure and interpretation of the French lyric sequence*, Charlottesville: University Press of Virginia, 1991.

Ferguson, Margaret W. *Trials of desire: Renaissance defences of poetry*, New Haven: Yale University Press, 1983.

Freccero, John, 'The fig tree and the laurel: Petrarch's poetics', *Literary theory / Renaissance texts*, ed. P. Parker and D. Quint, Baltimore: The Johns Hopkins University Press, 1986, 20–32.

Greene, Roland (ed.), 'Material poetry of the Renaissance / the Renaissance of material poetry', *Harvard library bulletin new series 3*, no. 2 (1992), 66–93.

Post-Petrarchism: origins and innovations of the Western lyric sequence, Princeton: Princeton University Press, 1991.

Unrequited conquests: love and empire in the colonial Americas, Chicago: University of Chicago Press, 1999.

Jeffreys, Mark, *New definitions of lyric: theory, technology, and culture*, New York: Garland, 1998.

Javitch, Daniel, 'The emergence of poetic genre theory in the sixteenth century', *Modern language quarterly*, 59 (1998), 139–70.

Jones, Ann Rosalind, *The currency of Eros: women's love lyric in Europe, 1540–1620*, Bloomington: Indiana University Press, 1990.

Kennedy, William J. *Authorizing Petrarch*, Ithaca: Cornell University Press, 1994.

Marotti, Arthur F. *Manuscript, print, and the English Renaissance lyric*, Ithaca: Cornell University Press, 1995.

Mazzaro, Jerome, *Transformations in the Renaissance English lyric*, Ithaca: Cornell University Press, 1970.

Navarrete, Ignacio, *Orphans of Petrarch: poetry and theory in the Spanish Renaissance*, Berkeley and Los Angeles: University of California Press, 1994.

Literary forms: Renaissance theatre and the theory of tragedy

Primary sources and texts

Aubignac, François Hédelin, abbé d', *Pratique du théâtre*, ed. P. Martino, Algiers: Carbonel; Paris: Champion, 1927.

Castelvetro, Lodovico, *Castelvetro on the art of poetry: an abridged translation of 'Poetica d'Aristotele vulgarizzata e sposta'*, trans. A. Bongiorno, Binghamton: Medieval and Renaissance texts and studies, 1984.

Heinsius, Daniel, *On plot in tragedy (De tragoediae constitutione)* (1611), trans. and ed. P. R. Sellin and J. J. McManmon, Northridge, CA: San Fernando Valley State College, 1971.

Racine, Jean, *Principes de la tragédie*, ed. E. Vinaver, Manchester and Paris: Nizet, 1951.

Rapin, René, *Réflexions sur la poétique d'Aristote, et sur les ouvrages des poètes anciens et modernes*, Paris: F. Muguet, 1674.

Secondary sources

Abbé, Derek van, *Drama in Renaissance Germany and Switzerland*, Melbourne: Melbourne University Press, 1961.

Hermenegildo, Alfredo, *La tragedia en el Renacimiento español*, Barcelona: Planeta, 1973.

Herrick, Marvin T. *Italian tragedy in the Renaissance*, Urbana: University of Illinois Press, 1965.

Lebègue, Raymond, *La tragédie française de la Renaissance*; 1944; reprint Brussels: Office de Publicité, 1954.

Marker, Frederick J., and Marker, Lise-Lone, *The Scandinavian theatre: a short history*, Oxford: Blackwell, 1975.

Reiss, Timothy J. *Towards dramatic illusion: theatrical technique and meaning from Hardy to 'Horace'*, New Haven: Yale University Press, 1971.

Tragedy and truth: studies in the development of a Renaissance and neoclassical discourse, New Haven: Yale University Press, 1990.

Rennert, Hugo Albert, *The Spanish stage in the time of Lope de Vega*; 1909; reprint New York: Dover, 1963.

Stäuble, Antonio, 'L'idea della tragedia nell'umanismo', in *La rinascita della tragedia nell'Italia dell'umanismo. Atti del IV Convegno di Studio Viterbo Giugni 1979*, Viterbo: Sorbini, 1980, pp. 48–66.

Stone, Donald, *French humanist tragedy: a reassessment*, Manchester: Manchester University Press, 1974.

Literary forms: Elizabethan theatrical genres and literary theory

Primary sources and texts

Alexander, Sir William, *The monarchic tragedies* (1604), in *Poetical works*, ed. L. E. Kastner and H. B. Charlton, Manchester: University of Manchester Press, 1921, 2 vols.

Aristotle, *Aristotle, on the art of poetry*, trans. I. Bywater, Oxford: Clarendon Press, 1909.

Bentley, G. E. *The Jacobean and Caroline stage*, Oxford: Clarendon Press, 1941–68, 7 vols.

Cannon, C. D. (ed.), *A warning for fair women: a critical edition*, The Hague: Mouton, 1975.

Cary, Lady Elizabeth, *The tragedy of Mariam, the fair queen of Jewry*, ed. B. Weller and M. Ferguson, Berkeley: University of California Press, 1994.

Chambers, E. K. *The Elizabethan stage*, Oxford: Clarendon Press, 1923, 4 vols.

Cunliffe, J. W. (ed.), *Early English classical tragedies*, Oxford: Clarendon Press, 1912.

Fletcher, John, *The faithful shepherdess*, in *Elizabethan and Stuart plays*, ed. C. R. Baskervill, V. B. Heltzel, and A. H. Nethercot, New York: Henry Holt & Co., *c.* 1934.

Greene, Robert, *Pandosto*, in Alexander Grosart, *Life and complete works in prose and verse*, London and Aylesbury: privately printed, 1881–6, 15 vols.

Gurr, Andrew, *The Shakespearian playing companies*, Oxford: Clarendon Press, 1996.

Heinsius, Daniel, *On plot in tragedy*, trans. P. R. Sellin and J. J. McManmon, Northridge, CA: San Fernando State College, 1971.

Lodge, Thomas, *A defence of poetry, music, and stage-plays* (1579), London: Shakespeare Society, 1853.

Smith, G. G. (ed.), *Elizabethan critical essays*, Oxford: Clarendon Press, 1904, 2 vols.

Spingarn, J. E. (ed.), *Critical essays of the seventeenth century*, Oxford: Clarendon Press, 1908–9, 3 vols. [Reprint Bloomington: Indiana University Press, 1957].

Secondary sources

Baldwin, T. W. *William Shakspere's small Latine and lesse Greeke*, Urbana: University of Illinois Press, 1944.
  Shakespeare's five-act structure, Urbana: University of Illinois Press, 1947.

Boas, Frederick S. *University drama in the Tudor age*, Oxford: Clarendon Press, 1914.

The Cambridge companion to English Renaissance drama, ed. A. R. Braunmuller and M. Hattaway, Cambridge: Cambridge University Press, 1990.

Doran, Madeleine, *Endeavors of art*, Madison: University of Wisconsin Press, 1954.

Herrick, Marvin T. *Comic theory in the sixteenth century*, Urbana: University of Illinois Press, 1950.

The Poetics of Aristotle in England, New Haven: Yale University Press, 1930.

Hunter, G. K. *English drama 1586–1642: the age of Shakespeare*, Oxford: Clarendon Press, 1997.

Nelson, Alan, *Early Cambridge theatres: college, university and town stages, 1464–1720*, Cambridge: Cambridge University Press, 1994.

Radcliff-Umstead, D. *The birth of modern comedy in Renaissance Italy*, Chicago: University of Chicago Press, 1969.

Ribner, Irving, *The English history play in the age of Shakespeare*, New York: Barnes and Noble, 1965.

Ristine, F. H. *English tragicomedy: its origin and history*, New York: Columbia University Press, 1910.

Salingar, Leo, *Shakespeare and the traditions of comedy*, Cambridge: Cambridge University Press, 1974.

Spingarn, Joel, *A history of literary criticism in the Renaissance*, New York: Columbia University Press, 1925.

Sweeting, Elizabeth J. *Early Tudor criticism, linguistic and literary*, Oxford: Blackwell, 1940.

Thompson, E. N. S. *The controversy between the puritans and the stage*, New York: Henry Holt and Co., 1903.

Wilson, F. P. and Hunter, G. K. *English drama, 1485–1585*, Oxford: Clarendon Press, 1968.

Witherspoon, A. M. *The influence of Robert Garnier on Elizabethan drama*, New Haven: Yale University Press, 1924.

Literary forms: defining comedy in the seventeenth century

Primary sources and texts

Bossuet, Jacques Bénigne, *Maximes et réflexions sur la comédie*, Paris: Anisson, 1694.

Collier, Jeremy, *A short view of the immorality and profaneness of the English stage*, facs. reprint Menston: Scolar Press, 1971.

Corneille, Pierre, *Comédies*, ed. J. Maurens, Paris: Flammarion, 1968.

Writings on the theatre, ed. H. T. Barnwell, Oxford: Blackwell, 1965.

Dennis, John, *The critical works of John Dennis*, ed. E. N. Hooker, Baltimore: The Johns Hopkins University Press, 1939–43, 2 vols.

Dryden, John, *Of dramatic poetry and other critical essays*, ed. G. Watson, London: J. Dent, 1962, 2 vols.

Guéret, Gabriel, *La promenade de Saint-Cloud*, ed. G. Monval, Paris: Librairie des Bibliophiles, 1888.

Jonson, Ben, *Timber, or discoveries made upon men and matter*, ed. R. S. Walker, Syracuse: Syracuse University Press, 1953.

Ben Jonson [Works], ed. C. H. Herford and P. and E. Simpson, Oxford: Clarendon Press, 1925–52, 11 vols. [Edition under reissue with corrections, 1986–].

Molière (Jean-Baptiste Poquelin), *Théâtre complet*, ed. G. Couton, Paris: Gallimard, 1971, 2 vols.

Nicole, Pierre, *Traité de la comédie: et autres pièces d'un procès du théâtre*, ed. L. Thirouin, Paris: Champion, 1998.

Rymer, Thomas, *The critical works*, ed. C. A. Zimansky, New Haven: Yale University Press, 1956.

Shadwell, Thomas, *The complete works*, ed. M. Summers, London: Fortune Press, 1927, 5 vols.

Spingarn, J. E. (ed.), *Critical essays of the seventeenth century*, Oxford: Clarendon Press, 1908–9, 3 vols. [Reprint Bloomington: Indiana University Press, 1957].

Secondary sources

Atkins, J. W. H. *English literary criticism: the Renascence*; 1947; reprint London: Methuen, 1968.

Baldwin, Charles Sears, *Renaissance literary theory and practice: classicism in the rhetoric and poetic of Italy, France, and England 1400–1600*, ed. D. L. Clark, New York: Columbia University Press, 1939.

Collinet, J-P. *Lectures de Molière*, Paris: Colin, 1974.

Guichemerre, R. *La comédie avant Molière: 1640–1660*, Paris: Colin, 1972.

Hume, Robert D. *Dryden's criticism*, Ithaca: Cornell University Press, 1970.

Krutch, J. W. *Comedy and conscience after the Restoration*; 1924; reprint New York: Columbia University Press, 1961.

Lebègue, R. *Le théâtre comique en France de Pathelin à Mélite*, Paris: Hatier, 1972.

Scherer, Colette, *Comédie et société sous Louis XIII*, Paris: Nizet, 1983.

Scherer, Jacques, *La dramaturgie classique en France*, Paris: Nizet, 1950.

Voltz, P. *La comédie*, Paris: Colin, 1964.

Literary forms: dialogue, essay, epigram, emblem, satire, humour

Primary sources and texts

Alberti, Leon Battista, *I libri della famiglia*, ed. R. Romano and A. Tenenti, 2nd edn revised by F. Furlan, Turin: Einaudi, 1994.

Alciato, Andrea, *Andreas Alciatus. The Latin works. The emblems in translation*, ed. P. M. Daly, V. W. Callahan, and S. Cuttler, Toronto: University of Toronto Press, 1985, 2 vols.

Bacon, Francis, *The essays*, ed. J. Pitcher, Harmondsworth: Penguin, 1985.
  The works of Francis Bacon, ed. J. Spedding, R. L. Ellis, and D. D. Heath, London: Longmans, 1857–74, 14 vols. [Facs. reprint Stuttgart and Bad Cannstatt: Frommann-Holzboog, 1989].

Bruni, Leonardo, *Dialogi ad Petrum Paulum Histrum*, ed. S. U. Baldassari, Florence: Olschki, 1994.

Casaubon, Isaac, *De satyrica Graecorum poesi et Romanorum satira* (1605), ed. P. E. Medine, New York: Scholars' Facsimiles and Reprints, 1973.

Castiglione, Baldesar, *The book of the courtier*, trans. C. S. Singleton, New York: Doubleday, 1959.
  Il libro del cortegiano, ed. B. Maier, 2nd edn, Turin: Unione Tipografico-Editrice Torinese, 1964.

Frank, Grace and Miner, Dorothy (ed.), *Proverbes en rime*, Baltimore: The Johns Hopkins University Press, 1937.

Galilei, Galileo, *Dialogi dei massimi sistemi*, ed. F. Flora, Milan: Mondadori, 1996.

Guazzo, Stefano, *La civil conversazione*, ed. A. Quondam, Modena: Panini, 1993, 2 vols.

Guilpin, Edward, *Skialetheia*; 1598; facs. reprint London: Oxford University Press, 1931.

Hall, Joseph, *Virgidemiae*, London: T. Creede for R. Dexter, 1597-9.

Harington, John [trans.], *Orlando furioso* (1591), ed. R. McNulty, Oxford: Clarendon Press, 1972; see Harington's Preface.

Hawkins, Henry, *Partheneia sacra*, introduction by K. J. Höltgen, Aldershot: Scolar Press, 1993.

Joubert, Laurent, *Traité du ris* (1579), edited and translated as *Treatise on laughter* by Gregory de Rocher, University, AL: Alabama University Press, 1990.

La Perrière, Guillaume de, *La morosophie*, intro. by A. Saunders, Aldershot: Scolar Press, 1993.

Le Roy, Pierre, *et al.*, *La satyre Ménippée: de la vertue du catholicon d'Espagne et de la tenue des estatz de Paris* (1594), ed. C. Marcilly, Paris: Garnier, 1889.

Marston, John, *The scourge of villanie*; 1599; facs. reprint Edinburgh: Edinburgh University Press, 1966.

Manso, Giambattista, *Del dialogo*, Venice: Deuchino, 1628.

Montaigne, Michel de, *The essays of Michel de Montaigne*, trans. and ed. M. A. Screech, London and New York: Penguin, 1991.

Pallavicino, Pietro Sforza, *Trattato dello stile e del dialogo*, Rome: Eredi de Corbelletti, 1646.

Puttenham, George (?), *The arte of English poesie* (1589), ed. G. D. Willcock and A. Walker, Cambridge: Cambridge University Press, 1936.

Rollenghagen, Gabriel, *Nucleus emblematum selectissimorum*, Paris: Aux Amateurs de Livres, 1989.

Sebillet, Thomas, *Art poétique françois*, ed. F. Gaiffe, new edn by F. Goyet, Paris: Nizet, 1988.

Sidney, Philip Sir, *A defence of poetry*, in *Miscellaneous prose of Sir Philip Sidney*, ed. K. Duncan-Jones and J. van Dorsten, Oxford: Oxford University Press, 1973.

Sigonio, Carlo, *Del dialogo*, ed. F. Pignatti, Rome: Bulzoni, 1993.

Tasso, Torquato, *Il discorso dell'arte del dialogo* (1585), ed. G. Baldassari, 'Il discorso tassiano "Dell'arte del dialogo"', *Rassegna della litteratura italiana* 75 (1971), 93-119.

  Tasso's 'Dialogues': a selection, with the 'Discourse on the art of dialogue', ed. C. Lord and D. Trafton, Berkeley, Los Angeles, London: University of California Press, 1982.

Webbe, William, *A discourse of English poetrie* (1586), in G. Gregory Smith (ed.), *Elizabethan critical essays*; 1904; reprint Oxford and New York: Oxford University Press, 1971, 2 vols.

Wilson, Thomas, *The arte of rhetorique*, ed. T. Derrick, New York and London: Garland, 1982.

Wither, George, *The workes*, London: J. Beale for T. Walkley, 1620.

Secondary sources

Angress, R. K. *The early German epigram: a study in Baroque poetry*, Lexington: The University Press of Kentucky, 1971.
Baumlin, James, 'Generic contexts of Elizabethan satire', in *Renaissance genres*, ed. B. Lewalski, Cambridge, MA: Harvard University Press, 1986, pp. 444–67.
Beaujour, Michel, *Miroirs d'encre*, Paris: Seuil, 1980.
Blanchard, Scott, *Scholars' bedlam: Menippean satire in the Renaissance*, Lewisburg: Bucknell University Press, 1995.
Cave, Terence, *The cornucopian text: problems of writing in the French Renaissance*, Oxford: Clarendon Press, 1979.
Colie, Rosalie L. *Paradoxia epidemica*, Princeton: Princeton University Press, 1966.
  The resources of kind: genre-theory in the Renaissance, ed. B. K. Lewalski, Berkeley, Los Angeles, and London: University of California Press, 1973.
Cox, Virginia, *The Renaissance dialogue: literary dialogue in its social and political contexts, Castiglione to Galileo*, Cambridge: Cambridge University Press, 1992.
Daly, Peter M. *Literature in the light of the emblem*, Toronto: University of Toronto Press, 1978.
De Caprio, Vincenzo, 'I cenacoli umanistici', in *Letteratura italiana. 1. Il letterato e le istituzioni*, ed. A. Asor Rosa, Turin: Einaudi, 1982, pp. 799–822.
Elliott, Robert C. *Power of satire: magic, ritual, and art*, Princeton: Princeton University Press, 1960.
Fournel, Jean-Louis, *Les dialogues de Sperone Speroni: libertés de la parole et règles de l'écriture*, Marburg: Hitzeroth Verlag, 1990.
Fowler, Alastair, *Kinds of literature: an introduction to the theory of genres and modes*, Cambridge, MA: Harvard University Press, 1982.
Friedrich, Hugo, *Montaigne*, ed. P. Desan and trans. D. Eng, Berkeley: University of California Press, 1991.
Fubini, Riccardo, 'All'uscita dalla scolastica medievale: Salutati, Bruni, e i "Dialogi ad Petrum Histrum" ', *Archivio storico italiano* 150 (1992), 1065–103.
Gill, R. B. 'A purchase of glory: the persona of late Elizabethan satire', *Studies in philology* 72 (1975), 408–18.
Girardi, Raffaelle, *La società del dialogo: retorica e ideologia nella letteratura conviviale del Cinquecento*, Bari: Adriatica Editrice, 1989.
Glauser, Alfred, *Montaigne paradoxal*, Paris: Nizet, 1972.
Grafton, Anthony (ed.), *Rome reborn: the Vatican library and Renaissance culture*, Washington, DC: Library of Congress, 1993.
Gray, Floyd, *La balance de Montaigne: exagium/essai*, Paris: Nizet, 1982.
  Montaigne bilingue: le latin des 'Essais', Paris: Champion, 1991.
Griffin, Dustin, *Satire: a critical reintroduction*, Lexington: University Press of Kentucky, 1994.
Griffiths, Gordon, Hankins, James, and Thompson, David (ed.), *The humanism of Leonardo Bruni: selected texts*, Binghamton: State University of New York Press, 1987.

Hankins, James, 'The myth of the Platonic academy of Florence', *Renaissance quarterly* 44 (1991), 429–75.

Herrick, Marvin T. *Comic theory in the sixteenth century*, Urbana: University of Illinois Press, 1964.

Hirzel, Rudolf, *Der Dialog: Ein literar-historischer Versuch*; 1895; reprint Hildesheim: Georg Ohms, 1963, 2 vols.

Jardine, Lisa, *Francis Bacon: discovery and the art of discourse*, Cambridge: Cambridge University Press, 1974.

Jones-Davies, M. T. (ed.), *La satire au temps de la Renaissance*, Paris: Touzot, 1986.

Kidwell, Carol, *Pontano: poet and prime minister*, London: Duckworth, 1991.

Kirk, Eugene, *Menippean satire: an annotated catalogue of texts and criticism*, New York and London: Garland Press, 1980.

Kuppersmith, William, *Roman satirists in seventeenth-century England*, Lincoln, NB: University of Nebraska Press, 1985.

Laurens, Pierre, *L'abeille dans l'ambre: célébration de l'épigramme*, Paris: Les Belles Lettres, 1989.

Lauvergnat-Gagnière, Christiane, *Lucien de Samosate et le lucianisme en France au XVIe siècle: athéisme et polémique*, Geneva: Droz, 1988.

Le Guern, Michel, 'Sur le genre du dialogue', in *L'automne de la Renaissance*, ed. J. Lafond and A. Stegmann, Paris: J. Vrin, 1981, pp. 141–8.

Marsh, David, *The Quattrocento dialogue: classical tradition and humanist innovation*, Cambridge, MA: Harvard University Press, 1980.

  Lucian and the Latins: humor and humanism in the early Renaissance, Ann Arbor: University of Michigan Press, 1998.

Mattioli, Emilio, *Luciano e l'umanesimo*, Naples: Istituto per gli studi storici, 1980.

Mayer, Charles-Albert, *Lucien de Samosate et la Renaissance française*, Geneva: Slatkine, 1984.

McCuaig, William, *Carlo Sigonio: the changing world of the late Renaissance*, Princeton: Princeton University Press, 1988.

Patrizi, Giorgio (ed.), *Stefano Guazzo e la 'Civil conversazione'*, Rome: Bulzoni, 1990.

Prescott, Anne Lake, 'Humanism in the Tudor jestbook', *Moreana* 24.95–6 (1987), 5–16.

Quondam, Amedeo, 'L'Accademia', in *Letteratura italiana. I. Il letterato e le istituzioni*, ed. A. Asor Rosa, Turin: Einaudi, 1982, pp. 823–98.

Rabil, Albert, Jr. (ed. and trans.), *Knowledge, goodness, and power: the debate over nobility among Quattrocento Italian humanists*, Binghamton: State University of New York Press, 1991.

Rawson, Claude (ed.), *English satire and the satiric tradition*, Oxford: Blackwell, 1984.

Robinson, Christopher, *Lucian and his influence in Europe*, London: Duckworth, 1979.

Russell, Daniel S. *The emblem and device in France*, Lexington: French Forum, 1985.

Schenkeveld, Dirk M. 'Oi kritikoi in Philodemus', *Mnemosyne* 21 (1968), 176–214.

Selden, Raman, *English verse satire 1590–1765*, London: George Allen and Unwin, 1978.

Sidwell, Keith, 'Lucian in the Italian Quattrocento', unpublished Ph.D. thesis, University of Cambridge, 1975.

Snyder, Jon R. *Writing the scene of speaking: theories of dialogue in the late Italian Renaissance*, Stanford: Stanford University Press, 1989.

Tateo, Francesco, *Tradizione e realtà nell'umanesimo italiano*, Bari: Dedalo Libri, 1967.

Thibaudet, Albert, *Physiologie de la critique*, Paris: Nouvelle Revue Critique, 1930.

Thompson, Craig R. *The translations of Lucian by Erasmus and St. Thomas More*, Binghamton: The Vail-Ballou Press, 1940.

Tomarken, Annette H. *The smile of truth: the French satirical eulogy and its antecedents*, Princeton: Princeton University Press, 1990.

Villey, Pierre, *Les sources et l'évolution des 'Essais' de Montaigne*, Paris: Hachette, 1908, 2 vols.

Welch, Marcelle Maistre, 'Montaigne critique littéraire', unpublished Ph.D. thesis, University of Michigan, 1972.

Wheeler, Angela, *English verse satire from Donne to Dryden: imitation of classical models*, Heidelberg: C. Winter, 1992.

Zappala, Michael O. *Lucian of Samosata in the two Hesperias: an essay in literary and cultural translation*, Potomac: Scripta Humanistica, 1990.

Theories of prose fiction*: England

Primary sources and texts

Barclay, John, *Barclay his Argenis*, trans. Kingesmill Long, London: Seile, 1625.

Cavendish, Margaret, *Natures pictures drawn by fancies pencil to the life*, London: for J. Martin and J. Allestrye, 1656.

Congreve, William, *Incognita* (1692), in *An anthology of seventeenth-century fiction*, ed. P. Salzman, Oxford: World's Classics, 1991.

Elizabethan critical essays, ed. G. G. Smith, London: Oxford University Press, 1959, 2 vols.

Hoskins, John, *Directions for speech and style*, ed. H. H. Hudson, Princeton: Princeton University Press, 1935.

Huet, Pierre-Daniel, *A treatise of romances and their originals*, London: R. Battersby, for S. Heyrick, 1672.

Osborne, Dorothy, *Letters to Sir William Temple*, ed. K. Parker, London: Penguin, 1987.

Sidney, Philip Sir, *A defence of poetry*, in *Miscellaneous prose of Sir Philip Sidney*, ed. K. Duncan-Jones and J. van Dorsten, Oxford: Clarendon Press, 1973.

Spingarn, J. E. (ed.), *Critical essays of the seventeenth century*, Oxford: Clarendon Press, 1908–9, 3 vols. [Reprint Bloomington: Indiana University Press, 1957].

Secondary sources

Davis, Lennard J. *Factual fictions*, New York: Columbia University Press, 1983.

Hunter, J. Paul, *Before novels*, New York: Norton, 1990.

Hutson, Lorna, *The usurer's daughter: male friendship and fictions of women in sixteenth-century England*, London: Routledge, 1994.

Lucas, Caroline, *Writing for women: the example of woman as reader in Elizabethan romance*, Milton Keynes: Open University Press, 1989.

Margolies, David, *Novel and society in Elizabethan England*, London: Croom, 1985.

Mayer, Robert, *History and the early English novel*, Cambridge: Cambridge University Press, 1997.

M'Keon, Michael, *The origins of the English novel 1600–1740*, Baltimore: The Johns Hopkins University Press, 1987.

Salzman, Paul, *English prose fiction, 1558–1700: a critical history*, Oxford: Clarendon Press, 1985.

Smith, Nigel, *Literature and revolution in England 1640–1660*, New Haven and London: Yale University Press, 1994.

Tieje, A. J. 'The expressed aim of the long prose fiction from 1579 to 1640', *Journal of English and Germanic philology* 11 (1912), 402–32.

Theories of prose fiction: France

Primary sources and texts

Amadis of Gaul [Books 1–4], trans. and ed. E. B. Place and H. C. Behm, Lexington: University Press of Kentucky, 1974–5.

Boileau-Despréaux, Nicolas, *Dialogue des héros de roman*, in *Œuvres complètes*, ed. F. Escal, Paris: Gallimard, 1966.

Charnes, abbé de, *Conversations sur la critique de 'La Princesse de Clèves'*; 1679; facs. reprint Tours: Université de Tours, 1973, ed. F. Weil.

Cholakian, Patricia F. and Rouben C. (ed.), *The early French novella: an anthology of fifteenth- and sixteenth-century tales*, Albany: State University of New York Press, 1972.

Des Périers, Bonaventure, *Novel pastimes and merry tales*, trans. and ed. R. and V. La Charité, Lexington: University Press of Kentucky, 1972.

Du Plaisir, *Sentiments sur les lettres et sur l'histoire avec des scrupules sur le style*, ed. P. Hourcade, Geneva: Droz, 1975.

Estienne, Henri, *L'Apologie pour Hérodote*, ed. P. Ristelhuber, Paris: Liseux, 1879, 2 vols.

Guéret, Gabriel, *La promenade de Saint-Cloud*, ed. G. Monval, Paris: Librairie des Bibliophiles, 1888.

Huet, Pierre-Daniel, *Traité de l'origine des romans*, Geneva: Slatkine, 1970.

Jourda, Pierre (ed.), *Conteurs français du XVIe siècle*, Paris: Gallimard, 1965.

Krailsheimer, A. J. (ed.), *Three sixteenth-century conteurs*, Oxford: Oxford University Press, 1966.

Langlois, F. *Le tombeau des romans, où il est discouru i) contre les romans ii) pour les romans*, Paris: C. Morlot, 1626.

Mareschal, André, *La Chrysolite, ou le secret des romans*, Paris: T. de Bray, 1627.

Marguerite de Navarre, *The Heptaméron*, trans. and ed. P. A. Chilton, Harmondsworth: Penguin, 1984.

Scudéry, Madeleine de, *Clélie*, Geneva: Slatkine, 1973.

Segrais, Jean-Regnault de, *Nouvelles françoises*, ed. R. Guichemerre, Geneva: Droz, 1990–2, 2 vols.

Sorel, Charles, *Le berger extravagant*, Geneva: Slatkine, 1972.

De la connoissance des bons livres ou examen de plusieurs auteurs, ed. L. Moretti Cenerini, Rome: Bulzoni, 1974.

Spingarn, J. E. (ed.), *Critical essays of the seventeenth century*, Oxford: Clarendon Press, 1908–9, 3 vols. [Reprint Bloomington: Indiana University Press, 1957].

Valincour, Jean-Baptiste-Henri du Trousset de, *Lettres à Madame la Marquise *** sur le sujet de 'La Princesse de Clèves'*, ed. A. Cazes, Paris: Bossard, 1925.

Vigneulles, Philippe de, *Les cent nouvelles de Philippe de Vigneulles (1471– 1523?)*, ed. C. H. and R. Livingston, and R. H. Ivy, Jr., Geneva: Droz, 1972.

Villiers, Pierre de, *Entretiens sur les contes de fées*, Paris: J. Collombat, 1699.

Secondary sources

Baker, M. J. 'France's first sentimental novel and novels of chivalry', *Bibliothèque d'humanisme et Renaissance* 36 (1974), 33–45.

Bessière, Jean, Daros, Philippe, Cazauran, Nicole (ed.), *La nouvelle: Boccace, Marguerite de Navarre, Cervantes*, Paris: Champion, 1996.

Clements, Robert J., and Gibaldi, Joseph, *Anatomy of the 'novella': the European tale collection from Boccaccio and Chaucer to Cervantes*, New York: New York University Press, 1977.

Coulet, H. *Le roman jusqu'à la révolution*, Paris. A. Colin, 1967, 2 vols.

Dallas, D. *Le roman français de 1660 à 1680*, Paris: J. Gamber, 1932.

Dauphine, James, and Périgot, Béatrice (ed.) *Conteurs et romanciers de la Renaissance: mélanges offerts à Gabriel-André Pérouse*, Paris: Champion, 1997.

Deloffre, F. *La nouvelle en France à l'âge classique*, Paris: Didier, 1968.

Engel, Vincent, and Guissard, Michel (ed.), *La nouvelle de langue française aux frontières des autres genres, du Moyen Age à nos jours*, Actes du colloque de Metz, June 1996, Ottignies [Belgium]: Quorum, 1997.

Fabre, J. *Idées sur le roman de Madame de La Fayette au marquis de Sade*, Paris: Klincksieck, 1979.

Ferrier, Janet M. *Forerunners of the French novel: an essay on the development of the 'nouvelle' in the later Middle Ages*, Manchester: Manchester University Press, 1954.

Frappier, Jean, 'Les romans de la table ronde et les lettres en France au XVIᵉ siècle', *Romance philology* 19 (1965–6), 178–93.

Gibaldi, Joseph. 'Towards a definition of the novella', *Studies in short fiction* 12 (1975), 91–7.

Godenne, R. *Histoire de la nouvelle française aux XVIIᵉ et XVIIIᵉ siècles*, Geneva: Droz, 1970.

La nouvelle, Paris: Champion, 1995.

Hardee, A. Maynor, 'Towards a definition of the French Renaissance novel', *Studies in the Renaissance* 15 (1968), 25–38.

Hipp, M.-T. *Mythes et réalités: enquête sur le roman et les mémoires (1660–1700)*, Paris: Klincksieck, 1976.

Jefferls, R. R. 'The "conte" as a genre in the French Renaissance', *Revue de l'Université d'Ottawa* 26 (1956), 435–50.

Kasprzyk, Krystina, *Nicolas de Troyes et le genre narratif en France au XVIe siècle*, Paris: Klincksieck, 1963.

Lever, M. *Le roman français au XVIIe siècle*, Paris: Presses Universitaires de France, 1981.

Romanciers du grand siècle, Paris: Fayard, 1996.

Mallinson, G. J. 'Fiction, morality, and the reader: reflections on the classical formula "plaire et instruire"', *Continuum* 1 (1989), 203–28.

McFarlane, I. D. *A literary history of France: Renaissance France (1470–1589)*, London and New York: E. Benn and Barnes and Noble, 1974; see esp. pp. 167–92, 234–59.

Molinié, G. *Du roman grec au roman baroque*, Toulouse: Le Mirail, 1982.

Norton, Glyn P. 'The Emilio Ferretti letter: a critical preface for Marguerite de Navarre', *Journal of medieval and Renaissance studies* 4 (1974), 287–300.

'Laurent de Premierfait and the fifteenth-century French assimilation of the *Decameron*: a study in tonal transformation', *Comparative literature studies* 9 (1972), 376–91.

'Narrative function in the *Heptaméron* frame-story', *La nouvelle française à la Renaissance*, ed. L. Sozzi and V.-L. Saulnier, Geneva and Paris: Slatkine, 1981, pp. 435–47.

Pellegrini, Carlo (ed.), *Il Boccaccio nella cultura francese*, Florence: Olschki, 1971.

Pérouse, Gabriel-A. *Nouvelles françaises du XVIe siècle: images de la vie et du temps*, Geneva: Droz, 1977.

Pizzorusso, A. *La poetica del romanzo in Francia (1660–1685)*, Rome: Sciascia, 1962.

Ratner, M. *Theory and criticism of the novel in France from L'Astrée to 1750*; 1938; reprint New York: Russell and Russell, 1971.

Serroy, J. *Roman et réalité: les histoires comiques au XVIIe siècle*, Paris: Minard, 1980.

Showalter, Jr., E. *The evolution of the French novel (1641–1782)*, Princeton: Princeton University Press, 1972.

Vaganay, Hugues, *Amadis en français: essai de bibliographie*; 1906; reprint Geneva: Slatkine, 1970.

Weddige, Hilkert, *Die Historien vom Amadis aus Frankreich: dokumentarische Grundlegung zur Entstehung und Rezeption*, Wiesbaden: F. Steiner, 1975.

Theories of prose fiction: Italy

Primary sources and texts

Alunno, Francesco, *Le ricchezze della lingua volgare . . . sopra il Boccaccio*, Venice: Aldus, 1551.

Bembo, Pietro, *Prose della volgar lingua*, ed. C. Dionisotti, Turin: Unione Tipografico-Editrice Torinese, 1966.

Bonciani, Francesco, *Lezione sopra il comporre delle novelle*, in B. Weinberg, *Trattati di poetica e retorica del Cinquecento*, 4 vols., Bari: Laterza, 1972, vol. III, pp. 135–73.

Castelvetro, Lodovico, *Alcuni difetti commessi da Giovanni Boccaccio nel Decamerone*, in *Opere varie critiche*; 1727; reprint Munich: W. Fink, 1969.
Quale sia la correzione di Girolamo Ruscello [sic] delle Novelle del Boccaccio, in *Opere varie critiche*; 1727; reprint Munich: W. Fink, 1969.
Ferretti, Emilio, Prefatory letter to Marguerite de Navarre, in *Le Décaméron de Messire Iehan Bocace Florentin*, trans. A. Le Maçon, Paris: E. Roffet, 1545.
Giraldi Cintio, Giovambattista, *Discorso intorno al comporre dei romanzi*, in *Discorsi . . . intorno al comporre dei romanzi, delle comedie, e delle tragedie, e di altre maniere di Poesie*, Venice: G. Giolito, 1554.
Giraldi Cinthio on romances, trans. and ed. H. L. Snuggs, Lexington: University Press of Kentucky, 1968.
Malatesta, Gioseppe, *Della poesia romanzesca, overo delle difese del Furioso, ragionamento secondo . . . delle difese del Furioso ragionamento terzo*, Rome: G. Faciotto, 1596.
Della nuova poesia overo delle difese del Furioso, Dialogo, Verona: Sebastiano dalle Donne, 1589.
Pigna, Giovanni Battista, *I romanzi*, Venice: V. Valgrisio, 1554.
Ridolfi, Luca Antonio, *Ragionamento sopra alcuni luoghi del Cento novelle del Decameron*, Lyons: Roville, 1557.
Ruscelli, Girolamo, *Vocabolario generale di tutte le voci usate dal Boccaccio*, Venice: G. Griffio, 1552.
Sperone Speroni, *De' romanzi*, first published in Speroni's *Opere*, Venice: D. Occhi, 1740, vol. v, pp. 521–8.

Secondary sources

Asor Rosa, Alberto, 'La narrativa italiana del Seicento', in *Letteratura italiana III, Le forme del testo. La prosa*, Turin: Einaudi, 1984, pp. 715–57.
Beer, Marina, *Romanzi di cavalleria: il 'Furioso' e il romanzo italiano del primo Cinquecento*, Rome: Bulzoni, 1987.
Bragantini, Renzo, *Il riso sotto il velame: la novella cinquecentesca tra l'avventura e la norma*, Florence: Olschki, 1987.
Cottino-Jones, Marga, *Il dir novellando: modello e deviazioni nella novella del '500*, Rome: Salerno, 1994.
Crocetti, Camillo Guerrieri, *G. B. Giraldi ed il pensiero critico del sec. XVI*, Milan, etc.: Albrighi, Segati & Co., 1832.
Eigen, Hella, *Die Überlieferung der 'Letteratura cavalleresca': ihre Stellung auf dem italienischen Buchmarkt des 15. Jahrhunderts*, Wiesbaden: O. Harrassowitz, 1987.
Ferrario, Giulio, *Storia ed analisi degli antichi romanzi di cavalleria e dei poemi romanzeschi d'Italia*, Milan: author's printing, 1828–9, 4 vols.
Guglielminetti, Marziano, *La cornice e il furto: studi sulla novella del '500*, Bologna: Zanichelli, 1984.
Hempfer, Klaus W. *Ritterepik der Renaissance: Akten des deutsch-italienischen Kolloquium, Berlin, 1987*, Stuttgart: F. Steiner, 1989.
Javitch, Daniel, *Proclaiming a classic: the canonization of 'Orlando furioso'*, Princeton: Princeton University Press, 1991.

Looney, Dennis, *Compromising the classics: romance epic narrative in the Italian Renaissance*, Detroit: Wayne State University Press, 1996.

Malato, E. (ed.), *La novella italiana: atti del convegno di Caprarola (1988)*, Rome: Salerno, 1989, 2 vols.

Picone, M., and Bendinelli Predelli, M. (ed.), *I cantari, struttura e tradizione: atti del convegno internazionale di Montréal (1981)*, Florence: Olschki, 1984.

Porcelli, Bruno, *La novella del Cinquecento*, Bari: Laterza, 1979.

Rodax, Yvonne, *The real and the ideal in the novella of Italy, France, and England: four centuries of change in the Boccaccian tale*, Chapel Hill: University of North Carolina Press, 1968.

* *Relevant critical material on theories of prose fiction in Spain is found below in the bibliographical section on National Developments.*

Contexts of criticism: metropolitan culture and socio-literary environments

Primary sources and texts

Ascham, Roger, *English works*, ed. W. A. Wright, Cambridge: Cambridge University Press, 1904.

Barbaro, Francesco, 'On wifely duties', in *The earthly republic: Italian humanists on government and society*, trans. and ed. B. G. Kohl and R. G. Witt, Philadelphia: University of Pennsylvania Press, 1978, pp. 179–228.

Birken, Sigmund von, *Teutsche Rede-bind- und Dicht-Kunst*; 1679; reprint Hildesheim and New York: Olms, 1973.

Bruni, Leonardo, 'Panegyric to the city of Florence', in *The earthly republic: Italian humanists on government and society*, trans. and ed. B. G. Kohl and R. G. Witt, Philadelphia: University of Pennsylvania Press, 1978, pp. 121–75.

Buchner, Augustus, *Anleitung zur deutschen Poeterey*, ed. M. Szyrocki, Tübingen: Niemeyer, 1966.

Buffet, Marguerite, *Nouvelles observations sur la langue française, avec l'éloge des illustres savantes tant anciennes que modernes*, Paris: J. Cusson, 1668.

Castiglione, Baldesar, *The book of the courtier*, trans. C. S. Singleton, Garden City: Anchor Books, 1959.

Celtes, Conrad, *Der Briefwechsel des Conrad Celtes*, ed. H. Rupprich, Munich: Beck, 1934.

Champier, Symphorien, *De la noblesse et ancieneté de la ville de Lyon*, Paris: A l'enseigne Saint Nicolas, 1529.

Dryden, John, *Essay of dramatick poesy*, in *The essays of John Dryden*, ed. W. P. Ker, Oxford: Oxford University Press, 1926, 2 vols.

Elyot, Sir Thomas, *The book named the governor*, ed. S. E. Lehmberg, London: Dent; New York: Dutton, 1962.

Fabricius, Georg [Goldschmied], *De re poetica libri IIII*, Antwerp: Plantin, 1565 [Expanded edition: *De re poetica libri VII*, Leipzig(?): Johann Steinman(?), 157?].

Filelfo, Francesco, *Epistolarum familiarium libri XXXVII*, Venice: Ioannes et Gregorius de Gregoriis, 1502.

[Fruchtbringende Gesellschaft], *Die Briefe der Fruchtbringenden Gesellschaft und Beilagen: Die Zeit Fürst Ludwigs von Anhalt-Köthen, 1617–1650*, ed. K. Conermann and D. Merzbacher, Die deutsche Akademie des 17. Jahrhunderts, Reihe I, Abt. A: Kritische Ausgabe der Briefe, Beilagen und Akademiearbeiten, Köthen, vol. I, Tübingen: Niemeyer, 1992.

[Fruchtbringende Gesellschaft], *Die ersten Gesellschaftsbücher der Fruchtbringen Gesellschaft (1622, 1624 und 1628)*, ed. K. Conermann, Die deutsche Akademie des 17. Jahrhunderts, Reihe II, Abt. A: Dokumente und Darstellungen, Köthen, vol. I, Tübingen: Niemeyer, 1992.

[Fruchtbringende Gesellschaft], *Der Fruchtbringenden Gesellschaft geöffneter Erzschrein: Das Köthener Gesellschaftsbuch Fürst Ludwig I. von Anhalt-Köthen 1617–1650*, ed. K. Conermann, Weinheim: VCH/Acta humaniora, 1985, 3 vols.

Gosson, Stephen, *Markets of bawdrie: the dramatic criticism of Stephen Gosson*, ed. A. Kinney, *Salzburg studies in English literature*, 4 (1972).

Gottsched, Johann Christoph, *Versuch einer critischen Dichtkunst*; 4th edn, 1751; reprint Darmstadt: Wissenschaftliche Buchgesellschaft, 1962.

Hardison, O. B., Jr. (ed.), *English literary criticism: the Renascence*, Englewood Cliffs: Prentice-Hall, 1963.

Harsdörffer, Georg Philipp, *Frauenzimmer Gesprächspiele*, ed. I. Böttcher, Deutsche Neudrucke: Reihe Barock 13, Tübingen: Niemeyer, 1968–9, 8 vols.

Harsdörffer, Georg Philipp, and Klaj, Johann, *Pegnesisches Schäfergedicht*, in *Die Pegnitz-Schäfer: Nürnberger Barockdichtung*, ed. E. Mannack, Stuttgart: Reclam, 1968.

L'Héritier, Marie-Jeanne, *L'apothéose de Mademoiselle de Scudéry*, Paris: J. Moreau, 1702.

Hoskins, John, *Directions for speech and style*, ed. H. H. Hudson, Princeton: Princeton University Press, 1935.

King, Margaret L. and Rabil, Jr., Albert (ed.), *Her immaculate hand: selected works by and about the women humanists of Quattrocento Italy*, Binghamton: State University of New York Press, 1983.

Klaj, Johann, *Redeoratorien und 'Lobrede der Teutschen Poeterey'*, ed. C. Wiedemann, Tübingen: Niemeyer, 1965.

La Force, Charlotte Rose Caumont de, *Les jeux d'esprit: promenade de la princesse de Conti à Eu* (1701), ed. M. de La Grange, Paris: Aubry, 1862.

Melanchthon, Philipp, *Opera quae supersunt omnia*, ed. C. G. Bretschneider, Brunswick and Halle (Saale): C. A. Schwetschke, 1834–60, 28 vols.

Micyllus, Jacob [Moltzer], *De re metrica libri tres*, Frankfurt: C. Egen, 1539.

Morhof, Daniel Georg, *Unterricht von der Teutschen Sprache und Poesie*; 1682; reprint Bad Homburg: Gehlen, 1969, ed. H. Boetius.

Opitz, Martin, *Buch von der deutschen Poeterey*, ed. C. Sommer, Stuttgart: Reclam, 1970.

Pasquier, Etienne, *Lettres historiques pour les années 1556–1594*, ed. D. Thickett, Geneva: Droz, 1966.

Petrarch, *Rerum familiarium libri I–VIII*, trans. A. S. Bernardo, Albany: State University of New York Press, 1975.

Poliziano, Angelo, *Angeli Politiani opera*; 1553; facs. reprint Turin: Bottega d'Erasmo, 1971, ed. I. Maïer, 3 vols.

Puttenham, George (?), *The arte of English poesie* (1589), ed. G. D. Willcock and A. Walker, Cambridge: Cambridge University Press, 1936.

Sévigné, Marie de Rabutin-Chantal, Marquise de, *Correspondance*, ed. R. Duchêne, Paris: Gallimard, 1972, 3 vols.

Sidney, Philip Sir, *An apology for poetry*, ed. F. G. Robinson, Indianapolis: Bobbs-Merrill, 1970.

Smith, G. Gregory (ed.), *Elizabethan critical essays*, Oxford: Clarendon Press, 1904, 2 vols.

Spanmüller, Jakob [Iacobus Pontanus], *Poeticarum institutionum libri III*, Ingolstadt: A. Sartorius, 1594.

Spingarn, J. E. (ed.), *Critical essays of the seventeenth century*, Oxford: Clarendon Press, 1908–9, 3 vols. [Reprint Bloomington: Indiana University Press, 1957].

Stow, John, *A survey of London*, ed. C. L. Kingsford; 1908; reprint Oxford: Clarendon Press, 1971, 2 vols.

Thomasius, Christian, *Der Studirenden Jugend Discours welcher Gestalt man denen Frantzosen in gemeinem Leben und Wandel nachahmen solle?*, in *Deutsche Schriften*, ed. P. von Düffel, Stuttgart: Reclam, 1970, pp. 7–49.

Thou, Jacques-Auguste de, *Historiarum sui temporis*, Frankfurt: N. Hoffmann, 1614–21.

Vadianus, Joachim, *De poetica et carminis ratione liber*, trans. and ed. P. Schäffer, Munich: W. Fink, 1973, 3 vols.

Zesen, Philipp, *Deutscher Helicon*, in *Sämtliche Werke*, ed. U. Maché, vol. IX, Berlin and New York: Walter de Gruyter, 1971.

Secondary sources

Asch, Ronald G., and Birke, Adolf (ed.), *Princes, patronage, and the nobility: the court at the beginning of the modern age c. 1450–1650*, London: German Historical Institute; Oxford and London: Oxford University Press, 1991.

Auberlen, Eckhard, *The commonwealth of wit: the writer's image and his strategies of self-representation in Elizabethan literature*, Tübingen: G. Narr, 1984.

Babelon, Jean-Pierre, *Paris au XVIᵉ siècle*, Paris: Hachette, 1986.

Backer, Dorothy, *Precious women*, New York: Basic Books, 1974.

Barish, Jonas, *The antitheatrical prejudice*, Berkeley: University of California Press, 1981.

Baron, Hans, *From Petrarch to Leonardo Bruni*, Chicago: University of Chicago Press, 1968.

Bates, Catherine, *The rhetoric of courtship in Elizabethan language and literature*, Cambridge: Cambridge University Press, 1992.

Bauer, Werner M. 'Humanistische Bildungszentren', in *Deutsche Literatur, eine Sozialgeschichte*, ed. I. Bennewitz and U. Müller, vol. II, *Von der Handschrift zum Buchdruck: Spätmittelalter, Reformation, Humanismus*, Reinbek: Rowohlt, 1991, pp. 262–73.

Bentley, Jerry, *Politics and culture in Renaissance Naples*, Princeton: Princeton University Press, 1987.

Bernstein, Eckhard, *Die Literatur des deutschen Frühhumanismus*, Stuttgart: Metzler, 1978.

Bircher, Martin, and van Ingen, Ferdinand, *Sprachgesellschaften, Sozietäten, Dichtergruppen*, Hamburg: E. Hauswedell, 1978.

Brennan, Michael, *Literary patronage in the English Renaissance: the Pembroke family*, London and New York: Routledge, 1988.

Butler, Martin, *Theatre and crisis, 1632–1642*, Cambridge: Cambridge University Press, 1984.

Cognasso, Francesco, 'Il ducato visconteo e la repubblica ambrosiana', in *Storia di Milano*, ed. G. Martini, 16 vols., Milan: Fondazione Treccani degli Alfieri, 1953–66, vol. VI, pp. 387–448.

Davis, Natalie Zemon, *Society and culture in early modern France*, Stanford: Stanford University Press, 1975.

DeJean, Joan, *Tender geographies: women and the origins of the novel in France*, New York: Columbia University Press, 1991.

Dickens, A. G. (ed.), *The courts of Europe: politics, patronage and royalty 1400–1800*, New York: McGraw-Hill, 1977.

Evans, Robert O. *Ben Jonson and the poetics of patronage*, Lewisburg: Bucknell University Press, 1989.

Fayolle, Roger, *La critique littéraire en France*, Paris: Colin, 1971.

Febvre, Lucien, and Martin, Henri-Jean, *L'apparition du livre*, Paris: Michel, 1971. *The coming of the book*, trans. D. Gerard, London: New Left Books, 1976.

Fraser, Russell, *The war against poetry*, Princeton: Princeton University Press, 1970.

Garin, Eugenio, 'La cultura milanese nella metà del xv secolo', in *Storia di Milano*, ed. G. Martini, 16 vols., Milan: Fondazione Treccani degli Alfieri, 1953–66, vol. VI, pp. 545–608.

Gascon, Richard, *Grand commerce et vie urbaine au XVIe siècle*, Paris: Presses Universitaires de France, 1971.

Grafton, Anthony, *Joseph Scaliger: a study in the history of classical scholarship*, Oxford: Clarendon Press; New York: Oxford University Press, 1983.

Hall, Vernon, *Renaissance literary criticism: a study of its social content*, New York: Columbia University Press, 1945.

Harth, Erica, *Cartesian women: versions and subversions of rational discourse in the old regime*, Ithaca and London: Cornell University Press, 1992.

Helgerson, Richard, *Self-crowned laureates: Spenser, Jonson, and the literary system*, Berkeley: University of California Press, 1983.

Hunter, G. K. *John Lyly, the humanist as courtier*, Cambridge, MA: Harvard University Press, 1962.

Javitch, Daniel, *Poetry and courtliness in Renaissance England*, Princeton: Princeton University Press, 1978.

Kent, F. W., Simons, Patricia, and Eade, J. C. (ed.), *Patronage, art and society in Renaissance Italy*, Oxford: Clarendon Press, 1987.

Ketelsen, Uwe-K. 'Literarische Zentren – Sprachgesellschaften', in *Deutsche Literatur, eine Sozialgeschichte*, ed. H. Steinhagen, vol. III, *Zwischen Gegenreformation und Frühaufklärung: Späthumanismus, Barock 1572–1740*, Reinbek: Rowohlt, 1985, pp. 117–37.

King, Margaret L. *Venetian humanism in an age of patrician dominance*, Princeton: Princeton University Press, 1985, pp. 98–157. *Women of the Renaissance*, Chicago: University of Chicago Press, 1991.

Klaniczay, Tibor, 'Celtis und die Sodalitas litteraria per Germaniam', in *Respublica Guelpherbytana*, Wolfenbütteler Beiträge zur Renaissance- und Barockforschung, ed. A. Buck and M. Bircher, Amsterdam: Rodopi, 1987, pp. 79–105.

Kleinschmidt, Erich, *Stadt und Literatur in der Frühen Neuzeit*, Cologne and Vienna: Böhlau, 1982.

Kristeller, Paul Oskar, *Renaissance thought: the classic, scholastic, and humanist strains*; 1955; reprint New York: Harper & Row, 1961.

Lefranc, Abel, *Histoire du Collège de France*, Paris: Hachette, 1898.

Lougee, Carolyn, *Le paradis des femmes: women, salons, and social stratification in seventeenth-century France*, Princeton: Princeton University Press, 1976.

Lytle, Guy Fitch, and Orgel, Stephen (ed.), *Patronage in the Renaissance*, Princeton: Princeton University Press, 1981.

Maclean, Ian, *Woman triumphant: feminism in French literature, 1610–52*, Oxford: Clarendon Press, 1977.

Manley, Lawrence, *Literature and culture in early modern London*, Cambridge: Cambridge University Press, 1995.

Martines, Lauro, *Power and imagination: city-states in Renaissance Italy*, New York: Vintage Books, 1979.

Society and history in English Renaissance verse, Oxford: Blackwell, 1985.

May, Steven, *Elizabethan courtier poets: the poems and their contexts*, Columbia: University of Missouri Press, 1991.

Monfasani, John, *George of Trebizond: a biography and a study of his rhetoric and logic*, Leiden: Brill, 1976.

Montgomery, Robert L. *The reader's eye: studies in didactic literary theory from Dante to Tasso*, Berkeley: University of California Press, 1979.

Ong, Walter J. *Ramus, method, and the decay of dialogue: from the art of discourse to the art of reason*; 1958; reprint New York: Octagon, 1974.

Patterson, Annabel, *Censorship and interpretation: the conditions of reading and writing in early modern England*, Madison: University of Wisconsin Press, 1984.

Peck, Linda Levy, *Court patronage and corruption in early Stuart England*, Boston: Unwin Hyman, 1990.

Picard, Roger, *Les salons littéraires et la société française, 1610–1789*, New York: Brentano's, 1943.

Rabil, Albert, Jr. *Laura Cereta: Quattrocento humanist*, Binghamton: State University of New York Press, 1981.

Rabil, Albert, Jr. (ed.) *Renaissance humanism: foundations, forms, and legacy*, Philadelphia: University of Pennsylvania Press, 1988, 3 vols.

Richter, Mario, 'La poetica di Bèze e le *Chrestiennes méditations*', *Aevum* (1964), 225–40.

Robin, Diana, *Filelfo in Milan: writings, 1451–1477*, Princeton: Princeton University Press, 1991.

Romier, Lucien, 'Lyons and cosmopolitanism at the beginning of the French Renaissance', in *French humanism, 1470–1600*, ed. W. L. Gundersheimer, London: Macmillan, 1969, pp. 90–109.

Salmon, J. H. M. *Society in crisis: France in the sixteenth century*, London: Benn, 1975.

Saunders, J. W. 'The social situation of seventeenth-century poetry', in *Metaphysical poetry*, ed. M. Bradbury, Bloomington: Indiana University Press, 1970. 'The stigma of print: a note on the social bases of Tudor poetry', *Essays in criticism* 1 (1951), 139–64.

Schöne, Albrecht (ed.), *Kürbishütte und Königsberg: Modellversuch einer sozialgeschichtlichen Entzifferung poetischer Texte*, Munich: Beck, 1975. *Stadt – Schule – Universität – Buchwesen und die deutsche Literatur im 17. Jahrhundert*, Munich: Beck, 1976.

Smuts, Malcolm, *Court culture and the origins of a royalist tradition in early Stuart England*, Philadelphia: University of Pennsylvania Press, 1987.

Stinger, Charles, *The Renaissance in Rome*, Bloomington: Indiana University Press, 1985.

Sweeting, Elizabeth J. *Early Tudor criticism, linguistic and literary*, Oxford: Blackwell, 1940.

Thomson, Patricia, 'The literature of patronage, 1580–1630', *Essays in criticism* 2 (1952), 267–84.

Wadsworth, James B. *Lyons 1473–1503: the beginnings of cosmopolitanism*, Cambridge, MA: Mediaeval Academy of America, 1962.

Whigham, Frank, *Ambition and privilege: the social tropes of Elizabethan courtesy theory*, Berkeley: University of California Press, 1984.

Wilson, N. G. *From Byzantium to Italy: Greek studies in the Italian Renaissance*, Baltimore: The Johns Hopkins University Press, 1992.

Witt, Ronald G. *Hercules at the crossroads: the life, works, and thought of Coluccio Salutati*, Durham, NC: Duke University Press, 1983.

Yates, Francis A. *The art of memory*, Chicago: University of Chicago Press, 1966.

Voices of dissent: the Ciceronian controversy

Primary sources and texts

Bembo, Pietro, *Le epistole 'De imitatione' di Giovanfrancesco Pico della Mirandola e di Pietro Bembo*, ed. G. Santangelo, Florence: Olschki, 1954. *Prose . . . nella quale si ragiona della volgar lingua*, Venice: G. Tacuino, 1525.

Castellesi, A. *De sermone Latino et modis Latine loquendi*, Rome: Mascohius, 1514.

Delminio, Giulio Camillo, *Della imitazione*, in *Trattati di poetica e retorica del Cinquecento*, ed. B. Weinberg, Bari: Laterza, 1970, vol. 1, pp. 161–85.

Dolet, Etienne, *L'Erasmianus sive Ciceronianus d'Etienne Dolet (1535)*, ed. E. V. Telle, Geneva: Droz, 1974.

Erasmus, Desiderius, *Dialogus cui titulus, Ciceronianus, sive, de optimo genere dicendi*, ed. A. H. T. Levi and trans. B. I. Knott, in *The collected works of Erasmus*, vol. XXVIII, Toronto: University of Toronto Press, 1986.

Poliziano, A. Letter to Paolo Cortesi, in *Prosatori latini del Quattrocento*, ed. E. Garin, Milan and Naples: Ricciardi, 1952, pp. 902–4.

Oratio super Flavio Quintiliano et Stati Sylvis, in *Prosatori latini del Quattrocento*, ed. E. Garin, Milan and Naples: Ricciardi, 1952, pp. 869–85.

Ramus, Petrus, *Peter Ramus's attack on Cicero: text and translation of Ramus's 'Brutinae quaestiones'*, trans. C. E. Newlands; intro. J. J. Murphy, Davis: Hermagoras, 1992.

Weinberg, Bernard (ed.), *Trattati di poetica e retorica del Cinquecento*, ed. B. Weinberg, Bari: Laterza, 1970–4, 4 vols.

Secondary sources

Chomarat, Jacques, *Grammaire et rhétorique chez Erasme*, Paris: Les Belles Lettres, 1981, 2 vols.

D'Amico, J. 'The progress of Renaissance Latin prose: the case of Apuleianism', *Renaissance quarterly* 37 (1984), 351–92.

D'Ascia, L. *Erasmo e l'umanesimo romano*, Florence: Olschki, 1991.

Fumaroli, Marc, *L'âge de l'éloquence: rhétorique et 'res literaria' de la Renaissance au seuil de l'époque classique*, Geneva: Droz, 1980.

Gmelin, H. 'Das Prinzip der Imitatio in den romanischen Literaturen der Renaissance', *Romanische Forschungen* 46 (1932), 98–173.

Grayson, C. *A Renaissance controversy: Latin or Italian?* Oxford: Clarendon Press, 1960.

Mouchel, C. *Cicéron et Sénèque dans la rhétorique de la Renaissance*, Marburg: Hitzeroth, 1990.

Pigman, G. W., III, 'Versions of imitation in the Renaissance', *Renaissance quarterly* 33 (1980), 1–32.

'Imitation and the Renaissance sense of the past: the reception of Erasmus' *Ciceronianus*', *Journal of Medieval and Renaissance studies* 9 (1979), 155–77.

Sabbadini, R. *Storia del Ciceronianismo e di altre questioni letterarie nell'età della Rinascenza*, Turin: Loescher, 1886.

Scott, I. *The imitation of Cicero as a model for style*, New York: Teachers College, Columbia University, 1910.

Voices of dissent: reorganizing the encyclopaedia, Vives and Ramus on Aristotle and the scholastics

Primary sources and texts

Ong, Walter J. *A Ramus and Talon inventory*, Cambridge, MA: Harvard University Press, 1958.

Ramus, Petrus, *Arguments in rhetoric against Quintilian: translation and text of Peter Ramus's Rhetoricae distinctiones in Quintilianum (1549)*, ed. J. J. Murphy, trans. C. Newlands, Dekalb: Northern Illinois University Press, 1986.

Aristolelicae animadversiones, Paris: J. Bogardus, 1543 [Reprint Stuttgart: F. Frommann, 1964].

Dialecticae institutiones, Paris: J. Bogardus, 1543 [Reprint Stuttgart: F. Frommann, 1964].

Dialecticae partitiones, Paris: J. Bogardus, 1543.

Vives, Juan Luis, *In pseudodialecticos*, ed. and trans. C. Fantazzi, Leiden: Brill, 1979.
   On education: a translation of the 'De tradendis disciplinis' of Juan Luis Vives, trans. F. Watson, Cambridge: Cambridge University Press, 1913.
   Opera omnia (1782–90); ed. G. Mayans; facs. reprint London: Gregg Press, 1964, 8 vols.

Secondary sources

Bonilla y San Martín, Adolfo, *Luis Vives y la filosofía de rinacimiento*, 2nd edn, Madrid: L. Rubio, 1929, 3 vols.
Grafton, Anthony, and Jardine, Lisa, *From humanism to the humanities: education and the liberal arts in fifteenth- and sixteenth-century Europe*, London: Duckworth; Cambridge, MA: Harvard University Press, 1986.
Hidalgo-Serna, 'Einleitung', *Über die Gründe des Verfalls der Künste*, trans. W. Sendner, Munich: W. Fink, 1990.
Kahn, Victoria, 'Habermas, Machiavelli, and the critique of ideology', *Publications of the modern language association of America* 105 (1990), 464–76.
   Rhetoric, prudence, and skepticism in the Renaissance, Ithaca: Cornell University Press, 1985.
Kristeller, Paul Oskar, *Renaissance thought: the classic, scholastic, and humanist strains*; 1955; reprint New York: Harper & Row, 1961.
Murphy, James J. 'Introduction', *Arguments in rhetoric against Quintilian: translation and text of Peter Ramus's 'Rhetoricae distinctiones in Quintilianum' (1549)*, trans. C. Newlands, Dekalb: Northern Illinois University Press, 1986.
Noreña, Carlos G. *Juan Luis Vives*, The Hague: M. Nijhoff, 1970.
   A Vives bibliography, Lewiston: Edwin Mellen Press, 1990.
Ong, Walter J. *Ramus, method, and the decay of dialogue: from the art of discourse to the art of reason*; 1958; reprint New York: Octagon, 1974.
Sharratt, Peter, 'Peter Ramus and the reform of the university: the divorce of philosophy and eloquence?', in *French Renaissance studies, 1540–70: humanism and the encyclopaedia*, ed. P. Sharratt, Edinburgh: University of Edinburgh Press, 1976, pp. 4–20.
   'Recent work on Peter Ramus (1970–1986)', *Rhetorica* 5 (1987), 7–58.
Sloan, Thomas O. 'The crossing of rhetoric and poetry in the English Renaissance', in *The rhetoric of Renaissance poetry from Wyatt to Milton*, ed. T. O. Sloan and R. B. Waddington, Berkeley: University of California Press, 1974, pp. 212–43.
Vasoli, C. *La dialettica e la retorica dell'umanesimo: 'invenzione' e 'metodo' nella cultura del XV e XVI secolo*, Milan: Feltrinelli, 1968.

Voices of dissent: the rise of the vernaculars

Primary sources and texts

Alberti, Leon Battista, *La prima grammatica della lingua volgare*, ed. C. Grayson, Bologna: Commissione per i testi di lingua, 1964.

Bembo, Pietro, *Prose . . . nella quale si ragiona della volgar lingua*, Venice: G. Tacuino, 1525.

Bovelles, Charles de, *Liber de differentia vulgarium linguarum*, Paris: R. Estienne, 1533.

Brerewood, Edward, *Enquiries touching the diversity of languages, and religions through the . . . world*, London: J. Bill, 1614.

Burton, Robert, *The anatomy of melancholy*, Oxford: J. Lichfield and J. Short for H. Cripps, 1624; [ed. F. Dell and P. Jordan-Smith, New York: Farrar and Rinehart, 1927].

Dante Alighieri, *Il convivio*, ed. G. Busnelli and G. Vandelli, Florence: F. le Monnier, 1968.

De vulgari eloquentia, trans. A. G. F. Howell, in *Latin works of Dante*, London: Temple Classics, 1904.

Du Bellay, Joachim, *La deffence et illustration de la langue françoyse*, ed. H. Chamard, Paris: Didier, 1948.

Montaigne, Michel de, *The complete works of Montaigne: Essays, Travel Journal, Letters*, trans. D. M. Frame, Stanford: Stanford University Press, 1967.

Nebrija, Antonio de, *Gramática castellana*, ed. P. Galindo Romeo and L. Ortiz Muñoz, Madrid: Junta del Centenario, 1946.

Peletier du Mans, Jacques, *L'art poëtique*, ed. A. Boulanger, Paris: Les Belles Lettres, 1930.

Speroni, Sperone, *I dialogi*, Venice: Aldus, 1542 [Contents include *Dialogo delle lingue*].

Dialogo delle lingue, ed. H. Harth, Munich: W. Fink, 1975.

Tolomei, Claudio, *Il Cesano . . . nel quale . . . si disputa del nome . . . si dee . . . chiamare la volgar lingua*, Venice: G. Giolito, 1555.

Trissino, Giovanni Giorgio, *Il Castellano: dialogo . . . della lingua italiana*, Milan: Daelli, 1864.

La quinta e la sesta divisione della Poetica (c. 1549), in *Trattati di poetica e retorica del Cinquecento*, ed. B. Weinberg, Bari: Laterza, 1970, vol. II, pp. 7–90.

Valla, Lorenzo, *Ars grammatica*, ed. P. Casciano, Milan: A. Mondadori, 1990.

Opera omnia, Basle: H. Petrus, 1540.

Varchi, Benedetto, *L'Hercolano: dialogo nel qual si ragiona generalmente delle lingue*, Venice: F. Giunti & Fratelli, 1570.

Webbe, Joseph, *An appeale to truth, in the controversy betweene art & use; about the best and most expedient course in languages*, London: George Latham, 1622.

Secondary sources

Baron, Hans, *The crisis of the early Italian Renaissance*, Princeton: Princeton University Press, 1955.

'The *querelle* of the Ancients and Moderns as a problem for Renaissance scholarship', *Journal of the history of ideas* 20 (1959), 3–22.

Brunot, Ferdinand, *Histoire de la langue française*, vol. II, Paris: A. Colin, 1906.

Dionisotti, Carlo, *Gli umanisti e il volgare fra Quattro e Cinquecento*, Florence: F. le Monnier, 1968.

Fubini, Riccardo, 'La coscienza del Latino negli umanisti', *Studi medievali* series 3, 2 (1961), 505–50.

Gerl, Hanna-Barbara, *Rhetorik als Philosophie: Lorenzo Valla*, Munich: W. Fink, 1974.

Gravelle, Sarah Stever, 'The Latin-vernacular question and humanist theory of language and culture', *Journal of the history of ideas* 49 (1988), 367–86.

Grayson, Cecil, *A Renaissance controversy: Latin or Italian?* Oxford: Clarendon Press, 1960.

Jones, Richard F. *The triumph of the English language*, Stanford: Stanford University Press, 1953.

Klein, Hans Wilhelm, *Latein und Volgare in Italien*, Munich: M. Hueber, 1957.

Migliorini, Bruno, *Storia della lingua italiana*, 3rd edn, Florence: Sansoni, 1961.

Ngugi wa Thiong'o, *Decolonising the mind: the politics of language in African literature*, London and Nairobi: James Currey / Heinemann, 1986.

Ong, Walter J. *Interfaces of the word: studies in the evolution of consciousness and culture*, Ithaca: Cornell University Press, 1977.

  Rhetoric, romance, and technology, Ithaca: Cornell University Press, 1971.

Percival, W. Keith, 'Grammatical tradition and the rise of the vernaculars', *Current trends in linguistics* 13 (1975), 231–75.

Villey, Pierre, *Les sources italiennes de la 'Deffense et illustration de la langue françoise' de Joachim du Bellay*, Paris: H. Champion, 1908.

Waswo, Richard, *Language and meaning in the Renaissance*, Princeton: Princeton University Press, 1987.

Voices of dissent: Ancients and Moderns*

Primary sources and texts

Boileau-Despréaux, Nicolas, *Satires*, *L'art poétique*, and *Réflexions critiques*, in *Œuvres complètes*, ed. A. Adam and F. Escal, Paris: Gallimard, 1966.

Bouhours, Dominique, *La manière de bien penser dans les ouvrages d'esprit*, Paris: Cramoisy, 1687.

Bruni, Leonardo, *Ad Petrum Paulum Histrum dialogus*, in *Prosatori latini del Quattrocento*, ed. E. Garin, Milan and Naples: Ricciardi, 1952, pp. 41–99.

Charpentier, François, *Deffense de la langue françoise pour l'inscription de l'arc de triomphe*, Paris: C. Barbin, 1676.

Desmarets de Saint-Sorlin, Jean, *La comparaison de la langue et de la poésie françoise avec la grecque et la latine, et des poètes grecs, latins, & françois*, Paris: T. Jolly, 1670.

Du Bellay, Joachim, *La deffence et illustration de la langue françoyse*, ed. H. Chamard, Paris: Didier, 1948.

Erasmus, Desiderius, *Ciceronianus*, ed. A. H. T. Levi, in the *Collected works of Erasmus*, vol. XXVIII, Toronto, Buffalo, and London: University of Toronto Press, 1986.

Fontenelle, Bernard Le Bovier de, *Entretiens sur la pluralité des mondes; Digression sur les anciens et les modernes*, ed. R. Shackleton, Oxford: Clarendon Press, 1955.

Perrault, Charles, *Paralelle des anciens et des modernes*; 1688–97; facs. reprint Munich: Eidos, 1964 [Also contains *Le siècle de Louis le Grand*].

Terrasson, Jean, *Dissertation critique sur l'Iliade d'Homère, où à l'occasion de ce poème on cherche les règles d'une poëtique fondée sur la raison, & sur les exemples des anciens et des modernes*, Paris: F. Fournier et A.-U. Coustelier, 1715, 2 vols.

Wooton, Edward, *Reflections upon ancient and modern learning*, London: J. Leake for P. Buck, 1694.

Secondary sources

Baron, Hans, 'The *querelle* of the Ancients and Moderns as a problem for Renaissance scholarship', *Journal of the history of ideas* 20 (1959), 3–22.

Black, Robert, 'Ancients and Moderns in the Renaissance: rhetoric and history in Accolti's *Dialogue on the preeminence of men of his own time*', *Journal of the history of ideas* 43 (1982), 3–32.

Curtius, Ernst Robert, *European literature and the Latin Middle Ages*, trans. W. R. Trask, London and Henley: Routledge & Kegan Paul, 1979, pp. 247–72.

Davidson, Hugh M. 'Fontenelle, Perrault and the realignment of the arts', in *Literature and history in the age of ideas: essays on the Enlightenment presented to George R. Havens*, ed. C. G. S. Williams, Columbus: Ohio State University Press, 1975, pp. 3–13.

DeJean, Joan, *Ancients against Moderns: culture wars and the making of a 'fin de siècle'*, Chicago: University of Chicago Press, 1997.

Gillot, Hubert, *La querelle des anciens et des modernes en France*, Paris: Champion, 1914.

Gombrich, Ernst, 'The Renaissance conception of artistic progress and its consequences', in *Norm and form: studies in the art of the Renaissance*, 4th edn, Chicago: University of Chicago Press, 1985, pp. 1–10.

Highet, Gilbert, *The classical tradition: Greek and Roman influences on Western literature*, New York: Oxford University Press, 1949, pp. 261–88.

Jones, Richard Foster, *Ancients and moderns: a study of the background of The Battle of the Books*, St Louis: Washington University Studies, 1936.

Kapitza, Peter K. *Ein bürgerlicher Krieg in der gelehrten Welt: Zur Geschichte des Querelle des Anciens et des Modernes in Deutschland*, Munich: W. Fink, 1981.

Keller, Abraham C. 'Ancients and moderns in the early seventeenth century', *Modern language quarterly* 11 (1950), 79–82.

Kortum, Hans, *Charles Perrault und Nicolas Boileau. Der Antike-Streit im Zeitalter der klassischen französischen Literatur*, Berlin: Rutten & Loening, 1966.

Levi, A. H. T. '*La Princesse de Clèves* and the *Querelle des Anciens et des Modernes*', *Journal of European studies* 10 (1980), 62–70.

Levine, Joseph M. *The Battle of the Books: history and literature in the Augustan age*, Ithaca and London: Cornell University Press, 1991.

'Giambattista Vico and the quarrel between the Ancients and the Moderns', *Journal of the history of ideas* 52 (1991), 55–79.

Lombard, A. *La querelle des Anciens et des Modernes: l'abbé Du Bos*, Neuchâtel: Attinger Frères, 1908.

Lorimer, J. W. 'A neglected aspect of the "Querelle des Anciens et des Modernes" ', *Modern language review* 51 (1956), 179–85.

Margiotta, Giacinto, *Le origini italiane della Querelle des Anciens et des Modernes*, Rome: Studium, 1953.

Pigman, G. W., III, 'Imitation and the Renaissance sense of the past: the reception of Erasmus' *Ciceronianus*', *Journal of Medieval and Renaissance studies* 9 (1979), 155–77.

Rigault, Hippolite, *Histoire de la querelle des Anciens et des Modernes*, Paris: Hachette, 1856.

Vasoli, Cesare, 'La première querelle des "anciens" et des "modernes" aux origines de la Renaissance', in *Classical influences on European culture*, ed. R. R. Bolgar, Cambridge: Cambridge University Press, 1976, pp. 67–80.

Wencelius, Léon, 'La querelle des Anciens et des Modernes et l'humanisme', *XVIIe siècle* 9–10 (1951), 15–34.

* *Relevant critical material on the Quarrel of Ancients and Moderns in England and Italy is also found below in the bibliographical section on National Developments.*

Voices of dissent: women as *auctores* in early modern Europe

Primary sources and texts

Anger, Jane, *Her protection for women* (1589), ed. S. G. O'Malley, in *The early modern Englishwoman: a facsimile library of essential works, 'Defences of women'*, Pt. I, *Printed writings, 1500–1640*, ed. B. Travistsky and P. Cullen, et al., 10 vols. (Aldershot: Scolar Press; Brookfield, VT: Ashgate, 1996–), vol. IV [unpaginated].

Crenne, Hélisenne de, *Œuvres*, Geneva: Slatkine, 1977.

Fonte, Moderata, *Il merito delle donne*, Venice: D. Imberti, 1600.

Gournay, Marie de, *Les advis, ou, les presens de la demoiselle de Gournay*, Paris: Jean du Bray, 1641.

Labé, Louise, *Euvres de Louize Labé lionnoize*, Lyons: Jean de Tournes, 1555.

Marguerite de Navarre, *L'Heptaméron*, ed. M. François, Paris: Garnier, 1967.

Marinelli, Lucrezia, *Le nobiltà et eccellenze delle donne: et i diffetti, et mancamenti de gli huomini*, Venice: G. B. Ciotti, 1600.

Roches, Madeleine and Catherine des, *Œuvres*, 2nd edn, Paris: Abel L'Angelier, 1579.
    Les missives de mesdames des Roches de Poitiers mere et fille, Paris: Abel L'Angelier, 1586.

Scudéry, Madeleine de, *Conversations nouvelles sur divers sujets*, Paris: C. Barbin, 1684.

Summers, M. (ed.), *The works of Aphra Behn*; 1915; reprint New York: Benjamin Blom, 1967, 6 vols.

Terracina, Laura, *Discorso sopra il principio di tutti i canti d'Orlando furioso*, Venice: D. Farri, 1560.

Travistsky, B., and Cullen, P. *et al.* (eds), *The early modern Englishwoman: a facsimile library of essential works*, Pt. I, *Printed writings, 1500–1640*, Aldershot: Scolar Press; Brookfield, VT: Ashgate, 1966– , 10 vols.

Secondary sources

Bauschatz, C. 'Marie de Gournay's gendered images for language and poetry', *Journal of Medieval and Renaissance studies* 25 (1995), 489–500.

Conti Odorisio, Ginevra, *Donna e società nel Seicento: Lucrezia Marinelli e Arcangela Tarabotti*, Rome: Bulzoni, 1979.

DeJean, Joan. *Tender geographies: women and the origins of the novel in France*, New York: Columbia University Press, 1991.

Harth, E. *Cartesian women: versions and subversions of rational discourse in the old regime*, Ithaca and London: Cornell University Press, 1992.

Jones, A. R. *The currency of Eros: women's love lyric in Europe, 1540–1620*, Bloomington: Indiana University Press, 1990.

Jordan, C. *Renaissance feminism: literary texts and political models*, Ithaca and London: Cornell University Press, 1990.

Kelly-Gadol, J. 'Early feminist theory and the *querelle des femmes*, 1400–1789', *Signs* 8 (Fall 1982), 4–28.

Reiss, T. J. *The meaning of literature*, Ithaca and London: Cornell University Press, 1992.

Structures of thought: Renaissance Neoplatonism

Primary sources and texts

Ficino, Marsilio, *Opera omnia*; 1576; reprint Turin: Bottega d'Erasmo, 1959, 1962, 1983, ed. P. O. Kristeller and M. Sancipriano, 2 vols.

Landino, Cristoforo, *Scritti critici e teorici*, ed. R. Cardini, Rome: Bulzoni, 1974.

Pico della Mirandola, Giovanni, *Opera omnia*; 1572; reprint Turin: Bottega d'Erasmo, 1971, ed. E. Garin, 2 vols.

Secondary sources

Allen, Michael J. B. *The Platonism of Marsilio Ficino*, Berkeley: University of California Press, 1984.

Plato's third eye: studies in Marsilio Ficino's metaphysics and its sources, Aldershot, Hampshire: Variorum, 1995.

Synoptic art: Marsilio Ficino on the history of Platonic interpretation, Florence: Olschki, 1998.

Cardini, Roberto, *La critica del Landino*, Florence: Sansoni, 1973.

Chastel, André, *Art et humanisme à Florence au temps de Laurent le Magnifique*, Paris: Presses Universitaires de France, 1961.

Marsile Ficin et l'art (1954), Geneva: Droz, 1975.

Coulter, James A. *The literary microcosm: theories of interpretation of the later Neoplatonists*, Leiden: Brill, 1976.

Field, Arthur, *The origins of the Platonic Academy of Florence*, Princeton: Princeton University Press, 1988.

Gombrich, Ernst H. 'Icones symbolicae: philosophies of symbolism and their bearing on art', in *Symbolic images: studies in the art of the Renaissance*, London: Phaidon, 1972, pp. 123–95.

Hankins, James, *Plato in the Italian Renaissance*, Leiden and New York: Brill, 1990, 2 vols.

Kallendorf, Craig, *In praise of Aeneas: Virgil and epideictic rhetoric in the early Italian Renaissance*; 1943; reprint Gloucester, MA: Peter Smith, 1964.

Kristeller, Paul Oskar, *The philosophy of Marsilio Ficino*, New York: Columbia University Press, 1943.

Lamberton, Robert, *Homer the theologian: Neoplatonist allegorical reading and the growth of the epic tradition*, Berkeley: University of California Press, 1986.

Sheppard, Anne D. R. *Studies in the 5th and 6th essays of Proclus' Commentary on the Republic*, Hypomnemata 61, Göttingen: Vandenhoeck and Ruprecht, 1980.

Tigerstedt, E. N. *Plato's idea of poetical inspiration*, Commentationes humanarum litterarum: societas scientiarum Fennica, 44, 2, Helsinki: no pub., 1969.
  'The poet as creator: origins of a metaphor', *Comparative literature studies* 5, 4 (1968), 455–88.

Tomlinson, Gary, *Music in Renaissance magic: towards a historiography of others*, Chicago: University of Chicago Press, 1993.

Trimpi, Wesley, *Muses of one mind: the literary analysis of experience and its continuity*, Princeton: Princeton University Press, 1983.

Walker, D. P. *The ancient theology: studies in Christian Platonism from the fifteenth to the eighteenth century*, Ithaca: Cornell University Press, 1972.

Warden, John (ed.), *Orpheus: the metamorphoses of a myth*, Toronto: University of Toronto Press, 1982.

Weinberg, Bernard, *A history of literary criticism in the Italian Renaissance*, Chicago: University of Chicago Press, 1961, 2 vols.

Wind, Edgar, *Pagan mysteries in the Renaissance*, rev. edn, New York: Norton, 1968.

Structures of thought: cosmography

Primary sources and texts

Colletet, Guillaume, *Traité de la poésie morale et sententieuse*, in *L'art poétique*, Paris: A. de Sommaville and L. Chamhoudry, 1658 [Facs. reprint, Geneva: Slatkine, 1970].

Landino, Cristoforo [Christophorus Landinus], *Comento sopra la Comedia di Dante* (1481), in *Scritti critici e teorici*, ed. R. Cardini, vol. 1, Rome: Bulzoni, 1974.

Salutati, Coluccio, *De laboribus Herculis*, ed. B. L. Ullman, Zurich: Thesaurus Mundi, 1951.

Tyard, Pontus de, *Le premier curieux*, ed. J. C. Lapp, Ithaca: Cornell University Press, 1950.
Tesauro, E. *Il cannocchiale Aristotelico*, Venice: Milocho, 1682 [1670; facs. reprint Bad Homburg: Gehlen, 1968, ed. A. Buck].

Secondary sources

Hallyn, F. *Le sens des formes: études sur la Renaissance*, Geneva: Droz, 1994 [See esp. section III, 'Poésie scientifique'].
Heninger, S. K., Jr. *Touches of sweet harmony: Pythagorean cosmology and Renaissance poetics*, San Marino, CA: Huntington Library, 1974.
Keller, L. *Palingène, Ronsard, Du Bartas: trois études sur la poésie cosmologique de la Renaissance*, Berne: Francke, 1974.
Roellenbleck, G. *Das epische Lehrgedicht Italiens im fünfzehnten und sechzehnten Jarhundert: ein Beitrag zur Literaturgeschichte des Humanismus und der Renaissance*, Munich: W. Fink, 1975.
Rostvig, M. S. 'Ars aeterna: Renaissance poetics and theories of divine creation', *Mosaïc* 3 (1969–70), 40–61.
Schmidt, Albert-Marie, *La poésie scientifique en France au seizième siècle*, Paris: A. Michel, 1938.
Tigerstedt, E. N. 'The poet as creator: origins of a metaphor', *Comparative literature studies* 5 (1968), 455–88.
Wilson, D. *French Renaissance scientific poetry*, London: Athlone Press, 1974.

Structures of thought: natural philosophy and the 'new science'

Primary sources and texts

Bacon, Francis, *The works of Francis Bacon*, ed. J. Spedding, R. L. Ellis, and D. D. Heath, new edn, London: Longmans, 1857–74, 14 vols. [Facs. reprint Stuttgart and Bad Cannstatt: Frommann-Holzboog, 1989].
Galilei, Galileo, *Dialogue concerning the two chief world systems*, trans. S. Drake, Berkeley: University of California Press, 1957.
Kepler, Johannes, *Somnium*, trans. E. Rosen, Madison: University of Wisconsin Press, 1967.
Palissy, Bernard, *Œuvres*, Paris: Blanchard, 1961.
Paré, Ambroise, *The apologie and treatise*, trans. T. Johnson, New York: Dover, 1968.

Secondary sources

Grafton, Anthony, *Defenders of the text: the traditions of scholarship in an age of science 1450–1800*, Cambridge, MA: Harvard University Press, 1991.
Panizza, Letizia (ed.), *Philosophical and scientific poetry in the Renaissance*, *Renaissance studies* 5 (1991).
Pantin, Isabelle, *La poésie du ciel en France dans la seconde moitié du seizième siècle*, Geneva: Droz, 1995.

Schatzberg, Walter, *et al.* (ed.), *The relations of literature and science: an annotated bibliography of scholarship 1880–1980*, New York: Modern Language Association of America, 1987.

Schmidt, Albert-Marie, *La poésie scientifique en France au seizième siècle*, Paris: Albin Michel, 1938.

Structures of thought: Stoicism and Epicureanism
Primary sources and texts

Del Rio, Martin, *Syntagma tragoediae latinae*, Antwerp: J. Moretus, 1593–4.

Dryden, John, 'A discourse concerning the original and progress of satire', in *Essays of John Dryden*, ed. W. P. Ker, 2 vols., Oxford: Clarendon Press, 1900, vol. II, pp. 15–114.

  'Preface to *Sylvae*', in *The works of John Dryden*, Berkeley and Los Angeles: University of California Press, 1956– , vol. III: *Poems 1685–1692*, ed. E. Miner, pp. 3–18.

Frachetta, Girolamo, *Breve spositione di tutta l'opera di Lucretio*, Venice: P. Paganini, 1589.

Lipsius, Justus, *Opera omnia*, Wessel: A. Hoogenhuysen, 1675, 4 vols.

Lucretius, *His six books 'De natura rerum'*, trans. T. Creech, Oxford: A. Stephens, 1682.

Secondary sources

Croll, M. W. *Style, rhetoric and rhythm*, ed. J. M. Patrick, *et al.*, Princeton: Princeton University Press, 1966.

Darmon, Jean-Charles, *Philosophie épicurienne et littérature au XVIIᵉ siècle en France: études sur Gassendi, Cyrano de Bergerac, La Fontaine, Saint-Evremond* (Paris: Presses Universitaires de France, 1998).

Fraisse, S. *L'influence de Lucrèce en France au seizième siècle*, Paris: Nizet, 1962.

Jones, H. *The Epicurean tradition*, London and New York: Routledge, 1989.

Morford, M. *Rubens and the circle of Lipsius*, Princeton: Princeton University Press, 1991.

Shifflet, Andrew, *Stoicism, politics, and literature in the age of Milton: war and peace reconciled*, Cambridge: Cambridge University Press, 1998.

Spanneut, M. *Permanence du stoïcisme*, Gembloux: Duculot, 1973.

Structures of thought: Calvinism and post-Tridentine developments
Primary sources and texts

Aubigné, Théodore Agrippa d', *Œuvres*, ed. H. Weber, J. Bailbé and M. Soulié, Paris: Gallimard, 1969.

Calvin, Jean, *Institution de la religion chrestienne* (1541), Geneva: J. Bourgeois, 1562.

Du Bartas, Guillaume de Salluste, sieur, *La sepmaine*, ed. Y. Bellenger, Paris: Nizet, 1980.

Mornay, Charlotte Arbaleste de, *The memoirs of Philippe du Plessis-Mornay, sieur Marly*, ed. de Witt, Paris: Jules Renouard, 1868–9.

Secondary sources

Breen, J. Quirinus, *John Calvin: a study in French humanism*, Grand Rapids: Eerdmans, 1931.

Cave, Terence, *Devotional poetry in France, c. 1570–1613*, London and New York: Cambridge University Press, 1968.

Cave, Terence, and Jeanneret, Michel, *Métamorphoses spirituelles: anthologie de la poésie religieuse française 1570–1630*, Paris: J. Corti, 1972.

Clément, Michèle, *Une poétique de crise: poètes baroques et mystiques (1570–1660)*, Paris: Champion, 1996.

Coats, Catharine Randall, *Subverting the system: d'Aubigné and Calvinism*, Kirksville, MO: Sixteenth Century Publishers, 1990.

Gilmont, Jean-François, *Crespin, un éditeur réformé du XVIᵉ siècle*, Geneva: Droz, 1981.

Millet, Olivier, *La pensée de Jean Calvin*, Geneva: Droz, 1993.

Pannier, Jacques, *Calvin écrivain, et sa place et son rôle dans l'histoire de la langue et de la littérature françaises*, Paris: Fischbacher, 1930.

Raitt, Jill, 'Theodore Beza, 1519–1605', in *Shapers of religious traditions in Germany, Switzerland and Poland*, New Haven: Yale University Press, 1981, pp. 75–101.

Soulié, Marguerite, *L'inspiration biblique dans la poésie religieuse de d'Aubigné*, Paris: Klincksieck, 1975.

Wencelius, Léon, *L'esthétique de Calvin*, Geneva: Slatkine, 1969.

Structures of thought: Port-Royal and Jansenism

Primary sources and texts

Arnauld, Antoine, and Nicole, Pierre, *La logique ou l'art de penser*, édition revue et augmentée, Paris: Savreux, 1664.
  La logique ou l'art de penser, ed. P. Clair and F. Girbal, Paris: Presses Universitaires de France, 1965.

Arnauld, Antoine, and Lancelot, C. *Grammaire générale et raisonnée de Port-Royal*, Geneva: Slatkine, 1980.

La Bruyère, Jean de, *Les caractères, ou les mœurs de ce siècle*, ed. R. Garapon, Paris: Garnier, 1962.

La Rochefoucauld, François, duc de, *Maximes, suivies des Réflexions diverses*, ed. J. Truchet, Paris: Garnier, 1983.

Nicole, Pierre, *Essais de morale*, Geneva: Slatkine, 1971, 4 vols.

Pascal, Blaise, *Œuvres complètes*, ed. L. Lafuma, Paris: Seuil, 1972.

Racine, J. *Œuvres complètes*, ed. R. Picard, Paris: Gallimard, 1966, 2 vols.

Secondary sources

Bénichou, P. *Morales du grand siècle*, Paris: Gallimard, 1948.

Cognet, L. *Le Jansénisme*, Paris: Presses Universitaires de France, 1961.

Goldmann, L. *Le dieu caché*, Paris: Gallimard, 1959.

Marin, L. *La critique du discours*, Paris: Editions de Minuit, 1975.

Melzer, S. *Discourses of the fall*, Berkeley: University of California Press, 1986.

Sedgwick, A. *Jansenism in seventeenth-century France*, Charlottesville: University Press of Virginia, 1977.

Neoclassical issues: combative criticism, Jonson, Milton, and classical literary criticism in England

Primary sources and texts

Davenant, Sir William, *Gondibert*, ed. D. F. Gladish, Oxford: Clarendon Press, 1971.

Dryden, John, *Essays*, ed. W. P. Ker, Oxford: Clarendon Press, 1900, 2 vols.

Heinsius, Daniel, *On plot in tragedy (De tragoediae constitutione)* (1611); trans. and ed. P. R. Sellin and J. J. M\u1d9cManmon, Northridge, CA: San Fernando Valley State College, 1971.

Jonson, Ben, *Ben Jonson* [Works], ed. C. H. Herford and P. and E. Simpson, Oxford: Clarendon Press, 1925–52, 11 vols. [Edition under reissue with corrections, 1986–].

Longinus, *Peri hupsous, or Dionysius Longinus of the heights of eloquence*, trans. John Hall, London: R. Daniel for F. Eaglesfield, 1652.

Milton, John, *Complete prose works*, ed. D. M. Wolfe, *et al.*, New Haven: Yale University Press, 1953–82, 8 vols.

  Poems, ed. J. Carey and A. Fowler, Harlow: Longmans, 1968.

Smith, G. Gregory (ed.), *Elizabethan critical essays*, Oxford: Clarendon Press, 1904, 2 vols.

Spenser, Edmund, *The Faerie Queene*, ed. A. C. Hamilton, London and New York: Longman, 1977.

Spingarn, J. E. (ed.), *Critical essays of the seventeenth century*, Oxford: Clarendon Press, 1908–9, 3 vols. [Reprint Bloomington: Indiana University Press, 1957].

Secondary sources

Greene, Thomas M. *The light in Troy: imitation and discovery in Renaissance poetry*, New Haven: Yale University Press, 1982.

Hardison, O. B., Jr. 'The orator and the poet: the dilemma of humanist literature', *Journal of Medieval and Renaissance studies* 1 (1971), 33–44.

  'The two voices of Sidney's *Apology for poetry*' in *Sidney in retrospect: selections from English literary Renaissance*, ed. A. F. Kinney, Amherst: University of Massachusetts Press, 1988, pp. 45–61.

Hathaway, Baxter, *The age of criticism: the late Renaissance in Italy*, Ithaca: Cornell University Press, 1962.

M\u1d9cPherson, D. 'Ben Jonson's library and marginalia: an annotated catalogue', *Studies in philology* 71 (1974), Appendix.

Manley, Lawrence, *Convention: 1500–1700*, Cambridge, MA: Harvard University Press, 1980.

Mueller, Martin, 'Sixteenth-century Italian criticism and Milton's theory of catharsis', *Studies in English literature* 6 (1966), 139–50.

Peterson, Richard S. *Imitation and praise in the poems of Ben Jonson*, New Haven and London: Yale University Press, 1981.

Pigman, G. W., III, 'Versions of imitation in the Renaissance', *Renaissance quarterly* 33 (1980), 1–32.

Samuel, Irene, 'The development of Milton's poetics', *Publications of the modern language association of America* 92 (1977), 231–40.

Sellin, Paul R. 'Sources of Milton's catharsis: a reconsideration', *Journal of English and Germanic philology* 60 (1961), 712–30.

'Milton and Heinsius: theoretical homogeneity', in *Medieval epic to the 'epic theatre' of Brecht: essays in comparative literature*, ed. R. P. Amato and J. M. Spalek, University of Southern California studies in comparative literature 1, Los Angeles: University of California Press, 1968, pp. 125–34.

Snyder, Susan, *Pastoral process: Spenser, Marvell, Milton*, Stanford: Stanford University Press, 1998.

Steadman, John M. *The walls of paradise: essays on Milton's poetics*, Baton Rouge and London: Louisiana State University Press, 1985.

Neoclassical issues: the rhetorical ideal in France

Primary sources and texts

Arnauld, Antoine and Nicole, Pierre, *La logique ou l'art de penser*, édition revue et augmentée, Paris: Savreux, 1664.

Aubignac, François Hédelin, abbé d', *Pratique du théâtre*, ed. P. Martino, Algiers: Carbonel; Paris: Champion, 1927.

Bary, R. *La rhétorique française*, Paris: Le Petit, 1659 [Re-edition of the 1653 edn].

Boileau-Despréaux, Nicolas, *L'art póetique*, in *Œuvres complètes*, ed. A. Adam and F. Escal, Paris: Gallimard, 1966.

Fénelon, François de Salignac de La Mothe-, *Dialogues sur l'éloquence en général et sur celle de la chaire en particulier, avec une lettre écrite à l'Académie française*, Paris: F. Delaulne, 1718.

Guéret, Gabriel, *Entretiens sur l'éloquence de la chaire et du barreau*, Paris: J. Guignard 1666.

Rapin, René, *Les comparaisons des grands hommes de l'antiquité; Les réflexions sur l'éloquence, la poétique, l'histoire et la philosophie*, Paris: F. Muguet, 1684, 2 vols.

Vaugelas, Claude Favre de, *Remarques sur la langue française*, Paris: Veuve J. Camusat et P. Le Petit, 1647.

Secondary sources

Bayley, Peter, *French pulpit oratory, 1598–1650: a study in themes and styles, with a descriptive catalogue of printed texts*, Cambridge: Cambridge University Press, 1980.

Davidson, Hugh M. *Audience, words, and art: studies in seventeenth-century French rhetoric*, Columbus: Ohio State University Press, 1965.
Pascal and the arts of the mind, Cambridge: Cambridge University Press, 1993.
France, Peter, *Racine's rhetoric*, Oxford: Clarendon Press, 1965.
Rhetoric and truth in France: Descartes to Diderot, Oxford: Clarendon Press, 1972.
Fumaroli, M. *L'âge de l'éloquence: rhétorique et 'res literaria' de la Renaissance au seuil de l'époque classique*, Geneva: Droz, 1980.
Fumaroli, M. (ed.), *Critique et création littéraire en France au XVIIᵉ siècle*, Paris: Editions du CNRS, 1977.
Genetiot, Alain, *Poétique du loisir mondain, de Voiture à La Fontaine*, Paris: Champion, 1997.
McKeon, Richard P. *Rhetoric: essays in invention and discovery*, ed. M. Backman, Woodbridge, CT: Ox Bow Press, 1987.
Murphy, James J. (ed.), *Renaissance eloquence: studies in the theory and practice of Renaissance rhetoric*, Berkeley: University of California Press, 1983.
Rubin, David Lee and McKinley, Mary (ed.), *Convergences: rhetoric and poetics in seventeenth-century France*, Columbus: Ohio State University Press, 1989.
Zobermann, Pierre, *Les cérémonies de la parole: l'éloquence d'apparat en France dans le dernier quart du XVIIᵉ siècle*, Paris: Champion, 1998.

Neoclassical issues: Cartesian aesthetics

Primary sources and texts

Alberti, Leon Battista, *On painting and sculpture: the Latin texts of 'De pictura' and 'De statua'*, ed. with trans., intro., and notes by C. Grayson, London: Phaidon, 1972.
Descartes, René *Compendium musicae*, in *Œuvres*, ed. C. Adam and P. Tannery, 2nd edn, 11 vols., Paris: Vrin/CNRS, 1974–86, vol. x.
Œuvres, ed. C. Adam and P. Tannery, 2nd edn, Paris: Vrin/CNRS, 1974–86, 11 vols.
Zarlino, Gioseffo, *Le istitutioni harmoniche*; 1558; reprint New York: Broude, 1965.

Secondary sources

Damisch, Hubert, *L'origine de la perspective*, new edn, Paris: Flammarion, 1993.
Kristeller, Paul Oskar, 'The modern system of the arts', in *Renaissance thought II: papers on humanism and the arts*, New York: Harper & Row, 1965, pp. 163–227.
Moyer, Ann E. *Musica scientia: musical scholarship in the Italian Renaissance*, Ithaca: Cornell University Press, 1992.
Palisca, Claude V. *Humanism in Italian Renaissance musical thought*, New Haven: Yale University Press, 1985.
Pirro, André, *Descartes et la musique*; 1907; reprint Geneva: Minkoff, 1973.

Reiss, Timothy J. *The discourse of modernism*, Ithaca: Cornell University Press, 1982.
  The meaning of literature, Ithaca: Cornell University Press, 1992.
White, John, *The birth and rebirth of pictorial space*, 3rd edn, Cambridge, MA:
  Harvard University Press, 1987.

Neoclassical issues: principles of judgement

Primary sources and texts

Aubignac, François Hédelin, abbé d', *Pratique du théâtre*, ed. P. Martino, Algiers:
  Carbonel; Paris: Champion, 1927.
Balzac, Jean-Louis Guez de, *Œuvres*, Paris: T. Jolly, 1665, 2 vols.
Boileau-Despréaux, Nicolas, *Œuvres complètes*, ed. A. Adam and F. Escal, Paris:
  Gallimard, 1966.
Bouhours, Dominique, *La manière de bien penser dans les ouvrages d'esprit*;
  1715; reprint Brighton: University of Sussex Library, 1971.
  Les entretiens d'Ariste et d'Eugène, présentation de Ferdinand Brunot, Paris: A.
  Colin, 1962.
Chapelain, Jean, *Opuscules critiques*, ed. A. C. Hunter, Paris: Droz, 1936.
Corneille, Pierre, *Œuvres complètes*, ed. G. Couton, Paris: Gallimard, 1980–7,
  3 vols.
La Bruyère, J. de, *Les caractères, ou les mœurs de ce siècle*, ed. R. Garapon, Paris:
  Garnier, 1962.
La Mesnardière, Hippolyte-Jules Pilet de, *La poëtique*; 1640; reprint Geneva:
  Slatkine Reprints, 1972.
Méré, Antoine Gombaud, chevalier de, *Lettres*, Paris: D. Thierry and C. Barbin,
  1682, 2 vols. paginated as one.
  Œuvres complètes, ed. C.-H. Boudhors, Paris: Fernand Roches, 1930, 3 vols.
Perrault, Charles, *Paralelle des anciens et des modernes*; 1688–97; facs. reprint
  Munich: Eidos, 1964, ed. H. R. Jauss.
Perrot d'Ablancourt, Nicolas, *Lettres et préfaces critiques*, ed. R. Zuber, Paris:
  Didier, 1972.
Rapin, René, *Les comparaisons des grands hommes de l'antiquité*; *Les réflexions
  sur l'éloquence, la poétique, l'histoire et la philosophie*, Paris: F. Muguet,
  1684, 2 vols.
Saint-Evremond, Charles Marguetel de Saint-Denis, seigneur de, *Lettres*, ed.
  R. Ternois, Paris: Didier, 1967–8, 2 vols.
  Œuvres en prose, ed. R. Ternois, Paris: Didier, 1962–9, 4 vols.
Valincour, Jean-Baptiste-Henri du Trousset de, *Lettres à Madame la Marquise ***
  sur le sujet de 'La Princesse de Clèves'*, ed. A. Cazes, Paris: Bossard, 1925.

Secondary sources

Bray, René, *La formation de la doctrine classique en France*, new edn, Paris: Nizet,
  1961.
Brody, Jules, *Boileau and Longinus*, Geneva: Droz, 1958.
Dens, Jean-Pierre, *L'honnête homme et la critique du goût*, Lexington: French
  Forum, 1981.

Fumaroli, Marc (ed.), *Critique et création littéraire en France au XVIIe siècle*, Paris: Editions du CNRS, 1977.

Gasté, Armand (ed.), *La querelle du Cid: pièces et pamphlets*, Paris: H. Welter, 1898.

Genetiot, Alain, *Poétique du loisir mondain, de Vorture à La Fontaine*, Paris: Champion, 1997.

Genette, Gérard, 'Vraisemblance et motivation', in *Figures II*, Paris: Seuil, 1969, pp. 71–99.

Jehasse, Jean, *Guez de Balzac et le génie romain*, Saint-Etienne: Publications de l'Université de Saint-Etienne, 1978.

Kibédi Varga, Aron (ed.), *Les poétiques du classicisme*, Paris: Aux Amateurs de Livres, 1990.

Moriarty, Michael, *Taste and ideology in seventeenth-century France*, Cambridge: Cambridge University Press, 1988.

Neoclassical issues: Longinus and the Sublime

Primary sources and texts

Boileau-Despréaux, Nicolas, *Œuvres complètes*, ed. A. Adam and F. Escal, Paris: Gallimard, 1966.

Catullus, *Catullus, et in eum commentarius M. Antonii Mureti*, Venice: P. Manutius, 1554.

La Fontaine, Jean de, *Œuvres diverses*, ed. P. Clarac, Paris: Gallimard, 1958.

Longinus, *Longinus on the Sublime: the Greek text edited after the Paris manuscript*, ed. W. R. Roberts, 1899; 2nd edn 1907; reprint Cambridge: Cambridge University Press, 1935.

Montaigne, Michel de, *Les essais de Michel de Montaigne*, ed. P. Villey; rev. edn V.-L. Saulnier, Paris: Presses Universitaires de France, 1965.

Ogier, François, *Apologie pour monsieur de Balzac*; 1627; reprint Saint-Etienne: Publications de l'Université de Saint-Etienne, 1977.

Patrizi [da Cherso], Francesco, *Della poetica*, ed. D. Aguzzi-Barbagli, Florence: Istituto Nazionale di studi sul Rinascimento, 1969–71, 3 vols.

Secondary sources

Aulotte, Robert, 'Sur quelques traductions d'une ode de Sappho au XVIe siècle', *Lettres d'humanité* (December 1958), 107–22.

Brody, Jules, *Boileau and Longinus*, Geneva: Droz, 1958.

Coleman, Dorothy Gabe, 'Montaigne and Longinus', *Bibliothèque d'humanisme et Renaissance* 47 (1985), 405–13.

Costil, Pierre, *André Dudith, humaniste hongrois, 1533–1589: sa vie, son œuvre et ses manuscrits grecs*, Paris: Les Belles Lettres, 1935.

Fumaroli, Marc, 'Rhétorique d'école et rhétorique adulte: remarques sur la réception européenne du traité "Du Sublime" au XVIe et au XVIIe siècle', *Revue d'histoire littéraire de la France* 86 (1986), 33–51.

Goyet, Francis, *Le Sublime du 'lieu commun': l'invention rhétorique dans l'Antiquité et à la Renaissance*, Paris: Champion, 1996.

Hartmann, Pierre, *Du sublime de Boileau à Schiller*, Strasburg: Presses Universitaires de Strasbourg, 1997.

Logan, J. L. 'Longinus', in *Ancient writers: Greece and Rome*, ed. T. J. Luce, 2 vols., New York: Scribner, 1982, vol. II, pp. 1063–80.

   'Montaigne et Longin: une nouvelle hypothèse', *Revue d'histoire littéraire de la France* 83 (1983), 355–70.

Magnien, Michel, 'Montaigne et le sublime dans les *Essais*', in *Montaigne et la rhétorique*, ed. J. O'Brien, M. Quainton, and J. J. Supple, Paris: Champion, 1995, pp. 27–48.

Rigolot, François, 'Louise Labé et la redécouverte de Sappho', *Nouvelle revue du seizième siècle* 1 (1983), 19–31.

Sedley, David L. 'Sublimity and skepticism in Montaigne', *Publications of the modern language association of America* 113 (1998), 1079–92.

Weinberg, Bernard, 'Une traduction française du *Sublime* de Longin vers 1645', *Modern philology* 59 (1962), 159–201.

   'Translations and commentaries of Longinus, *On the Sublime*, to 1600: a bibliography', *Modern philology* 47 (1950), 145–51.

A survey of national developments: England

Primary sources and texts

Bacon, Francis, *The new organon*, ed. F. H. Anderson, New York: Macmillan, 1960.

Behn, Aphra, *The works*, ed. J. Todd, 7 vols., Columbus: Ohio State University Press, 1992–6, vol. V, *The plays, 1671–5* (1996).

Carew, Thomas, *Poems*, ed. R. Dunlap, Oxford: Clarendon Press, 1949.

Certain sermons or homilies, Oxford: Oxford University Press, 1840.

Craig, D. H. (ed.), *Jonson: the critical heritage*, London: Routledge & Kegan Paul, 1990.

Davenant, Sir William, *Gondibert*, ed. D. F. Gladish, Oxford: Clarendon Press, 1971.

Dennis, John, *The critical works of John Dennis*, ed. E. N. Hooker, Baltimore: The Johns Hopkins University Press, 1939–43, 2 vols.

Dryden, John, *Essays*, ed. W. P. Ker, Oxford: Clarendon Press, 1900, 2 vols.

   Of dramatic poesy and other critical essays, ed. G. Watson, London: J. M. Dent, 1962, 2 vols.

Jonson, Ben, *Ben Jonson* [Works], ed. C. H. Herford and P. and E. Simpson, Oxford: Clarendon Press, 1925–52, 11 vols. [Edition under reissue with corrections, 1986–].

Marvell, Andrew, *Complete poems*, Harmondsworth: Penguin, 1972.

Milton, John, *Complete poems and major prose*, ed. M. Hughes, New York: Odyssey, 1957.

   Complete prose works (1624–1642), ed. D. M. Wolfe, vol. I, New Haven: Yale University Press, 1953.

Munro, John (ed.), *The Shak[e]speare allusion book*; 1909; reissued with preface by E. Chambers, London: Oxford University Press, 1932, 2 vols.

Rymer, Thomas, *The critical works*, ed. C. A. Zimansky, New Haven: Yale University Press, 1956.

Shawcross, John T. (ed.), *Milton: the critical heritage*, London: Routledge & Kegan Paul, 1970.

Smith, G. Gregory (ed.), *Elizabethan critical essays*, Oxford: Clarendon Press, 1904, 2 vols.

Spenser, Edmund, *Poetical works*, ed. J. C. Smith and E. de Sélincourt, London: Oxford University Press, 1970.

Spingarn, J. E. (ed.), *Critical essays of the seventeenth century*, Oxford: Clarendon Press, 1908–9, 3 vols. [Reprint Bloomington: Indiana University Press, 1957].

Spurgeon, Caroline F. E. *Five-hundred years of Chaucer criticism and allusion (1357–1900), Part 1*, Oxford: Oxford University Press, 1914.

Waller, Edmund, *Poems*, ed. G. T. Drury, London: Lawrence and Bullen, 1893.

Webbe, William, *A discourse of English poetrie* (1586), in G. Gregory Smith (ed.), *Elizabethan critical essays*; 1904; reprint Oxford and New York: Oxford University Press, 1971, 2 vols.

Secondary sources

Bate, Walter Jackson, *The burden of the past and the English poet*, Cambridge, MA: Harvard University Press, 1970.

Bentley, Gerald Eades, *Shakespeare and Jonson: their reputations in the seventeenth century compared*, Chicago: University of Chicago Press, 1945, 2 vols. in 1.

Fry, Paul H. *The reach of criticism: method and perception in literary theory*, New Haven: Yale University Press, 1983.

Kerrigan, William, *The prophetic Milton*, Charlottesville: University Press of Virginia, 1974.

Levine, Joseph M. *The Battle of the Books: history and literature in the Augustan age*, Ithaca and London: Cornell University Press, 1991.

Lewalski, Barbara K. *Protestant poetics and the seventeenth-century religious lyric*, Princeton: Princeton University Press, 1979.

Manley, Lawrence, *Convention, 1500–1750*, Cambridge, MA: Harvard University Press, 1980.

Maus, Katherine Eisaman, *Ben Jonson and the Roman frame of mind*, Princeton: Princeton University Press, 1984.

Monk, Samuel H. *The Sublime: a study of critical theories in XVIIIth-century England*, New York: Modern Language Association, 1935.

Pechter, Edward, *Dryden's classical theory of literature*, Cambridge: Cambridge University Press, 1975.

Peterson, Richard S. *Imitation and praise in the poems of Ben Jonson*, New Haven: Yale University Press, 1981.

Shifflet, Andrew, *Stoicism, politics, and literature in the age of Milton: war and peace reconciled*, Cambridge: Cambridge University Press, 1998.

Snyder, Susan, *Pastoral process: Spenser, Marvell, Milton*, Stanford: Stanford University Press, 1998.

Weinbrot, Howard D. *Britannia's issue: the rise of British literature from Dryden to Ossian*, Cambridge: Cambridge University Press, 1993.

Zwicker, Steven D. *Lines of authority: politics and English literary culture, 1649–1689*, Ithaca: Cornell University Press, 1993.

A survey of national developments: France

Primary sources and texts

Aubignac, François Hédelin, abbé d', *Pratique du théâtre*, ed. P. Martino, Algiers: Carbonel; Paris: Champion, 1927.

Balzac, Jean-Louis Guez de, *Œuvres*, Paris: T. Jolly, 1665, 2 vols.

Boileau-Despréaux, Nicolas, *Œuvres complètes*, ed. A. Adam and F. Escal, Paris: Gallimard, 1966.

Chapelain, Jean, *Opuscules critiques*, ed. A. C. Hunter, Paris: Droz, 1936.

Du Plaisir, *Sentiments sur les lettres et sur l'histoire avec des scrupules sur le style*, ed. P. Hourcade, Geneva: Droz, 1975.

La Mesnardière, Hippolyte-Jules Pilet de, *La poëtique*; 1640; reprint Geneva: Slatkine, 1972.

Mairet, Jean de, *La Silvanire*, Préface, in *Théâtre du XVIIe siècle*, ed. J. Schérer, J. Truchet, and A. Blanc, 3 vols., Paris: Gallimard, 1975–92, vol. I, pp. 479–88.

Ogier, François, *Tyr et Sidon*, Préface, in Jean de Schélandre, *Tyr et Sidon*, ed. J. W. Barker, Paris: Nizet, 1974, pp. 150–61.

Pellisson-Fontanier, Paul, *Discours sur les œuvres de M. Sarasin*, in Jean-François Sarasin, *Les œuvres de Monsieur Sarasin*, ed. G. Ménage, Paris: A. Courbé, 1656, pp. 1–72.

Sarasin, Jean-François, *Discours de la tragédie*, in Jean-François Sarasin, *Les œuvres de Monsieur Sarasin*, ed. G. Ménage, Paris: A. Courbé, 1656, pp. 243–84.

Sorel, Charles, *La bibliothèque françoise*, Geneva: Slatkine, 1970.

    De la connoissance des bons livres ou examen de plusieurs auteurs, ed. L. Moretti Cenerini, Rome: Bulzoni, 1974.

Valincour, Jean-Baptiste-Henri du Trousset de, *Lettres à Madame la Marquise *** sur le sujet de 'La Princesse de Clèves'*, ed. A. Cazes, Paris: Bossard, 1925.

Secondary sources

Bray, René, *La formation de la doctrine classique en France*, new edn, Paris: Nizet, 1961.

Cave, Terence, *Recognitions: a study in poetics*, Oxford: Clarendon Press, 1988.

Cristin, Claude, *Aux origines de l'histoire littéraire*, Grenoble: Presses Universitaires de Grenoble, 1973.

Fumaroli, Marc, *L'âge de l'éloquence: rhétorique et 'res literaria' de la Renaissance au seuil de l'époque classique*, Geneva: Droz, 1980.

Fumaroli, Marc (ed.) *Critique et création littéraire en France au XVIIe siècle*, Paris: Editions du CNRS, 1977.

Gasté, Armand (ed.), *La querelle du Cid: pièces et pamphlets*, Paris: H. Welter, 1898.

Genetiot, Alain, *Poétique du loisir mondain, de Voiture à La Fontaine*, Paris: Champion, 1997.

Jehasse, Jean, *Guez de Balzac et le génie romain*, Saint-Etienne: Publications de l'Université de Saint-Etienne, 1978.

  La renaissance de la critique, Saint-Etienne: Publications de l'Université de Saint-Etienne, 1976.

Kibédi Varga, Aron, *Rhétorique et littérature: études de structures classiques*, Paris: Didier, 1970.

Lough, John, *Writer and public in France from the Middle Ages to the present day*, Oxford: Clarendon Press, 1978.

Mortgat, Emmanuelle, and Méchoulan, Eric (ed.), *Ecrire au XVIIe siècle: une anthologie*, Paris: Presses Pocket, 1992.

Viala, Alain, *Naissance de l'écrivain: sociologie de la littérature à l'âge classique*, Paris: Editions de Minuit, 1985.

A survey of national developments: Italy

Primary sources and texts

Bembo, Pietro, *Prose della volgar lingua*, Venice: Tacuino, 1525 [Modern edition Padua: Liviana, 1967].

Bruno, G. *Dialoghi italiani*, Florence: Sansoni, 1958.

Castelvetro, Lodovico, *Poetica d'Aristotele vulgarizzata e sposta*, ed. W. Romani, Bari: Laterza, 1978–9, 2 vols.

Garin, E. (ed.), *Prosatori latini del Quattrocento*, Milan and Naples: Ricciardi, 1952.

Marino, Giambattista, *Epistolario: seguito da lettere di altri scrittori del Seicento*, ed. A. Borzelli and F. Nicolini, Bari: Laterza, 1911–12, 2 vols.

Pozzi, M. (ed.), *Trattatisti del Cinquecento*, Milan and Naples: Ricciardi, 1978.

Raimondi, E. (ed.), *Trattatisti e narratori del Seicento*, Milan and Naples: Ricciardi, 1960.

Tasso, Torquato, *Discorsi dell'arte poetica e del poema eroico*, ed. L. Poma, Bari: Laterza, 1964.

Trissino, Giovanni Giorgio, 'Sofonisba', in *Il teatro italiano*, 6 vols., Turin: Einaudi, 1977, vol. I, pp. 1–78.

Weinberg, Bernard (ed.), *Trattati di poetica e retorica del Cinquecento*, ed. B. Weinberg, Bari: Laterza, 1970–4, 4 vols.

Secondary sources

Aurigemma, M. 'La teoria dei modelli e i trattati d'amore', in *La letteratura italiana, storia e testi*, ed. C. Muscetta, 9 vols., Bari: Laterza, 1973, vol. IV.1, pp. 327–69.

Baldassarri, G. 'L'apologia del Tasso e *la maniera platonica*', in *Letteratura e critica: saggi in onore di Natalino Sapegno*, vol. IV, Rome: Bulzoni, 1977, pp. 223–51.

Battistini, A., and Raimondi, E. 'Retoriche e poetiche dominanti', in *Letteratura italiana*, ed. A. Asor Rosa, 9 vols., Turin: Einaudi, 1984, vol. III, pp. 5–339.

Burke, P. *Culture and society in Renaissance Italy (1420–1540)*, London: Batsford, 1973.

Chiari, A. 'La fortuna del Boccaccio', in *Questioni e correnti di storia letteraria*, ed. A. Momigliano, Milan: Marzorati, 1949, pp. 275–348.

Croce, F. 'Critica e trattatistica del Barocco', in *Storia della letteratura italiana*, ed. E. Cecchi and N. Sapegno, 8 vols., Milan: Garzanti, 1967, vol. V, pp. 473–518, 495–6, and 500–6.

'Le poetiche del Barocco in Italia', in *Momenti e problemi di storia dell'estetica*, 2 vols., Milan: Marzorati, 1959, vol. I, pp. 547–75.

Della Terza, D. '*Imitatio*: theory and practice: the example of Bembo the poet', *Yearbook of Italian studies* 1 (1971), 321–5.

Dionisotti, Carlo, *Geografia e storia della letteratura italiana*, Turin: Einaudi, 1977.

Gli umanisti e il volgare fra Quattro e Cinquecento, Florence: F. le Monnier, 1968.

Eisenstein, Elizabeth L. *The printing press as an agent of change: communications and cultural transformations in early-modern Europe*, Cambridge and New York: Cambridge University Press, 1979.

Herrick, Marvin T. *The fusion of Horatian and Aristotelian literary criticism 1531–1555*, Urbana: University of Illinois Press, 1946.

Jacobs, E. F. (ed.), *Italian Renaissance studies*, London: Faber and Faber, 1960.

Maggini, F. 'La critica dantesca dal '300 ai nostri giorni', in *Questioni e correnti di storia letteraria*, ed. A. Momigliano, Milan: Marzorati, 1949, pp. 123–66.

Mazzacurati, G. *La crisi della retorica umanistica nel Cinquecento*, Naples: Libreria Scientifica, 1961.

Migliorini, B. 'La questione della lingua', in *Questioni e correnti di storia letteraria*, ed. A. Momigliano, Milan: Marzorati, 1949, pp. 1–75.

Moretti, W., and Barilli, R. 'La letteratura e la lingua, le poetiche e la critica d'arte', in *La letteratura italiana, storia e testi*, ed. C. Muscetta, vol. IV.2, Bari: Laterza, 1973, pp. 487–571, 492–7.

Praz, Mario, *Studi sul concettismo*, Florence: Sansoni, 1946.

Spingarn, J. E. *A history of literary criticism in the Renaissance*, New York: Harbinger Books, 1963.

Tateo, Francesco, *Retorica e poetica fra Medioevo e Rinascimento*, Bari: Adriatica, 1960.

Ulivi, F. *L'imitazione nella poetica del Rinascimento*, Milan: Marzorati, 1959.

Vasoli, Cesare, 'L'estetica dell'umanesimo e del Rinascimento', in *Momenti e problemi di storia dell'estetica*, 2 vols., Milan: Marzorati, 1959, vol. I, pp. 325–433.

Weinberg, Bernard, *A history of literary criticism in the Italian Renaissance*, Chicago: University of Chicago Press, 1961, 2 vols.

A survey of national developments: Spain

Primary sources and texts

Calderón de la Barca, Pedro, *La vida es sueño*, ed. C. Morón Aroyo, Madrid: Cátedra, 1977.

Cervantes, Miguel de, *La ingeniosa historia de Don Quijote de la Mancha*, ed. M. de Riquer, Barcelona: Juventud, 1955, 2 vols.

Góngora y Argote, Luis de, *Fábula de Polifemo y Galatea*, ed. A. Parker, Madrid: Cátedra, 1983.

Gracián y Morales, Baltasar, *El criticón*, ed. A. Prieto, Madrid: Planeta, 1985.

Secondary sources

Brownlee, Marina S. *The poetics of literary theory: Lope de Vega's 'Novelas a Marcia Leonarda' and their Cervantine context*, Madrid: Porrúa, 1981.

Castro, Américo, *De la edad conflictiva: crisis de la cultura española en el siglo XVII*; 1961; reprint Madrid: Taurus, 1976.

Forcione, Alban K. *Cervantes, Aristotle, and the 'Persiles'*, Princeton: Princeton University Press, 1970.

Guillén, Claudio, *The anatomies of roguery: a comparative study in the origins and the nature of picaresque literature*, New York: Garland, 1987.

Maravall, José Antonio, *Culture of the Baroque*, trans. T. Cochran, Minneapolis: University of Minnesota Press, 1986.

Mariscal, George, *Contradictory subjects: Quevedo, Cervantes and seventeenth-century Spanish culture*, Ithaca: Cornell University Press, 1991.

Shergold, N. D. *A history of the Spanish stage from medieval times until the end of the seventeenth century*, Oxford: Clarendon Press, 1967.

Smith, Paul Julian, *Writing in the margin: Spanish literature of the Golden Age*, Oxford: Clarendon Press, 1988.

Terry, Arthur, *Seventeenth-century Spanish poetry: the power of artifice*, Cambridge: Cambridge University Press, 1993.

Vega Ramos, Maria Jose, *La teoria de la novella en el siglo XVI: la poetica neoaristotelica ante el Decameron*, Salamanca: J. Cromberger, 1993.

A survey of national developments: Germany

Primary sources and texts

Borinski, Karl, *Die Poetik der Renaissance*; 1886; reprint Hildesheim: Olms, 1967.

Lämmert, Eberhard (ed.), *Romantheorie: Dokumentation ihrer Geschichte in Deutschland 1420–1880*, Cologne and Berlin: Kiepenhauer & Witsch, 1971.

Lempicki, Sigmund von, *Geschichte der deutschen Literaturwissenschaft bis zum Ende des 18. Jahrhunderts*, 2nd rev. edn, Göttingen: Vandenhoeck & Ruprecht, 1968.

Secondary sources

Braungart, Georg, 'Rhetorik, Poetik, Emblematik', in *Deutsche Literatur. Eine Sozialgeschichte*, ed. H. A. Glaser, vol. III, 'Zwischen Gegenreformation und Frühaufklärung', Reinbek: Rowohlt, 1985, pp. 219–36.

Carlsson, Anni, *Die deutsche Buchkritik von der Reformation bis zur Gegenwart*, Berne and Munich: Francke, 1969.

Engelsing, Rolf, *Der Bürger als Leser. Lesergeschichte in Deutschland 1500–1800*, Stuttgart: Metzler, 1974.
Garber, Klaus, *Martin Opitz – 'der Vater der deutschen Dichtung'*, Stuttgart: Metzler, 1976.
Schöne, Albrecht, *Kürbishütte und Königsberg: Modellversuch einer sozialgeschichtlichen Entzifferung poetischer Texte*, Munich: Beck, 1975.
Szyrocki, Marian, *Poetik des Barock*; 1968; reprint Stuttgart: Reclam, 1977.
Wutenow, Ralph-Rainer, 'Literaturkritik, Essayistik und Aphoristik', in *Deutsche Literatur. Eine Sozialgeschichte*, ed. H. A. Glaser, vol. IV, 'Zwischen Absolutismus und Aufklärung', Reinbek: Rowohlt, 1980, pp. 120–47.

A survey of national developments: the Low Countries

Primary sources and texts

Brandt, George W. (ed.), *German and Dutch theatre, 1600–1848*, Cambridge: Cambridge University Press, 1993.
Gillis, M. A. 'To the Reader' [1566], in the appendix to Karel Porteman, 'The earliest reception of the *Ars emblematica* in Dutch', in *The European emblem*, ed. B. F. Scholz *et al.*, Leiden: Brill, 1990, pp. 33–53.
Heinsius, Daniel, *On plot in tragedy (De tragoediae constitutione)* (1611), trans. and ed. P. R. Sellin and J. J. McManmon, Northridge, CA: San Fernando Valley State College, 1971.
Hooft, P. C., 'Oration concerning the excellence of poetry' (*c.* 1610–15), trans. T. Hermans and L. Gilbert, *Dutch crossing* 47 (1992), 24–52.
Vondel, Joost van den, 'Introduction to Dutch Poetry' (1650), trans. T. Hermans and L. Gilbert, *Dutch crossing* 29 (1986), 50–63.

Secondary sources

Harmsen, Ton, *Onderwys in de tooneel-poëzy. De opvattingen over toneel van het Kunstgenootschap Nil Volentibus Arduum*, Rotterdam: Ordeman, 1989.
Ijsewijn, Jozef, 'Humanism in the Low Countries', in *Renaissance humanism: foundations, forms, and legacy*, ed. A. Rabil, Jr., vol. II, Philadelphia: University of Pennsylvania Press, 1988, pp. 156–215.
Meter, J. H. *The literary theories of Daniel Heinsius*, Assen: Van Gorcum, 1984.
Parente, James, *Religious drama and the humanist tradition: Christian theater in Germany and in the Netherlands*, Leiden: Brill, 1987.
Schenkeveld, Maria A. *Dutch literature in the age of Rembrandt: themes and ideas*, Amsterdam and Philadelphia: J. Benjamins, 1991.
Schenkeveld-Van der Dussen, M. A. (ed.), *Nederlandse literatuur, een geschiedenis*, Groningen: M. Nijhoff, 1993.
Smits-Veldt, Mieke, *Het Nederlandse Renaissance-toneel*, Utrecht: HES, 1991.
Samuel Coster, ethicus-didacticus, Groningen: Wolters-Noordhoff / Forsten, 1986.
Spies, Marijke, 'Developments in sixteenth-century Dutch poetics: from "Rhetoric" to "Renaissance"', in *Renaissance-Rhetorik / Renaissance Rhetoric*, ed. H. Plett, Berlin and New York: De Gruyter, 1993, pp. 72–91.

Index